THE WEST

Key Eras in the Transformation of the West

■ Map 1 Roman Empire at Its Greatest Extent, ca. 117 C.E.

Western civilization has undergone many transformations throughout its history. When the Roman Empire was at its greatest extent, the basic intellectual, religious, political, and geographic outlines of what we call the West today were drawn.

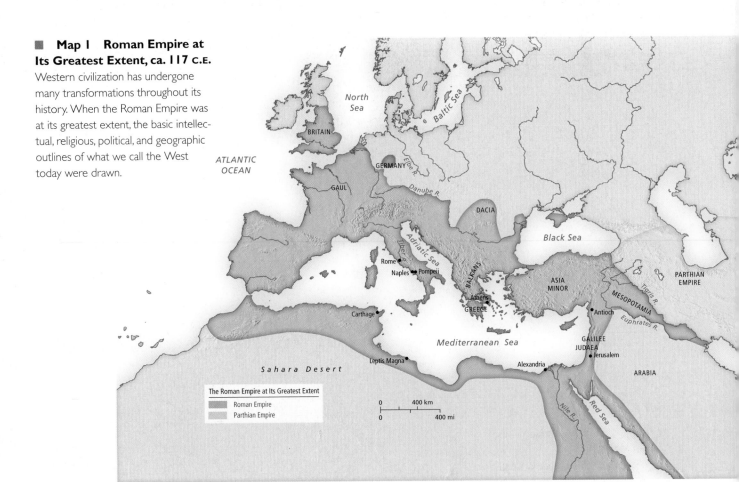

■ Map 2 Carolingian Empire

During the Carolingian Empire, Europe experienced greater political cohesion, as the Carolingian armies successfully re-unified most of the western European territories of the ancient Roman Empire, distinguishing it from the Byzantine Empire in the east.

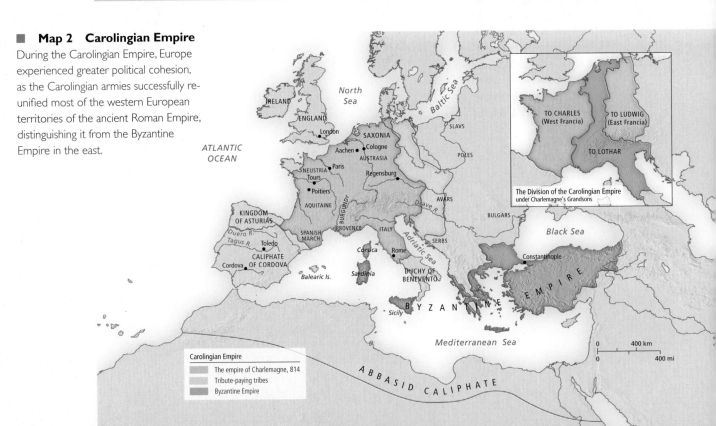

Map 3 Europe After the Congress of Vienna, 1815

The major European powers re-drew the map of Europe with the Congress of Vienna in 1815 after the defeat of Napoleon. This map shows the dismantlement of the massive empire France had acquired under his leadership.

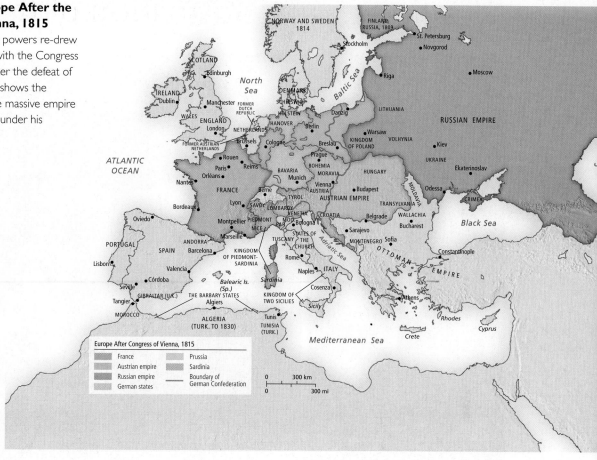

Europe After Congress of Vienna, 1815
- France
- Austrian empire
- Russian empire
- German states
- Prussia
- Sardinia
- Boundary of German Confederation

Map 4 Europe After World War I

The map of Europe changed dramatically after World War I with the collapse of the old authoritarian empires and the creation of independent nation-states in eastern Europe. What neither Map 3 nor Map 4 can show, however, is the expansion of "the West" beyond European borders to embrace cultures on other continents, including Australia, Africa, and North America.

Europe and the Middle East After World War I
- To Great Britain
- To France
- To Italy
- To Rumania
- To Denmark
- To Yugoslavia (Serbia and Montenegro)
- To Belgium
- To Greece
- Became independent
- 1914 boundaries
- New boundaries

THE WEST

ENCOUNTERS & TRANSFORMATIONS

CONCISE EDITION

BRIAN LEVACK
University of Texas at Austin

EDWARD MUIR
Northwestern University

MICHAEL MAAS
Rice University

MEREDITH VELDMAN
Louisiana State University

PEARSON
Longman

New York   San Francisco   Boston
London   Toronto   Sydney   Tokyo   Singapore   Madrid
Mexico City   Munich   Paris   Cape Town   Hong Kong   Montreal

Publisher: Priscilla McGeehon
Senior Acquisitions Editor: Janet Lanphier
Senior Development Editor: David Kear
Executive Marketing Manager: Sue Westmoreland
Media and Supplements Editor: Kristi Olson
Production Manager: Donna DeBenedictis
Project Coordination and Electronic Page Makeup: Elm Street Publishing Services, Inc.
Text Design: Pearson Education Development
Cover Designer/Manager: John Callahan
Cover and Frontispiece Art: Mansueti, Giovanni; traceable since 1485; died c. 1526/27. *Scenes from the life of Mark the Evangelist*, undated. Oil on canvas, 376 × 612 cm. From the cycle with scenes from the legend of St. Mark at S. Maria dei Crociferi. Venice, Gallerid dell' Accademia. Photo: akg-images/Cameraphoto
Cartography: Maps.com
Photo Researcher: Photosearch, Inc.
Manufacturing Buyer: Roy L. Pickering, Jr.
Printer and Binder: Quebecor World Dubuque
Cover Printer: Coral Graphic Services, Inc.

For permission to use copyrighted material, grateful acknowledgement is made to the copyright holders on pp. C-1–C-3, which are hereby made part of this copyright page.

Library of Congress Cataloging-in-Publication Data

The West : encounters, transformations / Brian Levack . . . [et al.].—Concise ed.
     p. cm.
     Includes bibliographical references and index.
     ISBN 0-321-27597-7 (single v. ed.) — ISBN 0-321-27632-9 (v. 1) — ISBN 0-321-27631-0
     (v. 2)
     1. Civilization, Western—History—Textbooks.   I. Levack, Brian P.

CB245.W455 2006
909'.09821—dc22

2005031672

Copyright © 2007 by Pearson Education, Inc.

Please visit us at www.ablongman.com/levackconcise

ISBN 0-321-27597-7 (single volume edition)
ISBN 0-321-27632-9 (volume I)
ISBN 0-321-27631-0 (volume II)

4 5 6 7 8 9 10—QWD—09 08 07

Brief Contents

Detailed Contents

CHAPTER 17

The West and the World: Empire, Trade, and War, 1650–1850 *357*

CHAPTER 18

Eighteenth-Century Society and Culture *381*

JUSTICE IN HISTORY

CHAPTER 28

The West in the Contemporary Era: New Encounters and Transformations   *597*

JUSTICE IN HISTORY

Documents

Maps

Justice in History Features

Preface

We wrote this textbook to answer questions about the identity of the civilization in which we live. Journalists, politicians, and scholars often refer to our civilization, its political ideologies, its economic systems, and its cultures as "Western" without fully considering what that label means and why it might be appropriate. The classification of our civilization as Western has become particularly problematic in the age of globalization. The creation of international markets, the rapid dissemination of ideas on a global scale, and the transmission of popular culture from one country to another often make it difficult to distinguish what is Western from what is not. *The West: Encounters & Transformations* offers students a history of Western civilization in which these issues of Western identity are given prominence. Our goal is neither to idealize nor to indict that civilization but to describe its main characteristics in different historical periods.

The West: Encounters & Transformations gives careful consideration to two basic questions. The first is how did the definition of the West change over time? In what ways did its boundaries shift and how did the distinguishing characteristics of its cultures change? The second question is, by what means did the West—and the idea of the West—develop? We argue that the West is the product of a series of cultural encounters that occurred both outside and within its geographical boundaries. We explore these encounters and the transformations they produced by detailing the political, social, religious, and cultural history of the regions that have been, at one time or another, a part of the West.

This concise edition is a condensed version of the successful *The West: Encounters & Transformations*. While we have compressed the text, eliminating details and extra examples, we have retained its broad thematic framework and its interpretations of Western history. In particular, we have retained our emphasis on the way the West has changed over the centuries as a result of a series of cultural encounters.

Defining the West

What is the West? How did it come into being? How has it developed throughout history? Many textbooks take for granted which regions or peoples of the globe constitute the West. They treat the history of the West as a somewhat expanded version of European history. While not disputing the centrality of Europe to any definition of the West, we contend that the West is not only a geographical realm with ever-shifting boundaries but also a cultural realm, an area of cultural influence extending beyond the geographical and political boundaries of Europe. We so strongly believe in this notion that we have written the essay "What Is the West?" to encourage students to think about their understanding of Western civilization and to guide their understanding of each chapter. Many of the features of what we call Western civilization originated in regions that are not geographically part of Europe (such as northern Africa and the Middle East), while ever since the fifteenth century various social, ethnic, and political groups from non-European regions (such as North and South America, eastern Russia, Australia, New Zealand, and South Africa) have identified themselves, in one way or another, with the West. Throughout the text, we devote considerable attention to the boundaries of the West and show how borderlines between cultures have been created, especially in eastern and southeastern Europe.

Considered as a geographical and cultural realm, "the West" is a term of recent origin, and the civilization to which it refers did not become clearly defined until the eleventh century, especially during the Crusades, when western European Christians developed a distinct cultural identity. Before that time we can only talk about the powerful forces that created the West, especially the dynamic interaction of the civilizations of western Europe, the Byzantine Empire, and the Muslim world.

Over the centuries Western civilization has acquired many salient characteristics. These include two of the world's great legal systems (civil law and common law), three of the world's monotheistic religions (Judaism, Christianity, and Islam), certain political and social philosophies, forms of political organization (such as the modern bureaucratic state and democracy), methods of scientific inquiry, systems of economic organization (such as industrial capitalism), and distinctive styles of art, architecture, and music. At times one or more of these characteristics has served as a primary source of Western identity: Christianity in the Middle Ages, science and rationalism during the Enlightenment, industrialization in the nineteenth and twentieth centuries, and a defense of individual liberty and democracy in the late twentieth century. These sources of Western identity, however, have always been challenged and contested, both when they were coming into prominence and when they appeared to be most triumphant. Western culture has never been monolithic, and even today references to the West imply a wide range of meanings.

Cultural Encounters

The definition of the West is closely related to the central theme of our book, which is the process of cultural encounters. Throughout *The West: Encounters & Transformations,* we examine the West as a product of a series of cultural encounters both outside the West and within it. We show that the West originated and developed through a continuous process of inclusion and exclusion resulting from a series of encounters among and within different groups. These encounters can be described in a general sense as external, internal, or ideological.

EXTERNAL ENCOUNTERS

External encounters took place between peoples of different civilizations. Before the emergence of the West as a clearly defined entity, external encounters occurred between such diverse peoples as Greeks and Phoenicians, Macedonians and Egyptians, and Romans and Celts. After the eleventh century, external encounters between Western and non-Western peoples occurred mainly during periods of European exploration, expansion, and imperialism. In the sixteenth and seventeenth centuries, for example, a series of external encounters took place between Europeans on the one hand and Africans, Asians, and the indigenous people of the Americas on the other. Two chapters of *The West:*

Encounters & Transformations. (Chapters 12 and 17) and a large section of a third (Chapter 23) explore these external encounters in depth and discuss how they affected Western and non-Western civilizations alike.

INTERNAL ENCOUNTERS

Our discussion of encounters also includes similar interactions between different social groups *within* Western countries. These internal encounters often took place between dominant and subordinate groups, such as between lords and peasants, rulers and subjects, men and women, factory owners and workers, masters and slaves. Encounters between those who were educated and those who were illiterate, which recur frequently throughout Western history, also fall into this category. Encounters just as often took place between different religious and political groups, such as between Christians and Jews, Catholics and Protestants, royal absolutists and republicans.

IDEOLOGICAL ENCOUNTERS

Ideological encounters involve the interaction between comprehensive systems of thought, most notably religious doctrines, political philosophies, and scientific theories about the nature of the world. These ideological conflicts usually arose out of internal encounters, when various groups within Western societies subscribed to different theories of government or rival religious faiths. The encounters between Christianity and polytheism in the early Middle Ages, between liberalism and conservatism in the nineteenth century, and between fascism and communism in the twentieth century were ideological encounters. Some ideological encounters had an external dimension, such as when the forces of Islam and Christianity came into conflict during the Crusades and when the Cold War developed between Soviet communism and Western democracy in the second half of the twentieth century.

   The West: Encounters & Transformations illuminates the variety of these encounters and clarifies their effects. By their very nature encounters are interactive, but they have taken different forms: they have been violent or peaceful, coercive or cooperative. Some have resulted in the imposition of Western ideas on areas lying outside the geographical boundaries of the West or the perpetuation of the dominant culture within Western societies. More often than not, however, encounters have resulted in a more reciprocal process of exchange in which both Western and non-Western cultures or the values of both dominant and subordinate groups have undergone significant transformation. Our book not only identifies these encounters but also discusses their significance by returning periodically to the issue of Western identity.

Coverage

································ ▬ ································

T he West: Encounters & Transformations offers both balanced coverage of political, social, and cultural history and a broader coverage of the West and the world.

BALANCED COVERAGE

Our goal throughout the text has been to provide balanced coverage of political, social, and cultural history and to include significant coverage of religious and military history as well. Political history defines the basic structure of the book, and some chapters, such as those on building the classical world, the age of confessional divisions, absolutism and state building, the French Revolution, and the coming of mass politics, include sustained political narratives. Because we understand the West to be a cultural as well as a geographical realm, we give a prominent position to cultural history. Thus we include rich sections on Hellenistic philosophy and literature, the cultural environment of the Italian Renaissance, the creation of a new political culture at the time of the French Revolution, and the atmosphere of cultural despair and desire that prevailed in Europe after World War I. We also devote special attention to religious history, including the history of Islam as well as that of Christianity and Judaism. Unlike many other textbooks, our coverage of religion continues into the modern period.

The West: Encounters & Transformations also provides extensive coverage of the history of women and gender. Wherever possible the history of women is integrated into the broader social, cultural, and political history of the period. But there are also separate sections on women in our chapters on classical Greece, the Renaissance, the Reformation, the Enlightenment, the Industrial Revolution, World War I, World War II, and the postwar era.

THE WEST AND THE WORLD

Our book provides broad geographical coverage. Because the West is the product of a series of encounters, the external areas with which the West interacted are of major importance. Three chapters deal specifically with the West and the World.

- Chapter 12, "The West and the World: The Significance of Global Encounters, 1450–1650"
- Chapter 17, "The West and the World: Empire, Trade, and War, 1650–1850"
- Chapter 23, "The West and the World: Cultural Crisis and the New Imperialism, 1870–1914"

These chapters present substantial material on sub-Saharan Africa, Latin America, the Middle East, India, and East Asia. Our text is also distinctive in its coverage of eastern Europe and the Muslim world, areas which have often been considered outside the boundaries of the West. These regions were arenas within which significant cultural encounters took place. Finally we include material on the United States and Australia, both of which have become part of the West. We recognize that most American college and university students have the opportunity to study American history as a separate subject, but treatment of the United States as a Western nation provides a different perspective from that usually given in courses on American history. For example, this book treats the American Revolution as one of four Atlantic revolutions, its national unification in the nineteenth century as part of a broader western European development, its pattern of industrialization as related to that of Britain, and its central role in the Cold War as part of an ideological encounter that was global in scope.

Organization

The chronological and thematic organization of our book conforms in its broad outline to the way in which Western civilization courses are generally taught. We have limited the number of chapters to twenty-eight, an effort to make the book more compatible with the traditional American semester calendar and to solve the frequent complaint that there is not enough time to cover all the material in the course. We have also made some significant changes in organization:

- Chapter 2, which covers the period from ca. 1600 to 550 B.C.E., is the first in a Western civilization textbook to examine the International Bronze Age and its aftermath as a period important in its own right because it saw the creation of expansionist, multiethnic empires, linked by trade and diplomacy.

- In Chapter 4 the Roman Republic, in keeping with contemporary scholarship, has been incorporated into a discussion of the Hellenistic world, dethroned slightly to emphasize how it was one of many competing Mediterranean civilizations.
- Chapter 12 covers the first period of European expansion, from 1450 to 1650. It examines the new European encounters with the civilizations of sub-Saharan Africa, the Americas, and East Asia. By paying careful attention to the characteristics of these civilizations before the arrival of the Europeans, we show how this encounter affected indigenous peoples as well as Europeans.
- Chapter 16 is devoted entirely to the Scientific Revolution of the seventeenth century in order to emphasize the central importance of this development in the creation of Western identity.
- Chapter 17, which covers the second period of European expansion, from 1650 to 1850, studies the growth of European empires, the beginning of global warfare, and encounters between Europeans and the peoples of Asia and Africa.
- Chapter 26 on World War II contains substantial sections on both the Holocaust and the atomic bomb. The development of techniques and technologies of mass killing, and the resulting moral and political debates, helped define the post-World War II West.

Features and Pedagogical Aids

In writing this textbook we have endeavored to keep both the student reader and the classroom instructor in mind at all times. The text includes the following features and pedagogical aids, all of which are intended to support the themes of the book.

WHAT IS THE WEST?

The West: Encounters & Transformations begins with an essay to engage students in the task of defining the West and to introduce them to the notion of cultural encounters. "What Is the West?" guides students through the text by providing a framework for understanding how the West was shaped. Structured around the six questions of What? When? Where? Who? How? and Why?, this framework encourages students to think about their understanding of Western civilization. The essay serves as a blueprint for using this textbook.

JUSTICE IN HISTORY

Found in every chapter, this feature is aimed at presenting a historically significant trial or episode in which different notions of justice (or injustice) were debated and resolved. The *Justice in History* features illustrate cultural encounters within communities as they try to determine the fate of individuals from all walks of life. Many famous trials dealt with conflicts over basic religious, philosophical, or political values, such as those of Socrates, Jesus, Joan of Arc, Charles I, Galileo, and Adolf Eichmann. Other *Justice in History* features show how judicial institutions, such as the ordeal, the inquisition, and revolutionary tribunals, handled adversarial situations in different societies. These essays, therefore, illustrate the way in which the basic values of the West have evolved through attempts to resolve disputes, contention, and conflict.

What Is the West?

MANY OF THE PEOPLE WHO INFLUENCE PUBLIC OPINION—POLITICIANS, teachers, clergy, journalists, and television commentators—frequently refer to "Western values," "the West," and "Western civilization." They often use these terms as if they do not require explanation. But what *do* these terms mean? The West has always been an arena within which different cultures, religions, values, and philosophies have interacted, and any definition of the West will inevitably arouse controversy.

The most basic definition of the West is of a place. Western civilization is now typically thought to comprise the regions of Europe, the Americas, Australia, and New Zealand. However, this is a contemporary definition of the West. The inclusion of these places in the West is the result of a long history of European expansion through colonization. In addition to being a place, Western civilization also encompasses a cultural history—a tradition stretching back thousands of years to the ancient world. Over this long period the civilization we now identify as Western gradually took shape. The many characteristics that identify any civilization emerged over this time: forms of government, economic systems, and methods of scientific inquiry, as well as religions, languages, literature, and art.

Throughout the development of Western civilization, the ways in which

JUSTICE IN HISTORY

The Trial of Joan of Arc

After only fifteen months as the inspiration of the French army, Joan of Arc fell into the hands of the English, who brought her to trial for witchcraft. The English needed to stage a kind of show trial to demonstrate to their own demoralized forces that Joan's remarkable victories had been the result not of military superiority but rather of witchcraft. In the English trial, conducted at Rouen in 1431, Joan testified that her mission to save France was in response to voices she heard that commanded her to wear men's clothing. On the basis of this evidence of a confused or double gender identity, the ecclesiastical tribunal de-

authority of divine commands. The problem the English judges faced was to demonstrate that the voices came not from God but from the Devil. If they could prove that, then they had evidence of witchcraft and sorcery. Following standard inquisitorial guidelines, the judges knew that authentic messages from God would always conform to church dogma. Any deviation from official doctrines would constitute evidence of demonic influence. Thus, during Joan's trial the judges demanded that she make theological distinctions that were alien to her. When they wanted to know if the voices were those of angels or saints, Joan seemed

Each *Justice in History* feature includes two pedagogical aids. "Questions of Justice" helps students explore the historical significance of the episode just examined. These questions can also be used in classroom discussion or as student essay topics. "Taking It Further" provides the student with a few references that can be consulted in connection with a research project.

PRIMARY SOURCE DOCUMENTS

In each chapter we have presented a number of excerpts from primary source documents in order to reinforce or expand upon the points made in the text and to introduce students to the basic materials of historical research.

MAPS AND ILLUSTRATIONS

Artwork is a key component of our book. We recognize that many students often lack a strong familiarity with geography, and so we have taken great care to develop maps that help sharpen their geographic skills. Complementing the book's standard map program, we include maps focusing on areas outside the borders of Western civilization. These maps include a small thumbnail globe that highlights the geographic area under discussion in the context of the larger world. Fine art and photos also tell the story of Western civilization and we have included over 200 images to help students visualize the past: the way people lived, the events that shaped their lives, and how they viewed the world around them.

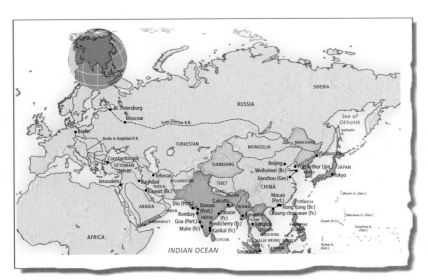

CHRONOLOGIES AND SUGGESTED READINGS

Each chapter includes a chronological chart and suggested readings. Chronologies outline significant events, such as "The Road to the Atom Bomb," and serve as convenient references for students. Each chapter concludes with an annotated list of suggested readings. These are not scholarly bibliographies aimed at the professor, but suggestions for students who wish to explore a topic in greater depth or to write a research paper. A comprehensive list of suggested readings is available on our book-specific website, www.ablongman.com/levackconcise.

GLOSSARY

We have sought to create a work that is accessible to students with little prior knowledge of the basic facts of Western history or geography. Throughout the book we have explained difficult concepts at length. For example, we present in-depth explanations of the concepts of Zoroastrianism, Neoplatonism, Renaissance humanism, the various Protestant denominations of the sixteenth century, capitalism, seventeenth-century absolutism, nineteenth-century liberalism and nationalism, fascism, and modernism. Key concepts such as these are identified in the chapters with a degree symbol (°) and defined as well in the end-of-text Glossary.

A NOTE ABOUT DATES AND TRANSLITERATIONS

In keeping with current academic practice, *The West: Encounters & Transformations* uses B.C.E. (before the common era) and C.E. (common era) to designate dates. We also follow the most current and widely accepted English transliterations of Arabic. Qur'an, for example, is used for Koran; Muslim is used for Moslem. Chinese words appearing in the text for the first time are written in *pinyin*, followed by the older Wade-Giles system in parentheses.

Supplements for Qualified College Adopters

COMPANION WEBSITE

www.ablongman.com/levackconcise

Instructors can take advantage of the Companion Website that supports this text. The instructor section includes teaching links and a link to the Instructor Resource Center.

INSTRUCTOR'S RESOURCE MANUAL

0-321-33880-4

Written by Sharon Arnoult, Midwestern State University, each chapter contains a chapter outline, significant themes, learning objectives, lesson enrichment ideas, discussion suggestions, and questions for discussing the primary source documents in the text.

TEST BANK

0-321-33879-0

Written by Susan Carrafiello, Wright State University, this supplement contains more than 1,200 multiple-choice and essay questions. All questions are referenced by topic and text page number.

TESTGEN-EQ COMPUTERIZED TESTING SYSTEM

0-321-33878-2

This flexible, easy-to-master computerized test bank on a dual-platform CD includes all of the items in the printed test bank and allows instructors to select specific questions, edit existing questions, and add their own items to create exams. Tests can be printed in several different fonts and formats and can include figures, such as graphs and tables.

HISTORY DIGITAL MEDIA ARCHIVE CD-ROM

0-321-14976-9

The Digital Media Archive CD-ROM contains electronic images and interactive and static maps, along with media elements such as video. These media assets are fully customizable and ready for classroom presentation or easy downloading into your PowerPoint presentations or any other presentation software.

Supplements for Students

COMPANION WEBSITE

www.ablongman.com/levackconcise
Providing a wealth of resources for students using *The West: Encounters & Transformations,* Concise Edition, this Companion Website contains chapter summaries, interactive practice test questions, and Web links for every chapter in the text.

RESEARCH NAVIGATOR AND RESEARCH NAVIGATOR GUIDE

0-205-40838-9
Research Navigator is a comprehensive Website comprising three exclusive databases of credible and reliable source material for research and for student assignments: EBSCO's ContentSelect Academic Journal Database, *The New York Times* Search-by-Subject Archive, and "Best of the Web" Link Library. The site also includes an extensive help section. The Research Navigator Guide provides students with access to the Research Navigator Website and includes reference material and hints about conducting online research. This supplement is free to qualified college adopters when packaged with the text.

MAPPING WESTERN CIVILIZATION: STUDENT ACTIVITIES

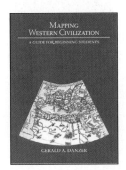

0-673-53774-9
Written by Gerald Danzer of the University of Illinois at Chicago, this free map workbook for students is designed as an accompaniment to Discovering Western Civilization Through Maps and Views. It features exercises designed to teach students to interpret and analyze cartographic materials as historical documents. The instructor is entitled to a free copy of the workbook for each copy of the text purchased from Longman.

WESTERN CIVILIZATION MAP WORKBOOKS

Volume I: 0-321-01878-8, Volume II: 0-321-01877-X
Prepared by Glee Wilson of Kent State University, these two volumes include map exercises designed to test and reinforce basic geographic literacy and to build critical thinking skills. Available shrink-wrapped at no cost with any Longman survey text.

STUDY GUIDE

Volume I: 0-321-33887-1, Volume II: 0-321-33888-1
Containing activities and study aids for every chapter in the text, each chapter of the *Study Guide* written by Carron Fillingim, Louisiana State University, includes a thorough chapter outline; timeline; map exercise; identification, multiple-choice, and thought questions; and critical-thinking questions based on primary source documents from the text.

STUDY CARD FOR WESTERN CIVILIZATION

0-321-29233-2
Colorful, affordable, and packed with useful information, Allyn & Bacon/Longman's Study Cards make studying easier, more efficient, and more enjoyable. Course information is distilled down to the basics, helping you quickly master the fundamentals, review a subject for understanding, or prepare for an exam. Because they're laminated for durability, you can keep these Study Cards for years to come and pull them out whenever you need a quick review.

MYHISTORYLAB (www.myhistorylab.com)

MyHistoryLab provides students with an online package complete with an electronic version of the comprehensive version of *The West,* numerous study aids, primary sources, and a chapter exam. With several hundred primary sources and images, as well as map activities with gradable quizzes and map workbook activities, the site offers students a unique, interactive experience that brings history to life. The comprehensive site also includes a History Bookshelf with more than fifty of the most commonly assigned books in history classes and a History ToolKit with tutorials and helpful links.

LONGMANWESTERNCIVILIZATION.COM (www.longmanwesterncivilization.com)

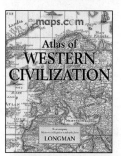

This Website provides the same resources as MyHistoryLab but without course management and the electronic textbook.

LONGMAN ATLAS OF WESTERN CIVILIZATION

0-321-21626-1

This 52-page atlas features carefully selected historical maps that provide comprehensive coverage for the major historical periods. Each map has been designed to be colorful, easy-to-read, and informative, without sacrificing detailed accuracy. This atlas makes history—and geography—more comprehensible.

A SHORT GUIDE TO WRITING ABOUT HISTORY, FIFTH EDITION

0-321-22716-6

Written by Richard Marius, late, of Harvard University, and Melvin E. Page, Eastern Tennessee State University, this engaging and practical text helps students get beyond merely compiling dates and facts; it teaches them how to incorporate their own ideas into their papers and to tell a story about history that interests them and their peers. Covering both brief essays and the documented resource paper, the text explores the writing and researching processes, identifies different modes of historical writing, including argument, and concludes with guidelines for improving style.

Penguin-Longman Partnership

The partnership between Penguin Books and Longman Publishers offers your students a discount on the following titles when qualified college instructors bundle them with any Longman survey text. Visit www.ablongman.com/penguin for more information.

AVAILABLE TITLES

Peter Abelard, *The Letters of Abelard and Heloise*
Dante Alighieri, *Divine Comedy: Inferno*
Dante Alighieri, *The Portable Dante*
Anonymous, *Early Irish Myths & Sagas*
Anonymous, *The Epic of Gilgamesh*

Anonymous, *The Song of Roland*
Anonymous, *Vinland Sagas*
Hannah Arendt, *On Revolution*
Aristophanes, *The Knights, Peace, The Birds, Assemblywomen, Wealth*
Aristotle, *The Politics*

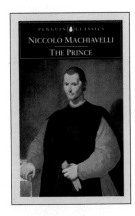

Louis Auchincloss, *Woodrow Wilson*
(Penguin Lives Series)
Jane Austen, *Emma*
Jane Austen, *Persuasion*
Jane Austen, *Pride and Prejudice*
Jane Austen, *Sense and Sensibility*
Edward Bellamy, *Looking Backward*
Richard Bowring, *Diary of Lady Murasaki*
Charlotte Brontë, *Jane Eyre*
Charlotte Brontë, *Villette*
Emily Brontë, *Wuthering Heights*
Edmund Barke, *Reflection on the
Revolution in France and on the
Proceedings in Certain Societies in
London Relative to that Event*
Benvenuto Cellini, *The Autobiography of
Benvenuto Cellini*
Geoffrey Chaucer, *The Canterbury Tales*
Marcus Tullius Cicero, *Cicero: Selected
Political Speeches*
Miguel de Cervantes, *The Adventures of
Don Quixote*
Bartolome de las Casas, *A Short Account of
the Destruction of the West Indies*
René Descartes, *Discourse on Method and
The Meditations*
Charles Dickens, *Great Expectations*
Charles Dickens, *Hard Times*
John Dos Passos, *Three Soldiers*
Einhard, *Two Lives of Charlemagne*
Olaudah Equiano, *The Interesting
Narrative and Other Writings*
M. Finley (ed.), *The Portable Greek
Historians*
Jeffrey Gantz (tr.), *Early Irish Myths and
Sagas*
Peter Gay, *Mozart* (Penguin Lives Series)
William Golding, *Lord of the Flies*
Kenneth Grahame, *The Wind in the
Willows*
Grimm & Grimm, *Grimms' Fairy Tales*
Thomas Hardy, *Jude the Obscure*
Herodotus, *The Histories*
Thomas Hobbes, *Leviathan*
Homer, *The Iliad*
Homer, *The Iliad* (Deluxe)
Homer, *Odyssey Deluxe*
Homer, *Odyssey: Revised Prose Translation*
The Koran
Lemisch, *B. Franklin*
Deborah Lipstadt, *Denying The Holocaust*
Primo Levi, *If Not Now, When?*
Machiavelli, *The Prince*
Bill Manley, *The Penguin Historical Atlas of
Ancient Egypt*

Karl Marx, *The Communist Manifesto*
Colin McEvedy, *The New Penguin Atlas of
Ancient History*
Colin McEvedy, *The New Penguin Atlas of
Medieval History*
John Stuart Mill, *On Liberty*
Jean-Baptiste Molière, *Tartuffe and
Other Plays*
Charles-Louis Montesquieu, *Persian
Letters*
Sir Thomas More, *Utopia and Other
Essential Writings*
Robert Morkot, *The Penguin Historical
Atlas of Ancient Greece*
Sherwin Nuland, *Leonardo Da Vinci*
George Orwell, *1984*
George Orwell, *Animal Farm*
Plato, *Great Dialogues of Plato*
Plato, *The Last Days of Socrates*
Plato, *The Republic*
Plutarch, *Fall of the Roman Republic*
Marco Polo, *The Travels*
Procopius, *The Secret History*
Jean-Jacques Rousseau, *The Social
Contract*
Sallust, *The Jugurthine Wars, The
Conspiracy of Cataline*
Chris Searre, *The Penguin Historical Atlas
of Ancient Rome*
Desmond Seward, *The Hundred Years War*
William Shakespeare, *Four Great
Comedies: The Taming of the Shrew, A
Midsummer's Night Dream, Twelfth
Night, The Tempest*
William Shakespeare, *Four Histories:
Richard II, Henry IV: Part I, Henry IV:
Part II, Henry V*
William Shakespeare, *Four Great Tragedies:
Hamlet, Macbeth, King Lear, Othello*
William Shakespeare, *Hamlet*
William Shakespeare, *King Lear*
William Shakespeare, *Macbeth*
William Shakespeare, *The Merchant of
Venice* (Pelican Series)
William Shakespeare, *The Merchant of
Venice* (Signet Classics)
William Shakespeare, *Othello*
William Shakespeare, *The Taming of
the Shrew*
William Shakespeare, *The Tempest*
William Shakespeare, *Twelfth Night*
Mary Shelley, *Frankenstein*
Aleksandr Solzhenitsyn, *One Day in the
Life of Ivan Denisovich*
Sophocles, *The Three Theban Plays*

St. Augustine, *The Confessions of St. Augustine*

Robert Louis Stevenson, *The Strange Case of Dr. Jekyll and Mr. Hyde*

Suetonius, *The Twelve Caesars*

Jonathan Swift, *Gulliver's Travels*

Tacitus, *The Histories*

Various, *The Penguin Book of Historical Speeches*

Voltaire, *Candide, Zadig and Selected Stories*

Carl von Clausewitz, *On War*

von Goethe, *Faust, Part 1*

von Goethe, *Faust, Part 2*

Edith Wharton, *Ethan Frome*

Willet, *The Signet World Atlas*

Gary Wills, *Saint Augustine* (Penguin Lives Series)

Virginia Woolf, *Jacob's Room*

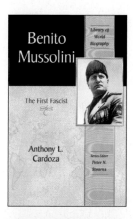

Longman Library of World Biography Series

Each interpretive biography in the new Library of World Biography series focuses on a figure whose actions and ideas significantly influenced the course of world history. Pocket-sized and brief, each book relates the life of its subject to the broader themes and developments of the time. Series titles include:

Ahmad al-Mansur: Islamic Visionary by Richard Smith, Ferrum College

Alexander the Great: Legacy of a Conqueror by Winthrop Lindsay Adams, University of Utah

Benito Mussolini: The First Fascist by Anthony L. Cardoza, Loyola University

Fukuzawa Yukichi: From Samurai to Capitalist by Helen M. Hopper, University of Pittsburgh

Ignatius of Loyola: Founder of the Jesuits by John Patrick Donnelly, Marquette University

Jacques Coeur: Entrepreneur and King's Bursar by Kathryn L. Reyerson, University of Minnesota

Kato Shidzue: A Japanese Feminist by Helen M. Hopper, University of Pittsburgh

Simon Bolivar: Liberation and Disappointment by David Bushnell, University of Florida

Vasco da Gama: Renaissance Crusader by Glenn J. Ames, University of Toledo

Zheng He: China and the Oceans in the Early Ming, 1405–1433 by Edward Dreyer, University of Miami

Acknowledgments

In writing this book we have benefited from the guidance of many members of the superb editorial staff at Longman. Our first acquisitions editor, Bruce Borland, encouraged us to write a book emphasizing the theme of cultural encounters, while Jay O'Callaghan, Erika Gutierrez, and Janet Lanphier helped us refine that theme as the book progressed. Dawn Groundwater, our senior development editor, gave us valuable line-by-line criticisms of all our chapters and helped us keep our audience in mind as we revised them. Priscilla McGeehon, publisher for the social sciences, facilitated the progress of the project at a number of crucial junctures. Heather Johnson superintended the copyediting and proofreading with skill and efficiency, while Jullie Chung helped us locate the most appropriate illustrations. Sue Westmoreland, the executive marketing manager for history, offered many creative ideas for promoting the book.

The authors wish to thank the following friends and colleagues for their assistance: Joseph Alehermes, Kenneth Alder, Karl Appuhn, Sharon Arnoult, Nicholas Baker, Paul-Alain Beaulieu, Paula Baskovits, Kamilia Bergen, Timothy Breen, Peter Brown, Peter Carroll, Patricia Crone, Tracey Cullen, Arthur Eckstein, Susanna Elm, Benjamin Frommer, Cynthia Gladstone, Dena Goodman, Matthias Henze, Stanley Hilton, Kenneth Holum, Mark Jurdjevic, Werner Kelber, Cathleen Keller, Anne Kilmer, Jacob Lassner, Robert Lerner, Nancy Levack, Richard Lim, David Lindenfeld, Sarah Maza, Laura McGough, Roderick McIntosh, Susan K. McIntosh, Glenn Markoe, William Monter, Randy Nichols, Scott Noegel, Monique O'Connell, Carl Petry, Michael Rogers, Karl Roider, Sarah Ross, Michele Salzman, Paula Sanders, Regina Schwartz, Ethan Shagan, Julia M. H. Smith, and James Sidbury.

We would also like to thank the many historians who gave generously of their time to review our manuscript at various stages of development. Their comments and suggestions have helped to improve the book. Thank you:

Joel D. Benson, *Northwest Missouri State University*

Marjorie K. Berman, *Red Rocks Community College*

Eric Bobo, *Hinds Community College*

Gregory S. Brown, *University of Nevada, Las Vegas*

Elspeth Carruthers, *University of Illinois-Chicago*

Jill Fehleison, *Quinnipiac University*

Rachel B. Goldman, *Rutgers University*

Ronald J. Granieri, *University of Pennsylvania*

Ann R. Higginbotham, *Eastern Connecticut State University*

Russell Jacobsen, *Crown College*

Gerritdina Justitz, *North Dakota State University*

Joy Kammerling, *Eastern Illinois University*

Shelly Lemons, *St. Louis Community College-Meramec*

Scott Lingenfelter, *College of DuPage*

Mark S. Malaszczyk, *Saint John's University*

Steven G. Marks, *Clemson University*

Ruth McClelland-Nugent, *Southern Illinois University*

Martin R. Menke, *Rivier College*

Sheila H. Moore, *Hinds Community College*

John E. Moser, *Ashland University*

Ronnie Peacock, *Community College of Aurora*

Sandra Pryor, *Old Dominion University*

Thomas Sayer, *Concordia University*

James M. Scarry, *Cleveland State University*

Constantina Scourtis Gaddis, *Onondaga Community College*

Ruth Suyama, *L.A. Mission College*

Janet A. Thompson, *Tallahassee Community College*

Nicholas Waddy, *Alfred State College*

Janet M.C. Walmsley, *George Mason University*

Daniel J. Walther, *Wartburg College*

Amy Woodson-Boulton, *Loyola Marymount University*

Amanda Wunder, *University of New Hampshire*

BRIAN LEVACK
EDWARD MUIR
MICHAEL MAAS
MEREDITH VELDMAN

Meet the Authors

Brian Levack grew up in a family of teachers in the New York metropolitan area. From his father, a professor of French history, he acquired a love for studying the past, and he knew from an early age that he too would become a historian. He received his B.A. from Fordham University in 1965 and his Ph.D. from Yale in 1970. In graduate school he became fascinated by the history of the law and the interaction between law and politics, interests that he has maintained throughout his career. In 1969 he joined the History Department of the University of Texas at Austin, where he is now the John Green Regents Professor in History. The winner of several teaching awards, Levack teaches a wide variety of courses on British and European history, legal history, and the history of witchcraft. For eight years he served as the chair of his department, a rewarding but challenging assignment that made it difficult for him to devote as much time as he wished to his teaching and scholarship. His books include *The Civil Lawyers in England, 1603–1641: A Political Study* (1973), *The Formation of the British State: England, Scotland and the Union, 1603–1707* (1987), and *The Witch-Hunt in Early Modern Europe* (1987 and 1995), which has been translated into eight languages.

His study of the development of beliefs about witchcraft in Europe over the course of many centuries gave him the idea of writing a textbook on Western civilization that would illustrate a broader set of encounters between different cultures, societies, and ideologies. While writing the book, Levack and his two sons built a house on property that he and his wife, Nancy, own in the Texas hill country. He found that the two projects presented similar challenges: It was easy to draw up the design, but far more difficult to execute it. When not teaching, writing, or doing carpentry work, Levack runs along the jogging trails of Austin, and he has recently discovered the pleasures of scuba diving.

Edward Muir grew up in the foothills of the Wasatch Mountains in Utah, close to the Emigration Trail along which wagon trains of Mormon pioneers and California-bound settlers made their way westward. As a child he loved to explore the broken-down wagons and abandoned household goods left at the side of the trail and from that acquired a fascination with the past. Besides the material remains of the past, he grew up with stories of his Mormon pioneer ancestors and an appreciation for how the past continued to influence the present. During the turbulent 1960s, he became interested in Renaissance Italy as a period and a place that had been formative for Western civilization. His biggest challenge is finding the time to explore yet another new corner of Italy and its restaurants.

Muir received his Ph.D. from Rutgers University, where he specialized in the Italian Renaissance and did archival research in Venice and Florence, Italy. He is now the Clarence L. Ver Steeg Professor in the Arts and Sciences at Northwestern University and former chair of the History Department. At Northwestern he has won several teaching awards. His books include *Civic Ritual in Renaissance Venice* (Princeton, 1981); *Mad Blood Stirring: Vendetta in Renaissance Italy* (Johns Hopkins, 1993 and 1998); and *Ritual in Early Modern Europe* (Cambridge, 1997).

Some years ago Muir began to experiment with the use of historical trials in teaching and discovered that students loved them. From that experience he decided to write this textbook, which employs trials as a central feature. He lives beside Lake Michigan in Evanston, Illinois. His twin passions are skiing in the Rocky Mountains and rooting for the Chicago Cubs, who manage every summer to demonstrate that winning isn't everything.

Michael Maas was born in the Ohio River Valley, in a community that had been a frontier outpost during the late eighteenth century. He grew up reading the stories of the early settlers and their struggles with the native peoples, and seeing in the urban fabric how the city had subsequently developed into a prosperous coal and steel town with immigrants from all over the world. As a boy he developed a lifetime interest in the archaeology and history of the ancient Mediterranean world and began to study Latin. At Cornell University he combined his interests in cultural history and the Classical world by majoring in Classics and Anthropology. A semester in Rome clinched his commitment to these fields—and to Italian cooking. Mass went on to get his Ph.D. in the Graduate Program in Ancient History and Mediterranean Archaeology at University of California at Berkeley.

He has traveled widely in the Mediterranean and the Middle East and participated in several archaeological excavations, including an underwater dig in Greece. Since 1985 he has taught ancient history at Rice University in Houston, Texas, where he founded and directs the interdisciplinary B.A. Program in Ancient Mediterranean Civilizations. He has won several teaching awards.

Maas's special area of research is Late Antiquity, the period of transition from the Classical to the Medieval worlds, which saw the collapse of the Roman Empire in western Europe and the development of the Byzantine state in the east. During his last sabbatical, he was a member of the Institute for Advanced Study in Princeton, New Jersey, where he worked on his current book, *The Conqueror's Gift: Ethnography, Identity, and Imperial Power at the End of Antiquity* (forthcoming). His other books include *John Lydus and the Roman Past: Antiquarianism and Politics in the Age of Justinian* (1992); *Readings in Late Antiquity: A Sourcebook* (2000); and *Exegesis and Empire in the Early Byzantine Mediterranean* (2003).

Maas has always been interested in interdisciplinary teaching and the encounters among different cultures. He sees *The West: Encounters & Transformations* as an opportunity to explain how the modern civilization that we call "the West" had its origins in the diverse interactions among many peoples of antiquity.

Meredith Veldman grew up in the western suburbs of Chicago in a close-knit, closed-in Dutch Calvinist community. In this immigrant society, history mattered: the "Reformed tradition" structured not only religious beliefs but also social identity and political practice. This influence certainly played some role in shaping Veldman's early fascination with history. But probably just as important were the countless World War II reenactment games she played with her five older brothers. Whatever the cause, Veldman majored in history at Calvin College in Grand Rapids, Michigan, and then earned a Ph.D. in modern European history, with a concentration in nineteenth- and twentieth-century Britain, from Northwestern University in 1988.

As Associate Professor of History at Louisiana State University, Veldman teaches courses in nineteenth- and twentieth-century British history and twentieth-century Europe, as well as the second half of "Western Civ." In her many semesters in the Western Civ. classroom, Veldman tried a number of different textbooks but found herself increasingly dissatisfied. She wanted a text that would convey to beginning students at least some of the complexities and ambiguities of historical interpretation, introduce them to the exciting work being done now in cultural history, and, most important, tell a good story. The search for this textbook led her to accept the offer made by Levack, Maas, and Muir to join them in writing *The West: Encounters & Transformations*.

The author of *Fantasy, the Bomb, and the Greening of Britain: Romantic Protest, 1945–1980* (1994), Veldman is also the wife of a Methodist minister and the mother of two young sons. They reside in Baton Rouge, Louisiana, where Veldman finds coping with the steamy climate a constant challenge. She and her family recently returned from Manchester, England, where they lived for three years and astonished the natives by their enthusiastic appreciation of English weather.

THE WEST

What Is the West?

M ANY OF THE PEOPLE WHO INFLUENCE PUBLIC OPINION—POLITICIANS, teachers, clergy, journalists, and television commentators—frequently refer to "Western values," "the West," and "Western civilization." They often use these terms as if they do not require explanation. But what *do* these terms mean? The West has always been an arena within which different cultures, religions, values, and philosophies have interacted, and any definition of the West will inevitably arouse controversy.

The most basic definition of the West is of a place. Western civilization is now typically thought to comprise the regions of Europe, the Americas, Australia, and New Zealand. However, this is a contemporary definition of the West. The inclusion of these places in the West is the result of a long history of European expansion through colonization. In addition to being a place, Western civilization also encompasses a cultural history—a tradition stretching back thousands of years to the ancient world. Over this long period the civilization we now identify as Western gradually took shape. The many characteristics that identify any civilization emerged over this time: forms of government, economic systems, and methods of scientific inquiry, as well as religions, languages, literature, and art.

Throughout the development of Western civilization, the ways in which people identified themselves changed as well. People in the ancient world had no such idea of the common identity of the West, only of being subjects of an empire. But with the spread of Christianity and Islam between the first and seventh centuries, the notion of a distinct civilization in these "Western" lands subtly changed. People came to identify themselves less as subjects of a particular empire and more as members of a community of faith—whether that community comprised followers of Christianity, Judaism, or Islam. These communities of faith drew lines of inclusion and exclusion that still exist today. Starting about 1,600 years ago, Christian monarchs began to obliterate polytheism (the worship of many gods) and marginalize Jews. From a thousand to 500 years ago, Christian authorities strove to expel Muslims from Europe. Europeans developed definitions of the West that did not include Islamic communities, even though Muslims continued to live in Europe and Europeans traded and interacted with the Muslim world. The Islamic countries themselves erected their

The Temple of Hera at Paestum, Italy: Greek colonists in Italy built this temple in the sixth century B.C.E. Greek ideas and artistic styles spread throughout the ancient world both from Greek colonists, such as those at Paestum, and from other peoples who imitated the Greeks.

3

own barriers, isolating themselves from the Christian West, even as they continued to look back to the common cultural origins in the ancient world that they shared with Jews and Christians. During the Renaissance in the fifteenth century, these ancient cultural origins became an alternative to religious affiliation for thinking about the identity of the West. From this Renaissance historical perspective Jews, Christians, and Muslims descended from the cultures of the ancient Hebrews, Greeks, and Romans. Despite all their differences, the followers of these religions shared a history. In fact, in the late Renaissance a number of thinkers imagined the possibility of rediscovering the single universal religion that they thought must have once been practiced in the ancient world. If they could just recapture that religion they could restore the unity they imagined had once prevailed in the West.

The definition of the West has also changed as a result of European colonialism, which began about 500 years ago. When European powers assembled large overseas empires, they introduced Western languages, religions, technology, and culture to many distant places in the world, making Western identity a transportable concept. In some of these colonized areas—such as North America, Argentina, Australia, and New Zealand—the European newcomers so outnumbered the indigenous people that these regions became as much a part of the West as Britain, France, and Spain. In other European colonies, especially in European trading outposts on the Asian continent, Western culture failed to exercise a widespread influence.

As a result of colonialism Western culture sometimes merged with other cultures, and in the process both were changed. Brazil, a South American country inhabited by large numbers of indigenous peoples, the descendants of African slaves, and European settlers, epitomizes the complexity of what defines the West. In Brazil, almost everyone speaks a Western language (Portuguese), practices a Western religion (Christianity), and participates in Western political and economic institutions (democracy and capitalism). Yet in Brazil all of these features of Western civilization have become part of a distinctive culture, in which indigenous, African, and European elements have been blended. During Carnival, for example, Brazilians dressed in indigenous costumes dance in African rhythms to the accompaniment of music played on European instruments.

For many people today, the most important definition of the West involves adherence to a certain set of values, the "Western" values. Values are the moral and philosophical principles that are held in esteem by a particular culture. The values typically identified as Western today include universal human rights, toleration of religious diversity,

■ **A Satellite View of Europe**

What is the West? Western civilization has undergone numerous transformations throughout history, but it has always included Europe.

equality before the law, democracy, and freedom of inquiry and expression. However, these values have not always been part of Western civilization. They came to be fully appreciated only very recently as the consequence of a long and bloody history. In fact, there is nothing inevitable about these values, and Western history at various stages exhibited quite different ones. For example, the rulers of ancient Rome extended the privileges of citizenship, the right to own property, and the ability to participate in trade to a select few inhabitants of their empire—thus only the privileged enjoyed the benefits of equality before the law. Most medieval Christians were completely convinced that their greatest contribution to society would be to make war against Muslims and heretics and to curtail as much as possible the actions of Jews. Equality was seldom valued in Western societies until quite recently. Western Christians enslaved Africans until about a century and a half ago. Some Muslims in Africa still enslave other Africans. Well into the twentieth century, women were excluded from voting and equal access to jobs. In Switzerland, in fact, women did not get the vote until 1971 and in one canton not until 1990. Also in the twentieth century, Nazi Germany and the Soviet Union demonstrated that history could have turned out very differently in the West. These totalitarian regimes in Europe accepted none of the Western values so prized today and terrorized their own populations and millions of others beyond their borders through massive abuses of human rights. The history of the West is riddled with examples of leaders who stifled free inquiry and who censored authors and journalists. These examples testify to the fact that the values of Western societies have always been contended, disputed, and fought over. In other words, they have a history. This text highlights and examines that history, demonstrating how hard values were to formulate in the first place and how difficult they have been to preserve.

The Shifting Borders of the West

The geographical setting of the West also has a history. This textbook begins about 10,000 years ago in the Mesopotamian region of southwestern Asia—what is now Iraq. The West begins with the domestication of animals, the cultivation of the first crops, and the establishment of long-distance trading networks in the Tigris, Euphrates, and Nile River valleys. Cities, kingdoms, and empires in those valleys gave birth to the first civilizations. By about 500 B.C.E., the civilizations that are the cultural ancestors of the modern West had spread from southwestern Asia and North Africa to include the entire Mediterranean basin—areas influenced by Egyptian, Hebrew, Greek, and Roman thought, art, law, and religion. By the first century C.E. the Roman Empire drew the map of what historians consider the heartland of the West: most of western and southern Europe, the coastlands of the Mediterranean Sea, and the Middle East.

The West is now usually thought to include Europe and the Americas. However, the borders of the West have in recent decades come to be less about geography than culture and identity. When Japan, an Asian country, accepted some Western values such as human rights and democracy after World War II, did it become part of the West? Most Japanese might not think so, but the spread of these "Western" values in a traditional Asian country that had never been colonized by a European power complicates the idea of what is the West. Or consider the Republic of South Africa, which until 1994 was ruled by the white minority, people descended from European immigrants. The oppressive regime violated human rights, rejected full legal equality for all citizens, and jailed or murdered those who questioned

the government. Only when that government was replaced through democratic elections and a black man became president did South Africa fully embrace what the rest of the West would consider Western values. To what degree was South Africa part of the West before and after these developments?

Russia long saw itself as a Christian country with a tradition of cultural, economic, and political ties with the rest of Europe. The Russians have intermittently identified with their Western neighbors, but their neighbors were not always sure about the Russians. After the Mongol invasions of the thirteenth and fourteenth centuries, much of Russia was isolated from the rest of the West; during the Cold War from 1949 to 1989, Russian communism and the Western democracies were polarized. When was Russia "Western" and when not?

Thus, when we talk about where the West is, we are almost always talking about the Mediterranean basin and much of Europe (and later, the Americas). But we will also show that countries that border "the West," and even countries far from it, might be considered Western in many aspects as well.

Asking the Right Questions

So how can we make sense of the West as a place and an identity, the shifting borders of the West, and Western civilization in general? In short, what has Western civilization been over the course of its long history—and what is it today?

Answering these questions is the challenge this book poses. There are no simple answers to any of these questions, but there is a method for finding answers. The method is straightforward. Always ask the *what, when, where, who, how,* and *why* questions of the text.

THE *WHAT* QUESTION

What is Western civilization? The answer to this question will vary

■ **The Astrolabe**
The mariner's astrolabe was a navigational device intended for use primarily at sea. The astrolabe originated in the Islamic world and was adopted by Europeans in the twelfth century—a cultural encounter that enabled Europeans to embark on long ocean voyages around the world.

according to time and place. In fact, for much of the early history covered in this book, Western civilization as we know it today did not exist as a single cultural entity. Rather, a number of distinctive civilizations were taking shape in the Middle East, northern Africa, and Europe, each of which contributed to what later became Western civilization. But throughout time the idea of Western civilization slowly began to form. Thus the understanding of Western civilization will change from chapter to chapter. The most extensive change in the place of the West was through the colonial expansion of the European nations between the fifteenth and twentieth centuries. Perhaps the most significant cultural change in the West came with acceptance of the values of scientific inquiry for solving human and philosophical problems, an approach that did not exist before the seventeenth century but became one of the distinguishing characteristics of Western civilization.

THE WHEN QUESTION

When did the defining characteristics of Western civilization first emerge, and for how long did they prevail? To make it possible to keep track of what happened when, each chapter includes a chronology of key events and developments. Dates have no meaning by themselves, but the connections *between* them can be very revealing. For example, dates show that the agricultural revolution that permitted the birth of the first civilizations unfolded over a span of about 10,000 years—which is more time than was taken by all the other events and developments covered in this textbook. Wars of religion plagued Europe for nearly 200 years before Enlightenment thinkers articulated the ideals of religious toleration. The American Civil War—the war to preserve the union, as President Abraham Lincoln termed it— took place at exactly the same time as other wars were being fought to achieve national unity in Germany and Italy. In

■ **Map 1   Core Lands of the West**
The geographical borders of the West have changed substantially throughout history.

other words, by paying attention to other contemporaneous wars for national unity the American experience seems less peculiarly an American event.

By learning when things happened, one can identify the major causes and consequences of events and thus see the transformations of Western civilization. For instance, the ability to produce a surplus of food through agriculture and the domestication of animals was a prerequisite for the emergence of civilizations. The violent collapse of religious unity after the Protestant Reformation in the sixteenth century led some Europeans to propose the separation of church and state two centuries later. And during the nineteenth century many Western states—in response to the enormous diversity among their own peoples—became preoccupied with maintaining or establishing national unity.

THE *WHERE* QUESTION

Where has Western civilization been located? Geography, of course, does not change very rapidly, but the idea of where the West is does. The location of the West is not so much a matter of changing borders but of how people identify themselves. The key to understanding the shifting borders of the West is to study how the peoples within the West thought of themselves. These groups include Muslims and the peoples of eastern Europe (such as the Soviet Union during the Cold War), which some people have wanted to exclude from the West. In addition, the chapters trace the relationships between the West (as it was constituted in different periods) and other, more distant civilizations with which it interacted. Those civilizations include not only those of East Asia and South Asia but also the indigenous peoples of sub-Saharan Africa, the Americas, and the Pacific islands.

THE *WHO* QUESTION

Who were the people responsible for making Western civilization? Sometimes they were anonymous, such as the unknown geniuses who invented the mathematical systems of ancient Mesopotamia. At other times the makers of the West were famous—saints such as Joan of Arc, creative thinkers such as Galileo Galilei, or generals such as Napoleon. But history is not made only by great and famous people. Humble people, such as the many millions who migrated from Europe to North America or the unfortunate millions who suffered and died in the trenches of World War I, can also influence the course of events.

Perhaps most often this book encounters people who were less the shapers of their own destinies than the subjects of forces that conditioned the kinds of choices they could make, often with unanticipated results. When during the eleventh century farmers throughout Europe began to employ a new kind of plow to till their fields, they were merely trying to do their work more efficiently. They certainly did not recognize that the increase in food they produced would stimulate the enormous population growth that made possible the medieval civilization of thriving cities and magnificent cathedrals. Answering the who question requires an evaluation of how much individuals and groups of people were in control of events and how much events controlled them.

THE *HOW* QUESTION

How did Western civilization develop? This is a question about processes—about how things change or stay the same over time. This book identifies these processes in several ways. First, the theme of encounters and transformations has been woven throughout the story. What is meant by encounters? When the Spanish *conquistadores* arrived in the Americas some 500 years ago, they came into contact with the cultures of the Caribs, the Aztecs, the Incas, and other peoples who had lived in the Americas for thousands of years. As the Spanish fought, traded with, and intermarried with the natives, each culture changed. The Spanish, for their part, borrowed from the Americas new plants for cultivation and responded to what they considered serious threats to their worldview. Many native Americans, in turn, adopted European religious practices and learned to speak European languages. At the same time, they were decimated by European diseases to which they had never been exposed. They also witnessed the destruction of their own civilizations and governments at the hands of the colonial powers. Through centuries of interaction and mutual influence, both sides became something other than what they had been.

The European encounter with the Americas is an obvious example of what was, in fact, a continuous process of encounters with other cultures. These encounters often occurred between peoples from different civilizations, such as the struggles between Greeks and Persians in the ancient world or between Europeans and Chinese in the nineteenth century. Other encounters took place among people living in the same civilization. These include interactions between lords and peasants, men and women, Christians and Jews, Catholics and Protestants, factory owners and workers, and capitalists and communists. Western civilization developed and changed through a series of external and internal encounters.

Also, features in the chapters formulate answers to the question of how Western civilization developed. For example, each chapter contains an essay titled "Justice in History." These essays discuss a trial or some other episode involving questions of justice. Some "Justice in History" essays illustrate how Western civilization was forged in struggles over conflicting values, such as the discussion of the trial of Galileo, which examines the conflict between religious and scientific concepts of truth. Others show how

■ **Cortés Meets Montezuma**

As the Spanish fought, traded, and intermarried with the native peoples of the Americas during the fifteenth and sixteenth centuries, each culture changed.

efforts to resolve internal cultural, political, and religious tensions helped shape Western ideas about justice, such as the essay on the auto-da-fé, which illustrates how authorities attempted to enforce religious conformity. At the end of each "Justice in History" feature are several questions tying that essay to the theme of the chapter.

THE WHY QUESTION

Why did things happen in the way they did in history? This is the hardest question of all, one that engenders the most debate among historians. To take one persistent example, why did Hitler initiate a plan to exterminate the Jews of Europe? Can it be explained by something that happened to him in his childhood? Was he full of self-loathing that he projected onto the Jews? Was it a way of creating an enemy so that he could better unify Germany? Did he really believe that the Jews were the cause of all of Germany's problems? Did he merely act on the deeply seated anti-Semitic tendencies of the German people? Historians still debate the answers to these questions. These questions raise issues about human motivation and the role of human agency in histor-

ical events. Can historians ever really know what motivated a particular individual in the past, especially when it is so notoriously difficult to understand what motivates other people in the present? Can any individual determine the course of history? The *what, when, where, who,* and *how* questions are much easier to answer, but the *why* question, of course, is the most interesting one, the one that cries out for an answer.

This book does not always offer definitive answers to the *why* question, but it attempts to lay out the most likely possibilities. For example, historians do not really know what disease caused the Black Death in the fourteenth century, which killed about one-third of the population in a matter of months. But they can answer many questions about the consequences of that great catastrophe. Why were there so many new universities in the fourteenth and fifteenth centuries? It was because so many priests had died in the Black Death, creating a huge demand for replacements. The answers to the *why* questions are not always obvious, but they are always intriguing, and finding them is the joy of studying history.

The Beginnings of Civilization, 10,000–2000 B.C.E.

I N 1991 HIKERS TOILING ACROSS A GLACIER IN THE ALPS BETWEEN AUSTRIA AND Italy made a startling discovery: a man's body stuck in the ice. They alerted the police, who soon turned the corpse over to archaeologists. The scientists determined that the middle-aged man had frozen to death about 5,300 years ago. Ötzi the Ice Man (his name comes from the Ötztal Valley where he perished) quickly became an international celebrity as the world's oldest freeze-dried human.

The scientists who examined Ötzi believe that he was a shepherd herding flocks of sheep and goats to mountain pastures when he died. A few grains of wheat on his clothing suggested that he lived in a farming community. Copper dust in his hair hinted that Ötzi may also have been a metalworker, perhaps looking for ores during his journey. An arrowhead lodged in his back indicated a violent cause of death, but the exact circumstances remain mysterious.

Ötzi's gear was state-of-the-art for his time. His possessions showed deep knowledge of the natural world. He wore leather boots insulated with dense grasses chosen for protection against the cold. The pouch around his waist contained stone tools and fire-lighting equipment. The wood selected for his bow offered special strength and flexibility. In his light wooden backpack Ötzi carried containers to hold burning embers, as well as dried meat and nutritious seeds to eat on the trail. The arrows in his quiver featured a natural adhesive that tightly bound bone and wooden points to the shafts. The most noteworthy find among Ötzi's possessions was his axe. Its handle was made of wood but its head was copper—a remarkable innovation at a time when most tools were made of stone. Ötzi was ready for almost anything—except the person who shot him in the back.

Chapter Outline

- Culture, Agriculture, and Civilization

- The Birth of Civilization in Southwest Asia

- The Emergence of Egyptian Civilization

- The Transformation of Europe

Wall Plaque: Sumerian King Ur-Nanshe of the city of Lagash in Mesopotamia carries a basket of bricks that will be used to build a temple. Cuneiform writing identifies the king and his project. In the lower right corner he drinks a beer to celebrate the completion of the temple.

■ **Ötzi the Ice Man**
This artist's recreation shows Ötzi in his waterproof poncho carrying his state-of-the-art tools.

Ötzi lived at a transitional moment, at the very end of what archaeologists call the Neolithic Age, or "New Stone Age," when people made refinements in tool-making techniques over those of previous ages. For example, Neolithic artisans carved remarkably delicate arrowheads and blades that could be used for a variety of tasks, from hunting to sewing. The Neolithic Age was a long period of revolutionary change lasting from about 10,000 to about 3000 B.C.E. that altered human existence on Earth forever. Even the most advanced technological developments of the twentieth century did not reshape human life as profoundly as did those of the Neolithic era.

This chapter traces humanity's first steps toward the civilizations that developed in Southwest Asia, Egypt, and Europe—regions that made crucial contributions to the development of Western civilization. First we will consider the most fundamental encounter of all—the relationship between humans and the natural world. Many thousands of years of human interaction with nature led to food production through agriculture and the domestication of ani-

mals. This revolutionary achievement let humans develop new, settled forms of communities: first villages, then cities, and eventually kingdoms and empires. Civilizations grew from the foundations of agriculture and the domestication of animals. The growth of civilization also depended on constant interaction among communities that lived far apart. Once people were settled in a region, they began trading for commodities that were not available in their homelands. As trade routes extended over long distances and interactions among diverse peoples proliferated, ideas and technology spread.

In this chapter we will address several major questions about humanity's first civilizations:

■ What is the link between the food-producing revolution of the Neolithic era and the emergence of civilizations?

■ What transformed the earliest settled communities in Southwest Asia into the first cities, kingdoms, and empires in history?

■ How did civilization take shape along the Nile River in Egypt?

■ How and why did food production and the use of metals transform the lives of the men and women who populated Europe in the Neolithic Age?

Culture, Agriculture, and Civilization

Anthropologists use the term culture° to describe all the different ways that humans collectively adjust to their environment and organize and transmit their experiences and knowledge to future generations. We can understand a people's culture as a web of interconnected meanings that enable them to understand themselves and their place in the world. Each culture is distinctive; thus we use labels—"Greek culture" or "American culture." Yet all cultures constantly borrow from their neighbors and change over time.

People often use *culture* and *civilization* interchangeably, yet in the history of human development, civilization has a specific definition. Archaeologists define civilization° as a society differentiated by levels of wealth and occupation in which people lived in cities. With cities, human populations achieved the critical mass necessary to develop specialized occupations, as well as a level of economic production high enough to sustain complex religious and cultural practices. As villages evolved into cities, their social organization grew more complicated. The labor of most people supported a small group of political and religious leaders. A city's leaders controlled the mechanisms of not only government and

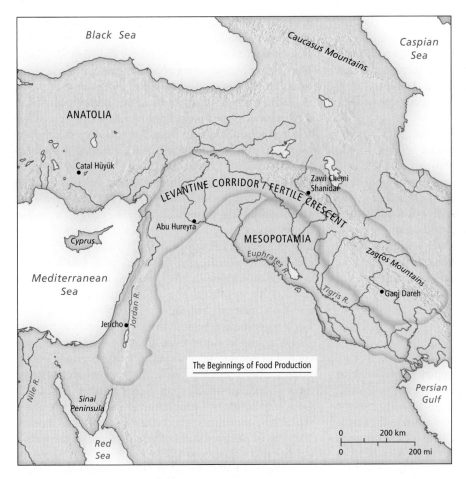

■ Map 1.1 The Beginnings of Food Production

This map shows early farming sites discovered by archaeologists where the first known production of food occurred in ancient Southwest Asia.

warfare but also the distribution of food and wealth. They augmented their authority by building temples to the gods and participating in religious rituals that linked divinity with kingship. Thus, in early civilizations three kinds of power—economic, political, and religious—converged.

THE FOOD-PRODUCING REVOLUTION

Food production made civilization possible. For the first thousands of millennia of their existence, modern humans, known as *Homo sapiens sapiens*° ("most intelligent people"), did not produce food. Between 200,000 and 100,000 years ago, *Homo sapiens sapiens* first appeared in Africa and began to spread to other continents. Scientists refer to this stage of human history as the Paleolithic Age, or Old Stone Age, because people made tools by cracking rocks and using their sharp edges to cut and chop. *Homo sapiens sapiens'* use of tools demonstrated adaptation to new environments and practical needs. They scavenged for wild food and became shrewd observers of the natural environment. They followed migrating herds of animals, hunting with increasing efficiency as their weapons improved. They also created beautiful works of art by carving bone and painting on cave

walls. By 45,000 years ago, these humans had reached most of Earth's habitable regions, except for Australia, the islands of the South Pacific, and North and South America.

The end of the last Ice Age about 15,000 years ago ushered in an era of momentous change: the food-producing revolution. As Earth's climate became warmer, causing changes in vegetation, humans began to interact with the natural environment in new ways. The warmer climate allowed cereal grasses to spread quickly over large areas; hunter-gatherers learned to collect these wild grains and grind them up for food. Some groups of hunter-gatherers settled in semipermanent camps near rivers and wetlands, where wild grains grew. When people learned that the seeds of wild grasses could be transplanted and grown in new areas, the domestication of plants was under way.

At the same time that people discovered the benefits of planting seeds, they also began domesticating pigs, sheep, goats, and cattle, which eventually replaced wild game as the main source of meat. Domestication° occurs when humans manipulate the breeding of animals in order to serve their own purposes—for example, making wool (lacking on wild sheep), laying extra eggs (not done by undomesticated chickens), and producing extra milk (wild cows produce only enough milk for their offspring). The first signs of goat domestication occurred about 8900 B.C.E. in the Zagros Mountains in Southwest Asia. Pigs, which adapt very well to human settlements because they eat garbage, were first domesticated around 7000 B.C.E. By around 6500 B.C.E domesticated cattle, goats, and sheep had become widespread.

Farming and herding required hard work, but the payoff was enormous. Even simple agricultural methods could produce about fifty times more food than hunting and gathering. Thanks to the increased food supply, more newborns survived past infancy. Populations expanded, and so did human settlements. With the mastery of food production, human societies developed the mechanisms not only to feed themselves, but also to produce a surplus, which could then be traded for other resources. Such economic activity allowed for economic specialization and fostered the growth of social, political, and religious hierarchies.

THE FIRST FOOD-PRODUCING COMMUNITIES

In Southwest Asia, where sufficient annual rainfall enabled crops to grow without irrigation, people began cultivating food in three separate areas. Archaeologists have named the first area the Levantine Corridor° (also known as the Fertile Crescent°)—a twenty-five-mile-wide strip of land that runs from Jericho in the Jordan River valley of modern Israel to the Euphrates River valley in today's Iraq. The second region was the hilly land north of Mesopotamia at the base of the Zagros Mountains in the western part of modern Iran. The third was Anatolia, or what is now the central region of Turkey. In each of these three regions, archaeological evidence reveals how societies made the revolutionary shift to food production (see Map 1.1).

The small settlement of Abu Hureyra near the center of the Levantine Corridor illustrates how agriculture developed over a long period at a single site. Humans first settled here around 9500 B.C.E. They fed themselves primarily by hunting gazelles and gathering wild cereals. But sometime between 8000 and 7700 B.C.E., they began to plant and harvest a small number of grains. Eventually they discovered that crop rotation—planting different crops in a field each year—resulted in a much higher yield. By 7000 B.C.E. Abu Hureyra had grown into a farming community, covering nearly thirty acres that sustained a population of about 400. A few generations later, the inhabitants of Abu Hureyra began herding sheep and goats to supplement their meat supply. These domesticated animals became the community's primary source of meat when the gazelle herds were depleted about 6500 B.C.E.

Families in Abu Hureyra lived in small dwellings built of mud brick containing several rooms. Archaeological evidence shows that many women in the community developed arthritis in their knees, probably from crouching for hours on end as they ground grains. Thus historians assume that while men hunted and harvested, women performed the labor of grinding grains and preparing food. The division of labor along gender lines indicates a growing complexity of social relations within communities.

To the south of Abu Hureyra, at the southwestern end of the Levantine Corridor, the farming village of Jericho offers a second example of how the food-producing revolution led to greater social complexity. Jericho began to develop rapidly after 8500 B.C.E. Located at an old hunting-gathering site along a stream in the Jordan River valley near modern Jerusalem, Jericho expanded to encompass nearly ten acres after its inhabitants started cultivating crops, including wheat, barley, lentils, and peas. They soon learned that if they let a field lie fallow for a season, the soil would be richer and more productive the following year. Archaeological evidence shows how Jericho's growing wealth enabled the community to evolve. The inhabitants developed more elaborate political, religious, and economic structures. Fairly sophisticated engineering projects, such as the digging of a nine-foot-deep ditch around the village as a flood control device and the erection of a massive stone wall to protect against attackers, indicate the emergence of some form of political organization. Other findings hint at religious beliefs. Jericho's people buried their dead within the settlement, sometimes under the floors of their houses. They placed plastered skulls of their deceased on the walls, a practice that may suggest worship of the family's ancestors.

Archaeological evidence also reveals that long-distance commerce played a part in the lives of these villagers. They exchanged agricultural goods for turquoise from the Sinai Peninsula, shells from the Mediterranean and Red Seas, and most important of all, obsidian from Anatolia. This volcanic stone was the most important commodity in the Neolithic Age because it could be used for making sharp-edged tools such as arrowheads, spear points, and sickles for harvesting crops.

The second region of village settlement, the lands at the foot of the Zagros Mountains north of Mesopotamia, reveals a different sort of development pattern from that exhibited in the Levantine Corridor. Archaeologists have unearthed a hunter-gatherer camp at Sawi Chemi Shanidar, dating to about 9000 B.C.E. In this settlement, the domestication of animals long predated the development of agriculture. The settlers herded animals, but they did not cultivate crops for more than a thousand years.

The third region of early settled communities, Anatolia, followed patterns more like those of the Levantine Corridor. Around 8500 B.C.E. a few simple settlements appeared. The villagers raised pigs and traded obsidian for materials from far away, such as the highly prized blue lapis lazuli stones from modern northeastern Afghanistan. A thousand years later, about 7400 B.C.E., Anatolians began cultivating a variety of crops, including wheat and lentils. They started herding sheep at roughly the same time as the

Abu Hureyra villagers, and domesticated dogs for hunting, herding, and protection. Many new villages sprang up in this region during the next millennium. The farmers lived in rectangular houses. More than mere huts, these houses featured plastered walls, hearths, courtyards, and ovens for baking breads.

Sometime after 6000 B.C.E. Anatolian communities grew more complex, with the emergence of religious beliefs and social hierarchies. For example, the Anatolian town of Çatal Hüyük consisted of thirty-two acres of tightly packed houses that the townspeople rebuilt more than a dozen times as their population expanded. Çatal Hüyük controlled the obsidian trade from Anatolia to the Levantine Corridor. The wealth from this trade fostered the emergence of social differences. The townspeople buried some of their dead with jewelry and other riches, a practice that indicates distinctions between wealthy and poor members of the society.

The long-distance obsidian trade sped up the development of communities in the Levantine Corridor, the Zagros Mountains, and Anatolia. These trade networks of the Neolithic Age laid the foundation for commercial and cultural encounters that would shape the development of civilizations for the next 5,000 years.

The Birth of Civilization in Southwest Asia

By 6000 B.C.E., settled communities that depended on farming and herding had become the norm throughout Southwest Asia. With better and more plentiful food, such communities expanded steadily. Prosperity further stimulated commerce, and merchants from different regions began traveling regularly to one another's villages to trade. Mesopotamia, the dry floodplain bounded by the Tigris and Euphrates Rivers, became the meeting place of peoples and ideas from across an enormous geographical area. Over time, these Mesopotamian village communities began to resemble one another and a more uniform culture developed. The development of this more uniform culture set the stage for the emergence of civilization in Southwest Asia.

SUMER: A CONSTELLATION OF CITIES IN SOUTHERN MESOPOTAMIA

About 5300 B.C.E. the villages in Sumer, an ancient name for southern Mesopotamia, began a dynamic civilization that would flourish for 3,000 years. At the height of this civilization, Sumerians (who called themselves "the black-headed people" because of their characteristic dark hair)

CHRONOLOGY	
150,000 YEARS AGO	Modern humans first appear in Africa
45,000 YEARS AGO	Modern humans spread through Africa, Asia, and Europe
13,000 YEARS AGO	Ice Age ends
10,000 YEARS AGO	Food production begins in Southwest Asia
7000 B.C.E.	Agriculture begins its very slow spread though Europe
3200 B.C.E.	First known written documents in cuneiform appear
3000 B.C.E.	Old Kingdom in Egypt begins
2500 B.C.E.	Sumerian civilization controls the Mesopotamian floodplain
2040 B.C.E.	Middle Kingdom in Egypt begins
1900 B.C.E.	Assyria grows powerful through trade and conquest
1800 B.C.E.	Babylonian civilization emerges; Hammurabi's Law Code prepared

lived in thriving cities governed by leaders who controlled agricultural production, regulated long-distance trade, and presided over the worship of the gods.

Sumerian civilization was linked to water. Over centuries, the Sumerians learned to control the unpredictable waters of the Tigris and Euphrates Rivers. Sumerians first dug their own small channels to divert floodwaters from the two great rivers to irrigate their dry lands. Then they discovered that by combining the labor force of several villages, they could build and maintain irrigation channels on a large scale. The lands irrigated by river water provided rich yields of crops that fed Sumer's growing population. Villages blossomed into cities that became the foundation of Sumerian civilization.

By 2500 B.C.E., about twelve major cities in Sumer had emerged that controlled the Mesopotamian floodplain in an organized fashion. Some cities achieved impressive dimensions. Uruk, for example, covered about two square miles by 2500 B.C.E. and had a population estimated at between 10,000 and 50,000 people, including the peasants living in the countryside, many of whom labored to provide food for the urban populations as well as for themselves.

These cities served as the economic centers of southern Mesopotamia. Craft specialists such as potters, toolmakers,

THE CLASH BETWEEN CIVILIZATION AND NATURE: THE TAMING OF ENKIDU

·················

The Sumerians saw their civilization as tightly linked to nature, as this passage from the tale of Gilgamesh suggests. This excerpt tells how Enkidu, Gilgamesh's companion, first became civilized. Originally living like a wild animal, Enkidu prevents hunters from trapping game. But city officials send him a prostitute who tames him by having sex with him for a week and introducing him to cooked food, beer, and clothing. As a result of this epic sexual encounter, Enkidu loses his ability to talk to the animals. The episode teaches that civilization imposes control on natural forces, transforming them in the process. In the figure of the prostitute we see nature controlled and regulated by the city—a metaphor for the Sumerians' civilization.

In the wilderness the goddess Aruru created valiant
Enkidu...
He knew neither people nor settled living...
He ate grasses like gazelles,
And jostled at the watering hole with the animals...
Then Shamhat [the prostitute] saw him—a primitive,
A savage fellow from the depths of the wilderness!...
Shamhat unclutched her bosom, exposed her sex,
And Enkidu took in her voluptuousness.

She was not restrained, but took his energy...
For six days and seven nights Enkidu stayed aroused,
And had intercourse with the prostitute,
Until he was sated with her charms.
But when he turned his attention to the animals,
The gazelles saw Enkidu and darted off,
The wild animals distanced themselves from his body...
Enkidu knew nothing about eating bread for food,
[nor] of drinking beer he had not been taught to.
The prostitute spoke to Enkidu, saying:
"Eat the food, Enkidu, it is the way one lives.
Drink the beer, as it is the custom of our land."
Enkidu ate the food until he was sated,
He drank the beer—seven jugs!—and became expansive
and sang with joy!
He was elated and his face glowed.
He splashed his shaggy body with water,
And rubbed himself with oil and turned into a human.
He put on some clothing and became like a warrior.
He took up weapons and chased lions so shepherds could
rest at night.
With Enkidu as their guard, the herders could lie down.

Source: Excerpts from Kovacs, Maureen Gallery, translator, *The Epic of Gilgamesh,* with an Introduction and Notes. Copyright © 1985, 1989 by the Board of Trustees of the Leland Stanford Junior University. All rights reserved. Used with the permission of Stanford University Press, www.sup.org.

---

and weavers gathered in these urban settings to purchase food, swap information, and sell their goods. By providing markets for outlying towns, the cities spun a web of economic interdependence. Long-distance trade, made easier by the introduction of wheeled carts drawn by oxen, enabled merchants to bring timber, ores, building stone, and luxury items unavailable in Mesopotamia from Anatolia, the Levantine Corridor, Afghanistan, and Iran. With the introduction of the potter's wheel, Sumerian artisans could mass-produce containers for trade and storage of grain and other commodities.

Within the cities, a small elite, headed by a king, controlled all economic resources. Centralized authorities directed the necessary labor for irrigation and water control, maintained warehouses for storing surplus grains, and distributed food to workers who labored on building projects for the king. The resources of Sumerian cities flowed in one direction: toward the support of the king and of the ziggurat, the monumental temple where everyone gathered to worship the city's main gods. Archaeological excavations reveal that the elite—priests, aristocrats, important civil administrators, and wealthy merchants—lived in luxurious houses near the temples, while everyone else crowded into small mud-brick houses with few comforts.

Control over the economic resources of their cities enabled kings to supply armies and lead them into battle. Sumerian kings frequently waged war against one another in an effort to increase their territory and power. This rivalry prevented Sumerian cities from uniting politically, but the kings maintained diplomatic relations with one another as well as with rulers throughout Southwest Asia and Egypt, primarily to protect their trading networks. Safe trade links helped tie the Sumerian cities together and fostered a common Sumerian culture.

Through trade and warfare and from the many diplomats, soldiers, travelers, and slaves who passed through Mesopotamia's cities, the Sumerians knew much about the natural resources, economic organization, and customs that characterized the foreign peoples around them. The world known to them extended from India in the east to the Caucasus Mountains in the north; to Egypt and Ethiopia in the south; and to the Mediterranean Sea in the west. Sumerians strongly believed that the gods favored them over all other peoples, and they developed intense prejudices against their neighbors, accusing them of cowardice, stupidity, and treachery.

Religion—powerfully influenced by Mesopotamia's volatile climate—played a central role in daily life. Sumerians

■ Cuneiform Texts

The clay tablet on the left, dating from about 3000 B.C.E., lists what are probably temple offerings under the categories day one, day two, and day three. The tablet below, was produced in Babylonia about 1750 B.C.E. It contains problems in geometry.

knew firsthand the famine and destruction that could result from sudden floods and storms. They envisioned each of these natural forces as a god who, like a human king or queen, had to be pleased and appeased. The all-powerful king Anu, the father of the gods, ruled the sky. Enlil was master of the wind and guided humans in the proper use of force. Enki ruled the Earth and rivers and guided human creativity and inventions. Inanna was the goddess of love, sex, fertility, and warfare. Sumerians believed that in order to survive they must continually demonstrate their subservience to the gods, and their practice of constantly feeding these deities with sacrifices was one way of doing so.

The Sumerian worldview revolved around religious belief. Each Sumerian city was protected by one god or goddess. The deity's temples served as the center of the city and the focus of religious life. In Uruk, for example, two enormous temples dominated the community: the Ziggurat of Anu (the supreme sky god) and the Temple of Heaven Precinct. This latter complex of buildings contained a colonnaded courtyard and a large limestone temple dedicated to Inanna (also known as Ishtar), the goddess of love and war and the city's special guardian. All Sumerian cities had similar temples that towered over the city, reminding all the inhabitants of the omnipresent gods who controlled their destiny.

Sumerians told exciting stories about their gods and heroes. One of the most popular figures in Sumerian ballads was the legendary king Gilgamesh of Uruk. Part god and part man, Gilgamesh—accompanied by his stalwart companion, Enkidu—embarked on many adventures that delighted Mesopotamian audiences for thousands of years. The tale describes how the gods created Enkidu to be Gilgamesh's companion and balance the king's rash dis-

position. Together the two men battled monsters and set out on long journeys in search of adventure. As a result of his travels, Gilgamesh became a wiser king and his subjects benefited from his new wisdom.

Sumerian culture exerted an enormous impact on the peoples of ancient Southwest Asia. Sumerians devised the potter's wheel, and also the wagon and the chariot, which proved essential for daily transportation and warfare. The Sumerians were skilled architects, as their ziggurats and city walls reveal. Their irrigation systems show their mastery of hydraulic engineering. They also developed detailed knowledge about the movement of the stars, planets, and the moon—especially as these movements pertained to agricultural cycles.

The Sumerians also made impressive innovations in mathematics. The first numerals (symbols for numbers) emerged around the same time as writing. Archaeologists have found many Sumerian tablets that show multiplication tables, square and cube roots, and exponents, as well as other practical information such as how to calculate compound interest on loans. Sumerian numeracy has left a lasting imprint on Western culture. The Sumerians divided the circle into 360 degrees and developed a counting system based on sixty in multiples of ten—a system still in use in the way we tell time.

Perhaps the Sumerians' most important cultural innovation was their development of writing. The Sumerians devised a unique script used to record their language. Historians call the symbols that were pressed onto clay tablets with sharp objects cuneiform°, or wedge-shaped, writing. The earliest known documents written in this language come from Uruk about 3200 B.C.E. Researchers believe, however, that the roots of cuneiform writing date back 10,000 years, when people began to cultivate crops and domesticate animals in Southwest Asia. To keep track of quantities of produce and numbers of livestock, villagers began using small clay tokens of different shapes to represent and record these quantities. The tokens took the uncertainty out of transactions, reducing conflict because parties to a transaction no longer had to rely simply on memory or spoken agreements. After several centuries, people stopped using tokens and simply impressed the shapes directly on a flat piece of clay or tablet with a pointed stick.

As commodities and trading became more complex, the number of symbols multiplied. By 3000 B.C.E. the number of symbols had been streamlined from about a thousand to approximately 500, but learning even 500 signs required intensive study. The scribes, the people who mastered these signs, became valued members of the community. Sumerian cuneiform writing spread, and other peoples of Mesopotamia and Southwest Asia began adapting it to record information in their own languages.

FROM AKKAD TO THE AMORITE INVASIONS

The political independence of Sumer's cities ended around 2340 B.C.E.. Conquered by a warrior who took the name Sargon ("true king"), Sumer's cities found themselves swallowed up by Mesopotamia's first great empire. Sargon came from Akkad, a region in Mesopotamia north of Sumer. Sargon's people, the Akkadians, had lived in Mesopotamia for more than a thousand years. The Akkadians began to migrate into Mesopotamia from their original homes somewhere in the Levantine Corridor during the late fourth millennium B.C.E. Their settlements grew in size, and although they intermingled with the native Sumerian population they preserved their own language and customs.

By bringing cities with very different languages, culture, and traditions under his rule, Sargon (r. ca. 2340–ca. 2305 B.C.E.) created a dynamic empire that endured for more than a century. The term empire° identifies a kingdom or any other type of state that controls foreign territories, either on the same continent or overseas. The realm that Sargon had established reached its greatest extent about 2220 B.C.E. Controlling a large empire posed new challenges for Akkadian rulers. To surmount them, Sargon and his successors imitated and expanded on the governing methods they observed in individual Sumerian cities. For example, to secure the loyalty of their many subjects, Akkadian kings presented themselves as symbols of unity in the form of semidivine figures. After a king's death, his subjects worshiped him as a god. Some monarchs claimed to be gods while they were alive.

Raising the revenues to meet the costs of running their enormous empire presented another problem for

Akkadian kings. The king paid for all the public buildings, irrigation projects, and temples throughout his realm, as well as for the immense army required to defend, control, and expand it. Monarchs generated revenues in several ways. One key source of revenue was the leasing out of the vast farmlands that belonged to the king. Kings also required conquered peoples to pay regular tribute in the form of trade goods, produce, and gold and silver. In addition, Akkadian kings depended on the revenue generated by commerce. They placed heavy taxes on raw materials imported from foreign lands. In fact, most Akkadian kings made long-distance trade the central objective of their foreign policy. They signed treaties with foreign kings and sent military expeditions as far as Anatolia and Iran to obtain timber, metals, luxury goods, and construction materials. Akkadian troops protected these international trade routes and managed the maritime trade in the Persian Gulf, where merchants brought goods by ship from India and southern Arabia.

The cities of Mesopotamia prospered under Akkadian rule. Even so, Akkadian rulers could not hold their empire together for reasons that historians do not completely understand. One cause was marauding tribes from the Zagros Mountains, who repeatedly infiltrated the kingdom and caused tremendous damage. Akkadian kings lost control of their lands and a period of anarchy began about 2103 B.C.E. "Who was king? Who was not king?" lamented a writer during this time of troubles. The kingdom finally collapsed about 2100 B.C.E.

With the fall of Akkad, the cities of Sumer regained their independence, but they were quickly reunited under Ur-Nammu (r. ca. 2112–ca. 2095 B.C.E.), king of the Sumerian city of Ur. Ur-Nammu established a powerful dynasty that lasted for more than a century. The kings of Ur strengthened the central government by turning formerly independent cities and their territories into provinces and appointing administrators to govern them.

Ur's kings also centralized economic production in their empire. The royal administration controlled most long-distance trade and developed a vigorous industry in woolen garments and leather goods. Ur's rulers supported thousands of artisans and laborers who were paid in beer and various agricultural products. The materials the artisans produced were traded throughout Southwest Asia. Wealth also flowed to the kings of Ur from farming and herding. The kings owned huge herds of livestock that grazed on royal estates, but ordinary people were not permitted to possess agricultural lands. Most of Ur's citizens worked either as tenant farmers on estates owned by the king and the political leaders, or as slaves. Each year government officials collected tens of thousands of cattle and hundreds of thousands of sheep and redistributed them to temples throughout the kingdom for use in sacrifices.

The most important innovation in Ur occurred in the realm of the law. Ur-Nammu compiled the first known col-

■ **Ziggurat of Ur**
Built of mud bricks, the Ziggurat of Ur was the focal point of religious life. This vast temple was built by King Ur-Nammu of the Third Dynasty (2113–2096 B.C.E.) and restored by the British archaeologist Sir Leonard Woolley in the 1930s.

lection of laws in ancient Mesopotamia. His laws reveal his determination to provide social justice for his subjects. The custom of writing down laws so that citizens and later generations could refer to them became a strong tradition in Western civilization.

The kings of Ur used political innovations, economic centralization, and legal codification to strengthen their hold over Sumer's cities; they did not, however, challenge or change the key facets of Sumerian culture. Ur's monarchs continued the long Mesopotamian tradition of building elaborate temple complexes featuring ziggurats, palaces, and tombs to demonstrate their piety. Like earlier Mesopotamian rulers, Ur's kings considered themselves gods. They placed their tombs in the temple complex of the moon god Nanna, Ur's special protector.

Despite their sophisticated government, the kings of Ur could not stave off political fragmentation. About 2000 B.C.E., seminomadic peoples known as Amorites began invading Mesopotamia from the steppes to the west and north. They seized fortified towns, taking food and supplies and causing widespread destruction. Their invasions destabilized the economy of Mesopotamia as well as of other regions of Southwest Asia. Peasants fled from the fields, and with no food or revenues, inflation and famine overcame the empire. Ur collapsed, and Mesopotamia shattered once again into a scattering of squabbling cities. Taking advantage of the political turmoil and attracted by the abundant food supplies, tribes of Amorites settled in Mesopotamian lands.

NEW MESOPOTAMIAN KINGDOMS: ASSYRIA AND BABYLONIA

Within a few generations, the Amorites absorbed the culture of the Mesopotamian urban communities they had conquered. Two new kingdoms, Babylonia and Assyria, emerged in the lands once controlled by Sumer and Akkad

and coexisted for more than two centuries. The phenomenon of invaders absorbing the culture of sophisticated communities they conquered and then creating something new would often be repeated as Western civilization evolved.

Ashur, the major city in Assyria, began as a trading hub on the upper Tigris River sometime before 2000 B.C.E. The discovery of bronze making may be one reason that Assyria's power began to expand. Bronze, an easily worked but very hard metal, became highly valued for both military and ornamental uses. By 1900 B.C.E. the Assyrians had established an extensive trading network in metals as well as agricultural products such as barley and wool that reached as far as Anatolia and Syria. They also controlled and operated about a dozen trading colonies throughout these regions.

By 1762 B.C.E., however, Assyria and all of Mesopotamia fell under the rule of King Hammurabi of Babylon, one of humanity's first great empire builders. The kingdom of Babylonia, a mixture of Sumerian and Amorite cultures, emerged about 1800 B.C.E. as the dominant power in southern Mesopotamia. To secure their rule and enrich their coffers, Babylonian kings embarked on the conquest of neighboring lands. Their capital city, Babylon, grew wealthy. Under the leadership of Hammurabi (r. 1792–1750 B.C.E.), Babylonia gained control of all of Mesopotamia, including the Assyrian realm. Impressed by his own victories, Hammurabi called himself "King of the Four Quarters of the World."

Hammurabi also called himself the "King of Justice," a well-deserved title because his historical legacy is a rigorous system of justice codified in law. The 282 civil, commercial, and criminal laws contained in the Law Code of Hammurabi unveil the social values and everyday concerns of Babylonia's rulers. For example, the irrigation system on which Babylonian agriculture depended is a frequent focus of the code. Many laws related specifically to damages and personal responsibility with regard to irrigation. Similarly, the code buttressed Babylon's social hierarchy by drawing

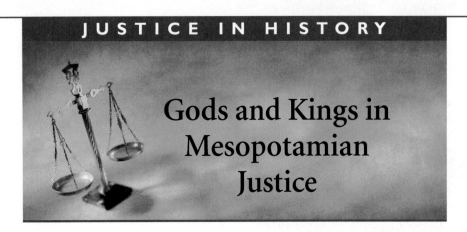

Gods and Kings in Mesopotamian Justice

Mesopotamian kings placed a high priority on ruling their subjects justly. Shamash, the sun god and protector of justice, named two of his children Truth and Fairness. In the preface to his law code, Hammurabi explained the relationship between his rule and divine justice:

> At that time, Anu and Enlil [two of the greatest gods], for the well-being of the people, called me by name, Hammurabi, the pious, god-fearing prince, and appointed me to make justice appear in the land [and] to destroy the evil and wicked, so that the strong might not oppress the weak, [and] to rise like Shamash over the black-headed people [the people of Mesopotamia].[1]

Courts in Mesopotamian cities handled cases involving property, inheritance, boundaries, sale, and theft. A special panel of royal judges and officials handled cases involving the death penalty, such as treason, murder, sorcery, theft of temple goods, or adultery. Mesopotamians kept records of trials and legal decisions on clay tablets so that others might learn from them and avoid additional lawsuits.

A lawsuit began when an individual brought a dispute before a court for trial and judgment. The court consisted of three to six judges chosen from among the town's leading men, who typically included merchants, scribes, and officials in the town assembly. The judges could speak with authority about the community's principles of justice.

Individuals involved in the dispute spoke on their own behalf and presented testimony through witnesses, written documents, or statements made by leading officials. Witnesses took strict oaths to tell the truth in a temple before the statue of a god. Once the parties presented all the evidence, the judges made their decision and pronounced the verdict and punishment.

Sometimes the judges asked the defendants to clear themselves by letting the god in whose name the oath was taken make the judgment. The accused person would then undergo an ordeal or test in which he or she had to jump into a river and swim a certain distance underwater. Individuals who survived were considered innocent. Drowning constituted proof of guilt and a just punishment rendered by the gods.

The following account of one such ordeal comes from the city of Mari, about 1770 B.C.E. In this case a queen was accused of casting spells on her husband. The maid whom she forced to undergo the ordeal on her behalf drowned, and we do not know whether the queen received further punishment:

> Concerning Amat-Sakkanim . . . whom the river god overwhelmed . . . : "We made her undertake her plunge, saying to her, 'Swear that your mistress did not perform any act of sorcery against Yarkab-Addad her lord; that she did not reveal any palace secret nor did another person open the missive of her mistress; that your mistress did not commit a transgression against her lord.' In connection with these oaths they had her take her plunge; the river god overwhelmed her, and she did not come up alive."[2]

This account illustrates the Mesopotamian belief that sometimes only the gods could make decisions about right and wrong. Kings willingly allowed the gods to administer justice in their kingdoms. In this way, divine justice and royal justice became part of the same system.

By contrast, the following trial excerpts come from a homicide case in which humans, not gods, made the final judgment. About 1850 B.C.E., three men murdered a temple official named Lu-Inanna. For unknown reasons they told the victim's wife, Nin-dada, what they had done. King Ur-Ninurta of the city of Isin sent the case to be tried in the city of Nippur, the site of an important court. When the case came to trial, nine accusers asked that the three murderers be executed. They also requested that Nin-dada should be put to death because she had not reported the murder to the authorities. The accusers said:

> They who have killed a man are not worthy of life. Those three males and that woman should be killed in front of the chair of Lu-Inanna, the son of Lugal-apindu, the religious official.

In her defense, two of Nin-dada's supporters pointed out that she had not been involved in the murder and therefore should be released:

■ The Law Code of Hammurabi

This stone copy of Hammurabi's code stands taller than seven feet. Written in Babylonian cuneiform script, it shows Hammurabi receiving the law directly from the sun god, Shamash, seated on a throne. The god wears a crown of horns, a scepter, and a ring, and has flames coming from his shoulders. Hammurabi stands because his status is lower than Shamash's. He raises his hand in a gesture of respect and speaks directly to the god.

Granted that the husband of Nin-dada, the daughter of Lu-Ninurta, has been killed, but what had the woman done that she should be killed?

The court agreed with this latter argument on the grounds that Nin-dada was justified in keeping silent because her husband had not provided for her properly. Then the members of the Assembly of Nippur faced the three murderers and said:

A woman whose husband did not support her . . . why should she not remain silent about him? Is it she who killed her husband? The punishment of those who actually killed him should suffice.

In accordance with the decision of the court, the defendants were executed.

This approach to justice—using witnesses, evaluating evidence, and rendering a verdict in a court protected by the king—demonstrates the Mesopotamians' desire for fairness. This court decision became an important precedent that later judges frequently cited. ■

Questions of Justice

1. How would a city benefit by letting a panel of royal officials make judgments about life-and-death issues? How would the king benefit?

2. These trials demonstrate that the enforcement of justice in Mesopotamia depended on the interaction of religious, social, and political beliefs. How does this interaction help us understand Mesopotamian civilization?

Taking It Further

Greengus, Samuel. "Legal and Social Institutions of Ancient Near Mesopotamia," in *Civilizations of the Ancient Middle East*, ed. Jack M. Sasson, vol. 1, pp. 469–484. 1995. Describes basic principles of law and administration of justice, with a bibliography of ancient legal texts.

Kuhrt, Amélie. *The Ancient Middle East: ca. 3000–330 B.C.*, vol. 1. 1995. An authoritative survey combining archaeological and textual evidence.

legal distinctions between classes of people. The crimes of aristocrats were treated more leniently than were the offenses of common people, while slaves were given no rights at all. At the same time, however, Hammurabi's Code introduced one of the fundamentals of Western jurisprudence: the idea that the punishment must suit the crime. One law reads: "If a man has opened his channel for irrigation and has been negligent and allowed the water to wash away a neighbor's field, he shall pay grain equivalent to the crops of his neighbors."[3] Through its introduction of such abstract principles as "an eye for an eye," Hammurabi's Code helped shape legal thought in Southwest Asia for a millennium. It is possible that it later influenced the laws of the Hebrews, and thus through the Hebrew Bible continues to mold ideas about justice to this day.

Babylonian society contained a private sector of merchants, craftspeople, farmers, and sailors. With no ties to the temples or the king, these free people grew prosperous. Merchants traveling by land and sea brought textiles and metals as well as luxury items such as gold and silver jewelry and gems from Anatolia, Egypt, Iran, Afghanistan, and lands along the Persian Gulf and Red Sea. This private sector enjoyed a degree of personal freedom unique in ancient Mesopotamia.

Nevertheless, Hammurabi and his successors imposed increasingly heavy taxes on their subjects. These financial demands provoked great resentment, and when Hammurabi died, many Babylonian provinces successfully revolted. The loss of revenue weakened the Babylonian imperial government. Successive kings tried to maintain their control by increasing the number of bureaucrats to enforce laws and to collect taxes, but such measures only made the government top-heavy. By 1500 B.C.E. it collapsed.

The Emergence of Egyptian Civilization

A s the civilizations of Mesopotamia rose and fell, another emerged far to the south: Egypt. A long and narrow strip of land in the northeast corner of the African continent, Egypt's lifeline is the Nile, the world's longest river, which flows north into the Mediterranean Sea from one of its points of origin in east Africa 4,000 miles away. The northernmost part of Egypt, where the Nile enters the Mediterranean, is a broad and fertile delta. In ancient times, Egypt controlled an 850-mile strip of land along the Nile. The river flooded annually from mid-July to mid-October, leaving behind rich deposits of silt ideal for planting crops. In its ancient days, the Nile abounded with fish, water birds, and game on the shore. The rich banks of

the Nile provided an ideal setting for agriculture and settled communities.

Historians organize the long span of ancient Egyptian history into four main periods: Predynastic (10,000–3000 B.C.E.), the Old Kingdom (3000–2200 B.C.E.), the Middle Kingdom (2040–1785 B.C.E.), and the New Kingdom (1600–1100 B.C.E., discussed in Chapter 2). Times of political disruption between the kingdoms are called intermediate periods. Despite these periods of disruption, the Egyptians maintained a remarkably stable civilization throughout millennia.

FROM THE PREDYNASTIC PERIOD TO THE OLD KINGDOM, CA. 3500–2200 B.C.E.

Like the peoples of Mesopotamia, the Egyptians were originally hunter-gatherers who slowly turned to growing crops and domesticating animals. Small villages, in which people could coordinate their labor most easily, appeared along the banks of the Nile between 5000 and 4000 B.C.E. By 3500 B.C.E., Egyptians could survive comfortably through agriculture and herding. With the transition to settled life complete, Egyptian society began to develop in many new ways. Small towns grew quickly in number along the Nile, and market centers connected by roads emerged as hubs where artisans and merchants exchanged their wares.

Toward the end of the Predynastic period, between 3500 and 3000 B.C.E., energetic trade along the Nile River resulted in a shared culture and unified way of life. Towns along the Nile grew into small kingdoms whose rulers constantly warred with one another, attempting to grab more land and extend their power. The big consumed the small, and by 3000 B.C.E., the towns had been absorbed into just two kingdoms: Upper Egypt in the south and Lower Egypt in the north. These two then united, forming what historians term the Old Kingdom.

With the unification of Egypt under one king, a new era dawned for this civilization. In the newly built capital city of Memphis, the Egyptian kings established themselves as the focal points of religious, social, and political life. Under the kings' careful supervision, the Old Kingdom stabilized and took on many of the characteristics of early civilizations we have seen in Mesopotamia, such as semidivine kingship, literate bureaucracies, a centralized economy, and strong support of long-distance trade.

Egyptian monarchs considered themselves gods as well as kings, and believed that Ra, the sun god and creator of the universe, had chosen them to rule as his representatives on Earth. In their role as religious leaders, kings claimed to control even the Nile and its life-giving floods. To the Egyptians, the presence of the kings meant that cosmic order reigned, and that the kingdom was protected against forces of disorder and destruction. The rulers steadily amassed more power, and by 2600 B.C.E. they owned the largest and richest agricultural lands.

The power of the kings was highly centralized. Authority began with the king and passed to his court officials and then to provincial governors who delegated power to the mayors of cities and villages. Administrators collected Egypt's surplus produce—coinage would not be used in Egypt for another 2,000 years—and then the kings' officials redistributed it throughout the kingdom. Surplus crops fed the armies that protected Egyptian territories and long-distance trade and the peasants who labored on public works such as temples, roads, and irrigation projects.

The job of keeping records of the kings' possessions and supervising food production fell to the scribes, who were trained in hieroglyph writing. This form of writing involved a set of several thousand signs called hieroglyphs, literally "sacred carvings." Hieroglyphs represent both sounds (as in our alphabet) and objects (as in a pictorial system). The hieroglyph system was very complex, all the more so because it diverged from the spoken Egyptian language. Consequently, learning hieroglyphs for literary or administrative purposes meant acquiring a second language and took years of schooling to master. It was worth the effort, however, for knowledge of hieroglyphs gave scribes great power. For 3,000 years, these royal bureaucrats kept the machinery of Egyptian government running despite the rise and fall of dynasties.

Like bureaucrats, priests in the king's service grew powerful. Priests came from elite families, often the king's, and their positions passed from father to son. They owned vast estates, including the temples to the god they served, and they became enormously wealthy. In addition, they often played a major role in political life. Kings sought their advice to ensure that in their leadership they were implementing the will of the gods.

Religious Beliefs in the Old Kingdom

Egypt's religion was polytheistic°; Egyptians believed that many gods controlled their destinies. Ra, the sun god, was one of the most important Egyptian deities. Embodying the power of Heaven over Earth, Ra had created the universe and everything in it. He journeyed across the sky every day in a boat, rested at night, and returned in the morning to resume his eternal journey. By endlessly repeating the cycle of rising and setting, the sun symbolized the harmonious

■ Narmer the Unifier of Egypt

Carved pieces of stone, called palettes, were originally crafted in the Predynastic period as holders for cosmetics, but they evolved into objects with important religious and symbolic functions. This sample shows King Narmer of Hierakonpolis, who lived about 3100 B.C.E. With his right hand he holds a mace and is about to smash the skull of an enemy. He stands on two dead enemies, as a servant behind him carries his sandals. A falcon god, Horus (Hierakonpolis means "City of the Falcon"), sits in a papyrus plant holding an enemy's severed head. Narmer wears the White Crown of Upper Egypt and a bull's tail, symbolizing his virility. On the other side, he wears the Red Crown of Lower Egypt, which he has conquered.

order of the universe that Ra established. The sun's reappearance at dawn every day gave Egyptians the hope of life after death.

Evil, however, constantly threatened the order of the universe in the form of Apopis, a serpent god whose coils could trap Ra's boat like a reef in the Nile. Ra's cosmic journey could continue only if proper worship and justice existed among humans. To make this possible, Ra created Egypt's kings, who shared in his divine nature and who ruled as his representatives on Earth.

Egyptians also worshiped Osiris, the son of the sky and the Earth, as god of the dead. According to Egyptian belief, Osiris was murdered by his brother Seth, god of chaos, after Osiris married their sister Isis, goddess of fertility. Seth cut Osiris into pieces and scattered them over the Earth, but Isis gathered the pieces and restored Osiris to life. The death and resurrection of Osiris symbolized the natural cycles of regeneration and rebirth that the Egyptians witnessed each spring as their fields bore new crops. After his regeneration, Osiris became king of the underworld, where he judged the dead. Egyptians associated this powerful deity with mummification, by which they tried to preserve bodies after death. Representations of Osiris appeared in pyramids, where the mummies of kings rested for eternity.

The Pyramids

With their emphasis on the afterlife, Egyptians took great pains to provide proper housing for the dead. Many tombs were built as monuments to the dead person's wealth and social status. These structures provided not only a resting place for the corpse but a symbolic entryway to the next life. Members of the elite were buried in expensive tombs filled with ivory furniture and other luxurious goods, but kings had the grandest tombs of all.

Burial customs in the Old Kingdom grew ever more elaborate. For the first several centuries of the Old Kingdom, kings built their tombs in the city of Abydos, the homeland of the first kings. The tombs consisted of an underground room with a special compartment for the royal corpse. The king's treasures filled nearby underground rooms. Above the ground sat a small palace featuring courtyards and halls suitable for a royal afterlife. The earliest of these tombs, dating to about 2800 B.C.E., contains the bones of animals and people sacrificed to accompany the ruler into the next world.

About 2680 B.C.E., architects began building a new kind of royal tomb. The defining feature was a great four-sided monument of stone in the shape of a pyramid. Elaborate temples in which priests worshiped statues of the king surrounded the monument. The structure also included compartments where the king could dwell in the afterlife in the same luxury he enjoyed during his life on Earth. King Djoser, the founder of the Old Kingdom, built the first pyramid complex at Saqqara near Memphis. Known today as the Step Pyramid, this structure rests above Djoser's burial place and rises high into the air in six steps, which represent a ladder to Heaven.

For the next 2,000 years, kings continued building pyramids for themselves and smaller ones for their queens, with each tomb becoming more architecturally sophisticated. The walls grew taller and steeper and contained hidden burial chambers and treasure rooms. The Great Pyramid at Giza, built around 2600 B.C.E. by King Khufu (or Cheops), stood as the largest human-made structure in the ancient world. It consists of more than two million stones that weigh an average of two and a half tons each. Covering thirteen acres, it reaches more than 481 feet into the sky.

Building the pyramid complexes was a long and enormously costly task. In addition to the architects, painters, sculptors, carpenters, and other specialists employed on the site throughout the year, stone masons supervised the quarrying and transportation of the colossal building blocks. Peasants, who were organized into work gangs and paid and fed by the king, provided the heavy labor when the Nile flooded their fields every year. As many as 70,000 workers out of a total population estimated at 1.5 million sweated on the pyramids every day. Entire cities sprang up around pyramid building sites to house the workmen, artisans, and farmers. The construction of enormous pyramids stopped after 2400 B.C.E., probably because of the expense, but smaller burial structures continued to be built for many centuries.

THE MIDDLE KINGDOM, CA. 2040–1785 B.C.E.

Around 2200 B.C.E. the Old Kingdom collapsed, due to economic decline, the deterioration of royal authority, and a cycle of terrible droughts that triggered a breakdown of law and order.

For 200 years, anarchy and civil war raged in Egypt during what historians call the First Intermediate Period. Finally, the governors of Thebes, a city in Upper Egypt, set out to reunify the kingdom. In 2040 B.C.E., Mentuhotep II consolidated his rule and established a vigorous new monarchy, initiating the Middle Kingdom (see Map 1.2).

Rulers in the Middle Kingdom defined a new role for themselves. They still viewed themselves as gods, but their rule became less despotic. Although they continued building large temple complexes to house themselves in the afterlife, these structures were not as grandiose as the Old Kingdom pyramids. The highly centralized bureaucracy opened to men of any social standing, as long as they could read and write hieroglyphs. Wealth spread more widely.

The kings also launched many public-works projects for the benefit of their subjects. Amenemhet I (r. 1991–1962 B.C.E.) and his successors transformed the marshy Fayyum Oasis, fifty miles southwest of Memphis, into a well-irrigated agricultural community that yielded abundant crops even in dry years.

Greater concern for the lives and needs of ordinary people also characterized the religious life of the Middle Kingdom. Because it stressed moral conduct more than the performance of rituals open only to the wealthy, the religion of the Middle Kingdom comforted more people with the hope of a satisfying afterlife.

EGYPTIAN ENCOUNTERS WITH OTHER CIVILIZATIONS

During both the Old and Middle Kingdoms, Egypt's kings sought to protect the trade routes along which raw materials and luxury goods were imported. Rulers did not hesitate to use force when necessary to protect their commercial interests. Some of them sent their armies to make punitive attacks in the western desert and in Sinai to stop raiders from robbing trade caravans. Other kings tried to maintain good relations with the chief trading cities of Syria and Palestine in order to stimulate trade.

From the earliest years of the Old Kingdom, Egypt cultivated friendly ties with the Mediterranean port city of Byblos, north of Beirut in modern Lebanon. Exchanges between Byblos and Egypt benefited both sides. Egyptians imported timber from Byblos for the construction of tombs and learned many shipbuilding techniques. The people of Byblos gained technical skills, especially in masonry and engineering, from the Egyptians. They were also influenced

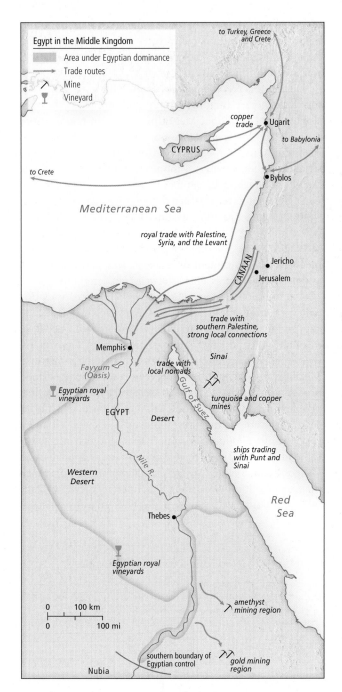

Map 1.2   Egypt in the Middle Kingdom
During the Middle Kingdom, Egyptian merchants traded extensively
with Southwest Asia and the cities of the eastern Mediterranean.
Turquoise and copper mines in the Sinai were heavily exploited.

imal skins. They also enslaved many Nubians and transported them for labor in Egypt. Agents of Egyptian rulers,
called Keepers of the Gateway of the South, tried to protect
the merchants by keeping the peace with the warlike
Nubian tribes. Slowly, Egyptian monarchs made their presence more permanent. About 1900 B.C.E., King Amenemhet
built ten forts at strategic locations where trade routes from
the interior of Africa reached the Nile River. Egyptian merchants placed the gold, ivory, and other natural resources
that reached these forts into boats, which they sailed northward along the Nile to Egypt. Egyptians came to depend on
these vast resources of Nubia.

Commercial connections between Egypt and other
African lands were less important. Egyptian merchants
traded with the land of Punt (modern Somalia) for spices
and rare woods, and they opened turquoise mines in the
Sinai. During the Old Kingdom, some merchants traded for
skins, ivory, incense, and slaves among the peoples living in
the Kingdom of Yam, located at the tributaries of the Nile
River in the interior of eastern Africa, but the Egyptians
abandoned trade with Africa south of Nubia during the
Middle Kingdom.

With the desert on both sides of the Nile Valley protecting Egypt from invasion by foreign enemies, the Egyptians
developed a distinctive culture characterized not only by
economic prosperity but also by a powerful sense of self-
confidence and optimism. Attracted by Egypt's stability and
prosperity, peoples from different lands sought to settle in
the Nile Valley. They took Egyptian names and assimilated
into Egyptian culture. The government settled these immigrants, as well as war captives, throughout the kingdom
where they could mix quickly with the local inhabitants.
This willingness to accept newcomers into their kingdom
lent Egyptian civilization even more vibrancy. During the
last years of the Middle Kingdom, many merchants and
large numbers of settlers moved into Egypt from Syria and
Palestine. Around 1750 B.C.E., one such group from Syria,
called the Hyksos, took control of Egypt and changed the
direction of Egyptian history. As we shall see in Chapter 2,
the Second Intermediate Period was marked by both foreign invasion and internal division.

by Egypt's religious beliefs. The Egyptian god of writing,
Thoth, became Taut in Byblos.

During the Old and Middle Kingdoms, Egyptian interactions with Nubia, the territory to the south, proved economically important. Egyptian merchants systematically
exploited Nubia's natural resources of gold, timber, and an-

The Transformation of Europe

The elements that produced civilization in Mesopotamia and Egypt began to appear about 10,000
years ago. Western history claims the cultures that
developed in these regions as remote ancestors. But in
Europe, the core territory of Western civilization today,
civilization developed later than in the floodplains of

Mesopotamia and the Levantine Corridor. Because the climate was colder and forests had to be cleared, food production was more difficult in Europe. Consequently Europeans made the transition from hunting and gathering to food production much more slowly. The food-producing revolution that had begun in Southwest Asia around 8000 B.C.E. spread to Europe a thousand years later when farmers, probably from Anatolia, ventured to northern Greece and the Balkans. It took another 4,000 years for the inhabitants of Europe to clear forests and to establish farms and grazing lands. By 2500 B.C.E., most of Europe's hunting and gathering cultures had given way to farming societies. New patterns of wealth, prestige, and inheritance had begun reshaping some communities but Europeans did not yet live in cities. Without the critical mass of people and possessions that accompanied city life, Europeans could not yet develop the specialized religious, economic, and political classes that characterize a "civilization." The transition to food production, however, laid the economic foundations of subsequent European cultures (see Map 1.3).

As farmers and herders spread across Europe, people adapted to different climates and terrain. A variety of cultures evolved from these differences. Archaeologists have named the different cultures of Neolithic Europe after some distinguishing feature of their pottery, tools, methods of constructing houses, or burial customs.

THE LINEAR POTTERY CULTURE

By 5000 B.C.E. one of the most important of these cultures, the Linear Pottery culture, had spread across Europe from modern-day Netherlands to Russia. Archaeologists call it the Linear Pottery culture because its people decorated their pottery with parallel lines. Their customs varied slightly in different regions, but they shared many similarities as well. For example, the Linear Pottery farmers lived in small villages of about sixty people. They built clusters of permanent family farmsteads made of timber and thatch, and rebuilt them over many generations. These farm families cultivated barley and other grains and kept sheep, goats, dogs, and, most important, cattle, which provided wealth and prestige. From gifts of jewelry and other luxury goods left in graves, archaeologists theorize that women were held in high esteem, perhaps because the people in these communities traced ancestry through them.

After about 4500 B.C.E., villages consisting of several hundred people began to appear in northern Europe, and a general trend toward cultural diversity accelerated. People in different regions used different kinds of pottery and probably spoke distinct languages.

As Linear Pottery settlements slowly spread, competition for farmlands and grazing lands stiffened. Archaeologists believe that men who controlled the livestock—the source of wealth and prestige—developed political authority. These early European elites tried to increase their influence

by seizing the lands and herds of others. Conflicts broke out among groups, and people fortified their villages with defensive works. These struggles marked the beginnings of warfare in Europe.

During this era, the peoples of the Linear Pottery communities began building communal tombs with huge stones called *megaliths*. Megaliths survive in regions from Scandinavia to Spain and on islands in the western Mediterranean. The best-known example of a megalithic structure is Stonehenge, a monument in England. People began to build Stonehenge about 3000 B.C.E. as a ring of pits. Later generations reconstructed it several times, adding large stones. Stonehenge took its final form about 1600 B.C.E., when builders positioned immense stones, each weighing several tons, in standing positions. Stonehenge possibly measured the movement of stars, the sun, and the planets, and perhaps served as a place for religious ceremonies.

Around 4500 B.C.E. early Europeans began experimenting with metallurgy, the art of using fire to shape metals such as copper into items such as tools or jewelry. Knowledge of metallurgy spread slowly across Europe from the Balkans, where people started to mine copper about the same time. Metallurgy would eventually prove as revolutionary as food production, but its beginnings were very modest. At first, people worked with copper only part of the year. Ötzi the Ice Man, for example, may have been both a shepherd and a coppersmith. Gradually, as copper tools and ornaments became more widely used, metalworkers became specialists. As villages became larger, wealthier inhabitants demonstrated their social status by wearing precious copper jewelry. Trade in metals flourished, changing Europe's economy by creat-

■ **Map 1.3 Neolithic Cultures in Europe**
During the Neolithic period, most of the peoples of Europe changed their way of life from hunting and gathering to food production. In the process, many new cultures developed.

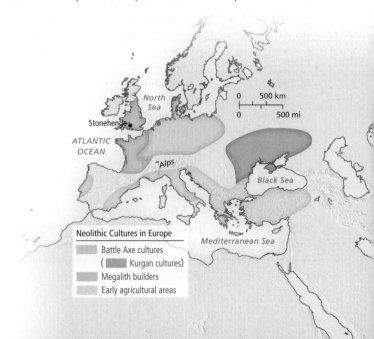

■ **Stonehenge**
This megalithic monument consists of two circles of standing stones with large blocks capping the circles. It was built without the aid of wheeled vehicles or metal tools, and the stones were dragged from many miles away.

ing long-distance commercial networks. In turn, these networks provided the basis for the meeting and blending of different cultural assumptions and ideas.

THE BATTLE AXE CULTURES

Between 3500 and 2000 B.C.E. the Battle Axe cultures gradually replaced the Linear Pottery cultures across Europe. Named for the stone and copper battle axes used in warfare, Battle Axe peoples cultivated many different types of crops and lived in rectangular single-family thatched dwellings. They may also have been the first peoples to domesticate the horse.

One of the better-understood Battle Axe cultures is that of the Kurgan peoples, who made their homes on the edges of the Russian steppes beginning about 3000 B.C.E. A warrior culture, the Kurgan people had to cross long distances to trade for the copper they needed for their weapons. They began to migrate from southern Russia about 3500 B.C.E., carrying their culture far to the west and south.

Scholars theorize that the Kurgan peoples brought with them a language that became the ancestor of the tongues spoken by half the world's population today. Historians call this language proto-IndoEuropean. The majority of the languages spoken in Europe, the Americas, and other lands colonized by Europeans, as well as Persian and Armenian spoken in Southwest Asia, share similarities in vocabulary and grammar inherited from this parent language. The Kurgan language and its offspring spread through Europe as a result of Kurgan migrations. The development of the IndoEuropean languages represents a foundation of Western civilization: the languages we speak.

TECHNOLOGY AND SOCIAL CHANGE

As the peoples of Europe developed their diverse cultures, their societies became socially stratified. One important tool that helped alter human relationships in early Europe was the plow, which became widely used around 2600 B.C.E. Once plow technology took hold, agricultural life in Europe underwent substantial changes over the course of a mere 200 years. The use of plows meant that fewer people were needed to cultivate Europe's heavy soils. With more people available to clear forest lands, new settlements sprang up and farming communities spread. The expansion of land under cultivation enabled farmers to move out from old family-controlled lands and start new homes. As a result, opportunities for individual initiative and the accumulation of wealth increased. Some farmers could afford trade goods of high prestige, and they passed their lands and possessions to their descendants, who used their inherited resources to acquire even more wealth. By exchanging these expensive and prestigious objects, men cultivated friendships and loyalty, established political and military ties, and formalized mutual obligations. Growing divisions resulted between rich and poor, the powerful and the weak.

Such changes were evident in western Europe between about 2600 and 2400 B.C.E. For the first time, individual graves played a prominent role in burial customs, which may indicate the emergence of new forms of authority based on the preeminence of individual men in the community, particularly those who controlled land and inheritances. The tombs contain weapons and luxury goods, suggesting not only that these individuals were wealthy and powerful men who could afford expensive symbols of their prestige and power, but also that they were warriors as well as or instead of farmers.

As warriors gained power, wealth, and influence in their communities, they emerged as political leaders, and they passed their wealth, political power, and social status down to their sons. These families came to dominate their soci-eties. Historians call these elite groups nobles or aristocrats. The presence of male-dominated groups, designated by birth, that controlled the greatest wealth and enjoyed the greatest privileges in society remained unchallenged in Europe until the eighteenth century, and it remains a defin-ing characteristic of Western civilization.

CONCLUSION
Civilization and the West

This chapter has described the change in human patterns of life from nomadic hunting and gathering to living in settled communities in which food was produced through agriculture and domestication of animals. This transformation took more than 8,000 years. The changes in food production led to the development of village settlements. Powerful elites emerged, and an individual's social status and gender defined what kind of work he or she performed. Soon human communities took on new characteristics. In Southwest Asia and Egypt, civilizations arose by about 3000 B.C.E. that were based on cities that devoted their re-sources to irrigation, warfare, and worship. The invention of writing enabled communities to record their laws and traditions. It also reinforced the long-distance trade that linked commu-nities together throughout Southwest Asia and beyond. Trade among these cities led to the en-counters of different peoples. They exchanged new food production technologies, advances in crafts, new approaches to government and administration, and stories and religious ideas.

These changes unfolded over many centuries and did not happen everywhere at the same time. Europe lagged behind Southwest Asia and Egypt in the development of cities and the emergence of civilization. By the end of the Neolithic Age, "the West" did not yet exist, but from the civilizations of Egypt and Southwest Asia, Western civilization would inherit such crucial components as systems of writing and numeracy, the idea of a law code based on ab-stract principles, and gender-based divisions of labor and power.

By 3000 B.C.E., the rulers of Egypt and Mesopotamia had spun a web of interrelated economies and shared political interests. Over the next millennium, cities such as Ur and Ashur grew powerful under the watchful eyes of ambitious kings who constantly fought with one another. But these kings did not yet possess the skills needed to rule vast empires for an extended period of time. As we will see in the next chapter, they would soon learn.

Suggestions for Further Reading

For a comprehensive list of suggested readings, please go to www.ablongman.com/levackconcise/chapter1

Andrews, Anthony P. *First Cities*. 1995. An excellent introduc-tion to the development of urbanism in Southwest Asia, Egypt, India, China, and the Americas.

Bogucki, Peter. *Forest Farmers and Stockherders: Early Agriculture and Its Consequences*. 1988. A clear synthesis of archaeological evi-dence from northern Europe.

Cunliffe, Barry, ed. *The Oxford Illustrated Prehistory of Europe*. 1994. An important synthesis of recent research by lead-ing archaeologists.

Fagan, Brian. *People of the Earth: An Introduction to World Prehistory*. 1998. A comprehensive textbook that introduces basic issues with a wealth of illustrations and explanatory materials.

Harris, David R., ed. *The Origins and Spread of Agriculture and Pastoralism in Eurasia*. 1996. A collection of detailed essays by noted experts that draw on the latest research.

Kemp, Barry J. "Unification and Urbanization of Ancient Egypt," in *Civilizations of the Ancient Middle East*, ed. Jack M. Sasson, vol. 2, pp. 679–690. 1995. Describes the emergence of towns and political unification of the early phases of Egyptian history.

Kuhrt, Amélie. *The Ancient Middle East: ca. 3000–330 B.C.,* vol. 1. 1995. An authoritative and up-to-date survey that combines archaeological and textual evidence in a lucid narrative with rich documentation.

Murnane, William J. "The History of Ancient Egypt: An Overview," in *Civilizations of the Ancient Middle East,* ed. Jack M. Sasson, vol. 2, pp. 691–718. 1995. A good place to start for a "big picture" of ancient Egyptian history.

Quirke, Stephen. *Ancient Egyptian Religion.* 1992. A brilliant synthesis and explanation of basic Egyptian beliefs and practices.

Redford, Donald B. *Egypt, Canaan, and Israel in Ancient Times.* 1993. A distinguished Egyptologist discusses 3,000 years of uninterrupted contact between Egypt and southwestern Asia.

Schmandt-Besserat, Denise. *How Writing Came About.* 1996. A highly readable and groundbreaking argument that cuneiform writing developed from a method of counting with tokens.

Shaw, I., ed. *The Oxford History of Ancient Egypt.* 2001. Provides excellent discussions of all aspects of Egyptian life.

Spindler, Konrad. *The Man in the Ice: The Discovery of a 5,000-Year-Old Body Reveals the Secrets of the Stone Age.* 1994. A leader of the international team of experts interprets the corpse of a Neolithic hunter found in the Austrian Alps.

Trigger, Bruce G. *Early Civilizations: Ancient Egypt in Context.* 1995. A leading cultural anthropologist examines Old and Middle Kingdom Egypt through comparison with the early civilizations of China, Peru, Mexico, Mesopotamia, and Africa.

Notes

.... ▬ ....

1. Samuel Greengus, "Legal and Social Institutions of Ancient Near Mesopotamia," in *Civilizations of the Ancient Middle East,* ed. Jack M. Sasson, vol. 1 (1995), 471.

2. Ibid., 474.

3. *Code of Hammurabi* (trans. J. N. Postgate), 55–56. Cited in J. N. Postgate, *Early Mesopotamia: Society and Economy at the Dawn of History* (1992), p. 160.

The International Bronze Age and Its Aftermath: Trade, Empire, and Diplomacy, 1600–550 B.C.E.

I N 1984, SCUBA-DIVING ARCHAEOLOGISTS BEGAN TO EXCAVATE THE WRECK OF A RICH merchant ship that sank about 1300 B.C.E. at Uluburun, off the southern coast of Turkey. Its cargo of raw materials and exotic luxury objects revealed a prosperous world of international trade and cultural exchange. A partial inventory includes ebony logs, ostrich eggshells, elephant tusks, and a trumpet carved from a hippopotamus tooth from Egypt. From Southwest Asia came exquisitely worked gold jewelry as well as nearly a ton of scented resin, perhaps intended for use as incense in religious worship. Finely painted storage jars from the island of Cyprus held pomegranates and probably olive oil. The archaeologists also recovered swords, daggers, and arrowheads, as well as hinged wooden writing boards with a thick wax surface on which business accounts could be recorded.

The most valuable portion of the cargo that the divers lifted from the ocean floor, however, consisted of 354 flat copper bars, each weighing about fifty pounds, and several bars of tin. When melted and mixed together, these metals produce bronze°. This alloy, which is much tougher than copper or tin by themselves, lends itself to the making of dishes, jewelry, tools, and especially weapons. The use of bronze ushered in a new era in the ancient world.

About 3200 B.C.E. people living in northern Syria and Iraq began making bronze. The technology spread slowly throughout Southwest Asia and into Egypt and Europe. Because deposits of tin and copper are not always present in the same areas, merchants traded over long distances to obtain the ores with which to forge the prized alloy. As they traded, they spread knowledge about bronze technology among diverse peoples. By 1600 B.C.E., when peoples throughout Southwest Asia, Egypt, and Europe had mastered bronze making, the International Bronze Age began (see Map 2.1).

Chapter Outline

- The Civilization of the Nile: The Egyptian Empire

- The Civilizations of Anatolia and Mesopotamia: The Hittite, Assyrian, and Babylonian Empires

- The Civilizations of the Mediterranean: The Minoans and Mycenaeans

- The End of the International Bronze Age and Its Aftermath

House of the Admiral: This lively wall painting, which may depict a religious celebration, comes from the so-called House of the Admiral on the island of Thera, midway between Crete and Greece. The painting is about twenty-two feet long and a foot and a half high. Created about 1500 B.C.E., before a volcanic explosion destroyed the settlement on Thera, the painting shows scenes of busy maritime activity outside a harbor town.

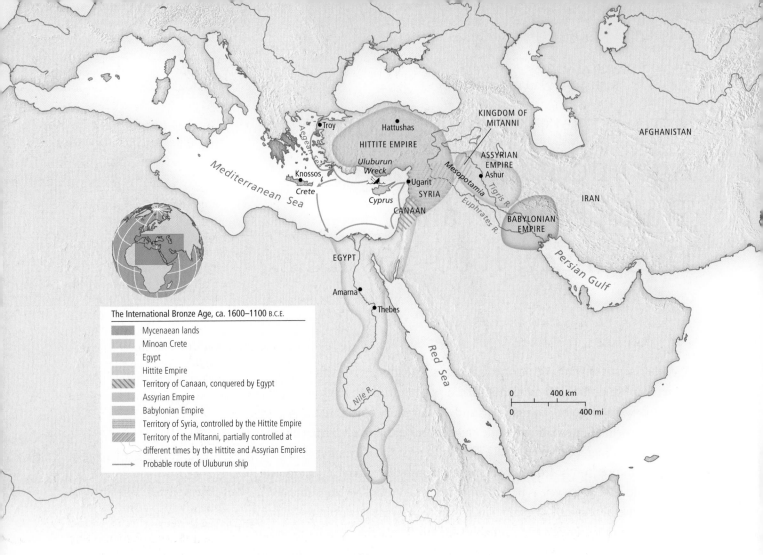

■ **Map 2.1 The International Bronze Age, ca. 1600–1100 B.C.E.**

For 500 years, networks of commerce and diplomacy tied together the distinct cultures of Egypt, Greece, Anatolia, and Southwest Asia.

The new international trade in bronze provides the key to understanding how four separate regions became linked in a large area of political and cultural influence and thus began to lay the foundations of Western civilization. Egyptians controlled the first region, which consisted of their territories along the Nile in northeast Africa and lands under their control in Southwest Asia. To the north, the Hittites dominated a second region in Anatolia (modern Turkey). To the east, Mesopotamia (modern Iraq) contained the kingdoms of the Assyrians and Babylonians. In the west, the fourth major region lay in the eastern Mediterranean where the Minoans on Crete and the Mycenaeans on mainland Greece developed maritime kingdoms. Several small mercantile kingdoms also developed on the eastern edge of the Mediterranean region, serving as buffers between the greater powers. These different cultures depended on an international trade network to obtain the metals and other goods they needed for everyday life. Their rulers encouraged this trade be-

cause they needed bronze to develop new weapons, especially horse-drawn chariots. Chariot fighting was expensive and therefore rulers constantly sought the acquisition of wealth and vital resources through not only trade but also conquest.

The use of horse-drawn chariots and the continued quest for new sources of wealth to finance them spurred rulers in Egypt, the Hittite kingdom, Assyria, and Babylonia to conquer large realms and construct enormous, multi-ethnic empires. Yet these same rulers recognized that constant warfare interrupted trade and interfered with the successful management of territories. Discovering the advantages of international cooperation for the first time, rulers during this period developed a system of diplomacy that produced long periods of peace—an unprecedented achievement. That the Uluburun cargo ship could stop at so many ports and take on board merchandise from so many different kingdoms illustrates the benefit of these peaceful times.

This chapter examines how the peoples of the International Bronze Age and its aftermath engaged in a series of commercial, technological, and cultural exchanges. To understand these changes we shall consider the following questions:

- How did Egypt during the New Kingdom use warfare and diplomacy to develop an empire that reached from Nubia to Mesopotamia?
- What were the political, religious, and cultural traditions of the Hittite Empire in Anatolia and the Assyrian and Babylonian Empires in Mesopotamia?
- What were the characteristics of the Mediterranean civilizations of Minoan Crete, Mycenaean Greece, Ugarit, and Troy, and what roles did they play in international trade and politics?
- What forces brought the International Bronze Age to a close and how did the Phoenicians, Assyrians, and Babylonians build new kingdoms and empires in its wake?

The Civilization of the Nile: The Egyptian Empire

Egypt played a central role in the economic, diplomatic, and cultural networks that shaped the International Bronze Age. A prosperous new phase of Egyptian history began when the Middle Kingdom ended about 1650 B.C.E. During the next 500-year period, Egyptians created a vast multiethnic empire stretching from Africa to Southwest Asia. Under the direction of talented and aggressive rulers, Egyptian imperial civilization reached its greatest height.

FROM THE HYKSOS ERA TO THE NEW KINGDOM

Egyptian history changed course abruptly at the end of the Middle Kingdom when the Hyksos, a people from northern Palestine whose name meant "peoples of foreign lands" in Egyptian, invaded Egypt and established a new regime in the northern Delta region. The Hyksos introduced to Egypt an advanced military technology that was revolutionizing warfare throughout Southwest Asia, Anatolia, and Greece. This technological innovation consisted of a chariot with wheels of bronze spokes. Two young men wearing bronze chain-mail armor rode into battle on each chariot, one driving the horses, the other shooting bronze-tipped arrows at the enemy. Troops of trained charioteers and bowmen easily outmaneuvered the traditional massed infantry forces and inflicted terrible casualties from a distance. Chariot warfare reshaped the economic policies and foreign relations of Egypt and all the other kingdoms and empires of the International Bronze Age. To meet the enormous expenses of training and supplying armies of charioteers, rulers carefully organized domestic resources and tried to acquire more wealth through trade and conquest.

About 1550 B.C.E. King Ahmose I (r. ca. 1569–ca. 1545 B.C.E.) mastered the new military tactics and technology and expelled the Hyksos from Egypt. Historians call the period of renewed Egyptian self-rule that began with Ahmose the New Kingdom (ca. 1550–1150 B.C.E.) Ahmose's new dynasty continued the highly centralized system of government that had been developed in the Middle Kingdom, but also added a powerful new force: a permanent, or standing, army. For the first time in Egyptian history, a ruler could count on the readiness of highly trained regiments of charioteers and infantrymen to go to war whenever he wished. Troops would also remain as garrisons in conquered lands. The standing army thus extended the ruler's reach and influence abroad. In this era, Egypt pushed its territorial boundaries into Asia, reaching as far as the Euphrates River.

During the New Kingdom, Egypt's kings first took the title *pharaoh,* which means "great house"—or master of all Egyptians. Pharaohs exercised wide-ranging and unrivaled political power. Egyptians believed that the gods entrusted their safekeeping to the pharaoh's care and that he had the final authority in matters of government, law, religion, and warfare. In return for the authority granted him by the gods, the pharaoh had the duty of maintaining peace and order in Egypt and bringing this order to the entire world. He did this by caring for the temples and cults of the gods, conquering Egypt's enemies, and ruling wisely.

Egypt during the New Kingdom developed a highly organized bureaucracy that helped the pharaoh maintain order. Egypt was divided into two major administrative regions: Upper Egypt in the south, governed from the city of Thebes, and Lower Egypt in the north, ruled from the city of Memphis. Regional administrators raised taxes and drafted men to work on the pharaoh's building projects. The chief minister of state, the vizier, superintended the administration of the entire kingdom. Every year the vizier decided when to open the canal locks on the Nile so that farmers' fields could be irrigated. He supervised the Egyptian treasury and the warehouses into which produce was paid as taxes.

Temples also played an essential part in the government of Egypt. Priests collected taxes, organized building projects, and administered justice among the many thousands of peasants who labored in the vast estates attached to the temples. The temple of Amun at Karnak, for example, controlled a workforce of nearly 100,000 people.

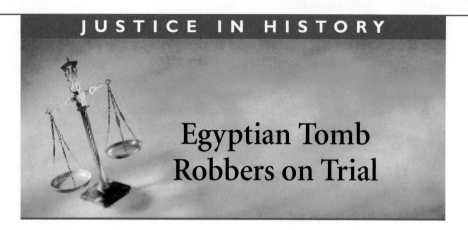

Egyptian Tomb Robbers on Trial

In New Kingdom Egypt a council called a *kenbet,* composed of the local governor and temple priests, combined the functions of prosecutor, judge, and jury. There was no counsel for the defendants. At the village level people might bring lawsuits against one another at the kenbet, and women and men alike represented themselves at trial. Another court, the Great Kenbet, handled all cases of property and taxation affecting state revenues as well as all offenses against the pharaoh and the government. This court consisted of high officials of the government and was headed by the pharaoh's chief administrator, the vizier.

One of the most serious crimes in Egypt was robbing tombs. People accused of this crime were interrogated by the authorities, who routinely used beatings and torture to extract confessions. The Great Kenbet then delivered a verdict. Conviction of tomb robbing carried the death penalty. Lesser crimes not related to tomb robbing could result in confiscation of property, beatings, forced labor, and body mutilation.

The following document comes from the trial record of tomb robbers in the Great Tombs of the pharaohs in the Valley of the Kings.[1] These tombs were situated a few miles from the Nile River at Thebes, where most of the New Kingdom pharaohs and their families were buried. The trials were conducted over a period of several summer days during the reign of Ramesses IX (r. 1125–1107 B.C.E.). The vizier, assisted by the overseer of the granary and treasury and two royal stewards, conducted the proceedings, which were written on a papyrus scroll unearthed in 1872 C.E. The account shows how justice was carried out in the New Kingdom.

> *Examination. The herdsman Bukhaaf of the temple of Amun was brought. The Vizier said to him, "When you were about that business in which you engaged and the god caught you and brought and placed you in the hand of pharaoh, tell me all the men who were with you in the Great Tombs." Bukhaaf replied, "As for me, I am a field worker of the temple of Amun. The woman came to the place where I was and she said to me, 'some men have found something that can be sold for bread; let's go so you may eat it with them.'" [Bukhaaf gives some misleading testimony that does not deceive the Kenbet.] Bukhaaf was examined with the stick [i.e., beaten]. "Stop, I will tell," he said. The Vizier said to him, "Tell the story of your going to attack the Great and Noble Tombs." Bukhaaf said, "It was Pewer, a workman of the City of the Dead [the Tombs] who showed us the tomb of Queen Hebrezet." The Vizier and the others said to him, "In what condition was the tomb that you went to?" Bukhaaf said, "I found it already open." He was examined with the stick again. "Stop," he said, "I will tell." The Vizier said to him, "Tell what you did." He said, "I brought away the inner coffin of silver and a shroud of gold and silver together with the men who were with me. And we broke them up and divided them among ourselves."*
>
> *[Bukhaaf's punishment is not recorded, but it was in all likelihood death.]*
>
> *On the third day of the trial of thieves, a carpenter Thewenani was examined for a different robbery. He proclaimed his innocence and swore a great oath, "If I speak untruth may I be mutilated and sent to Ethiopia."*

Despite several beatings and torture, Thewenani would not confess, and the vizier let him off with the warning that if he were accused again, he would be sentenced to death.

Later that day, Ese, the wife of the gardener Ker who had been implicated in stealing silver from the Great Tombs in still another case, was brought before the kenbet. She swore an oath to be truthful or be mutilated and placed on a stake. She denied any connection with the robbery, but one of the officials at the trial asked her how she had suddenly gotten rich enough to buy several slaves. Her answer that she had saved the money from selling the produce of her garden did not convince the kenbet, which brought in her slave to give testimony against her. Her fate is not recorded.

Why did Egyptian officials prosecute tomb robbers with such energy? They considered tomb robbing a serious crime for both religious and economic reasons. Egyptians were deeply concerned about the afterlife and stressed the proper treatment of the dead. They believed that when people died they were judged by the god Osiris. If they had lived good lives, their bodies would live again. The families of the deceased had the obligation to provide food and water at the graveside for the dead to eat. They also were required to remember the name of the dead. "Provide water for your father and mother who rest in the desert valley . . . Let the people know that you are doing it and then your son will do the same for you," advised one religious text.[2] In Egyptian eyes, robbing a tomb violated basic principles of religious behavior. It was a monstrous sacrilege.

The many gifts placed in a grave with the dead person were intended to make the deceased person's afterlife as comfortable as possible. Pharaohs and the wealthy elite of Egypt filled their tombs with luxury items of incalculable value—an irresistible lure for thieves. In addition to their profound desire to prevent sacrilege, Egyptian officials worried that plundering this treasure and putting it back into circulation would cause prices to fall and thereby derail the economy. From the point of view of Egyptian officials, tomb robbers deserved nothing less than death. Only this way would justice be served. ■

■ Judgment Day

Painted about 1285 B.C.E., this papyrus scroll shows the trial of a man called Hunefer on the day of judgment. The jackal-headed god Anubis leads Hunefer into the courtroom, where his heart is weighed against a feather on giant scales. Because the feather and the heart weigh the same, it means that the court decides that Hunefer has led a just life. The god of wisdom, Thoth, stands by the scale, records the result of the weighing, and leads Hunefer to the great god Osiris who judges and rules the dead. Hunefer can look forward to a peaceful eternity.

Questions of Justice

1. To what extent do both the living and the dead play a part in these trials?
2. The International Bronze Age witnessed the rise of strong, highly centralized states. What do these tomb raiders' trials reveal about the links among law, religion, and central state power?

Taking It Further

Goelet, Ogden. "Tomb Robbery Papyri," in *The Oxford Encyclopedia of Ancient Egypt,* ed. Donald B. Redford, vol. 3, pp. 417–418. 2001. Provides the latest analysis of the documents relating to the trials of tomb robbers as well as further bibliography.

Kruchten, Jean-Marie. "Law," in *The Oxford Encyclopedia of Ancient Egypt,* ed. Donald B. Redford, vol. 2, pp. 277–282. 2001. An excellent overview of Egyptian law with helpful suggestions for further reading.

■ Enemies of Egypt

These tiles found at the mortuary temple of Pharaoh Ramesses III were made around 1170 B.C.E. They depict Egypt's enemies with such great attention to details of clothing, hairstyle, and stereotyped physical features that we can know the ethnicity of the men. From left to right: a Libyan with tattooed arms, a Nubian with black skin, and a bearded Syrian. All wear handcuffs, a sign of their defeat and Egypt's triumph.

In the New Kingdom, women played an important role. Under Egyptian law, women and men had complete equality in matters of property, business, and inheritance. In addition to preparing foods, weaving cloth, and caring for livestock and children, women arranged burials and worshiped at tombs to ensure an afterlife for departed family members. Some women held priesthoods. The most powerful, the "God's Wife of Amun," was often a member of the royal family. This priestess had administrative responsibilities as well as the obligation to perform religious rituals. The wives of priests and officials formed musical groups called "Singers of Amun" that sang, clapped, and danced to the accompaniment of stringed instruments during religious rituals.

MILITARY EXPANSION AND DIPLOMATIC NETWORKS: BUILDING AN EMPIRE IN CANAAN AND NUBIA

During the New Kingdom, pharaohs conquered territories far beyond the borders of Egypt. The military power that came from chariot warfare technology made these conquests possible. A well-developed logistical system also contributed to Egypt's military strength. With food and supplies carefully prepared in advance by government ad-

ministrators, the Egyptian army regularly waged war far from home.

Egyptian attitudes toward non-Egyptians also encouraged the imperial expansion of the New Kingdom. Egyptians divided the world into two groups: themselves (whom they referred to as "The People") and everyone else. Egyptians were people who lived in the Nile Valley and spoke Egyptian. The other peoples known to the Egyptians were the Nubians, the Libyans, and the inhabitants of Southwest Asia. Egyptians believed that forces of chaos resided in foreign lands where the pharaoh had not yet imposed his will. Thus it was the pharaoh's responsibility to crush all foreign peoples and bring order to the world.

In their drive to establish order in the world, Egyptian rulers in the New Kingdom clashed with kingdoms in Anatolia, Syria, and Mesopotamia. Under the dynamic leadership of Thutmose I (r. 1504–1492 B.C.E.), the armies of Egypt conquered southern Palestine. A coalition of Syrian cities slowed further advance, but by the end of the reign of the great conqueror Thutmose III (r. 1458–1425 B.C.E.), Egypt had extended its control over all the lands between the Orontes River in Syria and the Euphrates in Mesopotamia. The western portion of this region, called Canaan (modern-day Lebanon, Israel, and parts of Jordan and Syria), provided the Egyptians with additional wealth, both because of Canaan's own natural resources and because Canaan was a vital trading center with ties to Mesopotamia and beyond.

The New Kingdom also expanded its territorial grip southward, seizing the populous and prosperous African land known in antiquity as Nubia or Kush (modern Sudan). Nubia was extremely rich in gold and other natural resources, while trade routes from central and eastern Africa that converged in Nubia further augmented its wealth. In order to gain control of these riches, Egyptian forces conquered Nubia about 1500 B.C.E. An Egyptian governor, called the King's Son of Kush, ruled the vast region in the pharaoh's name, but Egyptian control depended on the cooperation of Nubian princes who organized local labor and guaranteed the regular delivery of tribute. In return for this collaboration, the princes were permitted to govern their communities. To strengthen further their grip on Nubia, pharaohs encouraged Egyptians to migrate to Nubia and establish communities along the Nile River. These Egyptian colonies increased the population of Nubia and exploited the fertile river lands for the benefit of the pharaoh.

Although willing to use war to further their imperial interests, the pharaohs grew to prefer diplomatic means. Evidence of their diplomacy comes from an archive of documents discovered at Tell el-Amarna in 1887 C.E. Written in Akkadian, the Mesopotamian language used for international communication, these letters show that Egyptian pharaohs were in regular contact with the rulers of neighboring peoples, as well as with their own officials in Canaan and Syria. In their correspondence, the monarchs referred to themselves as "Great Kings" and addressed one another as "brother," despite their constant rivalry. By using these titles, the rulers recognized each other's authority and created a sense of international community. They cemented their ties by arranging marriages among the royal families and exchanging lavish gifts. By these means they could guard their frontiers and protect the merchants who crisscrossed their territories.

Egypt gained more than enormous wealth from its empire. The cultural encounter between Egyptians and the people they conquered resulted in an exchange of ideas and traditions. Egyptian speech, for example, adopted hundreds of Canaanite words. Many fairy tales about exotic lands modeled on Southwest Asia made their way into Egyptian literature. Numerous gods of conquered peoples entered Egyptian life as well. For example, Baal and Astarte, who were worshiped widely in Southwest Asia, became popular Egyptian divinities.

CHRONOLOGY

3200 B.C.E.	Bronze making begins in Northern Syria and Iraq
2000 B.C.E.	Minoans build first palaces on Crete
1650 B.C.E.	International Bronze Age begins; Hittite Kingdom emerges
1550 B.C.E.	New Kingdom begins in Egypt
1400 B.C.E.	Mycenaen Greece flourishes
1400 B.C.E.	Kassites gain control of Babylonia
1351 B.C.E.	Amenhotep IV (Akhenaten) begins his reign in Egypt
1244 B.C.E.	Tukulti-Ninurta I begins his reign; Assyria replaces Babylonia as dominant power in Mesopotamia
1200–1100 B.C.E.	Raiders of the Land and Sea appear; Hittite, Mycenaean, and other kingdoms of the Levant and Asia Minor collapse; Troy VIIa falls; International Bronze Age ends; Greek Dark Age begins
900 B.C.E.	Phoenician civilization develops
745 B.C.E.	Tiglath-Pileser III begins his reign; Neo-Assyrian imperial expansion underway
603 B.C.E.	Neo-Babylonian Empire replaces Neo-Assyrian as the most powerful in Southwest Asia

PHARAOHS: EGYPT'S DYNAMIC LEADERS

Egypt's success during the New Kingdom hinged in large part on the talents of its pharaohs. These rulers defined all aspects of Egyptian life, from empire building and trade to agriculture and worship.

Hatshepsut the Female Pharaoh and Thutmose III the Conqueror

One of the most remarkable rulers of the New Kingdom was Hatshepsut (1479–1458 B.C.E.), the first female pharaoh. With the aid of trusted advisers, Hatshepsut pursued policies of peace, though her armies waged war when necessary to secure Egypt's possessions in Southwest Asia.

Because pharaohs had always been men, all of the images of kingly power were male and the elaborate rituals of ruling presumed a male ruler. Hatshepsut carefully adapted her image to these expectations. For example, in the inscriptions and paintings of the great funerary temple that she built near Thebes, Hatshepsut is represented as a man, the son of the god Amun-Re. In more private contexts, she referred to herself as a woman. Several decades after Hatshepsut's death, her name was systematically removed from monuments throughout Egypt, probably to

■ **Hatshepsut as a Bearded Pharaoh**
Although she was a woman, tradition required that Hatshepsut be depicted as a man.

inform the gods that Egypt had returned to "proper" male kingship.

Thutmose III (r. 1458–1425 B.C.E.) succeeded his mother Hatshepsut and began a reign marked by military glory. He led his armies into Canaan seventeen times during his reign. In one of his greatest victories at Megiddo (in modern Israel) Thutmose captured more than 900 war chariots from his enemies. To maintain Egyptian authority throughout his empire, Thutmose established permanent garrisons in conquered territories, just as Ahmose had done when the territory had first been conquered. Thutmose cultivated a triumphant military atmosphere at court that was quite different from that of Hatshepsut, yet he also wrote literary works and pursued an interest in science. From Syria he brought back samples of the region's flowers and plants and had them painted on temple walls. Under his influence, Egyptian artists perfected their ability to capture detail, movement, and emotion in painting and sculpture.

The Amarna Period: Religious Ferment

Four decades after Thutmose III's reign, Egypt experienced a religious revolution, begun when Pharaoh Amenhotep III (r. 1388–1351 B.C.E.) turned away from traditional beliefs and practices. Amenhotep called the sun Aten and worshipped his physical form, the sun seen in the sky. The pharaoh's son, Amenhotep IV (r. 1351–1334 B.C.E.), changed his own name to Akhenaten ("One useful to Aten") and with his religious advisers took the revolutionary step of declaring that Aten was the only god. Thus the Egyptians in this period first developed monotheism°, the idea of a single, transcendent god for all humanity.

Full of religious enthusiasm, Akhenaten and his queen, Nefertiti, abandoned the capital of Thebes and built a new city where no temple had ever stood. Left open to the sun, the city received the first rays of light as each day dawned. Because the modern name for this site is Tell el-Amarna, historians refer to this period of religious ferment as the Amarna Period.

Akhenaten attacked the worship of other gods, closed down many temples, and appropriated their wealth and lands for himself. Paintings and sculptures no longer depicted Aten in the traditional way, as a falcon-headed god, but instead represented the deity as a simple disc with radiating beams of light. Akhenaten forbade the celebration of ancient public festivals to the other gods and even the mention of their names. His agents chiseled their names from monuments and buildings across the land.

Akhenaten gradually lost the support of the general population as well as that of the priests who administered the temples of other gods. The people of Egypt were unwilling to abandon the many traditional gods who played such an important role in their daily lives. After Akhenaten's death, the royal court returned to Memphis and then to Thebes. Akhenaten's monotheistic religion thus did not survive him.

The Battle of Kadesh and the Age of Ramesses

After Akhenaten's death, rule of Egypt passed through the hands of several men before Ramesses I took the throne in 1292 B.C.E. and established a new dynasty, the nineteenth in Egyptian history. The greatest king of the nineteenth dynasty was Ramesses II (r. 1279–1213 B.C.E.), who ruled for sixty-six years. Ramesses's efforts to restore Egyptian authority in Syria brought him into conflict with the king of the Hittites, Muwatallis, who wanted to conquer some of Egypt's possessions for himself. In 1274 B.C.E. the armies of Ramesses and Muwatallis clashed in a battle at the city of Kadesh in northern Syria. Muwatallis's huge Hittite army, with about 3,500 chariots and 37,000 infantry, caught the Egyptians by surprise, but in a last-minute counterattack led by the pharaoh himself, Egyptian troops rallied and pushed their enemy back. The battle ended in a stalemate, with heavy losses on both sides.

The Battle of Kadesh°, perhaps because of its indecisive outcome, resulted in a treaty between the two kings. Writing in Akkadian, the Egyptian and Hittite monarchs signed a treaty of friendship and cooperation in 1269 B.C.E. Ramesses formally abandoned Egyptian claims to the city of Kadesh and northern Syria. In return, the Hittite monarch acknowledged Egypt's right to control Canaan, establishing a boundary between the two states. The two powers also agreed to give one another aid and military assistance in case of invasion by a third party or in the event of internal rebellions. The Battle of Kadesh thus yielded nearly a century of peace between the Hittites and the Egyptians. During this period commerce flourished, benefiting both realms. With peace established with the Hittites, Egypt enjoyed many decades of prosperity under Ramesses II's rule.

The Civilizations of Anatolia and Mesopotamia: The Hittite, Assyrian, and Babylonian Empires

Egypt was only one of several large, highly centralized empires that developed during the International Bronze Age. As we can see on Map 2.1, Egypt's main rivals were the Hittite Empire in the north, and the Assyrian and Babylonian Empires in the east.

THE GROWTH OF HITTITE POWER: CONQUEST AND DIVERSITY

By about 1650 B.C.E., the Hittites had established control over the rich plateau of Anatolia. Like the Egyptians, the warlike Hittites were among the first people to use the new chariot warfare technology. For two centuries Hittite power gradually expanded across Anatolia and into western Mesopotamia, as well as southward into Syria where the Hittites stood face to face with the Egyptian Empire. As we saw earlier, Hittite conflict with Egypt culminated in the Battle of Kadesh in 1274 B.C.E. The stalemate at Kadesh led to a negotiated peace between the two empires and ushered in an era of prosperity.

At the top of the Hittite Empire was the Great King, who ruled in the name of the supreme God of Storms. Like Egyptian rulers, the Great King owned the land of all his subjects, and he gave agricultural estates to the noblemen who served as his officials. In return they supplied the soldiers and charioteers he demanded for the army. The Great King also strengthened ties of allegiance throughout his empire by requiring his officials and subordinate monarchs

to swear oaths of loyalty to the main Hittite gods. The Great King gave further unity to the empire by playing the role of chief priest of all the gods who were worshiped by the many different communities under his control. On special occasions, such as the New Year's Festival, Hittites worshipped their chief gods at the great outdoor sanctuary at Yazilikaya (to the northeast of the capital) under the direction of the king.

Hittite kings worked hard to provide uniform justice throughout their realm for rich and poor, male and female alike. This proved a complex undertaking because as the Hittite Empire expanded, it grew increasingly multiethnic, absorbing many smaller kingdoms with their own languages and cultural traditions. The many different peoples who made up the Hittite Empire were permitted to follow their own customs and laws. Administering justice thus required close cooperation between subject peoples' local authorities and the Great King's legal officials. The Hittite tongue served as the official language of law and government but the empire's cultural diversity and ties abroad forced the Hittites to keep records in other languages as well. The Hittites' use of cuneiform script, borrowed from nearby Mesopotamia, provides evidence of extensive cultural interaction with that region.

The Hittites spoke of their "thousand gods" because their religion drew from the empire's many subjects as well as from neighboring regions. The imperial government deliberately brought the statues of the gods of its subjects to its capital city of Hattushas and built many temples for them in an effort to promote the unity of all the people under the Great King's rule. Hittites believed that their gods were present in the form of their statues and that the gods wished to communicate with their human worshipers. Priests appointed by the Great King managed this "conversation" by making appropriate offerings to the deities at fixed intervals in an elaborate calendar of festivals and holy days. According to Hittite belief, properly worshiped gods would protect the empire as well as any individuals who might pray to them privately. In the Hittite afterlife, the souls of the deceased lived in a huge palace ruled by the Goddess of Death in the Underworld, located far below Earth's surface.

The expanding Hittite Empire played a prominent role in the network of trade and communication of the International Bronze Age. From the carefully kept inventory tablets that have survived, historians know that the Hittites made great profits by trading textiles, grains, and metals to markets as far away as Cyprus and the Aegean, Syria, and Mesopotamia.

THE MESOPOTAMIAN EMPIRES

During this period, two powerful empires emerged in Mesopotamia: Babylonia in the south and Assyria in the north. These kingdoms, which rivaled the Hittite Empire in wealth and power, had an equally vital place in the political, commercial, and cultural networks of the International Bronze Age.

The Kingdom of Babylonia

By about 1600 B.C.E. people known as Kassites infiltrated Mesopotamia as raiders, soldiers, and laborers. Their language and precise place of origin are unknown, but by 1400 B.C.E. they had gradually gained control of most of southern Mesopotamia. For the next 250 years, until about 1150 B.C.E., Kassite monarchs maintained order and prosperity in Babylonia, establishing the longest-ruling dynasty in ancient Southwest Asian history.

During these centuries, Babylonia enjoyed a golden age. Kassite kings politically unified Babylonia's many cities through a highly centralized administration that closely controlled both urban centers and countryside. These skilled monarchs won the loyalty of individuals of all ranks and temple priesthoods by giving them tracts of land. The Kassite kings gained a reputation for fair rule and for that reason were popular with their subjects. The government spent lavishly on temples, public buildings, and projects such as canals throughout the kingdom.

Under Kassite rule, Babylonia became renowned as a center of trade, culture, and learning. Science, medicine, and literature flourished during this period. With encouragement from the Kassite kings, who wished to demonstrate their full integration into Babylonian society, scribes systematically copied the works of earlier Mesopotamian cultures to preserve their intellectual legacy. Treatises on omens, astrology, and medicine gathered an enormous body of knowledge. Babylonian doctors earned fame throughout Southwest Asia. Gula, the goddess of healing known as the Great Physician, was the divine patron of a religious center where doctors received their training.

In literature, the Babylonian creation epic *Enuma Elish* tells the story of the origin of the world by Marduk, the god of Babylon and sole lord of the universe. The order that Marduk creates reflects the organized rule that the Kassite kings provided for Babylonia. Babylonian authors also wrote versions of the *Epic of Gilgamesh*, the Sumerian story about the establishment of civilization that we discussed in Chapter 1. These two great works were translated into many languages and entertained people throughout Southwest Asia for more than a thousand years.

The Kingdom of Assyria

Babylonia's chief rival for dominance in the Mesopotamian region during the International Bronze Age lay to the north: Assyria. Around 1350 B.C.E. Assyria recovered from more than a century of submission to the neighboring kingdom of Mittani in Syria. Under the skillful rule of Ashur-Uballit (ca. 1365–1330 B.C.E.) the Assyrian kingdom began a new phase of expansion. Like the rulers of the Egyptians and the Hittites, Ashur-Uballit and his successors

understood the value of close diplomatic ties with other great powers. As a letter found in Egypt reveals, he tried to win the favor of the pharaoh:

> *Thus speaks Ashur-Uballit, king of Assyria. May everything be well with you, your house, your land, your chariots and your troops. . . . I am sending you a beautiful chariot, two horses, and a bead of authentic lapis-lazuli [a valuable gemstone] as your greeting gift. . . .* [3]

Like their rivals, however, Ashur-Uballit and other Assyrian kings were also quite willing to go to war to safeguard their economic interests. To that end, Assyrian kings pushed westward, clashing with the Hittites over trade, metal ores, and timber. The Assyrians built a string of garrisons on their border with the Hittite kingdom and seized territories in northern Syria that had come under Hittite control. Assyrian kings also competed with Babylonia for control of copper, tin, horses, and other prized natural resources in the hilly lands to Mesopotamia's north and east. The mighty ruler Tukulti-Ninurta I (r. 1244–1208 B.C.E.) led his armies to victory over Babylonia and by the time of his death Assyria controlled all the lands extending from northern Syria to southern Iraq—the greatest reach Assyria would ever attain. Even though Babylonia would reassert its independence within the next twenty years, Assyria dominated Mesopotamian affairs for the next two centuries.

The Civilizations of the Mediterranean: The Minoans and the Mycenaeans

The Egyptian, Babylonian, and Assyrian Empires of the International Bronze Age were each rooted in civilizations that had emerged thousands of years before. In Europe, however, the cold climate and extensive forests slowed the development of city life and therefore of civilization. It was not until the International Bronze Age that two vigorous and distinctive civilizations developed in the eastern Mediterranean: the Minoan civilization of Crete and the Mycenaean civilization on mainland Greece.

Several smaller coastal cities and kingdoms situated on the eastern Mediterranean participated in the brisk trade that so characterized the International Bronze Age. These coastal kingdoms served as buffer states between Egypt, Mycenaean Greece, and the Hittite Empire. The two most prosperous, the mercantile kingdoms of Ugarit and Troy, played a "middleman" role in the trading and diplomatic networks that developed during these centuries.

MINOAN CRETE

About 2000 B.C.E. small urban communities on the island of Crete began to import copper and tin from the eastern Mediterranean. Sir Arthur Evans, the late-nineteenth-century British archaeologist who first discovered the remains of these communities, named them "Minoan," after the Cretan king Minos in Greek mythology. In the course of the second millennium B.C.E., the Minoans developed a busy merchant navy that traded with Greece, Egypt, and the coastal communities of the eastern Mediterranean. Crete became a thriving center of long-distance trade. Minoan civilization was the most brilliant in the Mediterranean until the sixteenth century B.C.E., when it was surpassed by that of the Mycenaeans.

Despite the rich array of artifacts and sites unearthed by archaeologists, the basic beliefs of Minoan religion remain a mystery. Historians do know that Minoans worshiped the powerful Mistress of Animals at some mountaintop shrines, and that in their homes they prayed to a goddess whom they always depicted as holding a snake. Statues show this Snake Goddess (or her priestess) wearing a many-tiered skirt, with breasts exposed and snakes coiled around her outstretched arms.

The Minoan economy revolved around four major urban administrative centers, called palaces, at Knossos, Phaistos, Mallia, and Zakros. The Knossos palace alone occupied three acres. At its center stood a courtyard surrounded by hundreds of rooms intended as living quarters for the governing and religious elite, administrative headquarters, shrines for religious worship, and warehouses for storing crops and wine. These warehouses, which could hold more than a quarter of a million gallons of wine or olive oil, show the Minoan rulers' tight control over the production of wealth on Crete. Palace administrators told farmers how much to grow and collected the produce from them, then gave back sufficient food for their subsistence. Palace officials also controlled the specialized artists who produced the crafts that were traded abroad.

The Minoan elites lived in great luxury in palaces connected to warehouses. Vivid frescoes (plaster painted while it is still wet) of sea creatures, flowers, court officials and acrobats in bright garments, and scenes of daily life adorned their walls. The residents enjoyed indoor plumbing and running water, comforts that most people in the West would not enjoy until the nineteenth century C.E. The palaces had no fortifications, suggesting that the Minoans felt quite safe on their island.

Like other monarchs, Minoan rulers carefully kept precise records of their wealth and possessions on clay tablets. Accountants recorded long lists of the livestock, produce, raw materials, and merchandise brought to the palace warehouses, as well as land holdings, debts, and payments made to the palace. These administrators used a form of writing known as Linear A, a simplified hieroglyphic script that

■ **Snake Goddess**

One of the most important divinities of Minoan civilization was the Snake Goddess. Here she (or her priestess) is captured in typical pose and dress: She grasps a snake in each outstretched hand and wears a tight-fitting, layered dress that exposes her breasts. A cat perches on her head.

developed on Crete around 1700 B.C.E., probably influenced by Egyptian writing. Linguists have not entirely deciphered the script.

Minoan mercantile documents found in ports along the eastern coast of the Mediterranean as well as the excavation of Minoan trading posts on the islands of the central Aegean Sea, on the island of Rhodes, and in other locations along the eastern Mediterranean coast reveal the international reach of Minoan travel and commerce. Minoan merchants sold their wares on the Greek mainland, and Minoan delegations brought rich gifts to the courts of Egyptian pharaohs. Exporting luxury goods—jewelry of precious metals and stones, painted vases, and delicate figures carved in the deep blue gemstone called lapis lazuli°— to eager foreign buyers made the Minoans wealthy.

About 1500 B.C.E. a volcano erupted on the island of Thera that lay between Crete and the Greek mainland. This enormous explosion destroyed the Minoan trading community on Thera; it also probably contributed to the weakening of Minoan Crete by destroying Minoan ships and affecting agriculture on Crete itself. Fifty years after the explosion on Thera, Minoan prosperity and power came to a sudden and unexplained end. All of the Cretan towns and palaces were destroyed except for Knossos, which fell about seventy-five years later. Excavations reveal that immediately after the destruction of the Minoan palaces, artifacts from mainland Greece appeared on Crete and throughout the Aegean. Graves on Crete began to contain Greek-style weapons and armor. Archaeologists do not know whether Mycenaean Greeks from the mainland caused the collapse of Minoan power or merely took advantage of it, but it is certain that invaders from Greece took control of Crete and its trade networks around this time. The international economy and the balance of maritime power in the eastern Mediterranean shifted from the island of Minoan Crete to the mainland of Mycenaean Greece.

MYCENAEAN GREECE

A German archaeologist, Heinrich Schliemann, first brought the Bronze Age civilization of mainland Greece to light in 1876 C.E. Determined to prove that the epic poems of the Greek poet Homer about the Trojan war were based in fact, Schliemann first dug at Troy (see next section) and then at the fortress of Mycenae, the home of the Greek king Agamemnon in Homer's *Iliad*. He made spectacular finds of golden treasures and sophisticated architecture at Mycenae, which archaeologists today believe was only one of perhaps six kingdoms on the Greek mainland. The name *Mycenaean* refers both to the kingdom of Mycenae and, more generally, to the culture of Greece during the International Bronze Age. Mycenaean civilization lasted from around 1600 to 1100 B.C.E.

THE MILLAWANDA LETTER

··················

About 1300 B.C.E., a Hittite king wrote the following letter to an unknown Mycenaean king, complaining of the behavior of a lesser ruler on the Aegean coast of Asia Minor who had defied the Hittite king's commands. The author's insistence on the formalities of diplomatic communication is striking. The letter indicates the significant role of international diplomatic relations among the great powers.

Millawanda was the Hittite name for the coastal town in Asia Minor where the Mycenaeans had established a stronghold. We do not know the location of the Mycenaean kingdom of Ahhijawa. We also do not know what was the previous trouble over the city of Wilusa (another name for Troy).

I have to complain of the insolent and treacherous conduct of . . . Tawagalawas. We came into contact in the land of Luqqa [in southwest Asia Minor]; and he offered to become a vassal of the Hittite Emperor . . . I order him, if he desires to become a vassal of mine, to make sure that no troops of his are to be found in Ijalanda [an unknown location] when I arrive there. And what do I find when I arrive at Ijalanda? The troops of Tawagalawas fighting on the side of my enemies. I defeat them, take many prisoners, devastate the district, scrupulously keeping the fortress of Atrija intact out of respect for my treaty with you. Now comes a Hittite subject, Pijamaradus, . . . who steals my 7000 prisoners, and makes off to your city Millawanda (Miletus). I command him to return to me: he disobeys. I write to you: you send a surly message, unaccompanied by gift or greeting. . . . So I go to fetch him. I enter your city Millawanda, for I have something to say to Pijamaradus, and it would be well that your subjects there should hear me say it. But my visit is not a success. I ask for Tawagalawas: he is not at home. I should like to see Pijamaradus: he has gone to sea. . . . Are you aware, and is it with your blessing, that Pijamaradus is going around saying that he intends to leave his wife and family, and incidentally my 7000 prisoners, under your protection, while he makes continual inroads into my territory? Kindly tell him either to settle down peacefully in your country, or to return to my country. Do not let him use Ahhijawa as a base for operations against me. You and I are friends. There has been no quarrel between us since we came to terms in the matter of Wilusa [Troy]: the trouble there was all my fault, and I promise you that it shall not happen again. As for my military occupation of your city Millawanda, please consider it a friendly visit. I am sorry that in the past you have had occasion to accuse me of being aggressive and of sending impolite messages: I was young then and carried away in the heat of action. I may add that I also have had harsh words from you, and I suggest that the fault may not lie with ourselves but with our messengers. Let us bring them to trial, cut off their heads, mutilate their bodies, and live henceforward in perfect friendship.

Source: From Denys L. Page, *History and the Homeric Iliad*, Copyright © 1959 by The Regents of the University of California. Reprinted by permission.

By 1400 B.C.E. a uniform Mycenaean civilization had reached its apex throughout southern Greece and in Mycenaean settlements abroad. The larger Mycenaean communities consisted of heavily fortified palaces with outlying agricultural lands. As on Crete, the Mycenaean palaces functioned as administrative centers of food collection and distribution. They also served as manufacturing centers that produced pottery, jewelry, tapestries, and other trade goods. Literate bureaucrats living in the palaces were essential in governing the Mycenaean kingdoms. Like their counterparts in Crete and Southwest Asia, they recorded long lists of livestock, slaves, farm produce, land holdings, taxes, and tribute taken from peasants and slaves. They also kept detailed records of imported and exported luxury goods and raw materials. These administrative records were written on clay tablets in a script known as Linear B, an early form of the Greek language still spoken today.

The most influential kingdom in southern Greece during this period was located at Mycenae, where kings governed from a citadel looking down on a broad agricultural plain. This center of power reveals much about in life in Bronze Age Greece. Thirty royal burials consisting of deep shafts arranged in two circles on the citadel and dating from 1600 to 1450 B.C.E. suggest a highly warlike people. The graves contain bronze swords, daggers, spearheads, and stone arrowheads and blades. The skeletons of the rulers buried in these graves stood nearly six feet tall, which made them tower over the general population. Apparently they enjoyed better nutrition than their subjects, whose graves reveal more diminutive skeletons. The many gold and silver drinking vessels and pieces of jewelry found in the graves further demonstrate that the Mycenaean leaders enjoyed tremendous luxury.

The Mycenaean kings relied on aristocratic warriors, who enforced the monarchs' decisions and served as military officers during wartime. As in Egypt, Anatolia, and Southwest Asia, elite warriors used light, fast-moving chariots pulled by horses. They also took their favorite weapons of war with them to the grave, suggesting that they valued military prowess very highly.

The Mycenaeans took advantage of the peaceful conditions in the eastern Mediterranean that diplomatic ties between Egypt and the Hittite Empire had helped create. With the collapse of Minoan Crete, they assumed control of commerce across the Aegean Sea and the eastern Mediterranean. During the fourteenth and thirteenth centuries B.C.E., Mycenaean merchants extended Minoan commercial routes, establishing strong links with Egyptians and the inhabitants of Ugarit and other coastal towns. Ships carried Mycenaean commodities in large clay vessels painted with distinctive designs as far west as Spain and northern Italy.

Mycenaean rulers also forged diplomatic ties with Egyptian monarchs. Ambassadors of Pharaoh Amenhotep III visited Crete and the Greek mainland, including Mycenae, where they presented ceremonial plaques bearing the pharaoh's name. In the interest of maintaining good relations and brisk commerce, Egyptian and Mycenaean rulers avoided war with each other during this period but Mycenaean relations with the Hittites were not quite so cordial. To extend and protect their trade routes, some Mycenaean Greeks settled on the coast of Asia Minor, a sphere of Hittite influence. There they engaged in trade, piracy, and warfare with surrounding communities. Hittite documents dating to the fourteenth century B.C.E. tell of meddling Mycenaean kings who slipped away to sea in their ships, out of the reach of landbound Hittite forces.

TWO COASTAL KINGDOMS: UGARIT AND TROY

Many independent cities existed along the border regions between Egypt, Mycenaean Greece, and the Hittite Empire. A string of these small communities stretched along the seacoast from the Aegean Sea to the Gaza Strip and served as a buffer between the three major powers. The two most notable of these cities were Ugarit and Troy.

Ugarit: A Mercantile Kingdom

Directly east of Cyprus on the Syrian coast lay the port city of Ugarit, which controlled a small but influential kingdom of about 2,000 square miles. Ugarit became a highly cultured city with international connections because of its rich natural resources. The fertile plain offered arable land for grapevines, olive trees, and grains, while the heavily forested surrounding hills provided timber for shipbuilding and construction. Perhaps Ugarit's greatest asset was a fine natural harbor that made the city a hub of international trade. Merchant ships like the one that sank at Uluburun sailed to Ugarit from Cyprus and the Aegean, the coast of western Anatolia, and Egypt. Caravans laden with goods arrived from Mesopotamia, the Hittite lands, and Canaan. People from all these places settled in Ugarit, whose population is estimated at 10,000 inhabitants. Another 25,000 people lived as farmers in the Ugarit countryside.

In Ugarit's spacious houses archaeologists have excavated numerous baked clay tablets containing legal, financial, literary, diplomatic, and religious texts written in Ugaritic, the local Semitic language. The tablets demonstrate the literacy of the Ugaritic elite. Young people studied their own language in school while also mastering foreign languages useful in trade and diplomacy. The tablets show an innovative alphabet. In it, each spoken sound was represented by just one letter or sign. This Ugaritic alphabet was the ancestor of all modern alphabets that follow the same principle of one sign per spoken sound.

Ugarit was always overshadowed by mighty Egypt to the south and the combative Hittite Empire to the north. To maintain Ugarit's independence, the port city's rulers had to be clever diplomats. Archaeologists have unearthed records of treaties made between the kings of Ugarit and Hittite, Assyrian, and other rulers in Southwest Asia. These treaties show that Ugarit played an influential role in international diplomacy.

Troy: A City of Legend

Troy, the best known and yet most mysterious of all Bronze Age cities, has captured the popular imagination for 3,000 years, but archaeology cannot explain the origins of the people who lived there, or even their language. Historians do know that like Ugarit, Troy was a city embedded in the intricate web of trade, diplomacy, and warfare that linked the societies of the International Bronze Age. Situated in northwest Asia Minor on a promontory overlooking a bay about six miles from the Aegean Sea, this city has become immortal as the site of the Trojan War in Homer's epic poems the *Iliad* and the *Odyssey*. Composed about 750 B.C.E., these stories are legends, not history. Still, they formed part of an enduring oral tradition that began in the International Bronze Age and reflect social conditions and perhaps even events that actually occurred.

Archaeologists have unearthed numerous distinct layers of occupation and construction in Troy, as generations of inhabitants rebuilt their city from about 3000 to 1200 B.C.E. Around 1700 B.C.E. the inhabitants of Troy VI (meaning the sixth major layer of occupation) constructed huge gateways and a royal palace consisting of many spacious mansions. A fortified citadel, Troy VI was built with monumental blocks of masonry similar to that used by the Hittites and the Mycenaeans, suggesting that techniques of military engineering had spread among these kingdoms. The Trojans prospered in the fifteenth and fourteenth centuries B.C.E. by trading with Mycenaean Greeks, Hittites, Cypriots, and merchants from Ugarit. But around 1270 B.C.E., an earthquake tumbled the mighty walls of Troy VI and the city went up in flames. The Trojans' prosperity and influence ended.

Heinrich Schliemann, the first archaeologist to excavate Troy, erroneously concluded that Troy VI was the city destroyed by Mycenaean Greeks in Homer's *Iliad*. Later archaeologists proved that Greeks had nothing to do with the city's collapse. Most archaeologists believe that if there is even a kernel of truth in Homer's stories about the Greek destruction of Troy, it must lie in the violent end of "Troy VIIa," the modest city built within the rubble of Troy VI's fortress walls by the survivors of the earthquake. This new version of the city also fell to ruin about 1190 B.C.E., probably as the result of warfare. Hittite royal documents indicate that at this time Mycenaeans were raiding the coastlands of Asia Minor in search of slaves and booty, and Linear B tablets from the Greek mainland list slaves captured on the Asia Minor coast. These records suggest that Troy VIIa may well have fallen prey to a Mycenaean attack. Some historians believe that in the centuries following Troy VIIa's destruction, the story of a Mycenaean raid slowly took on epic proportions as generations of Greek bards told and retold

■ **The "Death Mask of Agamemnon"**
Heinrich Schliemann, who excavated the tomb in which this gold mask was found, mistakenly jumped to the conclusion that it was the death mask of King Agamemnon, who led the Greek forces during the Trojan War, as told in Homer's *Iliad*. Later archaeologists have discovered that this king died several centuries before the period that Homer described.

it. Older tales recounting the glory of Troy VI may have augmented the legend of the Trojan War.

The End of the International Bronze Age and Its Aftermath

The intricate diplomatic, cultural, and economic interconnections between Egypt, Southwest Asia, Anatolia, and Greece broke between 1200 and 1100 B.C.E. These formerly vibrant civilizations plummeted into a dark age, marked by invasions, migrations, and the collapse of stable governments. The era of prosperity and international cooperation ended abruptly. In the aftermath of these turbulent events, however, the people of Southwest Asia from the Mediterranean coast to Mesopotamia gradually developed new and powerful kingdoms with distinctive cultures.

THE RAIDERS OF THE LAND AND SEA

Developments in Mycenaean Greece and the Hittite Empire were pivotal in bringing the International Bronze Age to an end. The collapse of Hittite and Mycenaean power contributed to migrations throughout the eastern Mediterranean. People fled their homes in search of new lands to settle. Overcoming all resistance, these displaced groups plundered cities and brought destruction to the entire eastern Mediterranean as they moved southward.

Warfare among the many competitive kingdoms of Mycenaean Greece probably began this chain of disasters. These conflicts resulted in the breakdown of the palace-centered economic system about 1150 B.C.E. When the Mycenaean kingdoms collapsed, the economy disintegrated as well. Literacy disappeared because without palace inventories to record, there was no need for scribes to learn Linear B. Trade and population declined rapidly, and many Greeks migrated to the coast of Asia Minor. The Greek language and some religious beliefs survived, but the crafts, artistic styles, and architectural traditions of Mycenaean life were forgotten. In contrast to the brilliance of Mycenaean civilization, the poverty and hardship of the era that followed merit the name "dark age."

For the Hittite Empire, a deadly combination of economic decline and invasions early in the twelfth century B.C.E. triggered the government's collapse. The subject kingdoms in the western regions of the Hittite Empire began to rebel, and peasants fled their lands. The Hittites became ever more dependent on foreign sources of grain, forcing their rulers to import larger supplies from Egypt and Syria. Rebellions occasionally blocked these shipments, worsening the Hittites' plight. By the first decade of the twelfth century B.C.E. an enemy force of uncertain origin stormed through the Hittite Empire and burned the capital city of Hattushas. With no effective leadership, Hittite power soon crumbled.

As Hittite and Mycenaean power collapsed, migrating peoples surged across the eastern Mediterranean. In Egyptian documents these people are referred to as Raiders of the Land and Sea°. They came from many places, impelled not only by political instability and economic decline, but also by earthquakes, plague, and climate change. The raiders included pirates and mercenaries, as well as migrating groups that traveled with their families and livestock in search of new lands.

The raiders' movements destabilized all the regions linked together by the trading and diplomatic networks of the International Bronze Age. Moving south through Syria and Palestine, the raiders destroyed Ugarit and other coastal cities. Bound together in a loose confederation, the raiders moved farther south toward Egypt in search of land and food. By 1170 B.C.E., the Egyptian Empire had lost control of Syria and Canaan. Groups of raiders settled on the Mediterranean coast and extended their power inland. Organized political life in Canaan disintegrated and the last of the Bronze Age cities collapsed by about 1100 B.C.E. (One group of raiders, the Peleset People, who settled on the coast of Canaan are known to us as the Philistines, a name that survives in the modern word *Palestine*.)

Egypt was able to marshal its military might and avoid total destruction at the hands of the Raiders of the Land and Sea, but it slipped into a long economic and military decline. Drought, poor harvests, and inflation ruined the Egyptian economy, while weak rulers struggled unsuccessfully to hold Egypt together. The bonds between Upper and Lower Egypt were severed, and the land of Egypt split once again into separate kingdoms.

In Mesopotamia, the kingdoms of Babylonia and Assyria also experienced an economic and political breakdown. Historians attribute this decline primarily to invasions by seminomadic peoples originating in Syria and the Iranian plateau. Their monarchs lost power and political influence, but the Assyrians and Babylonians nevertheless maintained their identity as distinct peoples throughout these troubled centuries.

After the International Bronze Age ended about 1100 B.C.E., two regions acquired special importance: the eastern coast of the Mediterranean, where the Phoenicians established a maritime culture, and Mesopotamia, where the kingdoms of Assyria and Babylonia revived. (We will examine the civilization of the Hebrews, which also emerged in the aftermath of the International Bronze Age, in Chapter 3.)

THE PHOENICIANS: MERCHANTS OF THE MEDITERRANEAN

Two hundred years after the International Bronze Age drew to a close, a dynamic maritime civilization took shape in the independent port cities that stretched along the eastern Mediterranean seaboard. Byblos, Tyre, and Sidon were the most powerful of these cities. These seafaring people, whom historians call Phoenicians, continued the commercial traditions of Ugarit and other small Bronze Age kingdoms. By following old Minoan and Mycenaean trade routes of the International Bronze Age, they created a large commercial sphere of influence. Hundreds of their ships crisscrossed the Mediterranean and ventured into the Atlantic Ocean in search of trade. By 950 B.C.E. they had established extensive trade and political connections with peoples of the Levant and spread their civilization into the Mediterranean world as far as North Africa, Italy, and Spain.

The search for metal ores motivated much of Phoenician commerce. Phoenician metal prospectors located deposits of precious ores in North Africa, Spain, Italy, Britain, and France. They traded with the local inhabitants in these regions who had been working the mines for centuries. In this way Phoenician traders established economic connections with lands that would later become the center of Western civilization. The enterprising Phoenicians also learned techniques of smelting metals for weapons, tools, and jewelry that had been developing in European lands since the International Bronze Age, and they transmitted this knowledge to Southwest Asian peoples. In return, they brought Asian and Egyptian artistic styles to western Mediterranean lands.

By 800 B.C.E., Carthage ("New City"), a colony located on the northern coast of modern Tunisia, had become the chief Phoenician city in the West. For this reason, Phoenician culture in the western Mediterranean is called Carthaginian. With its magnificent harbor and strategic location midway between the Levant and the straits of Gibraltar, Carthage controlled trade between the eastern and western Mediterranean. Its inhabitants developed a land-based empire on the North African coast and in Spain. Phoenicians were more interested in trading than settling, however. Their approach to trade facilitated good relations with the southern Mediterranean's native inhabitants, especially in Sicily and Italy.

Phoenician religion showed remarkable continuity through time and across the Mediterranean. Many of their gods and goddesses had also been worshiped by Southwest Asian peoples during the International Bronze Age. Even though the deities' names differed among many Phoenician cities, their roles as protectors and warriors remained the same. The chief gods were Baalat ("Lady of the Heavens") and her husband Baal ("Lord of the Heavens"), who represented the order of the natural world and protected the Phoenicians from danger. Phoenicians believed that Baal died every year and was reborn every spring. This myth celebrated the rebirth of nature and became very influential throughout the Mediterranean world. Many parents killed their firstborn son as an offering to the Lord and Lady of the Heavens at moments of crisis or as an offering for the fulfillment of a personal vow. Child sacrifice continued at Carthaginian settlements, often secretly, as late as 200 C.E. In the western Mediterranean, the Lady of the Heavens became associated with the practice of sacred prostitution, in which every sexual union between a priestess and a male believer symbolized the fertility and regenerative power of the Lady of the Heavens.

The Phoenicians' most lasting cultural contribution to the peoples of the Mediterranean world was the alphabet. The Phoenicians developed a system of writing based on that of Ugarit in which each letter represented a single sound. Thus the alphabet could be used to record the sounds of any language. The Phoenician alphabet spread throughout the Mediterranean world, where the Greeks and then the Romans adopted it. In this way it became the source of all alphabets and writing in the West.

Known mainly as accomplished sailors and merchants, the Phoenicians did not develop a large, centralized state. Their cities, therefore, became vulnerable to attack by larger empires and lost their independence in the fifth century B.C.E.. Their strong mercantile and seafaring culture, however, lasted into Roman times.

THE NEO-ASSYRIAN AND NEO-BABYLONIAN EMPIRES, 1050–550 B.C.E.

The decline of both Assyria and Babylonia at the end of the International Bronze Age did not result in their outright disappearance as kingdoms. Torn apart by invasions, they nevertheless managed to survive. Beginning in about 1050 B.C.E., new versions of the Assyrian and then the Babylonian imperial regimes began to regain effective control over their territories, re-establish their commercial power, and reconquer neighboring lands.

Neo-Assyrian Imperialism

After 1000 B.C.E., the Assyrian kings slowly reasserted their dominance in northern Mesopotamia. In 745 B.C.E., Tiglath-Pileser III (r. 745–727 B.C.E.) ascended the Assyrian throne and ushered in a century of rapid expansion. This Neo-Assyrian Empire was the first in history to control the Tigris, Euphrates, and Nile River valleys, where civilization had first emerged two millennia before (see Map 2.2). By 500 B.C.E., Nineveh, the Neo-Assyrian capital city, boasted at least 500,000 inhabitants.

Neo-Assyrian rulers, who called themselves "Kings of the Universe," developed a highly militarized empire. To terrify their victims and aid their conquests, they cultivated a reputation for extreme cruelty. Assyrian armies tortured, butchered, and enslaved the inhabitants of defeated cities. Then, after carting off everything of value, they burned the cities to the ground. News of their atrocities spread to

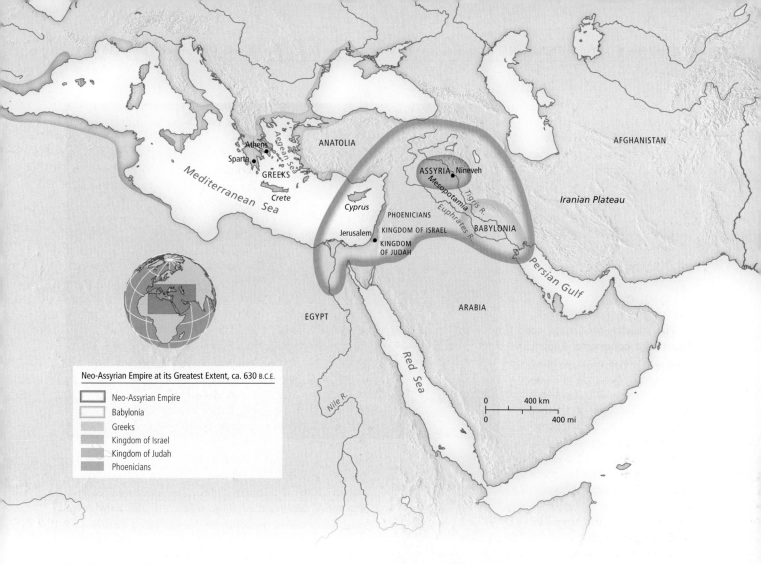

■ **Map 2.2   The Neo-Assyrian Empire at Its Greatest Extent, ca. 630 B.C.E.**
By 630 B.C.E., the Assyrians had recovered their strength and established the Neo-Assyrian Empire.
This huge realm included Mesopotamia, the Israelite kingdoms, Phoenicia, and parts of Egypt.

neighboring areas, which quickly and understandably surrendered.

Like their predecessors during the International Bronze Age, the Neo-Assyrian rulers grew wealthy from agriculture and trade. They also exploited their subjects more harshly than previously. Provincial administrators imposed crippling taxes and systematically drained away their subjects' resources. With these revenues, the kings could maintain armies of more than 100,000 men. At the same time, the government strengthened the economy by rebuilding cities, increasing the amount of land under cultivation, and building roads to improve trade and communications throughout the empire.

As the Assyrians conquered more and more peoples, they faced problems that have troubled empires ever since: How can subject peoples be controlled and what degree of cultural independence should they be permitted to retain? Assyrian solutions were thoughtful yet violent. Assyrian rulers permitted their subjects to continue their traditions

and religious practices without interference. If they rebelled against Assyrian authority, however, the army would crush them and deport entire populations to distant corners of the empire. Some Assyrian rulers depopulated entire regions. Perhaps as many as a million and a half people were forced from their homes by Assyrian deportation policies.

Ashurbanipal (r. 669–626 B.C.E.), the last strong ruler of the Neo-Assyrian Empire, attempted to create a uniform culture throughout his vast realm. At his command, scholars collected subject peoples' written knowledge, translated it into Akkadian, and distributed copies on clay tablets throughout Assyrian lands. Ashurbanipal did not succeed in imposing a standardized culture on the empire, but he was the first monarch to try to organize the diverse cultural inheritances of his many subject peoples.

Despite its prosperity and efficient administration, the Neo-Assyrian model of imperial rule failed to bring lasting unity to its peoples. Subject peoples who had endured brutal treatment at the hands of Assyrian administrators

■ **Ishtar Gate**

The magnificently tiled Ishtar Gate, right, provided a dramatic entrance to Babylon, the capital city of the Neo-Babylonian Empire. Babylonian artists used brightly colored tiles to create complicated three-dimensional depictions of animals, including lions, which represented royal power. The gate now rests in a museum in Berlin. An artist's reconstruction is shown below.

nursed a bitter resentment and revolted as soon as possible. The most significant of these rebels was the Babylonian king Nabopolassar in southern Mesopotamia (r. 625–605 B.C.E.). He allied himself with Persian kings and began a successful revolt against Assyrian rule. By 603 B.C.E., the Assyrian Empire collapsed again, this time for good.

The Neo-Babylonian Empire

After Nabopolassar acquired Assyrian territory, he built the Neo-Babylonian (or Chaldean) Empire into the most powerful in Southwest Asia, which lasted until 539 B.C.E. His son, the brilliant general Nebuchadnezzar II (r. 604–562 B.C.E.), conquered lands that had broken free when Assyrian rule collapsed. Babylonian armies seized Egypt, Syria, Phoenicia, and the kingdom of Judah, where they destroyed the city of Jerusalem and exiled many Jews to Babylon. (We will learn more about this exile in Chapter 3.)

With the wealth acquired from these conquests, Nebuchadnezzar made his capital city, Babylon, one of the most luxurious in the ancient world. A moat flooded with waters from the Euphrates River surrounded Babylon's eight miles of walls. The Ishtar Gate, which opened onto a grand avenue leading to the temple of Marduk, Babylon's greatest god, was decorated with glazed, brightly colored tiles. According to tradition, Nebuchadnezzar built the "Hanging Gardens of Babylon" for a favorite wife who missed her mountainous homeland. Splendid flowers and plants cascaded down the slopes of a terraced hillside that from a distance seemed to float in the air.

The Neo-Babylonian Empire comprised a constellation of wealthy cities in which life revolved around the uninterrupted worship of Marduk. At the center of each community stood a magnificent temple to the all-powerful god. The Babylonians considered proper worship essential for the prosperity of their communities. They looked to the king to provide the peaceful conditions in which they could worship their gods without interruption. The king, for his part, expected his subjects to obey his commands, and he counted on the priests to bolster his authority.

Religion not only gave the Babylonians a profound sense of spiritual security, it also expanded their scientific knowledge. The Babylonians believed that proper interpretation of the celestial bodies through astronomy could help them understand the will of the gods. Building on the Sumerians' mathematical and astronomical legacy, Babylonian astronomers patiently observed and recorded the movements of the stars, the planets, and the moon. They kept a continuous log of observations between 747 B.C.E. and 61 C.E., an astonishing achievement. Starting around 500 B.C.E., they had accumulated so much astronomical data that they could perform complicated mathematical computations to predict eclipses of the moon and sun. They also calculated the first appearance of the new moon every month, which enabled them to devise a calendar. These brilliant astronomers' calculations, which Persians and Greeks would later adopt, helped lay the foundation of Western science. From these able scientists, the West inherited the names of many constellations, the zodiac, and many complex mathematical models of astronomical phenomena.

CONCLUSION

The International Bronze Age and the Emergence of the West

The International Bronze Age and its aftermath marked two early but crucial phases in the formation of Western civilization. Within a large geographical area centered on the eastern Mediterranean but stretching far beyond its shores, an intricate network of political, commercial, and cultural ties was established among cities and kingdoms that had previously lived in relative isolation from each other. The forces that exposed the cultures of these areas to each other were the expansion of international trade; the development of a new military technology; the growth of large, multiethnic empires; and the establishment of diplomatic relations among rulers.

The encounters that took place among the peoples of these lands contributed to the emergence of Western civilization. Long before it was possible to identify what we now call the West, the exchange of commodities, the spread of religious ideas, the growth of common political traditions, the dissemination of scientific and technological techniques, and the borrowing of one language from another created a complex pattern of cultural diffusion over a vast geographical area.

During subsequent centuries the content of such cultural interaction would change, and the geographical area within which these exchanges took place would shift as well, first to the lands controlled by Persia, then to the Hellenistic world conquered by Alexander the Great, and later still to the sprawling Roman Empire. All these shifts took place as the result of imperial expansion and consolidation, a process that began with the formation of multiethnic empires discussed in this chapter. Each period of expansion, moreover, involved new cultural encounters among different peoples. In the next chapter we will continue to look at the aftermath of the International Bronze Age as we explore a series of encounters between Hebrews, Persians, and Greeks.

Suggestions for Further Reading

For a comprehensive list of suggested readings, please go to www.ablongman.com/levackconcise/chapter2

Bryce, Trevor. *The Kingdom of the Hittites.* 1998. The latest synthesis of Hittite history and culture.

Cline, Eric H. *Sailing the Wine-Dark Sea: International Trade and the Late Bronze Age Aegean* 1994. Essays by specialists on cultural and economic interconnections during the Bronze Age.

Cline, Eric H., and Diane Harris-Cline, eds. *The Aegean and the Orient in the Second Millennium: Proceedings of the 50th Anniversary Symposium, Cincinnati, 18–20 April 1997, Aegaeum 18.* 1998. A collection of papers by experts providing state-of-the-art discussions of all aspects of the connections among Bronze Age civilizations of the eastern Mediterranean and Middle East.

Dickinson, Oliver. *The Aegean Bronze Age.* 1994. Now the standard treatment of the complex archaeological data.

Dothan, Trude, and Moshe Dothan. *People of the Sea: The Search for the Philistines.* 1992. A highly popularized survey of the archaeological material.

Drews, Robert. *The End of the Bronze Age: Changes in Warfare and the Catastrophe ca. 1200 B.C.* 1993. A controversial but well-argued analysis that offers new solutions to the question of why the Bronze Age ended.

Fitton, J. Lesley. *The Discovery of the Greek Bronze Age.* 1996. A lucid and well-illustrated study of the archaeologists who brought the Greek Bronze Age to light in the nineteenth and early twentieth centuries.

Harding, A. F. *The Mycenaeans in Europe.* 1984. Exploration of the trade and cultural connections between Mycenaeans and the rest of Europe.

Hornung, Erik. *History of Ancient Egypt: An Introduction,* trans. David Lorton. 1999. A concise and lucid overview of Egyptian history and life.

Knapp, A. Bernard. *The History and Culture of Ancient Western Asia and Egypt.* 1988. A reliable archaeological and historical overview without excessive detail.

Kuhrt, Amélie. *The Ancient Middle East, ca. 3000–330 B.C.,* 2 vols. 1995. A magisterial overview, with excellent bibliography. The place to start for a continuous historical narrative of the region.

Macqueen, James G. *The Hittites and Their Contemporaries in Asia Minor.* 1986. This account stresses the interconnections of Hittites and other peoples.

Markoe, Glenn. *Phoenicians.* 2000. The best and most up-to-date treatment of Phoenician society by a noted expert.

Page, Denys. *History and the Homeric Iliad.* 1959. An entertaining and provocative examination of the historical context of the events described in Homer's *Iliad.*

Redford, Donald B. *Egypt, Canaan and Israel in Ancient Times.* 1992. An excellent, detailed synthesis of textual and archaeological evidence that emphasizes interconnections among cultures.

Schulz, Regine, and Matthias Seidel, eds. *Egypt: The World of the Pharaohs.* 1999. A sumptuously illustrated collection of essays on all aspects of Egyptian society and life by leading experts.

Traill, David. *Schliemann of Troy: Treasure and Deceit.* 1995. A fascinating discussion of the motivations and methods of the archaeologist who discovered the Bronze Age.

Walker, Christopher, ed. *Astronomy Before the Telescope.* 1996. A fascinating collection of essays about astronomy in the premodern period, which makes clear Western civilization's enormous debt to the Babylonians.

Wood, Michael. *In Search of the Trojan War.* 1985. A valuable introductory discussion of the archaeological and historical problems of placing Homer's Trojan War in its Bronze Age context.

Notes

1. T. Eric Peet, *The Great Tomb Robberies of the Twentieth Egyptian Dynasty* (2 vols. 1930, reprinted 1977). (Contains texts and translations of this and other trials.)
2. Regina Schulz and Matthias Seidel, eds., *Egypt: The World of the Pharaohs* (1998), 485.
3. Translated in A. Khurt, *The Ancient Middle East,* vol. I (1995), 350–351.

Building the Classical World: Hebrews, Persians, and Greeks, 1100–336 B.C.E.

I N THE SECOND HALF OF THE SIXTH CENTURY B.C.E., CYRUS THE GREAT, A PERSIAN king from southern Iran, created the largest empire the world had ever seen, with territories in Asia, the Middle East, Africa, and Europe. According to one of the many legends surrounding this celebrated ruler, Cyrus grew restless under the rule of another king. He summoned the Persian tribal leaders who owed him allegiance and instructed them to spend a day clearing land with sickles. When they finally stopped their backbreaking labor, he invited them to a magnificent banquet. After the men had devoured the last delicacy, Cyrus asked them which they enjoyed more, tasting the wonderful food or sweating in the fields. The chieftains shouted in unison that they preferred the wine and fine foods. Cyrus then proclaimed:

> *Men of Persia, follow me and I promise that you will enjoy this sort of luxury for the rest of your lives, but if you do not, your lives will be full of painful toil with no such rewards from your present masters.*[1]

Without hesitation the men joined Cyrus in his successful revolt. Under his able leadership the Persians went on to conquer more than twenty-three different peoples in territories ranging from the eastern Mediterranean coast to central Asia. Cyrus's successors added Egypt and parts of Greece and India to the Persian Empire. With its huge expanse and the stable government it provided to an enormous mix of cultures, the Persian Empire marked a turning point in the history of the ancient world.

Chapter Outline

- Hebrew Civilization and Religion
- Classical Persia: An Empire on Three Continents
- Greece Rebuilds, 1100–479 B.C.E.
- The Classical Age of Greece, 479–336 B.C.E.

Persian Art: Persian artists drew freely from the artistic traditions of their subject peoples. This illustration shows how they put their own stamp on the Babylonian art of ceramic tile. The tiles show two members of the elite imperial guard, known as the Immortals. The details of their uniforms appear in vivid color. Soldiers like these in Xerxes's army attacked the Greeks in the fifth century B.C.E.

This chapter examines the civilizations that developed during the six centuries following the collapse of the International Bronze Age around 1100 B.C.E. When long-distance trade in copper and tin broke down at that time, iron became the preferred metal for making tools and weapons throughout the ancient world. As a result of the widespread use of iron, archaeologists refer to the new period as the Iron Age. The main historical development during this period was a series of cultural encounters between the Persians and other peoples, particularly the Hebrews and Greeks. In the fifth and fourth centuries B.C.E. these encounters led to the formation of a world that has been so influential that we call it classical. For two centuries after Cyrus's death in 530 B.C.E., the Persian Empire prospered as its leaders methodically expanded their territory abroad and shrewdly managed their many subject peoples. The interaction of local cultures with Persian culture made an indelible impression on the history of the West. From their Assyrian and Babylonian subjects, the Persians inherited—and improved on—a political legacy of ruling a multiethnic empire. They also benefited from a scientific legacy that stretched back to the Sumerians. The Persians' capacity to borrow and adapt the most useful features of other cultures strengthened their own highly organized and justly administered empire.

Persian imperial power provided the backdrop for the development of two highly influential ideas in the Western tradition. These concepts came not from Persians themselves but from people who had been subject to their rule. The first idea was monotheism, the belief in only one god. This concept originated among the Hebrews, and it became a central tenet of their religion, Judaism, during this period. The tradition of biblical monotheism later became a central belief of Christianity and Islam as well.

The second idea was democracy°, the conviction that people should share equally in the government of their community, devise their own governing institutions, and select their own leaders. Democratic institutions originated in the Greek city-state of Athens in the sixth century B.C.E. Following surprising victories over the Persians in the fifth century B.C.E., Athens was free to develop its democratic institutions in an atmosphere of great economic stability and security.

At the same time, Athenian artists and thinkers began to flourish in the environment made possible by victories over the Persians. During the Classical Age of Greece, from 479 B.C.E. until 336 B.C.E., Athenians established philosophical schools that laid the foundations of Western philosophy and science, wrote dramas that grappled with fundamental moral questions, and created a distinctive Greek classical style in sculpture and architecture that has continued to be a source of inspiration in Western civilization up to the present day.

To understand how the classical world came together from so many cultural elements, this chapter will explore these questions:

- What political and religious beliefs and institutions gave Hebrew civilization its unique character, and what consequences came of its interactions with the Assyrians, Babylonians, and Persians?
- How did the Persian Empire bring these peoples of the Middle East together in a stable realm, and what elements of Persian religion and government have influenced Western thought?
- How did Greek city-states develop in the framework of a larger world dominated by Persia?
- What were the political, social, and intellectual innovations of Greece in the Classical Age?

Hebrew Civilization and Religion

One of the most influential civilizations in the West has been that of the Jews, a people who originated in the Middle East when the International Bronze Age came to an end. As we saw in Chapter 2, the Raiders of the Land and Sea destroyed many Canaanite cities around 1100 B.C.E. This disruption allowed different groups of seminomadic pastoralists, called *Hapiru* ("landless people"), to migrate into the hill country of Canaan, where they settled, herded their flocks, and began farming. Some historians think that this settlement was the origin of the biblical Hebrews, who gradually cohered into tribes and then kingdoms.

THE SETTLEMENT IN CANAAN

Around 1100 B.C.E. one small group of wandering Hapiru arrived in Canaan from Egypt, bringing with them the seeds of a powerful new religious belief. They gave allegiance to only one god. Belief in this one deity gave them a strong sense of identity and distinguished them from the Canaanite peoples, who worshiped many gods. These followers of one god became known as Hebrews, then Israelites, and later Jews. Many centuries later, their traditions explained that a leader called Moses had led them from slavery in Egypt to freedom in Canaan, and that he had received from God the laws known today as the Ten Commandments.

By absorbing new members and conquering other groups, a loose confederation of tribes gained control of most of Canaan during the eleventh century B.C.E. Impressed by the Hebrew victories, many Canaanites began to worship the Hebrew god and joined the Hebrew tribes. Gradually these various tribes came to believe that they all shared a common history and a common ancestor, Abraham, who had traveled to Canaan from his home in Mesopotamia long before Moses. According to biblical tradition, Abraham was the first person to worship only one god.

The most serious threat to the confederation of Hebrew tribes came from the Philistines, who controlled the Mediterranean coastal plain in Canaan and pushed relentlessly at the Hebrews living in the inland hills. Around 1050 B.C.E., a Philistine army defeated the Hebrew tribes in battle and captured the Ark of the Covenant, a chest that Hebrews believed contained the tablets on which the Ten Commandments were inscribed. According to traditions recorded in the Bible, the desperate Hebrews chose a king to give them stronger leadership, even though tribal tradition was hostile to the notion of kings. The tribes chose Saul to be the first king about 1020 B.C.E., and he retrieved the Ark from the Philistines. Some twenty years later, a popular warrior in Saul's court named David succeeded Saul as king and reigned from approximately 1000 to 962 B.C.E.

THE ISRAELITE KINGDOMS

By establishing a strong alliance among the Hebrew tribes of northern and southern Canaan, David defeated the Philistines permanently and built a prosperous kingdom. Called the Israelite monarchy by historians, this kingdom lay sandwiched between the empires of Egypt and Mesopotamia. By imitating the government institutions of these neighboring states, David transformed the nature of Israelite society. He set up a centralized bureaucracy run by professional soldiers, administrators, and scribes. Jerusalem, an old Canaanite city, served as the capital of his new kingdom. He moved the Ark of the Covenant to Jerusalem, bringing the worship of the Hebrew God under the control of the monarchy.

During the reign of David's son Solomon (ca. 962–922 B.C.E.), the kingdom of Israel enjoyed peace and prosperity. One of Solomon's greatest achievements was the construction of a grand temple in Jerusalem to serve as the house of God and a resting place for the Ark of the Covenant. The temple became the focal point of religious worship in his kingdom.

When Solomon died in 922 B.C.E., his heirs' inability to placate the northern Israelite tribes, who felt that Solomon had favored his own tribe of Judah at their expense, caused the Israelite kingdom to break into two parts. The kingdom of Israel, in the northern region of the former kingdom, established its capital at Shechem, while in the southern kingdom of Judah, the capital remained Jerusalem. During the next two centuries both of the two successor kingdoms struggled to survive under the shadow of the far more powerful neighboring empires of Assyria and Babylonia.

The Hebrew Prophets

During the period following the division of the Israelite kingdom, the gap between the rich and the poor in both kingdoms widened. Rapacious kings, greedy aristocrats, and high taxes meant that more and more debt-ridden peasants lost their farms to rich landholders. The poor found champions in the Hebrew prophets, who spoke out on behalf of the downtrodden with words they believed to be inspired by God. These social critics strongly censured what they saw as religious and moral decay among the landowners and kings, such as the worship of Canaanite gods, a practice that remained widespread. The prophet Elijah, who lived in the ninth century B.C.E., proclaimed that kings should not break the laws with impunity but should conform to the same laws as everyone else. The principle that kings and rulers are not above the law remained as a basic political idea in what eventually became the West. In the next century, another champion of social justice named Amos mocked the irony and hypocrisy of the royal court's celebrating lavish religious ceremonies in God's name while the poor starved. Isaiah, a prophet who lived in Jerusalem, demanded that people attempt to establish a just society in order to avert divine punishment. He had no patience for religious observance empty of personal commitment.

As Israel was reoccupied with internal problems, the neighboring Assyrian Empire was gathering power. As we saw in Chapter 2, Assyrian armies under the command of king Tiglath-Pileser conquered the Israelite kingdom in 733 B.C.E. Eleven years later, when the Israelite ruler refused to pay tribute, the Assyrians destroyed the kingdom and deported nearly 30,000 Israelites to Mesopotamia, a standard Assyrian practice with defeated enemies. The deported Israelites eventually forgot their cultural identity in their new homes and disappeared from the historical record, becoming known as the Lost Ten Tribes. The kingdom of Israel had come to an undignified end.

The kingdom of Judah, however, survived. By accepting the overlordship of the Assyrians and later the Babylonians, who had replaced the Assyrians as the dominant power in the Middle East by the late seventh century B.C.E., Judah escaped Israel's fate. After the destruction of the northern kingdom, a hunger for religious reform spread throughout Judah. People began to believe that God had destroyed the kingdom of Israel in anger, though they disagreed about the causes of his rage and how to appease him.

To regain God's favor, some of Judah's leaders insisted on the absolute primacy of the temple in Jerusalem as the place for religious worship. These reformers believed that God disapproved of his followers' worshiping him at many shrines instead of only one. By insisting on Jerusalem as the sole place of worship, the priests of Jerusalem increased their power. With the help of the king's soldiers, the temple priests in Jerusalem violently suppressed all other shrines to God scattered across the land. These developments enhanced a sense of Hebrew unity and identity.

Hebrew religious unity was not capable of protecting Judah from the military power of Babylonia. When Judah revolted against the Babylonians in 598 B.C.E., the

Babylonian king Nebuchadnezzar sent a large army to crush the rebellion. The next year he captured Jerusalem and deported Judah's king and high priests to Babylonia. Ten years later, when another revolt broke out, Babylonian forces burned Jerusalem to the ground and demolished Solomon's temple. Perhaps as many as 20,000 people were deported to Babylonia, an event historians call the Babylonian Exile°.

The Babylonian Exile

After the destruction of the Jerusalem temple in 587 B.C.E., the Hebrew exiles living in Babylonia struggled to maintain their cultural and religious identity. Sometime after 538 B.C.E., an anonymous author, known to biblical scholars as Second Isaiah, comforted the dispirited Hebrews in Babylonia. Trying to find meaning in the destruction of the kingdoms of Israel and Judah, he explained that God's primary interest lay in the spiritual realm, not in earthly kingdoms. The God described by Second Isaiah was a truly universal God who alone governed all Creation and shaped the lives of all the peoples of the world. This vision of a single, universal God not bound by time or place was perhaps the greatest legacy of Hebrew civilization to the West.

Second Isaiah promised that God would return his people to Jerusalem and that Cyrus the Great King of Persia, who had recently conquered the Babylonians, would serve as God's agent in this task. In 538 B.C.E., Cyrus instituted a policy permitting all peoples exiled by the Babylonians to return to their homelands. Many of the Hebrew exiles in Babylonia returned to their old homes, now governed by Persia, and attempted to revive traditional religious life in Jerusalem.

The Second Temple and Jewish Religious Practice

Nearly two generations passed before the Hebrews, with Persian assistance, finished building a new temple in Jerusalem, called the Second Temple, in 515 B.C.E. In the middle of the fifth century B.C.E., with the authority of the Persian king, a leader called Ezra the Scribe began to organize and regulate religious practices. For the next 500 years this restored temple worship would be the center of religious life. Historians call the Hebrews who lived after the completion of the Second Temple Jews. Henceforth, the people are known as Jews and their religion Judaism.

■ Isaiah Scroll

Discovered in a cave near the Dead Sea in 1947 and now housed in the Shrine of the Book in Jerusalem, this text of the biblical book of Isaiah was written between about 300 and 100 B.C.E., making it nearly a thousand years older than the next surviving manuscript of Isaiah. The two copies of the book of Isaiah differ in only a few minor details, demonstrating the care with which biblical texts were copied and passed on by generations of scribes.

The public role of Jewish women in organized worship was quite restricted. In the Second Temple period the Jews worshiped only one male god and denied all other deities. Women could not enter the most sacred portions of the temple where the main sacrifices were performed because according to religious law the blood of menstruation and childbirth made them ritually unclean. Many of these ancient attitudes regarding the place of women in religious and family life have survived to the present day, especially in the exclusion of women from the most sacred rituals and responsibilities in some forms of Judaism and Christianity.

The Hebrew Bible

After the Second Temple was built in 515 B.C.E., the Hebrew Bible (called the Old Testament by Christians) slowly took the shape it has today. Like many other peoples in the ancient Middle East, the Jews believed that their God had chosen them to serve him. They believed that historical events described in the Bible illustrate and interpret that relationship. The Bible provides a chronology of the world from the moment of its creation and gives an account of the early development of the Hebrew people. Drawn from a variety of oral and written sources, and composed many centuries after the events they describe, the biblical accounts condense and simplify a very complex process of migration, settlement, and religious development.

Many details in the Bible have been confirmed by non-Hebrew sources, but the Bible is primarily an expression of religious meaning through many different literary genres. It combines highly detailed narratives with folklore, prophecies, parables, stories, and poems. The Bible provides far more than the narration of events. It explains God's presence in human lives and establishes a moral vision of human existence. As a religious work the Hebrew Bible provides the basis of Judaism. In conjunction with the New Testament, written in the first century C.E., it is the foundational text of Christianity. Muslims also recognize both the Hebrew and Christian texts as holy writings, superseded only by the Qur'an. As a result no book has had more influence on the religious thought of the West.

Classical Persia:
An Empire on Three Continents

Persian history began about 1400 B.C.E., when small groups of people started migrating with their herds and flocks into western Iran from areas north of the Caspian Sea. Over five centuries these settlers slowly coalesced into two closely related groups, the Medes and the Persians.

CHRONOLOGY

CA. 1000–922 B.C.E.	David and Solomon rule the Israelite kingdom
721 B.C.E.	Assyrians destroy northern Israelite kingdom (Israel)
587 B.C.E.	Babylonians defeat southern Israelite kingdom (Judah)
538 B.C.E.	Cyrus of Persia permits Israelites to return to Palestine
CA. 507 B.C.E.	Cleisthenes's democratic reforms unify Attica
490 B.C.E.	Greeks stop Persian invasion at Marathon
478 B.C.E.	Delian League formed; Athenian Empire begins
431–404 B.C.E.	Peloponnesian War

By about 900 B.C.E. the Medes had established mastery over all the peoples of the Iranian plateau, including the Persians. In the sixth century, under the leadership of Cyrus the Great (r. 550–530 B.C.E.), Persia broke away from Medean rule and soon conquered the kingdom of the Medes. Under the guidance of this brilliant monarch and his successors, the Persians acquired a vast empire. They followed a monotheistic religion, Zoroastrianism, and governed their subjects with a combination of tolerance and firmness.

CYRUS THE GREAT AND PERSIAN EXPANSION

After ascending the Persian throne about 550 B.C.E., Cyrus embarked on a dazzling twenty-year career of conquering neighboring peoples. His military genius and organizational skills transformed the small kingdom near the Persian Gulf into a giant, multiethnic empire that stretched from India to the Mediterranean Sea.

Cyrus expanded his empire beyond Persia in several stages. In 547 B.C.E. he conquered Asia Minor, where he first came into contact with Greeks living on the westernmost coast and islands, a region called Ionia. Next he defeated the kingdom of Babylonia in 539 B.C.E., thus gaining control of the entire Mesopotamian region. After that he brought the region of present-day Afghanistan under his control and fortified it against the raids of the Scythian nomads who lived on the steppe lands to the north of his realm.

After Cyrus died in 530 B.C.E. his son Cambyses II (r. 529–522 B.C.E.) continued his father's policy of expansion by subduing Egypt and the wealthy Phoenician port cities. By the time of Cambyses's death in 522 B.C.E., Persia had become the mightiest empire in the world, with territorial possessions spanning Europe, Asia, the Middle East, and Africa (see Map 3.1).

A Government of Tolerance

The key to maintaining power in such a diverse empire lay in the Persian government's treatment of its many ethnic groups. The highly centralized Persian government wielded absolute power, but it rejected the brutal model of the Assyrian and Babylonian imperial system in favor of a more tolerant approach. Subject peoples were permitted to worship freely if they acknowledged the political supremacy of the Great King.

Zoroastrianism: An Imperial Religion

The Great Kings of Persia and the Persian people followed Zoroastrianism°, a monotheistic religion that still exists today. Its founder, the prophet Zoroaster, lived and preached sometime between 1500 and 1200 B.C.E. According to Zoroaster, Ahura Mazda (Lord Wisdom), the one and only god of all Creation, is the cause of all good things in the universe. Another eternal being, Angra Mainyu (or Ahriman), opposes him.

In Zoroastrian belief, Ahura Mazda will eventually triumph in this struggle with the forces of evil, leaving all Creation to enjoy a blissful eternity. Until then, the cosmic fight between Ahura Mazda's forces of light and Angra Mainyu's forces of darkness gives meaning to human existence and lays the foundation for a profoundly ethical way of life. Everyone has the responsibility of choosing between right and wrong actions.

■ **Map 3.1   The Persian Empire at Its Greatest Extent**

The Persian Empire begun by Cyrus about 550 B.C.E. grew to include all of the Middle East as far as India, Egypt, and northern Greece. This multiethnic, multireligious empire governed its many peoples firmly but tolerantly.

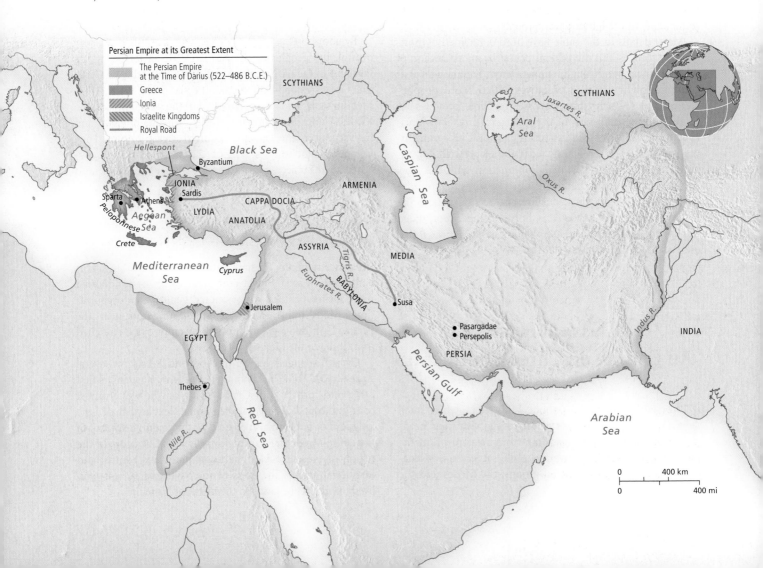

At the last Day of Judgment, sinners who have not obeyed Ahura Mazda's instructions will suffer eternal torment in a deep pit of terrible darkness. Those who have lived ethical lives will live eternally in a world purged of evil. In a period of transformation called "the Making Wonderful," the dead will be resurrected, and all will live together in the worship of Ahura Mazda.

The Great Kings of Persia believed themselves to be Ahura Mazda's earthly representatives. They committed their energies to fighting the forces of disorder active in the world. In this way, Zoroastrianism provided an ideological support for the Persian Empire's wars of conquest and consolidation at home. The Great Kings lavishly supported the Zoroastrian church, and although the Persian Empire tolerated other religions, Zoroastrianism became the official religion of the empire.

Zoroastrian beliefs have played an important role in shaping Western religious thought. They influenced the theology of the exiled Jews, and through Judaism they were in turn passed on to Christianity and Islam in later centuries. The idea of a final judgment followed by an afterlife in Heaven or Hell became a central concept in Christianity and Islam. Likewise, the idea of a final combat between the Devil and God, followed by the judgment of humanity and the establishment of the kingdom of God on Earth, is still important in many Christian communities.

THE ACHAEMENID DYNASTY

In 522 B.C.E., a Persian nobleman, Darius, seized the imperial throne by murdering one of the sons of Cyrus the Great and initiated the Achaemenid dynasty. Named for a legendary ancestor, Achaemenes, the new dynasty inaugurated an epoch of territorial expansion and cultural activity that lasted until the Macedonian conqueror Alexander the Great overwhelmed Persia in 330 B.C.E. Darius built a new capital city at Persepolis.

By 513 B.C.E. Darius had greatly expanded his empire. On his northeastern frontier he annexed portions of India as far as the Indus River. He built a canal in Egypt that linked the Mediterranean and Red Seas. But his conquests on the northwestern frontier of the Persian Empire had the greatest impact on Western civilization because they

■ **Scythian Nomads**
A Scythian nomad strings his bow. The Greek artist who made this vase pays scrupulous attention to the details of the Scythian's clothing, including his leggings, peaked cap, and tunic.

brought Persia into direct contact with the Greeks. The stage was now set for the confrontation between the Persians and the Greeks, a confrontation that demonstrated the limits of Persian imperialism.

Greece Rebuilds, 1100–479 B.C.E.

At the end of the International Bronze Age Greek civilization entered a period of bitter poverty and political instability. This period, known as the Dark Age, lasted until about 750 B.C.E., when the Archaic Age began. The Archaic Age was marked by economic growth at home and many Greek encounters with Phoenicians and Persians abroad. This period of revival set the stage for Greece's Classical Age, a time of great cultural achievement.

THE DARK AGE, CA. 1100–750 B.C.E.

Compared with the wealth and splendor of the Bronze Age Mycenaean communities, Greek life in the Dark Age was quite gloomy. Few new settlements were established on the mainland and urban life disappeared. Linear B writing dropped out of use entirely, and extensive maritime trade ended. A serious decline in agriculture led to a steep decrease in food production and population.

A slow economic recovery began in the Greek world about 850 B.C.E. Because of the harsh living conditions on the mainland during the Dark Age, many Greeks had abandoned their homes and moved to a region called Ionia that encompassed the coasts and islands of western Asia Minor. Relatively isolated from other Greek communities, these pioneers developed their own distinctive Ionian variation of the Greek language. By 800 B.C.E. the Ionian Greeks were regularly interacting with the Phoenicians in the eastern Mediterranean. These seafarers forged a connection between Greeks and the cultures of the Middle East that exerted a lasting impact on Greek society.

THE ARCHAIC AGE, CA. 750–479 B.C.E.

Between about 750 and 650 B.C.E., many fresh ideas poured into Greece from the Middle East through contact with the Phoenicians and other peoples. These encounters led to new economic practices (such as the use of coinage and charging interest on loans); new myths and literary themes (such as the story of the Great Flood); new ritual procedures for sacrificing animals; and new gods and goddesses (such as Dionysus, the god of wine).

By far the most valuable import from the Phoenicians was the alphabet, which was introduced in Greece sometime just before 750 B.C.E. The adoption of the alphabet was one of the developments that marked the beginning of the Archaic Age. Because an alphabet records sounds, not words, it can be adjusted easily for any language. Greeks quickly recognized the potential of the new system, and quickly adopted it throughout their communities. Greeks learned to write and read, first for business purposes and then for pleasure. They began to record their oral traditions, legends, and songs. At the same time, they began to compose an entirely new literature and write down their laws.

Homer's Epic Poems

Two of the greatest works of epic literature ever composed, the *Iliad* and the *Odyssey,* were soon written down in the new alphabet. A Greek poet named Homer, who probably lived around 750 B.C.E., is credited with composing these poems, but they were certainly not his personal invention. The stories of the *Iliad* and the *Odyssey* drew from a large and widely disseminated body of tales about the legendary Trojan War that wandering poets had recited for centuries. The poets had elaborated on the stories so much over time that historical accuracy was lost. Nevertheless, many details in the poems, especially about weapons and armor no longer used in Homer's day, suggest that the earliest versions of the poems were first recited in the International Bronze Age and may be very loosely based on events of that time.

The body of poems of which the *Iliad* and the *Odyssey* were a part tells how an army of Greek warriors sailed to Troy, a wealthy city on the northwest coast of Asia Minor, to recover a beautiful Greek princess, Helen, who had been stolen by a Trojan prince. After ten years of savage fighting, the Greeks finally stormed Troy and won the war, though their greatest fighters had died in battle. When the surviving heroes returned home to Greece, they were met with treachery and bloodshed.

The Polis

In addition to telling epic tales that glorified heroes of the past, Greeks in the Archaic Age experimented with new forms of social and political life. They developed a new style of community called the polis° (plural *poleis*), or city-state. A polis was a self-governing community consisting of an urban center with a defensible hilltop called an acropolis° and all the surrounding land farmed by citizens of the polis. Greek cities varied in size from a few square miles to several hundred. All contained similar institutions: an assembly in which the men of the community gathered to discuss and make decisions about public business; a council of male elders who offered advice on public matters; temples to gods who protected the polis and whose goodwill was necessary for the community's prosperity; and an open area in the center of town called an *agora,* which served as a market and a place for informal discussions.

Living in a polis provided an extremely strong sense of community. A person could be a citizen of only one polis, and every citizen was expected to place the community's interests above all other concerns. Even the women, who were citizens but not permitted to play a role in public life, felt powerful ties to their polis. While only citizens had full membership in a polis, enjoying the greatest rights and bearing the greatest responsibilities, every city had noncitizens from other communities. Some of these noncitizens had limited rights and obligations. Others were slaves, who had no rights at all.

Colonization and the Settlement of New Lands

A population boom during the Archaic Age forced Greeks to emigrate because the rocky soil of the mainland could not provide enough food. From about 750 to 550 B.C.E., cities such as Corinth and Megara on the mainland and Miletos in Ionia established more than 200 colonies overseas.

Greek emigrants traveled by boat to foreign shores. Many colonists settled on the Aegean coast north into the Black Sea region, which offered plentiful farmlands. The nearby settlement at Byzantium controlled access to the agricultural wealth of these Black Sea colonies. Greeks established many new cities in Sicily and southern Italy, as well as on the southern coast of France and the eastern coast of Spain. By 600 B.C.E. Greeks had founded colonies in North Africa in the region of modern Libya and on the islands of Cyprus and Crete. Greek merchants also set up a trading community on the Syrian coast and another in the Egyptian delta, with the pharaoh's permission.

New Greek cities like Syracuse and Tarentum in Italy, Massilia (Marseilles) in France, and Neapolis (Naples) in Italy gave land-hungry settlers the opportunity to prosper through farming, manufacturing, and trade. The colonists

Athenian

(front) (back)

Jewish Second Temple Period

(front) (back)

■ Athenian Coinage

The coins made in Athens displayed the head of Athena on one side, and her sacred bird, the owl, on the other side. The coin shown at the top dates to the height of the Athenian Empire, about 450 B.C.E. On the bottom, another coin of similar weight and appearance is called a Jehud (from the Persian name of the province of Judah). Minted near Jerusalem, its front shows a face based on Athena. Its back shows an owl and Hebrew writing. The similarities of these coins reveal the international influence of Athenian coinage and the importance of standard weights in long-distance trade.

obtained metal ores, timber, and slaves from the regions they settled and began growing wheat, olives, and grapes to make wine for export. Merchants carried the goods to markets all over the Mediterranean. The overseas world of the Greeks prospered, and a vibrant Greek culture with common language, gods, and social institutions spread throughout the Mediterranean and into the Black Sea area.

Although all of the Greek colonies maintained some formal religious ties with their mother city-states, or *metropoleis*, they were self-governing and independent. Some colonies failed, but others grew rich and populous enough to establish their own colonies. Because the Greek colonists seized territory by force and sometimes slaughtered the local inhabitants, relations with the people already living in these lands were often quite tense.

The Greek adoption of coinage spurred commercial activity among many Greek communities. Coinage first replaced barter as a medium of exchange in western Asia Minor about 630 B.C.E. as a form of portable wealth that could be used to buy goods and services. Minted from precious metals and uniform in weight, coins helped people

standardize the value of goods, a development that revolutionized commerce. When Athens became the dominant economic power in the Aegean during the second half of the fifth century B.C.E., Athenian coinage became the standard throughout the Greek world and far beyond.

Greek colonization played a critical role in shaping Western civilization by creating wealthy centers of Greek culture in Italy and the western Mediterranean. Sometimes overshadowed in the historical record by city-states of the Greek mainland, such as Athens, Sparta, and Corinth, the impressive new poleis spread Greek civilization, language, literature, religion, and art far beyond Greece itself.

Elite Athletic Competition in Greek Poleis

Athletic contests called panhellenic° games, because they drew participants from the entire Greek world, were a mainstay of aristocratic Greek culture in the Archaic Age. As many as 150 cities regularly offered aristocratic men the chance to win glory through competition in chariot racing, discus throwing, wrestling, foot racing, and other field events. Through sports the Greeks found a common culture that allowed them to express their Greek identity and honor the gods at the same time.

The Olympic games, which originated in 776 B.C.E., carried the most prestige. Every four years Greek athletes from southern Italy to the Black Sea gathered in the sacred grove of Olympia in central Greece to take part in games dedicated to Zeus, the chief Greek god. The rules required the poleis to call truces to any wars, even if they were in the middle of battle, and allow safe passage to all athletes traveling to Olympia. Records show the naming of champions at Olympia from 776 B.C.E to 217 C.E. The Roman emperor Theodosius I, who was a Christian, abolished the games in 393 C.E. because they involved the worship of Greek gods.

The Hoplite Revolution

The new wealth flowing through the panhellenic world transformed Greek life. For the first time, men who were not aristocrats could afford to purchase weapons of war. Called hoplites°, these men had the means to acquire helmets, shields, swords, shin guards, and thrusting spears. Hoplites developed a completely different method of fighting. Rather than galloping into battle on horseback or engaging in individual hand-to-hand combat to win personal glory, hoplites entered the battlefield as a phalanx°, fighting as a group that moved in unison. Standing shoulder to shoulder in rows eight men deep, each fighter relied on the man to his right to shield him while he struck forward with his sword or spear. Thus the hoplites' success depended on intense training and, above all, cooperation.

Hoplite fighting generated a sense of pride and common purpose that had political consequences, as hoplites demanded a political voice in the communities for which they fought. Their growing confidence directly challenged aristocratic families who traditionally held tight control over community decision making.

In many poleis, new political leaders arose to champion the cause of the hoplite citizenry. These political leaders were known as tyrants°, a word borrowed from the Middle East that originally did not have the negative connotation it carries today. Tyrants typically came from the ruling classes, but they found their political support among the hoplites and the poor who felt otherwise left out of the political life of the community. When tyrants seized power in a polis, they served the interests of the community as a whole, not just the aristocrats. They promoted overseas trade, built harbors, protected farmers, and began public-works projects to employ citizen workers and to beautify their cities. More important, the tyrants' authority enabled a broad range of Greek citizens to participate in government for the first time.

But tyrannies contained a fatal flaw. The power of the tyrant was handed down from father to son, and successors rarely inherited their fathers' qualities of leadership. As a result, the tyrannies often became oppressive and unpopular, especially among the hoplites and poor who had supported the tyrants in the first place. Few of them lasted more than two generations.

Two of the most important poleis on the Greek mainland, Sparta and Athens, dealt with tyranny in radically opposing ways. As a result, they created very different political and social systems for their citizens: Sparta became the model for an authoritarian, military society, while Athens was the model for democracy.

Sparta: A Militarized Society

Cut off from the rest of Greece by high mountain ranges to the west and north, Sparta dominated the Peloponnese, the southernmost part of Greece. Until about 700 B.C.E. Spartans lived very much like other Greeks except that their hoplite forces achieved political power without the aid of tyrants, whom they despised. Rapid expansion in the Peloponnese prompted Spartans to develop a highly militarized way of life. All political power rested with a corps of warrior hoplites that comprised the entire population of male citizens.

The Spartan social system grew more complex after 700 B.C.E. when the Spartans conquered Messenia, a fertile region in the western Peloponnese. To maintain control over the Messenians, who vastly outnumbered them, the Spartans brutally reduced the Messenians to the status of helots°, a level barely higher than beasts of burden. Helots paid half of their produce to their Spartan masters and could be murdered with impunity. Controlling the helots through terror became the Spartans' preoccupation.

In Sparta's social hierarchy free subjects stood one level above the helots. These individuals included merchants, craftsmen, and other tradesmen who lived in communities throughout Spartan territories. Free subjects paid taxes and served in the army when necessary, but they were not Spartan citizens.

The male and female citizens of Sparta stood at the top of the social pyramid. They devoted themselves completely to a military way of life. The greatest responsibility of all Spartan citizens was to fulfill the needs of the polis. From early childhood, boys trained to become soldiers and girls trained to become the mothers of soldiers. Boys left home at age 7 to live in barracks, where they began to master the skills of battle. They learned that their comrades-in-arms played a more important role in their lives than their own families.

After its conquest of Messenia, Sparta strengthened its presence further by organizing the Peloponnesian League, an informal alliance of most of the poleis in the Peloponnese. Spartans avoided wars far from home, but they and their allies joined with the Athenians and other Greeks in resisting Persia's aggression against Greece, as we will see shortly.

Athens: Toward Democracy

Athens, the best known polis of ancient Greece, made an incalculably rich contribution to the political, philosophical, artistic, and literary traditions of Western civilization. The first democracy in the ancient world, Athens developed principles of government that remain alive today. Athens's innovative form of government and the flowering of its intellectual life stemmed directly from its response to tyranny and Persian aggression.

In the eighth and seventh centuries B.C.E., the Athenians settled Attica, the territory surrounding their city, rather than sending colonists abroad. In this way, Athens gained more land and a larger population than any other polis. By the beginning of the sixth century, aristocrats controlled most of the wealth of Attica, and many of the Athenian peasants became heavily indebted to them, pledging their bodies as collateral on loans. They risked being sold into slavery abroad if they could not repay the debt.

With civil war between the debt-ridden peasantry and the aristocracy on the horizon, both segments of the population of Attica agreed to let Solon, an Athenian statesman known for his practical wisdom, reform the political system. In 594 B.C.E. Solon (ca. 650–570 B.C.E.) enacted several measures that limited the authority of the aristocracy and enabled all male citizens to participate more fully in Athenian public life. These reforms created the institutions of public political life from which democracy eventually developed.

Solon next organized the population into four classes based on wealth. Only men in the two richest classes could hold the highest administrative office of *archon* and be elected to the highest court, traditionally a base of aristocratic authority. From the third class, Solon created the *boule*, a council of 400 men who prepared the agenda for the general citizen assembly. Men from the fourth and poorest class, who could not afford hoplite weapons, could vote in the citizen assembly, though they could not be elected to any office. Men of any class could serve on a new court that Solon established. Women and slaves had no voice in government at all.

After a generation of internal peace, Athenian aristocrats began to chafe at their loss of power and rebelled against Solon's system. In ca. 560 B.C.E. a nobleman named Peisistratus (ca. 590–528 B.C.E.) seized power and ruled Athens as a tyrant. Like other tyrannies in Greece, Peisistratus's regime initially enjoyed widespread support. His sons, however, abused their power, and jealous aristocrats assisted by Sparta toppled the family's rule in 510.

Two years later, the assembly selected a nobleman named Cleisthenes to reorganize Athens. Building upon Solon's reforms, he set the basic institutions of democracy in place with a new council of 500 male citizens drawn from throughout Attica, which made decisions for the community. He ensured that every male citizen had a permanent voice in government, broke the power of aristocratic families, and set up the lasting, fundamental structures of Athenian democracy.

THE PERSIAN WARS, 490–479 B.C.E.

The strength of Cleisthenes's new system would be tested in the face of invasions by Persia in the fifth century B.C.E. Around 510 B.C.E. the Persian king Darius conquered the Ionian Greek poleis. The Persians ruled their new subjects fairly, but the Ionian Greeks nevertheless revolted in 499 B.C.E. When the Ionian Greek rebels asked Athens for assistance against the Persians, the Athenians sent an expeditionary force that helped the rebels burn Sardis, a Persian provincial capital. The Persians crushed the rebellion in 494 B.C.E., but they did not forget the role of Athens in it.

The Marathon Campaign

In 490 B.C.E., after four years of meticulous planning, a Persian army crossed the Aegean Sea in the ships of their Phoenician subjects. They landed at the beach of Marathon, some twenty-six miles from Athens. To save their city Athenian forces marched to Marathon, and with the aid of troops from a neighboring polis the outnumbered Greek army overcame the Persian forces, which withdrew from Greece. The surprising Greek victory at Marathon demonstrated that a well-trained hoplite force could defeat a far more numerous foe.

Athenian Naval Power and the Salamis Campaign

After Marathon, Athens embraced even more dramatic reforms. A new political leader named Themistocles persuaded his fellow citizens to spend the proceeds from a rich silver mine in Attica on a new navy and port. By 480 B.C.E. Athens possessed nearly 200 battleships, called triremes°. With three banks of oars manned by the poorest citizens of the polis, the triremes transformed Athens into a naval powerhouse. The entire male citizen body of Athens, not just the aristocrats and hoplites, could now be called to arms. The Athenian navy embodied Athenian democracy in action in which every male citizen had an obligation to defend his homeland.

The battle of Marathon had dealt a shameful blow to the Persians' pride that they resolved to avenge. In 480 B.C.E., Xerxes I, the new Persian Great King, launched a massive invasion of Greece. He brought an overwhelming force of some 150,000 soldiers, a navy of nearly 700 mostly Phoenician vessels, and ample supplies. His troops crossed from Asia into Europe by means of a bridge of boats over the Hellespont, while the navy followed a parallel path by sea in order to supply the troops. They intended to smash Athens.

Terrified by the magnitude of the Persian army, fewer than 40 of the more than 700 Greek poleis joined the defensive coalition that had formed in anticipation of the invasion. The Spartan king Leonidas led the coalition. Under his command, a Greek force stopped the Persians at the pass of Thermopylae until a traitor revealed an alternate path through the mountains. On the last day of the battle, Leonidas, his entire force of 300 valiant Spartans, and several thousand allies, died fighting.

Their sacrifice was not in vain. The disaster at Thermopylae gave the Athenians precious time to evacuate their city and to station their highly maneuverable fleet in the narrow straits of Salamis, just off the Athenian coast. In a stunning display of naval skill, the Athenian triremes defeated the Persian navy in a single day of heavy fighting. Xerxes withdrew most of his forces to Asia Minor, but left a large army in northern Greece.

Early in 479 B.C.E., a combined Greek army once again stopped the Persians at the battle of Plataea, north of Attica. In this battle a large contingent of Spartans led a decisive final charge. That same year, the combined naval forces of Greece defeated the Persian navy off the Ionian coast. Without a single substantial military success, Xerxes gave up the attempt to conquer Greece and returned to Persia.

The Classical Age of Greece, 479–336 B.C.E.

After the defeat of the Persians, the Greeks exhibited immense confidence in their ability to shape their political institutions and to describe and analyze their society and the world around them. In the political realm, the emboldened Athenians created a powerful empire that made them the dominant power in the Greek world. During this time democratic institutions flourished in Athens. The structures of Greek society provided many male citizens with the leisure time for debating public affairs in a democratic fashion, for attending plays, and for speculating about philosophical issues. The most distinctive feature of Athenian life during this period was its remarkable level of creativity, especially in drama, science, history writing, philosophy, and the visual arts.

THE RISE AND FALL OF THE ATHENIAN EMPIRE

With the Persian threat to Greece nearly eliminated, Athens began a period of rapid imperial expansion. This aggressive foreign policy soon set off waves of discord among the other Greek city-states that led to war and the eventual collapse of the Athenian Empire.

From Defensive Alliance to Athenian Empire

After the battle of Plataea, Athens reorganized its defensive alliance against Persia, creating the Delian League° named for the small island of Delos where the members met. By 469 B.C.E. the Delian League had driven the last Persians from the Aegean.

With the Persians ousted, the Athenians rapidly turned the Delian League into an empire organized for their own benefit. In subsequent decades the Athenians established military garrisons and intervened in the political life of many cities of the league by imposing heavy taxes and establishing many rules and financial regulations. Athenian policy had become indifferent to the original defensive purpose of the league, but the revenues generated by the league's exploitation simultaneously enabled democracy to flourish at home.

Democracy in the Age of Pericles

The chief designer of the Athenian Empire was Pericles, an aristocrat who dominated Athenian politics from 461 B.C.E. until his death in 429 B.C.E. During the so-called "Age of Pericles," Athenian democracy at home and empire abroad reached their peak.

During this period, the representative council of 500 men established by Cleisthenes continued to administer public business. The assembly made final decisions on issues of war, peace, and public policy by majority vote. Because men gained political power through debate in the assembly, a politician's rhetorical skills played an all-important role in convincing voters.

By the middle of the fifth century, Athens had about 1,500 officials in its bureaucracy. Now responsible for administrating the Delian League, boards of assessors determined the amount of money its members would pay. Many legal disputes arose among cities in the league, forcing Athens to increase the number of its courts. Because of the constant need for jurors and other office holders, Pericles began paying wages for public service, the first such policy in history. Jurors were chosen by lot, and trials lasted no more than a day to expedite cases, save money, and prevent jury tampering.

Additional reforms by Pericles gave Athenian women a more important role in society. Before 451 B.C.E., children born to Athenian men and their foreign wives attained full citizenship. Pericles's new law allowed citizenship only if both parents were Athenian citizens. As a result, Athenian citizen women took pride in giving birth to the polis's only legitimate citizens. Nevertheless, citizen women continued to be denied full freedom of action in public life.

MACEDONIA

PERSIAN
EMPIRE

• Sardis

ATTICA
• Athens

MESSENIA
• Sparta

Delos

0   50 km
0   50 mi

The Peloponnesian War
- Athens and its allies
- Sparta and its allies
- Neutral

■ **Map 3.2   The Peloponnesian War**
During this long conflict that lasted from 431 to 404 B.C.E., the forces of Athens and its allies struggled with Sparta and its allies for control of mainland Greece. Though Sparta defeated the Athenian Empire, Athens survived as an influential force in Greek social, political, and economic life.

The Peloponnesian War

Sparta and its allies felt threatened by growing Athenian power. Between 460 and 431 B.C.E., Athens and a few allies fought intermittently with Sparta and the Peloponnesian League. Full-scale war broke out between the two sides in 431 B.C.E., continuing until 404 B.C.E.(see Map 3.2). In the beginning of the conflict, called the Peloponnesian War, the Spartans repeatedly raided Attica in the hope of defeating Athenian forces in open battle. Thanks to Athens's fortifications and the two parallel five-mile-long walls connecting the city to its main port of Piraeus, the Athenians endured the devastating Spartan invasions.

In 421 B.C.E., Spartan and Athenian generals agreed to a fifty-year truce, but a mere six years later war broke out again, when the Athenian general Alcibiades, a nephew of Pericles, persuaded the Athenians to send an expeditionary force of 5,000 hoplites to invade Sicily and take its resources for the war effort. After two years of heavy fighting, the Athenian expedition ended in utter disaster. Soldiers from Syracuse in Sicily captured every Athenian ship and either slaughtered the Athenian soldiers or sold them into slavery.

The Collapse of Athenian Power

The Peloponnesian War dragged on for another ten years, but Athens never fully recovered from the catastrophic loss of men and ships in Sicily. The Spartans established a permanent military base within sight of Athens, which enabled them to control Attica. When 20,000 slaves in the Athenian silver mines escaped to freedom under the Spartans, Athens lost its main source of revenue. The final blow came when Lysander, the Spartan commander in chief, obtained money from Persia to build a navy strong enough to challenge Athenian sea power. At the battle of Aegospotami on the Hellespont, Lysander's navy sank every Athenian ship. Athens surrendered in 404 B.C.E.

The victorious Spartan forces pulled down the walls of Athens, but they refused to burn the city to the ground because Athens had been Sparta's valiant ally in the Persian Wars. Instead, the Spartans set up an oligarchy°, or government by a few. Led by the "Thirty Tyrants," a violent and conservative political faction, the oligarchy soon earned the hatred of Athenian citizens. Within a year they overthrew the tyrants and restored democracy.

THE SOCIAL AND RELIGIOUS FOUNDATIONS OF CLASSICAL GREECE

Amid the violence of the Classical Age, the Greek poleis developed a complex society, in which men and women had distinct roles to play and a set of religious practices that governed daily life. A hierarchy of gender roles determined individuals' access to public space, legal rights, and opportunities to work. In this emphatically patriarchal society, only men held positions of public authority, controlled wealth and inheritance, and enjoyed the right to participate in political life. Women were expected to engage in domestic activities, out of sight of non–family members. At the bottom of society were slaves of both genders, who had no rights at all.

Gender Roles

Greek women were expected to marry early in puberty, typically to men at least ten years older. Through marriage legal control of women passed from father to husband. Greek houses were small and usually divided into two parts. In the brighter front rooms husbands entertained their male friends at dinner and enjoyed active conversation and social interaction with other males. Wives spent the majority of their time in the more secluded portions of the home, supervising the household slaves, raising children, dealing with their mothers-in-law, and weaving cloth.

Greek men strictly monitored and closely controlled women's sexual activity. Because men considered females powerless to resist seduction, respectable women rarely ventured out in public without a chaperone. To the typical Greek husband, the ideal wife stayed out of public sight, dutifully obeyed him, and was satisfied by sexual relations with him three times a month. She was not supposed to mind if he had relations with prostitutes or adolescent boys.

Women who worked outside the home did so primarily in three capacities: as vendors of farm produce or cloth in the marketplace, as priestesses, and as prostitutes. The vendors, who used their skills as weavers to supplement the family income, came from the lower classes. Priestesses served the temples of goddesses. In classical Athens, more than forty publicly sponsored religious cults had female priests. These women gained high prestige in their communities. Greeks believed that some women possessed a special ability that made them excellent mediums through whom divinities often spoke. Such women served as oracles, as in the temple of Apollo at Delphi.

Prostitutes lived in all Greek cities, but unlike priestesses, their profession was considered shameful. In Athens, most prostitutes were slaves from abroad. Some women worked as elite courtesans called *hetairai*°. Because Greek men did not think it possible to have intellectual exchanges with their spouses, they hired hetairai to accompany them to social gatherings and to participate in stimulating conversations about politics, philosophy, and the arts. Like ordinary prostitutes, hetairai also were expected to be sexually available for pay. The Athenian orator Demosthenes famously summed up Greek attitudes toward women with these words: "We have hetairai for the sake of pleasure, regular prostitutes to care for our physical needs, and wives to bear legitimate children and be loyal custodians of our households."[2]

In classical Greece, where men considered women to be intellectually and emotionally inferior, some men believed that the best sort of friendship was found in male homosexual relationships. It was not uncommon for Greek men, especially prominent members of society, to have adolescent boys as lovers. In these relationships the older man often assumed the role of mentor to his younger companion. Some poleis institutionalized such relationships. In the city of Thebes, for example, the elite "Sacred Band" of 150 male couples led the city's hoplites into battle during the fourth century B.C.E. These men

■ **Male Homosexuality**
This painted vase displays a common homoerotic scene, the courting of an unbearded youth by an older man. The youth holds a garland that suggests athletic victory.

■ The Acropolis and the Parthenon

The Acropolis of Athens, crowned by the Parthenon, stood as a symbol of Athenian imperial culture.

were considered the best warriors because they would not endure the shame of showing cowardice to their lovers.

Slavery: The Source of Greek Prosperity

Unlike free citizens of a polis, slaves were totally under the control of other people and had no political or legal rights. Masters could kill them without serious penalty and could demand sexual favors at any time. Slavery existed in every polis at every social level.

Most information about Greek slavery comes from Athens, which was the first major slave society that is well-documented. Between about 450 and 320 B.C.E., the thriving polis had a total population of perhaps a quarter of a million people, one-third of whom were enslaved. In the Archaic Age most slaves had fallen into bondage for debt, but after Solon made the enslavement of Athenian citizens illegal in 594 B.C.E., the wealthy turned to sources outside Attica. Many slaves were captured during the Persian Wars, but most slaves were either the children of slaves or purchased from the thriving slave trade in people from around the Aegean.

Athenians and other Greeks relied on slaves to perform a wide variety of tasks. The city of Athens owned slaves who served as a police force, as public executioners, as clerks in court, and in other public capacities. Most slaves, however, were privately owned. Some labored as highly skilled artisans and businessmen who lived apart from their owners but were required to pay them a high percentage of their

profits. Every Greek household had male and female slaves who performed menial tasks. Some rich landowners owned gangs of slaves who worked in the fields. Others rented slaves to the polis to labor in the silver mines, where they were worked to death under hideous conditions.

Religion and the Gods

Religion permeated Greek life. It provided a structured way for Greeks to interact with the deities who exercised considerable influence over their lives. Greeks worshiped many gods, whom they asked for favors and advice. Every city kept a calendar of religious observances established for certain days. Festivals marked phases in the agricultural year, such as the harvest or sowing seasons, and initiation ceremonies marked an individual's transition from childhood to adulthood.

Although every polis had its own set of religious practices, people throughout the Greek world shared many ideas about the gods. The Greeks believed that the twelve greatest gods lived on Mount Olympus in northern Greece as a large and quite dysfunctional family. Zeus was the father and king; Hera was his sister and wife; and Aphrodite was the goddess of sex and love. The jealous clan also included Apollo, god of the sun, prophecy, and medicine; Ares, the god of war; and Athena, the goddess of wisdom. Greek mythology developed a set of stories about the Olympian gods that have passed into Western literature and art. Like the Greek language, these shared religious beliefs gave a common identity to Greeks. They also distinguished them from so-called barbarians who worshiped strange gods in ways the Greeks considered uncivilized.

INTELLECTUAL LIFE

In the Classical Age, Greeks investigated the natural world and explored the human condition with astonishing freshness and vigor. Their legacy in drama, science, philosophy, and the arts continued to inspire people in many subsequent periods of history.

Greek Drama

Greek men examined their society's values through public dramatic performances, which began in Athens in the early sixth century B.C.E. Fewer than fifty plays from the Greek classical period have survived, but they count among the most powerful examples of literature in the Western tradition.

Athenian tragedies told stories about the terrible suffering within human society. In many of these plays an important aristocrat or ruler is destroyed by a fatal personal flaw beyond his or her ability to control. With an unflinching gaze, playwrights examined conflicts between violent passion and reason and between the laws of the gods and those of human communities. Their dramas depicted the terrible consequences of vengeance, the brutality of war, and the relationship of the individual to the polis. In the plays of the three great Athenian tragedians—Aeschylus, Sophocles, and Euripides—characters learn vital lessons through their suffering, as does the audience.

In the plays of Sophocles (ca. 496–ca. 406 B.C.E.), humans are free to act, but they are trapped by their own weaknesses, their history, and the will of the gods. In *Antigone,* a young woman buries her outlaw brother in accordance with divine principles but in defiance of her city's laws, knowing that she will be executed for her brave act. In *Oedipus the King,* Oedipus unknowingly kills his father and marries his mother. When he learns what he has done, Oedipus blinds himself. Although he knows that a god caused his tragedy, he understands that he was the one who committed the immoral acts.

In addition to the tragedies, Greeks delighted in irreverent comedies. Performances of comedy probably began in the seventh century B.C.E. as lewd sketches associated with Dionysus, the god of wine and fertility. The playwright Aristophanes of Athens (ca. 450–388 B.C.E.) proved a master at presenting comedy as social commentary. No person, god, or institution escaped his mockery. Although fully committed to Athenian democracy, Aristophanes had no patience for hypocritical politicians or self-important intellectuals. His comic plays are full of raunchy sex and allusions to the day's issues, containing withering sarcasm, silly puns, and outrageous insults. Audiences howled at the fun,

GREEK VERSUS BARBARIAN

In the following excerpt Hippocrates of Kos (d. ca. 400 B.C.E.), known as the Father of Medicine, explains the forms of government of the Near East and the character of the people, whom he calls Asiatics. Like other Greeks of his time, Hippocrates believed in the superiority of Greek civilization. In this passage, he explains that the climatic zones in which people live determine the characteristics of their culture.

The small variations of climate to which the Asiatics are subject, extremes of both heat and of cold being avoided, account for their mental flabbiness and cowardice . . . They are less warlike than Europeans and tamer of spirit, for they are not subject to those physical changes and the mental stimulation that sharpen tempers and induce recklessness and hot-headedness . . . Such things appear to me to be the cause of the feebleness of the Asiatic race, but a contributory cause also lies in their customs; for the greater part is under monarchical rule . . . Even if a man be born brave and of stout heart, his character is ruined by this form of government.

Source: From Paul Cartledge, *The Greeks: A Portrait of Self and Others,* 1993. Reprinted by permission of Oxford University Press.

but these plays always carried a thought-provoking message as well.

Scientific Thought in Ionia

Greek science began about 600 B.C.E. in the cities of Ionia, when a handful of men began to ask new questions about the natural world. Living on the border between Greek and Persian civilizations, these Greek thinkers encountered the vigorous Babylonian scientific and mathematical traditions that still flourished in the Persian Empire. Inspired by these methods of carefully observing the natural world and systematically recording data, these Greek thinkers started pulling away from traditional Greek explanations for natural phenomena.

Greek thinkers rejected old notions of gods who arbitrarily inflicted floods, earthquakes, and other disasters on humanity. Instead, they looked for general principles that could explain each natural phenomenon. To these investigators, the natural world was orderly, knowable by means of careful inquiry, and therefore ultimately predictable. These scientists inquired about the physical composition of the natural world, tried to formulate the principles of why change occurs, and began to think about proving their theories logically.

The most important of these scientists from Ionia was Anaximander (ca. 610–547 B.C.E.). A student of Thales of Miletus (ca. 625–547 B.C.E.), Anaximander wrote a pioneering essay about natural science called *On the Nature of Things*. Anaximander became the first Greek to create a map of the inhabited world. He also argued that the universe was rational and symmetrical. In his view, it consisted of Earth as a flat disk at its center, held in place by the perfect balance of the limitless space around it.

Soon other investigators developed their own theories about the natural world. Heraclitus of Ephesus (ca. 500 B.C.E.) argued that fire, not gods, provided the true origin of the world. Leucippus of Miletus (fifth century B.C.E.) and Democritus of Abdera (ca. 460–370 B.C.E.) proposed that the universe consisted entirely of an endless number of material atoms. Too small to be seen, these particles floated everywhere. When the atoms collided or stuck together, they produced the elements of the world, including life itself. These atomists had no need for gods in their explanations of the natural world.

The Origins of Writing History

The Western tradition of writing history has its roots in the work of Herodotus (ca. 484–420 B.C.E.). In *Investigations* (the original Greek meaning of the word *history*), Herodotus attempted to explain the Persian Wars. For Herodotus, "the war between the Greeks and the non-Greeks" was just one episode in an unending cycle of violence between East and West, between barbarian and civilized, between oppressed and free.

Thucydides of Athens (d. ca. 400 B.C.E.) further advanced the science of writing history. His brilliant *History of the Peloponnesian War* stands as perhaps the single most influential work of history in the Western tradition because it provides a model for analyzing the causes of human events and the outcomes of individual decisions. In it he combines meticulous attention to accuracy and detail with a broad moral vision. To Thucydides, the Peloponnesian War represented a profound tragedy. Under the wise leadership of Pericles Athens had epitomized all that was good about a human community. Unfortunately, Athenians, like all humans, possessed a fatal flaw, the unrelenting desire to possess more. Never satisfied, they followed unprincipled leaders after Pericles's death, embarking on foolhardy adventures that eventually destroyed them.

The Origins of Philosophical Thought

During the fifth century B.C.E., a group of teachers known as sophists°, or wise men, traveled throughout the Greek-speaking world. They shared no common doctrines, and they taught everything from mathematics to political theory with the hope of instructing individuals in the best ways to lead better lives. The best-known among them was Protagoras (ca. 485–440 B.C.E.), who denied the existence of gods and absolute standards of truth. All human institutions, Protagoras argued, were created through human custom or law and not through nature. Thus, because truth is relative, an individual should be able to defend either side of an argument persuasively.

Socrates (469–399 B.C.E.), an Athenian citizen, challenged the sophists' notion that there were no absolutes to guide human life. He spent his days trying to help his fellow Athenians understand the basic moral concepts that governed their lives by relentlessly asking them questions. Because Socrates wrote nothing himself, historians know of his ideas chiefly through the accounts of his student Plato of Athens (ca. 428–347 B.C.E.), who made his teacher the central figure in his own philosophical essays.

Like Socrates, Plato rejected the notion that truth and morality are relative concepts. Plato taught that absolute virtues such as goodness, justice, and beauty do exist, but on a higher level of reality than human existence. He called these eternal, unchanging absolutes Forms°. In fact, in Platonic thought, the Forms represent true reality. Like shadows that provide only an outline of an object, life experience is merely an approximation of this true reality. Platonic theory emphasizes how the senses deceive us and how the truth is often hidden. Truth can be discovered only through careful, critical questioning rather than through observation of the physical world. As a result, Platonic thought emphasizes the superiority of theory over scientific investigation.

Plato and his student Aristotle (384–322 B.C.E.) stand as the two greatest thinkers of classical Greece. Aristotle founded his own school in Athens, called the Lyceum. Unlike his teacher, Aristotle did not envision the Forms as separate from matter. In his view, form and matter are completely bound together. For this reason, one can acquire knowledge of the Forms by carefully observing the world and classifying what one finds. Following this theory, Aristotle rigorously investigated a huge range of subjects, including animal and plant biology, mechanics, and physics. His many books made him the most influential natural scientist in the Western tradition before the modern period.

The Arts: Sculpture, Painting, and Architecture

Like philosophers and dramatists during the Classical Age, Greek sculptors, painters, and architects pursued ideal beauty and truth. Classical artists believed the human body was beautiful and an appropriate subject of their attention. They also valued the human capacity to represent in art the ideals of beauty, harmony, and proportion found in nature.

To create a statue that was an image of physical perfection, sculptors portrayed the best features of several human models while ignoring their flaws. They strove to depict the muscles, movement, and balance of the human figure in a way that was both lifelike in its imitation of nature

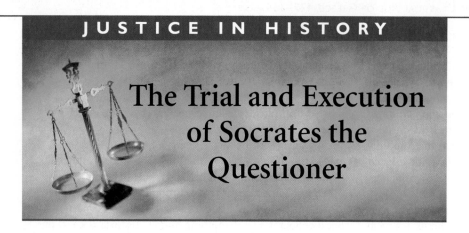

The Trial and Execution of Socrates the Questioner

In 399 B.C.E. the people of Athens tried and executed Socrates, their fellow citizen, for three crimes: for not believing in Athenian gods, for introducing new gods, and for corrupting the city's young men. The charges were paradoxical, for Socrates had devoted his life to investigating how to live ethically and morally. Although Socrates could have escaped, he chose to die rather than betray his most fundamental beliefs. Socrates wrote nothing down, yet his ideas and the example that he set by his life and death make him one of the most influential figures in the history of Western thought.

Born in Athens in 469 B.C.E., Socrates fought bravely during the Peloponnesian War. Afterward he openly defied the antidemocratic Thirty Tyrants whom the Spartans had installed in Athens. Socrates did not seek a career in politics or business. Instead he spent his time thinking and talking, which earned him a reputation as an eccentric. His friends, however, loved and deeply respected Socrates.

Socrates did not give lectures. Instead, he questioned people who believed they knew the truth. By asking them such questions as, "What is justice? Beauty? Courage?" and "What is the best way to lead a good life?" Socrates revealed that they—and most people—do not truly understand their most basic assumptions. Socrates did not claim to know the answers, but he did believe in the relentless application of rational argument in the pursuit of answers. This style of questioning, known as the Socratic method, infuriated complacent men because it made them seem foolish. But Socrates's method delighted people interested in taking a hard look at their most cherished beliefs.

Socrates attracted many followers. His brightest student was the philosopher Plato, to whom Socrates was not only a mentor, but a hero. Plato wrote a number of dialogues, or dramatized conversations, in which Socrates appears as a questioner, pursuing the truth about an important topic. Four of his dialogues—*Euthyphro, Apology, Crito,* and *Phaedo,* involve Socrates's trial and death.

The trial began when three citizens named Lycon, Meletus, and Anytus accused Socrates before a jury of 501 men. The accusers charged Socrates with corrupting the youth of Athens, failing to believe in the gods, and introducing new gods to the city. Socrates spoke in his own defense, but instead of showing any remorse, he boldly defended his method of questioning. Annoyed by Socrates's stubbornness, the jury convicted him.

Athenian law permitted accusers as well as defendants to suggest alternative penalties. When the accusers asked for death, Socrates responded with astonishing arrogance. He suggested instead that Athens pay him a reward for making the city a better place.

Outraged by this response from Socrates the jury chose death by an even wider margin. Socrates accepted their verdict calmly.

While Socrates sat in prison waiting for his execution, a friend named Crito offered to help him escape. Socrates refused to flee. He told Crito that only a man who did not respect the law would break it, and that such a man would indeed be a corrupting influence on the young. Socrates pointed out that he had lived his life as an obedient Athenian citizen and would certainly not break the law now. Human laws may be imperfect, he admitted, but they permit a society to function. Private individuals should never disregard them. To the end he remained a loyal citizen.

On his final day, with his closest friends around him, Socrates drank a cup of poison and died bravely. Plato wrote, "This is the way our dear friend perished. It is fair to say that he was the bravest, the wisest, and the most honorable man of all those we have ever known."[3]

Historians and philosophers have discussed Socrates's case since Plato's time. Were the accusations fair? What precisely was his crime? In the matter of corrupting Athens's youth, there is no doubt that at least two of his most fervent young followers, Alcibiades and Critias, had earned terrible reputations. Alcibiades had betrayed his city in the Peloponnesian War. Critias was

one of the most violent of the Thirty Tyrants. Many Athenians suspected Socrates of influencing them, even though these men represented everything he opposed.

Charges of impiety were harder to substantiate, but Athenians took them seriously. His fellow citizens knew that Socrates always participated in Athenian religious life. But during his defense Socrates admitted that his views were not exactly the same as those of his prosecutors. His claim to have a divine *daimon* or "sign" who sat on his shoulder and gave him advice was eccentric though not actually sacrilegious. Many Athenians thought this daimon was a foreign god rather than Socrates's metaphor for his own mental processes.

The reasons for the prosecution of Socrates lie much deeper than the official charges. His trial and execution emerged from an anti-intellectual backlash bred in the frustrations of Athens's defeat in the Peloponnesian War and in the Thirty Tyrants' rule. Even though Athenians had restored democracy, deep-seated resentments sealed Socrates's fate. In many societies throughout history, especially democratic ones like that of Athens that grant freedom to explore new ideas, people who fear change and creativity often strike out at artists, intellectuals, and innovators in times of stress. Athenians resented Socrates because he challenged them to think. He wanted them to live better lives, and they killed him. ■

Questions of Justice

1. What does this trial reveal about the nature of Athenian justice?
2. What does this trial tell us about the attitude of Athenians toward philosophy?

Taking It Further

Brickhouse, Thomas C., and Nicholas D. Smith. *Socrates on Trial.* 1989. A thorough analysis of Socrates's trial.

Stokes, Michael. *Plato: Apology, with Introduction, Translation, and Commentary.* 1997. The best translation, with important commentary.

and yet idealized in the harmony and symmetry of the torso and limbs. The balance between realism and idealism has continually inspired artists in the Western tradition.

Greek painters explored movement of the human body as well as colors and the optical illusion of depth. The figures that they depicted on vases and on walls became increasingly lively and realistic as the Classical Age unfolded. Artists portrayed every sort of activity from religious worship to erotic fun, but regardless of the subject, they shared a similar goal: to create a lifelike depiction of the human figure.

In a similar effort to capture ideals of perfection, Greek architects designed their buildings, especially temples, to be symmetrical and proportional. They used mathematical ratios that they observed in nature to shape their designs. The buildings they created show a grace, balance, and harmony that have inspired architects for more than two millennia.

CONCLUSION

Classical Foundations of the West

During the period from about 1100 to 336 B.C.E., several of the elements of what would later be considered the cultural inheritance of the West came into being. These elements came from the Hebrews, Persians, and Greeks and the encounters that took place among them. The legacy of the Hebrews has been their religious and ethical teachings, encapsulated in the Hebrew Bible. The Persians supplied a model for an efficient empire that was inherited by later conquerors, most notably Alexander the Great and his followers. They also established a model for future imperial systems, including the Roman Empire. By permitting forms of worship other than the official Zoroastrianism, the Persians limited dissent, and by allowing exiled peoples, such as the Hebrews, to return to their homes, they knitted together an efficient multiethnic, multireligious empire. Throughout that empire the older Middle Eastern traditions of science, mathematics, astronomy, and navigation (discussed in Chapter 2) passed on to the Greeks and then into the western Mediterranean, North Africa, and eventually Europe. Zoroastrian religious ideas of Heaven and Hell and the struggle between God and the Devil also found their way into other western religions, most notably Christianity.

The stumbling blocks for Persian imperial expansion to the West were the hoplite armies and fleets of the Greeks. When the Persians arrived on the shores of Greece, the institutions of the poleis were well established. However, the Greek victory strengthened those institutions and facilitated the further development of Athenian democracy. Under the political and cultural leadership of Athens, Greek civilization thrived, producing the most lasting artistic and philosophical contributions from the ancient world to the history of the West.

The military conflicts of this period demonstrated that well-trained, highly disciplined Greek hoplite troops were more than a match for the Persian army. In the next chapter, we will see how the kingdom of Macedonia to the north of Greece also learned this important lesson. After conquering Greece, the Macedonians, led by Alexander the Great, overwhelmed the entire Persian Empire. Alexander's conquests inaugurated a new era in history, the Hellenistic Age, in which classical Greek civilization spread over an enormous region.

Suggestions for Further Reading

······································· ▬ ·······································

For a comprehensive list of suggested readings, please go to www.ablongman.com/levackconcise/chapter3

Boardman, John. *Persia and the West: An Archaeological Investigation of the Genesis of Achaemenid Art.* 2000. A brilliantly illustrated study that stresses intercultural influences in every aspect of Persian art.

Boyce, Mary. *A History of Zoroastrianism.* Vol. 2. 1975. This authoritative examination provides a masterful overview of the religion of the Persian Empire.

Burkert, Walter. *The Orientalizing Revolution: Near Eastern Influence on Greek Culture in the Early Archaic Age,* trans. Margaret Pinder and Walter Burkert. 1993. Explains how the Semitic East influenced the development of Greek society in the Archaic Age.

Cohn, Norman. *Cosmos, Chaos, and the World to Come: The Ancient Roots of Apocalyptic Faith.* 1993. Expert critical analysis of apocalyptic religions in the West, including Zoroastrianism, ancient Judaism, Christianity, and other faiths.

Finkelstein, Israel, and Neil Asher Silberman. *The Bible Unearthed: Archaeology's New Vision of Ancient Israel and the Origin of the Sacred Texts.* 2001. An important archaeological interpretation that challenges the narrative of the Hebrew Bible and offers a reconsideration of biblical history.

Gottwald, Norman K. *The Hebrew Bible: A Socio-Literary Introduction.* 1985. Combines a close reading of the Hebrew Bible with the latest archaeological and historical evidence.

Just, Roger. *Women in Athenian Law and Life.* 1989. Provides an overview of the social context of women in Athens.

Kuhrt, Amélie. *The Ancient Near East, ca. 3000–330 B.C.* Vol. 2. 1995. This rich and comprehensive bibliography is a remarkably concise and readable account of Persian history with excellent discussion of ancient textual evidence. Many important passages appear in fluent translation.

Lindberg, David C. *The Beginnings of Western Science: The European Scientific Tradition in Philosophical, Religious, and Institutional Context, 600 B.C. to A.D. 1450.* 1992. This highly readable study provides an exciting survey of the main developments in Western science.

Markoe, Glenn. *Phoenicians.* 2000. The best and most up-to-date treatment of Phoenician society by a noted expert.

Murray, Oswyn. *Early Greece.* 1983. A brilliant study of all aspects of the emergence of Greek society between the Dark Age and the end of the Persian Wars.

Osborne, Robin. *Greece in the Making, 1200–479 B.C.* 1996. An excellent narrative of the development of Greek society with special regard to the archaeological evidence.

Stewart, Andrew. *Art, Desire, and the Body in Ancient Greece.* 1997. A provocative study that examines Greek attitudes toward sexuality and art.

Walker, Christopher, ed. *Astronomy Before the Telescope.* 1996. A fascinating collection of essays about astronomy in the premodern period that makes clear our enormous debt to the Babylonians.

Wieshöfer, Josef. *Ancient Persia from 550 B.C. to A.D. 650,* trans. Azizeh Azodi. 1996. A fresh and comprehensive overview of Persian cultural, social, and political history that relies on Persian evidence more heavily than on biased Greek and Roman sources.

Notes

······································· ▬ ·······································

1. Based on Herodotus, *History,* vol. 1, trans. Rex Warner (2000), 125–126.

2. Demosthenes, *Orations,* 59.122.

3. Plato, *Phaedo,* 1.118.

The Hellenistic Age, 336–31 B.C.E.

ONE EVENING AFTER DINNER IN 193 B.C.E., AT THE PALACE OF A GREEK KING in Asia Minor, two battle-hardened generals from different lands debated the identity of the greatest military commander of all time. Both generals came from aristocratic backgrounds. One had grown up in Rome; the other in Carthage, an imperial city on the coast of North Africa. They conversed in Greek, the language of diplomacy and culture that was used throughout the Mediterranean and the Middle East. The Carthaginian was Hannibal, a military genius who had led the armies of Carthage in a savage war against Rome between 218 and 201 B.C.E., and who now lived in exile. The Roman, who was visiting Asia Minor as part of a diplomatic mission, was Publius Cornelius Scipio Africanus. This equally brilliant general had ended the bloodiest war in Rome's history by defeating Hannibal. When Scipio asked Hannibal who he thought was the world's greatest general, Hannibal named the legendary Macedonian conqueror Alexander the Great. With a smile Scipio then asked his former foe, "What if *you* had defeated *me?*" "In that case," replied the Carthaginian in a flattering tone, "I would be the greatest general of them all."

This anecdote illuminates some fundamental elements of a period that historians call the Hellenistic Age. First, it reveals a cosmopolitan, Greek-based culture in which a Carthaginian general, whose native tongue was a Semitic language, and a Latin-speaking Roman aristocrat could easily communicate. Second, these two warriors shared knowledge of the history of Mediterranean lands, politics, and diplomatic etiquette. Most of all, both admired Alexander the Great, who had made their cosmopolitan world possible. Scipio, Hannibal, and doubtless their host sought to imitate the Macedonian king. Alexander and the

Celt and Wife: This dramatic statue epitomizes the mixing of cultures in the Hellenistic Age. The statue is a Roman copy in marble of a bronze original made at Pergamum in Asia Minor by a Greek sculptor. The artist tells the tragic story of a defeated Celt. Rather than be captured alive, he has just killed his wife and is at the precise moment of taking his own life. In typically Hellenistic style, the artist combines anatomical accuracy with psychological agony.

civilization he had inaugurated had set the standard for success in the minds of men from very different cultural backgrounds.

The Hellenistic period began when Alexander (r. 336–323 B.C.E.) conquered the Persian Empire, extending Greek culture as far east as present-day Afghanistan and India. Greeks called themselves *Hellenes,* and thus historians use the terms *Hellenism* and *Hellenistic* to describe the complex cosmopolitan civilization that developed in the wake of Alexander's conquests. This civilization offered a rich variety of goods, technologies, and ideas to anyone who knew or was willing to learn Greek. Greek became the common tongue used in trade, politics, and intellectual life.

Political borders did not limit Hellenistic civilization. After Alexander died, the empire he had built fragmented into smaller kingdoms that often fought one another. Despite the instability and warfare, however, Hellenistic culture thrived within the kingdoms that developed after Alexander's death. It also spread far beyond the lands conquered by Alexander, mainly in the western Mediterranean, where it had a profound effect on the civilizations of North Africa, Europe, and especially Rome. Romans, Jews, Persians, Celts, Carthaginians, and other peoples all absorbed elements of Greek culture—its philosophy, religion, literature, and art. Hellenism gave a common culture of science and learning to diverse peoples speaking different languages and worshiping different gods. Hellenism thus gave a cultural unity to a vast area stretching from Europe in the west to Afghanistan in the east. Large portions of this cultural realm ultimately became what historians call the West.

The spread of Hellenistic culture over this vast area involved a series of cultural exchanges. Greek culture offered great prestige and possessed a powerful intellectual appeal to non-Greek peoples, but it also posed a threat to their local, traditional identities. Instead of simply accepting Greek culture, these non-Greek peoples engaged in a process of cultural adaptation and synthesis. In this way Hellenism, which throughout this period remained open to outside influences, absorbed foreign scientific knowledge, religious ideas, and many other cultural traditions. These elements then entered the mainstream of Hellenistic culture and were transmitted to the greater Hellenistic world. Some of the basic components of Western civilization originated in these cultural encounters between Greek and non-Greek peoples. These include the seven-day week, beliefs in Hell and Judgment Day, the study of astrology and astronomy, and technologies of metallurgy, agriculture, and navigation.

The Hellenistic era and the age of independent Hellenistic kingdoms came to a close in 31 B.C.E., when the Roman politician and military commander Octavian (later known as Augustus) won control of the Mediterranean world, the Middle East, Egypt, and parts of Europe. This political development did not, however, put an end to the influence of Hellenistic culture. By forging a new, more resilient civilization in which Greeks, Romans, and many other peoples intermingled in peace, the Romans created their own version of Hellenism and introduced it to western Europe.

To understand the Hellenistic Age, this chapter will explore four questions:

- How did Alexander the Great create an empire in which Greek civilization flourished in the midst of many diverse cultures?
- What were the distinguishing features of Hellenistic society and culture, and what was the result of encounters between Greeks and non-Greeks?
- How did the Roman Republic come to dominate the Mediterranean world during the Hellenistic Age, and how did Roman rule over the Hellenistic East affect Rome's development?
- What political and social changes brought the Roman Republic to an end?

The Warlike Kingdom of Macedon

The Hellenistic Age had its roots in Macedon, a kingdom to the north of Greece that was rich in timber, grain, horses, and fighting men. Macedonians spoke a dialect of Greek, but their customs and political organization differed from those of the urbanized Greek communities that lay to their south. Unlike democratic Athens, Macedon had a hereditary monarchy. Because independent-minded nobles resented their rule, Macedonian kings had to wage war continuously to keep their precarious position on the throne.

UNITY AND EXPANSION UNDER KING PHILIP

Until the fourth century B.C.E. Macedon shrewdly avoided Greek affairs. During the Persian Wars (490 and 480–479 B.C.E.), Macedonian kings pursued a cautious and profitable policy of friendship with the Persian invaders. During the convulsions of the Peloponnesian War (431–404 B.C.E.) and its turbulent aftermath, Macedon refrained from exploiting Athens, Sparta, and the other Greek cities as they bled to exhaustion. The lack of Greek entanglements, however, could not ease the tensions between kings and nobles. In 399 B.C.E. Macedon slipped into a forty-year period of anarchy. Just as Macedon was on the verge of disintegration, King Philip II (382–336 B.C.E.) stepped forward and transformed the Macedonian kingdom. A ruthless opportunist

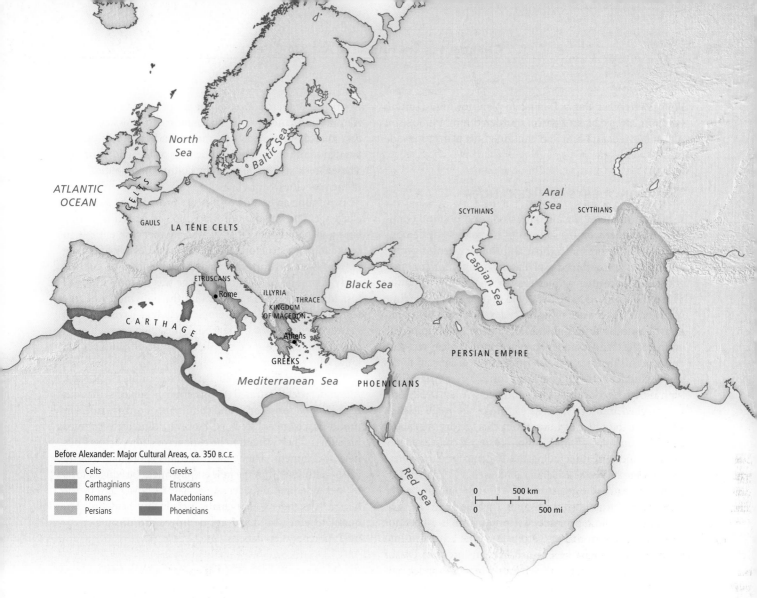

■ **Map 4.1 Before Alexander: Major Cultural Areas, ca. 350 B.C.E.**
During the Hellenistic Age, Greek culture influenced many cultures. This map shows the realms of the Persians, Celts, Romans, Carthaginians, and Phoenicians, whose societies would participate in the Hellenistic Age.

with a gift for military organization, Philip consolidated his power by eliminating his rivals, killing many of them in battle. He unified the unruly nobles who controlled different regions of Macedon by demonstrating the advantages of cooperation under his leadership. Philip led the nobles to victory after victory over hostile frontier tribes. He shared his plunder with the nobles and common soldiers alike. The Macedonians embraced his leadership (see Map 4.1).

Philip created a new army in which the nobles had a special role as cavalry armed with heavy lances. Called the Companions, they formed elite regiments bound to their king by oaths of loyalty. Philip reorganized the infantry, or foot soldiers, into military units called phalanxes. Armed with lances nearly fourteen feet long, the infantry held off the enemy while the cavalry galloped in to strike a fatal blow. This new strategy gave Philip's armies an enormous tactical advantage over traditional hoplite formations.

With Macedon firmly under his control, its borders secure and his army eager for loot, Philip stood poised to strike at Greece. Recognizing that Philip represented a threat to Greek liberty, the brilliant Athenian orator Demosthenes organized resistance among the city-states. In 338 B.C.E., however, Philip crushed the allied armies of the Greek *poleis* at the battle of Chaeronea in central Greece. In this confrontation Philip's 18-year-old son Alexander led the Companions in a charge that won the day for the Macedonians.

Philip next cast his eyes on the Persian Empire. In 337 B.C.E. he cloaked himself in the mantle of Greek culture and announced that he would lead his armies and the forces of Greece against the empire to the east to avenge Persia's invasion of Greece in the previous century. Philip's shrewd linking of classical Greek civilization with Macedonian force now became a rallying cry for imperialist expansion under

Philip's direction. But as Philip laid plans for his assault on Persia in 336 B.C.E., an assassin murdered him. Philip's son Alexander replaced him and continued his plans to invade the east.

THE CONQUESTS OF ALEXANDER

A man of immense personal charisma and political craftiness, Alexander won the support of his soldiers by demonstrating fearlessness in combat and military genius on the battlefield. He combined a predatory instinct for conquest and glory with utter ruthlessness in the pursuit of power. These traits proved to be the key to his success. By the time of his death, at the age of just 33, Alexander had won military victories as far east as India, creating a vast empire.

In 334 B.C.E. Alexander marched into Persian territory and won his first great victory in battle over Persian forces at the Granicus River, giving him control over Asia Minor with its rich Greek coastal cities and fleets. A few weeks later he marched into Syria, where he broke the main Persian army near the town of Issus. From this victory Alexander gained control of the entire eastern coast of the Mediterranean Sea, including the Phoenician cities where the Persians had established naval bases.

In 332 B.C.E. the maritime city of Tyre succumbed to Alexander's siege, and soon after that he marched into Egypt, where the inhabitants welcomed him as a liberator from their Persian masters. From Egypt he advanced into Mesopotamia, where he crushed Persian forces of Darius once again near the Tigris River. From there Alexander ventured southeast to Persepolis, the Persian capital, which he captured in January 330 B.C.E. He plundered the city and burned it to the ground. The enormous wealth Alexander acquired from Persepolis paid for all of his military activities for the next dozen years and invigorated the entire Macedonian economy. Darius, the Great King of Persia, escaped the destruction of his capital but was soon murdered by his own nobles. The once-powerful Persian Empire lay in ruins.

Alexander had fulfilled his father's pledge to gain vengeance against Persia, but he had no intention of slowing down his march of conquest (see Map 4.2). He pushed past the tribesmen of the harsh Afghan mountain ranges to penetrate Central Asia. In 327 B.C.E. he entered the territory that is modern Pakistan, where he defeated the Indian king. Then the tide of fortune slowly turned against him. When his exhausted armies refused to follow him into India, he had little choice but to begin a long and arduous return westward. Most of his soldiers died on the way, and Alexander himself suffered nearly fatal wounds. While recuperating at Babylon in 323 B.C.E., where he had begun to plan further conquests, Alexander succumbed to fever after a drinking bout. He had never lost a battle.

In strategic locations through the lands he had conquered, Alexander established cities as garrisons for his troops. More than a dozen of these cities received the name Alexandria in his honor. Thousands of Greeks migrated east to settle in the new cities to take advantage of the expanded economic opportunities for trade and farming. These Greek settlers became the cultural and political elite of the new cities.

Governing an empire of this size proved to be a difficult challenge. The kingdom of Macedon was geared to seizing land and plundering cities. It was another task entirely to create the infrastructure and discipline necessary for ruling an immense territory that had little linguistic or cultural unity. Alexander understood that he was no longer king of just Macedon. He recognized that the only model of rule suitable to such a diverse empire was that devised by his Persian predecessors: a Great King presiding over a hierarchy of nobles who governed Persian territory, and subject kings who ruled non-Persian regions.

By adopting the elaborate Persian role of the Great King, Alexander demonstrated to his foreign subjects that his regime stood for security and continuity of orderly rule. His proud Macedonian soldiers, however, ultimately stymied his efforts. They wanted to be conquerors, not partners in a new government. They failed to understand that men of other cultures within the new empire might be equally loyal to Alexander and thus deserve a share of power and public honor. Alexander's charismatic personality held his conquests together, but his death destroyed any dreams of cooperation between Persians and Greeks.

CHRONOLOGY

509 B.C.E.	Roman Republic established
336–323 B.C.E.	Alexander the Great reigns
264–241 B.C.E.	First Punic War
218–201 B.C.E.	Second Punic War
149–146 B.C.E.	Third Punic War
133–122 B.C.E.	Reforms of the Gracchi
90–88 B.C.E.	Rome fights "Social War" with Italian allies
60 B.C.E.	First Triumvirate is established
58–49 B.C.E.	Julius Caesar conquers Celts in Gaul
49–44 B.C.E.	Civil war in Rome; Caesar is victorious, then slain
43 B.C.E.	Second Triumvirate is formed
31 B.C.E.	Octavian defeats Antony and Cleopatra; end of the Roman Republic

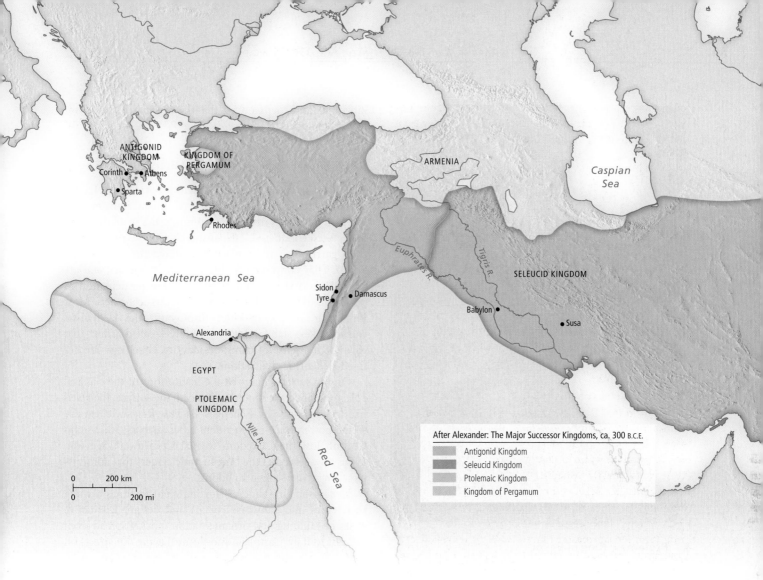

■ **Map 4.2   The Roman Conquest of the Mediterranean During the Republic**
Armies of the Roman Republic conquered the Mediterranean world during the Hellenistic Age,
overcoming the Carthaginian Empire, the Hellenistic successor kingdoms, and many Celtic peoples in
Spain and Gaul.

SUCCESSOR KINGDOMS: DISTRIBUTING THE SPOILS

Alexander left no adult heir, and the Macedonian nobles who served as his generals fought viciously among themselves for control of his conquered territory. Eventually these generals created a number of kingdoms out of lands Alexander had acquired. One general, Ptolemy, established the Ptolemaic dynasty in Egypt, which would last until 30 B.C.E. The largest portion of Alexander's conquests, comprising the bulk of the old Persian Empire, fell to his general Seleucus. Smaller kingdoms, such as Bactria Pergamum in Asia Minor, were carved out of the area Alexander had conquered.

Following the example of Macedon itself, the Hellenistic successor states all acquired a monarchical form of government, in which a king ruled with the support of the army and highly regimented bureaucracies. The members of the administrative hierarchy were all Greeks and Macedonians;

indigenous people were not recruited into the ruling elite. Greek was the language of rule in the successor kingdoms.

The king towered over Hellenistic society, holding authority over all his subjects and bearing ultimate responsibility for their welfare. Following the example of Alexander, Hellenistic monarchs earned legitimacy by leading their troops into wars of conquest. A king embodied the entire community that he ruled. He was at once the ruler, father, protector, savior, source of law, and god of all his subjects. Monarchs earned the loyalty of their subjects and glorified their own rule by establishing cities, constructing public buildings, and rewarding their inner circle.

In addition to the loyalty of their subjects, Hellenistic kings also depended on permanent professional armies to wage the military campaigns so essential to maintaining their authority and to defending their territories. Hellenistic kings fought wars over much larger territories than those that had led to squabbles among Greek city-states in previous centuries. The conquest of such territories required an

79

■ **Ptolemaic King of Egypt**
This golden ring depicts Ptolemy VI, who ruled Egypt from 176 to 145 B.C.E. Although he and his court spoke only Greek, he is depicted as a pharaoh wearing a double crown, the age-old symbol of Egyptian monarchy. The image on the ring demonstrated the integration of old and new political symbols in Egypt during the Hellenistic Age.

increase in the size of field armies. The Athenian hoplites had numbered about 10,000 in the fifth century B.C.E., but in the Hellenistic Age kings routinely mustered armies of between 60,000 and 80,000 men. Many soldiers came from military colonies established by the kings. In return for land, the men of these Greek-speaking colonies were obliged to serve generation after generation in the king's army and to police the native, non-Greek populations.

Hellenistic Society and Culture

Chronic warfare among Hellenistic monarchs made political unity among the Hellenistic kingdoms impossible. Nevertheless, the social institutions and cultural orientation of Greek-speaking people in all these kingdoms gave them a unity that their monarchs could not have even hoped to achieve.

CITIES: THE HEART OF HELLENISTIC LIFE

Alexander and his successors seized dozens of Greek city-states scattered across the eastern Mediterranean and founded dozens of new urban communities in all the territories they conquered. Hellenistic cities were much more than garrisons put in place to enforce the conquerors' power. They continued traditions of learning, art, and architecture, as well as traditions of citizen participation in public life that had flourished in the classical *poleis*. Most important, people in cities throughout the Hellenistic world spoke a standard version of Greek called Koine° that gave them a sense of common identity. Greek city life defined Hellenistic civilization.

On the surface, many of the institutions of the classical *poleis* remained the same, but beneath the surface, the *poleis* had undergone radical changes. Because kings wielded absolute power, once-independent cities such as Athens and Corinth lost their freedom to make peace or wage war. Cities now served as the bureaucratic centers that administered their rulers' huge kingdoms.

Hellenistic kings and aristocrats spent fortunes turning their cities into showcases of art and design. Distinctive styles of building and ornamentation quickly spread from the east to Italy, Carthage, and Rome. Laying out streets on a grid plan became standard in the Mediterranean world, lending a sense of order to urban space. Stone theaters for plays and spectacles, council halls, and roofed colonnades called *stoas* sprang up everywhere, as did baths with heated pools and gymnasium complexes with athletic facilities and classrooms.

The freestanding sculpture that decorated public spaces in Hellenistic cities took classical Greek forms in new directions. Turning away from representations of ideal perfection, Hellenistic artists delighted in exploring the movement of the human body and varieties of facial expression. Artists enjoyed portraying the play of fabrics across the human body to accentuate the contours of male and female flesh. Sometimes painted in bright colors, these statues explored human frailty and homeliness as often as they celebrated beauty and lofty emotions.

As we saw in Chapter 3, citizenship in the city-states of classical Greece was a carefully limited commodity that gave people a sense of identity, guaranteed desirable rights and privileges, and demanded certain responsibilities. Citizenship lost its political force because individual cities had lost their political autonomy. In a sharp break with earlier practice, important individuals sometimes gained the honor of citizenship in more than one city, something that Greeks in the Classical Age would have found inconceivable.

Hellenistic cities contained more diverse populations than had classical *poleis*. Alexandria, in Egypt, the largest and most cosmopolitan of Greek cities, boasted large communities of Macedonians, Greeks, Jews, Syrians, and Egyptians. Although these groups lived in different areas of town and often fought violently with one another, they all participated to varying degrees in the Hellenistic culture of the city. For example, Alexandrian Jews who spoke Greek translated the Hebrew Bible into Greek, a version called the Septuagint°, so that they could more easily read and understand it.

In some older cities such as Babylon and Jerusalem, deep-seated cultural and religious traditions prevented the complete penetration of Greek civilization. Many traditional customs and forms of religious worship, such as the Babylonian worship of the great god Marduk, continued untouched by the Greek way of life. Even the Greek language found limited use in local government. In Mesopotamian cities, for example, local administrators continued to use the local language, Aramaic. The leading families of these cities learned Greek, however, so they could communicate with the members of the king's government and gain political influence.

NEW OPPORTUNITIES FOR WOMEN

Women in the upper levels of Hellenistic society had the opportunity to wield considerably more power than was conceivable for aristocratic women in the classical Greek period. The wives of Hellenistic kings emerged as models of the new, more powerful Hellenistic woman. As public benefactors, these women built sanctuaries and public works, sponsored charioteers at the Olympic games, and provided dowries for poor brides.

To a lesser extent, opportunities for nonaristocratic Greek women also increased during the Hellenistic Age. In Alexandria young women received education in dancing, music, rudimentary reading and writing, and scholarship and philosophy. Often the daughters of scholars became scholars in their own right. Although their work is lost, we know that women wrote about astronomy, musical theory, and literature, and many female poets competed for honors. A few Hellenistic women distinguished themselves as portrait painters, architects, and harpists. Despite these accomplishments, women still had fewer rights and opportunities than men, and they remained under the supervision of their male relatives.

HELLENISTIC LITERATURE, PHILOSOPHY, AND SCIENCE

The Hellenistic Age witnessed the continuation of some trends in classical Greek scholarship while promoting some striking innovations in literature, philosophy, and science.

Literature: Poetry and History Writing

Much Hellenistic literature has vanished, but some surviving works give a glimpse of creativity and originality, which often combined urbanity and thoughtful scholarship. Hellenistic poets turned to frivolous themes because the repressive political climate discouraged questioning of authority. Light comedy became immensely popular, especially in the hands of the playwright Menander of Athens (ca. 300 B.C.E.). This clever author delighted audiences with escapist, frothy tales of temporarily frustrated love and happy endings. These plays, known now as New Comedy, developed from the risqué satires of classical Athens. They featured vivid street language and a cast of stock characters: crotchety parents, naive young men and silly young women, tricky slaves, and wicked pimps.

Theocritus (ca. 300–ca. 260 B.C.E.), who came from Syracuse but wrote in Alexandria in the 270s B.C.E., invented a new genre called pastoral poetry. His verses described idyllic life in the countryside, but his coarse herdsmen reflect the sadness and tensions of city life. Of all the Hellenistic poets, Theocritus has had the most wide-ranging and enduring influence, providing a model for pastoral verse in Rome, Shakespeare's England, and even nineteenth-century Russia. The other great poet from Alexandria, Callimachus (ca. 305–240 B.C.E.), combined playfulness with extraordinary learning in works ranging from *Collections of Wonders of the World* to his moving love poems, the *Elegies*. His poetry provides the best example of the erudite style known as Alexandrianism, which demonstrated a command of meter and language and appealed more to the intellect than to the emotions.

Powerful Hellenistic monarchs influenced the writing of history. Kings wanted flattering accounts of their deeds, not the probing, critical independence of mind that Thucydides had offered in the classical period. Some writers resisted these pressures, however. Hieronymous of Cardia, a professional administrator who lived to age 104, described nearly three generations of political intrigue that followed Alexander's death. His conclusion? Fortune, not the efforts of mighty kings, determines the affairs of men.

Philosophy: The Quest for Peace of Mind

The study of philosophy continued to flourish in the Hellenistic world. Plato's Academy and Aristotle's Lyceum remained in operation in Athens, drawing intellectually curious men from around the Mediterranean. In this environment several new schools of philosophy arose. Three of them in particular—the Epicureans, the Stoics, and the Cynics—shared the common goal of overcoming what they called disturbance, thereby acquiring an inner tranquility or peace of mind.

The first of these philosophical schools, the Epicureans°, was founded by Epicurus of Samos (341–271 B.C.E.). Because Epicurus believed that "the entire world lives in

■ **Comedy Mosaic from Pompeii**
Brilliant decorative mosaics have survived in great numbers from the Hellenistic world. Often derived from Greek paintings, which have entirely disappeared, these scenes give a vivid glimpse into everyday life. This mosaic is based on a scene from a comedy performed in a theater. We can almost hear the music as street entertainers play and dance in front of a rich man's house.

pain," he urged people to gain tranquility in their troubled souls through the rational choice of pleasure. The word *epicurean* today denotes a person of discriminating taste who takes pleasure in eating and drinking, but the pleasure Epicurus sought was intellectual, a perfect harmony of body and mind. To achieve this harmony Epicurus recommended a virtuous and simple life, characterized by plain living and withdrawal from the stressful world of politics and social competition. Epicurus also reassured his students that they should fear neither death nor the gods. There was no reason to fear death because the soul was material; hence there was no afterlife. Nor was there any reason to fear the gods, who lived in a happy condition far from Earth, unconcerned with human activity. With these fears assuaged, humans could find inner peace.

The main rival to Epicureanism was Stoicism°, the school established by Zeno of Citium (ca. 335–ca. 263 B.C.E.) at Athens in 300 B.C.E. Stoics believed that all human beings have an element of divinity in them and therefore participate in one single indissoluble cosmic process. They could find peace of mind by submitting to that cosmic order, which Stoics identified with nature or fate. Thus the word *stoic* today carries the meaning of a person who responds to pain or misfortune without showing passion or feeling. Stoics believed that wise men did not allow the vicissitudes of life to distract them. Rather than calling for withdrawal from the world, like the Epicureans, Stoicism encouraged people to participate actively in public life. Because Stoicism accepted the status quo, many kings and aristocrats embraced it. They wanted to believe that their success formed part of a cosmic, divine plan. Stoicism remained influential well into the time of the Roman Empire.

The members of the Cynic° movement took a different approach to gaining peace of mind. Cynics taught that the key to happiness was the elimination of all needs and desires. To achieve this goal, Cynics rejected all pleasures and possessions, leading a life of asceticism. Diogenes (ca. 412–324 B.C.E.), the chief representative of the school, made his home in an empty barrel. Cynics manifested contempt for the customs and conventions of society, including wealth, social position, and prevailing standards of morality. The word *cynic* today usually refers to a person who sneeringly denies the sincerity of human motives and actions. Some Cynics took the doctrine of Diogenes to extremes by satisfying, rather than denying, their simplest natural needs. Their behavior, which included public masturbation and defecation, repelled so many people that their philosophy failed to have a lasting impact.

Explaining the Natural World: Scientific Investigation

While Athens remained the hub of philosophy in the Hellenistic Age, the Ptolemaic kings made Alexandria the preeminent center of scientific learning by sponsoring scientific research and lectures on the natural world. In addition to summarizing the work of previous scholars, Hellenistic scientists sought to depict the world as it actually was. This emphasis on realism involved the rejection of some of the more speculative notions that had characterized classical Greek science.

In mathematics, Euclid (ca. 300 B.C.E.) produced a masterful synthesis of the knowledge of geometry in his great work, the *Elements,* which remained the standard geometry textbook until the twentieth century. Euclid demonstrated how one could attain knowledge by rational methods alone—by mathematical reasoning through the use of deductive proofs and theorems. Equally famous as a theorist and engineer was Archimedes of Syracuse (ca. 287–212 B.C.E.), who calculated the value of *pi* (the ratio of a circle's circumference to its diameter) and measured the diameter of the sun.

Astronomy advanced as well during the Hellenistic Age. In their research, Hellenistic investigators borrowed from the long tradition of precisely recorded observation of the heavens that Babylonian and Egyptian scholars had established. Heraclides of Pontus (ca. 390–310 B.C.E.) anticipated a sun-centered theory of the universe when he observed that Venus and Mercury orbit the sun, not Earth. Aristarchus of Samos (ca. 310–230 B.C.E.) established the idea that the planets revolve around the sun while spinning on their own axes. The sun-centered view never caught on, however, because of fierce opposition from the followers of Aristotle, whose Earth-centered theories had become canonical.

The Hellenistic medical tradition continued to flourish in the Roman Empire. Galen (129–199 C.E.), the greatest doctor of antiquity, organized Hellenistic medical knowledge. He produced accurate, realistic descriptions of human anatomy and formulated a theory regarding the motion of the blood from the liver to the veins that was not replaced until William Harvey discovered the circulation of the blood in the seventeenth century (see Chapter 16).

ENCOUNTERS WITH FOREIGN PEOPLES

During the Hellenistic Age, Greeks encountered large numbers of foreign peoples, and the effects of these interactions laid some of the foundations of the West. The encounters took place when Greeks explored the unknown regions in Africa and Europe; when Hellenistic culture met with resistance from Babylonians, Egyptians, and Hebrews; and when Celtic peoples migrated to the boundaries of the Hellenistic world.

Exploring the Hellenistic World

A spirit of inquiry—combined with hunger for trade and profit—drove men to explore and map the unknown world during the Hellenistic Age. Explorers backed by monarchs ventured into the Caspian, Aral, and Red Seas. By the second century B.C.E., Greeks had established trading posts along the coasts of modern Eritrea and Somalia, where merchants bought goods, particularly ivory, transported from the interior of Africa.

The most ambitious and successful of all Hellenistic explorers was Pytheas of Marseilles (ca. 310–306 B.C.E.). Setting out from the Greek city of Gades (the modern Spanish port of Cadiz), he sailed around Britain and reported the existence of either Iceland or Norway. He may even have reached the Vistula River in Poland. Throughout his journeys Pytheas contributed much to navigational knowledge by recording astronomical bearings and natural wonders such as the Northern Lights.

As these explorers expanded geographical horizons, Greeks developed a lively though condescending interest in the different peoples of the world. Greeks considered themselves culturally superior to non-Greek-speaking peoples, including Jews, Babylonians, Celts, steppe nomads, and sub-Saharan Africans who lived beyond the borders of Hellenistic kingdoms. Greeks considered all of these peoples inferior barbarians.

Resistance to Hellenistic Culture

Despite this curiosity among educated Greeks about foreign customs, a great barrier of mutual incomprehension and suspicious resentment separated Greeks and their subjects. Language was one such barrier. In most kingdoms, administrators conducted official business only in Greek. Few Greek settlers in the cities or even in far-flung, isolated military colonies ever bothered to learn the local languages, and only a small percentage of the local populations learned Greek. Many communities preferred to ignore their Greek rulers completely. In Babylonia, for example, age-old patterns of urban life centering on temple worship continued outside the influence of Greek culture. Some non-Greeks, however, hoped to rise in the service of their Greek masters. They made an effort to learn Greek and to assimilate into Hellenistic culture. Their collaboration with Greek rulers alienated them from their own people and provoked divisions within native societies.

Celts on the Fringes of the Hellenistic World

In addition to the Greek culture that spread throughout the Mediterranean and Near East, Celtic civilization flourished in Europe during the Hellenistic Age. Celtic peoples emerged in continental Europe north of the Alps about 750 B.C.E. The Celts, who lived in tribes that were never politically unified on a large scale, shared common dialects, metal- and pottery-making techniques, and agricultural and home-building methods. They are the ancestors of many peoples of northern and central Europe today.

Through trade and war, Celts played an influential role on the northern margins of the Hellenistic world from Asia Minor to Spain. Trading routes were established as early as the eighth century B.C.E., but commerce was often interrupted by war. The military activities of Celtic tribes restricted the expansion of Hellenistic kingdoms, thereby pressuring them to strengthen their military capacities.

Archaeologists call the first Celtic civilization in central Europe Hallstatt culture, because of excavations in Hallstatt, Austria. Around 750 B.C.E., Hallstatt° Celts started to spread from their homeland into Italy, the Balkans, Ireland, Spain, and Asia Minor, conquering local peoples on the way. These people left no written records,

so we know little of their political practices. The luxury goods and weapons left in their graves, however, indicate a stratified society led by a warrior elite. Hallstatt sites were heavily fortified, suggesting frequent warfare among communities. Men gained status through competitive exchange of gifts, raiding, and valor in battle.

In the middle of the fifth century B.C.E. a new phase in Celtic civilization began, called La Tène° culture, which takes its name from a site in modern Switzerland. More weapons appeared in tombs than in the Halstatt period, indicating intensified warfare. La Tène Celts developed new centers of wealth and power, especially in the valleys of the Rhine and Danube Rivers. They also founded large, fortified settlements in these regions as well as in present-day France and England.

La Tène craftsmen benefited from new trade routes across the Alps to northern Italy, the home of Etruscan merchants and artisans. Greek styles in art reached the Celts through these Etruscan intermediaries, but Celtic artists developed their own distinctive style of metalwork and sculpture. Many Celtic communities began to use coinage, which they adopted from the Greeks.

For about a century relations between the Celtic and Mediterranean peoples centered on trade, but around 400 B.C.E. overpopulation in central Europe instigated massive migrations of Celtic tribes. In 387 B.C.E. one migrating group of Celts sacked the city of Rome. Some Celts migrated to lands that are Slavic today (Slovakia and southern Poland), while others established new homes in the Po Valley in northern Italy, as well as Spain, Britain, and Ireland. Other groups of Celts invaded the Balkans, plundered Greece, and finally settled in Asia Minor, where they established a kingdom, called Galatia, known for the bravery and cruelty of its soldiers.

Rome's Rise to Power

During the Hellenistic Age, Rome expanded from being a relatively small city-state with a republican form of government into a vast and powerful empire. As it conquered

■ **Celtic Warriors**

These two Celtic statuettes of fighting men reveal the impact of Hellenistic art on native traditions. The first warrior, who stands stiffly and without a well-articulated anatomy, is the product of Celtic artistic traditions untouched by Greek art. The second figure shows the influence of Greek styles. He is well-balanced to throw a spear. His muscles are clearly understood and he turns convincingly in space.

■ **View of the Forum from Capitoline Hill**

This view down into the Forum valley was taken from the site of the Temple to Jupiter, Rome's mightiest god. All victory processions after a successful war would have ended at this temple, where sacrifices were made. Now tourists visit the remains of buildings from which Rome ruled an international empire.

the peoples who ringed the Mediterranean—the Carthaginians, the Celts, and the Hellenistic kingdoms of Alexander's successors—Rome incorporated these newcomers into the political structure of the republic. Trying to govern these sprawling territories with institutions and social traditions suited for a city-state overwhelmed the Roman Republic° and led to the establishment of a new form of government, the Roman Empire, by the end of the first century B.C.E.

ROMAN ORIGINS AND ETRUSCAN INFLUENCES

Interaction with outsiders shaped the story of Rome from its very beginning. Resting on low but easily defensible hills covering a few hundred acres above the Tiber River, Rome lies at the intersection of north-south and east-west trade routes that had been used in Italy since the Neolithic Age. Romans used these same routes to develop a thriving commerce with other peoples, many of whom they eventually conquered and absorbed into their Roman polity.

Settlements began in Rome about 1000 B.C.E., and control of the Tiber river crossing and trade allowed Rome to grow quickly. The Roman language, Latin, was one of at least 140 distinct languages and dialects spoken by Italy's frequently warring communities. Throughout this early period of Roman history, according to Roman legend, kings exercised political authority. During these years Romans also developed their military skills in order to defend themselves against their neighbors. Nevertheless, the Romans had amicable relations with some neighbors—particularly the Etruscans, who lived northwest of Rome.

In the sixth and seventh centuries B.C.E., Etruscan culture strongly influenced that of Rome. Like the Romans, the Etruscans° descended from indigenous prehistoric Italian peoples. By 800 B.C.E., they were firmly established in Etruria (modern Tuscany), and by the sixth century B.C.E. they controlled territory as far south as the Bay of Naples and east to the Adriatic Sea.

Etruscans carried on a lively trade with Greek merchants. Commerce became the conduit through which Etruscans and later Romans absorbed many aspects of

Greek culture. The Etruscans, for example, adopted the Greek alphabet and accepted many Greek myths, which they later transmitted to the Romans.

During the sixth century B.C.E., the Etruscans ruled Rome, influencing its religion and temple architecture. Although the Etruscans and Romans spoke different languages, a common culture deriving from native Italian, Etruscan, and Greek communities gradually evolved, especially in religious practice. The three main gods of Rome—Jupiter, Minerva, and Juno—were first worshiped in Etruria. (The Greek equivalents were Zeus, Athena, and Hera.)

THE BEGINNINGS OF THE ROMAN STATE

By about 600 B.C.E. Romans had prospered sufficiently to drain the marsh that lay at the center of their city. This created a public space that would be called the Forum°. At the same time they began to construct temples and public buildings, including the first senate house, where the elders met to discuss community affairs. Under the rule of its kings, some of whom were of Etruscan origin, Rome became an important military power in Italy. Only free male inhabitants of the city who could afford their own weapons voted in the citizen assembly, which made public decisions with the advice of the senate. Poor men could fight but not vote. Thus began the struggle between rich and poor that would plague Roman life for centuries.

About 500 B.C.E., when Rome had become a powerful city, with perhaps as many as 35,000 inhabitants, the Romans put an end to kingship and began a new system of government that historians call the Roman Republic. According to legend, in 509 B.C.E. a courageous aristocrat named Brutus overthrew the tyrannical Etruscan king, Tarquin the Arrogant. After the coup, Roman aristocrats established several new institutions in place of the kingship that structured political life for 500 years. An assembly comprising Rome's male citizens managed the city's legislative, judicial, and administrative affairs. As in the Greek *poleis*, only men participated in battle and public life. Each year, the assembly elected two chief executives called consuls, who could apply the law but whose decisions could be appealed. A body of elders, called the Senate, comprising about 300 Romans who had held administrative offices, advised the consuls, though they had no formal authority.

Hatred of kings, which became a staple of Roman political thought, prevented any one man from becoming too prominent. A relatively small group of influential families held real power within the political community, by both holding offices and working behind the scenes. As explained in Chapter 3, this kind of government is known as an oligarchy, or "the rule of the few."

Tensions between the rich and the poor shaped political and social life at Rome during the first two centuries of the Republic. At the top of the social hierarchy stood the patricians°, aristocratic clans whose high status extended to the days of the kings. These men, including the legendary Brutus, had been responsible for toppling the monarchy. Other rich landowners and senators with lesser pedigrees, as well as the prosperous farmers who made up the army's phalanxes, joined the patricians in resisting the plebeians°, the poorest segments of society. The plebeians demanded more political rights, such as a fair share of distributed public land and freedom from debt bondage. These efforts of poor Romans to acquire a political voice, called the Struggle of the Orders°, accelerated during the fifth century B.C.E., when Rome experienced a severe economic recession.

A victory in the plebeians' struggle came in 494 B.C.E., when they won the right to elect two tribunes each year as their spokesmen. Tribunes could veto magistrates' decisions and so block arbitrary judicial actions by the patricians. About 450 B.C.E., the plebeians took another major step forward with the publication of the Law of the Twelve Tables. The plebeians pressed for codification and public display of the law to ensure that aristocrats would not interpret the law arbitrarily or apply it to the disadvantage of the poor. In 445 B.C.E., a new law permitted marriage between plebeians and patricians.

Plebeians became fully integrated within the Roman government in 367 B.C.E., when politicians agreed that one of each year's two consuls should come from the plebeian class. The last concession to the plebeians came in 287 B.C.E., when the decisions of the Plebeian Assembly became binding on the whole state. The plebeians acquired their political strength and full acceptance in the political arena by simple extortion: They threatened to leave the army if the aristocratic elite failed to meet their demands. Without the plebeians, who constituted the bulk of the Roman army, the Republic could not protect itself from invaders or conquer new lands.

ROMAN TERRITORIAL EXPANSION

During the period of the Republic, Rome conquered and incorporated all of Italy, the vast Carthaginian Empire in northern Africa and Spain, and many of the lands inhabited by Celtic people to the north and west of Italy (see Map 4.2). As a result of these conquests, the Roman state found it necessary to change the methods of government established in the fifth century B.C.E.

Winning Control of Italy

The new political and military institutions that developed in Rome enabled the Romans to conquer the entire Italian peninsula. Romans began to expand their realm by allying with neighboring cities in Latium (the region of central Italy where Rome was situated). In 493 B.C.E. Rome successfully led a loose coalition of Latin-speaking cities called the Latin League against fierce hill tribes who coveted Latium's rich farmlands. Rome and its allies next confronted the Etruscans. In 396 B.C.E. they overcame the Etruscan city of Veii through a combination of military might and shrewd political maneuvering.

The next major step in Rome's expansion came in 338 B.C.E., when Roman troops smashed a three-year revolt of its Latin allies, who had come to resent Rome's overlordship. The peace settlement set the precedent for Rome's future expansion: Rome permitted defeated peoples to become citizens, giving them either partial or full citizenship. The conquered allies were permitted to continue their own customs and were not forced to pay tribute. Rome asked for only two things in return: loyalty and troops. All allied communities had to contribute soldiers to the Roman army in wartime. With the huge new pool of troops, Rome became the strongest power in Italy.

The Struggle with Carthage

By the third century B.C.E., imperial Carthage dominated the western Mediterranean region. From the capital city of Carthage located on the north African coast near modern Tunis, Carthaginians held rich lands along the African coast from modern Algeria to Morocco, controlled the natural resources of southern Spain, and dominated the sea lanes of the entire region. Phoenician traders had founded Carthage in the eighth century B.C.E., and the city's energetic merchants carried on business with Greeks, Etruscans, Celts, and eventually Romans. By the fourth century B.C.E. the Carthaginian Empire was playing an integral role in the economy of the Hellenistic world.

Rome and Carthage were old acquaintances. Eager for widespread recognition at the beginning of the Republic, Roman leaders signed a commercial treaty with Carthage. Several centuries of wary respect and increasing trade followed. In 264 B.C.E., just as Rome established power throughout the Italian peninsula, a war between Greek cities in Sicily drew Rome and Carthage into conflict as allies of the warring cities. Rome invaded Sicily, setting off the First Punic War, so called because the word *Punic* comes from the Latin word for "Phoenician." This war between Rome and Carthage lasted from 264 to 241 B.C.E.

Toward the end of the war Carthage signed a treaty in which it agreed to surrender Sicily and the surrounding islands and to pay a war indemnity over the course of a decade. Rome, however, wrecked the agreement by seizing Corsica and Sardinia, over which Carthage had lost effective control, and demanded larger reparations. Roman bad faith stoked Carthaginian hatred and desire for revenge.

War did not resume for another two decades, but the rapid growth of Carthaginian power in Spain led to renewed conflict with Rome. The Second Punic War (218–201 B.C.E.) erupted when the Carthaginian general Hannibal, 25 years old and eager for vengeance, captured Saguntum, a Spanish town with which Rome had formal ties of friendship. In an imaginative and daring move,

Hannibal then launched a surprise attack on Italy by crossing the Alps and invading from the north. With an army of nearly 25,000 men and eighteen elephants, he crushed the Roman armies sent against him. In the first major battle, at the Trebia River in the Po Valley, 20,000 Romans died. At Lake Trasimene in Etruria in 216 B.C.E., another 25,000 Romans fell. In the same year at Cannae, 50,000 men perished in Rome's worst defeat ever.

Despite these staggering losses, the Romans persevered and eventually defeated the Carthaginian general. They succeeded, first of all, because Hannibal lacked sufficient logistical support from Carthage to capitalize on his early victories and take the city of Rome. Second, most of Rome's allies in Italy proved loyal. They had often seen Romans prevail in the past and knew that the Romans took fierce revenge on disloyal friends. A third reason for Hannibal's defeat was the indomitable Roman spirit. The Romans simply refused to concede defeat, even after suffering devastating casualties.

Because the war against Hannibal had claimed so many Roman lives, many vengeful Romans agitated for the total destruction of Carthage. In particular, the statesman Marcus Porcius Cato (234–149 B.C.E.), who ended every public utterance with the demand "Carthage must be destroyed!", goaded Romans to violate the peace treaty and resume war with its old adversary. The Third Punic War (149–146 B.C.E.) resulted in the destruction of Carthage. Survivors were enslaved, and the city was burned to the ground and plowed under with salt. Its territories were reorganized as the Roman province of Africa.

Conflict with the Celts

Celtic peoples in western Europe fiercely resisted Roman military expansion. Not until the reign of Augustus (31 B.C.E.–14 C.E.) did the Romans bring the Celtic people in the Iberian peninsula under complete control. The most bitter conflict with the Celts began in 58 B.C.E., when the Roman general Julius Caesar invaded the part of Gaul that lies across the Alps. There he found numerous Celtic tribes with sophisticated political systems dominated by warrior aristocrats. After eight years of bloody conquest and massacre, Caesar conquered Gaul, turning the region into several Roman provinces that within a century became an integral part of the Roman Empire.

ROME AND THE HELLENISTIC WORLD

By the end of the Punic Wars, Rome had become involved in the affairs of the vigorous Hellenistic kingdoms of the East. Initially reluctant to take direct control of these regions, Roman leaders gradually changed their policies. After waging three successful wars against Macedon between 215 and 168 B.C.E., they assumed responsibility for maintaining order and gradually established absolute control over the entire eastern Mediterranean region.

Roman involvement in the Hellenistic world led to a complex encounter between Greek and Roman culture. It is often said that captive Greece took her captors captive. Hellenistic influence on Roman literature became strikingly apparent in the writing of history. In the second century B.C.E., the Greek historian Polybius made a major contribution to the writing of Roman history. Taken to Rome from Greece as a hostage in the 160s B.C.E., Polybius came to realize the futility of opposing Roman force. His *History*, written in the analytical tradition of the Greek historian Thucydides, traces Rome's astounding rise to world dominance in a mere fifty-three years and includes moralizing attacks on the abuse of power.

Hellenistic culture also had a major impact on Roman drama. Two Roman playwrights, Plautus (ca. 250–184 B.C.E.) and Terence (ca. 190–159 B.C.E.), took their inspiration from Hellenistic New Comedy and injected some fun into Roman literature. Their surviving works offer entertaining glimpses into the pitfalls of everyday life while also reinforcing the aristocratic values of the rulers of Rome's vast new domains.

Many educated Romans found Greek philosophy extremely attractive. The Hellenistic ethical philosophy that held the greatest appeal to Romans was Stoicism, because it encouraged an active public life. Stoic emphasis on the mastery of human difficulties appealed to aristocratic Romans' sense of duty and dignity. The great Roman orator and politician Marcus Tullius Cicero (106–43 B.C.E.) in particular combined Stoic ideas in a highly personal yet fully Roman way. He stressed moral behavior in political life while urging the attainment of a broad education. Cicero's high-minded devotion to the Republic won him the enmity of unscrupulous politicians, and he was murdered in 43 B.C.E. for his defense of Roman republican liberty.

The massive infusion of Hellenistic art into Rome following the Macedonian wars inevitably affected public taste. The most prestigious works of art decorated public shrines and spaces throughout the city. Many treasures went to private collectors. Greek artists soon moved to Rome to enjoy the patronage of wealthy Romans. Although copyists made replicas of Greek masterpieces, distinctively Roman artistic styles also emerged, just as they did in

■ **Magna Mater**
Romans worshiped Magna Mater (The Great Mother) after her cult was introduced in Rome during the Second Punic War against Hannibal. People had worshiped this goddess throughout the eastern Mediterranean since remote antiquity. This statue expresses her majestic power.

rhetoric, literature, philosophy, and history writing. In portrait sculpture, especially, a style developed that unflinchingly depicted all the wrinkles of experience on a person's face. In this way the venerable Roman tradition of carving ancestral busts merged with Greek art.

LIFE IN THE ROMAN REPUBLIC

During the Hellenistic Age, Rome prospered from the acquisition of new territories. A small number of influential families dominated political life, sometimes making decisions about war from which they could win wealth and prestige. The Roman Republic remained strong because these ruling families took pains to limit the amount of power any one man or extended political family might attain.

Patrons and Clients

The ruling families of Rome established political networks that extended their influence through all levels of Roman society. These relationships depended on the traditional Roman institution of patrons and clients°. By exercising influence on behalf of a social subordinate, a powerful man (the patron) would bind that man (the client) to him in anticipation of future support. In this way complex webs of personal interdependency influenced the entire Roman social system. The patron-client system operated at every level of society, and it was customary for a man of influence to receive his clients on matters of business at his home the first thing in the morning. In a modest household the discussion might involve everyday business such as shipping fish, arranging a marriage, or making a loan. But in the mansion of a Roman aristocrat a patron might be more interested in forging a political alliance. When several patron-client groups joined forces, they became significant political factions under the leadership of one patron.

Pyramids of Wealth and Power

Like its political organization, Rome's social organization demonstrated a well-defined hierarchy. By the first century B.C.E., a new, elite class of political leaders had emerged in Rome, composed of both the old noble families and those families of plebeian origin who had been able to attain membership in the Senate through their service in public offices. The men of this leadership class dominated the Senate and formed the inner circle of government. From their ranks came most of the consuls. They set foreign and domestic policy, led armies to war, held the main magistracies, and siphoned off the lion's share of the Republic's resources.

Beneath this elite group came the equestrian class. Equestrians normally abstained from public office, but were often tied to political leaders by personal obligation. Next in rank came the plebeians, the mass of citizens who lived in Rome and throughout Italy. As we have seen, the Plebeian Assembly had gradually come under the control of plebeian politicians who were the clients of aristocratic patrons. These plebeian politicians and their patrons had little interest in the condition of the poor. This left ordinary plebeians with no direct way to express their political will. Rome's Italian allies had even fewer rights than the plebeians, despite their service in the Roman armies. Although millions of allies inhabited lands controlled by Rome, only a privileged few of the local elites received Roman citizenship. The rest could only hope for the goodwill of Roman officials.

At the bottom of the Roman hierarchy were slaves. By the first century B.C.E., about two million slaves captured in war or born in captivity lived in Italy and Sicily. Romans considered the slaves pieces of property, "talking tools," whom their owners could exploit at will. The brutal inequities of this system led to violence. In 135 B.C.E. more than 200,000 slaves in Sicily began an ill-fated struggle for freedom that lasted three years. Between 104 and 101 B.C.E. 30,000 slaves took up arms in another unsuccessful rebellion. The most destructive revolt occurred in Italy during the years from 74 to 71 B.C.E., when an army of more than 100,000 slaves led by the Thracian gladiator Spartacus (gladiators were slaves who fought to the death for the public) battled eight Roman legions totaling about 50,000 men before being crushed by the superior Roman military organization.

The Roman Family

A Roman *familia* typically included not just the husband, wife, and unmarried children, but also their slaves and often freedmen and others who were dependent on the household. Legitimate marriages required the agreement of both husband and wife. Women usually married at puberty, and men did so in their twenties. Because few babies survived infancy, most families had only two or three children.

The Roman family mirrored the patterns of authority and dependency found in the political arena. Just as a patron commanded the support of his clients regardless of their status in public life, so the male head of the household directed the destiny of all his subordinates within the *familia*. The head of the family, or *paterfamilias,* held power of life and death over his wife, children, and slaves, though few men exercised this power. In reality, women and grown children often had a great deal of independence, and aristocratic women often exerted a strong influence in political life, though always from behind the scenes.

With very few exceptions Roman women remained legally dependent on a male relative. In the most common form of marriage, a wife remained under the formal control of the *paterfamilias* to whom she belonged before her marriage—in most cases, her father. In practice this meant that the wife retained control of her own property and the inheritance she had received from her father.

Beginnings of the Roman Revolution

··─··

The inequalities of wealth and power in Roman society led to the disintegration of the Republic. The rapid acquisition of territories and enormous wealth overseas heightened those differences. Roman reformers' attempts to face the new economic realities met with fierce resistance from those who profited the most from imperial rule: politicians, governors, high military personnel, and businessmen. These men sought personal glory and political advantage even if it came at the Republic's expense. Their quest for political prominence through military adventure, coupled with deep-seated flaws of political institutions, eventually overwhelmed the Republic's political structure and brought about a revolution—a decisive, fundamental change in the political system.

THE GRACCHI

During the second century B.C.E., more and more citizen farmers in Italy lost their fields to powerful landholders, who replaced them with slaves on their estates. As a result, the slave population of Italy increased dramatically. Some members of the political elite feared the danger inherent in these developments. If citizen farmers failed to meet the property requirements for military service and pay for their own weapons, as they traditionally had done, Rome would lose its supply of recruits for its legions.

Two young brothers, Tiberius and Gaius Gracchus, attempted some reforms. As a tribune, Tiberius (162–133 B.C.E.) convinced the Plebeian Assembly to pass a bill limiting the amount of public land that one man could possess and requiring that the excess land from wealthy landholders be redistributed in small lots to poor citizens. While the land redistribution was in progress, conservative senators arranged for assassins to club Tiberius Gracchus to death.

A decade later, when Tiberius's brother Gaius became tribune in 123 B.C.E., he turned his attention to the problem of extortion by corrupt governors in the provinces. Gaius Gracchus attempted to stop these abuses. He also tried to speed up land redistribution. But when he attempted to give citizenship to Rome's Italian allies in order to protect them from having their land confiscated by Romans, he lost the support of the Roman people, who did not wish to share the benefits of citizenship with non-Romans. In 121 B.C.E. Gaius committed suicide to avoid being murdered by a mob sent by his senatorial foes.

The ruthless suppression of the Gracchi (the Latin plural form of *Gracchus*) and their supporters lit the fuse of political and social revolution at Rome. By attempting to effect change through the Plebeian Assembly, the Gracchi unwittingly paved the way for less scrupulous aristocrats to seek power by falsely claiming to represent the interests of the poor. The introduction of assassinations into the public debate signaled the end of political consensus among the oligarchy. Rivalry among the elite combined with the desperation of the poor in an explosive blend, with the army as the wild card. If an unscrupulous politician were to join forces with poverty-stricken soldiers, the Republic would be in peril.

THE SOCIAL WAR

The next major crisis in Roman political life occurred in 90 B.C.E., when Rome's loyal allies in Italy launched a revolt against Rome known as the Social War (from the Latin word *socii*, which means "allies"). The confederation of allies demanded not independence but participation in the Roman Republic. They wanted full citizenship rights because they had been partners in all of Rome's wars and thus felt entitled to share in the fruits of victory. The allies lost this war, but once they were defeated, Rome granted all their demands anyway. Peoples of the entire Italian peninsula obtained Roman citizenship and quickly became a potent force in Roman political life. Their presence in the political arena tilted the political scales away from the wealthy in Rome toward the population of Italy in general.

Two years later another crisis arose when the aristocrat and consul Lucius Cornelius Sulla (138–78 B.C.E.) engaged in a bitter political struggle with Gaius Marius (157–86 B.C.E.), a general who had eliminated the property requirement for enlistment in the army. The final stage in this long struggle occurred in 82 B.C.E., when Sulla, returning from Asia Minor at the head of a loyal army, seized Rome in a battle that killed about 60,000 Roman soldiers. After murdering 3,000 of his political opponents, the Senate named him dictator, thereby giving him complete power. With the support of the aristocratic Senate, whose power he hoped to restore, Sulla crippled the political power of the plebeians. Surprisingly, however, Sulla resigned as dictator in 80 B.C.E. He was unwilling to destroy the Republic's institutions for the sake of his own ambition. Nevertheless, he had set a precedent for using armies in political rivalries.

THE FIRST TRIUMVIRATE

The Roman Republic's final downward spiral of social turmoil was provoked by three men: Pompey (Gnaeus Pompeius, 106–48 B.C.E.), Marcus Licinius Crassus (ca. 115–53 B.C.E.), and Gaius Julius Caesar (100–44 B.C.E.). Pompey, the general who suppressed a revolt in Spain, and

Crassus, the wealthiest man in Rome who had been one of Sullas's lieutenants, joined forces to crush the slave revolt of Spartacus in 71 B.C.E. Backed by their armies, they then coerced the Senate into naming them consuls in 70 B.C.E.

During their consulship, Pompey and Crassus made modest changes to Sulla's reforms. They permitted the tribunes to propose laws again and let equestrians serve on juries. After their year in office they retired without making further demands. Pompey continued his military career. He received a special command in 67 B.C.E. to clear pirates from the Mediterranean in order to protect Roman trade. The following year Pompey crushed another rebellion in Asia Minor. He reorganized Asia Minor and territories in the Middle East, creating new provinces and more client kingdoms subservient to Rome.

When Pompey returned to Rome he asked the Senate to grant land to his victorious troops. The Senate, jealous of his success and afraid of the power he would gain as the patron of so many troops, would not comply. To gain land for his soldiers and have his political arrangements in Asia Minor and the Middle East ratified, Pompey made an alliance with two men even more ambitious and less scrupulous than he: his old ally Crassus and Gaius Julius Caesar, the ambitious descendant of an ancient patrician family. The three formed an informal alliance historians call the First Triumvirate°. With their influence now combined, no man or institution could oppose them. Caesar obtained the consulship in 59 B.C.E., despite the objections of many senators. By using illegal means that would return to haunt him, he directed the Senate to ratify Pompey's arrangements in the Middle East and Asia Minor and to grant land to his troops. He arranged for Crassus's clients, the equestrian tax collectors, to have their financial problems resolved at public expense.

As a reward for his efforts on behalf of the triumvirate, the perpetually debt-ridden Caesar arranged to receive the governorship of the Po Valley and the Illyrian coast for five years after his consulship ended. As he set out for his governorship, he assumed command of Transalpine Gaul (northwest of the Alps) when its governor died. This put Caesar in a position to operate militarily in all of Gaul—and ultimately to conquer it.

THE RUINOUS EFFECTS OF CONQUEST

Roman conquests in Italy damaged the economy of newly captured rural areas. The following description by the Roman historian Appian describes the process of Roman settlement in newly taken territories in Italy, and the consequences of that settlement. The reforms of the Gracchi were intended to correct some of these problems.

The Romans, as they subdued the Italian peoples successively in war, seized a part of their lands and built towns there, or established their own colonies in already existing towns, using them as garrisons. Of the land thus acquired by war they assigned the cultivated part forthwith to settlers, or leased or sold it. Since they had no leisure as yet to allot the part which then lay desolated by war (this was generally the greater part), they proclaimed that in the meantime those who were willing to work it might do so for a share of the yearly crops—a tenth of the grain and a fifth of the fruit. From those who kept flocks, a tax was fixed for the animals, both oxen and small cattle. This they did in order to multiply the Italian race, which they considered to be the most laborious of peoples, so that so that they might have plenty of allies at home. But the very opposite happened; for the rich, getting possession of the greater part of the undistributed lands, and being emboldened by the lapse of time to believe that they would never be dispossessed, and adding to their holding the small farms of their poor neighbors, partly by purchase and partly by force, came to cultivate vast tracts instead of single estates, using for this purpose slaves as laborers and herdsmen, lest free laborers be drawn from agriculture into the army. . . . Thus the governing class became enormously rich and number of slaves multiplied throughout the country, while the Italian peoples dwindled in numbers and strength . . .

Source: From *A History of Rome through the Fifth Century, Volume 1, The Republic*, edited by A. H. M. Jones (New York: Walker and Company, 1968), p. 104.

JULIUS CAESAR AND THE END OF THE REPUBLIC

Caesar's determination to conquer Gaul lay in pursuing personal advantage. He knew that he would win glory, wealth, and prestige in Rome by conquering new lands, and so he promptly began a war (58–50 B.C.E.) against the Celtic tribes of Transalpine Gaul. In eight years Caesar conquered the area of modern France and Belgium, turning these territories into Roman provinces. He even briefly invaded

Britain. His intrusion into Celtic lands led to their eventual Romanization.

In Rome, a group of senators grew fearful of Caesar's power, ambitions, and arrogance. They appealed to Pompey for assistance, and he brought the armies loyal to him to the aid of the Senate against Caesar. The Senate then asked Caesar to lay down his command in Gaul and return to Rome. Facing trial and certain conviction if he were to return to Rome, Caesar refused. In 49 B.C.E. he left Gaul and marched south with his loyal troops against the forces of

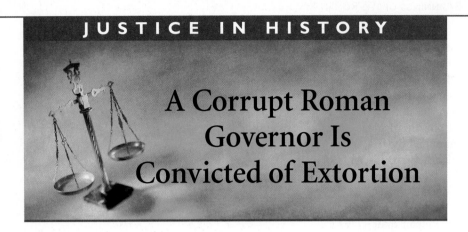

A Corrupt Roman Governor Is Convicted of Extortion

Governors sent by the Roman Senate to rule the provinces wielded absolute power, which often corrupted them. One such man was Gaius Verres, who was convicted in 70 B.C.E. in a court in Rome for his flagrant abuse of power while governor of Sicily. The courtroom drama in which Verres was found guilty reveals one of the deepest flaws of the Roman Republic: the unprincipled exploitation of lands under Roman control. It also reveals one of Rome's greatest strengths: the presence of men of high ethical standards who believed in honest government and fair treatment of Roman subjects. The trial and its result reveals Republican Rome at its best and worst.

While governor from 73 to 71 B.C.E., Verres had looted Sicily with shocking thoroughness. In his pursuit of gold and Greek art, Verres tortured and sometimes killed Roman citizens. His outraged victims employed the young and ambitious lawyer Marcus Tullius Cicero (106–43 B.C.E.) to prosecute Verres. They could not have chosen a better advocate.

The prosecution of Verres marks the beginning of Cicero's illustrious career as one of the most active politicians and certainly the greatest orator of the Republic. Cicero also stands as one of the most influential political philosophers of Western civilization, one who hated the corruption of political life and opposed tyranny in any

form. His many works have influenced political thinkers from antiquity to the present.

In the Roman Republic, only senators and equestrians between ages 30 and 60 could serve on juries for civil crimes like those committed by Verres. All adult male citizens had the right to bring a case to court, but women had less freedom to do so. After swearing oaths of good faith, accusers read the charges in the presence of the accused, who in turn agreed to accept the decision of the court.

When trials began, the prosecutor was expected to be present, but the accused could decline to attend. The prosecution and the defense both produced evidence, then cross-examined witnesses. Since a Roman lawyer could discuss any aspect of the defendant's personal or public life, character assassination became an important—and amusing—rhetorical tool.

After deliberating, the jury delivered its verdict and the judge gave the penalty required by law, generally fines or periods of exile. No provisions for appeal existed, but pardon could be obtained by a legislative act.

Cicero worked this system to his advantage in his prosecution of Verres. He nimbly quashed an attempt to delay the trial until 69 B.C.E., when the president of the court would be a crony of Verres. Then, with a combination of ringing oratory and irrefutable evi-

dence of Verres's crimes, Cicero made his case. The following excerpt from his speech shows Cicero's mastery of persuasive rhetoric:

Judges: at this grave crisis in the history of our country, you have been offered a peculiarly desirable gift . . . For you have been given a unique chance to make your Senatorial Order less unpopular, and to set right the damaged reputation of these courts. A belief has taken root which is having a fatal effect on our nation—and which to us who are senators, in particular, threatens grave peril. This belief is on everyone's tongue, at Rome and even in foreign countries. It is this: that in these courts, with their present membership, even the worst criminal will never be convicted provided that he has money. . . . And at this very juncture Gaius Verres has been brought to trial. Here is a man whose life and actions the world has already condemned—yet whose enormous fortune, according to his own loudly expressed hopes, has already brought him acquittal! Pronounce a just and scrupulous verdict against Verres and you will keep the good name which ought always to be yours. . . . I spent fifty days on a careful investigation of the entire island of Sicily; I got to know every document, every wrong suffered either by a community or an individual. . . .

For three long years he so thoroughly despoiled and pillaged the province that its restoration to its pre-

■ **Republican Portrait of Cicero**

This portrait of Cicero captures his uncompromising personality. The style of depicting every wrinkle conforms both to Hellenistic interest in psychological portraiture and traditional Roman directness. In the Republican period this type of portraiture was enormously popular.

vious state is out of the question. . . . All the property that anyone in Sicily still has for his own today is merely what happened to escape the attention of this avaricious lecher, or survived his glutted appetites. . . . It was an appalling disgrace for our country.

. . . In the first stage of the trial, then, my charge is this. I accuse Gaius Verres of committing acts of lechery and brutality against the citizens and allies of Rome, and many crimes against God and man. I claim that he has illegally taken from Sicily sums amounting to forty million sesterces. By the witnesses and documents, public and private, which I am going to cite, I shall convince you that these charges are true.[1]

Cicero's speech was persuasive and the jury found Verres guilty. Verres went into exile in Marseilles to avoid his sentence, but he did not avoid punishment altogether. Justice—relentless and ironic—caught up with him some years later during the civil wars that followed Julius Caesar's death. Mark Antony, who was also a connoisseur of other people's wealth, wanted Verres's art collection for himself and so put Verres's name on a death list to obtain it. The former governor of Sicily was murdered in 43 B.C.E.

In his prosecution of Verres, Cicero delivered more than an indictment of one corrupt man; for a brief moment he revealed some of the deepest, fatal flaws of the Roman Republic. The trial inspired some short-term reforms, but not until the reforms of the emperor Augustus did the relationship between Roman administrators and provincial populations become more fair. ■

Questions of Justice

1. What does Verres's trial reveal about weaknesses in the Roman Republic?
2. Cicero's speech illustrates his disdain for corruption and tyranny. What are the tensions between personal morality and the requirements of governing a large empire?

Taking It Further

Rawson, Elizabeth. *Cicero, A Portrait.* 1975. This book gives a balanced account of Cicero's life.

Gruen, Erich S. *The Last Generation of the Roman Republic.* 1974. A magisterial analysis of the Republic's decline, with emphasis on legal affairs.

the Senate, thereby deliberately plunging Rome into civil war. In 45 B.C.E., having finally defeated those forces, he returned to Italy. The following year he had himself proclaimed dictator for life and assumed complete control over all aspects of government, flagrantly disregarding the precedents of the Republic.

Once in power, Caesar permanently ended the autonomy of the Senate. He enlarged this assembly from 600 (its size at the time of Sulla) to 900 men, and then filled it with his supporters. He adjusted the chaotic Republican calendar by adding one day every leap year, creating a year of 365.25 days. The resulting "Julian" calendar lasted until the sixteenth century C.E. He regularized gold coinage and urban administration and planned a vast public library.

Caesar seriously miscalculated by assuming he could win the support of his enemies by not executing them and by making administrative changes that disregarded Republican precedent. These changes earned Caesar the resentment of traditionalist senators who failed to recognize that the Republic could never be restored. On March 15, 44 B.C.E., a group of idealistic senators, led by Cassius and Brutus, stabbed Caesar to death at a Senate meeting. The assassins claimed that they wanted to restore the Republic, but in reality they had only unleashed another brutal civil war.

Marcus Antonius (Mark Antony), who had been Caesar's right-hand man, stepped forward to oppose the conspirators. He was soon joined by Octavian, Caesar's grandnephew and legal heir. Though Octavian was only 19, he gained control of some of Caesar's legions and compelled the Senate to name him consul. Marcus Lepidus, commander of Caesar's cavalry, joined Mark Antony and Octavian to form the Second Triumvirate°. The new trio coerced the Senate into granting them power to rule Rome legally.

Antony, Octavian, and Lepidus soon began to struggle among themselves for absolute authority. After Lepidus dropped out of the contest, Antony and Octavian agreed to separate spheres of influence. Octavian took Italy and Rome's western provinces, while Antony took the eastern provinces. This division of power did not last. In Egypt, Antony joined forces with Cleopatra VII, the last descendent of the Hellenistic monarch Ptolemy. Octavian responded to this alliance by launching a vicious propaganda campaign against the couple, accusing Antony of surrendering Roman values and territory to a foreign seductress. The inevitable war broke out in 31 B.C.E. At the battle of Actium, in Greece, Octavian's troops defeated Antony and Cleopatra's land and naval forces.

The 32-year-old Octavian now stood as absolute master of the Roman world. He had a clear vision of the problems that had destroyed the Republic, and from its ashes he planned to rebuild the Roman state. Under the leadership of Octavian, who came to be known as the emperor Augustus, Rome created a new political system, the Roman Empire, in which Octavian had unprecedented power over a vast geographical area.

The new world order that Octavian created brought an end to the Hellenistic Age. Rome now ruled all the lands that Alexander the Great had conquered, except for Persia and the territories farther to the east, and Hellenistic culture would now have to accommodate the realities of Roman rule. As we will see in the next chapter, Octavian succeeded where Alexander had failed: He created a world empire that had the infrastructure it needed to endure, and the peaceful conditions that enabled its culture to flourish and spread.

CONCLUSION

Defining the West in the Hellenistic Age

During the Hellenistic Age the cultural and geographical boundaries of what would later be called the West began to take shape. These boundaries encompassed the regions where Hellenistic culture penetrated and had a lasting influence. The lands within the empire of Alexander the Great, all of which lay to the east of Greece and Egypt, formed the core of this cultural realm, but the Hellenistic world also extended westward across the Mediterranean, embracing the lands ruled by Carthage from North Africa to Spain. Hellenism also reached the edges of the lands inhabited by Celtic peoples. Most of all, Hellenistic culture left a distinctive mark on Roman civilization in Italy. In all these locations Greek culture interacted with those of the areas it penetrated, and the synthesis that resulted became one of the main foundations of Western civilization.

During the period of the Roman Empire, which will be the subject of the next chapter, a new blend of Hellenistic and Latin cultures, in which Hellenism was an important but not always the dominant component, took shape. The geographical arena within which this culture flourished was that of the vast Roman Empire, covering a large part of Europe, North Africa, and the Middle East. The culture that characterized this empire gave a new definition to what we now call the West.

Suggestions for Further Reading

For a comprehensive list of suggested readings, please go to www.ablongman.com/levackconcise/chapter4

Boardman, John, Jasper Griffin, and Oswyn Murray, eds. *Greece and the Hellenistic World, The Oxford History of the Classical World.* 1988. A synthesis of all aspects of Hellenistic life, with excellent illustrations and bibliography.

Cohn, Norman. *Cosmos, Chaos, and the World to Come: The Ancient Roots of Apocalyptic Faith.* 1993. This brilliant study explains the development of ideas about the end of the world in the cultures of the ancient world.

Cornell, T. J. *The Beginnings of Rome: Italy and Rome from the Bronze Age to the Punic Wars (ca. 1000–264 B.C.).* 1996. A synthesis of the latest evidence with many important new interpretations.

Crawford, Michael. *The Roman Republic.* 2nd ed. 1992. This overview by a leading scholar lays a strong foundation for further study.

Cunliffe, Barry. *The Ancient Celts.* 1997. This source analyzes the archaeological evidence for the Celtic Iron Age, with many illustrations and maps.

Cunliffe, Barry, ed. *The Oxford Illustrated Prehistory of Europe.* 1996. A collection of well-illustrated essays on the development of European cultures from the end of the Ice Age to the Classical period.

Gardner, Jane F. *Women in Roman Law and Society.* 1986. Explains the legal position of women in the Roman world.

Green, Peter. *Alexander to Actium: The Historical Evolution of the Hellenistic Age.* 1990. A vivid interpretation of the world created by Alexander until the victory of Augustus.

Gruen, Erich S. *The Hellenistic World and the Coming of Rome.* 1984. An extremely important study of how Rome entered the eastern Mediterranean world.

Kuhrt, Amélie, and Susan Sherwin-White, eds. *Hellenism in the East: The Interaction of Greek and Non-Greek Civilizations from Syria to Central Asia After Alexander.* 1987. These studies help us understand the complexities of the interaction of Greeks and non-Greeks in the Hellenistic world.

Pollitt, J. J. *Art in the Hellenistic Age.* 1986. A brilliant interpretation of the development of Hellenistic art.

Notes

1. From *Selected Works* by Cicero, translated by Michael Grant (Penguin Classics 1960, second revised edition 1971). Copyright © Michael Grant 1960, 1965, 1971. Reproduced by permission of Penguin Books Ltd.

Enclosing the West: The Early Roman Empire and Its Neighbors, 31 B.C.E.–235 C.E.

I N THE MIDDLE OF THE SECOND CENTURY C.E., AELIUS ARISTIDES, AN ARISTOCRATIC Greek writer who held Roman citizenship, visited Rome, where he gave a long public oration in honor of the imperial capital. His words reveal what the Roman Empire meant to a wealthy, highly educated man from Rome's eastern provinces: "Rome is to the whole world what an ordinary city is to its suburbs and surrounding countryside . . . you have given up the division of nation from nation . . . you have separated the human race into Roman and non-Romans."

Aristides's description of the empire as one grand city with a unified culture set off from the "non-Romans" in the world is an exaggeration. Nevertheless, it points to the key element of the Romans' success—a willingness to share their culture with their subjects and to assimilate them into the political and social life of the empire. Aristides understood that Roman culture flourished primarily in cities, and he believed that Roman urban life was the mark of civilization. In Aristides's opinion, Rome's destiny was to bring civilization to the rest of the world. His satisfied view of the Roman Empire demonstrates how successfully Rome had created a sense of common purpose among its elite citizens.

During its first two and a half centuries of existence, the Roman Empire brought cultural unity and political stability to an astonishingly diverse area stretching from the Atlantic Ocean to the Persian Gulf. Imperial rule disseminated Roman culture throughout not only the Mediterranean region and the Middle East, but also northwestern Europe. Within imperial Rome's parameters—intellectual, religious, political, and geographic—the basic outlines of what we call the West today were drawn.

This chapter examines the Roman Empire at the height of its power (ca. 31 B.C.E.–235 C.E.). We will see how its encounters with far-flung subject populations helped shape its development. Autocratic and exploitative, the

Chapter Outline

- The Imperial Center

- Life in the Roman Provinces: Assimilation and Resistance

- The Frontier and Beyond

- Society and Culture in the Imperial Age

Marcus Aurelius: The emperor Marcus Aurelius (r. 161–180) raises his right hand in a gesture of command, compelling the viewer to obey. A triumph of the art of bronze casting, this statue conveys the majesty of the Roman Empire.

Roman imperial system nonetheless provided the climate for rich developments in social, religious, and political life. Military force maintained the imperial system, but the stability and prosperity that accompanied Roman rule persuaded many subject peoples of its benefits. The new regime established a stable governing system that brought a nearly unbroken peace to the Mediterranean world for more than two centuries. Historians call this era the *Pax Romana*°, the "Roman peace". In these centuries Roman culture slowly took root across western Europe, North Africa, and the Middle East, transforming the lives of local populations. In the eyes of millions of people during these years, Rome ceased to be an unfamiliar and predatory occupying power. Many of its subjects came to regard Rome as a civilizing agent that provided unity and common culture. Others, particularly the slaves whose labor fueled the Roman economy and the small farmers whose taxes supported the Roman state, experienced Rome as an oppressive ruler.

This chapter analyzes imperial Rome's constantly evolving political and cultural community as three concentric circles of power—the imperial center, the provinces, and the frontiers and beyond. The imperial center served as the site of the main agents of control—the emperor, the Roman senate, and the army. In the second circle, provincial populations struggled with the challenges raised by the imposition of Roman culture and politics and in the process contributed to the construction of a new imperial culture. The outermost circle of the empire, its frontier zones and the lands beyond, included Romans living within the empire's borders as well as those peoples who lived on the other side, but who nonetheless interacted with Rome through trading and warfare. Finally, the chapter examines Roman society and culture during the imperial age. Four questions guide this exploration:

- How did the Roman imperial system develop and what roles did the emperor, senate, army, and Rome itself play in this process?
- How did provincial peoples assimilate to or resist Roman rule?
- How did Romans interact with peoples living beyond the imperial borders?
- What was the social and cultural response to the emergence and consolidation of empire?

The Imperial Center

After civil wars left the Roman Republic in ruins, a new political system emerged from its ashes. Rome continued to acquire and rule huge territories far from Italy. Its form of government, however, changed from a republic, in which members of an oligarchy competed for power that they shared by serving in elected offices, to an empire, in which one man, the emperor, held absolute power for life. During this transformation, the city of Rome, the center of imperial operations, became the model for social life, political processes, and architectural styles throughout the empire.

IMPERIAL AUTHORITY: AUGUSTUS AND AFTER

As we saw in Chapter 4, Julius Caesar's heir, Octavian, wrenched the state from the spiral of civil war and claimed that he had restored normal life to the Republic. Nothing could have been further from the truth. Behind a carefully crafted façade of restored Republican tradition and practice, Octavian created a Roman version of a Hellenistic monarchy, like those of Alexander the Great's successors in the eastern Mediterranean.

In 23 C.E. Octavian renounced the consulship and shrewdly arranged for the Senate to grant him unprecedented power, but disguised by Republican trappings. He could now legally intercede in all government activities and military affairs. He selected or approved all provincial governors and assumed direct control over particularly rich or particularly troublesome provinces. Other generals continued to lead the legions into battle, but always in his name. Other magistrates continued to administer the state in accordance with the traditional responsibilities of their office, but no one was chosen without Octavian's approval.

To mask his tyranny, Octavian never wore a crown. Following his instructions, the powerless Senate honored him with the invented title "Augustus." This title had no previous associations with kingship, but it implied a uniquely exalted, godlike authority in the community. Later rulers, accepting the trappings of monarchy more openly than Augustus, used the title *imperator,* or emperor.

The Problem of Succession

Following the example of the Hellenistic world, Augustus established a hereditary monarchy. When he died in 14 C.E., his stepson Tiberius (r. 14–37 C.E.) took control of the empire without opposition. The hereditary principle staved off the instability that would have come with open competition for the throne. In the Julio-Claudian dynasty inaugurated by Augustus, which lasted almost 100 years, every ruler came from Augustus's extended family. Nero, the last of Augustus's family line, committed suicide in 68 C.E. after civil war had broken out and the Senate declared him a public enemy. Because he left no heirs, four generals vied for the throne.

During this "Year of the Four Emperors" (69 C.E.), Rome learned what the historian Tacitus later called the "secret of empire"—that troops far from the imperial city could choose emperors. Four different emperors took the throne in quick succession as different Roman armies competed to seat their commanders. The winner of this contest was the general Titus Flavius Vespasianus, or Vespasian (r. 69–79 C.E.), the first Roman emperor who did not come from the highest nobility.

The Flavian dynasty that Vespasian established lasted twenty-five years until the death of his last son, Domitian (r. 81–96 C.E.). To avoid the chaos of another succession crisis, the Senate cooperated with the army in choosing a new emperor, the elderly Nerva (r. 96–98 C.E.). They hoped that this elderly, highly respected man who had no sons would ensure a smooth transition to the next regime, and so he did. Under pressure from the restless military establishment, Nerva adopted the vigorous general Trajan (r. 98–117 C.E.) as his son and heir, and thus inaugurated the era historians call the Antonine Age. For almost a century, Rome enjoyed competent rule to a large degree because Nerva's practice of adopting highly qualified succes-

sors continued. Historians consider the Antonine age a high point of Roman peace and prosperity.

This peaceful time ended with yet another imperial murder. Marcus Aurelius (r. 161–180 C.E.) abandoned the custom of picking a highly qualified successor, and instead was followed to the throne by his incompetent, cruel, and eventually insane son Commodus (r. 180–192 C.E.). In 192 C.E., several senators arranged to have Commodus strangled, triggering another civil war. A senator from North Africa, Septimius Severus, emerged victorious from this conflict and assumed the imperial throne in 193 C.E. The Severan dynasty he established lasted until 235 C.E. When Severus Alexander (r. 222–235 C.E.) attempted to negotiate with the German tribes by offering them bribes, his own troops killed him because they wanted the cash for themselves. Fifty years of political and economic crisis followed. As we will see in the next chapter, the imperial

■ **Map 5.1   The Roman Empire at Its Greatest Extent**

The Roman Empire reached its greatest extent during the reign of Trajan (98–117 C.E.). Stretching from the north of Britain to the Euphrates River, the empire brought together hundreds of distinct ethnic groups.

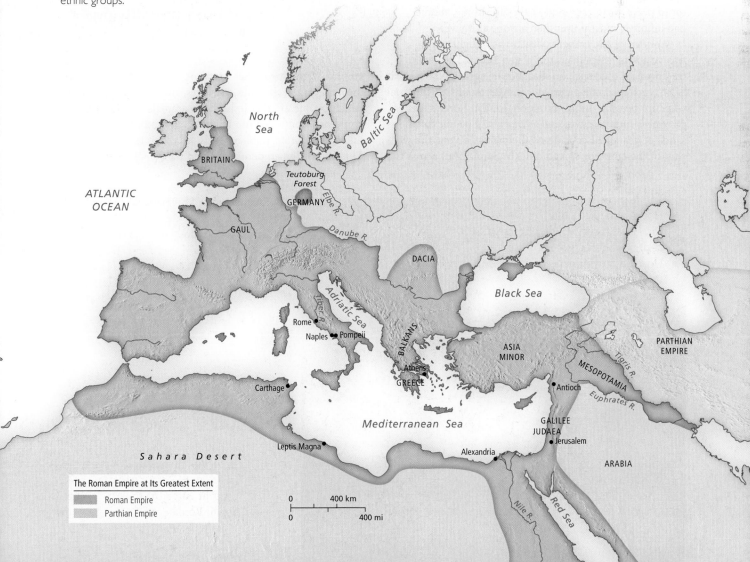

structure that emerged after this time of crisis differed significantly from the Augustan model.

The Emperor's Role: The Nature of Imperial Power

Under the Augustan imperial system, four main responsibilities defined the emperor's role. First, the emperor both protected and expanded imperial territory. Only the emperor determined foreign policy, made treaties, and waged war. The emperor's second responsibility was to administer justice and to provide good government throughout his dominions. In theory all citizens could appeal to the emperor directly for justice. Third, as *Pontifex Maximus,* or High Priest, the emperor supervised the public worship of the great gods of Rome, particularly Jupiter. Emperors and subjects alike believed that in order to fulfill Rome's destiny to rule the world, they must make regular sacrifices to the gods. Finally, the emperor became a symbol of unity for all the peoples of the empire. He served as the focal point around which all life in the empire revolved. Inevitably, he seemed more than human, even worthy of worship, for he was the guarantor of peace, prosperity, and victory for Rome, and he had infinitely more power than anyone else alive.

Worship of the emperor began with Augustus. He was reluctant to call himself a god because Roman tradition opposed such an idea, but he permitted his spirit to be worshiped in a paternal way. After Augustus, imperial worship became more pronounced. In Rome's eastern provinces such as Egypt and Syria, where people for thousands of years had considered their kings divine, the worship of the emperor spread quickly. Soon, cities across the

CHRONOLOGY	
31 B.C.E.–68 C.E.	Julio-Claudian dynasty rules Rome
CA. 4 B.C.E.–30 C.E.	Life of Jesus
9 C.E.	Romans abandon their conquests in Germany
66–70 C.E.	Jewish revolt crushed; Jerusalem and temple destroyed
69 C.E.	"Year of the Four Emperors"
69–96 C.E.	Flavian dynasty rules Rome
CA. 100 C.E.	New Testament completed
117 C.E.	Rome reaches greatest territorial extent under Trajan
138–192 C.E.	Antonine dynasty rules Rome
193–235 C.E.	Severan dynasty rules Rome
212 C.E.	Antonine Decree grants citizenship to all free inhabitants of the Roman Empire
235 C.E.	Fifty years of political and military turmoil begin

empire worshiped the emperor on special occasions through games, speeches, sacrifices, and free public feasts in which people ate the flesh of the animals sacrificed in the emperor's honor. Within magnificent temples, priests conducted elaborate public rituals to venerate the emperor. This cult of the emperor provided a focus of allegiance for

■ Aqueducts: The Pont du Gard

The graceful aqueduct known today as the Pont du Gard was built about 14 C.E. to carry water to the city of Nîmes, in the south of France, from its surrounding hills. Romans were highly sophisticated hydraulic engineers, and waterworks like this aqueduct were a common feature of all the large cities of the empire.

■ Augustus: A Commanding Presence

This imposing statue of Augustus dating to 19 B.C.E. depicts him as a warrior making a gesture of command. His face is ageless, the carving on his armor celebrates peace and prosperity, and his posture is balanced and forceful.

the diverse peoples of the empire and so served as a unifying force.

Emperors made their presence felt throughout the empire by building and restoring roads, temples, harbors, aqueducts, and fortifications. Sporting victories also brought the emperor into his subjects' lives. At the Circus Maximus in Rome, a chariot racetrack where a quarter of a million people could gather to cheer their favorite charioteer, as well as in racetracks throughout the empire, enthusiastic crowds shared the pleasure of the competition with the emperor or his representatives who sponsored the race. Although most people would never see their ruler, he was in their prayers and their public spaces every day.

THE AGENTS OF CONTROL

The emperor stood at the heart of the imperial system devised by Augustus. The imperial center also included two very important agents of control: the Roman Senate and the army.

To maintain the illusion that he had saved rather than destroyed the Republic, Augustus took pains to show respect for the Senate. He allowed its members to compete among themselves for promotion and honor in his service. Augustus emphasized integrity in the service of the state and sent able senators to govern provinces, thereby reducing corruption. He also gave the Senate legislative powers that had once belonged to the popular assemblies—but he retained the right to veto any legislation for himself. Thus the basic machinery of government inherited from the Republic continued to operate—but in conformity with the emperor's wishes.

Deprived of its autonomy, the Senate became an administrative arm of imperial rule. Senators served as provincial governors, army commanders, judges, and financial officers. They managed the water and grain supplies of the city of Rome, and some of them served on the emperor's advisory council. Aristocratic senators learned to serve the empire faithfully even if they disliked the emperor. Emperors

often brought new men into the Senate from the provinces as a reward for their support, with the belief that Rome grew strong through admitting the best of its provincials to the highest levels of government. Broadening Senate membership in this way enabled more and more of the romanized elites of the empire to feel they had a stake in the imperial enterprise. By the end of the third century C.E. more than half of Rome's senators came from outside of Italy.

While the emperor's relationship with the Senate was of primary importance, other social ranks also played crucial roles in imperial administration. Many members of the equestrian class served in government positions. In addition, many emperors employed freedmen (former slaves) on their administrative staffs and benefited from their loyalty and competence.

Like the Senate, the Roman army was a crucial component of the imperial center. Soldiers enforced peace in the provinces, defended the borders, and conquered new lands to win glory for the emperor. The emperor, in turn, relied on the army's support to remain in power. The army could make or break an emperor—something that every ruler understood. Augustus created a highly efficient professional army that would be the bulwark of the empire for nearly two and a half centuries. The strength of the army was augmented by subject peoples who had not been granted citizenship, the prerequisite for service in the legions. These subjects served as auxiliary troops. The combined legions and auxiliaries brought the military strength of the Roman army to 300,000 men.

THE CITY OF ROME

At the center of the imperial system stood the city of Rome. As Rome grew, it became the model for cities throughout the empire. Its public spaces and buildings provided a stage for the acting out of basic principles of imperial rule.

The center of political and public life in the city of Rome was the Forum, an area filled with many imposing buildings—administrative headquarters, law courts, and the Senate House. Roman laws were inscribed on gleaming

■ **Arch of Titus**

A triumphal arch built at the end of the first century c.e. honors the recently deceased Titus for crushing the Jewish revolt of 66–70 c.e. Marble reliefs inside the arch represent the loot from the Temple of Jerusalem in the triumphal parade.

bronze tablets and placed on the outer walls of these buildings, testimony to the principles of order that formed the framework of the Roman state. Basilicas, a kind of colonnaded hall in which Romans conducted public business ranging from finance to law courts, crowded against the sides of the Forum. Because public and religious life intertwined, the Forum also contained many grand temples of the gods who controlled Rome's destiny. Just as the Forum lay at the physical center of Rome, so the political and religious power it represented lay at the center of the imperial system.

The Forum particularly highlighted the emperor's power. Emperors built arches in the Roman Forum to celebrate their triumphs. After a victorious military campaign, emperors would parade through the Forum on the Sacred Way, pass under the arches, and finish at the temple of Jupiter. Delighted crowds would see defeated kings pass by in chains and marvel at huge floats piled high with loot.

The might of the emperor was on display throughout the city of Rome. Emperors spent gigantic sums on public waterworks and entertainment. They built colossal bathhouses and aqueducts that carried water into Rome from outlying hills. The Colosseum, built by Vespasian and Titus, replaced Nero's private pleasure pond and provided a spot in the very heart of the city where as many as 50,000 happy spectators could watch the slaughter of men and animals at the emperor's expense. Emperors built and maintained theaters, libraries, parks, and markets for the public's enjoyment. The camp of the Praetorian Guard lay at a discreet distance from the Forum, a reminder that the emperor could summon crippling force to suppress dissent.

In stark contrast to the gleaming homes and public buildings were the filthy slums of the poor. The impoverished majority of Rome's inhabitants lived in apartment buildings up to six stories high. Lacking proper foundations, these buildings often collapsed and could easily become firetraps. Unlike the Forum, then, these slums reveal the poverty rather than the splendor of Rome.

Life in the Roman Provinces: Assimilation and Resistance

Beyond the city of Rome and the imperial center lay the second concentric circle of power, the Roman provinces. In these diverse regions some people assimilated readily to Roman ways; others fiercely resisted.

Anyone could adopt the practices of Roman daily life, while formal grants of Roman citizenship gave many people the legal rights and privileges that Roman citizens enjoyed.

Social unrest always boiled beneath the surface of the Roman peace. Yet of the many revolts against Roman authority, only one ever succeeded. Roman military efficiency kept most subject peoples in check, but so, too, did the more positive aspects of Roman rule. Many provincial people came to think of themselves as Roman, with both the Roman army and the Roman law serving as significant unifying forces.

During the reign of Augustus large portions of present-day Germany and the Danube River basin came under Roman rule. His successors continued to add new lands to the empire. Claudius conquered Britain in 43 C.E., and by 117 C.E. Trajan had conquered Dacia (modern Romania), Mesopotamia, and parts of Arabia bordering the Red Sea. At this point the empire reached its greatest territorial extent. Trajan's successor, Hadrian, abandoned Mesopotamia because it was too expensive to control. Instead of conquest, Hadrian focused on consolidation. He organized Rome's frontier with a series of carefully planned fortifications, including the renowned wall that still crosses the north of Britain and bears his name.

THE CITIES AND THE COUNTRYSIDE

The Roman term *civitas*° denoted a city with its surrounding lands and villages. More than a thousand cities dotted the imperial map, connected by more than 40,000 miles of roads. Some urban hubs, such as Carthage and Alexandria, teemed with several hundred thousand people. In these immense provincial cities, governors and their staffs represented the Roman order in grand fashion. All cities had gladiator arenas; bathhouses; a forum; a council house; and temples to its gods, to Rome, and to the emperor.

A city council modeled on the Roman Senate presided over each city's affairs. City councilors had many responsibilities, which they viewed as great honors. City councils managed the grain supply, arranged for army recruitment, supervised the marketplaces, administered justice in local law courts, and most important of all, collected taxes for the central government. Councilors paid out of their own pockets for the upkeep of public works, aqueducts, and baths. They funded religious festivals and celebrations of the imperial cult. In addition, they sponsored gladiatorial games, wild-beast slaughters, chariot races, and other forms of public amusement. As provincial officials performed their public responsibilities on behalf of their hometowns, they imitated the efforts of that greatest patron of all, the emperor himself.

Control of the countryside was the key to the prosperity of the imperial system. Landholdings varied greatly in size and distribution. Augustus, for example, personally owned the entire province of Egypt. Like Augustus, wealthy Roman investors owned properties in many different areas, some bridging entire continents.

Peasants performed the agricultural labor that made the landowners rich. The circumstances of peasant life varied greatly throughout the empire. Some peasants owned small farms sufficient to maintain their families, perhaps with the assistance of seasonal wage laborers or a few slaves. Others rented their lands from landlords to whom they owed payment in the form of produce, coin, or labor. Extremely fierce penalties for inability to pay rents ranged from enslavement to other forms of bondage. All landowning peasants faced one constant threat—the possibility that a more powerful landowner might seize their fields by force. In addition to this relentless exploitation, the specters of famine, natural disasters, and debt constantly threatened the peasants' very survival.

AGRICOLA THE GENERAL

The historian Tacitus wrote a biography of his father-in-law, the general and administrator Gnaeus Julius Agricola (49–93 C.E.). Agricola had a glittering military career under the Flavian emperors. As commander in chief of Roman forces in Britain from 78 to 83 C.E., he subdued most of the island and advanced deep into Scotland. Agricola encouraged urbanization and Mediterranean customs such as public bathing and chariot racing. In the following selection, Tacitus considers the implications of deliberate "romanization."

The following winter passed without disturbance, and was employed in salutary measures. For, to accustom to rest and repose through the charms of luxury a population scattered and barbarous and therefore inclined to war, Agricola gave private encouragement and public aid to the building of temples, courts of justice and dwelling houses, praising the energetic and reproving the indolent. Thus an honourable rivalry took the place of compulsion. He likewise provided a liberal education for the sons of the chiefs, and showed such a preference for the natural powers of the Britons over the industry of the Gauls that they who lately disdained the tongue of Rome now coveted its eloquence. Hence, too, a liking sprang up for our style of dress and the toga became fashionable. Step by step they were led to things which dispose to vice, the lounge, the bath, the elegant banquet. All this in their ignorance they called civilization, when it was but a part of their servitude.

Source: From Tacitus, "Agricola 21" in *Complete Works of Tacitus*, edited by Moses Hadas, translated by Alfred John Church and William Jackson Brodribb, (New York: The Modern Library, 1942).

Despite these hardships, the peasantry during the empire's first three centuries managed to produce enough surplus crops to maintain the imperial system. Indeed, agricultural productivity during this era was remarkable, considering the low crop yields, the difficulty and expense of transportation, and the rudimentary farming technology of the time. Some historians estimate that Europe did not see a comparable level of agricultural productivity again until the seventeenth century.

REVOLTS AGAINST ROME

Conquest by Roman armies could be a long and brutal ordeal. After the shock of military defeat and surrender to Roman generals came the imposition of the administrative structures of Roman rule and the mechanisms of economic exploitation. Conquered lands were quickly organized into provinces. A governor ruled over each province and orchestrated the flow of slaves, timber, metals, horses, spices, and other treasures back to Rome. Not surprisingly, resentment simmered among conquered peoples. Revolts against Roman authority often followed soon after a subject people's initial defeat, while freedom was still a living memory. A brief look at some of the major rebellions reveals that tribal elites required more than one generation after conquest to embrace the imperial system and become fully integrated into the Roman world.

Arminius and the Revolt in Germany

In 9 C.E. Arminius, chieftain of a Germanic tribe called the Cherusci, led the only successful revolt against Roman rule. As a young man serving in an auxiliary regiment in the Roman army, Arminius earned Roman citizenship, learned to speak Latin, and gained the rank of equestrian. Arminius seemed to be a real friend of Rome, but his tribal ties proved stronger than his Roman loyalties when Lucius Varus, the newly appointed governor, imposed economic exploitation and taxation upon the Cherusci too quickly. Arminius and his followers lured the unsuspecting Varus into a trap in the Teutoburg Forest and slaughtered three entire Roman legions. A relief army under the command of the future emperor Tiberius contained the disaster, but nevertheless, when Augustus died in 14 C.E., all of Rome's legions were on the west side of the Rhine. No emperor ever again attempted to conquer Germany.

One lasting result of Arminius's successful revolt is the linguistic distinction that still cuts across Europe. Whereas French and Italian derive from Latin, German does not because the tribes living between the Rhine and Elbe Rivers managed to throw off the Roman yoke in 9 C.E.

Boudica's Revolt in Britain

Fifty years after Arminius's victory, a major uprising broke out in Britain, led by Boudica, the queen of the Iceni. The revolt had a long, complex history. In the decades following the initial conquest of the island by the emperor Claudius in 43 C.E., the Romans consolidated their power by encouraging those tribes not under Roman control to ally themselves with Rome as client states. Under King Prasutagus, the Iceni became Roman clients. Before King Prasutagus died in 60 C.E., he named the Roman emperor his co-heir with his wife, Boudica, and his daughters. The emperor Nero, however, pushed Boudica aside and established direct Roman rule. Emboldened by their new power, the agents of the tyrannical Roman governor abused Boudica and raped her daughters.

The queen led her forces into open rebellion. Boudica destroyed a legion and leveled several cities, but resistance ended quickly after Roman forces routed the Iceni and the queen took her own life. The peoples of Britain learned that resistance to Rome was futile. The Romans learned a lesson as well: Subject peoples should be treated more justly. The next Roman governor of Britain adopted more lenient administrative policies.

Jewish Revolts

Augustus had created the province of Judaea and annexed it to the Empire in 6 C.E. With Roman rule came heavy taxation that caused Judaea's economy to decline. Sixty years of Roman mismanagement combined with a desire for independence sparked a massive revolt in Judaea in 66 C.E. Jews formed their own government, appointed regional military commanders, abolished debt, and issued their own coinage imprinted with messages of freedom. In 70 C.E. Roman imperial forces captured Jerusalem, destroyed the Temple, and enslaved an estimated two million people.

Despite their overwhelming defeat, Jewish communities continued to resist Rome. During Trajan's reign, minor revolts broke out in the eastern Mediterranean (115–118 C.E.). Revolt erupted again in 132–135 C.E.. The last major Jewish uprising occurred in Palestine in the fourth century C.E. All were suppressed. The continuation of Jewish opposition to Roman rule, however, demonstrates that a population with a strong sense of religious identity rooted in a set of sacred texts could resist—and survive—the overwhelming power of Rome. Within a few generations most conquered peoples assimilated fully into Roman society. The Jews never did so.

FORCES OF ROMANIZATION

How did conquered peoples absorb Roman cultural and social values? As we saw earlier, the city served as a crucial force of romanization° in the provinces of the empire. Urban centers served as models of civic life, and through both their architecture and their ceremonies tied provincial peoples more tightly to Rome.

The army constituted a second important romanizing force. During the Republic, soldiers tended to be drawn from the city of Rome and surrounding regions. In the course of the first two and a half centuries of imperial rule, however, the number of troops from Italy steadily diminished as territories under Roman rule increased. Auxiliary troops regularly received Roman citizenship at the end of their service—a significant draw for provincials of all social ranks.

The army introduced provincial recruits to Roman religion and social organization. At the same time, army bases in far-flung regions provided the first taste of Roman culture and language to provincial peoples. The architecture of army camps and fortification, as well as weapons, armor, and tactics, followed the same conventions across the empire. Moreover, most soldiers retired near the bases in which they had been stationed. Towns full of former military personnel helped transmit Roman culture and values to provincial peoples. Latin, the language of command and army administration, provided another common bond. Inscriptions on soldiers' tombstones reveal that a simplified version of Latin developed in the army; this Latin dialect became the ancestor of French, Spanish, and other Romance languages.

Like the Roman army, Roman law constituted a third strong force for romanization. As the Roman Empire expanded during the first and second centuries C.E., conditions of peace and prosperity encouraged the spread of both Roman-style cities and Roman citizenship and thus the dominance of Roman law. Then, in 212 C.E., Emperor Aurelius Antoninus (r. 211–217 C.E.), nicknamed Caracalla, issued what became known as the *Antonine Decree°*. This ruling granted citizenship to all free men and women within the empire, presumably to increase the tax base. By formally eliminating the distinction between Roman conquerors and subject peoples, the Antonine Decree enabled Roman law to embrace the entire population. This legal uniformity further strengthened provincial loyalty to Rome. Provincial allegiances to their own traditions and laws that had coexisted with Roman imperial law for centuries began to diminish.

Not all citizens, however, were equal under the law. In the first century C.E. the wealthy upper class, generally called *honestiores,* and the poor, called *humiliores,* acquired different legal rights. For example, *honestiores* convicted of crimes were spared the most gruesome punishments, such as being crucified or being thrown to wild animals in the arena.

Roman law served to enhance the emperor's authority. During the Republic, magistrates or citizen assemblies had official authority to issue laws. In the imperial era, the control of law shifted into the emperor's hands. Whether the emperor was issuing a decree on his own initiative or making a general policy in response to an inquiry from a provincial administrator, his decisions had the same status as any law issued by a citizen assembly during the Republic.

As in the Republic, however, legal experts, or jurists, continued to help shape the law. Combining legal scholarship, teaching, and administrative careers, these legal experts advised the emperor, and collected and analyzed earlier laws and legal opinions. Papinian, Paul, and Ulpian, who lived in the early third century C.E., were the greatest of these specialists. They wrote hundreds of books of commentary that shaped the interpretation of Roman law for centuries. Collected and organized during the reign of Justinian in the sixth century C.E., their opinions were passed on to the jurists of medieval and Renaissance Europe. Roman law remains the foundation of Italian, French, and Spanish legal traditions today.

The Frontier and Beyond

.... ▬ ....

The third concentric circle of the Roman world consisted of the frontier—the outermost regions of the empire and beyond. Boundaries and border zones took shape on the edges of the empire as cultural distinctions emerged between "civilized" Romans and "barbarians" living across the borders.

FRONTIER ZONES: CIVILIZATION AND BARBARISM

In Virgil's *Aeneid* (ca. 26–19 B.C.E.), the god Jupiter promised that Romans would have empire without limits. By the early second century C.E., however, the empire's edges were clearly demarcated. Regularly spaced military bases and fortresses marked the northern border. Armed naval forces patrolled the Rhine and Danube, and the great wall of Hadrian stretched across the north of Britain. In the East, another line of military defenses extended from the Black Sea to the Nile. In North Africa, a perimeter of fortifications marked the limits of cultivable land along the empire's southernmost edge. For the Romans, these boundaries symbolized a cultural division between civilization and barbarism. In the Romans' view, all peoples who did not live under Roman rule were barbarians and therefore hostile. Romans used this distinction to help define their place in the world and to justify their conquest and absorption of other peoples.

ROMAN ENCOUNTERS WITH GERMANIC PEOPLES

The Rhine and Danube Rivers became the symbolic boundary between the Romans and their northern enemies. Most of Rome's legions were stationed along this boundary. The peoples living north of these two rivers posed the greatest threat to Rome during the first two and a half centuries C.E. of the empire. Called "Germans" by the Romans, these peoples spoke different dialects and lacked political unity. Led by aristocratic warriors, they often fought bitterly among themselves. Some tribes fragmented into pro- and anti-Roman factions. Occasionally tribes formed loose confederations under the leadership of charismatic warlords in order to defend themselves from Roman aggression or to invade the empire themselves.

During long periods of peace, however, the people on either side of the border had the opportunity to interact with one another through trade and military service. Because of their extensive trade with Roman merchants, many Germanic aristocrats developed a taste for Mediterranean luxuries, including wine and jewelry. By the second century C.E. some chose to live in Roman-style villas in imitation of Roman aristocrats. Many Germanic men also gained exposure to Roman civilization when they served in the Roman army as auxiliary troops. As members of the Roman army, they fought wherever they were sent in the empire, even if that meant warfare with other Germanic tribes to the north. Discharged after the standard twenty-five years of service, many of these men returned to their homes with Roman coin in their purses, a smattering of Latin, and knowledge of the riches and power of the Roman Empire.

By the end of the second century C.E. the weight of different peoples pressing on Rome's northern borders began to crack the imperial defenses. With the end of the Severan dynasty in 235 C.E., the empire entered a period of unrelieved disasters that lasted nearly fifty years. Invading groups from north of the Rhine and Danube Rivers pushed into the empire as far south as central Italy in search of plunder and land on which to settle. The Romans ultimately marshaled the military resources to repel the invaders and restore the empire's security late in the third century C.E. As we will see in the next chapter, however, the restored Roman Empire differed radically from the system Augustus inaugurated.

ROMAN ENCOUNTERS WITH ASIANS AND AFRICANS

Trade and diplomacy, rather than war, structured much of Rome's encounters with the peoples in Asia and Africa. Merchants risked great dangers to bring silk and other luxury goods westward from China in their caravans. Trade between India and Rome was also brisk and highly profitable in the first several centuries C.E. Archaeologists have discovered thousands of Roman coins in India and even in Thailand, evidence of commerce's far-flung reach.

Far more important were Rome's relations with its

most formidable rival, the mighty Parthian Empire. Parthia's realm encompassed the ancient Persian Empire, stretching from the Euphrates River to the Indus River (covering modern Iraq, Iran, and Pakistan). Unlike the poorly organized and politically unstable Germanic tribes the Romans confronted in western Europe, Parthia was highly structured and enormously powerful.

Augustus inaugurated a new Roman policy toward Parthia, just as he initiated changes in so many other aspects of Roman rule. Glory-seeking Roman generals of the late Republic had found Parthia an attractive but dangerous target. Augustus, however, used diplomatic rather than military means to deal with the Parthians. After Augustus, most Roman emperors opted for diplomacy over open conflict with Parthia because they knew they could not conquer and assimilate such a vast territory. Trajan, however, proved an exception. He conquered the Parthian provinces of Armenia and Mesopotamia in ambitious campaigns in 115–116 C.E., when Parthia was weakened by civil war. Trajan's triumph proved short-lived. His successor, Hadrian, abandoned these conquests because he knew that they overextended Rome's resources.

The most important result of the rivalry between Parthia and Rome was the exchange of products, ideas, and technology between their peoples. Romans highly prized Parthian steel and leather. The Romans also adopted some military technology and tactics from Parthia, particularly the use of heavily armed cavalry. By the fourth century C.E. these units constituted the core of Roman military might. Religious ideas also flowed between Rome and Parthia. Jewish scholars in the Roman Empire maintained close ties with the Jewish academies in the Parthian province of

■ **Wineship**

Wine merchants hurry their cargo to thirsty customers somewhere on the Rhine River. Because grapes could not be cultivated in this northern region, wine was a luxury there. Common people drank beer. This energetic but unsophisticated sculpture of the second century C.E. was found in Germany.

Babylonia. It was Christianity, however, that was most directly influenced by the Parthian-Roman religious interchange. Mani (216–276 C.E.), a Persian religious leader and founder of a religion called Manichaeism, preached that an eternal conflict between forces of light and darkness caused good and evil to intermingle. God's soul had become trapped in matter, and Jesus, the son of God, had come to Earth to retrieve God's soul. Mani taught that all those who followed Jesus and turned their back on earthly possessions would be redeemed. These ideas, particularly the association of the material world with evil, deeply influenced Christianity as it developed in the Roman Empire.

Rome's many encounters with Parthia helped shape its diplomacy, its commerce, and aspects of its religious life. In contrast, Rome had few interactions with the peoples of sub-Saharan Africa. Roman coins found deep in the interior of Africa suggest that the Romans may have traded with the peoples there. To the Romans, however, "Africa" was one of their provinces bordering the Mediterranean Sea—the region we know as North Africa today—not the vast continent that lay to the south. Only in the European Middle Ages would the name Africa come to stand for the entire land mass of the continent. The Romans used the word *Aethiopians* ("the People with Burned Faces") to refer to the peoples who lived south of the Sahara desert. From the Egyptians they learned of a place of fabulous wealth and exotic creatures. It would take many centuries, however, before European peoples viewed Africa as anything other than a fantasyland.

Society and Culture in the Imperial Age

The same central theme that characterized Roman politics after Augustus also characterized Roman society in the imperial age—the illusion of continuity with the Republic, masking fundamental change. The social pyramid described in Chapter 4 remained intact—aristocrats at the top, followed by plebeians and peasants, freedmen, and slaves. Important changes, however, occurred within the pyramid as imperial rule altered social and economic relationships. The shift from republic to empire had a profound influence on Roman culture and religious belief as well.

THE UPPER AND LOWER CLASSES

Roman emperors recognized three social groups, or orders, as having aristocratic status. The first order, the senators of Rome, occupied a place of honor at the very top of the social pyramid. Below the senators stood the equestrians. The equestrian order flourished in the imperial age. Many equestrians continued to follow business careers as they had during the Republic, but the expansion of the empire provided them with new opportunities in the diplomatic, fiscal, and military services. The third aristocratic order consisted of the city councilors. Like senators and equestrians, they were expected to be wealthy, of respectable birth, and of good moral character. In many cities, the sons of freedmen (men who had once been slaves) were permitted to be city councilors.

Women in the senatorial and equestrian ranks possessed far more freedom than was usual in the ancient world. By 250 C.E., the form of marriage by which a woman passed from the control of her father to that of her husband had almost entirely died out. Women now tended to remain, at least theoretically, under the control of their father or legal guardian. This practice gave a married woman more freedom, in large part because her husband no longer controlled her dowry. Some women used this freedom to move more into the public view, taking part in banquets, attending the gladiatorial battles at the Colosseum, and presiding over literary salons. At the highest level of society some women possessed real political power, though expressed behind the scenes. For example, Livia, married to Augustus for fifty-two years, possessed a great deal of influence during his reign.

The three aristocratic orders represented only a tiny fraction of the empire's population. Below them came the plebeians—Rome's poor but free underclass of citizens. Disease kept the plebeian birth rate and life expectancy very low. Probably more than a quarter of all infants died within their first five years, and a third of those who survived were dead by age 10. The average Roman man died at age 45, and the average woman at age 34. Yet plebeians benefited in some ways from imperial rule. In the city of Rome, for example, they received a daily allotment of free grain. (Approximately half of Rome's population of one million depended on the daily gifts of grain.) With little incentive to work and deprived of the rights and responsibilities of political participation, the plebeians enjoyed much leisure time. By the first century C.E., Romans had approximately 100 days designated as holidays. The plebeians demanded a steady diet of bloody entertainment, such as the gladiatorial combats in the Colosseum and the chariot races in the Circus Maximus. Thus plebeian life in the city of Rome was degraded into "bread and circuses": free grain and free entertainment.

SLAVES AND FREEDMEN

Slaves made up a huge percentage of Roman society, at the very bottom of the social order. Of Rome's approximately one million inhabitants, an estimated 400,000 were slaves during the early empire. When Augustus took control of Rome, slaves constituted 35 to 40 percent of the total population of Italy. Everyone accepted that humans could be reduced to property. As far as we know, no Roman citizen ever objected to slavery as an institution.

The victims of a brisk international trade in humans, most slaves entered the empire through conquest. Others were enslaved from birth, having been born of a slave mother. There was never a shortage of slaves, and sometimes after a successful military campaign, such as Trajan's defeat of the Dacians in 106 C.E., the market was glutted.

Ownership of slaves reflected a person's status. The emperor himself owned tens of thousands of slaves who labored on his estates throughout the empire. Rich men, too, possessed them in huge numbers. Even poor artisans and teachers might hold one or two. Former slaves who had gained their freedom (freedmen) also owned slaves. Slaves were permitted to earn money, with the result that even some slaves owned slaves.

Slaves used for domestic service or in commerce and crafts were the most fortunate. Many slaves worked on the great plantations, or latifundia°, as part of large slave gangs. The absentee owners cared little for the welfare of these slaves. Latifundia slaves often labored in chains and slept in underground prisons. The slaves sent to work in the mines experienced even worse conditions. For them, only a wretched death lay ahead. Female slaves were spared the horrors of working in the fields and mines, but they were valued far less than were male slaves. Dehumanized by their enslavement and stripped of their identity when taken from family and home, slaves lived in fear of their masters, who could abuse them physically or sexually with impunity. Violence lay at the heart of this institution, for ultimate control of slaves rested on force. In the face of such brutality, slaves had few options. They could try to escape, but if caught were branded on the forehead. Slave revolts never succeeded.

Despite their utter lack of freedom, many slaves formed emotional and sexual relationships with one another. Epitaphs on graves demonstrate that they used conventional terms of affection and marriage bonds such as husband and wife, although Roman law did not recognize these informal slave marriages. Some slave owners permitted slave marriages because they understood that slaves with families would be less likely to rebel. Complete submissiveness and the goodwill of their masters were necessary to hold a slave family together.

Slavery was not, however, necessarily a permanent condition. Slaves might obtain their freedom through manumission. Through this carefully regulated legal procedure, a master granted freedom to a slave as a reward for faithful service or docile behavior, or even out of genuine affection. The freedmen constituted an important class in Roman society. Freedmen made up only about 5 percent of Rome's population, but their enterprise and ambition marked them as some of the more successful members of Roman society.

Many former slaves worked in commerce or as skilled laborers, teachers, and doctors. A freed slave had only partial citizen rights, but his or her children became full Roman citizens who could freely marry other citizens.

Slavery remained a part of Mediterranean economic and social life until the early Middle Ages, but in the second century C.E. the role of slaves in the economy began to diminish. As Roman emperors concentrated on consolidating rather than expanding the borders of the empire, the supply of slaves dwindled, and the cost of slaves rose. Thus, slave owning may have become less economically viable.

LITERATURE AND EMPIRE

As in the Republic, in the empire Roman writers looked to Greek Hellenistic culture for their models. The fact of empire, however, was inescapable. No author could avoid the political facts of life, whether he cynically ignored them, enthusiastically embraced them, or cautiously probed their limits.

Writers during the reign of Augustus embodied the tensions and uncertainties of living in a society that had exchanged freedom for stability. Livy (59 B.C.E.–12 C.E.) wrote a massive history of Rome, called *From the Foundation of the City,* that traced Rome from its origins until his own time. Though less than a fifth of this work survives, we see that Livy presented Rome's rise to world mastery as a series of instructive moral and patriotic lessons. He showed how Rome grew to world power through vanquishing many enemies. Although proud of Rome's greatness, Livy also believed that with power came decadence. He expressed the hope that Augustus would restore Rome's glory and put an end to what he perceived as its moral and political decline.

The tragic career of Ovid (43 B.C.E.–17 C.E.) demonstrates the risks of offending an emperor. Ovid's brilliant love elegies had made him the darling of Rome. Then in 8 C.E., his erotic poem "The Art of Love," along with an obscure scandal involving Augustus's family, earned him the hostility of the prudish emperor. Augustus exiled Ovid to a squalid village on the Black Sea, where he died in sorrow.

The poet Horace (65–8 B.C.E.), son of a wealthy freedman, walked a more careful path. He avoided political entanglements and maintained close ties to Augustus. His poetry on public themes praised Augustus for bringing peace and the hope of a moral life to the world. Throughout his work, Horace urged serene appreciation of life's transient joys. In his most famous verse (*Odes* I.11.6ff) he sings, "Be wise, taste the wine, and since our time is brief, be moderate in your aspirations. Even as we speak, greedy life slips away from us. Grasp each day (*carpe diem*) and do not pin your hopes on tomorrow."

Virgil stands as the greatest of the Roman poets. Drawing on Hellenistic poetic forms, Virgil first wrote of the wisdom, safety, and serenity found in an idealized country life—with the terrible uncertainties of civil war providing a silent backdrop. Later, at Augustus's request Virgil composed the *Aeneid°*, an epic poem that legitimized and celebrated the emperor's reign. Ostensibly the poem was about the mythic foundation of the Roman state by the hero Aeneas, a Trojan prince fleeing the destruction of his native city by the Greeks. Through a series of cinematic "flash-forwards," Virgil presented the entire history of the Roman people as culminating in the reign of Augustus. In the *Aeneid,* the emperor brings to completion the nearly unendurable efforts of his Trojan ancestor. Yet Virgil was not just a propagandist for the imperial regime. Virgil praised those aspects of peace and fulfillment of duty that he genuinely valued, but questioned the costs of warfare and the demands of empire on human beings.

Seneca (ca. 4 B.C.E.–41 C.E.), who combined philosophical interests with literary skill, accepted the imperial system, but he acknowledged how hard it was to control one's human weaknesses and live a truly moral life. His integrity and rhetorical brilliance earned him the unenviable task of being Nero's tutor when the emperor was still an impressionable 12-year-old boy. For eight years Seneca guided Nero, and the empire enjoyed good government. As Nero matured, however, he found other, less decent advisers. Appalled by his student's descent into corruption, Seneca plotted to kill Nero. When he was caught, he killed himself instead.

Tacitus (ca. 56–ca. 118 C.E.) wrote about the first century of the Augustan age. Sardonic and terse, his historical accounts displayed a deep understanding of human psychological reaction to the harsh political realities of early imperial tyranny. Although Tacitus's career flourished under the tyrannical Domitian, he hated political oppression and he never abandoned his love for the best of Roman ideals. In the *Agricola,* his biography of his father-in-law, a general instrumental in the conquest of Britain, Tacitus affirmed that good men could serve their country honorably, even under bad rulers.

Scientific writing made great strides in the early centuries of the Roman Empire. Claudius Ptolemy of Alexandria maintained the high standards of the Hellenistic science tradition. Writing in the second half of the second century C.E., Ptolemy composed definitive works in many fields. Using the division of spheres into units of 60 first developed by the Sumerians and perfected by the Babylonians, Ptolemy's *Almagest* proved the theories and tables necessary to compute the positions of the sun, the moon, and five known planets. He accepted the Greek theory that the sun revolves around the Earth. Western astronomers used his maps of the heavens for nearly 1,500 years. His *Geography* gave readings in longitude and latitude and provided information for drawing a world map, which remained the basis of cartography until the sixteenth century. Translated from Greek into Arabic, Ptolemy's books became standard in the medieval Islamic world. Eventually they were translated into Latin and so passed back into use in western Europe during the Middle Ages.

RELIGIOUS LIFE

Religious expression in the Roman Empire took many forms. The imperial government made no effort to impose uniform belief, so subject peoples freely worshiped many gods and maintained their traditional religious rituals. Within many religious cultures, trends that first appeared in the Hellenistic Age continued, but important new developments also occurred, including the transformation of Judaism after the destruction of Jerusalem and the rise of Christianity.

Polytheism in the Empire

Syncretism°, the practice of equating two gods and fusing their cults, was a common feature of imperial religious life. Like many other Mediterranean peoples, the Romans often identified a foreign god with one of their own deities. For example, Julius Caesar described the Gallic god of commerce as Mercury, because Mercury served the same function in Roman religion. Romans did not care that other people throughout the empire might worship Jupiter or Juno or any other Roman god in different ways. Syncretism, then, helped unify the diverse peoples and regions under Roman rule. Through syncretism, shared religious experiences spread across the empire.

The anonymity of life in big cities contributed to the spread of religions that offered a measure of identity and community and a kind of salvation as well. Religions that promised victory over death or liberation from the abuses and pain of daily existence possessed a wide appeal. The goddess Isis, for example, who originated in Egypt, offered freedom from the arbitrary abuses of fate and life after death to her many followers throughout the empire. Her cult particularly attracted women. Because she was often depicted holding her baby son Horus, she represented the universal mother. Another popular religion that promised salvation to its initiates was that of Mithras, a sun god. Limited to men, worship of Mithras took place in underground chambers in which small groups held banquets, recited sacred lessons about the celestial journey of the soul after death, and made sacrifices to the god. Because this religion stressed both physical courage and performance of duty, it appealed especially to soldiers and administrators.

The most important religion of an eastern god whose worship spread throughout the Roman Empire was that of the Unconquered Sun. Originating in Syria, this deity came to be associated with Apollo and Helios, two Greco-Roman sun gods. When Elagabalus, the high priest of the Syrian sun god, became Roman emperor (r. 218–222 C.E.), he built a

■ **Mummy Wrapping from Egypt**

This painted linen cloth wrapped an Egyptian mummy buried during the second century C.E. It shows the Egyptian god Osiris (on the left) and the jackal-headed god Anubis (on the right). Between them is the deceased man, dressed in Roman clothing. His portrait has been carefully painted and added separately. The wrapping and portrait demonstrate the continuity of ancient Egyptian religion during Roman imperial rule.

huge temple dedicated to his god in Rome, and designated December 25 as a special day of worship to the deity. Within fifty years, the Unconquered Sun became the chief god of imperial and official worship. Only the rise of Christianity would displace the worship of the Unconquered Sun.

Gnosticism, which originated in the Hellenistic Age, continued its influence in the Roman Empire, affecting Judaism, Christianity, and many polytheistic religions. Gnostics believed that the material world of daily life is incompatible with the supreme god. They thought that sparks of divinity (sometimes considered the human soul) were imprisoned within the body. Only a redeemer sent from the supreme god could release these divine sparks.

The Origins of Rabbinic Judaism

Following the Roman devastation of Judaea and the destruction of the Temple in Jerusalem in 70 C.E., a new kind of community-based religious life began to develop among Jews in Judaea and other lands. Since the sixth century B.C.E., communities of Jews had lived outside Palestine, but after the Romans ransacked Judaea, the Diaspora° ("dispersion of population") came to characterize Jewish life. Jerusalem could not longer serve as Judaism's religious focus, and the entire religious practice of ritual animal sacrifice centered on the Temple disappeared. So, too, did the priesthood. The rabbi ("my master" in Hebrew) replaced the priest in the role of religious instructor and community guide. Scholars trained in the Jewish law, rabbis interpreted and taught the Torah, the first five books of the Hebrew Bible. By 200 C.E., synagogues emerged as communal centers in which rabbis studied Jewish law and passed judgment on disputes. Gradually synagogues developed into centers where the Jewish community would celebrate the Sabbath and pray together.

The greatest product of the rabbinic tradition was the Mishnah, a collection of legal opinions, legal decisions, and homilies to explain the law to unlearned people. Jewish teachers had begun accumulating this material in Hellenistic times, but it was completed around 220 C.E. The Mishnah consists of sixty-three books, each dealing with a particular aspect of law, ranging from matters of ritual purity to calendrical issues to civil and criminal law. Among the many moral principles stressed by the Mishnah, saving life was paramount. According to the Mishnah, no person could save his or her own life by causing another's death, and no person could be sacrificed for the welfare of the community. Moreover, to save a life, any person could break any Jewish religious law, except those forbidding idolatry, adultery, incest, or murder. In Jewish thought, saving one life symbolized saving humanity. A radical idea slowly emerged from this principle: Since all humans are made in God's image, they should all have equal rights. This idea contributed to the gradual decline of slave holding among Jews.

In addition to the rabbis who led individual Jewish communities, an official called the Patriarch represented the Jews as a whole to the emperor. The Romans appointed the Patriarch and gave him the highest political authority in Jewish affairs in the empire. The Patriarch's responsibilities included collecting taxes for Rome and choosing judges for Jewish courts. The Romans gave the Patriarch the rank of senator, as the representative of all the Jews in the empire. This arrangement, a clear example of how Roman authorities let local populations manage their own laws, continued until Christianity became the official religion of the empire in the fifth century C.E. Christian emperors then began persecuting Jews and limiting their participation in public life.

The Emergence of Christianity

The emergence of Christianity forced the Romans to deal with an entirely new community within the empire. Christianity was more than a new set of religious beliefs; Christians had a new sense of shared identity, a new sense of history, and a new perception of the Roman system. The number of Christians gradually grew until they came to dominate the religious life of the empire. Within 400 years of the death of its founder, Christianity became the official imperial religion.

The founder of Christianity was a Jew named Yeshua ben Yosef, known today as Jesus of Nazareth (ca. 4 B.C.E.– ca. 30 C.E.). Born in Galilee in northern Palestine during the reign of Augustus, Jesus grew to manhood in the Jewish community. Around age 30 he began to travel through Palestine with a band of followers, urging men and women to repent their sins because God would soon come to rule the Kingdom of Heaven on Earth. Jesus' followers believed him to be the messiah, an important figure in Jewish prophetic writings whose coming would inaugurate a new age of freedom for God's people. Like many other contemporary Jewish teachers, Jesus insisted that having the right intent in carrying out God's law mattered more than outward performance, that men and women should regard themselves and others as God's children, and that they should recognize God as their loving Father.

In 30 C.E. Jesus entered Jerusalem to preach his message. He dared to challenge some of the Jewish elites who controlled the Jewish Temple under Roman supervision, and caused a near-riot. This dangerous act led the Roman authorities to arrest, try, and convict him as a revolutionary. Sentenced to death, Jesus died by crucifixion, the usual form of capital punishment in the Roman Empire for noncitizens.

Jesus' followers, however, insisted that he still lived, that he rose from the dead three days after being executed, and that he appeared to them a number of times in the forty days between his resurrection from the dead and his ascent into heaven. They proclaimed him as not only the Jewish messiah, but as the Son of God who died on the cross as part of the divine plan. In Christian theology, Jesus' brutal death at the hands of the Romans became a loving sacrifice: The sinless Son of God endured the punishment that sinful men and women had earned. Christians, then, regarded Jesus as their savior, as the God whose intervention in human history rescued them from their sins and whose spirit continued to guide them in their earthly lives.

Jesus recorded none of his ideas in writing, but his followers transmitted his teachings orally for several years after his death and then in the 50s and 60s C.E. began to write them down. By about 120 C.E. they had compiled an authoritative body of texts that recorded Jesus' life and words, which Christians call the New Testament. Christians held that Jesus' teachings contained in the New Testament built on the teachings of the Hebrew Bible—the "Old" Testament. Consequently, they tended to interpret the Hebrew Bible in light of Christianity. For example, Christians read the prophetic writings of the Hebrew Bible as predictions of Jesus' birth, death, and resurrection.

For many decades after Jesus' death, his followers still thought of themselves as Jews. The word *Christian* (which comes from the Greek word *Christos,* meaning "the anointed one" or "messiah") was first used in the Syrian city of Antioch in the second half of the first century C.E. Christianity, however, eventually diverged from Judaism. Most scholars agree that the work and teaching of Paul of Tarsus (d. ca. 65 C.E.) played a crucial role in this development. An educated Jew, Paul fiercely opposed the new Christian teachings until he had a vision of Jesus calling him to Christian service. Paul became as ardent in his advocacy of Christianity as he had been in his opposition. The most effective early Christian missionary, he traveled throughout Asia Minor, inaugurating and developing Christian communities. Even more important, Paul wrote letters that circulated among these communities. These letters, written in the 50s C.E., constitute our earliest written Christian documents and articulate key doctrines of the Christian faith—doctrines that helped divide Christianity from Judaism.

In Paul's writings, the Christian view of Jesus' crucifixion as a divine sacrifice to atone for human sin was first fully developed. Paul taught that the only way a man or a woman could join God after death for an eternity of peace and happiness was by belief in Jesus as the Son of God and as the savior of humanity. Paul preached this message to the Jews of the Diaspora and, significantly, to non-Jews. Paul encouraged Christian converts from outside Judaism to abide by certain Jewish laws, but he did not require that they be circumcised, a key Jewish initiation rite, or that they follow Jewish dietary restrictions.

Paul was executed as a troublemaker by the Romans in 65 C.E.; five years later the Roman Army razed the Jewish Temple, destroyed Jerusalem, and devastated Judaea. After the fall of the Temple, Judaism and Christianity took their own distinctive paths. As we have seen, the destruction of the Jerusalem Temple in 70 C.E. forced Jews to abandon religious practice based on ritual sacrifice and to substitute a synagogue-centered faith that emphasized study of the Torah. In contrast, Christian theology centered on sacrifice. Through the ritual or "sacrament" of the Eucharist (Holy Communion), Christians recalled Jesus' sacrifice of himself on the cross.

For all their fundamental differences of belief, Christianity and Judaism shared some characteristics that distinguished them from other religions of antiquity. Both Christianity and Judaism combined a statement of belief with a social ethic. Their ethical systems embodied values that strengthened the religious community. Both, for

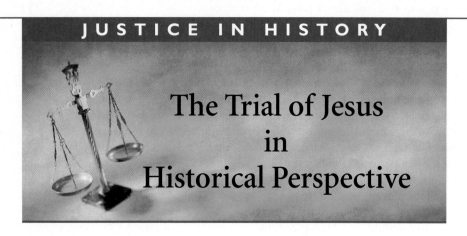

The Trial of Jesus in Historical Perspective

In 30 C.E. Roman authorities in the city of Jerusalem in the Roman province of Judaea tried and executed a Jewish teacher known today as Jesus of Nazareth or Jesus Christ, whose teachings lie at the foundation of Christianity, the faith of hundreds of millions of people in the world today. Although an insignificant event at the time, the trial of Jesus and its interpretation made and continues to make a profound impact on Western civilization.

Information about Jesus' trial comes from the New Testament books of Matthew, Mark, Luke, and John. These narratives, called the Gospels, were written thirty to sixty years after Jesus' death. They relate that during three years of teaching and miraculous healing in the provinces of Galilee and Judaea, Jesus earned the resentment of certain segments of the Jewish religious leadership by disregarding aspects of Jewish religious law. According to the Gospels, when Jesus entered the Temple precinct in Jerusalem, he angered the temple elites by denouncing their hypocrisy and by overturning the tables of money changers. The priests then conspired to kill him. They paid one of Jesus' followers to reveal his whereabouts, arrested him on either the night before or the night of the Passover feast, and tried him immediately before the Sanhedrin, the highest Jewish court, which met that same night in the house of the Jewish high priest. The Sanhedrin found Jesus guilty of the crime of blasphemy for claiming to be the messiah, the Son of God.

Lacking the authority to put Jesus to death, the Jewish leaders brought Jesus before Pontius Pilate, the Roman governor, and demanded that he execute Jesus. Pilate hesitated, but the priests persuaded him by insisting that Jesus threatened the emperor's authority with his claim to be King of the Jews. Pilate's soldiers crucified Jesus, but according to the Gospel accounts, the real blame for Jesus' death lay with the Jews who had demanded his execution. In all four Gospels, Jewish crowds in Jerusalem reject Jesus and cry out, "Crucify him!" to a reluctant Pontius Pilate.

The Gospel accounts of Jesus' arrest, trial, and crucifixion offer some difficulties for historians: Details of these narratives conflict with what scholars understand about the conduct of trials by Jewish authorities and Roman provincial administrators. For example, the evidence that we have indicates that the Sanhedrin did not hold trials at night; it did not meet in the house of the High Priest; and it did not convene on a Jewish feast day or the night before a feast. A far more important difference, however, is that according to Jewish law Jesus would not have blasphemed or committed a crime by claiming to be the messiah. Originating in ceremonies of anointing kings, the word *messiah* had many interpretations in Judaism as a kingly figure of power—but not as a god.

If scholars' understanding of first-century Judaism and Jewish life is correct, and Jesus had not committed a crime under Jewish law by claiming to be the messiah, what then was his offense? Why did some members of the priestly elite oppose him? The Gospels point to the probable answer: These documents highlight the importance of Jesus' confrontation with the Jewish elites in the Temple. Jesus had committed a very dangerous act by denouncing the priests in Jerusalem. These men, especially the High Priest himself, owed their positions of power to the Roman overlords

■ **The Scales of Justice**

The goddess Aequitas represented the idea of fairness in Roman justice.

Early Christian Symbols
Early Christian symbols decorate this Roman tombstone. The anchor represents hope, while the fish stand for Jesus. The Greek word for fish, *icthus*, is an anagram of the Greek words for "Jesus Christ Son of God and Savior."

and were responsible for maintaining order. These Jewish elites saw Jesus as an agitator who posed a threat to their authority. Jesus was first brought before the Sanhedrin, the Jewish court permitted by the Romans to deal with affairs within the Jewish community. The Romans had appointed all seventy-one members of the court, including Caiaphas, the high priest who led it. These court members knew that if they could not control Jesus, the Romans would certainly replace them. The Sanhedrin could not punish Jesus under Jewish law, but it could send him before Roman magistrates on a charge that the Romans would not hesitate to prosecute—stirring up rebellion.

Jesus' popularity with the common people and the disturbance in the Temple precinct would have been enough to arouse Roman suspicion. Roman officials usually responded to real or imagined threats to the political order by crucifixion. In the eyes of Pontius Pilate, a cautious magistrate, Jesus constituted a threat to public order, and so deserved execution. He would not have been reluctant to kill him.

Why, then, do the Gospels tend to shift the blame for Jesus' death from Pontius Pilate, who most certainly or-dered Jesus' execution, and place it on the Jewish community? We know that the Gospel narratives began to be written down in an atmosphere of growing hostility and suspicion between Jews and Christians. Moreover, after Roman armies destroyed the Jerusalem Temple in the Jewish rebellion of 66–70 C.E., Christians wanted to disassociate themselves from Jews in Roman eyes, hoping to persuade Roman authorities to think of them not as rebels but rather as followers of a lawful religion. Such concerns may have shaped the Gospel writers' tendencies to emphasize the role of the Jewish leaders in Jesus' death and to deemphasize Pilate's responsibility.

The Gospels also relate that before he died Jesus predicted the destruction of the Jewish Temple in Jerusalem. Many early Christians came to believe that the fall of the Temple and the savage repression of the Jewish rebellion served as divine punishment for the Jews who had caused Jesus' death. These interpretations of Jesus' trial and execution, and of the destruction of the Jewish community in Palestine, helped poison Christian–Jewish relations for two millennia. From the first century C.E. through the twentieth, important segments of the Christian community blamed "the Jews" for Jesus' crucifixion.

Questions of Justice

1. What does the trial of Jesus show about Roman methods of provincial administration—and about the limitations of these methods? Who had power in Judaea?

2. In Christian theology, Jesus died for the sins of the world. In theological terms, then, all sinners—all human beings—bear responsibility for Jesus' death. Why, then, does it matter if the Gospels place the blame for Jesus' crucifixion on the Jewish leaders and crowds?

Taking It Further

Crossan, John Dominic. *Who Killed Jesus: Exposing the Roots of Anti-Semitism in the Gospel Story of the Death of Jesus.* 1997. A highly engaging investigation.

Johnson, Luke Timothy, John Dominic Crossan, and Werner H. Kelber. *The Jesus Controversy.* 1999. Three experts discuss the problems of finding who Jesus "really was."

Sherwin-White, A. N. *Roman Society and Roman Law in the New Testament.* 1963. A leading Roman historian puts the New Testament in its Roman context.

example, protected the underprivileged—widows, orphans, and the poor—in their communities. Both religious communities also had an internal organization that did not depend on Rome. Their leaders (bishops for Christians and rabbis for Jews) gave judgments based on law that was separate from the Roman justice system. Finally, both Judaism and Christianity were monotheistic. Jews and Christians believed that that there is only one God, with whom contact is direct and immediate. To the Romans, who believed in many gods, this monotheism was the strangest aspect of the two faiths. Worshiping only one god made no sense to Romans, with their tradition of making sacrifices to many gods.

The Spread of Christianity

Christianity drew many of its first converts from socially marginalized groups, such as women, noncitizens, and slaves. Indeed, Jesus' message was revolutionary in the way it overturned conventional boundaries of class, gender, and ethnicity. Paul's writings in the New Testament illustrate this perspective. Paul encouraged a communal life in which all followers of Jesus were equal in the eyes of God. As he wrote to a small Christian community in Galatia in Asia Minor, "For in Christ Jesus . . . there is no longer Jew or Greek, there is no longer slave or free, there is no longer male or female." Paul therefore urged the entry of gentiles (non-Jews) into the Christian community, and taught that Jesus' teachings would one day unify all of humanity.

Christianity continued to attract the poor and outcast, but by the middle of the second century C.E., an important change occurred within the ranks of Christian adherents. Many new converts to the faith were men and women who had already been educated in Greek philosophy. They began to analyze and understand Christianity in the terms with which they were familiar: the abstract ideas of the Greek and Hellenistic philosophical traditions. Rather than dismiss Plato's teachings as the ideas of an unbeliever, for example, they argued that his ideas about the supremacy of the soul and what it meant to lead a good life anticipated the teachings of Jesus. Because it eventually led to Christianity's assimilation of much of classical culture, this encounter between Christians and the intelligentsia of the Mediterranean world transformed the Christian faith. As Christians developed methods of analyzing biblical texts drawn from philosophy and rhetoric, the language of Christianity fused with that of Greek and Latin intellectual life.

Much of this development centered on the works of a group of Christian writers called Apologists°. The Apologists publicly defended their faith to learned non-Christian audiences (just as Socrates had defended his beliefs in Plato's *Apology*—hence the name *Apologists*). In the process, they helped shape the integration of Christian teachings and Hellenistic learning. Origen (ca. 184–255 C.E.), the most profound thinker among the Apologists, was as much a classical scholar as a churchman. He laid the groundwork for the integration of classical Greek philosophy and culture with Christianity. This complex step was of unparalleled importance in the development of Western civilization because it not only enhanced the appeal of Christianity among educated believers but also ensured the transmission of many Greek philosophical ideas to what would become Western culture.

The Apologists faced stiff opposition from within the Christian community because many churchmen viewed classical learning with deep suspicion. Tertullian (ca. 160–240 C.E.), Origen's influential contemporary, argued forcefully for the separation of Christianity from the learning and culture of the non-Christian world. He worried that the mingling of religious cults so common in his day might corrupt Christianity. Tertullian summed up his opposition to classical culture: "What has Athens to do with Jerusalem? What is there in common between the philosopher and the Christian?" Christians like Tertullian mistrusted the power of the human intellect and stressed the need to remain focused on Jesus' teachings. Yet Tertullian could not stop the integration of Christianity with classical learning. By the third century C.E. Christians could no longer ignore the Mediterranean world in which they lived.

And that world could no longer ignore them. Many of Christianity's core concepts, such as its ideas about personal salvation, the equality of individual men and women before God, and the redemption of humanity from sin, distinguished it from the empire's polytheistic faiths. Most strikingly, Christianity firmly rejected the existence of multiple gods and sought to convince followers of other religions that they stood in error. In addition, Christians' close community life and failure to engage in the public life of Roman culture won them suspicion. By the second half of the first century C.E., many Roman officials perceived Christians as potential enemies of the state because they refused to join in the worship of the emperor. Christians endured persecution and many who refused to renounce their religious beliefs were executed. Christians believed that these victims of religious persecution had died gloriously and called them martyrs, or witnesses for their faith.

In their vision of all humanity united under a single God and their desire to replace other forms of religious expression with the worship of this one God, Christians were truly revolutionary. Christians eventually succeeded in displacing all polytheist religions within the Roman Empire. Although polytheism still exists in many parts of the world today, it is nearly absent from the West. As a consequence, a fundamental part of how many peoples understood the world changed radically.

CONCLUSION
Rome Shapes the West

·······························■·······························

The map of the Roman Empire outlined the heart of the regions included in the West today. Rome was the means by which cultural and political ideas developed in Mediterranean societies and spread into Europe. This quilt of lands and peoples was acquired mostly by conquest. An autocratic government held the pieces together. Although Roman authorities permitted no dissent in the provinces, they allowed provincial peoples to become Roman. Being Roman meant that one had specific legal rights of citizenship, not that one belonged to a particular race or ethnic group. Thus, in addition to expanding the boundaries of the empire and patrolling its borders, the Roman army brought a version of Roman society to subject peoples. By imitating Roman styles of architecture and urban life, the cities, too, helped spread Roman civilization. Moreover, the elites of these cities helped funnel the resources of the countryside into the emperor's coffers and so sustained the imperial system.

For two and a half centuries the *Pax Romana* inaugurated by Augustus fostered a remarkable degree of cultural uniformity within the empire's boundaries. Rome's civilization, including its legal system, its development of cities, and its literary and artistic legacy, made it the foundation of Western civilization as we know it today. The legal precedents established by Roman jurists remain valid in much of Europe. Latin and Greek literature of the early Roman Empire has entertained, instructed, and inspired readers in the West for nearly 2,000 years. Until very recently all educated people in the West could read Latin and looked to the works of the Romans for their model in prose style. Many of our public buildings and memorial sculptures continue to adhere to the artistic and architectural models first outlined in Rome. The Roman Empire was the most important and influential model of an imperial system for Europeans until modern times. Of equal importance, the monotheism and ethical teachings of Judaism and Christianity have been prominent forces in shaping Western ideals and attitudes.

A debilitating combination of economic weakness, civil war, and invasions by northern peoples would almost destroy the Roman Empire in the third century C.E. How the Roman Empire recovered and was transformed in the process is the story of the next chapter.

Suggestions for Further Reading

·······························■·······························

For a comprehensive list of suggested readings, please go to www.ablongman.com/levackconcise/chapter5

Beard, Mary, John North, and Simon Price. *Religions of Rome.* 2 vols. 1995. The first volume contains essays on polytheist religions, and the second contains translated ancient sources.

Gardner, Jane F. *Women in Roman Law and Society.* 1987. Discusses issues pertaining to women in Rome.

Garnsey, Peter, and Richard Saller. *The Roman Empire: Economy, Society, and Culture.* 1987. Stresses the economic and social foundations of the Roman Empire.

Hornblower, Simon, and Antony Spawforth, eds. *The Oxford Classical Dictionary.* 3rd ed. 1996. This encyclopedia treats all aspects of Roman culture and history.

Markus, Robert. *Christianity in the Roman World.* 1974. An excellent study of the growth of Christianity.

Romm, James. *The Edges of the Earth in Ancient Thought: Geography, Exploration, and Fiction.* 1992. An exciting introduction to the Roman understanding of real and imaginary peoples.

Talbert, Richard, ed. *The Barrington Atlas of the Classical World.* 2000. This atlas contains the best maps available.

Webster, Graham. *The Roman Imperial Army.* 3rd ed. 1985. Discusses military organization and life in the empire.

Wiedemann, Thomas. *Emperors and Gladiators.* 1992. An important study of the ideology and practice of gladiatorial combat.

Wolfram, Herwig. *The Roman Empire and Its Germanic Peoples.* 1997. Examines the interrelation of Romans and Germans over several centuries.

Woolf, Greg. *Becoming Roman: The Origins of Provincial Civilization in Gaul.* 1998. The best recent study of romanization.

Late Antiquity: The Age of New Boundaries, 250–600

D URING THE LAST WEEK OF AUGUST IN 410, AN EVENT OCCURRED THAT stunned the Roman world. A small army of landless warriors—no more than a few thousand men—led by their king, Alaric, forced their way into the city of Rome and plundered it for three days. For more than a year Alaric had been threatening the city of Rome in an attempt to extort gold and land for his people. When his attempts at extortion failed, he resorted to attacking the city directly. Because Alaric's followers, the Visigoths, were Christian, they spared Rome's churches and took care not to violate nuns. But that left plenty of loot—gold, silver, and silks—for them to cart away.

For these warriors and their families, who had first invaded the Roman Empire from their homelands in southern Russia thirty years earlier, pillaging the most opulent city in the Mediterranean world was a pleasant interlude in a long struggle to secure a permanent home. For the Romans, however, the looting of Rome was an unfathomable disaster. They could scarcely believe that their capital city, the gleaming symbol of world rule, had fallen to an army of so-called barbarians, one of many Germanic tribes who migrated into the Roman Empire. "If Rome is sacked, what can be safe?" lamented the churchman Jerome when he heard the news in far-off Jerusalem. His remark captures the outrage and astonishment felt by Roman citizens everywhere, Christian and non-Christian alike, who believed that their empire was divinely protected and would last forever.

To understand how the Visigoths managed to sack Rome, we must examine late antiquity, the period between about 250 and 600, which bridged the classical world and the Middle Ages. During this critical era in the development of

Chapter Outline

- Crisis and Recovery in the Third Century

- Christianizing the Empire

- New Christian Communities and Identities

- The Breakup of the Roman Empire

The Vienna Genesis: Written in silver ink on purple-dyed parchment, this sumptuous manuscript of the first book of the Bible, now in a museum in Vienna, Austria, was created in the sixth century, probably for a member of the imperial court in Constantinople. The Greek text at the top portion of the page tells the story of Susanna at the Well, which is illustrated at the bottom of the page. Though the illustration tells a biblical story, certain details reflect conditions in late antiquity, such as fortified cities and the growing importance of camels in travel and commerce. The seated, seminude female in the lower left is derived from polytheist religion. She personifies the stream from which the more modestly dressed Susanna gathers water.

Western civilization, the Roman Empire underwent radical transformation. After its recovery from a half century of near-fatal civil war, foreign invasion, and economic crisis, Rome experienced a hundred years of political reform and economic revival. Yet by the middle of the fifth century, the political unity of the Mediterranean world had come to an end. The Roman Empire collapsed in western Europe. In its place, new Germanic kingdoms developed in Italy, Gaul, Britain, Spain, and North Africa. These kingdoms would serve as the foundation of western medieval Europe.

In contrast, the Roman Empire in the East managed to hold together and prosper. Rome's eastern provinces formed the nucleus of what historians call the Byzantine Empire, based in the city of Constantinople (modern Istanbul in Turkey). Until their empire fell to the Turks in 1453, the inhabitants of this eastern realm considered themselves Romans. The Byzantine Empire served as the most important cultural center in Europe throughout the Middle Ages. In both Byzantium (where Roman political administration was maintained) and the new kingdoms of the West (where it was not), Rome's cultural legacy continued, although in very different ways.

Late antiquity witnessed not only the collapse of the Roman Empire in the West but also the emergence of Christianity as the dominant religion throughout the imperial realm. From there it spread beyond the imperial borders, bringing new notions of civilization to the people of Europe, North Africa, and the Middle East. In this era one did not have to be Roman to be Christian, but it was necessary to be Christian to be civilized. Once Christianity became dominant, the cultural boundaries between Christians, Jews, and polytheists hardened.

To explore this complex age of consolidation, transformation, and cultural transmission, we will consider the following questions:

- How did the Roman Empire successfully reorganize following the instability of the third century?
- How did Christianity become the dominant religion in the Roman Empire, and what impact did it exert on Roman society?
- How did Christianity transform communities and enrich religious experience inside and outside the empire?
- How and why did the Roman Empire in the West disintegrate?

Crisis and Recovery in the Third Century

In the years between 235 and 284, the Roman Empire staggered under waves of political and economic turmoil. Rival generals competed for the throne, chronic civil war shook the empire's very foundation, and invaders hungry for land and plunder broke through the weakened imperial borders. The economy collapsed and the imperial administration broke down. But in 284, a new emperor seized power and halted the process of decline, shoring up the empire with drastic administrative and social reforms and religious persecution.

THE BREAKDOWN OF THE IMPERIAL GOVERNMENT

In 235, the assassination of Emperor Severus Alexander, the last member of the Severan dynasty, sent the imperial administration into a tailspin. Military coup followed military coup as ruthless generals with nicknames like "Sword-in-Hand" competed for the throne. In the latter half of this century, not one of more than four dozen emperors and would-be emperors died a natural death. Gallienus clung to the throne longest: His reign lasted fifteen years (253–268). Most emperors held power for only a few months. Preoccupied with merely staying on the throne, they neglected the empire's borders, leaving them vulnerable to attack.

This situation had dire consequences for the empire. Foreign invaders attacked both eastern and western provinces throughout late antiquity. To the Romans' deep shame, Emperor Valerian was captured in battle by the Great King of Persia in 260. War bands from across the Rhine River reached as far south as Italy, forcing the emperor Aurelian to build a great wall around the city of Rome in 270. Many other cities across the empire constructed similar defenses. The Roman military system and the Roman economy buckled under the pressure of invasions and civil war. Inflation spun out of control and coins lost their value. The government paid soldiers in produce and supplies rather than cash. Not surprisingly, resentment boiled among the troops.

The seat of power now shifted from Rome to provincial cities. Unlike their predecessors, the soldier-emperors of this era, who came mostly from frontier provinces, had little time to cultivate the support of the Roman Senate. Instead, they held court in cities close to the embattled frontiers. Towns far from Rome, such as York in Britain or Trier in Gaul, had long functioned as military bases and supply distribution centers. Now they served as imperial capitals whenever the emperor resided there.

With the emperor on the move and with armies slipping from imperial control, political power fragmented. Political decentralization injured the empire further. Some cities and provinces took advantage of the weakened government to try to break away from Roman control. In the early 260s and 270s a large portion of Gaul known as the Gallic Empire briefly established independence. A few years later, Zenobia, the queen of Palmyra (r. 267–272), a city in Syria that had grown wealthy from the caravan trade, rebelled

■ Subjugation of Valerian

Persian kings built their tombs in a cliff six miles north of Persepolis, the old Persian capital. Here at Naqsh-i Rustam, a carving depicts the Great King Shapur I (239–272) on horseback holding the arm of his prisoner, the Roman emperor Valerian. The previous Roman emperor, Philip (known as "the Arab"), kneels in supplication. Shapur bragged about his accomplishments: "When I first came to rule, the Roman emperor Gordian gathered an army from the whole empire of the Romans, Goths, and Germans and came to Mesopotamia against my empire. . . . and we annihilated the Roman army. Then the Romans proclaimed Philip the new emperor . . . and he came to plead with me, and he paid 500,000 gold pieces as ransom and became our tributary . . . And when I marched against Carrhae and Edessa [Roman cities in Syria], the Emperor Valerian advanced against us . . . We fought a great battle . . . and I captured the Emperor Valerian myself with my own hands."

against Rome, and a bitter war ensued. The emperor Aurelian's troops finally crushed Palmyra in 272 and led Zenobia in chains through the streets of Rome in a triumphal procession. Such triumphs, however, were few and far between in these years.

DIOCLETIAN'S REFORMS

Diocletian (r. 284–305) stepped in to rescue the empire near the end of the third century. Diocletian launched a succession of military, administrative, and economic reforms that had far-reaching consequences. Not since the reign of Augustus had the Roman Empire been so fundamentally transformed.

After ruling alone for two years, Diocletian recognized that the enormous responsibilities of imperial rule overburdened a single ruler, and so he took the dramatic step of dividing the empire into two parts. In 286 he chose a co-ruler, Maximian, to govern the western half of the empire, while he continued to rule in the East. Maximian maintained a separate administrative system and his own army. Then, in 293, Diocletian and Maximian subdivided their territories by appointing two junior-level emperors. These junior rulers administered their territories in the eastern and western parts of the empire with their own bureaucracies and armies.

Through this system of government, called the tetrarchy°, Diocletian hoped not only to make the imperial government more efficient, but also to put an end to the bloody cycle of imperial assassinations. Although he had gained the throne by murdering his predecessor, he knew that the empire's survival depended on a reliable succession strategy. To that end, Diocletian dictated that the junior emperors were to step into the senior emperors' place when they retired. Then they themselves were to select two new talented and reliable men to be junior emperors and their eventual replacements. Thus supreme power was to be handed down from capable ruler to capable ruler, and the constant cycle of assassinations and civil wars was to be broken.

■ **The Tetrarchs**

Stolen by crusaders during the Middle Ages from its original site near Constantinople, this statue of the tetrarchs now is built into a wall of the cathedral of San Marco in Venice. To depict their solidarity and readiness for war, the tetrarchs are presented as fierce soldiers in military uniform, holding their swords with one hand and clasping their colleague's shoulder with the other. Each pair of figures shows one junior emperor and one senior emperor, who has more worry lines in his forehead as a sign of his greater responsibilities.

To restore Roman military power that had been weakened during the crises of earlier decades, Diocletian reorganized the Roman army. He nearly doubled its size to about 400,000 men. In order to protect the empire from invaders, he stationed these troops along the borders of the empire and built military roads from Britain in the West to the Euphrates River in the East. At the same time, Diocletian sought to reduce the army's involvement in political affairs. Although he was a soldier himself, he recognized that the army had played a disruptive role in earlier decades by constantly engaging in civil wars. He reduced the size of each legion in order to limit its commander's power as well as to increase its maneuverability. He placed the legions under new, loyal commanders. With these military reforms effected, Diocletian was able to secure the empire's borders once again and suppress internal revolts (see Map 6.1).

Reorganizing the army was only one part of Diocletian's vision of reform. To restore efficient government, he also embarked on a thorough reorganization of the empire's administrative system. He redrew the map of the realm, drastically reducing the size of provinces and setting up separate civilian and military bureaucracies within each. These changes further reduced the risk of rebellion by limiting the power of any single civilian official. This administrative overhaul resulted in a significant expansion of the numbers of bureaucrats and military commanders.

Maintaining the bloated civilian and military apparatus created by the tetrarchy, especially in an era of rampant inflation, demanded full use of the empire's financial resources as well as far-reaching economic reforms. To halt the declining value of money, Diocletian attempted to freeze wages and prices by imperial decree. He also increased taxes and endeavored to make tax collection more effective through the establishment of a regular—and deeply resented—census to register all taxpayers. The new tax system generated enough revenues to fund the now enormous machinery of government.

This tax system was, however, riddled with loopholes and inequities. Senators, army officers, and other influential citizens were undertaxed or not taxed at all, and rich landowners often used bribery and force to fend off imperial tax collectors. Consequently the greatest burden fell on those least able to bear it: the peasants. Fewer rich men controlled more of the empire's land and the wealth it generated than ever before. The emperor himself was the wealthiest of all, adding to his possessions through confiscation of lands owned by cities and private individuals.

Diocletian did nothing to address the widening social and economic division in his empire; instead, he attempted to reinforce the cultural unity of the empire through religious persecution. In 303, he and his junior emperor Galerius initiated an attack on Christians in the eastern part of the empire, which was under their rule. The two emperors believed that failure to worship the traditional Roman gods had angered the deities and brought hardship to the empire. In what is now known as the Great Persecution°. Diocletian and Galerius forbade Christians to assemble for worship and ordered the destruction of all churches and sacred books. Several thousand women and men refused to cooperate and were executed.

Diocletian's reforms stabilized and preserved the Roman Empire. They also had three unintended consequences that altered the character of the empire. First, the quality of urban life slowly deteriorated under his reorganized imperial government. As we saw in Chapter 5, cities played an essential role in imperial Rome's economic, religious, and cultural life: Romans saw themselves as civilized because they lived in cities. The number of Roman cities remained largely unchanged, but the weight of the new tax system and the costly bureaucracy of the increasingly centralized imperial government transformed many traditions of urban daily life. To finance imperial projects, emperors confiscated most city-owned lands and revenues, resulting in a reduction of funds to spend on civic life:

games, chariot races, public buildings, and maintenance of urban infrastructure.

Furthermore, the city councilors, who had the responsibility of raising the tax revenues required by the central government, were frustrated. They knew that failure to provide the imperial government with the sums it demanded could lead to public flogging with lead-tipped whips—a punishment as humiliating as it was painful. Once considered a great honor, holding civic office began to lose its appeal. Because a position in the imperial bureaucracy granted immunity from service in city government, with its crushing fiscal obligations, many ambitious men turned to the imperial bureaucracy to win the honors, status, and power that used to come with positions in the city government. Meanwhile, both the wealth and numbers of city aristocrats, the traditional leaders and patrons of their communities, dwindled.

The second unintended consequence of Diocletian's reforms was the failure to centralize government within the

---

■　**Map 6.1　The Roman Empire in Late Antiquity**

Following the reforms of Diocletian, the Roman Empire enjoyed a century of stable government, with the same borders as in earlier centuries.

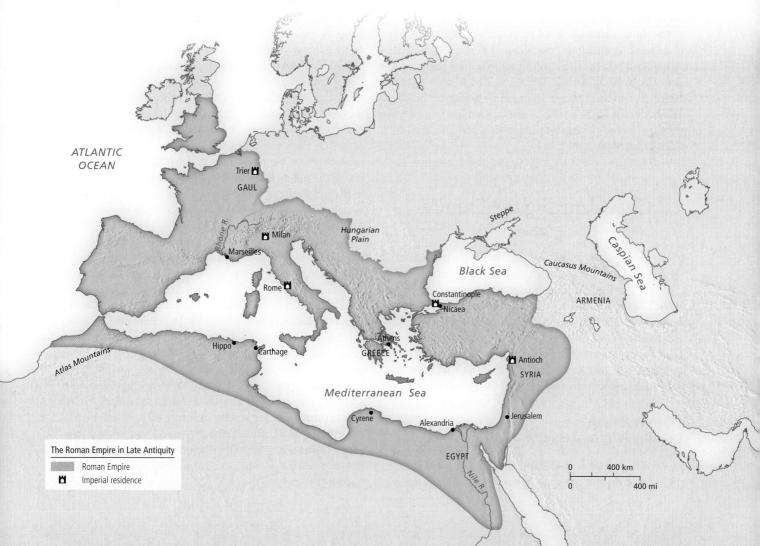

western provinces of the empire, where political power fragmented into the hands of local rich men. As some men grew richer and more powerful, poor people turned to them for protection against other landowners and ruthless imperial tax collectors. In return for this protection, peasants gave their wealthy patrons ownership of the farms on which they continued to work. These peasants, called *coloni*, lost the right to leave their farms and move elsewhere. Coloni had to perform labor for their landlords and had only limited control of their own possessions, although they could not be evicted and were still considered free Roman citizens.

The imperial government supported this form of near-slavery because it benefited the biggest landholders—including the emperor—who needed a stable workforce tied to the land to make agriculture profitable. The coloni system also promised the emperor a reliable source of tax revenues. But over time, landowners began to develop private armies to protect their vast country estates and the peasants who labored on them. This usurpation of the role of the central government weakened the authority of the emperor and his administration in the western provinces. In contrast, the eastern provinces of the empire remained prosperous into the sixth century. Private estates grew in size, but the imperial administrators maintained tight control of the economy.

The final unintended consequence of Diocletian's reforms was that the center of power in the empire shifted decisively to the East, where wealth and political might were increasingly concentrated. Diocletian's own style of rule contributed to this process. He not only delegated the government of the western (and by implication less important) provinces to his co-emperor, Maximian, but also lived for much of his reign in the East.

Christianizing the Empire

When Diocletian died, he left the eastern provinces of the empire, at least, stronger militarily, administratively, and economically than they had been for nearly a century. The steps he had taken to eradicate Christianity, however, turned out to be a failure. The new faith gathered momentum despite the hostility of Diocletian and other polytheist emperors. Eventually, it captured the imagination of an ambitious young Roman who would become the empire's first Christian emperor.

CONSTANTINE: THE FIRST CHRISTIAN EMPEROR

In 305, Diocletian stepped down from the imperial throne and insisted that his co-emperor in the West, Maximian, re-tire as well. Diocletian expected a peaceful succession to occur. It did, but just barely. The two junior emperors, Galerius and Constantius, took Diocletian's and Maximian's places. Just one year later, Constantius died in Britain. Abandoning the principles of the tetrarchy, the troops stationed in Britain proclaimed in 306 Constantius's son, Constantine (ca. 280–337), to be his replacement. The ambitious young general set out to claim sole rule of the Roman Empire. In 312 he smashed the army of Maxentius, his last rival in the West, at the battle of the Milvian Bridge over the Tiber River at Rome. Twelve years later he defeated Licinius, the tetrarch ruling in the East. Constantine then joined the empire together with himself as absolute ruler. Thus both the four-part rule of the empire and the system of succession that Diocletian implemented came to an end.

In other ways, however, Constantine continued along Diocletian's reformist path. Under Constantine the empire's eastern and western sectors retained separate administrations. To overcome the dangers of decentralization Constantine installed new officials called praetorian prefects in each sector. These rulers were directly accountable to the emperor. He also retained Diocletian's emphasis on a large field army, but ensured that heavily armored cavalry troops were trained for rapid deployment to trouble spots.

Moreover, Constantine, like Diocletian, did little to ease the economic burden weighing down the peasants and poor townsfolk. The imperial bureaucracy remained immense, the army remained huge, and so taxes remained high. To reinforce the economic structures of the empire, Constantine tried to reform the coinage system. He recognized that the existing coins had become so debased that they were effectively worthless, so he created a new gold coin—the *solidus*. (Seventy-two *solidi* equaled one pound of gold.) The creation of the *solidus* stabilized the economy by restoring the value of currency. The new coin ended the inflationary spiral that had contributed so much to the political and social turmoil of the third century and remained the standard coin in the Mediterranean world for 800 years.

To glorify his name and monarchy, Constantine founded a new capital city, Constantinople, the "City of Constantine," on the site of the Greek city Byzantium in 324. Constantine's choice of location reveals a shrewd eye for strategy. The city lay at the juncture of two military roads that linked Europe and Asia and controlled access to the Black Sea. From this convenient spot the emperor could monitor the vast resources of the empire's eastern provinces. Constantinople became a heavily fortified New Rome. In response to the threat of attack by Vandal pirates, the emperor Theodosius II erected massive defensive walls around the city in 413. In future centuries these fortifications would protect the city—and indeed, the empire—from ruin on several occasions. The city rapidly grew in size, reaching perhaps several hundred thousand inhabitants by the early sixth century.

Unlike Diocletian, Constantine embraced the new religion of Christianity. Most emperors had associated themselves with a divine protector. Constantine chose the sun god Apollo as his first divine companion. But the night before the pivotal battle at the Milvian Bridge in 312, Constantine experienced a revelation, which he interpreted as a sign from the Christian God. After triumphing in battle, Constantine attributed his success to Christ's favor. Later in his reign, writers described Constantine's victory as a miracle. Though it was not unusual for an emperor to embrace a new god, Constantine's particular choice made a difference. Because monotheistic Christianity repudiated rival gods and alternative forms of worship, Constantine's conversion led to the eventual Christianization of the entire empire. Constantine did not order his subjects to accept Christianity or forbid polytheist worship. He did, however, encourage widespread and public practice of his new faith. Before Constantine Christian worship had been conducted in the privacy of homes, but he lavished funds on church buildings. He obtained the gold for his new solidus coinage by looting the treasures that had been stored for centuries in polytheist temples. Now yoked to the imperial office, Christianity quickly gained strength across the empire and became a potent challenge to traditional modes of religious expression.

THE SPREAD OF CHRISTIANITY

Before the fourth century Christianity had spread through traveling missionaries who established congregations in most cities of the empire. After Constantine, successive emperors promoted Christianity, which grew rapidly throughout the empire during the fourth century. With imperial support, church leaders transformed the face of cities by building churches and leading attacks on the institutions and temples of polytheist worship.

The Rise of the Bishops

Much of the early growth of Christianity occurred in cities. In imitation of Roman urban administration, the Christian community developed its own administrative structures and leadership hierarchy. Just as an imperial official directed each city's political affairs with a staff of assistants, so each city's Christian community came to be led by a bishop who in turn had a staff of priests and administrators. Just as a provincial governor controlled the political affairs of all of the cities and rural regions in his province, so the bishop of the main city of a province held authority over the other bishops and priests in the province. This main or head bishop came to be called a *metropolitan* (because he resided in the chief city, the metropolis, of the province) in the east, an *archbishop* in the west. Through this hierarchy of metropolitans/archbishops, bishops, and priests, the scattered Christian communities were linked into what emerged as the Christian Church.

With its sophisticated administrative structure, the Church grew quickly and bishops emerged as important powers in their cities. A bishop's main task was to supervise the religious life of his *see,* which comprised not only the city itself but also its surrounding agricultural regions. Such supervision involved explaining Christian principles and teaching the Bible to these communities, as well as caring for the general welfare of orphans, widows, sick people, prisoners, and travelers. Constantine incorporated bishops into the imperial government by permitting them to act as judges in civil actions. Litigants could choose to be tried before a bishop rather than a civil judge. The decisions of a bishop had the same legal authority as those made by civil judges and could not be appealed. Through these changes, the Church began functioning almost as an administrative arm of the government, although it still had its own internal organization. Indeed, when Roman rule collapsed in western Europe in the fifth century, the Church survived the crisis and stepped in to fill the vacuum of public leadership.

By 400 Rome had become the most important see in western Europe, and the bishop of Rome was called the "pope"—the papa or father of the other western bishops. By the middle of the fifth century the emperor formally recognized the pope's claim to preeminence and the right of appeal over other bishops. A number of factors explain why the office of the bishop of Rome evolved into the papacy°. Together with Jerusalem, Rome was a site of powerful symbolic importance to Christians. Both the Apostle Peter, the first among Jesus' disciples, and Paul of Tarsus, the traveling teacher who took a leading role in spreading Christianity beyond its Jewish origins, died as martyrs in Rome. Early Christians considered Peter to have been the first bishop of Rome who passed on his authority to all subsequent popes.

In this way popes claimed to be the chief bishops of the Christian world. They insisted that their spiritual authority took precedence over rival bishops in four other imperial cities: Constantinople, Jerusalem, Alexandria in Egypt, and Antioch in Syria. The bishops of these leading religious centers, however, also claimed spiritual descent from Jesus' apostles. They did not accept papal authority and often quarreled bitterly with the pope over matters of faith and politics. The tensions among these bishops led to deep divisions between the eastern and western parts of the empire that have lasted until the present day.

Christianity and the City of Rome

The spread of Christianity transformed the appearance of Roman cities. Constantine set an example of public and private spending on churches, hospitals, and monastic communities that conformed to Christian values. The first churches in Rome were built to honor Christian martyrs of earlier centuries, including the great basilicas built over the presumed burial sites of Sts. Peter and Paul. Constantine financed the construction of St. Peter's Basilica, an enormous

■ A Female Priest

This foot-high ivory panel shows a female priest making a sacrifice at an altar to an unnamed god or goddess. *Symmachorum* means "of the family of the Symmachi," an aristocratic Roman clan in which some members defended the old gods in the face of Christianity. This elegant plaque commemorates some now-forgotten event in the family's life.

structure with five aisles punctuated with marble columns. Its altar rested over Peter's grave. (Today the papal cathedral of St. Peter stands on that same spot, in the heart of the Vatican, the city of the pope.) The construction of these churches signaled that Jesus' disciples Peter and Paul had replaced Rome's mythical founders Romulus and Remus as the city's sacred patrons. In other places, too, Christian saints took the place of traditional gods and heroes as protectors of city life. With the construction of Christian churches, spending on traditional buildings such as temples, bathhouses, and public entertainment facilities such as the circuses gradually declined.

With the proliferation of new Christian houses of worship in Rome and other cities came new religious festivals and rituals that gradually replaced traditional celebrations. Christians marked the anniversaries of the martyrdom of saints on the calendar. Sometimes a Christian holiday (a holy day) competed with a non-Christian holiday. For example, Rome's churchmen designated December 25 as the birthday of Christ to challenge the popular festival of the Unconquered Sun, which fell on the same day.

One additional development in the Christian shaping of time was the use of the letters A.D. as a dating convention. A.D. stands for *anno domini*, or "in the year of our Lord," referring to the year of Jesus' birth. It began in 531, when Dionysius Exiguus, a monk in Rome, established a simple system for determining the date of Easter every year. He began his calendar with the birth of Jesus in the year 1 (zero was unknown in Europe at this time) and started counting from there. Although he was a few years off in his determination of the year of Jesus' birth, his system slowly came into general use by the tenth century. In modern societies where Christianity is not universal, the abbreviation A.D. has been replaced by C.E.—meaning "in the Common Era"—to designate years (as is done in this textbook): In both systems, however, the year 1 still refers to Jesus' birth.

Regardless of what designation is used—A.D. or C.E.—the Christian system has become the standard dating convention used around the world.

Old Gods Under Attack

To Christians, the diverse range of religious expression in the Roman Empire was intolerable. They labeled all polytheistic worship with the derogatory term paganism° and made a determined effort to eradicate it. Christians attacked polytheism on two fronts: public practice and private belief.

During the fourth century bishops and monks, often in collusion with local administrators, led attacks on polytheist shrines and holy places. Because polytheism was not a single, organized religion, it offered no systematic opposition to government-supported Christian attacks. The most vocal opponents to this Christianization of the empire lived in Rome. In sharp contrast to the pious court at Constantinople, the conservative aristocracy of the city of Rome clung hard to the old gods, but in 391 polytheist worship became illegal.

The pace of conversion accelerated in the fifth and sixth centuries. Emperor Justinian (r. 527–565) sponsored programs of forced conversion in the countryside of Asia Minor, where tens of thousands of his subjects still followed ancient ways. Eradicating polytheism in the Roman Empire meant far more than the substitution of one religion for another. Polytheism lay at the heart of every community, influencing every activity, every habit of social life, in the pre-Christian world. To replace the worship of the old gods required a true revolution in social and intellectual life.

New Christian Communities and Identities

T he spread of Christianity produced new kinds of identities based on faith and language. Christianity solidified community loyalties and allegiances by providing a shared belief system and new opportunities for participation in religious culture. Yet at the same time, Christianity opened up new divisions and gave rise to new hostilities.

THE CREATION OF NEW COMMUNITIES

Christianity fostered the growth of large-scale communities of faith by providing a well-defined set of beliefs and values. These basic beliefs and values had to be integrated with daily life and older ways of thinking. Christianity required followers to study and interpret the Bible, the religion's sacred text. The religion also demanded allegiance to one God and a complex set of doctrines, and it dictated a distinctive lifestyle of self-restraint especially in sexual behavior. Weaving these elements into daily life resulted in a strong sense of Christian identity and common purpose. This new Christian identity competed with and at times replaced older identities linked to Roman citizenship or shaped by regional or urban loyalties.

Christian Doctrine and Heresy

The foundations of Christian doctrine were found in two texts: the Hebrew Bible, which Christians called the Old Testament, and Jesus' teachings, contained in the New Testament. Both testaments contained powerfully evocative narratives, moral teachings, poems, and parables, the precise meanings of which were not always self-evident. The Church soon ran into difficulties over interpretation of these texts, as Church leaders disagreed about the meanings of many biblical passages. Councils of bishops met frequently to try to resolve doctrinal differences and produce statements of the faith that all parties could accept. Two theological questions generated the most disagreement: the nature of the Trinity and the nature of Jesus Christ.

Christians believe that one God created and governs Heaven and Earth. This monotheistic foundation, however, undergirded a complex theological system in which the one God was understood to exist in three distinct "persons," each fully and absolutely God—God the Father, God the Son, and God the Holy Spirit—or the Holy Trinity. Church leaders argued about the precise relation of the three persons to one another and within the Trinity. Were the Son and the Holy Spirit of the same essence as the Father? Were they equally divine? Did the Father exist before the Son?

These debates over the Trinity were intimately connected to the second issue of contention with the early Church—the question of the nature of Jesus. At one extreme, some Christian scholars believed that Jesus was entirely divine and had no human nature. This emphasis on Jesus' divinity made his death on the cross and his resurrection irrelevant, for God could not suffer and die. It also severed the links between Jesus and his human followers by emphasizing that Jesus was entirely "transcendent" or "other," entirely beyond human comprehension or human limitations. At the other extreme, some Christians taught that Jesus was entirely human and not at all divine, thus challenging both the belief in the Trinity and what most other Christians understood as Jesus' mission on Earth.

The questions of the nature of the Trinity and the nature of Jesus erupted in the first great Christian controversy of late antiquity: the dispute between the Arians and the Athanasians. The Arians asserted that God the Father created Jesus, so Jesus could not be equal to or of the same essence as God the Father. Arians argued that the Trinitarian idea that Jesus as God the Son was both fully divine and fully human was illogical. The Athanasians were horrified by what they saw as the Arians' attempt to degrade Jesus' divinity. They preached that Christian truths were beyond human logic, and that Jesus was fully God, equal to and of the same substance as God the Father, yet also fully human.

The Arian-Athanasian dispute resulted in perhaps the most influential of the many church meetings held in late antiquity: the Council of Nicaea. In 325, Emperor Constantine summoned the bishops to Nicaea, a town near Constantinople, to reach a decision about the relationship among the divine members of the Holy Trinity. The bishops produced the Nicene Creed, which is still recited in Christian worship today. The creed states that God the Son (Jesus Christ) is identical in nature and essence to God the Father, the Athanasian belief. More than a century later, the Council of Chalcedon of 451 reinforced the Nicene Creed. The assembled bishops agreed that Jesus was both fully human and fully divine, and that these two natures were entirely distinct though united.

The Nicene Creed and the decisions of the Council of Chalcedon became the correct, or orthodox°, interpretation of Christian teaching because they had the support of most bishops and the imperial court. Still, some bishops and other religious leaders continued to debate conflicting interpretations of the Bible, and many ordinary Christians continued to hold beliefs that clashed with those defined as orthodox. People who held the orthodox point of view considered such alternative doctrines to be false beliefs, or heresies°, and they labeled the supporters of these doctrines *heretics.*

The doctrinal differences between orthodox and unorthodox or heretical Christian groups created and helped cement different communal and ethnic identities in late antiquity. Several geographic zones of Christians emerged that held different interpretations of Christian doctrine. A central zone based in Constantinople and including North Africa, Gaul, Italy, and the Balkans contained Christians called Chalcedonians°, or orthodox. (In the Latin-speaking western provinces they were also called Catholics.) These believers followed the decision of the Council of Chalcedon in 451 that defined Christ's divine and human natures as equal but entirely distinct. In late antiquity, the emperors in Constantinople and the popes in Rome—as well as most of the population of the Roman Empire—were Chalcedonian Christians. Although the Christians in this zone agreed on fundamental matters of doctrine, they differed culturally by producing Bibles, delivering sermons, and conducting religious ceremonies in their native languages—Greek in the eastern part of the central zone, Latin in the western. About 410, the churchman Jerome finished a new Latin translation of the Bible that replaced earlier Latin versions. This translation, called the Vulgate Bible, became the standard Bible in western European churches for many centuries. The western Church's use of Latin made it possible for other Latin texts from Roman antiquity to survive that might otherwise have been lost. The Church's use of Latin ensured the survival of Roman legal, scientific, and literary traditions, even after Roman rule had evaporated in western Europe.

In the eastern zone of the empire most of the Christians were Anti-Chalcedonians, also known by the derogatory term of Monophysites (literally "one nature"). They believed that Jesus Christ had only one nature rather than two. He was entirely divine and never human, even though he took on a human body while on Earth. Anti-Chalcedonian communities had developed by the end of late antiquity in Armenia, Egypt (where they were known as Copts), and Syria. These groups produced Bibles and a vast Christian literature in Armenian, Egyptian (written with Greek characters), and Syriac. The Syriac churches dominated in the eastern zone.

A third zone of Christians living in the western provinces of the Roman Empire in late antiquity comprised Arian Christians. As described earlier, Arians° believed that Jesus was not equal to or of the same essence as God the Father. Most people who followed Arian Christianity were Goths and other Germanic settlers who converted to Arian Christianity while they lived north of the Danube and in southern Russia. When they migrated into the Roman Empire in the fifth century, they seized political control of Rome's western provinces. Because of religious differences with the Roman Christians who followed Chalcedonian Christianity, the two groups did not intermarry, and the Arians were able to maintain their ethnic identity in the face of the much larger Roman population whom they ruled. Because a Gothic priest named Ulfila had created a Gothic alphabet and used it to translate the Bible, Gothic culture thrived in the western zone despite its minority status.

The Monastic Movement

Near the end of the third century, a new Christian spiritual movement took root in the Roman Empire. Known today as asceticism°, this movement called for Christians to subordinate their physical needs and temporal desires to a quest for spiritual union with God. Asceticism both challenged the emerging connection between the political and religious hierarchies and rejected the growing wealth of the Church.

The founder of the ascetic movement was Antony, an Egyptian Christian. Around 280 Antony sold all his property and walked away from his crowded village near the Nile into the desert in search of spiritual union with God. A few decades later, Athanasius, the Bishop of Alexandria, Egypt, composed a biography, the *Life of Antony,* telling how Antony overcame all the temptations the Devil could conjure up, from voluptuous naked women to opportunities for power and fame. Vividly describing the struggle between asceticism ("the discipline") and the demonic lures of everyday life ("the household"), Athanasius's work became one of the most influential books in Western literature. It captured the spiritual yearnings of many thousands of men and women, inspiring them to imitate Antony by following "the discipline" to seek spiritual communion with God.

Over time many Egyptian ascetics began to construct communities for themselves. The result was the monastic movement°. Monastic communities soon multiplied in the eastern provinces of the Roman Empire, especially near Jerusalem in Palestine, where Jesus had lived centuries earlier. Drawing from earlier monastic rules written in Greek, Benedict of Nursia (ca. 480–547) wrote a Latin *Rule* that became the foundation for monasticism in western Europe. Benedict built a monastery on Monte Cassino near Naples in 529. Benedict emphasized voluntary poverty and a life devoted to prayer. Fearing that the Devil could easily tempt an idle monk, Benedict stressed manual labor. He therefore ordered that all monks perform physical labor for parts of every day when they were not sleeping or praying. Since the first monks were Roman aristocrats who held manual labor in contempt, Benedict's orders were quite radical.

In the western Roman Empire monasticism played a central role in preserving classical learning and thus allowing its integration into Christian culture in later centuries. Much of the responsibility for the preservation of the classical intellectual tradition lay with the many monasteries of the Benedictine Order, which followed Benedict's *Rule*. Benedict himself was wary of classical teaching, but he wanted the monks and nuns under his supervision to be able to read religious books. Basic education at the very least had to become part of monastic life. Benedictine monasteries provided an education not only to their inhabitants but also to any eager scholar from the surrounding communities. The Benedictine definition of "manual labor" expanded to include the copying of ancient manuscripts, and Benedictine monasteries developed significant libraries. As monasteries that adhered to Benedict's *Rule* spread throughout Europe, they served as centers of education and also succeeded in preserving much Latin literature.

The monastic movement opened new avenues for female spirituality. In monastic communities, men and women lived separately to reduce sexual temptation, but within the confines of these communities, gender was irrelevant. It was just one more difficult physical boundary to cross over on the path to finding God. By joining monastic communities and leaving the routines of daily life behind, women could gain independence from the obligations of male-dominated society. In all the lands where Christianity was followed, ascetic women created communities of their own. They lived as celibate sisterhoods of nuns, dedicated to spiritual quest and service to God.

Monasticism also reinforced negative ideas about women and sexuality in the Church. During late antiquity an increasingly negative view of women emerged in the writings of churchmen. Christian writers branded women as disobedient, sexually promiscuous, innately sinful, and naturally inferior to men. In ascetic thought, women were linked to the corrupt world of the flesh against which the Christian must exercise unceasing vigilance. Male ascetics preached and practiced sexual abstinence as an important self-denying discipline.

Jews in a Christian World

Until Christianity became the official religion of the Roman Empire, Jews had been simply one among hundreds of religious and ethnic groups who lived under Roman rule. Prior to the fourth century, Jews had enjoyed full citizenship rights and appeared in all professions and at all levels of society.

Christianity slowly erased all this. According to Christian belief, Jews had been the chosen people of God until the appearance of Jesus, who displaced them from God's plan. Christians criticized Jews for failing to accept that Jesus' teachings had supplanted those of the Hebrew Bible, and blamed them collectively for Jesus' crucifixion. Christians viewed the Diaspora (the dispersion of Jews around the world after the destruction of Jerusalem by the Roman army in 70) as God's way of punishing the Jews.

With the advance of Christianity within the empire, conditions for Jews declined. Beginning in the fourth century, Roman laws began to discriminate against Jews, forbidding them to marry Christians, own Christian slaves, or accept converts into their faith. With the support of Christian imperial officials, Church leaders sometimes forced entire communities of Jews to convert to Christianity on pain of death. In 429, Roman officials abolished the office of Jewish patriarch, the head of the Jewish community who enjoyed the status of a Roman prefect. The Roman emperors had long recognized the patriarch as leader of the many Jews who were dispersed throughout the empire, and had given the patriarch certain legal and administrative duties. With the office abolished, the Roman treasury now collected for itself the special taxes that had been paid by Jews for the patriarch's administration. The end of the Patriarchate shows that Jews had lost their status as a religious community in the eyes of the empire.

Individual Jewish communities continued to administer their own affairs under the leadership of rabbis—men who served as teachers and interpreters of Jewish law. With the completion of the Mishnah°, the final organization and transcription of Jewish oral law, by the end of the third century and the production of the Jerusalem and Babylonian Talmuds°, or commentaries on the law, by the end of the fourth and fifth centuries, respectively, rabbis and their courts now dominated Jewish community life.

ACCESS TO HOLINESS: CHRISTIAN PILGRIMAGE

Christianity not only created new communities and condemned others, it also offered new avenues of participation in religious culture. In late antiquity, Christians of all social ranks began to make religious journeys, or pilgrimages°. Their goal was to visit sacred places, especially places where holy objects, known as relics°, were housed. They believed these relics were inherently holy because they were physical objects associated with saints and martyrs, or with Jesus himself. The most highly valued relics were the bones from the venerated person. Christians believed that contact with such relics could cure them of an illness, heighten their spiritual awareness, or improve their lives. Palestine became a frequent destination of Christian pilgrims because it contained the greatest number of sacred sites and relics associated with events described in the Bible and particularly with Jesus' life and death. Between the fourth and seventh centuries, thousands of earnest Christian pilgrims flocked to Palestine to visit holy sites and pray for divine assistance and forgiveness for their sins.

Palestine did not have a monopoly on holy places, however. Pilgrims traveled to places throughout the Roman world wherever saints had lived and died and where their relics rested. Their pilgrimages contributed to the growth of a Christian view of the world in several ways. Because pilgrimage was a holy enterprise, Christian communities gave hospitality and lodging to religious travelers. This fostered a shared sense of Christian community among people from many lands. Christians envisioned a Christian "map" dominated by spiritually significant places. Travel guides that explained this "spiritual geography" became popular among pilgrims. Most of all, pilgrims who returned home enriched in their faith and perhaps cured in mind or spirit inspired their home communities with news of a growing Christian world directly linked to the biblical lands they heard about in church.

CHRISTIAN INTELLECTUAL LIFE

During the first three centuries after Jesus' death, when Christians were marginalized and at times persecuted in Roman society, many church leaders strongly criticized classical learning. Churchmen argued that the learning of pagan intellectuals was false wisdom, that it distracted Christians from what was truly important—contemplation of Jesus Christ and the eternal salvation he offered—and therefore that it corrupted young Christians.

Classical learning and the educational system that kept it alive posed a challenge to Christian educators because it emphasized the power of reason over faith. In particular, Greek philosophy taught that every belief should be doubted and questioned before it can be accepted as true. How should Christians reconcile classical teachings with the doctrines of their faith, particularly when the two conflicted? Did the classics of Greek and Roman literature constitute a threat to Christianity? Could Christians learn anything of value from non-Christian cultures? Should educated men turn their backs on classical learning in order to avoid being corrupted by it?

After Constantine's conversion in 312, the Church became an increasingly influential voice in the empire and classical learning no longer seemed as threatening to Christians as it had before. Many church leaders now came from the empire's urban elite, where they had benefited from classical learning. Christian officials grudgingly approved secular education as churchmen recognized that the traditional curriculum in classical rhetoric, grammar, and literature still had practical value because it was useful for the administration of the church and the law. Such training became an integral part of Christian life, at least among the Roman upper classes.

Writing in Greek and Latin, churchmen now drew freely from classical texts and methods of discussion, even though they considered the Christian scriptures the sole source of truth. Christianity not only influenced the way people saw themselves in relation to philosophy and faith, it also shaped their view of the Roman Empire's role in human history. Eusebius, the bishop of Caesarea in Palestine from 313 to 339 and an adviser to Constantine, developed a theory of history that linked the development of the Roman Empire to a divine plan for humanity's salvation. The *Pax Romana*, according to Eusebius, provided the perfect, indeed the divinely ordained, conditions for the rapid spread of Christian teaching and the rapid growth of the Christian Church. In Eusebius's view, Constantine's conversion to Christianity marked the next step in God's plan.

The career of Augustine (354–430) shows how a classical education could serve Christian purposes. Born to parents of modest means, Augustine attended traditional Roman schools as a youth. His talent and schooling had prepared him for a high position in public life. After his conversion to Christianity, Augustine became the influential bishop of the city of Hippo Regius in North Africa. He recounted his spiritual experiences and conversion in the *Confessions* (397), a partial autobiography written in middle age. Drawing on the ideas of the Greek philoso-

pher Plato and Christian scriptures, Augustine in the *Confessions* meditated on the meaning of life, especially on sin and redemption. To modern readers his sins seem petty things, but for him the real message was the power of redemption that made possible eternal life. His conversion to Christianity had been at first a matter of spiritual illumination, and Augustine showed how incomplete an intellectual conversion was without a spiritual one as well. To further his spirituality he had to cleanse himself of the desires of the flesh, which led him to renounce sexuality completely. Using his episcopal office as a platform from which to defend Christianity from polytheist philosophers and to define all aspects of the Christian life, Augustine displayed a sincere respect for certain aspects of Roman cultural and intellectual accomplishments—especially rhetoric and history. But he always believed Christianity was superior.

Augustine's confidence in the superiority of Christianity was profoundly challenged in 410 when the Visigoths plundered the city of Rome itself. Augustine was prompted to reexamine the conventional Christian notions, derived from the writings of Eusebius, about Rome's place in the history of the world. In his book *The City of God*, completed in 423, Augustine developed a new interpretation of history. Though Augustine admired the Romans for their many virtues, he concluded that Rome played no significant role in salvation history and that the sack of Rome had no special meaning for Christians. Augustine's theory disconnected Christian ideas of human destiny from the fate of the Roman Empire. In his view, the Roman Empire was just one among many that had existed and that would exist before Jesus' return. Because of their successful blending of ancient and Christian wisdom and their rhetorical power, Augustine's writings have been second only to the Bible in their influence on Christian thought.

The Breakup of the Roman Empire

During the fifth century, the Roman Empire split into two parts: the Latin-speaking provinces in western Europe, and the largely Greek- and Syriac-speaking provinces in the east. As the Roman government lost control of its western domains, independent Germanic kingdoms emerged in its place. The eastern provinces remained under the control of the Roman emperor, whose capital city was not Rome, but Constantinople. These surviving eastern provinces of the Roman Empire came to be called Byzantium after the fall of the Roman Empire in the West.

THE FALL OF ROME'S WESTERN PROVINCES

Why did Roman rule remain strong in the eastern Mediterranean while collapsing in western Europe? This is one of the most hotly debated subjects in European history. Edward Gibbon, an eighteenth-century writer whose *Decline and Fall of the Roman Empire* has influenced historians of Rome, criticized the Catholic Church for diverting able men away from public service and into religious life. Other historians attributed Rome's collapse in the west to enormous waves of so-called barbarian invasions. The reason the Romans lost their western provinces is, unfortunately, more complicated and less dramatic than any of these one-dimensional explanations.

Loss of Imperial Power in the West

The rather undramatic explanation is that the end of Roman rule in western Europe came in a haphazard and gradual fashion as the cumulative result of unwise decisions, weak leadership, and military failure. In the fourth century, the sudden appearance in southern Russia of the Huns, a fierce nomadic people from central Asia, set in motion a series of events that helped bring about the eventual collapse of Roman rule in western Europe. In 376, in what is now south Russia, an army of Huns drove a group of Visigoths from their farmlands. The refugees gained permission from the Roman emperor Valens to cross the Danube and settle in the Balkans in return for supplying troops to the Roman army. In the past, Roman rulers had frequently made this sort of arrangement with newcomers eager to settle in the empire. The Roman officials in charge of this resettlement, however, flagrantly exploited the refugees by charging them exorbitant fees for food and supplies. The situation grew so intolerable that in 378 the Visigoths revolted. At the battle of Adrianople in Thrace they killed Valens and destroyed an entire Roman army.

The Visigoths' successful rebellion wounded the empire, but not fatally. Rome's response to the disaster, however, sowed the seeds for a serious loss of imperial power in the West. Necessity forced the new emperor, Theodosius the Great (r. 379–395), to permit Visigothic soldiers to serve in the Roman army under their own Visigothic commanders. But this precedent of allowing independent military forces of dubious loyalty operate freely within the empire was a terrible mistake. The consequences of Theodosius's decision to allow the Visigoths their own commanders became all too clear in the mid-390s when Alaric, the Visigoths' king, turned on his Roman masters and began to attack and plunder Roman cities.

In 409 he demanded that parts of northern Italy and the western coast of the Balkans be turned over to him. When the Roman Senate refused, Alaric and his men sacked the city. Disbelieving senators and citizens alike could only watch as the Visigoths rampaged through their streets.

The Visigoths' sack of Rome not only dealt a psychological blow to the empire's inhabitants, it also led indirectly to the loss of many of Rome's western provinces. To fight Alaric, legions withdrew from the empire's northwestern defenses, leaving the frontier in Britain and along the Rhine vulnerable. The military situation in the western provinces became chaotic. By 410 Rome entirely abandoned its control of Britain, leaving the inhabitants defenseless against the Saxons, a Germanic tribe originally from the shores of the North Sea near modern Denmark. Crossing the Rhine frontier, small bands of marauding tribes roamed through Gaul, while the Vandals and their allies raided all the way to Spain and North Africa.

Although the invading bands were small, the imperial government in the West no longer possessed the administrative capacity to marshal its military resources and push the invaders out. Instead, it turned to diplomacy, offering the invaders a place within the Roman Empire in return for which they would pay taxes and fight with Rome. Within a matter of a few decades, however, invaders throughout the western provinces shook off their subordinate status to Rome. Thus, encroaching bands of Germanic peoples gradually established independent kingdoms in the regions of Britain, Gaul, Spain, and North Africa (see Map 6.2). The empire was not invaded by overwhelming numbers of savage invaders. In fact, their numbers were puny compared to the millions of Roman provincials they pitted themselves against, but Roman authorities lacked both the organization and the strength to defeat them.

Even though most of the western provinces had fallen to invaders by 450, the Romans managed to hold on to Italy for a short while longer. The city of Rome remained the home of the Senate, while the emperor of the western provinces resided in Ravenna, a town on Italy's northeast coast. Military strongmen, however, held the real power in Italy, although they were formally subordinate to the emperor. These soldiers were usually not Romans by birth, but they adopted Roman culture and fought for Rome's advantage. In 476 one of these strongmen, a Germanic general named Odovacar, ended the charade of obedience to the emperor. He deposed the last emperor in the west, a boy named Romulus Augustulus. Odovacar then assumed full power over the Italian peninsula, naming himself king of Italy. For many historians the year 476 symbolizes the end of the Roman Empire in the West. In actuality, however, 476 is a date of little significance. The Romans' control of their western provinces had all but slipped away decades earlier.

■ **Map 6.2 Germanic Kingdoms, ca. 525**

In little more than a century after their entry into the Roman Empire, different Germanic peoples had established several powerful kingdoms in western Europe.

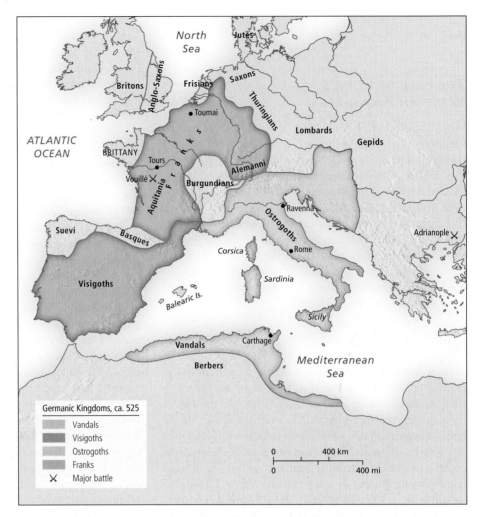

Cultural Encounters After the End of Roman Rule

By the mid-fifth century, when the fighting between Germanic invaders and the Romans ended, the two sides had to learn to live with one another. The rulers of the Germanic tribes of Vandals, Ostrogoths, and Visigoths possessed military power but were vastly outnumbered by the Romans. For example, only 40,000 Vandals controlled North Africa, which had a population of several million Romans. Although the Romans had no military power, they dominated urban life and agricultural production. The Romans continued to enjoy urban life and education but were ruled by Germanic masters who when they took over had been nomads with a very different religion and culture. Both sides faced challenges in adapting to the new situation.

In Britain the Germanic settlers were polytheists who nearly snuffed out the Roman Christians. In Gaul, North Africa, Italy, and Spain, the new settlers followed Arian Christianity, a creed that viewed Jesus Christ as subordinate to God the Father. The Romans, on the other hand, followed orthodox Christianity and thus saw the invaders as heretics. Although this religious difference caused considerable friction between the two peoples, it also worked to their mutual advantage. Roman law forbade intermarriage between orthodox and Arian Christians, so the settlers remained a distinct minority in their new domains. This enabled them to maintain a separate Arian clergy and separate churches and hence a distinct identity in the midst of the vastly superior numbers of Roman provincials they ruled.

Of all the former empire's western provinces, Italy prospered the most under Germanic rule, particularly under the long reign of Theodoric the Ostrogoth (r. 493–526). Theodoric sought to create an atmosphere of mutual respect between Ostrogoths and Romans by maintaining two separate administrations—one for his Ostrogoths, the other for the Romans—so that both communities could manage their own affairs under his supervision. Theodoric united Visigothic kingdoms in Spain and Gaul with his own in Italy, ultimately wielding great influence throughout west-

A ROMAN ARISTOCRAT LEARNS GOTHIC

·····················

Sidonius Apollinaris was a Roman aristocrat who lived in Gaul in the fifth century when Germanic kingdoms replaced Roman imperial rule. In this letter, he gently teases a Roman friend, Syagrius, who has been trying to find a place in the new power structure in the kingdom established in southern Gaul by the Burgundians, a Germanic tribe. Syagrius served as a legal adviser at the Burgundian court, where separate legal systems were enforced for Burgundians and Romans. Syagrius was one of a long succession of Romans who kept Roman culture and law working for several generations after the empire fell in the West—but he had to learn a new language:

Sidonius sends greetings to his friend, Syagrius:

You are the great-grandson of a consul . . . and you are descended from a poet . . . and the culture of his descendants has not declined one bit from his standard . . . I am therefore inexpressibly amazed that you have quickly acquired a knowledge of the German tongue with such ease. And yet I remember that your boyhood had a good schooling in liberal studies and I know for certain that you often declaimed with spirit and eloquence before your professor of oratory. This being so, please tell me how you have managed to absorb so swiftly into your inner being the exact sounds of an alien race, so that now after reading Vergil under the schoolmaster's cane and toiling and working through the rich fluency of . . . Cicero, you burst forth like a young falcon from an old nest. You have no idea what amusement it gives me, and others too, when I hear that in your presence the barbarian is afraid to perpetrate a barbarism in his own language. The bent elders of the Germans are astounded at you when you translate letters, and they adopt you as umpire and arbitrator in their mutual dealings . . . Only one thing remains, most clever of men: continue with undiminished zeal, even in your hours of ease, to devote some attention to reading; and like the man of refinement that you are, observe a just balance between the two languages: retain your grasp of Latin, lest you be laughed at, and practice the other, in order to have the laugh on them. Farewell.

Source: Reprinted by permission of the publishers and Trustees of the Loeb Classical Library from *Sidonius Poems and Letters, Volume II,* Loeb Classical Library Volume LCL 420, translated by W. B. Anderson, Cambridge, Mass.: Harvard University Press, 1935. The Loeb Classical Library® is a registered trademark of the President and Fellows of Harvard College.

ern Europe. Italy prospered under his rule, and the communities of Ostrogoths and Romans lived together amicably.

Throughout the western provinces links to the Roman Empire in the East began to weaken. Most of the invaders had brought their traditional practice of pledging fidelity and obedience to a local chieftain, and this tradition began to erode loyalty to the far-off Roman emperor in Constantinople. By pledging themselves to a Germanic king, men gained a place in the "tribe" of their new chieftain, who rewarded them with gifts and the opportunities to win prestige, honor, and land. Thus service to the empire gradually gave way to oaths of loyalty to local chieftains. Over time, new warrior-based aristocracies took shape in which landowning noblemen forged ties of personal loyalty to their local king.

Roman culture did not abruptly end with the last vestiges of Roman rule. It remained a vital presence in most regions, but it took different forms in the various lands now ruled by Germanic leaders. In Britain, Roman culture perhaps fared the worst and little of it survived into later ages. There the Germanic language the Saxon invaders and their Angle allies spoke took hold and began developing into the English spoken today. In Gaul, North Africa, Italy, and Spain, the Germanic settlers quickly learned the tongues of the Romans they ruled. Within several centuries these Latin-based "Romance" (based on the Roman speech) languages grew into the early versions of French, Italian, Spanish, and Portuguese. Latin continued as the language of literacy, and the settlers borrowed heavily from Roman literary forms. Writing in Latin, they produced histories of their tribal kingdoms in imitation of Roman historians. They also developed law codes composed in Latin influenced by Roman models.

THE BIRTH OF BYZANTIUM

Despite the profound alterations wrought by Christianity and Rome's loss of the western provinces, the Roman Empire endured in the eastern Mediterranean without interruption. Constantinople, the imperial city founded by Constantine in 324, became the center of a remodeled empire that over several centuries acquired both Christian and Roman characteristics. Historians have named this realm the Byzantine Empire, or Byzantium, although the inhabitants of the realm continued to think of themselves as Romans for a thousand years.

Christianity and Law Under Justinian

The most important amalgamation of Christian and Roman traditions took place during the reign of the emperor

Justinian (r. 527–565). He combined a powerful intellect, an unshakable Christian faith, and a driving ambition to reform the empire. Justinian inaugurated a number of changes that highlighted his role as a Christian emperor. First of all, he emphasized the position of the emperor at the center of society in explicitly Christian terms. He was the first emperor to use the title "Beloved of Christ" and he amplified the emperor's role in Church affairs. He ruthlessly purged non-Christians and heretical Christians from public life so that only men who were orthodox Christians could hold government offices.

Justinian's plan was to impose his version of Christian orthodoxy, based on the decrees of the Council of Chalcedon, on the entire empire. In the East this meant snuffing out the survivals of polytheist worship and the Monophysite heresy. After he reconquered the western domains of the empire, it meant combating the Arian Christian Vandals and Ostrogoths living there. In the East he was relatively successful, but his ruthless persecutions so alienated the populations of Syria and Egypt that they became ready converts to Islam in the following century (see Chapter 7). In the West the bishops of North Africa and Italy deeply resented Justinian's attempts to meddle in their affairs even when disagreements about doctrinal matters were relatively minor. As a result a bitter division arose between Christian churches in the eastern and western Mediterranean over the rights of bishops to resist imperial authority on religious matters.

Justinian attempted to create a Christian society by using Roman law coupled with military force. Unlike rulers of Rome's early empire, who permitted subject peoples to maintain their own customary laws, Justinian suppressed local laws throughout his realm. He envisioned all of his subjects obeying only Roman law—law that he defined and that God approved.

Thus, in his God-given mission as emperor-legislator, Justinian reformed Roman law. In an effort to simplify the vast body of civil law, he ordered his lawyers to sort through all the laws that had accumulated over the centuries and determine which of them should still be enforced. This monumental effort, which was completed in 534, is known as the *Code of Justinian*. Justinian also ordered the collection of other legal books, commentaries, and the new laws he had promulgated, which when put together with the *Code* constitute what is now called the *Corpus of Civil Law°*. The body of Roman law was passed down to later generations primarily through this compilation, which became a pillar of European civilization.

Justinian's Wars: Short-Term Success, Long-Term Failure

Besides reorganizing Byzantium's legal system, Justinian devoted himself to returning the empire to greatness through war. Throughout most of his reign he fought on two fronts:

CHRONOLOGY	
286	Diocletian begins imperial reforms
306–337	Reign of Constantine, first Christian emperor
324	Constantinople founded
378	Battle of Adrianople; Visigoths enter empire
391	Polytheist worship forbidden by Roman law
CA. 400	Jerusalem Talmud completed
410	Jerome completes Vulgate Bible
476	Romulus Augustulus, last Roman emperor in western Europe, is deposed
493	Theodoric the Ostrogoth rules Italy
CA. 500	Babylonian Talmud completed
527–565	Reign of Justinian
529	Benedict founds monastery at Monte Cassino
542	Plague strikes empire

in the East against the Persian Empire and in the West against Rome's fallen provinces. He wanted to reestablish imperial control over these western territories, now ruled by Germanic kings. Between 533 and 554 Justinian's armies snatched back North Africa from the Vandals, seized Sicily and Italy from the Ostrogoths, and won parts of Spain from the Visigoths. Although Justinian managed to realize many of his ambitions in the West, he did so at such a terrible cost to the treasury and devastation to the conquered provinces that while the Byzantine Empire temporarily expanded, it was permanently weakened financially.

The short-term success but ultimate failure of Justinian's ambitions in the western provinces was due to two factors. First, although the defeat of the Vandal kingdom in North Africa proved relatively easy, the Ostrogoths in Italy proved to be much sterner foes. The fighting between Justinian's troops and Ostrogoth armies in Italy lasted some two decades. Justinian's armies eventually wrestled Italy back under imperial control, but the long-term effects of the protracted reconquest had disastrous consequences for Justinian's empire. Between pouring precious financial resources into the Italy campaign and maintaining his grip on North Africa, Justinian was draining his empire's resources dry. The Byzantine hold on Italy would gradually slip away after Justinian's death. Second, Justinian's reconquest of Italy took decades because the population of the empire was decimated by the bubonic plague. The first on-

slaught in 542 took the lives of perhaps half the population of Constantinople—about a quarter of a million people. An estimated one-third of the entire population of the empire's inhabitants succumbed to the dreaded disease. With the population reduced by the plague, Justinian's army could not recruit the large number of soldiers it needed to fight on several fronts; the protracted battle for Italy was the result. After Justinian, Byzantine emperors lacked the resources to attempt to reconquer the Mediterranean world.

Although Justinian's greatest military successes were in the western Mediterranean, his most dangerous enemy was the Persian Empire on his eastern flank. This huge, multiethnic empire, under the rule of the Sasanian dynasty (ca. 220–633), had been Rome's main rival throughout late antiquity. Justinian fought several brutal wars with Persia. The emperor gave top priority to the struggle on his eastern frontier by supplying more than half of the Byzantine troops, led by his best generals. He also provided more financial resources to the struggle in the East than to the wars of reconquest in the West. By the time of Justinian's death, the two superpowers had established an uneasy coexistence, but the disputed territories between them remained unresolved. From then on the Byzantines firmly focused their attention toward the threats from the East.

Justinian succeeded in creating a Christian-Roman society, united under one God, one emperor, and one law. On the basis of the unified culture created by Justinian, the Byzantine Empire would survive in some form for nearly a millennium. While in the western provinces of the former Roman Empire, learning faded nearly away and once-great cities withered into tiny hamlets, Constantinople remained the principal center of learning and the greatest city in the world.

■ **The Cathedral of Holy Wisdom (Haghia Sophia)**
When Justinian entered his newly completed cathedral of Holy Wisdom (Haghia Sophia) in Constantinople, he boasted, "Solomon, I have outdone you!" He meant that his church was bigger than the Jerusalem temple built by the biblical king Solomon. For centuries Haghia Sophia was the largest building in Europe. In 1453 the church became a mosque. Today it is a public museum.

■ **Persian Coins and the Religion of Zoroaster**
This silver Persian coin depicts the Sasanian Great King Ohrmazd II (r. 302–309). He wears an elaborate crown. On the coin's other side two Zoroastrian priests tend a fire altar. Zoroastrianism was the state religion of the Persian Empire in late antiquity.

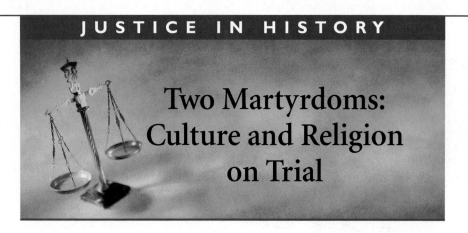

Two Martyrdoms: Culture and Religion on Trial

Between the reigns of Diocletian (r. 284–305) and Justinian (r. 527–565), the status of Christians changed dramatically. Christians went from being a religious minority persecuted by the imperial government to a majority that persecuted non-Christians with the Roman government's backing. One thing did not change during this period, however. Whether polytheist or Christian, emperors used force to compel their subjects to believe and worship in prescribed ways, hoping to keep the empire in the gods' good graces. To ensure religious conformity, emperors used the Roman judicial system. A comparison of the trials of a Christian soldier named Julius in 303 and Phocas, an aristocrat in Constantinople accused of paganism in 529 and 545, illustrates the objectives and methods of the Roman government's religious prosecution.

In 303 officials arrested a veteran soldier named Julius and brought him before the prefect Maximus. The following excerpt comes from a description of the trial:[1]

"Who is this?" asked Maximus. One of the staff replied: "This is a Christian who will not obey the laws." "What is your name?" asked the prefect. "Julius," was the reply. "Well, what say you, Julius?" asked the prefect. "Are these allegations true?" "Yes, they are," said Julius. "I am indeed a Christian. I do not deny that I am precisely what I am." "You are surely aware," said the prefect, "of the emperors' edicts which order you to sacrifice to the gods?" "I

am aware of them," answered Julius. "I am indeed a Christian and cannot do what you want; for I must not lose sight of my living and true God." . . . "If you think it a sin," answered the prefect Maximus, "let me take the blame. I am the one who is forcing you, so that you may not give impression of having consented voluntarily. Afterwards you can go home in peace, you will pick up your ten-year bonus, and no one will ever trouble you again. . . . If you do not respect the imperial decrees and offer sacrifice, I am going to cut your head off." "That is a good plan," answered Julius, "Only I beg . . . that you execute your plan and pass sentence on me so that my prayers may be answered. . . . I have chosen death for now so that I might live with the saints forever." The prefect Maximus then delivered the sentence as follows: "Whereas Julius has refused to obey the imperial edicts, he is sentenced to death."

After Constantine's conversion to Christianity in 312, persecution of Christians stopped, and Christian officials began to attack polytheism with the government's support. The emperor Justinian severely enforced laws against polytheists, executing anyone who sacrificed animals to non-Christian gods. During Justinian's reign, the imperial government launched three major persecutions of polytheists. In the first episode of persecution in 528–529, one year after Justinian ascended to the throne, a handful of government officials were charged with the crime of worshiping pagan gods.

One of these men was Phocas the Patrician, an aristocratic lawyer with an illustrious career in the emperor's service. After serving as the chief of protocol at court, he was sent to Antioch with funds to rebuild the city after a ruinous earthquake in 526. Cleared of charges of practicing paganism in 529, he continued to enjoy Justinian's trust and earn further promotions. In 532 he served for a year as Praetorian prefect, the most powerful position in the realm after the emperor. During this time, Phocas was responsible for raising revenues and administering the empire. He assisted in the construction of the new Cathedral of Holy Wisdom (Haghia Sophia; see illustration on page 135) in Constantinople by raising revenues. He also spent his personal funds in supporting smaller churches and ransoming hostages captured by Byzantium's enemies. Justinian next made him a judge and sent him on a mission to investigate the murder of a bishop. Then, in 545–546, during the second wave of persecution, despite his publicly recognized activities in support of the church and his faithful service to Justinian, Phocas was arrested again. He was among the doctors, teachers, and government officials suddenly charged with being pagans. A contemporary historian described a time of terror in Constantinople, when officials accused of worshiping the old gods in secret were driven from public office, had their property confiscated by the emperor, and were executed. In a panic, some of the accused men took their own lives. Phocas was one of

them. Rather than undergo the humiliation of public execution, Phocas committed suicide. The furious emperor ordered that Phocas's body be buried in a ditch like an animal, without prayer or ceremony of any sort.

Phocas thus missed the third purge of 562, when polytheists were arrested throughout the empire, paraded in public, imprisoned, tried, and sentenced. Zealous crowds threw thousands of non-Christian books into bonfires in the empire's cities.

The official reason for persecuting Christians such as Maximus was relatively simple: Christians refused to obey the law by making sacrifices to the Roman gods. But why did the later Christian governments use such a heavy hand in persecuting polytheists? Men like Phocas who were attacked as pagans were highly educated in the traditional learning of the Greco-Roman world. Indeed, it was this learning that was really on trial. Phocas and other victims had a deep commitment to traditional Roman culture; their "paganism" was not the furtive worship of old gods such as Zeus or Apollo. Rather, Phocas was considered a pagan because he was loyal to classical philosophy, literature, and rhetoric, without any Christian overlay or interpretation. In Justinian's eyes, this sort of classical learning had no place in a Christian empire. ■

Questions of Justice

1. Why did both polytheist and Christian governments of Rome think it was necessary to persecute adherents of non-official religions?

Taking It Further

Helgeland, John. *Christians in the Military: The Early Experience.* 1985. An introduction to the persecutions of Christians in the Roman army and their depiction in Christian literature.

Maas, Michael. *John Lydus and the Roman Past: Antiquarianism and Politics in the Age of Justinian.* 1992. This book explains how Justinian's policies about religion also involved an encounter with the empire's classical heritage.

CONCLUSION

A Transformed World

The transformation of the Roman world in late antiquity helped create the West as we understand it today. Christianity became the dominant religion throughout the Roman Empire. It assimilated much of classical culture and became the official religion by 400. During late antiquity Europe split into two parts. After Roman rule in the West collapsed, Germanic rulers established new kingdoms in the old Roman provinces. These kingdoms spoke Romance languages derived from Latin, and used Latin in church and law. In the eastern Mediterranean, the Roman Empire developed in new ways. Christianity and Roman civilization merged to create the vibrant Byzantine civilization. Greek remained the dominant tongue of daily life and Christian worship.

When Islam emerged as a powerful religious and political entity at the end of the late antique period, as we will see in the next chapter, its adherents were by definition excluded from the European communities of Christian believers. As a result, the North African, Southwest Asian, and Balkan lands that Islamic conquerors seized from the Byzantine Empire lost their place in the roster of "Western" communities, while those lands not conquered by Islam became the bastion of a medieval civilization that defined itself primarily as European and Christian.

Suggestions for Further Reading

For a comprehensive list of suggested readings, please go to www.ablongman.com/levackconcise/chapter6

Bowersock, G. W. *Hellenism in Late Antiquity.* 1990. Explains the important role of traditional Greek culture in shaping late antiquity.

Bowersock, G. W., Peter Brown, and Oleg Grabar, eds. *Late Antiquity: A Guide to the Postclassical World.* 1999. An indispensable handbook containing synthetic essays and shorter encyclopedia entries.

Brown, Peter. *The Cult of the Saints: Its Rise and Function in Late Antiquity.* 1981. A brilliant and highly influential study.

Brown, Peter. *The Rise of Western Christendom: Triumph and Diversity.* 1996. An influential and highly accessible survey.

Cameron, Averil. *The Later Roman Empire.* 1993. *The Mediterranean World in Late Antiquity.* 1997. Excellent textbooks with bibliography and maps.

Clark, Gillian. *Women in Late Antiquity: Pagan and Christian Life-Styles.* 1993. The starting point of modern discussion; lucid and reliable.

Harries, Jill. *Law and Empire in Late Antiquity.* 1999. Explores the presence and practice of law in Roman society.

Lee, A. D. *Information and Frontiers: Roman Foreign Relations in Late Antiquity.* 1993. An exciting and original investigation.

Maas, Michael. *Readings in Late Antiquity: A Sourcebook.* 2000. Hundreds of ancient sources in translation illustrating all aspects of late antiquity.

Markus, Robert. *The End of Ancient Christianity.* 1995. Excellent introduction to the transformation of Christianity in late antiquity.

Rich, John, ed. *The City in Late Antiquity.* 1992. Important studies of changes in late antique urbanism.

Thompson, E. A. *The Huns,* rev. Peter Heather. 1996. The best introduction to major issues.

Notes

1. John Helgeland, *Christians in the Military: The Early Experience* (1985), p. 64–65.

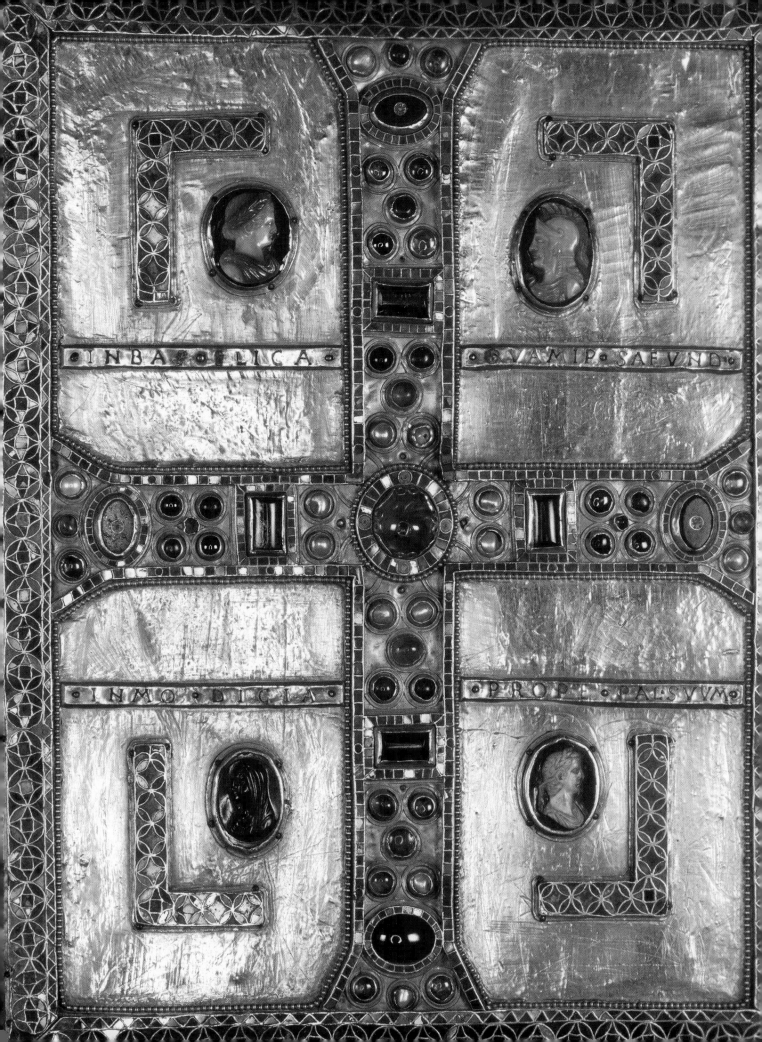

Byzantium, Islam, and the Latin West: The Foundations of Medieval Europe

ONE GRAY DAY IN CENTRAL GERMANY IN 740, AN ENGLISH MONK NAMED Boniface swung his axe at an enormous oak tree. This was the sacred Oak of Thor, where German men and women had prayed for centuries to one of their mightiest gods. Some local Christians cheered and applauded the monk. But an angry crowd of men and women gathered as well, cursing Boniface for attacking their sacred tree. Then something extraordinary occurred. Though Boniface had only taken one small chop, the entire tree came crashing down, split neatly into four parts. Boniface's biographer, a monk named Willibald, explained the strange event as God's judgment against "pagan" worshipers. In Willibald's account of the incident, the hostile crowd was so impressed by the miracle that they immediately embraced Christianity. As the news spread, more and more Germans accepted the faith, and Boniface's fame grew.

Whether or not the miracle at the Oak of Thor actually occurred, Boniface, a missionary who worked closely with the pope in Rome, played a leading role in spreading Christianity among the peoples of northern Europe. The Christian missionaries who traveled to lands far beyond the Mediterranean world brought Latin books and established monasteries. Through Christianity and the literacy that spread from these monastic centers, the monks established cultural ties among the new Germanic converts to Roman learning and the late antique world.

But Boniface was not Roman. He was English, a descendant of the Germanic settlers called the Anglo-Saxons, who took control of much of Britain after the Roman legions abandoned it in the early fourth century. Boniface's England (as southern Britain is called after the Anglo-Saxon settlements) was just one of the former Roman provinces in western Europe that had been settled and eventually ruled by Germanic tribes. In England Roman culture had been overwhelmed

Chapter Outline

- Byzantium: The Survival of the Roman Empire
- The New World of Islam
- The Birth of Latin Christendom

Theodolinda's Gospel Book: Pope Gregory the Great gave a valuable copy of the Gospels to the Lombard queen Theodolinda when her son was christened in 603. Jewels, enamels, and Roman cameos decorated the book's covers, a sign of the pious devotion given to the Bible.

139

and was reintroduced only indirectly through Christianity. In Spain, Italy, and France, in contrast, the Germanic settlers grafted their societies onto a still-living Roman stalk. The intermingling of these cultures produced Christian kingdoms on a Roman foundation. Historians refer to these continental kingdoms plus Britain as Latin Christendom.

The Latin Christendom that came to dominate western Europe was only one of three major civilizations that emerged on the ruins of the late antique Roman world and that constituted the West during this period. Far from where Boniface chopped down the Oak of Thor was the Byzantine Empire, which consisted of the eastern provinces of the Roman Empire. Byzantium inherited from ancient Rome a vibrant Christian culture that spread through the Balkans and influenced eastern Europe and eventually Russia. As the dominant Christian power in the eastern Mediterranean, Byzantium was a center of learning and an intermediary between the peoples of western Europe and the Middle East for a thousand years.

During this same period, another religion—Islam—created a third major civilization. In the century after the death of its founder, the prophet Muhammad, in 632, Muslims (believers in Islam) burst from their home in Arabia to conquer an empire stretching from Spain to central Asia. Muslims rejected Christianity and did not adopt Roman law. Nevertheless they absorbed some Roman institutions of imperial government, which played a fundamental role in shaping their empire.

These three civilizations—Latin Christendom, Byzantium, and Islam—and the interactions among them forged a new era in western history, called the Middle Ages (ca. 550–ca. 1500), or the West's medieval period. We consider all three of these medieval civilizations parts of Western civilization because they emerged in North Africa, the middle East and Europe, the core lands of the West. Moreover, all three drew from Rome's cultural, administrative, and religious legacy, although in different ways. Finally, these civilizations all centered on monotheistic religions that shared basic beliefs about God that ultimately derived from the Hebrew Bible. However, because of the conflicts among these three medieval civilizations, cultural and political boundaries developed between them that are still visible today. Byzantium and Latin Christendom grew apart even if they still accepted one another as fellow Christians. After the early adherents to Islam attacked neighboring countries, including Christian ones, in an attempt to spread the faith of Muhammad, Christians (both Byzantine and Latin) and Muslims came to consider one another adversaries. However, the adversarial relationship between the two religious camps has never been continuous, and for most of their histories Christians and Muslims have traded with one another and managed to get along.

To understand how these three civilizations formed the foundation of medieval Europe, we will explore three questions:

- How did the often embattled Byzantine Empire manage to survive and preserve Christian Roman civilization?
- How did Islam develop in Arabia, and how did its followers create a vast empire so quickly?
- How did Latin Christendom—the new kingdoms of western Europe—blend Rome's legal and governmental legacies with its Germanic heritage and how did Christianity spread in these new kingdoms?

Byzantium: The Survival of the Roman Empire

The emperor Justinian (r. 527–565) tried to restore the glory of the Roman Empire by reconquering former Roman provinces so that his realm extended from southern Spain to the Persian frontier. After Justinian's death in 565, the Byzantine Empire began losing territory to surrounding enemies. In response, emperors reorganized Byzantium militarily. Several important Roman institutions, however, continued in the medieval period: the emperor with his imperial bureaucracy, the army, and the Orthodox Church. These institutions gave strength to the Byzantine Empire and helped it endure many challenges.

AN EMBATTLED EMPIRE

By 750, the Byzantine Empire was reduced to a much smaller regional power struggling for survival against many enemies. Some of the threats came from the north from nomadic tribes, such as the Slavs, Avars, and Bulgars who migrated into the Balkans and permanently settled within the borders of the empire. These peoples became the ancestors of some of the current inhabitants of the region. In the West the Byzantines faced the Germanic tribe of the Lombards, who had formed a powerful kingdom that eroded the imperial rule over northern Italy reestablished by Justinian. To the East they confronted their old rival, the Persian Empire. And from the South an entirely new threat rose out of the Arabian peninsula from the armies of Islam. The encounters between these diverse enemies and Byzantium were usually hostile, and their encirclement of Byzantium forced important changes in Byzantine administration and military policy.

By the end of the sixth century the deluge began as the nomadic Slavs, Avars, and Bulgars had all begun to appear on the borders of Byzantium. The Slavic societies had formed from a blending of many cultures and ethnic groups. Within a few decades or so after the Slavs migrated into eastern Europe and the Balkans were themselves overwhelmed by the Avars, a nomadic people with a bone-chilling reputation for cruelty and ferocity in warfare. From their base in the plains of present-day Hungary, the Avars extended their territory into central Europe, creating an empire by forcing conquered peoples, including Slavs, to serve in their armies (see Map 7.1).

By 600, Slavic and Avar groups had seized most Byzantine lands from the Danube to Greece. In 626, Slav and Avar forces attacked Constantinople from the Northwest, while their Persian allies approached from the East. The capital city survived their combined assault, but it took the Byzantines nearly four centuries to reassert control over the Balkans. Fast on the heels of the Slavs and Avars came the Bulgars, who established rule over the largely Slavic inhabitants of the territory between the Danube River, the Black Sea, and the Balkans. The Bulgars

destroyed old Roman cities there and expelled Christians. Between the late seventh and ninth centuries, the Slavs and Bulgars merged into an independent Slavic-speaking kingdom called Bulgaria, which frequently waged war with Byzantium.

Byzantium also faced threats to its western territories and by the middle of the eighth century lost hold of all its possessions in southern Spain, North Africa, and Italy. At the end of the sixth century as a response to persistent turmoil in the West, the Byzantine emperors had reorganized the region into two new administrative units called *exarchates*. Because of their distance from Constantinople and the weight of the local problems they confronted, the two exarchates remained quasi-independent of the rest of the Byzantine Empire. The Exarchate of Carthage administered southern Spain and North Africa, but it failed to resist the onslaught of enemies. Southern Spain fell to the

■   **Map 7.1   The Byzantine Empire, ca. 600**

By 600 the Byzantine Empire consisted of Anatolia, Greece, part of the Balkans, Syria, Egypt, and some territories in North Africa and Spain. Until the rise of Islam, the Persian Empire remained its greatest enemy.

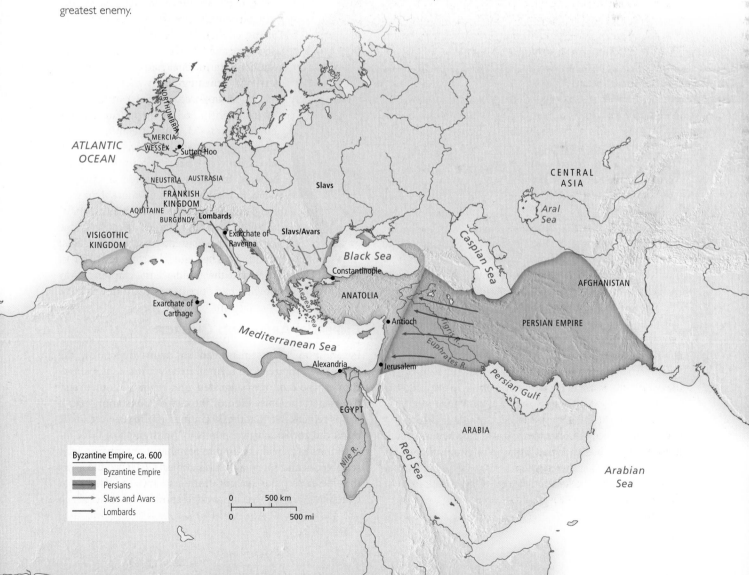

Visigoths in the 630s, and North Africa lasted until 698 when it was lost to Muslim armies. The Exarchate of Ravenna administered the Byzantine possessions in Italy and Sicily, including the city of Rome, where because of his prestige the support of the pope was important for implementing Byzantine policies. But in 751 the Germanic Lombards captured Ravenna, put an end to the exarchate, and eliminated forever the tenuous vestiges of authority the Byzantines had managed to preserve in Italy since the conquests of Justinian.

On the eastern front, Persia continued to threaten Byzantium after Justinian's death. The two powers fought intermittently for the rest of the sixth century. In 602 the struggle entered a new and final phase when the Persian ruler Chosroes II launched a series of devastating attacks against Byzantium. In 614 Chosroes seized Antioch, the richest Roman city in Syria. Then he captured Jerusalem, the holiest Christian city in the Byzantine Empire.

Motivated by a desire to avenge these losses, the Byzantine emperor Heraclius (r. 610–641) devoted his life to crushing the Persians once and for all. This resourceful and tenacious emperor spent most of his reign locked in a life-and-death struggle against Persia. After years of desperate fighting, Heraclius finally defeated Chosroes on Persian territory. Heraclius's victory over Persia, however, exacted a huge toll. It left the Byzantines (and the Persians) too exhausted to resist the sudden onslaught of a new enemy, the Muslim Arab armies.

The military vigor of the Muslim armies derived from the new religion of Islam that appeared in the Arabian peninsula in the seventh century. Islam is discussed in detail later in this chapter, but for the Byzantines the Muslim armies represented a new and what would prove to be a persistent threat. After the 630s, Islamic armies attacked the Byzantine Empire continually from the East, raiding deep into Anatolia (modern Turkey) and sometimes threatening Constantinople itself. The Byzantines were forced to abandon the wealthy province of Syria and lost Egypt. Although an enormous Arab force besieged Constantinople itself between 716 and 718, the strength of Constantinople's walls saved the capital. Unfazed, Arab troops soon resumed their annual raids into Byzantine territory, defeating nearly every Byzantine army that opposed them. From the death of Justinian in 565 to the collapse of the empire in 1453, the Byzantines faced threats from all sides and were frequently at war with neighboring countries and rebellious provinces. They were probably at war with Islamic armies no more than with others, but the Muslims represented a singular threat to Byzantium largely because Arabic armies were so persistently successful against the Byzantines. They quickly conquered all of North Africa and the middle East, chipping away huge parts of what had once been Byzantine territory.

■ **King David Plate**

Nine silver plates made in Constantinople about 630 illustrate scenes from the career of the biblical king David. The largest plate (about 20 inches in diameter) shows David battling the giant Goliath. Though the subject matter is biblical, the style of representing clothing, human bodies, and spatial relationships comes directly from the classical tradition. The artist may have intended to show a connection between the warrior king of the Bible and the emperor Heraclius, who defeated the mighty Persian emperor Chosroes II.

EMPEROR, ARMY, AND CHURCH

In addition to assaults from so many directions, the Byzantine Empire faced turmoil from within. As it lost territories, the economy stagnated, and religious controversy threatened the unity even of the city of Constantinople. It seems remarkable that the Byzantine Empire survived at all, but it did and its survival points to the strength of three institutions that held the empire together: the emperor, who set policies and safeguarded his subjects' welfare; the army that defended the realm's frontiers; and the Orthodox Christian Church, which provided spiritual guidance. Each of these institutions displayed a certain rigidity that meant they adapted slowly to changes, but this weakness was also their strength because Byzantine institutions created stability in a world of turmoil. The Byzantine system also created new more flexible military institutions that made it possible to respond to armed threats on the frontiers without direct authorization from Constantinople. Despite terrible losses, Byzantium survived.

Imperial Administration and Economy

Based in the capital city of Constantinople, the emperor stood at the very center of Byzantine society. His authority, which his people believed had been granted by God, reached to every corner of the empire. This supreme ruler governed with the assistance of a large bureaucracy that he tightly controlled.

Men fortunate enough to obtain a position in the imperial government acquired considerable wealth and influence. For this reason leading provincial families sent their sons to Constantinople in search of positions in the imperial hierarchy. Through this method of recruitment Constantinople remained in close touch with the outlying regions of the empire.

In response to the many external threats, Byzantine society came to be organized for constant preparation for war. Emperors relied on their armies to protect Constantinople, the nerve center of the shrinking Byzantine state, and defend against invaders. By about 650, emperors abandoned the late antique system of provinces and reorganized their forces in Asia Minor into four military districts called themes, each with its own army and administration commanded by a general chosen by the emperor. These military forces remained strong enough to keep the empire from collapsing in spite of devastating losses to Islamic armies throughout the seventh century.

By 750 the themes developed considerable independence from Constantinople and were the basis of further reorganization of the agricultural economy and procedures for recruitment. Soldiers and sailors who were once paid in cash from the emperor's tax revenues now were granted land on which to support themselves. Fighting men had to provide their own weapons from their income as farmers, and the theme system enabled the various parts of the empire to function without direct support from the imperial treasury. Despite the rigid nature of the imperial bureaucracy, the theme system created some measure of defensive flexibility for the empire. While it could no longer launch large-scale offensive conquests, as was possible in the time of Justinian, Byzantium could at least attempt to defend its shrinking borders.

By the end of the seventh century, when the rich provinces of Egypt and Syria and the wealthy cities of Alexandria, Antioch, Jerusalem, and many others had fallen to the Arabs, the Byzantine economy stumbled. Thousands of refugees from lands conquered by Muslims streamed into the empire and strained its dwindling resources. In conquered provinces, Muslim rulers monopolized trade revenues and prevented Byzantine merchants from participating in long-distance commerce. Cut off from foreign markets, Byzantines stopped manufacturing goods for export. As the economy shriveled, the standard of living in most Byzantine cities steeply declined. Until the late tenth century when the economy revived, Byzantium stagnated, but it did not disappear.

The Church and Religious Life

Most Byzantines identified themselves as Orthodox Christians, meaning that like the emperor they accepted the doctrines established by the first seven church councils, especially the Council of Chalcedon in 451 that defined Christ's human and divine natures as being united in one divine "person" without any separation, division, or change. This distinguished Byzantine Christians from other Christian communities that interpreted the nature of Christ differently, as we saw in Chapter 6. After Justinian the widespread acceptance of Chalcedonian Christianity gave Byzantium religious unity.

One of the institutional strengths of the Orthodox Church was that like the empire itself, the clergy had a hierarchical organization. The patriarch, or chief bishop, of Constantinople led the Orthodox Church, administering several thousand clergymen in the capital and directing church affairs throughout the empire. Emperors generally controlled the patriarchs, and often they worked closely together, serving Byzantium's spiritual needs. The patriarch helped impose religious unity throughout Byzantium by controlling the network of bishops based in cities.

During the seventh and eighth centuries, Christian instruction under the supervision of the Church replaced the traditional Roman educational system. By about 600, city leaders had stopped paying schoolmasters to offer traditional instruction because they lacked funds. Learning so declined that by the seventh century most Byzantines could neither read nor write. Pious Christians also developed a deep suspicion of classical learning, with its references to ancient gods and customs frowned on by the Church. Those few who learned how to read did so by studying the Bible, not the classics of Greek antiquity. As a result of the general decline in learning, the Church monopolized intellectual life. Unlike late antiquity when the Church felt threatened by those educated in ancient Greek philosophy, now Christianity monopolized all culture and thought.

Icons and the Iconoclastic Controversy

Despite that monopoly, a divisive controversy erupted within the Church itself in the eighth century. As enemies tore at the borders of the empire, Byzantines wondered why God was punishing them so severely. Their answer was that somehow they were failing God. Convinced that only appeasing God could save them, Emperor Leo III (r. 717–741) took action. His most important move was to challenge the use of icons°, the images of God and saints found everywhere in Byzantine worship.

Byzantine theologians understood icons as vehicles through which the divine presence could make itself accessible to believers. Churchmen cautioned that God and saints do not actually reside within the icons, and so believers should not worship the images themselves. Rather, they should consider icons as doorways to a spiritual world, enabling believers to encounter a holy presence. Thus Byzantines treated icons with great love and respect.

Some Byzantine religious thinkers in the eighth century, however, advised Emperor Leo that icon veneration should be halted because too many people believed icons were divine themselves. They confused the image of the icon with what it represented and worshiped icons just as polytheists had worshiped statues in their temples. Besides following the advice of these theologians, Leo decided to act after a volcanic eruption destroyed the island of Santorini, proving in his mind that God had been angered by icon veneration. Leo forbade the presence and veneration of holy images (except for crucifixes) throughout the empire, but public resistance and even riots forced him to move very carefully. The prohibition and destruction of icons, known as iconoclasm° (image breaking), sparked a bitter controversy that divided Byzantine society until 842.

Leo's iconoclasm backfired because the veneration of icons was such a vital part of popular religious life. He found it difficult to enforce iconoclasm outside Constantinople. Revolts broke out in Greece and southern Italy when imperial messengers arrived with orders to destroy images. The iconoclastic controversy affected international politics as well. Outraged by the Byzantine emperor's prohibition of icons, the Roman pope, the dominant religious and by now political figure in the West, excommunicated Leo. In retaliation Leo deprived the pope of political authority over southern Italy, Sicily, and Illyricum (the Balkan coast of the Adriatic Sea), a political authority the popes claimed they had inherited from long-gone Roman emperors of the West. The Roman popes never forgave the emperor for this slight. This conflict contributed to a growing rift between Greek Orthodox and Latin Christianity.

After years of turmoil, two Byzantine empresses who sympathized with their subjects' religious convictions restored icons to churches. In 787, the empress Irene called a general church council that reversed Leo's ruling. After a brief renewal of iconoclasm, in 843 the empress Theodora introduced a religious ceremony for commemorating images, which Orthodox Christians still celebrate annually.

■ **An Icon That Survived Iconoclasm: St. Peter in the Monastery at Mount Sinai**
This image of St. Peter, painted sometime during the sixth century, is in the Monastery of St. Catherine on Mount Sinai in Egypt. Because Egypt was in Muslim hands when the iconoclastic controversy broke out, this image survived.

Icons remain an integral part of Orthodox worship today. The iconoclastic controversy may have widened the gap between Greek Orthodox and Latin Christianity, but its resolution created even greater religious unity within the Byzantine world. A common religious culture not only unified the Byzantines, but it provided solace and a spiritual connection to Byzantium for the many Christians who found themselves in the former Byzantine territories that had been conquered by Islamic rulers.

■ **Map 7.2 The Expansion of Islam: The Umayyad Caliphate, ca. 750**
By about 750 the Umayyad caliphate had reached its greatest extent. It provided political unity to territories stretching from central Asia to Spain. Islam became the dominant religion in this vast empire.

The New World of Islam

·····················■·····················

The Muslim armies that battered Byzantium created a thriving civilization that transformed the Mediterranean world. Islam originated in the early seventh century among the inhabitants of the Arabian peninsula. Through conquest and expansion, Muslims created a single Islamic Empire stretching from Spain to central Asia by 750 (see Map 7.2).

Before the emergence of Islam, Arabs were mostly a tribal people from the Arabian peninsula and the Middle East who spoke Arabic, a semitic language related to Hebrew. Despite their shared language, Arab communities took different forms and were not unified into a single

state. Those living in the interior of the Arabian peninsula led a nomadic life herding camels. On the edges of the desert they raised goats and sheep. In south Arabia, they farmed, lived in towns, and developed extensive commercial networks. During the late Roman Empire some Arabs had lived within the empire while others traded there, an experience that gave them extensive knowledge of both Roman civilization and Christianity.

Before the rise of Islam in the seventh century, most Arabs worshiped many gods, including natural objects such as the sun and certain rocks or trees. But there were also some Jewish and Christian Arabs whose ideas about monotheism, Heaven and Hell, and the judgment of individuals after death were in circulation and helped open the way to the teachings of a prophet who was thought to speak directly for God.

THE RISE OF ISLAM

Islam is based on the Qur'an and the sayings of the prophet Muhammad (ca. 570–632). Muhammad was born in 570 to the powerful Hashimite clan of the Quraysh tribe in the cosmopolitan and wealthy west Arabian trading city of Mecca. This city was the site of the Kaaba, a sacred stone where polytheist Arabs worshiped various deities. As a young man Muhammad married a widowed businesswoman, Khadija, and worked as a caravan merchant. In this profession he earned a reputation as a skilled arbitrator of disputes, which were common among the feuding tribes of Arabia. At about age 40, Muhammad reported that while he was meditating in solitude, an angel appeared before him, saying, "Muhammad, I am Gabriel and you are the Messenger of God. Recite!" According to Muhammad's account, the angel gave him a message to convey to the people of Mecca. Muhammad's message was a call to the Arabs to worship the one true God (the God of Abraham) and to warn of the fires of Hell if they failed to answer that call. Muhammad continued to report what he considered revelations for the rest of his life. They were written down as the Qur'an (meaning "recitation"), the holy book of Islam. Though Muhammad won some followers among friends and family, the people of Mecca initially did not accept his monotheist message and some were openly hostile to him.

In 622, Muhammad and his followers moved from Mecca to Medina, a city 200 miles to the north. Aware of Muhammad's skill as a mediator, several feuding tribes in Medina had invited him to settle their long-lasting disputes. Muhammad's emigration to Medina, known as the *Hijra,* marks a historical turning point in the development of Islam. For the first time Muhammad and his followers lived as an independent community. Accepted by his followers as the prophet of God, Muhammad strictly regulated the internal affairs of his new community and its relations with outsiders, creating a society that was political as well as religious. At the center of this Islamic community lay the mosque°, the place where his followers gathered to pray and hear Muhammad recite the Qur'an.

Initially, Muhammad and his followers enjoyed good relations with the Jews who controlled the markets in Medina. But as his influence among the Arab tribes grew, he became involved in a series of disputes with the Jewish tribes, who refused to accept him as a prophet. Muhammad expelled some Jewish tribes, massacred the men, and enslaved the women and children of others. With Jewish opposition eliminated and control of Medina secured, Muhammad turned to his old enemies in Mecca and attempted to convince them of his divine mission. After a series of military engagements with the Meccans, he led an army against Mecca itself, which surrendered in 630.

Using a combination of force and negotiation, Muhammad drew many Arab tribes into his new religious community. His authority rested on both his success as a military leader who was successful at raiding caravans and defeating enemy tribes and his reputation as a prophet. By the time of his death in 632 he had unified most of Arabia under Islam. Muhammad created a tightly controlled community that was inspired by his teachings.

Islam as Revealed to Muhammad

Islam teaches that Allah (which means "God" in Arabic) revealed his message to Muhammad, the last in a line of prophets. Such prophets included Abraham, Moses, and David, all pivotal biblical figures in the Jewish tradition who transmitted divine instruction to humanity, and Jesus Christ, whom Muslims accept as a prophet but not the son of God. Muslims claimed Abraham as their ancestor because he was the father of Ishmael, whom they consider the father of the Arab peoples. Thus, Islam evolved out of the same religious tradition as Judaism and Christianity.

Muhammad taught his followers basic principles that eventually came to be called the five Pillars of Islam°. *Islam* means "submission," and by performing these acts of faith Muslims demonstrate submission to the will of God. First, all Muslims must acknowledge that there is only one God and that Muhammad is his prophet. Second, they must state this belief in prayer five times a day. On Fridays, the noon prayers must be recited in the company of other believers. Muslims may say their prayers anywhere. Third, Muslims must fast between sunrise and sunset during Ramadan, the ninth month of the Muslim calendar. Fourth, Muslims must give generous donations of money and food to the needy in their community. Islam expects its followers to be kind to one another, especially to orphans and widows, and to work for the good of the entire Islamic community. Fifth, Muslims must make a pilgrimage to Mecca at least once in their lives if it is possible. As the focus of prayer and pilgrimage, Mecca quickly became the center of the Muslim world. With the spread of Islam to Persia, Asia, and parts of Europe in the seventh century, Muslims from many different lands encountered one another in Mecca, developing a shared Islamic identity.

While the Qur'an contains many examples of proper behavior for the community to follow, Muslims also looked to the prophet Muhammad's example as a guide. Muhammad taught his followers to struggle for the good of the Muslim community. This struggle is called *jihad.* Islam teaches that the duty of *jihad* should be fulfilled by the heart, the tongue, the hand, and the sword. The *jihad* of the heart consists of a spiritual purification by doing battle with the Devil and avoiding temptations to do evil. *Jihad* of the tongue requires believers to propagate the faith; *jihad* of the hand requires them to correct moral wrongs. The fourth way to fulfill one's duty is to employ the sword by waging war against unbelievers and enemies of Islam. Because Jews and Christians also believed in a divine revelation, they were given a special dispensation with regard to *jihad* of the sword. They could either convert to Islam or submit to

■ **The Kaaba in Mecca**

In pre-Islamic times, Arabs worshiped a large black stone at the Kaaba shrine in the center of Mecca. When Muhammad established Islam in Mecca in 629, he rejected the polytheist past and transformed the Kaaba into the holiest place in the Islamic world, revered as the house of God. Muslim teachers interpreted polytheist rituals that continued under Islam, such as walking around the Kaaba seven times, as symbols of the Muslim believer's entry into God's presence. Muslims from all over the world make pilgrimages to the Kaaba. These journeys foster a sense of shared religious identity among them, no matter where their homelands lie.

Islamic rule by paying special taxes. If they rejected both options, they became subject to *jihad* of the sword. Most modern Muslim scholars understand *jihad* as waging war with one's inner self, but some Muslims have revived the concept of *jihad* of the sword in support of military engagements and terrorism.

The Islamic Community After Muhammad

Muhammad had demonstrated a remarkable talent for leadership during his lifetime, but he did not choose anyone to succeed him. His death in 632 caused a profound crisis among his followers. Would the Islamic community stay united under a single new leader or break up into smaller groups? After many deliberations, Muslim leaders chose the prophet's father-in-law, Abu Bakr, to lead them. Abu Bakr (r. 632–634) became the first caliph, or successor to Muhammad. The form of Islamic government that evolved under his leadership is called the caliphate°.

Most Muslims supported Abu Bakr, but some opposed him. One group claimed that Muhammad's son-in-law and cousin, Ali, should have become the first caliph instead. Other Arab tribes rejected not only Abu Bakr's succession, but Islam itself. They rebelled, claiming that their membership in the Islamic community had been valid only when Muhammad was alive. Abu Bakr crushed these forces in a struggle called the Wars of Apostasy (a word meaning renunciation of a previous faith). By the time of his death in 634, Abu Bakr had brought most of Arabia back under his control, but the disputes between his followers and those of Ali led to a permanent split within Islam between the majority Sunni, who followed Abu Bakr, and the minority Shi'ites, who followed Ali.

In the course of the wars among Muslims after the death of Muhammad, Abu Bakr created a highly trained Muslim army eager to spread the faith and gain additional wealth and power. Under the leadership of the second caliph, Umar (r. 634–644), Muslim forces moved north from the Arabian peninsula and invaded rich territories of the Byzantine and Persian Empires. Within just a decade Islamic troops had conquered Egypt, Syria, and all of Persia as far east as India. Meanwhile, Muslim navies seized Cyprus, raided in the eastern Mediterranean, and defeated a large Byzantine fleet. Muslim armies were racing across North Africa without serious opposition when civil war broke out in 655 and temporarily halted their advance.

Two groups struggled for control of the caliphate during this six-year civil war. On one side were Muhammad's son-in-law Ali, who had become caliph in 656, and his supporters, the Shi'ites. On the other side was the wealthy Umayyad family who opposed him. In 661 the Umayyads arranged Ali's assassination and took control of the caliphate, creating a new dynasty that would last until 750. The Umayyads established Damascus in Syria as their new capital city, which shifted Islam's power center away from Mecca.

THE UMAYYAD CALIPHATE

The Umayyad dynasty produced brilliant administrators and generals. At the end of the civil war in 661, these talented leaders consolidated their control of conquered

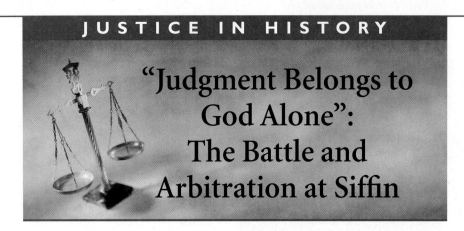

"Judgment Belongs to God Alone": The Battle and Arbitration at Siffin

On a spring day in 657, two Muslim armies confronted each other at Siffin, a village on the Euphrates River in Mesopotamia. The armies were commanded by men who had been long-time rivals, the Caliph Ali (r. 656–661) and Muawiya, the governor of Syria. Their rivalry stemmed from Muawiya's refusal to accept Ali's authority as caliph. The Battle of Siffin became a defining moment in the development of the Islamic state. Basic Islamic ideas about divine judgment were put to the test, leading to passionate debate about how God makes his judgment known to Muslims.

Ali had taken power after the assassination of his predecessor, Caliph Uthman, in 656. The murder went unpunished, but many people considered Ali responsible because when he became caliph he appointed officials known to have taken part in the murder and because he had never disavowed the crime. Uthman belonged to the influential Umayyad clan, and his supporters and family felt an obligation to avenge their kinsman's death. Chief among Ali's opponents was Muawiya, a leading member of the Umayyad clan. Muawiya maintained a strong army and powerful support in Syria.

The immediate provocation of the confrontation between Muawiya and Ali was Uthman's murder, but the men's quarrel also stemmed from tensions about status and membership in the Muslim community. The earliest converts to Islam and their descendants believed that their association with Muhammad entitled them to greater status than the many new non-Arab converts to the religion, most of whom supported Ali. Resenting Ali's popularity among the newer members of the Islamic community, the early converts supported Muawiya. Further support for Muawiya came from many tribal leaders who opposed the caliph's growing authority.

The new converts to Islam also had complaints. In their view, the earliest Muslims, including the Umayyad clan, unfairly enjoyed a privileged position in the Islamic community even though all Muslims were supposed to be treated equally.

When Ali and Muawiya confronted each other at Siffin, they hesitated to fight because many of their soldiers felt strongly that Muslims should not shed the blood of other Muslims. As one of Ali's followers said,

> It is one of the worst wrongs and most terrible trials that we should be sent against our own people and they against us. . . . Yet, if we do not assist our community and act faithfully toward our leader, we deny our faith, and if we do that, we abandon our honor and extinguish our fire.[1]

So for three months, the armies engaged in only occasional skirmishes.

Finally, in July 657, real fighting broke out. Ali encouraged his men with these words: "Be steadfast! May God's spirit descend on you, and may God make you firm with conviction so that he who is put to flight knows that he displeases his God . . . "

The furious battle came to a sudden halt in July when Muawiya's soldiers held up pages of the Qur'an on the ends of their spears and appealed for arbitration. When Ali's men saw this symbolic gesture, they stopped fighting and demanded that their leader settle his differences with Muawiya peacefully through arbitration.

Mediation of conflicts by third-party arbitrators frequently occurred among Arab tribes. Muhammad himself had earned renown as a skilled mediator before Islam was revealed to him. However, the arbitration between Ali and Muawiya failed to resolve the conflict. The two men and their armies separated without having reached an agreement. Ali continued to rule as caliph, but his authority declined rapidly because many Arabs interpreted his willingness to go to arbitration as a sign of weakness. In 661 Ali was assassinated.

In contrast, Muawiya's power grew after the Battle of Siffin. He openly claimed the caliphate for himself and began making deals with the tribal leaders for their support in order to form his own coalition. After Ali's assassination, Muawiya became caliph.

The fact that the arbitration at Siffin occurred at all had long-lasting consequences. Most important, a small but influential Muslim faction emerged when the two leaders first confronted one another. They objected to Ali's initial agreement to arbitration, arguing that God was the only true arbitrator. They believed that Ali should pull out of the arbitration and submit to God's judgment, which they believed could be known only through battle. These Muslims wanted to fight Muawiya in order to find out what God wanted. This splinter group became known as the Kharijites or "seceders." The Kharijites expressed their view in the phrase, "Judgment belongs to God alone."

The Kharijites went one step further in their beliefs. They declared not only that Ali was wrong to accept human arbitration, but that he and his supporters should no longer be considered Muslims. In their view, Ali and his supporters had committed an unpardonable grave sin by accepting arbitration. The Kharijites claimed that they were the only true Muslims. Small in numbers, they established several independent communities in the Islamic Empire and turned their

back on Islamic society. They lived as bandits until the tenth century, when they disappeared from the historical record.

Other Muslims who disagreed with the Kharijites proclaimed that neither the Kharijites nor any other human being could know whether sinners were still Muslims in the eyes of God. In their opinion, believers would discover God's judgment on these matters only at the End of Days, when God will judge all humanity. ◼

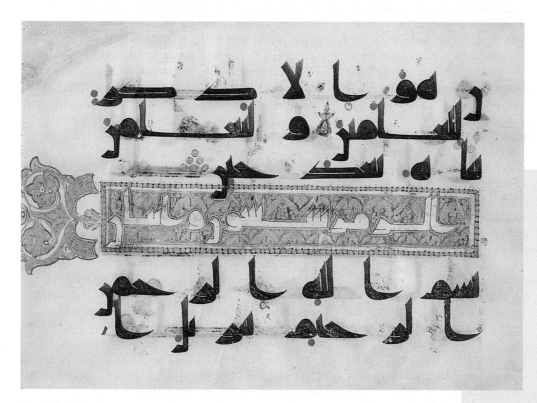

◼ The Qur'an

Muslim artists devised elaborate Arabic scripts to enhance the beauty of the Qur'an, the holiest text of their faith. This page of the Qur'an, dating to the Umayyad caliphate, is written in the elegant and highly decorative Kufic script.

Questions of Justice

1. During this early period of the Islamic Empire, how did different Arab beliefs about how God makes his judgment known influence the sense of the proper forms of human justice?

Taking It Further

Watt, W. M. *The Formative Period of Islamic Thought.* 1973. This account discusses the formation of sects and political groups in early Islamic history.

territories and established peaceful conditions in the empire. Then they resumed wars of conquest to spread the Islamic state's power and to gain wealth.

Conquests

The Umayyads viewed the world as consisting of two parts: the "House of Islam," which contained the territories under their political control, and the "House of War," which included all non-Muslim lands, which they hoped to conquer. By the early 700s, Muslim armies had rolled west across North Africa as far as the Atlantic Ocean, invaded much of Spain, and overthrown the Visigothic kingdom in just one battle. From Spain they attacked France, but in 732, Charles Martel "the Hammer," leading a Frankish army, stopped their advance into Europe at the Battle of Poitiers.

Umayyad caliphs attempted to conquer the Christian kingdom of Nubia south of Egypt to obtain its gold and spread Islam. The Nubians successfully repelled the Muslim invaders. While struggling with the Nubians, Umayyad armies continued to strike at the Byzantine Empire, but after the last massive land and sea attacks failed in 717, they gave up attempts at conquest and settled for annual raids to gain plunder.

Umayyad armies moved eastward with equal speed and success. They reached the territories of modern Pakistan and India and even penetrated central Asia, where they captured the caravan city of Samarkand. During the Umayyad caliphate, this city served as a commercial hub on the trade route to China. In 751, just after the death of the last Umayyad caliph, Muslim armies defeated Chinese troops of the expansionist Chinese Tang dynasty at the Battle of Talas in central Asia. Despite their victory, the Muslims decided to halt their expansion and did not advance farther into Chinese-controlled areas in central Asia.

Like the Battle of Poitiers, which marked the limit of the Umayyads' expansion into western Europe, the Battle of Talas marked the limit of Muslim military expansion into central Asia. For the next four centuries, these borders would define the Islamic world.

Governing the Islamic Empire

Drawing heavily on the administrative systems of the Byzantine and Persian provinces they had conquered, the Umayyads developed a highly centralized and authoritarian regime that changed the political character of the Muslim community. The first Umayyad caliph, Muawiya (r. 661–680), established a hereditary monarchy to ensure orderly succession of power. This was a major change in the caliphate. Unlike the first four caliphs, who ruled by virtue of their prestige (as did Arab tribal chiefs) and more importantly by the consent of the community, the Umayyads made the caliphate a dictatorial institution with no community consent.

To control their vast empire, Umayyad rulers developed a new administrative system. They designed new provinces that replaced old Roman and Persian administrative units and developed a professional bureaucracy based in the capital of Damascus to meet their expanding financial needs and to ensure that the taxes collected in the provinces came to the central treasury.

To unify their empire, the Umayyads made Arabic the official language of their empire. Arabic gradually replaced the languages of the conquered peoples. Only in Iran did Persian survive as a widely spoken language, and even there Arabic served as the language of government. In the Umayyad caliphate, the Arabic language functioned as Latin had done in the early Roman Empire: It provided a common language for diverse subject peoples. By 800 Arabic had become the essential language of administration and international commerce in lands from Morocco to central Asia.

Arab armies had conquered enormous territories but were only a small minority among the huge non-Muslim populations whose great wealth and manpower resources they controlled. The Umayyad caliphs vastly expanded the earlier Muslim policy of establishing garrison cities in conquered lands to hold down the more numerous local populations. Arab settlers from the Arabian peninsula migrated to newly conquered lands in great numbers. They established themselves first in the garrison towns where government officials were based, and then they became a significant presence in major cities, such as Alexandria, Jerusalem, and Antioch. Arabs also founded many new cities such as Fustat, which later became Cairo, Egypt.

Revenues once earmarked for gymnasiums and other public buildings during the Roman Empire now went to local mosques. These centers of Islamic urban culture replaced the forums and agoras of the Roman and Greek world as the chief public space for men. Mosque schools provided education for boys. Muslims gathered at mosques for religious worship and public festivals. In their capacity as administrative centers, mosques provided courtrooms, assembly halls, and treasuries for the community.

Islam sharply defined the differences between Muslims and non-Muslims. The conquerors understood themselves as a community of faith. Only individuals who converted to Islam could gain full participation in the Islamic community. Their ethnicity did not matter. Therefore Muslims defined their new subjects by their religion, something Egyptians, Assyrians, Persians, Greeks, and Romans before Constantine had never done. The Qur'an (2:256) states that "there is no compulsion in religion," meaning that monotheists (Jews, Christian, and Zoroastrians) cannot be forced to convert to Islam. Islamic law called them "Peoples of the Book" because each of these religious communities had a sacred book. They had lower status than Muslims, and they had to pay a special tax for non-Muslims. Jewish communities in particular flourished throughout Umayyad lands, notably in Spain and Mesopotamia. Jews found their subordinate but protected status under Islam preferable to

THE PACT OF UMAR: ISLAM ENCOUNTERS THE GREAT FAITHS OF THE ANCIENT MIDDLE EAST

....

Islam recognized Christians, Jews, and Zoroastrians as "Peoples of the Book" because they were monotheists and because their religions were based on holy texts. The Pact of Umar, issued by the Caliph Umar I (r. 634–644), introduced the idea that Muslim authorities would protect them, though with restrictions. This letter was sent by the Christians of Syria to Umar I, spelling out the restrictions they accepted.

When Umar . . . may God be pleased with him, accorded a peace to the Christians in Syria, we wrote to him as follows:

In the name of God, the Merciful and Compassionate.

This is a letter to the servant of God Umar, Commander of the Faithful, from the Christians of such-and-such a city. When you came against us, we asked you for safe-conduct for ourselves, our descendants, our property, and the people of our community, and we undertook the following obligations toward you:

We shall not build, in our cities or in their neighborhood, new monasteries, churches, convents, or monks' cells, nor shall we repair, by day or night, such of them as fall in ruins or are situated in the quarters of the Muslims.

We shall not give shelter in our churches or in our dwellings to any spy, nor hide him from the Muslims.

We shall not teach the Qur'an to our children.

We shall not manifest our religion publicly nor convert anyone to it.

We shall not prevent any of our kin from entering Islam if they wish it.

We shall show respect toward the Muslims, and we shall rise from our seats when they wish to sit.

We shall not seek to resemble the Muslims by imitating any of their garments, the headgear, the turban, footwear, or the parting of the hair.

We shall not mount our saddles, nor shall we gird swords nor bear any kind of arms nor carry them on our persons.

We shall not engrave Arabic inscriptions on our seals.

We shall not sell fermented drinks.

We shall not display our crosses or our books in the roads or markets of the Muslims. We shall only use clappers in our churches very softly. We shall not raise our voices in our church services or in the presence of Muslims, nor shall we raise our voices when following our dead (in funeral processions). We shall not show lights on any of the roads of the Muslims or in their markets. We shall not bury our dead near the Muslims.

We shall not take slaves who have been allotted to the Muslims.

We shall not build houses overtopping the houses of the Muslims.

We accept these conditions for ourselves and for the people of our community, and in return we receive safe-conduct.

If we in any way violate these undertakings for which we ourselves stand surety, we forfeit our covenant, and we become liable to the penalties for contumacy [resistance to authority] and sedition.

Source: From *Islam: From the Prophet Muhammad to the Capture of Constantinople, Volume 2: Religion and Society,* edited by Bernard Lewis, translated by Bernard Lewis, copyright © 1987 by Bernard Lewis. Used by permission of Oxford University Press, Inc.

---

the open persecution they suffered in many Christian kingdoms. Muslims viewed polytheists differently. Polytheists had the choice of conversion to the Muslim faith or death.

Commercial Encounters

The economic system of the Muslim world changed under Umayyad rule. Long-distance overland trade rapidly expanded due to the peaceful conditions established by the Umayyads. Although Muslim merchants could travel safely from Morocco to central Asia and earn great sums, such long-distance expeditions were expensive. The Qur'an approves of mercantile trading, and Islamic law permitted letters of credit, loans, and other financial instruments that made commerce over huge distances possible long before they were known in Christian Europe. Umayyad rulers further stimulated international commerce by creating new silver and gold coins that Muslim merchants, as well as businessmen as far away as western Europe, Scandinavia, and Russia, used to pay for goods.

Camels played a significant role in the expanding Islamic economy because they made long-distance trade extremely profitable. Merchants had used domesticated camels throughout the Arabian peninsula for many centuries, but the caliphate's huge size and peaceful conditions brought new opportunities for long-distance camel-borne trade. Camels can carry heavy cargoes through harsh terrain for long periods, and they require little water. Because these "ships of the desert" do not need paved roads, caravan routes did not have to follow Roman road systems. New trade routes suited for camels developed from Morocco to central Asia. Camel-based commerce proved so successful that between 700 and 1500, paved roads, as well as the carts and wagons that traveled on them, nearly disappeared. Furthermore, because of long-distance camel caravans, the

Mediterranean Sea, the great superhighway of the Roman Empire, lost its primary place in international trade. The revenues earned from the camel caravans helped make the Umayyad caliphate extremely rich.

Arab merchants stretched their commercial networks deep into Asia and Africa. They sailed past Zanzibar and India to Canton in southern China, following sea routes established by Persian navigators. Arab traders also sailed down the coast of East Africa to obtain slaves and natural resources brought from the interior. Muslim cities marketed a remarkable variety of exotic luxuries from panther skins from India to paper and silk from China.

Throughout the formative period of Islam and the Umayyad caliphate, Muslims took firm hold of territories stretching from North Africa to central Asia, creating a single political realm there for the first time in history. The inhabitants of the Arabian peninsula, with their trade connections to Asia and Africa, joined the peoples of the Middle East and the Mediterranean in an intricate system of commerce and government.

The Birth of Latin Christendom

By 750, several new kingdoms had emerged in the lands that once constituted the western part of the Roman Empire. Various Anglo-Saxon kings controlled most of England. The Visigoths ruled in Spain; the Franks in modern-day France, Germany, and the Netherlands; and the Lombards in Italy. These territories were not politically united as they had been under the Roman Empire, but they shared enough in common that historians refer to these kingdoms collectively as Latin Christendom.

GERMANIC KINGDOMS ON ROMAN FOUNDATIONS

Historians describe these new kingdoms of Christendom as Germanic because the peoples who established them were the descendants of Germanic tribes who had migrated into the western Roman Empire during its final centuries. Although most of these kingdoms borrowed from Roman law while establishing government institutions, they maintained their own cultural identity and relied on their own methods of rule. Thus, they were able to unify the kingdoms in three ways. First, in the Germanic kingdoms personal loyalty rather than legal rights unified society. Kinship obligations to a particular clan of blood relatives, rather than citizenship as in the Roman Empire, defined a person's place in society and his or her relationship to rulers. A sec-

ond unifying force was Latin Christianity, or Catholicism, which became the dominant religion in the kingdoms. The common faith linked rulers with their subjects. A third unifying force was Latin, which served as the language of worship, learning, and diplomacy in these kingdoms.

From Tribes into Kingdoms

By the time the Roman Empire collapsed in the West during the fifth century, numerous Germanic tribes had settled in the lands of the former empire. These tribes became the nucleus for new kingdoms as Germanic chiefs transformed themselves into kings. Roman civilization had suffered more completely in Britain during the fifth century than it did on the European continent, largely because of Britain's great distance from Rome and the small number of Romans who had settled there. As seen in Chapter 6, about 400, the Roman economic and administrative infrastructure of Britain fell apart, and the last Roman legions left the island to fight on the continent. Raiders from the coast of the North Sea called Angles and Saxons (historians refer to them as Anglo-Saxons) took advantage of Britain's weakened defenses and launched invasions.

Because the small bands of Anglo-Saxon settlers fought as often among themselves as they did with the Roman Britons, the island remained fragmented politically during the first few centuries of the invaders' rule. But by 750, three warring kingdoms managed to seize enough land to coalesce and dominate Britain: Mercia, Wessex, and Northumbria.

Neither Roman legal traditions nor the Latin language survived as strongly in Britain as on the continent, but both were reintroduced by Christian missionaries. Although Roman law influenced the Anglo-Saxons, Latin remained a minority language known only by churchmen. We can see evidence of this in the English language, which derives primarily from the Germanic languages spoken by the Anglo-Saxon settlers of Britain. In contrast, the Romance (or Roman-based) languages of French, Spanish, and Italian developed from Latin spoken in Rome's former provinces on the Continent, where Roman civilization was more deeply rooted.

The largest and most powerful kingdom on the continent of western Europe became that of the Franks, which evolved out of the encounter between Roman and Frankish cultures. In the course of the fifth century, as Roman imperial control of western Europe disintegrated, Frankish power grew. One group among the Franks, called Salians, gradually gained preeminence among the Frankish people. The Salians' leading family were the Merovingians. A crafty Merovingian war chief named Childeric ruled a band of Salian Franks from about 460 until his death in about 481 and laid the foundations for the Merovingian kingdom. His energetic and ruthless son Clovis (r. 481–511) made the Franks the leading power in the former Roman province of northern Gaul, which became the base of power for the Frankish kingdom. He also murdered many

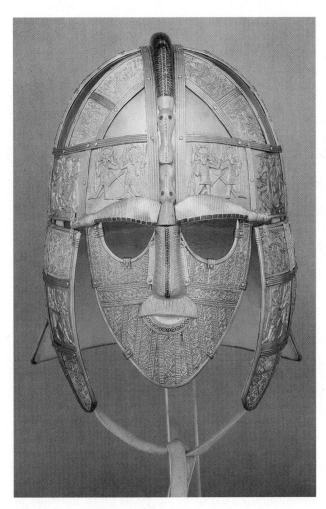

■ **Sutton Hoo: An Anglo-Saxon Proclaims His Power**

Dating from around 625, this magnificent iron helmet with face mask and decorations in gold, silver, and precious stones was found in a ship under a massive mound at Sutton Hoo in eastern Britain. The helmet is based on Roman ceremonial helmets of the late empire, but is in keeping with the armor of Anglo-Saxon warrior kings. An extremely rich array of military equipment, jewelry, and coins were also found in the mound. Although some scholars have speculated that the mound was the burial site of an Anglo-Saxon king, in fact there is no evidence that anyone was buried in the ship or that it belonged to a king.

of his relatives and other Frankish chieftains whom he considered rivals.

Clovis's wife, Clotild, followed Latin or Catholic Christianity, the religion accepted by most of the inhabitants of the former Roman Empire in western Europe. Historians refer to this version of Christianity as Latin Christianity because its followers used a Latin Bible and performed church services in Latin. Catholic Christianity, like the Greek-based Orthodox Christianity in the Byzantine Empire, teaches the full equality of the Father,

the Son, and the Holy Spirit in the Trinity. In contrast to Catholic Christianity was Arian Christianity. Arians believed that Christ was divine, but inferior to God the Father in rank, authority, and glory.

The theological distinction between Catholic and Arian Christians in western Europe was a crucial political issue that divided the Catholic subjects from their Germanic rulers who were usually Arians. Around 500, perhaps influenced by his wife's beliefs, the polytheist Clovis converted to Catholic Christianity rather than the Arian Christianity favored by other Germanic kings. About 3,000 warriors, the core of his army, joined their king in this change to the new faith. Clovis had practical reasons to convert as well. He intended to attack the Visigothic kingdom in southern Gaul. The Visigoths followed Arian Christianity, but their subjects, the Roman inhabitants of the region, followed Catholic Christianity. By converting to Catholicism, Clovis won the support of the Visigoths' subjects. With their help Clovis and his Frankish army crushed the Visigothic king Alaric II, who died at the battle of Vouillé in the summer of 507. Clovis now controlled almost all of Gaul as far as Spain. He and his immediate successors also conquered other Germanic tribes, including those in Switzerland, southwest Germany, Burgundy, and Provence.

Despite these successes, the Merovingian dynasty gradually grew weak as a result of conflicts among kings, their quarrelsome sons, and independent-minded aristocrats. As a result of these squabbles, Clovis's kingdom split into four separate realms, which were repeatedly reunified and split again. Merovingian kings still ruled in these kingdoms, but they had become so ineffectual that real power passed to the official in charge of the royal household called the "Mayor of the Palace." One of these mayors, Charles Martel "the Hammer" (r. 714–741), established his personal power by regaining control over regions that had slipped away from Merovingian rule and by defeating an invading Muslim army at Poitiers in 732. Martel's son, Pepin the Short (r. 741–768), dethroned the last of the Merovingian monarchs and in 751 made himself king of the Franks. As we will see in Chapter 8, the new royal house established by Charles Martel came to be called the Carolingian dynasty and spread Frankish dominion over much of western Europe.

In contrast to the Frankish kings who after Clovis accepted Catholic Christianity, during the sixth century the Visigothic kings adhered to Arian Christianity. Controlling southern Gaul and most of Spain, these kings attempted to convert the indigenous population to Arianism. Because most of the population in southern Gaul accepted the Roman Church, the Arianism of the Visigothic kings created hostility among the population. When the Frankish king Clovis invaded southern Gaul in 507, many Catholics welcomed him and provided the Franks with military assistance. Defeated, the Visigothic kings retreated to Spain, where they concentrated on unifying the people through the spread of Arianism and the acceptance of Roman law, which influenced the Visigothic law codes. However, in 711 invading armies of Muslims from North Africa vanquished the last Visigothic king. As a result, most of Spain, except for a small Christian enclave in the north, became part of the Umayyad caliphate.

Just as the Anglo-Saxons dominated Britain, the Franks northern Gaul, and the Visigoths Spain, between 568 and 774, a Germanic tribe known as the Lombards controlled most of northern and central Italy. As we have seen, Justinian's wars in Italy and a devastating plague drained the Byzantine Empire's strength. Without imperial troops to defend Italy, the peninsula became vulnerable to invasion. The Romans living in Italy put up a feeble resistance to the invading Lombards. Within three years the Lombards controlled all of northern Italy, Tuscany, and parts of southern Italy in the region of Spoleto, near Naples. By 700, the Lombard kings had asserted their authority by developing a royal bureaucracy of judges and legal officials, compensating somewhat for the weaknesses of the Lombard system evident in the initial conquest, which had granted most authority to local officials, known as dukes. But like the Visigoths in Spain they too were weakened by internal political disputes. In 774 the Frankish king Charlemagne crushed the Lombard kingdom.

The Growth of the Papacy

The Byzantine emperors maintained a tenuous hold on the city of Rome and its surrounding lands during the violent sixth century. Strapped for cash and troops, however, distant Byzantine rulers proved unequal to the task of defending the city from internal or external threats. In the resulting power vacuum, the popes stepped in to manage local affairs and became, in effect, princes who ruled over a significant part of Italy.

Gregory the Great (r. 590–604) stands out as the most powerful of these popes. Gregory pleaded in vain for military assistance from Byzantium, but finally in desperation turned to the Frankish kingdoms in western Europe for protection. Through clever diplomacy, Gregory successfully cultivated the goodwill of the Christian communities of western Europe by offering religious sanction to the authority of friendly kings. He encouraged Christian missionaries to spread the faith in England and Germany. Gregory had set the stage for a dramatic increase in papal power, both because he was politically pragmatic and because he was a model of religious integrity.

DIFFERENT KINGDOMS, SHARED TRADITIONS

With the exception of England, where Anglo-Saxon invaders drove out the Roman population, the leaders of the new Germanic kingdoms faced a common problem: How should the Germanic minority govern subject peoples who vastly outnumbered them? These rulers found a solution to this problem by blending Roman and Germanic traditions. For example, the kings served as administrators of the civil order in the style of the Roman emperor, issuing laws and managing a bureaucracy. They also served as war leaders in the Germanic tradition, leading their men into battle in search of glory and loot. As the Germanic kings defined new roles for themselves, they discovered that Christianity could bind all their subjects together into one community of believers. The merging of Roman and Germanic traditions could also be traced in the law, which eventually erased the distinctions between Romans and Germans, and in the ability of women to own property, a right far more common among the Romans than the Germans.

Roman and Germanic Legacies

In imitation of Roman practice, the monarchs of Latin Christendom designated themselves the source of all law and believed that they ruled with God's approval. Kings controlled all appointments to civil, military, and religious office. Accompanied by troops and administrative assistants, they also traveled throughout their lands to dispense justice, collect taxes, and enforce royal authority. In particular, they relied on literate Roman aristocrats and Christian bishops for administration on the local level. These aristocratic and ecclesiastical officials were based in cities and administered law courts, but as the populations in the cities declined and most cities disappeared they became far less influential than they had been in the late centuries of the Roman Empire.

At the same time the kingdoms of Latin Christendom developed from Germanic war bands led by chieftains. By rewarding warriors with land and loot taken in war, as well as with revenues skimmed from subject peoples, chieftains created political communities of loyal men and their families, called clans or kin groups°. Though these followers sometimes came from diverse backgrounds, they all owed military service to the clan chiefs. Because leadership in Germanic society was hereditary, networks of loyalty and kinship expanded through the generations, creating ethnic groups, such as Franks and Lombards, who were led by a common king.

The new Latin Christian kingdoms had highly hierarchical societies geared for warfare. The clan consisted of all the households and blood relations loyal to the clan chief, and a warrior who protected them and spoke on their behalf before the king on matters of justice. Clan chieftains in turn swore oaths of loyalty to their king and agreed to fight for him in wars against other kingdoms. The clan leaders formed a new aristocracy among the Germanic peoples. The new Germanic aristocrats intermarried with the preexisting Roman elites of wealthy landholders, thus maintaining control of most of the land. These people stood at the very top of the social order, winning the loyalty of their followers by providing gifts and parcels of land. Under the weight of this new upper class, the majority of the population, the ordinary farmers and artisans, slipped into a deepening dependence on these nobles.

Though this social hierarchy showed some similarities to societies in earlier Roman times, the new kingdoms' social groups were defined by law in a fundamentally different way. Unlike Roman law, which defined people by citizenship rights and obligations, the laws of the new kingdoms defined people by their *wergild*°. A Germanic concept, *wergild* referred to what an individual was worth in case he or she suffered some grievance at the hands of another. If someone injured or murdered someone else, *wergild* was the amount of compensation in gold that the wrongdoer's family had to pay to the victim's family. If proper *wergild* was not paid, the injured party's kin group felt obligated to gain vengeance for their loss, which frequently led to vicious feuding.

Unity Through Law

Within the kingdoms of Latin Christendom, rulers achieved unity by merging Germanic and Roman legal principles. Germanic law differed from Roman law on issues of family and property. Clovis's *Law Code* or *Salic Law,* published between 508 and 511, allowed Romans who were his subjects to switch to Frankish law. Eventually the Frankish king's policies eroded distinctions among Romans, Franks, and other ethnic groups within his realm. By 750, most Romans had chosen to abandon their legal identity as Romans and live according to Frankish law, and the distinction between Roman and Frank lost all meaning. A similar process occurred in other Germanic kingdoms.

The merging of Roman and Germanic law prompted Germanic rulers to reconsider the question of a woman's right to inherit land. In the Roman Empire, women had inherited land without difficulty. Indeed, perhaps as much as 25 percent of the land in the entire realm had been owned by women. In many Germanic societies, however, men could inherit land and property far more easily than women. Attitudes about female inheritance began to shift when the Germanic settlers established their homes in previously Roman provinces and began to marry Roman women who owned property. Germanic rulers adopted the custom of female inheritance because it enabled the new settlers to keep the property that their Roman wives had inherited and brought to the marriage. Despite some limitations, the new laws transformed women's lives. A woman who received an inheritance of land could live more independently, support herself if her husband died, and have a say in the community's decisions.

THE SPREAD OF LATIN CHRISTIANITY IN THE NEW KINGDOMS OF WESTERN EUROPE

As Latin Christianity slowly spread through the new kingdoms, churchmen sought to quicken the pace. Following the biblical command to evangelize, they believed that they had a moral responsibility to convert all the people of the world to their faith. They sent out missionaries to explain the religion to nonbelievers and challenge the worship of polytheist gods. Their hard work paid off. Although pockets of paganism survived for several more centuries, by 750 most of those living in the new kingdoms had become Christians.

Converting the Irish and Anglo-Saxons

Though the Romans had conquered most of Britain during the imperial period, they never attempted to bring Ireland into their empire. Thus the island off Britain's west coast had had only minimal contact with early Christianity. Little is known for certain of how Christianity came to Ireland. There were probably missionaries who traveled with traders from the Roman Empire, but the earliest firm date is 431, when Palladius was supposedly sent to administer to those in Ireland who were already Christians. Subsequent missionary history in Ireland is dominated by the figure of St. Patrick (d. ca. 492 or 493), whose later biographers improbably gave him credit for converting all the Irish to Christianity. A ninth-century record describes his capture from a Roman villa in Britain by Irish raiders, who sold him into slavery in Ireland. Patrick learned Irish during his years in captivity. He managed to escape to Britain, where he was ordained into the priesthood and sent back to Ireland as a missionary. A great deal of confusion exists regarding Patrick's life, and some scholars argue that tradition merged the experiences of the two missionaries, Palladius and Patrick. However, by the end of the fifth century Christianity had a firm foothold in Ireland.

But Ireland was still a rural place without cities to house bishops or schools to teach the Latin necessary to read the Bible. Irish churchmen found solutions to these problems in monasteries, places where priests could receive training and men and women from the surrounding communities could learn to read Latin and absorb the basics of Christian education. By 750, the Irish scholars produced by these monasteries gained a high reputation for their learning in their own lands as well as across western Europe.

Irish monasteries sent out dozens of missionaries, who in turn founded new monasteries in England, France, and Germany. Columba (521–597), for instance, founded several new monasteries in Ireland as well as one on the island of Iona, off Scotland's western coast. From this thriving community missionaries began to bring Christianity to the peoples of Scotland. The offshoot monastery of Lindisfarne in northern England also became a dynamic center of learning and missionary activity. During the seventh century, missionaries based there carried Christianity to many other parts of England. They also began converting the people of Frisia on the North Sea, in the area of the modern Netherlands.

Besides the Irish monks who went to Anglo-Saxon England, Pope Gregory the Great (r. 590–604) and his

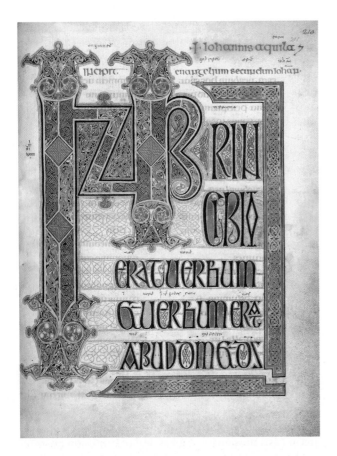

Eadfrith, a monk and later bishop of the Lindisfarne monastery in England, completed the writing and illustration of this Gospel book by 698 to honor a saint whose relics had come to the altar that year. A monk wrote an Anglo-Saxon translation of the book between the lines of Latin sometime during the tenth century. The artist painted soft, bright colors into elaborate interconnected designs that characterize Celtic art, showing continuity of Celtic artistic traditions through the Roman and early medieval periods. The page shown here is the first page of the Gospel of John and was the most complicated of Eadfrith's designs.

successors sent other missionary monks from Rome. Through missionary efforts Gregory hoped to save souls and in so doing forged a Christian community not just in England but throughout Europe. Gregory understood that the first step in creating that new community was to convert as many people as possible to the faith; deep learning about the religion could come later. To that end he instructed missionaries to permit local variations in worship and to accommodate harmless vestiges of pre-Christian worship practices. "Don't tear down their temples," Gregory advised; "put a cross on the roofs!"

Following Gregory's pragmatic suggestion, missionaries in England accepted certain Anglo-Saxon calendar conventions that stemmed from polytheist worship. For example, in the Anglo-Saxon calendar, the weekdays took their names from old gods: Tuesday derived from Tiw, a war god; Wednesday from Woden, king of the gods; Thursday from Thor, god of thunder; and Friday from Freya, goddess of agriculture. Anglo-Saxon deities eventually found their way into the Christian calendar as well. Eostre, for example, a goddess whose festival came in April, gave her name to the Christian holiday Easter.

Monastic Intellectual Life

The missionaries from Rome were members of the vigorous monastic movement initiated by Benedict of Nursia

(ca. 480–547) from his monastery at Monte Cassino in Italy (see Chapter 6). So that their contemplations might not depart from the path of truth, Benedict had encouraged monks to seek guidance in the Bible, in the writings of the renowned theologians, and in works of spiritual edification. Thus, monks had to be literate in Latin. They needed training in the Latin classics, which required books.

Medieval monasteries set aside at least two rooms—the scriptorium° and the library—to meet the growing demand for books. In the scriptorium, scribes laboriously copied Latin and Greek manuscripts as an act of religious devotion. Monks preferred to read Christian texts with a spiritual message, so these books were the most frequently copied. In many monasteries, however, monks preserved non-Christian texts. By doing so, they kept knowledge of Latin and classical learning alive. Indeed, many of the surviving works by authors of the Classical Age were copied and passed on by monks in the sixth and seventh centuries.

Monks did far more than merely copy ancient texts, however. Some wrote original books of their own. At the English monastery at Jarrow, for example, Bede (d. 735) became the most distinguished scholar in eighth-century Europe. He wrote many books, including the *History of the English Church and People*. This work provides an invaluable source of information about the early Anglo-Saxon kingdoms.

Monks shared their expanding knowledge with Christians outside the monastery walls. They established schools at monasteries where boys (and in some places girls) could learn to read and write. Outside Italy where some public schools survived, most of the very few literate people who lived between 550 and 750 gained their education at monastery schools. The men trained in these schools played an important role in society as officials and bureaucrats. Their skills in reading and writing were necessary for keeping records and writing business and diplomatic letters.

Jews in a Christian World

For Jews during this era, quality of life varied in the different western European kingdoms. Jews continued to work in every profession, own land, serve in the army, and engage in trade. The vast majority of monarchs protected the Jewish minorities living in their kingdoms. Thus many Jews prospered in the Frankish, Visigothic, and Lombard realms (no Jews lived in England during this period). But Christian churchmen still blamed Jews collectively for Jesus' death and especially feared that Christians might be tempted to convert to Judaism. Some bishops advocated persecuting Jews, but only a few rulers were willing to follow their advice.

Leading churchmen in the western kingdoms also developed theological reasons for wanting Jews to convert to Christianity. Pope Gregory urged conversion because he believed that Christ would return to Earth only when Jews embraced Christianity. Nevertheless, Gregory advocated the use of persuasion and kindness to encourage conversion, rather than force or terror. On numerous occasions he intervened to stop Christians from committing violence against Jews. Other Christian writers, such as the Isidore of Seville (in Spain), further developed the idea that Jews had a place in Christian society because of their role in bringing about Christ's return and then the Day of Judgment. Highly ambivalent, Christians both persecuted and protected Jews.

CHRONOLOGY

481–511	Clovis rules kingdom of Franks
565	Death of Justinian
568–774	Lombards control northern and central Italy
CA. 570	Muhammad born in Mecca
622	Muhammad flees to Medina (the Hijra)
661–750	Umayyad dynasty rules Muslim empire from Damascus
698	Muslim armies take Byzantine Exarchate of Carthage in North Africa
711	Muslim armies defeat last Visigoth king in Spain
732	Charles Martel defeats Muslim forces at Poitiers in France
751	Lombards take Exarchate of Ravenna in Italy; Abbasid dynasty begins; Carolingian dynasty begins in France

CONCLUSION

Three Cultural Realms

The death of the Byzantine emperor Justinian I in 565 marked the last time the territory spanning from Spain to Carthage to Constantinople would be united under one imperial ruler. The Persian Empire still menaced Byzantium's eastern frontier, and except for Italy and some coastal areas of Spain, western Europe was now ruled by Germanic kings. During the next two centuries western Europe, the Mediterranean world, and the Middle East as far as India and central Asia were utterly reconfigured politically and culturally. By about 750, three new realms had come into sharp focus: the Christian Byzantine Empire based at Constantinople; the vast Umayyad caliphate created by Muhammad's Islamic followers; and Latin Christendom in western Europe, which was fragmented politically but united by Christianity. Each of these regions was constituted as a community of religious faith and had, at best, a limited toleration of other faiths. The cultural foundations they established as well as the divisions that emerged among them are still shaping the West today.

These three cultural realms of the West each borrowed from the heritage of ancient Rome, especially its network of cities, which survived most completely in the Mediterranean and the Middle East. They were each influenced by the religious traditions of antiquity, especially the emphasis on monotheism in Judaism. They each adapted parts of Roman law but reshaped it to suit changing needs and new cultural influences. The heritage of Rome remained strongest in Byzantium. Indeed, the Byzantines continued to call themselves Romans. But between the sixth and eighth centuries these three cultural realms came to be distinguished by the language that dominated intellectual life and by the forms of monotheism practiced. In Byzantium the Greek language and Orthodox Christianity with its distinctively elaborate ceremonies defined the culture. By the end of the Umayyad caliphate, the Arabic language was becoming widespread and many Islamic beliefs and practices were becoming standard over a wide area. In western Europe, many languages were spoken but Latin became the universal language of the Church and government. None of these cultural realms, however, had yet achieved the level of uniformity and monolithic authority they would achieve during the subsequent centuries of the Middle Ages.

The year 750 saw the end of the Umayyad caliphate and the limit of Muslim expansion in western Europe and central Asia. After that the Byzantine Empire struggled for survival. In the Latin West, the Merovingian dynasty lost control of the Frankish kingdom. In the next chapter we will see how the Carolingian dynasty that succeeded the Merovingians led the Franks to predominance in western Europe. We will also discover how the Abbasid caliphate inaugurated a new, rich period in Islamic life, and how Byzantium began to reassert itself politically and culturally.

Suggestions for Further Reading

For a comprehensive list of suggested readings, please go to www.ablongman.com/levackconcise/chapter7

Bowersock, Glen, Peter Brown, and Oleg Grabar, eds. *Late Antiquity: A Guide to the Post-Classical World.* 1999. Interpretive essays combined with encyclopedia entries make this a starting point for discussion.

Brown, Peter. *The Rise of Western Christendom: Triumph and Diversity* A.D. *200–1000.* 2001. A brilliant interpretation of the development of Christianity in its social context.

Brown, Thomas S. *Gentlemen and Officers: Imperial Administration and Aristocratic Power in Byzantine Italy,* A.D. *554–800.* 1984. The basic study of Byzantine rule in Italy between Justinian and Charlemagne.

Bulliet, Richard W. *The Camel and the Wheel.* 1990. A fascinating investigation of the importance of the camel in history.

Cohen, Jeremy. *Living Letters of the Law: Ideas of the Jew in Medieval Christianity.* 1999. A masterful investigation of early medieval Judaism.

Cook, Michael. *Muhammad.* 1996. A short, incisive account of Muhammad's life that questions the traditional picture.

Cormack, Robin. *Writing in Gold: Byzantine Society and Its Icons.* 1985. An expert discussion of icons in the Byzantine world.

Crone, Patricia, and Michael Cook. *Hagarism: The Making of the Islamic World.* 1977. A challenging view of the origins of Islam.

Donner, Fred M. *The Early Islamic Conquests.* 1981. Discusses the first phases of Islamic expansion.

Geary, Patrick J. *The Peoples of Europe in the Early Middle Ages.* 2002. Discusses the emergence of the new kingdoms of Europe, stressing the incorporation of Roman elements.

Hourani, George. *Arab Seafaring in the Indian Ocean in Ancient and Early Medieval Times.* 1995. The standard discussion of Arab maritime activity.

Lawrence, C. H. *Medieval Monasticism.* 2001. An fine introduction to the phenomenon of Christian monasticism.

Mayr-Harting, Henry. *The Coming of Christianity to Anglo-Saxon England.* 1991. How a Germanic people were converted to Christianity.

Moorhead, John. *The Roman Empire Divided, 400–700.* 2001. The best recent survey of the period.

Robinson, Francis, ed. *The Cambridge Illustrated History of the Islamic World.* 1977. Many excellent and well-illustrated articles that will be useful for beginners.

Strayer, Joseph B., ed. *Dictionary of the Middle Ages.* 1986. An indispensable reference work.

Treadgold, Warren. *A History of the Byzantine State and Society.* 1997. A reliable narrative of Byzantine history.

Webster, Leslie, and Michelle Brown, eds. *The Transformation of the Roman World,* A.D. *400–900.* 1997. A well-illustrated synthesis with maps and bibliography.

Wickham, Chris. *Early Medieval Italy: Central Government and Local Society, 400–1000.* 1981. Examines the economic and social transformation of Italy.

Notes

1. Al-Tabari, *The History of Al-Tabari.* Vol. 17, *The First Civil War,* trans. and annotated G. R. Hawting (1985), 50.

Empires and Borderlands: The Early Middle Ages

I N 860 FIERCE RUS TRIBESMEN ABOARD A FLEET OF SLEEK DRAGON SHIPS RAIDED the villages along the shores of the Black Sea and then stomped up to the gates of Constantinople, ready for pillage and rape. Taken by surprise, the Byzantines were gripped with panic. The Byzantine patriarch Photius called upon the people to repent of their sins to avoid God's wrath, and when the Rus unexpectedly broke camp and departed, it was interpreted as an act of divine intervention.

The Rus inhabited the river valleys of present-day Ukraine and Russia in eastern Europe. Accustomed to the rough life of long winter treks, grubby little villages, and constant danger, they were dazzled by the sight of the Great City, with its half a million inhabitants, the gilded cupolas of its churches, the marble palaces of the aristocrats and emperor, the cavernous wharves and warehouses of its merchants, and the twelve miles of protective fortifications and walls. The people of Constantinople were equally astonished by the sight of the Rus merchants—sun-worn, fur-clad, and armed to the teeth—whom they met with fascination and fear. The usual purpose of these repeated visitations was trade.

In the merchant stalls of Constantinople, traders from many cultures met, haggled, and came to know something of one another. None perhaps were more unlike each other than the rough Rus and the refined Byzantines, but their mutual desires for profit kept them in a persistent, if tentative, embrace. These

Chapter Outline

- The Carolingians

- Invasions and Recovery in the Latin West

- Byzantium and Eastern Europe

- The Dynamism of Islam

Reliquary Bust of Charlemagne, ca. 1350: This bust was made more than 500 years after the death of Charlemagne, which means it is unlikely to be an accurate portrait of him. Medieval portraits, however, were not intended to represent the individuals as they actually looked but to represent their status or spiritual qualities. The majesty of this work, which housed some of the bones of Charlemagne, encouraged veneration of the great ruler considered a saint by many during the Middle Ages.

repeated interactions among very different peoples who traded, competed, and fought with one another offer clues for understanding the medieval world, also known as the Middle Ages.

The term *Middle Ages* refers to the period between the ancient and modern civilizations, from ca. 550 to 1500. The culture of that period rested on the foundations of three great civilizations: the Latin-Christian kingdoms of western Europe; the Greek Christianity of Byzantium; and the Arabic-speaking Islamic caliphates of the Middle East, North Africa, and Spain. The dynamic interactions among these three civilizations, distinguished by religion and language, lay at the heart of medieval culture. But the great civilizations also encountered barbarian peoples outside Christian and Islamic civilization—traders, raiders, and nomads from the North and East.

During the Early Middle Ages, the period from ca. 550 to 1050, the most important innovation was that a distinctive Latin Christian culture began to emerge in western Europe. The Carolingian Empire, which lasted from 800 to 843 and controlled much of western Europe, re-established the Roman Empire in the West for the first time in more than 300 years and sponsored a revival of interest in antiquity called the Carolingian Renaissance. The Carolingian Empire's collapse was followed by a period of anarchy as Europe faced wave after wave of hostile invaders. Only during the late tenth and eleventh centuries did the kingdoms of western Europe become strong enough to resist the invaders and to convert many of them to Christianity. At the same time the strength of the Byzantine empire was sapped by other invaders and internal strife, but it too revived and experienced a remarkable Renaissance under the Macedonian dynasty (867–1056). The most energetic of the three civilizations during this period was Islam, which threatened militarily both the Latin Christian kingdoms and Byzantium, supported important philosophical and scientific work, and produced a thriving economy.

During the eleventh century, the first signs appeared of a shift in the balance of military and cultural power away from Byzantium and the Islamic states toward the kingdoms of western Europe. The principal task of this and the following chapter is to trace how that happened. This chapter will address four questions:

- How did the Carolingian Empire contribute to establishing a distinctive western European culture?
- After the collapse of the Carolingian Empire, how did the Western kingdoms consolidate in the core of the European continent and how did Roman Catholicism spread to its periphery?
- Why did Byzantium revive after a series of invasions and then decline?
- What were the sources of dynamism and weakness within the Islamic states?

The Carolingians

Among the successor kingdoms to the Roman Empire in the West, as we saw in Chapter 7, none was more powerful militarily than the kingdom of the Franks, which encompassed much of the ancient Roman province of Gaul. However, the kingdom had a fatal flaw. It was considered the private property of the royal family, and according to Frankish custom, a father was obliged to divide his estates among his legitimate sons. As a result, whenever a king of the Franks died, the kingdom was divided up. Even the greatest Frankish king, Charlemagne, whose father Pepin had established the Carolingian dynasty, could not prevent the division through inheritance of the vast empire he had assembled through military conquests.

THE LEADERSHIP OF CHARLEMAGNE

During his reign, Charlemagne (r. 768–814) engaged in almost constant warfare, especially against polytheistic tribes that when defeated were usually compelled to accept Christianity. He went to war eighteen times against the Germanic tribe the Saxons, whose forced conversion only encouraged subsequent rebellions. The causes for Charlemagne's persistent warfare were complex. He believed he had an obligation to spread Christianity. He also needed to control his borders from incursions by hostile tribes. Perhaps most important, however, was his need to satisfy his followers, especially the members of the aristocracy, by providing them with opportunities for plunder and new lands. As a result of these wars, he established a network of subservient kingdoms that owed tribute to the Frankish empire (see Map 8.1).

The extraordinary expansion of the Frankish empire represented a significant departure from the small, loosely governed kingdoms that had prevailed in the wake of the collapse of the Roman Empire. Charlemagne's empire covered all of western Europe except for southern Italy, Spain, and the British Isles. His military ambitions had brought the Franks into direct confrontation with other cultures—the polytheistic German tribes, Scandinavians, and Slavs; the Orthodox Christians of Byzantium; and the Muslims in Spain. These confrontations were usually hostile and violent, characterized as they were by the imposition of Frankish rule and faith.

Coronation of Charlemagne as Emperor

Charlemagne's coronation as Roman emperor at the hands of Pope Leo III (r. 795–816) conferred extraordinary authority on the Frankish kingdom. On Christmas

Day 800 in front of a large crowd at St. Peter's Basilica, Pope Leo presided over a ceremony in which Charlemagne became the first Roman emperor in the West since the fifth century.

The coronation exemplified two of the most prominent characteristics of the Carolingians. The first was the conscious imitation of the ancient Roman Empire, especially the late Roman Christian empire of Constantine. Charlemagne's conquests approximated the former territory of the western Roman Empire, and the churches built during his reign were modeled after the fourth- and fifth-century basilicas of Rome. The second characteristic of Carolingian rule was the obligation of the Frankish kings to protect the Roman popes, an obligation that began under Charlemagne's father Pepin. In exchange for this protec-

tion, the popes offered the Carolingian monarchs the legitimacy of divine sanction.

The imperial title bestowed on Charlemagne tremendous prestige and tremendous risk. With the imperial crown came the rulership of northern Italy and theoretical superiority over all other rulers in the West. But it made dangerous enemies of the Byzantine emperors. They had been calling themselves Roman emperors since the fourth century and justly claimed to be the true heirs of the legal authority of the ancient Roman Empire. To them Charlemagne was nothing more than a usurper of the imperial crown. In their minds the pope had no right to crown anyone emperor. Instead of reuniting the eastern and western halves of the ancient Roman Empire, the coronation of Charlemagne drove them further apart.

■ **Map 8.1 Carolingian Empire**
Charlemagne's conquests were the greatest military achievement of the Early Middle Ages. The Carolingian armies successfully reunified all western European territories of the ancient Roman Empire except for southern Italy, Spain, and Britain. However, the empire was fragile due to Frankish inheritance laws that required all legitimate sons to inherit lands from their father. By the time of Charlemagne's grandsons the empire began to fragment.

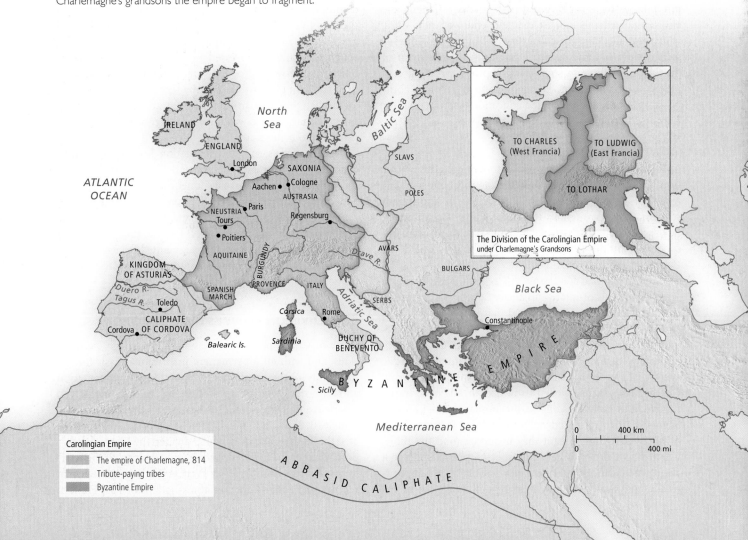

Carolingian Rulership

Even the discerning and strong rulership of Charlemagne depended more on personal than institutional forms of rule. Personal loyalty to the Carolingian monarch, expressed in an oath of allegiance, provided the strongest bonds unifying the realm, but betrayals were frequent. The Carolingian system required a monarch with outstanding personal abilities and unflagging energy, such as Charlemagne possessed, but a weak monarch threatened the collapse of the entire empire. Until the reign of Charlemagne, royal commands had been delivered orally, and there were few written records of what decisions had been made. Charlemagne's decrees (capitularies) gradually came to be written out. The written capitularies began to strengthen and institutionalize governmental procedures through written aids to memory.

The Carolingians reorganized government around territorial units called counties°, each administered by a count. In many respects, however, the Church provided the most vital foundations for the Carolingian system of rulership. Because Carolingian monarchs took responsibility for the welfare of Christianity, they took charge of the appointment of bishops and reorganized church administration into a strict hierarchy of archbishops who supervised bishops who, in turn, supervised parish priests. Charlemagne also revitalized the monasteries and endowed new ones, which provided the royal court with trained personnel— scribes, advisers, and spiritual assistants. Most laymen of the time were illiterate, so monks and priests wrote the emperor's letters for him, kept government records, composed histories, and promoted education—all essential for Carolingian rule.

The Carolingian Renaissance

In addition to organizing efficient political administration, Charlemagne sought to make the royal court an intellectual center. He gathered around him prominent scholars from throughout the realm and other countries. Under Charlemagne's patronage, these scholars were responsible for the flowering of culture that is called the Carolingian Renaissance.

The Carolingian Renaissance° ("rebirth") was one of a series of revivals of interest in ancient Greek and Latin literature. Charlemagne understood that both governmental efficiency and the propagation of the Christian faith required the intensive study of Latin, which was the language of the law, learning, and the Church. The Latin of everyday speech had evolved considerably since antiquity. During Charlemagne's time, spoken Latin had already been transformed into early versions of the Romance languages of Spanish, Italian, and French. Distressed that the poor Latin of many clergymen meant they misunderstood the Bible, Charlemagne ordered that all prospective priests undergo a rigorous education and recommended the liberal application of physical punishment if a pupil was slow in his lessons. However, due to the lack of properly educated teachers the Carolingian reforms did not penetrate very far into the lower levels of the clergy, who taught by rote the rudiments of Christianity to the nonliterate peasants.

The most significant accomplishments of the Carolingian Renaissance emanated from the palace school established in Aachen. The man most fully responsible for the intellectual vitality of the palace school was the English poet and cleric Alcuin of York (ca. 732–804). Charlemagne himself joined his sons, his friends, and his friends' sons as a student, and under Alcuin's guidance the court became a lively center of discussion and exchange of knowledge. They debated issues such as the existence or nonexistence of Hell, the meaning of solar eclipses, and the nature of the Holy Trinity. After fifteen years at court, Alcuin became the abbot of the monastery of St. Martin at Tours, where he expanded the library and produced a number of works on education, theology, and philosophy.

A brilliant young monk named Einhard (ca. 770–840) who studied in the palace school quickly became a trusted friend and adviser to Charlemagne. Based on twenty-three years of service to Charlemagne and research in royal documents, Einhard wrote the *Life of Charlemagne* (830–833), which describes Charlemagne's family, foreign policy, conquests, administration, and personal attributes. In Einhard's vivid Latin prose, Charlemagne comes alive as a great leader, a lover of hunting and fighting, who unlike his rough companions possessed a towering sense of responsibility for the welfare of his subjects and the salvation of their souls. In Einhard's biography, Charlemagne appears as an idealist, the first Christian prince in medieval Europe to imagine that his role was not just to acquire more possessions but to better humankind.

Charlemagne's rule and reputation had lasting significance for western Europe. Around 776 an Anglo-Saxon monk referred to the vast new kingdom of the Franks as the Kingdom of Europe, reviving the Roman geographical term *Europa*. Thanks to the Carolingians, Europe became more than a geographical expression. It became the geographical center of a new civilization that supplanted the Roman civilization of the Mediterranean and transformed the culture of the West.

THE DIVISION OF WESTERN EUROPE

None of Charlemagne's successors possessed his personal skills, and without a permanent institutional basis for administration, the empire was vulnerable to fragmentation and disorder. After years of fighting among themselves, Charlemagne's three grandsons—Charles the Bald (d. 877), Lothar (d. 855), and Ludwig the German (d. 876)—negotiated the Treaty of Verdun, which divided the Frankish kingdom. Charles the Bald received the western part of the territories, the kingdom of West Francia. Ludwig the German received the eastern portion, the kingdom of East Francia.

Lothar obtained the imperial title as well as the central portion of the kingdom, the "Middle Kingdom," which extended from Rome to the North Sea (see Map 8.1). In succeeding generations, the laws of inheritance created further fragmentation of these kingdoms, and during the ninth and tenth centuries the descendants of Charlemagne died out or lost control of their lands. By 987 none were left.

Invasions and Recovery in the Latin West

Despite Charlemagne's campaigns of conquest and conversion, the spread of Christianity throughout western Europe remained uneven and incomplete. By 900, Latin Christianity was limited to a few regions that constituted the heartland of western Europe—the Frankish lands, Italy, parts of Germany that had been under Carolingian rule, the British Isles, and a fringe in Spain. During the ninth and tenth centuries, hostile polytheistic tribes raided deep into the tightly packed Christian core of western Europe. Despite these attacks Christianity survived, and many of the polytheist tribes eventually accepted the Christian faith. These conversions were not always the consequence of Christian victories in battle, as had been the case during late antiquity and the Carolingian period. More frequently they resulted from organized missionary efforts by monks and bishops.

THE POLYTHEIST INVADERS OF THE LATIN WEST

Some of the raiders during the eighth to eleventh centuries plundered what they could from the Christian settlements of the West and returned home. Others seized lands, settled down, and established new principalities. The two groups who took advantage of the weakness of the Latin West most often during this period were the Magyars and Vikings.

Settling in the middle of the Danube River basin, the Magyars mounted raiding parties that ranged far into western Europe. Between 898 and 920 they sacked settlements in the prosperous Po River valley of Italy and then descended on the remnant kingdoms of the Carolingian Empire. Wherever they went they plundered for booty and took slaves for domestic service or sale. The kings of western and central Europe were powerless against these fierce raiders, who were unstoppable until 955 when the Saxon king Otto I (who later became emperor) destroyed a band of marauders on their way home with booty. After 955, the Magyars raids subsided, and in 1000 their king converted to Latin Christianity, which tied his people to the culture of the West.

The most devastating of the eighth- to eleventh-century invaders of western European settlements were the Vikings, also called Norsemen or Northmen. (These Viking warriors were ethnically related to the Rus who harassed Constantinople at the same time.) During this period, Danish, Norwegian, and Swedish Viking warriors sailed on long-distance raiding expeditions from their homes in Scandinavia. Every spring the long Viking dragon ships sailed forth, each carrying 50 to 100 warriors avid for loot.

■ **A Norman Ship, Possibly Based on a Viking Design, Used in the Invasion of England in 1066**
Note the single sail, the horses and warriors in the hold of the ship, and the tiller, which was mounted on the starboard side toward the stern. Stern-mounted rudders, which gave the helmsman much greater control of the direction of the ship, were gradually introduced during the twelfth century.

By the middle of the ninth century, the Vikings began to maintain winter quarters in the British Isles and on the shores of the weak Carolingian kingdoms—locations that enabled them to house and feed ever-larger raiding parties. These raiders soon became invading armies that took land and settled their families on it. As a result, the Vikings moved from disruptive pillaging to permanent occupation, which left a lasting mark on Europe. The most significant influence of the Vikings outside Scandinavia was in the British Isles. In 865 a great Viking army conquered large parts of northeastern England, creating a loosely organized network of territories known as the Danelaw. The Danish and Norse conquests in the British Isles left deep cultural residues in local dialects, geographical names, personal names, social structure, and literature.

After the mid-ninth century, the kings of Scandinavia (Norway, Denmark, and Sweden) began to assert control over the bands of raiders who had constituted the vanguard of the Viking invasions. By the end of the tenth century, the great age of Viking raiding by small parties ended. The Scandinavian kings established a firm hold over the settled population and converted to Christianity, bringing their subjects with them into the new faith. Henceforth, the descendants of the Viking raiders settled down to become peaceable farmers and shepherds.

THE RULERS IN THE LATIN WEST

As a consequence of the disintegration of the Carolingian order and the subsequent invasions, people during the ninth and tenth centuries began to seek protection from local warlords who assumed responsibilities once invested in royal authorities.

Lords and Vassals

The society of warlords derived from Germanic military traditions in which a great chief attracted followers who fought alongside him. The relationship was voluntary and egalitarian. By the eighth century, however, the chief had become a lord° who dominated others, and his dependents were known as vassals°.

The bond of loyalty between lord and vassal was formalized by an oath. The oath established a personal relationship in which the lord reciprocated the vassal's loyalty and willingness to obey the lord with protection and in some cases with a land grant called a fief°. Lords frequently called on their vassals for military assistance to resist invaders or to fight with other lords. The fief supplied the vassal with an income to cover the expenses of armor and weapons and of raising and feeding horses, all of which were necessary to be an effective mounted soldier, known by the twelfth century as a knight°. This connection between lord-vassal relations and the holding of a fief is called feudalism°.

During the ninth and tenth centuries, the lords often became the only effective rulers in a particular locality. After the collapse of public authority during the invasions and the dissolution of the Carolingian Empire, lordship implied political and legal jurisdiction over the inhabitants of the land. These lords came to exercise many of the powers of the state, such as adjudicating disputes over property or inheritance and punishing thieves and murderers.

The mixture of personal lord-vassal obligations, property rights conveyed by the fief, and legal jurisdiction over communities caused endless complications. The king's vassals were also lords of their own vassals, who in turn were lords over lesser vassals down to the level of simple knight. In theory such a system created a hierarchy of authority that descended from the king, but reality was never that simple. In France, for example, many of the great lords enjoyed as much land as the king, which made it very difficult for the king to force them to enact his will. Many vassals held different fiefs from different lords, which created a confusion of loyalties, especially when two lords of the same vassal went to war against one another.

The Western European Kingdoms After the Carolingians

At a time when the bonds of loyalty and support between lords and vassals were the only form of protection from invaders and marauders, lordship was a stronger social institution than the vague obligations all subjects owed to their kings. To rule effectively, a king was obliged to be a strong lord, in effect to become the lord of all the other lords, who in turn would discipline their own vassals. Achieving this difficult goal took several steps. First, the king had to establish a firm hand over his own lands, the royal domain. With the domain supplying food, material, and fighting men, the king could attempt the second step—establishing control over lords who lived outside the royal domain. To hold sway over these independent-minded lords, kings sometimes employed force but frequently offered lucrative rewards by giving out royal prerogatives to loyal lords. These prerogatives included the rights to receive fines in courts of law, to collect taxes, and to perform other governmental functions. As a result, some medieval kingdoms, such as France and England, began to combine in the hands of the same people the personal authority of lordship with the legal authority of the king, creating feudal kingship.

The final step in the process of establishing royal authority was to emphasize the sacred character of kingship. With the assistance of the clergy, kings emulated the great Christian emperors of Rome, Constantine and Justinian. Medieval kings became quasi priests who demanded obedience from their subjects who believed kings represented the majesty of God on Earth. The idea slowly began to take hold that the kingdom had an eternal existence separate

■ A Medieval Windmill
The peasant on the left is carrying a sack of grain for milling. The entire mill was built on a pivot so that it could be rotated to catch the wind.

from the mortal person of the king and that it was superior to its component parts—its provinces, tribes, lords, families, bishoprics, and cities.

The kingdoms of East and West Francia, which arose out of the remnants of the Carolingian Empire, produced kings who attempted to expand the power of the monarchy and enhance the idea of kingship. In East Francia the greatest of the kings, Otto I the Great (936–973), combined deep Christian piety with formidable military ability. More than any other tenth-century king, he supported the foundation of missionary bishoprics in polytheist Slavic and Scandinavian lands, thereby pushing the boundaries of Christianity beyond what they had been under Charlemagne. As Charlemagne had done earlier, Otto was crowned emperor in 962, reviving the Roman Empire in the West, which by the 1030s consisted of most of the Germanic duchies, north-central Italy, and Burgundy. In later centuries these regions collectively came to be called the Holy Roman Empire.

Like East Francia, West Francia included many groups with separate ethnic and linguistic identities, but the kingdom had been Christianized much longer because it had been part of the Roman Empire. Thus West Francia, although highly fragmented, possessed the potential for greater unity by using Christianity to champion the authority of the king.

Strengthening the monarchy became the crucial goal of the Capetian dynasty, which succeeded the last of the Carolingian kings. Hugh Capet (r. 987–996) was elevated king of West Francia in an elaborate coronation ceremony in which the prayers of the archbishop of Reims offered divine sanction to the new dynasty. The term *France* at first applied only to Capet's feudal domain, a small but rich region around Paris, but through the persistence of the Capetians West Francia became so unified that the name France came to refer to the entire kingdom.

Anglo-Saxon England had never been part of the Carolingian Empire, but because it had long been Christian, England shared in the culture of the Latin West. England suffered extensive damage at the hands of the Vikings. Alfred the Great (r. 871–899) finally defeated the Viking Danes in 879. As king of only Wessex (not of all England), Alfred consolidated his authority and issued a new law code.

During the late ninth and tenth centuries, Anglo-Saxon England experienced a cultural revival under royal patronage. King Alfred proclaimed that the Viking invasions had been God's punishment for the neglect of learning, without which God's will could not be known. Alfred accordingly promoted the study of Latin. He also desired that all men of wealth learn to read the language of the English people. Under Alfred a highly sophisticated literature appeared in Old English. This literature included poems, sermons, commentaries on the Bible, and translations of important Latin works.

TWO WORLDS: MANORS AND CITIES

After the end of the invasions of the ninth and tenth centuries, the population of western Europe recovered dramatically. Technological innovations created the agricultural revolution° that increased the supply of food. With more food available, people were better nourished than they had been in more than 500 years. As a result of more and better food, the population began to grow. In the seventh century all of Europe was home to only about 14 million inhabitants. Much of the land cultivated in the ancient world had reverted to wild forests, simply because there were not enough people left to farm it due to the deaths

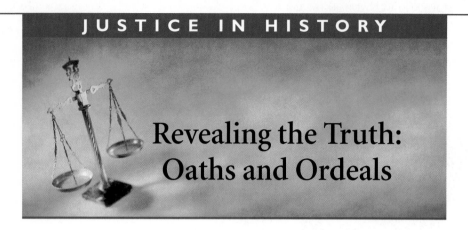
Revealing the Truth: Oaths and Ordeals

No participant in a lawsuit or criminal trial today would dream of entering the courtroom without an accompanying pile of documents to prove the case. In modern society we trust written over oral evidence because we are aware of how easily memories can be distorted. In an early medieval court, however, the participants usually arrived with nothing more than their own sworn testimony and personal reputations to support their cause. Papers alleging to prove one thing or another meant little in a largely illiterate society. Unable to read and perhaps aware that the few who could read might deceive them, most people trusted what they had personally seen and heard. Count Berthold of Hamm expressed the opinion of many when, after being presented with documents opposing his claim to a piece of land, he "laughed at the documents, saying that since anyone's pen could write what they liked, he ought not to lose his rights over it."

To settle disputes, medieval courts put much more faith in confession or in eyewitness testimony than in documents. In 1124 Pope Calixtus II pronounced that "we put greater faith in the oral testimony of living witnesses than in the written word."

Under normal trial procedures, a man would give his oath that what he was saying was true. If he was an established and respected member of the community, he would also have a number of "oath-witnesses" testify for his reliability, although not to the truth or falsehood of his evidence. The court would also hear from witnesses in the case. This system worked well enough when two local men, known in the community, were at odds. But what happened when there was a trial involving a person who had a bad reputation, was a known liar, or was a stranger? What would happen in a case with no witnesses?

In these instances, medieval courts sometimes turned to trial by ordeal to settle the matter. The judicial ordeal was used only as a last resort, as a German law code of 1220 declared: "It is not right to use the ordeal in any case, except that the truth may be known in no other way." The wide range of situations and people handed over to the ordeal makes clear that in the eyes of the medieval courts, the ordeal was a fallback method when all else failed to reveal the truth.

What was a trial by ordeal? There were several types. The most common was trial by fire. The accused would plunge his or her arm into a cauldron of boiling water to retrieve a coin or a jewel, or alternately would pick up a red-hot iron and walk nine paces. A variation of this method was to walk over hot coals or red-hot plowshares. After the accused suffered this ordeal, his or her hand or foot would be bound for three days and then examined. If the wound was healing "cleanly," meaning without infection, the accused was declared innocent. If not, he or she was adjudged guilty. Another common form of the ordeal was immersion in cold water, or "swimming," made famous in later centuries by its use in witch trials. The accused would be thrown into a river or lake. If the water "rejected" her and she floated, then she was guilty. If the water "embraced" her and she sank, then she was innocent. The obvious complication that a sinking person, even though innocent, may have also been a drowning person did not seem to deter use of trial by water.

The ordeal was especially widespread in judging crimes such as heresy and adultery and in assigning paternity. In 1218, Inga of Varteig carried the hot iron to prove that her son, born out of wedlock, was the son of deceased King Hakon III, which if true would change the line of succession in Norway. The ordeal was also used to decide much more pedestrian matters. In 1090, Gautier of Meigné claimed a plot of land from the monks of St. Auban at Angers, arguing that he had traded a horse in return for the property. He too carried a hot iron to prove his claim.

The belief that an ordeal could effectively reveal guilt or innocence in a judicial matter was based on the widespread conviction that God constantly and actively intervened in earthly affairs and that his judgment could be seen immediately. To focus God's attention on a specific issue, the participants performed the ordeal in a ritual manner. A priest was usually present to invoke God's power and to bless the implements employed in the ordeal. In

■ **Trial by Ordeal**

In this twelfth-century miniature, a person is being subjected to submersion in cold water as a way to test the veracity of his or her testimony. If the accused sank, innocence was declared. If the accused floated, guilty was the judgment.

one typical formula, the priest asked God "to bless and sanctify this fiery iron, which is used in the just examination of doubtful issues." Priests would also inform the accused, "If you are innocent of this charge . . . you may confidently receive this iron in your hand and the Lord, the just judge, will free you." The ritual element of the judicial ordeal emphasized the judgment of God over the judgment of men.

During the eleventh and twelfth centuries, the use of the ordeal waned. The recovery of Roman law, the rise of literacy and written documents in society at large, and a greater confidence in the power of courts to settle disputes all contributed to the gradual replacement of the ordeal with the jury trial or the use of torture to elicit a confession from the accused. In England the common law began to entrust the determination of the truth to a jury of peers who listened to and evaluated all the testimony. The jury system valued the opinions of members of the community over the reliability of the ordeal to reveal God's judgment. These changes mark a shift in medieval society toward a growing belief in the power of secular society to organize and police itself, leaving divine justice to the afterlife. But the most crucial shift came from within the Church itself, which felt its spiritual mission compromised by the involvement of priests in supervising ordeals. In 1215 the Fourth Lateran Council forbade priests from participating, and their absence made it impossible for the ordeal to continue as a formal legal procedure. ■

Questions of Justice

1. Why was someone's reputation in the community so significant for determining the truth in a medieval trial? How do reputations play a role in trials today?

2. What do oaths and the trial by ordeal reveal about the relationship between human and divine justice during the Middle Ages?

Taking It Further

Bartlett, Robert. *Trial by Fire and Water: The Medieval Judicial Ordeal.* 1986. Associates the spread of the trial by ordeal with the expansion of Christianity. The best study of the ordeal.

van Caenegen, R. C. *An Historical Introduction to Private Law.* 1992. A basic narrative from late antiquity to the nineteenth century that traces the evolution of early medieval trial procedures.

■ **A Heavy *Carruca* Plow**
At the center of the two-wheeled plow is a sturdy timber from which the coulter projects just in front of the plowshare, which is hidden by the earth.

from plague and the Germanic invasions. By 1300 the population had exploded to 74 million. From the seventh to the fourteenth centuries, then, the population grew many times over, perhaps as much as 500 percent. The most dramatic signs of population growth began after the year 1000.

The Medieval Agricultural Revolution

At the beginning of the eleventh century, most people lived in small villages or isolated farmsteads. Peasants literally scratched out a living from a small area of cleared land around the village by employing a light scratch plow that barely turned over the soil. The farms produced mostly grain, which was consumed as bread, porridge, and ale or beer. Vegetables were rare, meat and fish uncommon. Over the course of the century, the productivity of the land was greatly enhanced by a number of innovations that came into widespread use.

The invention of new labor-saving devices ushered in the power revolution. These included the water and wind mills used to grind grain and turn saws to mill timber. The exploitation of power of animals also became more efficient with the introduction of a new type of horse collar, which increased the animal's pulling power.

The centerpiece of the agricultural revolution was the heavy plow, which had several distinctive advantages over previous lighter scratch plows. The heavy plow cut through and lifted the soil, aerating it and bringing to the surface minerals vital for plant growth. After the introduction of the new plow, the three-field crop rotation system was gradually introduced. In the three-field system one field was planted in the fall with grain; one was planted in the spring with beans, peas, or lentils; and one lay fallow. Both fall and spring plantings were harvested in the summer, after which all the fields shifted. The three-field rotation system produced extraordinary advantages: the amount of

land under cultivation was vastly increased; beans planted in the spring rotation returned nitrogen to the soil; and the crop rotation combined with animal manure reduced soil exhaustion from excessive grain planting.

The agricultural revolution had a significant effect on society. First, villagers learned to cooperate—by pooling draft animals for plow teams, redesigning their fields, coordinating the three-field rotation of crops, and timing the harvest schedule. To accomplish these cooperative ventures, they created village councils and developed habits of collective decision making that were essential for stable community life. Second, the system produced not only more food, but better food. Beans and other vegetables grown in the spring planting were rich in proteins.

Manors and Serfs

The medieval agricultural economy bound landlords and peasants together in a unit of management called the manor. A manor referred to the holding of a single lord and the community of farmers who worked it. A single village might be divided up to serve several small manors, or a large manor might draw from several villages. Some lords possessed several manors and traveled from one to another throughout the year. The lord of the manor usually had his own large house or stone castle and served as the presiding judge of the community. However, most lords probably did not dictate what happened at the sessions of the manor court, which probably functioned as a kind of village meeting in most cases. Although the lord was clearly the social superior of the peasants on his manor, he could not rule effectively without their cooperation.

During the Middle Ages the most common status for farm workers, who constituted the vast majority of the populace, was that of serf. Serfs° were tied to a specific manor, which they could not leave. They had certain legal rights,

■ **A Silver Crucifix from Birka, Sweden, ca. 900**

The Viking fascination with silver was exploited by early missionaries, who had local silversmiths adapt the symbolism of Christianity to traditional Scandinavian art forms. Such objects assisted in the conversion of the Swedes.

such as the right to a certain portion of what they produced, but they were obliged to subject themselves to the lord's will. In theory, at least, the relationship between the lord and his serfs was reciprocal. The lord supplied the land, sometimes tools and seed, and protection from invaders and bandits. In return serfs supplied the labor necessary to work the land.

The Growth of Cities

Before the eleventh century the vast majority of people in Europe lived on manors, in rural villages, or perhaps in small market towns of a few thousand people. The cities that survived from the ancient world remained small, except in the Mediterranean. When the population began to grow as a consequence of the agricultural revolution, migrants from the manors and villages swelled the market towns into cities and repopulated the few cities that had survived from antiquity.

The newly thriving cities proved to be troublesome for the lords, bishops, and kings who usually had legal authority over them. As the population grew and urban merchants became increasingly rich, the cities in which they lived enjoyed even greater resources than the rural lords. In many places the citizens of the new enlarged towns attempted to rid themselves of their lords to establish self-rule or, at least, substantial autonomy for their city. In the cities of north-central Italy, for example, the prominent townsmen began to chafe at the violent authority the rural lords held over them. The lords taxed or even stole the wealth that the townsmen earned through manufacturing and trade. The lords made life unsafe and unbearable, fighting among themselves and abusing the unarmed townsmen. To counter the power of the lords, townsmen formed sworn defensive associations called communes°, which quickly became the effective government of the towns. The communes evolved into city-states, which were self-governing cities that became small states by seizing control of the surrounding countryside. Perhaps as many as a hundred or more cities in north-central Italy formed communes after 1070.

As a result of the population explosion after the year 1000, growing cities became one of the defining features of medieval life. Most of these cities were modest in size—with populations numbering in the tens of thousands rather than hundreds of thousands—but they became important as centers of trade and manufacturing.

THE SPREAD AND REFORM OF CHRISTIANITY IN THE LATIN WEST

As the core of the Latin West became politically stronger and economically more prosperous during the tenth and eleventh centuries, Christianity spread among the previously polytheistic tribes in northern and eastern Europe. Through conversion, Latin Christianity became the dominant religion in Europe and came to distinguish itself more firmly from the Orthodox Christianity of Byzantium. Latin Christianity and Greek Orthodoxy gradually grew apart during the Middle Ages, primarily over theological differences and disputes about the ultimate authority in the Church.

Conversions

Among the polytheistic tribes on the northern and eastern frontiers of the Latin West in Scandinavia, the Baltic Sea region, and parts of eastern Europe, the first Christian conversions usually took place when a king or chieftain accepted Christianity. His subjects were expected to follow. Teaching Christian principles and forms of worship required much more time and effort. Missionary monks usually arrived after a king's conversion, but these monks tended to take a tolerant attitude about variations in the liturgy. Because most Christians were isolated from one another, new converts tended to practice their own local forms of worship and belief. Missionaries and Christian princes discovered that the most effective way to combat this localizing tendency was to found bishoprics.

In central Europe Latin forms of Christianity spread. From the middle of the tenth century along the eastern frontiers of Germany, a line of newly established bishoprics became the base for the conversion of the polytheist Slavic tribes. Over a period of about sixty years, these German bishoprics pushed the Latin form of Christianity deep into east-central Europe. This effort ensured that the Poles, Bohemians (Czechs), and Magyars (Hungarians) looked to the West and the pope for their cultural models and religious leadership.

The first bishoprics in Scandinavia were also established in the last half of the tenth century. Whereas Germans were primarily responsible for the spread of Christianity among the Slavs of central Europe, it was English missionaries who evangelized Scandinavia. Denmark had the first completely organized church in Scandinavia, represented by the establishment of nine bishoprics by 1060. The diffusion into Sweden, Norway, and Iceland came later after the strong kingdoms developed in those countries and a pro-Christian dynasty could assist the spread of the new religion.

The Task of Church Reform

As Christianity expanded, its spiritual mission suffered from its success in the violent and materialistic world of secular affairs. Over the centuries many wealthy and pious people had made large donations of land to the Church. As a result the Church became immensely wealthy. Such wealth tempted the less pious to corruption, and some of the Roman popes who had benefited from the wealth of the Church were reluctant to promote reforms that would have reduced corruption. Even those who wanted to eliminate corruption were slow to assemble the administrative machinery necessary to enforce their will across the unruly lands of Latin Christianity.

The idea and energy for the reform of the Church came out of the monasteries. Monks thought the best way to clean up corruption in the Church would be to improve the morals of individuals. If men conducted themselves with a sense of moral responsibility, the whole institution of the Church could be purified. The model for self-improvement was provided by monks themselves, who set an example for the rest of the Church and for society at large. The most influential of the reform-minded monasteries was that of Cluny° in Burgundy, which was established in 910. Cluny itself became the center of a far-reaching reform movement that was sustained in more than 1,500 Cluniac monasteries.

The success of Cluny and other reformed monasteries provided the base from which reform ideas spread beyond the isolated world of monks to the rest of the Church. The first candidates for reform were parish priests and bishops. Called the *secular clergy* (in Latin *saeculum,* meaning "secular") because they lived in the secular world, they differed from the regular clergy (in Latin *regula,* those who followed a "rule") who lived in monasteries apart from the world. The lives of many secular clergy differed little from their lay neighbors. (*Laypeople* or *the laity* referred to all Christians who had not taken religious vows to become a priest, monk, or nun.) The Roman Church had repeatedly forbidden priests to marry, but the prohibitions had been ineffective until Cluniac reform stressed the ideal of the sexually pure priest. The other objective of the clerical reform movement was the elimination of the corrupt practices of simony and lay investiture. Simony° was the practice of buying and selling church offices. Lay investiture° took place when nobles, kings, or emperors actually installed churchmen and gave them their symbols of office ("invested" them). Through this practice, the powerful laity dominated the clergy and usurped the property of the

Church for their own use. The movement to eradicate simony and lay investiture attempted to get the emperor and all other lords to keep their hands off Church offices and lands.

Byzantium and Eastern Europe

In late antiquity Constantinople and Rome had been the capitals of the two halves of the Roman Empire. Once joined in a common Christian culture, eastern and western Christians had grown so far apart that by the late ninth century they began to constitute separate civilizations. There were still cultural exchanges among them as merchants, pilgrims, and scholars crossed back and forth, but Church leaders and rulers disagreed on what they considered vitally important issues. They held different opinions about religious matters, such as the dating of Easter, the rituals of the liturgy, the role of images in worship, and the authority of the bishop in Rome, whom Orthodox Christians refused to recognize as pope. To Orthodox Christians, the pope was just one bishop among many Christian bishops. As the popes found protection from the Frankish kings and Carolingian emperors during the eighth and ninth centuries, their ties with the Byzantine emperor loosened. After the imperial coronation of Charlemagne, the eastern (Byzantine) and the western (Carolingian and later German) emperors became rival claimants to the authority of ancient Rome.

The East and West also spoke different languages. In the East, Greek was the language of most of the population, and Latin had been largely forgotten by the end of the sixth century. In the West, Latin or local dialects of Latin prevailed; except in southern Italy and Sicily, only a few knew some Greek.

BYZANTIUM

Like western Europe, the Byzantine Empire suffered from a long period of instability provoked by wave after wave of invaders. During the eighth and early ninth centuries Byzantium was prey to a series of invasions by Muslim armies and by the Bulgars, who were a confederation of several groups of nomads from the steppes of central Asia. Resisting these invaders sapped the strength of the empire and its emperors.

The Macedonian Dynasty

Byzantium's weakness in the face of external enemies ceased during the Macedonian dynasty (867–1056), a line of emperors that lasted six generations. Before the Macedonians the Byzantine Empire had had no law of succession, which meant that there was always potential for instability when an emperor died as the powerful families struggled over who would become the new emperor. But after Basil I (r. 867–886) murdered his way to the throne he kept his family in power by naming his sons co-emperors and encouraging the principle of dynastic succession. Under the Macedonian emperors, Byzantine armies attacked the Arabs, and a missionary effort converted the Bulgars, the Russians, and many of the Slavic tribes. Whereas on the eastern borders the only option against the Muslims was a military one, in the polytheistic Balkans missionary efforts helped create new alliances. By conversion the Byzantines brought the southern Slavs and the Bulgars into their sphere of influence. The Bulgars, however, proved to be inconstant allies, and on several occasions threatened Constantinople itself.

As we saw at the beginning of this chapter, the Rus also threatened Constantinople by sailing down the Dneiper River from Kiev to the Black Sea. After resisting a series of assaults from the Rus, the Byzantines sought to break down their hostility through diplomatic contacts and trade. Through conversions among members of the ruling families, Byzantine missionaries spread Christianity and Greek culture, making the Rus less isolated and more open to Byzantine influence. By the end of the tenth century the Rus had converted en masse and accepted the subordination of their church to the patriarch of Constantinople. As a result the Rus remained culturally connected to Byzantium, a connection that helped determine the forms of worship within Russian Orthodoxy.

Under the Macedonian dynasty, the economy of Constantinople thrived. Home to more than half a million people by the tenth century, the city became a great marketplace where goods from as far away as China and the British Isles were exchanged. It was also the center for the production of luxury goods, especially silk cloth and brocades, which were traded throughout Europe, Asia, and northern Africa. During this period aristocratic families, the Church, and monasteries became immensely rich, and devoted themselves to embellishing the city with magnificent buildings, mosaics, and icons, creating the Macedonian Renaissance°.

Great creative energies were devoted to defining the religious dogmas of Orthodoxy and creating unity within the Byzantine Church. The patriarch Photius (ca. 810–ca. 893) became the most eminent scholar in the history of Byzantium. Photius maintained a huge library, which became a major center for the study of ancient Greek literature based on the rare manuscripts he had collected. Photius was the author of several important works, including the *Library,* an encyclopedic compendium of classical, late antique, and early Byzantine writers in both theology and secular literatures. By summarizing and analyzing these writers, Photius pioneered the book review, and his summaries remain especially vital because many of these books have been lost since his time. In addition to writing, Photius was deeply involved in church politics. Elected patriarch while still a layman, he was twice deposed from office due to the shifts of political winds in Constantinople. A bitter critic of the Latin Christians, Photius is often blamed for widening the gap between the two main branches of Christianity.

The quasi-sacred office of the emperor came to be magnified in elaborate court ceremonies under the Macedonian dynasty. The historian Emperor Constantine VII Porphyrogenetus (r. 912–959) wrote *On the Administration of the Empire,* an important source for Byzantine history. He also wrote the *Book of Ceremonies,* which became a model for royal ceremony throughout the Christian world and was adapted in kingdoms across Europe from Spain to Russia. The accumulation of ancient manuscripts and the compilations of ancient philosophy created an important cultural link between the medieval and the ancient worlds. In these accomplishments the Macedonian Renaissance surpassed the Carolingian Renaissance in the West.

Instability and Decline

Despite the achievements of the Macedonians, new threats loomed on the horizon. Under the Macedonian emperors, Byzantium had never been completely free from the external threat of invasions. The extent to which the empire succeeded in meeting these threats had depended on two factors—the political stability guaranteed by the Macedonian dynasty and the organization and recruitment of the army through the military districts of the themes.

Emperor Basil II died in 1025 and left no direct heirs. But members of his family continued to rule until 1056, largely because of the general assumption that the peace and prosperity of the empire depended on the dynasty. Basil's successors, however, were not the strong leaders that had distinguished the earlier Macedonian dynasty. Administration of the empire was highly centralized, with a tangled bureaucracy that supervised everything from diplomatic ceremony to the training of lowly craftsmen. Without energetic leadership, the Byzantine bureaucracy quickly degenerated into routine and failed to respond to new challenges.

The early Macedonian emperors' success in checking invasions had been largely the result of Byzantium's superior military capacities, guaranteed by the theme system. In the themes, free, tax-paying soldier-farmers lived in villages under the supervision of a military commander who was also civil administrator. By the eleventh century the independence of these soldier-farmers was threatened by deteriorating economic conditions. Every time a crop failed or a drought or famine struck, starving soldier-farmers in the themes were forced to surrender their land and their independence to one of the prosperous aristocrats who offered them food. As the great landowners acquired more land, the small farmers who were the backbone of the army began to disappear or lose their freedom. Because only free landholders could perform military service, the concentration of land in the hands of a few was disastrous for the army. The late Macedonian emperors lacked the ability to initiate reforms that would have arrested this dangerous trend.

To make matters worse, after 1025 Byzantium faced formidable new enemies. In the West the Normans, who were distant descendants of Viking settlers, advanced on southern Italy and Sicily, crushing Byzantine power in Italy forever. In the East Byzantium faced an even more dangerous enemy. In 1071, the Seljuk Turks, who had converted to Sunni Islam in the previous century, captured the Byzantine emperor himself at the battle of Manzikert in Armenia. After their victory the Seljuks advanced across Asia Minor and threatened the very survival of Byzantium. The situation looked bleak indeed, and over the succeeding centuries, western European armies and the Turks ate away at Byzantium until its final collapse in 1453.

BORDERLANDS IN EASTERN EUROPE

In much of the Balkan peninsula during the seventh through ninth centuries, the dissolution of Byzantine power created a power vacuum among peoples who were Christians and still considered themselves subjects of the Roman Empire. The peninsula was also home to substantial numbers of the more recently arrived polytheist Slavic and Bulgar peoples who had never been subject to Rome. During the ninth through eleventh centuries, most of these tribes converted to one form or another of Christianity, and the patterns of those conversions have had lasting consequences to this day. The religious dividing line between those who adhered to Latin Christianity, which is now called Roman Catholicism, and those who followed Orthodox rites cut directly through Slavic Europe.

The various Slavic tribes in eastern Europe were extremely fragmented politically. The intricate distribution of ethnic and linguistic groups made this region more diverse than western Europe and complicated state building in the East. Throughout this region, tribal loyalties had long dominated society and prevented sophisticated political development. But by about 1000 the new kingdoms of Bulgaria, Kievan Rus, and Poland began to solidify as certain dominant families made dynastic claims to rule over clusters of tribes (see Map 8.2). Bulgaria and Kievan Rus became bastions of Orthodox Christianity, Poland of Roman Catholicism.

The Bulgarian khan (the head of a confederation of clans) Boris I (r. 852–889) accepted Orthodox Christianity from Byzantium in 865. His conversion illustrates the politics of the period. During the ninth century Christianity had acquired a powerful allure among the polytheistic tribes, not the least because Christian rulers considered so-called pagans legitimate objects of aggression, and their acceptance of Christianity opened the possibility for diplomatic ties and alliances. For Boris, therefore, conversion was a way to ward off Byzantine attacks, and he brilliantly negotiated for a Bulgarian Church that recognized the ultimate authority of the patriarch of Constantinople but was essentially autonomous.

The autonomy of the Bulgarian Church was further guaranteed later in the ninth century by the adoption of a Slavic rather than Latin or Greek liturgy. This was made possible by the missionary work in neighboring Moravia of St. Cyril (ca. 826–869) and his brother St. Methodius (815–885), who had invented an alphabet to write the Slavic language. They translated a church liturgy into a version of the Slavic language, now known as Old Church Slavonic. The acceptance of the Slavonic liturgy gradually led the ethnically and linguistically mixed peoples of Bulgaria to identify with Slavic culture and language. From a string of monasteries established by the Bulgarians, the Old Church Slavonic liturgy spread among the Serbs, Romanians, and Russians, creating cultural ties among these widespread peoples that have survived to the present.

Like the Bulgars, the Rus eventually adopted a Slavic language and Slavic customs. From among the merchant-warriors of the Rus arose the forebears of the princes of Kiev, who by the end of the tenth century ruled a vast forest domain through a loose collective of principalities. The term *Rus* (later *Russian*) came to be applied to all the lands ruled by the princes of Kiev.

The zenith of Kievan Rus was under Vladimir the Great (r. 980–1015) and his son Iaroslav the Wise (r. 1019–1054). A ruthless fighter, Vladimir consolidated into a single state the provinces of Kiev and Novgorod, a city in the far north that had grown rich from the fur trade. A polytheist by birth, Vladimir had seven wives and took part in human sacrifices. However, when offered a military alliance with Byzantium in 987, he abandoned his other wives, married the Byzantine emperor's sister, and accepted conversion to Orthodox Christianity. He then forced the inhabitants of Kiev and Novgorod to be baptized and had their pagan idols cast into the rivers. The Byzantine Church established administrative control over the Rus Church by appointing an Orthodox archbishop for Kiev. The liturgy was in Old Church Slavonic, which provided a written language and the stimulus for the literature, art, and music at the foundations of Russian culture. The religious and political connection between the Rus and Byzantium influenced the course of Russian history; it also limited the eastward spread of Roman Catholicism.

Unlike Bulgaria and Kievan Rus, Poland favored Roman Catholicism, an association that helped create strong political and cultural ties to western Europe. The Slavic Poles inhabited a flat plain of forested land with small clearings for farming. First exposed to missionaries tied to Saint Methodius, Poland resisted Christianity until Prince Mieszko (ca. 960–992) created the most powerful of the Slav states and accepted Latin Christianity in 966 in an attempt to build political alliances with Christian princes. To solve the problem of German religious and political interference in his lands, Mieszko subordinated his country to the Roman pope with the Donation of Poland (ca. 991). Thus began Poland's long and special relationship with the papacy. Mieszko's successor, Boleslaw the Brave (992–1025), expanded his territories through conquest, making Poland one of the largest European kingdoms. Boleslaw's immediate successors, however, allowed the central authority of the government to slip away into the hands of the local nobility and even lost the title of king.

By the eleventh century the three great Christian kingdoms of eastern Europe had been established, but Bulgaria, Kievan Rus, and Poland rested on shaky foundations. All three were subject to dissolution whenever a succession crisis or a weak king opened the door for the nobility to seize power. Bulgaria and Kiev became bastions of Old Slavonic Orthodoxy. Poland had become the principal Catholic state among the Slavs.

The Dynamism of Islam

The principal reason for the rapid spread of Islam was the capacity of the prophet Muhammad's message to unify many diverse communities in Arabia. Especially during its early centuries, Islam disseminated Muhammad's message by both force and persuasion. Islamic rule quickly spread from Arabia into Persia, Egypt, Palestine, Syria, and beyond. During the eighth and ninth centuries, Islam penetrated areas of Europe.

THE ABBASID CALIPHATE

One of the Islamic Empire's continuing problems was how to sustain political unity over time. The fundamental problem arose from disagreements about succession. After Muhammad's death in 632, the ruler of the Islamic state was called the caliph°. The first cracks in the unity of Islam broke open over the proper succession to the caliphate. To this day the principal sectarian divisions within Islam between the Shi'ites and the Sunnis derive

■ **Map 8.2   The Expanding States of Eastern and Northern Europe**
Eastern Europe during the Early Middle Ages was home to a very diverse population of tribes and fledgling states. Within this diversity the states of Bulgaria, Kievan Rus, and Poland emerged by the beginning of the eleventh century.

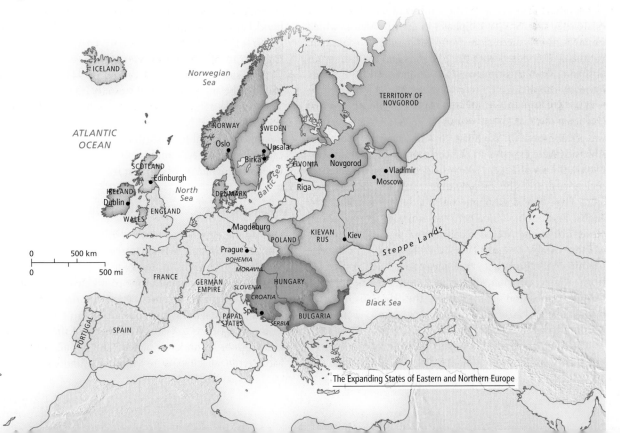

The Expanding States of Eastern and Northern Europe

from conflicts over succession that emerged after the death of Muhammad.

As we saw in Chapter 7, after the assassination of Muhammad's son-in-law and first cousin Ali, the caliphate fell under the control of the Umayyad clan, who governed a vast Islamic Empire between 661 and 750. The Umayyads, however, were never firmly in control of the entire Islamic world and faced a series of rebellions, especially from the Shi'ites, the followers of Ali, and the Abbasid clan, who were descendants of Muhammad's uncle. These two groups—the Shi'ites and the Abbasids—were briefly allied in mutual hostility to the Umayyads. However, after the last Umayyad caliph died in a battle in 750, the Abbasids seized the caliphate and Shi'ite support for the Abbasids collapsed. Abbasid victory made permanent the split within Islam between the minority Shi'ites and the majority Sunni. While the Shi'ites and Sunni both considered the caliphate a hereditary office restricted to members of Muhammad's Hashimite clan of the Quraysh tribe, the Shi'ites believed that only direct descendants of Muhammad through his daughter Fatima and son-in-law Ali should rule the Islamic community. The Sunni, in contrast, devised a more flexible theory of succession that allowed them to accept the Abbasid caliphs and in later generations even foreign caliphs. The caliphate developed into an office that combined some governmental and some religious responsibilities.

Once they had secured the caliphate, the Abbasids engaged in a campaign to exterminate the entire Umayyad family. The only Umayyad to escape their extermination order, Abd al-Rahman I (r. 756–788), fled to Spain where he founded what would later become the Umayyad caliphate of Córdoba (756–1031). In the tenth century the Fatimids established the Shi'ite caliphate in North Africa, which claimed direct succession from Muhammad's daughter, Fatima, and opposed both the Abbasids and the Umayyads of Spain. From this time on, the Muslim world split apart into rival caliphates.

The Abbasid caliphate (750–945) quickly altered the character of the Muslim world. In 762–763 a new capital was established in Baghdad. In this new location, the Abbasids were exposed to the ceremonial and administrative traditions of Persia, which helped expand the intellectual horizons of the caliphs, their courtiers, and bureaucrats. The Abbasid caliphate continued to be dominated by Arabs, and Arabic remained the language of the court. Nevertheless, the Abbasids considered all Muslims equals, whether Arabs or not. This belief fostered a distinctive Islamic civilization that fused ideas and practices derived from Arabic, Persian, Byzantine, and Syrian cultures. Despite opposition from purists, the Abbasids married non-Arabs and recruited Turks, Slavs, and even non-Muslims to serve as palace guards.

The Abbasid caliphs expanded their control over society, but they were far from despots. The caliph was first and foremost an emir—that is, the commander of a professional army. He was also responsible for internal security, which meant suppressing rebellions, supervising officials, and making sure taxes were honestly collected. But the caliph did not become involved in other public institutions, such as the mosques, hospitals, and schools. The principal exception was the office of market inspector, through which the caliph guaranteed fair business practices. In this commitment to the integrity of markets and trade, the Islamic caliphate was considerably more advanced than either Byzantium or the Latin kingdoms of western Europe.

The period of Abbasid greatness lasted about a century (754–861), and its eclectic nature is reflected in its literature. The famous *Arabian Nights,* stories written down for the Caliph Harun al-Rashid (r. 786–809), were based on Hellenistic, Hebrew, Indian, and Arab legends. The *Arabian Nights* and the rich tradition of Arabic poetry, which often recounted tales of thwarted love, in turn influenced Western Christian poetry of courtly love.

Philosophical and scientific inquiry thrived under Caliph al-Mamun (r. 813–833), who had an astronomical observatory built in Baghdad and who appreciated the work of al-Kindi (who died sometime after 870), the first outstanding Islamic philosopher. Al-Kindi grappled with questions specific to Islam but also with the works of Aristotle and problems in astrology, medicine, optics, arithmetic, cooking, and metallurgy—topics that made him well known outside the Islamic world. The work of the Arabic translators in the ninth and tenth centuries created a crucial cultural link between the ancient and medieval worlds. The Muslims supplied Arabic translations of ancient Greek texts to a later generation of Jews and Christians in Spain, who translated them into Latin. These secondhand and third-hand Latin translations of ancient philosophy and science became the core of the university curriculum in western Europe during the twelfth century.

Abbasid political power ceased in 945 when a clan of rough tribesmen from northwestern Iran seized Baghdad. The Abbasid caliphs remained figureheads, and there were occasional attempts to reinvigorate the caliphate, but its greatness as a ruling institution had ceased. However, the caliphate remained a vital symbol of Islamic unity and survived as a formal institution, at least, for another 300 years.

ISLAMIC CIVILIZATION IN EUROPE

During the eighth and ninth centuries the Muslim armies chipped away at Christian territories in Europe. Unlike their fellow Muslims in the Middle East and North Africa, most of the Muslims in Europe conducted themselves more as raiders than conquerors. They plundered and pillaged but did not stay long and did not attempt a mass conversion of Christians to Islam. The effects of these raids, however, cannot be underestimated. The populations of many Mediterranean cities were vulnerable and diminished al-

■　Mosque of Córdoba

The great mosque was one of the wonders of the world during the tenth century. Since Islam prohibited the depiction of the human body, mosques were embellished with geometrical forms and quotations from the Qur'an. The repetition of multiple arches creates an intricate pattern that changes as the viewer moves about in the space.

most to the point of disappearing as urban life became impossible. The only hope for survival was to disperse into the countryside, where families could live off the land and find protection with one of the many local lords who built castles for defense.

The significant exceptions to the pattern of raiding were in Sicily and Spain. These areas became the principal borderlands through which Arabic learning and science filtered into Catholic Europe. These borderlands became zones of particularly intense cultural interaction, where several languages were spoken and where in accord with Muslim toleration for other monotheist religions Christians and Jews were allowed to observe their own faiths. Although small, Muslim Sicily and Spain were among the most dynamic places in Europe during the eighth to early eleventh centuries. No Christian city in western Europe could rival Córdoba in size and prosperity. Even within the Muslim world, which enjoyed many splendid cities, the only city

comparable to Baghdad was Córdoba. A German nun visiting Córdoba in Muslim Spain during the tenth century thought the city embodied "the majesty and adornment of the world, the wondrous capital . . . radiating in affluence of all earthly blessings."[1] During the tenth century the caliphate of Córdoba became the most important intellectual capital in western Europe, renowned for the learning of both its Muslim and Jewish scholars. Córdoba's fame derived from the extensive authority and magnificent building projects encouraged by the caliph Abd al-Rahman III (r. 912–961) and his three successors.

With an ethnically mixed population of more than 100,000, Córdoba boasted 700 mosques, 3,000 public baths, 5,000 silk looms, and 70 libraries. The caliph alone possessed a library housing more than 400,000 volumes. The streets of the city were paved and illuminated at night, the best houses enjoyed indoor plumbing, and the rich enjoyed country villas as vacation retreats. (In contrast, the city of Rome did not erect streetlamps for another thousand years.)

The lasting influence of the golden age of Córdoba can be found in the legacy of the poets, scientists, physicians, astronomers, and architects who thrived under the caliphs' patronage. Despite some tensions among Muslims and Jews, many of the prominent intellectuals in the caliphs' court were Arabized Jews. Typical of the many non-Muslims who served Arab rulers, the Jew Samuel ibn Nagrela (993–1055) rose to the position of vizier (minister) of the neighboring Muslim kingdom of Granada. An able Hebrew poet, biblical commentator, and philosopher, Samuel ibn Nagrela was also an effective commander of Muslim armies. His brilliant career reflected the value Muslims placed on learning and skill.

During the early eleventh century, after a series of succession disputes that led to the murder of several caliphs,

A HUMBLE CHRISTIAN MONK MEETS THE CALIPH OF CÓRDOBA

························

In 953 the German emperor Otto I sent the abbot John of Gorze on a diplomatic mission to the court of Abd al-Rahman III, the caliph of Córdoba, in order to enlist his help in stamping out piracy in the western Mediterranean. Unfortunately for John, because the letters he carried from the emperor were overtly hostile to Islam, he was put under house arrest for three years. The caliph also could not understand the commitment to poverty and filth required of a Christian monk and interpreted John's refusal to dress elegantly as a calculated slight. However, John's pious sincerity eventually changed the caliph's mind. In recognition of the power of John's convictions, the caliph extended him a sign of exceptional respect by allowing him to kiss the royal hand.

John, released from almost three years of cloistered seclusion, was ordered to appear in the royal presence. When he was told by the messengers to make himself presentable to royalty by cutting his hair, washing his body, and putting on clean clothes, he refused, lest they should tell the caliph that he had changed in his essential being beneath a mere change of clothes. The caliph then sent John ten pounds in coin, so that he might purchase clothing to put on and be decent in the royal eyes, for it was not right for people to be presented in slovenly dress.

John could not at first decide whether to accept the money, but eventually he reasoned that it would be better spent for the relief of the poor, and sent thanks for the caliph's generosity and for the solicitude he had deigned to show him. The monk added in his reply: "I do not despise royal gifts, but it is not permitted for a monk to wear anything other than his usual habit, nor indeed could I put on any garment of a color other than black." When this was reported to the caliph, he remarked: "In this reply I perceive his unyielding firmness of mind. Even if he comes dressed in a sack, I will most gladly receive him." . . .

When John arrived at the dais where the caliph was seated alone—almost like a godhead accessible to none or to very few—he saw everything draped with rare coverings, and floor-tiles stretching evenly to the walls. The caliph himself reclined upon a most richly ornate couch. As John came into his presence, the caliph stretched out a hand to be kissed. The hand-kissing not being customarily granted to any of his own people or to foreigners, and never to persons of low and middling mark, the caliph none the less gave John his hand to kiss.

Source: From Colin Smith, *Christians and Moors in Spain, Volume 1* (Aris and Phillips, 1988).

---

the caliphate of Córdoba splintered into numerous small states. The disunity of Muslim Spain provided opportunities for the stubborn little Christian states of Navarre, Aragon, and Castile to push against the frontiers of their opulent Muslim neighbors. During the reign of Alfonso VI (r. 1072–1109), Castile became the dominant military power on the peninsula. Forcing Muslims to pay tribute to him to finance further wars and gathering assistance from French knights eager for plunder and French monks ardent for converts, Alfonso launched a massive campaign known as the Spanish Reconquest that led to the capture of Toledo in 1085. After the time of Alfonso VI, the Reconquest lost steam, and a few surviving remnants of Muslim power managed to hang on in Spain for another 400 years.

LEGENDS OF THE BORDERLANDS

From the late eighth to the eleventh centuries, Muslim and Christian armies grappled in innumerable violent engagements. The border regions between their respective lands became militarized through building of fortresses and castles, assignment of territory to lords and generals willing to defend the borders, and settlement by soldier-farmers who

served as infantrymen when required. The borderlands, however, were more than just places of conflict. During times of peace, Christians and Muslims traded with and even married one another, and in the confused loyalties typical of the times, soldiers and generals from both faiths frequently switched sides. One of the lasting fruits of these borderland societies were legends of great heroes. These legends began as stories recited in verse to entertain the aristocrats whose ancestors had fought in the borderlands, and several of these oral legends were eventually refashioned into epic poems that became extremely popular and much imitated. There were French, Byzantine, and Spanish versions of borderland epics, each strongly influencing language and culture.

The Song of Roland, an Old French epic poem that dates from around 1100, tells a story about the Battle of Roncesvalles, which took place in 778. The actual historical battle had been a minor skirmish between the soldiers of Charlemagne returning from a campaign in Spain against Basques who massacred the rear guard of the Frankish army in revenge for Charlemagne's brutal destruction of their homes. *The Song of Roland,* however, transforms this sordid episode into a great epic battle. It replaces the

Basques with Muslims—the recurring enemies of the Christian Franks—and explores the psychology of family betrayal, a personality clash among friends, and the folly of heedless courage. In the climax of the poem, the hero Roland, seeking renown for his valor, rejects his companion Oliver's advice to blow a horn to alert Charlemagne of a Muslim attack. The battle is hopeless, and when the horn is finally sounded it is too late to save Roland or Oliver. For those who heard and cherished the poem, the disagreement between the prudent Oliver and the reckless Roland expressed the complicated values of bravery and loyalty, the most important values in medieval French society. In this poem the borderland conflicts between Christians and Muslims became a primal source for medieval aristocratic culture.

The epic tenth-century Greek poem *Digenes Akritas* describes the heroic feats of soldiers during the late eighth century on the eastern frontier of the empire, where Byzantine and Arab populations both fought and cooperated in a complex symbiosis. The father of the hero of the poem was an Arab soldier who abducted the daughter of a Byzantine general, married her, and converted to Christianity. The son of this mixed marriage was Digenes ("two-blooded"), a man of two peoples and two religions, who became a border fighter. This greatest Byzantine hero, who lived between two cultures, was the poetic embodiment of the engagement between Byzantium and Islam at a time when the former seemed clearly in the ascendant. Like *The Song of Roland* for the French, the legends surrounding *Digenes Akritas* had a profound influence on Greek literature. Later writers referred to it and retold its stories again and again.

In the border wars of eleventh-century Spain, the most effective soldier was Rodrigo Díaz de Vivar (ca. 1043–1099), known to history as El Cid (from the Arabic word for "lord"). Fighting for Alfonso VI, the king of Castile, El Cid was the most famous figure of the Spanish Reconquest. He is remembered in legend as a heroic Christian knight fighting for God; however, El Cid did not in fact live out this role during his life. After a quarrel with Alfonso, El Cid went over to the Muslim side. For nearly ten years, this most prestigious of the Christian warriors defended the Muslim king of Saragossa. During this period of fighting his fellow Christians, El Cid added to his reputation as a general who had never suffered defeat. Even when the Almoravids invaded from North Africa and threatened the very existence of Christian Spain, El Cid did not come to the rescue of the Christian kingdoms. Instead he undertook a private adventure to carve out a kingdom for himself in Muslim Valencia. Under El Cid the city was partially Christianized and Christian immigrants began to move there, but Christian rule did not survive his death.

Soon after El Cid's death and despite his inconstant loyalty to Castile and Christianity, he was elevated to the status of the great hero of Christian Spain. Legend soon supplanted historical truth. The popularity of the twelfth-century epic poem *The Poem of My Cid* transformed this cruel, vindictive, and utterly self-interested man into a model of Christian virtue and self-sacrificing loyalty.

Similar to the western American frontier, the medieval borderlands created legends of heroism and epic struggles. The borderlands were a wild frontier into which desperate men fled to hide or to make opportunities for themselves. Like Digenes Akritas, many were the products of mixed ancestry because of Christian and Muslim abductions and marriages. The borderlands produced a class of professional warriors, such as El Cid, who took advantage of the perpetual conflicts of the Christian and Muslim kingdoms to enrich themselves and their followers. The meeting of Christians and Muslims that took place there stimulated medieval poetry and the values of knightly valor that characterized the Middle Ages.

CONCLUSION

An Emerging Unity in the Latin West

The most lasting legacy of the Early Middle Ages was the distinction between western and eastern Europe, established by the patterns of conversion to Christianity. Slavs in eastern Europe, such as the Poles, who were converted to Catholicism looked to Rome as a source for inspiration and eventually considered themselves part of the West. Those who converted to Orthodox Christianity, such as the Bulgarians and Russians, remained Europeans certainly but came to see themselves as culturally distinct from their Western counterparts. The southern border of Christian Europe was defined by the presence of the Islamic caliphates, which despite recurrent border wars with Christian kingdoms greatly contributed to the cultural vitality of the West during this period.

During this same period, however, a tentative unity began to emerge among western European Christians, just as Byzantium fell into decline and Islam divided among competing caliphates. That ephemeral unity was born in the hero worship of Charlemagne and the resurrection of the Roman Empire in the West, symbolized by his coronation in Rome. The collapse of the Carolingian Empire created the basis for the European kingdoms that dominated the political order of Europe for most of the subsequent millennium. These new kingdoms were each quite distinctive, and yet they shared a heritage from ancient Rome and the Carolingians that emphasized the power of the law on one hand and the intimate relationship between royal and ecclesiastical authority on the other. The most distinguishing mark of western Europe became the practice of what would come to be called Roman Catholicism, a distinctive form of Christianity identifiable by the use of the Latin language and the celebration of the church liturgy in Latin.

By about 1050, three social institutions had emerged that became characteristic of Latin medieval society for the next 400 years or more. The first was the system of personal loyalties associated with lordship and vassalage. All medieval kings were obliged to build their monarchies upon the social foundations of lordship. The second institution was the agricultural economy built on manors, which took advantage of the productive capacities of the agricultural revolution. The third institution distinctive to Latin medieval society was cities. Their demographic revival was a product of the agricultural revolution, which produced a surplus rural population that migrated to and energized the cities.

By the end of the eleventh century, emerging western Europe had recovered sufficiently from the many destructive invaders and had built new political and ecclesiastical institutions that enabled it to assert itself on a broader stage. The first move was sensational: The leaders of the Roman Church declared their intention to achieve what the Byzantines had failed to do—recapture Jerusalem from Islam. As we shall see in the next chapter, with the beginning of the Crusades at the end of the eleventh century, western Europeans began an aggressive engagement outside of their own continent.

Suggestions for Further Reading

···································· ▬ ····································

For a comprehensive list of suggested readings, please go to www.ablongman.com/levackconcise/chapter8

Bartlett, Robert. *The Making of Europe: Conquest, Colonization and Cultural Change: 950–1350.* 1993. The best, and often greatly stimulating, analysis of how Latin Christianity spread in post-Carolingian Europe.

Franklin, Simon, and Jonathan Shepard. *The Emergence of Rus: 750–1200.* 1996. The standard text for this period.

Gimpel, Jean. *The Medieval Machine: The Industrial Revolution of the Middle Ages.* 1976. A short, lucid account of the power and agricultural revolutions.

Hollister, C. Warren. *Medieval Europe: A Short History.* 1997. This concise, crisply written text presents the development of Europe during the Middle Ages by charting its progression from a primitive rural society, sparsely settled and impoverished, to a powerful and distinctive civilization.

Jones, Gwyn. *A History of the Vikings.* 2001. A comprehensive, highly readable analysis.

Reynolds, Susan. *Fiefs and Vassals: The Medieval Evidence Reinterpreted.* 1994. The most important reexamination of the feudalism problem.

Riché, Pierre. *The Carolingians: A Family Who Forged Europe.* 1993. Translated from the 1983 French edition, this book traces the rise, fall, and revival of the Carolingian dynasty and shows how it molded the shape of a post-Roman Europe that still prevails today. This is basically a family history, but the family dominated Europe for more than two centuries.

Stenton, Frank M. *Anglo-Saxon England.* 2001. This classic history covers the period ca. 550–1087 and traces the development of English society from the oldest Anglo-Saxon laws and kings to the extension of private lordship.

Treadgold, Warren T. *A Concise History of Byzantium.* 2001. The best short survey.

Notes

·······································

1. Quoted in Jane S. Gerber, *The Jews of Spain: A History of the Sephardic Experience* (1992), 28.

The West Asserts Itself: The High Middle Ages

OUSAMA, A TWELFTH-CENTURY ARAB NOBLEMAN, MADE A BUSINESS TRIP TO Jerusalem, which at the time was occupied by Christian crusaders. To fulfill the obligation of his Muslim faith to pray daily, Ousama went to the Al-Aksa mosque, the oldest Muslim shrine in Jerusalem. He was struck by the contrast between those crusaders who had resided in Jerusalem for some time and had an understanding of Islam and those who had just arrived and "show themselves more inhuman." Some of the old-timers had even befriended him and made certain he had a place to pray. But the newcomers were far from friendly. He reported, "One day I went into [the mosque] and glorified Allah. I was engrossed in my praying when one of the Franks [as Muslims called all western Europeans] rushed at me, seized me and turned my face to the East, saying, 'That is how to pray!'" At that time Christians were supposed to pray facing the rising sun in the East. Muslims pray facing Mecca to the south of Jerusalem. On two occasions the Templars, members of a Christian military order who guarded the mosque, had to expel the zealous Frank from the mosque so Ousama could return to his prayers. The Templars apologized to Ousama, saying, "He is a stranger who has only recently arrived from Frankish lands. He has never seen anyone praying without turning to the East."

An uneasy familiarity developed among the Christians and Muslims in Jerusalem during this period. It was possible for an Arab such as Ousama to describe the Templars as his "friends," and they in turn protected him from the intolerance of the newly arrived Europeans. This peculiar mixture of friendliness and intolerance cut both ways. Ousama recounted another scene he witnessed at the Dome of the Rock, the place from which it was believed that Muhammad ascended to heaven but which the crusaders had transformed into a Christian church. A Templar approached a Muslim and asked if he would like to see God as a child. When the Muslim answered "yes," the Templar displayed a painting of

Gothic Architecture: Interior view of stained-glass windows in Sainte-Chapelle, upper chapel, interior toward east, Paris.

the Virgin Mary with the Christ child on her lap. The Muslim was shocked at the Christian's idolatry of referring to an image as God. "May Allah raise himself high above those who speak such impious things!" Ousama exclaimed.

Throughout the Middle Ages, Muslims and Christians mixed mutual curiosity with militant hostility. Their tentative appreciation of each other was undermined by grotesque misunderstandings. The complexity of the relationship became especially clear in spiritual centers such as the mosques and churches of Jerusalem.

The cultural exchanges and clashes among the Catholic West, the Orthodox East, and the Muslim South were punctuated by the battles of the Crusades. Based on the efforts of the knights who fought in the Crusades and European merchants, the Catholic West began to assert itself both militarily and economically in Byzantium and in the Muslim world. As a result, western Europeans more sharply distinguished themselves from the Orthodox and Muslim worlds. The West became more exclusively Latin and Catholic.

The consolidation of a distinctive Western identity and the projection of Western power outside Europe for the first time was made possible by internal European developments. Several vigorous kings created political stability in the West by consolidating their authority through financial and judicial bureaucracies. At the same time, the West experienced a period of creative ferment unequaled since antiquity. The Roman Catholic Church played a central role in encouraging intellectual and artistic activity, but there was also a flourishing literature in the languages of the common people—French, German, and Italian.

During the twelfth and thirteenth centuries western Europe, in particular, was profoundly transformed. To understand this transformation, this chapter will address several fundamental questions:

- What were the causes and consequences of the Crusades?
- How did the Catholic Church consolidate its hold over the Latin West?
- How did the western European monarchies strengthen themselves?
- What made western European culture distinctive?

The West in the East: The Crusades

On a chilly November day in 1095 in a bare field outside of Clermont, France, Pope Urban II (r. 1088–1099) delivered a landmark sermon to the assembled French clergy and laypeople eager to hear the pope. In stirring words Urban recalled that Muslims in the East were persecuting Christians and that the holy places in Palestine had been ransacked. He called upon the knights "to take up the cross" to defend their fellow Christians in distress.

Urban's appeal for a Crusade was stunningly successful. When he finished speaking, the crowd chanted back, "God wills it." The news of Urban's call for a holy war in the East spread like wildfire, and all across France and the western part of the German Empire knights prepared for the journey to Jerusalem.

Urban's call for a Crusade gave powerful religious sanction to the western Christian military expeditions against Islam. From 1095 until well into the thirteenth century, there were recurrent, large-scale crusading expeditions as Christian knights from the Latin West attempted to take, retake, and protect Christian Jerusalem (see Map 9.1). But the ideal of going on a Crusade lasted long after the thirteenth century into modern times.

To people in the eleventh century, the very idea of Jerusalem had a mystical allure. Enhancing this allure was a widespread confusion between the actual earthly city of Jerusalem in Palestine, where Jesus had been crucified more than a millennium before, and the fantastic heavenly city of Jerusalem with walls of dazzling precious stones as promised in the Bible (Revelation 21:10ff). Many of the crusaders probably could not distinguish between the earthly and the heavenly cities and thought that when they abandoned their homes for Jerusalem, they were marching directly to Paradise. The promise of an eternal reward was reinforced by a special offer Pope Urban made in his famous sermon at Clermont to remit all penance for sin for those who went on the Crusade. Moreover, a penitential pilgrimage to a holy site such as Jerusalem provided a sinner with a pardon for capital crimes such as murder.

There was a significant difference between a pilgrim and a crusader, however. A pilgrim was always unarmed. A crusader carried weapons and was willing not just to defend other pilgrims from attack but to launch an assault on those he considered heathens. The innovation of the Crusades was to create the idea of armed pilgrims who received special rewards from the Church. The merger of a spiritual calling and military action was strongest in the knightly orders. The Templars, Hospitallers, and Teutonic Knights were soldiers who took monastic vows of poverty, chastity, and obedience. But rather than isolating themselves to pray in a monastery, they went forth, sword in hand, to defend the Christian Church.

CRUSADING WARFARE

The original impulse for the Crusades° was the threat that Muslim armies posed to Christian peoples, pilgrims, and holy places in the eastern Mediterranean. By the middle of the eleventh century the Seljuk Turks, who had converted to Islam, were putting pressure on the Byzantine Empire. Pope

Urban's appeal for a Crusade in 1095 came in response to a request for military assistance from the Byzantine emperor Alexius Comnenus. The crusaders landed in the Middle East and struck out to capture Jerusalem itself from the Muslims. In achieving this goal, the First Crusade (1095–1099) was strikingly successful.

In 1099, after a little more than a month's siege, the crusaders scaled the walls of Jerusalem and took possession of the city, which was also holy to Muslims and Jews and previously largely inhabited by them. The Christian triumph led to the establishment of the Latin principalities, which were devoted to maintaining a Western foothold in the Holy Land. The Latin principalities included all of the territory in contemporary Lebanon, Israel, and Palestine.

The subsequent crusades never achieved the success of the first. In 1144 Muslims captured the northernmost Latin principality, the county of Edessa—a warning to

Westerners of the fragility of a defensive system that relied on a few scattered fortresses strung along a thin strip of coastline. In response to the loss of Edessa, Christians launched the Second Crusade. In 1187, the sultan of Egypt and Syria, Saladin (1137–1193), recaptured Jerusalem for Islam. In response to this dispiriting loss, the Third Crusade (1189–1192) assembled the most spectacular army of European chivalry ever seen, led by Europe's three most powerful kings: German emperor Frederick Barbarossa, Philip Augustus of France, and Richard the Lion-Heart of England. After Frederick drowned wading in a river en route and Philip went home, Richard the Lion-Heart negotiated a truce with Saladin. The Fourth Crusade proved a particular disaster. In 1199, Pope Innocent III called for yet another Crusade to recapture Jerusalem, but instead the crusaders and the Venetian fleet were diverted to intervene in a disputed imperial

■ **Map 9.1   The Major Crusades**

During the first three Crusades, Christian armies and fleets from western Europe attacked Muslim strongholds and fortresses in the Middle East in an attempt to capture and hold Jerusalem. The Fourth Crusade never arrived in the Middle East, as it was diverted to besiege Constantinople. The routes to the Holy Land on this map are approximate.

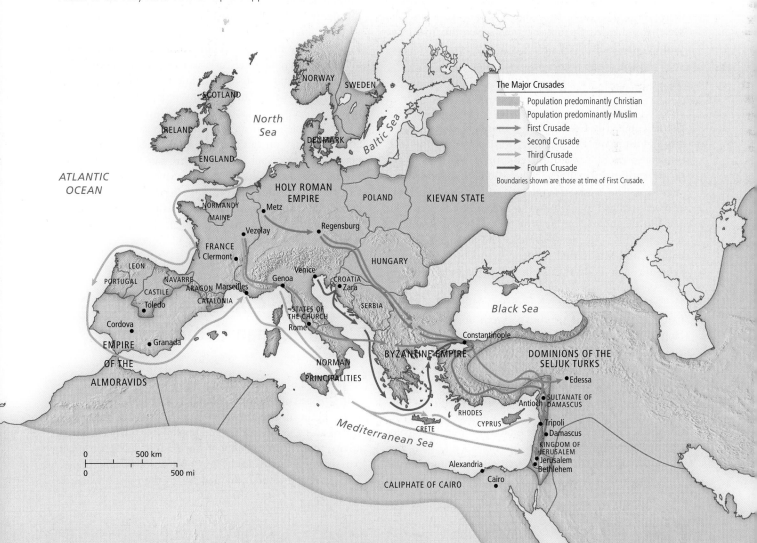

succession in Byzantium. They besieged and captured Constantinople. After the conquest the crusaders and Venetians divided up among themselves the Byzantine Empire, which they held until 1261.

THE SIGNIFICANCE OF THE CRUSADES

Despite the capture of Jerusalem during the First Crusade, the crusaders could not maintain control of the city and for more than a century wasted enormous efforts on what proved to be a futile enterprise. Neither did any of the Latin principalities in the Middle East survive for very long. The crusaders who resided in these principalities were obliged to learn how to live and trade with their Muslim neighbors, but few of them learned Arabic or took seriously Muslim learning. The strongest Islamic cultural and intellectual influences on Christian Europe came through Sicily and Spain rather than via returning crusaders.

The most important immediate consequence of the Crusades was not the tenuous Western possession of the Holy Land but the expansion of trade and economic contacts the expeditions facilitated. No one profited more from the Crusades than the Italian cities that provided transportation and supplies to the crusading armies. During the Crusades, Genoa, Pisa, and Venice were transformed from small ports of regional significance into hubs of international trade. Genoa and Venice established their own colonial outposts in the eastern Mediterranean, and both vied to monopolize the rich commerce of Byzantium. Profits from this trade helped galvanize the economy of western

Europe, leading to an era of exuberant economic growth during the twelfth and thirteenth centuries.

Long after the thirteenth century, the crusading ideal was kept alive in Christian Europe. Active crusading military orders were fighting Turks as late as 1798, and some of those orders still exist. A crusading tax survived in Spain and parts of Latin America into very modern times. In many respects the Crusades established the idea that Christian rulers had an obligation to use military force against attacks on faithful Christians and Christian holy places. The principal threat in Christian eyes came from Muslim armies. At the same time, Muslims perceived the Crusades as an attempt to conquer territory that rightfully belonged to them. As we shall see shortly, not only Muslims but even other Christians who dissented from official doctrines could become the objects of a Crusade.

The Consolidation of Roman Catholicism

The late eleventh through thirteenth centuries witnessed one of the greatest periods of religious vitality in the history of Roman Catholicism. Manifest by the rise of new religious orders and remarkable intellectual creativity, the religious vitality of the era was due in no small part to the effective leadership of a series of able popes. They gave the Church the benefits of the most advanced, centralized government in Europe. However, the papacy's successful intervention in worldly affairs helped undermine its spiritual authority, opening the way to the degradation of the papacy in the fourteenth century.

THE POPE BECOMES A MONARCH

There were many bishops in Christianity, but as one monk put it, "Rome is . . . the head of the world." The task of the medieval popes was to make this theoretical claim to authority real—in short, to make the papacy a religious monarchy. In the last half of the eleventh century under a series of dynamic reformers, the papacy firmly reasserted itself as the head of the Roman Catholic world. The most successful of these reformist popes was Gregory VII (r. 1073–1085).

Gregory's greatness lay in his leadership over the internal reform of the Church. Every year he held a church council in Rome where he decreed against simony (the buying and selling of church offices) and against priests who married and attempted to bequeath church property to their children. Gregory centralized authority over the Church itself by sending out papal legates, representatives who delivered orders to local bishops, and attempted to free it from external influence by asserting the superiority of the pope over all other authorities. Gregory's theory of papal supremacy led him into direct conflict with the German Emperor Henry IV (r. 1056–1106). The issue was lay investiture, the power of kings and emperors to pick their own candidates for ecclesiastical offices, especially bishoprics.

The struggle between Pope Gregory and Emperor Henry is now known as the Investiture Controversy°, so named because Henry was controlling Church appointments by reserving for himself the right to bestow or "invest" the symbols of ecclesiastical office. To correct this abuse Gregory deposed Henry from the imperial throne and excommunicated him from the Church. Excommunication° prohibited the emperor from participating in the sacraments and forbade any social contact whatsoever with the surrounding community. Henry's friends started to abandon him, rebellion broke out in Germany, and the most powerful German lords called for a meeting to elect a new emperor. Backed into a corner, Henry plotted a clever counterstroke.

Early in the winter of 1077 Pope Gregory set out to cross the Alps to meet with the German lords. When Gregory reached the Alpine passes, however, he learned that Emperor Henry was on his way to Italy. In fear of what the emperor would do, Gregory retreated to the castle of Canossa, where he expected to be attacked. Henry surprised Gregory, however, by arriving not with an army but as a supplicant asking the pope to hear his confession. As a priest Gregory could hardly refuse to hear the confession of a penitent sinner, but he nevertheless attempted to humiliate Henry by making him wait for three days, kneeling in the snow outside the castle. Henry's presentation of himself as a penitent sinner posed a dilemma for Gregory. The German lords were waiting for Gregory to appear in his capacity as the chief justice of Christendom to judge Henry, but Henry himself was asking the pope to act in his capacity as priest to grant absolution for sin. The priest in Gregory won out over the judge, and he absolved Henry.

Even after the deaths of Gregory and Henry, the Investiture Controversy continued to poison relations between the popes and emperors, but Gregory VII's vision of papal supremacy over all kings and emperors persevered.

How the Popes Ruled

The most lasting accomplishment of the popes during the twelfth and thirteenth centuries derived less from dramatic confrontations with emperors than from the humdrum routine of the law. Beginning with Gregory VII, the papacy became the supreme court of the Catholic world by claiming authority over a vast range of issues. To justify these claims, Gregory and his assistants conducted massive research of old laws and treatises. These were organized into a body of legal texts called canon law°.

Canon law came to encompass many kinds of cases, including all those involving the clergy, disputes about church property, and donations to the Church. The law of the Church also touched on many of the most vital concerns of the laity—all those who were not priests, monks, or nuns—including annulling marriages, legitimating bastards, prosecuting bigamy, protecting widows and orphans, and resolving inheritance disputes. Most of the cases originated in the courts of the bishops, but the bishops' decisions could be appealed to the pope and cardinals sitting together in the papal consistory. The consistory could make exceptions from the letter of the law, called dispensations, giving it considerable power over kings and aristocrats who wanted to marry a cousin, divorce a wife, legitimate a bastard, or annul a will. By the middle of the twelfth century, Rome was awash with legal business. The functions of the canon law courts became so important that those who were elected popes were no longer monks but trained canon lawyers, men very capable in the ways of the world.

The pope also presided over the curia°, the administrative bureaucracy of the Church. The cardinals served as ministers in the papal administration and were sent off to foreign princes and cities as ambassadors, or legates. Because large amounts of revenue were flowing into the coffers of the Church, Rome became the financial capital of the West.

The Pinnacle of the Medieval Papacy: Pope Innocent III

The most capable of the medieval popes was Innocent III (r. 1198–1216). Innocent possessed a clear-sighted concept of the papal monarchy. To him the pope was the overlord and moral guide of the Christian community, with authority over the entire world. He recognized the right of kings to rule over the secular sphere, but he considered it his duty to prevent and punish sin, a duty that gave him wide latitude to meddle in the affairs of kings and princes.

Innocent provided the papacy with a strong territorial base of support so that the popes could act with the same freedom as kings and princes. Innocent is generally considered the founder of the Papal State in central Italy, an independent state that lasted until 1870 and survives today in a tiny fragment as Vatican City. By calling the Fourth Crusade, he kept alive the crusading ideal. He also expanded the definition of crusading by calling for a Crusade to eliminate heresy within Christian Europe. He asserted the power of the papacy over political affairs by assuming the right to veto imperial elections and by demanding that several of the kings of Europe pay homage to him as their lord.

Innocent's greatest accomplishment was to codify the rites of the liturgy and to define the dogmas of the faith. This monumental task was the achievement of the Fourth Lateran Council, held in Rome in 1215. This council issued decrees that reinforced the celebration of the sacraments as the centerpiece of Christian life. It did more than any other council to fulfill the goal of uniformity of rites in Catholicism, and its influence survives to this day.

Innocent was a crafty, intelligent man who in single-minded fashion pursued the greater good of the Church as he saw it. His policies, however, had ruinous results in the hands of his less able successors. Their blunders undermined the pope's spiritual mission. They went beyond defending the Papal State and embroiled all Italy in a series of bloody civil wars. By the fourteenth century the pope's position as a monarch superior to all others collapsed under the weight of immense folly and hypocrisy.

DISCOVERING GOD IN THE WORLD

Even before the First Crusade, Catholic Europe began to experience an unprecedented spiritual awakening. Many laypeople who had previously been Christians in name only began to attend church services and to show genuine enthusiasm for the Church. The most vital indication of spiritual renewal was the success of new religious orders, which satisfied a widespread yearning to discover the hand of God in the world.

The New Religious Orders

In the early thirteenth century, two religious figures from Spain and Italy formulated a new kind of religious order composed of mendicant friars°. From the very beginning the friars wanted to distinguish themselves from monks. Instead of working in a monastery to feed themselves as did monks, friars ("brothers") wandered from city to city and throughout the countryside begging for alms (*mendicare*

means "to beg", hence *mendicant*). Unlike monks who remained in a cloister, friars tried to help ordinary laypeople with their problems by preaching and administering to the sick and poor.

The Spaniard Dominic (1170–1221) founded the Dominican Order to convert Muslims and Jews and to combat heresy among Christians, against whom he began his preaching mission while traveling through southern France. The ever-perceptive Pope Innocent III recognized Dominic's talents while he was visiting Rome and gave his new order provisional approval. Dominic believed that conversion could be achieved through persuasion and argument. Famed for their preaching skills, Dominicans were equally successful at moving the illiterate masses and debating sophisticated opponents.

From the beginning, the Dominican order synthesized the contemplative life of the monastery and the active ministry of preaching to laypeople. In contrast to traditional monastic orders, the Dominican order was organized like an army. Each province was under the supervision of a master general, and each Dominican was ready to travel wherever needed to preach and convert.

The Franciscan order enjoyed a similar success. The Italian Francis of Assisi (1182–1226) was less an organizer than an intensely spiritual man and a visionary. The son of a prosperous merchant, Francis as a young man rebelled against the selfishness of his father's materialistic world. In a famous episode, he stripped naked in the town square as a symbol of his rejection of all possessions. Dressed in rags, he begged for food, preached repentance in the streets, and ministered to outcasts and lepers. Without training as a priest or license as a preacher, Francis at first seemed like a devout eccentric or even a dangerous heretic, but his rigorous imitation of Jesus began to attract like-minded followers. In 1210 Francis and his ragged brothers showed up in the opulent papal court of Innocent III seeking approval of a new religious order. Innocent was impressed by Francis's sincerity and his willingness to profess obedience to the pope. Innocent's provisional approval of the Franciscans was a brilliant stroke, in that it gave the papacy a way to manage the widespread enthusiasm for a life of spirituality and purity.

Both the Dominican and Franciscan orders spread rapidly. Liberated from the obligation to live in a monastery, the mendicant friars traveled wherever the pope ordered them, making them effective agents of the papal monarchy. They preached Crusades. They pacified the poor. They converted heretics and non-Christians through their inspiring preaching revivals. They established Catholic colonies along the frontiers of the West and beyond.

The Flowering of Religious Sensibilities

During the twelfth and thirteenth centuries the widespread enthusiasm for religion exalted spiritual creativity. Experimentation pushed Christian piety in new directions, not just for aristocratic men, who dominated the Church hierarchy and the monasteries, but for women and laypeople from all social levels.

Catholic worship concentrated on the celebration of the Eucharist°. The Eucharist, which was the crucial ritual moment during the Mass, celebrated Jesus' last meal with his apostles. The Eucharistic rite consecrated wafers of bread and a chalice of wine as the body and blood of Christ. After the consecration, the celebrating priest distributed to the congregation the bread, called the host. Drinking from the chalice, however, was a special privilege of the priesthood. More than anything else, belief in the miraculous change from bread to flesh and wine to blood, along with the sacrament of baptism, distinguished Christian believers from others. As simple as it was as a ritual observance, belief in the Eucharistic miracle presented a vexing and complex theological problem—why the host still looked, tasted, and smelled like bread rather than flesh, and why the blood in the chalice still seemed to be wine rather than blood. After the Fourth Lateran Council in 1215, Catholics solved this problem with the doctrine of transubstantiation°. The doctrine rested on a distinction between the outward appearances of the object, which the five senses can perceive, and the substance of an object, which they cannot perceive. When the priest spoke the words of consecration during the Mass, the bread and wine were changed into the flesh and blood of Christ in substance ("transubstantiated") but not in outward appearances. Thus, the substance of the Eucharist literally became God's body, but the senses of taste, smell, and sight perceived it as bread.

Veneration of the Eucharist enabled the faithful to identify with Christ because believers considered the consecrated Eucharistic wafer to be Christ himself. By eating the host, they had literally ingested Christ, making his body part of their bodies. Eucharistic veneration became enormously popular in the thirteenth century and the climax of dazzling ritual performance.

During this period public veneration of saints also shifted away from local patron saints and toward more universal figures. Christians had always honored the Virgin Mary, but beginning in the twelfth century her immense popularity provided Catholics with a positive female image that contradicted the traditional misogyny and mistrust associated with Eve. Clerics and monks had long depicted women as deceitful and lustful in luring men to their moral ruin. In contrast, the veneration of the Virgin Mary promoted the image of a loving mother who would intervene with her son on behalf of sinners at the Last Judgment. Theologians still taught that the woman Eve had brought sin into the world, but the woman Mary offered help in escaping the consequences of sin.

Mary became a model with whom women could identify, presenting a positive image of femininity. In images of her suckling the Christ child, she became the perfect em-

THE SONG OF BROTHER SUN

Francis of Assisi is known, among other things, as a nature mystic, which means he celebrated God's creation through a love of nature. In one of the most renowned celebrations of nature ever written, "The Song of Brother Sun," Francis transforms the inanimate forces of nature into his spiritual brothers and sisters.

Be praised, my Lord, with all Your creatures,
Especially Sir Brother Sun,
By whom You give us the light of day!
And he is beautiful and radiant with great splendor.
Of You, Most High, he is a symbol!

Be praised, my Lord, for Sister Moon and the Stars!
In the sky You formed them bright and lovely and fair.

Be praised, my Lord, for Brother Wind
And for the Air and cloudy and clear and all Weather,
By which You give sustenance to Your creatures!

Be praised, my Lord, for Sister Water,
Who is very useful and humble and lovely and chaste!

Be praised, my Lord, for Brother Fire,
By whom You give us light at night,
And he is beautiful and merry and mighty and strong!

Be praised, my Lord, for our Sister Mother Earth,
Who sustains and governs us,
And produces fruits with colorful flowers and leaves!

Source: From *The Little Flowers of St. Francis* by St. Francis of Assisi, translated by Raphael Brown, copyright © 1958 by Beverly Brown. Used by permission of Doubleday, a division of Random House, Inc.

bodiment of the virtue of charity, the willingness to give without any expectation of reward. Through the image of the nursing Virgin Mary, the ability to nurture became associated not just with Mary but with Christ himself.

In contrast to the early Christian saints who were predominantly martyrs and missionaries, during the twelfth and thirteenth centuries saints exhibited sanctity more through nurturing others, especially by feeding the poor and healing the sick. Nurturing was associated with women, and many more women became saints during this period than during the entire first millennium of Christianity.

Saints, however, were exceptional people. Most Christians contented themselves with the sacraments, especially baptism, penance, and the Eucharist; perhaps a pilgrimage to a saint's shrine; and a final attempt for salvation by making a pious gift to the Church on their deathbed. The benevolent process of discovering God also stimulated a related malevolent process of attempting to detect the influence of the Devil in the world. To eradicate the Devil's influence, Christians made some people the outcasts of Western society.

CREATING THE OUTCASTS OF EUROPE

As churchmen and kings sought to enforce religious unity and moral reform during the twelfth and thirteenth centuries, they were disturbed by peoples who did not seem to fit into official notions of Christian society. Some of these people, such as heretics and Jews, actively rejected church authority. The papacy began a dramatic wave of military expeditions against heretical lords in order to deprive them of their lands and to inquire into the beliefs that they had allowed to flourish in their territories. Follow-up campaigns attempted to convert, control, or suppress these religious minorities, who were made social outcasts.

The Heretics: Cathars and Waldensians

In its efforts to defend the faith, the Church during the first half of the thirteenth century began to authorize bishops and other clerics to conduct inquisitions (formal inquiries) into specific instances of heresy or perceived heresy. The so-called heretics tended to be faithful people who sought a form of religion purer than the Church provided. During the thirteenth and early fourteenth centuries, inquisitions and systematic persecutions targeted the Cathars and Waldensians, who at first had lived peacefully with their Catholic neighbors.

The Cathars were especially strong in northern Italy and southern France. The name *Cathar* derives from the Greek word for "purity." Heavily concentrated around the French town of Albi, the Cathars were also known as Albigensians. They departed from Catholic doctrine, which held that God created Earth, because they believed that an evil force had created all matter. To purify themselves, an elite few—known as "perfects"—rejected their own bodies as corrupt matter, refused to marry and procreate, and in extreme cases gradually starved themselves. These purified perfects provided a dramatic contrast to the more worldly Catholic clergy. For many, Catharism became a form of protest against the wealth and power of the Church. By the 1150s the Cathars had organized their own churches, performed their own rituals, and even elected their own bishops. Where they became deeply rooted, as in the south of France, they practiced their faith openly until Pope Innocent III authorized a Crusade against them.

The Waldensians were the followers of Peter Waldo (d. ca. 1184), a merchant of Lyons, France, who had abandoned all his possessions and taken a vow of poverty. Desiring to imitate the life of Jesus and live in simple purity, the Waldensians preached and translated the Gospels into their own language so that laypeople who did not know Latin could understand them. The Waldensians created an alternative church that became widespread in southern France, Rhineland Germany, and northern Italy.

Catholic authorities, who were often the objects of strong criticisms from the Cathars and Waldensians, grew ever more hostile to them. Bishops declared heretics liable to the same legal penalties as those guilty of treason, which authorized the political authorities to proceed against them. In 1208 Pope Innocent III called the Albigensian Crusade, the first of several holy wars launched against heretics in the south of France. The king of France was only too happy to fight the Albigensian Crusade because he saw it as a means of expanding royal power in a region of France where his authority was weak. To eradicate the remaining Cathars and Waldensians, several kings and popes initiated inquisitions. By the middle of the thirteenth century the Cathars had been converted or exterminated except for a few isolated pockets in the mountains, which were stamped out by later inquisitors. The Waldensians were nearly wiped out by inquisitorial campaigns, but a few scattered groups have managed to survive to this day, mostly by retreating to the relative safety of the high Alps and later to the Americas.

Systematic Persecution of the Jews

Before the Crusades, Christians and Jews had lived in relative harmony in Europe. In fact, during the Carolingian period the Frankish kings and emperors had protected Jewish communities from the occasional hostility of bishops who sought to expel them. The Crusades, however, fomented increased violence against Jews. Discrimination and assaults against Jews soon became far more common than ever before. In 1182 Jews were expelled from France and allowed to return only under dire financial penalties. In England the monarchy discriminated against the Jews, opening the way for the massacre and mass suicide of the entire Jewish community of York in 1190. The 1215 decrees of the Fourth Lateran Council, which were the centerpiece of Innocent III's pontificate, attempted to regulate the activities of the Jews of Europe. These decrees prohibited Jews from holding public offices and required them to wear distinctive dress.

Christians justified their persecution of Jews during the twelfth and thirteenth centuries in two ways. First, they depicted Jews as the enemies of Christ. This bias was based on the belief that Jews were members of a conspiratorial organization devoted to the destruction of Christianity. Second, jurists began to consider Jews as royal serfs because they lived in a Christian kingdom at the king's sufferance. By classifying Jews as serfs, the law deprived them of the rights of private property. As the jurist Bracton put it, "The Jew can have nothing of his own, for whatever he acquires he acquires not for himself but for the king; for the Jews live not for themselves but for others and so they acquire not

■ **Burning of Heretics During the Early Thirteenth Century**
These were followers of Amalric of Bène, whose body was dug up and burned in 1210. King Philip II of France supervises the burning.

for themselves but for others."[1] This precept, which was promulgated in Spain, England, and the German Empire, justified the repeated royal confiscations of Jewish property. Especially when faced with a fiscal shortfall, kings were inclined to solve their financial problems by expropriating the property of the Jewish community. As a result of these policies, most Jews were desperately poor. Since they were prohibited from owning land or joining craft guilds, Jews were forced to seek other means of support. Because Christians were barred from loaning money at interest, running pawn shops and banking were some of the few economic activities open to European Jews.

One of the ways medieval Catholic society became unified was by ostracizing certain groups of people from within its midst. The cleansing of Christian Europe was a tragedy for its victims, but it gave both church and government officials a greater sense of unity and control.

Strengthening the Center of the West

D uring the twelfth and thirteenth centuries, Catholic western Europe became the supreme political and economic power in the Christian world, eclipsing Byzantium—an achievement that made it a potent rival to the Islamic states. One reason was stronger political unity.

The kings of France and England, in particular, achieved unprecedented power over their own dominions. A second reason was economic. From the city-states in Italy to the cities on the shores of the Baltic Sea, Europe was bound together by an extensive trading network controlled by sophisticated merchants. As a result, by the thirteenth century Europeans enjoyed a high level of prosperity.

THE MONARCHIES OF WESTERN EUROPE

During the High Middle Ages, France and England began to exhibit the fundamental characteristics of unified kingdoms. Several developments explain how these kingdoms strengthened themselves. First, they formed political units that persisted. These units had borders that survived despite changes in rulers and dynasties. Second, these kingdoms developed lasting, impersonal institutions that managed finances and administration. We can blame this period for the rise of bureaucracies. Third, they established a system for resolving disputes and rendering justice in which the final authority was the king—the principle of sovereignty. Fourth, the medieval monarchies resolved that the fundamental loyalty of subjects should be to the laws of the state, a loyalty greater than the obligations of a vassal to a lord or even a son to a father. Stable borders, permanent bureaucracies, sovereignty, and the rule of law were the foundations on which France and England became the most powerful kingdoms in Europe during the twelfth and thirteenth centuries (see Map 9.2).

Expansion of Power: France

France enjoyed a continuous succession of kings who ruled for long periods of time, produced male heirs, and avoided succession disputes. In the turbulent Middle Ages, dynastic continuity was a key ingredient in building loyalty and avoiding chaos. The vigorous Philip I (r. 1060–1108) initiated a succession of extremely effective kings. Unpopular with the clergy because of his alleged adultery, Philip took charge of his own domain, the Ile-de-France, an area roughly the size of Vermont but with the fertile soil of Illinois. In the royal domain he countermanded the arbitrary justice of local lords by extending royal justice. By focusing his attention on establishing himself as the undisputed lord of his own domain, Philip provided his descendants with a powerful lordship upon which they built the French monarchy.

More than a century later King Philip's namesake, King Philip II Augustus (r. 1180–1223) proved himself a shrewd realist who outmaneuvered his vassal, the English king John, to recover much of western France for himself. To administer his domain and newly acquired lands, Philip introduced new royal officials, the *baillis,* paid professionals who were often trained in Roman law. Directly responsible to the king, they had full administrative, judicial, and military powers in their districts. Philip tolerated considerable regional diversity, but the *baillis* laid the foundation for a bureaucracy that centralized French government. Many historians consider Philip Augustus the most important figure in establishing the unity of the French state.

Lord of All Lords: The King of England

When William I, the Conqueror (r. 1066–1087), seized England in 1066, he claimed all the land. The new king kept about one-fifth of the land under his personal rule and parceled out the rest to the loyal nobles, monasteries, and the churches. This policy ensured that every bit of England

■ **Map 9.2   Western European Kingdoms in the Late Twelfth Century**

The kings of England occupied Ireland as well as much of western France. France itself was consolidated around the Ile-de-France, the area around Paris. The kingdoms of Germany, Bohemia, Burgundy, and Italy were ruled by the German emperors.

was held as a fief, directly or indirectly, from the king, a principle of lordship enforced by an oath of loyalty to the crown required of all vassals. About 180 great lords from among the Norman aristocracy held land directly from the king, and hundreds of lesser nobles were vassals of these great lords. William accomplished what other kings only dreamed about: He had truly made himself the lord of all lords. William's hierarchy of nobles transformed the nature of the English monarchy, giving the Norman kings far greater authority over England than any of the earlier Anglo-Saxon kings had enjoyed and creating a more unified realm than any kingdom on the continent.

The legacy of the conquest provided William's successors with a decided advantage in centralizing the monarchy. Nevertheless, the system required the king's personal attention. King Henry II (r. 1154–1189) proved himself an indefatigable administrator and calculating realist who made England the best-governed kingdom in Europe at the time. Reacting to the anarchy that prevailed when he ascended to the throne, he strengthened the government of England and extended English authority—with varying degrees of success—over Ireland, Wales, and Scotland.

The greatest innovations of Henry's rule were judicial. His use of sheriffs to enforce the royal will produced the legends of Robin Hood, the bandit who resisted the nasty sheriff of Nottingham on behalf of the poor. But in reality the sheriffs probably did more good than harm in protecting the weak against the powerful. In attempting to reduce the jurisdiction of the nobles, Henry made it possible for almost anyone to obtain a writ that moved a case to a royal court. To make justice more available to those who could not travel to Westminster, just outside London where the royal court usually sat, Henry introduced a system of itinerant circuit court° judges who visited every shire in the land four times a year. When this judge arrived, the sheriff was required to assemble a group of men familiar with local affairs to report the major crimes that had been committed since the judge's last visit. These assemblies were the origins of the grand jury° system, which persists to this day as the means for indicting someone for a crime.

For disputes over the possession of land, sheriffs assembled a group of twelve local men who testified under oath about the claims of the disputants and the judge made his decision on the basis of their testimony. These assemblies were the beginning of trial by jury°. The system was later extended to criminal cases and remains the basis for rendering legal verdicts in common-law countries, including Britain, the United States, and Canada.

The royal powers assembled by Henry met strong reaction under King John (r. 1199–1216). In 1204 John lost to King Philip II of France the Duchy of Normandy, which had been one of the foundations of English royal power since William the Conqueror. After the French defeated King John at the Battle of Bouvines in 1214, the barons of England grew tired of being asked to pay for wars the king lost. In 1215 some English barons forced John to sign Magna Carta° ("great charter," in reference to its size), in which the king pledged to respect the traditional feudal privileges of the nobility, towns, and clergy. Contrary to widespread belief, Magna Carta had nothing to do with asserting the liberty of the common people or guaranteeing universal rights. It addressed only the privileges of a select few rather than the rights of the many. Subsequent kings, however, swore to uphold it, thereby accepting the fundamental principle that even the king was obliged to respect the law. After Magna Carta the lord of all lords became less so.

English government boasted two important innovations under King Edward I (r. 1272–1307). The first was the foundation of the English Parliament (from the French "talking together"). Edward called together the clergy, barons, knights, and townsmen in Parliament in order to raise large sums of money for his foreign wars. The members of Parliament had little choice but to comply with the king's demands, and all they received in return was Edward's explanation of what he was going to do with their money. The English Parliament differed from similar assemblies on the Continent in that it more often included representatives of the "commons." The commons consisted of townsmen and prosperous farmers who lacked titles of nobility but whom the king summoned because he needed their money. The second governmental innovation during Edward's reign consisted of an extensive body of legal reforms. Edward curtailed the power of the local courts, which were dominated by rural landlords and aristocrats. He began to issue statutes that applied to the entire kingdom. Under Edward, lawyers began to practice at the Inns of Court in London, where they transformed customary legal practices into the common law that still survives as the foundation of Anglo-American law.

A Divided Regime: The German Empire

Heir to the old Carolingian kingdom of East Francia, the German Empire suffered from the division between its principal component parts in Germany and northern Italy. Germany itself was an ill-defined region, subdivided by deep ethnic diversity and powerful dukes who ruled their lands with a spirit of fierce independence. As a result, emperors could not rule Germany directly but only by demanding homage from the dukes who became imperial vassals. In northern Italy, the other part of the emperor's dominion, he did not even enjoy these extensive ties of vassalage and could rely only on vague legal rights granted by the imperial title and his ability to keep an army on the scene.

The century between the election of Frederick I (r. 1152–1190), known as Barbarossa or "red-beard," and the death of his grandson Frederick II (r. 1212–1250)

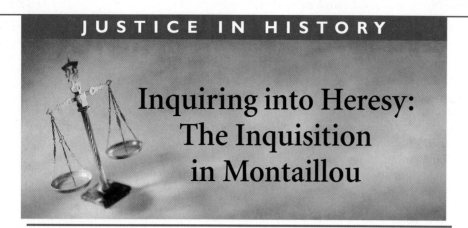

Inquiring into Heresy: The Inquisition in Montaillou

In 1208 Pope Innocent III issued a call for a Crusade against the Cathars or Albigensians. Fighting on behalf of French King Philip II, Simon de Montfort decisively defeated the pro-Cathar barons of southern France at Muret in 1213. Catharism retreated to the mountains, where it was kept alive by a clandestine network of adherents. The obliteration of these stubborn remnants required methods more subtle than the blunt instrument of a Crusade. It required the techniques of inquisitors adept at interrogation and investigation.

Against the Cathar underground, the inquisition conducted its business through a combination of denunciations, exhaustive interrogations of witnesses and suspects, and confessions. Because its avowed purpose was to root out doctrinal error and to reconcile heretics to the Church, eliciting confessions was the preferred technique. But confessed heretics could not receive absolution until they informed on their friends and associates.

One of the last and most extensively documented inquisition cases against Catharism took place in Montaillou, a village in the Pyrenees Mountains, near the border of modern-day France and Spain. The Montaillou inquisition began in 1308, a century after the launch of the Albigensian Crusade and long after the heyday of Catharism.

However, the detailed records of the inquisitors provide a revealing glimpse into Catharism and its suppression as well as the procedures of the inquisition. The first to investigate Montaillou was Geoffrey d'Ablis, the inquisitor of Carcassone. In 1308 he had every resident over age 12 seized and imprisoned. After the investigation, the villagers suffered the full range of inquisitorial penalties for their Cathar faith. Some were burned at the stake or sentenced to life in prison. Many who were allowed to return to Montaillou were forced to wear a yellow cross, the symbol of a heretic, sewn to the outside of their garments.

Unfortunately for these survivors, Montaillou was investigated again from 1318 to 1325 by the most fearsome inquisitor of the age, Jacques Fournier, who was later elected Pope Benedict XII. Known as an efficient, rigorous opponent of heresy, Fournier forced virtually all the surviving adults in Montaillou to appear before his tribunal. When the scrupulous Fournier took up a case, his inquiries were notoriously lengthy and rigorous. Both witnesses and defendants spoke of his tenacity, skill, and close attention to detail in conducting interrogations. If Fournier and his assistants could not uncover evidence through interrogation and confession, they did not hesitate to employ informers and spies to obtain the necessary information. When Pierre Maury, a shepherd who had been sought by the inquisitors for many years, returned to the village for a visit, an old friend received him with caution: "When we saw you again we felt both joy and fear. Joy, because it was a long time since we had seen you. Fear, because I was afraid lest the Inquisition had captured you up there: if they had they would have made you confess everything and come back among us as a spy in order to bring about my capture."[2]

Fournier's success in Montaillou depended on his ability to play local factions against each other by encouraging members of one clan to denounce the members of another. Fournier's persistence even turned family members against one another. The clearest example of this convoluted play of local alliances and animosities, family ties, religious belief, and self-interest is the case of Montaillou's wealthiest family, the Clergues.

Bernard Clergue was the count's local representative, which made him a kind of sheriff, and his brother Pierre was the parish priest. Together they represented both the secular and religious arms of the inquisition in Montaillou. In his youth, Pierre had Cathar sympathies, and he reportedly had kept a heretical book or calendar in his home. Nevertheless, at some time before 1308, he and Bernard betrayed the local Cathars to the inquisition. In the proceedings that followed, they had the power to either protect or expose their neighbors and family members. When one of his relatives was summoned to appear before the inquisition, Bernard warned her to "say you fell off the ladder in your house; pre-

Heretics Besiege the Church

In this fifteenth-century painting the Church is symbolized by a castle, which is defended by the pope and bishops. Many of the heretics attacking the Church wear blindfolds, which symbolize their inability to see the truth.

tend you have broken bones everywhere. Otherwise it's prison for you."[3] Pierre relentlessly used his influence for his own and his family's benefit. A notorious womanizer, Pierre frightened women into sleeping with him by threatening to denounce them to the inquisition. Those he personally testified against were primarily from other prominent Montaillou families who represented a challenge to the Clergues' power. As one resident bitterly testified, "the priest himself cause[s] many inhabitants of Montaillou to be summoned by the Lord Inquisitor of Carcassone. It is high time the people of the priest's house were thrust as deep in prison as the other inhabitants of Montaillou."[4]

Despite the Clergues' attempted misuse of the inquisitorial investigation for their own purposes, the inquisitor Fournier persevered according to his own standards of evidence. In 1320 he finally had Pierre Clergue arrested as a heretic. The sly priest died in prison. ■

Questions of Justice

1. How did the methods of the inquisition help create outcasts from Catholic society? How did these methods help consolidate Catholic identity?

2. The primary function of the inquisition was to investigate what people believed. What do you think the inquisitors thought justice to be?

Taking It Further

Lambert, Malcolm. *The Cathars.* 1998. The best place to investigate the Cathar movement in the full sweep of its troubled history.

Le Roy Ladurie, Emmanuel. *Montaillou: The Promised Land of Error,* trans. Barbara Bray. 1978. The best-selling and fascinating account of life in a Cathar village based on the records of Fournier's inquisition.

Moore, R. I. *The Formation of a Persecuting Society: Power and Deviance in Western Europe, 950–1250.* 1987. Places the harassment of heretics in the broader context of medieval persecutions.

represented the great age of the medieval German Empire, a period of relative stability preceded and followed by disastrous phases of anarchy and civil war. Both of these Hohenstaufen emperors, however, faced hostility from the popes whose own monarchic pretensions clashed with imperial rule in Italy.

Barbarossa projected enormous personal charisma that helped him awe recalcitrant vassals. He became a careful student of the imperial dignities encoded in Roman law, surrounded himself with experts in that law, and considered himself the heir of the great emperors Constantine, Justinian, and Charlemagne. To set himself on a firmer financial footing, Barbarossa launched a series of expeditions across the Alps to subdue the enormously wealthy Italian cities that were technically part of his realm, even though they acted as if they were independent. The campaign proved a disaster. It galvanized papal opposition to him and forced the Italian city-states to put aside their rivalries to form an anti-imperial coalition, the Lombard League. At the Battle of Legnano in 1176 the league decisively defeated the German imperial army, forcing Barbarossa to recognize the autonomy of the city-states.

Barbarossa's young grandson, Frederick II, turned the traditional policy of the German emperors upside down. Instead of residing in Germany and attempting to influence Italian affairs from afar, Frederick, who loved the warm climate and engaging society of the South, lived in Sicily and left Germany alone.

Frederick II proposed to rule through a professional imperial bureaucracy, to employ itinerant inspectors to check corruption, and to introduce uniform statutes based on Roman law. In effect, he sought a level of uniformity similar to what France and England had achieved during this period, and he was probably subject to similar influences derived from ancient Roman political theory and law. However, the popes' enduring antagonism to these plans and Frederick's own despotic tendencies undermined these ambitious and potentially fruitful reforms.

After Frederick II's death, his successors lost their hold on both Italy and Germany. During the nearly constant warfare and turmoil of the late thirteenth century, the exceedingly inappropriate name of "Holy Roman Empire" came into general use for the German Empire. The term suggested a universal empire ordained by God and descended from ancient Rome, but the lofty claims embedded in the name found no basis in the crude reality of the rebellious, disunited lands of Germany and Italy.

THE ECONOMIC BOOM YEARS

The kingdoms of the medieval West thrived on an economic base of unprecedented prosperity. What made possible the twelfth- and thirteenth-century economic boom? As we saw in Chapter 8, the agricultural and power revolutions of the eleventh century certainly provided the necessary foundations, but three other factors also proved crucial.

First, there were advances in transportation networks. Trade in grain, woolen cloth, and other bulk goods depended on the use of relatively cheap water transportation for hauling goods. Where there were neither seaports nor navigable rivers, goods had to be hauled cross-country by pack train, a very expensive enterprise. To address the problem and to facilitate transportation and trade, new roads and bridges were built, and old Roman roads that had been neglected for a thousand years were repaired.

The most lucrative trade was the international commerce in luxury goods. Because these goods were lightweight and high-priced, they could sustain the cost of long-distance transportation across land. Italian merchants virtually monopolized the European luxury trade. The Genoese distributed rare alum—the fixing agent for dyeing cloth—from the west coast of Asia Minor to the entire European cloth industry. Venetians and Genoese imported cotton from the Middle East. Raw silk, transported aboard camel caravans from China and Turkestan, was sold at trading posts on the shores of the Black Sea and in Constantinople to Italian merchants who earned enormous profits selling shimmering silk fabric to the ladies and gentlemen of the western European aristocracy. The silk trade was quite small in quantity, but it was of great value to international commerce because silk was so highly prized. Rubies, pearls, coral, and diamonds were also easily transported for fantastic profits. Marco Polo of Venice, for example, specialized in trading jewels, which he sewed into the linings of his clothing for safety when he trekked across Asia from Venice to China and back. During the thirteenth century, Polo was one of countless European merchants crisscrossing the caravan routes of Asia and north Africa.

Even the bulk commodities the Italians brought from the East were valuable enough to sustain the high transportation costs. Known by the generic term "spices," these included hundreds of exotic items: True spices such as pepper, sugar, cloves, nutmeg, ginger, saffron, mace, and cinnamon were used to enhance the otherwise boring, bland medieval cuisine; for dyeing cloth indigo was used for blue and madder root for red; medicinal herbs including opiates were used as pain relievers.

The second factor responsible for the economic boom of the twelfth and thirteenth centuries was the creation of new business techniques that long-distance trade necessitated. For example, the expansion of trade and new markets required a moneyed economy. Coins had almost disappeared in the West for nearly 400 years during the Early Middle Ages, when most people lived self-sufficiently on manors and bartered for what they could not produce for themselves. By the thirteenth century Venice and Florence were minting their own gold coins, which became the medium for exchange across much of Europe.

Merchants engaged in long-distance trade began to develop the essential business tools of capitalism during this period. They created business partnerships, uniform accounting practices, merchants' courts to enforce contracts and resolve disputes, letters of credit (used like modern traveler's checks), bank deposits and loans, and even insurance policies. The Italian cities established primary schools to train merchants' sons to write business letters and keep accounts—a sign of the growing professional character of business. Two centuries earlier an international merchant had been an itinerant peddler who led pack trains over dusty and muddy tracks to customers in small villages and castles. But by the end of the thirteenth century an international merchant could stay at home behind a desk, writing letters to business partners and ship captains and enjoying the profits from his labors in the bustling atmosphere of a thriving city.

The third factor in the economic prosperity of the period was cities. Cities both facilitated the commercial boom and were the primary beneficiaries of it. All across Europe, especially in Flanders, the Netherlands, and north-central Italy, cities exploded in size. Exact population figures are hard to come by, but there is ample evidence of stunning growth. Between 1160 and 1300 Ghent had to expand its city walls five times to accommodate all its inhabitants. During the thirteenth century the population of Florence grew by an estimated 640 percent.

Urban civilization, one of the major achievements of the Middle Ages, was an outgrowth of commerce. From urban civilization came other achievements. All the cities built large new cathedrals to flaunt their accumulated wealth and to honor God. New educational institutions, especially universities, trained the sons of the urban, commercial elite in the professions.

Medieval Culture: The Search for Understanding

Cultural encounters during the High Middle Ages took many forms. Some were direct exchanges, as when Christians and Muslims in crusader Jerusalem discovered their different ways of praying. Other encounters were more indirect, as when medieval thinkers read the books of ancient philosophers and so were confronted with challenging ideas that did not fit easily into their view of the world. During the twelfth and thirteenth centuries, this second kind of encounter, based on the re-

CHRONOLOGY

1073–1085	Reign of Pope Gregory VII
1095–1099	First Crusade
1198–1216	Reign of Pope Innocent III
1202–1204	Fourth Crusade; culminates in capture of Constantinople by Western crusaders
1208–1213	Albigensian Crusade
1215	Magna Carta; Fourth Lateran Council promulgates dogma of transubstantiation
1221	Death of Dominic
1226	Death of Francis of Assisi

newed availability of works of classical Greek philosophy, opened creative possibilities, especially in theology. The Greek philosophers had been dead for nearly 1,500 years, but the medieval thinkers who discovered ancient philosophy experienced a profound cultural shock. First Muslim and then Jewish and Christian writers struggled to reconcile the rational approach of Aristotle and other Greek philosophers with the faith demanded by Islam, Judaism, and Christianity. Some suffered from a crisis of faith. Others confronted the challenge presented by ancient philosophy and attempted to reconcile reason and faith by creating new philosophical systems.

REVIVAL OF LEARNING

In 1050 education was available only in monasteries and cathedral schools, and the curriculum was very basic, usually only reading and writing. These two kinds of schools had different educational missions. Monastic education trained monks to read the books available in their libraries as an aid to contemplating the mysteries of the next world. In contrast, the cathedral schools, which trained members of the ecclesiastical hierarchy, emphasized the practical skills of rational analysis that would help future priests, bishops, and royal advisers solve the problems of this world. By 1100 the number of cathedral schools had grown significantly and the curriculum expanded to include the study of the ancient Roman masters, Cicero and Virgil, who became models for clear Latin composition.

Scholasticism: A Christian Philosophy
In addition to teaching Latin grammar, cathedral schools recognized a growing need for training in logic as well.

Students tended to gather around popular lecturers in the cathedral schools where they were trained in scholasticism, which emphasized the critical methods of reasoning.

Scholasticism° literally means "of the schools," but the term also refers to a broad philosophical and theological movement that dominated medieval thought. In this broader sense, scholasticism refers to the use of logic learned from Aristotle to interpret the meaning of the Bible and the writings of the Church fathers, who created Christian theology in its first centuries. Books were scarce in the cathedral schools because the only means of duplication before the invention of the printing press was hand copying onto expensive sheepskin parchment. So the principal method of teaching and learning was the lecture. Teachers read out loud Latin texts, and students were obliged to memorize what they heard. In the classroom the lecturer would recite a short passage, present the comments of other authorities on it, and draw his own conclusions. He would then move onto another brief passage and repeat the process. Students heard the same lectures over and over again until they had thoroughly memorized the text under discussion. In addition to lectures, scholastics engaged in disputations. Participants in a disputation presented oral arguments for or against a particular thesis, a process called dialectical reasoning. Disputants were evaluated on their ability to investigate through logic the truth of a thesis. Disputations required several skills—verbal facility, a prodigious memory so that apt citations could be made, and the ability to think quickly. The process we know today as debate originated with these medieval disputations. Lectures and disputations became the core activities of the scholastics, who considered all subjects, however sacred, appropriate for reasoned examination.

Universities: Organizing Learning

From the cathedral schools arose both scholasticism and the first universities. Initially the universities were little more than guilds (trade associations), organized by either students or teachers to protect their interests. As members of a guild, students bargained with their professors and townspeople as would other tradesmen over costs and established minimum standards of instruction. The guild of the law students at Bologna received a charter in 1158, which probably made it the first university. Some of the early universities were professional schools, such as the medical faculty at Salerno, but true to their origins as cathedral schools, most emphasized theology over other subjects.

The medieval universities formulated the basic educational practices that are still in place today. They established a curriculum, examined students, conferred degrees, and conducted graduation ceremonies. Students and teachers wore distinctive robes, which are still worn at graduation ceremonies. Teachers were clergymen—that is, they "professed" religion—hence the title of professor for a university instructor. In their first years students pursued the liberal arts curriculum, which consisted of the *trivium* (grammar, rhetoric, and logic) and the *quadrivium* (arithmetic, geometry, astronomy, and music). This curriculum is forerunner of the arts and sciences faculties and distribution requirements in modern universities. Medieval university students devoted many years to rigorous study and rote memorization. Completion of a professional doctorate in law, medicine, or theology typically required more than ten years.

Medieval universities did not admit women, in part because women were barred from the priesthood and most university students were training to become priests. (Women did not attend universities in significant numbers until the nineteenth century.) There was also a widespread fear of learned women who might think on their own. The few women who did receive advanced educations had to rely on a private tutor.

The Ancients: Renaissance of the Twelfth Century

The scholastics' integration of Greek philosophy with Christian theology represents a key facet of the Twelfth-Century Renaissance°, a revival of interest in the ancients comparable in importance to the Carolingian Renaissance of the ninth century and the Italian Renaissance of the fifteenth. Between about 1140 and 1260 a flood of new Latin translations of the Greek classics came from Sicily and Spain, where Christians had close contacts with Muslims and Jews. Muslim philosophers had translated into Arabic the Greek philosophical and scientific classics, which were readily available in the Middle East and North Africa. These Arabic translations were then translated into Latin, often by Jewish scholars who knew both languages. Later a few Catholic scholars traveled to Byzantium, where they learned enough Greek to make even better translations from the originals.

As they encountered the philosophy of the ancients, Muslim, Jewish, and Christian thinkers faced profoundly disturbing problems. The principles of faith revealed in the Qur'an of Islam and the Hebrew and Christian Bibles were not easily reconciled with the philosophical method of reasoning found in Greek works, especially those by Aristotle. These religious thinkers recognized the superiority of Greek thought over their own. They worried that the power of philosophical reasoning undermined religious truth. As men of faith they challenged themselves to demonstrate that philosophy did not contradict religious teaching, and some of them went even further to employ philosophical reasoning to demonstrate the truth of religion. They always faced opposition within their own religious faiths, however, especially from people who thought philosophical reason was an impediment to religious faith.

Avicenna (980–1037), an Iranian physician, was the first Muslim thinker to confront the questions raised by Greek philosophy, such as how to prove the existence of God or account for the creation of the world. Avicenna's commentaries on Aristotle deeply influenced the Catholic scholastics, who quoted him extensively. Avicenna attempted a rational proof of the existence of God based on the "necessary existent." Without God nothing exists; therefore, if we exist, so must God.

Following Avicenna's lead, Averroës (1126–1198) became the most powerful Muslim philosopher. He rose to become the chief judge of Córdoba, Spain, and an adviser to the caliph. In *The Incoherence of the Incoherence* (1179–1180), Averroës argued that the aim of philosophy is to explain the true, inner meaning of religious revelations. This inner meaning, however, should not be disclosed to the unlettered masses, who must be told only the simple, literal stories and metaphors of Scripture. Although lively and persuasive, Averroës's defense of philosophy failed to stimulate further philosophical speculation within Islam. Once far superior to that of the Catholic world, Islamic philosophy and science went into a steep decline as mysticism and rote learning were favored over rational debate. Averroës received a more sympathetic hearing among Jews and Catholics than among Muslims.

Within Judaism, many had attempted unsuccessfully a reconciliation of Greek philosophy with Hebrew law and scripture. Success was achieved by a contemporary of Averroës, also from Córdoba—the Jewish philosopher, jurist, and physician Moses Maimonides (1135–1204). His most important work in religious philosophy was *The Guide for the Perplexed* (ca. 1191), which synthesized Greek philosophy, science, and Judaism. Widely read in Arabic, Hebrew, and Latin versions, the book stimulated both Jewish and Christian philosophy.

For medieval Catholic philosophers, one of the most difficult tasks was reconciling the biblical account of the divine creation with Aristotle's teaching that the universe was eternal. Even in this early clash between science and religion, creationism was the sticking point. Following the lead established by Avicenna, Averroës, and Maimonides, the great project of the scholastics became to demonstrate the fundamental harmony between Christian faith and the philosophical knowledge of the ancients.

The most effective resolution of the apparent conflict between faith and philosophy was found in the work of Thomas Aquinas (1225–1274), whose philosophy is called Thomism°. A Dominican friar, Aquinas avoided distracting controversies and academic disputes to concentrate on his two great summaries of human knowledge—the *Summary of the Catholic Faith Against the Gentiles* (1261) and the *Summary of Theology* (1265–1274). In both of these massive scholastic works, reason fully confirmed Christian faith. Encyclopedias of knowledge, they rigorously examined whole fields through dialectical reasoning.

Building on the works of Averroës, Aquinas solved the problem of reconciling philosophy and religion by drawing a distinction between *natural truth* and *revealed truth.* For Aquinas, natural truth meant the kinds of things anyone can know through the operation of human reason; revealed truth referred to the things that can be known only through revelation, such as the Trinity and the incarnation of Christ. Aquinas argued that these two kinds of truths could not possibly contradict one another because both came from God. Apparent contradictions could be accommodated by an understanding of a higher truth. On the issue of creation, for example, Aquinas argued that Aristotle's understanding of the eternal universe was inferior to the higher revealed truth of the Bible that God created the universe in seven days.

The most influential of the scholastic thinkers, Aquinas asserted that to achieve religious truth one should start with faith and then use reason to reach conclusions. He was the first to understand theology systematically in this way, and in doing so he raised a storm of opposition among Christians who were threatened by philosophical reason. Like the work of Avicenna and Maimonides before him, Aquinas's writings were at first prohibited by the theological faculties in universities. Nevertheless, his method remains crucial for Catholic theology to this day.

Just as scholastic theologians looked to ancient Greek philosophy as a guide to reason, jurists revived ancient Roman law, especially at the universities of Bologna and Pavia in Italy. In the law faculties, students were required to learn the legal work of the emperor Justinian—the text of the *Body of the Civil Law,* together with the commentaries on it. The systematic approach of Roman law provided a way to make the legal system less arbitrary for judges, lawyers, bureaucrats, and advisers to kings and popes. Laws had long consisted of a contradictory mess of municipal regulations, Germanic customs, and feudal precepts. Under Roman law, judges were obliged to justify their verdicts according to prescribed standards of evidence and procedure. The revival of Roman law in the twelfth century made possible the legal system that still guides most of continental Europe.

COURTLY LOVE

In addition to the developments in philosophy, theology, and the law, the Twelfth-Century Renaissance included a remarkable literary output in the vernacular languages, the tongues spoken in everyday life. The new vernacular literature was created by poets called troubadours°. The troubadour poets included women as well as men, and their literature reflected an entirely new sensibility about the relationships between men and women. The troubadours wrote poems of love, meant to be sung to music; their literary movement is called courtly love°. They composed in Provençal, one of the languages of southern France, and the first audience for their poems was in the courts of southern France. These graciously elegant poems clearly show influences from Arabic love poetry and especially from Muslim mystical literature in which the soul, depicted as feminine, seeks her masculine God/lover. The troubadours secularized this theme of religious union by portraying the ennobling possibilities of the love between a woman and a man. In so doing, they popularized the idea of romantic love, one of the most powerful concepts in all of Western history.

An innovative aspect of the courtly love poems of the troubadours was their idealization of women. The male troubadours, such as Chrétien de Troyes (1135–1183), placed women on a pedestal and treated men as the "love vassals" of beloved women to whom they owed loyalty and service. Female troubadours, such as Marie de France (dates unknown), did not place women on a pedestal but idealized emotionally honest and open relationships between lovers. The troubadours typically saw women as holding power over men or acting as their equals. From southern France, courtly love spread to Germany and elsewhere throughout Europe. Based on a now-lost version in Old French, Gottfried von Strassburg recomposed in German the romance of Tristan and Iseult. At first the two lovers struggle to resist temptation and to doubt the other's love, but they find themselves unable to keep away from one another. His resistance is motivated by a sense of honor and hers by "maiden shame," but the power of love triumphs over prudence and the two consummate the relationship.

■ **Romanesque Cathedral Architecture**
The rounded arches, the massive columns, the barrel vaults in the ceilings, and the small windows were characteristic of the Romanesque style. The pointed arch over the apse is a later Gothic addition.

THE CENTER OF MEDIEVAL CULTURE: THE GREAT CATHEDRALS

When tourists visit a European city today, they usually want to see its cathedral. Most of these imposing structures were built between 1050 and 1300 and symbolize the soaring ambitions and imaginations of their largely unknown builders. These buildings became multimedia centers for the arts—incorporating architecture, sculpture, stained glass, and painting in their structure and providing a setting for the performance of music and drama. The medieval cathedrals took decades, sometimes centuries, to build at great cost and sacrifice. They are magnificent examples of the pious devotion to God of the people who built them and of the principles of medieval Christian civilization.

The Romanesque° style spread throughout western Europe during the eleventh century and the first half of the

twelfth century because the master masons who understood sophisticated stone construction techniques traveled from one building site to another, bringing with them a uniform style. The principal innovation of the Romanesque was the arched stone roofs, which were more aesthetically pleasing and less vulnerable to fire than the flat roofs they replaced. The high stone roofs of Romanesque churches and cathedrals required the support of massive stone pillars and thick walls. As a result, windows were small slits that imitated the slit windows of castles. Romanesque churches had a dark, yet cozy appearance, which was sometimes enlivened by painted walls or sculpture. Romanesque churches and cathedrals were the first architectural expression of the new and growing medieval cities, proud and wealthy places. In such a building, God became a fellow townsman, an associate in the grand new project of making cities habitable and comfortable.

of stained glass, transforming the interior spaces into a mystical haven from the outside world. At different times of the day, the multicolored windows converted sunlight into an ever-changing light show that offered sparkling hints of the secret truths of God's creation. See, for example, the image on page 182. The light that passed through these windows symbolized the light of God. The windows themselves contained scenes that were an encyclopedia of medieval knowledge and lore. In addition to Bible stories and the lives of saints, these windows depicted common people at their trades, animals, plants, and natural wonders. These windows celebrated not only the promise of salvation but all the wonders of God's creation. They drew worshipers out of the busy city in which they lived and worked toward the perfect realm of the divine.

Interior of a Gothic Cathedral

Narrow columns and the pointed arches characterized the Gothic style.

Flying Buttresses of Chartres Cathedral

The flying buttress did more than hold up the thin walls of Gothic cathedrals. The buttress created an almost lacelike appearance on the outside of the building, magnifying the sense of mystery evoked by the style.

More than a century after the urban revival began, during the late twelfth and thirteenth centuries, the Gothic° style replaced the Romanesque. The innovation of this style was pointed arches, which superseded the rounded arches of the Romanesque. These narrow pointed arches drew the viewer's eye upward toward God and gave the building the appearance of weightlessness that symbolized the Christian's uplifting reach for heaven. The neighborly solidity of the Romanesque style was abandoned for an effect that stimulated a mystical appreciation of God's utter otherness, the supreme divinity far above mortal men and women. The Gothic style also introduced the innovation of the flying buttress, an arched construction on the outside of the walls that redistributed the weight of the roof. This innovation allowed for thin walls, which were pierced by windows much bigger than was possible with Romanesque construction techniques.

The result was stunning. The stone work of a Gothic cathedral became a skeleton to support massive expanses

CONCLUSION

Asserting Western Culture

During the twelfth and thirteenth centuries, western Europe matured into its own self-confident identity. Through penal laws and discrimination, heretical groups within Europe were systematically transformed into outcasts or eliminated altogether. The processes of creating outcasts within Europe and defining what it meant to be a Catholic accompanied the external assertion of Latin power. The West looked both inward and outward as it measured itself, defined itself, and promoted itself. The most dramatic outward assertion of Western identity was the series of Crusades, when European power was extended outside the continent for the first time since the fall of the Roman Empire in the West.

Less a semibarbarian backwater than it had been even in the time of Charlemagne, western Europe cultivated modes of thought that revealed an almost limitless capacity for creative renewal and critical self-examination. That capacity, first evident during the Twelfth-Century Renaissance, is what has most distinguished the West ever since. Part of the reason for this creative capacity rested in the cultivation of critical methods of thinking based on applying the logic of ancient Greek philosophy to the Bible and on defending the conclusions drawn through disputations. These methods were codified in scholasticism. No medieval thinker followed these critical methods consistently, and they repeatedly caused alarm among some believers. However, this tendency to question basic assumptions is among the greatest achievements of Western civilization. The western European university system, which was based on teaching methods of critical inquiry, differed from the educational institutions in other cultures, such as Byzantium or Islam, that were devoted to passing on received knowledge. This distinctive critical spirit connects the cultures of the ancient, medieval, and modern West.

Suggestions for Further Reading

For a comprehensive list of suggested readings, please go to www.ablongman.com/levackconcise/chapter9

Bartlett, Robert. *The Hanged Man: A Story of Miracle, Memory, and Colonialism in the Middle Ages.* 2004. This engrossing account captures well how medieval peoples understood those from other cultures.

Bony, Jean. *French Gothic Architecture of the Twelfth and Thirteenth Centuries.* 1983. With many beautiful illustrations, this is a good way to begin an investigation of these magnificent buildings.

Colish, Marcia L. *Medieval Foundations of the Western Intellectual Tradition, 400–1400.* 1997. The best general study.

Keen, Maurice. *Chivalry.* 1984. Readable and balanced in its coverage of this sometimes misunderstood phenomenon.

Lambert, Malcolm. *Medieval Heresy: Popular Movements from the Gregorian Reform to the Reformation.* 2nd ed. 1992. The best general study of heresy.

Lawrence, C. H. *The Friars: The Impact of the Early Mendicant Movement on Western Society.* 1994. The best general study of the influence of Dominicans and Franciscans.

Moore, R. I. *The Formation of a Persecuting Society: Power and Deviance in Western Europe, 950–1250.* 1987. A brilliant analysis of how Europe became a persecuting society.

Morris, Colin. *The Papal Monarchy: The Western Church from 1050 to 1250.* 1989. A thorough study that should be the beginning point for further investigation of the many fascinating figures in the medieval Church.

Mundy, John H. *Europe in the High Middle Ages, 1150–1309.* 3rd ed. 1999. A comprehensive introduction to the period.

Riley-Smith, Jonathan Simon Christopher. *The Crusades: A Short History.* 1990. Exactly what the title says.

Riley-Smith, Jonathan Simon Christopher. *The Oxford Illustrated History of the Crusades.* 2001. An utterly engaging, comprehensive study.

Strayer, Joseph R. *On the Medieval Origins of the Modern State.* 1970. Still the best short analysis.

Notes

1. A. F. Pollock and F. W. Maitland, *The History of English Law,* vol. 1 (1895), 468.

2. Cited in Emmanuel Le Roy Ladurie, *Montaillou: Promised Land of Error,* trans. Barbara Bray (1978), 130.

3. Ibid., 56.

4. Ibid., 63.

non essent regestrantes que non
et futuris ministrantes que per

The West in Crisis:
The Later Middle Ages

THE FOURTEENTH CENTURY DAWNED WITH A CHILL. IN 1303 AND THEN AGAIN during 1306–1307, the Baltic Sea froze over. No one had ever heard of that happening before, and the freezings foretold worse disasters. The cold spread beyond its normal winter season, arriving earlier in the autumn and staying later into the summer. Then it started to rain and did not let up. The Caspian Sea began to rise, flooding villages along its shores. In the summer of 1314 all across Europe, crops rotted in sodden fields. The meager harvest came late, precipitating a surge in prices for farm produce and forcing King Edward II of England to impose price controls. But capping prices did not grow more food.

In 1315 the situation got worse. In England during that year, the price of wheat rose 800 percent. Preachers compared the ceaseless rains to the Great Flood in the Bible, and floods did come, overwhelming dikes in the Netherlands and England, washing away entire towns in Germany, turning fields into lakes in France. Everywhere crops failed.

Things got much worse. Torrential rains fell again in 1316, and for the third straight year the crops failed, creating the most severe famine in recorded European history. The effects were most dramatic in the far North. In Scandinavia agriculture almost disappeared, in Iceland peasants abandoned farming and turned to fishing and herding sheep, and in Greenland the European settlers began to die out. Already malnourished, the people of Europe became susceptible to disease and starvation. Desperate people resorted to desperate options. They ate cats, rats, insects, reptiles, animal dung, and tree leaves. Stories spread that some ate their own children. In Poland the starving were said to cut down criminals from the gallows for food.

By the 1340s, nearly all of Europe was in an endless cycle of disease and famine. Then came the deadliest epidemic in European history, the Black Death, which killed at least one-third of the total population. The economy collapsed.

Chapter Outline

- A Time of Death
- A Cold Wind from the East
- Economic Depression and Social Turmoil
- A Troubled Church and the Demand for Religious Comfort
- An Age of Warfare
- The Culture of Loss

A Time of Death: Burying the plague victims of Tournai, 1349. The fourteenth and early fifteenth centuries were a time of famine, war, and plague.

Trade disappeared. Industry shriveled. Hopeless peasants and urban workers revolted against their masters, demanding relief for their families. Neither church nor state could provide it. The popes left the dangerous streets of Rome for Avignon, France, where they were obliged to extort money to survive. The two great medieval kingdoms of France and England became locked in an interminable struggle that depleted royal treasuries and wasted the aristocracy in a series of clashes that historians call the Hundred Years' War. European culture became obsessed with death.

Of all the frightening elements of these disasters, perhaps most frightening was that their causes were hidden or completely unknowable given the technology and medical understanding that became available only a century ago. In many respects, the West was held captive by the climate, economic forces that no one completely understood, and microbes that would not be identified for another 550 years. During the twelfth and thirteenth centuries the West had asserted itself against Islam through the Crusades and spread Catholic Christianity to the far corners of Europe. During the fourteenth and early fifteenth centuries, however, the West drew into itself due to war, plague, and conflicts with the Mongol and Ottoman Empires. Western European contact with Russia became more intermittent, and the Byzantine Empire, once the bastion of Orthodox Christianity, fell to the Muslim armies of the Ottomans.

This chapter explores the multiple interlocking crises of the fourteenth and fifteenth centuries. It addresses six questions:

- What caused the deaths of so many Europeans?
- How did forces outside Europe, in particular the Mongol and Ottoman Empires, influence conditions in the West?
- How did disturbances in the rudimentary global economy of the Middle Ages precipitate almost complete financial collapse and widespread social discontent in Europe?
- Why did the church fail to provide leadership and spiritual guidance during these difficult times?
- How did incessant warfare transform the most powerful medieval states?
- How did European culture offer explanations and solace for the otherwise inexplicable calamities of the times?

A Time of Death

I n the course of just two generations the population of Europe dropped from 74 million to 52 million. The raw numbers, however, hardly touch the magnitude of human suffering, which fell disproportionately on the poor, the very young, and the old. Death by starvation and disease became the fate of uncomprehending millions. The demographic crisis of the fourteenth century was the greatest natural disaster in Western civilization since the epidemics of antiquity. How did it happen?

MASS STARVATION

A crisis in agriculture produced the Great Famine. By the fourteenth century no more land was available for clearing, which meant that an ever-growing population tried to survive on a fixed amount of farming land. Because of the limitations of medieval agriculture, the ability of farmers to produce food could not keep up with unchecked population growth. At the same time there may have been a change in climate, known as the "Little Ice Age." The mean annual temperatures dropped just enough to make it impossible to grow crops in the more northerly parts of Europe and at high elevations. The result was less land available for cultivation and a harsher climate that shortened the growing season.

The imbalance between food production and population set off a dreadful cycle of famine and disease. Insufficient food resulted in either malnutrition or starvation. Those who suffered from prolonged malnutrition were particularly susceptible to epidemic diseases, such as typhus, cholera, and dysentery. By 1300, children of the poor faced the probability of extreme hunger once or twice during their childhood.

THE BLACK DEATH

Following on the heels of the Great Famine, the Black Death arrived in Europe in the spring of 1348 with brutal force. Experts still dispute the cause of the Black Death, but most follow the traditional theory that the bubonic plague° was the most likely culprit. According to this theory, the infection (*Pasteurella pestis*) causes inflamed swellings called buboes (hence, "bubonic" plague) in the glands of the groin or armpit, internal bleeding, and discoloration of the skin, which suggested the name "Black Death." The symptoms of bubonic plague were exceptionally disgusting, according to one quite typical contemporary description: "all the matter which exuded from their bodies let off an unbearable stench; sweat, excrement, spittle, breath, so fetid as to be overpowering; urine turbid, thick, black or red. . ."[1]

However, there are problems with the traditional theory that the Black Death was caused by bubonic plague. The Black Death spread much more rapidly from person to person than the bubonic plague does in modern epidemics, and many of the reported symptoms from the fourteenth century do not match the symptoms observed in modern plague victims. It is distinctly possible that the cause of the

Black Death was a disease unknown to us or one that has changed over time.

Modern estimates indicate that during the late 1340s and early 1350s from India to Iceland, about one-third of the population perished. In Europe this would have meant that about 20 million people died, with the deaths usually clustered in a matter of a few weeks or months after the disease first appeared in a particular locale. The death toll, however, varied erratically from place to place, ranging from about 20 to 90 percent. So great was the toll that entire villages were depopulated or abandoned. In the Mediterranean basin, where the many port cities formed a network of contagion, the disease reappeared between 1348 and 1721 in one port or another about every fifteen to twenty years. Some of the later outbreaks were just as lethal as the initial 1348 catastrophe.

Whatever the cause of the Black Death, contemporaries thought that it came to Europe from Asia. Modern research has suggested that the homeland of the *Pasteurella pestis* bacillus is an extremely isolated area in central Asia, from which the plague could have spread during the fourteenth century. However, even if the Black Death was not caused by the *Pasteurella pestis* bacillus, the fate of the West was ensnared in a unified web that stretched from China to Iceland. The strongest strands in that web were those of merchant traders and armies. During the Later Middle Ages, no army was as important for the fate of Europe as the mounted warriors of the distant Mongol tribes, whose relentless conquests drove them from Outer Mongolia across central Asia toward Europe.

A Cold Wind from the East

The Mongols and Turks were nomadic peoples from central Asia. Closely related culturally but speaking different languages, these peoples exerted an extraordinary influence on world history despite a rather small population. Map 10.1 shows the place of origin of the Mongols and Turks and where they spread across a wide belt of open, relatively flat land stretching from the Yellow Sea between China and the Korean peninsula to the Baltic Sea and the Danube River basin in Europe.

THE MONGOL INVASIONS

Between 1206 and 1258, the Mongols transformed themselves from a collection of disunited tribes with a vague ethnic affinity to the most extensive empire in the history of the world. The epic rise of the previously obscure Mongols was the work of a Mongol chief who succeeded in uniting the various quarreling tribes and transforming them into a

world power. In 1206 he was proclaimed Genghis Khan (ca. 1162–1227) ("Very Mighty King"), the supreme ruler over all the Mongols. Genghis broke through the Great Wall of China, destroyed the Jin (Chin) empire in northern China, and occupied Beijing. His cavalry swept across Asia as far as Azerbaijan, Georgia, northern Persia, and Russia. Eventually, Mongol armies conquered territories that stretched from Korea to Hungary and from the Arctic Ocean to the Arabian Sea. The Mongol success was accomplished through a highly disciplined military organization, tactics that relied on extremely mobile cavalry forces, and a sophisticated intelligence network. During the Russian campaign in the winter of 1223, the Mongol cavalry moved with lightning speed across frozen rivers to accomplish the only successful winter invasion of Russia in history. Although the Russian forces outnumbered the Mongol armies and had superior armor, they were crushed in every encounter with the Mongols.

The Mongol invasions completely altered the composition of Asia and much of eastern Europe—economically, politically, and ethnically. Once they had conquered new territories, they established the Mongol Peace by reopening the caravan routes across Asia, which had been closed for a thousand years, making trans-Eurasian trade possible and merchants safe from robbers. The most famous of the many who traversed this route were the Venetian merchants from the Polo family, including Marco Polo, who arrived at the court of the Great Khan in China in 1275. Marco Polo's book about his travels offers a vivid and often remarkably perceptive account of the Mongol Empire during the Mongol Peace. It also illustrates better than any other source the cultural engagement of the Christian West with the Mongol East during the late thirteenth century, an encounter in which both sides demonstrated an abiding fascination with the other's religion and social mores.

Mongol power climaxed in 1260. In that year the Mongols suffered a crushing defeat in Syria at the hands of the Mamluk rulers of Egypt, an event that ended the Mongol reputation for invincibility. Conflicts and succession disputes among the various Mongol tribes made them vulnerable to rivals and to rebellion from their unhappy subjects. The Mongol Empire did not disappear overnight, but its various successor kingdoms never recaptured the dynamic unity forged by Genghis Khan. During the fourteenth century the Mongol Peace came to an end. The collapse of the Mongol Peace broke the thread of commerce across Eurasia and stimulated the European search for alternative routes to China that ultimately resulted in the voyages of Christopher Columbus in 1492.

THE RISE OF THE OTTOMAN TURKS

The Mongol armies were never very large, so the Mongols had always augmented their numbers with Turkish tribes.

The result was that outside Mongolia, Turks gradually absorbed the Mongols. Turkish replaced Mongolian as the dominant language, and the Turks took over the government of the central Asian empires that had been scraped together by the Mongol conquests. In contrast to the Mongols, many of whom remained Buddhists, the Turks became Muslims and created an exceptionally dynamic, expansionist society of their own.

Among the Turkish peoples, the most successful state builders were the Ottomans. Named for Osman I (d. 1326), who brought it to prominence, the Ottoman dynasty endured for more than 600 years, until 1924. The nucleus of the Ottoman state was a small principality in Anatolia (a portion of present-day Turkey), which in the early fourteenth century began to expand at the expense of its weaker neighbors, including the Byzantine Empire (see Map 10.2).

The Ottoman state was built not on national, linguistic, or ethnic unity, but on a purely dynastic network of personal and military loyalties to the Ottoman prince, called the sultan. Thus the vitality of the empire depended on the energy of the individual sultans. The Ottomans thought of themselves as *ghazis*, warriors for Islam devoted to destroying polytheists, including Christians. (To some Muslims in

■   **Map 10.1   The Mongol Empire, 1206–1405**

The Mongols and Turks were nomadic peoples who spread out across Asia and Europe from their homeland in the region of Mongolia. The Mongol armies eventually conquered vast territories from Korea to the borders of Hungary and from the Arctic Ocean to the Arabian Sea.

■ **Map 10.2 The Ottoman Empire**

The Ottoman state expanded from a small principality in Anatolia, which is south of the Black Sea. From there the Ottomans spread eastward into Kurdistan and Armenia. In the West they captured all of Greece and much of the Balkan peninsula.

this period the Christian belief in the Trinity and veneration of numerous saints demonstrated that Christians were not true monotheists.)

When Mehmed II, "The Conqueror" (r. 1451–1481), became the Ottoman sultan, he began to obliterate the last remnants of the Byzantine Empire. During the winter of 1451–1452, the sultan ordered the encirclement of Constantinople, a city that had once been the largest in the world but now was reduced from perhaps a million people to fewer than 50,000. The final assault came in May 1453 and lasted less than a day. When the city fell, the Ottoman army plundered, raped, and enslaved the populace. The last Byzantine emperor, Constantine XI, was never found amid the multitude of the dead. The fall of Constantinople ended the Christian Byzantine Empire, the continuous remnant of the ancient Roman Empire. But the idea of Rome was not so easily snuffed out. The first Ottoman

sultans residing in Constantinople continued to be called "Roman emperors."

Although the western European princes had done little to save Byzantium, its demise was a profound shock, rendering them vulnerable to the Ottoman onslaught. For the next 200 years the Ottomans used Constantinople as a base to threaten Christian Europe. Hungary and the eastern Mediterranean empire of Venice remained the last lines of defense for the West, and at various times in succeeding centuries the Ottomans launched expeditions against the great capitals of Europe, including Vienna and Rome.

The Ottoman conquests created a lasting Muslim presence within the borders of Europe, especially in Bosnia and Albania. In succeeding centuries Christian Europe and the Muslim Ottoman Empire would be locked in a deadly competitive embrace, but they also benefited from innumerable cultural exchanges and regular trade.

Economic Depression and Social Turmoil

Adding insult to injury in this time of famine, plague, and conquest, the West began to suffer a major economic depression during the fourteenth century. The causes of this economic catastrophe were complex, but the consequences were obvious. Businesses went bust, banks collapsed, guilds were in turmoil, and workers rebelled. At the same time, the effects of the depression were unevenly felt. The economic conditions for many peasants actually improved since there was a labor shortage in the countryside due to the loss of population. Forced to pay their peasants more for their labor and crops, landlords saw their own fortunes decline. Finding it harder to pay the higher prices for food, urban workers probably suffered the most since their wages did not keep up with the cost of living.

THE COLLAPSE OF INTERNATIONAL TRADE AND BANKING

The Mongol Peace during the thirteenth century had stimulated vast, lucrative trade in exotic luxury items between Europe and Asia. When the Mongol Empire began to break up in the fourteenth century, the trade routes were cut off or displaced. As a result, trade dwindled. Alternative routes would have taken merchants through Constantinople, but Ottoman pressure on Byzantium endangered these routes.

The financial infrastructure of medieval Europe was tied to international trade in luxury goods. The successful, entrepreneurial Italian merchants who dominated the luxury trade deposited their enormous profits in Italian banks. The Italian bankers lent money to the aristocracy and royalty of northern Europe to finance the purchases of exotic luxuries and to fight wars. The whole system was mutually reinforcing, but it was very fragile. With the disruption of supply sources for luxury goods, the financial networks of Europe collapsed, precipitating a major and lasting depression. By 1346 all of the major banks in Italy, which was the banking center of Europe, crashed. With the bank crash, virtually all sources of credit dried up all across Europe.

REBELLIONS FROM BELOW

The luxury trade that brought exotic items from Asia to Europe represented only half of the economic equation. The other half was the raw materials and manufactured goods that Europeans sold in exchange, principally woolen cloth. The production of woolen cloth depended on a highly sophisticated economic system that connected shepherds in England, the Netherlands, and Spain with woolen cloth manufacturers in cities. The manufacture of cloth and other commodities was organized by guilds. The collapse of the luxury trade reduced the demand for the goods produced by the guilds, depriving guildsmen and urban workers of employment at a time when the cost of food was rising. Frustrated and enraged, workers rebelled.

An Economy of Monopolies: Guilds

Central to the political and economic control of medieval cities were the guilds°. Guilds were professional associations devoted to protecting the special interests of a particular trade or craft and to monopolizing production and trade in the goods the guild produced. There were two dominant types of guilds. The first type, merchant guilds, attempted to monopolize the local market for a particular commodity. There were spice guilds, fruit and vegetable guilds, and apothecary guilds. The second type, craft guilds, regulated the manufacturing processes of artisans, such as carpenters, bricklayers, woolen-cloth manufacturers, glass blowers, and painters. These guilds were dominated by master craftsmen who ran their own shops. Working for wages in these shops were the journeymen, who knew the craft but could not yet afford to open their own shops. Under the masters and journeymen were apprentices, who worked usually without pay for a specific number of years to learn the trade.

When the economy declined during the fourteenth century, the urban guilds became lightning rods for mounting social tension. Guild monopolies produced considerable conflict, provoking anger among those who were blocked from joining guilds and thus excluded from the economic and political benefits available to guild members, and among young journeymen who earned low wages. These tensions exploded into dangerous revolts.

"Long Live the People, Long Live Liberty"

Economic pressures erupted into rebellion most dramatically among woolen-cloth workers in the urban centers in Italy, the Netherlands, and France. The most famous revolt involved the Ciompi, the laborers in the woolen-cloth industry of Florence, Italy, where guilds were a powerful force in city government. The Ciompi, who performed the heaviest jobs such as carting and the most noxious tasks such as dyeing, had not been allowed to have their own guild and were therefore deprived of the political and economic rights of guild membership.

Fueling the Ciompi's frustration was the fact that by the middle of the fourteenth century woolen-cloth production in Florence dropped by two-thirds, leaving many workers unemployed. In 1378 the desperate Ciompi rebelled. A crowd chanting, "Long live the people, long live liberty," broke into the houses of prominent citizens, released political prisoners from the city jails, and sacked the rich convents that housed the pampered daughters of the wealthy. Over the course of a few months, the rebels managed to force their way onto the city council, where they demanded tax and economic reforms and the right to form their own guild. The Ciompi revolt is one of the earliest cases of workers demanding political rights. The disenfranchised workers did not want to eliminate the guilds' monopoly on political power; they merely wanted a guild of their own so that they could join the regime. That was not to be, however. After a few weeks of success, the Ciompi were divided and defeated.

Worker and peasant rebellions also broke out during the fourteenth century in France, the Netherlands, and England, but none of them met with lasting success. However, they revealed for the first time in the West a widespread impulse among the lower classes to question and protest the existing social and economic order. The universal failure of lower-class rebellion was due, in part, to the lack of any clear alternative to the existing economic and political system. The Ciompi had just wanted to join the existing guild system.

A Troubled Church and the Demand for Religious Comfort

In reaction to the suffering and widespread death during the fourteenth century, many people naturally turned to religion for spiritual consolation and for explanations of what had gone wrong. But the spiritual authority of the Church was so dangerously weakened during this period that it failed to satisfy the popular craving for solace. The moral leadership that had made the papacy such a powerful force for reform during the eleventh through thirteenth centuries was completely lacking in the fourteenth. Many laypeople gave up looking to the pope for guidance and found their own means of religious expression, making the fourteenth and fifteenth centuries one of the most religiously creative epochs in Christian history. Some of the new religious movements, especially in England and Bohemia, veered onto the dangerous shoals of heresy, threatening the fragile unity of the Church.

THE BABYLONIAN CAPTIVITY OF THE CHURCH AND THE GREAT SCHISM

Faced with anarchy in the streets of Rome as local aristocrats engaged in incessant feuding, a succession of seven consecutive popes chose to reside in the relative calm of Avignon, France. This period of voluntary papal exile is known as the Babylonian Captivity of the Church° (1305–1378), a biblical reference recalling the captivity of the Jews in Babylonia (587–539 B.C.E.). The popes' supposed subservience to the kings of France during this period dangerously politicized the papacy, destroying its

ability to rise above the petty squabbles of the European princes. The enemies of the kings of France just did not trust the popes who were residing in France and who were themselves French. The loss of revenues from papal lands in Italy lured several popes into questionable financial schemes, which included accepting kickbacks from appointees to church offices, taking bribes for judicial decisions, and selling indulgences°. Indulgences were certificates that allowed penitents to atone for their sins and reduce their time in purgatory by paying money.

When Pope Urban VI (r. 1378–1389) was elevated to the papacy in 1378 and announced his intention to reside in Rome, a group of disgruntled French cardinals returned to Avignon and elected a rival French pope. The Church was then divided over allegiance to Italian and French claimants to the papal throne, a period called the Great Schism° (1378–1417). During the Great Schism the kings, princes, and cities of Europe divided their allegiances between the rival candidates. The Church was split not because of doctrinal differences but because competing systems of political alliances sustained the Schism. The French king and the allies of France supported the French pope. The enemies of France gave aid and comfort to the Italian pope.

The Great Schism created the need for a mechanism to sort out the competing claims of rival popes. That need led to the Conciliar Movement°. The conciliarists argued that a general meeting or council of the bishops of the Church had authority over the pope, could be called to order by a king, and could pass judgment on a standing pope or order a conclave to elect a new one. Several general councils were held during the early fifteenth century to resolve the schism and initiate reforms, but solutions were difficult to achieve because politics and the affairs of the Church were so closely intertwined. The Council of Constance (1414–1417) finally succeeded in restoring unity to the Church and also in formally asserting the principle that a general council is superior to the pope and should be called frequently. The Council of Basel (1431–1449) approved a series of necessary reforms, although these were never implemented due to the hostility to conciliarism by Pope Eugene IV (r. 1431–1447). The failure of even the timid reforms of the Council of Basel opened the way for the more radical rejection of papal authority during the Protestant Reformation of the sixteenth century. The Conciliar Movement, however, was not a complete failure because it provided a model for how reform could take place. This model would later become central to the Catholic Reformation and the foundation of modern Catholicism (see Chapter 13).

THE SEARCH FOR RELIGIOUS ALTERNATIVES

The popes' loss of moral authority during the Babylonian Captivity and the Great Schism opened the way for a remarkable variety of reformers, mystics, and preachers, who appealed to lay believers crying out for a direct experience of God and a return to the message of the original apostles of Christ. Some of these movements were heretical, but the weakened papacy was unable to control them, as it had successfully done during the thirteenth-century crusade against the Albigensians.

Protests Against the Papacy: New Heresies

For most Christians during the fourteenth century, religious life consisted of witnessing or participating in the seven sacraments, which were formal rituals celebrated by duly consecrated priests usually within the confines of churches. After baptism, which was universally performed on infants, the most common sacraments for lay adults were penance and communion. Both of these sacraments emphasized the power of the clergy over the laity and therefore were potential sources for resentment. The sacrament of penance required the layperson to confess his or her sins to a priest, who then prescribed certain penalties to satisfy the sin. At communion, it was believed, the priest changed the substance of an unleavened wafer of bread, called the Eucharist, into the body of Christ and a chalice of wine into his blood, a miraculous process called transubstantiation. Priest and lay recipients of communion both ate the wafer, but the chalice was reserved for the priest alone. More than anything else, the reservation of the chalice for priests profoundly symbolized the privileges of the clergy. Since medieval Catholicism was primarily a sacramental religion, reformers and heretics tended to concentrate their criticism on sacramental rituals, especially of their spiritual value compared to other kinds of worship such as prayer.

The most serious discontent about the authority of the popes, the privileges of the clergy, and the efficacy of the sacraments appeared in England and Bohemia (a region in the modern Czech Republic). An Oxford professor, John Wycliffe (1320–1384), criticized the power and wealth of the clergy, played down the value of the sacraments for encouraging ethical behavior, and exalted the benefits of preaching, which promoted a sense of personal responsibility. During the Great Schism, Wycliffe rejected the authority of the rival popes and asserted instead the absolute authority of the Bible, which he wanted to make available to the laity in English rather than in Latin, which only priests understood.

Wycliffe's ideas found their most sympathetic audience outside England among a group of reformist professors at the University of Prague in Bohemia, where Jan Hus (1369–1415) regularly preached to a large popular following. Hus's most revolutionary act was to offer the chalice of consecrated communion wine to the laity, thus symbolically diminishing the special status of the clergy. When Hus also preached against indulgences, which he said converted the sacrament of penance into a cash transaction, Pope John XXIII excommunicated him. Hus attended the Council of Constance to defend his ideas. Despite a promise of safe conduct from the Holy Roman emperor (whose jurisdiction included Bohemia and Constance),

Hus was imprisoned, his writings were condemned, and he was burned alive as a heretic.

Imitating Christ: The Modern Devotion

In the climate of religious turmoil of the fourteenth and fifteenth centuries, many Christians sought deeper spiritual solace than the institutionalized Church could provide. By stressing individual piety, ethical behavior, and intense religious education, a movement called the Modern Devotion° became highly influential. Promoted by the Brothers of the Common Life, a religious order established in the Netherlands, the Modern Devotion was especially popular throughout northern Europe.

The Modern Devotion was also spread by the best-seller of the late fifteenth century, the *Imitation of Christ*, written in 1441 by a Common Life brother, probably Thomas à Kempis. By emphasizing frequent private prayer and moral introspection, the *Imitation* provided a spiritual manual to guide laypeople in the path toward spiritual renewal that had traditionally been reserved for monks and nuns.

The moral and financial degradation of the papacy during the fourteenth and early fifteenth centuries was countered by the persistent spirituality of the laity, manifest in the Modern Devotion. As a result, throughout Europe laypeople took responsibility, not only for their own behavior, but for the spiritual and material welfare of their entire community and of the Church itself. Lay spirituality remained deeply traditional rather than innovative. These pious people founded hospitals for the sick and dying, orphanages for abandoned children, and confraternities that engaged in a wide range of charitable good works—from providing dowries for poor women to accompanying condemned criminals to the gallows.

An Age of Warfare

Western Europe was further weakened during the fourteenth century by prolonged war between its two largest and previously most stable kingdoms, England and France. The Hundred Years' War° (1337–1453) was a struggle over England's attempts to assert its claims to territories in France. The prolonged conflict drained resources from the aristocracies of both kingdoms, deepening and lengthening the economic depression. The Hundred Years' War sowed the seeds of a military revolution that by the sixteenth century transformed the kingdoms of western Europe. In that transformation monarchies, ruled by relatively weak kings and strong aristocracies, evolved into modern states, ruled by strong monarchs who usurped many of the traditional privileges of the aristocracy in order to centralize authority and strengthen military prowess.

THE FRAGILITY OF MONARCHIES

The most dangerous threat to the kings of France and England during the fourteenth and fifteenth centuries came less from worker and peasant rebellions than from members of the aristocracy, who were fiercely protective of their jurisdictional privileges over their lands. The privilege of jurisdiction allowed aristocrats to act as judges for crimes committed in their territories, a privilege that was a crucial source of their power. In both kingdoms, royal officials asserted the legal principle that aristocratic jurisdictions originated with the crown and were subordinate to it. The problem behind this controversy was inherent in the system of rule in France and England—overlapping, conflicting, and sometimes contradictory jurisdictions and loyalties produced by many generations of inheritance. The system bred strife and limited the power of the monarch. Thus the Hundred Years' War was both a conflict between two kingdoms and a series of civil wars between aristocratic factions and imperiled monarchs.

Medieval monarchies depended on the king to maintain stability. Despite the remarkable legal reforms and bureaucratic centralization of monarchies in England and France during the twelfth and thirteenth centuries (see Chapter 9), weak or incompetent kings were all too common during the fourteenth. Weak kings created a perilous situation made worse by disputed successions. The career of Edward II (r. 1307–1327) of England illustrates the peril. Edward was unable to control the vital judicial and financial sinews of royal power. He continued the policy of his father, Edward I, by introducing resident justices of the peace who had replaced the inadequate system of itinerant judges who traveled from village to village to hear cases. In theory, these justices of the peace should have prevented the abuses of justice typical of aristocratic jurisdictions, but even though they were royal officials who answered to the king, most of those appointed were also local landowners who were deeply implicated in many of the disputes that came before them. As a result, justice in England became notoriously corrupt and the cause of discontent. Edward II was so incompetent in dealing with the consequences of corrupted justice that he provoked a civil war in which his own queen joined his aristocratic enemies to depose him.

The French monarchy was no better. In fact, the French king was in an even weaker constitutional position than the English monarch. In France the king had effective jurisdiction over only a small part of his realm. Many of the duchies and counties of France were quasi-independent principalities, paying only nominal allegiance to the king, whose will was ignored with impunity. In these regions the administration of justice, the collection of taxes, and the recruitment of soldiers all remained in the hands of local lords. To explain why he needed to raise taxes, Philip IV, "The Fair" (r. 1285–1314), created a representative assembly, the Estates General, which met for the first time in

■ **Royal Justice**
English kings were preoccupied with extending their prerogatives over the judiciary as a way to express royal power. Despite the corruption of the many lower courts, the Court of the King's Bench attempted to assert a level of uniform procedures and royal control of justice.

1302, but he still had to negotiate with each region and town individually to collect the taxes. Given the difficulty of raising taxes, the French kings resorted to makeshift solutions that hurt the economy, such as confiscating the property of vulnerable Jewish and Italian merchants and debasing the coinage to increase the value of scarce silver. Such a system made the finances of the kingdom of France especially shaky because the king lacked a dependable flow of revenues.

THE HUNDRED YEARS' WAR

The Hundred Years' War revealed the fragility of the medieval monarchies. The initial cause of the war involved disputes over the duchy of Aquitaine. The king of England also held the title of duke of Aquitaine, who was a vassal of the

French crown, which meant that the English kings technically owed military assistance to the French kings whenever they asked for it. A long succession of English kings had reluctantly paid homage as dukes of Aquitaine to the king of France, but the unusual status of the duchy was a continuing source of contention.

The second cause of the war derived from a succession crisis over the French crown. When King Charles IV died in 1328, his closest surviving relative was none other than the archenemy of France, Edward III (r. 1327–1377), king of England. To the barons of France, the possibility of Edward's succession to the throne was unthinkable, and they excluded him because his relation to the French royal family was through his mother. Instead the barons elected to the throne a member of the Valois family, King Philip VI (r. 1328–1350), and at first Edward reluctantly accepted the decision. However, when Philip started to hear judicial appeals from the duchy of Aquitaine, Edward changed his mind. He claimed the title of king of France for himself, sparking the beginning of more than a century of warfare.

The Hundred Years' War (1337–1453) was not a continuous formal war but a series of occasional pitched battles, punctuated by long truces and periods of general exhaustion. In terms of its potential for warfare, France, far richer and with three times the population, held the advantage over sparsely populated England. In nearly every battle the French outnumbered the English, but the English were usually victorious because of superior discipline and the ability of their longbows to break up cavalry charges. As a rule, the English avoided open battle, preferring raids, sieges of isolated castles, and capturing French knights for ransom. For many Englishmen the objective of fighting in France was to get rich by looting. Because all the fighting took place on French soil, France suffered extensive destruction and significant civilian casualties from repeated English raids.

In the early phases of the war, the English enjoyed a stunning series of victories. At Agincourt in 1415, King Henry V (r. 1413–1422) and England's disease-racked army of 6,000 were cut off by a French force of about 20,000. In the ensuing battle the English archers repelled a hasty French cavalry charge and the fleeing, terrified horses trampled the French men-at-arms as they advanced. The English lost only a few hundred, but the French suffered nearly 10,000 casualties. After Agincourt, the French never again dared challenge King Henry in open battle, and were forced to recognize him as the heir to the French throne.

By 1429 the English were on the verge of final victory. They occupied Paris and Rheims, and their army was besieging Orleans. The Dauphin (title of the heir to the throne) Charles was penniless and indecisive. Even his own mother denied his legitimacy as the future king. At this point a 17-year-old illiterate peasant from Burgundy, Joan of Arc [Jeanne d'Arc, ca. 1412–1431], following "divine voices," went to Orleans to lead the French armies.

Under her inspiration Orleans was relieved, French forces began to defeat the English, much of the occupied territory was regained, and the Dauphin was crowned King Charles VII (r. 1429–1461) in the cathedral of Rheims. After Joan failed to recapture Paris, however, her successes ceased. The final success of the French came from the leadership of King Charles and the general exhaustion of the English forces.

Charles VII reorganized the French army and gradually chipped away at the English holdings in France, eventually taking away Aquitaine in 1453. The English lost all their possessions in France except Calais, which was finally surrendered in 1558. There was no peace treaty, just a fading away of war in France, especially after England stumbled into civil war—the War of the Roses (1455–1485).

The Hundred Years' War had broad consequences. First, nearly continuous warfare between the two most powerful kingdoms in the West exacerbated other conflicts as well. Scotland, the German princes, Aragon, Castile, and most importantly Burgundy were drawn into the conflict at various stages, making the English-French brawl a European-wide war at certain stages. The squabble between France and England made it much more difficult to settle the Great Schism that split the Church during the same period. Second, the war devastated France, which eventually regained control of most of its territory but still suffered the most from the fighting. During the century of the war, the population dropped by half, due to the ravages of com-

■ **Siege Warfare**
English soldiers pillaging and burning a French town.

bat, pillage, and plague. Agriculture languished after the English repeatedly mounted raids that destroyed crops and sacked peasant villages. Third, the deaths of so many nobles and destruction of their fortunes diminished the international luxury trade; merchants and banks as far away as Italy went broke; and the Flemish woolen industry was disrupted, causing further economic damage. Finally, the war helped make England more English. Before the war the Plantagenet dynasty in England was more French than English. The monarchs possessed extensive territories in France and were embroiled in French affairs. English aristocrats also had business in France, spoke French, and married their French cousins. After 1450 the English abandoned the many French connections that had stretched across the English Channel since William the Conqueror sailed from Normandy to England in 1066. Henceforth, the English upper classes cultivated English rather than French language and culture.

THE MILITARY REVOLUTION

The "military revolution," whose effects first became evident during the Hundred Years' War, refers to changes in warfare that marked the transition from the late medieval to the early modern state. The heavily armored mounted knights, who had dominated European warfare and society since the Carolingian period, were gradually supplanted by foot soldiers as the most effective fighting unit in battle. Infantry units were composed of men who fought on foot in disciplined ranks, which allowed them to break up cavalry charges by concentrating firepower in deadly volleys. Infantry soldiers could fight on a greater variety of terrains than mounted knights, who needed even ground and plenty of space for their horses to maneuver. The effectiveness of infantry units made battles more ferocious but also more decisive, which was why governments favored them. Infantry, however, put new requirements on the governments that recruited them. Armies now demanded large numbers of well-drilled foot soldiers who could move in disciplined ranks around a battlefield. Recruiting, training, and drilling soldiers made armies much more complex organizations than they had been, and officers needed to possess a wide range of management skills. Governments faced added expenses as they needed to arrange and pay for the logistical support necessary to feed and transport those large numbers. The creation of the highly centralized modern state resulted in part from the necessity to maintain a large army in which infantry played the crucial role.

Infantry used a variety of weapons. The English demonstrated the effectiveness of longbowmen during the Hundred Years' War. Capable of shooting at a much more rapid rate than the French crossbowmen, the English longbowmen at Agincourt protected themselves behind a hurriedly erected stockade of stakes and rained a shower of

CHRONOLOGY	
1206–1258	Mongol armies advance undefeated across Eurasia
1281–1326	Reign of Osman I
1305–1378	Babylonian Captivity of the Church
CA. 1310–1320	Famines begin
1320–1384	John Wycliffe
1337–1453	Hundred Years' War
1348	Black Death in Europe
1369–1415	Jan Hus
1378–1417	Great Schism
CA. 1412–1431	Joan of Arc
1453	Fall of Constantinople to Turks
1455–1485	War of the Roses in England

deadly arrows on the French cavalry to break up charges. In the narrow battlefield, which was wedged between two forests, the French cavalry had insufficient room to maneuver, and when some of them dismounted to create more room, their heavy armor made them easy to topple over and spear through the underarm seam in their armor. Some English infantry units deployed ranks of pikemen who created an impenetrable wall of sharp spikes.

The military revolution of the fourteenth and fifteenth centuries also introduced gunpowder to European warfare. Arriving from China with the Mongol invasions, gunpowder was first used in the West in artillery. Beginning in the 1320s huge wrought-iron cannons were used to shoot stone or iron against fortifications during sieges. By the early sixteenth century bronze muzzle-loading cannons were used in field battles. With the introduction during the late fifteenth century of the first handgun and the harquebus (a matchlock shoulder gun), properly drilled and disciplined infantrymen could deliver very destructive firepower. Gun shot pierced plate armor, whereas arrows bounced off. The slow rate of fire of these guns, however, necessitated carefully planned battle tactics.

The military revolution precipitated a major shift in European society as well as in battlefield tactics. The successful states were those that created the financial base and bureaucratic structures necessary to put into the field a well-trained professional army composed of infantry units and artillery. Armies now required officers who were capable of drilling infantry or understanding the science of warfare in order to serve as an artillery officer. The traditional landed aristocrats, accustomed to commanding armored

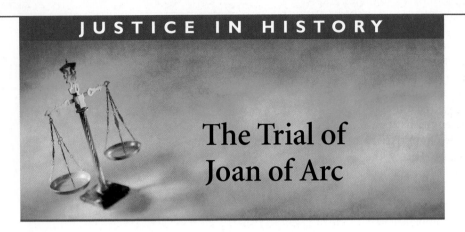

The Trial of Joan of Arc

After only fifteen months as the inspiration of the French army, Joan of Arc fell into the hands of the English, who brought her to trial for witchcraft. The English needed to stage a kind of show trial to demonstrate to their own demoralized forces that Joan's remarkable victories had been the result not of military superiority but rather of witchcraft. In the English trial, conducted at Rouen in 1431, Joan testified that her mission to save France was in response to voices she heard that commanded her to wear men's clothing. On the basis of this evidence of a confused or double gender identity, the ecclesiastical tribunal declared her a witch and a relapsed heretic. The court sentenced her to be burned at the stake.

Political motivations governed the 1431 English trial for witchcraft, but Joan's testimony provides some clues to her own identity conflicts. One of the most compelling questions arising from the trial is why the English tried Joan as a heretic in a church court rather than in a military one as a prisoner of war. The answer can be found in the two pieces of evidence against Joan that ultimately resulted in her condemnation: the spiritual "voices" she claimed to hear and her cross-dressing in men's clothing.

From the beginning of her emergence onto the political scene, Joan's voices intrigued all who came into contact with her. Joan claimed that she was guided by the voices of St. Catherine, St. Margaret, and the Archangel Michael. To Joan, these voices had the authority of divine commands. The problem the English judges faced was to demonstrate that the voices came not from God but from the Devil. If they could prove that, then they had evidence of witchcraft and sorcery. Following standard inquisitorial guidelines, the judges knew that authentic messages from God would always conform to church dogma. Any deviation from official doctrines would constitute evidence of demonic influence. Thus, during Joan's trial the judges demanded that she make theological distinctions that were alien to her. When they wanted to know if the voices were those of angels or saints, Joan seemed perplexed and responded, "This voice comes from God . . . I am more afraid of failing the voices by saying what is displeasing to them than answering you."[2] The judges kept pushing, asking if the saints or angels had heads, eyes, and hair. Exasperated, Joan simply replied, "I have told you often enough, believe me if you will."

The judges reformulated Joan's words to reflect their own rigid scholastic categories and concluded that her "veneration of the saints seems to partake of idolatry and to proceed from a pact made with devils. These are less divine revelations than lies invented by Joan, suggested or shown to her by the demon in illusive apparitions, in order to mock at her imagination while she meddled with things that are beyond her and superior to the faculty of her condition."[3] In other words, Joan was just too naive and uneducated to have authentic visions. But the English judges were on dangerous ground because during the previous fifty years there had been a number of notable female mystics, including St. Catherine of Siena and St. Bridget of Sweden, whose visions had been accepted as authentic by the pope. The English could not take the chance that they were executing a real saint. They had to prove Joan was a witch by showing that her visions were theologically unsound. But that they could not do.

If they could not convict her for bad theology, the English needed evidence for superstitious practices. In an attempt to do that, they drew up seventy charges against her. Many of these consisted of allegations of performing magic, such as chanting spells, visiting a magical tree at night, and invoking demons. They attempted to prove bad behavior by insinuating that a young man had refused to marry her on account of her immoral life. They asserted that her godmother was a notorious witch who had taught her sorcery. None of these ploys worked, however, because Joan consistently denied these charges. She did, however, admit to one allegation: she cross-dressed as a man.

Some of the charges against her and many of the questions she was asked concerned how she dressed:

> The said Joan put off and entirely abandoned women's clothes, with her hair cropped short and round in the fashion of young men, she wore shirt, breeches, doublet, with hose joined together, long and fastened to the said doublet by twenty points, long leggings laced on the outside, a short mantle reaching to the knee, or thereabouts, a close-cut cap, tight-fitting boots or buskins, long spurs, sword, dagger, breastplate, lance and other arms in the style of a man-at-arms.[4]

The judges explained to her that "according to canon law and the Holy Scriptures" a woman dressing as a man or a man as a woman is "an abomination before God."[5] She replied simply and consistently that "everything that I have done, I did by command of the

■ Joan of Arc

Joan of Arc appears before King Charles VII and his council. In this miniature taken from a chronicle of the period, Joan appears dressed in full armor and sword in the lower right corner. The label next to her knee reads, "La Pucelle," which means "The Young Girl." There are no contemporary portraits of Joan, and this image is clearly a generalized one of a young woman in armor rather than a portrait taken from the real Joan.

voices" and that wearing male dress "would be for the great good of France."[6] When they asked her to put on a woman's dress in order to take the Eucharist on Easter Sunday, she refused, saying the miracle of the Eucharist did not depend on whether she wore a man's or a woman's clothing. On many occasions she had been asked to put on a woman's dress and refused. "And as for womanly duties, she said there were enough other women to do them."[7]

After a long imprisonment and psychological pressure from her inquisitors, Joan confessed to charges of witchcraft, signed a recantation of her heresy, and agreed to put on a dress. She was sentenced to life imprisonment on bread and water. Why did she confess? Some historians have argued that she was tricked into confessing because the inquisitors really wanted to execute her but could not do so unless she was a *relapsed* heretic. To be relapsed she had to confess and then somehow return to her heretical ways. If that was the inquisitors' intention, Joan soon obliged them. After a few days in prison, Joan threw off the

women's clothes she had been given and resumed dressing as a man. As a witness put it, "The said Catherine and Margaret [instructed] this woman in the name of God to take and wear a man's clothes, and she had worn them and still wears them, stubbornly obeying the said command, to such an extent that this woman had declared she would rather die than relinquish these clothes."[8]

Joan was willing to be burned at the stake rather than disobey her voices. Why? Historians will never know for sure, but dressing as a man may have been necessary for her to fulfill her role as a military leader. The men who followed her into battle and trusted her voices accepted the necessity of this mutation of gender. In her military career, Joan had adopted the masculine qualities of chivalry: bravery, steadfastness, loyalty, and a willingness to accept pain and death. She made herself believable by dressing as a knight. A number of soldiers who had served with her testified that although they knew Joan was a woman, they had never felt any sexual desire for her, which suggests that she seemed androgynous to them. It was precisely Joan's gender ambiguity that the inquisitors found a dangerous sign of Satan's hand. And it was Joan's refusal to abandon her ambiguous gender identity that provided the inquisitors with the evidence they needed.

Joan's condemnation was much more than another example of men's attempt to control women. The inquisitors needed evidence of demonic influence, which to their minds Joan's transgressive gender behavior supplied. Joan's confused gender identity threatened the whole system of neat hierarchical distinctions upon which scholastic theology rested. To the theologians, everything in God's creation had its own proper place and anyone who changed his or her divinely ordained position in society presented a direct affront to God.

The English verdict and Joan's tragic fate greatly wounded French pride. In 1456 at her mother's instigation the French clergy reopened her case in a posthumous trial that sought to rehabilitate her in the eyes of the church. To these churchmen, she was an authentic visionary and a saint who listened to a direct command from God. To the French people ever since, she has become a national symbol of pride and of French unity against a foreign invader. In our own time, Joan has been characterized as many things—a saint, a madwoman, a female warrior, a woman exercising power in a male world, and a woman openly transgressing gender categories by dressing in men's clothes. ■

Questions of Justice

1. In medieval ecclesiastical trials such as this one, what kinds of evidence were presented and what kind of justice was sought?

2. What did Joan's claim that she heard voices reveal about her understanding of what constituted the proper authority over her life?

Taking It Further

Joan of Arc. *In Her Own Words,* trans. Willard Trask. 1996. The record of what Joan reputedly said at her trials.

Warner, Marina. *Joan of Arc: The Image of Female Heroism.* 1981. A highly readable feminist reading of the Joan of Arc story.

knights, found that noble lineage was not as important as technical skills and talents.

The Culture of Loss

During the fourteenth and early fifteenth centuries, the omnipresence of violence and death became a common theme in the arts, and strangely the subject matter for jokes, fancy-dress masquerades, and wild dances. The preoccupation with death revealed an anxious attachment to fleeting life.

This widespread anxiety had many manifestations. Some aristocrats sought escape from the terror by indulging in a beautiful fantasy life of gallant knights and beautiful ladies. Others went on long penitential pilgrimages to the shrines of saints or to the Holy Land. During the fourteenth century the tribulations of the pilgrim's travels became a metaphor for the journey of life itself, stimulating creative literature.

REMINDERS OF DEATH

In no other period of Western civilization has the idea of death constituted such a pervasive cultural theme as during the fourteenth and fifteenth centuries. The religious justification for this preoccupation was the Reminder of Death, a theme in a contemporary book of moral guidance advising the reader that "when he goes to bed, he should imagine not that he is putting himself to bed, but that others are laying him in his grave."[9] Reminders of Death became the everyday theme of preachers, and popular woodcuts represented death in simple but disturbing images. These representations emphasized the transitory nature of life, admonishing that every created thing perishes. The Reminder of Death tried to encourage ethical behavior in this life by showing that in everyone's future was neither riches, nor fame, nor love, nor pleasure, but only the decay of death.

The most macabre Reminder of Death was the Dance of Death. First appearing in a poem of 1376, the Dance of Death evolved into a street play, performed to illustrate sermons that called for repentance. It also appeared in church murals, depicting a procession led by a skeleton that included representatives of the social orders, from children and peasants to pope and emperor. All were being led to their inevitable deaths.

In earlier centuries, tombs had depicted death as serene: On top of the tomb was an effigy of the deceased, dressed in the finest clothes with hands piously folded and eyes open to the promise of eternal life. In contrast, during the fourteenth century tomb effigies began to depict putrefying bodies or naked skeletons, symbols of the futility of human status and achievements. These tombs were disturbingly

■ **Tomb Effigy of a Knight**
This effigy above the tomb of Jean d'Alluy shows the deceased as if he were serenely sleeping, still dressed in the armor of his worldly profession.

graphic Reminders of Death. Likewise, poems spoke of the putrid smell of rotting flesh, the livid color of plague victims, the cold touch of the dead. Preachers loved to personalize death. They would point to the most beautiful young woman in the congregation and describe how she would look while rotting in the grave, how worms would crawl through the empty sockets that once held her alluring eyes.

Late medieval society was completely frank about the unpleasant process of dying, unlike modern societies that hide the dying in hospitals and segregate mourning to funeral homes. Dying was a public event, almost a theatrical performance. The last rites of the Catholic Church and the Art of Dying served to assist souls in their final test before God and to separate the departed from their kin. According to the Art of Dying, which was prescribed in numerous advice books and illustrations, the sick or injured person should die in bed, surrounded by a room full of people, including children. It was believed that a dying person watched a supernatural spectacle visible to him or her alone as the heavenly host fought with Satan and his demon minions for the soul. The Art of Dying compared the deathbed

■ **Decomposing Cadaver**
The tomb effigy of Jean de Lagrange.

contest to a horrific game of chess in which the Devil did all he could to trap the dying person into a checkmate just at the moment of death. In the best of circumstances, a priest arrived in time to hear a confession, offer words of consolation, encourage the dying individual to forgive his or her enemies and redress any wrongs, and perform the last rites.

ILLUSIONS OF A NOBLE LIFE

Eventually death arrived for everyone, peasant and noble alike, a fact that the Reminders of Death were designed to keep foremost in the minds of all Christians. Some people, especially among the nobility, sought to ignore this fundamental truth through escapist fantasies. These fantasies shielded nobles not only from the inevitability of death but also from all the other perils of the age—the worker and peasant rebellions, the economic depression that depleted their wealth, and the military revolution that challenged their monopoly on soldierly valor. During the Later Middle Ages, many nobles indulged in chivalric escapism and idealized their class as the remedy for evil times. They thought God had placed them on Earth to purify the world.

Much of the attraction of chivalry derived from its fanciful vision of the virtues of the ascetic life, the life that practices severe self-discipline and abstains from physical pleasures. The ideal medieval knight was as much a self-denying ascetic as the ideal medieval monk. The highest expression of the chivalric ideal was the knight-errant, a warrior who roamed in search of adventure. He was poor and free of ties to home and family, a man who lived a life of perfect freedom but whose virtue led him to do the right thing. In reality most knights were hardly ascetics but rich, propertied men who were completely involved in the world and who indulged in all of its pleasures.

The ideal of the ascetic knight-errant was pursued in an elaborately developed dream culture that occupied much of the time and cultural energy of the aristocracy. The dream world of the noble life especially animated the duchy of

Burgundy, a quasi-independent principality that paid nominal allegiance to the French king. Burgundy set the chivalric standards for all of Europe during the fifteenth century. Famous for his lavish lifestyle, Duke Philip the Good (r. 1419–1467) was a notorious rake who seduced numerous noble ladies and produced many illegitimate children, but he also epitomized the ideals of chivalry in his love of horses, hunting, and court ceremonies. He was an extravagant patron of the arts, which made him famous throughout Europe. Musicians, manuscript illuminators, painters, tapestry makers, and historians thrived with his support and made Burgundy the center of European aristocratic fashion.

The dukes of Burgundy sustained their power through their personal ties to the nobility and elites of the cities of their dominions. They were constantly on the move, visiting palaces, castles, and towns. They created a kind of theater state, staging elaborate entry ceremonies to the towns they visited; celebrating with fantastic splendor every event in the ducal family, such as marriages and births; entertaining the nobles with tournaments and the people with elaborate processions; and guaranteeing the loyalty of the nobles by inviting them to join the Order of the Golden Fleece, which occupied its members by training for a crusade.

PILGRIMS OF THE IMAGINATION

During the Middle Ages, a pilgrimage offered a religiously sanctioned form of escape from the omnipresent suffering and peril. Pious Christians could go on a pilgrimage to the Holy Land, Rome, or the shrine of a saint, such as Santiago de Compostela in Spain or Canterbury in England. The usual motive for a pilgrimage was to fulfill a vow or promise made to God, or to obtain an indulgence, which exempted the pilgrim from some of the time spent in punishment in Purgatory after death. The pilgrimage became the instrument for spiritual liberation and escape from difficulties. As a result, going on a pilgrimage became a compelling model for creative literature, especially during the fourteenth century. Not all of these great works of literature were fictional pilgrimages, but many evoked the pilgrim's impulse to find a refuge from the difficulties of daily life or to find solace in the promise of a better life to come.

■ Peasants and a Ducal Castle in Burgundy

Peasants sowing wheat and shearing sheep in the rich agricultural region that made possible the expensive court life of the duchy of Burgundy. One of the many great castles of the dukes appears in the background.

Dante Alighieri and *The Divine Comedy*

In *The Divine Comedy* an Italian poet from Florence, Dante Alighieri (1265–1321), imagined the most fantastic pilgrimage ever attempted, a journey through Hell, Purgatory, and Paradise. A work of astounding originality, *The Divine Comedy* remains the greatest masterpiece of medieval literature. Little is known about Dante's early life except that somehow he acquired an encyclopedic education that gave him expertise in Greek philosophy, scholastic theology (the application of logic to the understanding of Christianity; see Chapter 9), Latin literature, and the newly fashionable poetic forms in Provençal, the language of southern France. Dante was involved in the dangerous politics of Florence, which led to his exile under pain of death if he ever re-

turned. During his exile Dante wandered for years, suffering grievously the loss of his home: "bitter is the taste of another man's bread and . . . heavy the way up and down another man's stair" (*Paradiso,* canto 17). While in exile, Dante sustained himself by writing his great poetic vision of human destiny and God's plan for redemption.

In the poem Dante himself travels into the Christian version of the afterlife, but the poetic journey displays numerous non-Christian influences. The passage through Hell, for example, derived from a long Muslim poem reconstructing Muhammad's *miraj,* a night journey to Jerusalem and ascent to heaven. Dante's poem can be read on many levels—personal, historical, spiritual, moral, theological—as it recounts an allegorical pilgrimage to visit the souls of the departed. Dante connects his personal suffering with the historical problems of Italy, the warnings of the dead who had sinned in life, and the promise of rewards to those who had been virtuous. Dante's trip, initially guided by the Latin poet Virgil, the epitome of ancient wisdom, starts in Hell. While traveling deeper into its harsh depths, Dante is warned of the harmful values of this world by meeting a cast of sinful characters who inhabit the world of the damned. In Purgatory his guide becomes Beatrice, Dante's deceased beloved, who stands for the Christian virtues. In this section of the poem, he begins the painful process of spiritual rehabilitation where he comes to accept the Christian image of life as a pilgrimage. In Paradise he achieves spiritual fulfillment by speaking with figures from the past who have defied death.

The lasting appeal of this long, complex, and difficult poem is a wonder. Underlying the appeal of *The Divine Comedy* is perhaps its optimism, which expresses Dante's own cure to his depressing condition as an exile. The power of Dante's poetry established the form of the modern Italian language. Even in translation the images and stories can intrigue and fascinate.

Geoffrey Chaucer and *The Canterbury Tales*

Geoffrey Chaucer (ca. 1342–1400) was the most outstanding English poet prior to William Shakespeare. As a courtier and diplomat, Chaucer was a trusted adviser to three successive English kings. But he is best known for his literary output, including *The Canterbury Tales.*

In *The Canterbury Tales* a group of thirty pilgrims tell stories as they travel on horseback to the shrine at Canterbury. By employing the pilgrimage as a framing device for telling the stories, Chaucer was able to bring together a collection of people from across the social spectrum, including a wife, indulgence hawker, miller, town magistrate, clerk, landowner, lawyer, merchant, knight, abbess, and monk. The variety of characters who told the tales allowed Chaucer to experiment with many kinds of literary forms, from a chivalric romance to a sermon. The pilgrimage combined the considerations of religious morality

DANTE DESCRIBES HELL

In The Divine Comedy, *Dante imagined a series of circles in Hell into which were cast those guilty of a certain class of sin. In the eighth circle Dante and his guide Virgil came upon those guilty of fraud. They suffered for all eternity in the depths of stinking, filthy caverns in the ground. Dante and Virgil followed a path through Hell, and at this point the path led to a series of arches that spanned the caverns.*

Here we heard people whine in the next chasm,
and knock and thump themselves with open palms,
and blubber through their snouts as if in a spasm.

Steaming from that pit, a vapor rose
over the banks, crusting them with a slime
that sickened my eyes and hammered at my nose.

That chasm sinks so deep we could not sight
its bottom anywhere until we climbed
along the rock arch to its greatest height.

Once there, I peered down; and I saw long lines
of people in a river of excrement
that seemed the overflow of the world's latrines.

I saw among the felons of that pit
one wraith who might or might not have been tonsured—
one could not tell, he was so smeared with shit.

He bellowed: "You there, why do you stare at me
more than at all the others in this stew?"
And I to him: "Because if memory
serves me, I knew you when your hair was dry.
You are Alessio Interminelli da Lucca.
That's why I pick you from this filthy fry."

And he then, beating himself on his clown's head:
"Down to this have the flatteries I sold
the living sunk me here among the dead."

And my Guide prompted then: "Lean forward a bit
and look beyond them, there—do you see that one
scratching herself with dungy nails, the strumpet
who fidgets to her feet, then to a crouch?
It is the whore Thais . . .

with the fun of a spring vacation more concerned with the pleasures of this world than preparing for the next, which was the avowed purpose of going on a pilgrimage. In this intertwining of the worldly and the spiritual, Chaucer brought the abstract principles of Christian morality down to a level of common understanding.

Margery Kempe and the Autobiographical Pilgrimage

As the daughter of a town mayor, Margery Kempe (1373–1440) was destined for a comfortable life as a middle-class wife in provincial England. After her first child was born, however, she experienced a bout of depression during which she had a vision of Christ. She began to experience more visions and felt a calling to lead a more spiritual life. As a married woman she could not become a nun, which would have been the normal course for a woman with her spiritual inclinations. Instead, she accepted her marital duties and bore fourteen children.

At the age of about 40 she persuaded her husband to join her in a mutual vow of chastity and embarked on her own religious vocation. Always a bit of an eccentric, Kempe became a fervent vegetarian at a time when meat was scarce but highly desired. She also developed an insatiable wanderlust, undertaking a series of pilgrimages to Jerusalem, Rome, Germany, Norway, Spain, and numerous places in England. On these pilgrimages she sought out mystics and recluses for their spiritual advice. Her own devotions took the form of loud weeping and crying, which alienated many people who feared she might be a heretic or a madwoman. Toward the end of her life she dictated an account of her difficult dealings with her husband, her spells of madness, her ecstatic visions, and her widespread travels as a pilgrim. For Kempe the actual experience of undertaking pilgrimages made it possible for her to examine the course of her own life, which she understood as a spiritual pilgrimage. Her *Book* (1436) was the earliest autobiography in English.

Christine de Pisan and the Defense of Female Virtue

The work of the poet Christine de Pisan (1364–1430) did not evoke a spiritual pilgrimage like Dante's, Chaucer's, or Kempe's but was a thoughtful and passionate commentary on the tumultuous issues of her day. At age 15 Pisan married a notary of King Charles V of France, but by age 25 she was a widow with three young children. In order to support her family, she turned to writing and relied on the patronage of the royalty and wealthy aristocrats of France, Burgundy, Germany, and England.

Christine de Pisan championed the cause of women in a male-dominated society that was often overtly hostile to them. Following the fashion of the times, she invented a new chivalric order, the Order of the Rose, whose members took a vow to defend the honor of women. She wrote a defense of women for a male readership and an allegorical autobiography. But she is most famous for the two books she wrote for women readers, *The Book of the City of Ladies* and *The Book of Three Virtues* (both about 1407). In these she recounted tales of the heroism and virtue of women and offered moral instruction for women in different social roles. In 1415 she retired to a convent where in the last year of her life she wrote a masterpiece of ecstatic lyricism that celebrated the early victories of Joan of Arc. Pisan's book turned the martyred Joan into the heroine of France.

CONCLUSION

Looking Inward

Unlike the more dynamic, outward-looking thirteenth century, Europeans during the fourteenth and early fifteenth centuries turned their attention inward to their own communities and their own problems. Europe faced one calamity after another, each crisis compounding the misery. In the process the identity of the West became more defensive and the fragility of Christianity itself was laid bare. The process of changing Western identities can be seen in two ways. First, as a result of the Western encounters with the Mongol and Ottoman Empires, the political and religious frontiers of the West shifted. These two empires redrew the map of the West by ending the Christian Byzantine Empire and by leaving Christian Russia on the margins of the West. With the Mongol invasions, the eastward spread of Christianity into Asia ended. The Ottoman conquests left a lasting Muslim influence inside eastern Europe, particularly in Bosnia and Albania. Peoples who were predominantly Christian and whose political institutions were a heritage of the ancient Roman Empire now survived under the domination of Asiatic empires and in a tenuous relationship with the rest of the Christian West. Most of the new subjects of these empires remained Christian, but their Mongol and Ottoman masters destroyed their political autonomy. The Ottoman Empire remained hostile to and frequently at war with the Christian West for more than 200 years.

Second, in western Europe people reinforced their identity as Christians and became more self-conscious of the country in which they lived. At the same time Christian civilization was becoming eclipsed in parts of eastern Europe, however, it revived in the Iberian peninsula where the Muslim population, once the most extensive in the West, suffered discrimination and defeat. A stronger sense of self-identification by country can be most dramatically seen in France and England as a consequence of the Hundred Years' War. The French rallied around a saintly national heroine, Joan of Arc. After dropping claims to France after the Hundred Years' War, the English aristocracy stopped speaking French and adopting the customs of the French court. They became less international and more English. The Western countries became more self-consciously characterized by an attitude of "us" versus "them."

Except for the very visible military conquests of the Mongols and the Ottomans, the causes of most of the calamities of the fourteenth century were invisible or unknown. No one recognized a climate change or understood the dynamics of the population crisis. No one could see the plague bacillus. No one grasped the role of the Mongol Empire in the world economy or the causes for the collapse of banking and trade. Unable to distinguish how these forces were changing their lives, western Europeans only witnessed their consequences. In the face of these calamities, European culture became obsessed with death. However, calamity also bred creativity, manifest in the passionate intensity of life. The search for answers to the question, "Why did this happen to us?" produced a new spiritual sensibility and a rich literature. Following the travails of the fourteenth century, moreover, there arose in the fifteenth a new, more optimistic cultural movement—the Renaissance. Gloom and doom was not the only response to troubles. During the Renaissance some people began to search for new answers to human problems in a fashion that would transform the West anew.

Suggestions for Further Reading

....

For a comprehensive list of suggested readings, please go to www.ablongman.com/levackconcise/chapter10

Cohn, Samuel. *The Black Death Transformed: Disease and Culture in Early Renaissance Europe.* 2003. A well-argued case that the Black Death was not caused by the bubonic plague.

Duby, Georges. *France in the Middle Ages, 987–1460: From Hugh Capet to Joan of Arc.* 1991. Traces the emergence of the French state.

Gordon, Bruce, and Peter Marshall, eds. *The Place of the Dead: Death and Remembrance in Late Medieval and Early Modern Europe.* 2000. A collection of essays that shows how the placing of the dead in society was an important activity that engendered considerable conflict and negotiation.

Herlihy, David. *The Black Death and the Transformation of the West.* 1997. A pithy, readable analysis of the epidemiological and historical issues surrounding the Black Death.

Holmes, George. *Europe: Hierarchy and Revolt, 1320–1450.* 1975. Excellent examination of rebellions.

Huizinga, Johan. *The Autumn of the Middle Ages,* trans. Rodney J. Payton and Urlich Mammitzsch. 1996. A new translation of the classic study of France and the Low Countries during the fourteenth and fifteenth century. Dated and perhaps too pessimistic, Huizinga's lucid prose and broad vision still make this an engaging reading experience.

Imber, Colin. *The Ottoman Empire, 1300–1481.* 1990. The basic work that establishes a chronology for the early Ottomans.

Jordan, William C. *The Great Famine: Northern Europe in the Early Fourteenth Century.* 1996. The most comprehensive book on the famine.

Lambert, Malcolm. *Medieval Heresy: Popular Movements from the Gregorian Reform to the Reformation.* 1992. Excellent general study of the Hussite and Lollard movements.

Le Roy Ladurie, Emmanuel. *Times of Feast, Times of Famine: A History of Climate since the Year 1000,* trans. Barbara Bray. 1971. The book that introduced the idea of the Little Ice Age and promoted the study of the influence of climate on history.

Lynch, Joseph H. *The Medieval Church: A Brief History.* 1992. A pithy, elegant survey of ecclesiastical institutions and developments.

Morgan, David O. *The Mongols.* 1986. Best introduction to Mongol history.

Sumption, Jonathan. *The Hundred Years' War: Trial by Battle.* 1991. First volume goes only to 1347. When it is completed it will be the best comprehensive study.

Swanson, R. N. *Religion and Devotion in Europe, c. 1215– c. 1515.* 1995. The best up-to-date textbook account of late medieval religious practice.

Notes

....

1. Cited in Philip Ziegler, *The Black Death* (1969), 20.
2. Trial record as quoted in Marina Warner, *Joan of Arc* (1981), 122.
3. Ibid., 127.
4. Ibid., 143.
5. *The Trial of Joan of Arc,* trans. W. S. Scott (1956), 134.
6. Ibid., 106.
7. Ibid., 135.
8. Warner, *Joan of Arc,* 145.
9. Ziegler, *The Black Death,* 156.

The Italian Renaissance and Beyond: The Politics of Culture

FOR FIFTEEN YEARS NICCOLÒ MACHIAVELLI WORKED AS A DIPLOMAT AND POLITical adviser, a man always at the center of the action in his hometown of Florence. But in 1512 there was a change of regimes in the city-state of Florence. Distrusted by the new rulers and suspected of involvement in an assassination plot, he was abruptly fired from his job, imprisoned, tortured, and finally ordered to stay out of town. Exiled to his suburban farm, impoverished, and utterly miserable, Machiavelli survived by selling lumber from his wood lot to his former colleagues, who regularly cheated him. To help feed his family he snared birds; to entertain himself he played cards in a local inn with the innkeeper, a butcher, a miller, and two bakers. As he put it, "caught this way among these lice I wipe the mold from my brain [by playing cards] and release my feeling of being ill-treated by Fate."

In the evenings, however, Machiavelli transformed himself into an entirely different person. He entered his study, removed his mud-splattered clothes, and put on the elegant robes he had once worn as a government official. And then, "dressed in a more appropriate manner I enter into the ancient courts of ancient men and am welcomed by them kindly." Machiavelli was actually reading the works of the ancient Greek and Latin historians, but he described his evening reading as a conversation: He asked the ancients about the reasons for their actions, and in reading their books he found answers. For four hours, "I feel no boredom, I dismiss every affliction, I no longer fear poverty nor do I tremble at the thought of death: I become completely part of them."[1]

Machiavelli's evening conversations with the long-dead ancients perfectly expressed the sensibility of the Italian Renaissance. This wretched man,

Chapter Outline

■ The Cradle of the Renaissance: The Italian City-States

■ The Influence of Ancient Culture

■ Antiquity and Nature in the Arts

■ The Early Modern European State System

The Birth of Venus (1480): Sandro Botticelli's depiction of the birth of the ancient goddess of love exemplifies the Renaissance fascination with the culture of antiquity.

disillusioned with his own times and bored by his empty-headed neighbors, found in the ancients the stimulating companions he could not find in life. For him the ancient past was more alive than the present. In this sense Machiavelli was very much a Renaissance man, because feeling part of antiquity is what the Renaissance is all about. For those who were captivated by it, the ancient past and the examples of leadership and beauty it offered seemed to be a cure for the ills of a decidedly troubled time.

The word Renaissance°, which means "rebirth," is a term historians invented to describe a movement that sought to imitate and understand the culture of antiquity. The fundamental Renaissance principle was the need to keep everything in balance and proportion, an aesthetic ideal derived from ancient literature. In political theory, this meant building a stable society on the foundations of well-balanced individuals who conformed to a rigorous code of conduct. In the arts it meant searching for the underlying harmonies in nature, which typically meant employing geometry and the mathematics of proportion in drawing, painting, sculpting, and designing buildings. Renaissance artists thought geometry unlocked the secrets of nature and revealed the hidden hand of God in creation. Most historians date the Renaissance from about 1350 to 1550.

The Renaissance helped refashion the concept of Western civilization. From the fifth to the fourteenth centuries, the West identified itself primarily through conformity to Roman Catholicism, which meant the celebration of uniform religious rituals in Latin and obedience to the pope. The Renaissance added a new element to this identity. Although by no means anti-Christian, Renaissance thinkers began to think of themselves as the heirs of pre-Christian cultures—Hebrew, Greek, and Roman. In this sense, they began to imagine a Western civilization that was more than just Christian.

Through reading the texts and viewing the works of art of the long-dead ancients, people during the Italian Renaissance gained historical and visual perspective on their own world and cultivated a critical attitude. To understand what was distinctive about their insights, this chapter will address four questions:

■ In what ways did the political and social climate peculiar to the Italian city-states help create Renaissance culture?

■ How did Renaissance thinkers create historical perspective and devise methods of criticism for interpreting texts?

■ How did various attempts to imitate antiquity in the arts alter perceptions of nature?

■ How did the monarchies of western Europe gather the strength to become more assertive and more effective?

The Cradle of the Renaissance: The Italian City-States

In comparison with the rest of Europe and other world civilizations, Renaissance Italy was distinguished by the large number and political autonomy of its thriving city-states. The Netherlands and parts of the Rhine Valley were as thoroughly urbanized, but only in Italy did cities have so much political power.

Italian city-states first established themselves as independent republics during the late eleventh and twelfth centuries. The governmental practices of these city-states produced the political theory of republicanism°, a state in which government officials were elected by the people or a portion of the people. The Renaissance theory of republicanism was first articulated by Marsilius of Padua (1270–1342) in *The Defender of the Peace,* a book that relied on the precedents established by the ancient Roman republic. Marsilius recognized two kinds of government—principalities and republics. Principalities relied on the descending principle that political authority came directly from God and trickled down through kings and princes to the rest of humanity. According to this principle, the responsibility of government was to enforce God's laws. Marsilius, however, rejected the idea that the task of the political world was to express the will of God. His ascending principle of republicanism suggested that laws derive not from God but from the will of the people, who freely choose their own form of government and who are equally free to change it. In Marsilius's theory, citizens regularly expressed their will through voting.

During the fourteenth century, most city-states abandoned or lost their republican institutions and came to be ruled by princes. The reasons for the transformation of these republics into principalities were related to the economic and demographic turmoil created by the international economic collapse and the Black Death discussed in Chapter 10. Two of the largest republics, however, survived without losing their liberty to a prince. The Renaissance began in these two city-states, Florence and Venice (see Map 11.1). Their survival as republics, which made them exceptions to the rule by the fifteenth century, helps explain the origins of the Renaissance.

THE RENAISSANCE REPUBLICS: FLORENCE AND VENICE

In an age of despotic princes, Florence and Venice were keenly aware of how different they were from other cities, and they feared they might suffer the same fate as their neighbors if they did not defend their republican institutions and liberty. In keeping alive the traditions of republican self-government, these two cities created an environment of competition and freedom that stimulated creative ingenuity. Although neither of these cities were democracies, nor were they particularly egalitarian, they were certainly more open to new ideas than cities ruled by princes. In Florence and Venice a few great families called the *patriciate* controlled most of the property, but these patricians competed among themselves to gain recognition and fame by patronizing great artists and scholars. This patronage by wealthy men and women made the Renaissance possible. Because the tastes of these patricians dictated what writers and artists could do, understanding who they were helps explain Renaissance culture.

Florence Under the Medici

The greatest patron during the early Renaissance was the fabulously rich Florentine banker Cosimo de' Medici (1389–1464). Based on his financial power, Cosimo effectively took control of the Florentine republic in 1434, ushering in a period of unprecedented domestic peace and artistic splendor called the Medicean Age (1434–1494). Cosimo's style of rule was exceedingly clever. Instead of making himself a prince, which the citizens of Florence would have opposed, he managed the policies of the republic from behind the scenes. He seldom held public office, but he made himself the center of Florentine affairs through shrewd negotiating, the quiet fixing of elections, and the generous distribution of bribes, gifts, and jobs. Cosimo's behind-the-scenes rule illustrated a fundamental value of Renaissance culture—the desire to maintain appearances. In this case, the appearance of the Florentine republic was saved, even as the reality of Florentine liberty was subverted.

Cosimo's brilliant patronage of intellectuals and artists mirrored a similar ambition to maintain appearances. It helped make Cosimo appear a pious, generous man who modeled himself after the great statesmen of the ancient Roman republic. Cosimo appreciated intelligence and merit wherever he found it. He frequented the discussions of prominent scholars, some of whom became his lasting friends. Intrigued by what he learned from them, he personally financed the search for and acquisition of manuscripts of ancient Latin and Greek literature and philosophy for new libraries he helped establish. In return for his financial support, many Florentine scholars dedicated their works to Cosimo. He took particular interest in the revival of the ancient Greek philosopher Plato, and he set up the neo-Platonic philosopher Marsilio Ficino (1433–1499) with a house and steady income.

Cosimo's most significant patronage of the arts clustered in the neighborhood where he lived. He rebuilt the nearby monastery of San Marco. He personally selected Fra Angelico, a monk, to paint the austere yet deeply emotive frescoes throughout the monastery. As the centerpiece of his neighborhood beautification plans, Cosimo built for his own family a magnificent new palace, which he filled with innumerable objects of beauty and exquisite paintings.

Cosimo's grandson Lorenzo the Magnificent (r. 1469–1492) expanded the family's dominance in Florentine politics through what has been called "veiled lordship." Lorenzo never took the title of prince but behaved very much like one by intervening publicly in the affairs of the state. In contrast to his grandfather's commitment to public patronage, Lorenzo's interest in the arts concentrated on building private villas, collecting precious gems, and commissioning small bronze statues, the kinds of things that gave him private pleasure rather than a public reputation. A fine poet

■ **Map 11.1 Northern Italy in the Mid-Fifteenth Century**

During the Renaissance the largest city-states, such as Milan, Venice, and Florence, gained control of the surrounding countryside and smaller cities in the vicinity, establishing regional territorial states. Only Venice and Florence remained republics. Milan and Savoy were ruled by dukes. The Gonzaga family ruled Mantua and the Este Modena and Ferrara. The states of the Church were ruled by the pope in Rome.

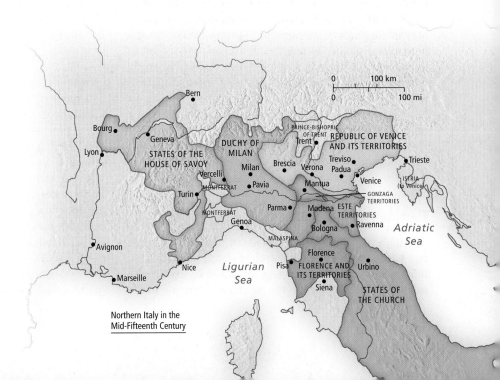

Northern Italy in the Mid-Fifteenth Century

and an intellectual companion of the most renowned scholars of his age, Lorenzo created a lasting reputation as a well-rounded, accomplished Renaissance man.

Venice, the Cosmopolitan Republic

Venice resembled Florence in that it survived into the Renaissance period with its republican institutions intact, but it was far more politically stable. Situated in the midst of a vast lagoon, Venice's streets consisted of broad channels in which great seagoing merchant ships were moored and small canals choked with private gondolas for local transportation. To protect their fragile city from flooding, the Venetians recognized that they had to cooperate among themselves, and thus the imperative for survival helped create a republic that became a model of stability and ecological awareness. The Venetians, for example, created the world's first environmental regulatory agencies, which were responsible for hydrological projects, such as dikes and dredging canals, and for forestry management to prevent soil erosion and the consequent silting up of the lagoon.

Venice was among the first European powers to have colonies abroad. To guarantee its merchant ships access to the eastern Mediterranean and Constantinople, Venice conquered a series of ports, including a significant number in Greece. Its involvement in international trade and governing distant colonies made Venice unusually cosmopolitan. Many Venetian merchants spent years living abroad and some settled in the colonies. Moreover, people from all over Europe flocked to the city of Venice—Germans, Turks, Armenians, Albanians, Greeks, Slovenes, Croats, and Jews—each creating their own neighborhood communities and institutions. Venetian households owned Russian, Asian, Turkish, and African slaves, all of whom contributed to the remarkable diversity of the city.

The defining characteristic of Venetian government was its social stability, a trait that made it the envy of other more troubled cities and the source of imitation by republican-minded reformers throughout Europe. Whereas the Florentine republic was notoriously unstable and subject to quiet subversion by the Medicis, Venice boasted a largely unchanging republican constitution that lasted from 1297 to 1797. Thus Venice is the longest-surviving republic in history. It was, however, a very exclusive republic. Out of a total population of nearly 150,000, only a small political elite of 2,500 nobles enjoyed voting privileges. From this elite and from Venice's many wealthy religious institutions came the resources to patronize Renaissance artists.

PRINCES AND COURTIERS

Although the Renaissance began in the relative freedom of republics, such as Florence, it soon spread to principalities, those states ruled by one man, the prince. In contrast to the multiple sources of support for the arts and learning in the

republics, patronage in the principalities was more constricted, confined to the prince and members of his court. The terms *lord* and *prince* refer to rulers who possessed formal aristocratic titles, such as the Marquis of Mantua, the Duke of Milan, and the King of Naples. Most Renaissance princes came from local aristocratic families who seized control of the government by force and established a dynasty that continued to rule the city.

The Ideal Prince, the Ideal Princess

Federico II da Montefeltro (1422–1482), Duke of Urbino, succeeded in achieving the lasting fame and glorious reputation that so many princes craved. Federico was a mercenary captain. From among the peasants of the duchy he recruited an army, which he hired out to the highest bidder. He soon earned a European-wide reputation for his many victories and enriched the duchy with the income from mercenary contracts and plunder. Federico epitomized the ideal Renaissance prince—a father figure to his subjects, astute diplomat, brilliant soldier, generous patron, avid collector, and man of learning. This was a prince who combined the insights of contemplative study with active involvement in the affairs of the world.

Federico's rule was paternalistic. He was concerned for the welfare of his subjects and personally listened to their complaints and adjudicated their disputes. His military adventures tripled the size of his duchy. Conquests brought the prosperity that financed his expensive building projects and his collection of Latin manuscripts. Federico's personal library surpassed that of any contemporary university library in Europe, and his wide-ranging reading interests showed his openness to the latest developments in learning. Because of Federico, the small mountainous duchy of Urbino acquired a cultural importance far greater than its size warranted.

The best candidate for the ideal princess was Isabella d'Este (1474–1539), the Marchioness of Mantua. Such was her fame as a patron that she was known during her lifetime as "the first lady of the world." Enjoying an education that was exceptional for a girl in the fifteenth century, she grew up in the court at Ferrara, where she was surrounded by famous painters and poets and where she cultivated the friendship of foreign ambassadors and leading intellectuals of the time. Such was her fame that her own clothing designs established the fashion for all of Europe. But her influence went far beyond that. When her husband was absent and after his death, she ruled Mantua by herself, earning a reputation for her just decisions and witty charm. She gained renown for her ability as a tenacious negotiator and behind-the-scenes diplomat. An avid reader and collector, she personally knew virtually all the great artists and writers of her age. Her influence spread far beyond Mantua, in part through her voluminous correspondence, which is estimated to include 12,000 letters.

The Ideal Courtier

The Renaissance republics developed a code of conduct for the ideal citizen. The code encouraged citizens to devote their time and energies to public service. The code insisted that the most valuable services of the citizen were to hold public office, to pay taxes honestly, and to help beautify the city through patronage of the arts. In similar fashion the Renaissance principalities created a code for the ideal courtier. A courtier was a man or woman who lived in or regularly visited the palace of a prince. Courtiers helped the prince's household function by performing all kinds of services, such as taking care of the family's wardrobe, managing servants, educating children, providing entertainment, keeping accounts, administering estates, going on diplomatic missions, and fighting battles. To best serve the princely family in whatever was needed, a courtier had to cultivate a wide range of skills. Men trained in horsemanship, sword play, and all kinds of sports, which were useful for keeping in shape for war. Women learned to draw, dance, play musical instruments, and engage in witty conversation. Both men and women needed to be adept at foreign languages so that they could converse with visitors and diplomats. According to the ideal, men should also know Latin and Greek, which were the foundations of a formal education. Some of the women in the courts also learned these ancient languages.

The stability and efficiency of the princely states depended on the abilities of the courtiers, who performed many of the functions that elected officials did in the republics. It was also extremely important to prevent conflicts among the courtiers; otherwise the peace of the state would be compromised. The most influential guide to how a courtier should behave was *The Book of the Courtier* (composed between 1508 and 1528) by the cultivated diplomat Baldassare Castiglione (1478–1529). Underlying the behavior and conversation of the ideal courtier described in this book were two general principles that governed all courtly manners—nonchalance and ease.

Nonchalance is the ability to do something that requires considerable training and effort while making it appear to be natural and without effort. The need to maintain appearances, which we first saw in the disguised rulership of Cosimo de' Medici in Florence, became one of the distinguishing traits of Italian Renaissance culture. According to Castiglione, all human action and communication should be moderate and balanced, creating the effect of ease. In effect, *The Book of the Courtier* translated the ideals of harmony and proportion so admired in Renaissance culture into a plan for human comportment. By using courtly manners, human beings governed the movements of the body according to an almost mathematical ideal of proportion.

Through *The Book of the Courtier* and its many imitators, the Renaissance ideal of courtly manners began to be widely disseminated during the sixteenth century due to the capacity of the newly invented printing press to produce inexpensive copies of the same text. Written in a lucid Italian that

■ Courtiers Waiting on a Princely Family

The man at the far right is posing in a nonchalant manner. Members of the prince's family on the left congregate around him as he conducts business from the throne, which is just a chair with a dog resting underneath. In this scene the prince confers with a messenger who has brought him a letter.

made for lively reading, the book was translated into Latin, English, French, and Spanish and absorbed into the literature of Europe. By studying these books, any young man or woman of talent and ambition could aspire to act and speak like a great aristocrat. The courtly ideal was completely accessible to anyone who could read, and many of its precepts were incorporated into the educational curriculum.

The Papal Prince

The Renaissance popes were the heads of the Church; they also had jurisdiction over the Papal State in central Italy. Thus they combined the roles of priest and prince. The Papal State was supposed to supply the pope with the income to run the affairs of the Church, but as we saw in Chapter 10, during the period when the popes left Rome and resided in Avignon (France) and during the Great Schism of 1305–1417, the popes lost control of the Papal State. After 1418 the popes saw that they had two main tasks—regain the revenues of the Papal State and rebuild the city of Rome, which had become a neglected ruin. To collect the taxes and revenues due them, many popes were obliged to use military force to bring the rebellious lords and cities into obedience. The popes also engaged in squabbles with the neighboring states that had taken advantage of the weakness of the papacy during the schism.

These military and diplomatic adventures thrust the popes into some very nasty quarrels—a situation that undermined the popes' ability to provide moral leadership. Pope Alexander VI (r. 1492–1503) financed his son Cesare Borgia's attempts to carve out a principality for himself along the northern fringe of the Papal State. He also married off his daughter, Lucrezia Borgia, in succession to several different Italian princes who were useful allies in the pope's military ambitions. Alexander's successor, Pope Julius II (r. 1503–1513), continued to pursue military advantage in the Papal State. He took his princely role so seriously that he donned armor, personally led troops during the siege of Bologna, and rather presumptuously rewarded himself with a triumphal procession, an honor that had been granted in ancient Rome to victorious generals such as Julius Caesar.

Many of the Renaissance popes were embarrassed by the squalor of the city of Rome, an unfit place to serve as the capital of the Church. By the late fifteenth century a number of popes were ambitious to create a capital they felt worthy for Christendom. The most clear-sighted of the builders of Rome was Pope Leo X (r. 1513–1521), the second son of Lorenzo the Magnificent. Educated by the circle of scholars who surrounded the Medicis, Leo was destined for a clerical career at a young age. He received a doctorate in canon law and was made a cardinal at age 17. During Leo's pontificate, Rome was transformed into one of the centers of Renaissance culture. Leo's ambition can best be measured in his project to rebuild Saint Peter's Basilica as the largest church in the world. He tore down the old

Basilica, which had been a major pilgrimage destination for more than a thousand years, and planned the great church that still dominates Rome today.

The Influence of Ancient Culture

The need in Renaissance Italy to provide effective models for how citizens and courtiers should behave stimulated a reexamination of ancient culture. The civilizations of ancient Greece and Rome had long fascinated the educated classes in the West. In Italy where most cities were built around or on top of the ruins of the ancient past, the seduction of antiquity was particularly pronounced. During the fourteenth and fifteenth centuries many Italian thinkers and artists attempted to foster a rebirth of ancient cultures. At first they merely attempted to imitate the Latin style of the best Roman writers. Then scholars tried to do the same thing with Greek, stimulated in part by direct contact with Greek-speaking refugees from Byzantium. Artists trekked to Rome to fill their notebooks with sketches of ancient ruins, sculptures, and medallions. Wealthy collectors hoarded manuscripts of ancient philosophy, built libraries to house them, bought up every piece of ancient sculpture they could find, and dug up ruins to find more antiquities to adorn their palaces. Patrons demanded that artists produce new works that imitated the styles of the ancients and that displayed a similar concern for rendering natural forms. Especially prized were lifelike representations of the human body.

Patrons, artists, and scholars during the Renaissance not only appreciated the achievements of the past but began to understand the enormous cultural distance between themselves and the ancients. That insight made their perspective historical. They also developed techniques of literary analysis to determine when a particular text had been written and to differentiate authentic texts from ones that had been corrupted by the mistakes of copyists. That ability made their perspective critical.

PETRARCH AND THE ILLUSTRIOUS ANCIENTS

The founder of the historical critical perspective that characterized the Renaissance was Francesco Petrarca (1304–1374), known in English as Petrarch. In contrast to the medieval thinkers who admired the ancients and treated their words as repositories of eternal wisdom, Petrarch discovered that the ancients were mere men much like himself. More than anything else, that insight might distinguish what was new about the Italian Renaissance, and Petrarch was the first to explore its implications.

Petrarch's early fame came from his poetry, in both his native Italian and in Latin. In an attempt to improve his

Latin style, Petrarch engaged in a detailed study of the best ancient Roman writers and searched to find old manuscripts that were the least corrupted by copyists. In that search he was always watching for anything by the Roman orator Cicero (106–43 B.C.E.), who was the Latinist most revered for literary style. In 1345 Petrarch briefly visited Verona to see what he could find in the library of a local monastery. While thumbing through the dusty volumes, he excitedly happened upon a previously unknown collection of letters Cicero had written to his friend Atticus.

As Petrarch began to read the letters, however, he suffered a profound shock. Cicero had a reputation as the greatest sage of the Romans, a model of good Latin style, of philosophical sophistication, and most of all of high ethical standards. But in the letters Petrarch found not sage moral advice but gossip, rumors, and crude political calculations. Cicero looked like a scheming politician, a man of crass ambition rather than grand philosophical wisdom. Although Petrarch could never forgive Cicero for being less than what he had avowed in his philosophical writings, he had discovered the human Cicero rather than just the idealized Cicero, a man so human you could imagine having a conversation with him.

And having a conversation was precisely what Petrarch set out to do. Cicero, however, had been dead for 1,388 years. So Petrarch wrote a letter to Cicero's ghost. Adopting Cicero's own elegant Latin style, Petrarch lambasted the Roman for going against the moral advice he had given others. Petrarch quoted Cicero back to Cicero, asking him how he could be such a hypocrite.

> *Your letters I sought for long and diligently; and finally, where I least expected it, I found them. At once I read them, over and over, with the utmost eagerness. And as I read I seemed to hear your bodily voice, O Marcus Tullius [Cicero's given names], saying many things, uttering many lamentations, ranging through many phases of thought and feeling. I long had known how excellent a guide you have proved for others; at last I was to learn what sort of guidance you gave yourself. . . . Now it is your turn to be the listener.*[2]

Petrarch went on to lecture Cicero for his false dealings, his corruption, and his moral failures. The point of the exercise of writing a letter to a dead man was to compare the ideals Cicero had avowed in his philosophical work and the reality he seemed to have lived. Making comparisons is one of the elementary techniques of a critical method, and it became the hallmark of Petrarch's mode of analysis. Petrarch's letter reduced the stature of the ancients a bit, making them less like gods and more like other men who made mistakes and told lies. Petrarch ended this remarkable, unprecedented letter with a specific date, given in both the Roman and Christian ways, and a description of Verona's location in a way an ancient Roman would understand—as if he were making it possible for Cicero to find and answer him. This concern for historical precision typified the aspect that

was most revolutionary about Petrarch's approach. No longer a repository of timeless truths, the ancient world became a specific time and place, which Petrarch perceived to be at a great distance from himself. The ancients had ceased to be godlike; they had become historical figures. After his letter to Cicero, Petrarch wrote a series of letters to other illustrious ancients in which he revealed the human qualities and shortcomings of each.

Petrarch and his follower Lorenzo Valla (1407–1457) developed critical methods by editing classical texts, including parts of Livy's history of Rome, which was written about the time of Jesus. Petrarch compared different manuscript versions of Livy's work in an attempt to establish exactly the original words, a method very different from the medieval scribe's temptation to alter or improve a text as he saw fit. Petrarch strived to get the words right because he wanted to understand exactly what Livy had meant, a method now called the philological approach. Philology° is the comparative study of language, devoted to understanding the meaning of a word in a particular historical context. Valla elaborated on Petrarch's insights into philology to demonstrate that words do not have fixed meanings but take on different meanings depending on who is using them and when they were written. It was obvious, for example, that the word *virtue* had meant something quite different to the polytheist Livy than it did to readers in the fourteenth and fifteenth centuries, who understood virtue in Christian terms. A concern for philology gave Petrarch and his followers access to the individuality of a writer. In the particularity of words, Petrarch discovered the particularity of actual individuals who lived and wrote many centuries before.

An interest in the meaning of words led Petrarch to study the rhetoric° of language. Rhetoric refers to the art of persuasive or emotive speaking and writing. From his studies of rhetoric, Petrarch became less confident about the ability of language to represent truth than he was about its capacity to motivate readers and listeners to action. He came to think that rhetoric was superior to philosophy because he preferred a good man over a wise one, and rhetoric offered examples worthy of emulation rather than abstract principles subject to debate. Petrarch wanted people to behave morally, not just talk or write about morality. And he believed that the most efficient way to inspire his readers to do the right thing was to write moving rhetoric.

THE HUMANISTS: THE LATIN POINT OF VIEW

Those who followed Petrarch's approach to the classical authors were the Renaissance humanists°. The Renaissance humanists studied Latin and sometimes Greek texts on grammar, rhetoric, poetry, history, and ethics. (The term *humanist* in the Renaissance meant something very different from what it means today—someone concerned with human welfare and dignity.) The humanists sought to resurrect a form of Latin that had been dead for more than a

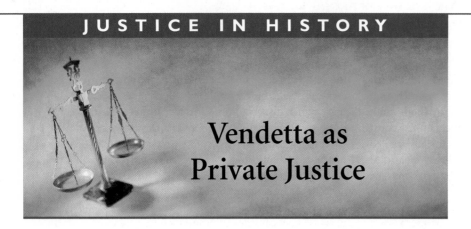

Vendetta as Private Justice

During the fourteenth and fifteenth centuries, the official justice provided by the law courts competed with the private justice of revenge. Private justice was based on the principle of retaliation. When someone was murdered or assaulted, it became the obligation of the victim's closest male relatives to avenge the injury by harming the perpetrator or one of his relatives to a similar degree. A son was obliged to avenge the death of his father, a brother the injury of his brother. Given the weakness of most governments, the only effective justice was often private justice or, as the Italians called it, *vendetta*. As the most significant source of disorder during the Renaissance, vendetta was a practice that all governments struggled to eradicate.

One of the attributes that distinguished an act of private justice from a simple violent crime was that avengers committed their acts openly and even bragged about what they had done. A criminal covered his tracks. An avenger did not. Therefore, the violence of an act of revenge was carried out in public so there would be witnesses, and often it was performed in a highly symbolic way in order to humiliate the victim as much as possible.

In Renaissance Italy private justice took many forms, but always such acts sought to do more than create another victim. They sought to deliver a message. After a period of disorder in 1342, the Florentines granted extraordinary judicial powers to a soldier of fortune, Walter of Brienne, known as the Duke

of Athens. But Walter offended many Florentines by arresting and executing members of prominent families. In September of that year a crowd led by these families besieged the government palace and captured the duke's most hated henchmen, the "conservator" and his son. Even though the conservator had been the highest judge of Florence, the Florentines repudiated his authority by obtaining revenge. An eyewitness reported what happened next:

> The son was pushed out in front, and they cut him up and dismembered him. This done, they shoved out the conservator himself and did the same to him. Some carried a piece of him on a lance or sword throughout the city, and there were those so cruel, so bestial in their anger, and full of such hatred that they ate the raw flesh.[3]

This story of revenge in the most sophisticated city in Europe on the eve of the Renaissance illustrates the brutality of private justice, especially the need to make a public example of the victim.

Another account from nearly 200 years later tells of the murder of Antonio Savorgnan, a nobleman from Friuli who had killed a number of his enemies the previous year. Rather than attempting to have Antonio arrested as they could have, the murderers avenged their dead relatives through private justice. One eyewitness recounted that Antonio was attacked while leaving church, and then, "It was by divine miracle that Antonio Savorgnan was wounded: his head opened, he fell down, and he never spoke another

word. But before he died, a giant dog came there and ate all his brains, and one cannot possibly deny that his brains were eaten."[4] This time a dog did the avengers' work for them. Perhaps the strangest detail in both of these accounts is that the writers wanted readers to believe that the victim had been eaten, either by humans or by a dog. Why was this an important message to get across?

The eating of a victim was one way avengers signaled that they were killing as an act of private justice. In both of the killings just described, the killers were retaliating for the murder of one of their close relatives and symbolically announcing to others that the attack was not an unjustifiable crime but a legitimate act of revenge. To convey that message, avengers could not ambush their opponent in the dark of night but were obliged to confront him openly in broad daylight before witnesses. There had to be the appearance, at least, of a fair fight. Murderers symbolized their revenge in several ways: They butchered the corpse as if it were the prey of a hunt or fed the remains to hunting dogs or even ate it themselves in what appeared to be a frenzy of revenge.

One of the major objectives of any government, whether a tiny city-state or a great monarchy, was to substitute public justice for private justice; but the persistence of tradition was strong. During the sixteenth century as governments sought to control violence and as the Renaissance values of moderation spread, a different kind of pri-

Questions of Justice

1. How did the persistence of private justice present a challenge to the emerging states of the Renaissance?

2. In what ways did private justice reflect Renaissance values, such as the value of keeping appearances?

Taking It Further

Muir, Edward. *Mad Blood Stirring: Vendetta in Renaissance Italy.* 1998. A study of the most extensive and long-lasting vendetta in Renaissance Italy. It traces the evolution of vendetta violence into dueling.

Weinstein, Donald. *The Captain's Concubine: Love, Honor, and Violence in Renaissance Tuscany.* 2000. A delightfully engaging account of an ambush and fight among two nobles over a woman who was the concubine of the father of one of the fighters and the lover of the other. It reveals the disturbing relationship between love and violence in Renaissance society.

vate justice appeared—the duel. Traditionally, the duel had been a means of solving disputes among medieval knights, but during the sixteenth century duels became much more common, even among men who had never been soldiers. Dueling required potential combatants to conform to an elaborate set of rules: The legitimate causes for a challenge to a duel were few, the combatants had to recognize each other as honorable men, the actual fight took place only after extensive preparations, judges who were experts on honor had to serve as witnesses, and the combatants had to swear to accept the outcome and abstain from fighting one another in the future.

The very complexity of the rules of dueling limited the violence of private justice, and that meant that fewer fights actually took place. Dueling, in effect, civilized private justice. Although dueling was always against the law, princes tended to wink at duels because they kept conflicts among their own courtiers under control. At the same time, governments became far less tolerant of other forms of private justice, especially among the lower classes. They attempted to abolish feuds and vendettas and insisted that all disputes be submitted to the courts. ■

thousand years and was distinct from the living Latin used by the Church, law courts, and universities—which they thought was mediocre compared to ancient Latin. In this effort, humanists acquired a difficult but functional skill that opened a wide variety of employment opportunities to them and gave them great public influence. They worked as schoolmasters, secretaries, bureaucrats, official court or civic historians, and ambassadors. Many other humanists were wealthy men who did not need a job but were fascinated with the rhetorical capabilities of the new learning to persuade other people to do what they wanted them to do.

Because humanists could be found on different sides of almost all important questions of the day, the significance of their work lies less in what they said than in how they said it. They wrote about practically everything: painting pictures, designing buildings, planting crops, draining swamps, raising children, managing a household, and educating women. They debated the nature of human liberty, the virtues of famous men, the vices of infamous ones, the meaning of Egyptian hieroglyphics, and the cosmology of the universe.

How did the humanists' use of Latin words and grammar influence the understanding of this vast range of subjects? Their approach was entirely literary. When they wanted to design a building, they read ancient books on architecture instead of consulting masons and builders. By studying the ancients, humanists organized experience into new categories that changed people's perceptions of themselves, the society they lived in, and the universe they inhabited. Humanist writing revealed what might be called the *Latin point of view*. Each language organizes experience according to the needs of the people who speak it, and all languages make arbitrary distinctions, dividing up the world into different categories. People who have studied a foreign language have run across these arbitrary distinctions when they learned that some expressions can never be translated exactly.

The humanists' recovery of the Latin point of view contributed new words, new sentence patterns, and new rhetorical models that often altered their own perceptions in very subtle ways. For example, when a fifteenth-century humanist examined what the ancient Romans had written about painting, he found the phrase *ars et ingenium. Ars* referred to skills that can be learned by following established rules and adhering to models provided by the best painters. Thus, the ability of a painter to draw a straight line, to mix colors properly, and to identify a saint with the correct symbol are examples of *ars* or what we would call craftsmanship. The meaning of *ingenium* was more difficult to pin down, however. It referred to the inventive capacity of the painter, to his ingenuity. The humanists discovered that the ancients had made a distinction between the craftsmanship and the ingenuity of a painter. As a result, when humanists and their pupils looked at paintings, they began to make the same distinction and began to admire the genius of artists

whose work showed ingenuity as well as craftsmanship. Ingenuity came to refer to the ability of the painter to arrange his figures in a novel way, to employ unusual colors, or to create emotionally exciting effects that conveyed piety, sorrow, or joy as the subject demanded. So widespread was the influence of the humanists that the most ingenious artists demanded higher prices and became the most sought after. In this way, creative innovation was encouraged in the arts, but it all started very simply with the introduction of new words into the Latin vocabulary of the people who paid for paintings. A similar process of establishing new categories altered every subject the humanists touched.

The humanist movement spread rapidly during the fifteenth century. Leonardo Bruni (ca. 1370–1444), who became the chancellor of Florence (the head of the government's bureaucracy), employed humanist techniques to defend the republican institutions and values of the city. Bruni's defense of republican government is called civic humanism°. He argued that the truly ethical man should devote himself to active service to his city rather than to passive contemplation in scholarly retreat or monastic seclusion. Thus Bruni formulated the ethic of responsible citizenship that remains today as necessary to sustain a free society. Given the supreme value Christianity had long placed on the passive contemplation of divine truth, Bruni's assertion that active public service constituted an even higher vocation was radical indeed.

The humanists guaranteed their lasting influence through their innovations in the educational curriculum. The objective of humanist education was to create well-rounded male pupils (girls were not usually accepted in humanist schools) who were not specialists or professionals, such as the theologians, lawyers, and physicians trained in universities, but critical thinkers who could tackle any problems that life presented. It was a curriculum well suited for the active life of civic leaders, courtiers, princes, and churchmen. The influence of the humanist curriculum persists in the general-education requirements of modern universities, which require students, now of both sexes, to obtain intellectual breadth before they specialize in narrow professional training.

Historians have identified a few female humanists from the Renaissance. Because they were so unusual, learned humanist women were often ridiculed. Jealous men accused the humanist Isotta Nogarola (1418–1466) of promiscuity and incest, and other women insulted her in public. A famous male schoolmaster said that Nogarola was too feminine in her writings and should learn how to find "a man within the woman."[5] Laura Cereta (1475–1506), who knew Greek as well as Latin and was adept at mathematics, answered the scorn of a male critic with rhetorical insult worthy of Petrarch himself:

I would have been silent, believe me, if that savage old enmity of yours had attacked me alone. . . . But I cannot tolerate your hav-

A HUMANIST LAMENTS THE RUINS OF ROME

·················

In 1430 the distinguished humanist Poggio Bracciolini (1380–1459) was working in Rome as a papal secretary. In this account he describes his and a friend's response to seeing the ruins of the once-great city of Rome. Poggio's lament and those of other humanists stimulated popes to commit themselves to the rebuilding of the city, but the enthusiasm to return Rome to its ancient splendor had some unfortunate side effects. Many of the building materials for the new Rome were pillaged from the ruins of the old Rome. As a result, much of the destruction of the ancient city of Rome occurred during the Renaissance.

Not long ago, after Pope Martin left Rome shortly before his death for a farewell visit to the Tuscan countryside, and when Antonio Lusco, a very distinguished man, and I were free of business and public duties, we used to contemplate the desert places of the city with wonder in our hearts as we reflected on the former greatness of the broken buildings and the vast ruins of the ancient city, and again on the truly prodigious and astounding fall of its great empire and the deplorable inconstancy of fortune. And once when we had climbed the Capitoline hill, and Antonio, who was a little weary from riding, wanted to rest, we dismounted from our horses and sat down together within the very enclosures of the Tarpeian ruins, behind the great marble threshold of its very doors, as I believe, and the numerous broken columns lying here and there, whence a view of a large part of the city opens out.

Here, after he had looked about for some time, sighing and as if struck dumb, Antonio declared, "Oh, Poggio, how remote are these ruins from the Capitol that our Vergil celebrated: 'Golden now, once bristling with thorn bushes.' How justly one can transpose this verse and say: 'Golden once, now rough with thorns and overgrown with briars.'"

Source: "The Ruins of Rome" by Poggio Bracciolini, translated by Mary Martin McLaughlin, from *The Portable Renaissance Reader,* by James B. Ross and Mary Martin McLaughlin, editors, copyright 1953, renewed © 1981 by Viking Penguin Inc. Used by permission of Viking Peguin, a division of Penguin Group (USA) Inc.

ing attacked my entire sex. For this reason my thirsty soul seeks revenge, my sleeping pen is aroused to literary struggle, raging anger stirs mental passions long chained by silence. With just cause I am moved to demonstrate how great a reputation for learning and virtue women have won by their inborn excellence, manifested in every age as knowledge, the [purveyor] of honor. Certain, indeed, and legitimate is our possession of this inheritance, come to us from a long eternity of ages past.[6]

These few humanist women can be seen as among the first feminists. They advocated female equality and female education but also urged women to take control of their own lives. Nogarola answered her critics in a typical humanist fashion by reinterpreting the past. Thinking at this time suggested that all women were the daughters of Eve, who in her weakness had submitted to the temptation of the serpent, which led to the exile of humanity from the Garden of Eden. Nogarola pointed out that Eve had been no weaker than Adam, who also ate of the forbidden fruit, and therefore women should not be blamed for the Fall from God's grace. Cereta was the most optimistic of the women humanists. She maintained that if women paid as much attention to learning as they did to their appearances, they would achieve equality. Despite the efforts of Cereta and other female humanists, progress in women's education was extremely slow. The universities remained closed to talented women. The first woman to earn a degree from a university did so in 1678, and it took another two hundred years before very many others could follow her example.

Through the influence of the humanists, the Latin point of view permeated Renaissance culture. They educated generations of wealthy young gentlemen and a few young women whose appreciation of antiquity led them to pay to collect manuscripts of ancient literature, philosophy, and science. These patrons were also responsible for encouraging artists to imitate the ancients. What began as a narrow literary movement became the stimulus to see human society and nature through entirely new eyes. As we shall see in Chapter 13, some humanists, especially in northern Europe, applied these techniques with revolutionary results to the study of the Bible and the sources of Christianity.

Antiquity and Nature in the Arts

················· ▬ ·················

More than any other age in Western history, the Italian Renaissance is identified with the visual arts. The unprecedented clusters of brilliant artists active in a handful of Italian cities during the fifteenth and sixteenth centuries overshadow any other contribution of Renaissance culture. Under the influence of the humanists, Renaissance artists began to imitate the sculpture, architecture, and painting of the ancients. At first they concerned themselves with merely copying ancient styles and poses. But soon they attempted a more sophisticated form of imitation. They wanted to understand the principles that made it possible for the artists of classical Greece and Rome to make their figures so lifelike. That led them to observe more directly nature itself, especially the anatomy of the human body. Renaissance art was driven by the passionate desire of artists and their patrons both to imitate ancient models and to imitate nature. These twin desires produced a certain creative tension in their work because the ancients, whose works of art often depicted gods and goddesses, had idealized and improved upon what they observed in nature. Renaissance artists sought to depict simultaneously the ideal and the real—an impossible goal, but one that sparked remarkable creativity.

Just as humanists recaptured antiquity by collecting, translating, and analyzing the writings of classical authors, so Renaissance artists made drawings of surviving classical medals, sculpture, and architecture. Collected in sketchbooks, these drawings often served as patterns from which the apprentices in artists' workshops learned how to draw. Because artists believed that the classical world enjoyed an artistic tradition vastly superior to their own, these sketches became valuable models from which other artists could

learn. Two of the most influential Florentine artists, the architect Filippo Brunelleschi (1377–1446) and the sculptor Donatello (1386–1466), may have gone to Rome together as young men to sketch the ancient monuments. No Roman paintings survived into the fifteenth century (Pompeii, which proved to have a treasure trove of Roman art buried under layers of volcanic ash, had not yet been excavated), and no Renaissance artist ever saw a Greek building, so the only examples of ancient art to copy were the ruins of Roman buildings and a few surviving Roman statues. As a result, architecture and sculpture led the way in the imitation of ancient art, but Renaissance artists imposed their own sensibilities on the ancients as much as they imitated them.

The Renaissance style evolved in Florence during the first few decades of the fifteenth century. In 1401 the 24-year-old Filippo Brunelleschi entered a competition to design bronze relief panels for the north doors of the Baptistery. He narrowly lost to the even younger Lorenzo Ghiberti (1378–1455). Look at the illustrations on the opposite page. The rules of the competition required both

■ The Competition Panels of the Sacrifice of Isaac

These two panels were the finalists in a competition to design the cast bronze doors on the north side of the Baptistery in Florence. Each demonstrates a bold new design that attempted to capture the emotional trauma of the exact moment when an angel arrests Abraham's arm from sacrificing his son Isaac (Genesis 22:1–12). Both artists went on to be closely associated with the new style of the Renaissance. The panel on the left, by Filippo Brunelleschi, lost to the one on the right, by Lorenzo Ghiberti. Notice how the Ghiberti relief better conveys the drama of the scene by projecting the elbow of Abraham's upraised arm outward toward the viewer. As a result the viewer's line of sight follows the line of the arm and knife directly toward Isaac's throat.

■ **Linear Perspective**
In these panels Ghiberti broke out of the Gothic frame that had inhibited him in the panels on the north doors. Now he was free to explore the full potential of the newly discovered principles of linear perspective.

artists to fit their relief panels within a fancy decorative frame in the Gothic style, which had been in fashion for nearly 300 years. However, both competition relief panels seem constrained by the curves and angles of the frame. For example, some of the figures in the Brunelleschi panel project outside it as if trying to escape the restraints of the style. Ghiberti's relief shows the two characteristic elements of the early Renaissance style: The head of Isaac is modeled after a classical Roman sculpture, and the figures and horse on the left are depicted as realistically as possible. In these elements, Ghiberti was imitating both antiquity and nature.

Ghiberti worked on the north doors for twenty-one years and won such renown as a result that when he finished he was immediately offered a new commission to complete panels for the east portal. These doors, begun in 1425, took twenty-seven years to finish. In the east doors, Ghiberti substituted a simple square frame for the Gothic frame of the north doors, thereby liberating his composition. In the illustration above, which depicts the biblical story of Jacob and Esau, the squares in the pavement set up an underlying geometry to the scene. The background architecture of rounded arches and crisp-angled columns in the classical style creates the illusion of depth in the relief.

This illusion is achieved through linear perspective°, that is, the use of geometrical principles to depict a three-dimensional space on a flat, two-dimensional surface. The rigorous geometry of the composition provided the additional benefit of allowing Ghiberti to divide up the space to depict several different scenes within one panel. In the panels of the east doors, he created the definitive Renaissance interpretation of the ancient principles of the harmony produced by geometry. Michelangelo later remarked that the doors were fit to serve as the "gates of paradise."

After failing to win the competition for the Baptistery doors, Brunelleschi turned to architecture. In his own time, Brunelleschi was considered to have revived ancient Roman principles, but it is evident now that he was less a student of antiquity than an astutely original thinker. In his buildings he employed a proportional system of design that is best seen in his masterpiece, the Pazzi Chapel, shown below. He began with a basic geometric unit represented by each of the small rectangles clustered in groups of four on the upper third of the façade of the chapel. The height of each of these was approximately the height of an average man. All the other dimensions of the building were multiples of these basic rectangles. Thus, the building was formed from

■ The Geometry of Renaissance Architecture

Filippo Brunelleschi designed the Pazzi Chapel in Florence to match the geometrical proportions of the human body.

the proportions of a human being. Brunelleschi employed what he saw as the natural dimensions of humanity and transformed them into principles of architectural geometry. The result was a stunning impression of harmony in all the spaces of the building.

Later sculptors and architects built on the innovations of Ghiberti and Brunelleschi. Florence became renowned for its tradition of sculpture, producing the two greatest Renaissance masters of the art, Donatello and Michelangelo Buonarroti (1475–1564). In their representations of the human form, both of these sculptors demonstrated the Renaissance preoccupation with the relationship between the ideal and the natural.

Conceptions of both the ideal and the natural are evident in the work of the most important painter of the early Florentine Renaissance, Masaccio (1401–ca. 1428), who worked in fresco. A common form of decoration in churches, fresco was the technique of applying paint to wet plaster on a wall. In his great fresco cycle for the Brancacci chapel painted in the 1420s, Masaccio depicted street scenes from Florence complete with portraits of actual people,

including himself. These were examples of naturalism. On some other figures—Jesus, St. Peter, and St. John—he placed heads copied from ancient sculptures of gods. These were examples of idealized beauty, which were especially suitable for saints. In Masaccio's frescoes, both realistic and idealized figures appeared in the same work. The realistic figures helped viewers identify with the subject of the picture by allowing them to recognize people they actually knew. The idealized figures represented the saintly, whose superior moral qualities made them appear different from average people.

Masaccio developed the technical means for employing linear perspective in painting. To achieve the effect of perspective, he organized the entire composition around the position he assumed a viewer would take while looking at the picture. Once he established the point of view, he composed the picture to direct the viewer's gaze through the pictorial space. In *The Tribute Money,* shown oppposite, he drew the spectator's eye to the head of Jesus, who is the figure in the middle pointing with his right hand. In addition, Masaccio recognized that the human eye perceives an object when light shines on it to create lighted surfaces and shadows. He used this understanding in creating a painting technique called *chiaroscuro* ("light and shade"). There is a single source of light in the painting coming from the same direction as the light in the room. That light defines figures and objects in the painting through the play of light and shadow. The strokes of Masaccio's paintbrush tried to duplicate the way natural light plays upon surfaces.

The techniques developed by Masaccio came to complete fulfillment in the career of Leonardo da Vinci (1452–1519). So compelling was Leonardo's curiosity and desire to tackle new problems that many of his paintings remained unfinished. He was a restless experimenter, never settling on simple solutions. Because of experiments Leonardo made with paint, his *Last Supper* fresco in Milan has seriously deteriorated. His mature works, such as *Mona Lisa*, completely reconciled the technical problems of representing human figures with realistic accuracy and the spiritual goal of evoking deep emotions. Unlike some of his predecessors, who grouped figures in a painting as if they were statues, Leonardo managed to make his figures appear to interact and communicate with one another.

The technique of painting with oils achieved new levels among painters in the Netherlands and in Flanders (in present-day Belgium, but at the time a province in the Duchy of Burgundy). By carefully layering numerous coats of tinted oil glazes over the surface of the painting, these

The Tribute Money: Combining Natural and Idealized Representations

In this detail of a fresco of Christ and his Apostles, Masaccio mixed naturalism and idealized beauty. The figure on the right with his back turned to the viewer is a tax collector, who is depicted as a normal human being. The head of the fourth figure to the left of him, who represents one of the apostles, was copied from an ancient statue that represents ancient ideals of beauty.

painters created a luminous surface that gave the illusion of depth. The use of glazes enabled painters to blend brushstrokes in a way that made them virtually imperceptible. As a result Flemish and Dutch painters excelled in painting meticulous details, such as the textures of textiles, the reflections of gems, and the features of distant landscapes. Jan van Eyck (ca. 1395–1441) was the most famous Flemish painter. He worked as a court painter for the Duke of Burgundy, for whom he undertook many kinds of projects including decorating his palaces and designing stage sets and ornaments for festivals. His oil paintings were so famous that he was much praised by the Italian humanists, and numerous Italian patrons, including the Medicis, bought his works.

The Early Modern European State System

The civic independence that had made the Italian Renaissance possible was profoundly challenged during the Italian Wars (1494–1530). During these wars France, Spain, and the Holy Roman Empire attempted to carve up the peninsula for themselves, and the Italian city-states were thrown into turmoil. By 1530 the Italian city-states, with the exception of Venice, had lost their independence to the triumphant king of Spain. The surrender of the rich city-states of Italy was the first and most prominent sign of a major transformation in the European sys-

tem of states. The age of city-states was over because they could never muster the level of materiel and manpower necessary to put and keep a large army in the field. Only the large monarchies of the West could do that.

MONARCHIES: THE FOUNDATION OF THE STATE SYSTEM

During the last half of the fifteenth century, the monarchies of western Europe began to show signs of recovery from the turmoil of the fourteenth and early fifteenth centuries, which had been marked by famine, plague, revolts, and the Hundred Years' War. The early modern European state system was the consequence of five developments. First, governments established standing armies. As a result of the military revolution that brought large numbers of infantrymen to the field of battle and gunpowder cannons to besiege cities and castles, governments were obliged to modernize their armies or face defeat. Since the ninth century, kings had relied on feudal levies, in which soldiers were recruited to fulfill their personal obligation to a lord, but by the late fifteenth century governments began to organize standing armies. These armies enjoyed high levels of professionalism and skill, but they were very expensive to maintain because the soldiers had to be regularly paid. Moreover, the new artillery was costly, and improvements in the effectiveness of artillery bombardments necessitated extensive improvements in the walls of castles, fortresses, and cities. As a result, kings were desperate for new revenues.

The need for revenues led to the second development, the systematic expansion of taxation. Every European state struggled with the problem of taxation. The need to tax efficiently produced the beginnings of a bureaucracy of tax assessors and collectors in many states.

People naturally resisted the burden of new taxes, and monarchs responded to the resistance. This tension led to the third development. Monarchs attempted to weaken the institutional seats of resistance by abolishing the tax-exempt privileges of local communities and ignoring regional assemblies and parliaments that were supposed to approve new taxes. During the twelfth and thirteenth centuries, effective government was local government, and kings seldom had the power to interfere in the affairs of towns and regions. During the fifteenth century, however, kings everywhere attempted to eliminate or erode the independence of towns and regional parliaments in order to raise taxes more effectively and to express the royal will throughout the realm.

The fourth development, closely linked to the third, can be seen in monarchs' attempts to constrain the independence of the aristocracy and the Church. In virtually every kingdom, the most significant threats to the power of the king were the powerful aristocrats. In England a civil war among aristocrats almost tore the kingdom apart. Kings everywhere struggled to co-opt or force submission from these aristocrats. Likewise, the autonomy of the Church threatened monarchial authority, and most monarchs took measures to oblige churchmen to act as agents of government policy.

The fifth development in the evolution of the European state system was the institution of resident ambassadors. During the Italian Wars, the kings of Europe began to exchange permanent, resident ambassadors who were responsible for informing their sovereign about conditions in the host country and representing the interests of their country abroad. Resident ambassadors became the linchpins in a sophisticated information network that provided intelligence about the intentions and capabilities of other kings, princes, and cities. These ambassadors typically enjoyed a humanist education, which helped them adapt to many strange and unpredictable situations, understand foreign languages, negotiate effectively, and speak persuasively. Ambassadors cultivated courtly manners, which smoothed over personal conflicts. For the development of the new state system, gathering reliable information became just as important as maintaining armies and collecting taxes.

France: Consolidating Power and Cultivating Renaissance Values

With the largest territory in western Europe and a population of more than 16 million, France had the potential to become the most powerful state in Europe if the king could figure out how to take advantage of the kingdom's size and resources. By 1453 the Hundred Years' War between France and England had come to an end. With the inspiration of Joan of Arc and with the reform of royal finances by the merchant-banker Jacques Coeur, King Charles VII (r. 1422–1461) expelled the English and regained control of his kingdom. Under Charles, France created its first professional army. Equally important, during the Hundred Years' War the Pragmatic Sanction of Bourges° (1438) guaranteed the virtual autonomy of the French Church from papal control, giving the French king unparalleled opportunities to interfere in religious affairs and to exploit Church revenues for government purposes.

Louis XI (r. 1461–1483), called the "Spider King" because of his fondness for secret intrigue, took up the challenge of consolidating power over the great nobles of his kingdom, who thwarted his state building and threatened his throne. Against these powerful rivals, Louis turned to an equally powerful new weapon—the *taille*. During the final years of the Hundred Years War, in order to support the army, the Estates General (France's parliament) granted the king the *taille*, the right to collect an annual direct tax. After the war, the tax continued and Louis turned it into a permanent source of revenue for himself and his successors. Armed with the financial resources of the *taille*, Louis took on his most rebellious vassal, Charles the Bold, the Duke of Burgundy, and in 1477 professional Swiss infantrymen in the pay of Louis defeated the plumed knights of Burgundy. Charles was killed in battle, and only his daughter Mary's hurried marriage to the Habsburg Archduke Maximilian bought the protection Burgundy needed from the Holy Roman Empire and prevented France from seizing all of the duchy.

The monarch most responsible for the spread of Renaissance culture in France was Francis I (r. 1515–1547), a sportsman and warrior who thrilled to the frenzy of battle. Much of his early career was devoted to pursuing French interests in the Italian Wars, until he was captured in battle in 1525 in Italy. Thereafter he focused more on patronizing Italian artists and humanists at his court and importing Italian Renaissance styles. He had the first Renaissance-style chateau built in the Loire Valley and hired artists, including Leonardo da Vinci. As a result of Francis's patronage, Italy was no longer the exclusive center of Renaissance culture.

Spain: Unification by Marriage

In the early fifteenth century the Iberian peninsula was a diverse place, lacking political unity. It was home to several different kingdoms—Portugal, Castile, Navarre, and Aragon, which were all Christian, and Granada, which was Muslim. Each kingdom had its own laws, political institutions, customs, and languages. Unlike France, the Christian kingdoms of medieval Iberia were poor, underpopulated, and preoccupied with the reconquest, the attempt to drive the Muslims from the peninsula. There was little reason to assume that this region would become one of the greatest powers in Europe, the rival of France.

That rise to power began with a wedding. In 1469 Isabella, who later would become Queen of Castile (r. 1474–1504), married Ferdinand, who later would be King of Aragon (r. 1479–1516). The objective of this arranged marriage was to solidify an alliance between the two kingdoms, not to unify them, but in 1479 Castile and Aragon were combined into the kingdom of Spain. Of the two, Castile was the larger, with a population of perhaps six million, and the richer because of the government-supported sheep-raising industry called the *Mesta*. Aragon had less than a million people and was a hybrid of three very distinct regions that had nothing in common except that they shared the same king. Together Isabella and Ferdinand, each still ruling their own kingdoms, at least partially subdued the rebellious aristocracy and built up a bureaucracy of well-educated middle-class lawyers and priests to manage the administration of the government.

The Christian kings of Iberia had long aspired to making the entire peninsula Christian. In 1492 the armies of Isabella and Ferdinand defeated the last remaining Iberian Muslim kingdom of Granada. While celebrating the victory over Islam, the monarchs made two momentous decisions. The first was to rid Spain of Jews as well as Muslims. Isabella and Ferdinand decreed that within six months all Jews must either convert to Christianity or leave. To enforce conformity to Christianity among the converted Jews who did not leave, the king and queen authorized an ecclesiastical tribunal, the Spanish Inquisition, to investigate the sincerity of conversions. The second decision was Isabella's alone. She financed a voyage by a Genoese sea captain, Christopher Columbus, to sail west into the Atlantic in an attempt to reach India and China. Isabella's intention seems to have been to outflank the Muslim kingdoms of the Middle East and find allies in Asia. As we shall see in the next chapter, Columbus's voyage had consequences more far-reaching than Isabella's intentions, adding to the crown of Castile immense lands in the Americas.

Despite the diversity of their kingdoms, Isabella and Ferdinand made Spain a great power. The clever dynastic marriages they arranged for their children allowed Spain to encircle rival France and established the framework for the diplomatic relations among European states for the next century and a half (see Map 11.2). Their eldest daughter and, after her death, her sister were married to the king of Portugal. Their son and another daughter, Joanna, married offspring of Mary of Burgundy and the Emperor Maximilian I of the Holy Roman Empire. Joanna's marriage produced a son, Charles V, who amassed extraordinary power. He succeeded to the Habsburg lands of Burgundy, inherited the crowns of Castile and Aragon (r. 1516–1556), was elected Holy Roman Emperor (r. 1519–1558), ruled over the Spanish conquests in Italy, and was the Emperor of the Indies, which included all of Spanish Central and South America. This was the greatest accumulation of territories by a European ruler since Charlemagne. The encirclement

CHRONOLOGY

1304–1374	Francesco Petrarca, first humanist
CA. 1370–1444	Leonardo Bruni, chancellor of Florence
1377–1446	Filippo Brunelleschi, Florentine sculptor and architect
1378–1455	Lorenzo Ghiberti, Florentine sculptor
1386–1466	Donatello, Florentine sculptor
1401–CA. 1428	Masaccio, Florentine fresco painter
1475–1564	Michelangelo Buonarroti, Florentine sculptor, painter, architect, poet
1479	Unification of Spain
1492	Conquest of Granada; expulsion of the Jews from Spain; voyage of Christopher Columbus
1494–1530	The Italian Wars
1508	Baldassare Castiglione begins writing *The Book of the Courtier*

of France was completed with the wedding of Isabella and Ferdinand's daughter Catherine of Aragon to the Prince of Wales and after his death to his brother, King Henry VIII (r. 1509–1547) of England.

England: From Civil War to Stability Under the Tudors

At the end of the Hundred Years' War in 1453, the English crown was defeated. Thousands of disbanded mercenaries were let loose in England and enlisted with one quarreling side or the other in feuds among aristocratic families. The mercenaries brought to England the evil habits of pillage, murder, and violence they had previously practiced in the wars with France. King Henry VI (r. 1422–1461) suffered from bouts of madness that made him unfit to rule and unable to control the disorder. Under the tensions caused by defeat and revolt, the royal family fractured into the two houses of Lancaster and York, which fought a vicious civil war, now known as the Wars of the Roses (1455–1485) from the red and white roses used to identify members of the two opposing sides.

After decades of bloody conflict, the cynical but able Richard III (r. 1483–1485) usurped the throne from his twelve-year-old nephew Edward V and had Edward and his brother imprisoned in the Tower of London, where they were murdered, perhaps on Richard's orders. Richard's apparent cruelty and his scandalous intent to marry Edward's

The Dynastic Marriages That Encircled France

The Empire of Charles V

Boundary of the Holy Roman Empire

■ **Map 11.2   The Dynastic Marriages That Encircled France**
Through skillfully arranging the marriages of their sons and daughters, Ferdinand of Aragon and
Isabella of Castile managed to completely surround the rival kingdom of France with a network of
alliances.

young sister, now heir to the throne, precipitated open defections against him. When Henry Tudor challenged
Richard, many nobles flocked to Henry's banner. At the
Battle of Bosworth Field (1485), Richard was slain and his
crown discovered on the field of battle. His naked corpse
was dragged off and buried in an unmarked grave.

When Henry Tudor became King Henry VII (r. 1485–
1509), there was little reason to believe that exhausted
England could again become a major force in European
events. It took years of patient effort for Henry to become
safe on his own throne. He revived the Court of Star
Chamber as an instrument of royal will to punish unruly
nobles who had long bribed and intimidated their way out
of trouble with the courts. Because the king's own hand-
picked councilors served as judges, Henry could guarantee
that the court system became more equitable and obedient
to his wishes. Henry confiscated the lands of the rebellious
lords, thereby increasing his own income, and he prohibited all private armies except those that served his interests.

By managing his administration efficiently, eliminating
unnecessary expenses, and staying out of war, Henry governed without the need to call on Parliament for increased
revenues.

THE ORIGINS OF
MODERN POLITICAL THOUGHT

The revival of the monarchies of western Europe and the
loss of the independence of the Italian city-states forced a
rethinking of politics. As in so many other fields, the
Florentines led the way. The Florentine Niccolò Machiavelli
(1469–1527) is best known as the father of modern political
theory. Trained as a humanist, he lacked the personal
wealth and family connections that allowed others to move
as a matter of birthright in high social and political circles.
As we saw in the story that opened this chapter, Machiavelli
had worked as a diplomat and military official but had been
exiled for complicity in a plot against the Medici family,

who had retaken Florence in 1512. While in exile he wrote a book of advice for the Medicis in the vain hope that they would give him back his job. They probably never read his little book, *The Prince* (1513), but it became a classic in political thought. In it he encouraged rulers to understand the underlying principles of political power, which differed from the personal morality expected of those who were not rulers. He thought it was important for a prince to appear to be a moral person, but Machiavelli pointed out that the successful prince might sometimes be obliged to be immoral in order to protect the interests of the state. How would the prince know when this might be the case?

Machiavelli's answer was that "necessity" forced political decisions to go against normal morality. The prince "must consider the end result," which meant that his highest obligation was preserving the very existence of the state, which had been entrusted to him and which provided security for all citizens of the state. This obligation was higher even than his obligation to religion.

Machiavelli's *The Prince* has sometimes been considered a blueprint for tyrants. However, as his more learned and serious work, *The Discourses of the First Decade of Livy* (1516–1519), makes clear, Machiavelli himself preferred a free republic over a despotic princely government. In some ways, *The Discourses* is an even more radical work than *The Prince* because it suggests that class conflict is the source of political liberty: "In every republic there are two different inclinations: that of the people and that of the upper class, and . . . all the laws which are made in favor of liberty are born of the conflict between the two."[7] In this passage, Machiavelli suggested that political turmoil was not necessarily a bad thing, because it was by provoking conflict that the lower classes prevented the upper classes from acting like tyrants.

In all his works, Machiavelli sought to understand the dynamics behind political events. To do this, he theorized that human events were the product of the interaction between two forces. One force was fortune, a term derived from the name of the ancient Roman goddess Fortuna. Fortune stood for all things beyond human control and could be equated with luck or chance. Machiavelli depicted fortune as extremely powerful, like an irresistible flood that swept all before it or the headstrong goddess who determined the fate of men. Fortune controlled perhaps half of all human events. The problem with fortune was its changeability and unpredictability: "since Fortune changes and men remain set in their ways, men will succeed when the two are in harmony and fail when they are not in accord." How could a ruler or even a simple citizen put himself in harmony with fortune and predict its shifts? The answer could be found in the characteristics of the second force, virtue, which he understood as deriving from the Roman concept of *virtus*, literally "manliness." The best description of virtue could be found in the code expected of an ancient Roman warrior: strength, loyalty, and courage. If a man possessed these traits he was most likely to be able to confront the unpredictable. As Machiavelli put it, "I am certainly convinced of this: that it is better to be impetuous than cautious."[8] The man possessing virtue, therefore, looked for opportunities to take control of events before they took control of him. In that way he put himself in harmony with fortune.

CONCLUSION

The Politics of Culture

·· ▬ ··

The Renaissance began simply enough as an attempt to imitate the Latin style of the best ancient Latin authors and orators. Within a generation, however, humanists and artists pushed this narrowly technical literary project into a full-scale attempt to refashion human society on the model of ancient cultures. Reading about the ancients and looking at their works of art provoked comparisons with contemporary Renaissance society. The result was the development of a critical approach to the past and present. The critical approach was accompanied by an enhanced historical sensibility, which transformed the idea of the West from one defined primarily by religious identification with Christianity to one forged by a common historical experience.

During the sixteenth century, western Europeans absorbed the critical-historical methods of the Renaissance and turned them in new directions. As we shall see in the next chapter, Spanish and Portuguese sailors encountered previously unknown cultures in the Americas and only vaguely known ones in Africa and Asia. Because of the Renaissance, those who thought and wrote about these strange new cultures did so with the perspective of antiquity in mind. As we shall see in Chapter 13, in northern Europe the critical historical methods of the humanists were used to better understand the historical sources of Christianity, especially the Bible. With that development, Christianity began to take on new shades of meaning, and many thoughtful Christians attempted to make the practices of the church conform more closely to the Bible. The humanist approach to religion led down a path that permanently divided Christians into contending camps over the interpretation of Scripture, breaking apart the hard-won unity of the Roman Catholic West.

Suggestions for Further Reading

For a comprehensive list of suggested readings, please go to www.ablongman.com/levackconcise/chapter11

Baxandall, Michael. *Painting and Experience in Fifteenth Century Italy: A Primer in the Social History of Pictorial Style.* 1988. A fascinating study of how the daily social experiences of Florentine bankers and churchgoers influenced how these individuals saw Renaissance paintings and how painters responded to the viewers' experience. One of the best books on Italian painting.

Brown, Patricia Fortini. *Art and Life in Renaissance Venice.* 1997. A delightful study about how art fit into the daily lives and homes of the Venetian upper classes.

Brucker, Gene. *Florence: The Golden Age, 1138–1737.* 1998. A brilliant, beautifully illustrated history by the most prominent American historian of Florence.

Burke, Peter. *The Italian Renaissance.* 1999. A concise and readable synthesis of the most recent research.

Hale, J. R. *Renaissance Europe, 1480–1520.* 2000. A witty, engaging, and enlightening study of Europe during the formation of the early modern state system. Strong on establishing the material and social limitations of Renaissance society.

King, Margaret L. *Women of the Renaissance.* 1991. The best general study of women in Renaissance Europe. It is especially strong on female intellectuals and women's education.

Kohl, Benjamin G., and Alison Andrews Smith, eds. *Major Problems in the History of the Italian Renaissance.* 1995. A useful collection of articles and short studies of major historical problems in the study of the Renaissance.

Martines, Lauro. *Power and Imagination: City-States in Renaissance Italy.* 1988. An excellent general survey that is strong on class conflicts and patronage.

Nauert, Jr., Charles G. *Humanism and the Culture of Renaissance Europe.* 1995. The best survey of humanism for students new to the subject. It is clear and comprehensive.

Skinner, Quentin. *Machiavelli: A Very Short Introduction.* 2000. This is the place to begin in the study of Machiavelli. Always clear and precise, this is a beautiful little book.

Vasari, Giorgio. *The Lives of the Artists.* 1998. Written by a sixteenth-century Florentine who was himself a prominent artist, this series of artistic biographies captures the spirit of Renaissance society.

Notes

1. *The Portable Machiavelli,* trans. and ed. Peter Bondanella and Mark Musa (1979), 67–69.
2. Francesco Petrarca, "Letter to the Shade of Cicero," in Kenneth R. Bartlett, ed., *The Civilization of the Italian Renaissance: A Sourcebook* (1992), 31.
3. Giovanni Villani, *Cronica,* vol. 7 (1823), 52. Translation by the authors.
4. Agostino di Colloredo, "Chroniche friulane, 1508–18," *Pagine friulane* 2 (1889), 6. Translation by the authors.
5. Quoted in Margaret L. King, *Women of the Renaissance* (1991), 197.
6. "Laura Cereta to Bibulus Sempronius: Defense of the Liberal Instruction of Women," in Margaret King and Alfred Rabil, eds., *Her Immaculate Hand: Selected Words by and About the Women Humanists of Quattrocento Italy* (1983), 82.
7. *The Portable Machiavelli,* 183.
8. Ibid., 161–162.

The West and the World: The Significance of Global Encounters, 1450–1650

O
N A HOT OCTOBER DAY IN 1492, CHRISTOPHER COLUMBUS AND HIS MEN, dressed in heavy armor, clanked onto the beach of an island in the Bahamas. The captain and his crew had been at sea sailing west from the Canary Islands for five weeks, propelled by winds they thought would take them straight to Asia. As the ships under Columbus's command vainly searched among the islands of the Caribbean for the rich ports of Asia, Columbus thought he must be in India and thus called the natives he met "Indians." At another point he thought he might be among the Mongols of central Asia, which he described in his journal as the "people of the Great Khan." Both of Columbus's guesses about his location were incorrect, but they have left a revealing linguistic legacy in terms still in use: "Indians" for the native Americans, and both "cannibals" and "Caribbean" from Columbus's inconsistent spellings of Khan. Columbus believed that the people he called the Cannibals or Caribs ate human flesh. But he got that information—also incorrect—from their enemies. Thus began one of the most lasting misunderstandings from Columbus's first voyage.

Historians know very little about the natives' first thoughts of the arrival of their foreign visitors, but they know that the effects of the arrival were catastrophic. Within a few generations the Caribs almost completely died out, replaced by African slaves who worked the plantations of European masters.

Western civilization at the end of the fifteenth century hardly seemed on the verge of encircling the globe with outposts and colonies. Its kingdoms had barely been able to reorganize themselves sufficiently for self-defense, let alone world exploration and foreign conquest. Nevertheless, by 1500 Europeans could be found fighting and trading in Africa, the Americas, and Asia. A mere fifty years

The Encounter of Three Cultures: On this wooden bottle painted in the Incan style about 1650, an African drummer leads a procession, followed by a Spanish trumpeter and an Incan official. The mixing of cultures that occurred after the arrival of the Spanish and Portuguese is what distinguished the Americas from other civilizations.

later, Europeans had destroyed the two greatest civilizations in the Americas, had begun the forced migration of Africans to the Americas through the slave trade, and had opened trading posts throughout South and East Asia.

Before 1500 the West, identified by its languages, religion, agricultural technology, literature, folklore, music, art, and common intellectual tradition that stretched back to pre-Christian antiquity, was largely confined to Europe and the Middle East. After 1500 European travelers and missionaries began to export Western culture and technology to the rest of the world, especially after large numbers of European settlers moved to the Americas.

After the sixteenth century, European culture could be found in many distant lands, and western European languages and forms of Christianity were adopted by or forced on other peoples. The West was now more of an idea than a place, a certain kind of culture that thrived in many different environments. The process was not all one-way, however: Western Europeans came under the influence of the far-flung cultures they visited, transforming Europe into the most cosmopolitan corner of the Earth. The European voyages integrated the globe biologically and economically. Microbes, animals, and plants that had once been isolated were now transported throughout the world. Because the Europeans possessed the ships for transport and the guns for coercion, they became the dominant players in international trade, even in places thousands of miles from the European homeland.

To understand the European encounters with the world during the fifteenth and sixteenth centuries, this chapter will address four central questions:

- Why did the European incursions into sub-Saharan Africa lead to the vast migration of Africans to the Americas as slaves?
- How did the arrival of Europeans in the Americas transform native cultures and life?
- Why was the European encounter with Asian civilizations far less disruptive than those in Africa and the Americas?
- How was the world tied together in a global biological and economic system?

Europeans in Africa

Geographers of the ancient world, writing in Greek and Latin, had accumulated a substantial knowledge about all of North Africa, but they were almost completely ignorant of the region south of the Sahara desert. In fact, the interior of sub-Saharan Africa had been governed for centuries by highly developed kingdoms and boasted numerous wealthy cities. By the fifteenth century, Muslim contacts with sub-Saharan Africa made it clear that the region was a rich source of gold and slaves. In search of these, Europeans, especially the Portuguese, began to journey down the west coast of Africa. Enabled by new developments in ship technology, the Europeans were capable of making long sea voyages. European settlers founded colonies in the Atlantic islands off the west coast of Africa, establishing precedents for colonies that would later be installed in the Americas.

EUROPEAN VOYAGES ALONG THE AFRICAN COAST

Although sub-Saharan Africa represented something of a mystery to most Europeans, merchants from Italy, Catalonia, Castile, and Portugal had long shown interest in the ports of the Maghreb, the collective name for the present-day regions of Morocco, Algeria, and Tunisia on the Mediterranean coast of North Africa. There they brought wool and woolen textiles, wine, dye stuffs, and clandestine items such as weapons, which they traded for various commodities, most significantly gold. Since at least the mid-thirteenth century, the Maghreb had been famous as the northern terminus of the gold caravans from Mali. In the thirteenth and fourteenth centuries, European traders obtained gold in the Maghreb in exchange for silver mined in Europe. They then resold the gold in the ports along the northern shore of the Mediterranean for more silver than they had originally paid to buy the gold. With the handsome silver profits made in the gold trade, merchants provided a steady supply that encouraged the general adoption of gold coinage throughout much of southern Europe. Gold was highly prized in Europe largely because it was rare in comparison to silver, and by the laws of supply and demand the commodity that is scarce is more valuable.

To gain more direct access to the sources of gold, European traders occasionally crossed the Sahara with camel caravans—the "ships of the desert." The efficient camel caravans created a vast trading network that stretched from Mali and Morocco in the west of Africa into central Asia, completely bypassing the Mediterranean. But Europeans had little hope of regularly using the "sea of sand" routes across North Africa because of the hostility of Muslim inhabitants who were wary about foreign interlopers, especially Christian ones. The alternative for Europeans was to outflank the Muslims by crossing the sea of water, but their galleys were adapted to the relatively calm waters of the Mediterranean and were ill-suited for the voyage on the heavy seas of the Atlantic (see Map 12.1).

The disadvantages of Mediterranean galleys were surmounted during the fifteenth century through changes in the technology of ocean sailing. The Iberian peninsula (the land of present-day Portugal and Spain), situated be-

Long before the arrival of the Portuguese via sea routes, caravans of camels crisscrossed the Sahara desert during the fourteenth century, linking the sources of gold in Mali with the Maghreb (the coast of northwest Africa) and the seaports of the Mediterranean. The greatest medieval Arabic traveller, Ibn Battuta (1304–ca. 1369), crossed the Sahara and spent more than a year in Mali. He left the most extensive account of medieval West Africa.

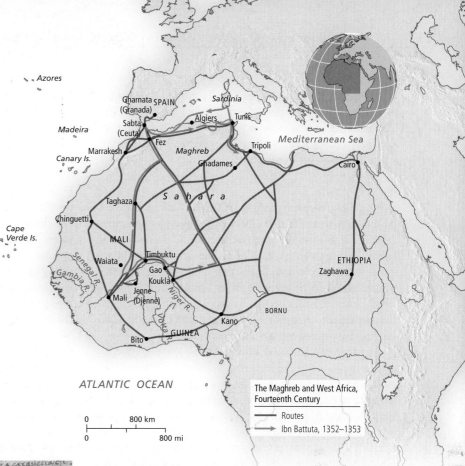

An Early Caravel

The caravel was typical of the hybrid ship developed during the fifteenth century on the Iberian peninsula. The ship on the lower right is rigged with a lateen sail on its main mast.

tween the Mediterranean and the Atlantic, was uniquely located to develop a hybrid ship that combined features of Mediterranean and Atlantic designs. The initial impulse for developing the shipping technology was to facilitate trade between the Mediterranean and northern Europe via the Atlantic. The resulting changes, however, also made possible much more ambitious voyages into the unknown southern regions.

The Iberians modified the cog design, the dominant ship in the Atlantic, by adding extra masts and creating a new kind of rigging that combined the square sails of Atlantic ships, suitable for sailing in the same direction as the wind was blowing, with the triangular "lateen" sails of Mediterranean galleys, which permitted sailing into the wind. The result was a ship that could sail in a variety of winds, carry large cargoes, be managed by a small crew, and be defended by guns mounted in the castle superstructure. These hybrid three-mast ships, called caravels°, appeared about 1450, and for the next 200 years Europeans sailed ships of this same basic design on long ocean voyages to the very ends of the Earth.

Also assisting European navigators were other technological innovations, the fruit of late medieval Mediterranean seafaring. The compass provided an approximate indicator of direction, and the astrolabe and naked-eye celestial navigation made it possible to estimate latitudes. Books of sailing directions, called portolanos°, included charts and descriptions of ports and recorded the location of dangerous shoals and safe harbors for future voyages. The advances in maritime technology made it possible for Europeans motivated by economic need and religious fervor to sail wherever they wanted.

New Colonialism

During the fifteenth century, European colonialism departed somewhat from the patterns of the past. Mediterranean colonies established during the Crusades of the twelfth and thirteenth centuries had relied on native inhabitants to produce commodities that could be expropriated by the colonizers. These were either aristocratic colonies in which a few warriors occupied castles to dominate the native population or mercantile colonies built around a trading post for foreign merchants.

As Europeans ventured into the Atlantic more frequently and expanded their contacts with sub-Saharan Africa, they established new patterns of colonization. In search of fertile lands for agriculture, Castile and Portugal founded colonies in the Canary Islands, the Madeira archipelago, the Azores, and the Cape Verde Islands. The climate of these islands was similar to the Mediterranean and invited the cultivation of typical Mediterranean crops, such as grains and sugar cane, but the islands lacked a native labor force. When Europeans arrived, the Canaries were seriously underpopulated and the other islands were uninhabited. In response to the labor shortage, two new types of colonies emerged, both of which were later introduced into the Americas.

The first new type of colony during this period was the settler colony°. The settler colony derived from the medieval, feudal model of government, in which a private person obtained a license from a king to seize an island or some part of an island. The king supplied financial support and legal authority for the expedition. In return the settler promised to recognize the king as his lord and occasionally to pay a fee after the settlement was successful. The kings of Castile and Portugal issued such licenses for the exploitation of Atlantic islands. The actual expeditions to colonize these islands were private enterprises, and adventurers from various parts of Europe vied for a license from any king who would grant them one. For example, the first European settlement in the Canary Islands was led by a Norman knight, Jean de Béthencourt, who could not obtain sufficient support from the king of France and thus switched loyalties to the king of Castile.

After the arrival of the Europeans, all the natives of the Canaries, called the Guanches, were killed or died off from European diseases, creating the need for settler families from Europe to till the land and maintain the Castilian claim on the islands. These peasants and artisans brought with them their traditional family structures, customs, language, religion, seeds, livestock, and patterns of cultivation. Wherever settler colonies were found, whether in the Atlantic islands or the Americas, which the Europeans called the New World, they Europeanized the landscape and remade the lands they cultivated in the image of the Old World.

The second new type of colony was the plantation colony°. Until the occupation of the Cape Verde Islands in the 1460s, the Atlantic island colonies had relied on European settlers for labor. However, the Cape Verdes attracted few immigrants because of the rigors of the tropical climate, and yet the islands seemed especially well suited for growing the lucrative sugar cane crop. The few permanent European colonists there tended to be exiled criminals, and the Cape Verdes became a haven for lawless ruffians who were disinclined to work. Because there was no indigenous population to exploit on the Cape Verdes, the few European colonizers began to look elsewhere for laborers and voyaged to the African coast where they bought slaves who had been captured from inland villages. These slaves worked as agricultural laborers in the Cape Verdes sugar cane fields. Thus, in the Cape Verdes began the tragic conjunction between African slavery and the European demand for sugar. When sugar began to replace honey as the sweetener of choice for Europeans, the almost insatiable demand was supplied by sugar cultivated by slaves in plantation colonies, first in the Atlantic islands and later in the West Indies and American mainland. Over the next 300 years, this pattern for plantation colonies was repeated for other valuable agricultural commodities, such as indigo for dyes, coffee, and cotton, which were grown to sell in European markets. The first loop of what would eventually become a global trading circuit was now completed.

The Portuguese in Africa

The first European voyages along the African coast during the fifteenth century were launched by the Portuguese. The sponsor of these voyages was Prince Henry the Navigator (1394–1460). As governor of Algarve, the southernmost province of Portugal, Henry established a headquarters at Sagres and financed numerous exploratory voyages. Driven by the quest for fame and a profound faith in astrology, Henry had two objectives above all else: In order to enhance his reputation, he wanted to steal the Canary Islands from his archrival, the king of Castile, and to reward the men who sailed his ships, he desperately needed to get his hands on more gold.

The first Portuguese expeditions along the African coast were prompted by Henry's desire to capture the Canaries. He tried armed force, negotiations with the inhabitants, and entreaties to the pope, all with no success. He even purchased phony titles to the Canaries in a transparent attempt to fool the Castilians that he was really the lord of the islands. In the mid-1450s, however, Henry's disappointment over the Canaries subsided as it became evident that gold from Mali could be obtained farther south from bases near the Senegal and Gambia rivers. Although the many voyages of Henry's sailors did not fulfill his dreams of conquest and enormous riches, he and other members of his family did help colonize Madeira and the Azores. As a source of sugar, Madeira became a valuable colony (see Map 12.2).

After Henry's death, Portuguese exploration of the African coast accelerated. In only six years, a private merchant of Lisbon commissioned voyages that added 2,000 miles of coastline that was known to the Portuguese. In 1482 the exploration policy that had been a loose and haphazard enterprise under private contractors was transformed. That year the Portuguese royal house took control of trade with Africa; they required that all sailings be authorized and all cargoes inventoried, and they built a permanent fortress at Elmina near the mouth of the Volta River in modern Ghana in West Africa. At Elmina, Portuguese traders found local sources of gold and opportunities to obtain more upriver. Rather than establishing new settler or plantation colonies, the Portuguese on the African coast relied on trading posts that supplied gold, ivory, pepper, and slaves.

Europeans in the Americas

Like the Europeans who sailed along the African coast, the first European voyagers to the Americas coveted gold and an alternative route to India and China. The European impulse to reach Asia by sailing west came from the fact that the Ottoman Empire, which was pushing into the Mediterranean after the conquest of Constantinople in 1453, blocked the traditional trade routes through the Middle East and across the Black and Red Seas. Europeans relied on Asian sources for medicines, spices, and all kinds of luxury goods, which were unavailable elsewhere. Those who gained access to the source of these lucrative goods could make enormous profits. The desire to profit from this trade impelled men to take great risks to find an alternative route to East Asia. In the short run, the Americas proved to be an impediment to achieving these goals because the two continents stood in the way of getting to Asia. But in the

■ **Map 12.2 Europeans in the World, Fifteenth and Sixteenth Centuries**
During the fifteenth and sixteenth centuries European sailors opened sea lanes for commerce across the Atlantic, Pacific, and Indian Oceans. Dates indicate first arrival of Europeans.

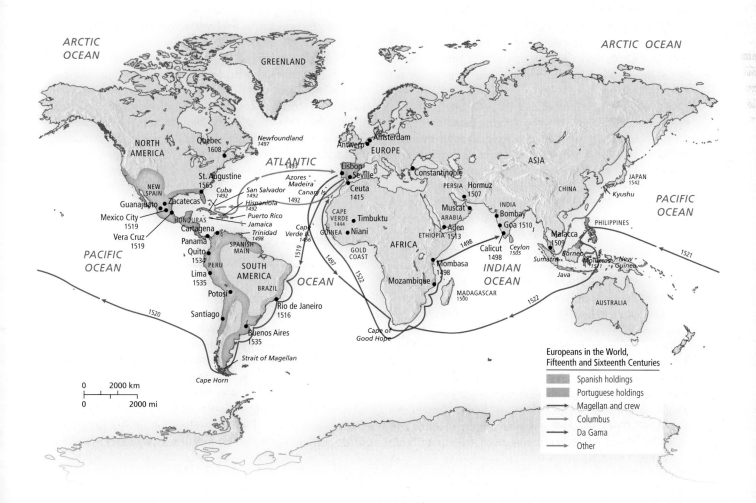

long run, the European voyages to the Americas brought unimaginable consequences.

THE AMERICAS BEFORE THE CONQUISTADORES

Prior to their contact with Europeans, the peoples of the Americas displayed remarkable cultural variety. Nomadic hunters spread across the sub-Arctic regions, western North America, and the Amazon jungles, while farming settlements prevailed in much of South America and eastern North America. Some of these North American cultures, such as the Anasazi and Iroquois, developed highly sophisticated forms of political organization, but none matched the advanced civilizations of Mesoamerica and the central Andes to the south. On the eve of the arrival of Europeans, two great civilizations, the Aztecs of central Mexico and the Incas of highland Peru, had built extensive empires that dominated their neighbors.

The Aztec Empire of Mexico

Mesoamerica (the region known today as Mexico and Central America) had been the home of a series of highly urbanized, politically centralized cultures: the Mayans (300–900), the Toltecs (900–1325), and finally the Aztecs (1325 to the Spanish conquest in 1522). The Aztecs found safety from incessant warfare with neighboring tribes on an island in Lake Texcoco, where they established the city of Tenochtitlán, now Mexico City. From their base at Tenochtitlán the Aztecs followed a brilliantly successful policy of divide and conquer, first allying with powerful neighbors to attack weaker groups, then turning against former allies.

The Aztec king, Montezuma I (r. 1440–1469), consolidated an empire that stretched across most of central Mexico. In order to provide food for his people during a severe famine between 1450 and 1454, Montezuma first conquered the breadbasket of Mexico, the rich coastal region of the Totonacs. In repeated attacks, swarms of Aztec warriors took city after city, captured the local chief whenever possible, burned the temple, and extorted tribute payments from the population. With the riches gained from conquest, Montezuma transformed Tenochtitlán from a dusty town of mud houses to a great imperial capital built of stone with a grand botanical garden that displayed plants taken from various climates.

The Aztecs excelled in the perpetual state of war that had long been the dominant fact of life in Mexico, and as a result they attributed great religious value to war. They practiced the concept of the "flowery war," a staged occurrence when states agreed to a predetermined time and place for a battle, the only objective of which was to take prisoners for temple sacrifice. Sustaining the gods' hunger for human sacrifices became the most notorious feature of Aztec religion. The rituals of sacrifice permeated Aztec society. It has

been estimated that 10,000 victims were sacrificed each year, with the number rising to 50,000 on the eve of the Spanish conquest.

The Incan Empire of the Andes

At about the same time the Aztecs were thriving in Mexico, the Incas expanded their empire in Peru and developed a comprehensive imperial ideal. Whereas the Aztecs created a loosely linked empire based on tribute payments, the Incas employed a more direct form of rulership. As they pushed out from their base in the south Andes during the fifteenth century, they imposed their authority on conquered peoples.

The first Incan emperor, Pachacuti Inca Yupanqui (r. 1438–1471), founded the empire around 1438 when he spread Incan rule beyond the valley of Cuzco. By the end of the fifteenth century, the Incas had begun to integrate by force the distinctive cultures of the various conquered regions. In this way, they created a mountain empire 200 miles wide and 2,000 miles long, stretching from modern-day Chile to Ecuador and comprising a population of about ten million. From his capital at Cuzco, the Incan emperor lived in luxury and established an elaborately hierarchic political structure. His authority was carried through layers of aristocrats down to officials who were responsible for every ten families in every village. These families supplied food and tribute for the empire, worked on roads and bridges, and served in the army. State-owned warehouses of food guaranteed the peasants freedom from starvation and provided for the sick and elderly.

A superb network of roads and bridges covered more than 18,000 miles and made it possible to communicate with relays of runners who could cover as much as 140 miles a day. Troops could also be quickly dispatched to trouble spots via these roads. Despite this well-organized imperial system, the Incan Empire became overly centralized and decisions could be made only by the emperor himself, a fatal flaw that, as we shall see, allowed the Spanish invaders to crush it very quickly.

THE MISSION OF THE EUROPEAN VOYAGERS

The European arrival in the Americas was the result of a mistake promoted by Christopher Columbus's (1451–1506) stubborn sense of mission. Columbus believed that he had been predestined to fulfill biblical prophecies. If he could reach China, he could outflank the Ottoman Turks and recapture Jerusalem from the Muslims who had held it since 1187, an achievement that would usher in the Second Coming of Christ. In trying to convince Queen Isabella of Castile to finance his mission to voyage to China by sailing west, he later admitted that to make his case he ignored navigational data and, instead, relied "entirely on holy, sacred Scripture and certain prophetic texts by certain saintly

■ **The Aztec Rite of Human Sacrifice**
Human victims had their hearts cut out by a priest at the top of the stairs to a temple.

persons, who by divine revelation have had something to say on this matter."[1]

It had long been recognized that it was theoretically possible to reach China, Columbus's goal, by sailing west. Most educated people, and certainly all those influenced by the Renaissance humanists, agreed the world was round. The problem was not a theoretical one about the shape of the Earth but a practical one about getting around it. During Columbus's life the most widely accepted authority on the circumference of the Earth was the ancient Greek geographer Ptolemy, who had estimated that the distance across the Atlantic Ocean from Europe to Asia was more than 10,000 miles. The practical problem was that no ship in Columbus's day could hope to sail that far without landfalls along the way for finding provisions and making repairs. In fact, Ptolemy had underestimated the size of the Earth by 25 percent, but Columbus decided that Ptolemy had overestimated the distance. Columbus also imagined that the wealthy island of Japan lay farther east of the Asian continent than it actually does, thus further minimizing the distance of the voyage. His extremely inaccurate estimate of how close China was seems to have been more the result of wishful thinking and religious fervor than geographical expertise, and the experts uniformly advised against financing Columbus's voyage. When the Spanish defeated the Muslim kingdom of Granada in 1492, which completed the Christian reconquest of the Iberian peninsula, Queen Isabella succumbed to the religious enthusiasm of the moment and relented. She offered Columbus a commission for the voyage in the hope that it would ensure a final Christian victory over Islam.

On August 3, 1492, Columbus set sail with three small ships—the Niña, Pinta, and Santa Maria—and a crew of ninety men and boys. After refitting in the Canary Islands, the modest convoy entered unknown waters guided only by Columbus's faith in finding China, which was, in fact, many thousands of miles farther west than he thought it would be. At two in the morning on the moonlit night of October 12, a lookout spied land, probably Watling Island in the Bahamas. In all, Columbus made four voyages across the Atlantic (1492, 1493, 1498, 1502), exploring the Caribbean Islands, the coast of Central America, and part of the coast of South America. He never abandoned the belief that he had arrived in Asia.

Soon after Columbus returned to Spain from his first voyage, the Spanish monarchs who had sponsored him tried to obtain a monopoly to explore the western Atlantic. They appealed to Pope Alexander VI, who was himself a Spaniard and sympathetic to their request. In an effort to give the Spanish a firm legal monopoly to the lands across the Atlantic, the pope confirmed in 1493 the right of Spanish sailors to explore all lands to the west as long as they did not infringe on the rights of another Christian ruler. Since all involved still thought Columbus had arrived in China, the obvious other Christian ruler was the king of Portugal, whose sailors had already pushed far enough south down the African coast to realize that they could eventually reach China by sailing east. The pope ordered a line of demarcation drawn along a north-south line 100 leagues (about 300 miles) west of the Azores and Cape Verde Islands. Spain received all lands west of the line; Portugal obtained the lands to the east. This line of demarcation seemed to limit the Portuguese to Africa, which alarmed them and led to direct negotiations between the Portuguese and the Spaniards. The result of the negotiations was the Treaty of Tordesillas in 1494, which moved the line of demarcation to 370 leagues (about 1,110 miles) west of the Cape Verde Islands, a decision that granted to Portugal all of Africa, India, and Brazil.

Despite Columbus's persistent faith that he had found a route to the East Indies, other voyagers began to suspect, even before Columbus's death, that he had not found Asia at all and that other routes had to be explored. Another Italian, the Florentine Amerigo Vespucci (1454–1512), met Columbus, helped him prepare for the third voyage, and later made at least two voyages of his own across the Atlantic. From his voyages, Vespucci recognized something of the immensity of the South American continent and was the first to use the term "New World." Because he used the term and because the account of his voyages got into print before Columbus's, Vespucci's given name, Amerigo (America), came to be attached to the New World rather than Columbus's. By the 1520s, Europeans had explored the Americas extensively enough to recognize that the New World was nowhere near India or China.

After the Treaty of Tordesillas, explorers followed two distinct strategies for finding a sea route to East Asia. The first strategy was the continued Portuguese pursuit of routes to the south and east around Africa. Between 1487 and 1488, Bartholomew Dias (ca. 1450–1500) reached the Cape of Good Hope at the southern tip of the African continent. This discovery made it evident that passage to India could be achieved by sailing south, rounding the tip of Africa, and crossing the Indian Ocean. Political and financial problems in Portugal, however, prevented a follow-up to Dias's voyage for ten years. Between 1497 and 1499, Vasco da Gama (ca. 1460–1524) finally succeeded in sailing from Lisbon to India around the Cape of Good Hope. This celebrated voyage included a great looping westward course far out into the Atlantic to escape the doldrums, an area in the ocean where the winds died. As a consequence of the route opened by da Gama, the Portuguese were the first Europeans to establish trading posts in Asia. They reached the Malabar coast of India in 1498 and soon found their way to the Spice Islands and China. By the middle of the sixteenth century, the Portuguese had assembled a string of more than fifty trading posts° and forts from Sofala on the east coast of Africa to Nagasaki in Japan.

The second strategy for reaching Asia consisted of Spanish attempts to pursue Columbus's proposed route west. The problem faced by those sailing under the Spanish flag was to find a way around the barrier presented by the American continents. A Portuguese sailor named Ferdinand Magellan (ca. 1480–1521), who had previously sailed to Asia aboard Portuguese ships, persuaded the king of Spain to sponsor a voyage to Asia sailing west around South America. That venture (1519–1522), which began under

Magellan's command, passed through the strait named after him at the tip of South America and crossed the Pacific in a voyage of extreme hardship as his men suffered from thirst and hunger and died of scurvy. Magellan himself was killed by natives in the Philippines. After three years at sea, only 18 survivors from the original 240 in Magellan's fleet reached Seville, Spain, having sailed around the world for the first time. Contemporaries immediately recognized the epic significance of the voyage, but the route opened by Magellan was too long and arduous for the Spanish to employ as a reliable alternative to the Portuguese route around Africa.

In the course of three centuries (about 1480–1780), European navigators linked the previously isolated routes of seaborne commerce, opened all the seas of the world to trade, and encountered many of the cultures and peoples of the world. For the first hundred years or so, the Portuguese and Spanish effectively maintained a monopoly over these trade routes, but gradually English, Dutch, and French sailors all made their way around the globe. In the Americas, inadvertently made known to Europeans by Christopher Columbus, the Spanish immediately began settlements and attempted to subdue the indigenous populations.

THE FALL OF THE AZTEC AND INCAN EMPIRES

Following the seafaring captains, such as Columbus and Magellan, came the conquistadores°. They were Spanish adventurers, usually from impoverished minor noble families, who launched their own expeditions with little or no legal authority, hoping to acquire sufficient riches to impress the king to give them official sanction for additional conquests. Those conquistadores who did acquire legal authority from the crown received the privilege to conquer new lands in the name of the king of Spain and to keep a portion of those territories for themselves. In return they were obliged to turn over to the king one-fifth—the "royal fifth"—of everything of value they acquired, an obligation enforced by a notary sent along with the conquistadores to keep a record of everything valuable that was found. The conquistadores also extended Spanish sovereignty over new lands and opened the way for missionaries to bring millions, at least nominally, into the Christian fold.

All conquistadores were required to read a document, called the *requerimiento°*, to the natives before making war on them. The document briefly explained the principles of Christianity and commanded the natives to accept them immediately along with the authority of the pope and the sovereignty of the king of Spain. If the natives refused, they were warned that they would be forced through war to subject themselves "to the yoke and obedience of the Church and of Their Highnesses. We shall take you and your wives and your children, and shall make slaves of

■ **Spanish Conquistadores Land on an Island in the New World**
The armored Spaniards are met by the naked inhabitants who offer them jewels and gold. As one of
their first acts, the Spaniards erect a cross, symbolizing the Christian conquest of the New World.

them, and as such shall sell and dispose of them as Their
Highnesses may command. And we shall take your goods,
and shall do you all the mischief and damage that we can."[2]
The *requerimiento* revealed the conflicting motives behind
the Spanish conquest. On the one hand, the Spanish were
sincerely interested in converting the natives to Christianity.
On the other, the conquistadores were trying to justify the
immorality of their actions by suggesting that the natives
had brought the attack on themselves by refusing to obey
the Spanish king.

Hernán Cortés and the Conquest of Mexico

Among the first and most successful of the conquistadores
was Hernán Cortés (1485–1547). After a number of bloody
battles in Mexico, Cortés set off with 450 Spanish troops,
15 horses, and 4,000 native allies to conquer the great
capital of the Aztec Empire, Tenochtitlán, a city of at least
300,000 and defended by thousands of warriors. As Cortés
approached, Montezuma II was slow to set up a strong defense, because he suspected Cortés might be the white god,
Quetzalcoatl, who according to prophecies would arrive
one day from the east. The result was disastrous for the
Aztecs. Montezuma knew his reign was doomed unless he
could gain the assistance of other gods to drive Quetzalcoatl

away. Thus, rather than an ardent military campaign, the
king's defense primarily took the form of human sacrifices,
which failed.

By 1522 Cortés controlled a territory in New Spain—
as Mexico was renamed—larger than Old Spain itself.
Aztec culture and its religion of human sacrifice disappeared as Franciscan friars arrived to evangelize the surviving population.

Francisco Pizarro and the Conquest of Peru

In 1531 Francisco Pizarro (ca. 1478–1541) left Panama
with a small expedition of 180 men and 30 horses. Pizarro's
goal was to conquer Peru, known to be a land rich with
gold. Gathering additional recruits along the way, he sailed
to northern Peru and sent out spies who discovered that
the Incan emperor, Atahuallpa, could be found in the highland city of Cajamarca. When Pizarro and his forces arrived
there, the central square was empty, but Atahuallpa was en-
camped nearby with a large army. Pizarro treacherously invited Atahuallpa to come for a parlay, but instead took him
captive. The news of the capture plunged the overly centralized Incan Empire into a crisis because no one dared
take action without the emperor's orders. In an attempt to

■ **Spaniards Attacking Tenochtitlán, 1519**
Notice how the Spaniards had placed cannons on the bows of these small ships, which were built to sail on the lake.

most native peoples, some of whom—in the Caribbean, northern Argentina, and central Chile—completely disappeared through the ravages of conquest and diseases, which will be discussed shortly. Whereas Spanish became the language of government and education, some native traditions survived and a mixed-blood European immigrant and native population called *mestizos* gradually appeared. Through this process, Spanish America became the first lasting outpost of Western civilization outside of Europe.

The basic form of economic and social organization in Spanish America was the encomienda° system, which was created as an instrument to exploit native labor. An encomienda was a royal grant awarded for military or other services that gave the conquistadores and their successors the right to gather tribute from the Indians in a defined area. In return, the encomendero (the receiver of the royal grant and native tribute) was theoretically obliged to protect the natives and teach them the rudiments of the Christian faith. Because the encomiendas were very large, only a small number of Spanish settlers were actually encomenderos. In greater Peru, which included modern Peru, Ecuador, and Bolivia, there were never more than 500 encomenderos. By the seventeenth century these encomiendas had evolved to become great landed estates called haciendas°.

There were only a few prosperous encomenderos, but the stories about those who rose from rags to riches in the New World were so compelling that during the sixteenth century alone more than 200,000 Spaniards migrated there. Only one in ten of Spanish immigrants were women, and for a long time the colonies suffered from a shortage of Spanish women. Although native Americans were usually excluded from Spanish society, many native women who were the mistresses and even wives of Spaniards partially assimilated to European culture and helped pass it on to their offspring. These native women learned Spanish and were converted to Christianity, and because of their origins they could mediate between the dominant Spanish and the subordinate native population.

Wherever they went in the Americas, the Spaniards brought African slaves with them. Most of the slaves remembered little about their original African cultures, however, because many had been born in Spain, the Caribbean, or the Cape Verde Islands, and Spanish had become their native

satisfy the Spaniards' hunger for gold and to win his freedom, Atahuallpa had a room filled with gold and silver for the conquistadores, but the treasure merely stimulated their appetite for more. In July 1533 Pizarro executed the emperor, and by the following November he had captured the demoralized Incan capital of Cuzco.

The conquest of Peru vastly increased the size of the Spanish Empire and began to satisfy the craving for gold that had impelled Columbus and the conquistadores in the first place. Through the collection of the royal fifth, gold and silver flowed into the royal coffers in Spain. The discovery in 1545 of the fabulous Peruvian silver mine of Potosí (in what is now in southern Bolivia) coincided with the introduction of the mercury amalgamation process that separated silver from ore. Mercury amalgamation enabled the Spaniards to replace surface gathering of silver ore with tunneling for ore, a procedure that led to greatly elevated yields of precious metals. For a century the silver of Peru helped provide otherwise impoverished Spain with the resources to become the most powerful kingdom in Europe.

SPANISH AMERICA: THE TRANSPLANTING OF A EUROPEAN CULTURE

With the defeat of the Aztec and Incan empires, the process of transplanting Spanish society to the Americas began in earnest. The arrival of Europeans was a catastrophe for

WHAT MONTEZUMA BELIEVED ABOUT THE SPANISH

·················

After Cortés arrived in Tenochtitlán, he had an interview with Montezuma, the Aztec emperor. The following letter to Emperor Charles V includes a speech Montezuma suppos-edly gave to Cortés in which the Aztec emperor surrendered authority to the Spanish because he assumed that Charles was an ancient god or ruler the Aztecs believed would return from the East. Just as Columbus was inspired by Christian prophecies to sail into the unknown, Montezuma was en-couraged by Aztec prophecies to accept Cortés's invasion as a fulfillment of a religious obligation.

Long time have we been informed by the writings of our ancestors that neither myself nor any of those who inhabit this land are natives of it, but rather strangers who have come to it from foreign parts. We like-wise know that from those parts our nation was led by a certain lord (to whom all were subject), and who then went back to his native land, where he remained so long delaying his return that at his coming those whom he had left had married the women of the land and had many children by them and had built themselves cities in which they lived, so that they would in no wise return to their own land nor acknowledge him as lord; upon which he left them. And we have always believed that among his de-scendants one would surely come to subject this land and us as rightful vassals. Now seeing the regions from which you [i.e., Cortés] say you come, which is from where the sun rises, and the news you tell of this great king and ruler [Emperor Charles V] who sent you hither, we believe and hold it certain that he is our natural lord: especially in that you say he has long had knowledge of us. Wherefore be certain that we will obey you and hold you as lord in place of that great lord of whom you speak, in which service there shall be neither slackness nor deceit: and throughout all the land, that is to say all that I rule, you may command anything you desire, and it shall be obeyed and done, and all that we have is at your will and pleasure. And since you are at your own land and house, rejoice and take your leisure from the fatigues of your journey and the battles you have fought; for I am well informed of all those that you have been forced to engage in on your way here. . . .

Source: From Hernán Cortés, "The Second Letter to Emperor Charles V" from Anthony Pagden, ed., *Letters from Mexico.* Copyright © 1986 by Yale University. Reprinted with the permis-sion of Yale University Press.

---

language. At every stage from initial explorations to the building of new cities, Africans participated in helping make the Americas Spanish. Unlike in the West Indies and the coastal regions where they became plantation workers, blacks in the interior of South America often fought and worked as partners with the Spanish, not as full equals but as necessary auxiliaries for and beneficiaries of the conquest.

The king of Spain was represented in the Americas by the two viceroys, who were the highest colonial officials. One in Mexico City governed the West Indies, the mainland north of Panama, Venezuela, and the Philippines; the other in Lima, Peru, had authority over all of Spanish South America, excluding Venezuela. However, the vast territory of Spanish America and the enormous cultural diversity within it precluded any rigorous centralized control either from Spain or from the viceregal capitals.

In Spanish America the church was a more effective presence than the state. Driven by the same religious fervor as Columbus, Catholic missionaries trekked into the far-thest reaches of Spanish America, converting the native populations to Christianity with much more success than in Africa or Asia. Greed had enticed the conquistadores, but an ardent desire to spread the gospel of Christianity spurred the missionaries. As heirs to the long Christian struggle against Islam and, in particular, the reconquest of the Iberian peninsula from the Muslims, the missionaries found in the Americas an exceptional opportunity to ex-pand Christianity. The most zealous missionaries were members of religious orders—Franciscans, Dominicans, and Jesuits—who were distinguished from the parish priests by their autonomy and special training for mission-ary work. Instead of answering to a bishop who had author-ity over a defined region, members of religious orders were organized like an army, followed the commands of the head of their order in Rome, and were willing to travel anywhere in the world.

PORTUGUESE BRAZIL: THE TENUOUS COLONY

In 1500 Pedro Cabral sighted the Brazilian coast, claiming it for Portugal under the Treaty of Tordesillas. While the Spaniards busied themselves with the conquest of Mexico and Peru, the Portuguese largely ignored Brazil, which lacked any obvious source of gold or temptingly rich civilizations to conquer. Instead, the Portuguese concen-trated on developing their lucrative empire in Asia.

The impetus for the colonization of Brazil was the growing European demand for sugar. The Brazilian cli-mate was perfectly suited for cultivating sugar cane. Between 1575 and 1600, Brazil became the Western world's leading producer of sugar, luring thousands of poor

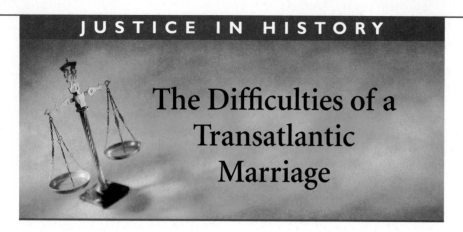

The Difficulties of a Transatlantic Marriage

In 1557 Francisco Noguerol de Ulloa, a Spanish conquistador who had fought in Peru, returned home to Spain. During his nearly two decades in the New World, he had amassed a sizable fortune and earned a great reputation for himself. He expected to enjoy his wealth and fame in a peaceful retirement, but instead almost immediately upon his return he was arrested on the charge of bigamy. During his long stay in Peru, he had neither seen nor heard from the Spanish woman he had married before he left, and when his sisters wrote to him that she had died he thought he was free to marry again. So he did. But when he returned to Spain, his first wife, Dona Beatriz, who was alive and well, heard about his second marriage and filed suit against him for bigamy.

The chance to escape Beatriz had impelled Francisco across the Atlantic in the first place. Many Spanish conquistadores were trying to flee troubles at home, such as a bad marriage. Francisco had married Beatriz under pressure from his widowed mother for the usual reasons parents forced their children into arranged marriages. Beatriz came with a large dowry and provided useful alliances for Francisco's mother and sisters, who felt vulnerable because of Francisco's father's untimely death.

But the marriage was a failure from the beginning. According to Francisco, they had never slept together, and in the eyes of the Church, at least, an unconsummated marriage was not a real marriage. Certainly Francisco and Beatriz never lived together, and she bore him no children. However, his lack of affection for his wife did not prevent him from accepting large payments for her dowry or from writing to his in-laws to ask for money when in his early years abroad he ran into difficulties in Peru. Even a letter of consolation on the death of his wife's sister included a request for more money. Francisco may never have had an affectionate or sexual relationship with Beatriz, but he certainly had a financial one.

Peru eventually rewarded Francisco with a great fortune. For his military prowess and devotion to the Spanish crown, he was granted one of the largest and most productive encomiendas in Peru, a vast tract of land that included the labor of thousands of Incas and a retinue of personal slaves, including a harem of female domestics. Once the false news of Beatriz's death spread throughout Peru, Francisco came to be regarded as the most eligible bachelor in the entire colony. Although many women were eager to become his wife, Francisco did not remarry for years after the news of his first wife's death.

Francisco's second wife, Dona Catalina, shared at least two attributes with his first wife: wealth and social prominence. Born into a respectable Castilian family, she was herself the widow of one of the most powerful Spaniards in Peru. She controlled her own vast fortune in property and other assets, which meant that she could bring a substantial dowry to her new husband. Her reputation as a woman of modesty and virtue was impeccable; she also possessed one vital asset that Beatriz apparently lacked—great beauty. Catalina was known as the "crown jewel of all the women of those parts." It is no wonder that Francisco chose her as his new wife. This time he consummated the marriage.

This case reveals much about the nature of marriage in imperial Spain, and the relative power of men and women in Spanish and colonial society. Marriage was the union of two families, not just two people. Social standing counted for more than affection in the choice of a spouse. Francisco, in fact, had to defend himself against the charge that he had fallen in love with Catalina and had, therefore, abandoned Beatriz so that he could marry Catalina. Love was not an acceptable reason for marriage, let alone an acceptable reason for leaving one marriage for another. In his trial and subsequent litigation, he never claimed to love his new wife and in fact denied that he knew her well at all before the wedding. As an honorable and respectable widow, she had lived a secluded life that would have made it impossible for Francisco to have had much contact with her at all, or so he said.

To escape Beatriz, Francisco had to prove that the marriage had never been a real marriage. To this end, he and his lawyers highlighted the fact that he had never consummated his first marriage, a fact that would have automatically invalidated it as a legal marriage according to the canon law of the Church. To keep Francisco as her husband, Beatriz had to prove that they had had sex together at least once. Francisco's belief that Beatriz was dead had no legal bearing on the case because she was not.

Despite Francisco's arguments that the marriage had never been valid, the judges initially decided in favor of Beatriz. Francisco was sentenced to pay a heavy fine to Beatriz, to serve time in jail, and to separate from his second wife, whom he was forbidden to ever see again. Perhaps most galling of all, he was obliged to resume marital relations with Beatriz, with whom he had certainly never lived before. Beatriz won the case largely because of the legal protection women enjoyed in sixteenth-century Spain. Husbands had obligations toward their wives that the courts consistently enforced.

One of the most important protections women had was the dowry itself. A man could enjoy the income from his wife's dowry, but legally she still had certain claims to it. If he died before she did—which was quite likely given the difference in age between men and women at first marriage—

she had a claim on his estate to have the entire sum of her dowry restored to her, not to his family or his heirs but only to her. Beatriz supplied the court with extensive evidence of receipts for dowry payments, signed by Francisco himself. The judges respected the legal protections for women and would not allow Francisco to squander the dowry or relegate it entirely for himself. Francisco's repeated requests to his in-laws for more money made him look like an opportunistic fortune hunter rather than a valuable family ally. The court's judgment in favor of Beatriz

had less to do with the emotions of love than the defense of the dowry system and its role in maintaining social stability.

Catalina did not accept lightly the loss of the man she considered her husband. She needed to protect her own dowry from Beatriz's claims. Catalina filed a countersuit to assert that much of Francisco's assets were profits earned from her own dowry, which could not, therefore, be transferred to Beatriz. Catalina was fighting not just for her dowry but for her good name and her marriage, and the courts eventually found a way to recognize the rights of both women—Beatriz to her dowry portion and Catalina to her honorable marriage to Francisco.

In the end, it was the women who resolved the legal struggle that surrounded Francisco. For both women, the courts and the dowry system served as a powerful form of protection for their financial well-being and their honor. Despite the overwhelming authority of men in Spanish society, women were not passive pawns. They found ways to assert control over their own lives. It is revealing that the distance between the Old and New Worlds had little bearing on the status of or legal protections for these women. Far from becoming a lawless frontier, early colonial Peru was for Spaniards at least, an extension of Spanish society. ◼

◼ A Spanish Couple

Francisco Noguerol de Ulloa and Catalina would have dressed much like this aristocratic couple out for a stroll.

Questions of Justice

1. In what ways did the sixteenth-century Spanish legal system protect the rights of women?
2. What does this case reveal about how Spanish society was transported to the New World?

Taking It Further

Cook, Alexandra Parma, and Noble David Cook. *Good Faith and Truthful Ignorance: A Case of Transatlantic Bigamy.* 1991. A detailed study of the Noguerol de Ulloa case.

young men from Portugal and the Azores who took native women as wives, thereby producing a distinctive mestizo population. In the coastal regions, the land was cleared for vast sugar cane plantations. Sugar cane production required back-breaking, dangerous labor to weed and especially to cut the cane.

The Portuguese increasingly looked to Africans to perform the hard labor of sugar cane production that they were unwilling to do themselves. As a result, the Brazilian demand for slaves intensified the Portuguese presence in West Africa and the African presence in Brazil. In the search for ever more slaves, Portuguese slave buyers enlarged their area of operations in Africa south to Angola, where in 1575 they founded a trading post. This post became the embarkation point for slave traders who sailed directly to Brazil and sold slaves in exchange for low-grade Brazilian tobacco, which they exchanged for more slaves when they returned to Angola.

As in Spanish America, Portuguese authorities felt responsible for converting the natives to Christianity. In Brazil, the Jesuits took the lead during the last half of the sixteenth century by establishing a school for the training of missionaries on the site of the present city of São Paulo. São Paulo became the headquarters for the "Apostle of Brazil," José de Anchieta, who worked among the indigenous peoples. In the seventeenth century, Father Antonio Vieira established a string of missions in the Amazon valley. Once converted, natives were resettled into villages called aldeias°, which were similar to Spanish missions. By papal decree Indians who had settled in aldeias were considered Christian and could not be enslaved. Restrictions on enslaving Indians created a perceived labor shortage and further stimulated the demand for African slaves.

More rural, more African, and less centrally governed than Spanish America, Brazil during its colonial history remained a plantation economy in which the few dominant white European landowners were vastly outnumbered by their African slaves. In certain areas a racially mixed population created its own vibrantly hybrid culture that combined native, African, and European elements, especially in the eclectic religious life that combined Catholic with polytheistic forms of worship.

NORTH AMERICA: THE LAND OF LESSER INTEREST

Compared with Central and South America, North America outside Mexico held little attraction for Europeans during the sixteenth century. European experience in North America consisted of a number of exploratory missions and several failed attempts at colonization. By 1600, when hundreds of thousands of Europeans and Africans had settled in the Caribbean and Central and South America, only a handful of Europeans could be found in North America outside Mexico.

The principal attractions of North America were the cod fisheries in the waters off Newfoundland, which every spring lured ships from England, and the hope of finding a Northwest Passage to China and India through or around the continent to the North. An Italian captain in the employ of England, Giovanni Caboto, known in English as John Cabot (ca. 1450–ca. 1498), landed in North America in 1497 and established the basis for an English claim in the New World, but no one bothered to follow up on the claim. In 1524 the French king sent another Italian navigator, Giovanni da Verrazano (ca. 1485–1528), to find a passage around North America, which resulted in the first geographical description of the coast from North Carolina to Newfoundland.

In the competition for the Americas, the English arrived late, devoting themselves at first to preying on Spanish shipping rather than building their own colonies.

During the reign of Queen Elizabeth I (r. 1558–1603), English efforts finally turned to establishing colonies in the Americas. Two prominent courtiers, Humphrey Gilbert and his stepbrother, Walter Raleigh, sponsored a series of voyages intended to found an English colony called Virginia in honor of Elizabeth, "The Virgin Queen." The shift of English interest from piracy to colonization was made possible by Elizabeth's success in strengthening the monarchy, building up the fleet, and encouraging investments in New World colonies. In 1585 the first English colonists in the Americas landed on Roanoke Island off the coast of North Carolina, but they were so poorly prepared that their attempt and a second one in 1587 failed. The inexperienced and naive English settlers did not even make provisions for planting crops.

The successful English colonies came a generation later. Learning from past mistakes, the colonists of Jamestown in Virginia, who landed in 1607, brought seeds for planting, built fortifications for protection, and established a successful form of self-government. From these modest beginnings, the English gradually established vast plantations along the rivers of Virginia. There they raised tobacco to supply the new European habit of smoking, which had been picked up from native Americans. In 1620 religious refugees from England settled in Massachusetts Bay, but in contrast to Central and South America, most of North America by 1650 remained only marginally touched by Europeans.

Europeans in Asia

ndia, the Malay peninsula, Indonesia, the Spice Islands, and China were the ultimate goal of the European explorers during the fifteenth and sixteenth centuries. They were eventually reached by many routes—by the Portuguese sailing around Africa, by the Spanish sailing around South America, and by the Russians trekking across the vastness of Siberia. Trade between Europe and Asia was very lucrative. Europeans were especially dependent on Asian sources for luxury goods such as silk, spices for cooking and preserving food, and medicines for pain relief and healing.

In contrast to the trade in Africa and America, Europeans failed to monopolize trade in Asia. The Europeans were just one among many trading groups, some working under government sponsorship, such as the Portuguese, and others working alone, such as the Chinese.

In 1497–1499 Vasco da Gama opened the most promising route for the Portuguese around Africa to South and East Asia. But the sailing distances were long, limiting the number of people who could be transported to Asia, and the Asian empires were well equipped to defend themselves against European conquest. As a result, European engagement with Asia was slight for 300 years. Because Europeans lacked the support system provided by colonial conquest, few Europeans settled in Asia, and even missionary work proved much more difficult than in the Americas.

Unlike Brazil, where the Portuguese established colonial plantations, in Asia they established trading posts along the coasts of India, China, and the Spice Islands. When the Portuguese first arrived at a location with a safe harbor and easy access to the hinterland, they built a fort and forced, bribed, or tricked the local political authority, usually a chieftain, to cede the land around the post to Portugal. The agents sent to trade in Asia were called factors and their trading posts were called factories. But they were not factories in the modern sense of sites for manufacturing; they were safe places where merchants could trade and store their merchandise. The factors lived in the factories with a few other Portuguese traders, a small detachment of troops, and servants recruited from the local population. Nowhere did Portuguese authority extend very far into the hinterland. The traditional political structures of local chieftains remained, and the local elites usually went along with the arrangement because they profited by reselling European wares, such as cloth, guns, knives, and many kinds of cheap gadgets. The factors acquired silks, gold, silver, raw cotton, pepper, spices, and medicines. Some of these outposts of the Portuguese Empire survived until late in the twentieth century, but their roots remained exceedingly shallow. Through the trading post empires, commercial rivalries among European states extended abroad to Asia. Competition over these trading posts foreshadowed the beginnings of a global economy dominated by Europeans. It also demonstrated the Europeans' propensity to transform European wars into world wars.

In addition to trade, the Portuguese and other European powers sought to spread Christianity among the local Asian populations. Franciscan, Dominican, and later Jesuit missionaries preached to the indigenous peo-

CHRONOLOGY

1394–1460	Life of Prince Henry the Navigator of Portugal
CA. 1438	Founding of Incan empire in Peru by Pachacuti Inca Yupanqui
1440–1469	Reign of Montezuma I of the Aztec Empire
1450s	Appearance of new European ship design, the caravel
CA. 1450	European slave trade in Africa begins
1492–1502	Voyages of Christopher Columbus
1497–1499	Vasco da Gama reaches India via Cape of Good Hope
1519–1522	Spanish conquer Mexico; Ferdinand Magellan's crew circumnavigates the globe

ples. To accomplish conversions, they tried persuasion, because without the backing of a full-scale conquest as in the Americas, resorting to force was usually not an option. The missionaries frequently drew the ire of local rulers, who viewed the converts as traitors—a situation that led to the persecution of some of the new Christians. To accomplish their task of conversion, Christian missionaries had to learn the native languages and something of the native culture and religion. In this effort, the Jesuits were particularly dedicated; they sent members of their order to the Chinese imperial court, where they lived incognito for decades, although they made few converts. Jesuits also traveled to Japan, where they established an outpost of Christianity at Nagasaki. With the exception of the Spanish Philippines, which was nominally converted to Catholicism by 1600, Christian missionaries in Asia were far less successful than in the Americas. Perhaps one million Asians outside the Philippines had been converted during this period, but many of these conversions did not last. Christians were most successful in converting Buddhists and least effective among Muslims, who almost never abandoned their faith.

The significance of the European trading post empires lies less in the influence of Europe on Asia than in the influence of Asia on Europe. Asian products from spices and opium to silk cloth and oriental rugs became commonplace items in middle- and upper-class European households. European collectors became fascinated with Chinese porcelains, lacquered boxes, and screen paintings. At the same time, Asians began to visit Europe, a tradition begun when four Japanese converts to Christianity arrived in Lisbon in 1586 and made a celebrated tour of Europe.

The Beginnings of the Global System

As a result of the European voyages of the fifteenth and sixteenth centuries, a network of cultural, biological, and economic connections formed along intercontinental trading routes. These connections created a global system that has been sustained ever since. Today's global economy, based on the Internet, air transportation, and free trade, operates much more efficiently and quickly than its predecessors, but it is merely an extension and elaboration of a system that first appeared on a global scale during the sixteenth century. For many thousands of years, Europe, northern Africa, and Asia had been in contact with each other, but the system that took form during the sixteenth century began to encompass most of the globe, including sub-Saharan Africa and the Americas. Unlike earlier international trading systems that linked Europe and Asia, the new global system was dominated by Europeans. They turned large parts of the Americas into plantations that used African slave labor to grow crops for European consumers. This system transformed human society by bringing into contact elements that had previously been separate and isolated—regional cultures, biological systems, and local economies.

THE COLUMBIAN EXCHANGE

The most dramatic changes were at first produced by the trade of peoples, plants, animals, microbes, and ideas between the Old and New Worlds—a process known as the Columbian Exchange°. For the native Americans, the importation of Europeans, Africans, and microbes had devastating consequences—threatening indigenous religions, making native technology irrelevant, disrupting social life, and destroying millions of lives. For Europeans, the discovery of previously unknown civilizations profoundly shook their own understanding of human geography and history. Neither the ancient philosophers nor the Bible, which was understood to be an accurate history of humankind since the creation of the world, had provided a hint about the peoples of the Americas.

The Slave Trade

The growing population of Europe developed a taste for exotic products such as sugar, tobacco, coffee, and indigo dye. The European colonizers who sought to supply the demand for these goods needed agricultural workers, first for the colonies in the Atlantic islands and then for plantations in the Americas. In the Americas, European diseases decimated the indigenous population, creating a labor shortage. Europeans also found it difficult to enslave the native peoples, who knew the territory and could easily escape.

The flourishing demand for labor was supplied by the population of Africa. The institution of slavery was well established in Africa long before the beginning of the transatlantic slave trade dominated by Europeans. Muslim slavers had been capturing sub-Saharan Africans for centuries, and Africans had enslaved one another. However, Europeans greatly increased the demand for slaves. Once Europeans started to buy up slaves in the coastal trading posts, enterprising African chieftains sent slave-hunting expeditions into the interior. As a consequence, the slave-trading states of the Guinea coast gained power at the expense of their neighbors and spread the unwelcome web of the slave trade deep into the African interior. The slave hunters sold captives to the Europeans for transportation across the Atlantic. Following the Portuguese in the trade came the Dutch, English, French, and Danes, who eventually established their own trading posts to obtain slaves.

During the nearly 400 years of the European slave trade (ca. 1500–1870), more than ten million Africans were transported to the Americas, the result of which was that large slices of the Americas were transformed into outposts of sub-Saharan African cultures. Blacks came to outnumber the native Americans and constituted the majority of the colonial population in most of the Caribbean, and broad parts of coastal Central America, Venezuela, Guyana, and Brazil. Much of the male population of Angola was transported directly to Brazil, a forced migration that resulted in a dramatic excess of females over males in the most heavily depopulated areas of Angola. In the process, Portuguese Brazil became the single largest recipient of African slaves. It was the destination of 3.6 million Africans—nearly ten times the number brought to all of English-speaking North America.

The slave ships that sailed the infamous Middle Passage across the Atlantic were so unhealthy, with Africans "stacked like books on a shelf," that a significant portion of the human cargo died en route. The physical and psychological burdens that slavery placed on its victims can scarcely be imagined, in large part because few slaves were ever allowed to learn to read and write, and thus direct records of their experiences are rare. Documents from ship surgeons, overseers, and slave masters, however, indicate that slaves were subjected to unhealthy living conditions, back-breaking work, and demoralization.

The plantations of the New World mixed together Africans from different cultures and language groups, making it difficult for slaves to build the solidarity necessary to rebel successfully. In a few places, runaways established their own self-governing communities, such as the Saramakas of Surinam or the Cimarrón republic in Peru, but most found

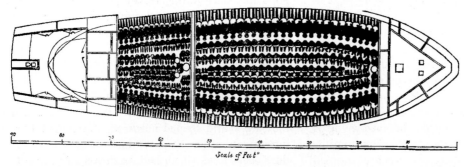

Scale of Feet

PLAN OF A SLAVE VESSEL.

THE SLAVE TRADE.

THE motion in the House of Lords made by Lord Denman, on Tuesday night, has naturally revived the interest of the measures for the extinction of this vile traffic of "man-selling and man-stealing." The close of the session is marked by these humane exertions, as was its commencement, in the comprehensive speech of Lord George Bentinck, in the House of Commons, on February 3. His Lordship then held in his hand a communication from Captain Pilkington, of the Royal Navy, on the subject of the slave-trade, accompanied with a plan of one of the slave vessels (which we now Engrave). They were sit-

entertainment enlivened by some most exquisite performances on the national instrument, the harp, much to the delight of all assembled. From the dinner-table the company retired at an early hour to the School-rooms, where the *conversazioni* were held.

WEDNESDAY.

On Wednesday, as the Geological and Natural History Sections were unable to finish the business before them, they each held meetings; but as a great number of members had left Swansea that morning by the *Lord Beresford* steamer, and others were examining the works in the neighbourhood, the Sections were very slightly attended, and the papers communicated were of small general interest.

A dinner, given by Lewis W. Dillwyn, Esq., who is himself one of the oldest members of the Royal Society, may be regarded as the close of the proceedings.

The last General Meeting was held in the afternoon, when it appeared, that, notwithstanding the inferiority of Swansea as respects population, this meeting has added considerably to the funds of the Association.

In concluding our notice of an Association which numbers among its members all the most eminent men in every department of physical and natural science, we cannot but express our satisfaction at the business-like character of this meeting. It is true that it has not startled the word by the announcement of any great discovery; but it will be found, upon examination, to present a fair average rate of progress. The vulnerable points have been less apparent than hitherto; and by the exclusion from the sections of all subjects which were not purely scientific, and by particularly avoiding those communications which have frequently been introduced as mere trading advertisements, of which we witnessed but one, that on gutta percha, which in our opinion should not have been required, the Association has placed itself upon exalted ground, and en-

Water Line

■ The Middle Passage

As human cargo, slaves were packed together for the long voyage from a slave-trading post in Africa to the plantation colonies of the Americas.

escape impossible because they had no place to go and certainly no way to return to their homeland. Despite these crushing hardships, and even within the harsh confines of white-owned plantations, black slaves created their own institutions, family structures, and cultures.

Biological Exchanges

Europeans certainly perpetuated atrocities in the New World, including the intentional genocide of whole peoples. Nevertheless, the introduction of new diseases to the Americas and the disruption of traditional economies led to a form of unintentional genocide that resulted in the deaths of millions. The European, Asian, and African continents, on the one hand, and the Americas, on the other, had been isolated from each other for so long that they had become two biologically distinct worlds. After the voyages of Christopher Columbus they were rejoined in ways that— for good or for ill—made them more alike culturally and, especially, biologically.

How did a few thousand Europeans so easily conquer the civilizations of the Americas, which were populated by millions of people? After all, the Aztecs, Incas and others

put up a stubborn resistance to the conquistadores, and yet the Europeans triumphed time after time. The answer: epidemics. Along with their gunpowder weapons, the conquistadores' most effective allies were the invisible microbes of Old World diseases, such as smallpox. A native of the Yucatán peninsula recalled the better days before the conquest:

There was then no sickness; they had no aching bones; they had then no high fever; they had then no smallpox; they had then no burning chest; they had then no abdominal pain; they had then no consumption; they had then no headache. At that time the course of humanity was orderly. The foreigners made it otherwise when they arrived here.[3]

Nearly every chronicler of the New World conquests was stunned by the toll that epidemic disease had on the natives soon after their initial contact with Europeans. Between 1520 and 1600, Mexico suffered fourteen major epidemics, and Peru suffered seventeen. By the 1580s the populations of the Caribbean islands, the Antilles, and the lowlands of Mexico and Peru had almost completely died off. Historians estimate the deaths in the tens of millions. The preconquest population of Mexico, which has been estimated at about 19 million, dropped in eighty years to 2.5 million. Even the infrequent contacts between European fishermen and fur traders with natives on the coast of what is now Canada led to rapid depopulation.

The most deadly culprit was smallpox, but measles, typhus, scarlet fever, and chicken pox also contributed to the devastation. All of these were dangerous and even life-threatening to Europeans and Africans alike, but from exposure, people of the Old World had either died young or survived the illness with a resistance to infection from the disease. However, native Americans had never been exposed to these diseases, and as a population completely lacked immunities to them. As a result, all it took was for one infected person to arrive from the Old World to kill off many millions in the New World. After Cortés's men were first driven from Tenochtitlán, a Dominican friar reported that a new ally appeared: "When the Christians were exhausted from war, God saw fit to send the Indians smallpox, and there was a great pestilence in the city. . . . "[4] The epidemic undoubtedly impaired the fighting ability of the Aztecs. The Spaniards' immunity to the very diseases that killed off so many Indians reinforced the impression that the Europeans were favored agents of the gods or gods themselves. As a Mayan put it, "we were born to die."[5]

The exchange of other forms of life was less obviously disastrous. Following the Europeans came a flood of European animals and plants. With the conquistadores came pigs, cattle, goats, sheep, donkeys, and horses—all previously unknown in the New World. Pigs that escaped from the first Spanish ships to land in Florida were the ancestors of the ubiquitous wild razorback pigs of the southern United States. Vast areas of Mexico and Peru depopulated of humans were repopulated with enormous herds of sheep. The cattle herded by the present-day gauchos of Argentina derive from Iberian stock. The characteristic Latin American burro came from Europe as did the horse, which came to be so prized by the plains Indians of North America. Sheep, cattle, and horses, in particular, completely changed the way of life of the native American peoples.

From Europe came the lucrative plantation crops of sugar, cotton, rice, and indigo, crops that required a large supply of field hands. European varieties of wheat, grapes, and olives soon appeared as major crops in Mexico and elsewhere. In exchange, the Americas offered new crops to the Old World such as tobacco, cocoa, paprika, American cotton, pumpkins, beans, maize (corn), and potatoes. European peasant farmers discovered that maize and the potato provided an attractive substitute for wheat. In many places, the potato replaced wheat as the staple in the diet of the poor. By yielding more calories per acre than wheat or virtually any other traditional grain, the potato made it possible to support more people on a given amount of land. With the spread of the potato as a food source, European populations began to increase rapidly, a trend that created population pressures, which in turn stimulated additional European migrations to the Americas.

The Problem of Cultural Diversity

For Christians and Jews, the Bible remained the unchallenged authority on the origins of the whole world, but the New World created numerous problems for biblical interpretation. The book of Genesis told of Creation and the Great Flood, which had destroyed all people and all animals except those saved in Noah's ark. The New World brought into question that vision of a single creation and cleansing flood simply because it could not explain why the plants and animals of the Americas were so different. If the only animals on Earth were those Noah preserved, then why were they different on the two sides of the Earth? About the New World a French writer asked, "How falls it out that the nations of the world, coming all of one father, Noah, do vary so much from one another, both in body and mind?"[6] Thinkers argued either that there must have been more than one creation or that the Great Flood must have covered only Palestine rather than the entire Earth.

The greatest conceptual challenge to Christian Europe were the New World peoples themselves. If these people were not the children of God's Creation, then how did they get there? If they were God's children, then why were they so different from Europeans? In the terms available to sixteenth-century thinkers, there were three possible ways to answer these questions. One was to assume that the native Americans were subhumans, demons, or some strange form of animal life. This answer was the most convenient one to those who sought to exploit the natives. Often with little or no foundation, these Europeans believed that the natives practiced devil worship, incest, sexual promiscuity, polygamy, sodomy, and cannibalism—all signs of their demonic nature. In this extreme form of European belief, the natives did not even possess a human soul and were neither capable of converting to Christianity nor worthy of human rights.

A second answer to why the peoples of the New World were so different sprung from a belief that the natives were complete innocents. The native peoples lived in a kind of earthly Paradise, unspoiled by the corruption of European society. Some of the early English explorers of Virginia found the natives "most gentle, loving and faithful, void of any guile or treason," and one missionary found them "all the more children of God owing to their very lack of capacity and skill."[7]

The most influential spokesman during the sixteenth century for this idea of native innocence was the powerful advocate of human rights Bartholomew de Las Casas (1474–1566), the bishop of arid, impoverished Chiapas in

Mexico. Throughout his career, Las Casas forcefully argued against the enslavement and ill treatment of the native Americans, which was chronicled in his most important published work, *The Brief Relation of the Destruction of the West Indies* (1542). Through Las Casas's influence, Spanish royal policy toward the Indians became more peaceful and sympathetic.

The third response to the question of how to explain the "differentness" of New World peoples neither dehumanized them nor assumed them innocent but simply recognized their differences as the natural consequence of human diversity. Advocates of this position proposed some form of cultural toleration. The inconvenient facts of the New World brought to the forefront the inadequacy of traditional moral standards for judging the behavior of other people. Deciding whether a particular people were bad or good raised questions about the criteria for making such judgments, and these questions introduced the principle of cultural relativism. Cultural relativism° recognized that many (but not necessarily all) standards of judgment are specific to particular cultures rather than the fixed truths established by natural or divine law.

The most eloquent voice during the sixteenth century for toleration based on cultural relativism was Michel de Montaigne (1533–1592), the brilliant French essayist. After a career as a hardworking public official, he retired at age 38 to his estate to a life of study and contemplation. Among his many interests, he especially loved to read about travels to the New World. His essay "On Cannibals" pointed to the hypocrisy of Christians who condemned the alleged cannibalism of the native Americans but justified the torture and murder of other Christians over some minor theological dispute. Montaigne argued that a truly ethical, truly Christian person was not a rigid follower of biblical laws but was capable of understanding and tolerating cultural differences. The discovery in the New World that non-Christians could lead moral lives, love their families, practice humility and charity, and benefit from highly developed religious institutions shook the complacent sense of European superiority.

THE CAPITALIST GLOBAL ECONOMY

During the sixteenth century a truly global economy began to take shape as a consequence of the European encounters with the rest of the world. As the Europeans sailed the oceans of the world in search of profits, they pioneered a new form of economic organization—agrarian capitalism°. In agrarian capitalism Europeans organized the production of certain kinds of commercial crops, such as sugar, tobacco, and indigo, which were raised for sale to an expanding population in Europe. With land expropriated from native peoples in the Atlantic islands, the Americas, and parts of Asia, European capitalists began to raise commercial crops on an unprecedented scale. Unlike other forms of capitalism, which relied on workers who were paid a wage, agrarian capitalism relied on slave labor, mostly provided by transplanted Africans.

Agrarian capitalism depended on the creation of European empires—the settler colonies, plantation colonies, and trading post empires of the Portuguese, Spanish, Dutch, French, Danes, English, and Russians. These empires, however, were very different from those of the ancient world, medieval Europe, preconquest Americas, and Asia. In ancient Rome, medieval Byzantium, and early modern China, for example, imperial governments promoted monopolies and inhibited free access to the market and thus stymied the development of capitalism. These empires produced economic stagnation instead of growth. But in the European global empires of the sixteenth century, the organization of trade and the division of labor took place outside the authority of any one state, a fact that made it impossible for a single imperial government to monopolize completely economic resources. It was the competition among imperialist states, rather than control by a single powerful empire, that was new.

The creation of the European empires during the sixteenth century made it possible for capitalists to maximize their profits through regional specialization. Western Europe became the *core* of the global economy, the center of a complex variety of economic activities and institutions—banking, insurance, trade companies, gun manufacture, shipbuilding, and cloth production. In Europe agriculture was more and more devoted exclusively to producing food, and the labor supply was free—neither serfs, as had been the case in the Middle Ages, nor slaves, as was the case in parts of the Americas. The distant colonies, especially in Spanish and Portuguese America, became the *periphery* devoted to raising single cash crops, such as sugar, tobacco, cotton, coffee, or indigo for dyes. Agriculture in the periphery was produced on large estates by slaves.

The capitalist global economy has steadily and relentlessly expanded throughout the world since the sixteenth century. Much of the subsequent history of Western civilization can be understood only in terms of the triumph of capitalism and the economic integration of a world dominated by Westerners. The capitalist global economy has yielded many benefits in enhancing the material well-being of the middle classes of the West, increasing the available food supply of the world, and stimulating technological innovation. But there have been costs. Since the sixteenth century, the gap between rich and poor individuals and rich and poor countries has widened, and societies on the agrarian periphery have found it enormously difficult to break out of their disadvantaged position in the world economy.

CONCLUSION

The Significance of the Global Encounters

The world was forever changed by the European voyages from about 1450 to 1650. The significance of these encounters lay not so much in the Europeans' geographical discoveries as in the scale of permanent contact these voyages made possible among previously isolated peoples of the world. Vikings had been to the Americas before Columbus, and the Chinese had earlier engaged in long-distance voyages of reconnaissance as far as the east coast of Africa. But none of these early voyages had created a lasting economic system or lasting cultural contacts. The European voyages of the fifteenth and sixteenth centuries did.

As a result of the Portuguese slaving enterprises on the coast of West and Central Africa, millions of Africans were uprooted, transported in chains to a strange land, and forced to toil in subhuman conditions on plantations. There they grew crops for the increasingly affluent European consumers and generated profits often used to buy more slaves in Africa, parts of which became depopulated in the process. In Europe until at least the middle of the nineteenth century, every cup of coffee, every puff of tobacco, every sugar candy, and every cotton dress of indigo blue came from the sweat of a black slave.

Many of the native Americans lost their lives, their land, and their way of life as a result of European encounters. The most isolated of them retained their languages and religion, but other groups were assimilated to the point of nearly complete cultural loss. Everywhere in the Americas, native peoples suffered from the invasion of Old World microbes even more than from the invasion of Old World conquerors. The destruction of the Aztec and Incan Empires were certainly the most dramatic, but everywhere native peoples struggled to adapt to an invasion of foreign beings from a foreign world.

Asia was far less altered by contact with Europeans. European civilization remained on the cultural periphery of Asia. But European access to Asian luxury goods remained a crucial component in the expanding global economy that became one of the first fruits of European capitalism.

Coming to terms with the variety of world cultures became a persistent and absorbing problem in Western civilization. Most Europeans retained confidence in the inherent superiority of their civilization, but the realities of the world began to chip away at that confidence, and economic globalization profoundly altered Western civilization itself. Westerners began to confront the problem of understanding "other" cultures and in so doing changed themselves. The West came to mean less a place in Europe than a certain kind of culture that was exported throughout the world through conversion to Christianity, the acquisition of Western languages, and the spread of Western technology.

Suggestions for Further Reading

For a comprehensive list of suggested readings, please go to www.ablongman.com/levackconcise/chapter12

Chaudhuri, K. N. *Trade and Civilization in the Indian Ocean: An Economic History from the Rise of Islam to 1750.* 1985. Arguing for the long-term unity of trade routes, the book lays out the importance of Asian merchants to maritime trade networks from the South China Sea to the Mediterranean.

Clendinnen, Inga. *Aztecs: An Interpretation.* 1991. A provocative, sometimes disturbing book that directly confronts the implications of human sacrifice and cannibalism among the Aztecs and offers an explanation for it by analyzing Aztec religion.

Crosby, Alfred W. Jr., *The Columbian Exchange: Biological and Cultural Consequences of 1492.* 1973. The most significant study on the implications of the biological exchanges for the cultural history of both the Old and New Worlds. It has the benefit of being an exciting book to read.

Curtin, Philip D. *African History: From Earliest Times to Independence.* 1995. An excellent survey by one of the most distinguished comparative historians.

Elvin, Mark. *The Pattern of the Chinese Past: A Social and Economic Interpretation.* 1973. An excellent overview of Chinese history that covers Chinese responses to Western encounters.

Fernández-Armesto, Felipe. *Before Columbus: Exploration and Colonization from the Mediterranean to the Atlantic, 1229–1492.* 1987. Engagingly written and original in scope, this is the best single account of early European colonization efforts.

Fernández-Armesto, Felipe. *Columbus.* 1991. The 500th anniversary of Columbus's voyage in 1492 provoked a wide-ranging reappraisal of his motives and career. This pithy, engaging book is by far the most convincing in revising Columbus's image, but it deflated much of the Columbus myth and caused considerable controversy.

Oliver, Roland. *The African Experience from Olduvai Gorge to the 21st Century.* 2000. A highly readable general survey.

Pagden, Anthony. *European Encounters with the New World: From Renaissance to Romanticism.* 1993. A fascinating examination of how Europeans interpreted their encounters with America.

Parry, J. H. *The Age of Reconnaissance.* 1982. An analysis of European shipping technology and the causes behind European explorations. It covers all the major voyages.

Parry, J. H. *The Spanish Seaborne Empire.* 1990. The standard study on the subject. It brings together an enormous range of material and presents it clearly and cogently.

Phillips, William D. Jr., and Carla Rahn Phillips. *The Worlds of Christopher Columbus.* 1992. A balanced analysis of Columbus's attempts to find financing for his voyage that pays equal attention to his personal ambition, Christian zeal, and navigational skills.

Notes

1. Christopher Columbus, quoted in Felipe Fernández-Armesto, *Columbus* (1991), 154.
2. Sir Arthur Helps, *The Spanish Conquest in America,* vol. 1 (1900), 1, 264–267.
3. *The Book of Chilam Balam of Chumayel,* ed. and trans. Ralph L. Roy (1933), 83.
4. *The Conquistadores: First-Person Accounts of the Conquest of Mexico,* ed. and trans. Patricia de Fuentes (1963), 159.
5. *The Annals of the Cakchiquels and Title of the Lords of Totnicapán,* trans. Adrian Recinos, Dioniscio José Chonay, and Delia Goetz (1953), 116.
6. Quoted in ibid., 207. Spelling has been modernized.
7. Quoted in ibid., 369.

The Reformations of Religion, 1500–1560

O N OCTOBER 31, 1517, AN OBSCURE MONK-TURNED-UNIVERSITY-PROFESSOR nailed on the door of the cathedral in Wittenberg, Germany, an announcement containing ninety-five theses or debating propositions. Martin Luther had no hint of the ramifications of this simple act—as common then as posting an announcement for a lecture or concert on a university bulletin board now. But Luther's seemingly harmless deed would spark a revolution. Within weeks all Germany was ablaze over what was widely seen as Luther's daring attack on the pope. Within a few short years Wittenberg became the European center for a movement to reform the Church. As the pope and high churchmen resisted Martin Luther's call for reform, much of Germany and eventually most of northern Europe and Britain broke away from the Catholic Church in a movement called the Protestant Reformation, which dominated European affairs from 1517 until 1560.

Martin Luther was successful because he expressed in print what many felt in their hearts—that the Church was failing in its most fundamental obligation to help Christians achieve salvation. In contrast, many Catholics considered the Protestants dangerous heretics who offended God with their errors and whose heresies made salvation impossible. Moreover, many Catholics had long recognized the need for reforms in the Church and had been diligently working on achieving them. To them the intemperate Martin Luther only made matters worse.

The division between Protestants and Catholics split the West into two distinctive religious cultures. The result was that the hard-won unity of the West, which had been achieved during the Middle Ages through the expansion of Christianity to the most distant corners of the European continent and through

Chapter Outline

- Causes of the Reformation
- The Lutheran Reformation
- The Diversity of Protestantism
- The Catholic Reformation
- The Reformation in the Arts

The Imitation of Christ: In Albrecht Dürer's self-portrait at age 28, he literally shows himself imitating Christ's appearance. The initials AD are prominently displayed in the upper left-hand corner. They stand for Albrecht Dürer but also for *anno domini,* "the year of our Lord."

the leadership of the papacy, was lost. Catholics and Protestants continued to share a great deal of the Christian tradition, but fateful issues divided them: their understanding of salvation, the function of the sacraments in promoting pious behavior, the celebration of the liturgy in Latin, and obedience to the pope. After the Reformation of the sixteenth century, the common Christian culture was permanently severed by the Protestants' refusal to accept the authority of the pope on these issues.

This chapter will explore the reformations of religion undertaken by both Protestants and Catholics by addressing five central questions:

- What caused the religious rebellion that began in German-speaking lands and spread to much of northern Europe?
- How did the Lutheran Reformation create a new kind of religious culture?
- How and why did Protestant denominations multiply to such an extent in northern Europe and Britain?
- How did the Catholic Church reform itself during the same period?
- How did the religious turmoil of the sixteenth century transform the role of the visual arts in public life?

Causes of the Reformation

The Protestant Reformation was the culmination of nearly 200 years of turmoil within the Church. As we saw in Chapter 10, during the fourteenth and fifteenth centuries the Church was especially hampered by the contradiction between its divine mission and its obligations in this world. On the one hand, the Church taught that its mission was otherworldly, as the source of spiritual solace and the guide to eternal salvation. On the other hand, the Church was thoroughly of this world. It owned vast amounts of property, maintained a far-reaching judicial bureaucracy to enforce canon (Church) law, and was headed by the pope, who was also the territorial prince of the Papal State in central Italy. Whereas from the eleventh to the thirteenth centuries the popes had been the source of moral reform and spiritual renewal in the Church, by the fifteenth century they had become part of the problem. The problem was not so much that they had become corrupt but that they were unable to respond effectively to the demands of ordinary people who were increasingly concerned with their own salvation and the effective government of their communities.

Three developments, in particular, contributed to the demand for religious reform: the search for the freedom of private religious expression, the print revolution, and the

Northern Renaissance interest in the Bible and sources of Christianity. While the papacy's moral authority precipitously declined, lay Christians were drawn to new forms of worship. Particularly influential were the Modern Devotion, which was promoted by the Brothers of the Common Life, and the *Imitation of Christ,* written by a Common Life brother about 1441. By emphasizing frequent private prayer and moral introspection, the *Imitation* provided a kind of spiritual manual that helped laypeople follow the same path toward spiritual renewal that traditionally had been reserved for monks and nuns. The goal was to imitate Christ so thoroughly that Christ entered the believer's soul. For example, the 1500 self-portrait of Albrecht Dürer (1471–1528), a work influenced by the Modern Devotion, portrayed the artist as if he were Christ himself. This portrait is the opening image in this chapter.

The Modern Devotion and other trends in private devotion quickly spread in large part due to the invention of the printed book. Two fifteenth-century inventions revolutionized the availability of books. First, movable metal type was introduced around 1450, and after that time printed books first began to appear. Perhaps the very first was a Bible printed by Johannes Gutenberg in Mainz, Germany. Equally important, cheap manufactured paper replaced expensive sheepskins. These two developments reduced the cost of books to a level that made them available even to artisans of modest incomes.

Among the first to take advantage of the intellectual influence made possible by printed books were the humanists. As we saw in Chapter 11, the humanists were writers devoted to rediscovering the lost works of antiquity and developing the study of philology, of how the meanings of words change over time. The humanists who specialized in subjecting the Bible to philological study are called the Christian humanists°. In examining the sources of Christianity, their goal was not to criticize Christianity or the Church but to understand the precise meaning of its founding texts, especially the Bible and the writings of the Church fathers, who wrote in Greek and Latin and commented on the Bible during the early centuries of Christianity. The Christian humanists sought to correct what they saw as mistakes in interpreting Christian doctrine and by spreading what they saw as the proper interpretation to improve the moral behavior of all Christians.

By far the most influential of the Christian humanists was a Dutchman, Desiderius Erasmus (ca. 1469–1536). Exploiting the potential of the relatively new printing industry, Erasmus became the most inspiring moral critic of his times. During times of war he eloquently called for peace; he published a practical manual for helping children develop a sense of morality; and he laid out easy-to-follow guidelines for spiritual renewal in the *Handbook for the Militant Christian.* He was most popular for his biting criti-

Albrecht Dürer, *The Knight, Death, and the Devil*

This engraving of 1513 illustrates Erasmus's *Handbook for the Militant Christian* by depicting a knight steadfastly advancing through a frightening landscape. A figure of death holds an hourglass, indicating that the knight's time on Earth is limited. A devil follows behind him threateningly. His valiant horse and loyal dog represent the virtues that a pious Christian must acquire.

cisms of the Church that revealed a genuine spiritual sorrow shared by many of his readers:

> I could see that the common body of Christians was corrupt not only in its affections but in its ideas. I pondered on the fact that those who profess themselves pastors and doctors for the most part misuse these titles, which belong to Christ, for their own advantage. . . . Is there any religious man who does not see with sorrow that this generation is far the most corrupt there has ever been?[1]

Erasmus's lasting fame, however, rests on his perceptive philological analysis of the Bible and other early Christian texts. To the Christian humanists, the test for the legitimacy of any religious practice was whether it could be found in the Bible and whether it promoted moral behavior. The Christian humanists' preoccupation with textual criticism focused attention on the sources of Christianity, and some were profoundly shaken by the deep disparity they perceived between the Christianity of the New Testament and the state of the Church in their own time.

But Erasmus was also an eloquent popularizer. He demonstrated to a large public how individuals could apply to their daily lives previously obscure trends in humanist learning and how a better understanding of the Bible could purify faith and combat corruption within the Church. Erasmus remained a loyal Catholic, but his work helped popularize some of the principles that came to be associated with the Protestant reformers.

The Lutheran Reformation

The Protestant Reformation began with the protests of Martin Luther against the pope and certain Church practices. Luther and his followers would not have succeeded without the support of local political authorities, who had their own grievances against the pope and the

Holy Roman Emperor. The Lutheran Reformation first spread in Germany and later Scandinavia with the assistance and encouragement of local authorities: the town magistrates and the territorial princes. Luther's ideas also had a magnetic appeal to a wide spectrum of the population, especially women and peasants.

MARTIN LUTHER AND THE BREAK WITH ROME

Martin Luther (1483–1546) suffered a grim childhood and uneasy relationship with his father, a miner who wanted his son to become a lawyer. During a break from the University of Erfurt where he was studying law, Luther was thrown from his horse in a storm and nearly died. That frightening experience impelled him to become a monk, a decision that infuriated his father because it meant that young Luther abandoned a promising professional career. By becoming a monk, Luther replaced the control of his father with obedience to his superiors in the Augustinian Order. They sent him back to the University of Erfurt for advanced study in theology and then transferred him from the lovely garden city of Erfurt to Wittenberg in Saxony, a scruffy town "on the edge of beyond," as Luther described it. At Wittenberg Luther began to teach at an undistinguished university, far from the intellectual action. Instead of lamenting his isolation, Luther brought the world to his university by making it the center of the religious reform movement.

As a monk, Luther had been haunted by a deep lack of self-worth: "In the monastery, I did not think about women, or gold, or goods, but my heart trembled, and doubted how God could be gracious to me. Then I fell away from faith, and let myself think nothing less than that I had come under the Wrath of God, whom I must reconcile with my good works."[2] Obsessed by the fear that no amount of charitable good works, prayers, or religious ceremonies would compensate for God's contempt of him, Luther suffered from anxiety attacks and prolonged periods of depression. He understood his psychic turmoil and shaky faith as any monk would—the temptations of the Devil, who was a very powerful figure in Luther's life.

Over several years, while preparing and revising his university lectures on St. Paul, Luther gradually reexamined the theology of penance. The sacrament of penance provided a way to confess sins and receive absolution for them. If a penitent had lied, for example, he could seek forgiveness for the sin by feeling sorry about it, confessing it to a priest, and receiving a penalty, usually a specified number of prayers. Penance took care of only those penalties the Church could inflict on sinners; God's punishment for sins would take place in Purgatory (a place of temporary suffering for dead souls) and at the Last Judgment. But Catholic theology held that penance in this world would reduce punishment in the next. In wrestling with the concept of penance, Luther long meditated on the meaning of a difficult passage in St. Paul's Epistle to the Romans (1:17): "The just shall live by faith." Luther came to understand this passage to mean that eternal salvation came not from performing the religious good works of penance but as a gift from God. That gift was called "grace" and was completely unmerited. Luther called this process of receiving God's grace "justification by faith alone°," because the ability to have faith in Christ was a sign that one had received grace.

Luther's emphasis on justification by faith alone left no room for human free will in obtaining salvation, because Luther believed that faith could come only from God's grace. This did not mean that God controlled every human action, but it did mean that humans could not will to do good. They needed God's help. Those blessed with God's grace would naturally perform good works. This way of thinking about God's grace had a long tradition going back to St. Augustine, the Church father whose work profoundly influenced Luther's own thought. In fact, many Catholic thinkers had embraced a similar position, but they did not draw the same conclusions about free will that Luther did. In the turmoil of the Reformation Luther's interpretation of St. Augustine separated Lutheran from Catholic theology. The issue of free will became one of the most crucial differences between Protestants and Catholics. Based on his rejection of free will, Luther eventually concluded that the sacraments of the Church could work only if the person receiving them had received God's grace. One could not will them to work. He abandoned all but two of the sacraments because sacraments were examples of vain works that deluded people into thinking they could earn salvation by performing them. He was obliged to retain communion and baptism because they were clearly authorized by the Bible, but disputes over the meaning of these two sacraments created divisions within the Protestant Reformation movement itself.

For Luther this seemingly bleak doctrine of denying the human will to do good liberated him from his persistent fears of damnation. He no longer had to worry whether he was doing enough to please God or could muster enough energy to fight the Devil. All he had to do was trust in God's grace. After this breakthrough, Luther reported that "I felt myself to be born anew, and to enter through open gates into paradise itself. From here, the whole face of the Scriptures was altered."[3]

In 1517 Luther became embroiled in a controversy that led to the separation of him and his followers from the Roman Catholic Church. In order to finance the building of a new St. Peter's Basilica in Rome, Pope Leo X had issued a special new indulgence. An indulgence was a particular form of penance whereby a sinner could remove years of punishment in Purgatory after death by performing a good work here on Earth. For example, pilgrims to Rome or Jerusalem were often in search of indulgences, which were concrete measures of the value of their penances. Indulgences formed one of the most intimate bonds between the Church and the laity because they offered a means for the forgiveness of specific sins.

During the fourteenth century popes in need of ready cash had begun to sell indulgences. But Pope Leo's new indulgence went far beyond the promise of earlier indulgences by offering a one-time-only opportunity to escape penalties in Purgatory for all sins. Moreover, the special indulgence could apply not only to the purchaser but to the dead already in Purgatory. The new indulgence immediately made all other indulgences worthless because it removed all penalties for sin whereas others removed only some.

A group of the Wittenbergers asked Martin Luther for his advice about buying the new indulgence. Luther responded less as a pastor offering comforting advice to his flock than as a university professor keen for debate. He prepared in Latin ninety-five theses—arguments or talking points—about indulgences that he announced he was willing to defend in an academic disputation. Luther had a few copies printed and according to Lutheran tradition dramatically posted one on the door of Wittenberg Cathedral. In fact, his posting of the theses makes a good story, but there is no evidence that he actually did so. It was just standard practice for debates. The Ninety-Five Theses were hardly revolutionary in themselves. They argued a simple point that salvation could not be bought and sold, a proposition that was sound, conservative theology, and explicitly accepted the authority of the pope even as they set limits on that authority. On that point, Luther was merely following what the Church councils of the fifteenth century had decreed. Luther's tone was moderate. He simply suggested that Pope Leo may have been misled in issuing the new indulgence. No one showed up to debate Luther, but someone translated the Ninety-Five Theses into German and printed them, and within a few weeks, a previously unknown professor from an obscure university was the talk of the German-speaking lands.

After Pope Leo rejected Luther's objections to indulgences and threatened to excommunicate him, Luther abandoned his moderate tone and launched an inflammatory pamphlet campaign. Some pamphlets were first written in Latin for learned readers, but all soon became available in Luther's acerbic German prose, which delighted readers. *Freedom of a Christian* (1520) argued that the Church's emphasis on good works had distracted Christians from the only source of salvation—God's grace, which was manifest in the faith of the Christian. It proclaimed the revolutionary doctrine of the "priesthood of all believers°," which reasoned that all those of pure faith were themselves priests, a doctrine that undermined the authority of the Catholic clergy over the laity. The most inspirational pamphlet, *To the Christian Nobility of the German Nation* (1520), called on the German princes to reform the Church and to defend Germany from exploitation by the corrupt Italians who ran the Church in Rome. When Pope Leo ordered Luther to retract his writings, Luther responded with a defiant demonstration in which he and his students burned the pope's decree and all of the university library's books of Church law. The die was cast.

The pope demanded that Luther be arrested, but Luther's patron, Frederick the Wise, the Elector of Saxony (a princely title indicating that he was one of those who elected the emperors of the Holy Roman Empire) answered by defending the professor. Frederick refused to make the arrest without first giving Luther a hearing at the Imperial Diet (parliament), which was set to meet at the town of Worms in 1521. Assembled at the Diet of Worms were haughty princes, grave bishops, and the resplendent young Emperor Charles V (r. 1519–1558), who was presiding over his first Imperial Diet. The emperor ordered Luther to disavow his writings, but Luther refused to do so. For several days the diet was in an uproar, divided by friends and foes of Luther's doctrines. Just before he was to be condemned by the emperor, Luther disappeared, and rumors flew that he had been assassinated. For days no one knew the truth. Frederick the Wise had kidnapped Luther for his own safety and hidden him in the castle at Wartburg, where for nearly a year he labored in quiet seclusion translating the New Testament into German.

THE LUTHERAN REFORMATION IN THE CITIES AND PRINCIPALITIES

Luther had escaped arrest and execution at the hands of the emperor, but he could not control his own followers and allies. The Reformation quickly became a vast, sprawling movement far beyond the control of any individual, even in Luther's own Wittenberg. One of the characteristics of the Protestant Reformation was that once reformers rejected the supreme authority of the papacy, differences about forms of worship or biblical interpretation led to division within the movement and eventually to the formation of separate churches.

In its early phases the Reformation spread most rapidly among the educated urban classes. During the sixteenth century, fifty of the sixty-five German imperial cities, at one time or another, officially accepted the Protestant Reformation. Besides these large imperial cities, most of the 200 smaller German towns with a population of more than 1,000 experienced some form of the Protestant movement. During the 1520s and 1530s, the magistrates (mayors and other office holders) of these towns took command of the Reformation movement by seizing control of the local churches. The magistrates implemented Luther's reform of worship, disciplined the clergy, and stopped the drain of revenues to irresponsible bishops and the distant pope.

The German princes of the Holy Roman Empire had their own reasons to resent the Church. They wanted to appoint their own nominees to ecclesiastical offices and to diminish the legal privileges of the clergy. During the 1520s Luther's enormous popularity gave many German princes the opportunity they had been waiting for. Despite his steadfast Catholicism, Emperor Charles V was in no position to resist their demands. During most of his reign, Charles faced a two-front war—against France and against the Ottoman Turks. Charles could ill afford additional trouble with the German princes because he desperately needed their military assistance. At the first Imperial Diet of Speyer in 1526, Charles granted the princes territorial sovereignty in religion by allowing them to decide whether they would enforce the imperial edict of the Diet of Worms against Luther and his followers. To preserve the empire from external enemies, Charles was forced to allow its internal division along religious lines.

The Appeal of the Reformation to Women and Peasants

As divisive as Reformist theology was to imperial politics, it had a particular appeal to people who were habitually excluded from the political world, especially women and peasants. In the early days of the movement, women felt that Luther's description of "the priesthood of all believers" meant that women as well as men could participate fully in the religious life of the Church. Women understood Luther's phrase "the freedom of a Christian" as freeing them from the restrictive roles that had traditionally kept them silent and at home. Moreover, Luther and the other major reformers saw positive religious value in the role of wife and mother. Abandoning the Catholic Church's view that celibate monks and nuns were morally superior to married people, Luther declared marriage holy and after considerable resistance and delay set an example by taking a wife, the ex-nun Katherine von Bora. The wives of the reformers often became partners in the Reformation, taking particular responsibility for organizing charities and administering to the poor.

The Reformation appealed to many peasants simply because it offered them a simplified, purified religion and, most important, local control of the church. However, other peasants understood the Reformation in more radical terms as licensing social reforms that Luther himself never supported.

In June 1524 a revolt of peasants broke out in many parts of Germany. Over the next two years, the rebellion spread as peasants rose up against their feudal lords to demand the adoption of Lutheran reforms in the Church, a reduction of feudal privileges, the abolition of serfdom, and the self-government of their communities.

These peasants were doing exactly what they thought Luther had advocated when he wrote about the "freedom of the Christian." They interpreted his words to mean complete social as well as religious freedom. However, Luther had not meant anything of the sort. To him the freedom of the Christian referred to inner, spiritual freedom, not liberation from economic or political bondage. Instead of supporting the rebellion begun in his name, Luther and nearly all the other reformers backed the feudal lords and condemned in uncompromising terms the violence of the peasant armies. In *Against the Thieving, Murderous Hordes of Peasants* (1525), Luther expressed his own fear of the lower classes and revealed that despite his acid-tongued attacks on the pope, he was fundamentally a conservative thinker who was committed to law and order. He urged that the peasants be hunted down and killed like rabid dogs. And so they were. Between 70,000 and 100,000 peasants died, a slaughter far greater than the Roman persecutions of the early Christians. To the peasants, Luther's conservative position on social and economic issues felt like betrayal, but it enabled the Lutheran Reformation to retain the support of the princes, which was essential for its survival.

Lutheran Success

Soon after the crushing of the Peasants' Revolt, the Lutheran Reformation faced a renewed threat from its Catholic opponents. In 1530 Emperor Charles V bluntly commanded all Lutherans to return to the Catholic fold or face arrest. Enraged, the Lutherans refused to comply. The following year the Protestant princes formed a military alliance, the Schmalkaldic League, against the emperor. Renewed trouble with France and the Turks prevented a military confrontation between the league and the emperor for fifteen years, giving the Lutherans enough breathing space to put the Reformation on a firmer basis in Germany by training ministers and educating the laity in the new religion. In the meantime Lutheranism spread beyond Germany into Scandinavia, where it received support from the kings of Denmark and Sweden as it had among the princes of northern Germany.

After freeing himself yet again from foreign wars and failing to effect a compromise solution in Germany, Charles V turned his armies against the Protestants. However, in 1552 the Protestant armies defeated in battle the Catholic forces of the emperor, and Charles was forced to relent. In 1555 the Religious Peace of Augsburg° established the principle of *cuius regio, eius religio,* which means "he who rules determines the religion of the land." Protestant princes were permitted to retain all church lands seized before 1552 and to enforce Protestant worship, but Catholic princes were also allowed to enforce Catholic worship in their territories. Those who disagreed with the religion of their ruler would not be tolerated; their options were to change religious affiliations or to emigrate elsewhere. With the Peace of Augsburg the religious division of the Holy Roman Empire became permanent, and the legal foundations were in place for the development of the two distinctive religious cultures—Protestant and Catholic.

The Diversity of Protestantism

The term *Protestant* originally applied only to those followers of Luther who *protested* the decisions of the second Imperial Diet of Speyer in 1529, which attempted to force them back into the Catholic fold, but the term came to describe much more than that small group. It designated all western European Christians who refused to accept the authority of the pope. Protestantism encompassed innumerable churches and sects. Many of these have survived since the Reformation; some disappeared in the violence of the sixteenth century; others have sprung up since, especially in North America, where Protestantism has thrived.

The varieties of Protestantism can be divided into two types. The first type was the product of the Magisterial Reformation°, which refers to the churches that received official government sanction. These included the Lutheran churches (Germany and Scandinavia); the Reformed and Calvinist churches (Switzerland, Scotland, the Netherlands, and a few places in Germany); and the Anglican church (England and later its colonies). The second type was the

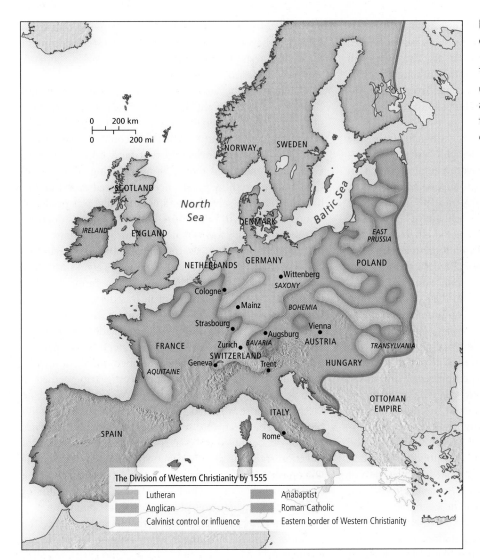

■ **Map 13.1 The Division of Western Christianity by 1555**
The West, which had been culturally unified by Christianity for more than a thousand years, split apart during the sixteenth century. These religious divisions persist to this day.

The Division of Western Christianity by 1555

Lutheran		Anabaptist	
Anglican		Roman Catholic	
Calvinist control or influence		Eastern border of Western Christianity	

product of the Radical Reformation° and includes the movements that failed to gain official recognition and were at best tolerated, at worst persecuted. This strict division into Magisterial and Radical Protestantism broke down in eastern Europe, where the states were too weak to enforce religious conformity. In eastern Europe religious variety prevailed over rigid conformity, at least for the sixteenth century (see Map 13.1).

THE REFORMATION IN SWITZERLAND

The independence of Switzerland from the Holy Roman Empire meant that from the beginning of the Reformation local authorities could cooperate with the reformers without opposition from the emperor, as was the case in Germany prior to 1555 when the Religious Peace of Augsburg established the principle that he who rules establishes the religion of the land. Except for the leading cities of Zürich, Basel, and Geneva, Switzerland remained an impoverished land of peasants who could not fully support

themselves from the barren mountainous land. To supplement their meager incomes, young Swiss men fought as mercenaries in foreign armies, often those of the pope. The strain created by the mercenary's life stimulated the desire for sweeping reforms in Switzerland.

Zwingli's Zürich
Ulrich Zwingli (1484–1531) had served as a chaplain with the Swiss mercenaries serving the pope in Italy. In 1520, after being named the People's Priest of Zürich, Zwingli criticized his superior bishop for recruiting local young men to die in the papal armies. That same year he began to call for reform of the Church, advocating the abolition of the Roman Catholic mass, the marriage of priests, and the closing of monasteries. One of the novel features of Zwingli's reform was the strict emphasis on preaching the Word of Scripture during Church services, in contrast to the emphasis on ritual in the traditional Catholic liturgy. He ordered the removal of all paintings and statues from churches because they were too powerful a distraction

from concentrating on the preaching. Zwingli was certainly influenced by the writings of Erasmus, but he denied that Luther had any effect on him at all. The Zwinglian Reformation began independently of the Lutheran Reformation and created a separate reform center from which initiatives spread throughout Switzerland, southern Germany, and England.

Two features distinguished the Zwinglian from the Lutheran Reformation. One was Zwingli's desire to have reformed ministers participate in governmental decisions. In Lutheran Germany, church and state supported each other, but they remained legally separate, and the prince alone had the authority to determine the religion of the land. In Zürich, the moral Christian and the good citizen were one and the same, and Zwingli worked with the magistrates of the city council, who step-by-step legalized the Reformation and enforced conformity through its police powers.

Luther and Zwingli also differed in their understanding of the nature of the Eucharist, the communion sacrament that reenacted Christ's Last Supper with his apostles. Luther believed that Christ's body was spiritually present in the communion bread. "You will receive," as he put it, "as much as you believe you receive."[4] This emphasis on the inner, spiritual state of the believer was very characteristic of Luther's introspective piety. In contrast to Luther, Zwingli could not accept the idea of Almighty God making himself present in a humble piece of bread. To Zwingli the Eucharistic bread was just a symbol that stood for the body of Christ. The problem with the symbolic interpretation of the Eucharist was that the various reformers could not agree with Zwingli on exactly what the Eucharist symbolized. As early as 1524, it became evident that each reformer was committed to a different interpretation, and these different interpretations became the basis for different Protestant churches.

In 1529 Count Philip of Hesse (1504–1567) tried to forge a military alliance between the Protestants of Germany and Switzerland against the Catholics. The theological disputes over the Eucharist blocked full cooperation, however. Philip brought together Luther, Zwingli, and the other principal reformers for a formal discussion at the new Protestant university of Marburg. But Luther adamantly refused to compromise and shrugged off Zwingli's tearful pleas for cooperation. The failure of the Marburg Colloquy marked the permanent rupture of the Reformation movement.

Calvin's Geneva

In the next generation the momentum of the Reformation shifted to Geneva, Switzerland, under the leadership of John Calvin (1509–1564). Calvin arrived in French-speaking Geneva as a religious refugee in 1536, and came to support the city's long struggle for independence from the Duke of Savoy, who had been rejected as the city's lord a few years before. Calvin worked with the Genevan magistrates who attempted to build a holy community that was independent of the dictates of the city's Catholic bishop. But Calvinism spread far beyond its Swiss home, becoming the dominant form of Protestantism in France, the Netherlands, Scotland, and New England.

Calvin's theology extended the insights of Luther and Zwingli to their logical conclusion. This pattern was most obvious in his understanding of justification by faith. Luther had argued that the Christian could not earn salvation through good works and that faith came only from God. Calvin reasoned that if an all-knowing, all-powerful God knew everything in advance and caused everything to happen, then the salvation of any individual was predetermined or, as Calvin put it, "predestined." Calvin's doctrine of predestination° was not new. In fact, it had long been discussed among Christian theologians. But for Calvin two considerations made it crucial. First was Calvin's certainty that God was above any influence from humanity. The "majesty of God," as Calvin put it, was the principle from which everything else followed. Second, Calvin and other preachers had noticed that in a congregation attending a sermon, only a few listened and paid attention to what was preached, while the vast majority seemed unable or unwilling to understand. The reason for this disparity seemed to be that only the Elect could truly follow God's Word. The Elect were those who had received God's grace and would be saved. The Elect were known only to God, but Calvin's theology encouraged the converted to feel the assurance of salvation and to accept a "calling" from God to perform his will on earth. God's calling° gave Calvinists a powerful sense of personal direction, which committed them to a life of moral activity, whether as preacher, wife, or shoemaker.

Calvin composed an elegant theological treatise, the *Institutes of the Christian Religion,* first published in six chapters in 1535 but constantly revised and expanded until it reached eighty chapters in the definitive 1559 edition. Trained as a lawyer, Calvin wrote a tightly argued and reasoned work, like a trial attorney preparing a case. In Calvin's theology the parts fit neatly together like a vast, intricate puzzle. Calvin's work aspired to be a comprehensive reformed theology that would convince through reasoned deliberation, and it became the first systematic presentation of Protestant doctrine. Whereas Luther spun out his sometimes contradictory ideas in a series of often polemical pamphlets, Calvin devoted himself to perfecting his comprehensive theology of Protestantism and using it as the foundation for a holy community of the Elect.

Given its emphasis on building a holy community, Calvinism helped transform the nuclear family into a social unit for training and disciplining children, a family in which women had a vital educational function that in turn encouraged women's literacy. Calvinist communities also began to allow divorce for women who had been abused by their husbands. Calvinist women and men were both disciplined and liberated—disciplined to avoid physical and material pleasures, and liberated from the necessity to do good works but guided by God's grace to do them anyway.

THE REFORMATION IN BRITAIN

Great Britain, as the island kingdom is known today, did not exist in the sixteenth century. The Tudor dynasty, which began in 1485 with Henry VII, ruled over England, Wales, and Ireland, but Scotland was still a separate kingdom with its own monarch and church institutions. These countries had distinctive political traditions, culture, and language, and as a result their Reformation experiences differed considerably. The Tudors imposed the Reformation as a matter of royal policy, and they were mostly successful in England and Wales. But they hardly made a dent in the religious culture of Ireland, which was a remarkable exception to the European pattern of conformity to the religion of the ruler. There the vast majority of the population were Catholics, a faith different from that of their Protestant monarch. Scotland, also an exception to the rule, wholeheartedly accepted the Protestant Reformation against the will of its Catholic queen and most of the clergy.

The Tudors and the English Reformation

In 1527 the rotund, self-absorbed, but crafty King Henry VIII (r. 1509–1547) announced that he had come to the pious conclusion that he had gravely sinned by marrying his brother's widow, Catherine of Aragon. By this time the couple had been married for eighteen years, their only living child was the princess Mary, and at age 42 Catherine was unlikely to give birth to more children. Henry let it be known that he wanted a son, mostly to secure the English throne for the Tudor dynasty. He also had his eye on the most engaging woman of the court, Anne Boleyn, who was less than half Catherine's age. In the past popes had usually been cooperative when a powerful king needed an annulment, but Pope Clement VII (r. 1523–1534) was in no position to oblige Henry. At the time of the marriage, the papal curia had issued a dispensation for Henry to marry his brother's widow, a practice that is prohibited in the Bible. In effect, Henry was asking the papacy to admit it had made a mistake. In addition, at the moment when Henry's petition for divorce arrived, Clement was under the control of Catherine's nephew, the Emperor Charles V, whose armies had recently captured and sacked the city of Rome. In 1531 Henry gave up trying to obtain papal approval and definitively separated from Catherine. Eighteen months later he secretly married Anne Boleyn. England's compliant Archbishop Thomas Cranmer (1489–1556) pronounced the marriage to Catherine void and the one to Anne valid. But the marriage to Anne did not last. When she began to displease him, Henry had her arrested, charged with incest with her brother and adultery with other men. She was convicted and beheaded.

The English separation from the Roman Catholic Church, which took place in 1534 through Acts of Supremacy and Succession, passed at Henry's request by the English Parliament, has often been understood as a by-product of Henry's capricious lust and the plots of his brilliant minister, Thomas Cromwell (ca. 1485–1540). It is certainly true that Henry's desire to rid himself of Catherine led him to reject papal authority and to establish himself as the head of the Church of England. It is also certainly true that Henry was an inconstant husband: Of his six wives, two were divorced and two beheaded. However, the English Reformation cannot be explained simply as the consequence of royal whim or the machinations of a single minister.

The English Reformation began as a declaration of royal independence from papal supervision rather than an attempt to reform the practices of the Church. Under Henry VIII the English Reformation could be described as Catholicism without the pope. Protestant doctrine, at first, had little role in the English Reformation, and Henry had himself been one of the most vociferous critics of Martin Luther. Royal supremacy established control over the Church by granting to the king supervising authority over liturgical rituals and religious doctrines. Thomas Cromwell, who worked out the practical details for parliamentary legislation, was himself a Protestant, and no doubt his religious views emboldened him to reject papal authority. But the principal theorist of royal supremacy was a Catholic, Thomas Starkey (ca. 1499–1538). A sojourn in Italy had acquainted Starkey with Italian Renaissance political theory, which emphasized concepts of civic liberty. In fact, even many English Catholics found the change acceptable as long as it meant only abandoning submission to the pope in distant Rome. Those who opposed cutting the connection to Rome suffered for their opposition. Bishop John Fisher (ca. 1469–1535) and Sir Thomas More (1478–1535), the humanist friend of Erasmus and former chancellor of England, were both executed for their refusal to go along with the king's decision.

With this display of despotic power, Henry seized personal control of the English church and then closed the monasteries and confiscated their lands. He redistributed the monastic lands to the nobility in an effort to purchase their support and to make money for the crown. Henry's officials briefly flirted with some Protestant reforms, but theological innovations were largely avoided. The Reformation of Henry VIII was more significant for consolidating the dynastic power of the Tudors than for initiating wide-ranging religious reform. On the local level many people embraced the Reformation for their own reasons, often because it gave them a sense of control over the affairs of their community. Others went along simply because the power of the king was too strong to resist.

Henry's six wives bore three surviving children. As each succeeded to the throne, the official religion of England

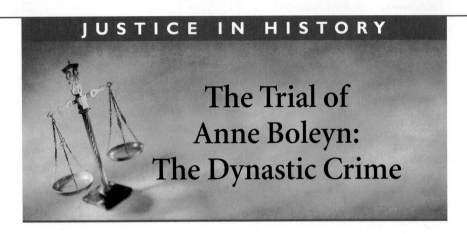

The Trial of Anne Boleyn: The Dynastic Crime

Anne Boleyn, the first of Henry VIII's wives to be executed, was beheaded in the Tower of London's courtyard in May 1536, just a few hundred feet from the hall in which she had celebrated her coronation three years earlier. She had been tried by a court of peers and unanimously convicted of high treason. The evidence against her was for adultery, but the alleged adultery of a queen was considered treason because it put in question the paternity of potential heirs to the throne. Queen Anne insisted on her innocence until the end, but her final address to the crowd did not protest her execution. Instead, she said, "According to the law and by the law I am judged to die, and therefore I will speak nothing against it."[5] To twenty-first-century observers, Anne seems to accept her unjust fate passively. To sixteenth-century observers, however, she died "boldly," and her refusal to admit guilt and to accept the law was one of the best indicators of her innocence.

To understand Anne Boleyn's scaffold statement, it is necessary to look at the idea of a "fair trial" in sixteenth-century England. She was condemned for high treason because of her supposed adultery with five men, including her own brother. But her supposed lovers were in other places when the adulteries were alleged to have taken place—evidence that casts doubt on their truth. She was unable to present this evidence, which today would serve as an alibi for the defendant, because

she heard the charges against her for the first time at the actual trial. The queen enjoyed no counsel for the defense, had no opportunity to call witnesses on her own behalf, and had no protection against self-incrimination. Because she was the queen of England, her trial was unusual, but these procedures were standard in the sixteenth century.

It was widely known that the king wished her death, but because her trial followed the accepted legal procedures, it was considered a fair trial by the standards of the sixteenth century. When Anne married Henry, who had recently divorced Catherine of Aragon, Anne's most important role was to provide the king with a male heir. Anne soon gave birth to a daughter, Elizabeth, but she then suffered two miscarriages. Some historians argue that Henry wanted to get rid of Anne in favor of her younger rival, Jane Seymour, but others have suggested that because the fetus of Anne's second miscarriage was deformed, she was suspected of witchcraft. Henry

himself stated that he had been seduced by witchcraft, which was why God had not permitted him to have a son. He considered the marriage null and void because Anne's witchery had coerced him into the liaison. As far as Henry was concerned, Anne's failure to bear him a son was evidence of some sort of wrongdoing on her part. It remained only to construct a case against her.

The king and his prosecutors assembled a large number of statements about Anne's infidelity, which shocked

■ **Portrait of King Henry VIII**

This portrait by Hans Holbein the Younger depicts Henry as he looked shortly after Queen Anne's execution.

■ **Portrait Sketch of Anne Boleyn**

This portrait of Anne Boleyn may be by Hans Holbein the Younger. It was probably painted while Anne was queen of England.

observers of the trial. John Husee wrote, "I think verily, if all the books and chronicles . . . which against woman hath been penned, contrived, and written since Adam and Eve, those same were, I think, verily nothing in comparison of that which hath been done and committed by Anne the Queen." James Spelman commented, "All the evidence was of bawdery and lechery, so that there was no such whore in all the realm."[6]

The quantity and offensive nature of the evidence was part of a propaganda campaign Henry orchestrated to convince the members of the nobility and the English people that Anne's execution was justified.

Despite the careful orchestration of the trial, the preponderance of the evidence, and the procedures that denied her systematic defense, Anne Boleyn managed to convince a number of observers that she was innocent. Charles Wriothesley recounted, "She made so wise and discreet answers to all things laid against her, excusing herself through her words so clearly as though she had never been faulty to the same."[7] Most telling was the opinion of Chapuys, the ambassador of Emperor Charles V to Henry's court. Chapuys had previously been hostile to Anne, but he considered the whole trial a sham. After the jury returned a guilty verdict, Anne herself shrewdly ob-

served, "I believe you have reasons . . . upon which you have condemned me: but they must be other than those that have been produced in court."[8]

The trial of Anne Boleyn was a classic example of the triumph of judicial form over the substance of evidence. Since Henry and the prosecutors had followed the proper trial procedures, they believed they were above reproach on legal grounds. Anne had been justly condemned even if the evidence against her had been faked. ■

Questions of Justice

1. Assuming that the evidence against Anne was false, why was it deemed necessary for the alleged treason of a queen to be defined as adultery rather than something else, such as witchcraft or heresy?

2. What do these charges tell us about the nature of early modern conceptions of kingship?

Taking It Further

Guy, John. *Tudor England*. 1990. Taking account of recent scholarship, this is the best general history of the period. It includes illuminating portraits of the principal figures.

Warnicke, Retha M. *The Rise and Fall of Anne Boleyn: Family Politics at the Court of Henry VIII*. 1991. Based on a careful examination of all the available evidence, Warnicke shows how the trial was a consequence of Henry VIII's desire to preserve his dynasty.

gyrated wildly. Because his youngest child, Edward, was a male, Henry designed him successor to the throne. His two daughters, Mary and Elizabeth, were to succeed only in the event that Edward died without an heir, which he did. Only ten years old when he followed his father to the throne, King Edward VI (r. 1547–1553) was the pawn of his Protestant protectors, some of whom pushed for a more thorough Protestant Reformation in England than Henry had espoused. After Edward's premature death, his half-sister, Queen Mary I (r. 1553–1558), daughter of Henry and Catherine of Aragon, attempted to bring England back to obedience to the pope. Her unpopular marriage to the king of Spain and her failure to retain the support of the nobles, who were the foundation of Tudor government, damaged the Catholic cause in England.

Mary's successor and half-sister, Elizabeth Tudor, the daughter of Henry and Anne Boleyn, was an entirely different sort. Queen Elizabeth I (r. 1558–1603), raised as a Protestant, kept her enemies off balance and her quarrelsome subjects firmly in hand with her tremendous charisma and shrewd political judgments.

Between 1559 and 1563, Elizabeth repealed the Catholic legislation of Mary and promulgated her own Protestant laws, collectively known as the Elizabethan Settlement, which established the Church of England, known as the Anglican Church (Episcopalian in the United States). The touchstone of the Elizabethan Settlement was the Thirty-Nine Articles (finally approved by Parliament in 1571), which articulated a moderate version of Protestantism. It retained the ecclesiastical hierarchy of bishops as well as an essentially Catholic liturgy translated into English. This "middle way" between Roman Catholicism and militant Calvinism was ably defended by the moderate Calvinist Richard Hooker (1553–1600), whose *Laws of Ecclesiastical Polity* emphasized how the law as promulgated by the royal government manifested the divine order.

Scotland: The Citadel of Calvinism

While England groped its way toward moderate Protestantism, neighboring Scotland became one of the most thoroughly Calvinist countries in Europe. In 1560 the parliament of Scotland, with encouragement from Queen Elizabeth of England, overthrew Roman Catholicism against the will of Mary Stuart, Queen of Scots (1542–1587).

The Scots Confession of 1560, written by a panel of six reformers, established the new church. John Knox (ca. 1514–1572) breathed a strongly Calvinist air into the church through his many polemical writings and the official liturgy he composed in 1564, the *Book of Common Order.* Knox emphasized faith and individual Christian conscience over ecclesiastical authority, a priority that discouraged compromise among the Scots. Instead of the episcopal structure in England, which granted bishops the authority over doctrine and discipline, the Scots Church (Kirk in Scottish) established a Presbyterian form of organization, which gave

organizational authority to the pastors and elders of the congregations, all of whom had equal rank. As a result the Presbyterian congregations were more independent and subject to local variations than the episcopal structure allowed in the Anglican Church.

THE RADICAL REFORMATION

The magisterial reformers in Germany, Switzerland, England, and Scotland managed to obtain official sanction for their religious reforms, often at the cost of some compromise with governmental authorities. As a result of those compromises, the magisterial reformers were challenged by radicals from among their own followers who demanded faster, more thorough reform. In most places the radicals represented a small minority, perhaps never more than 2 percent of all Protestants. But their significance outstripped their small numbers, in part because they forced the magisterial reformers to respond to their arguments and because their enemies attempted to eradicate them through extreme violence.

The radicals can be divided into three categories: Anabaptists, who attempted to construct a holy community on the basis of literal readings of the Bible; Spiritualists, who abandoned all forms of organized religion to allow individuals to follow the inner voice of the Holy Spirit; and Unitarians, who advocated a rational religion that emphasized ethical behavior over ceremonies.

The Anabaptists: The Holy Community

For Anabaptists, the Bible was a blueprint for reforming not just the church but all of society. Because the Bible reported that Jesus was an adult when he was baptized, the Anabaptists rejected infant baptism and adopted adult baptism (Anabaptism° means to rebaptize). An adult, they believed, could accept baptism as an act of faith, unlike an oblivious infant. Anabaptists saw the sacraments of baptism and communion as symbols of faith, which had no purpose or meaning unless the recipient was already a person of faith. Adult baptism reserved for the faithful few allowed the creation of a pure church, isolated from the sinfulness of the world.

Because they did not want the faithful to be tainted by contact with the sinful, Anabapists advocated the complete separation of Church and state. Anabaptists sought to obey only God and completely rejected all established religious and political authorities; they required adherents to refuse to serve in government offices, swear oaths, pay taxes, or fight in armies. Anabaptists sought to live in highly disciplined "holy communities," which excommunicated errant members and practiced simple services based on scriptural readings. Because the Anabaptist communities consisted largely of uneducated peasants, artisans, and miners, a dimension of economic radicalism colored the early

Anabaptist movement. For example, some Anabaptist radicals advocated the elimination of all private property and the sharing of wealth. On the position of women, however, Anabaptists were staunchly conservative, denying women any public role in religious affairs and insisting that they remain under the strict control of their fathers and husbands.

Because the Anabaptists promoted such a radical reorganization of society along biblical lines, they provoked a violent reaction. In Zürich the city council decreed that the appropriate punishment was for all Anabaptists to be drowned in the local river where they had been rebaptizing themselves. By 1529 it became a capital offense in the Holy Roman Empire to be rebaptized, and during the sixteenth century perhaps as many as 5,000 Anabaptists were executed for the offense, a persecution that tended to fragment the Anabaptists into isolated, secretive rural communities. The Amish and Mennonites in North America are remnants of sixteenth-century Anabaptists. Inspired by the early Anabaptists, the modern Baptists in Britain and America owe their foundation to later developments of the seventeenth century.

Spiritualists: The Holy Individual

Whereas the Anabaptists radicalized the Swiss Reformation's emphasis on building a godly community, the Spiritualists° radicalized Luther's commitment to personal introspection. Perhaps the greatest Spiritualist was the aristocratic Caspar Schwenckfeld (1490–1561), who was a friend of Luther's until he broke with the reformer over what he considered the weak spirituality of established Lutheranism. Schwenckfeld believed that depraved humanity was incapable of casting off the bonds of sin, which only a supernatural act of God could achieve. This separation from sinfulness was revealed through an intense conversion experience, after which the believer gained spiritual illumination. Schwenckfeld called this illumination the "inner Word," which he understood as a living form of the Scriptures written directly on the believer's soul by the hand of God. Schwenckfeld also prized the "outer Word," that is, the Scriptures, but he found the emotional experience of the inner Word more powerful than the intellectual experience that came from reading the Bible. Spiritualists reflected an inner peace evident in their calm physical appearance, lack of anxiety, and mastery of bodily appetites—a state Schwenckfeld called the "castle of peace."

Unitarians: A Rationalist Approach

The universal acceptance of the Trinity among Christians changed in the middle of the sixteenth century with the emergence of numerous radical sects that rejected the divinity of Christ. They were called Arians, Socinians, Anti-Trinitarians, or Unitarians°. Distinctive to Christian theology—in comparison to other monotheistic religions, such as Judaism and Islam—is the doctrine of the Trinity, which posits that the one God has three identities—God the Father, God the Son, and God the Holy Spirit. The doctrine of the Trinity made it possible for Christians to believe that God the Son "took on flesh" in what is called the "incarnation." At a particular moment in history, God became the human being Jesus Christ. The doctrine of the Trinity was officially established as Christian dogma at the Council of Nicea in 325, in response to the Arian heresy, which had denied that Christ was "co-eternal" with God the Father. The Trinitarian Christians thought the Arian doctrine denied Christ's full divinity.

During the sixteenth-century Reformation various forms of the Arian doctrine were revived. The Italian Faustus Socinus (1539–1604) taught a rationalist interpretation of the Scriptures and argued that Jesus was a divinely inspired man, not God-become-man. Socinus's followers thus rejected the doctrine of the Trinity, which they found contrary to simple common sense and without support in Scripture. Socinus's ideas remain central to Unitarianism—the specific rejection of Trinitarian doctrine and the general emphasis on rationality.

The Anabaptists and Unitarians shared some early connections and similarities, but the two groups soon parted ways. Both Anabaptists and Unitarians followed the logic of their own beliefs and were unwilling to compromise with other Protestants. Anabaptists isolated themselves in their own communities and avoided contact with outsiders to avoid pollution from sinners and persecution from the authorities. Unitarians were more open to public debate, and in eastern Europe they attracted support from the powerful.

THE FREE WORLD OF EASTERN EUROPE

During the sixteenth century eastern Europe offered a measure of religious freedom and toleration unknown elsewhere in Europe. As a result, eastern Europe was open to considerable religious experimentation and attracted refugees from the oppressive princes of western Europe. Such religious toleration was made possible by the relative weakness of the monarchs in Bohemia, Hungary, Transylvania, and especially Poland-Lithuania, where the great land-owning aristocrats exercised nearly complete freedom on their estates. All of these kingdoms had Catholic monarchs, but the Reformation radicalized the aristocrats who dominated the parliaments, enabling Protestantism to take hold even against the wishes of the monarch.

No other country was as tolerant of religious diversity as Transylvania (now in Romania), largely because of the weak monarchy, which could not have enforced religious uniformity even if the king had wanted to do so. In Transylvania, Unitarianism took hold more firmly than anywhere else. In 1572 the tolerant ruler Prince István Báthory (r. 1571–1586) granted the Unitarians complete legal equality to establish their own churches along with Catholics, Lutherans, and Calvinists—the only place in Europe where equality of religions was achieved. Transylvania was also home to significant communities of Jews, Armenian Christians, and Orthodox Christians.

The sixteenth century was the golden age of the Polish-Lithuanian Commonwealth, which was by far the largest state in Europe. It escaped both the Ottoman invasions and the religious wars that plagued the Holy Roman Empire. From the Lutheran cities in the German-speaking north to the vast open plains of Great Poland, where Calvinism took hold among the independent-minded nobility, religious lines often had been drawn along ethnic or class divisions. When Sigismund August (r. 1548–1572) became king, he declared, "I am not king of men's conscience," and inaugurated extensive toleration of Protestant churches, even while the vast majority of peasants remained loyal to Orthodoxy or Catholicism. Fleeing persecution in other countries, various Anabaptist groups and Unitarians found refuge in Poland. This extensive religious diversity in Poland later disappeared during the Catholic Reformation.

The Catholic Reformation

The Catholic Reformation, also known as the Counter Reformation, profoundly revitalized the Catholic Church and established an institutional and doctrinal framework that persisted into the late twentieth century. The Catholic Reformation° was a series of efforts to purify the Church; these efforts were not necessarily just a reaction to the Protestant Reformation but evolved out of late medieval spirituality, driven by many of the same impulses that stimulated the Protestants. The most important of these efforts was the creation of new religious orders, especially the Society of Jesus, whose members are known as the Jesuits. They promoted a vast educational program that improved understanding of the faith and a missionary effort that spread Christianity throughout the world. However, the Church also responded to the challenge of the Protestant Reformation by establishing the Holy Office of the Inquisition, promulgating the *Index of Forbidden Books,* and implementing the decrees of the Council of Trent (1545–1563).

THE RELIGIOUS ORDERS IN THE CATHOLIC REFORMATION

The most dramatic and effective manifestation of the Catholic Reformation was the founding of new religious orders. By far the most influential new order was the Society of Jesus. In 1540 Ignatius Loyola (1491–1556) and a group of kindred spirits organized the Society with Loyola as the first general of what came to be called the Jesuits.

The dynamic personality and intense spirituality of Loyola gave the new order its distinctive commitment to moral action in the world. Loyola's most impressive personal contribution to religious literature was the *Spiritual Exercises* (1548), which became the foundation of Jesuit practice. Republished in more than 5,000 editions in hundreds of languages, The *Exercises* prescribe a month-long retreat devoted to a series of meditations in which the participant mentally re-experiences the spiritual life, physical death, and miraculous resurrection of Christ. Much of the power of the *Exercises* derives from the systematic employment of each of the five senses to produce a defined emotional, spiritual, and even physical response. Participants in the *Exercises* seem to hear the blasphemous cries of the soldiers at Christ's crucifixion, feel the terrible agony of His suffering on the cross, and experience the blinding illumination of His resurrection from the dead. Those who participated in the *Exercises* considered the experience life-transforming and usually made a steadfast commitment to serve the Church.

The Jesuits distinguished themselves from other religious orders by extending their personal spirituality to minister to others. They did not wear clerical clothing, and on foreign missions they devoted years to learning about the language and culture of the peoples they hoped to convert. Jesuits became famous for their loyalty to the pope, and some took a special fourth vow (in addition to the three traditional vows of poverty, chastity, and obedience) to go on a mission if the pope requested it. Many traveled as missionaries to distant parts of the globe, such as China and Japan. In Europe and the Americas the Jesuits established a vast network of colleges; most were similar to modern high schools but some became universities. These colleges offered free tuition, which made them open to the poor who had few other opportunities for education. The Jesuit colleges combined a thorough training in languages, humanities, and sciences accompanied by religious instruction and moral guidance. They became especially popular because the Jesuit fathers were much more likely to pay personal attention to their students than professors in the established universities.

Creating a ministry that was active in the world was much more difficult for the female orders than for the Jesuits and the other male orders. Women who sought to reinvigorate old orders or found new ones faced hostility from ecclesiastical and civic authorities, who thought women had to be protected by either a husband or the cloister wall. Women in convents were supposed to be entirely separated from the world, "as if they were dead," but this principle was at odds with the desires of many devout women who wanted to help make the world a better place.

The first task of those who were ardently religious was to reform convent life. The most famous model was provided by Teresa of Avila (1515–1582), who wrote a strict new rule for the long-established Carmelites, requiring mortifications of the flesh and complete withdrawal from the world. Teresa described her own mystical experiences in her *Autobiography* (1611) and in the *Interior Castle* (1588), a compelling masterpiece in the literature of mysticism. Teresa advocated a very cautious brand of mysticism, which was checked by regular confession and skepticism about extreme acts of self-deprivation. For example, she recognized that a nun who fell into an apparent rapture after extensive fasting was probably just having hallucinations from the hunger. During the Catholic Reformation, the many orders of nuns created their own distinctly female culture, producing a number of learned women and social reformers who had considerable influence in the arts, education, and charitable work such as nursing.

PAUL III, THE REFORMING POPE

Despite the many earlier attempts at reform and the Protestant threat, the Church was slow to initiate its own reforms because of resistance among bishops and cardinals of the Church hierarchy who worried that reform would threaten their income. More than twenty years after Luther's defiant stand at the Diet of Worms in 1521, Pope Paul III (r. 1534–1549) finally launched a systematic counterattack.

In 1542 on the advice of an archconservative faction of cardinals, Paul III reorganized the Roman Inquisition, called the Holy Office. The function of the Inquisition was to inquire into the beliefs of all Catholics primarily to discover indications of heresies such as those of the Protestants. Jews, for example, were exempt from its authority, although Jews who had converted or been forced to convert to Christianity did fall under the jurisdiction of the Inquisition. There had been other inquisitions, but most had been local or national. The Spanish Inquisition was controlled by the Spanish monarchs, for example. In contrast, the Holy Office came under the direct control of the pope and cardinals and termed itself the Universal Roman Inquisition. Its effective authority did not reach beyond northern and central Italy, but it set the tone for the entire Catholic Reformation Church.

A second effort to stop the spread of Protestant and other ideas deemed heretical led to the first *Index of Forbidden Books,* drawn up in 1549 in Venice, the capital of the publishing industry in Italy. The *Index* censored or banned many books that the Church considered detrimental to the faith and the authority of the Church. Most affected by the strictures were books about theology and philosophy, but books of moral guidance were also prohibited or butchered by the censors, such as the works of Erasmus, and classics of literature, such as Giovanni Boccaccio's *The Decameron*. The official papal *Index* of 1559 prohibited translations of the Bible into vernacular languages such as

CHRONOLOGY	
1517	Luther posts the Ninety-Five Theses
1519–1558	Reign of Emperor Charles V
1520	Zwingli declared the People's Priest in Zürich
1524–1525	German peasants' revolt
1534	Parliament in England passes the Acts of Supremacy and Succession
1534–1549	Pontificate of Pope Paul III
1535	First edition of John Calvin's *Institutes of the Christian Religion*
1540	Founding of the Society of Jesus
1542	Reorganization of the Roman Inquisition or Holy Office
1545–1563	Meetings of the Council of Trent
1555	The Religious Peace of Augsburg
1559–1563	Elizabethan Settlement of the Anglican Church

Italian. The prohibition of vernacular Bibles was especially important because the Church insisted that laypeople required a trained intermediary in the person of a priest to interpret and explain the Bible. The Church's protective attitude about biblical interpretation clearly distinguished the Catholic from the Protestant attitude of encouraging widespread Bible reading.

THE COUNCIL OF TRENT

By far the most significant of Pope Paul III's contributions to the Catholic Reformation was his call for a general council of the Church, which began to meet in 1545 in Trent on the border between Italy and Germany. The Council of Trent established principles that guided the Catholic Church for the next 400 years.

Between 1545 and 1563 the council met under the auspices of three different popes in three separate sessions, with as much as ten years between sessions. The objective of these sessions was to find a way to respond to the Protestant criticisms of the Church, to reassert the authority of the pope, and to launch reforms that would guarantee a well-educated and honest clergy. The decrees of the Council of Trent, which had the force of legislation for the entire Church, defied the Protestants by refusing to yield any ground on the traditional doctrines of the Church. The decrees confirmed the efficacy of all seven of the traditional sacraments, the reality of Purgatory, and the spiritual value of indulgences. In order to provide better supervision of the Church, bishops were ordered to reside in their dioceses or regions. Trent decreed that every diocese should have a seminary to train priests, providing a practical solution to the problem of clerical ignorance.

The Council of Trent represented a dramatic reassertion of the authority of the papacy, the bishops, and the priesthood. The actual implementation of the decrees varied considerably from country to country and from diocese to diocese, however. The model for enforcing the decrees was Archbishop Carlo Borromeo (archbishop, 1565–1584) of Milan. His energetic visitations of his diocese and attention to administrative detail became an example for others. Despite the hopes of some council participants, it had no effect whatsoever in luring Protestants back into the Catholic fold.

The Reformation in the Arts

Most of the paintings and sculptures created before and during the sixteenth century were destined for churches or had some kind of religious function. But with the tensions brought about during the Reformation, one of the major issues dividing Protestants and Catholics was defining the proper role of the arts in Christian worship. Except among the most radical Protestants, who entirely rejected any role for the arts in religious worship, the difference between the two was more one of degree than of kind. Catholics considered religious images, properly regulated, vital for devotion. Protestants, however, were uneasy about religious art because they worried about confining divine truths within any kind of visual representation.

PROTESTANT ICONOCLASM

Protestants sometimes initiated reform by vandalizing churches through acts of iconoclasm, the removing, breaking, or defacing of religious statues, paintings, and symbols such as crucifixes. The destruction of religious works of art more often than not took place even when the reformers themselves discouraged or denounced it. Nevertheless, in town after town in the thrall of reform enthusiasm, laypeople destroyed religious art, including some of the greatest masterpieces of the Middle Ages and Renaissance. Their violence against property was seldom matched by violence against people. Protestant mobs were much more likely to rip down an altar painting than to attack a priest.

Three factors likely explain iconoclasm. One was that people feared the power of such images. Guillaume Farel, the reformer of Geneva before Calvin, told how his parents had taken him as a child to the shrine of the Holy Cross at

■ Iconoclasm in the Netherlands

This engraving shows statues being hauled down by the men on the left of the church pulling ropes. Note that one statue is already lying on the ground. On the right side of the church, men are breaking the stained glass windows with clubs.

Ego sum Papa.

Ego sum Papa
(Jch bin der Papst).

Französischer Holzschnitt gegen den
lasterhaften Papst Alexander VI.

■ **Anti-Catholic Propaganda**

This woodcut, titled *I Am the Pope,* satirizes the papacy by depicting Pope Alexander VI as a monster. Alexander was infamous for allegedly conducting orgies in the Vatican. This kind of visual propaganda was an effective way to undermine support for the papacy.

Tallard, France. A priest stationed at the shrine told the pilgrims that the cross shook violently during storms. What Farel remembered most about the cross was his fear, reinforced by the apprehension of his parents. The implication was that images possessed great powers that could be used both to protect and to destroy. The problem with religious images, therefore, was not that they were idols, which were by definition without power. They were dangerous because they were perceived to be too powerful.

A second reason for iconoclasm was that religious images devoured financial resources that could be better spent on the poor. Ulrich Zwingli was especially articulate on this point. He hoped that the assets devoted to paying for paintings and statues could be transformed into "food of the poor." In this sense iconoclasm was part of a pious project

to redirect the energy of Christians toward solving the social problems of the community. Great paintings were given to hospitals to serve as fuel, and crucifixes were sold as lumber with the proceeds going to the indigent.

Many reformers spoke of a third concern about images. They worried that a church filled with works of art distracted worshipers from paying attention to the Word of Scripture. They found the meaning of images too ambiguous, too subject to misinterpretation. Instead they wanted to ensure that their preaching provided the interpretation of Scripture. In effect, they wanted to substitute the Word of God for the image of God. In many reformed Dutch churches, for example, the walls were stripped bare of images and whitewashed. Passages of scripture were then painted on the walls in place of the images.

Although skeptical of the role of images in churches, propagandists for the Protestant Reformation had no such reservation about woodcuts and engravings, which could be reproduced in multiple copies and cheaply sold to thousands of people. These images, the visual by-product of the printing revolution, promoted the Reformation to the masses in a simple graphic way by lampooning the pope and ridiculing the wealth of the clergy. These images were the prototype for modern political cartoons. Also popular were portraits of the reformers. Many a pious Lutheran household replaced an image of the Madonna with an engraving of Martin Luther and his wife, Katherine von Bora.

CATHOLIC REFORMATION ART

The Catholic Church retained a strong commitment to the religious value of the arts. However, the Catholic Reformation recognized that abuses had taken place in works of art that depicted events that did not appear in Scripture and placed artists under much closer surveillance than before. The Council of Trent enjoined artists to avoid representing impieties of any sort and to use their art to teach correct doctrine and to move believers to true piety. Religious art had to convey a message simply, directly, and in terms that unlettered viewers could understand. The best Catholic art employed dramatic theatrical effects in lighting and the arrangement of figures to represent deep emotional and spiritual experiences. Through contemplating these pictures, viewers were supposed to create similar experiences within themselves. In this sense an aesthetic and a spiritual appreciation of art were inseparable.

The Council of Trent forced a re-evaluation of previous trends in the arts and a number of existing works of art. The Italian Renaissance, in particular, had glorified the human body, often represented in the nude. In earlier generations churchmen and popes had not objected to the display of naked figures in churches and chapels because after all the human body was God's finest creation. However, after the Council of Trent many influential

■ **The Last Judgment**
In this fresco by Michelangelo, the figure with the raised hand in the upper center is Christ. On his right sits the Virgin Mary. Both figures were painted over with clothing to hide their nudity.

ecclesiastics disapproved this practice in the strongest terms. Michelangelo's *The Last Judgment,* a fresco painted in the Sistine Chapel in the Vatican in Rome between 1534 and 1541, came under severe attack the year after the last session of Trent. The polemical *Dialogue on the Errors of Painters* criticized Michelangelo for subordinating the representation of Christian truths to his own stylistic interests in the human nude.

Since artists' livelihoods depended on the patronage of aristocrats and high ecclesiastical officials, most quickly fell into line with the new requirements. Artistic rebels were rare in the late sixteenth-century Catholic world. In 1577 the pope founded a new academy in Rome to create guidelines for artists in promoting Christianity, and the Jesuits proved very influential in defining a new path for artists. Many prominent artists across Europe enthusiastically embraced the Catholic Reformation. Some became friends of Jesuits, undertook commissions for Jesuits, and practiced the *Spiritual Exercises,* thereby suffusing a Jesuit sensibility throughout Catholic culture.

■ The Inquisition Criticizes a Work of Art

This painting was originally intended to represent the Last Supper when Christ introduced the mass to his apostles. Because there are many figures in it who are not mentioned in the biblical account and the supper appears as if it were a Renaissance banquet, the artist, Paolo Veronese, was obliged to answer questions from the Inquisition. Ordered to remove the offending figures, Veronese instead changed the name of the painting to depict the less theologically controversial supper in the house of Levi.

THE INQUISITION INTERROGATES PAOLO VERONESE

....

In 1572 the prominent painter Paolo Veronese was called before the Inquisition in the city of Venice to answer questions about a painting of the Last Supper that he had created for the refectory of the friars of Santi Giovanni e Paolo. Paintings of the Last Supper were particularly sensitive during the controversies of the Reformation because Catholics believed that Christ had instituted the mass at the Last Supper.

[The inquisitor] said to him, "Who do you think was really present at that supper?"

He answered, "I believe that Christ and his apostles were present. But if there is space left over in the picture I decorate it with figures of my own invention."

Said to him, "Did anyone commission you to paint Germans and clowns and the like in that picture?"

He answered, "No, my lords; my commission was to adorn that picture as I saw fit, for it is large and can include many figures, or so I thought."

It was said to him, "When you, the painter, add these decorations to your pictures, is it your habit to make them appropriate to the subject and to proportion them to the principal figures, or do you really do as the fancy takes you, without using any discretion or judgment?"

He answered, "I make the pictures after proper reflection, within the limits of my understanding."

He was asked, "Did he think it proper to depict at the Lord's last supper clowns, drunkards, Germans, dwarfs, and other lewd things?"

He answered, "No, my lords."

He was asked, "Why, then, did you paint them?"

He answered, "I did them on the understanding that they are not within the place where the supper is being held."

He was asked, "Do you not know that in Germany and other places infected with heresy they are accustomed, by means of outlandish paintings full of indecencies and similar devices, to abuse, mock and pour scorn on the things of the Holy Catholic Church, in order to teach false doctrine to foolish and ignorant people?"

He answered, "I agree, my lord, that it is bad; but I must say again that I am obliged to follow the example of my predecessors." [He was referring here to Michelangelo's Last Judgment in the Sistine Chapel of the Vatican.]

The inquisitors ordered Veronese to correct the painting, but he merely changed its name from The Last Supper *to* The Feast in the House of Levi. *It now hangs in the Accademia Gallery in Venice.*

Source: From *Venice: A Documentary History, 1450–1630,* edited by David Chambers and Brian Pullan, with Jennifer Fletcher. Published by Blackwell Publishers (Oxford, 1992). Reprinted by permission.

CONCLUSION
Competing Understandings

During the Reformation the West was permanently divided into two discordant religious confessional cultures of Protestant and Catholic. The religious unity of the West achieved during the Middle Ages had been the fruit of many centuries of diligent effort by missionaries, monks, popes, and crusading knights. That unity was lost through the conflicts between, on the one hand, reformers, city magistrates, princes, and kings who wanted to control their own affairs and, on the other, popes who continued to cling to the medieval concept of the papal monarchy. In the West, Christians no longer saw themselves as dedicated to serving the same God as all other Christians. Instead, Catholics and Protestants emphasized their differences.

The differences between these two cultures had lasting implications for how people understood and accepted the authority of the Church and the state, how they conducted their family life, and how they formed their own identities as individuals and as members of a larger community. The next chapter will explore all of these themes.

As the result of intransigence on the part of both confessional cultures, the division had tragic consequences. From the late sixteenth century to the late seventeenth century, European states tended to create diplomatic alliances along this ideological and religious divide, they allowed disputes about doctrine to prevent peaceful reconciliation, and they conducted wars as if they were a fulfillment of God's plan. Even after the era of religious warfare ended, Protestant and Catholic confessional cultures remained ingrained in all aspects of life, influencing not just government policy but painting, music, literature, and education. This division completely reshaped the West into a place of intense religious and ideological conflict and by the eighteenth century undermined the very idea that the West was necessarily a Christian civilization.

Suggestions for Further Reading

For a comprehensive list of suggested readings, please go to www.ablongman.com/levackconcise/chapter13

Bireley, Robert. *The Refashioning of Catholicism, 1450–1700: A Reassessment of the Counter Reformation.* 1999. A fair reappraisal of the major events by one of the most prominent historians of Catholicism in this period.

Bossy, John. *Christianity in the West, 1400–1700.* 1985. A short study not of the institutions of the Church but of Christianity itself, this book explores the Christian people, their beliefs, and their way of life. The book demonstrates considerable continuities before and after the Reformation and is especially useful in understanding the attitudes of common lay believers as opposed to the major reformers and Church officials.

Cameron, Euan. *The European Reformation.* 1995. The most comprehensive general survey, this bulky book covers all the major topics in considerable detail. It is excellent in explaining theological issues.

Hsia, R. Po-chia. *The World of Catholic Renewal 1540–1770.* 1998. An excellent survey of the most recent research.

Koenigsberger, H. G., George L. Mosse, and G. Q. Bowler. *Europe in the Sixteenth Century,* 2nd ed. 1989. A good beginner's survey. Strong on political events.

McGrath, Alister E. *Reformation Thought: An Introduction,* 3rd. rev. ed. 1999. Indispensable introduction for anyone seeking to understand the ideas of the European Reformation. Drawing on the most up-to-date scholarship, McGrath offers a clear explanation of these ideas, set firmly in their historical contexts.

Muir, Edward. *Ritual in Early Modern Europe.* 2nd ed. 2005. A broad survey of the debates about ritual during the Reformation and the implementation of ritual reforms.

Oberman, Heiko A. *Luther: Man Between God and the Devil,* trans. Eileen Walliser-Schwarzbart. 1992. First published to great acclaim in Germany, this book argues that Luther was more the medieval monk than history has usually regarded him. Oberman claims that Luther was haunted by the Devil and saw the world as a cosmic battleground between God and Satan. A brilliant, intellectual biography that is sometimes challenging but always clear and precise.

O'Malley, John. *Trent and All That: Renaming Catholicism in the Early Modern Era.* 2000. O'Malley works out a remarkable guide to the intellectual and historical developments behind the concepts of Catholic reform and, in his useful term, Early Modern Catholicism. The result is the single best overview of scholarship on Catholicism in early modern Europe, delivered in a pithy, lucid, and entertaining style.

Ozment, Steven. *The Age of Reform, 1250–1550: An Intellectual and Religious History of Late Medieval and Reformation Europe.* 1986. Firmly places the Protestant Reformation in the context of late medieval spirituality and theology, particularly strong on pre-Reformation developments.

Reardon, Bernard M. G. *Religious Thought in the Reformation,* 2nd ed. 1995. A good beginner's survey of the intellectual dimensions of the Reformation.

Scribner, R. W. *For the Sake of the Simple Folk: Popular Propaganda for the German Reformation.* 1994. The innovative and fascinating study of the Lutheran use of visual images.

Scribner, R. W. *The German Reformation.* 1996. A short and very clear analysis of the appeal of the Reformation by the leading social historian of the period. Pays attention to what people actually did rather than just what reformers said they should do.

Notes

1. *Correspondence of Erasmus,* trans. R. A. B. Mynors and D. F. S. Thomson, annotated by Wallace K. Ferguson (1974–1994), no. 858, 167–177.
2. Quotation from Gordon Rupp, *Luther's Progress to the Diet of Worms* (1964), 29.
3. Ibid., 33.
4. Quoted in Heiko A. Oberman, *Luther: Man Between God and the Devil,* trans. Eileen Walliser-Schwarzbart (1989), 240.
5. E. W. Ives, *Anne Boleyn* (1986), 398.
6. Quoted in Margery Stone Schauer and Frederick Schauer, "Law as the Engine of State: The Trial of Anne Boleyn," *William and Mary Law Review,* vol. 22 (1980), 68.
7. Quoted in Ives, 387.
8. Quoted in Schauer and Schauer, 70.

The Age of Confessional Division, 1550–1618

O N JULY 10, 1584, A CATHOLIC EXTREMIST NAMED FRANÇOIS GUION, WITH a brace of pistols hidden under his cloak, surprised William the Silent, the Prince of Orange, as he was leaving the dining hall of his palace and shot him at point-blank range. William had been the leader of the Protestant nobility in the Netherlands, which was in revolt against the Catholic king of Spain. Guion masqueraded as a Protestant for seven years in order to ingratiate himself with William's party, and before the assassination he had consulted three Catholic priests who had confirmed the religious merit of his plan. Spain's representative in the Netherlands, the Duke of Parma, had offered a reward of 25,000 crowns to anyone who killed William, and at the moment of the assassination four other fanatics were in Delft trying to gain access to the Prince of Orange.

The murder of William the Silent exemplified an ominous figure in Western civilization—the religiously motivated assassin. There had been many assassinations before the late sixteenth century, but the assassins tended to be motivated by the desire to gain political power or to avenge a personal or family injury and less often by religious differences. In the wake of the Reformation the idea that killing a political leader of the opposing faith would serve God's plan became all too common. The assassination of William illustrated patterns of violence that have become the modus operandi of the political assassin—the use of deception to gain access to the victim, the vulnerability of leaders who wish to mingle with the public, the lethal potential of easily concealed pistols (a new weapon at that time), the corruption of politics through vast sums of money, and the obsessive hostility of zealots against their perceived enemies. The widespread acrimony among the varieties of Christian faith created a climate of religious extremism during the late sixteenth and early seventeenth centuries. After the Protestant

St. Bartholomew's Day Massacre: This Protestant painter, François Dubois, depicted the merciless slaughter of Protestant men, women, and children in the streets of Paris in 1572. The massacre was the most bloody and infamous in the French Wars of Religion and created a lasting memory of atrocity.

and Catholic Reformations, the various forms of Christianity came to be called confessions because their adherents believed in a particular confession of faith, or statement of religious doctrine.

Religious extremism was just one manifestation of an anxiety that pervaded European society at the time—a fear of hidden forces controlling human events. In an attempt to curb that anxiety, the European monarchs created confessional states. The combined effort of state and church sought to discipline common people, persecute deviants of all sorts, and combat enemies through a religiously driven foreign policy. During this age of confessional division, European countries polarized along confessional lines, and governments persecuted followers of minority religions, whom they saw as threats to public security. Anxious believers everywhere were consumed with pleasing an angry God, but when they tried to find God within themselves many Christians seemed only to find the Devil in others. The bloody history of confessional conflicts during the sixteenth and seventeenth centuries, in fact, eventually stimulated the formation of the modern ethical principles of religious toleration, separation of church and state, and human rights during the eighteenth century.

The religious controversies of the age of confessional division redefined the West. During the Middle Ages, the West came to be identified with the practice of Latin Catholic Christianity. The Reformation of the early sixteenth century broke up the unity of medieval Christian Europe by dividing westerners into Catholic and Protestant camps. During the late sixteenth and seventeenth centuries, governments reinforced religious divisions and attempted to unify their peoples around a common set of beliefs. By the end of the eighteenth century, these confessional religious identities changed in some places into more secular political ideologies, such as the belief in the superiority of a republic over a monarchy, but the assumption that all citizens of a state should believe in some common ideology remained. The period from about 1500 to 1750—the Early Modern period in European history—produced the lasting division of the West into national camps that were based on either religious confessions or ideological commitments.

The pervasive anxiety of the late sixteenth and early seventeenth centuries raises several questions that this chapter will explore:

- How did the expanding population and price revolution exacerbate religious and political tensions?
- How did religious and political authorities attempt to discipline the people?
- How did religious differences provoke violence and start wars?
- How did the countries of eastern Europe during the late sixteenth century become enmeshed in the religious controversies that began in western Europe during the early part of the century?

The Peoples of Early Modern Europe

In the sixteenth century the population began to rebound from the catastrophic losses of the Black Death in the fourteenth and fifteenth centuries, but the sudden swell brought dramatic and destabilizing consequences that contributed to a pervasive anxiety. The expanded population transformed the balance of power, as northern Europe recovered its population more successfully than southern Europe. As the population grew, young men and women flocked to the cities, creating enormous social strains and demands on local governments. Perhaps most disruptive was the price revolution, which brought inflation that ate away at the buying power of everyone from working families to kings and queens. The anxiety produced by these circumstances lasted into the seventeenth century.

THE POPULATION RECOVERY

During a period that historical demographers call the "long sixteenth century" (ca. 1480–1640), the population of Europe began to grow consistently again for the first time since the late thirteenth century. In 1340, on the brink of the Black Death, Europe had about 74 million inhabitants, or 17 percent of the world's total. By 1400 the population of all of Europe had dropped to 52 million (less than one-fifth of the population of the United States today), or 14 percent of the world's total. Over the course of the long sixteenth century, Europe's population grew from 60.9 million to 77.9 million, just barely surpassing the pre-Black Death level.

Two stunning facts emerge from the population figures for the larger European countries during the sixteenth century. The first is the much greater rate of growth in northern Europe compared to southern Europe. England grew by 83 percent, Poland grew by 76 percent, and even the tiny, war-torn Netherlands gained 58 percent. During the same period Italy grew by only 25 percent and Spain by 19 percent. These trends signal a massive, permanent shift of demographic and economic power from the Mediterranean countries of Italy and Spain to northern, especially northwestern, Europe. The second fact to note from these data is the overwhelming size of France, which was home to about a quarter of Europe's population. Once France recovered from its long wars of religion, its demographic superiority overwhelmed competing countries and made it the dominant power in Europe, permanently eclipsing its chief rival, Spain. Because the Holy Roman Empire and especially its core regions in the German-speaking lands lacked political unity, it was unable to take advantage of its position as the second-largest state.

What explains the growth in the population and the economy? To a large extent, it was made possible by the transformation from subsistence to commercial agriculture in certain regions of Europe. Subsistence farmers, called peasants, had worked the land year in and year out, raising grains for the coarse black bread that fed their families, supplemented only by beer, grain porridge, and occasionally vegetables. Meat was rare and expensive. Peasants consumed about 80 percent of everything they raised, and what little was left over went almost entirely to the landlord as feudal dues and to the church as tithing—the obligation to give to God one-tenth of everything earned or produced. Peasant families lived on the edge of existence. In a bad year some starved to death, usually the vulnerable children and old people. But during the sixteenth century, in areas with access to big cities, subsistence agriculture gave way to commercial crops, especially wheat, which was hauled to be sold in town markets. Profits from this market agriculture stimulated farmers to raise even greater surpluses in the agricultural regions around the great cities—London, Antwerp, Amsterdam, Paris, Milan, Venice, Barcelona, and in scattered places in Germany. Commercial crops and the cash income they produced meant fewer starving children and a higher standard of living for those who were able to take advantage of the new opportunities. As commercial agriculture spread, the population grew because the rural population was better fed and more prosperous.

THE REGULATED CITIES

By the 1480s cities began to grow, largely through migration from the more prosperous countryside, but the growth was uneven with the most dramatic growth occurring in the cities of the North, especially London, Antwerp, and Amsterdam. The surpluses of the countryside, both human and agricultural, flowed into the cities during the sixteenth century. Compared to even the prosperous rural villages the cities must have seemed incomparably rich. Half-starved vagabonds from the countryside would have marveled at shops piled high with food (white bread, fancy pies, fruit, casks of wine, roasting meats); they would have wistfully passed taverns full of drunken, laughing citizens; and they would have begged for alms in front of magnificent, marble-faced churches.

Every aspect of the cities exhibited dramatic contrasts between the rich and poor, who lived on the same streets and often in different parts of the same houses. Around 1580 Christian missionaries brought a Native American chief to the French city of Rouen. Through an interpreter he was asked what impressed him the most about European cities, so unlike the villages of North America. He replied that he was astonished that the rag-clad, emaciated men and women who crowded the streets did not grab the plump, well-dressed rich people by the throat.

The wretched human surplus from the farms continuously replenished and swelled the populations of the cities, which were frequently depleted by high urban death rates. As wealthy as the cities were, they were unhealthy places: Human waste overflowed from open latrines because there were no sewage systems; garbage, manure, dead animals, and roaming pigs and dogs made the streets putrid and dangerous; and water came from polluted rivers or sat stale in cisterns for months. Under such conditions, entire neighborhoods could be wiped out in epidemics. Both ends of the lifespan were vulnerable: One in three babies died in the first year of life; old people did not last long in cold, drafty houses. When the plague struck, which it continued to do about every twenty years until 1721, the rich escaped to their country retreats while the poor died in the streets or in houses locked up and under quarantine.

To deal with the consequences of commerce and massive immigration, European cities attempted to regulate the lives of their inhabitants. Ringing bells measured each working day, and during the sixteenth century many cities erected a large mechanical clock in a prominent place so that busy citizens could keep to their schedules. Municipal officers inspected the weights and measures in the city market, regulated the distribution of produce to guarantee an abundant food supply, and repaired the streets and city walls. However talented or enterprising, new arrivals to the city had very limited opportunities. They could hardly start up their own business because all production was strictly controlled by the guilds. Recall from Chapter 10 that guilds were associations of merchants or artisans organized to protect their interests. Guilds rigidly regulated their membership; they required an apprenticeship of many years, prohibited technological innovations, guaranteed certain standards of workmanship, and did not allow branching out into new lines. A member of the goldsmiths' guild could not make mirrors; a baker could not sell fruit on the side; a house carpenter could not lay bricks. Given the limited opportunities for new arrivals, immigrant men and women begged on the streets or took charity from the public dole. The men picked up any heavy-labor jobs they could find. Both men and women became servants, a job that paid poorly but at least guaranteed regular meals.

The more comfortable classes of the cities enjoyed large palaces and luxurious lifestyles. They hired extensive staffs of servants, feasted on meat and fine wines, and purchased exotic imports such as silk cloth, spices from the East, and, in the Mediterranean cities, slaves from eastern Europe, the Middle East, or Africa. The merchants whose fortunes came from cloth manufacturing, banking, and regional or international trade maintained their status by marrying within their own class, providing municipal offices to those whose fortunes had fallen, and educating their children in the newly fashionable humanist schools. The wealthy of the cities were the bastions of social stability. They possessed the financial resources and economic skills to protect themselves from the worst consequences of economic instability, especially the corrosive wave of price inflation that struck the West after about 1540.

THE PRICE REVOLUTION

Price inflation became so pervasive during the last half of the sixteenth century that it contributed to the widespread fear that events were being controlled by hidden forces. The phenomenon that historians call the Price Revolution° refers to the fact that after a long period of falling or stable prices that stretched back to the fourteenth century, Europe experienced sustained price increases, beginning around 1540. The inflation lasted a century, forcing major economic and social changes that permanently altered the face of Western society. During this period overall prices across Europe multiplied five- or sixfold.

What caused the inflation? The basic principle is simple. The price paid for goods and services is fundamentally the result of the relationship between *supply* and *demand.* If the number of children who need to be fed grows faster than the supply of grain, the price of bread goes up. This happens simply because those mothers who can afford it will be willing to pay a higher price to save their children from hunger. If good harvests allow the supply of grain to increase at a greater rate than the demand for bread, then prices go down. The equation gets somewhat more complicated when taking into account two other factors that can influence price. One factor is the *amount of money in circulation.* If the amount of gold or silver available to make coins increases, there is more money in circulation. When more money is circulating, people have more money to buy more things, which creates the same effect as an increase in demand—prices go up. The other factor is called the *velocity of money in circulation,* which refers to the number of times money changes hands to buy things. When people buy commodities with greater frequency, it has the same effect as increasing the amount of money in circulation or of increasing demand—again, prices go up.

The precise combination of these factors in causing the great Price Revolution of the sixteenth century has long been a matter of considerable debate. Most historians would now agree that the primary cause of inflation was population growth, which increased demand for all kinds of basic commodities, such as bread and woolen cloth for clothing. As Europe's population finally began to recover, more people needed and desired to buy more things. This explanation is most obvious for commodities that people need to survive, such as grain to make bread. These commodities have what economists call *inelastic demand,* that is, consumers do not have a great deal of discretion in purchasing them. Everybody has to eat. The commodities that people could survive without if the price is too high, such as dancing shoes and lace collars, are said to have *elastic demand.* In England between 1540 and 1640 overall prices rose by 490 percent. More telling, however, is that the price of grain (inelastic demand) rose by a stunning 670 percent, whereas the price of luxury goods (elastic demand) rose much less, by 204 percent.

Monetary factors also contributed to inflation. The Portuguese brought in significant amounts of gold from Africa, and newly opened mines in central Europe increased the amount of silver by fivefold as early as the 1520s. The discovery in 1545 of the fabulous silver mine of Potosí (in present-day Bolivia) brought to Europe a flood of silver, which Spain used to finance its costly wars. As inflation began to eat away at royal incomes, financially strapped monarchs all across western Europe debased their money because they believed, mistakenly, that producing more coins containing less silver would buy more. In fact, the minting of more coins meant each coin was worth less and would buy less. In England, for example, debasement was the major source of inflation during the 1540s and 1550s.

Probably the most serious consequence of the Price Revolution was that the hidden force of inflation caused widespread human suffering. During the late sixteenth and early seventeenth centuries, people felt their lives threatened, but they did not know the source and so they imagined all kinds of secret powers at work, especially supernatural ones. The suspicion of religious differences created by the Reformation provided handy, if utterly false, explanations for what had gone wrong. Catholics suspected Protestants, Protestants suspected Catholics, both suspected Jews, and they all worried about witches. Authorities sought to relieve this widespread anxiety by looking in all the wrong places, by disciplining the populace, hunting for witches, and battling against enemies from the opposite side of the confessional divide.

Disciplining the People

The first generation of the Protestant and Catholic Reformations had been devoted to doctrinal disputes and to either rejecting or defending papal authority. Subsequent generations of reformers in the last half of the sixteenth and the early seventeenth centuries faced the formidable task of building the institutions that would firmly establish a Protestant or Catholic religious culture. Leaders of all religious confessions attempted to revitalize the Christian community by disciplining nonconformists and enforcing moral rigor. Members of the community came to identify responsible citizenship with conformity to a specific Christian confession.

Whether Lutheran, Calvinist, Catholic, or Anglican, godly reformers sought to bring order to society and attacked popular culture. They reformed or abolished wild festivals, they imprisoned town drunks, they decreased the number of holidays, and they tried to regulate sexual behavior. Many activities that had once been accepted as normal came to be considered deviant or criminal. The process of better ordering society required that the common people accept a certain measure of discipline. Discipline required cooperation between church and secular authorities, but it was not entirely imposed from above. Many people wholeheartedly cooperated with moral correction and even encouraged reformers to go further. Others passively, actively, or resentfully resisted it.

ESTABLISHING CONFESSIONAL IDENTITIES

Between 1560 and 1650 religious confessions° reshaped European culture, and loyalty to a single confession governed the relationships between states. A confession consisted of the adherents to a particular statement of religious doctrine—the Confession of Augsburg for Lutherans, the Helvetic Confessions for Calvinists, the Thirty-Nine Articles for Anglicans, and the decrees of the Council of Trent for Catholics. Based on these confessions of faith, the clergy disciplined the laity, exiled nonconformists, and promoted distinct religious institutions, beliefs, and culture.

The process of establishing confessional identities did not happen overnight; it lasted for centuries and had far-reaching consequences. During the second half of the sixteenth century, Lutherans turned from the struggle to survive within the hostile Holy Roman Empire to establishing a confessional identity in the parts of the empire where Lutheranism was the chosen religion of the local prince. They had to recruit Lutheran clergy and provide each clergyman with a university education, which was made possible by scholarship endowments from the Lutheran princes of the empire. Once established, the Lutheran clergy became a branch of the civil bureaucracy, received a government stipend, and enforced the will of the prince. Calvinist states followed a similar process, but where they were in a minority, as in France, Calvinists had to go it alone, and the state often discriminated against them. In those places confessional identities were established in opposition to the state and the dominant confession.

Catholics responded with their own aggressive plan of training new clergymen, educating the laity, and reinforcing the bond between church and state. Just as with the Lutheran princes, Catholic princes in the Holy Roman Empire associated conformity to Catholicism with loyalty to themselves, making religion a pillar of the state. Everywhere in western Europe (except for Ireland, a few places in the Holy Roman Empire, and for a time France) the only openly practiced religion was the religion of the state.

POLICING THE FAMILY

One matter on which Calvinists, Lutherans, and Catholics agreed was that the foundation of society should be the au-

thority fathers had over their families. In this respect, their views were very traditional. According to an anonymous treatise published in 1586 in Calvinist Nassau, the three pillars of Christian society were the church, the state, and the household. This proposition made the father's authority a reflection of the authority of clergy and king—a position that all the confessions would have accepted. The enforcement of patriarchy required the policing of gender roles.

However, regional differences in the structure of the family itself meant that despite the near universal acceptance of the theory of patriarchy, the reality of the father's authority varied a great deal. Since the early Middle Ages in northwestern Europe—in Britain, Scandinavia, the Netherlands, northern France, and western Germany—couples tended to wait to marry until their mid- or late twenties, well beyond the age of sexual maturity. When these couples married, they established their own household separate from either of their parents. Husbands were usually only two or three years older than their wives, and that proximity of age tended to make those relationships more cooperative and less authoritarian than the theory of patriarchy might suggest. In northwestern Europe the couple had to be economically independent before they married, which meant both had to accumulate savings or the husband needed to inherit from his deceased father before he could marry. By contrast, in southern Europe, men in their late twenties or thirties married teenaged women over whom they carried a certain authority by virtue of their age. In the South patriarchy meant husbands ruled over wives. In eastern Europe, both spouses married in their teens and resided in one of the parental households for many years, which placed both spouses for extended periods under the authority of the husband's parents.

The marriage pattern in northwestern Europe required prolonged sexual restraint by young men and women until they were economically self-sufficient. In addition to individual self-control, sexual restraint required social control by church and secular authorities who seem to have been more vigilant about regulating sexual behavior than in southern and eastern Europe. Their efforts seem to have been generally successful. For example, in sixteenth-century Geneva, where the elders were especially wary about sexual sins, the rates of illegitimate births were extremely low.

The northwestern European families also tended to be smaller. Married couples in northwestern European began to space their children through birth control and family planning. These self-restrained couples practiced withdrawal, the rhythm method, or abstinence. When mothers no longer relied on wet nurses and nursed their own infants, often for long periods, they also reduced their chances of becoming pregnant. Thus, limiting family size became the social norm in northwestern Europe, especially among the educated and urban middle classes. Protestant families tended to have fewer children than Catholic families, but Catholics in this region also practiced some form of birth

■ **The Ideal Family**

During the late sixteenth century, idealized depictions of harmonious family life became very popular. This etching, which was sold in multiple copies at modest prices much as a wall poster would be today, depicts a prosperous peasant family.

control, even though Church law prohibited all forms except abstinence.

The moral status of marriage also demonstrated regional variations during the early modern period. Protestants no longer considered husbands and wives as morally inferior to celibate monks and nuns, and the wives of preachers in Protestant communities certainly had a respected social role never granted to the concubines of priests. But the favorable Protestant attitude toward marriage did not necessarily translate into a positive attitude toward women. In Germany the numerous books of advice, called the Father of the House literature, encouraged families to subordinate the individual interests of servants, children, and the mother to the dictates of the father, who was encouraged to be just but who had to be obeyed. Even if a wife was brutally treated by her husband, she could neither find help from authorities nor expect a divorce.

Although families had always cherished their children, during the Reformation both Protestant and Catholic preachers placed even greater emphasis on the welfare, education, and moral upbringing of children. Protestants contributed to this process by emphasizing the family's responsibility for their children's moral guidance and religious education. One of the obligations of Protestant fathers was to read and teach the Bible in the home. This directive may have been more a theoretical ideal than a practical reality, but the rise in literacy among both boys and girls in Protestant countries attests to the increased importance of education.

Discipline also played a large role in the sixteenth-century family. Parents had always demonstrated love toward their children by indulging them with sweets and toys and protecting them from danger. But during the sixteenth century some authors of advice books and many preachers began to emphasize that parental love must be tempered by strict discipline. In effect, the clergy attempted to impose their own authoritarian impulses on the emotional lives of the family. The Protestant emphasis on the majesty of God and a belief in original sin translated into a negative view of human nature, especially in young children. Calvinist theologians who held such a view placed a special emphasis on family discipline.

In order to break the will of their infants, mothers were encouraged to wean them early and turn them over for a strict upbringing by their fathers. The ideal father was to cultivate both love and fear in his children by remaining unemotional and firm. He was to be vigilant to prevent masturbation, to discourage frivolity, and to toughen little children by not allowing them to eat too much, sleep too long, or stay too comfortably warm. Although discouraged from being unnecessarily brutal, the godly father was never to spare the rod on either his children or his wife.

SUPPRESSING POPULAR CULTURE

The family was not the only institution that sixteenth-century educated reformers sought to discipline. Their efforts also targeted many manifestations of traditional popular culture. The reformers or puritans, as they came to be called in England, wanted to purify both the church and society, to remake it into a "godly community" by encouraging and even enforcing moral behavior, particularly on undisciplined youths and members of the lower classes. The suppression of popular culture had two aspects. One was a policing effort, aimed at ridding society of presumably un-Christian practices. The other was a missionary enterprise, an attempt to bring the Protestant and Catholic

■ The Battle Between Carnival and Lent

In this allegory, called *The Battle Between Carnival and Lent* (1559) by Pieter Brueghel the Elder, the festive season of Carnival is represented by a fat man riding a wine barrel. He is engaged in a mock joust with an emaciated figure representing Lent, the season for fasting. Behind Carnival, people engage in games, drinking, dancing, and flirtations. Behind Lent, a procession of the pious leads back into a church.

Reformations to the people through instruction and popular preaching.

Overall the reformers sought to encourage an ethic of moderation, which valued thrift, modesty, chastity, and above all self-control. This ethic was neither Protestant nor Catholic but was promoted by clerics of all religious confessions. The traditional popular culture they so distrusted stressed other values such as spontaneity and emotional freedom, values that were hardly subject to control and could have dangerous, often violent consequences.

The festival of Carnival° came under particularly virulent attack. The most popular annual festival, Carnival took place for several days or even weeks before the beginning of Lent and included all kinds of fun and games—silly pantomimes, bear baiting, bullfights, masquerades, dances, lots of eating and drinking, and illicit sex. Pieter Brueghel the Elder's painting *The Battle Between Carnival and Lent* (1559) illustrates the role of festivals in the popular culture. In the painting, a fat man riding on a wine barrel engages in a mock joust with an emaciated, stooped figure of uncertain gender who rides a wheeled cart pulled by a monk and nun. The two figures in the painting symbolize the two festival seasons. The fat man represents Carnival, a time of joyous, gluttonous, drunken feasting; the lean one represents Lent, a period of sexual abstinence and fasting that precedes Easter. During the sixteenth century contemporaries understood the contrast between Carnival, which was devoted to bodily pleasure, and Lent, during which the bodily desires were ignored to enable repentance, as the battle between two divergent ideas of society. The battle was not just a symbol but a reality that took place through the attempts to suppress popular culture.

What Catholics reformed, Protestants abolished. Martin Luther had been relatively tolerant of popular culture, but later reformers were not. The most famous German Carnival, the *Schembartlauf* of Nuremberg, was abolished;

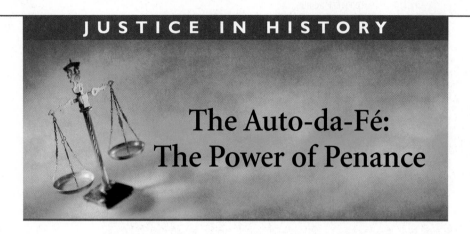

The Auto-da-Fé:
The Power of Penance

Performed in Spain and Portugal from the sixteenth to eighteenth centuries, the auto-da-fé merged the judicial processes of the state with the sacramental rituals of the Catholic Church. An *auto* took place at the end of a judicial investigation conducted by the inquisitors of the Church after the defendants had been found guilty of a sin or crime. The term *auto-da-fé* means "theater of faith," and the goal was to persuade or force a person who had been judged guilty to repent and confess. Organized through the cooperation of ecclesiastical and secular authorities, autos-da-fé brought together an assortment of sinners, criminals, and heretics for a vast public rite that dramatized the essential elements of the sacrament of penance: contrition, by which the sinner recognized and felt sorry for the sin; confession, which required the sinner to admit the sin to a priest; and satisfaction or punishment, by which the priest absolved the sinner and enacted some kind of penalty. The auto-da-fé transformed penance, especially confession and satisfaction, into a spectacular affirmation of the faith and a manifestation of divine justice.

The *auto* symbolically anticipated the Last Judgment, and it provoked deep anxiety among those who witnessed it about how God would judge them. By suffering bodily pain in this life the soul might be relieved from worse punishments in the next. The sinners, convicts, and heretics, now considered penitents, were forced to march in a procession that went through the streets of the city from the cathedral to the town hall or place of punishment. These processions would typically include some thirty or forty penitents, but in moments of crisis they could be far larger. In Toledo in 1486 there were three *autos*—one parading 750 penitents and two displaying some 900 each.

A 1655 *auto* in Córdoba illustrates the symbolic character of the rites. Soldiers bearing torches that would light the pyre for those to be burned led the procession. Following them came three bigamists who wore on their heads conical miters or hats painted with representations of their sin, four witches whose miters depicted devils, and three criminals with harnesses around their necks to demonstrate their status as captives. The sinners carried unlit candles to represent their lack of faith. Criminals who had escaped arrest were represented in the procession by effigies made in their likeness, and those who had died before punishment were carried in their coffins. The marching sinners appeared before their neighbors and fellow citizens stripped of the normal indicators of status, dressed only in the emblems of their sins. Among them walked a few who wore the infamous *sanbenitos,* a kind of tunic or vest with a yellow strip down the back, and a conical hat painted with flames. These were the *relajados,* the unrepentant or relapsed sinners who were going to be "relaxed" (released into the hands of the secular authorities) at the culminating moment of the *auto* when they were strangled and burned.

The procession ended in the town square at a platform from which penances were performed as on the stage of a theater. Forced to their knees, the penitents were asked to confess and to plead for readmission into the bosom of the church. For those who did confess, a sentence was announced that would rescue them from the pains of Purgatory and the flames of the *auto.* The sentence required them to join a penitential procession for a certain number of Fridays, perform self-flagellation in public, or wear a badge of shame for a prescribed period of time. Those who failed to confess faced a more immediate sentence.

The most horrendous scenes of suffering awaited those who refused to confess or who had relapsed into sin or heresy, which meant their confession was not considered sincere. If holdouts confessed prior to the reading of the sentence, then the *auto* was a success, a triumph of the Christian faith over its enemies, and everything that could possibly elicit confessions was attempted, including haranguing, humiliating, and torturing the accused until their stubborn will broke. If the accused finally confessed after the sentence was read, then they would be strangled before burning, but if they held out to the very end, they would be burned alive. From the ecclesiastics' point of view, the refusal to confess was a disaster for the entire Church because the flames of the pyre opened a window into Hell. They would certainly prefer to see the Church's authority acknowledged through confession than

■ **Auto-da-Fé in Lisbon**

A procession conducted the sinners, many with hats or aprons identifying their sins, to a stage and pyre where relapsed heretics were burned.

to see the power of Satan manifest in such a public fashion.

It is reported that crowds witnessed the violence of the autos-da-fé with silent attention in a mood of deep dread, not so much of the inquisitors, it seems, as for the inevitability of the final day of divine judgment that would arrive for them all. The core assumption of the auto-da-fé was that bodily pain could save a soul from damnation. As one contemporary witness put it, the inquisitors removed "through external ritual [the sinners'] internal crimes." It was assumed that the public ritual framework for the sacrament of penance would have a salutary effect on those who witnessed the *auto* by encouraging them to repent before they too faced divine judgment. ■

Questions of Justice

1. How did the auto-da-fé contribute to the formation of an individual and collective sense of being a Catholic?
2. In the auto-da-fé, inflicting physical pain was more than punishment. How was inflicting pain understood to be useful in promoting social and religious justice?

Taking It Further

Flynn, Maureen. "Mimesis of the Last Judgment: The Spanish *Auto de fe*," *Sixteenth Century Journal* 22 (1991): 281–297. The best analysis of the religious significance of the auto-da-fé.

Flynn, Maureen. "The Spectacle of Suffering in Spanish Streets," in Barbara A. Hanawalt and Kathryn L. Reyerson, eds., *City and Spectacle in Medieval Europe*. 1994. In this fascinating article Flynn analyzes the spiritual value of physical pain.

in England the great medieval pageants of York, Coventry, Chester, Norwich, and Worcester disappeared; in Calvinist Holland, the Christmas tradition of giving children gifts was strongly denounced.

HUNTING WITCHES

The most catastrophic manifestation of the widespread anxiety of the late sixteenth and seventeenth centuries was the great witch-hunt°. The judicial prosecution of alleged witches in either church or secular courts dramatically increased about the middle of the sixteenth century and lasted until the late seventeenth, when the number of witchcraft trials rapidly diminished and stopped entirely in western Europe.

Many people of the sixteenth and seventeenth centuries believed in the power of demonic magic. The practitioner of this kind of magic—usually but not always a female witch—called on evil spirits to gain access to power. Demonic magic was generally understood as a way to work harm by ritual means. Belief in the reality of harmful magic and of witches had been widespread for centuries, and there had been occasional witch trials throughout the Middle Ages. Systematic witch-hunts, however, began only when ecclesiastical and secular authorities showed a willingness

to employ the law to discover and punish accused witches. The Reformation controversies of the late sixteenth century and the authorities' willingness to discipline deviants of all sorts certainly intensified the hunt for witches. Thousands of people were accused of and tried for practicing witchcraft. About half of these alleged witches were executed, most often by burning. Cases of alleged witchcraft rarely occurred in a steady flow, as one would find for other crimes. Typically, witchcraft trials took place during localized hunts when a flareup of paranoia multiplied allegations against vulnerable members of the community. Most allegations were against women, in particular young unmarried women and older widows, but men and even young children could be accused of witchcraft as well.

People in many different places—from shepherds in the mountains of Switzerland to Calvinist ministers in the lowlands of Scotland—thought they perceived the work of witches in human and natural events. The alleged demonic magic of witchcraft appeared in two forms: *maleficia* (doing harm) and *diabolism* (worshiping the devil). The rituals of *maleficia* consisted of a simple sign or a complex incantation, but what made them *maleficia* was the belief that the person who performed them intended to cause harm to someone or something. There were many kinds of *maleficia*, including coercing an unwilling lover by sprin-

■ **The Witches' Sabbath**

The myth of the witches' sabbath depicted witches paying homage to an enthroned Satan. The typical sabbath motifs included the ability to fly and cannibalism of Christian babies, as shown on the lower right. The figures walking on their hands reveal a world literally turned upside down.

kling dried menstrual blood in his food, sickening a pig by cursing it, burning a barn by marking it with a hex sign, bringing wasting diarrhea to a child by reciting a spell, and killing an enemy by stabbing a wax statue of him. Midwives and women who specialized in healing were especially vulnerable to accusations of witchcraft. The intention behind a particular action they might have performed was often obscure, making it difficult to distinguish between magic designed to bring beneficial results, such as the cure of a child, and *maleficia* designed to bring harmful ones. With the high infant mortality rates of the sixteenth and seventeenth centuries, performing magical rituals for a sick baby could be very risky. The logic of witchcraft beliefs implied that a bad ending must have been caused by bad intentions.

While some people may have attempted to practice *maleficia,* the second and far more serious kind of ritual practice associated with demonic magic, *diabolism,* almost certainly never took place. Diabolism was a fantasy that helped explain events that could not otherwise be explained. The theory behind diabolism asserted that the witch had sold her soul to the Devil, whom she worshiped as her god. These witches had made a pact with the Devil, worshiped the Devil in the ritual of the witches' sabbath, flew around at night, and sometimes changed themselves into animals. The two core beliefs of the pact with the Devil and the witches' sabbath created the intellectual and legal conditions for the great witch-hunt of the sixteenth and seventeenth centuries.

A pact with the devil was believed to give the witch the ability to accomplish *maleficia,* in exchange for which she was obliged to serve and worship Satan. The most influential witchcraft treatise, *The Hammer of Witches* (1486), had an extensive discussion of the ceremony of the pact. After the prospective witch had declared her intention to enter his service, Satan appeared to her, often in the alluring form of a handsome young man who offered her rewards, including a demonic lover, called an *incubus.* To obtain these inducements, the witch was obliged to renounce her allegiance to Christ, usually signified by stomping on the cross. The Devil rebaptized her in a disgusting substance, guaranteeing that her soul belonged to him. To signify that she was one of his own, the Devil marked her body in a hidden place, creating a sign, which could easily be confused with a birthmark or blemish. To an inquisitor or judge almost any mark on the skin might confirm guilt.

Between about 1550 and 1650, approximately 100,000 people in Europe were tried for witchcraft. About 50,000 of these were executed. Approximately half of the trials were in the German-speaking lands of the Holy Roman Empire. Prosecutions were also extensive in Switzerland, France, Scotland, Poland, Hungary, Transylvania, and Russia. As the product of collective beliefs and collective paranoia, witchcraft beliefs could be applied to all kinds of people, but allegations were most commonly lodged against poor, older women in small rural villages.

The Confessional States

The Religious Peace of Augsburg of 1555 provided the model for a solution to the religious divisions produced by the Reformation. According to the principle of *cuius regio, eius religio* (he who rules determines the religion of the land), each prince in the Holy Roman Empire determined the religion to be followed by his subjects, and those who disagreed were obliged to convert or emigrate elsewhere. Certainly, forced exile was economically and personally traumatic for those who emigrated, but it preserved what was almost universally believed to be the fundamental principle of successful rulership—one king, one faith, one law. In other words, each state should have only one church. Except in the notoriously weak states of eastern Europe and a few small troubled principalities in the Holy Roman Empire, hardly anyone thought it desirable to allow more than one confession in the same state.

The problem with this political theory of religious unity, of course, was the reality of religious divisions created by the Reformation. In some places there were as many as three active confessions—Catholic, Lutheran, and Calvinist—in addition to the minority sects, such as the Anabaptists, and the Jewish communities. The alternative to religious unity would have been religious toleration, but hardly anyone in a position of authority was willing to advocate that. Wherever there were significant religious minorities within a state, the best that could be hoped for was a condition of anxious tension, omnipresent suspicion, and periodic hysteria (see Map 14.1). The worst possibility was civil war in which religious affiliations and political rivalries were intertwined in such complicated ways that finding peaceful solutions was especially difficult. Between 1560 and 1648 several religious civil wars broke out, including the French Wars of Religion, the Dutch revolt against Spain, the Thirty Years' War in Germany, and the English Civil War. (The latter two will be discussed in Chapter 15.) The sharp confessional divisions that assasinations and civil wars engendered also stimulated writers, poets, and dramatists to examine the human condition. Perhaps no period in the history of the West produced as many great works of literature as the late sixteenth and early seventeenth centuries.

THE FRENCH WARS OF RELIGION

By 1560 Calvinism had made significant inroads into predominantly Catholic France. Pastors sent from Geneva had been especially successful in the larger provincial towns, where their evangelical message appealed to enterprising merchants, professionals, and skilled artisans. Some 10 percent or more of the population had become Calvinists, or Huguenots° as French Protestants were called. The political strength of the Huguenots was greater than their numbers

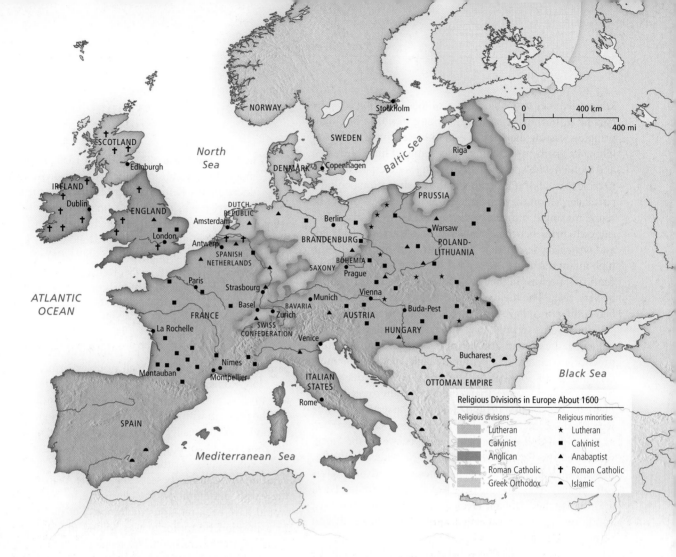

■ **Map 14.1 Religious Divisions in Europe About 1600**

After 1555 the religious borders of Europe became relatively fixed, with only minor changes in confessional affiliations to this day.

might indicate, because between one-third and one-half of the lower nobility professed Calvinism. Calvinism was popular among the French nobility for two reasons. One involved the imitation of social superiors. When a high aristocrat converted to Protestantism, he tended to bring his noble clientele into the new faith as well, who converted through loyalty to their patron or through the patron's ability to persuade those who were financially dependent on him. As a result of a few aristocratic conversions in southwest France, Calvinism spread through "a veritable religious spider's web,"[1] as one contemporary put it.

Even more important than networks of male patrons was the influence of powerful aristocratic women. The sister of King Francis I of France (r. 1515–1547), Marguerite of Angoulême (1492–1549), married the king of Navarre (an independent kingdom situated between France and Spain) and created a haven in Navarre for Huguenot preachers and theologians. Her example drew other aristocratic ladies to the Huguenot cause, and many of the Huguenot leaders during the French Wars of Religion were the sons and grandsons of these early female converts.

Marguerite's daughter, Jeanne d'Albret, sponsored Calvinist preachers for several years before she publicly announced her own conversion in 1560, and her son, Henry Bourbon, became the principal leader of the Huguenot cause during the French Wars of Religion° and the person responsible for eventually bringing the wars to an end.

The Origins of the Religious Wars

Like all civil wars, the French Wars of Religion exhibited a bewildering pattern of intrigue, betrayal, and treachery. Three distinct groups constituted the principal players. The first group was the royal family, consisting of Queen Catherine de Médicis and her four sons by Henry II—King Francis II (r. 1559–1560), King Charles IX (r. 1560–1574), King Henry III (r. 1574–1589), and Duke Francis of Alençon (1554–1584)—and her daughter, Marguerite Valois (1553–1615). The royal family remained Catholic but on occasion reconciled themselves with the Huguenot opposition, and Marguerite married into it. The second group was the Huguenot faction of nobles led by the Châtillon family and the Bourbon family who ruled

Navarre. The third group was the hard-line Catholic faction led by the implacable Guise family. These three groups vied for supremacy during the successive reigns of Catherine de Médicis's three sons, none of whom proved to be effective monarchs.

In 1562 civil war broke out in earnest. For nearly forty years a series of religious wars sapped the strength of France. Most of the battles were indecisive, which meant neither side sustained military superiority for long. Both sides relied for support on their regional bases: The Protestant strength was in the Southwest, the Catholic in Paris and the North. Besides military engagements, the French Wars of Religion were characterized by political assassinations and massacres.

Massacre of St. Bartholomew's Day

After a decade of bloody yet inconclusive combat, the royal family tried to resolve the conflict by making peace with the Protestants, a shift of policy signified by the announcement of the engagement of Marguerite Valois, daughter of Henry II and Catherine de Médicis, to Henry Bourbon, the son of the Huguenot King of Navarre. At age 19, Marguerite—or Queen Margot, as she was known—was already renowned for her brilliant intelligence. But she was renowned also for her wanton morals, and to complicate the situation further, on the eve of the wedding she was having an affair with another Henry, the young new Duke of Guise, who was the leader of the intransigent Catholic faction. The marriage between Marguerite and Henry of Navarre was to take place in Paris in August 1572, an event that brought all the Huguenot leaders to the heavily armed Catholic capital for the first time in many years. The gathering of all their enemies in one place presented too great a temptation for the Guises, who hatched a plot to assassinate the Huguenot leaders. Perhaps because she had become jealous of the Huguenots' growing influence on her son, King Charles IX, the mercurial Catherine suddenly switched sides and became implicated in the plot.

Catherine somehow convinced the weak-willed king to order the massacre of the Huguenot nobles gathered in Paris. On August 14, 1572, St. Bartholomew's Day, the people of Paris began a slaughter. Between 3,000 and 4,000 Huguenots were butchered in Paris and more than 20,000 others were put to death throughout the rest of France. Henry of Navarre saved his life by pretending to convert to Catholicism, while most of his companions were murdered.

Catherine's attempted solution for the Huguenot problem failed to solve anything, however. Henry of Navarre escaped his virtual imprisonment in the royal household, set Marguerite up in an isolated castle, returned to Navarre and his faith, and reinvigorated Huguenot resistance. Two Huguenot political thinkers laid out a theory justifying political revolution: François Hotman in *Francogallia* (1573) and Théodore de Bèze in *Right of Magistrates* (1579). They argued that since the authority of all magistrates, including

THE ST. BARTHOLOMEW'S DAY MASSACRE: PAINFUL MEMORIES

The Duke of Sully (1560–1641) became an ambassador and finance minister for the French king Henry IV and was the principal architect of the Edict of Nantes, which provided a measure of religious toleration for Protestants in France after 1589. During the St. Bartholomew's Day Massacre he was 12 years old, but he never forgot what he witnessed. Sully was one of the few members of Henry of Navarre's personal entourage to survive the massacre.

Intending on that day to wait upon the king my master [Henry of Navarre, later King Henry IV of France], I went to bed early on the preceding evening; about three in the morning I was awakened by the cries of people, and; the alarm-bells, which were everywhere ringing. . . . I was determined to escape to the College de Bourgogne, and to effect this I put on my scholar's gown, and taking a book under my arm, I set out. In the streets I met three parties of the Life-guards; the first of these, after handling me very roughly, seized my book, and, most fortunately for me, seeing it was a Roman Catholic prayer-book, suffered me to proceed, and this served me as a passport with the two other parties. As I went along I saw the houses broken open and plundered, and men, women, and children butchered, while a constant cry was kept up of, "Kill! Kill! O you Huguenots! O you Huguenots!" This made me very impatient to gain the college, where, through God's assistance, I at length arrived, without suffering any other injury than a most dreadful fright.

Source: From "The Saint Bartholomew's Day Massacre" in Bayle St. John, ed., *Memoirs of the Duke of Sully, Vol. 1* (London: George Bell and Sons, 1877).

even low-ranking nobles, came directly from God, the Huguenot nobles had the right and obligation to resist a tyrannical Catholic king. During the same period, Catholic moderates known as the *politiques* rejected the excesses of the Guises and argued for an accommodation with the Huguenots.

The wars of religion continued until the assassination of King Henry III, brother of the late Charles IX. Both Charles and Henry had been childless, a situation that made Henry Bourbon of Navarre the rightful heir to the throne, even though he was a Huguenot. Henry Bourbon became King Henry IV (r. 1589–1610) and recognized that predominantly Catholic France would never accept a Huguenot king, and so in 1593 with his famous quip, "Paris is worth a mass," Henry reconverted to the ancient faith, and most opposition to him among Catholics collapsed. Once he returned to Catholicism he managed to have the pope annul his childless marriage to Marguerite so that he could marry Marie de' Médicis and obtain her huge dowry. Affable, witty, generous, and exceedingly tolerant, "Henry the Great" became the most popular king in French history, reuniting the war-torn country by ruling with a very firm hand. With the Edict of Nantes° of 1598, he allowed the Huguenots to build a quasi state within the state, giving them the right to have their own troops, church organization, and political autonomy within their walled towns, but they were banned from the royal court and the city of Paris.

Despite his enormous popularity, Henry too fell victim to fanaticism. After surviving eighteen attempts on his life, in 1610 the king was fatally stabbed by a Catholic fanatic who took advantage of the opportunity presented when the royal coach unexpectedly stopped behind a cart loading hay. Unlike the aftermath of the St. Bartholomew's Day massacre, Catholics all over France mourned Henry's death and considered the assassin mad. Henry's brilliant conciliatory nature and the horrors of the religious wars had tempered public opinion.

PHILIP II, THE KING OF PAPER

France's greatest rivals were the Habsburgs, who possessed vast territories in the Holy Roman Empire, controlled the elections for emperor, and had dynastic rights to the throne of Spain. As archenemies of the Protestant Reformation, they had regularly helped finance the Catholic cause during the French Wars of Religion. During the late sixteenth century, Habsburg Spain took advantage of French weakness to establish itself as the dominant power in Europe. When the great Emperor Charles V (who had been both Holy Roman Emperor and king of Spain) abdicated his thrones in 1556, the Habsburg possessions in the Holy Roman Empire and the emperorship went to his brother, Ferdinand I, and the balance of his vast domain to his son, Philip II (r. 1556–1598). Philip's inheritance included Milan, Naples, Sicily, the Netherlands, scattered outposts on the north coast of Africa, colonies in the Caribbean, Central America, Mexico, Peru, the Philippines, and most important of all, Spain. In 1580 he also inherited Portugal and its far-flung overseas empire, which included a line of trading posts from West Africa to the Spice Islands and the vast colony of unexplored Brazil.

Ruling over these enormous territories was a gargantuan task that Philip undertook with obsessive seriousness. From the rambling palace of El Escorial, which was also a mausoleum for his father and a monastery, Philip lived in semi-monastic seclusion and ruled as the "King of Paper," an office-bound bureaucrat rather than the rule-from-the-saddle warrior his father had been and many of his contemporary monarchs remained. Philip kept himself to a rigid daily work discipline that included endless committee meetings and long hours devoted to poring over as many as 400 documents a day, which he annotated extensively in his crabbed hand. Because of his inability to delegate authority and his immersion in minutiae, Philip tended to lose his grasp of the larger picture, especially the shaky finances of Spain.

This grave, distrustful, rigid man saw himself as the great protector of the Catholic cause and committed Spain to perpetual hostility toward Muslims and Protestants. On the Muslim front he first bullied the Moriscos, the descendants of the Spanish Muslims. The Moriscos had received Christian baptism, but they were suspected of secretly practicing Islam, and in 1568 Philip issued an edict that banned all manifestations of Muslim culture and ordered the Moriscos to turn over their children to Christian priests to educate. The outraged Moriscos of Granada rebelled but were soundly defeated. At first dispersed throughout Spain, the surviving Moriscos were eventually expelled from the country in 1609. Philip hardened his policy toward the Moriscos because he feared, not unreasonably, that they would become secret agents on Spanish soil for his great Mediterranean rivals, the Ottoman Turks.

Philip once said he would rather lose all his possessions and die a hundred times than be the king of heretics. His attitude toward Protestants showed that he meant what he said. Through his marriage to Queen Mary I of England (r. 1553–1558), Philip encouraged her persecutions of Protestants, but they got their revenge. After Mary's death her half-sister, Queen Elizabeth I, refused his marriage proposal and in 1577 signed a treaty to assist the Protestant Netherlands, which was in rebellion against Spain. To add insult to injury, the English privateer Sir Francis Drake (ca. 1540–1596) conducted a personal war against Catholic Spain by raiding the Spanish convoys bringing silver from the New World. In 1587 Drake's embarrassing successes culminated with a daring raid on the great Spanish port city of Cadiz where, "singeing the king of Spain's beard," he destroyed the anchored Spanish fleet and many thousands of tons of vital supplies. Philip retaliated by building a huge fleet of 132 ships armed with 3,165 cannons, which sailed from Portugal to rendezvous with the Spanish army stationed in the Netherlands and launch an invasion of England in 1588. As the Invincible Armada, as it was called, passed through the English Channel, it was met by a much smaller English fleet, assembled out of merchant ships refitted for battle. Unable to maneuver as effectively as the English in the fluky winds of the channel and mauled by the rapid-firing English guns, the Spanish Armada° suffered heavy losses and was forced to retreat to the north, where it sustained further losses in storms off the coasts of Scotland and Ireland. Barely more than half of the fleet finally straggled home. The defeat severely shook Philip's sense of invincibility.

The reign of Philip II illustrated better than any other the contradictions and tensions of the era. No monarch had at his grasp as many resources and territories as Philip, and yet defending them proved extremely costly. The creaky governmental machinery of Spain put a tremendous burden on a conscientious king such as Philip, but even his unflagging energy and dedication to his duties could not prevent military defeat and financial disaster. Economic historians remember Philip's reign for its series of state bankruptcies and for the loss of the Netherlands, the most precious jewel in the crown of Spain.

THE DUTCH REVOLT

The Netherlands boasted some of Europe's richest cities, situated amid a vast network of lakes, rivers, channels, estuaries, and tidal basins that periodically replenished the exceptionally productive soil through flooding. The Netherlands consisted of seventeen provinces, each with its own distinctive identity, traditions, and even language. The southern provinces were primarily French-speaking; those in the north spoke a bewildering variety of Flemish dialects. In 1548 Emperor Charles V annexed the northern provinces that had been part of the Holy Roman Empire to the southern provinces he had inherited from his father. His decision meant that when his son, Philip II, became king of Spain, all of the Netherlands was included with the Spanish crown. With his characteristic bureaucratic mentality, Philip treated Dutch affairs as a management problem rather than a political sore spot, an attitude that subordinated the Netherlands to Spanish interests. Foreign rule irritated the Dutch, who had long enjoyed ancient privileges including the right to raise their own taxes and muster their own troops.

Consolidating the Netherlands under the Spanish crown deprived the Dutch princes of the right to choose the official religion of their lands, a right they would have enjoyed had the provinces remained in the Holy Roman Empire where the Religious Peace of Augsburg granted princes religious freedom. Philip's harsh attitude toward Protestants upset the Netherlands' delicate balance among Catholic, Lutheran, Calvinist, and Anabaptist communities. Huguenot refugees from the French Wars of Religion heightened the anti-Catholic fanaticism of the local Calvinists, who in 1566 occupied many Catholic churches and destroyed paintings and statues.

In response to the rapidly deteriorating situation in the Netherlands, Philip issued edicts against the heretics and strengthened the Spanish Inquisition. Philip also dispatched 20,000 Spanish troops under the command of the Duke of Alba (1508–1582), a veteran of the Turkish campaigns in North Africa and victories over the Lutheran princes of the Holy Roman Empire. Alba directly attacked the Protestants. Alba himself boasted that during the campaign against the rebels, he had 18,000 people executed, in addition to those who died in battle or were massacred by soldiers. The Prince of Orange, William the Silent (1533–1584), accompanied into exile 60,000 refugees, who constituted about 2 percent of the population. While abroad William began to organize resistance to Alba.

Alba's replacement, the shrewd statesman and general, the Duke of Parma (r. 1578–1592), ultimately subdued the southern provinces, which remained a Spanish colony. The seven northern provinces, however, united in 1579 and declared independence from Spain in 1581. William the Silent became the *stadholder* (governor) of the new United Provinces, and after his assassination his 17-year-old son, Maurice of Nassau, inherited the same title.

The Netherlands' struggle for independence transformed the population of the northern provinces from mixed religions to staunch Calvinism. The Dutch Revolt° became ensnared in the French Wars of Religion through Huguenot refugees, and the alliance with England, which provided much-needed financial and moral support, reinforced the Protestant identity of the Dutch. The international Protestant alliance created by the Dutch Revolt and centered in the Netherlands withstood both Philip's fury and Parma's calm generalship. The failure of the Spanish Armada to land Parma's men in England guaranteed the survival of an independent Netherlands. The Dutch carried on a sporadic and inconclusive war against Spain until the end of the Thirty Years' War in 1648, when the international community recognized the independent Republic of the United Provinces.

LITERATURE IN THE AGE OF CONFESSIONAL DIVISION

Churches and monarchs everywhere demanded religious conformity in word and deed, a situation that would seem to stifle creativity, and yet the late sixteenth and early seventeenth centuries were one of the most remarkable periods in the history of creative literature. During this period the native or vernacular languages of western Europe (Italian, French, Portuguese, Spanish, and English) became literary languages, replacing Latin as the dominant form of expression, even for the educated elite.

The greatest masters of French prose during this crucial period were François Rabelais (ca. 1483–1553) and Michel de Montaigne (1533–1592). Trained as a lawyer, Rabelais became a friar and priest but left the Church under a cloud of heresy to become a physician. Rabelais's satirical masterpiece, a series of novels recounting the fantastic and grotesque adventures of Gargantua and Pantagruel, combined an encyclopedic command of humanist thought with stunning verbal invention that has had a lasting influence on humorous writers to this day.

After a modestly successful legal career, Montaigne retired to the family chateau to discover himself by writing essays, a literary form well suited to reflective introspection. In his essays, Montaigne struggled with his lasting grief over the premature death from dysentery of a close friend, reflected on his own experience of the intense physical pain of illness, and diagnosed the absurd causes of the French Wars of Religion. Montaigne's essays are a profound

■ **Queen Elizabeth I of England**
Elizabeth presided over the greatest age of English literature.

series of meditations on the meaning of life and death, presented in a calm voice of reason to an age of violent fanaticism.

During the reign of Elizabeth I (r. 1558–1603), the Renaissance truly arrived in England. The principal figure of the Elizabethan Renaissance was a professional dramatist, William Shakespeare (1564–1616). In a series of theaters, including the famous Globe on the south side of the Thames in London, Shakespeare wrote, produced, and acted in comedies, tragedies, and history plays. Shakespeare's enormous output of plays, some of which made veiled allusions to the politics of Elizabeth's court, established him not only as the most popular dramatist of his time but the greatest literary figure in the English language. The power of his plays derives from the subtle understanding of human psychology found in his characters and the stunning force of his language. For Shakespeare, as for Montaigne, the source of true knowledge was self-knowledge.

States and Confessions in Eastern Europe

In contrast to the confessional states of western Europe where rulers demanded religious conformity, the weak states of eastern Europe during the early sixteenth century were less successful in linking religious conformity to political loyalty. Whereas in the West the religious controversies stimulated writers to investigate deeply the human condition but made them cautious about expressing nonconforming religious opinions, writers and creative people in the East during this period were able to explore a wide range of ideas in a relatively tolerant atmosphere.

During the last decades of the sixteenth and early seventeenth centuries, however, dynastic troubles compromised the relative openness of the eastern states, enmeshing them in conflicts among themselves that had an increasingly strong religious dimension. In the Holy Roman Empire the weakness of the mad Emperor Rudolf permitted religious conflicts to fester, setting the stage for the disastrous Thirty Years' War (1618–1648) that pitted Catholic against Protestant states.

THE DREAM WORLD OF EMPEROR RUDOLF

The Holy Roman Empire was a very loose confederation of semi-independent, mostly German-speaking states, many of which ignored imperial decrees that did not suit them. The crippling weakness of the imperial system became most evident during the reign of Rudolf II (r. 1576–1612). Soon after his election to the imperial throne, Rudolf moved his court from bustling Vienna to the lovely quiet of Prague in Bohemia. Fearful of noisy crowds and impatient courtiers, standoffish toward foreign ambassadors who presented him with difficult decisions, paranoid about scheming relatives, and prone to wild emotional gyrations from deep depression to manic grandiosity, Rudolf was hardly suited for the imperial throne. In fact, many contemporaries, who had their own reasons to underrate him, described him as hopelessly insane.

Incapable of governing, Rudolf transmuted the imperial ideal of universality into a strange dream world. In Prague he gathered around him a brilliant court of humanists, musicians, painters, physicians, astronomers, astrologers, alchemists, and magicians. These included an eclectic assortment of significant thinkers—the great astronomers Tycho Brahe and Johannes Kepler, the notorious occult philosopher Giordano Bruno, the theoretical mathematician and astrologer John Dee, and the remarkable inventor of surrealist painting Giuseppe Arcimboldo. As Chapter 16 will explain, many of these figures are considered the immediate forerunners of the Scientific Revolution, but Rudolf also fell prey to fast-talking charlatans. This weird court, however, was less the strange fruit of the emperor's hopeless dementia than the manifestation of a striving for universal empire. Rudolf sought to preserve the cultural and political unity of the empire, to eradicate religious divisions, and to achieve peace at home. Rudolf's court in Prague was perhaps the only place left during the late sixteenth century where Protestants, Catholics, Jews, and even radical heretics such as Bruno could gather together in a common intellectual enterprise. The goal of such gatherings was to discover the universal principles that governed nature, principles that would provide the foundations for a single unifying religion and a cure for all human maladies. It was a noble, if utterly improbable, dream.

While Rudolf and his favorite courtiers isolated themselves in their dream world, the religious conflicts within the empire reached a boiling point. Without a strong emperor, the Imperial Diets were paralyzed by confessional squabbles. In the following decade, more than 200 religious revolts or riots took place.

THE RENAISSANCE OF POLAND-LITHUANIA

As the major power in eastern Europe, Poland-Lithuania engaged in a tug-of-war with Sweden over control of the eastern Baltic and virtually constant warfare against the expansionist ambitions of Russia (see Map 14.2). The most remarkable achievement of Poland-Lithuania during this contentious time was its unparalleled and still controversial

■ **Map 14.2   Poland-Lithuania and Russia**

These countries were the largest in Europe in the size of their territories but were relatively underpopulated compared to the western European states.

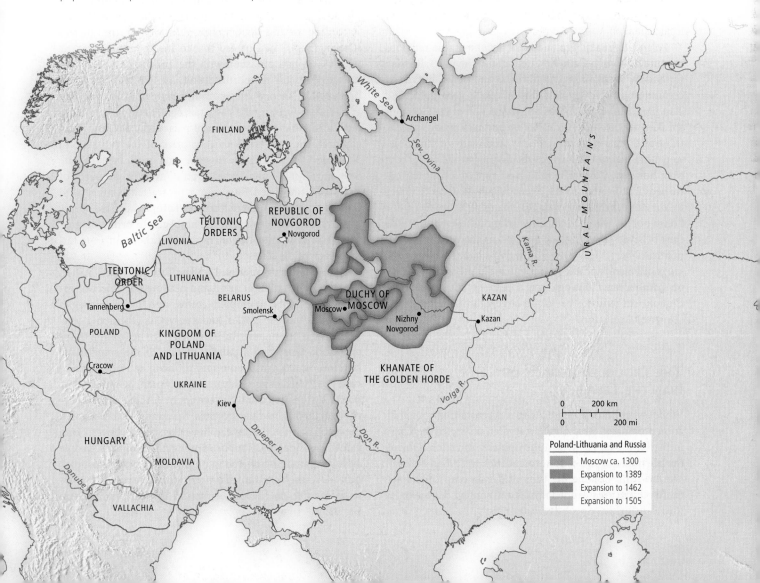

experiments in government. Poland-Lithuania had an elected king but called itself a republic. The king was a figurehead, and Poland-Lithuania was a republic in the sense that it was effectively governed by assemblies of nobles.

Very loosely joined since 1336, Poland and Lithuania created a constitutional union in 1569, creating a confederation in which Poland supplied the king, but the Grand Duchy of Lithuania was considered an equal partner and allowed to retain its own laws, administration, and army. The novel feature of the confederation was how the nobles reserved power for themselves through their control of regional assemblies, which in turn dominated the central parliament called the Sejm. These nobles elected the king and treated him, at best, as a hired manager. They resisted all attempts to exert royal power by asserting the legal right to form local armed assemblies against the king and by exercising the principle of unanimity in the Sejm, which prevented the king or a strong faction from dominating affairs. In the last half of the seventeenth century Poland-Lithuania fell into chaos under this system, but for nearly three-quarters of a century it worked well enough—at least for the nobles. The rule of the nobles in Poland-Lithuania came at a great cost to the Polish peasants, however, who were ruthlessly forced into serfdom and deprived of their legal rights.

Poland-Lithuania contained an incomparable religious mixture of Roman Catholics, Lutherans, Calvinists, Russian Orthodox, Anabaptists, Unitarians, and Jews, but these communities were strongly divided along geographic and class lines. Lutheranism was a phenomenon of the German-speaking towns, the peasants of Poland remained Catholic, those in Lithuania were Orthodox, and many of the nobles were attracted to Calvinism. During the late sixteenth century, however, Christians in Poland almost completely returned or converted to the Roman Catholic faith. The key to the transformation was the changing attitude of the Polish nobles, who had tolerated religious diversity because they believed that religious liberty was the cornerstone of political liberty. However, a growing alliance between the kings of Poland and the Jesuits enhanced the social prestige of Catholicism. Through the spread of elite education, Catholicism returned to Poland largely through persuasion rather than coercion.

THE TROUBLED LEGACY OF IVAN THE TERRIBLE

While Poland experimented with a decentralized confederation dominated by nobles that severely restricted the king's initiative, Russia evolved in the opposite direction. During the late fifteenth and sixteenth centuries, the grand dukes of Moscow who became the tsars of Russia eclipsed the authority of the great landed nobles and snuffed out the inde-

pendence of the towns. The authoritarian tendencies of the tsars harmed the Russian peasants, however, just as royal weakness harmed the Polish peasants. After 1454 Moscow's creation of military fiefs (*pomestye*) to supply soldiers against the Tartars (Mongol tribes) allowed the nobles to push the peasants back into serfdom. Refusing to accept enserfment, the peasants fled the fields in massive numbers, depopulating central Russia as they found refuge among the Cossack colonies along the borders to the southeast.

Russia was already well integrated into the European diplomatic community and engaged in trade with its Western neighbors. But for more than 300 years Russia had been under the "Tartar Yoke," a term describing the Mongolian tribes that overran the country, pillaging and depopulating it. Ivan III, "The Great" (1462–1505), succeeded in gradually throwing off the Tartar Yoke by refusing to continue to pay tribute to the Mongols. Ivan married Zoë, the niece of the last Greek emperor of Constantinople. The marriage gave him the basis for claiming that the Russian rulers were the heirs of Byzantium and the exclusive protectors of Orthodox Christianity, the state religion of Russia. Following the Byzantine tradition of imperial autocracy, Ivan practiced Byzantine court ceremonies, and his advisers developed the theory of the Three Romes. According to this theory, the authority of the ancient Roman Empire had passed first to the Byzantine Empire, which God had punished with the Turkish conquest, and then to Moscow as the third and last "Rome." Ivan celebrated this theory by assuming the title of tsar (or "Caesar"). With his wife's assistance, he hired Italian architects to rebuild the grand ducal palace, the Kremlin. Ivan captured the vast northern territories of the city-state of Novgorod, expanding the Russian state north to the White Sea and east to the Urals. Ivan's invasion of parts of Lithuania embroiled Russia in a protracted conflict with Poland that lasted more than a century. Like his fellow monarchs in western Europe, Ivan began to bring the aristocrats under control by incorporating them into the bureaucracy of the state.

Ivan III's grandson, Ivan IV, "The Terrible" (1533–1584), succeeded his father at age 3 and became the object of innumerable plots, attempted coups, and power struggles among his mother, uncles, and the boyars (the upper-level nobles who dominated Russian society). The trauma of his childhood years and a painful disease of the spine made him inordinately suspicious and prone to acts of impulsive violence. When at age 17 Ivan was crowned, he reduced the power of the dukes and the boyars by forcing them to exchange their hereditary estates for lands that obligated them to serve the tsar in war. In weakening the boyars, Ivan gained considerable support among the common people and was even remembered in popular songs as the people's tsar. Nevertheless, Ivan distrusted everyone. He often arrested people on charges of treason just for taking a trip abroad. In a cruel revenge on his enemies among the boyars, he began a reign of terror in which he personally committed horrendous atrocities. His massacre in 1570 of the inhabitants of Novgorod, whom he suspected of harboring Polish sympathies, contributed to his reputation as a bloody tyrant. By setting aside half of the realm as his personal domain, he created a strong financial base for the army, which led to military successes in the prolonged wars against Poland, Lithuania, and Sweden. During his reign, however, the Polish threat and boyar opposition to his rule revealed signs of the fragility of Russian unity.

During the "Time of Troubles°" (1604–1613), Russia fell into chaos. Boyar families struggled among themselves for supremacy, the Cossacks from the South led a popular revolt, and Poles and Swedes openly interfered in Russian affairs. Finally, the Time of Troubles ended when in 1613 the national assembly elected Tsar Michael Romanov, whose descendants ruled Russia until they were deposed in 1917. During the seventeenth century the Romanovs gradually restored order to Russia, eroded the independence of local governments, and strengthened the institution of serfdom. By the end of the seventeenth century Russia was strong enough to reenter European affairs as a major power.

CHRONOLOGY

1548	Annexation of the northern provinces of the Netherlands to the Spanish crown
1569	Constitutional Union of Poland and Lithuania
1572	Massacre of St. Bartholomew's Day
1576-1612	Reign of Emperor Rudolf II
1581	Seven northern provinces of the Netherlands declare independence from Spain
1584	Assassination of William the Silent
1588	Defeat of the Spanish Armada
1593	King Henry IV of France converts to Catholicism
1598	Edict of Nantes grants Protestants religious toleration
1604–1613	Time of Troubles in Russia
1609	Expulsion of the Moriscos from Spain

CONCLUSION

The Divisions of the West

During the late sixteenth and early seventeenth centuries, hidden demographic and economic pressures eroded the confidence and security of many Europeans, creating a widespread sense of unease. Most people retreated like confused soldiers behind the barricades of a rigid confessional faith, which provided reassurance that was unavailable elsewhere. To compensate for the absence of predictability in daily life, societies everywhere imposed strict discipline—discipline of women, children, the poor, criminals, and alleged witches.

The union between religion and political authority in the confessional states bolstered official religious faith with the threat of legal or military coercion. Where different religious confessions persisted within one state—most notably France and the Netherlands—the result was riots, assassinations, and civil war. The West had become divided along religious lines in two ways. The first kind of division was within countries with religiously mixed populations, where distinctive religious communities competed for political power and influence. In these countries religion became the cornerstone to justify patriotism or rebellion, loyalty or disloyalty to the monarch. The second kind of division was international. The confessional states formed alliances, crafted foreign policies, and went to war, with religion determining friend and foe. The West split into religiously driven camps.

Suggestions for Further Reading

For a comprehensive list of suggested readings, please go to www.ablongman.com/levackconcise/chapter14

Anderson, M. S. *The Origins of the Modern European State System, 1494–1618.* 1998. The best short study for students new to the subject of the evolution of the confessional states in Europe. This book is very good at establishing common patterns among the various states.

Burke, Peter. *Popular Culture in Early Modern Europe.* 1994. This wide-ranging book includes considerable material from eastern Europe and Scandinavia, as well as the more extensively studied western European countries. Extraordinarily influential, it showed how much could be learned from studying festivals and games.

Davies, Norman. *God's Playground: A History of Poland,* rev. ed., 2 vols. 1982. By far the most comprehensive study of Polish history, this is particularly strong for the sixteenth and seventeenth centuries. Davies offers a Polish-centered view of European history that is marvelously stimulating even if he sometimes overstates his case for the importance of Poland.

Dukes, Paul. *A History of Russia: Medieval, Modern, Contemporary, ca. 882–1996,* 3rd ed. 1998. A comprehensive survey that synthesizes the most recent research.

Evans, R. J. W. *Rudolf II and His World: A Study in Intellectual History, 1576–1612.* 1973. A sympathetic examination of the intellectual world Rudolf created. Evans recognizes Rudolf's mental problems but lessens their significance for understanding the period.

Holt, Mack P. *The French Wars of Religion, 1562–1629.* 1996. A lucid short synthesis of the events and complex issues raised by these wars.

Hsia, R. Po-chia. *Social Discipline in the Reformation: Central Europe 1550–1750.* 1989. An excellent, lucid, and short overview of the attempts to discipline the people in Germany.

Levack, Brian P. *The Witch-Hunt in Early Modern Europe,* 2nd ed. 1995. The best and most up-to-date short examination of the complex problem of the witch-hunt. This is the place to begin for students new to the subject.

Ozment, Steven E. *Ancestors: The Loving Family in Old Europe.* 2001. This comprehensive study of family life demonstrates that families were actually far more loving than the theory of patriarchy would suggest.

Parker, Geoffrey. *The Dutch Revolt,* rev. ed. 1990. The classic study of the revolt by one of the most masterful historians of the period. This study is especially adept at pointing to the larger European context of the revolt.

Parker, Geoffrey. *The Grand Strategy of Philip II.* 1998. Rehabilitates Philip as a significant strategic thinker.

Wiesner, Merry E. *Women and Gender in Early Modern Europe.* 1993. This is the best short book for students new to the subject.

Notes

1. Quoted in R. J. Knecht, *The French Wars of Religion, 1559–1598,* 2nd ed. (1996), 13.

Absolutism and State Building in Europe, 1618–1715

IN 1651 THOMAS HOBBES, AN ENGLISH PHILOSOPHER LIVING IN EXILE IN FRANCE, was convinced that the West had descended into chaos. As he looked around him, Hobbes saw nothing but political instability, rebellion, and civil war. The turmoil had begun in the late sixteenth century, when the Reformation sparked the religious warfare described in the last chapter. In 1618 the situation deteriorated when another cycle of internal political strife and warfare erupted. The Thirty Years' War (1618–1648) wreaked economic and social havoc in Germany, decimated its population, and forced governments throughout Europe to raise large armies and tax their subjects to pay for them. The entire European economy suffered as a result.

During the 1640s, partly as a result of that devastating conflict, the political order of Europe virtually collapsed. In England a series of bloody civil wars led to the destruction of the monarchy and the establishment of a republic. In France a civil war over constitutional issues drove the royal family from Paris. In Spain the king faced rebellions in no fewer than four of his territories. Europe was in the midst of a profound and multifaceted crisis.

Hobbes proposed a solution to this crisis. In 1651 he published a book, *Leviathan,* about the origin and exercise of political power. He argued that if people were left to their own devices in a hypothetical state of nature, in which government did not exist, they would find themselves in constant conflict. In these circumstances, life would soon become, in Hobbes's famous words, "solitary, poor, nasty, brutish, and short." The only way for people to find peace in this dangerous world would be to agree with their neighbors to form a political society, or a state, by surrendering their independent power to a ruler who would make laws, administer justice, and maintain order. In this state the ruler would not share power with others. His subjects, having agreed to submit to his rule, could not resist or depose him.

Louis XIV: Portrait of Louis XIV in military armor, with his plumed helmet and his crown on the table to the right. The portrait was painted during the period of French warfare. In the background is a French ship.

Non est potestas Super Terram quæ   Comparetur   ei Iob. 41. 24.

The term used to designate the type of government Hobbes advocated is absolutism°. In the most general terms, absolutism means a political arrangement in which one ruler possesses complete and unrivaled power. The political history of the West during the seventeenth and early eighteenth centuries can be written largely in terms of the efforts made by European monarchs to introduce absolutism. Those efforts were accompanied by policies intended to make the states they ruled wealthier and more powerful. These policies encountered serious resistance, but in most European countries the advocates of state building and absolutism prevailed. By the end of the seventeenth century the West comprised a number of large states, governed by rulers who had achieved unrivaled powers and who commanded large, well-equipped armies. The West had entered the age of absolutism, which lasted until the outbreak of the French Revolution in 1789.

Not only did the West acquire a clear political identity during the seventeenth century, but its geographical boundaries also began to shift. Russia, which Europeans thought of as part of the East, began a program of imitating Western governments and became a major player in European diplomacy and warfare. At the same time Russia's southern neighbor, the Ottoman Empire, which had long straddled the boundary between East and West, was increasingly viewed by Europeans as part of a remote, Asian world.

To understand absolutism and state building in Europe, this chapter will address the following questions:

■ What did absolutism mean, both as a political theory and as a practical program, and how was absolutism related to the growth of the power of the state?

■ How did the encounters that took place in France and Spain during the seventeenth century result in the establishment of absolutism, and how powerful did those two states become in the seventeenth century?

■ What was the nature of royal absolutism in central and eastern Europe, and how did the policies of the Ottoman Empire and Russia help establish the boundaries of the West during this period?

■ Why did absolutism fail to take root in England and the Dutch Republic during the seventeenth century?

The Nature of Absolutism

Seventeenth-century absolutism had both a theoretical and a practical dimension. Theoretical absolutists included writers like Hobbes who described the nature of power in the state and explained the conditions for its acquisition and continuation. Practical absolutists were the rulers who took concrete political steps to subordinate all other political authorities within the state to themselves. Efforts to introduce royal absolutism in Europe began in the late sixteenth and early seventeenth centuries, but only in the late seventeenth century, after the Thirty Years' War and the political turmoil of the 1640s, did many European rulers consolidate their political positions and actually achieve absolute power.

The word *absolutism* usually conjures up images of despotic kings terrorizing every segment of the population, ruling by whim and caprice, and executing their subjects at will. Nothing could be further from the truth. Absolute monarchs succeeded in establishing themselves as the highest political authorities within their kingdoms, but they never attained unlimited power. Nor could they exercise power in a completely arbitrary manner. Theoretical absolutists never sanctioned this type of arbitrary rule, and the laws of European states never permitted it. Even if European monarchs had wished to act in this way, they usually could not because they did not have the political or judicial resources to impose their will on the people. The exercise of royal power in the seventeenth century, even when it was considered absolute, depended on the tacit consent of noblemen, office holders, and the members of local political assemblies. Kings usually could not afford to risk losing the support of these prominent men by acting illegally or arbitrarily, and when they did, they found themselves faced with rebellion.

THE THEORY OF ABSOLUTISM

When seventeenth-century political writers referred to the monarch as having absolute power, they usually meant that he possessed the highest legislative power in his kingdom. In particular, they meant that he did not share the power to make law with representative assemblies like the English Parliament. The French magistrate Jean Bodin (ca. 1530–1596), who was one of the earliest proponents of absolutist theory, argued in *Six Books of a Commonweal* (1576) that absolute power consisted of several attributes, the most important of which was the power to make law. Absolute monarchs, therefore, were rulers who could make law by themselves.

Many absolutists (although not Hobbes) claimed that kings received their power directly from God and therefore ruled by divine right. This meant that they were accountable only to God, not to their subjects. Absolutists also claimed that kings were above the law. This meant that when monarchs acted for reason of state, that is, for the benefit of the entire kingdom, they were not strictly bound by the laws of their kingdoms. It did not mean kings or queens could act arbitrarily, illegally, or despotically. Absolute rulers were always expected to observe the individual rights and liberties of their subjects as well as the moral law established by God.

THE PRACTICE OF ABSOLUTISM

What steps did the European monarchs who claimed absolute power take to establish and maintain themselves as the supreme authorities within the state? The first strategy they employed was the elimination or the weakening of national representative assemblies, such as Parliament in England. In France, which is considered to have been the most absolutist state in seventeenth-century Europe, the monarchy stopped summoning its national assembly, the Estates General, in 1614.

The second strategy of absolute monarchs was to subordinate the nobility to the king and make them dependent on his favor. The political and social power of the nobility often led them to participate in rebellions and conspiracies against the king. Monarchs who aspired to a position of un-

rivaled power in their kingdoms therefore took steps to keep the nobility in line, not only by suppressing challenges to their authority but also by appointing men from different social groups as their chief ministers. At the same time, however, the king could not afford to alienate the same men, upon whom he still relied for running his government and maintaining order in the localities. Absolute monarchs, therefore, offered nobles special privileges, such as exemption from taxation, in exchange for their recognition of the king's superiority and their assistance in maintaining order in the localities. In this way nobles became junior partners in the management of the absolutist state.

The final strategy of absolute monarchs was to gain effective control of the administrative machinery of the state and to use it to enforce royal policy throughout their kingdoms. Absolute monarchs were by nature state builders. They established centralized bureaucracies that extended the reach of their governments down into the smallest towns and villages and out into the most remote regions of their kingdoms. The business conducted by these centrally controlled bureaucracies included collection of taxes, recruitment of soldiers, and operation of the judicial system. In these ways the policies pursued by absolute monarchs had an impact on the lives of all royal subjects, not just noblemen and royal councilors.

WARFARE AND THE ABSOLUTIST STATE

Much of the growth of European states in the seventeenth century can be related in one way or another to the conduct of war. During the period from 1600 to 1721, European powers were almost constantly at war. The entire continent was at peace for only four of those years. To meet the demands of war, rulers kept men under arms at all times. By the middle of the seventeenth century, after the Thirty Years' War had come to an end, most European rulers had acquired such standing armies. These armies not only served their rulers in foreign wars but also helped them maintain order and enforce royal policy at home. Standing armies thus became one of the main props of royal absolutism.

During the seventeenth and early eighteenth centuries European armies became larger, in many cases tripling in size. In the 1590s Philip II of Spain had acquired mastery of Europe with an army of 40,000 men. By contrast, in the late seventeenth century Louis XIV of France needed an army of 400,000 men to become the dominant power on the continent. The increase in the size of these forces can be traced to the invention of gunpowder and its more frequent use in the fifteenth and sixteenth centuries. Gunpowder led to the widespread use of the musket, a heavy shoulder firearm carried by a foot soldier. The use of the musket placed a premium on the recruitment and equipment of large armies of infantry, who marched in square columns with men holding long pikes (long wooden shafts with pointed metal heads) to protect the musketeers from enemy attacks. As the size of these armies of foot soldiers grew, the role of mounted soldiers, who had dominated medieval warfare, was greatly reduced.

The cost of recruiting, training, and equipping these mammoth armies was staggering. In the Middle Ages individual lords often had sufficient financial resources to assemble their own private armies. By the beginning of the seventeenth century the only institution capable of putting the new armies in the field was the state itself. The same was true for navies, which now consisted of heavily armed sailing ships, each of which carried as many as 400 sailors. To build these large armies and navies, as well as to pay the increasing cost of waging war itself (which rose 500 percent between 1530 and 1630), the state had to identify new methods of raising and collecting taxes. In times of war as much as 80 percent of the revenue taken in by the state went for military purposes.

The equipment and training of military forces and the collection and allocation of the revenue necessary to subsidize these efforts stimulated the expansion and refinement of the state bureaucracy. Governments found it necessary to employ thousands of new officials to supervise the collection of new taxes, and in order to make the tax collection system more efficient, governments often introduced entirely new administrative systems. Rulers of European states recognized that the exercise of absolute power greatly facilitated the utilization of state power for these purposes.

The Absolutist State in France and Spain

T he two European countries in which royal absolutism first became a political reality were France and Spain. The histories of these two monarchies in the seventeenth century followed very different courses. The kingdom of France, especially during the reign of Louis XIV (r. 1643–1715), became a model of state building and gradually emerged as the most powerful country in Europe. The Spanish monarchy, on the other hand, struggled to introduce absolutism at a time when the overall economic condition of the country was deteriorating and its military forces were suffering a series of defeats. Spain established the forms of absolutist rule, but the monarchy was not able to match the political or military achievements of France in the late seventeenth century.

THE FOUNDATIONS OF FRENCH ABSOLUTISM

Efforts to make the French monarchy absolute began in response to the disorder that occurred during the wars of religion in the late sixteenth century. The first significant steps toward the achievement of absolutism were taken during the reign of Louis XIII (r. 1610–1643). During the king's youth, when his mother, Marie de' Médici, assumed the leadership of the government, aristocratic factions vied for supremacy at court. This factional conflict exposed the main weakness of the monarchy, which was the rival power of the great noble families of the realm. The statesman who addressed this problem most directly was Louis's main councilor, Cardinal Armand Jean du Plessis de Richelieu (1585–1642), who became the king's chief minister in 1628. Richelieu was arguably the greatest state builder of the seventeenth century. He directed all his energies toward centralizing the power of the French state in the person of the king.

Richelieu's most immediate concern was bringing the independent nobility to heel and subordinating their local power to that of the state. This he accomplished by suppressing several conspiracies and rebellions led by noblemen and by restricting the independent power of the provincial assemblies and the eight regional parlements°, which were the highest courts in the country. His great administrative achievement was the strengthening of the system of the intendants°. These paid crown officials, who were recruited from the professional classes and the lower ranks of the nobility, became the main agents of French local administration. Responsible only to the royal council, they collected taxes, supervised local administration, and recruited soldiers for the army.

The most challenging task for Richelieu, as for all French ministers in the early modern period, was increasing the government's yield from taxation, a task that became more demanding during times of war. Richelieu managed to increase the yield from the *taille*, the direct tax on land, as much as threefold during the period 1635–1648. He supplemented the taille with taxes on office holding. Even then, the revenue was insufficient to meet the extraordinary demands of war.

The minister who succeeded Richelieu on his death in 1642 was his protégé Jules Mazarin (1602–1661), a diplomat of Italian birth who dominated the government of Louis XIV when the king was still a boy. Mazarin continued the policies of his predecessor, but he was unable to prevent civil war from breaking out in 1648. This challenge to the French state, known as the *Fronde* (a pejorative reference to a Parisian game in which children flung mud at passing carriages) began when the members of the Parlement of Paris, the most important of all the parlements, refused to register an edict of the king. This act of resistance led to demands that the king sign a document limiting royal authority. Barricades went up in the streets of Paris, and the royal family was forced to flee the city. The Fronde entered a more violent phase in 1650 when the Prince de Condé and his noble allies waged war against the government and even formed an alliance with France's enemy, Spain. Only after Condé's military defeat in 1653 did the entire rebellion collapse.

The Fronde stands as the great crisis of the seventeenth-century French state. It revealed the strength of the local, aristocratic, and legal forces with which the king and his ministers had to contend. These forces managed to disrupt the growth of the French state, drive the king from his capital, and challenge his authority throughout the kingdom. But in the long run they could not destroy the achievement of Richelieu and Mazarin. By the late 1650s the damage had been repaired and the state had resumed its growth.

ABSOLUTISM IN THE REIGN OF LOUIS XIV

The man who presided over the development of the French state for the next fifty years was the king himself, Louis XIV, who assumed direct control of his government after the death of Mazarin in 1661. In an age of absolute monarchs, Louis towered among his contemporaries. He is widely regarded as the most powerful king of the seventeenth century. This reputation comes as much from the image he conveyed as from the policies he pursued. Artists, architects, dramatists, and members of his immediate entourage helped the king project an image of incomparable majesty and authority. At Versailles, about ten miles from Paris, Louis constructed a lavishly furnished palace that became his main residence and the center of the glittering court that surrounded him. The palace was built in the baroque° style, which emphasized the size and grandeur of the structure while also conveying a sense of unity and balance among its diverse parts. The baroque style, criticized by contemporaries for its exuberance and pomposity, appealed to absolute monarchs who wished to emphasize their unrivaled position within society and their determination to impose order and stability on their kingdoms.

The image of magnificence and power that Louis conveyed in art and ceremony mirrored and reinforced his more tangible political accomplishments. His greatest achievement was to solve the persistent problem of aristocratic independence and rebellion by securing the complete loyalty and dependence of the old nobility. This he achieved first by requiring the members of these ancient families to come to Versailles for a portion of every year, where they stayed in apartments within the royal palace itself. At Versailles Louis involved them in the elaborate cultural activities of court life and in ceremonial rituals that emphasized their subservience to the king. At the same time, he excluded the nobles from holding important offices in the government of the realm, a strategy designed to prevent them from building an independent power base within the bureaucracy. This policy of taming the nobility and depriving them of central administrative power could work only if they received something in return. Like all the absolute monarchs of western Europe, Louis gave members of the nobility wealth and privileges in exchange for their loyalty to the crown. In this way the monarchy and the nobility served each other's interests.

In running the actual machinery of government Louis built upon and perfected the centralizing policies of Richelieu and Mazarin. After the death of Mazarin in 1661

■ **Versailles Palace, Center of the Court of Louis XIV after 1682**

The palace was constructed between 1669 and 1686. Its massiveness and grandeur and the order it imposed on the landscape made it a symbol of royal absolutism.

the king, now 23 years old, became his own chief minister, presiding over a council of state that supervised the work of government. The provincial intendants became even more important than they had been under Richelieu and Mazarin, especially in providing food, arms, and equipment for royal troops. They also were enlisted to secure the cooperation of the local judges, city councils, and parish priests as well as the compliance of the local population.

Even more beneficial to the French state was the determination of Jean Baptiste Colbert (1619–1683), the king's financial minister, to use the country's economic resources for its benefit. The theory underlying this set of policies was mercantilism°, which held that the wealth of the state depended on its ability to import fewer commodities than it exported. Its goal was to secure the largest possible share of the world's monetary supply. In keeping with those objectives, Colbert increased the size of France's merchant fleet, founded overseas trading companies, and levied high tariffs on France's commercial rivals. To make France economically self-sufficient he encouraged the growth of the French textile industry, improved the condition of the roads, built canals throughout the kingdom, and reduced some of the burdensome tolls that impeded internal trade.

The most intrusive exercise of the power of the state during Louis XIV's reign was the decision to enforce religious uniformity. The king always considered the existence of a large Huguenot minority within his kingdom an affront to his sense of order. Toleration was divisive and dangerous, especially to someone who styled himself as "Most Christian King." Even after Richelieu had leveled the walls of the fortified Huguenot towns, the problem of religious pluralism remained. In 1685 Louis addressed this problem by revoking the entire Edict of Nantes, which had granted freedom of worship and full civil rights to Huguenots in 1598. Protestant churches were closed and often destroyed, while large numbers of Huguenots were forced to emigrate to the Netherlands, England, and Protestant German lands. Few exercises of absolute power in the seventeenth century caused more disruption in the lives of ordinary people than this attempt to realize the king's ideal of "one king, one law, one faith."

LOUIS XIV AND THE CULTURE OF ABSOLUTISM

A further manifestation of the power of the French absolutist state was Louis's success in influencing and transforming French culture. Kings had often served as patrons of the arts by providing income for artists, writers, and musicians while endowing cultural and educational institutions. Louis took this type of royal patronage to a new level, making it possible for him to control the dissemination of ideas and the very production of culture itself. The architects of the palace at Versailles, the painters of historical scenes that hung in its hallways and galleries, the composers

CHRONOLOGY

1618	Bohemian revolt against Habsburg rule; beginning of the Thirty Years' War
1628	Cardinal Richelieu becomes chief minister of Louis XIII of France
1642–1646	Civil War in England, ending with the capture of King Charles I
1643	Accession of Louis XIV of France
1648–1653	The Fronde in France
1648	Treaty of Westphalia, ending the Thirty Years' War
1649	Execution of Charles I of England and the beginning of the Republic
1682	Accession of Tsar Peter the Great of Russia (r. 1682–1725)
1685	Revocation of the Edict of Nantes
1688–1689	Glorious Revolution in England and Scotland

of the plays and operas that were performed in its theaters, the sculptors who created busts of the king to decorate its chambers, and the historians and pamphlet writers who celebrated the king's achievements in print all benefited from Louis's direct financial support.

Much of Louis's patronage went to cultural institutions, thereby enabling the king to influence a wider circle of artists and have a greater effect on the cultural life of the nation. He took over the Academy of Fine Arts in 1661, founded the Academy of Music in 1669, and chartered a theater company, the *Comédie Française,* in 1680. In 1666 Louis extended his patronage to the sciences with the founding of the Royal Academy of Sciences, which benefited the state by devising improvements in ship design and navigation.

Of all the cultural institutions that benefited from Louis XIV's patronage, the *Académie Française* had the most enduring impact on French culture. This academy, a society of literary scholars, had been founded in 1635 with the support of Cardinal Richelieu. Its purpose was to standardize the French language and serve as the guardian of its integrity. In 1694, twenty-two years after Louis became the academy's patron, the first official French dictionary appeared in print. This achievement of linguistic uniformity, in which words received authorized spellings and definitions, reflected the pervasiveness of Louis's cultural influence as well as the search for order that became the defining characteristic of his reign.

Louis introduced order and uniformity into every aspect of his own life and that of his country. He followed a precise routine in ordering his daily life, introduced ceremonies that ordered the life of his court, and insisted on the court's adoption of table manners that followed strict rules of politeness. He created a bureaucracy that was organized along rational, orderly principles, and he sought to ensure that all his subjects would practice the same religion. The establishment of a clearly defined chain of command in the army, which Louis's minister the Marquis de Louvois introduced, gave organizational cohesion and hierarchical order to the large military force the king and his ministers assembled. Nearly all areas of French public life were transformed by the king's desire to establish order and uniformity and his use of the power of the state to enforce it.

THE WARS OF LOUIS XIV, 1667–1714

The seventeenth-century French state was designed not only to maintain internal peace and order but also to wage war against other states. Colbert's financial and economic policies, coupled with the military reforms of the Marquis de Louvois, had laid the foundations for the creation of a formidable military machine. Louis deployed this armed force against an array of European powers in four separate wars between 1667 and 1714. His goal in these wars was the acquisition of German and Spanish territories in the Rhineland along the eastern borders of his kingdom. Louis dreamed of establishing a "universal monarchy," reminiscent of the empires of ancient Rome, Charlemagne in the ninth century, and Charles V in the sixteenth century.

In order to prevent Louis from acquiring this empire, Great Britain, the Dutch Republic, Spain, and Austria formed a coalition against him. Matched by the combined military forces of these allies, forced to wage war on many different fronts (including North America), and unable to provide adequate funding of the war on the basis of its system of taxation, France felt compelled to conclude peace in 1697. The Treaty of Ryswick marked the turning point in the expansion of the French state and laid the groundwork for the establishment of a balance of power° in the next century, an arrangement whereby various countries form alliances to prevent any one state from dominating the others.

The Treaty of Ryswick, however, did not mark the end of French territorial ambition. In 1701 Louis went to war once again, this time as part of an effort to place a French Bourbon candidate, his grandson Duke Philip of Anjou, on the Spanish throne. This plan threatened to give Louis effective control of all Spanish territory and thus realize the "absolute empire" of his dreams. The British, Dutch, and Austrians formed an alliance against France and Spain, and after a long and costly conflict, known as the War of the Spanish Succession (1701–1713), the members of this coalition were able to dictate the terms of the Treaty of Utrecht (1713). Philip, who suffered from fits of manic depression

and went days without dressing or leaving his room, was allowed to remain on the Spanish throne as Philip V (r. 1700–1746), but only on the condition that the French and Spanish crowns would never be united. Spain ceded its territories in the Netherlands and in Italy to the Austrian Habsburg Monarchy and its strategic port of Gibraltar at the entrance to the Mediterranean to the British. The treaty not only confirmed the new balance of power in Europe but also resulted in the transfer of large parts of French Canada, including Newfoundland and Nova Scotia, to Great Britain.

The loss of French territory in North America, the strains placed on the taxation system by the financial demands of war, and the weakening of France's commercial power as a result of this conflict made France a less potent state at the time of Louis's death in 1715 than it had been in the 1680s. Nevertheless the main effects of a century of French state building remained, including a large, well-

■ Map 15.1   French Territorial Acquisitions, 1679–1714

The main acquisitions were lands in the Spanish Netherlands to the north and Franche Comté, Alsace, and Lorraine to the east. Louis thought of the Rhine River as France's natural eastern boundary, and territories acquired in 1659 and 1697 allowed it to reach that limit.

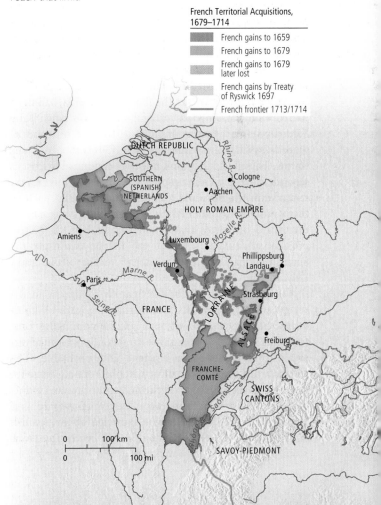

French Territorial Acquisitions, 1679–1714

- French gains to 1659
- French gains to 1679
- French gains to 1679 later lost
- French gains by Treaty of Ryswick 1697
- French frontier 1713/1714

integrated bureaucratic edifice that allowed the government to exercise unprecedented control over the population and a military establishment that remained the largest and best equipped in Europe.

ABSOLUTISM AND STATE BUILDING IN SPAIN

The history of Spain in the seventeenth century is almost always written in terms of failure, since the country endured a long period of economic decline that began in the late sixteenth century with a precipitate drop in the size of its population and stretched well into the eighteenth century. The monarchy became progressively weaker during the seventeenth century, as it was occupied by a succession of ineffective kings who exercised far less power than their French counterparts. To make matters worse, Spain in the seventeenth century suffered a long series of military defeats, most of them at the hands of the French, and it lost the position it had held in the sixteenth century as the major European power. By the early eighteenth century Spain was a shadow of its former self, and its culture reflected uncertainty, pessimism, and nostalgia for former imperial greatness. None of this failure, however, should obscure the fact that Spain, like France, underwent a period of state building during the seventeenth century, and that its government, like that of France, gravitated toward absolutism.

The Spanish monarchy in 1600 ruled more territory than did France, and the various kingdoms and principalities that it comprised possessed far more independence than even the most remote and peripheral French provinces. The center of the monarchy was the kingdom of Castile, with its capital at Madrid. This kingdom, the largest and wealthiest territory within the Iberian peninsula, had been united with the kingdom of Aragon in 1479 when King Ferdinand II of Aragon (r. 1479–1516), the husband of Queen Isabella of Castile (r. 1474–1504), ascended the throne. These two kingdoms, however, continued to exist as separate states after the union, each having its own representative institutions and administrative systems. Each of them, moreover, contained smaller, semiautonomous kingdoms and provinces that retained their own distinctive political institutions. Outside the Iberian peninsula the Spanish monarchy ruled territories in the Netherlands, Italy, and the New World.

The great challenge for the Spanish monarchy in the seventeenth century was to integrate the various kingdoms and principalities of Spain into a more highly centralized state while at the same time making the machinery of that state more efficient and profitable. The statesman who made the most sustained efforts at realizing these goals was the energetic and authoritarian Count-Duke of Olivares (1587–1645), the contemporary and counterpart of Richelieu during the reign of the Spanish king Philip IV (1621–1665). The task Olivares faced was more daunting than anything the French cardinal had ever confronted. As a result of decades of warfare, the Spanish monarchy in the 1620s was penniless, the kingdom of Castile had gone bankrupt, and the entire country had already entered a period of protracted economic decline.

To deal with these deep structural problems Olivares proposed a reform of the entire financial system, the establishment of national banks, and a new system of taxation. At the same time he tried to address the problem of ruling a disparate and far-flung empire, making all the kingdoms and principalities within the monarchy contribute to national defense on a proportionate basis. His ultimate goal was to unify the entire peninsula in a cohesive Spanish national state, similar to that of France. This policy involved suppression of the individual liberties of the various kingdoms and principalities and direct subordination of each area to the king himself. It was, in other words, a solution based on the principles of absolutism.

Olivares was unable to match the state-building achievement of Richelieu in France. His failure, which was complete by the time he fell from office in 1643, can be attributed to three factors. The first was the opposition he confronted within Castile itself, especially from the cities, over the question of taxation. The second, a problem facing Spain throughout the seventeenth century, was military failure, in this case the losses to France during the final phase of the Thirty Years' War. That defeat aggravated the financial crisis and prevented the monarchy from capitalizing on the prestige that usually attends military victory. The third and most serious impediment was opposition to the policy of subordinating the outlying Spanish regions to the kingdom of Castile. The kingdoms and provinces on the periphery of the country were determined to maintain their individual laws and liberties, especially the powers of their own representative assemblies, in the face of the pressures to centralize power in Madrid.

Provincial resistance to a policy of Castilian centralization lay at the root of the Spanish crisis of the seventeenth century. This crisis did not throw Castile itself into a state of civil war. Unlike Paris during the Fronde, Madrid itself remained peaceful. Throughout the 1640s the crown managed to maintain order within its main kingdom, probably because it had learned the art of negotiating directly with the thousands of towns and villages that ran local government. Instead, the Spanish crisis took the form of separatist revolts in Portugal, Catalonia, Sicily, and Naples. With the exception of Portugal, which recovered its sovereignty in 1640, the monarchy met this test and managed to maintain control of its provincial and Italian territories. In the aftermath of the revolts, however, the monarchy failed to bring the areas within the sphere of effective central government control.

The relative weakness of the Spanish monarchy, especially in comparison with that of France, became most apparent in the late seventeenth century, the age of Louis XIV. In two important respects the Spanish government failed to match the achievement of the French. First, it could never escape the grip that the old noble families had on the central administration. The unwillingness of the monarchy to recruit ministers and officials from the mercantile and professional groups within society (which were small to begin with in Spain) worked against the achievement of bureaucratic efficiency and made innovation virtually impossible. Second, unlike the French government during Colbert's ministry, the Spanish government failed to encourage economic growth. The hostility of the aristocratic ruling class to mercantile affairs prevented the country from stemming its own economic decline and the government from solving the formidable financial problems facing it.

The mood that prevailed within the upper levels of Castilian society in the seventeenth century reflected the failure of the government and the entire nation. The contrast between the glorious achievements of the monarchy during the reign of Philip II (r. 1555–1598) and the somber realities of the seventeenth century led most members of the ruling class to retreat into that past, a nostalgia that only encouraged further economic and political stagnation. The work of Miguel de Cervantes (1547–1616), the greatest Spanish writer of the seventeenth century, reflected this change in the Spanish national mood. In 1605 and 1615 Cervantes published (in two parts) *Don Quixote,* the story of an idealistic wandering nobleman who pursued dreams of an elusive military glory. This work served as a commentary on a nobility that had lost confidence in itself.

Absolutism and State Building in Central and Eastern Europe

The forces that led to the establishment of absolutism and state building in France and Spain also made an impact on central and eastern Europe. In Germany the Thirty Years' War led to the establishment of two absolutist states, Prussia and the Austrian Habsburg Monarchy. Further to the East, the Ottoman and Russian Empires, both of them on the margins of the West, also developed absolutist political systems that shared many of the same characteristics as those in western and central Europe.

GERMANY AND THE THIRTY YEARS' WAR, 1618–1648

Before 1648 the main political power within the geographical area known as Germany was the Holy Roman Empire. This large political formation was a loose confederation of kingdoms, principalities, duchies, ecclesiastical territories, and cities, each of which had its own laws and political institutions. The emperor, who was elected by a body of German princes, exercised immediate jurisdiction only in his own dynastic possessions and in the imperial cities. The empire was not in any sense a sovereign state, even though it had long been a major force in European diplomacy.

The Thirty Years' War permanently altered the nature of this vast and intricate political structure. That war began as a conflict between Protestant German princes and the Catholic emperor over religious and constitutional issues. The incident that triggered it in 1618 was the so-called Defenestration of Prague, when members of the predominantly Protestant Bohemian legislature, known as the Diet, threw two royal officials out a castle window as a protest against the religious policies of their recently elected king, the future emperor Ferdinand II. The Diet proceeded to depose Ferdinand, a Catholic, and elect a Protestant prince. The war soon broadened into a European-wide struggle over the possession of German and Spanish territory, as the Danes, Swedes, and French successively entered the conflict against the emperor and his Spanish Habsburg relatives. For a brief period in the late 1620s England also entered the conflict against Spain. The war, which was fought mainly on German soil, had a devastating effect on the region. More than one million soldiers marched across German lands, sacking towns and exploiting the resources of local communities. Germany lost up to one-third of its population, while the destruction of property retarded the economic development of the region for more than fifty years.

The political effects of the war were no less traumatic. By virtue of the Treaty of Westphalia, which ended the war in 1648, the empire was permanently weakened and the German territories within the empire developed more institutional autonomy. Two of these German states soon surpassed all the others in size and military strength and became major European powers. The first was Brandenburg-Prussia, a collection of various territories in northern Germany that was transformed into the kingdom of Prussia at the beginning of the eighteenth century. The second state was the Austrian Habsburg Monarchy, which in the eighteenth century was usually identified simply as Austria. The Habsburgs had long dominated the Holy Roman Empire and continued to secure election as emperors after the Treaty of Westphalia. In the late seventeenth century, however, the Habsburg Monarchy acquired its own institutional identity, distinct from that of the empire. It consisted of the lands that the Habsburgs controlled directly in the southeastern part of the empire and other territories that lay outside the boundaries of the empire. Both Prussia and Austria developed their own forms of absolutism during the second half of the seventeenth century.

■ **Map 15.2 Europe After the Treaty of Westphalia, 1648**
The Holy Roman Empire no longer included the Dutch Republic, which was now independent of Spain. Some of the lands of the Austrian Habsburg Monarchy and Brandenburg-Prussia lay outside the boundaries of the Holy Roman Empire. Italy was divided into a number of small states in the north, while Naples, Sicily, and Sardinia were ruled by Spain.

THE GROWTH OF THE PRUSSIAN STATE

In 1648, at the end of the Thirty Years' War, Prussia could barely have claimed the status of an independent state, much less that of an absolute monarchy. The core of the Prussian state was Brandenburg, which claimed the status of an electorate, since its ruler cast one of the ballots to elect the Holy Roman Emperor. The lands that belonged to the elector of Brandenburg lay scattered throughout northern Germany and stretched into eastern Europe. The Hohenzollern family, in whose line the electorate of Brandenburg passed, also owned or controlled lands that lay scattered throughout northern Germany and stretched into eastern Europe.

The Great Elector Frederick William (r. 1640–1688) began the long process of turning this ramshackle structure

into a powerful and cohesive German state. His son King Frederick I (r. 1688–1713) and grandson Frederick William I (r. 1713–1740) completed the transformation. The key to their success was to secure the compliance of the traditional nobility, who in Prussia were known as Junkers°. The Great Elector Frederick William achieved this end by granting the Junkers a variety of privileges, most notably the legal confirmation of their rights over the serfs.

With the loyalty of the Junkers secure, Frederick William went about the process of building a powerful Prussian state. A large administrative bureaucracy, centralized under a General Directory in Berlin, governed both financial and military affairs throughout the elector's lands. The taxes that the government collected, especially from the towns, went in large part to fund a standing army, which had come into being in the late 1650s. Commanded by officers drawn

A GERMAN WRITER DESCRIBES THE HORRORS OF THE THIRTY YEARS' WAR

In 1669 the German writer H. J. C. Grimmelshausen (1625–1676) published an imaginary account of the adventures of a German vagabond, to whom he gave the name Simplicissimus. The setting of the book was the Thirty Years' War in Germany, which Grimmelshausen had experienced firsthand. At age 10 Grimmelshausen, like the character Simplicissimus in the book, was captured by Hessian troops and later became a camp follower. In this chapter Simplicissimus describes how the palace of his father was stormed, plundered, and ruined.

The first thing that these troops did was, that they stabbed their horses; thereafter each fell to his appointed task, which task was either more or less than ruin and destruction. For though some began to slaughter and to boil and to roast, so that it looked as if there should be a merry banquet forward, yet others there were who did but storm through the house above and below the stairs. . . . All that they had no mind to take with them they cut in pieces. Some thrust their swords through the hay and straw as if they had not enough sheep and swine to slaughter; and some shook the feathers out of the beds and in their stead stuffed in bacon and other dried meat and provisions as if such were better and softer to sleep upon. Others broke the stove and the windows as if they had a never-ending summer to promise. Housewares of copper and tin they beat flat, and packed such vessels, all bent and spoiled, in with the rest. Bedsteads, tables, chairs and benches they burned, though there lay many cords of dry wood in the yard. . . .

Our maid was so handled in the stable that she could not come out; which is a shame to tell of. Our man they laid bound upon the ground, thrust a gag into his mouth, and poured a pailful of filthy water into his body; and by this, which they called a Swedish draught, they forced him to lead a party of them to another place where they captured men and beasts, and brought them back to our farm, in which company were my dad, my mother, and our Ursula.

And now they began first to take the flints out of their pistols and in place of them to jam the peasants' thumbs in and so to torture the poor rogues as if they had been about the burning of witches. For one of them they had taken they thrust into the baking oven and there lit a fire under him, although he had as yet confessed no crime; as for another, they put a cord round his head and so twisted it tight with a piece of wood that the blood gushed from his mouth and nose and ears. In a word each had his own device to torture the peasants, and each peasant had several torture.

Source: Reprinted from *The Adventurous Simplicissimus: Being the Description of the Life of a Strange Vagabond Named Melchior Sternfels Von Fuchshaim* by H. J. C. Grimmelshausen. Published by the University of Nebraska Press.

from the nobility, this army quickly became the best trained fighting force in Europe. Prussia became a model military state, symbolized by the transformation of the royal gardens into an army training ground during the reign of Frederick William I.

As this military state grew in size and complexity, its rulers acquired many of the attributes of absolute rule. Most significantly they became the sole legislators within the state. The main representative assembly in the electorate, the Diet of Brandenburg, met for the last time in 1652. The elevation of Frederick I's status to that of king of Prussia in 1701 marked a further consolidation of power in the person of the ruler. His son's style of rule, which included physical punishment of judges whose decisions displeased him, suggested that the Prussian monarchy not only had attained absolute power but could occasionally abuse it.

THE AUSTRIAN HABSBURG MONARCHY

The Austrian Habsburgs were much less successful than the Hohenzollerns in building a centralized, consolidated state along absolutist lines. The various territories that made up the Austrian Habsburg Monarchy in the late seventeenth century were larger and more diverse than those that belonged to the king of Prussia. In addition to the collection of duchies that form present-day Austria, it embraced two subordinate kingdoms, which were themselves composed of various semiautonomous principalities and duchies. The first of these, lying to the north, was the kingdom of Bohemia, which had struggled against Habsburg control for nearly a century. The second, lying to the southeast, was the kingdom of Hungary, including the large semiautonomous principality of Transylvania. In 1713 the monarchy also acquired the former Spanish Netherlands and the Italian territories of Milan and Naples.

The Austrian Habsburg monarchs of the seventeenth and early eighteenth centuries never succeeded in integrating these ethnically, religiously, and politically diverse lands into a unified, cohesive state similar to that of France. In governing its Austrian and Bohemian lands, however, this decentralized Habsburg monarchy did nonetheless acquire some of the characteristics of absolutist rule. After defeating the Bohemians at the Battle of White Mountain in 1620 during the Thirty Years' War, Emperor Ferdinand II

(r. 1618–1637) exiled many of the Protestant nobility and then undertook a deliberate expansion of his legislative and judicial powers in the areas under his immediate control.

A policy of severe religious repression accompanied this increase in the emperor's authority. Like Cardinal Richelieu of France, Ferdinand assumed that Protestantism served as a justification for rebellion, and he therefore decided that its practice could not be tolerated. Protestants in all the emperor's territories were forced to take a Catholic loyalty oath, and Protestant education was banned. Protestant towns were destroyed at exactly the same time that Richelieu was razing the fortifications of the Huguenot town of La Rochelle. These efforts at reconversion continued right through the seventeenth century. They amounted to a policy of religious or "confessional" absolutism.

While the Habsburgs succeeded in imposing some elements of absolutist rule on the Austrians and the Bohemians in the early seventeenth century, they encountered much more resistance when they attempted to follow the same course of action with respect to Hungary. Hungarians had a long tradition of limited, constitutional rule in which the national Diet had exercised powers of legislation and taxation. Habsburg emperors made some limited inroads on these traditions, but they were never able to break them. They also were unable to achieve the same degree of religious uniformity that they had imposed on their other territories. In Hungary the Habsburgs encountered the limits of royal absolutism.

THE OTTOMAN EMPIRE: BETWEEN EAST AND WEST

In the seventeenth and early eighteenth centuries the southeastern border of the Habsburg Monarchy separated the kingdom of Hungary from the Ottoman Empire. This militarized frontier marked not only the political boundary between two empires but a deeper cultural boundary between East and West.

As we have seen in previous chapters, the West is not just a geographical but also a cultural realm, and the people who inhabit this realm, although distinct from one another, share many of the same religious, political, legal, and philosophical traditions. The Ottoman Turks, who posed a recurrent military threat to the Habsburg monarchy and who reached the gates of Vienna in 1683, were generally thought of as not belonging to this Western world. Because the Ottoman Turks were Muslims, Europeans considered them infidels who were bent on the destruction of Christendom. Ottoman emperors, known as sultans, were considered despots who ruled over their subjects as slaves. The sultans were also depicted in Western literature as cruel and brutal tyrants.

These stereotypes of the Turks served the function of giving Europeans a sense of their own Western identity. Turks became a negative reference group with whom Europeans could favorably compare themselves. The realities of Ottoman politics and culture, however, were quite different from the ways in which they were represented in European literature. Turkish despotism, the name Europeans gave to the Ottoman system of government, existed only in theory. Ever since the fourteenth century Ottoman writers had claimed for the sultan extraordinary powers, including the right to seize the landed property of his subjects at will. In practice, however, he never exercised unlimited power. His prerogatives were limited by the spirit of Muslim law, and he shared power with the grand vizier, who was his chief executive officer. There was little difference between the rule of the sultans and that of European absolute monarchs.

Ottoman Turks and Europeans frequently went to war against each other, but there was a constant pattern of diplomatic, economic, and cultural interaction between them. The Turks had formed diplomatic alliances with the French against the Austrian Habsburgs on a number of occasions. Europeans and Ottomans often borrowed military technology from each other, and they also shared knowledge of administrative techniques. Trade between European countries and the Ottoman Empire remained brisk throughout this period. Communities of Turks and other Muslims lived in European cities, while numerous European merchants resided in territories under Ottoman control.

These encounters between Turks and Europeans indicate that the militarized boundary between the Habsburgs and the Ottoman Empire was much more porous than its fortifications would suggest. Military conflict and Western contempt for Muslim Turks disguised a much more complex process of political and cultural interaction between the two civilizations. Europeans tended to think of the Ottoman Empire as "oriental," but it is more accurate to view it as a region lying between the East and the West.

RUSSIA AND THE WEST

The other seventeenth-century power that marked the boundary between East and West was the vast Russian Empire, which stretched from its boundary with Poland in the west all the way to the Pacific Ocean in the east. Until the end of the seventeenth century, the kingdom of Muscovy and the lands attached to it seemed, at least to Europeans, part of the Asiatic world. Dominated by an Eastern Orthodox branch of Christianity, Russia drew very little upon the cultural traditions associated with western Europe. Unlike its neighboring Slavic kingdom of Poland, it had not absorbed large doses of German culture. It also appeared to Europeans to be another example of "oriental despotism," a state in which the ruler, known as the tsar, could rule his subjects at will.

During the reign of Tsar Peter I, known as Peter the Great (r. 1682–1725), Russia underwent a process of westernization, bringing it more into line with the culture of European countries and becoming a major European power. This policy began after Peter visited England, Holland, northern Germany, and Austria in 1697 and 1698. Upon his return he directed his officials and members of the upper levels of Russian society to adopt Western styles of dress and appearance, including the removal of men's beards. Beards symbolized the backward, Eastern, Orthodox culture from whose grip Peter hoped to extricate his country. Young Russian boys were sent abroad for their education. Women began to participate openly in the social and cultural life of the cities, in violation of Orthodox custom. Smoking was permitted despite the Church's insistence that Scripture condemned it. The calendar was reformed and books were printed in modern Russian type. Peter's importation of Western art and the imitation of Western architecture complemented this policy of enforced cultural change. Westernization, however, involved more than a change of manners and appearance. It also involved military and political reforms that changed the character of the Russian state.

During the first twenty-five years of his reign Peter had found himself unable to achieve sustained military success against his two great enemies, the Ottoman Turks to the south and the Swedes to the west. During the Great Northern War with Sweden (1700–1721) Peter introduced a number of military reforms that eventually turned the tide against his enemy. These reforms were based on the knowledge he had acquired of military technology, organization, and tactics of western European states, especially Prussia and, ironically, Sweden itself. Having introduced a program of conscription, Peter assembled a large standing army of more than 200,000 men, which he trained and disciplined in the Prussian manner.

This new military state also acquired many of the centralizing and absolutist features of western European monarchies. Efforts to introduce absolutism in Russia had begun during the reigns of Alexis (r. 1645–1676) and Fedor (r. 1676–1682), who had achieved limited success in strengthening the central administration, controlling the nobility, and brutally suppressing peasant rebellions. Peter built upon his predecessors' achievement. He created an entirely new structure for managing the empire, appointing twelve governors to superintend Russia's forty-three separate provinces. He brought the Orthodox Church under state control. By establishing a finely graded hierarchy of official ranks in the armed forces, the civil administration,

■ **Peter the Great at the Battle of Poltava (1709), at Which Russia Defeated Swedish Forces**
Standing 6 feet 7 inches tall, at a time when the average male height was 5 feet 8 inches, Peter was great in military and political achievements as well as in stature.

and the court, Peter not only improved administrative efficiency but also made it possible for men of nonaristocratic birth to attain the same privileged status as the old landowning nobility.

The most visible sign of Peter's policy of westernization was the construction of the port city of St. Petersburg on the Gulf of Finland, which became the new capital of the Russian Empire. One of the main objectives of Russian foreign policy during Peter's reign had been to secure "a window to Europe" on the Baltic, which would open up trade with the West and allow Russia to become a Western naval power. By draining a swamp at the estuary of the Neva River, Peter laid the basis for the construction of an entirely new city, which was designed with the assistance of French and Italian architects in a style characteristic of European cities. Construction began in 1703, and within twenty years St. Petersburg had a population of 100,000 people. With his new capital city now looking westward, and an army and central administration reformed on the basis of Prussian and French example, Peter could enter the world of European diplomacy and warfare as both a Western and an absolute monarch.

Resistance to Absolutism in England and the Dutch Republic

The kingdom of England and the northern provinces of the Netherlands stand out as the two great exceptions to the dominant pattern of political development in seventeenth-century Europe. Both of these countries successfully resisted the establishment of royal absolutism, and neither underwent the rigorous centralization of power and the dynamic growth of the state that usually accompanied the establishment of absolutist rule. In England the encounter between the proponents and opponents of absolute monarchy was more pronounced than in any other European country. It resulted in the temporary destruction of the monarchy in 1649 and the establishment of parliamentary supremacy after the Glorious Revolution of 1688. In the northern provinces of the Netherlands, known as the Dutch Republic, an even more emphatic rejection of absolutism occurred. During their long struggle to win their independence from Spain, the Dutch established a republican, decentralized form of government, but that did not prevent them from acquiring considerable military strength and dominating the world's economy during the seventeenth century.

THE ENGLISH MONARCHY

At various times in the seventeenth century English monarchs tried to introduce royal absolutism, but the political institutions and traditions of the country stood as major obstacles to their designs. The most important of these traditions was the making of law and the levying of taxes by the two Houses of Parliament, the House of Lords and the House of Commons, with the king holding the power to sign or veto the bills they passed.

In the early seventeenth century the perception began to arise, especially among certain members of the House of Commons, that this tradition of parliamentary government was under attack. The first Stuart king, James I (r. 1603–1625), aroused some of these fears in a number of speeches and published works in which he emphasized the height of his independent royal power, which was known in England as the prerogative°. James also spoke often about his divine right to rule, and he claimed that the main function of Parliament was simply to give the king advice, rather than to make law. These statements had the effect of antagonizing members of Parliament, leading them to defend their privileges, including the right they claimed to discuss foreign policy and other affairs of state.

James's son, Charles I (r. 1625–1649), believed in absolutism every bit as much as his father, but unlike James, Charles actually put his theories into practice. His efforts to force his subjects to lend money to the government during a war with Spain (1625–1629) and his imprisonment of men who refused to make these loans led Parliament to pass the Petition of Right in 1628. This document declared boldly that subjects possessed fundamental rights that kings could not violate under any circumstances, even when the country was at war.

In 1629 Charles dismissed Parliament and did not summon it again for eleven years. During this period, known as the personal rule°, Charles used his prerogative to bring in new revenues, thus taxing the people without the consent of Parliament. At the same time the king's religious policy fell under the control of William Laud, the archbishop of Canterbury. Laud's determination to restore many of the rituals associated with Roman Catholicism alienated large numbers of Puritans—the more extreme English Protestants—and led to a growing perception that the king's government was engaged in a conspiracy to destroy both England's "ancient constitution" and its Protestant religion.

This period of absolutism might have continued indefinitely if Charles had not once again been faced with the financial demands of war. In 1636 the king tried to introduce a new religious liturgy in his northern kingdom of Scotland. Perceiving the liturgy to be "popish," the Scots signed a National Covenant in 1638, pledging themselves to defend the integrity of their Protestant religion; abolished episcopacy (government of the church by bishops) in favor of a Presbyterian system of church government; and mobilized a large army. To secure the funds to fight the Scots, Charles was forced to summon his English Parliament in 1640, thus ending the period of personal rule and his efforts to rule as an absolute monarch.

THE ENGLISH CIVIL WARS AND REVOLUTION

Tensions between the reconvened English Parliament and Charles led to the first revolution of modern times. The Short Parliament, called in April 1640, lasted only two months, but a Scottish military victory against the English in that year forced the king to call a second parliament. The Long Parliament, which met in November 1640, impeached many of the king's ministers and judges and abolished the courts that had been active in the prosecution of Puritans. Parliament declared the king's nonparliamentary taxes illegal, and it enacted a law limiting the time between the meetings of Parliament to three years.

This legislation did not satisfy the king's critics in Parliament. Their suspicion that the king was conspiring against them created a poisoned political atmosphere in which neither side trusted the other. In August 1642 a civil war began between the forces raised by Parliament and those loyal to the king. Parliament, which benefited from the creation in 1645 of a well-trained, efficient fighting force, the New Model Army, won this war in 1646 and took Charles prisoner. The king's subsequent negotiations with the Scots and the English Presbyterians, both of whom had originally fought against him, led to a second civil war in 1648. In this war, which lasted only a few months, the New Model Army once again defeated Royalist forces.

This military victory led to a series of revolutionary changes in the English system of government. Believing that Charles could never be trusted, a small group of radicals in Parliament, following the wishes of the army, set up a court to try Charles in January 1649. The trial resulted in Charles's conviction and execution. Shortly thereafter the House of Commons destroyed the House of Lords and the monarchy itself and set up a republic.

The republican government established in 1649 did not last. In 1653 Oliver Cromwell (1599–1658), the commander-in-chief of the army, dissolved the Long Parliament and had himself proclaimed Protector of England, Scotland, and Ireland. Cromwell had been a leader of the revolution, but he also sought to achieve a settlement that would give the country the political stability it desperately needed. The establishment of the Protectorate, in which Cromwell shared legislative power with Parliament, represented an effort to return to a more traditional system of government. After Cromwell's death in 1658 and the brief rule of his son Richard, the Protectorate collapsed and the army restored the monarchy in 1660.

LATER STUART ABSOLUTISM AND THE GLORIOUS REVOLUTION

Charles II (r. 1660–1685) and his brother James II (r. 1685–1688) were both absolutists who admired the political achievement of their cousin, Louis XIV of France. Neither of them, however, attempted to rule indefinitely without Parliament, as Charles I had. Their main objective was to destroy the independence of Parliament by packing it with their own supporters and use the prerogative to weaken the force of the parliamentary statutes to which they objected.

The main political crisis of Charles II's reign was the attempt by a group of members of Parliament, known by their opponents as Whigs, to exclude the king's brother, James, from the throne on the grounds that he was a Catholic. Charles opposed this strategy because it violated the theory of hereditary divine right, according to which God sanctioned the right of the king's closest heir to succeed him. Those members of Parliament who supported Charles on this issue, whom the Whigs called Tories, thwarted the designs of the Whigs in three successive parliaments between 1679 and 1681.

An even more serious political crisis occurred after James II succeeded to the throne in 1685. James began to exempt his fellow Catholics from the penal laws, which prevented them from worshiping freely, and from the Test Act of 1673, which had denied them the right to hold office under the crown. These efforts by the monarchy to grant toleration and political power to Catholics revived the traditional English fears of absolutism and popery. Not only the Whigs but also the predominantly Anglican Tories became alarmed at the king's policies. The birth of a Catholic son to James by his second wife, the Italian princess Mary of Modena, in June 1688 created the fear that the king's religious policy might be continued indefinitely. A group of seven Whigs and Tories drafted an invitation to William III of Orange, the captain general of the military forces of the Dutch Republic and James's nephew, to come to England to defend their Protestant religion and their constitution. William was married to James's daughter, the Protestant Princess Mary, and as the king's nephew he also had a claim to the throne himself.

Invading with an international force of 12,000 men, William forced James to abdicate the throne and flee to France. The Convention, a special parliament convened by William in 1689, offered the crown to William and Mary while at the same time securing their assent to the Bill of Rights. This document, which is considered a cornerstone of the English constitution, corrected many of the abuses of royal power at the hands of James and Charles, especially the practice of exempting individuals from the penalties of the laws made by Parliament. By proclaiming William king and by excluding Catholics from the throne, the Bill of Rights also destroyed the theory of hereditary divine right.

The events of 1688–1689, which are known as the the Glorious Revolution, were decisive in defeating once and for all the absolutist designs of the Stuart kings and in guaranteeing that Parliament would form a permanent and regular place in English government. For the English aristocracy, the peers and gentry who sat in Parliament, the revolution guaranteed that they would occupy a paramount position within English politics and society for more than a hundred years. The revolution also had profound effects on British and European diplomacy, since it quickly brought England and Scotland into a war against Louis XIV of France, the great antagonist of William III. The main reason William had come to England and secured the crown in the first place was to secure British entry into the European alliance he was building against France.

The Glorious Revolution prompted the publication of a genuinely revolutionary political manifesto, John Locke's *Two Treatises of Government* (1690). Like Hobbes, Locke argued that men left the state of nature and agreed to form a political society in order to protect their property and prevent the chaos that characterized a state of war. But unlike Hobbes, Locke asserted that the government they formed

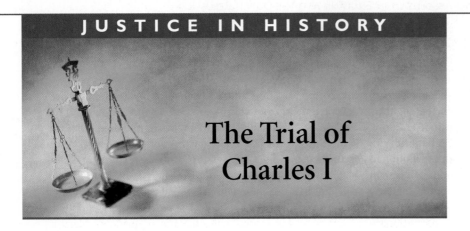

The Trial of Charles I

In January 1649, after the New Model Army had defeated Royalist forces in England's second civil war and purged Parliament of its Presbyterian members, the few remaining members of the House of Commons voted by a narrow margin to erect a High Court of Justice to try King Charles I. This trial, which resulted in Charles's execution, marked the only time in European history that a monarch was tried and executed while still holding the office of king.

The decision to try the king formed part of a deliberate political strategy. The men who arranged the proceeding knew that they were embarking on a revolutionary course by declaring that the House of Commons, as the elected representative of the people, was the highest power in the realm. They also knew that the republican regime they were establishing did not command a large body of popular support. By trying the king publicly in a court of law and by ensuring that the trial was reported in daily newspapers (the first such trial in history), they hoped to prove the legitimacy of their cause and win support for the new regime.

The decision to bring the king to justice created two legal problems. The first was to identify a crime upon which the trial would be based. For many years members of Parliament had insisted that the king had violated the ancient laws of the kingdom. The charge read that he had "wickedly designed to erect an unlimited and tyrannical power" and had waged war against his people in two civil wars.

His prosecutors claimed that those activities amounted to the crime of treason. The problem was that treason in England was a crime committed by a subject against the king, not by the king against his subjects. In order to try the king for this crime, his accusers had to construct a new theory of treason, according to which the king had attacked his own political body, which they identified with the kingdom or the state.

The second problem was to make the court itself a legitimate tribunal. According to English constitutional law, the king possessed the highest legal authority in the land. He appointed his judges, and the courts represented his authority. Parliament could vote to erect a special court, but the bill authorizing it would become law only if the king agreed to it. In this case the House of Commons had set up the court by its own authority, and it had named 135 men, most of whom were army officers, to serve as its judges. The revolutionary nature of this tribunal was difficult to disguise, and Charles made its illegality the basis of his defense. When asked how he would plead, he challenged the legitimacy of the court.

"By what power am I called hither?" he asked. "I would know by what authority—I mean lawful authority. There are many unlawful authorities in the world—thieves and robbers by the highways. And when I know what lawful authority, I shall answer. Remember I am your king, your lawful king. . . . I have a trust committed to me by God by old and lawful descent; I will not betray it to answer to a new unlawful authority."

By taking this position Charles put himself on the side of the law, and by refusing to enter a plea he also prevented his prosecutors from presenting the evidence against him.

The arguments that King Charles and John Bradshawe, the president of the court, presented regarding the legitimacy of the court reflected the main constitutional conflict in seventeenth-century England. On the one hand was the doctrine of divine-right absolutism, according to which the king received his authority from God. He was therefore responsible to God alone, not to the people. His subjects could neither try him in a court of law nor fight him on the battlefield. "A king," said Charles, "cannot be tried by any superior jurisdiction on earth." On the other hand was the doctrine of popular sovereignty, which held that political power came from the people. As Bradshawe said in response to Charles's objection, "Sir, as the law is your superior, so truly Sir, there is something that is superior to the law, and that is indeed the parent or author of law, and that is the people of England." This trial, therefore, involved not only a confrontation between Charles and his revolutionary judges but an encounter between two incompatible political ideologies.

In 1649 the advocates of popular sovereignty triumphed over those of divine right. Charles was convicted as a

■ **Trial of Charles I at Westminster Hall, January 1649**

The king is sitting in the prisoner's box in the foreground, facing the commissioners of the High Court of Justice. His refusal to plead meant that a full trial could not take place.

"tyrant, traitor, murderer, and public enemy of the good people of this nation." The verdict was never in doubt, although only 67 of the 135 men originally appointed as judges voted to convict the king, and a mere 59 signed the death warrant. The trial succeeded only to the extent that it facilitated the establishment of the new regime. With Charles gone, Parliament could move ahead with the abolition of the monarchy and the establishment of a republic. But in dramatic terms the trial was a complete failure. Charles, a small shy man with a nervous stammer, was expected to make a poor impression, but he spoke eloquently when he refused to plead, and he won support from spectators in the gallery. In the greatest show trial of the seventeenth century, the royal defendant stole the show.

When Charles's son, Charles II, was restored to the throne in 1660, royalists finally had their revenge against the judges of this court. Those who could be found alive were hanged, disemboweled, and quartered. For those who were already dead, there was to be another type of justice. In 1661 Royalists exhumed the badly decomposed corpses of Bradshawe, Henry Ireton, and Oliver Cromwell, the three men who bore the largest responsibility for the execution of the king. The three cadavers were hanged and their skulls were placed on pikes on top of Westminster Hall. This macabre ritual served as the Royalists' way of vilifying the memory of the judges of this illegal and revolutionary trial, and their unpardonable sin of executing an anointed king.

■

Questions of Justice

1. The men who brought King Charles to trial often spoke about bringing him to "justice." How is justice best understood in this context?

2. How does this trial reveal the limitations of divine-right absolutism in England?

Taking It Further

Peacey, Jason, ed. *The Regicides and the Execution of Charles I.* 2001. A collection of essays on various aspects of this episode and the men who signed the death warrant.

Wedgewood, C. V. *The Trial of Charles I.* 1964. Presents a full account and analysis of the trial by one of the great historical stylists of the twentieth century.

■ **The Landing of William of Orange's Fleet in England, November 1688**
The declared objective of this expedition was "for the restoration of the Constitution and the True Religion of England, Scotland and Ireland." After arriving in England, James II fled the country. William and his wife Mary became king and queen of England and Scotland in February 1689.

was based on trust and that governments that acted against the interests of the people could be dissolved. In these circumstances the people could establish a new regime.

THE DUTCH REPUBLIC

In many respects the United Provinces of the Netherlands, known as the Dutch Republic, forms the most striking exception to the pattern of state building in seventeenth-century Europe. It was the only major European state to maintain a republican form of government throughout the entire seventeenth century. As a state it also failed to conform to the pattern of centralization and consolidation that became evident in almost all European monarchies. The Dutch Republic never acquired much of a centralized bureaucracy. The provinces formed little more than a loose confederation of sovereign republican states. Each of the provinces sent deputies to the States General, where unanimity was required on all important issues.

Political power in the Dutch Republic lay mainly with wealthy merchants and bankers. Their political power reflected the highly commercial character of the Dutch economy. In the early seventeenth century the Dutch began to dominate European and world trade, serving as middlemen and shippers for all the other powers of Europe. As part of this process Dutch trading companies, such as the Dutch East India Company, began to establish permanent outposts in India, Indonesia, North America, the Caribbean, South America, and South Africa.

To support their dynamic mercantile economy, Dutch cities developed financial institutions favorable to trade. An Exchange Bank in Amsterdam, which had a monopoly on the exchange of foreign currencies, allowed merchants to make international transactions by adding sums to or deducting sums from their accounts whenever they imported or exported goods. A stock market, also situated in Amsterdam, facilitated the buying and selling of shares in commercial ventures.

This bourgeois republic also made a distinct contribution to European culture during the seventeenth century, known as its Golden Age. The Dutch cultural achievement was greatest in the area of the visual arts, where Rembrandt van Rijn (1606–1669), Franz Hals (ca. 1580–1666), and Jan Steen (1626–1679) formed only part of an astonishing con-

■ **The Amsterdam Stock Exchange in 1668**

Known as the Bourse, this multipurpose building served as a gathering point for merchants trading in different parts of the world. The main activity was the buying and selling of shares of stock in trading companies during trading sessions that lasted for two hours each day.

centration of artistic genius in the cities of Amsterdam, Haarlem, and Leiden. Dutch painting of this era reflected the social and political climate in which painters worked. Dutch artists of the Golden Age produced intensely realistic portraits of merchants and financiers, such as Rembrandt's famous *Syndics of the Clothmakers of Amsterdam* (1662). Realism became one of the defining features of Dutch painting, evident in the numerous street scenes, still lifes, and landscapes that Dutch artists painted and sold to a largely bourgeois clientele.

In the early eighteenth century the Dutch Republic lost its position of economic superiority to Great Britain and France, which developed even larger mercantile empires of their own and began to dominate world commerce. A long period of war against France, which ended in 1713, took its toll on Dutch manpower and wealth, and the relatively small size of the country and its decentralized institutions made it more difficult for it to recover its position in European diplomacy and warfare. But in the seventeenth century this highly urbanized and commercial country showed that a small, decentralized republic could hold its own with the absolutist states of France and Spain as well as with the parliamentary monarchy of England.

CONCLUSION

The Western State in the Age of Absolutism

Between 1600 and 1715 three fundamental political changes, all related to each other, helped redefine the West. The first was the dramatic and unprecedented growth of the state. During these years all Western states grew in size and strength. They became more cohesive as the outlying provinces of kingdoms were brought more firmly under central governmental control. The administrative machinery of the state became more complex and efficient. The armies of the state could be called upon at any time to take action against internal rebels and foreign enemies. The income of the state increased as royal officials collected higher taxes, and governments became involved in the promotion of trade and industry and in the regulation of the economy. By the beginning of the eighteenth century one of the most distinctive features of Western civilization was the prevalence of these large, powerful, bureaucratic states. There was nothing like them in the non-Western world.

The second change was the introduction of royal absolutism into these Western states. From one end of the European continent to the other, efforts were made to establish the monarch as a ruler with complete and unrivaled power. These efforts achieved varying degrees of success, and in two states, England and the Dutch Republic, they ended in failure. Nevertheless, during the seventeenth and eighteenth centuries the absolutist state became the main form of government in the West. For this reason historians refer to the period of Western history beginning in the seventeenth century as the age of absolutism.

The third change was the conduct of a new style of warfare by Western absolutist states. The West became the arena where large armies, funded, equipped, and trained by the state, engaged in long, costly, and bloody military campaigns. The conduct of war on this scale threatened to drain the state of its financial resources, destroy its economy, and decimate its civilian and military population. Western powers were not unaware of the dangers of this type of warfare. The development of international law and the attempt to achieve a balance of power among European powers represented efforts to restrict the conduct of seventeenth-century warfare. These efforts, however, were not completely successful, and in the eighteenth and nineteenth centuries warfare in the West entered a new and even more dangerous phase, aided by the technological innovations that the scientific and industrial revolutions made possible. To the first of those great transformations, the revolution in science, we now turn.

Suggestions for Further Reading

For a comprehensive list of suggested readings, please go to www.ablongman.com/levackconcise/chapter15

Aylmer, G. E. *Rebellion or Revolution.* 1986. A study of the nature of the political disturbances of the 1640s and 1650s.

Beik, William. *Louis XIV and Absolutism: A Brief Study with Documents.* 2000. An excellent collection of documents.

Collins, James B. *The State in Early Modern France.* 1995. The best general study of the French state.

Elliott, J. H. *Richelieu and Olivares.* 1984. A comparison of the two contemporary absolutist ministers and state builders in France and Spain.

Harris, Tim. *Politics under the Later Stuarts.* 1993. The best study of Restoration politics, including the Glorious Revolution.

Hughes, Lindsey. *Russia in the Age of Peter the Great.* 1998. A comprehensive study of politics, diplomacy, society, and culture during the reign of the "Tsar Reformer."

Israel, Jonathan. *The Dutch Republic: Its Rise, Greatness and Fall, 1477–1806.* 1996. A massive and authoritative study of the Dutch Republic during the period of its greatest global influence.

Parker, David. *The Making of French Absolutism.* 1983. A particularly good treatment of the early seventeenth century.

Parker, Geoffrey. *The Military Revolution.* 1988. Deals with the impact of the military revolution on the world as well as European history.

Rabb, Theodore K. *The Struggle for Stability in Early Modern Europe.* 1975. Employs visual as well as political sources to illustrate the way in which Europeans responded to the general crisis of the seventeenth century.

Schama, Simon. *The Embarrassment of Riches: An Interpretation of Dutch Culture in the Golden Age.* 1987. Contains a wealth of commentary on Dutch art and culture during its most influential period.

Wilson, Peter H. *Absolutism in Central Europe.* 2000. Analyzes both the theory and the practice of absolutism in Prussia and Austria.

The Scientific Revolution

I N 1609 GALILEO GALILEI, AN ITALIAN MATHEMATICIAN AT THE UNIVERSITY OF Padua, introduced a new scientific instrument, the telescope, which revealed a wealth of knowledge about the stars and planets that filled the night skies. Having heard that a Dutch artisan had put together two lenses in such a way that magnified distant objects, Galileo built his own such device and directed it toward the heavens. Anyone who has looked through a telescope or seen photographs taken from a satellite can appreciate Galileo's excitement at what he saw. Objects that appeared one way to the naked eye looked entirely different when magnified by his new "spyglass," as he called it. The Milky Way, the pale glow that was previously thought to be a reflection of diffused light, turned out to be composed of a multitude of previously unknown stars. The surface of the moon, long believed to be smooth, uniform, and perfectly spherical, now appeared to be full of mountains, craters, and other irregularities. The sun, which was also supposed to be perfect in shape and composed of matter that could not be altered, was marred by spots that appeared to move across its surface. When turned toward Jupiter, the telescope revealed four moons never seen before. Venus, viewed over the course of many months, appeared to change its shape, much in the way that the moon did in its various phases. This latter discovery provided evidence for the relatively new theory that the planets, including Earth, revolved around the sun rather than the sun and the planets around the Earth.

Galileo shared the discoveries he made not only with fellow scientists but with other Europeans. In 1610 he published *The Starry Messenger,* a treatise in which he described his discovery of the new moons of Jupiter. Twenty-two years later he included the evidence he had gained from his telescope in another book, *Dialogue Concerning the Two Chief World Systems,* to support the claim that the Earth orbited the sun. He also staged a number of public demonstrations of his new astronomical instrument, the first of which took place on top of one of the

Chapter Outline

- The Discoveries and Achievements of the Scientific Revolution

- The Search for Scientific Knowledge

- The Causes of the Scientific Revolution

- The Intellectual Effects of the Scientific Revolution

- Humans and the Natural World

The Telescope: The telescope was the most important of the new scientific instruments that facilitated discovery. This engraving depicts an astronomer using the telescope in 1647.

city gates of Rome in 1611. To convince those who doubted the reality of the images they saw, Galileo turned the telescope toward familiar landmarks in the city. Interest in the new scientific instrument ran so high that a number of amateur astronomers acquired telescopes of their own.

Galileo's observations and discoveries formed one facet of the development that historians call the Scientific Revolution. A series of remarkable achievements in astronomy, physics, chemistry, and biology formed the centerpieces of this revolution, but its effects reached far beyond the observatories and laboratories of seventeenth-century scientists. The Scientific Revolution brought about fundamental changes in Western thought, altering the way in which Europeans viewed the natural world, the supernatural realm, and themselves. It stimulated controversies in religion, philosophy, and politics and brought about changes in military technology, navigation, and economic enterprise. The revolution added a new dimension to Western culture and provided a basis for claims of Western superiority over people in other lands. For all these reasons the Scientific Revolution marked a decisive turning point in the history of Western civilization, and it set the West apart from contemporary civilizations in the Middle East, Africa, and Asia.

In this chapter we will explore the scope and development of the Scientific Revolution and the changes it brought about in Western thought and culture. Five questions will structure our exploration of this subject:

- What were the scientific achievements and discoveries of the late sixteenth and seventeenth centuries that historians refer to as the Scientific Revolution?
- What methods did scientists use during this period to investigate nature, and how did they think nature operated?
- Why did the Scientific Revolution take place in western Europe at this particular time?
- How did the Scientific Revolution influence the development of philosophical and religious thought in the seventeenth and early eighteenth centuries?
- How did the Scientific Revolution change the way in which seventeenth- and eighteenth-century Europeans thought of their relationship to the natural world?

The Discoveries and Achievements of the Scientific Revolution

Unlike political revolutions, such as the English Revolution of the 1640s discussed in the last chapter, the Scientific Revolution developed gradually and over a long period of time. It began in the middle and later decades of the sixteenth century and continued into the early years of the eighteenth century. Even though it took a relatively long time to unfold, it was revolutionary in the sense that it brought about a radical transformation of human thought, just as political revolutions have produced fundamental changes in systems of government. The most important changes in seventeenth-century science took place in the fields of astronomy, physics, chemistry, and biology.

ASTRONOMY: A NEW MODEL OF THE UNIVERSE

The most significant change in astronomy was the acceptance of the view that the sun, not the Earth, was the center of the universe. Until the middle of the sixteenth century, most natural philosophers—as scientists were known at the time—subscribed to the writings of the Greek astronomer Claudius Ptolemy (100–170 C.E.). Ptolemy's observations and calculations had given considerable support to the cosmology° (a theory regarding the structure and nature of the universe) proposed by the Greek philosopher Aristotle (384–322 B.C.E.). According to Ptolemy and Aristotle, the center of the universe was a stationary Earth, around which the moon, the sun, and the other planets revolved in circular orbits. Beyond the planets a large sphere carried the stars, which stood in a fixed relationship to each other, around the Earth from east to west once every twenty-four hours, thus accounting for the rising and setting of the stars. Each of the four known elements—earth, water, air, and fire—had a natural place within this universe, with the heavy elements, earth and water, being pulled down toward the center of the Earth and the light ones, air and fire, hovering above it. All heavenly bodies, including the sun and the planets, were composed of a fifth element, called ether, which unlike matter on Earth was thought to be eternal and could not be altered, corrupted, or destroyed.

This traditional view of the cosmos had much to recommend it, and some educated people continued to subscribe to it well into the eighteenth century. The authority of Aristotle, predominant in late medieval universities, was reinforced by the Bible, which in a few passages referred to the motion of the sun. The motion of the sun could be confirmed by simple human observation. We do, after all, see the sun "rise" and "set" every day, while the idea that the Earth rotates at a high speed and revolves around the sun contradicts the experience of our senses. Nevertheless, the Earth-centered model of the universe failed to provide an explanation for many patterns that astronomers observed in the sky, most notably the paths followed by planets. In the sixteenth century natural philosophers began to consider alternative models of the universe.

The first major challenge to the Ptolemaic system came from a Polish cleric, Nicolaus Copernicus (1473–1543),

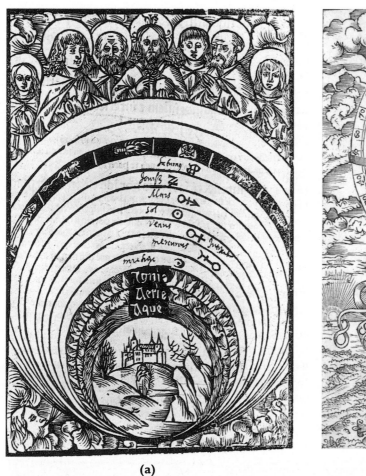

(a)

(b)

◼ Two Views of the Ptolemaic or Pre-Copernican Universe

(a) In this sixteenth-century engraving the Earth lies at the center of the universe and the elements of water, air, and fire are arranged in ascending order above the Earth. The orbit that is shaded in black is the firmament or stellar sphere. The presence of Christ and the saints at the top reflects the view that Heaven lay beyond the stellar sphere. (b) A medieval king representing Atlas holds a Ptolemaic cosmos. The Ptolemaic universe is often referred to as a two-sphere universe: The inner sphere of the Earth lies at the center and the outer sphere encompassing the entire universe rotates around the Earth.

who in 1543 published *The Revolutions of the Heavenly Spheres,* in which he proposed that the center of the universe was not the Earth but the sun. The book was widely circulated, but it did not win much support for the sun-centered theory of the universe. The mathematical arguments Copernicus presented in the book were so abstruse that only the most erudite astronomers could understand them. Even those who could appreciate his detailed plotting of planetary motion were not prepared to adopt the central thesis of his book. In the late sixteenth century the great Danish astronomer Tycho Brahe (1546–1601) accepted the argument of Copernicus that the planets revolved around the sun but still insisted that the sun continued to revolve around the Earth.

Significant support for the Copernican model of the universe among scientists began to materialize only in the seventeenth century. In 1609 a German astronomer, Johannes Kepler (1571–1630), confirmed the central position of the sun in the universe. In his treatise *New Astronomy,* Kepler also demonstrated that the planets, including the Earth, followed elliptical rather than circular orbits and that the planets moved in accordance with a series of physical laws. Kepler's book, however, did not reach a large audience, and his achievement was not fully appreciated until many decades later.

Galileo Galilei (1564–1642) was far more successful than Kepler in gaining support for the sun-centered model of the universe. Galileo had the literary skill, lacking in Kepler, of being able to write for a broad audience. Using the evidence gained from his observations with the telescope, and presenting his views in the form of a dialogue between the advocates of the two competing worldviews, he demonstrated the plausibility and superiority of Copernicus's theory.

The publication of Galileo's *Dialogue Concerning the Two Chief World Systems—Ptolemaic and Copernican* in 1632 won many converts to the sun-centered theory of the universe, but it lost him the support of Pope Urban VIII (r. 1623–1644), who had been one of his patrons. Urban believed that by naming the character in *Dialogue* who defended the Ptolemaic system Simplicio (that is, a simple person), he was mocking the pope himself. In the following year Galileo was tried before the Roman Inquisition, an ecclesiastical court whose purpose was to maintain theological orthodoxy. The charge against him was that he had challenged the authority of Scripture and was therefore guilty of heresy, the denial of the theological truths of the Roman Catholic Church. (See "Justice in History: The Trial of Galileo" later in this chapter.)

PHYSICS: THE LAWS OF MOTION AND GRAVITATION

Galileo made his most significant contributions to the Scientific Revolution in the field of physics, which deals with matter and energy and the relationship between them. In the seventeenth century the main branches of physics were mechanics (the study of motion and its causes) and

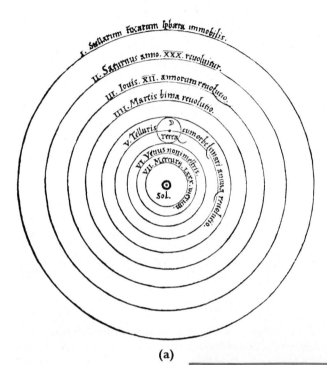

(a)

■ **Two Early Modern Views of the Sun-Centered Universe**

(a) The depiction by Copernicus. Note that all the orbits are circular, rather than elliptical, as Kepler was to show they were. The outermost sphere is that of the fixed stars. (b) A late-seventeenth-century depiction of the cosmos by Andreas Cellarius in which the planets follow elliptical orbits. It illustrates four different positions of the Earth as it orbits the sun.

(b)

optics (the study of light). Galileo's most significant achievement in physics was to formulate a set of laws governing the motion of material objects. His work, which laid the foundation of modern physics, effectively challenged the theories of Aristotle regarding motion.

According to Aristotle, whose views dominated science in the late Middle Ages, the motion of every object except the natural motion of falling toward the center of the Earth required another object to move it. If the mover stopped, the object fell to the ground or simply stopped moving. One of the problems with this theory was that it could not account for the continued motion of a projectile, such as a discus or a javelin, after it left the hand of the person who threw it. Galileo's answer to that question was that an object continues to move or to lie at rest until something external to it intervenes to change its motion. In addition to this theory of inertia, Galileo formulated a mathematical law of motion that explained how the speed and acceleration of a falling object are determined by the distance it travels during equal intervals of time.

The greatest achievements of the Scientific Revolution in physics belong to English scientist Sir Isaac Newton (1642–1727). Newton was one of those rare geniuses whose research changed the way future generations viewed the world. During the 1680s Newton formulated a set of mathematical laws that governed the operation of the entire physical world. In 1687 he published his theories in *Mathematical Principles of Natural Philosophy*. The centerpiece of this monumental work was the universal law of gravitation°, which demonstrated that the same force holding an object to the Earth also holds the planets in their orbits. Newton established that any two bodies attract each other with a force that is directly proportional to the product of their masses and inversely proportional to the square of the distance between them. This law represented a synthesis of the work by Kepler on planetary motion, Galileo on inertia, the English physicist Robert Hooke (1635–1703) on gravity, and the Dutch scientist Christian Huygens (1629–1695) on centrifugal force. Newton's *Mathematical Principles* superseded the works of all these scientists by establishing the existence of a single gravitational force and by giving it precise mathematical expression. At the same time it revealed the unity and order of the entire physical world. It provided, in Newton's words, "a system of the world."

CHEMISTRY: DISCOVERING THE ELEMENTS OF NATURE

At the beginning of the seventeenth century, the branch of science today called chemistry had little intellectual respectability. It was not even an independent discipline,

CHRONOLOGY

1543	Copernicus publishes *The Revolutions of the Heavenly Spheres,* challenging the traditional Earth-centered cosmos
1609	Johannes Kepler publishes *New Astronomy,* identifying elliptical orbits of the planets
1620	Sir Francis Bacon publishes *The New Organon,* arguing for the necessity of rigorous experimentation
1628	William Harvey publishes *On the Motion of the Heart and Blood in Animals,* demonstrating the circulation of the blood
1632	Galileo publishes *Dialogue Concerning the Two Chief World Systems,* leading to his trial
1633	Galileo tried by the Roman Inquisition
1637	René Descartes publishes *Discourse on the Method*
1662	Founding of the Royal Society of London
1687	Newton publishes his *Mathematical Principles of Natural Philosophy*

since it was considered a part of either medicine or alchemy°, the magical art of attempting to turn base metals into precious ones. The most famous chemist of the sixteenth century was the Swiss physician and natural magician Paracelsus (1493–1541), who rejected the theory advanced by the Greek physician Galen (129–200 C.E.) that diseases were caused by the imbalance of the four "humors" or fluids in the body—blood, phlegm, black bile, and yellow bile. The widespread medical practice of drawing blood from sick patients to cure them was based on Galen's theory. Paracelsus began instead to treat his patients with chemicals, such as mercury and sulfur, to cure certain diseases. Paracelsus is often dismissed for his belief in alchemy, but his prescription of chemicals to treat specific diseases helped give chemistry a respectable place within medical science.

During the seventeenth century chemistry became a legitimate field of scientific research, largely as the result of the work of the English natural philosopher Robert Boyle (1627–1691). Boyle destroyed the prevailing idea that all basic constituents of matter share the same structure. He contended that the arrangement of their components, which Boyle identified as corpuscles or atoms, determines their characteristics. Boyle also conducted experiments on the volume, pressure, and density of gas and the elasticity of air. His most famous experiments, undertaken with the help of an air pump, proved the existence of a vacuum. Largely as a result of Boyle's discoveries, chemists won acceptance as legitimate members of the company of scientists.

BIOLOGY: THE CIRCULATION OF THE BLOOD

The English physician William Harvey (1578–1657) made one of the great medical discoveries of the seventeenth century by demonstrating in 1628 that blood circulates throughout the human body. Harvey challenged the traditional theory regarding the motion of the blood advanced by Galen and perpetuated by medieval philosophers. According to this traditional theory, blood originated in the liver, where it was converted from food and then flowed outward through the veins, providing nourishment to the organs and the other parts of the body. A certain amount of blood was also drawn from the liver into the heart, where it passed from one ventricle to the other and then traveled through the arteries to different parts of the body. During its journey this arterial blood was enriched by a special *pneuma* or "vital spirit" that originated in the atmosphere and was necessary to sustain life. When this enriched blood reached the brain, it became the body's "psychic spirits," which eventually traveled to the nerves and influenced human behavior.

During the late sixteenth century a succession of Italian scientists called specific aspects of Galen's theory into question. It was Harvey, however, who proposed an entirely new framework for understanding the motion of the blood. Through a series of experiments on human cadavers and live animals in which he weighed the blood that the heart pumped every hour, Harvey demonstrated that the blood circulates throughout the body, traveling outward from the heart through the arteries and returning to the heart through the veins. The heart, rather than sucking in blood, performed the essential function of pumping it by means of its contraction and constriction. The only gap in Harvey's theory was the question of how blood goes from the ends of the arteries to the ends of the veins. The answer to this question came in 1661, when scientists, using another new magnifying instrument known as a microscope, could see the capillaries connecting the veins and arteries.

The Search for Scientific Knowledge

The natural philosophers who made these various scientific discoveries worked in different academic disciplines, and each followed his own procedures for discovering scientific truth. In the sixteenth and seventeenth centuries there was no such thing as a single "scientific method." Many natural philosophers, however, shared similar views regarding the way in which nature operated and the means by which humans could acquire knowledge of it. In searching for scientific knowledge, these scientists engaged in extensive observation and experimentation, used a process of deductive reasoning to solve scientific problems, expressed their theories in mathematical terms, and argued that nature operated like a machine. Taken together, these common features of scientific research ultimately defined a distinctly Western approach to solving scientific problems.

OBSERVATION AND EXPERIMENTATION

The most prominent feature of scientific research in sixteenth- and seventeenth-century Europe was the extensive observation of nature, combined with the testing of hypotheses by means of rigorous experimentation. This was primarily a process of induction°, in which theories emerged only after the systematic accumulation and analysis of large amounts of data. It assumed a willingness to abandon all preconceived notions, whether they were those of Aristotle, Galen, or medieval philosophers, and to base scientific conclusions on experience and observation.

The English philosopher Francis Bacon (1561–1626) promoted this empirical, experimental approach in his book *New Organon* (1620), in which he complained that all previous scientific endeavors, especially those of ancient Greek philosophers, relied too little on experimentation. Two English scientists who followed this approach rigorously were Robert Boyle, who performed a succession of experiments with an air pump to prove the existence of a vacuum, and Robert Hooke, whose experiments with a pendulum provided one of the foundations for Newton's theory of universal gravitation.

DEDUCTIVE REASONING

The second feature of sixteenth- and seventeenth-century scientific research was the application of deductive reasoning to scientific problems. Unlike the inductive experimental approach, which found its most enthusiastic practitioners in England, the deductive approach had its most zealous advocates on the European continent. The men who took this approach were just as determined as Bacon and Boyle to replace the testimony of human authorities with what they discovered from nature itself. Their main method, however, was to establish basic scientific truths or propositions from which other ideas or laws could be deduced logically. The French philosopher and mathematician René Descartes (1596–1650) became the champion of this methodology. In his *Discourse on the Method* (1637) he recommended that in solving any intellectual problem a person should first establish fundamental principles or truths and then proceed deductively from those ideas to more specific conclusions.

The model for deductive reasoning was mathematics, in which one also moves logically from certain premises to conclusions by means of equations. Rational deduction°

proved to be an essential feature of scientific methodology, although some scientists relied too heavily on it at the expense of a more experimental approach. The limitations of an exclusively deductive approach became apparent when Descartes and his followers deduced a theory of gravitation from the principle that objects could influence each other only if they actually touched. The theory, as well as the principle upon which it was based, lacked an empirical foundation, which is one based on observation and experience, and eventually had to be abandoned.

MATHEMATICS AND NATURE

The third feature of scientific research in the sixteenth and seventeenth centuries was the application of mathematics to the study of the physical world. The mathematical treatment of nature was undertaken by scientists working in both the experimental and the deductive traditions. Descartes shared with Galileo, Kepler, and Huygens the conviction that nature had a geometrical structure and that it could therefore be understood in mathematical terms. The physical dimensions of matter, which Descartes claimed were its only properties, could of course be expressed mathematically. Galileo claimed that mathematics was the language in which philosophy was written in "the book of the universe."

In the seventeenth century Isaac Newton's work provides the best illustration of the application of mathematics to scientific problems. Newton used observation and experimentation to confirm his theory of universal gravitation, but the work in which he presented his theory, *Mathematical Principles of Natural Philosophy,* was written in the language of mathematics. Just as Newton had synthesized previous work in physics to arrive at the law of universal gravitation, he also combined the experimental and deductive approaches to acquire scientific truth. His approach to solving scientific problems, which became a model for future scientific research, involved generalization on the basis of particular examples derived from experiments and the use of deductive, mathematical reasoning to discover the laws of nature.

THE MECHANICAL PHILOSOPHY

Much of the scientific experimentation and deduction undertaken in the seventeenth century proceeded on the assumption that the natural world operated as if it were a machine made by a human being. This philosophy of nature, which is often referred to as the mechanical philosophy°, cannot be attributed to a single person, but its most comprehensive statement can be found in the work of Descartes. The scholastic philosophers of the fourteenth and fifteenth centuries insisted that nature was fundamentally different from a machine or any other object built by humans. Descartes, Kepler, Galileo, and Bacon all denied that as-

■ **René Descartes**
Although Descartes was a scientist who made contributions to the study of biology and optics, he is best known for the method he proposed to attain certain knowledge and his articulation of the mechanical philosophy.

sumption, arguing that nature operated in a mechanical way, just like a clock or some other piece of machinery.

According to mechanists—scientists who subscribed to the mechanical philosophy—nature consisted of many machines, some of them extremely small. The human body was itself a machine, and the center of that human machine, the heart, was in Harvey's words "a piece of machinery in which, though one wheel gives motion to another, yet all the wheels seem to move simultaneously." To Descartes, the only part of a human being that was not a machine was the mind, which was completely different from the body and the rest of the material world. Unlike the body, the mind was an immaterial substance that could not be measured mathematically. Because Descartes made this sharp distinction between the mind and the human body, we speak of his philosophy as being dualistic°.

The mechanical philosophy presented just as bold a challenge to those philosophers known as Neoplatonists° as it did to the scholastics. Neoplatonists believed that the natural world was animistic—that is, it possessed a soul (known to them as a world soul) and was charged with various occult forces and spirits. The English natural philosopher William Gilbert (1544–1603), who wrote extensively on the phenomenon of magnetism, adopted a Neoplatonic worldview when he declared that the Earth and other planets were actually alive. Kepler clearly recognized the incompatibility of this outlook with that of the mechanical philosophy when he insisted that the machine of the universe was not similar to "a divine animated being."

Descartes and other mechanists argued that matter was completely inert or dead. It had neither a soul nor any innate purpose. Its only property was extension, or the physical dimensions of length, width, and depth. Without a spirit or any other internal force directing its action, matter simply responded to the power of the other bodies with which it came in contact. According to Descartes, all physical phenomena could be explained by reference to the dimensions and the movement of particles of matter. He once claimed, "Give me extension and motion and I will construct the universe." Even the human body contained no "vital spirits." The only difference between the human body and other machines was that the mind (or soul) could move it, although how it did so was a matter of great controversy, as we shall see in a later section.

The view of nature as a machine implied that it operated in a regular, predictable way in accordance with unchanging laws of nature. Scientists could use reason to discover what those laws were and thus learn how nature performed under any circumstances. The scientific investigations of Galileo and Kepler were based on those assumptions, and Descartes made them explicit. The immutability of the laws of nature implied that the entire universe was uniform in structure, an assumption that underlay Newton's formulation of the laws of motion and of universal gravitation. Newton's theory of gravity denied Descartes's view of matter as inert, but he nonetheless accepted his view that the universe operated like a machine.

The Causes of the Scientific Revolution

....

Why did the Scientific Revolution take place at this particular time, and why did it originate in western European countries? What prompted natural philosophers in Italy, France, England, and the Dutch Republic to develop new ways of looking at the world? There are no simple answers to these questions. We can, however, identify a number of developments that inspired this remarkable set of scientific discoveries. Some of these developments were internal to science, in the sense that they arose out of earlier investigations conducted by natural philosophers in the Middle Ages, the Renaissance and the early sixteenth century. Others were external to the development of science, arising out of the religious, political, social, and economic life of Europe during the early modern period.

DEVELOPMENTS WITHIN SCIENCE

The three internal causes of the Scientific Revolution were the research into motion conducted by scholastic natural philosophers in the fourteenth century, the scientific investigations conducted by humanists at the time of the Renaissance, and the collapse of the dominant conceptual frameworks that had governed scientific inquiry and research for centuries.

Late Medieval Science

Modern science can trace some of its origins to the fourteenth century, when the first significant modifications of Aristotle's scientific theories began to emerge. These challenges came not only from theologians, who objected that Aristotle was a pagan philosopher, but also from natural philosophers, who refined some of the basic ideas of Aristotle's physics.

The most significant of these refinements was the theory of impetus. Aristotle, as we have seen, had argued that an object would stop as soon as it lost contact with the object that moved it. The scholastic philosophers who modified this principle claimed that objects in motion acquire a force that stays with them after they lose contact with the mover. The theory of impetus did not bring about a full-scale demolition of Aristotle's mechanics, but it did begin to call Aristotle's authority into question. The theory of impetus was known in Galileo's day, and it influenced some of his early thought on motion.

Renaissance Science

Renaissance natural philosophers made tangible contributions to the rise of modern science despite the fact that the Renaissance, the revival of classical antiquity in the fifteenth and sixteenth centuries, was not conducive to the type of scientific research that Galileo, Descartes, Boyle, and Newton conducted. Renaissance humanism was mainly a literary and artistic movement, and humanists were not particularly interested in scientific knowledge. Humanism also cultivated a tradition of deferring to the superior wisdom of classical authors, whereas the new science defined itself largely in opposition to the theories of the ancients, especially Aristotle, Ptolemy, and Galen.

The natural philosophers of the Renaissance did nonetheless make a number of important contributions to the birth of modern science. Many of the discoveries of the late sixteenth and seventeenth centuries drew their inspiration from Greek scientific works that had been recovered in their original form during the Renaissance. Copernicus found the original idea of his sun-centered universe in the writings of Aristarchus of Samos, a Greek astronomer of the third century B.C.E. whose work had been unknown during the Middle Ages. The theory that matter was divisible into small measurable particles known as atoms was inspired at least in part by the recovery of the texts of ancient philosophers, most notably Democritus, who flourished around 480 B.C.E.

The Renaissance philosophy of Neoplatonism, despised by mechanists, also played an important role in the Scientific Revolution. In addition to the belief that the natural world had a soul, Neoplatonists adopted a geometric view of the universe and therefore encouraged the application of mathematics to the study of the natural world. Kepler developed his third law of planetary motion by applying to the cosmos the Neoplatonic idea of a harmony between numbers. The Neoplatonic tendency to think in terms of large, general categories also encouraged scientists such as Kepler, Galileo, and Newton to discover universal laws of nature. Even alchemy, which many Neoplatonists practiced during the Renaissance, involved natural philosophers in experiments that gave them a limited sense of control over the operations of nature. The followers of Paracelsus, whose alchemy was tinged with Neoplatonic mysticism, were firm advocates of the observation of nature and experimentation.

Some of the most prominent natural philosophers of the seventeenth century were influenced to some extent by the cultural traditions that we associate with the Renaissance. Kepler became involved in the study of magic at the court of the Holy Roman Emperor Rudolf II. From his reading in Neoplatonic sources, Kepler acquired his belief that the universe was constructed according to geometric principles. Bacon gained some of his enthusiasm for experimentation from his interest in natural magic°, which was the use of magical words and drawings to manipulate forces in the physical world without calling on supernatural beings for assistance. Newton was fascinated by the subject of magic and studied alchemy intensively.

These contributions of the Renaissance to the new science were so important that some historians have identified the sixteenth century, when learned magic was in vogue and when the mechanical philosophy had not yet taken hold, as the first stage of the Scientific Revolution, to be followed by the mechanical phase when the discoveries of Galileo, Boyle, and Newton took center stage. Modern science resulted not so much from the victory of the mechanical philosophy over its Neoplatonic predecessor but from this encounter between these two worldviews.

The Collapse of Paradigms

The second internal cause of the Scientific Revolution was the collapse of the intellectual frameworks that had governed the conduct of scientific research since antiquity. The key to understanding this development is the recognition that scientists in all historical periods do not strive to introduce new theories but prefer to work within an established conceptual framework, or what the scholar Thomas Kuhn

has referred to as a paradigm°. Scientists strive to solve puzzles that are presented by the paradigm. Every so often, however, the paradigm that has governed scientific research for an extended period of time collapses because it can no longer account for many different observable phenomena. A scientific revolution occurs when the old paradigm collapses and a new paradigm takes its place.

The revolutionary developments we have studied in astronomy can be explained at least in part by the collapse of the Ptolemaic paradigm, in which the sun and the planets revolved around the Earth. Whenever ancient or medieval astronomers confronted a new problem as a result of their observations, they tried to accommodate the results to the Ptolemaic model. In the process they had to refine the basic concept that Ptolemy had presented. By the sixteenth century the paradigm had been modified or adjusted so many times that it no longer made sense. As scientists gradually added numerous "epicycles" of planetary motion outside the prescribed spheres, and as they identified numerous "eccentric" or noncircular orbits around the Earth, Ptolemy's paradigm of a harmoniously functioning universe gradually became a confused collection of planets and stars following different motions. Faced with this situation, Copernicus began to look for a simpler and more plausible model of the universe. The sun-centered theory that he proposed became the new paradigm within which Kepler, Galileo, and Newton all worked.

In the field of biology a parallel development occurred when the old paradigm constructed by Galen, in which the blood originated in the liver and was drawn into the heart and from there traveled through the arteries to the brain and nerves, also collapsed. By the seventeenth century the paradigm of Galen could no longer satisfactorily explain the findings of medical scholars, such as the recognition that blood could not easily pass from one ventricle of the heart to the other. It was left to Harvey to introduce an entirely new paradigm, in which the blood circulated through the body. As in astronomy, the collapse of the old paradigm led to the Scientific Revolution, and Harvey's new paradigm served as a framework for subsequent biological research.

DEVELOPMENTS OUTSIDE SCIENCE

A number of nonscientific developments also encouraged the development and acceptance of new scientific ideas. These developments outside science include the spread of Protestantism, the patronage of scientific research, the invention of the printing press, and military and economic change.

Protestantism

The growth of Protestantism in the sixteenth and seventeenth centuries encouraged the rise of modern science. Catholics as well as Protestants engaged in scientific research, and some of the most prominent European natural philosophers, including Galileo and Descartes, were devout Catholics. Protestantism, however, encouraged the emergence of modern science in two indirect ways.

First, Protestant countries proved to be more receptive than Catholic ones to new scientific ideas. Protestant churches, for example, did not prohibit the publication of books that promoted novel scientific ideas on the grounds that they were heretical, as the Papal Index did. The greater willingness of Protestant governments, especially those of England and the Dutch Republic, to tolerate the expression of unorthodox ideas helps to explain why the main geographical arena of scientific investigation shifted from the Catholic Mediterranean to the Protestant North Atlantic in the second half of the seventeenth century.

The second connection between Protestantism and the development of science was the emphasis Protestant writers placed on the idea that God revealed his intentions not only in the Bible but also in nature itself. Protestants claimed that individuals had a duty to discover what God had revealed to them in this way, just as it was their duty to read Scripture to gain knowledge of God's will. Kepler's claim that the astronomer was "as a priest of God to the book of nature," a reference to the Protestant idea of the priesthood of all believers, serves as an explicit statement of this Protestant outlook.

Patronage

Although the intellectual problems that scientists grappled with may have inspired them to pursue their research and conduct experiments, they could not have succeeded without some kind of financial and institutional support. Only with the acquisition of an organizational structure could science acquire a permanent status, develop as a discipline, and give its members a professional identity. The universities, which today are known for their support of scientific research, did not serve as the main source of that support in the seventeenth century. One reason was that most universities, which were predominantly clerical institutions, had a vested interest in the defense of scholastic theology and Aristotelian science. They were therefore unlikely to provide the type of free academic atmosphere in which new scientific ideas might flourish. Moreover, within the university the only subject that allowed for the exploration of nature was that of philosophy. As long as science was considered a branch of philosophy, it could not establish its autonomy as a discipline and gain recognition as a legitimate pursuit in its own right.

Given limited support from the universities, scientists became dependent upon the patronage of wealthy and politically influential individuals. For the most part this patronage came from the kings, princes, and great noblemen who ruled European territorial states. During the seventeenth century, scientists found this type of patronage in two different types of institutions. The first were the courts of Italian and German princes. Galileo, for example, was the

beneficiary of the patronage of the Grand Duke of Tuscany Cosimo II de' Medici, the Roman aristocrat Prince Federico Cesi, and even Pope Urban VIII. These patrons, who were eager to display their interest in and support of learning, were actually responsible for securing Galileo's university appointments.

The second type of scientific institutions that provided patronage to scientists were academies in which groups of scientists could share ideas and work collectively. One of the earliest of these institutions was the Academy of the Lynxes in Rome, founded in 1603 by Prince Cesi. Galileo became a member of this academy in 1611, and it published many of his works. In 1657 Cosimo II founded a similar institution, the Academy of Experiment, in Florence. These academies offered a more regular source of patronage than scientists could acquire from individual positions at court, but they still served the function of glorifying their founders, and they depended on patrons for their continued existence. The royal academies established in the 1660s, however, especially the Royal Academy of Sciences in France and the Royal Society in England, reduced that dependence on their patrons. These academies were established by the crown, but they operated with a minimum of royal intervention. The royal academies also acquired a permanent location that made possible a continuous program of work.

The mission of the Royal Society in England was the promotion of scientific knowledge through a program of experimentation. It also served the political purpose of placing the results of scientific research at the service of the state, as we shall see shortly. This had been Francis Bacon's objective in his *New Organon,* and many of the members of the society, including Robert Boyle and Robert Hooke, were committed to the implementation of Bacon's plans. The research that members of the Royal Society did on both ship construction and military technology gave some indication of this commitment. These attempts to use scientific technology to strengthen the power of the state show that two of the most important developments of the seventeenth century, the growth of the modern state and the emergence of modern science, were related.

The Printing Press

The scientific academies and societies of the seventeenth century gave natural philosophers an opportunity to discuss their findings among themselves, but these scientists also needed to communicate the results of their research to scientists in more distant localities. The introduction and spread of printing throughout Europe made it much easier for scientists to share their discoveries with others who were working on similar problems. During the Middle Ages, when books were handwritten, the dissemination of scientific knowledge was limited by the number of copies that could be made of a manuscript. Moreover, errors could easily creep into the text as it was being copied. The advent and

■ **The Frontispiece of Thomas Sprat's *The History of the Royal Society of London* (1667)**
Fame places a laurel on a bust of Charles II, the patron of the society, while the president of the society, Lord Brouncker, sits to the left, pointing to the king's name. The late Sir Francis Bacon, whose emphasis on experimentation defined the purpose of the society, sits to the right and points to the navigational devices and firearms that he had predicted would lead to European control of the globe. They are sitting in a room filled with books and scientific instruments, including a telescope. In the background the Thames River, the gateway to the British Empire, suggests a further link between science and empire.

spread of printing helped to correct this problem: Scientific achievements could be preserved in a much more accurate form and presented to a broader audience. The availability of printed copies also made it much easier for other scientists to correct or supplement the data that the authors supplied. In this way the entire body of scientific knowledge became cumulative, as it is today.

It remains uncertain how large a role printed materials played in the development of science. Scientists certainly read the work of others, but they also devoted large amounts of time to their own experiments, and those experiments in the long run were more important than books in the development of scientific knowledge. Printing may have accomplished more by making members of the nonscientific community aware of the latest advances in physics and astronomy than by leading scientists themselves to make new discoveries. In this way printing helped to make science an integral part of the culture of educated Europeans.

Military and Economic Change

The Scientific Revolution occurred at roughly the same time that both the conduct of warfare and the European economy were undergoing dramatic changes. As territorial states increased the size of their armies and their military arsenals, they naturally demanded more accurate weapons with longer range. Some of the work undertaken by physicists during the seventeenth century, especially concerning the trajectory and velocity of missiles, gravitation, and air resistance, had the specific intention of improving military weaponry. Members of the Royal Society in England conducted extensive scientific research on these topics, and in so doing followed Francis Bacon's recommendation that scientists place their research at the service of the state.

The practical needs of capitalist enterprise also had a bearing on the direction of scientific research. The seventeenth century was a formative period in the emergence of a new capitalist economy, one in which private individuals engaged in trade, agriculture, and industry in order to realize ever-increasing profits. Some of the questions discussed at the meetings of the Royal Society suggest that its members undertook research with the specific objective of making such capitalist ventures more productive and profitable. The research did not always produce immediate results, but ultimately it increased economic profitability and contributed to the growth of the English economy in the eighteenth century. Knowledge of the displacement of water by ships led to improvements in methods of ship construction, which benefited merchants engaged in overseas trade. The study of mechanics led to new techniques to ventilate mines and raise coal or ore from them, thus making mining more profitable.

The Intellectual Effects of the Scientific Revolution

The Scientific Revolution had a profound impact on the intellectual life of educated Europeans. The discoveries of Copernicus, Kepler, Galileo, and Newton, as well as the assumptions upon which their work was based, influenced the way in which they approached intellectual problems, understood religion, and viewed the supernatural realm.

SKEPTICISM AND INDEPENDENT REASONING

One of the most significant intellectual effects of the Scientific Revolution was the encouragement it gave to the habit of skepticism, the tendency to doubt what we have been taught and are expected to believe. This skepticism formed part of the method that seventeenth-century scientists adopted in their efforts to solve philosophical problems.

In *Discourse on the Method*, Descartes showed the extremes to which this skepticism could be taken by doubting the reality of his own sense perceptions and even his own existence. He eventually found a way out of this dilemma when he realized that the very act of doubting proved his existence as a thinking being. As he wrote in words that have become famous, "I think, therefore I am." Upon this foundation Descartes went on to prove the existence of God and the material world, thereby conquering the skepticism with which he began his inquiry. In the process, however, Descartes had promoted an approach to solving intellectual problems that asked people to question the authority of others and to think clearly and systematically for themselves. The effects of this method began to become apparent in the late seventeenth century, when Descartes's methodology was invoked in challenging a variety of orthodox opinions regarding the supernatural world.

Some of the most radical of those opinions came from the mind of Baruch Spinoza (1632–1677), who grew up in Amsterdam in a community of Spanish and Portuguese Jews who had fled the Inquisition. Although educated in the Orthodox Jewish manner, Spinoza also studied Latin and read the works of Descartes and other Christian writers of the period. From Descartes, Spinoza had learned "that nothing ought to be admitted as true but what has been proved by good and solid reason." This skepticism and independence of thought led to his excommunication from the Jewish community at age 24, at which time he changed his first name from its Jewish form, Baruch, to Benedict.

Spinoza's independence of thought led him to conclude that there was only one substance in the universe, which he equated with nature or God. This pantheism, in which all matter became spirit and was comprehended within God, challenged not only the ideas of Descartes regarding the separation of the mind and the body but also a fundamental tenet of Christianity—the distinction between God as pure spirit and the material world that God had created. In his most famous book, *A Treatise on Religion and Political Philosophy* (1670), Spinoza developed these ideas and also called for complete freedom from intellectual restraints.

Spinoza's skeptical approach to solving philosophical and scientific problems revealed the radical intellectual potential of the new science. The freedom of thought that Spinoza advocated, as well as the belief that nature followed immutable laws and could be understood in mathematical terms, served as important links between the Scientific Revolution and the Enlightenment of the eighteenth century. Those connections will be studied more fully in Chapter 18.

SCIENCE AND RELIGION

The most profound intellectual effects of the Scientific Revolution occurred in the area of religious thought. The claims of the new science presented two challenges to traditional Christian belief. The first involved the apparent contradiction between the sun-centered theory of the universe and biblical references to the sun's mobility. Since the Bible was considered the inspired word of God, the Church took everything it said, including any passages regarding the operation of the physical world, as literally true. The Bible's reference to the sun moving across the sky served as the basis of the official papal condemnation of sun-centered theories in 1616 and the prosecution of Galileo in 1633.

The second challenge to traditional Christian belief was the implication that if the universe functioned as a machine, on the basis of immutable natural laws, then God apparently played a very small role in its operation. This position, which was adopted by the late-seventeenth- and eighteenth-century thinkers known as deists°, was considered a denial of the Christian belief that God superintended the operation of the world and was continually active in its governance.

Although the new science and seventeenth-century Christianity appeared to be on a collision course, a number of scientists and theologians insisted that there was no conflict between them. One argument they made was that religion and science were separate disciplines that had very different concerns. Religion dealt with the relationship of humans with God, while science explained how nature operated. As Galileo wrote in one of his letters, "The Holy

Ghost teaches us how to go to Heaven, not how the heavens go." Scripture was not intended to explain natural phenomena, but to convey religious truths that could not be grasped by human reason. In making these points Galileo was pleading for the separation of religion and science by freeing scientific inquiry from the control of the Church.

Another argument for the compatibility of science and religion was the claim that the mechanical philosophy, rather than relegating God to the role of a retired engineer, actually manifested his unlimited power. In a mechanistic universe God was still the formulator of the laws of nature that guaranteed its regular operation. According to Boyle and Newton, moreover, God played a supremely active role in governing the universe by keeping all matter constantly in motion.

As the new science became more widely accepted, and as the regularity and immutability of the laws of nature became more apparent, religion itself began to undergo a transformation. Instead of denying the validity of the new science, many theologians, especially Protestants, accommodated scientific knowledge to their religious beliefs. Many clergymen who accepted the new science argued that since God worked through the processes of nature, human beings could acquire theological knowledge of him by engaging in scientific inquiry. For them religion and science were not so much separate but complementary forms of knowledge, each capable of illuminating the other.

The most widespread effect of the new science on religion was a new emphasis on the compatibility of reason and religion. In the Middle Ages scholastic theologians such as Thomas Aquinas had tried to reconcile the two, arguing that there was a body of knowledge about God, called natural theology, that could be obtained without the assistance of revelation. Now, however, with the benefit of the new science, theologians and philosophers began to expand the role that reason played in religion. In the religious writings of the English philosopher John Locke, the role of reason became dominant. In *The Reasonableness of Christianity* (1695), Locke argued that reason should be the final arbiter of the existence of the supernatural and it should also determine the true meaning of the Bible.

The new emphasis on the reasonableness of religion is often viewed as evidence of a broader trend toward the secularization of European life, a process in which religion gave way to more worldly concerns. In one sense this secular trend was undeniable. By the dawn of the eighteenth century, theology had lost its dominant position at the universities, the sciences had become autonomous academic disciplines, and religion had lost much of its intellectual authority.

Religion had not, however, lost its relevance. Throughout the eighteenth century it remained a vital force in the lives of most European people. Religious books continued to be published in great numbers. Many of those who accepted the new science continued to believe in a providen-

tial God and the divinity of Christ. Moreover, a small but influential group of educated people, following the lead of the French mathematician, physicist, and religious philosopher Blaise Pascal (1623–1662), insisted that although reason and science have their place, they represent only one sphere of truth. In his widely circulated book *Reflections,* which lay unfinished at his death but was published in 1670, Pascal argued that religious faith occupied a higher sphere of knowledge that reason and science could not penetrate. Pascal had been an advocate of the new science, but on the question of the relationship between science and religion, he presented arguments that could be used against Spinoza, Locke, and all those who considered reason the ultimate arbiter of truth.

MAGIC, DEMONS, AND WITCHCRAFT

The new science not only changed many patterns of religious thought but also led to a denial of the reality and effectiveness of magic. Magic is the use of a supernatural, occult, or mysterious power to achieve extraordinary effects in the physical world or to influence the course of human events. The effects can be beneficial or harmful. In the sixteenth and seventeenth centuries men and women believed in and practiced two forms of magic. Natural magic, such as the practice of alchemy, involved the manipulation of occult forces that were believed to exist in nature. Demonic magic°, on the other hand, involved the invocation of evil spirits so that one might gain access to their supernatural power. The men who were most committed to the mechanical philosophy denied the effectiveness of both types of magic. By claiming that matter was inert, they challenged the central notion of natural magic, which is the belief that material objects are animated by occult forces, such as a sympathy for another object. If matter was not alive, it contained no forces for a magician to manipulate.

The denial of the reality of demonic magic was based on a rejection of the powers of demons. Seventeenth-century scientists did not necessarily deny the existence of angelic or demonic spirits, but the mechanical philosophy posed a serious challenge to the belief that those spirits could influence the operation of the physical world. The belief in demons experienced a slow death. Many scientists struggled to preserve a place for them in the physical world, arguing that demons, like God, could work through the processes of nature. Ultimately, however, the logic of the mechanical philosophy expelled them from the worldview of the educated classes. By the beginning of the eighteenth century, scientists and even some theologians had labeled the belief in demons as superstition, which originally had meant false or erroneous religion but which was now redefined to mean ignorance of mechanical causes. As Thomas Sprat, an English clergyman, declared in his history of the Royal Society, "Experiments have proven demons don't exist."

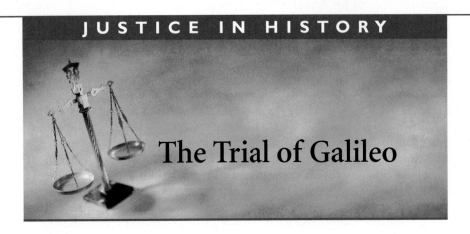

The Trial of Galileo

The events leading to the trial of Galileo for heresy in 1633 began in 1616, when a committee of eleven theologians reported to the Roman Inquisition that the sun-centered theory of Copernicus was heretical. Those who accepted this theory were declared to be heretics not only because they called the authority of the Bible into question but because they denied the exclusive authority of the Catholic Church to determine how the Bible should be interpreted. The day after this report was submitted, Pope Paul V instructed Cardinal Robert Bellarmine, a theologian who was on good terms with Galileo, to warn him to abandon his Copernican views. Galileo had written extensively in support of the sun-centered thesis, especially in his *Letters on Sunspots* (1613) and his *Letter to the Grand Duchess Christina* (1615), although he had never admitted that the theory was proved conclusively. Now he was being told that he should not hold, teach, or defend in any way the opinion of the sun's stability or the Earth's mobility. If he were to ignore that warning, he would be prosecuted as a heretic.

During the next sixteen years Galileo published two books. The first, *The Assayer* (1623), was an attack upon the views of an Italian philosopher regarding comets. The book actually won Galileo considerable support, especially from the new pope, Urban VIII, who was eager to be associated with the most fashionable intellectual trends. Urban took Galileo under his wing and

made him the intellectual star of his court. Urban even went so far as to declare that support for Copernicanism was not heretical but only rash.

The patronage of the pope may have emboldened Galileo to exercise less caution in writing his second book of this period, *Dialogue Concerning the Two Chief World Systems* (1632). This treatise was ostensibly an impartial presentation of the rival Ptolemaic and Copernican cosmologies, but in its own quiet way it served the purpose of promoting Copernicanism. Galileo sought proper authorization from ecclesiastical authorities to put the book in print, but he eventually allowed it to be published in Florence before it received official approval from Rome.

The publication of *Dialogue* precipitated Galileo's fall from the pope's favor. Urban, who at this time was coming under criticism for leniency with heretics, ordered the book taken out of circulation in the summer of 1632 and appointed a commission to investigate Galileo's activities. After receiving the report from the committee a few months later, he turned the matter over to the Roman Inquisition, which charged Galileo with heresy.

The Roman Inquisition had been established in 1542 to preserve the Catholic faith. Its main concern was the prosecution of heresy. Like the Spanish Inquisition, this Roman ecclesiastical court has acquired a reputation for being harsh and arbitrary, for administering torture, for proceeding in secrecy, and for denying the accused

the right to know the charges in advance of the trial. There is some validity to these criticisms, although the Roman Inquisition did not torture Galileo or deny him the opportunity to present a defense. The most unfair aspect of the proceeding, and of inquisitorial justice in general, was the determination of the outcome of the trial by the same judges who had brought the charges against the accused and conducted the interrogation. This meant that in a politically motivated trial such as Galileo's, the verdict was a foregone conclusion. To accept Galileo's defense would have been a sign of weakness and a repudiation of the pope.

Although the underlying substantive issue in the trial was whether Galileo was guilty of heresy for denying the sun's motion and the Earth's immobility, the more technical question was whether by publishing *Dialogue* he had violated the prohibition of 1616. In his defense Galileo claimed that the only reason he had written *Dialogue* was to present "the physical and astronomical reasons that can be advanced for one side or the other." He denied holding Copernicus's opinion to be true.

In the end the court determined that by publishing *Dialogue*, Galileo had violated the injunction of 1616. He had disseminated "the false opinion of the Earth's motion and the sun's stability" and he had "defended the said opinion already condemned." Even Galileo's efforts "to give the impression of leaving it undecided and labeled as probable" was still a very serious error,

■ **The Trial of Galileo, 1633**

Galileo is shown here presenting one of his four defenses to the Inquisition. He claimed that his book, *Dialogue Concerning the Two Chief World Systems,* did not endorse the Copernican model of the universe.

since there was no way that "an opinion declared and defined contrary to divine Scripture may be probable." The court also declared that Galileo had obtained permission to publish the book in Florence without divulging to the authorities there that he was under the injunction of 1616.

Throughout the trial every effort was made to distance the pope from his former protégé. There was real fear among the members of the papal court that since the pope had been Galileo's patron and had given him considerable latitude in developing his ideas, he himself would be implicated in Galileo's heresy. Every step was taken to guarantee that information regarding

the pope's support for Galileo did not surface. The court made sure, for example, that no one from the Medici court, which had provided support for Galileo, would testify on Galileo's behalf. The trial tells us as much about the efforts of Urban VIII to save face as about the Catholic Church's hostility to the new science.

Galileo was required to formally renounce his views and to avoid any further defense of Copernicanism. After making this humiliating submission to the court, he was sent to Siena and later that year was allowed to return to his villa in Arcetri near Florence, where he remained under house arrest until his death in 1642. ■

Questions of Justice

1. Galileo was silenced because of what he had put into print. Why had he published these works, and why did the Church consider his publications a serious threat?

2. Is a court of law an appropriate place to resolve disputes between science and religion? Why or why not?

Taking It Further

Finocchiaro, Maurice, ed. *The Galileo Affair: A Documentary History.* 1989. A collection of original documents regarding the controversy between Galileo and the Roman Catholic Church.

Sharratt, Michael. *Galileo: Decisive Innovator.* 1994. A study of Galileo's place in the history of science that provides full coverage of his trial and papal reconsiderations of it in the late twentieth century.

The denial of the power of magic, together with the rejection of the belief in the power of demonic spirits, also explains why many educated Europeans began to deny the reality of witchcraft in the later half of the seventeenth century. Witches were individuals, mostly women, who stood accused of using magic to harm their neighbors, their animals, or their crops. They were also accused of having made a pact with the Devil, the means by which they received their magical powers. In many cases it was claimed that witches worshipped the Devil collectively at nocturnal orgies known as sabbaths. To someone who subscribed to the mechanical philosophy, this entire set of beliefs about witches was highly questionable. Demons could not intervene in the operation of the physical world, much less make pacts with human beings and copulate with them at the sabbath.

The skeptical views that many educated people acquired regarding witchcraft and magic were usually not shared by people who remained illiterate. For them magic and witchcraft remained very real, and they continued to suspect and accuse their neighbors of engaging in diabolical practices until the early nineteenth century. All of this served to highlight a widening gap between the views of the educated and those of the common people. In the late seventeenth century members of the educated classes began to develop unprecedented contempt for the ignorance and superstition of the common people. The education of the upper classes in the new science and in Descartes's philosophy only aggravated what was already a noticeable trend.

The development of two separate realms of culture became one of the main themes of eighteenth-century history, and it contributed directly to the formation of class divisions. On the one side were the educated upper classes who prided themselves on their rational and enlightened views; on the other were the illiterate peasants who continued to believe in magic, witchcraft, and what the educated referred to as "vulgar superstition."

Humans and the Natural World

The spread of scientific knowledge not only redefined the views of educated people regarding the supernatural realm, but it also led them to reconsider their relationship to nature. This process involved three separate but related inquiries. The first was to determine the place of human beings in a sun-centered universe; the second to investigate how science and technology had given human beings greater control over nature; and the third to reconsider the relationship between men and women in light of new scientific knowledge regarding the human mind and body.

THE PLACE OF HUMAN BEINGS IN THE UNIVERSE

The astronomical discoveries of Copernicus and Galileo offered a new outlook regarding the position of human beings in the universe. The Earth-centered Ptolemaic cosmos that dominated scientific thought during the Middle Ages was also human-centered. Not only was the planet that human beings inhabited situated at the center of the universe, but on Earth humans occupied a privileged position: They were the absolute physical and moral center of this universe.

The acceptance of a sun-centered model of the universe began to bring about a fundamental change in these views of humankind. Once it became apparent that the Earth was not the center of the universe, human beings began to lose their privileged position in nature. The Copernican universe was neither Earth-centered nor human-centered. Scientists such as Descartes continued to claim that human beings were the greatest of nature's creatures, but their habitation of a tiny planet circling the sun inevitably reduced the sense of their own importance. Moreover, as astronomers began to recognize the incomprehensible size of the cosmos, the possibility emerged that there were other habitable worlds in the universe, calling into further question the unique status of humankind.

In the late sixteenth and seventeenth centuries a number of literary works explored the possibility of other inhabited worlds and forms of life. In *Lunar Astronomy* (1634), a work that combined science and fiction, Kepler described various species of moon dwellers, some of whom were rational and superior to humans. The most ambitious and fascinating of all these books was a fictional work by the French dramatist and poet Bernard de Fontenelle, *Conversations on the Plurality of Worlds* (1686). This work, which became immensely popular throughout Europe, was more responsible than any purely scientific discovery of the seventeenth century for leading the general reading public to call into question the centrality of humankind in Creation.

THE CONTROL OF NATURE

The Scientific Revolution bolstered the confidence human beings had in their ability to control nature. By disclosing the laws governing the operation of the universe, the new science gave humans the tools they needed to make nature serve their own purposes more effectively than it had in the past. This confidence in human mastery over nature found its most articulate expression in the writings of Francis Bacon. Instead of accepting the traditional view that humans were either passively reconciled with nature or victimized by it, Bacon believed that knowledge of the laws of nature could restore the dominion over nature that humans had lost in the biblical Garden of Eden. Bacon believed that nature existed for human beings to control and exploit for their own benefit. His famous maxim, "knowledge is power," conveyed his confidence that science would give human beings this type of control over nature.

Later in the seventeenth century the members of the Royal Society proclaimed their intention to make scientific knowledge "an instrument whereby mankind may obtain a dominion over things." This optimism regarding human control of nature found support in the belief that God permitted such mastery, first by creating a regular and uniform universe and then by giving people the rational faculties by which they could understand nature's laws.

Many scientists of the seventeenth century emphasized the practical applications of their research, just as scientists often do today. Descartes, who used his knowledge of optics to improve the grinding of lenses, contemplated ways in which scientific knowledge might improve the drainage of marshes, increase the velocity of bullets, and use bells to make clouds burst. Members of the Royal Society discussed the possibility of making labor-saving machines. These efforts to apply scientific knowledge to practical problems encouraged the belief, which has persisted to the present day, that science could improve human life.

WOMEN, MEN, AND NATURE

The new scientific and philosophical ideas of the seventeenth century challenged ancient and medieval notions regarding women's physical and mental inferiority to men. At the same time the new science left other traditional ideas about the roles of men and women unchallenged.

Until the seventeenth century, a woman's sexual organs were thought to be imperfect versions of a man's, an idea that made woman an inferior version of man and in some respects a freak of nature. During the sixteenth and seventeenth centuries, a body of scientific literature advanced the new idea that women had sexual organs that were perfect in their own right and served distinct functions in reproduction. Another traditional biological idea that came under attack during this period was Aristotle's view that men made a more important contribution to reproduction than did women. The man's semen was long believed to contain the form of the body as well as the soul, while the only contribution the woman was believed to have made to the process was the formless matter upon which the semen acted. By the beginning of the eighteenth century, a scholarly consensus had emerged that recognized equal contributions from both sexes to the process of reproduction.

Some seventeenth-century natural philosophers also called into question ancient and medieval ideas regarding women's mental inferiority to men. In this regard Descartes supplied a theory that presupposed intellectual equality between the sexes. In making a radical separation between the

■ **Astronomers in Seventeenth-Century Germany**
Elisabetha and Johannes Hevelius working together with a sextant in a German astronomical observatory. More than 14 percent of all German astronomers were female. Most of them cooperated with their husbands in their work.

mind and the human body, Descartes found no difference between the minds of men and women. As one of his followers wrote in 1673, "The mind has no sex." A few upper-class women provided solid evidence to support this revolutionary claim of female intellectual equality. Princess Elisabeth of Bohemia, for example, carried on a long correspondence with Descartes during the 1640s and challenged many of his ideas on the relationship between the body and the soul. The privately educated English noblewoman Margaret Cavendish (1623–1673) wrote scientific and philosophical treatises and conversed with the leading philosophers of the day.

Although seventeenth-century science laid the theoretical foundations for a theory of sexual equality, it did not challenge other traditional ideas that compared women

ELISABETH OF BOHEMIA CHALLENGES DESCARTES

....

Elisabeth of Bohemia, the daughter of King Frederick of Bohemia and granddaughter of King James I of England, engaged in a long correspondence with Descartes regarding his philosophy. Privately educated in Greek, Latin, and mathematics, Elisabeth was one of a small group of noblewomen who participated in the scientific and philosophical debates of the day. The letter concerns the relationship between the soul (or mind), which Descartes claimed was immaterial, and the body, which is entirely composed of matter. One of the problems for Descartes was to explain how the mind can move the body to perform certain functions. In the letter Elisabeth plays a deferential, self-effacing role but in the process exposes one of the weaknesses of Descartes's dualistic philosophy.

The Hague, 20 June 1643

Monsieur Descartes,

. . . The life I am forced to lead does not leave me the disposition of enough time to acquire a habit of meditation according to your rules. So many interests of my family that I must not neglect, so many interviews and civilities that I cannot avoid, batter my weak spirit with such anger and boredom that it is rendered for a long time afterward useless for anything else. All of which will excuse my stupidity, I hope, not to have been able to understand the idea by which we must judge how the soul (not extended and immaterial) can move the body by an idea we have in another regard of heaviness, nor why a power—which we have falsely attributed to things under the name of a quality—of carrying a body toward the center of the Earth when the demonstration of a contrary truth (which you promised in your Physics) confirms us in thinking it impossible. The idea of a separate independent quality of heaviness—given that we are not able to pretend to the perfection and objective reality of God—could be made up out of ignorance of that which truly propels bodies towards the center of the Earth. Because no material cause represents itself to the senses, one attributes heaviness to matter's contrary, the immaterial, which nevertheless I would never be able to conceive but as a negation of matter and which could have no communication with matter.

I confess that it is easier for me to concede the matter and the extension of the soul than to concede that a being that is immaterial has the capacity to move a body and to be moved by it. For if the former is done by giving information, it is necessary that the spirits which make the movement be intelligent, which you do not accord to anything corporal. And although, in your meditations, you show the possibility of the soul being moved by the body, it is nevertheless very difficult to comprehend how a soul, as you have described it, after having had the faculty and habit of good reasoning, would lose all that by some sort of vapors, or that being able to subsist without the body and having nothing in common with it, would allow itself to be so ruled by the body.

Source: From *The Princess and the Philosopher: Letters of Elisabeth of the Palatine to René Descartes* by Andrea Nye. Copyright © 1999 by Rowman & Littlefield Publishers, Inc. Reprinted by permission.

---

unfavorably to men. Most educated people continued to ground female behavior in the humors, claiming that because women were cold and wet, as opposed to hot and dry, they were naturally more deceptive, unstable, and melancholic than men. They also continued to identify women with nature itself, which had always been depicted as female. Bacon's use of masculine metaphors to describe science and his references to "man's mastery over nature" therefore seemed to reinforce traditional ideas of male dominance over women. His language also reinforced traditional notions of men's superior rationality. In 1664 the secretary of the Royal Society, which excluded women from membership, proclaimed that the mission of that institution was to develop a "masculine philosophy."

The new science provided the theoretical foundations for the male control of women at a time when many men expressed concern over the "disorderly" and "irrational" conduct of women. In a world populated with witches, rebels, and other women who refused to adhere to conventional standards of proper feminine behavior, the adoption of a masculine philosophy was associated with the reassertion of patriarchy.

CONCLUSION
Science and Western Culture

The Scientific Revolution was a uniquely Western phenomenon. It had no parallel in the Eastern world. During the Middle Ages the Islamic civilizations of the Middle East produced a rich body of scientific knowledge that had influenced the development of science in western Europe, but by the time of the Scientific Revolution Islamic science had entered a period of decline. Other civilizations, most notably in China and India, also possessed impressive scientific traditions, but they too failed to undergo a transformation similar to that which occurred in western Europe in the seventeenth century.

In all these non-Western civilizations, religious traditions had prevented philosophers from undertaking an objective study of the natural world. Either nature was viewed as an entirely secular (that is, not religious) entity and hence not worthy of study on its own terms, or it was viewed as something so heavily infused with spiritual value that it could not be subjected to rational analysis. Only in Europe did religious and cultural traditions allow the scientist to view nature as both a product of supernatural forces and something that was separate from the supernatural realm. Nature could therefore be studied objectively without losing its religious significance. Only when nature was viewed in this dual way, as both the creation of God and as something independent of the deity, could it be subjected to mathematical analysis and brought under human domination.

The Scientific Revolution gave the West a new source of identity. The West could be distinguished not only by its Christianity, its capitalist economic system, its large bureaucratic states, and its massive standing armies, but also by the scientific content of its education, its approach to the natural world, and its science-based technology. By the beginning of the eighteenth century, modern science became an essential component of Western culture. It also laid the foundations of the Enlightenment, another distinctively Western phenomenon, which will be discussed in Chapter 18.

The rise of Western science and technology had profound implications for the encounters that took place between Western and non-Western peoples in Africa, Asia, and the Americas. By the eighteenth century, European science provided explicit support for European empires, which will be discussed in Chapters 17 and 23. Science gave Western states the military and navigational technology that allowed them to establish their control over non-Europeans. Knowledge of botany and agriculture allowed Western powers to develop the resources of the areas they colonized and to use these resources for the improvement of their own societies. Most important, the possession of scientific knowledge and technology encouraged people in the West to think of themselves as superior to the people they subjugated or controlled. Scientific theories regarding biological and physiological differences between the people who inhabited the West and natives of other countries also contributed to those attitudes. Western imperialism had its roots in the Scientific Revolution of the seventeenth century.

Suggestions for Further Reading

For a comprehensive list of suggested readings, please go to www.ablongman.com/levackconcise/chapter16

Biagioli, Mario. *Galileo, Courtier: The Practice of Science in the Culture of Absolutism.* 1993. Argues that Galileo's desire for patronage determined the type of research he engaged in and the scientific questions he asked.

Cohen, H. Floris. *The Scientific Revolution: A Historiographical Inquiry.* 1995. A thorough account of all the different interpretations of the causes and significance of the Scientific Revolution.

Dear, Peter. *Discipline and Experience: The Mathematical Way in the Scientific Revolution.* 1995. Explains the importance of mathematics in the development of seventeenth-century science.

Debus, Allen G. *Man and Nature in the Renaissance.* 1978. Deals with the early history of the Scientific Revolution and develops many of its connections with the Renaissance.

Drake, Stillman, ed. *Discoveries and Opinions of Galileo.* 1957. Includes four of Galileo's most important writings, together with a detailed commentary.

Easlea, Brian. *Magic, Witch-Hunting and the New Philosophy.* 1980. Relates the end of witch hunting to the spread of the mechanical philosophy.

Kuhn, Thomas S. *The Copernican Revolution.* 1957. The most comprehensive and authoritative study of the shift from an Earth-centered to a sun-centered model of the universe.

Popkin, Richard. *The History of Scepticism from Erasmus to Spinoza.* 1979. Discusses skepticism as a cause as well as an effect of the Scientific Revolution.

Schiebinger, Londa. *The Mind Has No Sex? Women in the Origins of Modern Science.* 1989. Explores the role of women in all aspects of scientific endeavor.

Shapin, Steven. *The Scientific Revolution.* 1996. A study of the origins of the modern scientific worldview that emphasizes the social influences on the production of knowledge and the social purposes for which scientific knowledge was intended.

Shapin, Steven, and Simon Schaffer. *Leviathan and the Air Pump.* 1989. Study of the difference between Robert Boyle and Thomas Hobbes regarding the value of experimentation.

Thomas, Keith. *Man and the Natural World: A History of the Modern Sensibility.* 1983. A study of the shifting attitudes of human beings toward nature during the period from 1500 to 1800.

Webster, Charles. *The Great Instauration: Science, Medicine and Reform, 1626–1660.* 1975. Explores the relationship between Puritanism and the Scientific Revolution in England.

Westfall, Richard S. *Never at Rest: A Biography of Isaac Newton.* 1980. A superb biography of the most influential scientist in the history of the West.

The West and the World: Empire, Trade, and War, 1650–1850

IN 1789 OLAUDAH EQUIANO, A FREED SLAVE LIVING IN GREAT BRITAIN, PUBLISHED an autobiographical account of his experiences in captivity. In this narrative Equiano recounted his seizure in the Gambia region of Africa and his transportation on a slave ship to the British Caribbean colony of Barbados. He described the unmerciful floggings to which the Africans on his ship were subjected, the unrelieved hunger they experienced, and the insufferable heat and smells they endured in the hold of the ship. He witnessed the suicide of those who threw themselves into the sea in order to avoid further misery. He was terrified that his white captors would eat him, and he wished for a merciful death.

Once the ship had reached its destination Equiano related how the Africans were herded into pens where white plantation owners examined, purchased, and branded them. The most moving part of Equiano's narrative is his account of the cries he heard as family members were sold to different masters. "O you nominal Christians," wrote Equiano, "might not an African ask you, learned you this from your God? Is it not enough that we are torn from our country and friends to toil for your luxury and lust of gain? Must every tender feeling be sacrificed to your avarice? Surely this is a new refinement in cruelty, which, while it has no advantage to atone for it, thus aggravates distress and adds fresh horrors to the wretchedness of slavery."

The journey that Equiano was forced to take across the Atlantic Ocean and the emotions he described were experienced by millions of African men and women during the period from 1650 to 1850. The forced emigration of Africans from their homelands, their sale to white landlords, and their subjection to inhumane treatment number among the abiding horrors of Western civilization. To understand how these horrors could have occurred, especially at the hands of

Chapter Outline

- European Empires in the Americas and Asia

- Warfare in Europe, North America, and Asia

- The Atlantic World

- Encounters Between Europeans and Asians

- The Crisis of Empire and the Atlantic Revolutions

Samuel Scott, *A Thames Wharf* (1750s): British merchants conducted a brisk trade with Asia and the Americas in the eighteenth century.

men who proclaimed a commitment to human freedom, we must study the growth of European empires during these centuries.

As European states grew in size, wealth, and military power in the sixteenth and seventeenth centuries, the most powerful of them acquired large overseas empires. By the end of the seventeenth century the British, French, and Dutch had joined the Portuguese and the Spanish as overseas imperial powers. As we discussed in Chapter 12, the first stage of empire building, which lasted from 1500 until about 1650, had many different motives: the search for gold and silver, the mission to Christianize the indigenous populations, the desire of some colonists to escape religious persecution, the urge to plunder, the efforts of monarchs to expand the size of their dominions, and the desire to profit from international trade.

During the second stage of empire building, which lasted from roughly 1650 to 1850, the economic motive for acquiring overseas possessions became dominant. More than anything else, imperial policy was shaped by the desire for profit within a world economy. As far as the governments of western Europe were concerned, all colonies were economic enterprises. They supplied the parent country, often referred to as the metropolis°, with agricultural products, raw materials, and minerals. Overseas colonies also provided the metropolis with markets for its manufactured goods.

The growth of these empires marked a significant transformation of the West. As European powers gained control of distant lands, the geographical boundaries of the cultural realm we call the West expanded dramatically. This geographical expansion resulted in the spread of Western ideas, political institutions, and economic systems to Asia and the Americas. At the same time, encounters between Europeans and non-Western peoples, especially those of Asia, brought about significant changes in the cultures of the West.

To understand the relationship between empire, trade, and war during this period, and their impact on the changing definition of the West, this chapter will address five main questions:

- How did the composition and the organization of European empires change during the seventeenth and eighteenth centuries?
- In what ways did the wars waged by European powers during this period involve competition for overseas possessions and trading routes?
- How did European empires create an Atlantic economy in which the traffic in slaves was a major feature?
- What cultural encounters took place between European and Asian peoples during this period of empire building, and how did these encounters change Western attitudes toward outsiders?
- Why did European powers begin to lose control of some of their colonies, especially those in the Americas, between 1775 and 1825?

European Empires in the Americas and Asia

The main political units in Europe during this period are usually referred to as states°. A state is a consolidated territorial area that has its own political institutions and recognizes no higher authority. Thus we refer to France, England (which became Great Britain after its union with Scotland in 1707), Prussia, the Dutch Republic, and Portugal as states. As we have discussed in Chapter 15, most of these states acquired larger armies and administrative bureaucracies during the sixteenth and seventeenth centuries, mainly to meet the demands of war. Consequently they became more highly integrated and cohesive political structures.

Many European states formed the center or core of much larger political formations known as empires°. The main characteristic of an empire in the seventeenth and eighteenth centuries was that it comprised many different kingdoms or territorial possessions outside the geographical boundaries of the state itself. These imperial territories were controlled by the metropolis, but they were not fully integrated into its administrative structure. Some of the territories that formed a part of these empires were located in Europe. The Austrian Habsburg monarchy, for example, had jurisdiction over a host of separate kingdoms and principalities in central and eastern Europe, including Hungary and Bohemia. This arrangement made Austria an empire, a designation it formally acquired in 1806. In like manner the Spanish monarchy, which also was an empire, controlled many different kingdoms and provinces in the Iberian peninsula as well as territories in southern Italy and the Netherlands. On the eastern and southeastern periphery of Europe the Russian and Ottoman empires controlled vast expanses of land not only in Europe but also in the adjacent areas of Asia. As in previous centuries, the Russian and Ottoman empires marked the ever-shifting and often blurred boundaries between East and West.

Beginning in the fifteenth century, as the result of transoceanic voyages of exploration and the establishment of overseas colonies, western European states acquired, settled, or controlled territories in the Americas, Africa, and Asia. The earliest of the European overseas empires were established by the Spanish and the Portuguese. During the period we are considering here, three rising European powers—Great Britain, France, and the Dutch Republic—began to rival the older empires. By the end of the period the British had emerged as the dominant imperial power.

THE RISE OF THE BRITISH EMPIRE

The fastest-growing of these new European overseas empires was that of Great Britain. England had begun its overseas empire in the late twelfth century, when it conquered the neighboring island of Ireland, but only in the seventeenth century did it begin to acquire lands in the New World and Asia.

By 1700 the English empire in the Americas included a number of colonies on the North American mainland, a vast territory in the northern part of Canada, and a cluster of islands in the Caribbean, most notably Barbados, Jamaica, and the Bahamas. These West Indian colonies developed an economy that used slave labor, and therefore blacks brought there from Africa soon outnumbered Europeans by a significant margin. In the colonies on the mainland of North America, however, most of the colonists were white. This was true even in the southern colonies, where slave labor was also introduced. Only in South Carolina, which was settled by Caribbean planters, did the black population exceed 50 percent.

During the seventeenth century the English also established a number of trading posts, known as factories°, along the coast of India. The first of these factories was Surat, which was settled in 1612, and it was soon followed by Madras (1640), Bombay (1661), and Calcutta (1690). There were significant differences between these outposts and the colonies in the Caribbean and the North American mainland. The number of British settlers in India, most of whom were members of the East India Company, remained extremely small, and they did not establish large plantations like those in the Caribbean colonies and the southern mainland colonies. Consequently they did not introduce slave labor into these countries. In contrast to the situation in North America and the Caribbean, the British in India had to deal with a large native population. At first they had contact with that population only when they were engaged in trade. In the second half of the eighteenth century, however, the British began to gain direct political control of Indian provinces, and by 1850 they controlled a large portion of the South Asian subcontinent.

In addition to their settlements in America and India, the British acquired influence and ultimately political control of the area from Southeast Asia stretching down into the South Pacific. In the late seventeenth century the British began to challenge the Dutch and the Portuguese for control of the trade with Indonesia, and in the second half of the eighteenth century British merchants established a thriving trade with the countries on the Malay peninsula. In the late eighteenth century the British also began to explore the South Pacific, which remained the last part of the inhabited world that Europeans had not yet visited and settled. In 1770 the British naval officer and explorer Captain James Cook (1728–1779) claimed the entire eastern coast of Australia for Great Britain, and in 1788 the British established a penal colony in the southeastern corner of the continent at Botany Bay.

The British Empire of the late seventeenth and eighteenth centuries possessed little administrative coherence; it was a hodgepodge of colonies, factories, and territories that had different relationships to the royal government in Britain (see Map 17.1). In India the provinces brought under British control were run by a trading corporation that exercised many functions of government. Some colonies in America, such as Maryland and Pennsylvania, operated under charters granted to members of the aristocracy. Most of the colonies on the North American mainland and in the Caribbean had their own legislatures. None of these colonies, however, sent representatives to the British Parliament. The only bond of unity among all the colonists is that they, like British subjects living in England or Scotland, owed their allegiance to the monarch and were under the monarch's protection. All of these colonists were therefore British subjects.

THE SCATTERED FRENCH EMPIRE

French colonization of North America and India paralleled that of Great Britain, but it never achieved the same degree of success. As the British were establishing footholds in the West Indies and the mainland of North America, the French acquired their own islands in the Caribbean and laid claim to large sections of Canada and the Ohio and Mississippi River valleys in the present-day United States. In the West Indies the French began the process of colonization by introducing indentured servants for periods of three years, but in the eighteenth century they began to follow the British and Spanish pattern of importing slaves to provide the labor for the sugar plantations.

The parallel between French and British overseas expansion extended to India, where in the early eighteenth century the French East India Company established factories at Pondicherry, Chandenagar, and other locations. The French fought the British in India both on land and at sea at different critical times between 1744 and 1815. The British ultimately prevailed in this struggle, and by the turn of the nineteenth century the French presence in India had been reduced to a few isolated factories.

The waning of French influence in India coincided with a series of territorial losses in the New World. Defeats suffered at the hands of the British during the Seven Years' War (1756–1763) resulted in the transfer of French Canada and the territory east of the Mississippi River to Great Britain. During that conflict France also ceded the vast region of Louisiana between the Mississippi River and the Rocky Mountains to Spain. France regained Louisiana in 1801 but then promptly sold the entire territory to the United States in 1803. The following year the French Caribbean colony of Saint Domingue became independent, although France retained possession of its other West Indian colonies.

THE COMMERCIAL DUTCH EMPIRE

The tiny Dutch Republic acquired almost all of its overseas possessions in the first half of the seventeenth century, at about the same time that the British and French were establishing their first colonies in Asia and the New World.

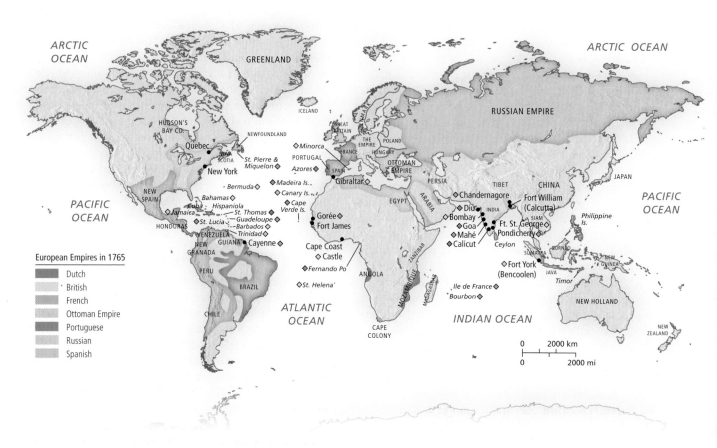

■ **Map 17.1   European Empires in 1763**

This map shows the overseas possessions of Britain, France, the Dutch Republic, Spain, and Portugal. Russian overseas expansion into North America had not yet begun.

The formation of the Dutch empire went hand in hand with the explosive growth of the Dutch economy in the seventeenth century. At that time the Dutch Republic became the center of a global economy, and its overseas colonies in the New World, Asia, and Africa helped the republic maintain its commercial supremacy. Dutch overseas settlements, just like the port cities of the metropolis, were dedicated almost exclusively to serving the interests of trade.

The Dutch were more eager than other European powers to use military and naval power to acquire and fortify trading depots. They seized two trading posts from the Portuguese on the West African coast in 1637, and in 1641 they also acquired from Portugal the African islands of São Tomé and Principe. In 1624 the Dutch, operating through their West Indian Company, seized the northern coast of Brazil, and after its return to Portugal in 1654 they acquired two small West Indian islands and a number of small plantation colonies on the Guiana coast of South America, mainly in present-day Suriname. From these small settlements in Africa and the Caribbean the Dutch traded with the Spanish, Portuguese, French, and British colonies.

Through these ports the Dutch brought more than 500,000 slaves to Brazil, the Spanish colonies, and the French and British West Indies.

In addition to their African and Caribbean possessions, the Dutch established a presence in three other parts of the world. In the early seventeenth century they settled a colony in the Hudson River valley on the North American mainland. They named the colony New Netherland and its main port, at the mouth of the river, New Amsterdam. In 1664 the Dutch lost the colony to the English, who renamed the colony and the port New York. The second area was in Asia, where the Dutch East India Company established a fort at Batavia (now Jakarta in Indonesia) and factories in India, China, and Japan. These possessions allowed the Dutch to engage in trade throughout Asia. The third area was the southern tip of Africa, where in 1652 the Dutch settled a colony at the Cape of Good Hope, mainly to provide support for ships engaged in commerce with the East Indies. In this colony 1,700 Dutch settlers, most of them farmers known as boers°, developed an agricultural economy on plantations that employed slave labor. The loss of this colony to the British at the end of the eighteenth century

■ **The Dutch Factory of Batavia in Indonesia, ca. 1665**

The Dutch Republic dominated the Asian trade in the seventeenth century. Batavia (now Jakarta) was the most important of their settlements in Southeast Asia. The efforts of the Dutch to transplant their culture is evident in this building's Dutch style of architecture.

reflected a more general decline of Dutch military and imperial strength.

THE VAST SPANISH EMPIRE

Of all the European overseas empires, the lands under the control of the Spanish monarchy were the most extensive. At the height of its power in 1650, the Spanish Empire covered the western part of North America from California to Mexico and from Mexico down through Central America. It also included Florida and the Caribbean islands of Cuba, San Domingo, and Puerto Rico. It embraced almost all of South America except Brazil, which was under Portuguese control. In Asia the main Spanish possessions were the Philippine Islands, named for the future King Philip II in 1542 and conquered with little bloodshed after 1564. The Philippines served as the main base from which the Spanish engaged in trade with other Asian countries.

Spanish overseas possessions were integrated into a much more authoritative imperial system than were those of the British. Until the eighteenth century a hierarchy of councils, staffed by men appointed by the crown, exercised political control of the various large territories or viceroyalties into which the empire was divided. Like other European empires, the Spanish colonial empire was designed to serve the purposes of trade. Until the eighteenth century a council in Seville directed Spanish ships from the southwestern Spanish port of Cadiz to selected ports on the eastern coasts of Spanish America, from which they were redirected to other ports. The ships returned to Spain carrying the gold and silver that had been extracted from the mines of Mexico and Peru.

The Bourbon kings of Spain, who were installed on the throne in 1700, introduced a number of political reforms that were intended to increase the volume of the colonial trade and prevent the smuggling that had always threatened to undermine it. On the one hand, they opened up the colonial trade to more Spanish and American ports and permitted more trade within the colonies. On the other hand, the Bourbons, especially Charles III (r. 1759–1788), brought the viceroyalties under the direct control of Spanish royal officials and increased the efficiency of the tax collection system. The Bourbon reforms made the empire more manageable and profitable, but they also created tension between the Spanish-born bureaucrats and the creoles°, the people of Spanish descent who had been born in the colonies.

THE DECLINING PORTUGUESE EMPIRE

Portugal had been the first European nation to engage in overseas exploration and colonization. During the late fifteenth and sixteenth centuries they had established colonies in Asia, South America, and Africa (see Chapter 12). By the beginning of the eighteenth century, however, the Portuguese Empire had declined in size and wealth in relation to its rivals. The Portuguese continued to hold a few ports in India, most notably the small island of Goa. They also retained a factory at Macao off the southeastern coast of China. In the New World the major Portuguese plantation colony was Brazil, which occupied almost half the land mass of South America and which supplied Europe with sugar, cacao (from which chocolate is made), and other agricultural commodities. Closely linked to Brazil were the Portuguese colonies along and off the West African coast. These possessions were all deeply involved in the transatlantic trade, especially in slaves. The Portuguese also had a series of trading stations and small settlements on the southeastern coast of Africa, including Mozambique.

The contraction of the Portuguese Empire in the seventeenth and eighteenth centuries resulted in the transfer of land to other European countries. A relatively weak European power, Portugal did not fare well in the fierce military conflicts that ensued in South America and Asia over control of the colonial trade. Portugal's main military and economic competition came from the Dutch, who seized many of its Asian, African, and South American

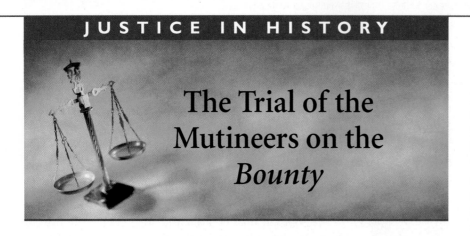
The Trial of the Mutineers on the *Bounty*

In December 1787 a British ship named the *Bounty,* under the captainship of William Bligh, left Portsmouth, England, on a momentous journey to Tahiti, an island in the South Pacific that Captain James Cook had first visited in 1769. The goal of the voyage of the *Bounty* was neither exploration nor colonial expansion but to bring home breadfruit trees that Cook had discovered on his second trip to the island in 1773. The trees, so it was hoped, would be introduced to the West Indies as a source of food for the slaves and hence the survival of the plantation economy. The voyage of the *Bounty* was therefore part of the operation of the new global economy that European expansion had made possible. The total size of the crew, all of whom had volunteered for service, was forty-six. The master's first mate, who became the main leader of a mutiny against Bligh, was Fletcher Christian.

The mutiny did not take place until after the ship had remained at Tahiti for a number of months, loaded its cargo of more than a thousand breadfruit plants, and begun its return voyage. The main reason for the mutiny was Captain Bligh's abusive and humiliating language. Unlike many other officers who faced the task of maintaining order on their ships and commanding the obedience of their crews, Bligh did not flog his men. In that regard Bligh's behavior was mild. Instead he went into tantrums and verbally abused them, belittling them and calling them scoundrels. Just before the mutiny Bligh called Fletcher Christian

a cowardly rascal and falsely accused him of stealing from him. On the morning of April 28, 1788, Christian arrested Bligh at bayonet point, tied his hands behind his back, and threatened him with instant death if he should speak a word. Claiming that "Captain Bligh had brought all this on himself," Christian and his associates put Bligh and eighteen other members of the crew into one of the ship's small launch boats and set them adrift, leaving them to reach a nearby island by their own power.

The mutineers sailed on to the island of Tubuai, where after a brief stay they split into two groups. Nine of them, headed by Christian and accompanied by six Tahitian men and twelve women, established a settlement on Pitcairn Island. The remaining sixteen mutineers returned to Tahiti. All but two of these men were apprehended in

1791 by Captain Edwards of the H.M.S. *Pandora,* which had been sent to Tahiti with the objective of arresting them and returning them to England for trial. At the beginning of its return voyage the *Pandora* was shipwrecked, and four of the prisoners drowned. The rest reached England aboard another ship in 1792. They were promptly charged before a navy court-martial with taking the *Bounty* away from its captain and with desertion, both of which were offenses under the Naval Discipline Act of 1766.

The trial took place aboard a British ship, H.M.S. *Duke,* in Portsmouth harbor in September 1792. The proceeding had all the markings of a state trial, one initiated by the government for offenses against the crown. Mutiny and desertion represented challenges to the state itself. During the second period of imperial expansion navies became major instruments of state power. Even when ships were used for purposes of exploration rather than naval combat, they served the interests of the state. The captain of the ship represented the power of the sovereign at sea. Because of the difficulty of maintaining order in such circumstances, he was given absolute authority. He could use whatever means necessary, including the infliction of corporal

■ **Sextant**

Eighteenth-century ships like the *Bounty* used this instrument to determine nautical position by means of the stars.

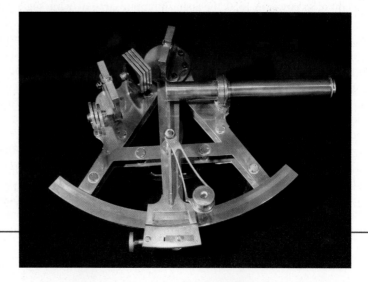

**The Mutineers Casting Bligh Adrift in the Launch,
Engraving by Robert Dodd (1790)**

This was the central act in the mutiny led by Fletcher Christian. Captain Bligh is standing in the launch in his nightclothes. Some of the breadfruit trees loaded on the ship at Tahiti can be seen on the top deck.

punishment, to preserve order. To disobey or challenge him was interpreted as an act of rebellion.

The trial was based on the assumption that the mutiny was illegal and seditious. The only question was the extent of individual involvement in the act itself. The degree of involvement was measured by evidence of one's co-operation with Christian or his loyalty to Bligh. The mere fact that some men had remained with Christian on the *Bounty* did not prove that they had supported the mutiny. Four of those men gave little evidence of having voluntarily cooperated with Christian, and those four men were eventually acquitted. The testimony of Captain Bligh, who declared that those four crew members had been reluctant to put him in the launch boat, was decisive in securing their nonguilty verdicts.

The remaining six men were convicted and sentenced to die by hanging. Three of those men were eventu-

ally spared their lives. Peter Heywood and James Morrison were well connected to influential people in the navy and the government and received royal pardons. William Muspratt, one of only three mutineers to hire a lawyer, entered a protest against the procedures of the court. In a court-martial, unlike a criminal trial at the common law, a prisoner could not call witnesses in his own defense. At the time of his conviction Muspratt protested that he had been "debarred calling witnesses whose evidence I have reason to believe would have tended to prove my innocence." The difference between the two systems of criminal justice, he claimed, "is dreadful to the subject and fatal to me." On this ground Muspratt was reprieved.

The three men who were executed died as model prisoners, proclaiming the illegality of their rebellion. Although the government had executed only a small minority of the mutineers, by securing their conviction

and dramatizing it with a widely publicized hanging, it had upheld its authority and thus reinforced the power of the crown.

Questions of Justice

1. How would you characterize the different ideals of justice used by the mutineers and the British admiralty court as the bases of their actions?

2. What does the journey of the *Bounty* tell us about the role of the British navy in the process of imperial expansion? What problems were inherent in using British ships for these purposes?

Taking It Further

Rutter, Owen, ed. *The Court-Martial of the "Bounty" Mutineers.* 1931. Contains a full transcript of the trial.

■ **Rio de Janeiro, the Major Slave Port in Brazil, Receiving Slaves**
More slaves went to Brazil than to any other country in the Americas. The trade continued until 1851, and only in 1888 was the institution of slavery abolished.

colonies, and who acquired many Portuguese trading routes. Most of those losses took place in Asia between 1600 and 1670. The Portuguese Empire suffered further losses when the crown relinquished Bombay and the northern African port of Tangier to the English as part of the dowry for the Portuguese princess Catherine of Braganza when she married King Charles II in 1661.

Brazil remained by far the most important of the Portuguese possessions during the late seventeenth and eighteenth centuries. The colony suffered from an unfavorable balance of trade with Portugal, but it expanded in population and wealth during this period, especially after the discovery of gold and diamonds led to large-scale mining in the interior. The slave trade increased in volume in order to provide additional labor in the mines and on the sugar plantations. In the first quarter of the nineteenth century, as the British slave trade declined and came to an end, Portuguese ships carried 871,600 slaves to Brazil. Between 1826 and 1850 the number increased to an astonishing 1,247,700. As a result of this massive influx of Africans, slaves accounted for approximately 40 percent of the entire Brazilian population by the beginning of the nineteenth century.

THE RUSSIAN EMPIRE IN THE PACIFIC

The only eastern European state that established an overseas empire during the eighteenth century was Russia. Between the fifteenth and the early eighteenth centuries Russia had gradually acquired a massive overland empire stretching from St. Petersburg in the west across the frigid expanse of Siberia to the Pacific Ocean. The main impulse of Russian expansion had been the search for exotic furs that were in high demand in the colder climes of Russia and northern Europe. During the reign of the Empress Catherine the Great (r. 1762–1796), Russia entered a period of further territorial expansion. On its western frontier it took part in the successive partitions of Poland between 1772 and 1795, while to the south it held the Crimean region within the Ottoman Empire between 1783 and 1792.

During the late eighteenth and early nineteenth centuries Russia also extended its empire overseas. Russian traders and explorers crossed the northern Pacific, where they encroached upon the hunting grounds of the native Aleuts in Alaska. The Russian-American Company, established in 1789, built a number of trading posts along the Pacific seaboard from Alaska down to Fort Ross in northern

California. These claims led to a protracted territorial dispute with Spain, which had established a string of missions and settlements on the California coast as far north as San Francisco. In this way the two great European empires of Russia and Spain, advancing from opposite directions, confronted each other on the western coast of North America. Russian expansion into Alaska and California also led to territorial disputes with the United States, which was engaged in its own process of territorial expansion westward toward the Pacific during the nineteenth century.

Warfare in Europe, North America, and Asia

Until the middle of the seventeenth century, European states engaged each other in battle almost exclusively within their own continent. The farthest their armies ever traveled was to the Middle East to fight the Turks or to Ireland to conquer the native Celts. The acquisition of overseas empires and the conflicts that erupted between European powers over the control of global trade brought those European conflicts to new and distant military theaters. Wars that began over territory in Europe were readily extended to America in one direction and to Asia in the other. The military forces that fought in these imperial battles consisted not only of metropolitan government troops but also those of the colonists. These colonial forces were often supplemented by the troops drawn from the local population, such as when the French recruited Native Americans to fight with them against the British in North America.

Wars fought overseas placed a premium on naval strength. Ground troops remained important, both in Europe and overseas, but naval power increasingly proved to be the crucial factor. All of the Western imperial powers either possessed or acquired large navies. Great Britain and the Dutch Republic rose to the status of world powers on the basis of sea power, while the French strengthened their navy considerably during the reign of Louis XIV. The Dutch used their naval power mainly against the Portuguese and the British, while the British directed theirs against the French and the Spanish as well as the Dutch. The overwhelming success that the British realized in these conflicts resulted in the establishment of British maritime supremacy.

MERCANTILE WARFARE

An increasingly important motive for engaging in warfare in the late seventeenth and eighteenth centuries was the protection and expansion of trade. The theory that underlay and inspired these imperial wars was mercantilism. As we discussed in Chapter 15, mercantilists believed that the wealth of the state depended on its ability to import fewer commodities than it exported and thus to acquire the largest possible share of the world's monetary supply. In order to achieve this goal, mercantilists encouraged domestic industry and placed heavy customs duties or tariffs on imported goods. Mercantilism was therefore a policy of protectionism°, the shielding of domestic industries from foreign competition. Mercantilists also sought to increase the size of the country's commercial fleet, establish colonies in order to promote trade, and import raw materials from the colonies to benefit domestic industry. The imperial wars of the seventeenth and eighteenth centuries, which were fought over the control of colonies and trading routes, thus formed part of a mercantilist policy.

The first of the great mercantile wars that involved conflict overseas arose between England and the Dutch Republic, the two emerging commercial giants of Europe, in the middle and late seventeenth century (1652–1654, 1664–1667, 1672–1675). The two countries were engaged in heated competition for control of the transatlantic trade, and the Dutch resented the passage of English laws, known as the Navigation Acts, that excluded them from trade with the English colonies. The Dutch claimed the right to trade with all ports in the world as well as to fish in the waters off British shores. Not surprisingly, many of the engagements in these wars took place at sea and in the colonies.

Shortly after the first Anglo-Dutch War, England also went to war against Spain (1655–1657). This conflict also reflected the new emphasis on mercantile objectives. The war resulted in the British acquisition of a profitable Caribbean colony, Jamaica, in 1655. The Anglo-Spanish tensions that surfaced in this conflict continued into the eighteenth century. In 1762, during another war against Spain, armed forces from Britain and the North American colonies seized the Cuban port of Havana as part of an effort to monopolize the Caribbean trade. The following year, however, Britain returned the city to Spain in exchange for Florida. This acquisition gave the British control of the entire North American eastern seaboard.

ANGLO-FRENCH MILITARY RIVALRY

Anglo-Spanish conflict paled in comparison with the bitter commercial rivalry between Great Britain and France during the eighteenth century. Anglo-French conflict was one of the few consistent patterns of eighteenth-century European warfare. It lasted so long and had so many different phases that it is known as the second Hundred Years' War, a recurrence of the bitter period of warfare between England and France from the middle of the fourteenth to the middle of the fifteenth century. The rivalry was marked by periodic naval and military engagements not only in Europe but in Asia and North America as well.

The Wars of the Spanish and Austrian Successions, 1701–1748

The Anglo-French rivalry of the eighteenth century had its roots in the war of the Spanish Succession (1701–1713). As we saw in Chapter 15, the proposed succession of a Bourbon to the Spanish throne threatened to create a massive French-Spanish empire that would have deprived British merchants of much of their valuable colonial trade. The war between France and Britain in North America, known by British colonists as Queen Anne's War, was settled in Britain's favor. The Treaty of Utrecht of 1713 kept the French and Spanish empires in America separate, and the French conceded their Canadian territories of Newfoundland and Nova Scotia to the British. The treaty marked the emergence of Britain as Europe's dominant colonial and maritime power.

The next phase of Anglo-French warfare, the War of the Austrian Succession (1740–1748), formed part of a European conflict that engaged the forces of Austria, Prussia, and Spain as well as those of Britain and France. In this conflict European dynastic struggles once again intersected with competition for colonial advantage overseas. The ostensible cause of this war was the impetuous decision by the new king of Prussia, the absolutist Frederick II (r. 1740–1786), to seize the large German-speaking province of Silesia from Austria upon the succession of Maria Theresa (r. 1740–1780) as the ruler of the hereditary Habsburg lands. Frederick's aggression enticed other European powers to join the conflict. When France declared war on Austria, Britain entered the war against France, mainly to keep France from acquiring Austria's possessions in the Netherlands.

The colonial phase of this war, known in British North America as King George's War, opened in 1744, when the French supported the Spanish in a separate war that Spain had been waging against Britain since 1739 over the Caribbean trade. The main military engagement of this war was the seizure of the French port and fortress of Louisbourg on Cape Breton Island in Canada by 4,000 New England colonial troops and a large British fleet.

The Seven Years' War, 1756–1763

European and colonial rivalries became even more entangled in the next round of Anglo-French warfare, known as the Seven Years' War (1756–1763) in Europe and the French and Indian War (1754–1763) in North America. The fighting in the North American theater of the war was particularly brutal and inflicted extensive casualties. In their struggle to gain control of eastern port cities and interior lands, the British and the French secured alliances with different Indian tribes. This colonial war also had an Asian theater, in which French and British forces, most of them drawn from

CHRONOLOGY

A Century of Anglo-French Warfare

1701–1713	War of the Spanish Succession (Queen Anne's War in North America): Spain is allied with France
1740–1748	War of the Austrian Succession (Europe): France is allied with Spain, Prussia, and Russia; Britain is allied with Austria
1756–1763	Seven Years' War (Europe): France is allied with Austria; Britain is allied with Prussia
1775–1783	American War of Independence: France is allied with United States against Britain in 1778
1792–1815	French Revolutionary and Napoleonic Wars: Britain is allied at various times with Austria, Prussia, Spain, and the Dutch Republic; warfare at various times in the West Indies as well as in India

the trading companies of their respective countries, vied for mercantile influence and the possession of factories along the coast of the Indian Ocean. This conflict led directly to the British acquisition of the Indian province of Bengal in 1765.

The Treaty of Paris, which ended this round of European and colonial warfare in 1763, had more profound implications in the colonies than in Europe. As a result of British naval victories, all of French Canada east of the Mississippi, including the entire province of Quebec, with its predominantly French population and French system of civil law, passed into British control (see Map 17.2). Even more important, the treaty secured British naval and mercantile superiority in the Atlantic, Caribbean, and Indian oceans.

The American and French Revolutionary Wars, 1775–1815

Despite the British victory over the French in 1763, the long conflict between the two countries continued into the early nineteenth century. During the American Revolution (1775–1783), which we shall consider later, the North American colonists secured French military aid. During that war a British fleet attacked the French colony of Martinique, while the French dispatched an expedition against the British at Savannah that included hundreds of Africans and mulattos, or people of mixed race, drawn from the population of the West Indies. In India further conflicts between the French and British occurred, mainly between 1781 and 1783. These simultaneous military engagements in various parts of the world turned this phase of Anglo-French conflict into the first truly global war.

Anglo-French rivalry entered yet another phase between 1792 and 1815, during the era of the French Revolution (see Chapter 19). Even during this later phase of the French-British rivalry the British pursued imperial objectives. They expanded their empire in India and consolidated their territory there under the governorship of Richard Wellesley (1760–1842). In 1795, in the midst of the war against France, the British also acquired the Dutch colony at the Cape of Good Hope, giving them a base for their claims to much larger African territories in the nineteenth century.

The Atlantic World

.... ▬ ....

By the beginning of the eighteenth century, the territorial acquisitions of the five European maritime powers had moved the geographical center of the West from the European continent to the Atlantic Ocean itself. Rather than separating large geographical land masses, the Atlantic became a unifying geographical entity. The boundaries of this new Western world were the four continents that bordered the Atlantic: Europe, Africa, North America, and South America. The main thoroughfares that linked

■ **Map 17.2   British Possessions in North America and the Caribbean After the Treaty of Paris**
The British acquisition of French territory marked a decisive moment in the expansion of the British Empire.

them were maritime routes across the Atlantic and up and down its coasts. Until the end of the eighteenth century, the main points of commercial and cultural contact between the four continents were the coastal areas and ports that bordered on the ocean. Within this Atlantic world arose new patterns of trade and economic activity, new interactions between ethnic and racial groups, and new political institutions. The Atlantic world also became the arena in which political and religious ideas were transmitted across the ocean and developed within a new environment.

THE ATLANTIC ECONOMY

The exchange of commercial goods and slaves between the western coasts of Europe, the African coasts, and the ports of North and South America created an economic enterprise that became one of the most active in the entire world (see Map 17.3). The ships that had brought the slaves from Africa to the Americas used the profits gained from their transactions to acquire precious metals and

■ **A Satire Against Coffee and Tobacco**

A seventeenth-century satirical depiction of two European women smoking tobacco and drinking coffee. Turkey, represented by the figure to the right, was the main source of these products in the seventeenth century. An African servant, to the left, pours the coffee.

agricultural products for the European market. They then returned to western European Atlantic ports, where the goods were sold.

This Atlantic economy was fueled ultimately by the demand of a growing European population for agricultural products that could not be obtained in Europe and were more costly to transport from Asia. Sugar was the most important of these commodities, but tobacco, cotton, rice, cacao, and coffee also became staples of the transatlantic trade. At the same time the North and South American colonists created a steady demand for manufactured goods, especially cutlery and metal tools, that were produced in Europe.

Two of the commodities that were imported from the colonies, tobacco and coffee, were criticized for the harmful effects they had on the human body. Tobacco was the target of a number of attacks written in the seventeenth century. Even at that early date critics recognized the adverse physical effects of this product, which had been used widely among Native Americans. "Tobacco, that outlandish weed," read one popular rhyme, "It spends the brain and spoils the seed." Critics also believed that it had a hallucinatory effect on those who inhaled its smoke.

Coffee was another stimulant that originally came exclusively from the Middle East but later began to be shipped from Haiti and after 1809 from Brazil. Like tobacco, coffee was controversial because of the effects it had on the human body. In the late seventeenth and eighteenth centuries it was believed to be a source of political radicalism, probably because the coffeehouses where it was consumed served as gathering places for political dissidents. Contemporaries also identified coffee's capacity to produce irritability and depression.

THE ATLANTIC SLAVE TRADE

The slave trade became the very linchpin of the Atlantic economy, and all five Western European imperial powers—Britain, France, the Dutch Republic, Spain, and Portugal—engaged in it. The trade arose to meet the demand of plantation owners in the New World for agricultural labor. In the seventeenth century, after the indigenous Indian population had been ravaged by disease and the indentured whites who emigrated from Europe in search of a more secure future had gained their freedom, this demand became urgent. Slave labor possessed a number of advantages over that of free labor. Slaves could be disciplined more easily, they could be forced to work longer hours, and they could be used to build a plantation economy in which the growing, harvesting, and processing of sugar and other agricultural commodities could be directed by one authority.

The slave trade formed the crucial link in the triangular pattern of commercial routes that began when European vessels traveled to ports along the western coast of Africa. There they exchanged European goods, including guns, for

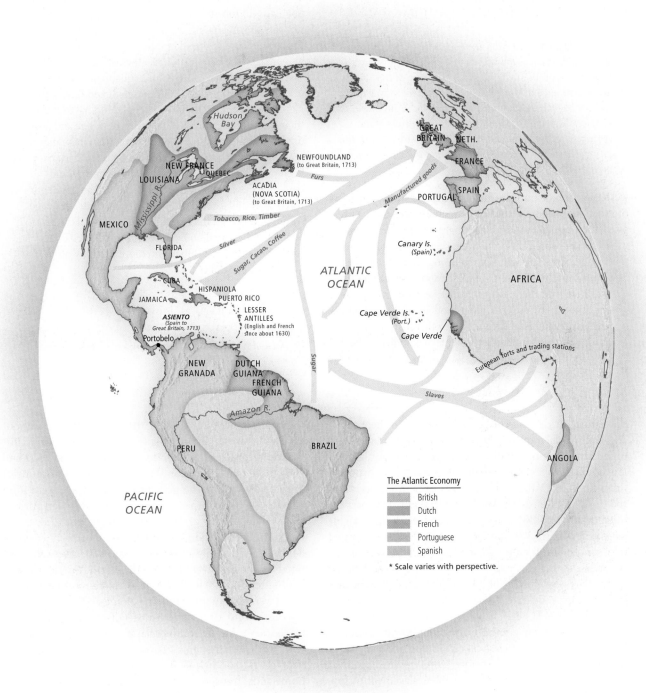

Hudson Bay

NEW FRANCE
QUEBEC
LOUISIANA

NEWFOUNDLAND
(to Great Britain, 1713)

ACADIA
(NOVA SCOTIA)
(to Great Britain, 1713)

GREAT BRITAIN
NETH.

FRANCE

Furs

Manufactured goods

PORTUGAL
SPAIN

Mississippi R.

MEXICO

FLORIDA

Tobacco, Rice, Timber

Silver

Sugar, Cacao, Coffee

CUBA

JAMAICA

HISPANIOLA
PUERTO RICO

LESSER
ANTILLES
(English and French
since about 1630)

ATLANTIC
OCEAN

Canary Is.
(Spain)

AFRICA

Cape Verde Is.
(Port.)

Cape Verde

ASIENTO
(Spain to
Great Britain, 1713)

Portobelo

NEW
GRANADA

DUTCH
GUIANA
FRENCH
GUIANA

Sugar

European forts and trading stations

Amazon R.

Slaves

PERU

BRAZIL

ANGOLA

PACIFIC
OCEAN

The Atlantic Economy

British
Dutch
French
Portuguese
Spanish

* Scale varies with perspective.

■ **Map 17.3 The Atlantic Economy in the Mid-Eighteenth Century**

Commodities and African slaves were exchanged between the four continents of North America,
South America, Europe, and Africa.

A FORMER SLAVE PROTESTS AFRICAN SLAVERY

....

In 1787 Quobna Ottobah Cugoano (1757–1791), a former slave, published an abolitionist treatise, Thoughts and Sentiments on the Evil and Wicked Traffic of the Slavery and Commerce of the Human Species. *Like the narrative written by Olaudah Equiano quoted at the beginning of this chapter, Cugoano's account describes the horrors of the African slave trade that he himself had experienced. In this passage Cugoano deplores the effect that the slave trade had on his native Africa.*

That base traffic of kid-napping and stealing men was begun by the Portuguese on the coast of Africa, and as they found the benefit of it for their own wicked purposes, they soon went on to commit further depredations. The Spaniards followed their infamous example, and the African slave trade was thought most advantageous for them, to enable themselves to live in ease and affluence by the cruel subjection and slavery of others. The French and English, and some other nations in Europe, as they founded settlements or colonies in the West Indies or in America, went on in the same manner, and joined hand in hand with the Portuguese and Spaniards to rob and pillage Africa as well as to waste and desolate the inhabitants of the western continent. But the European depredators and pirates have not only robbed and pillaged the people of Africa themselves; but, by their instigation, they have infested the inhabitants with some of the vilest combinations of fraudulent and treacherous villains, even among their own people, and have set up their forts and factories as a reservoir of public and abandoned thieves and as a den of desperadoes, where they may ensnare, entrap and catch men. So that Africa has been robbed of its inhabitants, its freeborn sons and daughters have been stole, and kid-napped and violently taken away and carried into captivity and cruel bondage. And it may be said in respect to that diabolical traffic which is still carried on by the European depredators, that Africa has suffered as much and more than any other quarters of the globe.

Source: Quobna Ottobah Cugoano, *Thoughts and Sentiments on the Evil and Wicked Traffic of the Slavery and Commerce of the Human Species* (London, 1787).

---

slaves that African merchants had captured in the interior and had marched to the sea. At these ports the slaves were branded with initials indicating to which nation they belonged. They were then crowded into ships that transported them across the Atlantic to the coast of South America, to the Caribbean, or as far north as Maryland. This was the often deadly Middle Passage, the second leg of the triangular journey, which was completed when the ships returned to their point of origin. Once they had arrived in the Americas, the slaves were sold to plantation owners in the tropical areas of the Caribbean and the south Atlantic and in the more moderate climates of the North American mainland.

Slavery has been present throughout world history. It was a major feature of classical civilization and it was also present in medieval Europe before 1200. As Islam expanded in the ninth century, Arabs began the enslavement of foreign peoples, including black slaves from east Africa, and they continued that traffic into the early modern period. In the sixteenth and seventeenth centuries Barbary pirates in the Mediterranean captured approximately 850,000 white Europeans during sea raids and forced them into slavery in Muslim North Africa.

Within this long history of world slavery, the African slave trade conducted by Europeans is unique in two respects. The first distinction is its size. This involuntary transportation of Africans to the New World is without parallel in world history. It is the largest transoceanic migration recorded in written documents. Between 1519 and 1867 more than 11 million slaves were shipped from Africa to the New World. The peak years of the trade were from 1751 to 1800, when nearly four million slaves left African shores. Nine out of every ten slaves were sent to Brazil or the Caribbean region, including the northern coast of South America. Only about 4 percent of all slaves were destined for the British colonies on the North American mainland (after 1776 the United States), and almost all of those slaves were sent to the southern colonies.

The second distinctive feature of the European slave trade was its highly commercial nature. Acting in concert with African chieftains, European slave traders seized people who had performed no acts of aggression in their homelands, transported them overseas, and sold them to the highest bidders. In this way African slaves were turned into commercial commodities and treated in a manner that deprived them of all human dignity. Slavery in the Americas has acquired a reputation for being particularly exploitative and barbaric, and this has much to do with its commercial character.

Differences in the treatment and survival of slaves in the various parts of the New World had more to do with economic conditions, climate, and population trends than with the nationality or the religion of the slave masters. The crucial factor was the nature of the labor to which the slaves were subjected. Slaves who worked on plantations, especially the sugar plantations, usually died within a few years. Most were worked to death. As long as the slave trade was still open, it was more profitable simply to replace those who died with new slaves than to try to extend the life of those the plantation owners already had.

Another factor influencing the treatment and survival of slaves was the ratio of the black to the white populations. When that ratio was high, as in all the Caribbean colonies, the codes regulating slave life were particularly harsh and created a reign of terror within the slave community. Yet another factor was climate. The absence of tropical diseases in the more temperate zone of the North American colonies provides the best explanation why in these colonies the numbers of births equaled and eventually exceeded the number of deaths long before they did in the Caribbean and South American colonies.

Not until the late eighteenth century did the enslavement of black Africans become a source of widespread moral concern. The movement to end the slave trade and slavery itself arose almost simultaneously in all European countries. It was inspired mainly by religious zeal, especially from evangelical Protestants in Great Britain and the Jesuits in Spain and Portugal. Societies were formed to campaign for the legislative prohibition of the transportation and sale of slaves. These appeals found support from European capitalists, especially in Britain, who no longer considered slavery economically advantageous. Goods produced by free labor, especially by machine, made slavery appear less cost-effective than in the past.

By the first decade of the nineteenth century opposition to slavery began to achieve limited success, and by 1851 it had brought about an end to the entire slave trade. The United States refused to allow any of its ports to accept slave ships after 1808, the same year in which the British parliament legislated an end to the trade within its empire. The Dutch ended their slave trade in 1814, the French in 1815, and the Spanish in 1838. Liberation of the slaves generally came later. The British dismantled the system within their empire between 1834 and 1838. Slavery persisted until 1848 in the French Caribbean, 1863 in the southern United States, 1886 in Cuba, and 1888 in Brazil.

CULTURAL ENCOUNTERS IN THE ATLANTIC WORLD

European countries had always possessed some ethnic diversity, but the emigration of people from many different parts of Europe and Africa to America, followed by their intermarriage, created societies of much greater complexity. Even the composition of the white European communities in the colonies was more varied than in the metropolis. In the British colonies, for example, English, Scots, and Irish were joined by large numbers of Germans, French, and Swiss.

The ethnicity of colonial populations was more varied in Latin American colonies than in North America. The higher proportion of Africans in those colonies, more extensive patterns of intermarriage, and the free status achieved by large numbers of blacks and mulattos created highly stratified societies by the end of the eighteenth century. In these colonies divisions arose not only between the recently arrived Europeans and the creoles, but between the various groups considered by Europeans to be below them. The social structure of Brazil was more complex than that of any other country in the New World. At the top of the social hierarchy were Portuguese bureaucrats and below them was a large and wealthy group of planter creoles. These two elite groups dominated a lower-class social hierarchy of mestizos (people of mixed white and Indian ancestry), indigenous people, mulattos, freed blacks, and slaves.

THE TRANSMISSION OF IDEAS

The Atlantic Ocean became a corridor for the transmission of political ideas. Political ideologies that developed in Europe spread from the Old World to the New World mainly by the large volume of printed works that were exported during the eighteenth century. The ancient idea that a republic was the best form of government, which had found widespread support in Renaissance Italy and in seventeenth-century England, appealed to many political leaders in colonial North America. Eighteenth-century French and Scottish ideas regarding the rights of man and the responsibility of the government to bring about the improvement of society found fertile ground in many parts of North and South America. At the time of the French Revolution, which will be discussed in Chapter 19, ideals of liberty and equality were spread not only throughout Europe but in the Americas as well. Legal ideas embodied in English common law, French civil law, and Spanish customary law were also transported to the New World and became the legal foundation of the new societies that were formed there.

The traffic in political ideas also flowed from the Americas to Europe. Political ideologies that were formed out of British and European ideas of liberty at the time of the American Revolution were sent back to European countries in a new form, where they inspired reform and revolution in Britain, France, and Ireland. These same ideas of liberty exerted a powerful influence in the Caribbean colonies and in South America. In Haiti, where French and American ideas of liberty inspired a revolution in the 1790s, radical ideas of racial equality developed within the new republic and then spread outward to other colonies and the United States.

Encounters Between Europeans and Asians

The period from 1650 to 1850 was decisive in the development of European empires in Asia. Like the American colonies, these overseas possessions formed important components of the empires of European states and were also essential to the operation of the global economy. European dominance of world trade was exercised not only in the Atlantic world but also in the Middle East and Asia.

The main difference between European empires in the East and in the West during the period from 1650 to 1850 is that in Asia European powers initially did not try to acquire and govern large land masses and subjugate their populations. Europeans first came to Asia to trade, not to conquer. When Europeans used military force in Asia, it was almost always against rival European powers, not the indigenous population. When European countries eventually used force against Asians, they discovered that victory was much more difficult than it had been in the New World. Establishment of European hegemony in Asia, therefore, took longer and was achieved more gradually than in the Americas.

POLITICAL CONTROL OF INDIA

Despite their original intentions, Europeans eventually began to acquire political control over large territories in Asia and subject Asians to European rule. The first decisive steps in this process took place in India during the second half of the eighteenth century. Until that time the British in India, most of whom were members of the British East India Company, remained confined to the factories that were established along the Indian coast. The main purpose of these factories was to engage in trade not only with Europe but also with other parts of Asia. In conducting this trade the British had to deal with local Indian merchants and to compete with the French, the Portuguese, and the Dutch, who had established factories of their own. They also found it advantageous to make alliances with the provincial governors, known as nawabs°, who controlled the interior of the country. It became customary for each European power to have its own candidate for nawab, with the expectation that he would provide favors for his European patrons once he took office.

Military Conflict and Territorial Acquisitions, 1756–1856

In 1756 this pattern of trading and negotiating resulted in armed military conflict in the city of Calcutta in the northeastern province of Bengal. The British had established a factory at Calcutta in 1690, and they continued to carry on an extensive trade there with Indian merchants, many of whom were Hindus. The nawab of Bengal, the Muslim Siraj-ud-Daulah, had contempt for all Europeans, especially the British, and he was determined that he would not be beholden to any of them. He was also deeply hostile to the Hindu merchants who were trading with the British. In June 1756 he sent an army of 50,000 Muslims against Calcutta, burning and plundering the city and beginning a siege of the British East India Company's Fort William, which was manned by 515 troops in the service of the company.

During this siege the shooting death of a Bengali guard led to an incident that became permanently emblazoned on the emerging imperial consciousness of the British people. Officers in the nawab's army crammed the entire remaining British contingent, a total of 146 men and women, into the fort's lockup or prison, known as the Black Hole of Calcutta. The British prisoners were stifled by the insufferable heat and a lack of water and air. Only twenty-two men and one woman survived.

The deaths of these British men and women in the Black Hole of Calcutta led the British to seek swift and brutal retribution against the nawab. In 1757 a force of 800 British troops and 2,000 native Indian soldiers known as sepoys° retook Calcutta and routed Siraj-ud-Daulah's army of 50,000 men at the battle of Plassey. A few years later the British East India Company secured the right to collect taxes and thus exercised political control over the entire province of Bengal. The enormous revenue from these taxes enabled the company to acquire a large army, which the British then used to gain control of other provinces in India as well as to defeat their French rivals.

The Sepoy Mutiny, 1857–1858

The British annexation of additional Indian provinces in the early nineteenth century set the stage for a major rebellion, known as the Sepoy Mutiny, against British rule in 1857. The British annexation of the state of Oudh, which many sepoys considered their homeland, created deep resentment against the British. The incident that provoked the mutiny was the issue of rifle cartridges coated with beef fat, which violated Hindu law, and pork fat, which violated Muslim law. Such insensitivity to native Indian culture struck a raw nerve. The cities of Delhi and Lucknow came under siege, and dreadful atrocities, including the hacking to death of British women and children, occurred. After suppressing the mutiny, the British government abolished the British East India Company and assumed direct rule of India.

CHANGING EUROPEAN ATTITUDES TOWARD ASIAN CULTURES

This second phase of European imperialism in Asia played a crucial role in the formation of Western identity. The

■ **Brighton Pavilion**

This building, designed by John Nash, reflected the incorporation of Eastern styles into English architecture, and was inspired by the description of Kubla Khan's palace in Samuel Taylor Coleridge's poem "Kubla Khan" (1816).

steadily increasing numbers of European merchants, missionaries, writers, and colonial administrators who had contact with these lands gained a clearer sense of who they were once they compared themselves to Indians, Chinese, and Polynesians. Until the seventeenth century Europeans thought of "the East" mainly as the Middle East, an area that was largely subsumed within the Ottoman Empire. Europeans expressed a generally negative view of the culture of this region (see Chapter 15), and over the years that perception had not changed. The political system of the Ottoman Empire was considered despotic and its religion, Islam, the antithesis of Christianity. The Far East, comprising South Asia (India), East Asia (China, Japan), and Southeast Asia (Burma, Siam, Indonesia), generally did not enter into these perceptions of "the Orient." There was little contact with this part of the world, and the little that was known about it was shrouded in mystery. During this period Europeans viewed the Far East mainly as an exotic land, rich in spices, silk, and other luxury commodities.

As European contacts with Asians became more frequent, Europeans developed more informed impressions of these distant lands and peoples. Some of those impressions were negative, especially when the power of Asian rulers was discussed, but many other characterizations of the East were positive. Interest in and admiration for both Indian and Chinese culture were most widespread during the middle years of the eighteenth century. The systematic study of Asian languages, especially Chinese and Sanskrit, began during this period. A preference for things Asian became characteristic of Enlightenment thinkers like Voltaire (1694–1778), who regarded Asian cultures as superior to those of a corrupt Europe. Voltaire also found the East unaffected by the superstition and the fanaticism that characterized Western Christianity, which he loathed. To him, the main philosophical tradition of China, Confucianism, which embodied a strict moral code, was a more attractive alternative.

This mid-eighteenth-century admiration of Asian culture coincided with a period of widespread Asian influences on Western art, architecture, and design. Eastern themes began to influence British buildings, such as in the Brighton Pavilion, designed by John Nash. French architects built pagodas (towers with the roof of each story turning upward) for their clients. Chinese gardens, which unlike classical European gardens were not arranged geometrically, became popular in England and France.

A new form of decorative art that combined Chinese and European motifs, known in French as *chinoiserie*°, became highly fashionable. Wealthy French people furnished their homes with Chinese wallpaper and hand-painted folding screens. The demand for Chinese porcelain, known in English simply as china, was insatiable. Vast quantities of this porcelain, which was technically and aesthetically superior to the stoneware produced in Germany and England, left China for the ports of western Europe. Even the dress of Europeans was influenced by Asian styles. A style of Indian nightwear, known as pajamas, became popular in England. Even a new sport, polo, which had originated to India, made its entry into upper-class European society at this time.

During the late eighteenth and early nineteenth centuries the European idealization of Asian culture came under direct attack. As the European presence in Asia became larger and more powerful, as the British began to exercise more control in India, and as merchants began to monopolize the Asian trade, Western images of the East became more unfavorable. Instead of being viewed as a repository of ancient ethical wisdom, Chinese philosophy was labeled as irrational when compared with that of the West. Confucianism fell out of favor, and Eastern religion in general was despised as being inferior to Christianity. Enlightenment thinkers such as Montesquieu and Diderot, whose thoughts will be discussed more fully in Chapter 18, ranked Asian political systems below those of the more "advanced" countries of Europe.

The Crisis of Empire and the Atlantic Revolutions

During the period from 1780 to 1825, European empires experienced a crisis that marked the end of the second stage of European overseas expansion. As a result of this crisis British, French, and Spanish governments lost large segments of their empires in the Americas. New states and nations were carved out of the older sprawling empires. The crisis was to some extent administrative. Having acquired large expanses of territory overseas, European states were faced with the challenging problem of governing them from a distance. They not only had to rule large areas inhabited by non-European peoples (Indians and African slaves), but they also faced the difficulty of maintaining the loyalty of people of European descent who were born in the colonies.

THE AMERICAN REVOLUTION, 1775–1783

The first Atlantic revolution was the revolt of the thirteen North American colonies and the establishment of their independence from British rule. During the second half of the eighteenth century, a number of tensions arose between the British government and its transatlantic colonies. All of these overseas colonies had developed traditions of self-government, and all of them had their own representative assemblies. At the same time the colonies were controlled by various governmental bodies responsible to the British Parliament, such as the Board of Trade. The colonies had their own militias, but they also received protection from British troops when conflicts developed with the French or other hostile powers.

The crisis that led to this revolution had its roots in the situation that emerged at the end of the French and Indian War. In order to maintain the peace agreed to in 1763, the government stationed British troops on the frontiers of the colonies. It argued that since the troops were protecting the colonists, they should contribute financially to their own defense. To this end the government began imposing a number of new taxes on the colonists. The taxes raised the central constitutional issue of whether Parliament had the power to legislate for British subjects in lands that did not elect members of that Parliament.

The passage of a series of British parliamentary statutes, known in the colonies as the Intolerable Acts, led to organized resistance to British rule, and in 1775 military conflict broke out at Lexington and Concord in Massachusetts. In 1776 thirteen of the colonies on the North American mainland approved a Declaration of Independence from Great Britain. A long revolutionary war, in which the colonists received assistance from France in 1778, ended with the defeat of British troops at Yorktown in 1781 and the recognition of the republic of the United States of America in the Treaty of Paris in 1783.

The case that the American colonists made for independence drew on the theories of John Locke, the seventeenth-century Whig political philosopher who justified resistance against a tyrannical regime. The revolution also found support in English common law, especially the principle that men could not be deprived of their rights without their own consent, and in the ideas of the Enlightenment that proclaimed the natural rights of all men. Republican theories, drawn from ancient Greece and Rome, gave colonists a model of a community of virtuous men joined in a commitment to the body politic, which they defined in colonial terms.

THE HAITIAN REVOLUTION, 1789–1804

The second successful revolution in the Atlantic world took place in the French Caribbean colony of Saint Domingue, known later as Haiti, which occupied the western portion of the island of Hispaniola. This revolution resulted in the establishment of the colony's independence, but the revolt was directed not so much against French rule as against the island's white planters. Just like their counterparts in

Spanish and British Caribbean colonies, these planters, known in Haiti as colons°, had little desire for national independence. They wished to remain within the protective custody of the French state. Since they formed a distinct minority of the total population, they did not think of themselves as constituting a separate national community. Any resistance to imperial rule, moreover, would have required that they arm their slaves in order to make the movement succeed, and that would have threatened their control of the black population.

The real threat of revolution in all the Caribbean colonies came not from the wealthy but from the subordinate members of the population. In Saint Domingue the revolution began in 1789 with a rebellion of people defined legally as free coloreds, most of whom were mulattos. The development that triggered this revolt, organized under the leadership of Vincent Ogé, was the refusal of the white planters, who were creoles, to give the free coloreds representation in the revolutionary French National Assembly as well as in local assemblies in Saint Domingue.

The free colored rebellion of 1789 led directly to a massive slave revolt in 1791. At that time slaves constituted about 90 percent of the population. Their uprising took place after the French National Assembly voted to abolish slavery in France but not in the French colonies. Spanish and British armies, frightened that this slave rebellion would spread to their colonies, occupied Saint Domingue and massacred thousands of slaves, many of them after they surrendered. In 1795, however, the Spanish withdrew from Saint Domingue and in 1798 the British, having lost as many as 40,000 soldiers, were also forced to leave. The man who had assumed the leadership of the slave revolt, the freed slave Toussaint L'Ouverture, then proceeded to conquer the entire island in 1801, abolish slavery, and proclaim himself the governor-general of an autonomous province.

In 1801, after Napoleon had assumed control of the French government and the idealism of the French Revolution had evaporated, a French army of 20,000 men occupied Saint Domingue. When it was learned that the French were planning to reintroduce slavery, however, two black generals, Jean-Jacques Dessalines and Henri Christophe, whom the French had enlisted to suppress the revolt, united freed blacks and slaves against the French forces. In 1803 these united forces drove the French out of the colony, and in 1804 they established an independent state of Haiti.

This new state of Haiti was far different from the United States, in that it was governed entirely by people of color and it banned slavery. It proclaimed racial equality by defining all Haitians as black. The plantation system was destroyed and the land was redistributed among free blacks; foreigners were forbidden to hold property. The Haitian revolution was the most radical and egalitarian of the Atlantic revolutions of the late eighteenth and early nine-

teenth centuries. Its unqualified declaration of human equality and its abolition of slavery served as an inspiration to abolitionist movements in other countries, including the United States, throughout the nineteenth century.

THE IRISH REBELLION, 1798–1799

Within the British Empire the country that was most directly inspired by the success of the American Revolution was the kingdom of Ireland. Unlike the residents of the thirteen colonies in North America, the Gaelic people of Ireland had long thought of themselves as a distinct nation. The English, however, had begun a conquest of this Irish nation in the twelfth century, and during the next 500 years they had struggled to rule it effectively. One of their methods was to settle English landlords on Irish lands.

In the early seventeenth century James VI of Scotland (who had also become James I of England in 1603) had settled both Scottish Presbyterians, later known as the Scots Irish, as well as English Anglicans, in the northern Irish province of Ulster. These Protestants of Scottish and English descent had become the core of the ruling establishment throughout Ireland, especially after Catholic rebellions in 1641–1649 and again in 1689–1690 had failed.

In the eighteenth century Irish Protestants began to resent their subservient relationship to the British government. Just like the American colonists, they recognized the way in which the Irish economy was serving British rather than Irish interests, and they resented the control that Britain had over the Irish parliament. A reform association known as the Society of United Irishmen, led by the Protestant Ulsterman Wolfe Tone, succeeded in building common ground between Protestants and Catholics. The United Irishmen demanded the repeal of the laws that denied Catholics the right to hold office and sit in the Irish parliament. In 1798 the United Irishmen aligned themselves with lower-class Catholic peasants known as Defenders, and these Irish groups staged an unsuccessful rebellion against British rule with the intention of establishing an Irish republic. The revolt, which was marred by atrocities on both sides, resulted in the death of 30,000 people.

The British government recognized that its arrangement for ruling Ireland, in which the nationalist republican movement had originated, could no longer work. It decided therefore to bring about a complete union between Great Britain and Ireland. By the terms of this arrangement, which took effect in 1801, Ireland's parliament ceased to meet; instead the Irish were to elect a limited number of representatives to sit in the British parliament. Ireland thus became a part of the United Kingdom, just as Scotland had done in 1707. The forces of Irish nationalism could not be contained, however, and during the nineteenth century new movements for Irish independence arose.

■ **Símon Bolívar Presenting the Flag of Liberation to Soldiers After the Battle of Carabobo, 1821**

Bolívar was the man most directly responsible for liberating South American countries from Spanish rule. He liberated his native Venezuela in 1821 and defeated Spanish forces in Peru in 1824.

NATIONAL REVOLUTIONS IN SPANISH AMERICA, 1810–1824

The final set of revolutions against European imperial powers occurred between 1810 and 1824 in a number of Spanish American colonies. Like the American Revolution, these struggles turned colonies into new states and led to the building of new nations. The first of these revolutions began in Mexico in 1810; others soon arose in Argentina, Colombia, Chile, and Peru. In these revolutions creoles played a leading role. The main sources of creole discontent were the Bourbon reforms, which had favored commercial interests, thereby threatening the position of many creole elites. The creoles also faced increasingly heavy taxation, as the Spanish government sought to make them support the expenses of colonial administration.

During the late eighteenth century Spanish creole discontent had crystallized into demands for greater political autonomy, similar to the objectives of British North American colonists. South American creoles began to think of themselves as Spanish Americans and sometimes simply as Americans. Like British American colonists, they also read and were inspired by the works of Enlightenment political philosophers. Nevertheless, the Spanish creole struggle against imperial rule did not commence until thirty years after the North American colonies had won their independence. One reason for this slow development

of revolutionary action was that Spanish American creoles still looked to the Spanish government to provide them with military support against the threat of lower-class rebellion.

The development that eventually precipitated these wars for national independence was the collapse of the Spanish monarchy after a French army invaded Spain in 1808 (see Chapter 19). In an effort to reconstitute the political order in their colonies, creoles sought to establish greater autonomy. Once the monarchy was restored, this demand for autonomy led quickly to armed resistance. This resistance began in Mexico, but it soon spread throughout Spanish America and quickly acquired popular support.

The man who took the lead in these early revolts against Spanish rule was the fiery Venezuelan aristocrat Símon Bolívar (1783–1830). Educated in the ideas of the Enlightenment, Bolívar led uprisings in his homeland in 1812 and 1814 and eventually defeated the Spanish there in 1819. Unlike most creoles, Bolívar was not afraid to recruit free coloreds and blacks into his armies. His hatred of European colonial governors knew few boundaries. At one point he reportedly commanded his soldiers to shoot and kill any European on sight. Bolívar carried the struggle for liberation to Peru, which became independent in 1824, and created the state of Bolivia in 1825. He was more responsible than any one individual for the liberation of Spanish America from Spanish rule. Independent states were established in Argentina in 1816, Chile in 1818, Colombia in 1819, and Mexico in 1821. By then the Spanish, who in the sixteenth century had the largest empire in the world, retained control of only two colonies in the Western Hemisphere: Puerto Rico and Cuba.

CONCLUSION

The Rise and Reshaping of the West

During the second period of European empire building, from 1650 until 1850, the West not only expanded geographically but also acquired a large share of the world's resources. By dominating the world's carrying trade, and by exploiting the agricultural and mineral resources of the Americas, Western states gained control of the world economy. The slave trade, with all its horrors, formed an important part of this economy and served as one of the main sources of Western wealth.

Western economic power laid the foundations for Western political control. In Asia European states assumed political control over territories slowly and reluctantly, as Britain's gradual and piecemeal acquisition of territory in India revealed. In the Americas, European powers acquired territory with relative ease, and European possessions in the New World soon became part of the West. By 1700, the geographical center of the West had become the Atlantic Ocean.

To some extent the American territories that were brought under European political control also became culturally part of the West. The European colonists who settled in the Americas preserved the languages, the religions, and many of the cultural traditions of the European countries from which they came. When some of the British and Spanish colonies in the Americas rebelled against European regimes in the late eighteenth and early nineteenth centuries, the identity of the colonists who led the resistance remained essentially Western. Even the political ideas that inspired national resistance to European regimes had their origins in Europe.

The assertion of Western political and economic power in the world cultivated a sense of Western superiority. The belief that Europeans, regardless of their nationality, were superior to those from other parts of the world originated in the encounters that took place between Europeans and both African slaves and the indigenous peoples in the Americas. In the late eighteenth century a conviction also developed, although much more slowly, that the West was culturally superior to the civilizations of Asia. This belief in Western superiority became even more pronounced when the economies of Western nations began to experience more rapid growth than those of Asia as a result of the Industrial Revolution.

Suggestions for Further Reading

For a comprehensive list of suggested readings, please go to www.ablongman.com/levackconcise/chapter17

Bailyn, Bernard. *Ideological Origins of the American Revolution.* 1967. A probing analysis of the different intellectual traditions on which the American colonists based their arguments for independence.

Blackburn, Robin. *The Making of New World Slavery: From the Baroque to the Modern, 1492–1800.* 1997. Places European slavery in a broad world perspective.

Boxer, C. R. *The Dutch Seaborne Empire, 1600–1800.* 1965. A thorough account covering the entire period of Dutch expansion.

Davis, Ralph. *The Rise of the Atlantic Economies.* 1973. A readable study of economic development on both sides of the Atlantic.

Eltis, David. *The Rise of African Slavery in the Americas.* 2000. An analysis of the different dimensions of the slave trade based on a database of slave ships and passengers.

Goody, Jack. *The East in the West.* 1996. Challenges the idea that Western cultures are more rational than those of Asia.

Greene, Jack P. *Peripheries and Center: Constitutional Development in the Extended Polities of the British Empire and the United States 1607–1788.* 1986. A study of the composition of the British Empire and its disintegration in North America.

Kamen, Henry. *Empire: How Spain Became a World Power.* 2003. Explains how Spain established the most extensive empire the world had ever known.

Langley, Lester D. *The Americas in the Age of Revolution, 1750–1850.* 1996. A broad comparative study of revolutions in the United States, Haiti, and Latin America.

Liss, Peggy K. *The Atlantic Empires: The Network of Trade and Revolutions, 1713–1826.* 1983. Places the American Revolution in a broader comparative setting and includes material on early Latin American independence movements.

Mungello, D. E. *The Great Encounter of China and the West, 1500–1800.* 1999. Studies China's acceptance and rejection of Western culture as well as the parallel Western reception of China.

Pagden, Anthony. *Lords of All the World: Ideologies of Empire in Spain, Britain and France ca. 1500–ca. 1800.* 1996. Discusses the theoretical foundations of the Atlantic empires.

Said, Edward. *Orientalism.* 1979. A study of the way in which Western views of the East have assumed its inferiority.

Eighteenth-Century Society and Culture

I N 1745 THOMAS BROWN AND ELEVEN OTHER MEN LIVING ON THE ESTATE OF THE Earl of Uxbridge, an English nobleman, were jailed for up to one year for shooting deer and rabbits on the earl's land. All twelve defendants were poor. Brown eked out a living as a coal miner in the earl's mines and rented a cottage and five acres of land from him. Like many of his fellow villagers, Brown supplemented his family's diet by shooting game from time to time, usually as he was walking to work through the earl's vast estate. This poaching violated a set of English parliamentary statutes known as the game laws, which restricted the shooting or trapping of wild animals to the members of the landed class.

The earl and other noblemen defended the game laws on the grounds that they were necessary to protect their property. The laws, however, served the even more important purpose of maintaining social distinctions between landowners and the common people. Members of the landed class believed that only they should have the right to hunt game and to serve deer, pheasants, and hares at lavish dinners attended by their social equals. For a poor person like Thomas Brown, who was described in a court document as "a rude disorderly man and a most notorious poacher," to enjoy such delicacies was a challenge to the social order.

This mid-eighteenth-century encounter between the Earl of Uxbridge and his tenants, which took the form of a criminal prosecution, reflected the tensions that simmered beneath the calm surface of eighteenth-century European society. These tensions arose between the members of the aristocracy, a small but wealthy governing elite, and the masses of tenants and laborers who formed the overwhelming majority of the European population. The aristocracy occupied a dominant position in eighteenth-century society. They controlled an enormous portion of the wealth in their countries, much of it in land. They staffed the state bureaucracies, the legislative assemblies, the military officer corps, and the

First Lecture in the Salon of Madame Geoffrin, 1755: The speaker is lecturing on Voltaire's *The Orphan of China* before a predominantly aristocratic audience of men and women.

judiciaries of almost all European states. They dominated and set the tone of high cultural life in Europe. Together with the monarchy and the church, with which they were socially and politically linked, the aristocracy formed what today is often referred to as "the Establishment."

By 1800 the social and political dominance of the aristocracy had begun to wane. Their legitimacy as a privileged elite was increasingly called into question. In a few countries political power began to pass from them to different social groups. The aristocracy did not surrender all their power, but they lost their stranglehold over society. This change began during a period of political stability between 1750 and the outbreak of the French Revolution in 1789.

The decline of the aristocracy was the result of a series of cultural encounters. The first were the tense and occasionally violent interactions between landowners and peasants who resented repressive upper-class rule. The second were criticisms of the aristocracy and the demands for reform that came from the increasingly literate, politically active people from the middle ranks of society, such as merchants, financiers, industrialists, and skilled artisans. The third was the cultural and intellectual movement known as the Enlightenment. Even though many of the Enlightenment's most prominent thinkers came from the ranks of the aristocracy, they advanced a set of political, social, economic, and legal ideas that ultimately inspired the creation of a more egalitarian society.

The aristocracy did not relinquish power willingly or quickly. Although they faced severe criticism and challenges to their dominance, they managed to preserve much of their wealth and maintain at least some of their political influence. To insulate themselves from criticisms from less powerful social groups, they adopted many of the values of the people who occupied the middle ranks of society and subscribed to many of the ideas of the Enlightenment, including those that criticized their own class. Internal encounters between different social groups, just like external encounters between Western and non-Western peoples, rarely result in total domination of one group over the other. Instead both parties change their thinking and behavior as a result of their interaction.

This chapter will address four main questions about eighteenth-century society and culture:

- What social groups belonged to the aristocracy and how did they exercise their power and influence during the eighteenth century?
- How did subordinate social groups, most notably the rural peasantry and those who lived in the towns, challenge the aristocracy during the late eighteenth century?
- What were the main features of Enlightenment thought and how did it present a threat to the old order?

- What impact did the Enlightenment have on Western culture and politics?

The Aristocracy

During the eighteenth century a relatively small, wealthy group of men dominated European society and politics. This social and ruling elite is often referred to as the aristocracy°, a term derived from a Greek word meaning the people who were the most fit to rule. In the eighteenth and nineteenth centuries the term *aristocracy* began to be applied not just to those few men who exercised political power but to the wealthiest members of society, especially those who owned land.

Within the aristocracy those who received official recognition of their hereditary status, including their titles of honor and special legal privileges, were known as the nobility°. In the Middle Ages the nobility consisted mainly of warriors who prided themselves on their courage and military skill. Over the course of many centuries these military functions became less important, although many noblemen, especially in central and eastern Europe, continued to serve as military officers in the armies of the state during the eighteenth century.

By the eighteenth century most European aristocracies included a relatively small group of titled noblemen (such as dukes and counts) who possessed great wealth and political influence and a much larger group of lesser aristocrats, occasionally referred to as gentry, who sometimes did not even bear hereditary titles. In Spain a vast gulf separated a few hundred titled noblemen, the *titulos,* and thousands of sometimes poverty-stricken *hidalgos.* In Britain a few hundred titled noblemen, known as peers, took precedence over some 50,000 families that belonged to the gentry. In Poland the nobility, known as the *szlachta,* was divided between a tiny, powerful group of magnates and some 700,000 noblemen of much more modest means who constituted more than 10 percent of the entire population.

The aristocracy was not completely closed to outsiders. Commoners could gain entrance to it, especially its lower ranks, on the basis of acquired wealth or government service. It was not unusual for lawyers, wealthy merchants, or accomplished state servants to accumulate wealth during their careers, use that wealth to purchase land, and then receive recognition of their new status in the form of a title of nobility. Many of the men to whom Peter the Great of Russia gave titles of nobility in the early eighteenth century were commoners. In France, where the old "nobility of the sword" could be distinguished from the "nobility of the robe" who ascended through state service, more than 20

■ **Marriage into the Nobility**

This painting by William Hogarth, in a series titled *Marriage à la Mode*, depicts the negotiation of a marriage contract between an English earl and a wealthy London merchant. The earl, seated to the left and pointing to his family tree, is negotiating with the merchant sitting across the table. The marriage will take place between the earl's vain son, sitting to the far right, and the distracted daughter of the merchant, sitting next to him. The two individuals who are about to be married have no interest in each other. The earl has incurred large debts from building the large mansion depicted in the rear, and he intends to use the dowry to recover financially. By virtue of this transaction the daughter will enter aristocratic society.

percent of mid-eighteenth-century noblemen could not trace their noble status back further than two generations.

It was also possible for prosperous farmers to enter the aristocracy by purchasing land, hiring manual laborers to perform agricultural work, and then adopting the leisured lifestyle, dress, and manners of aristocrats. These men did not bear titles, but they expected to be regarded as having the same status as other members of the lesser aristocracy. Occasionally women of nonnoble birth gained entry into aristocratic society by marriage. This usually occurred when a nobleman who was greatly in debt arranged to marry his son to the daughter of a wealthy merchant in order to secure the dowry from the father of the bride. The dowry became the price of the daughter's admission to the nobility.

The aristocracy was never a very large social group. The number of titled nobles was almost always less than 1 percent of the total population, and even when lesser nobles or gentry are taken into account, their total numbers usually amounted to no more than 4 percent. Only in Poland and Hungary did the percentages climb to more than 10 percent. Because of the small size of this social group, many nobles knew each other, especially those who were members of the same political assembly or who served together at court. The aristocracy was in fact the only real class° in European society before the early nineteenth century, in the sense that they formed a cohesive social group with similar economic and political interests, which they were determined to protect.

THE WEALTH OF THE ARISTOCRACY

The aristocracy was without question the wealthiest social group in all European countries, and during the eighteenth century many members of this group became even wealthier. The most prosperous aristocratic families lived in stupendous luxury. They built magnificent homes on their country estates and surrounded them with finely manicured gardens. In the cities, where service at court demanded more of their time, they built spacious palaces, entertained guests on a lavish scale, and purchased everything from expensive clothes to artistic treasures. They consumed the best food and wines they could find at home or abroad. This ostentatious display of wealth was intended to confirm their social importance and status.

Most of the income that supported the lifestyle of the aristocracy came directly or indirectly from land. In all European countries the aristocracy owned at least one-third of all the land, and in some countries, such as England and Denmark, they owned more than four-fifths of it. Even in the Italian states, where many of the nobility had come from families of merchants, they controlled large estates. Land provided the aristocracy with either feudal dues or rents from the peasants who lived and worked on their estates. Since noblemen did not engage in manual labor themselves, it is not surprising that they later came to be seen as unproductive parasites living off the labor of others.

During the first half of the eighteenth century the collective wealth of the European aristocracy reached new heights. In eastern Europe that increase in wealth derived mainly from the dramatic increase in the size of the population. With more serfs under their control, the landed nobility could increase the wealth they gained from their labor and dues. In western European countries, most notably Britain and France, the members of the aristocracy increasingly participated in other forms of economic activity. They operated rural industries such as mining and forestry. They entered the financial world by lending money to the government, thus serving the state in the process. They became involved in urban building projects and in the economic development of overseas colonies. Those who came from old families considered these pursuits to be beneath the status of a nobleman, but by investing at a distance nobles could give the impression that they were not actually engaged in the sordid transactions of the marketplace.

The members of the eighteenth-century aristocracy are often described as social and economic conservatives who were unable or unwilling to act in an entrepreneurial manner. The financial and commercial projects that many noblemen engaged in suggest that this reputation of the aristocracy is not fully deserved. Even on their landed estates, the aristocracy often behaved in a capitalistic manner during the seventeenth and eighteenth centuries. Many members of the aristocracy, both titled and untitled, adopted capitalist techniques of estate management to make their lands more productive. In England a nobleman, Charles Townshend, became widely known as "Turnip Townshend" when he introduced a crop rotation that included the lowly turnip. This type of agrarian entrepreneurship accounts for the accumulation of many great eighteenth-century aristocratic fortunes.

THE POLITICAL POWER OF THE ARISTOCRACY

The mid-eighteenth century marked the apex of political power for the aristocracy in Europe. Having recovered from the economic and political turmoil of the mid-seventeenth century, when they suffered economic losses and experienced a temporary eclipse of their power, noblemen pursued various strategies to increase or preserve their share of local and national political power. In England, where royal power was greatly restricted as a result of the Glorious Revolution, the aristocracy gained political dominance. A small group of noblemen sat in the House of Lords, while the gentry formed the large majority of members of the House of Commons. After 1689 the English king could not rule without the cooperation of these two Houses of Parliament.

A similar situation prevailed in Poland and Hungary, where only the nobility were represented in the legislative assemblies of those countries. In Sweden and most German states the nobility formed a separate group that voted by themselves within the representative assemblies of those kingdoms.

In absolute monarchies, where rulers had succeeded in restricting independent aristocratic power, members of the aristocracy exercised political power by controlling the institutions through which royal power was exercised. As we have seen in Chapter 15, absolute monarchs appeased the aristocracy by giving them control over provincial government and by recruiting them to occupy offices in the central bureaucracy of the state. The large bureaucracy of the eighteenth-century French state, for example, was run mainly by noblemen of the robe, a privileged group of approximately 2,000 officials who owed their noble status to their appointment to office rather than to heredity. In Russia during the early eighteenth century, tsars granted the nobility privileges and strengthened their powers over their serfs in order to secure the assistance the tsars needed to administer the Russian state at the local level.

The aristocracy exercised political power not only through bureaucratic institutions and provincial governments, but also through the judiciary. Members of the aristocracy often served as judges of the central law courts of their kingdoms. In England noblemen and gentry served as the judges of almost all the common law courts, hearing cases both at the center of government at Westminster and in the provinces. In France noblemen staffed the nine regional *parlements* that registered royal edicts and acted as a court of appeal in criminal cases. The nobility controlled the central tribunals of the German kingdoms and principalities. At the local level the nobility exercised either a personal jurisdiction over the peasants who lived on their lands or an official jurisdiction as magistrates, such as the justices of the peace in each English county.

THE CULTURAL WORLD OF THE ARISTOCRACY

During the eighteenth century the aristocracies in western and central European countries followed a lifestyle that emphasized their learning, refinement, and appreciation of the fine arts. The tradition of providing for their children's education either at the universities or in private academies was well established by this time. Even more important, aristocratic families began to acquire the manners and social graces that would be acceptable at court. By the early eighteenth century the aristocracy, especially its upper ranks, had become the backbone of what was then called "polite society."

The homes of the eighteenth-century aristocracy reflected their preference for classicism°, a style in art, architecture, music, and literature that emphasizes proportion, adherence to traditional forms, and a rejection of emotion and enthusiasm. The classicism of the eighteenth century marked a step away from the more dynamic, imposing baroque style, which had flourished in the seventeenth century. Classicism celebrated the culture of ancient Greece and Rome. The revival of that culture in the eighteenth century in art and architecture is often referred to as neoclassicism°. The residences of the eighteenth-century aristocracy built in the classical style were perfectly proportioned and elegant without being overly decorated. Their Greek columns and formal gardens, lined with statues of classical figures, served as symbols of their cultural heritage. The classical architecture of the eighteenth century reflected the quiet confidence of the aristocracy that they, like their Greek and Roman forebears, occupied a dominant position in society.

Eighteenth-century music, which is likewise referred to as classical, reflected a concern for formal design, proportion, and concise melodic expression. The two greatest composers of the eighteenth century, Franz Joseph Haydn (1732–1809) and Wolfgang Amadeus Mozart (1756–1791), whose music was played before predominantly aristocratic audiences, became the greatest composers in this tradition. Classical music appealed less to the emotions than either the baroque music of the seventeenth century or the romantic music of the nineteenth century. The dominance of classicism in music as well as architecture during the eighteenth century reflected broader cultural currents in European intellectual life, when science and philosophy placed the highest value on the rationality and order of all material and human life.

■ Chiswick House

This house was built by Lord Burlington as library and reception hall on his estate near London about 1725. Symmetrical, balanced, and restrained, the building embodies many of the features of classicism. Chiswick House was modeled on the architecture of the Italian Andrea Palladio (1518–1580), who in turn drew his inspiration from the buildings of ancient Rome.

Challenges to Aristocratic Dominance

Starting around the middle of the eighteenth century, the aristocracy endured increasingly acrimonious challenges to their power and criticisms of their values and lifestyles. They gradually lost the respect that they commanded from the lower ranks of society. By the end of the century European aristocracies had been significantly weakened. Their values had been called into question, while their political power and privileges had been eroded. A claim of nobility began to be viewed more as a sign of vanity than as a natural right to rule.

ENCOUNTERS WITH THE RURAL PEASANTRY

One set of challenges to the aristocracy came from the peasants and serfs who lived and worked on landed estates. This was the social group over whom the aristocracy exercised the most direct control. The control was most oppressive in central and eastern Europe, where the rural masses were serfs and therefore had no personal freedom. The plight of the serfs was relieved only partially by the elimination of some of the burdens of serfdom. In Prussia and Austria these obligations were abolished by royal edict. The monarchs who instituted these reforms may have been responding to the demands of philosophes°, the intellectuals and writers of the age, who condemned the institution of serfdom for its cruelty and inefficiency. A more powerful motive, however, was the desire of monarchs to collect taxes from a peasantry that was spending the greater part of its income on financial duties owed to aristocratic landowners. Since the peasants still remained overburdened by financial obligations, emancipation did little to improve their lot.

In western Europe, where serfdom had for the most part given way to tenant ownership and leasehold tenure, the condition of the rural masses was only marginally better. After 1720, famines became less common than they had been in the late seventeenth century, making it possible for peasants to eke out an existence. But other economic pressures, including the elimination of common pasture rights and an increase in taxation, continued to weigh down on them. Over the course of the eighteenth century the number of peasants owning small plots of land declined. Consequently the number of landless laborers who worked for wages increased. By 1789 almost half the peasants in France had no land at all.

As economic pressures on the peasants mounted, conflict between them and the aristocracy increased. Peasant resistance to their landlords could take a number of different forms. In some countries, most notably France, peasants could bring their grievances before village assemblies. These democratic institutions often succeeded in upholding peasants' demands, especially when royal officials in the provinces, who wished to collect their own taxes from the peasants, sided with them against the nobility.

Another option was to file a lawsuit against the lord, often with the assistance of the royal government. In Burgundy numerous peasant communities hired lawyers to take their seigneurs° or lords to court in order to prevent the imposition of new financial dues or the confiscation of communal village land. In these lawsuits, which became very common in the second half of the eighteenth century, peasants challenged not only the imposition of seigneurial dues but the very institution of aristocratic lordship. The language used by the peasants' lawyers in these cases inspired much of the rhetoric employed in the abolition of feudal privilege at the time of the French Revolution (see Chapter 19).

Peasants occasionally took more direct action against their landlords. In eastern France the number of incidents of rural violence against the property of seigneurs who tried to collect new duties increased toward the end of the eighteenth century. In Ireland a group known as the Whiteboys maimed cattle and tore down fences when landowners denied tenants their common grazing rights. Other forms of peasant action included poaching on the estates of landowners who claimed the exclusive right to hunt or trap game on their lands.

In western Europe these acts of resistance were largely confined to individual villages. The reduction in the incidence of famine in the eighteenth century provides one possible explanation for this pattern of isolated, localized resistance. Without recurrent subsistence crises, the plight of the rural masses was not sufficiently desperate to provoke widespread rebellion.

In eastern European countries, however, the deteriorating economic condition of the peasantry led to large-scale rebellion. The largest of these uprisings took place in Russia between 1773 and 1774. Pretending to be the murdered Tsar Peter III (d. 1762), the Cossack Emelian Pugachev (1726–1775) set out to destroy the Russian government of Catherine the Great and the nobility that served it. Pugachev assembled an army of 8,000 men, which staged lightning raids against government centers in the southern Urals. When these troops marched into the agricultural regions of the country they inspired as many as three million serfs to revolt. Pugachev promised to abolish serfdom, end taxation, and eliminate the lesser aristocracy. The rebellion took a heavy toll, as the serfs and soldiers murdered 3,000 nobles and officials. Responding to the fears of the aristocracy, Russian government troops brutally suppressed the uprising. Pugachev was transported to Moscow in an iron cage, where he was hanged, quartered, and burned.

Neither Pugachev nor the serfs who joined his rebellion envisioned the creation of a new social order. They still spoke in conservative terms of regaining ancient freedoms that had been lost. But this massive revolt reflected the depth of tension that prevailed between landlord and peasant, between nobleman and serf in the apparently stable world of the eighteenth century.

THE SOCIAL POSITION OF THE BOURGEOISIE

In the cities and towns the most serious challenges to the aristocracy came not from the urban masses, who posed an occasional threat to all urban authorities, but from the bourgeoisie°. This social group was more heterogeneous than the aristocracy. It consisted of untitled people of property who lived in the cities and towns. Prosperous merchants and financiers formed the upper ranks of the bourgeoisie, while members of the legal and medical professions, second-tier government officials, and emerging industrialists occupied a social niche just below them. The bourgeoisie also included some skilled artisans and shopkeepers, sometimes referred to as the "petty bourgeoisie," who were far more prosperous than the large mass of urban laborers.

The size of the bourgeoisie grew as the urban population of Europe expanded during the eighteenth century. This social group was far more numerous in the North Atlantic countries of France, the Dutch Republic, and Britain than in the states of central and eastern Europe. In England the bourgeoisie accounted for about 15 percent of the total population in 1800, whereas in Russia they constituted no more than 3 percent.

Because it was possible for some members of the bourgeoisie to achieve upward social mobility and join the ranks of the aristocracy, the social and economic boundaries separating these wealthy townsmen from the lower ranks of the nobility could become blurred. In French towns it was often difficult to distinguish between wealthy financiers and noble bureaucrats. The middle and lower ranks of the bourgeoisie, however, gradually emerged as a social group that acquired its own social, political and cultural identity, distinct from that of the aristocracy.

THE BOURGEOIS CRITIQUE OF THE ARISTOCRACY

At the core of bourgeois identity lay a set of values that contrasted with those attributed to the aristocracy, especially the noblemen and noblewomen who gathered at court. Not all members of the bourgeoisie shared these values, nor did all members of the nobility embody those attributed to them. Nonetheless, the bourgeois critique of aristocratic society, which flourished mainly among the lower or petty bourgeoisie rather than the great merchants and financiers, contributed to the formation of bourgeois identity and helped to erode respect for the traditional aristocracy.

The bourgeois critique of the aristocracy consisted of three related themes. First was the allegation that the aristocracy lived a life of luxury, hedonism, and idleness that contrasted with the thrifty, sober, hardworking petty bourgeoisie. Unlike the aristocracy, the bourgeoisie did not usually display their wealth. Second, court nobles were accused of being sexually promiscuous and immoral, while their wives were depicted as vain flirts. The predominance of arranged marriages within the nobility had in fact induced many noble husbands and wives to seek sexual partners outside marriage, a practice that was widely tolerated within aristocratic circles. By contrast, the bourgeoisie tended to enter into marriages in which both partners remained faithful to each other. Third, the members of the aristocracy were considered participants in a decadent international culture that often ignored or degraded the more wholesome, patriotic values of the bourgeoisie.

This critique of the aristocracy had profound political implications. It laid the foundation for the demands for equal political rights and the advancement of careers on the basis of talent rather than inherited wealth. These demands came mainly from people in the middle ranks of society: holders of minor political offices, shopkeepers, and even skilled artisans.

Criticism of aristocratic values and demands for liberty and equality received support from intellectuals who are usually identified with the movement known as the Enlightenment°. Not all of these thinkers and writers came from the middle ranks of society. Many of them were members of the aristocracy or the beneficiaries of aristocratic patronage. Nevertheless their goal was to bring about the reform of society, and that inevitably led to a critique of aristocratic values and practices.

The Enlightenment

·····························■·····························

The Enlightenment was the defining intellectual and cultural movement of the eighteenth century. Contemporaries used the word *Enlightenment* to describe their own intellectual outlook and achievements. For Immanuel Kant (1724–1804), the renowned German philosopher and author of *Critique of Pure Reason* (1781), enlightenment was the expression of intellectual maturity, the attainment of understanding solely by using one's reason without being influenced by dogma, superstition, or another person's opinion. It was also the knowledge of human society and human nature that one achieved as a result.

The Enlightenment is often referred to as a French movement, and it is true that the most famous of the European writers and thinkers of the Enlightenment, known as philosophes, were French. But French philosophes were inspired by seventeenth-century English sources, especially the writings of Isaac Newton (1647–1727) and John Locke (1632–1704), while German, Scottish, Dutch, Swiss, and

Italian writers made their own distinctive contributions to Enlightenment thought. The men and women of the Enlightenment thought of themselves not so much as French, British, or Dutch but as members of an international Republic of Letters, a cosmopolitan literary republic that knew no geographical boundaries. The Republic of Letters was open to ideas from all lands, but its literary achievements bore a distinctly Western stamp, and the ideas its members promoted became essential components of Western civilization.

THEMES OF ENLIGHTENMENT THOUGHT

Since the Enlightenment spanned the entire European continent and lasted for more than a century, it is difficult to establish characteristics that all its participants shared. Enlightenment writers did, however, emphasize several intellectual themes that gave the entire movement a certain degree of unity and coherence.

Reason and the Laws of Nature

The first theme emphasized by Enlightenment thinkers was the elevation of human reason to a position of paramount philosophical importance. Enlightenment thinkers placed almost unlimited confidence in the ability of human beings to understand how the world operates. This confidence was closely associated with the belief that the operation of the entire universe was governed by natural laws that human reason could discover. The search for and discovery of laws governing such phenomena as gravitation and dynamics gradually led to the belief that all activity, including the behavior of human beings, was governed by similar laws.

The application of natural law to human society was the most novel and distinctive feature of Enlightenment thought. According to Enlightenment thinkers, scientific laws governed the functioning of society. There were even laws governing the passions and the operation of the human psyche. In his *Treatise of Human Nature* (1739–1740), the Scottish philosopher David Hume (1711–1776) offered a science of the human mind, which could be applied to politics and other human endeavors. Economics, too, received the same treatment. The Scottish economist Adam Smith (1723–1790), who described the operation of economic life in *The Wealth of Nations* (1776), believed that the economy was subject to inviolable laws, just like those that governed the movement of the heavens.

The search for natural laws governing all human life provides one explanation for the unprecedented interest of eighteenth-century writers in non-European cultures. During the Enlightenment a vast literature subjected the peoples of the world to detailed description, classification, and analysis. The first thorough, scholarly studies of Indian, Chinese, and Arab cultures were published during the middle and late eighteenth century. This cross-cultural scholarship, which was facilitated by the rapid growth of overseas empires after 1660, served the purpose of providing intellectuals with information enabling them to discover laws governing the behavior of all people.

Religion and Morality

The spread of scientific knowledge in the eighteenth century gave the people of the Enlightenment a new understanding of God and his relationship to humankind. The gradual recognition that the universe was of unfathomable size and that it operated in accordance with natural laws made God appear more remote than he had been viewed in earlier centuries. Most philosophes believed that God was still the creator of the universe and the author of the natural laws that governed it, but they did not believe that he was still actively involved in its operation. This belief that God had created the universe, given it laws, and then allowed it to operate in a mechanistic fashion is known as deism°. In deism there was no place for the traditional Christian belief that God became human in order to redeem humankind from original sin.

Enlightenment thinkers, especially those who were deists, believed that human beings could use reason to discover the natural laws God had laid down at the time of Creation. This inquiry included the discovery of the principles of morality, which no longer were to be grounded in Scripture. To observe the laws of God now meant not so much keeping his commandments but discovering what was natural and acting accordingly.

Enlightenment thinkers were highly critical of the superstitious and dogmatic character of contemporary Christianity, especially Roman Catholicism. They minimized the importance of religious belief in the conduct of human life and substituted rational for religious values. In *An Enquiry Concerning Human Understanding* (1748) Hume challenged the argument of Descartes that God implants a number of clear and distinct ideas in our minds, from which we are able to deduce other truths. Hume's position was that our understanding derives from sense perceptions, not innate ideas. Even more important, he denied that there was any certain knowledge, thereby calling into question the authority of revealed truth and religious doctrine.

Hume's writing on religion reflected his skepticism. Raised a Presbyterian, he nevertheless rejected the revealed truths of Christianity on the ground that they had no rational foundation. The concept of Providence (the belief that God directs and controls human affairs) was completely alien to his philosophical position. An avowed deist, he expressed contempt for organized religion, especially Catholicism in France and Anglicanism in England. Organized religion, according to Hume, "renders men tame and submissive, is acceptable to the magistrate, and seems inoffensive to the people, till at last the priest, having firmly established his authority, becomes the tyrant of human society."

Progress and Reform

Theories regarding the stages of human development, coupled with the commitment of philosophes to the improvement and ultimate transformation of society, contributed to a belief in the progress of civilization. Until the eighteenth century the very notion of progress was alien to even the most highly educated Europeans. Those who held political power had dedicated themselves to maintaining the social and political order, not its transformation. Now, however, the possibility of improvement began to dominate philosophical and political discussion. The Enlightenment was largely responsible for making this belief in progress, especially toward the attainment of social justice, a prominent feature of modern Western culture.

Using evidence gained from encounters with non-Western people, some Enlightenment thinkers argued that all civilizations progressed gradually from relatively simple to more complex economies and societies. David Hume, Adam Smith, and their fellow Scotsman Adam Ferguson (1723–1816) identified four stages of human development, from one in which people engaged in hunting and gathering to one in which they engaged in commerce. The Marquis de Condorcet (1743–1794) identified nine distinct epochs in human history, predicting that in the tenth and final epoch humankind would reach a state of perfection.

Another source of the Enlightenment's belief in progress was the conviction that corrupt institutions could be reformed, thereby allowing societies to advance to a higher level and realize their full potential. The judicial institutions of government were particularly susceptible to this type of reforming zeal. Campaigns arose to eliminate the administration of judicial torture as well as capital punishment. All of this was intended to establish a more humane, civilized society.

The intellectual inspiration of this movement for legal reform was the work of the Italian jurist Cesare Beccaria (1738–1794). In his *Essay on Crimes and Punishments* (1764), Beccaria argued that punishment should be used not to exact retribution for crimes but to rehabilitate the criminal and to serve the interests of society. He called for the abolition of capital punishment and the imprisonment of convicted felons. The prison, which prior to the eighteenth century had been little more than a jail or holding facility, was now to become a symbol of the improvement of society.

VOLTAIRE AND THE SPIRIT OF THE ENLIGHTENMENT

The philosophe who captured all the main themes as well as the spirit of the Enlightenment was the writer and philosopher François Marie Arouet (1694–1778), known universally by his pen name, Voltaire. Born into a French bourgeois family, Voltaire became one of the most prominent and prolific writers of the eighteenth century. He wrote plays and novels as well as poems, letters, essays, and history. These writings revealed his commitment to scientific rationality, his contempt for established religion, and his unflagging pursuit of liberty and justice.

Like many men of the Enlightenment, Voltaire developed a deep interest in science. He acquired much of his scientific knowledge from a learned noblewoman, Madame du Châtelet, a scientist and mathematician who translated the works of Newton into French and who became Voltaire's mistress. From Madame du Châtelet, Voltaire acquired not only an understanding of Newton's scientific laws but also a commitment to women's education and equality.

Voltaire's belief in a Newtonian universe—one governed by the universal law of gravitation—laid the foundation for his deism and his attacks on contemporary Christianity. In his *Philosophical Dictionary* (1764), he lashed out at established religion and the clergy, Protestant as well as Catholic. In a letter to another philosophe attacking religious superstition he pleaded, "Whatever you do, crush the infamous thing." In Voltaire's eyes Christianity was not only unreasonable; it was vulgar and barbaric. He condemned the Catholic Church for the slaughter of millions of indigenous people in the Americas on the grounds that they had not been baptized, as well as the executions of hundreds of thousands of Jews, witches, and heretics in Europe.

Voltaire's indictment of the Church for these barbarities was matched by his scathing criticism of the French government for a series of injustices, including his own imprisonment for insulting the regent of France. While living in England for three years, Voltaire became an admirer of English legal institutions, which he considered more humane and just than those of his native country. A tireless advocate of individual liberty, he became a regular defender of victims of injustice, including Jean Calas, a Protestant shopkeeper from Toulouse who had been tortured and executed for allegedly murdering his son because he had expressed a desire to convert to Catholicism. The boy had in fact committed suicide.

ENLIGHTENMENT POLITICAL THEORY

Enlightenment thinkers are known most widely for their political theories, especially those that supported the causes of liberty and reform. The men and women of the Enlightenment did not, however, share a common political ideology, nor did they agree on the most desirable type of political society. They did share a belief that politics was a science, which like the cosmos had its own natural laws. They also thought of the state in secular rather than religious terms. There was little place in Enlightenment thought for the divine right of kings. Nor was there a place for the Church in the government of the state. On other issues, however, there was little consensus. Three thinkers in particular illustrate the range of Enlightenment political thought: Montesquieu, Rousseau, and Paine.

A Case of Infanticide in the Age of the Enlightenment

A mid-eighteenth-century trial of a young French woman charged with killing her newborn child provides a window into the life of women who occupied the lower rungs of French society, in contrast to those who frequented the court and met in salons. The trial also raises the larger questions, debated in French and European judicial circles during the time of the Enlightenment, of how society should deal with the mothers of illegitimate children and whether the punishments prescribed for infanticide, or the killing of a young child, were proportionate to the crime.

In August 1742 Marie-Jeanne Bartonnet, a 21-year-old unmarried woman from a small French village in Brie, moved to Paris, where she took up residence with Claude le Queux, whom she had known in her youth, and Claude's sister. At that time Bartonnet was seven months pregnant. On October 22 Bartonnet caused a ruckus in the middle of the night when she went to the toilet and began groaning loudly and bleeding profusely. When her neighbors found her, and when she asked for towels for the blood, they suspected that she had had a miscarriage and called for a midwife. By the time the midwife arrived, it was clear that the delivery had already taken place and that the infant had fallen down the toilet to the cesspool five stories below. Suspecting that Bartonnet had killed the baby, the proprietress of the building reported her to the nearest judicial officer. The next day judicial authorities returned

to the building and found the dead infant in the cesspool. An autopsy revealed that the child's skull had been dented by either a blunt instrument or a fall. After a medical examination of Bartonnet revealed the signs of having just delivered a baby, she was arrested and imprisoned for the crime of infanticide.

Bartonnet came very close to being executed, but the strict procedures of French justice saved her from paying the ultimate price for her apparent crime. In the seventeenth and eighteenth centuries French criminal justice had established clear criteria for determining the guilt or innocence of a person accused of a crime. These procedures involved a systematic interrogation of the accused (only rarely under torture), the deposition of witnesses, the evaluation of physical evidence, and the confrontation of the accused with the witnesses who testified against her. There also was a mandatory review of the case, which involved a further interrogation of the defendant, before the Parlement of Paris, the highest court in northern France.

The interrogations of Bartonnet did not give her judges much evidence on which they could convict her. When asked the name of the village where she had lived in Brie, she told her interrogators, "It's none of your business." She denied that she had even known she was pregnant, refused to name the man with whom she had had intercourse, and claimed that she had mistaken her labor pains for colic or

diarrhea. She denied picking her baby off the floor of the toilet after the delivery and throwing it into the cesspool. When presented with the baby's corpse, she claimed she did not recognize it.

After this interrogation, Bartonnet was given the opportunity to challenge the testimony of the witnesses who had seen her the night of the delivery. The most damning testimony came from Madame Pâris, the wife of the proprietor, who had found Bartonnet on the toilet and thus could verify the circumstances of the clandestine delivery. Bartonnet's inability to challenge the testimony of Madame Pâris led directly to her initial conviction. After reviewing the entire dossier of evidence, the king's attorney recommended conviction for concealing her pregnancy, hiding her delivery, and destroying her child. French criminal procedure entrusted the decision of guilt or innocence to the judges themselves, and on November 27 they voted that Bartonnet should be executed by hanging.

Marie-Jeanne Bartonnet's fate, however, was not yet sealed. When her case went on appeal to the Parlement of Paris, Bartonnet repeated her statement that she had gone to the toilet but did not know whether she had given birth. Even though her execution was warranted by terms of an edict of 1557 that defined the crime of infanticide, the judges of this court voted to commute her sentence to a public whipping, banishment from the jurisdiction of the Parlement of Paris, and

confiscation of her property. The basis of this decision appears to have been the absence of any proof that she had deliberately killed her baby. Indeed, its injuries could have been caused by its fall down the drain pipe into the cesspool. There was also the persistent refusal of the defendant to make a confession. She may have been lying, but it is equally possible that once she had delivered the baby, which happened very quickly, she convinced herself that it had not happened.

Bartonnet's trial for infanticide stands at the end of a long period of intense prosecution of this crime. Trials of this sort declined as cities and towns built foundling hospitals for abandoned infants and as the moral outrage for illegitimacy was redirected from the pregnant mother to the illegitimate father. The new legal values promoted at the time of the Enlightenment, moreover, made it less likely that any woman or man would be executed for this or any other crime. ■

Questions of Justice

1. As in many trials, the facts of this case can be used to support different claims of justice. If you had been the prosecutor in this trial, what position would you have taken to prove the crime of infanticide? If you had been defending Marie-Jeanne Bartonnet, what arguments would you have used in her defense?

2. In his *Essay on Crimes and Punishments* (1764), Beccaria recommended that punishments be determined strictly in accordance with the social damage committed by the crime. What would Beccaria have said about the original sentence of death in this case? What would he have said about the modified sentence handed down by the Parlement of Paris?

Taking It Further

Michael Wolfe, ed. *Changing Identities in Early Modern France.* 1997. Gives a full account of Marie-Jeanne Bartonnet's trial for infanticide.

Baron de Montesquieu: The Separation of Powers

The most influential political writer of the Enlightenment was the French philosophe Charles-Louis de Secondat, Baron de Montesquieu (1689–1755). In *Spirit of the Laws* (1748), Montesquieu argued that there were three forms of government: republics, monarchies, and despotisms, each of which had an activating or inspirational force. In republics that force was civic virtue, in monarchies it was honor, and in despotisms it was fear. In each form of government there was a danger that the polity could degenerate: The virtue of republics could be lost, monarchies could become corrupt, and despotisms could lead to repression. The key to maintaining moderation and preventing this degeneration of civil society was the law of each country. Ideally the law of a country should provide for the separation and balance of political powers. Only in that way could degeneration be avoided and moderation ensured.

Montesquieu used his knowledge of the British political system, which he had studied firsthand while living in England for two years, to propose that the key to good government was the separation of executive, legislative, and judicial power. He was particularly concerned about the independence of the judiciary. Montesquieu's emphasis on the importance of a separation of powers became the most durable of his ideas. It had profound influence on the drafting of the Constitution of the United States of America in 1787.

Jean-Jacques Rousseau: The General Will

Also influential as a political theorist was the Swiss philosophe Jean-Jacques Rousseau (1712–1778), who as a young man moved from Geneva to Paris and became a member of a prominent intellectual circle. Rousseau does not conform to the model of the typical Enlightenment thinker. His distrust of human reason and his emotionalism separated him from Hume, Voltaire, and another great French philosophe, Denis Diderot (1713–1784). Instead of celebrating the improvement of society as it evolved into higher forms, Rousseau had a negative view of the achievements of civilization. Rousseau idealized the uncorrupted condition of human beings in the state of nature, providing support for the theory of the "noble savage."

Rousseau's political theories were hardly conventional, but they appealed to some segments of the reading public. In his *Discourse on the Origin of Inequality among Men* (1755) and *The Social Contract* (1762) he challenged the existing political and social order with an uncompromising

■ **Differences Among the Philosophes**

This satirical print shows Rousseau, to the left, and Voltaire engaged in heated debate. The two men were both major figures in the Enlightenment, but they differed widely in temperament and in their philosophical and political views. Rousseau was very much the rebel; unlike Voltaire, he distrusted reason and articulated highly egalitarian political principles.

attack on aristocracy and monarchy. He linked absolute monarchy, which he referred to as despotism, with the court and especially with the vain, pampered, conceited, and overdecorated aristocratic women who wielded political influence with the king and in the salons. As an alternative to this aristocratic, monarchical, and feminized society Rousseau proclaimed the sovereignty of the people. Laws were to be determined by the General Will, by which he meant the consensus of a community of citizens (but not necessarily the vote of the majority).

Thomas Paine: The Rights of Man

Of all the Enlightenment political theorists, the English publicist and propagandist Thomas Paine (1737–1809) was arguably the most radical. Paine's radicalism was cultivated mainly by his intense involvement in the political world of revolutionary America, where he became politically active in the 1770s. At the time of the French Revolution, Paine continued to call for the establishment of a republic in France and in his native country. In his most widely circulated work, *The Rights of Man* (1791), he linked the institution of monarchy with the aristocracy, which he referred to as "a seraglio [a harem] of males, who neither collect the honey nor form the hive but exist only for lazy enjoyment."

The title of *The Rights of Man* identified a theme that appeared in much Enlightenment writing. Like Diderot and Rousseau, Paine spoke the language of natural rights. Until the Enlightenment, rights were considered legal privileges acquired by royal charter or by inheritance. The new emphasis on natural law, however, led to the belief that simply by being a human being one acquired natural rights that could never be taken away. The American Declaration of Independence (1776) presented an eloquent statement of these inalienable rights, which included "life, liberty and the pursuit of happiness."

WOMEN AND THE ENLIGHTENMENT

The claim advanced by Enlightenment thinkers that all human beings are equal in a state of nature did not lead to a widespread belief that on the basis of natural law men and women are equal. Quite to the contrary, many philosophes, including Diderot and Rousseau, argued that women were different in nature from men and that they should be confined to an exclusively domestic role as chaste wives and mothers.

This patriarchal argument supported the emerging theory of separate spheres°, which held that men and women should conduct their lives in different social and political environments. The identification of women with the private, domestic sphere laid the foundation for the ideology of female domesticity, which became popular in bourgeois society in the nineteenth century. But it denied them the freedom that aristocratic women in France had acquired

CHRONOLOGY	
\multicolumn{2}{l}{**Literary Works of the Enlightenment**}

1748	Baron de Montesquieu, *Spirit of the Laws*
1748	David Hume, *An Enquiry Concerning Human Understanding*
1751	First volume of Diderot and d'Alembert's *Encyclopedia*
1759	Voltaire, *Candide*
1762	Jean-Jacques Rousseau, *The Social Contract* and *Emile, or on Education*
1764	Cesare Beccaria, *Essay on Crimes and Punishments*
1781	Immanuel Kant, *Critique of Pure Reason*
1791	Thomas Paine, *The Rights of Man*
1795	Marquis de Condorcet, *Progress of the Human Mind*

during the eighteenth century, especially those who participated in polite society. It also continued to deny them civil rights. Eighteenth-century women could not vote and could not initiate lawsuits on their own authority. They were not full members of civil society.

Only in the 1790s did writers begin to use the language and ideas of the Enlightenment to advance the argument for the full equality of men and women. The first of these appeals came from Condorcet, who published *On the Admission of Women to the Rights of Citizenship* in 1789. In that pamphlet he proposed that all women who own property be given the right to vote. A similar appeal came from the French dramatist and revolutionary activist Marie Olympe Aubrey de Gouges (1748–1793). At the very beginning of the French Revolution, de Gouges, the daughter of a butcher, proposed that the revolutionary manifesto adopted by the French National Assembly, *Declaration of the Rights of Man and Citizen* (1789), be extended to include women as well as men.

De Gouges's English contemporary, Mary Wollstonecraft (1759–1797), was the most famous of the Enlightenment's advocates of women's rights. Inspired by the events of the French Revolution, Wollstonecraft wrote *A Vindication of the Rights of Woman* (1792). This treatise, which embodies a stinging critique of eighteenth-century polite society, made an eloquent appeal for extending civil and political rights to women and even proposed that women elect their own representatives to legislatures. She also claimed that in order for women to become the full equals of men within marriage and in the political realm, the education of women must be made equal and identical to that of men.

MONTESQUIEU SATIRIZES EUROPEAN WOMEN

Montesquieu's first publication, The Persian Letters *(1721), is a clever satire on French society. The book consists of a series of letters written to and from two fictional Persian travelers, Usbek and Rica. Because the characters come from a radically different culture, Montesquieu was able to avoid official censure for presenting his irreverent views. The Persians refer to the king as a great magician who has the power to persuade men to kill one another though they have no quarrel, and to the pope as "an old idol worshipped out of habit." Montesquieu's satire was all the more biting because Europeans harbored deep contempt for the world of the Middle East, which they thought of as a region ruled by oriental despots and inhabited by people with lax standards of sexual morality. In this passage from one of Usbek's early letters to one of his wives in the harem, Montesquieu presents a favorable image of the oriental harem to contrast with the aristocratic women of eighteenth-century France.*

Usbek to Roxana, at the seraglio in Ispahan

How fortunate you are, Roxana, to live in the gentle land of Persia and not in these poisoned regions where neither shame nor virtue are known! You live in my seraglio as in the bower of innocence, inaccessible to the assaults of mankind; you rejoice in the good fortune that makes it impossible for you to fall. No man has sullied you with lascivious glances; even your father-in-law, during the freedom of the festivals, has never seen your lovely mouth, because you have never failed to cover it with a sacred veil. . . .

If you had been raised in this country, you would not have been so troubled. Women here have lost all restraint. They present themselves barefaced to men, as if inviting conquest; they seek attention, and they accompany men to the mosques. On walks, even to their rooms; the service of eunuchs is unknown. In place of the noble simplicity and charming modesty which is the rule among you, one finds here a barbaric impudence, to which one cannot grow accustomed. . . .

When you enhance the brilliance of your complexion with lovely coloring, when you perfume all your body with the most precious essences, when you dress in your most beautiful garments, when you seek to distinguish yourself from your companions by the charm of your dancing or the delight of your song, when you graciously compete with them in beauty, sweetness and vivacity, then I cannot imagine that you have any other object than that of pleasing me. . . .

But what am I to think of European women? Their art in making up their complexions, the ornaments they display, the care they give to their bodies, their preoccupation with pleasing are so many stains on their virtue and outrages to their husbands.

Source: From Baron de Montesquieu, *The Persian Letters*, translated by George R. Healy (Hackett, 1999), Letter 26. Reprinted by permission of Hackett Publishing Company, Inc. All rights reserved.

THE ENLIGHTENMENT AND SEXUALITY

One facet of Enlightenment thought that had a profound effect on the position of women in society was the appeal for greater sexual permissiveness. Many philosophes, including Voltaire, Diderot, and Baron d'Holbach (1723–1789), remained openly critical of the strict standard of sexual morality enforced by Christian churches. The basic argument of the philosophes was that sexual activity should not be restricted because it was pleasurable and a source of happiness. The arbitrary prohibitions imposed by the Church contradicted human nature. European encounters with pagan natives of the South Pacific, who were reported to have enjoyed great sexual permissiveness, were used to reinforce this argument based on human nature. Diderot appealed to the sexual code of the Tahitians in his attack on Christian sexual morality.

Many philosophes, including Voltaire, practiced what they preached and lived openly with women out of wedlock. Other members of wealthy society adopted an even more libertine lifestyle. The Venetian adventurer and author Giacomo Casanova (1725–1798), who was expelled from a seminary for his immorality, gained fame for his life of gambling, spying, and seducing thousands of women. To one young Spanish woman, who resisted his advances in order to protect her virginity, he said: "You must abandon yourself to my passion without any resistance, and you may rest assured I will respect your innocence." Casanova's name soon became identified with sexual seduction.

The libertine values of a nobleman like Casanova is not surprising. Somewhat more remarkable was the growth of public sexual permissiveness among all social groups, including the rather prim and proper bourgeoisie and the working poor. Erotic literature, such as John Cleland's *Memoirs of a Woman of Pleasure* (1749), and pornographic prints achieved considerable popularity in an increasingly commercialized society. Voltaire and Diderot might not have approved of this literature or these practices, but their libertine, anti-Christian, materialist outlook helped to prepare the ground for their acceptance.

The Impact of the Enlightenment

The ideas of the Enlightenment spread to every country in Europe as well as to the Americas. They inspired programs of reform and radical political movements. Enlightenment thought, however, did not appeal to the entire population. It found a broad audience among the educated and the relatively prosperous, but it failed to penetrate the lower levels of society.

THE SPREAD OF ENLIGHTENED IDEAS

The ideas of the Enlightenment spread rapidly among the literate members of society, mainly by means of print. During the eighteenth century, print became the main medium of formal communication. The technology of printing allowed for the publication of materials on a scale unknown a century before. Pamphlets, newspapers, and books poured off presses, not only in the major cities but in provincial towns as well. Literacy rates increased dramatically throughout western Europe. The highly educated still constituted a minority of the population, but the better part of the aristocracy and many of those who occupied the middle ranks of society could read and write. By 1750 more than half the male population of France and England could read basic texts. The foundation of public libraries in all the major cities of western Europe made printed materials more widely available. In many bookshops, rooms were set aside for browsing in the hope that readers would eventually purchase the books they consulted.

One of the most widely circulated publications of the Enlightenment was the *Encyclopedia* compiled by the philosophe Denis Diderot and the mathematician Jean le Rond d'Alembert. This massive seventeen-volume work, which was published between 1751 and 1765, contained thousands of articles on science, religion, politics, and the economy. The entries in the *Encyclopedia* were intended not only to promote knowledge but also to advance the ideas of the Enlightenment. Included, for example, were two entries on natural law, which was described as being "perpetual and unchangeable." The entry on intolerance makes a passionate plea against religious persecution, while other articles praised the achievements of science and technology. Underlying the entire enterprise was the belief that knowledge was useful, that it could contribute to the improvement of human life. In these respects the *Encyclopedia* became the quintessential statement of the worldview of the Enlightenment.

Encyclopedias, pamphlets, newspapers, and novels were not the only means by which the ideas of the Enlightenment spread. A number of informal institutions promoted the exchange of ideas. Literary societies and book clubs, which proliferated in the major cities of western Europe, encouraged the public reading and discussion of the latest publications. Scientific societies sponsored lectures on the latest developments in physics, chemistry, and natural history. One of the most famous of these lectures demonstrated the power of electricity by charging a young boy, suspended from the ground, with static electricity. This "electrified boy," who was not harmed in the process, attracted objects from a stool placed below him.

Another set of institutions that promoted the ideas of the Enlightenment were the secret societies of men and women known as freemasons°. Freemasons strove to create a society based on reason and virtue, and they were committed to the principles of liberty and equality. Freemasonry first appeared in England and Scotland in the seventeenth century and then spread to France, the Dutch Republic, Germany, and as far east as Poland and Russia during the eighteenth century. Some of the most famous figures of the Enlightenment, including Voltaire, belonged to masonic lodges. In the 1770s there were more than 10,000 freemasons in Paris alone. The lodges were places where philosophes interacted with merchants, lawyers, and government leaders.

The most famous informal cultural institutions of the Enlightenment were the salons, the private sitting rooms of wealthy women where men and women were invited to discuss philosophy, science, literature, and politics. The salons were more socially exclusive than the literary and scientific societies and the masonic lodges, but they too encouraged the spread of Enlightenment ideas among members of both aristocratic and bourgeois society.

THE LIMITS OF THE ENLIGHTENMENT

The ideas of the Enlightenment spread rapidly across Europe, but their influence was limited. The market for books by philosophes like Voltaire and Rousseau was quite small. Diderot and d'Alembert's *Encyclopedia* sold a remarkable 25,000 copies by 1789, but that was exceptional, and many sales were to libraries. Most books on social and political theory, however, like scholarly works on science, did not sell very well. Rousseau's *The Social Contract* was a commercial failure.

Books on other topics had much better sales than the works of philosophes. Inspirational religious literature continued to be published in large quantities, indicating the limits of Enlightenment secularism. Novels, a relatively new genre of fiction that appealed to the bourgeoisie, were almost as successful. In France, books that were banned because of their pornographic content or their satirical attacks on the monarchy, the clergy, or ministers in the government also proved to be best-sellers in the huge underground French book market.

Among those who were illiterate or barely literate, Enlightenment ideas made even fewer inroads. The only exposure these people may have had to these ideas would be through the actions and attitudes of their social superiors. From the elitist perspective of the philosophes, the intellectual world of the illiterate was characterized by the superstition and ignorance that the philosophes were determined to eliminate.

The growing gap between a learned culture shared by philosophes and members of salons on the one hand and the popular culture of the lower classes on the other can be seen in the perpetuation of beliefs regarding magic and witchcraft among the uneducated. During the late seventeenth and eighteenth centuries, educated people in Europe gradually abandoned their belief in magic and witchcraft. As we have seen in Chapter 16, belief in the operation of a mechanical universe, religious skepticism, and rationalism had gradually eroded many beliefs regarding the operation of a supernatural realm, especially the possibility of demonic intervention in the natural world. Among the lower classes, however, this skeptical outlook found very little fertile ground. Popular belief in a world charged with supernatural and magical forces continued to lead villagers to accuse their neighbors of having harmed them by means of witchcraft. After European courts stopped prosecuting witches in the late seventeenth and early eighteenth centuries, local communities often took justice into their own hands and lynched the suspects themselves. It was left to the government to prosecute those who engaged in this illegal form of local justice.

ENLIGHTENED ABSOLUTISM

When we turn to Enlightenment political ideas, we confront an even more difficult task of determining the extent of their impact. The main figures of the Enlightenment were intellectuals—men of letters who did not occupy positions of great political importance and who did not devote much thought to the challenging task of putting their theories into practice. The audience for their books did not always include people with the power to implement their proposals. Nevertheless, Enlightenment thought did make its mark on eighteenth-century politics in two strikingly different ways.

The first was through the reforms enacted by those rulers who are often referred to as enlightened despots°. These rulers exercised absolute power and used that power to implement changes that Enlightenment thinkers had proposed. The term *despot* is misleading, since these enlightened rulers were rarely despotic in the sense of exercising power cruelly and arbitrarily. The connection between Enlightenment and royal absolutism is not as unnatural as it might appear. Many philosophes, including Voltaire, had little sympathy with democracy and social equality, and preferred to entrust absolute monarchs with the implementation of the reforms they advocated. Among the philosophes the prospect of a philosopher-king had widespread appeal.

■ Torture

The torture of a defendant as depicted in the published version of the criminal code promulgated by Empress Maria Theresa in 1769. This form of torture, the *strappado,* used a pulley to hang the accused from the ceiling. Weights could be attached to the feet to make the pain more excruciating. The purpose of judicial torture was to extract a confession. Torture was eliminated from the law codes of most continental European countries during the Enlightenment.

Rulers of central and eastern European countries were particularly receptive to Enlightenment thought. These monarchs had read widely in the literature of the Enlightenment and introduced Western intellectuals to their courts. The most famous of the enlightened absolutists was King Frederick II of Prussia, known as Frederick the Great (r. 1740–1786). Frederick, a deist who wrote poetry and was enamored of all things French, implemented a number of policies that reflected the ideals of the Enlightenment. The most noteworthy of these was the introduction of religious toleration throughout his predominantly Lutheran kingdom. Frederick also introduced a number of legal reforms with the intention of realizing the Enlightenment ideal of making the law both rational and humane. He authorized the codification of Prussian law (which was completed after his death in 1794), abolished judicial torture, and eliminated capital punishment. In order to provide for the training of future servants of the state, he began a system of compulsory education throughout the country.

In neighboring Austria two Habsburg rulers, Maria Theresa (r. 1740–1780) and her son Joseph II (r. 1780–1790), pursued reformist policies that gave them the reputation of being enlightened monarchs. The policies of Maria Theresa's that most clearly bore the stamp of the Enlightenment were her legal reforms. Inspired by Beccaria and Montesquieu, she established a commission to reform the entire corpus of Austrian law. A new code of criminal law was promulgated in 1769, and seven years later Maria Theresa issued an edict abolishing judicial torture. Joseph continued this program of legal reform by reorganizing the entire central court system and by eliminating capital punishment. He also revealed the influence of the Enlightenment by granting religious toleration, first to Protestants and Eastern Orthodox Christians in 1781, and then to Jews in 1782. With respect to social issues, he completed his mother's work of abolishing serfdom altogether.

The efforts of Catherine II of Russia (r. 1762–1796) to implement the ideas of the Enlightenment followed a different course from those of Maria Theresa and Joseph. Early in her reign, Catherine embarked on a program of reform similar to those of other enlightened absolutists. In 1767 she appointed a commission to codify Russian law on the basis of western European principles. Her recommendations to the commission included the abolition of torture and inhumane punishment and the establishment of religious toleration. She was eventually forced to disband the commission, which could not agree on a new code, but she later abolished torture and capital punishment on her own authority. Like Maria Theresa, she instituted a number of administrative and educational reforms, including the introduction of primary schooling in the provinces.

Catherine gained a reputation for being an enlightened European monarch, but her acceptance of traditional Russian culture and the need to maintain her rule prevented her from fully embracing the ideals of the Enlightenment. After putting down the Pugachev rebellion in 1774, she began to question the desirability of social reform, and the experience of the French Revolution in the 1790s led her to disavow the ideals of the Enlightenment.

On the issue of serfdom, which most Enlightenment thinkers wished to see abolished, Catherine would not

■ **Catherine the Great**

Catherine II of Russia on the day she succeeded in taking the throne from her husband, Peter III, at Peterhof in 1762. Catherine, who despised her husband, joined a conspiracy against him right after his accession to the throne. Catherine, like Peter, had a number of lovers, and her two children, including the future emperor Paul, were reputedly conceived by members of the nobility.

yield. She preserved that social system in order to secure the loyalty of the Russian nobility, and she extended it to Ukraine and parts of Poland after Russia incorporated those regions into the empire. Catherine also catered to the imperialistic ambitions of the Russians, gaining vast territories in eastern Europe, east Asia, and Alaska. Thus she expanded the Russian Empire at the very time when the ideals of the Enlightenment were leading some philosophes to call for the dissolution of large imperial structures.

THE ENLIGHTENMENT AND REVOLUTION

The Enlightenment also inspired movements for reform and revolution in western Europe and the Americas. The emphasis placed by Enlightenment thinkers on individual liberty, natural rights, and political reform put pressure on both monarchs and the traditional nobility either to make concessions or to relinquish power altogether.

In France the influence of the Enlightenment on the momentous changes that took place during the French Revolution (1789–1799) has been a matter of debate among historians. The complexity of the revolution, which will be discussed in Chapter 19, and the diversity of Enlightenment thought make this a particularly difficult debate to resolve. Many of the revolutionaries of the 1790s were steeped in the ideas of the Enlightenment, but these did not necessarily inspire the revolution itself. The French philosophes of the eighteenth century denounced the evils of the Old Regime and proposed many ideas about how governments should function, but they did not make serious efforts to introduce actual reforms, much less topple the government. Many philosophes had personal connections with aristocratic society, and very few shared the democratic and egalitarian ideas that came to the fore at the time of the Revolution.

We can nevertheless establish some connections between the ideas and programs of the philosophes and the events that transpired in France during the 1790s. Some of the figures of the Enlightenment contributed to the new critical spirit evident after 1750 or provided some inspiration for the creation of a new political culture once the revolution began. The towering reputation of Voltaire during the French Revolution—and the anger of conservatives who exhumed and burned his bones after it had ended—suggest that his passionate criticisms of the Old Regime and his pleas for human freedom at the very least helped to set the stage for the revolutionary events of the 1790s. The same is true of the radical Rousseau, whose democratic and republican ideas were used to justify some of the most important changes that took place during the revolution.

Yet another application of enlightened ideas to politics took place in the Americas. The advocates of colonial independence from their mother countries, such as Thomas Jefferson in Virginia and Símon Bolívar in Venezuela and Colombia, were all deeply influenced by the Enlightenment concepts of natural law, natural rights, liberty, and popular sovereignty. The Declaration of Independence, which was written by Jefferson, revealed its debt to the Enlightenment in its reference to the inalienable rights of all men and to the foundation of those rights in "the law of nature and Nature's God."

ENLIGHTENMENT AND WESTERN IDENTITY

The Enlightenment was a distinctly Western phenomenon. It arose in the countries of western Europe and then spread to central and eastern Europe (Germany, Austria, Poland, and Russia) and to the Americas. Most traditions that are identified today as "Western values" either had their origin or received their most cogent expression in the Enlightenment. In particular, the commitment to individual liberty, civil rights, toleration, and rational decision making all took shape in the West during this period.

It would be misleading, however, to make a simple equation between the ideas of the Enlightenment and the Western intellectual tradition. The ideals of the Enlightenment have never been fully accepted within Western societies. Ever since their original formulation, the ideas of the philosophes and publicists of the Enlightenment have been challenged by conservatives who argued that those ideas would lead to the destruction of religion and the social order. Nevertheless, the ideas and traditions of the Enlightenment, despite the challenges they have endured, have become deeply ingrained in Western law and politics. They are less often found embedded in the political and legal traditions of non-Western lands, and when they are, such as in the twentieth-century socialist legal system of China, their presence is more often the result of Western influence than the legacy of native Eastern thought.

The acquisition of Enlightenment values, even though they were never universally adopted, gave Europeans a clear sense of their own identity with respect to the rest of the world. Educated Europeans who prided themselves on being enlightened shared a similar mental outlook and a commitment to individual liberty, justice, and the improvement of civilization. For all of them religious faith was less important, both as an arbiter of morality and as a source of authority, than it was in these other cultures. The men and women of the Enlightenment all looked to the law as a reflection of natural law and as the guardian of civil liberty. Their writings helped their European and colonial public audiences think of themselves as even more distinct from non-Western people than they had in the past.

CONCLUSION

Change and Continuity in the Eighteenth Century

The eighteenth century is often viewed as a period of stability in the West. In political terms, that characterization makes some sense. During the years from 1700 to 1789 Europe stood between the turmoil of the mid-seventeenth century, which witnessed massive rebellions throughout Europe, and the upheaval of the French Revolution. In Great Britain, where Parliament had established its supremacy over the monarchy and where party factionalism ultimately resulted in the implementation of one-party rule by the Whigs, political peace was most apparent. A similar peace also dawned in countries where royal absolutism was in full force. In France, Spain, Prussia, Austria, and Russia, powerful central governments maintained tight control of the provinces and secured the suppression of the relatively few rebellions that broke out. In all these countries the political order remained intact. The aristocracy contributed to this stability. In their determination to preserve their own power, they placed financial burdens on their tenants, subjected the lower classes to harsh criminal prosecutions, and promoted a culture that celebrated the virtues of order and deference.

This picture of eighteenth-century stability is deceptive. Beneath the relatively placid surface of eighteenth-century European life, an array of historical forces was challenging the social and political order. These forces would ultimately bring about some of the most important transformations of the modern world. The growth of a wealthy and influential bourgeoisie, concentrated almost exclusively in the towns and cities, threatened to take power from the aristocracy and replace the values of that social elite with those of their own. The lower classes, beaten into submission by wealthy landlords and victimized by the brutalities of the criminal justice system, had developed their own strategies for denying the rulers the deference they expected and demanded. Finally, the thinkers of the Enlightenment, many of them drawn from the nobility itself, developed devastating critiques of both monarchy and aristocracy and set in motion movements for the reform of politics and the improvement of society. Instead of a stable and peaceful society, a picture emerges of a world in which all prevailing values and power structures were being challenged. These challenges all came to a head in the era of the French Revolution, to which we now turn.

Suggestions for Further Reading

For a comprehensive list of suggested readings, please go to www.ablongman.com/levackconcise/chapter 17

Alexander, John T. *Catherine the Great: Life and Legend.* 1989. A lively biography of the remarkable "enlightened despot."

Beckett, J. V. *The Aristocracy in England 1660–1914.* 1986. A comprehensive study of this landholding and governing elite. Makes the important distinction between the aristocracy and the nobility.

Darnton, Robert. *The Forbidden Best-Sellers of Pre-Revolutionary France.* 1995. A study of the salacious, blasphemous, and subversive books that sold more copies than those of the philosophes in eighteenth-century France.

Dewald, Jonathan. *The European Nobility 1500–1800.* 1996. A comprehensive study of this social class that emphasizes its adaptability.

Doyle, William. *The Old European Order, 1660–1800.* 2nd ed. 1999. The best general study of the period.

Houston, R. A. *Literacy in Early Modern Europe: Culture and Education.* 1991. The best survey of the subject for the entire period.

Lugee, Carolyn. *Le Paradis des Femmes: Women, Salons and Social Stratification in 17th-Century France.* 1976. A social study of the women of the salons.

Outram, Dorinda. *The Enlightenment.* 1995. A balanced assessment of the major historiographical debates regarding the Enlightenment.

Root, Hilton. *Peasants and King in Burgundy: Agrarian Foundations of French Absolutism.* 1979. A study of peasant communal institutions and their relationship with the crown as well as the nobility.

Williams, David, ed. *The Enlightenment.* 1999. An excellent collection of political writings with a long introduction.

The Age of the French Revolution, 1789–1815

O N JULY 12, 1789, THE FRENCH JOURNALIST CAMILLE DESMOULINS addressed an anxious crowd of Parisian citizens gathered outside the royal palace. Playing upon fears that had been mounting during the past two months, Desmoulins claimed that the royal government of Louis XVI was preparing a massacre of Parisians. "To arms, to arms," Desmoulins cried out, as he roused the citizens to their own defense. That night Parisians responded to his call by invading arsenals in the city in anticipation of an attack. The next day they declared themselves members of the National Guard, a volunteer militia of propertied citizens.

On the morning of July 14, crowds of Parisians moved into one of the suburbs of the city, where royal troops were stationed in an ancient fortress known as the Bastille. The Parisians feared that the troops in the Bastille would take violent action against them, and they also wanted to capture the ammunition stored inside the fortress, which served as both an arsenal and a prison. Negotiations with the governor of the Bastille were interrupted when some of the militia demanded the surrender of the troops. Shots were fired from both sides, and the exchange led to a full-scale assault upon the Bastille by the National Guard.

After three hours of fighting and the death of eighty-three people, the governor surrendered. He was then led by his captors, bearing the arms they had seized, to face charges before the officers of the city government. The crowd, however, crying for vengeance against their oppressors, attacked the soldiers and crushed some of them underfoot. The governor was stabbed hundreds of times, hacked to pieces, and decapitated. The chief magistrate of the city suffered the same fate for his reluctance to issue arms to its citizens. The crowd then placed

Chapter Outline

- The First French Revolution, 1789–1791

- The French Republic, 1792–1799

- Cultural Change in France During the Revolution

- The Napoleonic Era, 1799–1815

- The Legacy of the French Revolution

The Storming of the Bastille, July 14, 1789: The Bastille was attacked not because it was a symbol of the Old Regime, but because it contained weapons that the Parisian citizens needed to protect themselves from royalist troops.

the heads of the two men on spears and paraded through the city.

The storming of the Bastille was the first of many violent episodes that occurred during the sequence of events called the French Revolution. That revolution brought about some of the most fundamental changes in European political life since the end of Roman rule. It heralded the destruction of the Old Regime°, the eighteenth-century political order that had been dominated by an absolute monarch and a privileged nobility and clergy. A more radical phase of the revolution, beginning in 1792, resulted in the destruction of the French monarchy and the declaration of a republic. It also led to a period of state-sponsored terrorism in 1793 and 1794, during which one group of revolutionaries engaged in a brutal campaign to eliminate their real and imagined enemies.

The excesses of the revolution led to a conservative reaction. Between 1795 and 1799 a moderate republican government modified the egalitarianism of the revolution by limiting the right to vote to men of property. Between 1799 and 1814 the reaction continued under the direction of Napoleon Bonaparte, a military officer who assumed power in 1799, and then proclaimed himself emperor in 1804. Although Napoleon declared his loyalty to many of the principles of the revolution, his authoritarian rule undermined or reversed many of its achievements. In 1815 Napoleon fell from power and the monarchy was restored, marking the end of the revolutionary period. The ideas of the revolution, however, especially its commitment to democratic republicanism and its concept of the nation, continued to dominate politics in the West for the next hundred years.

In this chapter we shall address five questions regarding the age of the French Revolution:

- Why did the Old Regime in France collapse in 1789, and what revolutionary changes took place in French government and society during the next two years?
- How did a second, more radical revolution, which began with the establishment of the Republic in 1792, lead to the creation of a regime that used the power of the state to institute the Reign of Terror?
- In what ways did the political events of the revolution change French cultural institutions and create a new political culture?
- How did the authoritarian rule of Napoleon Bonaparte from 1799 to 1815 confirm and betray the achievements of the French Revolution, and what impact did his military conquests have on Europe and the world?
- What did the French Revolution ultimately achieve and in what ways did it change the course of European and Western history?

The First French Revolution, 1789–1791

The French Revolution consisted of two distinct transformations of the French political system. The first revolution, which began in 1789, resulted in a destruction of royal absolutism. The second and more radical revolution began in 1792 with the abolition of the monarchy and the formation of the French Republic.

THE BEGINNING OF THE REVOLUTION

The immediate cause of the revolution was a major economic crisis that bankrupted the monarchy and deprived it of its authority. The government of Louis XVI (r. 1774–1792) had inherited considerable debts from that of his grandfather, Louis XV (r. 1715–1774) as a result of protracted periods of warfare with Great Britain. The opening of a new phase of this warfare in 1778 pushed the government further into debt and put a strain on the entire French economy. As the crisis deepened, protests from the ranks of the nobility against royal policy became more vocal.

In 1787 the king proposed a new system of taxation that would include a direct tax on all landowners. Some nobles were willing to pay the taxes, but only if the king would summon the Estates General, a national legislative body that had not met since 1614. Louis resisted these pressures, since he did not want to give up the right to make law by his own authority. The deterioration of the government's financial condition, however, finally forced the king to yield. Louis announced that he would convene the Estates General in May 1789.

During the months leading up to the opening of this assembly, public debates arose over how the delegates should vote. The Estates General consisted of representatives of the three orders or social groups, known as estates, that made up French society: the clergy, the nobility, and the Third Estate. The Third Estate technically contained all the commoners in the kingdom (about 96 percent of the population). The elected representatives of the Third Estate, whose numbers had doubled by a recent order of the king, were propertied nonnoble members of lay society, including many lawyers and military officers.

Before the meeting a dispute arose among the representatives whether the three groups would vote by estate, in which case the first two estates would dominate the assembly, or by head, in which case the Third Estate would have numerical parity. Each side claimed that it was the best representative of the "nation," a term meaning the entire body of French people. The question of voting within the Estates General was not resolved when that body met at Versailles on May 5, 1789. After the king indicated that he would side with the clergy and nobility, the Third Estate took the dramatic step of declaring itself a National Assembly and asking members of the other estates to vote with them on the basis of "one man, one vote."

In response to this challenge, the king locked the Third Estate out of its meeting hall without explanation. The outraged members of the Third Estate went to a nearby indoor tennis court and took a solemn oath that they would not disband until the country had been given a constitution. One week later, after many clerics and noblemen had joined the ranks of the Third Estate, the king ordered the nobility and the clergy to join the National Assembly.

As this political crisis was reaching a climax, a major social crisis, triggered by a harvest failure in 1788, led to a breakdown of public order. The price of bread soared, reducing demand for manufactured goods and thus causing widespread unemployment among artisans. An increasing number of bread riots, peasant revolts, and urban strikes contributed to a sense of panic at the very time that the government's financial crisis deepened. In Paris the situation reached a critical point in June 1789. At this point the king, a man with little political sense, decided to send 17,000 royal troops to Paris to restore order. The arrival of the troops gave the impression that the government was planning an attack on the people of the city. It was in this atmosphere of public paranoia that Parisians formed the National Guard and stormed the Bastille.

With the fall of the Bastille the revolution had just begun. It moved into high gear two weeks later when the National Assembly responded to the outbreak of social unrest in the provinces. The scarcity of grain in the countryside gave rise to false rumors that the nobles were engaged in a plot to destroy crops and starve the people into submission. A widespread panic, known as the "Great Fear," gripped the entire country. Townspeople and armed peasants amassed in large numbers to defend themselves from hired agents of the nobility and save the harvest. In response to this panic, which reached its peak in the last two weeks of July, the National Assembly began to pass legislation that destroyed the Old Regime and created a new political order.

THE CREATION OF A NEW POLITICAL SOCIETY

Between August 1789 and September 1790 the National Assembly took three revolutionary steps. The first was the elimination of noble and clerical privilege. In August the assembly abolished the feudal dues that peasants paid their

CHRONOLOGY

1789

June 17	The Third Estate adopts the title of the National Assembly
July 14	The storming of the Bastille

1790

July 12	Civil Constitution of the Clergy

1791

October 1	Newly elected Legislative Assembly opens

1792

September 22	Abolition of the monarchy and establishment of the Republic

1793

January 21	Execution of Louis XVI

1795

October 26	End of the Convention; beginning of the Directory

1799

November 9–10	Napoleon's coup; Consulate is established

1804

December 2	Napoleon is crowned emperor of the French

1814

September	Congress of Vienna assembles

1815

June 18	Battle of Waterloo

lords, the private legal jurisdictions of noblemen, the collection of tithes by the clergy, and the exclusive rights of noblemen to hunt game on their lands. Ten months later the nobility lost their titles. Instead of a society divided into various corporate groups, each with its own privileges, France would now have only citizens, all of them equal at law. Social distinctions would be based on merit rather than birth.

The second step, taken on August 26, was the promulgation of the *Declaration of the Rights of Man and Citizen*. This document reveals the main influence of the Enlightenment on the revolution. It declared that all men, not just Frenchmen, had a natural right to liberty, property,

DECLARATION OF THE RIGHTS OF MAN AND CITIZEN (1789)

....

The passage of the Declaration of the Rights of Man and Citizen *by the National Assembly on August 26, 1789, is one of the earliest and most enduring acts of the French Revolution. A document of great simplicity and power, it was hammered out during many weeks of debate. Its concern with the natural rights of all people and equality before the law reflected the ideas of the Enlightenment.*

1. Men are born free and remain free and equal in rights. Social distinctions may be founded only on the common good.

2. The aim of all political association is the preservation of the natural and imprescriptible rights of man. These rights are liberty, property, security and resistance to oppression.

3. The principle of all authority rests essentially in the nation. No body nor individual may exercise any authority which does not emanate expressly from the nation.

4. Liberty consists in the freedom to do whatever does not harm another; hence the exercise of the natural rights of each man has no limits except those which assure to the other members of society the enjoyment of the same rights. These limits can only be determined by law. . . .

6. Law is the expression of the general will. Every citizen has the right to participate personally or through his representative in its formation. It must be the same for all, whether it protects or punishes. All citizens, being equal in the eyes of the law, are equally eligible to all dignities and to all public positions and occupations, according to their abilities, and without distinction except that of their virtues and talents.

7. No man may be indicted, arrested, or imprisoned except in cases determined by the law and according to the forms prescribed by law. . . .

10. No one should be disturbed for his opinions, even in religion, provided that their manifestation does not trouble public order as established by law.

11. The free communication of thoughts and opinions is one of the most precious of the rights of man. Every citizen may therefore speak, write, and print freely, but shall be responsible for any abuse of this freedom in the cases set by the law. . . .

17. Property being an inviolable and sacred right, no one may be deprived of it except when public necessity, determined by law, obviously requires it, and then on the condition that the owner shall have been previously and equitably compensated.

Source: From P.-J.-B. Buchez and P.-C. Roux, *Histoire parlementaire de la Révolution française.* (Paris: Paulin, 1834).

---

equality before the law, freedom from oppression, and religious toleration.

The third revolutionary step was a complete reorganization of the Church. In order to solve the problem of the national debt, the National Assembly placed land owned by the Church (about 10 percent of all French territory) at the service of the nation. The Civil Constitution of the Clergy of July 1790 in effect made the Church a department of the state, with the government paying the clergy directly. In order to retain their positions, the clergy were required to take an oath of loyalty to the nation.

In 1791 a newly elected Legislative Assembly—replacing the National Assembly—confirmed and extended many of these changes. A constitution, put into effect in October, formalized the end of royal absolutism. The king became a constitutional monarch, retaining only the power to suspend legislation, direct foreign policy, and command the armed forces. The constitution did not, however, give all men the right to vote. Only "active citizens," who paid the equivalent of three days' wages in direct taxes, had the right to vote for electors, who in turn chose representatives to the legislature.

The new constitution formally abolished hereditary legal privileges, thus providing equality of all citizens before the law. Subsequent legislation granted Jews and Protestants full civil rights and toleration. A law eliminating primogeniture (inheritance of the entire estate by the eldest son) gave all heirs equal rights to inherited property. The establishment of marriage as a civil contract and the right to end a marriage in divorce supported the idea of the husband and wife as freely contracting individuals.

This body of legislation amounted to nothing less than a revolution. The Old Regime had been destroyed and a new one had taken its place. Although the form of government remained a monarchy, the powers of that monarchy were drastically curtailed. Unlike the English revolutions of the 1640s and 1688, this revolution did not disguise the extent of the changes that had transpired by claiming that the revolution had recovered lost freedoms. It did not appeal to the French past at all. It promoted a new view of French society as a nation composed of equal citizens possessing natural rights, in place of the older concept of a society consisting of different corporate groups, each with its own privileges.

The French Republic, 1792–1799

Beginning in 1792 France experienced a second revolution that was much more radical than the first. During this revolution France was transformed from a constitutional monarchy into a republic. The state claimed far greater power than it possessed under the constitutional monarchy established in 1791, and it used that power to bring about a radical reform of French society.

THE ESTABLISHMENT OF THE REPUBLIC, 1792

During the first two years of the revolution it appeared that the building of a new French nation would take place within the framework of a constitutional monarchy. Absolutism had suffered an irreversible defeat, but there was little sentiment among the members of the Legislative Assembly, much less among the general population, in favor of abolishing the institution of monarchy. The only committed republicans—those supporting the establishment of a republic—in the Legislative Assembly belonged to a party known as the Jacobins°, who found support in political clubs in Paris and in other parts of the country. By the late summer of 1792 this group of radicals, drawing on the support of militant Parisian citizens known as *sans-culottes* (literally, those without breeches, the pants worn by noblemen), succeeded in bringing about the second, more radical revolution.

King Louis himself was in part responsible for this destruction of the monarchy. The success of constitutional monarchy depended on the king's willingness to play the new role assigned to him as a constitutional figurehead. He reluctantly agreed to wear the liberty cap with the tricolor cockade (a badge) to symbolize his acceptance of the revolution, but he could not disguise his opposition to the revolution, especially to the changes in the Church. This opposition led many people to suspect that he and his Austrian wife, Marie Antoinette, were encouraging the powers of Europe to invade France to restore the Old Regime.

The development that precipitated the downfall of the monarchy and led to the establishment of a republic was the decision of the Legislative Assembly to go to war. Exploiting xenophobic as well as revolutionary sentiment, a small group of republicans, headed by the eloquent orator Jacques-Pierre Brissot (1754–1793), convinced the assembly that France needed to take military action against

■ **Sans-Culottes**

Male and female dress of the *sans-culottes,* the armed Parisian radicals who supported the Republic. The men did not wear the breeches (*culottes*) that were in style among the members of the French nobility.

■ **The Attack on the Palace of the Tuileries**

On the night of August 10, 1792, Parisian crowds and volunteer soldiers attacked the royal palace in
Paris. The puffs of smoke in the building are coming from the Swiss guards, who were entrusted with
the defense of the royal family and the palace. The royal family escaped and took refuge in the
Legislative Assembly, but 600 of the Swiss guards were killed. Those that retreated were hunted down
in the streets of Paris and stripped of their uniforms, and their heads were placed on the ends of spears.

Austria and Prussia to prevent an invasion and preserve the
revolution. Brissot and his allies assured the assembly that a
large army of French citizens would not only win a quick
and decisive victory but would also inspire revolution
against "the tyrants of Europe" everywhere they went.

The Legislative Assembly declared war on Austria in
April 1792. Instead of a glorious victory, however, the war
resulted in a series of disastrous defeats at the hands of
Austrians and their Prussian allies in the Netherlands. This
military failure contributed to a mood of paranoia in Paris.
Fears arose that invading armies, in alliance with nobles,
would undermine the revolution. When the Austrians and
Prussians threatened to torch the entire city and slaughter
its population if anyone laid a hand on the royal family,
Parisian citizens immediately demanded that the king be
deposed.

On August 10 a radical republican committee overthrew
the Paris commune, the city government that had been installed in 1789, and set up a new, revolutionary commune. A

force of about 20,000 men, including volunteer troops from
various parts of the kingdom, invaded the Tuileries, the
royal palace in Paris. The attack on the Tuileries forced
the king to take refuge in the nearby Legislative Assembly.
The assembly promptly suspended the monarchy and
turned the royal family over to the commune. The assembly then ordered its own dissolution and called for the
election of a new legislative body that would draft a new
constitution.

The fall of the monarchy did nothing to allay the siege
mentality of the city, especially after further Prussian victories in early September escalated fears of a Prussian invasion. The feared foreign invasion, however, never material-
ized. On September 20, 1792, a surprisingly well-disciplined
and well-trained army of French citizens, inspired by the
principles of the revolution, repulsed the armies of
Austria and Prussia at Valmy. This victory saved the revolution. Delegates to a new National Convention, elected by
universal male suffrage°, had already arrived in Paris to

write a new constitution. On September 22 the convention declared that the monarchy was formally abolished and that France was a republic. France had now experienced a second revolution, more radical than the first, but dedicated to the same principles of liberty, equality, and fraternity.

THE JACOBINS AND THE REVOLUTION

By the time of its dissolution, the Jacobins had become the major political party in the Legislative Assembly. After the declaration of the Republic and the election of the National Convention, factional divisions began to develop within Jacobin ranks. The main split occurred between the followers of Brissot, known as Girondins°, and the radicals known as Montagnards°, or "the Mountain." The latter acquired their name because they occupied the benches on the side of the convention hall, where the floor sloped upward.

Both the Mountain and the Girondins claimed to be advancing the goals of the revolution, but they differed widely on which tactics to pursue. The Mountain took the position that as long as the state was endangered by internal and external enemies, the government needed to centralize authority in Paris. The Mountain thought of themselves as the representatives of the common people, especially the *sans-culottes* in Paris. Many of their leaders, including Georges-Jacques Danton (1759–1794), Jean-Paul Marat (1743–1793), and Maximilien Robespierre (1758–1794), were in fact Parisians. Their mission was to make the revolution even more egalitarian and to establish a republic characterized by civic pride and patriotism, which they referred to as the Republic of Virtue.

The Girondins, known as such because many of their leaders came from the southwestern *département* of Gironde, took a more conservative position than the Mountain on these issues. Favoring the economic freedom and local control desired by merchants and manufacturers, they were reluctant to support further centralization of state power. They were also afraid that the egalitarianism of the revolution, if unchecked, would lead to a leveling of French society and result in social anarchy.

The conflict between the Girondins and the Mountain became apparent in the debate over what to do with the deposed king. Louis had been suspected of conspiring with the enemies of the revolution, and the discovery of his correspondence with the Austrian government led to his trial for treason against the nation. The Girondins had originally expressed reluctance to bring him to trial, preferring to keep him in prison. Once the trial began, they joined the entire National Convention in voting to convict him, but they opposed his execution. This stance led the Mountain to accuse the Girondins of being secret collaborators with the monarchy. By a narrow vote the convention decided to put the king to death, and on January 21, 1793, Louis was executed at the Place de la Révolution. The instrument of death was the guillotine, an efficient and merciful but nonetheless terrifying decapitation machine inspired by the conviction that all criminals, not just those of noble blood, should be executed in a swift, painless manner.

The split between the Mountain and the Girondins became more pronounced as the republican regime encountered increasing opposition from foreign and domestic enemies. Early in 1793 Great Britain and the Dutch Republic allied with Prussia and Austria to form the First Coalition against France, and once again an invasion seemed imminent. At the same time internal rebellions against the revolutionary regime took place in various outlying provinces. In the minds of Robespierre and his colleagues, the Girondins were linked to these provincial rebels, whom they labeled as federalists° because they opposed the centralization of the French state and thus threatened the unity of the nation.

THE REIGN OF TERROR, 1793–1794

In order to deal with its domestic enemies, the republican government claimed powers that far exceeded those exercised by the monarchy in the age of absolutism. The convention passed laws that set up special courts to prosecute enemies of the regime and authorized special procedures that deprived those accused of their legal rights. These laws laid the legal foundation for the Reign of Terror°, a campaign to rid the state of its internal enemies. A Committee of Public Safety, consisting of twelve members entrusted with the executive power of the state, superintended this process. Although technically subordinate to the National Convention, the Committee of Public Safety became in effect a revolutionary dictatorship.

The man who emerged as the main figure on the Committee of Public Safety was Maximilien Robespierre. As a lawyer who defended indigent clients, Robespierre was elected to the Third Estate in 1789 and became a favorite of the *sans-culottes*, who called him "The Incorruptible." That he may have been, but he was also susceptible to the temptation to abuse power for partisan political purposes. Like Rousseau, whose work he admired, he was also willing to sacrifice individual liberty in the name of the collective General Will. Robespierre was primarily responsible for pushing the revolution to new extremes and for establishing the program of state repression that began in the autumn of 1793.

The most intense prosecutions of the Terror took place between October 1793 and June 1794, but they continued until August 1794. By that time the revolutionary courts had executed 17,000 people, while 500,000 had suffered imprisonment. Another 20,000 either died in prison or were killed without any form of trial. The most visible and alarming of the executions took place in Paris. The execution of Marie Antoinette and other royalists might have been justified on the basis of their active subversion of the regime, but trumped-up charges against Girondins exposed

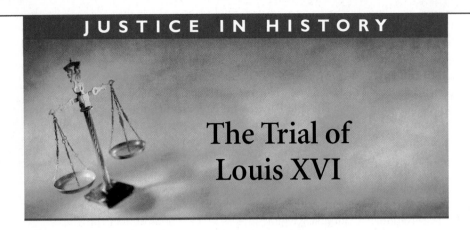

The Trial of Louis XVI

After the abolition of the monarchy and the proclamation of the French Republic in September 1792, the National Convention considered the fate of the deposed king. There was a broad consensus that Louis was guilty of treason against the nation and that he should answer for his crimes, but how he should do so was a matter of heated debate. The convention was divided between the Girondins and the Mountain. Of the two, the Girondins were more inclined to follow legal forms, whereas those of the Mountain considered themselves to be acting as a revolutionary tribunal that should adhere to standards of justice not specifically included in the law of the land. The convention thus became a forum where Louis's accusers expressed competing notions of revolutionary justice.

The most divisive and revealing issue was whether there should be a trial at all. The Mountain originally took the position that because the people had already judged the king on August 10, when the monarchy had fallen and the king taken prisoner, there was no need for a second judgment. They should proceed immediately to carrying out the death sentence. Robespierre argued that to have a trial would be counterrevolutionary, for it would allow the revolution itself to be brought before the court to be judged. A centrist majority, however, decided that the king had to be charged with specific offenses in a court of law and found guilty by due process before being sentenced.

A second issue, closely related to the first, was the technical legal question of whether the king could be subject to legal action. Even if the legislative branch of the government was considered the equal of the king in a constitutional monarchy, it did not possess authority over him. A further argument was that the king could not be tried for actions for which he had already suffered abdication. This claim was challenged on the most basic principle of the revolution—that the nation was higher than the king and his crimes were committed against that nation, which is the people. The king, moreover, was no longer king but was now a citizen and therefore subject to the law in the same way as anyone else.

The third issue was Louis's culpability for the specific charges in the indictment. These crimes included refusing to call the Estates General, sending an army to march against the citizens of Paris, and conducting secret negotiations with France's enemies. The journalist and deputy Jean-Paul Marat added that "he robbed the citizens of their gold as a subsidy for their foes" and "caused his hirelings to hoard, to create famine, to dry up the sources of abundance that the people might die from misery and hunger."

Nonetheless the king, who appeared personally to hear the indictment and then to respond to the charges on December 26, presented a plausible defense. He based it on the laws in force at the various times he was supposed to have committed his crimes. Thus he defended his sending of troops to Paris on the grounds that in June and July 1789 he could order troops wherever he wanted. In the same vein he argued that he had used force solely in response to illegal intimidation. These legalisms, however, only made the members of the convention more contemptuous of the king. His defense failed to persuade a single convention deputy. He was convicted of treason by a vote of 693–0.

This unanimous conviction of the king did not bring an end to the factional debates over the king's fate. Knowing that there was extensive support for the king in various parts of the country, the Girondins asked that the verdict be appealed to the people. Their argument was that the convention, dominated by the Mountain and supported by militants in Paris, had usurped the sovereignty of the people. Pierre-Victurnien Vergniaud, a lawyer from Bordeaux, pleaded that "To take this right from the people would be to take sovereignty from them, to transfer it . . . to the hands of the representatives chosen by the people, to transform their representatives into kings or tyrants." Vergniaud's motion to submit the verdict to the people for ratification lost by a vote of 424–283.

The last vote, the closest of all, determined the king's sentence. Originally it appeared that a majority might vote for noncapital punishment. The Marquis de Condorcet, for example, argued that although the king deserved death on the basis of the law of treason, he could not bring himself to vote for capital punishment on

MORT DE LOUIS CAPET 16ᵉ DU NOM, LE 21 JANVIER 1793.

■ Execution of Louis XVI, January 21, 1793

Although the king was convicted of treason by a unanimous vote, the vote to execute him carried by a slender majority of only twenty-seven votes.

principle. The radical response to this argument came from Robespierre, who appealed to the "principles of nature" in stating that the death penalty could be justified "only in those cases where it is vital to the safety of private citizens or of the public." Robespierre's impassioned oratory carried the day. By a vote of 361–334 the king was sentenced to "death within 24 hours" rather than the alternatives of imprisonment followed by banishment after the war or imprisonment in chains for life. The following day Louis was led to the guillotine.

All public trials, especially those for political crimes, are theatrical events, in that the various parties play specific roles and seek to convey certain mes-sages to their audiences. The men who voted to put Louis XVI on trial wanted to create an educational spectacle in which the already deposed monarch would be stripped of any respect he might still have commanded among the people. Louis was to be tried like any other traitor, and he was to suffer the same fate, execution by the guillo-tine. The attempt to strip him of all privilege and status continued after his death. His corpse, with his head placed between his knees, was taken to a cemetery, placed in a wooden box, and buried in the common pit. The revolu-tionaries were determined to guarantee that even in death the king would have the same position as the humblest of his former subjects. ■

Questions of Justice

1. How would you describe the stan-dard of justice that the members of the National Convention upheld in voting to execute the king? How did this standard of justice differ from the standard to which King Louis XVI appealed?

2. Evaluate the argument of Robespierre that the death penalty can be justified only in cases of public safety. Compare his argument to the Enlightenment critique of capital punish-ment presented by Cesare Beccaria. (See Chapter 17.)

Taking It Further

Jordan, David P. *The King's Trial: The French Revolution vs. Louis XVI.* 1979. The most thorough account of the trial.

Walzer, Michael (ed.). *Regicide and Revolution: Speeches at the Trial of Louis XVI.* 1974. A valuable collection of speeches with an extended commentary.

a process that that had spun completely out of control and was destroying republicans as well.

After the Committee of Public Safety executed Danton and others who had spoken out against the Terror, a group of moderate Jacobins in the convention organized a plot against Robespierre. Calling him a tyrant, they arrested him and hundreds of his followers and guillotined them on July 28, 1794. An equally swift retaliation was exacted against the Jacobins in the provinces, when members of the White Terror, so named for the white Bourbon flag they displayed, executed leaders of the local revolutionary tribunals. With these reprisals the most violent and radical phase of the French revolution came to an end.

THE DIRECTORY, 1795–1799

A desire to end the violence of the Terror allowed moderates in the National Convention to regain control of the state apparatus that Robespierre and his allies had used to such devastating effect. The Paris Commune was dismantled and the Committee of Public Safety abolished. In November 1794 the Jacobin clubs throughout the country, which had provided support for the Terror, were closed. The moderates who now controlled the government still hoped to preserve the gains of the revolution, while returning the country to more familiar forms of authority. A new constitution of 1795 bestowed executive power on a five-man Directorate, while an assembly consisting of two houses proposed and voted on all legislation. The franchise was limited to property holders, allowing only 2 million men out of an adult male population of 7 million to vote.

The establishment of the Directory formed part of a more general reaction against the culture of the republic. The austere, egalitarian dress of the *sans-culottes* gave way once again to fancy and opulent clothes, at least among the bourgeoisie. Low necklines, officially out of favor during the Reign of Terror, once again came back into fashion among wealthier members of society. France was still a republic, but it was no longer Robespierre's Republic of Virtue.

Some of the more entrepreneurial citizens of Paris welcomed the new regime, but opposition soon arose, mainly from Jacobins and *sans-culottes*. When the government relaxed the strict price controls that had been in effect under the Jacobins, the soaring price of bread and other commodities caused widespread social discontent among the population. By the end of 1798 inflation was running out of control. Collection of taxes was intermittent at best. Late in 1797 the Directory had been forced to cancel more than half the national debt, a step that further alienated wealthy citizens who had lent money to the government.

Military setbacks in 1798 and 1799 brought the situation to a critical point. An expedition to Egypt, which was intended to gain for France a foothold in the Middle East, had resulted in a number of victories against the Turks, but the British destroyed the French fleet at the Battle of the Nile in 1798. The next year a series of revolts against French rule in Italy and in the Austrian Netherlands pushed the French armies back to France's earlier boundaries. These military events produced a swing to the political left and raised the specter of another Jacobin coup.

In the face of this instability, Emmanuel-Joseph Sieyès (1748–1836), who had been elected as one of the directors two years earlier, decided to overthrow the government. The person Sieyès selected as his partner in this enterprise, and the man who immediately assumed leadership of the coup, was Napoleon Bonaparte (1769–1821), a 30-year-old general who in 1795 had put down a royalist rebellion in Paris with a "whiff of grapeshot."

Napoleon had already established impressive credentials as a military leader. In 1796 and 1797 he had won major victories in Italy, and those victories and his short-lived success in Egypt had made him enormously popular in Paris, where he was received as a hero when he assumed command of the armed forces in 1799. His popularity, his demonstrated military leadership, and his control of a large armed force made this "man on horseback" appear to have the best chance to replace the enfeebled civilian regime of the Directory.

Napoleon staged the coup against the Directory on November 9, 1799, and the following day France had a new government, known as the Consulate. Executive power was now to be vested in three consuls—Napoleon, Sieyès, and Roger Ducos (1754–1816), a former member of the National Convention who had voted to execute Louis XVI. It soon became clear, however, that Napoleon would be the dominant member of this triumvirate, and in the new constitution of December 1799 Napoleon was named First Consul. This appointment made him the most powerful man in France and for all practical purposes a military dictator. Republican forms of government were preserved in the new constitution, but they were easily manipulated to produce what the consuls desired. The French Republic had been replaced by a military dictatorship in all but name.

Cultural Change in France During the Revolution

The French Revolution was primarily a political revolution, but it also brought about profound changes in French culture. It transformed the cultural institutions of the Old Regime and created a new revolutionary culture.

■ **Jean Charles Tardieu, *The French Army Halts at Syene, Upper Egypt, on February 2, 1799***

This painting depicts a cultural encounter between French soldiers and Egyptians in the city of Syene (now Aswan) during the Egyptian campaign of 1798–1799. The soldiers are scribbling on the ruins of ancient Egypt, indicating a lack of respect for Egyptian culture.

THE TRANSFORMATION OF CULTURAL INSTITUTIONS

Between 1791 and 1794 most of the cultural institutions of the Old Regime were either destroyed or radically transformed, and new institutions under the control of the state took their place.

Schools

The confiscation of church property in 1790, followed by the abolition of the monastic religious orders, had a devastating effect on the traditional parish schools, colleges, and universities, most of which were run by the clergy. Without sufficient endowments, many of these schools were forced to close. During the Terror, schools suspected of having aristocratic associations and teaching counterrevolutionary doctrines came under further assault. Thousands of teachers lost their salaries and sought employment elsewhere. In September 1793 the universities were suppressed.

The government gradually realized that the entire educational process was collapsing. Recognizing the necessity of using education to encourage loyalty to the republican regime, the National Convention established a system of universal primary education. Instruction would be free, and the teachers would receive their salaries from the state. Unfortunately, the state did not have enough money to pay for the system, so the schools continued to languish.

The state was only slightly more successful in providing secondary education by converting abandoned colleges, monasteries, and libraries into "central schools," which were intended to provide a standardized form of state education. The system was improved significantly during the Napoleonic period, when the government established thirty-six secondary schools known as *lycées* while also allowing private and religious schools to continue to function.

Academies

The Parisian scientific and artistic academies established by Louis XIV were the epitome of privilege. They controlled their own membership, determined the recipients of their prizes, and had a monopoly of their particular branch of knowledge. They were also heavily aristocratic institutions; as many as three-quarters of their members were nobles or clergy.

During the revolution the academies were abolished as part of a general attack on corporate bodies. The work they did was taken over by various government committees. For example, the Commission on Weights and Measures, which had been part of the Academy of Science, became an independent commission. Its task had been to provide uniform weights and measures for the entire kingdom. In 1795 it established the meter, calculated as one ten-millionth of the distance from the North Pole to the equator, as the standard measure of distance.

The Royal Academy of Arts, dissolved by the National Convention in 1793, was replaced by the Popular and Republican Society of the Arts. The inspiration for this new republican society, which was open to artists of all social ranks, was Jacques-Louis David (1748–1825), the greatest painter of his generation. David presided over a revival of classicism in French painting, employing Greek and Roman motifs and exhibiting rationalism and lack of sentiment in his work.

Museums and Monuments

The day after the abolition of the monarchy the National Assembly created a Commission of the Museum, whose function was "to collect paintings, statues and other precious objects from the crown possessions" as well as from the churches and houses of the émigrés. The museum was to be located in the Louvre, a royal palace that also served as an art gallery. This museum was intended to be entirely historical and to have no relevance to contemporary politics.

The revolutionaries had more respect for these works of art than for the monuments honoring their former monarchs. In August 1793 the National Convention ordered the destruction of all the tombs of past French kings. One by one the tombs were opened and the corpses, embalmed in lead, were removed. The corpses were either left to disintegrate in the atmosphere or dragged unceremoniously to the cemetery, where they were thrown into the common pit. This disrespectful treatment of the remains of France's former kings was intended to erase the memory of monarchy.

THE CREATION OF A NEW POLITICAL CULTURE

As the state was taking over and adapting the cultural institutions of the Old Regime, revolutionaries engaged in a much bolder and original undertaking: the production of a new, revolutionary political culture. Its sole purpose was to legitimate and glorify the new regime. It symbolized the political values of that regime: liberty, equality, and fraternity in 1789 and republicanism after 1792. This culture was almost entirely political; all forms of cultural expression were subordinated to the realization of a pressing political agenda.

One of the main characteristics of this culture was that it was popular—it was shared by the entire populace, not simply by a small upper-class or literate elite. The fundamental political doctrine of the revolution was popular sovereignty°: the claim that the people were the highest political power in the state. The political culture that emerged—the textual and literary symbols spoken, written, and drawn to reflect this sovereignty of the people—would become the property of the entire population. The very words used to identify revolutionary institutions, such as the National Assembly and the National Guard, formed the texture of this new political culture.

The common people who embraced this new culture most enthusiastically were the *sans-culottes*—the radical shopkeepers, artisans, and laborers of Paris. The dress of these people influenced a change in fashion among the wealthier segments of society. A simple jacket replaced the ruffled coat worn by members of the upper classes, their powdered wigs gave way to natural hair, and they too now wore long trousers. They also donned the red liberty cap, to which a tricolor cockade was affixed. The tricolor, which combined the red and blue colors of Paris with the white symbol of the Bourbon monarchy, identified the adherents of the revolution.

Pamphlets, newspapers, brochures, and posters all promoted a distinctive revolutionary language, which became one of the permanent legacies of the revolution. Political leaders used the same rhetoric in their political speeches. *Sans-culottes* sang satirical songs and ballads, many of them to the same tunes well known in the Old Regime. The most popular of the songs of the revolutionary period was the *Marseillaise,* first sung by soldiers preparing for battle against the Austrians but soon adopted by the civilian population and sung at political gatherings.

The new revolutionary culture was emphatically secular. In its most extreme form, it was blatantly anti-Christian. In September 1793 the radical Jacobin and former priest Joseph Fouché inaugurated a program of de-Christianization°. Under his leadership, radical Jacobins closed churches and removed religious symbols such as crosses from cemeteries and public venues. In an effort to establish a purely civic religion, they forbade the public practice of religion and renamed churches "temples of reason."

This de-Christianization campaign became the official policy of the Paris Commune, and the National Convention issued a few edicts to enforce it. The program, however, did not win widespread support, and even some Jacobins claimed that in rejecting Christianity it had undermined a belief in God and the afterlife. In 1794 Robespierre attempted to modify the excesses of de-Christianization by launching the Cult of the Supreme Being. He promoted a series of festivals acknowledging the existence of a deity and the immortality of the soul. This new cult paid lip service to traditional religious beliefs, but it still served the secular purpose of promoting republican virtue.

The new secular revolutionary culture incorporated many elements of Christian culture. The new pageants and festivals designed to promote a civic religion were modeled on traditional Catholic processions. Revolutionaries co-opted some of the religious holy days for their own purposes. Meetings of revolutionaries often took on the atmosphere of religious revivals, as men and women wept in response to orations. Secular catechisms taught young children the virtues of republicanism in the same way that they had instructed them in Christian doctrine during the Old Regime.

In order to destroy all vestiges of the Old Regime, the government also instituted a new calendar in October 1793. The dates on the calendar began with September 22, 1792, the day the Republic was established. That became the first day of the year I, while the weeks now had ten days instead of seven. The calendar remained in effect until the last day of 1805.

The new revolutionary culture was disseminated widely, but it was always contested. Royalists trampled on the tricolor cockade and refused to adopt the new style of dress. This resistance from counterrevolutionary forces guaranteed that when the revolution was reversed, much of the new political culture would disappear. Like the political revolution, however, some elements of revolutionary culture, especially the rhetoric of the revolutionary press, could never be suppressed. Not only did these cultural innovations inspire revolutionaries for the next hundred years, but they also became part of the mainstream of Western civilization.

CULTURAL UNIFORMITY

One of the most striking features of the new revolutionary culture was its concern for standardization and simplicity. The division of France into *départements*, all roughly equal in size, population, and wealth, serves as one manifestation of this compulsion. The adoption of the metric system and the decimal system and the plan to establish one body of French law for the entire country, eventually brought to fruition by Napoleon, reflected the same impulse. So too did the efforts begun during the Terror to make French the official language in regions of the country that spoke Breton, Occitan, Basque, or other regional dialects.

The main source of this drive toward cultural uniformity was the desire to build a new French nation composed of equal citizens. Linguistic, legal, or administrative diversity only made the realization of that program more difficult. The quest for cultural and political standardization did not, however, originate during the revolution. Many of the projects of the 1790s, especially the desire to establish standard weights and measures, had begun during the Old Regime. They were often the product of the rationalism of the Enlightenment, which, as we have seen in Chapter 18, sought to make society conform to the operation of universal laws.

The Napoleonic Era, 1799–1815

The coup d'état on November 9, 1799, marked a turning point in the political history of France. The Consulate ushered in a period of authoritarian rule. Liberty was restricted in the interest of order; republicanism gave way to dictatorship. The French Revolution had apparently run its course. But the period between 1799 and 1815 was also a time of considerable innovation, especially in the realm of politics and diplomacy. Those innovations were primarily the work of one man, Napoleon Bonaparte, who controlled the French government for the next fifteen years.

NAPOLEON'S RISE TO POWER

Napoleon Bonaparte was born on the Mediterranean island of Corsica, which in 1770 came under French control. In 1779 the young Napoleon, whose native language was Corsican, received an appointment to a French military school. Displaying a natural gift for military science, he won a position in the artillery section of the national military academy in Paris.

The events of the revolution made possible Napoleon's rapid ascent to military prominence and political power. When the revolution broke out, Napoleon returned to Corsica, where he organized the National Guard. As the revolution became more radical he became a Jacobin, and he was commissioned to attack federalist and royalist positions in the south of France. In 1796 Napoleon was given command of the Army of Italy, and in 1799 he led the successful coup against the Directory and became First Consul.

Napoleon's personality was ideally suited to the acquisition and maintenance of political power. A man of unparalleled ambition, he was driven by an extraordinarily high assessment of his abilities. After one of his military victories he wrote, "I realized I was a superior being and conceived the ambition of performing great things." To the pursuit of his destiny he harnessed a determined and a stubborn will. Authoritarian by nature, he used intimidation as well as paternal concern to cultivate the loyalty of his subordinates. In an age dominated by high-minded causes, he exhibited an instinctive distrust of ideology and the doctrinaire pronouncements of philosophes like Rousseau. Napoleon's military training led him to take a pragmatic, disciplined approach to politics, in which he always sought the most effective means to the desired end.

Napoleon's acquisition of power was systematic and shrewd. Playing on the need for a strong leader, and using the army he controlled as his main political tool, he maneuvered himself into the position of First Consul in 1799. In 1802 he became consul for life, and two years later he crowned himself emperor of the French and his wife Josephine empress. The title of emperor traditionally denoted the height of monarchical power. It identified a ruler who not only ruled more than one kingdom or state but also did not share power with any other political authority.

NAPOLEON AND THE REVOLUTION

What was the relationship between Napoleon's rule and the French Revolution? Did Napoleon consolidate the gains of the revolution or destroy them? Napoleon always thought of himself as the heir of the revolution rather than its undertaker. He used the radical vocabulary of the revolution to characterize his domestic programs and his military campaigns. He presented himself as the ally of the common man against entrenched aristocratic privilege. He proclaimed a love for the French people and gave his support to the doctrine of popular sovereignty. He often referred to the rulers of other European countries as tyrants and presented himself as the liberator of their subjects.

This view of Napoleon as a true revolutionary, however, ignores the fact that his commitment to liberty was almost entirely rhetorical. Behind the appeals to the slogans of the revolution lurked an authoritarian will that was far stronger than that of any eighteenth-century absolute monarch. He used the language of liberty and democracy to disguise a thoroughgoing authoritarianism, just as he used the rhetoric of republicanism to legitimize his own dictatorial regime. When the empire was established he told his troops that they had the freedom to vote for or against the new form of government but then told them that if they voted against it, they would be shot.

A stronger case can be made for Napoleon's egalitarianism. He spoke of equality of opportunity. He supported the equality of all Frenchmen (but not Frenchwomen) before the law. This egalitarianism laid the foundation for the support he received from peasants, soldiers, and workers. It might be said that he brought both equality and political stability to France in exchange for political liberty.

Historians note two other ways Napoleon might be considered the heir of the revolution. The first is that he continued the centralization and growth of state power and the rational organization of the government that had begun in 1789. Each of the successive regimes between 1789 and 1815, even the Directory, had contributed to this pattern of state building, and Napoleon's contribution was monumental. The second was his continuation and extension of France's military mission to export the revolution to its European neighbors. The two achievements are related to each other, since it was the war effort that necessitated the further growth and centralization of state power.

NAPOLEON AND THE FRENCH STATE

Once Napoleon had gained effective control of the French state, he set about the task of strengthening it, making it more efficient, highly organized, and powerful. He settled the long struggle between Church and state, laid down an entirely new law code that imposed legal uniformity on the entire country, and made the civil bureaucracy more centralized, uniform, and efficient. All of this was done with the intention of making the state an effective instrument of social and political control.

Concordat with the Papacy

Napoleon's first contribution to the development of the French state, achieved during the Consulate, was to bring about a resolution of the bitter struggle between Church and state. A committed secularist, Napoleon was determined to bring the Church under the direct control of the state. This had been the main purpose of the Civil Constitution of the Clergy of 1790. Napoleon also realized, however, that this policy had divided the clergy between those who had taken an oath to the nation and those who had refused. Clerical independence had also become a major rallying cry of royalists against the new regime, thereby threatening the stability of the country.

Napoleon's solution to this problem was to reach an agreement with the Church that would satisfy clerics and royalists yet not deprive the state of its authority over the Church. The death of Pope Pius VI (r. 1775–1799), the implacable foe of the revolution, gave Napoleon the opportunity to address this problem. The new pope, Pius VII (r. 1800–1823), who was more sympathetic to liberal causes, was eager to come to terms with the French government. The Concordat, which Napoleon and Pius agreed to in 1801, gave something to both sides, although Napoleon gained more than he conceded. The pope agreed that all the clergy who refused to swear their loyalty to the nation would resign their posts. The pope would appoint new bishops, but only with the prior approval of Napoleon. The state would pay all clerical salaries, and the Church would abandon any claims it still had to the ecclesiastical lands seized by the state at the beginning of the revolution. These provisions represented formidable concessions to state power, but the pope did manage to secure a statement that Roman Catholicism was the religion of the majority of citizens, and Napoleon agreed to scrap the secular calendar introduced in 1793, thereby restoring Sundays and holy days.

The Civil Code

Napoleon's most enduring achievement in the realm of state building was the promulgation of a new legal code, the Civil Code of 1804, later known as the Napoleonic Code°. This body of law met a long-standing set of demands to reform the confusing and irregular body of French law. Ever since the Middle Ages, France had been governed by a multiplicity of laws. Efforts to produce a single, authoritative written code for all French people began during the revolution, but Napoleon completed the project and published the code.

The Civil Code, which consisted of more than 2,000 articles, reflected the values that were ascendant in Napoleonic French society. The ideals of the revolution were enshrined in the articles guaranteeing the rights of private property, the equality of all people before the law, and freedom of religion. The values it promoted, however, did not include the equality of the sexes. It granted men control of all family property. Women could not buy or sell property without the consent of their husbands. Only adult men could witness legal documents. All male heirs were entitled to inherit equal shares of a family estate, but daughters were excluded from the settlement.

The Civil Code had an impact on the law of several countries outside France. It became the basis for the codification of the laws of Switzerland, northern Italy, and the Netherlands, and it served as a model for the numerous codes that were compiled in the German territories controlled by France during the Napoleonic period. The Napoleonic Code also influenced the law of French-speaking North America, including the civil law of the state of Louisiana, which bears signs of its influence even today.

Administrative Centralization

Napoleon laid the foundation of modern French civil administration, which acquired the characteristics of rational organization, uniformity, and centralization. All power emanated from Paris, where Napoleon presided over a Council of State. This body consisted of his main ministers, who handled all matters of finance, domestic affairs, and war and oversaw a vast bureaucracy of salaried, trained officials. The central government also exercised direct control over the provinces, which lost the local privileges they had possessed under the Old Regime.

The men who served in the government of the French Empire belonged to one of two elaborate, hierarchical institutions: the civil bureaucracy and the army officer corps. The two were closely related, since the main purpose of the administrative bureaucracy was to prepare for and sustain the war effort. Both institutions were organized hierarchically, and those who held positions in them were trained and salaried. Appointment and promotion were based primarily on talent rather than birth.

The idea of "a career open to all talents," as Napoleon described it, ran counter to the tradition of noble privilege. This was one of the achievements of the revolution that Napoleon perpetuated during the empire. The new system did not amount to a pure meritocracy, in which advancement is determined solely by ability and performance, since many appointments were made or influenced by Napoleon

himself on the basis of friendship or kinship. The system did, however, allow people from the ranks of the bourgeoisie to achieve rapid upward social mobility.

NAPOLEON, THE EMPIRE, AND EUROPE

Closely related to Napoleon's efforts to build the French state was his creation of a massive European empire. The empire was the product of a series of military victories against the armies of Austria, Prussia, Russia, and Spain between 1797 and 1809. By the latter date France controlled, either directly or indirectly, the Dutch Republic, the Austrian Netherlands, Italy, Spain, and large parts of Germany and Poland. The instrument of these victories was the massive citizen army that Napoleon was able to assemble. Building on the *levée en masse* of 1793, which he supplemented with soldiers from the countries he conquered, Napoleon had more than one million men under arms by 1812.

Victories against Austria and Prussia in 1797 and against Austria in 1800 paved the way to French dominance of Europe. After concluding peace with Britain in 1802, Napoleon reorganized the countries that bordered on France's eastern and southeastern boundaries. In Italy he named himself the president of the newly established Cisalpine Republic, and he transformed the cantons of Switzerland into the Helvetic Republic.

Napoleon was far less successful at sea than on land. With no real experience in naval warfare, he could not match the dominance of the British navy, which retained its mastery of the seas throughout the entire revolutionary period. The most significant French naval defeat came in 1805, as Napoleon was preparing for an invasion of Britain. The British navy, under the command of the diminutive, one-eyed Admiral Horatio Nelson, won one of the most decisive battles in the history of naval warfare off the Cape of Trafalgar near Gibraltar. The British destroyed or captured half the French and Spanish ships that were preparing for an invasion of Britain.

The monumental naval defeat at Trafalgar did not prevent Napoleon from continuing his wars of conquest in central Europe. In October 1805 he defeated an Austrian army at Ulm, and in December of that year he overwhelmed the combined forces of Austria and Russia at Austerlitz. A defeat of Prussian forces at Jena and Auerstadt in 1806 gave him the opportunity to carve the new German kingdom of Westphalia out of Prussian territory in the Rhineland. In the East he created the duchy of Warsaw out of Polish lands controlled by Prussia. By 1807, in the words of one historian, Napoleon had "only allies and victims" on the Continent (see Map 19.1).

Napoleon inserted the last piece in this imperial puzzle by invading and occupying the kingdom of Spain in 1807. This campaign began as an effort to crush Portugal, the ally

■ Map 19.1 The Empire of Napoleon in 1812

By establishing dependent states in Spain, Italy, Germany, and Poland, France controlled far more territory than the areas technically within the French Empire.

of Britain. In May 1808, as French armies marched through Spain en route to Lisbon, the Portuguese capital, a popular insurrection against Spanish rule occurred in Madrid. This spontaneous revolt led to the abdication of King Charles IV and the succession of his son Ferdinand VII. Sensing that he could easily add one more territory to his list of conquests, Napoleon forced Ferdinand to abdicate and summoned his own brother, Joseph Bonaparte, who was then ruling the dependent kingdom of Naples, to become king of Spain.

Joseph instituted some reforms in Spain, but the abolition of the Spanish Inquisition and the closing of two-thirds of the Spanish convents triggered a visceral reaction from the Spanish clergy and the general populace. Fighting for Church and king, small bands of local guerillas subjected French forces to intermittent and effective sabotage. An invasion by British forces under the command of Arthur Wellesley, later the Duke of Wellington (1769–1852), in what has become known as the Peninsula War (1808–1813), strengthened Spanish and Portuguese resistance.

The reception of the French in Spain revealed that the export of revolution, which had begun with the French armies

of 1792, was a double-edged sword. The overthrow of authoritarian regimes in other European states won the support of progressive, capitalist, and anticlerical forces in those countries, but it also triggered deep resentment against French rule. The ideology of nationalism in Germany and Italy arose more because of a reaction against French rule than because the armies of France had tried to stimulate it.

THE DOWNFALL OF NAPOLEON

The turning point in Napoleon's personal fortunes and those of his empire came in 1810, when for the first time during his rule dissent became widespread. Despite the most stringent efforts at censorship, royalist and Jacobin literature poured off the presses. The number of military deserters and those evading conscription increased. When Napoleon annexed the Papal States, Pope Pius VII, who had negotiated the Concordat of 1801, excommunicated him.

Dissent at home had the effect of driving the megalomaniacal emperor to seek more glory and further conquests. In this frame of mind Napoleon made the ill-advised decision to invade Russia. The problem with a Russian invasion was that it stretched Napoleon's lines of communication too far and his resources too thin. Even before the invasion it was becoming increasingly difficult to feed, equip, and train the huge army he had assembled. The Grand Army that crossed from Poland into Russia in 1812 was not the efficient military force that Napoleon had commanded in the early years of the empire. Many of his best soldiers were fighting in the guerilla war in Spain. Casualties and desertions had forced Napoleon to call up new recruits who were not properly trained. Half the army, moreover, had been recruited from the population of conquered countries, making their loyalty to Napoleon uncertain.

The tactics of the Russians contributed to the failure of the invasion. Instead of engaging the Grand Army in combat, the Russian army kept retreating, pulling Napoleon further east toward Moscow. When Napoleon reached Moscow he found it deserted, and fires deliberately set by Muscovites had destroyed more than two-thirds of the city. Facing the onset of a dreaded Russian winter and rapidly diminishing supplies, Napoleon began the long retreat back to France. Skirmishes with Russians along the way conspired with the cold and hunger to destroy his army. During the entire Russian campaign his army lost a total of 380,000 men to death, imprisonment, or desertion.

Not to be discouraged, Napoleon soon began preparing for further conquests. Once again his enemies formed a coalition against him, pledging to restore the independence of the countries that had become his satellites or dependents. In 1813 allied forces inflicted a crushing defeat on him in the Battle of the Nations at Leipzig, Austrian troops defeated the French in northern Italy, and the British finally drove them out of Spain. As a result of these defeats, Napoleon's army was pushed back into France. A massive allied force advanced into Paris and occupied the city. Napoleon abdicated on April 6, 1814, and the allies promptly exiled him to the Mediterranean island of Elba.

This course of events led to the restoration of the Bourbon monarchy. By the terms of the first Treaty of Paris of May 1814, the allies restored the brother of Louis XVI, the Count of Provence, to the French throne as Louis XVIII (r. 1814–1824). Louis was an implacable foe of the revolution, and much of what he did was intended to undermine its achievements. The white Bourbon flag replaced the revolutionary tricolor. Catholicism was once again recognized as the state religion. Nonetheless, Louis accepted a Constitutional Charter that incorporated many of the

■ **Francisco Goya, *The Third of May, 1808***
This painting of the suppression of the popular revolt in Madrid in 1808 captures the brutality of the French occupation of Spain. A French unit executes Spanish citizens, including a monk in the foreground. Goya was a figure of the Enlightenment and a Spanish patriot.

changes made between 1789 and 1791. Representative government, with a relatively limited franchise, replaced the absolutism of the Old Regime. Equality before the law, freedom of religion, and freedom of expression were all reaffirmed. France had experienced a counterrevolution in 1814, but some of the political achievements of the previous twenty-five years were preserved.

Despite his disgrace and exile, Napoleon still commanded loyalty from his troops and from large segments of the population. The strength of his appeal became apparent in March 1815, when Napoleon escaped from Elba and landed in southern France. Promising to rid the country of the exiled royalists who had returned and to save the revolutionary cause that he claimed had been abandoned, he won over peasants, workers, and soldiers. Regiment after regiment joined him as he marched toward Paris. By the time he arrived, Louis XVIII had gone into exile once again, and Napoleon found himself back in power.

But not for long. The allied European powers quickly assembled yet another coalition. Napoleon marched an army of 200,000 men into the Austrian Netherlands, where the allies responded by amassing 700,000 troops. Near the small village of Waterloo, south of Brussels, British and Prussian forces inflicted a devastating defeat on the French army, which lost 28,000 men and went into a full-scale re-treat. Captured in the battle, Napoleon abdicated once again. He was exiled to the remote South Atlantic island of St. Helena, from which escape was impossible. He died there in 1821.

Even before the battle of Waterloo, the major powers of Europe had gathered in Vienna to redraw the boundaries of the European states that had been created, dismembered, or transformed during the preceding twenty-five years (see Map 19.2). Under the leadership of the Austrian foreign minister, Prince Clemens von Metternich (1773–1859), this conference, known as the Congress of Vienna°, worked out a settlement that was intended to preserve the balance of power in Europe and at the same time uphold the principle of dynastic legitimacy. By the terms of a separate Treaty of Paris (the second in two years) the boundaries of France were scaled back to what they had been in 1790, before it had begun its wars of expansion. To create a buffer state on the northern boundary of France, the Congress annexed the Austrian Netherlands to the Dutch Republic, which now became the kingdom of the Netherlands. In place of the defunct Holy Roman Empire, the Congress established a new German Confederation, a loose coalition of thirty-nine separate territories. The five major powers that had drawn this new map of Europe—Britain, Austria, Prussia, Russia, and France—agreed to meet annually to prevent any one country, especially France but also Russia, from achieving military dominance of the European Continent.

■ **Map 19.2 Europe After the Congress of Vienna, 1815**

The four most important territorial changes that took place in 1815 were the scaling back of the boundaries of France to their status in 1790, the Austrian acquisition of territory in western and northeastern Italy, the establishment of the new kingdom of the Netherlands, and the formation of the new German Confederation.

Europe After Congress of Vienna, 1815

- France
- Austrian empire
- Russian empire
- German states
- Prussia
- Sardinia
- Boundary of German Confederation

0   300 km
0   300 mi

The Legacy of the French Revolution

·······················■·······························

With the conclusion of the Congress of Vienna a tumultuous period of European and Western history finally came to an end. Not only had France experienced a revolution, but every country in Europe and America had felt its effects. Governments were toppled in countries as far apart as Poland and Peru. Added to this turbulence was the experience of incessant warfare. France was at war for more than twenty years during the period of the Republic and the empire, and it had brought almost all European powers into the struggle. With armies constantly in need of provisions and supplies, high taxation, galloping inflation, and food shortages inflicted economic hardship on a large portion of the European population.

The cost of all this instability and warfare in terms of human life is staggering. Within the space of one generation almost two million European soldiers were killed in action, wasted by disease, or starved or frozen to death. In France alone just under 500,000 soldiers died during the revolutionary wars of 1792–1802 and another 916,000 during the wars of the empire. Internal political disturbances took the lives of hundreds of thousands of civilians from all ranks of society, not only in France but throughout Europe. The violence was fed at all levels by unprecedented fears of internal and external subversion. Government officials, collaborators, counterrevolutionaries, and imagined enemies of the state were all executed. This spate of violence and death—much of it in the name of liberty—was inflicted almost entirely by the state or its enemies.

What was achieved at this extraordinary price? How did the France of 1815 differ from the France of 1788? What on balance had changed? For many years historians, especially those who believed that economic forces determined the course of history, claimed that as a result of the revolution the bourgeoisie, composed of merchants, manufacturers, and other commoners of substantial wealth, had replaced the nobility as the dominant social and political class in the country.

This assessment can no longer be sustained. The nobility certainly lost many of their privileges in 1789, and many of them went into exile during the revolutionary period; however, the position they had in French society in 1815 did not differ greatly from what it had been under the Old Regime. In both periods there was considerable blurring of the distinctions between nobility and bourgeoisie. Nor did the revolutionary period witness the emergence of a new class of industrial entrepreneurs. The only group who definitely profited from the revolution in the long run were men of property, regardless of which so-cial category or "class" they may have belonged to. Men of property emerged triumphant in the Directory, found favor during the Napoleonic period, and became the most important members of political society after the monarchy was restored.

It would be difficult to argue that *women* of any social rank benefited from the revolution. During the early years of the revolution, women participated actively in public life. They were involved in many demonstrations in Paris, including the storming of the Bastille and the march to Versailles to pressure the king to move to Paris. Women as well as men filled the ranks of the *sans-culottes*, and women donned their own female version of nonaristocratic dress. During the early years of the revolution, many women joined patriotic clubs, such as the Club of Knitters or the unisex Fraternal Society of Patriots of Both Sexes. In 1790 the Marquis de Condorcet had published *On the Admission of Women to the Rights of Citizenship,* and the following year Olympe de Gouges published *The Rights of Women,* in which she called for the granting of women's equal rights. Both of these advocates of women's rights had been influenced by Enlightenment thought, as we have discussed in Chapter 18.

The goal advanced by Condorcet and de Gouges was not to be realized. The radical Jacobins dealt it a terrible setback when they banned all women's clubs and societies on the grounds that their participation in public life would be harmful to the institution of the family. This action, coupled with the imprisonment and death of both de Gouges and Condorcet during the Terror, signaled an end to the extensive participation of women in political life, which had begun during the eighteenth century, especially in the salons. During the nineteenth century women were generally considered to occupy a separate sphere of activity from that of men. They were expected to exercise influence in the private sphere of the home, but not in the public sphere of politics. As we shall discuss in Chapter 20, the changes wrought by the Industrial Revolution reinforced this segregation of men and women by excluding many married women from the workforce.

The permanent legacy of the French Revolution lies in the realm of politics. First, the period from 1789 to 1815 triggered an enormous growth in the competence and power of the state. This was a trend that had begun before the revolution, but the desire of the revolutionaries to transform every aspect of human life in the service of the revolution, coupled with the necessity of utilizing all the country's resources in the war effort, gave the state more control over the everyday life of its citizens than ever before. Fifteen years of Napoleonic rule only accentuated this trend, and after 1815 many of those powers remained with the government.

An even more significant and permanent achievement of the French Revolution was the promotion of the doctrine of popular sovereignty. The belief that the people constituted the highest political authority in the state be-came so entrenched during the revolution that it could never be completely suppressed, either in France or in the other countries of Europe. Napoleon recognized its power when he asked the people to approve political changes he had already made by his own authority. He also arranged for such plebiscites to secure approval of the new states he had set up in Europe. After the restoration of the monarchy the doctrine of popular sovereignty was promoted mainly by the press, which continued to employ the new revolutionary rhetoric to keep alive the high ideals and aspirations of the revolution. The doctrine also contributed to the formation of two nineteenth-century ideologies, liberalism and nationalism, which will be discussed in Chapter 21.

The third permanent political change was the active participation of the citizens in the political life of the nation. This participation had been cultivated during the early years of the revolution, and it had been accompanied by the creation of a new political culture. Much of that culture was suppressed during the Napoleonic period, but the actual habit of participating in politics was not. The franchise was gradually expanded in Europe during the nineteenth century. The press spread political ideas to a large segment of the population. People from all walks of life participated in marches, processions, and demonstrations. All of this followed from the acceptance of the French revolutionary doctrine that the people are sovereign and have a right therefore to participate in the political life of the state.

CONCLUSION

The French Revolution and Western Civilization

The French Revolution was a central event in the history of the West. It began as an internal French affair, reflecting the social and political tensions of the Old Regime, but it soon became a turning point in European and Western history. Proclamations of the natural rights of humanity gave the ideals of the revolution widespread appeal, and a period of protracted warfare succeeded in disseminating those ideals outside the boundaries of France.

Underlying the export of French revolutionary ideology was the belief that France had become the standard-bearer of Western civilization. French people believed they were *la grande nation*, the country that had reached the highest level of political and social organization. They did not believe they had acquired this exalted status by inheritance. Unlike the English revolutionaries of the seventeenth century, they did not claim that they were the heirs of a medieval constitution. French republicans of the 1790s attributed none of their national preeminence to the monarchy, whose memory they took drastic steps to erase. They considered the secular political culture that emerged during the French Revolution to be an entirely novel development.

The export of French revolutionary political culture during the Republic and the empire brought about widespread changes in the established order. Regimes were toppled, French puppets acquired political power, boundaries of states were completely redrawn, and traditional authorities were challenged. Liberal reforms were enacted, new constitutions were written, and new law codes were promulgated. The Europe of 1815 could not be mistaken for the Europe of 1789.

The ideas of the French Revolution, like those of the Enlightenment that had helped to inspire them, did not go unchallenged. From the very early years of the revolution they encountered determined opposition, both in France and abroad. As the revolution lost its appeal in France, the forces of conservatism and reaction gathered strength. At the end of the Napoleonic period, the Congress of Vienna took steps to restore the legitimate rulers of European states and to prevent revolution from recurring. It appeared that the revolution would be completely reversed, but that was not the case. The ideas born of the revolution would continue to inspire demands for political reform in Europe during the nineteenth century, and those demands, just like those in the 1790s, would meet with fierce resistance.

Suggestions for Further Reading

For a comprehensive list of suggested readings, please go to www.ablongman.com/levackconcise/chapter19

Blanning, T. C. W. *The French Revolutionary Wars 1787–1802.* 1996. An authoritative political and military narrative that assesses the impact of the wars on French politics.

Chartier, Roger. *The Cultural Origins of the French Revolution.* 1991. Explores the connections between the culture of the Enlightenment and the cultural transformations of the revolutionary period.

Cobban, Alfred. *The Social Interpretation of the French Revolution.* 1971. Challenges the Marxist interpretation of the causes and effects of the revolution.

Doyle, William. *The Oxford History of the French Revolution.* 1989. An excellent synthesis.

Ellis, Geoffrey. *Napoleon.* 1997. A study of the nature and mechanics of Napoleon's power and an analysis of his imperial policy.

Furet, François. *The French Revolution, 1770–1814.* 1992. A provocative narrative that sees Napoleon as the architect of a second, authoritarian revolution that reversed the gains of the first.

Hardman, John. *Louis XVI: The Silent King.* 2000. A reassessment of the king that mixes sympathy with criticism.

Higgonnet, Patrice. *Goodness Beyond Virtue: Jacobins During the French Revolution.* 1998. Explores the contradictions of Jacobin ideology and its descent into the Terror.

Hunt, Lynn. *Politics, Culture and Class in the French Revolution.* 1984. Analyzes the formation of a revolutionary political culture.

Kennedy, Emmet. *The Culture of the French Revolution.* 1989. A comprehensive study of all cultural developments before and during the revolution.

Landes, Joan B. *Women and the Public Sphere in the Age of the French Revolution.* 1988. Explores how the new political culture of the revolution changed the position of women in society.

Lefebvre, Georges. *The Great Fear of 1789: Rural Panic in Revolutionary France.* 1973. Shows the importance of the rural unrest of July 1793 that provided the backdrop of the legislation of August 1789.

Schama, Simon. *Citizens: A Chronicle of the French Revolution.* 1989. Depicts the tragic unraveling of a vision of liberty and happiness into a scenario of hunger, anger, violence, and death.

The Industrial Revolution, 1760–1850

I N 1842 A 17-YEAR-OLD GIRL, PATIENCE KERSHAW, TESTIFIED BEFORE A BRITISH PARliamentary committee regarding the practice of employing children and women in the nation's mines. When the girl made her appearance, the members of the committee observed that she was "an ignorant, filthy, ragged, and deplorable-looking object, such as one of uncivilized natives of the prairies would be shocked to look upon." Patience, who had never been to school and could not read or write, told the committee that she was one of ten children, all of whom had at one time worked in the coal mines, although three of her sisters now worked in a textile mill. She went to the pit at five in the morning and came out at five at night. Her job in the mines was to hurry coal, that is, to pull carts of coal through the narrow tunnels of the mine. Each cart weighed 300 pounds, and every day she hauled eleven of them one mile. The carts were attached to her head and shoulders by a chain and belt, and the pressure of the cart had worn a bald spot on her head. Patience hurried coal for twelve hours straight, not taking any time for her midday meal, which she ate as she worked. While she was working, the men and boys who dug the coal and put it in the carts would often beat her and take sexual liberties with her. Patience told the committee, "I am the only girl in the pit; there are about 20 boys and 15 men. All the men are naked. I would rather work in a mill than a coal pit."

Patience Kershaw was one of the human casualties of an extraordinary development that historians usually refer to as the Industrial Revolution. This process, which brought about a fundamental transformation of human life, involved the extensive use of machinery in the production of goods. Much of that machinery was driven by steam engines, which required coal to produce the steam. Coal mining itself became a major industry, and the men who owned and operated the mines tried to hire workers, many of them children, at the lowest

Exhibit of Machinery at the Crystal Palace Exhibition in London in 1851: During the Industrial Revolution the manufacture of heavy machinery itself became an industry.

possible wage. It was this desire to maximize profits that led to the employment, physical hardship, and abuse of girls like Patience Kershaw.

The story of the Industrial Revolution cannot be told solely in terms of the exploitation of child or even adult workers. Many of its effects can be described in positive or at least morally neutral terms. The Industrial Revolution resulted in a staggering increase in the volume and range of products made available to consumers, from machine-produced clothing to household utensils. It made possible unprecedented and sustained economic growth. The Industrial Revolution facilitated the rapid transportation of passengers as well as goods across large expanses of territory, mainly on the railroads that were constructed in all industrialized countries. It brought about a new awareness of the position of workers in the economic system, and it unleashed powerful political forces intended to improve the lot of these workers.

The Industrial Revolution played a crucial role in redefining and reshaping the West. Until the late nineteenth century industrialization took place only in Western nations. During that century "the West" gradually became identified with those countries that had industrial economies. When some non-Western countries introduced mechanized industry in the twentieth century, largely in imitation of Western example, the geographical boundaries of the West underwent a significant alteration.

In this chapter we shall consider five basic questions:

■ To what economic and social developments does the term Industrial Revolution refer?
■ What social and economic changes made industrial development possible?
■ How did industrialization spread from Great Britain to the European continent and America?
■ What were the economic, social, and cultural effects of the Industrial Revolution?
■ What was the relationship between the growth of industry and Britain's dominance in trade and imperial strength during the middle years of the nineteenth century?

The Nature of the Industrial Revolution

The Industrial Revolution was a series of economic and social changes that took place in Great Britain during the late eighteenth and early nineteenth centuries and on the European continent and in the United States after 1815. The revolution consisted of four closely

---

CHRONOLOGY

Technological Innovations of the Industrial Revolution

1763	James Watts's rotative steam engine
1767	James Hargreaves's spinning jenny
1769	Richard Arkwright's water frame
1779	Samuel Crompton's mule
1787	Edmund Cartwright's power loom
1815	George Stephenson's steam locomotive
1846	Elias Howe's sewing machine

---

related developments: the introduction of new industrial technology, the utilization of mineral sources of energy, the concentration of labor in factories, and the development of new methods of transportation.

NEW INDUSTRIAL TECHNOLOGY

The Industrial Revolution ushered in the machine age, and to this day machines are the most striking feature of modern industrial economies. In the late eighteenth century such machines were novelties, but their numbers increased dramatically in the early nineteenth century. Machines were introduced in the textile, iron, printing, papermaking, and engineering industries and were used in every stage of manufacture. Machines extracted minerals that were used as either raw materials or sources of energy, transported those materials to the factories, saved time and labor in the actual manufacturing of commodities, and carried the finished products to market.

The most significant of the new machines were those used for spinning and weaving in the textile industry and the steam engine.

Textile Machinery

Until the late eighteenth century, the production of textiles throughout Europe, which involved both the spinning of yarn and the weaving of cloth, was done entirely by hand, on spinning wheels and hand looms respectively. This was the practice for wool, which was the main textile produced in Europe during the early modern period, as well as for a new material, cotton, which became immensely popular in the early eighteenth century, mainly because of its greater comfort. The demand for cotton yarn was greater than the quantities spinners could supply. To meet this demand a British inventor, James Hargreaves, in 1767 constructed a new machine, the spinning jenny, which greatly increased the amount of cotton yarn that could be spun and thus made available for weaving.

The spinning of yarn on the jenny required a stronger warp, the yarn that ran lengthwise on a loom. A power-driven machine, the water frame, introduced by the barber and wigmaker Richard Arkwright in 1769, made the production of this stronger warp possible. In 1779 Samuel Crompton, using tools he had purchased with his earnings as a fiddle player at a local theater, combined the jenny and the frame in one machine, called the mule. The mule, which could spin as much as 300 times the amount of yarn produced by one spinning wheel, became the main spinning machine of the early Industrial Revolution.

The tremendous success of the mule eventually produced more yarn than the weavers could handle on their hand looms. Edmund Cartwright, an Oxford-educated clergyman, supported by monies from his heiress wife, addressed that need with the invention of the power loom in 1787. The power loom, like the spinning jenny, the water frame, and the mule, met a specific need within the industry. It also gave the producer a competitive advantage by saving time, reducing the cost of labor, and increasing production. The net effect of all these machines was the production of more than 200 times as much cotton cloth in 1850 as in 1780.

The Steam Engine

The steam engine was even more important than the new textile machinery since it was used in almost every stage of the productive process, including the operation of textile machinery itself. The steam engine was invented by a Scottish engineer, James Watt, in 1763. It represented an improvement over the engine invented by Thomas Newcomen in 1709, which produced steam in a heated cylinder but was terribly slow and expensive to operate. Watt created a separate chamber where the steam could be condensed without affecting the heat of the cylinder. The result was a more efficient and cost-effective machine that could provide more power than any other source.

The steam engine soon became the workhorse of the Industrial Revolution. It raised minerals from mines and provided the intense blast of heat that was necessary to re-smelt pig iron into cast iron, which in turn was used to make industrial machinery, buildings, bridges, locomotives, and ships. Once the engine was equipped with a rotating device, it was used to drive the factory machinery in the textile mills, and it eventually powered the railroad locomotives that carried industrial goods to market.

Mineral Sources of Energy

Until the late eighteenth century, most economic activity, including the transportation of goods, was powered by either humans or beasts. Either people tilled the soil them-

selves, using a spade, or they yoked oxen to pull a plow. Either they carried materials and goods on their backs or they used horses to transport them. In either case the energy for these tasks came ultimately from organic sources, the food that was needed to feed farmers or their animals. If workers needed heat, they had to burn an organic material, wood or charcoal, to produce it. The amount of energy that could be generated in a particular region was therefore limited by its capacity to produce sufficient wood, charcoal, or food.

Organic sources of energy were renewable, in that new crops could be grown and forests replanted, but the long periods of time that these processes took, coupled with the limited volume of organic material that could be extracted from an acre of land, made it difficult to sustain economic growth. The only viable alternatives to these organic sources of energy before the eighteenth century were those that tapped the forces of nature: windmills and water wheels. The potential of those natural sources of energy was both limited and difficult to harness, and it could be tapped only in certain locations or at certain times. Moreover, those sources could not produce heat.

The decisive change in the harnessing of energy for industrial purposes was the successful use of minerals, originally coal but in the twentieth century oil and uranium as well, as the main sources of energy used in the production and transportation of goods. These minerals were not inexhaustible, but the supplies could last for centuries, and they were much more efficient than any form of energy produced from organic materials, including charcoal and peat. Coal produced the high combustion temperatures necessary to smelt iron, and unlike charcoal it was not limited by the size of a region's forests. Coal therefore became the key to the expansion of the British iron industry in the nineteenth century. Coal also became the sole source of heat for the new steam engine.

THE GROWTH OF FACTORIES

One of the most enduring images of the Industrial Revolution is that of the large factory, filled with workers, laboring amid massive machinery driven by either water or steam power. Mechanized factory production evolved out of forms of industry that had emerged during the early modern period (1500–1750), when two different types of industrial workplaces, the rural cottage and the large handicraft workshop, became the main locations where goods were produced.

Beginning in the sixteenth century, entrepreneurs began employing families in the countryside to spin and weave cloth and make nails and cutlery. By locating industry in the countryside rather than in the towns the entrepreneurs were able to pay lower wages, since the rural workers, who also received an income from farming, were willing to work for less

■ **Philippe Jacques de Loutherbourg, *Coalbrookdale by Night* (1801)**
This painting depicts the intense heat produced by the coal bellows used to smelt iron in
Coalbrookdale, an English town in the Severn Valley that was one of the key centers of industrial
activity at the beginning of the nineteenth century.

than the residents of towns. Another attraction of rural industry was that all the members of the family, including children, participated in the process. In this "domestic system" a capitalist entrepreneur provided the workers with the raw materials and sometimes the tools they needed. He later paid them a fixed rate for each finished product.

Rural household industry was widespread not only in certain regions of Britain but also in most European countries. In the late eighteenth century it gradually gave way to the factory system. The great attraction of factory production was mechanization, which became cost-efficient only when it was introduced in a central industrial workplace. In factories, moreover, the entrepreneur could reduce the cost of labor and transportation, exercise tighter control over the quality of goods, and increase productivity by concentrating workers in one location.

The second type of industrial workplace that emerged during the early modern period was the large handicraft workshop. Usually located in the towns and cities, rather than in the countryside, these workshops employed relatively small numbers of people with different skills who worked collectively on the manufacture of a variety of items, such as pottery and munitions. The owner of the workshop supplied the raw materials, paid the workers' wages, and gained a profit from selling the finished products.

The large handicraft workshop made possible a division of labor°—the assignment of one stage of production to each worker or group of workers. The effect of the division of labor on productivity was evident even in the manufacture of simple items such as buttons and pins. In *The Wealth of Nations* (1776), the economist Adam Smith (1723–1790) used a pin factory in London to illustrate how the division of labor could increase per capita productivity from no more than twenty pins a day to the astonishing total of 4,800.

Like the cottages engaged in rural industry, the large handicraft workshop eventually gave way to the mechanized factory. The main difference between the workshop and the factory was that the factory did not require a body of skilled workers. When production became mechanized, the worker's job was simply to tend to the machinery. The only skill factory workers needed was manual dexterity to operate the machinery. Only those workers who made industrial machinery remained craftsmen or skilled workers in the traditional sense of the word.

With the advent of mechanization, factory owners gained much tighter control over the entire productive process. Indeed, they began to enforce an unprecedented discipline among their workers, who had to accommodate themselves to the boredom of repetitive work and a

■ **Mule Spinning**
A large mechanized spinning mill in northern England, about 1835. The workers did not require any
great skill to run the machinery.

timetable set by the machines. Craftsmen who had been accustomed to working at their own pace now had to adjust to
an entirely new and more demanding schedule. "While the
engine runs," wrote one critical contemporary, "the people
must work—men, women, and children yoked together
with iron and steam."

NEW METHODS OF TRANSPORTATION

As industry became more extensive and increased its output, transport facilities, such as roads, bridges, canals, and
eventually railroads, grew in number and quality. Increased
industrial productivity has always depended on efficient
movement of raw materials to places of production and
transportation of finished products to the market. During
the early phase of the Industrial Revolution in Britain, water transportation supplied most of these needs. A vast network of navigable rivers and human-made canals, eventually more than 4,000 miles in length, was used to transport
goods in areas that did not have access to the coast. For
routes that could not be reached by water, the most common method of transportation was by horse-drawn carriages on newly built turnpikes or toll roads, many of them
made of stone so that they were passable even in wet
weather.

The most significant innovation in transport during the
nineteenth century was the railroad. Introduced as the
Industrial Revolution was gaining momentum, the railroad
provided quick, cheap transportation of heavy materials
such as coal and iron over long distances. Driven by coal-
burning, steam-powered locomotives, the railroads freed
transport from a dependence on animal power, especially
the horses that were used to pull coaches along turnpikes,
barges along canals, and even carts along parallel tracks in
mines. Railroads rapidly became the main economic thoroughfares of the industrial economy.

Transport facilities, unlike factories, can seldom be built
entirely by their individual owners. The cost of building
locomotives and laying railroad tracks is almost always too
great to come from the profits accumulated in the normal
conduct of one's business. The funds for these facilities
must come from private investment, governments, or international financial institutions. In Britain the capital for
the railroads came entirely from individual investors. In
other industrialized countries, with the exception of the
United States, governments played a more important role.
In Belgium, which was the second European country to experience an Industrial Revolution, and in Russia, which
was one of the last, the governments of those countries assumed the responsibility for building a national railroad
system.

Conditions Favoring Industrial Growth

The immediate causes of the Industrial Revolution were the competitive pressures that encouraged technological innovation, the transition to coal power, the growth of factories, and the building of the railroads. These developments, however, do not provide a full explanation for this unprecedented economic transformation. Certain social and economic conditions allowed industrialization to progress—a large population, improved agricultural productivity, the accumulation of capital, a group of people with scientific knowledge and entrepreneurial skill, and sufficient demand for manufactured goods. In this section we will look at the historical experience of Great Britain, which was the first country to industrialize, to see how these conditions made industrial economic development possible.

POPULATION GROWTH

Industrialization requires a sufficiently large pool of labor to staff the factories and workshops of the new industries. One of the main reasons why the Industrial Revolution occurred first in Britain is that its population during the eighteenth century increased more rapidly than that of any country in continental Europe. Between 1680 and 1820 the population of England more than doubled, while that of France grew at less than one-third that rate, and that of the Dutch Republic hardly grew at all. One of the reasons this growth took place was an increase in fertility. More people were marrying, and at a younger age, which increased the birth rate. The spread of rural industry seems to have encouraged this early-marriage pattern. Wage-earning textile workers tended to marry a little earlier than agricultural workers, probably because wage earners did not have to postpone marriage to inherit land or to become self-employed, as was the case with farm workers.

This increase in population facilitated industrialization in two ways. First, it increased demand for the goods that were being manufactured in large quantities in the factories. The desire for these products, especially the new cottons, played an important role in enlarging the domestic market for manufactured goods, as we shall see shortly. Second, it increased the supply of labor, freeing a substantial portion of the population for industry, especially for factory labor. At the same time, however, this increase was not so large as to have had a negative effect on industrialization. If population growth is too rapid, it can discourage factory owners from introducing costly machinery, because if labor is plentiful and cheap, it might very well cost less for workers to produce the same volume of goods by hand. Industrialization therefore requires a significant but not too

rapid increase in population—the exact scenario that occurred in Britain during the eighteenth century.

AGRICULTURAL PRODUCTIVITY

Between 1700 and 1800 British agriculture experienced a revolution, resulting in a substantial increase in productivity. A major reason for this increase was the consolidation of all the land farmed by one tenant into compact fields, whose boundaries were defined by hedges, bushes, or walls. The main benefit of this process of enclosure° was that it allowed individual farmers to exercise complete control over the use of their land. In the eighteenth and nineteenth centuries the number of these enclosures increased dramatically, as the British Parliament passed legislation that divided entire estates into a number of enclosed fields.

With control of their lands, farmers could make them more productive. The most profitable change was to introduce new crop rotations, often involving the alternation of grains such as rye or barley with root crops such as turnips or grasses such as clover. These new crops and grasses restored nutrients to the soil and therefore made it unnecessary to let fields lie fallow once every three years. Farmers also introduced a variety of new fertilizers and soil additives that made harvests more bountiful. Farmers who raised sheep took advantage of discoveries regarding scientific breeding that improved the quality of their flocks.

More productive farming meant that fewer agricultural workers were required to feed the population. This made it possible for more people to leave the farms to work in the factories and mines. The expanded labor pool of industrial workers, moreover, was large enough that factory owners did not have to pay workers high wages; otherwise the prospect of industrializing would have lost much of its appeal. The hiring of children and women to work in the factories and mines also kept the labor pool large and the costs of labor low.

CAPITAL FORMATION AND ACCUMULATION

The term capital° refers to all the assets used in production. These include the factories and machines that are used to produce other goods (fixed capital) as well as the raw materials and finished products that are sent to market (circulating capital). Mechanized industry involves the extensive and intensive use of capital to do the work formerly assigned to human beings. An industrial economy therefore requires large amounts of capital, especially fixed capital.

Capital more generally refers to the money that is necessary to purchase these physical assets. This capital can come from a number of different sources: It can come from individuals, such as wealthy landlords, merchants, or industrialists who invest the profits they have accumulated in industrial machinery or equipment. Alternatively, capital can come from financial institutions in the form of loans. Very often a number of individuals make their wealth available to an industrial firm by buying shares of stock in that company's operations.

In Great Britain the capital that was needed to achieve industrial transformation came almost entirely from private sources. Some of it was raised by selling shares of stock to people from the middle and upper levels of society, but an even larger amount came from merchants who engaged in domestic and international trade, landowners who profited from the production of agricultural goods (including those who owned plantations in America), and the industrial entrepreneurs who owned mines, ironworks, and factories. In Britain, where all three groups were more successful than in other parts of Europe, the volume of capital made available from these sources was substantial. These people could invest directly in industrial machinery and mines or, more commonly, make their wealth available to others indirectly in the form of loans from banks where they kept their financial assets.

TECHNOLOGICAL KNOWLEDGE AND ENTREPRENEURSHIP

The process of industrialization involves the application of technological knowledge to the manufacturing process. It also involves entrepreneurship, the ability to make business ventures profitable. The mechanization of industry demanded scientifically trained people not only to introduce new forms of machinery but also to mass-produce that machinery for other manufacturers. The development of new modes of transportation required the skill of an entire class of civil engineers who could design and construct locomotives, ships, canals, railroads, and bridges. At the same time, industrialization required a group of business experts who knew how to run the factories and market their products.

In the late seventeenth century England took the lead in making science an integral part of the nation's culture. In no other European country was so much attention given to the dissemination of scientific knowledge in public lectures, the meetings of local scientific societies, and the publication of scientific textbooks. Much of this popular scientific education focused on Newtonian mechanics and dynamics. To some extent the technological innovations and engineering achievements that took place in Britain during the Industrial Revolution can be considered the product of this unparalleled diffusion of scientific knowledge.

Industrial entrepreneurs, the people who actually ran the factories and superintended the industrial process, also needed a certain level of technological skill, but their talents lay much more in their ability to run a variety of capitalist enterprises for a profit. Britain had no shortage of this type of talent in the eighteenth century. Even before the advent of mechanization, a large group of merchant capitalists had organized the domestic system of rural industry and run

the large handicraft workshops in London and other cities and towns.

The invention and production of the steam engine readily illustrate the way in which technological and entrepreneurial skills reinforced and complemented each other. The partnership between the Scotsman James Watt, who invented the steam engine, and the Englishman Matthew Boulton represented a dynamic British alliance of science and capitalism. Of the two men, Watt had more scientific and mathematical knowledge, having taught himself geometry and trigonometry as well as having read textbooks on mechanics. He was familiar with the work of Joseph Black, the chemist at the University of Glasgow who studied steam, and he had acquired a knowledge of scientific instruments from his father's business as an outfitter of ships. He was also a shrewd businessman who figured out various ways to use his knowledge of engineering to turn a profit and acquire a competitive advantage over others. Boulton was the classic eighteenth-century English entrepreneur who manufactured a variety of small metal objects from toys and buttons to teakettles and watch chains. His contribution to the partnership was assembling workers with the requisite skills to mass-produce the engine.

DEMAND FROM CONSUMERS AND PRODUCERS

The conditions for industrialization that we have discussed so far all deal with supply°, that is, the amounts of capital, labor, food, and skill that are necessary to support the industrial process. The other side of the economic equation is demand°, that is, the desire of consumers to purchase industrial goods and of producers to acquire raw materials and machinery. Much of the extraordinary productivity of the Industrial Revolution arose from the demand for industrial products.

During the early years of industrialization, only about 35 percent of all British manufactured goods were exported. This statistic indicates that as the Industrial Revolution was taking hold, the domestic market was still the main source of demand for industrial products. The demand was especially strong among the bourgeoisie. Within that group a "consumer revolution" had taken place during the eighteenth century. This revolution was based on an unprecedented desire to acquire goods of all sorts, especially clothing and housewares, such as pottery, cutlery, furniture, and curtains. The consumer revolution was assisted by commercial manipulation of all sorts, including newspaper advertising, warehouse displays, product demonstrations, and the distribution of samples.

If this consumer revolution had been restricted to the middle class, it would have had only a limited effect on the Industrial Revolution. The bourgeoisie in the eighteenth century constituted at most only 20 percent of the entire population of Britain, and most of the goods they craved were luxury items rather than the types of products that could be easily mass-produced. A strong demand for manufactured goods could develop only if workers were to buy consumer goods such as knitted stockings and caps, cotton shirts, earthenware, coffeepots, nails, candlesticks, watches, lace, and ribbon. The demand for these products came from small cottagers and laborers as well as the middle class.

Demand for manufactured products from the lower classes was obviously limited by the amount of money that wage earners had available for non-essential goods, and real wages did not increase very much, if at all, during the eighteenth century. Nevertheless the income of families in which the wife and children as well as the father worked for wages did increase significantly both during the heyday of rural industry and during the early years of industrialization. With these funds available, a substantial number of workers could actually afford to buy the products that they desired. As the population increased, so too did this lower-class demand, which helped sustain an economy built around industrial production.

The Spread of Industrialization

The Industrial Revolution, like the Scientific Revolution of the sixteenth and seventeenth centuries, did not occur in all European countries at the same time. As we have seen, it began in Britain in the 1760s and for more than four decades was confined exclusively to that country (see Map 20.1). It eventually spread to other European and North American countries, where many industrial innovations were modeled on those that had taken place in Britain. Belgium, France, Germany, Switzerland, Austria, Sweden, and the United States all experienced their own Industrial Revolutions by the middle of the nineteenth century. Only in the late nineteenth century did countries outside the traditional boundaries of the West, mainly Russia and Japan, begin to industrialize. By the middle of the twentieth century, industrialization had become a truly global process, transforming the economies of a number of Asian and Latin American countries.

GREAT BRITAIN AND THE CONTINENT

Industrialization occurred on the European continent much later than it did in Great Britain. Only after 1815 did Belgium and France begin to industrialize on a large scale, and it was not until 1840 that Germany, Switzerland, and Austria showed significant signs of industrial growth. Other European countries, such as Italy and Spain, did not begin serious efforts in this direction until the late nineteenth century. It took continental European nations even longer

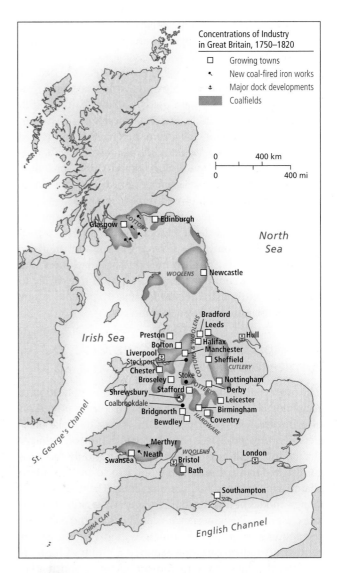

■ **Map 20.1   The Concentrations of Industry in Great Britain, 1750–1820**

The most heavily industrialized regions were in the north, where the population of cities such as Manchester, Liverpool, and Sheffield grew rapidly.

to rival the economic strength of Britain. Germany, which emerged as Britain's main competitor in the late nineteenth century, did not match British industrial output until the twentieth century.

Why did it take so long for other countries to industrialize? One explanation relates to the political situations in those countries. Well into the nineteenth century, most continental European countries had numerous internal political barriers that could impede the transportation of raw materials and goods from one part of the country to another. In Germany, for example, which was not politically united until 1871, scores of small sovereign territorial units charged tariffs whenever goods crossed their territorial boundaries. Only in 1834 was a customs union, the *Zollverein,* created to eliminate some of these barriers. In France, which had achieved a formal territorial unity during the reign of Louis XIV, local rights and privileges impeded internal trade until the early nineteenth century. This political situation was aggravated by the relatively poor state of continental roads and the inaccessibility of many seaports from production sites.

The contrast between the situation on the Continent and that which prevailed in Great Britain is striking. After 1707, when Scotland was united to England and freedom of internal trade was established between the two countries, the United Kingdom of Great Britain constituted the largest free trade zone in Europe. Thus raw materials and finished products could pass from one place within Great Britain to another, up to a distance of more than 800 miles, without payment of any internal customs or duties. The system of inland waterways was complete by 1780, and seaports were accessible from all parts of the country.

The industrial potential of many continental European countries was also weakened by the imposition of protective tariffs on goods imported from other countries. The purpose of this mercantilist policy was to develop national self-sufficiency and to maintain a favorable balance of trade, but it also had the negative effect of limiting economic growth. For example, in the Dutch Republic (the kingdom of the Netherlands after 1815) a long tradition of protecting established industries prevented that country from importing the raw materials and machines needed to develop new industries. Since protectionism invited retaliation from trading partners, it also tended to shrink the size of potential overseas markets.

A further obstacle to European industrialization was aristocratic hostility, or at least indifference, to industrial development. In Britain the aristocracy, which consisted of noblemen and gentry, were themselves often involved in capitalist enterprise and did not have the same suspicion of industry and trade that their counterparts in France and Spain often harbored. One British nobleman, the Duke of Devonshire, encouraged the exploitation of the copper mines on his estate, while the Duke of Bridgewater employed the engineer James Brindley to build a canal from the duke's coal mines in Worsley to Manchester in 1759.

A final reason for the slow industrialization of continental European countries was that they lacked the abundant raw materials that were readily accessible in Britain. The natural resources that Britain had in greatest quantities were coal and iron ore, both of which were indispensable to industrialization. The French and the Germans had some coal deposits, but they were more difficult to mine, and they were not located near ocean ports. Continental countries also lacked the access to other raw materials that Britain could import through its vast trading network, and in particular from its overseas colonies. With a large empire on four continents and the world's largest merchant marine,

Britain had abundant supplies of raw materials such as cotton as well as the capacity to import them cheaply and in large quantities.

FEATURES OF CONTINENTAL INDUSTRIALIZATION

During the first half of the nineteenth century, especially after 1830, Belgium, France, Switzerland, Germany, and Austria began to introduce machinery into the industrial process, use steam power in production, concentrate labor in large factories, and build railroads. This continental European version of the Industrial Revolution is usually described as an imitative process, one in which entrepreneurs or government officials simply tried to duplicate the economic success that Britain had achieved by following British example. Continental European nations did indeed rely to some extent on British industrial machinery. But each European nation, responding to its own unique combination of political, economic, and social conditions, followed its own course of industrialization.

One distinctive feature of continental European industrialization was that once countries like Belgium and Germany began to industrialize, their governments played a much more active role in encouraging and assisting in the process. In contrast to Britain, whose government allowed private industry to function with few economic controls, continental governments became active partners in the industrial process. They supplied capital for many economic ventures, especially the railroads and roads. In Prussia the government ran the mines. In a few cases continental European governments provided financial support for investors in an effort to encourage capital formation. In some places, such as Austria, the state eliminated the regulations of urban guilds that had restricted industrial development in rural regions.

A second major feature of continental European industrialization is that banks, particularly in Germany and Belgium, played a central role in industrial development. This was necessitated by the low level of capital formation on the Continent and the reluctance of entrepreneurs to take risks by investing money themselves. Banks in Germany and Belgium played a particularly active role in stimulating industry. Drawing on the resources of both small and large investors, these corporate banks became in effect industrial banks, building railroads and factories themselves in addition to making capital available for a variety of industrial ventures.

A third distinct feature of continental European industrialization is that the railroads actually contributed to the beginning of industrial development. In Great Britain the railroads were introduced sixty years after industrialization had begun and thus helped sustain a process of economic development that had been long afoot. By contrast the railroads on the Continent provided the basic infrastructure of its new economy and became a major stimulus to the development of all other industries. In Belgium, which was the first continental European nation to industrialize, the new government built a national railroad system during the 1830s and 1840s, not only to stimulate industry but also to unify the newly independent nation.

Of all the European countries that industrialized, only Belgium appears to have followed the British model closely by developing coal, iron, and textiles as the three main sectors of the new economy. Other countries tended to concentrate their activity in one specific area. France emphasized textiles, especially those like worsted woolens that did not compete with British cottons. France's coal production and consumption never matched that of Great Britain or Belgium, and after 1850 it fell behind that of Germany as well. In Germany the main economic advances, which did not begin until 1850, occurred mainly in the area of heavy industry, that is, coal, iron, and engineering rather than textiles.

INDUSTRIALIZATION IN THE UNITED STATES

Industrialization in the United States began during the 1820s, not long after Belgium and France had begun to experience their own industrial revolutions. It occurred first in the textile industry in New England, where factories using water-power produced goods for largely rural markets. New England also began producing two domestic hardware products—clocks and guns—for the same market. Between 1850 and 1880 a second region between Pittsburgh and Cleveland became industrialized. This region specialized in heavy industry, especially steelmaking and the manufacture of large machinery, and it relied on coal for fuel.

American industrialization conformed to many of the patterns established in Britain and on the European continent. As in Britain and France, the development of cottage industry preceded industrialization. Most of the industrial machinery used in the United States during the nineteenth century was modeled on imports from Britain. The most significant American technological innovation before 1900 was the sewing machine, which was patented by Elias Howe in 1846 and then developed and improved upon by Isaac Singer in the 1850s. This new machine was then introduced in Europe, where it was used in the production of ready-to-wear garments.

After 1865, when American industrialization began to spread rapidly across the entire country, American entrepreneurs made a distinctive contribution to the industrial process in the area of business organization, especially the operation of international firms. Toward the beginning of the twentieth century, American manufacturers streamlined the production process by introducing the assembly line, a division of labor in which the product passes from one operation to the next until it is fully assembled. The assembly line required the production of interchangeable parts, another American innovation, first used in the manufacture of rifles for the U.S. government.

Like Great Britain, the United States possessed vast natural resources, including coal. It also resembled Britain in the absence of governmental involvement in the process of industrialization. The main difference between the industrialization of the two countries is that during the nineteenth century labor in America was in relatively short supply. This placed workers in a more advantageous situation in dealing with their employers and prevented some of the horrors of early British industrialization from recurring on the other side of the Atlantic. Only with the influx of European immigrants in the late nineteenth century did the working conditions in America deteriorate and begin to resemble the early-nineteenth-century British pattern.

INDUSTRIAL REGIONALISM

Although we have discussed the industrialization of entire nations, the process usually took place within smaller geographical regions. There had always been regional specialization in agriculture, with some areas emphasizing crops and others livestock. During the Industrial Revolution, however, entire economies acquired a distinctly regional character. Regional economies began to take shape during the days of the domestic system, when merchants employed families in certain geographical areas, such as Lancashire in England, to produce textiles. In these regions there was a close relationship between agricultural and industrial production, in that members of the same household participated in both processes. Related industries, such as those for finishing or dyeing cloth, also sprang up close to where the cotton or wool yarn was spun and the cloth woven.

As industrialization spread outside Britain, this regional pattern became even more pronounced. In France the centers of the textile industry were situated near the northeastern border near Belgium and in the area surrounding Lyons in the east-central part of the country. Both of these areas had attracted rural household industry before the introduction of textile machinery. In Germany the iron industry was centered in the Ruhr region, where most of the country's coal was mined. Within the Habsburg Empire most industry was located in parts of Bohemia (now the Czech Republic). The region in Ireland that experienced the most significant measure of industrialization was the northern province of Ulster, a linen-producing area that became Europe's leading producer of ready-to-wear women's undergarments and men's shirts in the 1850s.

The development of regional economies did not mean that markets were regional. The goods produced in one region almost always served the needs of people outside that particular area. Markets for most industrial goods were national and international, and even people in small agricultural villages created a demand for manufactured goods. The French iron industry, for example, was centered in the

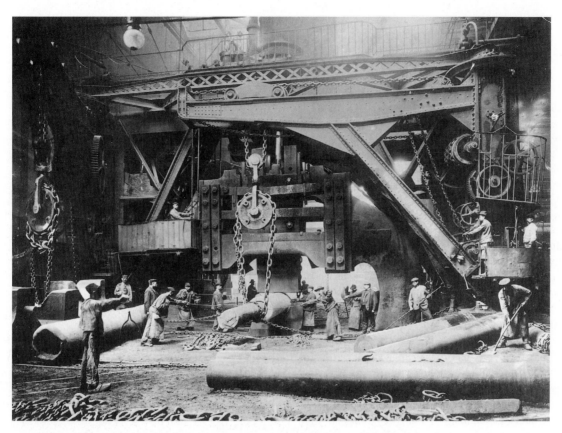

■ **A Colossal Steam-Driven Hammer, Nicknamed "Fritz," Installed by Alfred Krupp at His Steelworks in Essen in 1861**
Krupp's factory was located in the Ruhr region of Germany, the main center in that country for heavy industry.

eastern part of the country, but it catered to the needs of the wealthier segments of its own and other European populations, as did the iron industry in the Ruhr region in Germany and the textile industry in the north of England.

The development of regional industrial economies helps to explain the striking contrast that persisted well into the twentieth century between the parts of countries that had become heavily industrialized and those that retained at least many of the appearances of a preindustrial life. In Britain and the rest of Europe industrial machinery and factories were not introduced into every village. Some areas remained exclusively agricultural, while others continued a tradition of rural industry. This pattern was particularly evident in France, where mechanized industry was concentrated in a limited number of centers in the northeastern half of the country. In 1870 more than two-thirds of the French population still lived in rural areas. As economic growth and industrial development continued, however, agricultural regions eventually began to lose their traditional character. Even if industry itself did not arrive, the larger industrial economy made its mark. Agriculture itself became mechanized, while railroads and other forms of mechanized transport integrated these areas in a national economy.

The Effects of Industrialization

The Industrial Revolution had a profound impact on virtually every aspect of human life. It encouraged the growth of the population and the economy, affected the conditions in which people lived, changed family life, created new divisions within society, and transformed the traditional rural landscape. The changes that it brought about were most evident in Britain, but in time they have occurred in every country that has industrialized, including the United States.

POPULATION AND ECONOMIC GROWTH

The most significant of these changes was the sustained expansion of both the population and the economy. As we have seen, the Industrial Revolution in Britain was facilitated by a significant population increase in the eighteenth century. That growth had created a plentiful supply of relatively cheap labor, which in turn had helped to bring about

THOMAS MALTHUS WRITES ABOUT THE LIMITATION OF POPULATION

·················

Thomas Malthus was an English cleric who studied at Cambridge University and then took a position as a curate in a country parish in Surrey. In 1798 he published anonymously An Essay on the Principle of Population, *in which he advanced the argument that population tends to grow faster than the food supply, resulting in periodic subsistence crises that keep population in check. In the greatly expanded second edition of this book, published in 1803, Malthus distinguished between preventive and positive checks on the growth of population.*

The checks to population, which are constantly operating with more or less force in every society, and keep down the number to the level of the means of subsistence, may be classed under two general heads: the preventive and the positive.

The preventive check is peculiar to man and arises from that distinctive superiority in his reasoning faculties, which enables him to calculate distant consequences. . . . But man cannot look around him and see the distress which frequently presses upon those who have large families . . . These considerations are calculated to prevent a great number of persons in all civilized nations from pursuing the dictate of nature in an early attachment to one woman.

The positive checks to population are extremely various and include every cause, whether arising from vice or misery, which in any degree contributes to shorten the natural duration of human life. Under this head therefore may be enumerated all unwholesome occupations, severe labour and exposure to the seasons, extreme poverty, bad nursing of children, great towns, excesses of all kinds, the whole train of common diseases and epidemics, wars, pestilence, plague and famine.

On examining the obstacles to the increase of population which I have classed under the heads of preventive and positive checks, it will appear they are all resolvable into moral restraint, vice and misery. Of the preventive checks, the restraint from marriage, which if not followed by irregular gratifications may properly be termed moral restraint. Promiscuous intercourse, unnatural passions, violations of the marriage bed, and improper arts to conceal the consequences of irregular connexions clearly come under the head of vice. Of the positive checks, those which appear to arise unavoidably from the law of nature may be called exclusively misery; and those which we bring upon ourselves, such as wars, excesses and many others it would be in our power to avoid, are of a mixed nature. They are brought upon us by vice, and their consequences are misery.

Source: From Thomas Malthus, *An Essay on the Principle of Population, 2nd Edition,* 1803.

---

a marked increase in industrial output. As industry grew, population kept pace, and each provided a stimulus to the growth of the other.

Most contemporary observers in the late eighteenth century did not believe that this expansion of both the population and the economy could be sustained indefinitely. The most pessimistic of these commentators was Thomas Malthus (1766–1834), an English cleric who wrote *An Essay on the Principle of Population* in 1798. Malthus argued that population had a natural tendency to grow faster than the food supply. Thus, unless couples exercised restraint by marrying late and producing fewer children, the population would eventually outstrip the resources necessary to sustain it, resulting in poor nutrition, famine, and disease. These "positive checks" on population growth, which sometimes were initiated or aggravated by war, would drive population back to sustainable levels. These checks would also end periods of economic expansion, which generally accompany increases in population, by putting pressure on the food supply, raising the price of food, reducing employment, and lowering wages. Thus we might expect that the significant expansion of the population and the economy that took

place in eighteenth-century England would likewise reach its limits, just around the time that Malthus was writing.

This predicted cyclical contraction of both the population and the economy did not take place. Europe for the first time in its history managed to escape the "Malthusian population trap." Instead of being sharply reduced after 1800, the population continued to expand at an ever faster rate, doubling in Great Britain between 1800 and 1850 and following a similar pattern of rapid growth in all other countries that had industrialized. At the same time the economy, instead of contracting or collapsing, continued to grow and diversify.

It is not absolutely clear how Europe avoided the Malthusian trap in the nineteenth century. Part of the answer lies in the greater productivity of agriculture, but it was mainly developments in industry itself, especially the increased accumulation of capital, that kept Europe from succumbing to yet another cycle of depopulation and economic contraction. The accumulation of capital over a long period of time was so great that industry was able to employ large numbers of workers even during the 1790s and 1800s, when Europe was at war. Since they had income from wages, workers were willing to marry earlier and have larger families, and with lower food prices because of higher agricultural productivity they could afford to maintain a healthier diet and purchase more manufactured goods as well. Thus the Industrial Revolution itself, coupled with the changes in agriculture that accompanied it, proved Malthus wrong.

While the rapid growth of population in industrialized societies up until the late twentieth century is incontestable, the record of economic growth is not so clear. In order to claim that the Industrial Revolution has resulted in sustained economic growth, we have to take a broad view, looking at an overall pattern of growth and ignoring certain cyclical recessions and depressions. Nations that have industrialized, beginning with European countries in the nineteenth century, have all experienced a significant increase in both gross national product and per capita income over the long run. Economic growth in industrialized countries was not always rapid or continuous. During the first six decades of industrialization in Britain, for example, economic growth was actually fairly slow, mainly because so much capital went into subsidizing the long war against France (1792–1802; 1804–1815). Nevertheless, there still was steady growth, and the type of Malthusian economic contraction or collapse that had followed all previous periods of expansion did not occur. To that extent we can say that the Industrial Revolution has resulted in sustained economic growth in the West.

STANDARDS OF LIVING

Ever since the early years of the Industrial Revolution, a debate has raged over the effect of industrialization on the standard of living and the quality of life of the laboring population. The supporters of the two main schools of thought on this issue have been called the optimists and the pessimists. The optimists have always emphasized the positive effects of both the process of mechanization and the system of industrial capitalism that arose during the revolution. They have focused on the success that industrialized nations have achieved in escaping the Malthusian trap and in achieving sustained economic growth. The Industrial Revolution, so they argue, has resulted in an unprecedented rise in individual income, which has made it possible for the mass of a country's population to avoid poverty for the first time in human history.

The main yardstick that the optimists have used to measure the improvement in living standards is per capita real income, that is, income measured in terms of its actual purchasing power. Real income in Great Britain rose about 50 percent between 1770 and 1850 and more than doubled during the entire nineteenth century. These improvements, however, did not affect the lives of most workers for a long period of time—in Great Britain not until 1820, about sixty years after the beginning of industrialization. The increases

that occurred after that date, moreover, were only averages, concealing disparities among workers with different levels of skill. Only in the late nineteenth and twentieth centuries did industrialization raise the real income of all workers to a level that made the benefits of industrialization apparent.

Even if the pessimists concede a long-term increase in real income, it has never been substantial enough to persuade them that industrialization was on balance a positive good, at least for the working class. The pessimists have always stressed the negative effects of industrial development on the life of the lower classes. In their way of thinking, industrialization was an unmitigated disaster. The cause of this disaster in their eyes was not the process of mechanization but the system of industrial capitalism°. This form of capitalism is characterized by the ownership of factories by private individuals and by the employment of wage labor. Like earlier forms of mercantile and agricultural capitalism, it involved a systematic effort to reduce costs and maximize profits. In the pursuit of this goal, employers tried to keep wages as low as possible and to increase production through labor-saving technology, thus preventing workers from improving their lot.

Most of the evidence used to support the pessimist position has come from the early period of industrialization in Britain, when incomes were either stagnant or declining and when conditions in factories and industrial and mining towns were most appalling. It is difficult to measure these living standards statistically, but the weight of qualitative evidence suggests that they deteriorated during the nineteenth century. Working-class housing was makeshift and crowded, and there were few sanitary facilities. Poor drainage and raw sewage gave rise to a host of new hygienic problems, especially outbreaks of typhus and cholera. Between 1831 and 1866 four epidemics of cholera killed at least 140,000 people in Britain, most of whom lived in poorer districts.

While life in the city was bleak and unhealthy, working conditions in the factory were monotonous and demeaning. Forced to submit to a regimen governed by the operation of the machine, workers lost their independence as well as any control whatsoever over the products of their labor. They were required to work long hours, often fourteen hours a day, six days a week, with few breaks. Factory masters locked the doors during working hours, and they assessed fines for infractions such as opening a window when the temperature was unbearable, whistling while working, and having dirty hands while spinning yarn. Work in the mines was a little less monotonous, but it was physically more demanding and far more dangerous.

WOMEN, CHILDREN, AND INDUSTRY

During the early Industrial Revolution in Great Britain, large numbers of children and women were recruited into the workforce, especially the textile and mining industries.

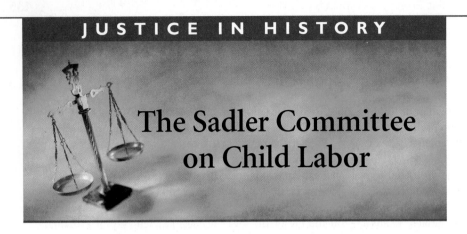

The Sadler Committee on Child Labor

The widespread use of child labor in Britain during the early decades of the Industrial Revolution led to efforts by social reformers and members of Parliament to regulate the conditions under which children worked. Parliament passed legislation restricting the number of hours that all children could work in textile mills in 1819 and 1829, but neither of these laws was enforced effectively, and they did not apply to all industries. Complaints of inhumane treatment, moral degradation, and exploitation of child workers continued to surface. In 1831 Michael Sadler (1780–1835), a Tory member of the British Parliament, introduced a bill in Parliament to limit the number of hours that all children could work to ten hours per day. Like many social reformers, Sadler was inspired by what he considered his Christian duty to protect dependent members of the community.

Sadler chaired the committee to which his bill was referred. In order to muster support for the bill, Sadler held hearings in which child workers themselves came before the committee to report on the conditions under which they lived and worked. The success of his bill was by no means guaranteed. Many members of Parliament were deeply committed to the policy of *laissez-faire,* according to which the government should not intervene in the operation of the economy, treating it instead as a self-regulating machine. Sadler had to convince his colleagues

that they should modify that policy in the case of children, on the grounds that the state was obliged to provide for the welfare of children when their parents were unable to do so. He also needed to make the members of Parliament and the broader public aware of the brutality of the conditions under which the children worked.

The hearings that took place were not a trial in the strict sense of the word, but they possessed many of the features of a judicial investigation, not unlike those conducted by grand juries in criminal cases. The committee's proceedings were intended to expose, condemn, and ultimately remedy misconduct by the factory owners. Procedurally the committee members had more latitude than did courts of law. Since these parliamentary committees were designed to extract information rather than to bring offenders to trial, they did not need to adhere to any established judicial guidelines. There was no cross-examination of witnesses, nor could factory owners present a defense. The witnesses in this investigation were chosen because Sadler knew they would reveal the evils of the factory system.

The testimony presented to the Sadler Committee produced abundant

■ Child Workers
These children are on their way to work in the Yorkshire textile mills.

evidence of the exploitation and physical abuse of child workers. Some of the most harrowing testimony came from the examination of a 17-year-old boy, Joseph Hebergam, on July 1, 1832. Hebergam revealed that he had begun the work of worsted spinning at age 7, that he worked at the factory from five A.M. until eight P.M., and that he had only thirty minutes for lunch at noon, leaving him to eat his other meals while standing on the job. In the factory there were three overlookers, one of whom was responsible for greasing the machinery and another for whipping the workers. The latter overlooker walked continually up and down the factory with whip in hand.

When asked where his brother John was working, Joseph replied that he had died three years before at age 16. Sadler then inquired into the cause of his brother's death. The boy responded,

"It was attributed to this, that he died from working such long hours and that it had been brought on by the factory. They have to stop the flies [part of the textile machinery] with their knees, because they go so swift they cannot stop them with their hands; he got a bruise on the shin by a spindle-board, and it went on to that degree that it burst; the surgeon cured that, then he was better; then he went to work again; but when he had worked about two months more his spine became affected, and he died." The witness went on to explain that his own severe labor had damaged his knees and ankles so much so that he found it painful to walk. His brother and sister would help carry him to the factory, but when they arrived late, even by as little as five minutes, the overlooker beat all three of them "till we were black and blue." At the request of the committee, Joseph then stood up to show the condition of his limbs. He reported the death of another boy who had sustained massive injuries when he was caught in the shaft of the machinery he was running. Joseph concluded his testimony by recounting how the factory owners had threatened him and his younger brothers with losing their jobs if they testified before the committee.

The hearings of the Sadler Committee were widely publicized, but they fell short of realizing their original objective. The bill, which eventually was approved by Parliament as the Factory Regulations Act of 1833, prohibited the employment of children under age 9 in all factories. Boys and girls were allowed to work up to nine hours a day from age 9 until their thirteenth birthdays, and up to twelve hours a day from age 13 until their eighteenth birthdays. The long-term effect of this legislation was to establish in Western industrialized countries the principle that early childhood was a period of life set aside for education rather than work. ∎

∎ **Child Labor in the Textile Industry**
Factory girls operate machinery in a textile mill under the tight supervision of the factory owner.

Questions of Justice

1. This investigation was concerned with the achievement of social justice rather than the determination of criminal culpability. What were the advantages of using legislative committees in such an undertaking?

2. Child labor was not a new phenomenon in the early eighteenth century. Why did the Industrial Revolution draw attention to this age-old practice?

Taking It Further

Horn, Pamela. *Children's Work and Welfare, 1780–1890.* 1996. An examination of the scale and nature of child employment in Britain and changing attitudes toward the practice.

In the woolen industry in the western part of England, for example, female and child labor together accounted for 75 percent of the workforce. Children under age 13 made up 13 percent of the cotton factory workforce, and those under age 18 made up 51 percent. This pattern of employment reflects the demands of industrialists, who valued the hand skills and dexterity that children possessed as well as the greater amenability of both children and women to the discipline of factory labor.

Female and child labor was both plentiful and cheap. Children received only one-sixth to one-third the wages of a grown man, while women generally took home only one-third to one-half of that adult male income. There was no lack of incentive for women and children to take one of these low-paying jobs. In a family dependent on wages, everyone needed to work, even when a large labor pool kept wages depressed.

The participation of both women and children in the workforce was not new. In an agricultural economy all members of the family contributed to the work, with parents and children, young and old, all being assigned specific roles. Rural industry also involved the labor of all members of the family. When people began working in the factories, however, they were physically separated from the home, making it impossible for workers to combine domestic and occupational labor.

As the workplace became distinct from the household, family life underwent a fundamental change, although this change did not occur immediately. During the early years of the Industrial Revolution, members of many families found employment together in the factories and mines. Gradually,

however, mothers found it impossible to care for their youngest children on the job, and most of them dropped out of the full-time workforce. The restriction of child labor by the British Factory Act of 1833 reinforced this trend and led to the establishment of a fairly common situation in which the male wage earner worked outside the home while his wife stayed home with the children.

CLASS AND CLASS CONSCIOUSNESS

As Europe became more industrialized and urbanized, and as the system of industrial capitalism became more entrenched, writers began to use a new terminology to describe the structure of society. Instead of claiming that society consisted of a finely graded hierarchy of ranks to which individuals belonged by virtue of their occupations or their legal status, they divided society into three classes that could be distinguished by the type of property people owned and the manner in which they acquired it. At the top of this new social hierarchy was the aristocracy, consisting of those who owned land and received their income in the form of rent. The middle class or bourgeoisie, which included the new factory owners, possessed capital and derived their income from profits, whereas the working class owned nothing but their own labor and received their income from wages.

Historians and social scientists disagree over the extent to which men and women in the nineteenth century were actually conscious of their membership in these classes. Some historians have claimed that the growth of wage labor, the exploitation of the working class, and conflicts

■ **Capital and Labor**
This cartoon, drawn by the illustrator Gustave Doré, depicts wealthy industrialists gambling with workers tied together as chips.

between capital and labor encouraged workers to think of themselves not so much as individuals who claimed a certain social status but as members of a large class of workers who shared the same relationship to the means of production. These historians have pointed to the growth of trade unions, political campaigns for universal male suffrage, and other forms of working-class organization and communication as evidence of this awakening of class consciousness.

Other historians have claimed that people were less conscious of their class position. True, at certain times in the early nineteenth century some workers thought of themselves as members of a class whose interests were in conflict with those of factory owners and financiers. It was much more common, however, for them to think of themselves primarily as practitioners of a particular craft, as members of a local community, or as part of a distinct ethnic minority, such as the Irish. When they demanded the right to vote, workers based their claim on their historic constitutional rights, not on the interests of all wage earners. When they demonstrated in favor of the ten-hour working day, they did so to improve the conditions in which they worked, not to advance the struggle of all workers against the middle class. The work experiences of laborers were too varied to sustain an awareness among most of them that they belonged to one homogeneous group.

THE INDUSTRIAL LANDSCAPE

As industry spread throughout Europe and reached into areas that previously had been untouched by mechanization, urban and rural areas underwent dramatic changes. The most striking of these changes took place in the new industrial towns and cities, some of which had been little more than country towns before the factories were built. Manchester, for example, grew from a modest population of 23,000 people in 1773 to a burgeoning metropolis of 105,000 by 1820. Large factories with their smokestacks and warehouses, ringed by long rows of houses built to accommodate the armies of new industrial workers, gave these cities an entirely new and for the most part a grim appearance.

Cities experienced the most noticeable changes in physical appearance, but the

countryside also began to take on a new look, mainly as a result of the transport revolution. The tunnels, bridges, and viaducts that were constructed to accommodate the railroad lines and the canals that were built to improve inland water transportation made an indelible imprint on the traditional terrain. In many ways this alteration of the landscape served as a statement of the mastery over nature that human beings had achieved at the time of the Scientific Revolution. The Industrial Revolution finally fulfilled the technological promise of that earlier revolution, and one of its effects was the actual transformation of the physical world.

Industry did not always form a blight on the landscape or offend aesthetic sensibilities. Some of the new industrial architecture, especially the viaducts and aqueducts that traversed valleys in the mountainous regions of the country, were masterpieces of modern engineering and architecture. Sir Walter Scott (1771–1832), the Scottish romantic novelist, claimed that the cast-iron Pont Cysyllte aqueduct in Wales, which carried the waters of the Caledonian Canal 127 feet above the River Dee, was the most beautiful work of art he had ever seen. The railroads also had the ability to inspire the artistic imagination, as they did in Joseph Turner's (1775–1851) romantic painting *Rain, Steam and Speed*, which captured the railroad's speed and beauty.

■ **Joseph M. W. Turner, *Rain, Steam and Speed: The Great Western Railway* (1844)**
This was one of the first oil paintings that had the railroad locomotive as its theme.

Industry, Trade, and Empire

As the middle of the nineteenth century approached, Britain towered above all other nations in the volume of its industrial output, the extent of its international trade, and the size of its empire. In industrial production it easily outpaced all its competitors, producing two-thirds of the world's coal, about half of its cotton cloth, half of its iron, and 40 percent of its hardware. Britain controlled about one-third of the world's trade, and London had emerged as the undisputed financial center of the global economy. Britain's overseas empire, which included colonies in Canada, the Caribbean, South America, India, Southeast Asia, and Australia, eclipsed that of all other European powers and would continue to grow during the second half of the century.

These three great British strengths—industry, trade, and empire—were closely linked. Britain's colonies in both Asia and in the Americas served as trading depots, while the promotion of trade led directly to the acquisition of new imperial possessions. Trade and empire in turn served the purposes of industry. Many of the raw materials used in industrial production, especially cotton, came from Britain's imperial possessions. At the same time, those possessions provided markets for Britain's mass-produced manufactured goods. Such imperial markets proved immensely valuable when France blockaded its ports during the Napoleonic wars and thereby cut into British trade with the entire European continent (see Chapter 19).

The great challenge for Britain during the nineteenth century was to find new markets for its industrial products. Domestic demand had been strong at the beginning of the Industrial Revolution, but by the 1840s British workers did not possess sufficient wealth to purchase the increasingly large volume of hardwares and textiles manufactured in the mills and factories. Britain therefore had to look overseas, including its own colonies, to find markets in which to sell the bulk of its industrial products. Three regions where Britain expanded its economic influence in the nineteenth century—East Asia, India, and Latin America—provide striking examples of the ways in which industry, trade, and empire were linked.

EAST ASIA: THE OPIUM WAR, 1839–1842

British conflict with China provides the best illustration of the way in which the British desire to promote trade led to the acquisition of new colonies. For three centuries the Chinese had tightly controlled their trade with European powers. By 1842, however, British merchants, supported by the British government, managed to break down these barriers and give Britain a foothold in China, allowing it to exploit the East Asian market.

The conflict arose over the importation of opium, a narcotic made from poppy seeds and produced in great quantities in India. This drug, which numbed pain but also had hallucinogenic effects and could cause profound lethargy, was in widespread use in Europe and had an even larger market in Asia. In China opium had became a national addiction by the middle of the eighteenth century, and the situation became much worse when British merchants increased the volume of illegal imports from India to China in the early nineteenth century. The Chinese government therefore decided to put an end to the opium trade.

Chinese efforts to stop British merchants from importing opium reached a climax in 1839, when the Chinese seized 20,000 chests of opium in the holds of British ships and spilled them into the China Sea. This incident led to the first Opium War (1839–1842), in which the British, who had the advantage of superior naval technology, attacked Chinese ports and forced the Chinese to come to terms. In a treaty signed in 1842 China ceded the island of Hong Kong to the British, reimbursed British merchants for the opium it had destroyed, and opened five Chinese ports to international trade. As part of this settlement, each of these ports was to be governed by a British consul who was not subject to Chinese law. In this way Britain expanded its empire, increased its already large share of world trade, and found new markets for British manufactured goods in East Asia.

INDIA: ANNEXATION AND TRADE

The interrelationship of industry, trade, and empire became even clearer in India, which became known as the jewel in Britain's imperial crown. As we have seen in Chapter 17, Britain gradually gained political control of India during the late eighteenth and nineteenth centuries. This control served the interests of British trade in two ways. First, it gave British merchants control of the trade between India and other Asian countries. Second, Britain developed a favorable balance of trade with India, exporting more goods to that country than it imported. Taxes paid to the British government by India for administering the country and interest payments on British loans to India increased the flow of capital from Calcutta to London. The influx of capital from India was in large part responsible for the favorable balance of payments that Britain enjoyed with the rest of the world until World War I. The capital that Britain received from these sources as well as from trade with China was funneled into the British economy or invested in British economic ventures throughout the world.

Control of India also served British interests by supplying British industries with raw materials while giving them access to the foreign markets they needed to make a profit. This promotion of British industry was done at the expense of the local Indian economy. The transportation of cotton grown in India to British textile mills, only to be returned to India in the form of finished cloth certainly retarded, if it did not destroy, the existing Indian textile industry. Resentment of this economic exploitation of India became one of the main sources of Indian nationalism in the late nineteenth century.

LATIN AMERICA: AN EMPIRE OF TRADE

British policy in Latin America developed differently from the way it had in China and India, but it had the same effect of opening up new markets for British goods. Great Britain was a consistent supporter of the movements for independence that erupted in South America between 1810 and 1824. Britain supported these movements not simply because it wished to undermine Spanish and Portuguese imperialism, but because it needed to acquire new markets for its industrial products. Britain did not need to use military force to open these areas to British trade, as it did in China. Once the countries became independent, they attracted large volumes of British exports. In 1840 the British cotton industry shipped 35 percent of all its exports to Latin American countries, especially to Argentina, Brazil, Uruguay, Mexico, and Chile. Britain also exported large amounts of capital to these Latin American countries by investing vast sums of money in their economies. Britain thus established an informal "empire of trade" in Latin America. These countries were not controlled by Britain, but they had the same economic relationship with Britain as did Canada, Australia, and other parts of the British Empire.

British investment and trade brought the newly independent nations of Latin America into the industrial world economy. In so doing, however, Britain assigned these countries to a dependent position in that economy, not unlike the position that India occupied in Asia about the same time. One effect of this dependence was to transform the small, self-sufficient village economies that had developed alongside the large plantations in Central and South America. Instead of producing goods themselves and selling them within their own markets, these villages now became suppliers of raw materials for British industry. At the same time the Latin American population became more dependent upon British manufactured goods. This transformation not only retarded or destroyed native Latin American industry but also created huge trade deficits for Latin American countries by the middle of the nineteenth century.

CONCLUSION
Industrialization and the West

B y 1850 the Industrial Revolution had begun to bring about some of the most dramatic changes in human life recorded in historical documents. Not since the Neolithic Age, when people began to live in settled villages, cultivate grains, and domesticate animals, did the organization of society, the patterns of work, and the landscape undergo such profound changes. In many ways the Industrial Revolution marked the watershed between the old way of life and the new. It gave human beings unprecedented technological control over nature, made employment in the home the exception rather than the rule, and submitted industrial workers to a regimentation unknown in the past. It changed family life, gave cities an entirely new appearance, and unleashed new and highly potent political forces, including the ideologies of liberalism and socialism, which shall be discussed in depth in the next chapter.

Industrialization changed the very definition of the West. In the Middle Ages the predominant cultural values of Western countries were those of Christianity, while in the eighteenth century those values were more often associated with the rational, scientific culture of the Enlightenment. Now, in the nineteenth century, the West was increasingly becoming identified with industrialization and the system of industrial capitalism it had spawned. In discussing the prospects of industrialization in the Ottoman Empire in 1856, a British diplomat wrote that "Europe is at hand, with its science, its labor, and its capital," but that the Qur'an and other elements of traditional Turkish culture "are so many obstacles to advancement in a Western sense." The Industrial Revolution was creating new divisions between the West and the non-Western world.

Until the late nineteenth century, industrialization took place only in nations that have traditionally formed a part of the West. Beginning in the 1890s, however, countries that lay outside the West or on its margins began to introduce industrial technology and methods. Between 1890 and 1910 Russia and Japan underwent a period of rapid industrialization, and in the second half of the twentieth century a number of countries in Asia and Latin America, as well as Turkey, followed suit. This process of industrialization and economic development is often described as one of westernization, and it has usually led to conflicts within those countries between Western and non-Western values. The industrialization of these nations has not always been fully successful, and even when it has, doubt remains as to whether those nations should now be included within the West. Industrialization outside Europe and the United States reveals once again that the composition of the West changes from time to time and that its boundaries are often difficult to define.

Suggestions for Further Reading

For a comprehensive list of suggested readings, please go to www.ablongman.com/levackconcise/chapter20

Ashton, T. A. *The Industrial Revolution,* reprint edition with preface by P. Hudson. 1992. The classic statement of the optimist position, identifying the benefits of the revolution.

Berg, Maxine. *The Age of Manufactures, 1700–1820: Industry, Innovation and Work in Britain.* 1994. A study of the process and character of specific industries, especially those employing women.

Brinley, Thomas. *The Industrial Revolution and the Atlantic Economy: Selected Essays.* 1993. Essays challenging the view that Britain's Industrial Revolution was a gradual process.

Deane, Phyllis. *The First Industrial Revolution.* 1967. The best study of technological innovation in Britain.

Gutmann, Myron. *Toward the Modern Economy: Early Industry in Europe, 1500–1800.* 1988. A study of cottage industry, especially in France.

Hobsbawm, E. J. *Industry and Empire.* 1968. A general economic history of Britain from 1750 to 1970 that analyzes the position of Britain in the world economy.

Jacob, Margaret. *Scientific Culture and the Making of the Industrial West.* 1997. An exploration of the spread of scientific knowledge and its connection with industrialization.

Morris. R. J. *Class and Class Consciousness in the Industrial Revolution, 1780–1850.* 1979. A balanced treatment of the link between industrialization and class formation.

Pollard, Sidney. *Peaceful Conquest: The Industrialization of Europe, 1760–1970.* 1981. A linking of coal supplies to economic development.

Rule, John. *The Vital Century, England's Developing Economy, 1714–1815.* 1992. A general economic history establishing the importance of early eighteenth-century developments.

Stearns, Peter. *The Industrial Revolution in World History,* 2nd ed. 1998. The best study of industrialization in a global context.

Teich, Mikulas, and Roy Porter, eds. *The Industrial Revolution in National Context: Europe and the USA.* 1981. Essays illustrating similarities as well as national differences in the process of industrialization.

Wrigley, E. A. *Continuity, Chance and Change: The Character of the Industrial Revolution in Britain.* 1988. Includes the best discussion of the transition from an advanced organic economy to one based on minerals.

Ideological Conflict and National Unification, 1815–1871

O N MARCH 18, 1871, THE PRESIDENT OF THE FRENCH GOVERNMENT, Adolphe Thiers, sent a small unit of troops to Paris to seize cannons that had been used against Prussian forces during their siege of the city a few months before. The artillery was in the possession of the National Guard, the citizen militia of Paris. Members of the National Guard felt that the government had abandoned them by recently concluding an armistice with the Prussians, who were still camped outside the city. They also believed that the government was determined to gain control of the city, which had refused to comply with its orders. When the troops reached the city, they encountered a hostile crowd of Parisians, many of whom were armed. The crowd surrounded the two generals who led the detachment, placed them up against a wall, and executed them.

This action led to a full-scale siege of Paris by government troops. In the city a committed group of radicals formed a new municipal government, the Paris Commune, which was a revival of the commune established during the French Revolution in 1792. The Commune took steps to defend the city against the government troops, and during its short life it implemented several social reforms. The Communards, as the members were known, set up a central employment bureau, established nurseries for working mothers, and recognized women's labor unions. For many decades the Commune served as a model of working-class government.

The Paris Commune lasted only a few weeks. On May 21 government troops poured through the gates of the city, and during the "bloody week" that followed they took the city street by street, demolishing the barricades and executing the Communards. The Communards retaliated by executing a number of hostages, including the archbishop of Paris. They also burned down the Tuileries Palace,

Chapter Outline

- New Ideologies in the Early Nineteenth Century

- Ideological Encounters in Europe, 1815–1848

- National Unification in Europe and America, 1848–1871

The Proclamation of the German Empire in the Hall of Mirrors at Versailles, January 21, 1871: King William I of Prussia, standing on the dais, is being crowned Emperor of Germany. At the center of the picture, dressed in a white uniform jacket, is Otto von Bismarck, the person most responsible for the unification of all German territory in one empire.

the hall of justice, and the city hall. During this one week at least 25,000 Communards were killed, and since many bodies were burned in the fires that consumed the city, the numbers were probably much higher.

The short life of the Paris Commune marks the climax of a tumultuous period of European history. Between 1815 and 1871 Europe witnessed numerous movements for reform, periodic uprisings, and several revolutions. The people who participated in these momentous developments, including the Communards of 1870, were inspired in large part by ideologies°, theories of society and government that lay at the basis of political programs. The ideologies that developed during this period—liberalism, conservatism, socialism, and nationalism—were the product of historical developments that had arisen in the West, and they endowed the West with a distinctive political culture. These four ideologies also provide a framework for understanding the complex and often confusing political and social history of the West from 1815 until 1871.

In this chapter we shall address three questions:

- What were the main features of the ideologies that inspired people to political action during those years?
- How did the encounters among the people who espoused these ideologies shape the political history of Europe between 1815 and 1848?
- How did liberal and conservative leaders use the ideology of nationalism as a tool to unite the people of various territories into nation-states between 1848 and 1871?

New Ideologies in the Early Nineteenth Century

In the wake of the French Revolution, four new ideologies—liberalism, conservatism, socialism, and nationalism—led thousands of Europeans to call for profound changes in the established political order. These ideologies had their roots in the works of eighteenth-century writers, but they developed into integrated systems of thought and inspired political programs in the first half of the nineteenth century.

LIBERALISM: THE PROTECTION OF INDIVIDUAL FREEDOM

Liberalism° is anchored in the beliefs that political, social, and economic freedoms are of supreme importance and that the main function of government is to protect those freedoms. The political agendas of nineteenth-century liberals varied from one country to another, but they all pursued three main objectives. The first objective was to establish and protect individual rights, such as the freedom of the press, freedom of religion, and freedom from arbitrary arrest and imprisonment. Liberals sought to guarantee these rights by having them enumerated in written constitutions. Opposed to aristocratic privilege, liberals supported the principle of equality before the law. As defenders of individual freedom they often campaigned to end slavery and serfdom.

The second objective of liberals was the extension of the franchise (the right to vote) to all property owners, especially those in the middle class. For the most part liberals were opposed to giving the vote to the lower classes, on the grounds that poor people, with little property of their own, could not be trusted to elect representatives who would protect property rights. Liberals also were opposed to giving the vote or any other form of political power to women. They justified the exclusion on the grounds that the proper arena for female activity was the home, where women occupied their natural domain. Liberals believed that only male property holders should be allowed to participate in public affairs.

The third objective of liberals was to promote free trade with other nations and to resist government regulation of the domestic economy. This economic dimension of liberal ideology, which is grounded in the writings of the Scottish economist Adam Smith and other advocates of free-market capitalism, is usually referred to as laissez-faire°, a phrase that means "let (people) do (as they choose)." Advocates of *laissez-faire* held that the government should intervene in the economy only if it is necessary to maintain public order and protect property rights.

Liberalism found its greatest strength among the urban middle class: merchants, manufacturers, and members of the professions. These people formed the group that felt most aggrieved by their exclusion from political life during the eighteenth and early nineteenth centuries and most eager to have government protect their property. Their substantial wealth provided the basis for their claim to acquire a share of political power, and as manufacturers and merchants they had the most to gain from an economy unfettered by government regulations.

CONSERVATISM: PRESERVING THE ESTABLISHED ORDER

Throughout human history people have demonstrated a desire to maintain the established order and to resist change. In the early nineteenth century, however, the ideals of the Enlightenment and the radical changes ushered in by the French Revolution led to the formulation of a new ideology of conservatism°, a set of ideas intended to prevent a recurrence of the revolutionary changes of the 1790s. The main goal of conservatives after 1815 was to preserve the monarchies and aristocracies of Europe against liberal and national movements.

The writer who most clearly articulated the principles of the new conservatism was the fiery, Irish-born parliamentary orator Edmund Burke (1729–1797). Burke had enormous respect for the existing social order, which he considered the handiwork of God. In his view society was a partnership between the living, the dead, and those who had yet to be born. On the basis of this view of the social order, Burke attacked the liberal and radical ideas that had inspired the French Revolution. In *Reflections on the Revolution in France* (1790), he asserted that equality was a dangerous myth; its effect would be to allow those at the bottom to plunder those at the top and thus destroy the social order. In Burke's view rights did not derive from human nature, as they did for the philosophes of the Enlightenment; rights were privileges that had been passed down through the ages and could be preserved only by a hereditary monarchy.

A fine line separates conservatism, which allows for gradual change, and reaction, which is the effort to reject any changes that have taken place and return to the old order. Early nineteenth-century conservatism provided an ideological foundation for the reactionary movements that arose throughout Europe after 1815. These movements had both national and international dimensions. In all western European countries, groups of influential and powerful individuals, usually nobles and churchmen, were determined to return to the days when they had more power. Internationally, the rulers of Europe, under the leadership of the Austrian foreign minister Clemens von Metternich, established a mechanism known as the Concert of Europe° to preserve the map of Europe as it was drawn at the Congress of Vienna (see Chapter 19). To do so meant taking concerted action against liberals and nationalists who attempted to unseat dynastic rulers.

Socialism: The Demand for Equality

Socialism, the third new ideology of the early nineteenth century, arose in response to the development of industrial capitalism and the liberal ideas that justified it. Socialism calls for the ownership of the means of production (such as factories, machines, and railroads) by the community, with the purpose of reducing inequalities of income, wealth, opportunity, and economic power. In small communities, such as some early nineteenth-century socialist settlements, ownership could be genuinely collective. In a large country, however, the only practical way to introduce socialism would be to give the ownership of property to the state, which represents the people.

The main appeal of socialism was the prospect of remedying the deplorable social and economic effects of the Industrial Revolution. Socialists did not object to the mechanization of industry as such. Like liberals, they wanted society to be as productive as possible. They did, however, object to the system of industrial capitalism that accompanied industrialization and the liberal economic theory that justified it.

The most radical form of nineteenth-century socialism was formulated by the German social philosopher Karl Marx (1818–1883). Marx was much more preoccupied than other socialists with the collective identity and political activities of the working class. Reading about working conditions in France during the early 1840s, Marx became convinced that workers in industrial society were the ultimate example of human alienation and degradation. In 1844 he began a lifetime association with another German-born philosopher, Friedrich Engels (1820–1895), who exposed the wretchedness of working class life in Manchester, England. Marx and Engels began to think of workers as part of a capitalist system, in which they owned nothing but their labor, which they sold to capitalist producers for wages.

Marx and Engels worked these ideas into a broad account of historical change in which society moved inevitably and progressively from one stage to another. They referred to the process by which history advanced as the dialectic°. Marx acquired the idea of the dialectic from the German philosopher Georg Wilhelm Friedrich Hegel (1770–1831), who believed that history advanced in stages as the result of the conflict between one idea and another. Marx disagreed with Hegel on the source of historical change, arguing that material or economic factors rather than ideas determined the course of history. Hence Marx's socialist philosophy became known as dialectical materialism°.

According to Marx and Engels, the first stage of the dialectic had taken place when the bourgeoisie, who received their income from capital, seized political power from the aristocracy, who received their income from land, during the English and French revolutions. Marx and Engels predicted that the next stage of this historical process would be a conflict between the bourgeoisie and the working class or proletariat°, which received its income from wages. This conflict, according to Marx and Engels, would result in the triumph of the working class. Led by a committed band of revolutionaries, the proletariat would take control of the state, establish a dictatorship so that they could implement their program without opposition, and usher in a classless society.

Marx and Engels issued this call to action in *The Communist Manifesto* (1848), which ended with the famous words, "Working men of all countries unite!" Marx's brand of socialism, communism°, takes its name from this book. Communism is a revolutionary ideology that advocates the overthrow of "bourgeois" or capitalist institutions and the transfer of political power to the proletariat. Communism differs from more moderate forms of socialism in its call for revolution, its emphasis on class conflict, and its insistence on complete economic equality.

KARL MARX AND FRIEDRICH ENGELS, *THE COMMUNIST MANIFESTO* (1848)

....

These excerpts from the final pages of The Communist Manifesto *summarize the communist plan for establishing a socialist society by means of revolution. They reveal Marx's view of history as a succession of class conflicts and his prediction that the proletariat will become the ruling class. The appeal for working-class solidarity and revolution illustrates the power of socialist ideology to inspire people to action.*

The history of all past society has consisted in the development of class antagonisms, antagonisms that have assumed different forms at different epochs. But whatever form they may have taken, one fact is common to all past ages, viz., the exploitation of one part of society by the other . . .

We have seen above that the first step in the revolution by the working class is to raise the proletariat to the position of ruling class, to win the battle of democracy. The proletariat will use its political supremacy to wrest, by degrees, all capital from the bourgeoisie, to centralize all means of production in the hands of the state, i.e., of the proletariat organized as the ruling class, and to increase the total of productive forces as rapidly as possible.

If the proletariat during its contest with the bourgeoisie is compelled by the force of circumstances, to organize itself as a class, if by means of a revolution it makes itself the ruling class, and as such sweeps away by force the old conditions of production, then it will, along with these conditions, have swept away the conditions for the existence of class antagonisms and of classes generally, and will thereby have abolished its own supremacy as a class. . . .

Communists disdain to conceal their views and aims. They openly declare that their ends can be attained only by the violent overthrow of all existing social conditions. Let the ruling classes tremble at a Communist revolution. The proletarians have nothing to lose but their chains. They have a world to win. WORKING MEN OF ALL COUNTRIES UNITE!

Source: From Karl Marx and Friedrich Engels, *The Communist Manifesto*, 1848, translated in English by Friedrich Engels in 1888.

NATIONALISM: THE UNITY OF THE PEOPLE

Nationalism, the fourth new ideology of the early nineteenth century, also took shape during and after the French Revolution. A nation° in the nineteenth-century sense of the word refers to a large community of people who possess a sense of unity based on a belief that they have a common homeland and share a similar culture. The ideology of nationalism° is the belief that the people who form this nation should have their own political institutions and that the interests of the nation should be defended and promoted at all costs.

The geographical boundaries of nations do not often correspond to the geographical boundaries of states, which are administrative and legal units of political organization. For example, in the early nineteenth century Germans often referred to their nation as comprising all people who spoke German. At that time, however, there were several German states, such as Prussia, Bavaria, and Baden. A primary goal of nationalists is to create a nation-state°, a single political entity that governs all the members of a particular nation. The doctrine that justifies this goal is national self-determination°, the claim that any group that considers itself a nation has the right to be ruled only by members of its own nation and to have all the members of the nation included in this state.

Nationalists emphasized the antiquity of nations, arguing that there had always been a distinct German, French, English, Swiss, or Italian people living in their respective homelands. This claim involved a certain amount of fiction, since in the past the people living in those lands possessed little cultural unity. There was little uniformity, for example, in the languages spoken by people who were identified as German, French, or Italian. Until the eighteenth century most educated Germans wrote in French, not German. Only a small percentage of Italians spoke Italian, and the main language of many Italian nationalists of the nineteenth century was French. Even after nation-states were formed, a large measure of linguistic, religious, and ethnic diversity has persisted within those states and has made true cultural unity impossible. The nation is therefore in a certain sense a myth—an imagined community to which nationalists believe they belong, but which in reality has never existed.

Nationalism was often linked to liberalism during the early nineteenth century, when both movements supported revolutionary programs to realize the goal of national self-determination. Liberals believed that representative government and a limited expansion of the franchise would provide a firm foundation for the establishment of the nation-state, both in nations like Spain with a long tradition of self-rule as well as in countries like Greece that were seeking their independence from autocratic rulers. In Germany and Italy, where there was no central state, nationalists and liberals joined together to create one. There was, however, a difference of emphasis between the two ideologies, even in the early years of the nineteenth century. Liberalism stressed individual freedom, whereas nationalism was more concerned with political unity. At times those different ideals came into conflict with each other. The liberal doctrine of free trade, for example, ran into conflict with the doctrine of economic nationalism, which encouraged the protection of national industries.

Nationalism was just as capable of supporting conservatism as liberalism in the early nineteenth century. Since the nation was often viewed as having deep roots in the distant past, some nationalists glorified the monarchical and hierarchical political arrangements that prevailed in the Middle Ages. In 1848 conservative Prussian landlords rallied around the cause of "God, King, and Fatherland." Later in the nineteenth century, nationalism became identified almost exclusively with conservatism when the lower middle classes began to prefer the achievement of national glory, either in warfare or in imperialistic pursuits, to the establishment of individual freedom.

CULTURE AND IDEOLOGY

As the four great ideologies of the Western world were developing during the nineteenth century, they were influenced by two powerful cultural traditions: scientific rationalism and romanticism. These two traditions represented two sharply divergent sides of modern Western culture.

Scientific Rationalism

Scientific rationalism is a manner of thinking that traces its origins to the Scientific Revolution and reached its full flowering in the Enlightenment. This tradition has provided a major source of Western identity ever since the late eighteenth century. It has stressed the powers of human reason and considered science superior to all other forms of knowledge. Scientific rationalism is essentially a secular tradition in that it does not rely on theology or Christian revelation for its legitimacy. The effort to construct a science of human nature, which was central to Enlightenment thought, belongs to this tradition, while the Industrial Revolution, which involved the application of scientific knowledge to production, was one of its products.

During the nineteenth century, scientific rationalism continued to have a powerful influence on Western thought and action. As scientific knowledge continued to grow, and as more people received a scientific education, the values of science and reason were proclaimed more boldly. Scientific knowledge and an emphasis on the importance of empirical data (that which can be tested) became essential components of much social thought. The clearest statement that science was the highest form of knowledge and would lead inevitably to human progress was the secular philosophy of positivism°.

The main elements of positivism were set forth by the French philosopher Auguste Comte (1798–1857). Like many thinkers in the Enlightenment tradition, Comte argued that human society passed through a succession of historical stages, each leading to a higher level. It had already passed through two stages, the theological and the metaphysical, and it was now in the third, the positive or scientific stage. Comte predicted that in the final positive stage of history the accumulation of factual or scientific knowledge would enable thinkers to discover the laws of human behavior and thus make possible the improvement of society.

Romanticism

The cultural tradition that posed the greatest challenge to scientific rationalism was romanticism°. This tradition originated as an artistic and literary movement in the late eighteenth century, but it soon developed into a more general worldview. The artists and writers who identified themselves as romantics recognized the limits of human reason in comprehending reality. Unlike scientific rationalists, they used intuition and imagination to penetrate deeper levels of being and to comprehend the entire cosmos. Romantic art, music, and literature therefore appealed to the passions rather than the intellect.

Romantics did not think of reality as being simply material, as did the positivists. For them it was also spiritual and emotional, and their purpose as writers and artists was to communicate that non-empirical dimension of reality to their audiences. Romantics also had a different view of the relationship between human beings and nature. Instead of standing outside nature and viewing it objectively, in the manner of a scientist analyzing data derived from experiments, they considered themselves a part of nature and emphasized its beauty and power.

As an art form, romanticism was a protest against the classicism that prevailed in the late eighteenth century. As we discussed in Chapter 18, classicism reflects a worldview in which the principles of orderliness and rationality prevail. Classicism is a disciplined style that demands adherence to formal rules that governed the structure as well as the content of literature, art, architecture, and music. By contrast romanticism allows the artist much greater freedom.

In literature the romantic protest against classicism led to the introduction of a new poetic style involving the use of imagery, symbols, and myth. Many romantic prose works explore the exotic, the weird, the mysterious, and even the satanic elements in human nature. Mary Shelley's introspective novel *Frankenstein* (1818), an early example of science fiction that embodies a critique of scientific rationalism, incorporates many of these themes.

Within the visual arts, romanticism also marked a rebellion against the classicism that had dominated eighteenth-century culture. Classicism emphasized formality and symmetry in art, and it celebrated the culture of an ideal Greek and Roman past. By contrast, romantic painters depicted landscapes that evoked a mood and an emotion rather than

■ **John Martin, *Sadak in Search of the Waters of Oblivion* (1812)**
This painting reflects the romantic concern with the fantastic or the bizarre as well as its intention to convey the power of nature.

an objective pictorial account of the surroundings. Romantic paintings were intended to evoke feeling rather than to help the viewer achieve intellectual comprehension.

Romantic music, which also appealed to the emotions, marked a similar but more gradual departure from the formal classicism that was triumphant during the eighteenth century. The inspirational music of Ludwig van Beethoven (1770–1827) marked the transition from classical to romantic forms. Beethoven's early work conformed to the conventions of classical music, but his later compositions, which were completed as he became progressively deaf and which defied traditional classical harmonies, were intended to evoke an emotional response. His famous "Ode to Joy," in his ninth and final symphony, remains unequaled in its ability to rouse the passions. In the view of one critic, Beethoven's music "opens the floodgates of fear, of terror, of horror, of pain, and arouses that longing for the eternal which is the essence of romanticism."

Romanticism, like the rational and scientific culture it rejected, had powerful political implications, leaving its mark on the ideologies of the modern world. In the early nineteenth century, romanticism appealed to many liberals because it involved a protest against the established order and emphasized the freedom of the individual. In France wealthy liberal bourgeoisie generally patronized romantic music and literature, while nobles and clerics denounced

them. Romanticism could, however, provide support for conservatism by idealizing the traditional social and political order of the Middle Ages and the central importance of religion in society.

Romanticism has a closer association with nationalism than with any other ideology. In the most general sense romanticism invested the idea of "the nation" with mystical qualities, thus inspiring devotion to it. Romantics also had an obsessive interest in the cultural, literary, and historical roots of national identity. This connection between romanticism and nationalism can be seen in the work of the German philosopher and literary critic Johann Gottfried von Herder (1744–1803), who was one of the leaders of a literary movement that encouraged subjectivity and a revolt against accepted classical standards. Herder promoted the study of German language, literature, and history with the explicit purpose of giving the German people a common sense of national unity. Like many romantics, Herder idealized the Middle Ages and cultivated many of the myths that surrounded that epoch in Germany's history.

Ideological Encounters in Europe, 1815–1848

The four new ideologies of the nineteenth century—liberalism, conservatism, socialism, and nationalism—interacted in a variety of ways, sometimes reinforcing each other and at other times leading to direct and violent political conflict. During the years between 1815 and 1831 the main ideological encounters occurred between liberalism, sometimes infused with nationalism, and conservatism. In 1815, at the time of the Congress of Vienna, it appeared that conservatism would carry the day. The determination of Metternich, the Austrian minister, to employ all the resources of the Concert of Europe to suppress any signs of revolutionary activity made the future of liberalism and nationalism appear bleak. The power of the new ideologies, however, could not be completely contained. Liberal and nationalist revolts took place in three distinct periods: the early 1820s, 1830, and 1848. During the latter two periods the demands of workers, sometimes expressed in socialist terms, added to the ideological mixture. In all these encounters conservatives had their say, and in most cases they emerged victorious.

LIBERAL AND NATIONALIST REVOLTS, 1820–1825

Between 1820 and 1825 a sequence of revolts in Europe revealed the explosive potential of liberalism and nationalism and the determination of conservatives to crush those ideologies. These revolts also reflected the strength of movements for national self-determination. The three most significant revolts took place in Spain, Greece, and Russia.

The Liberal Revolt of 1820 in Spain

The earliest clash between liberalism and conservatism occurred in Spain, where liberals ran into determined opposition from their king, Ferdinand VII (r. 1808–1833). Ferdinand had been restored to power in 1814 after his forced abdication in 1808. In 1812, during the rule of Joseph Bonaparte, the Spanish *cortes* —the representative assembly in that kingdom—had approved a liberal constitution. This constitution provided a foundation for a limited monarchy and the protection of Spanish civil liberties. In keeping with the ideas of the French Revolution, it also declared that the Spanish nation, not the king, possessed sovereignty. The tension began when King Ferdinand declared that he would not recognize this constitution. Even worse for the disheartened liberals was Ferdinand's decision to reestablish the Spanish Inquisition, invite exiled Jesuits to return, and refuse to summon the *cortes*. In 1820, when the Spanish Empire in the New World had already begun to collapse (see Chapter 17), liberals in Madrid, in alliance with some military officers, seized power.

This liberal revolt proved to be a test for the Concert of Europe. Metternich urged intervention, and although the British refused because they wanted to protect their trading interests with the Spanish colonies, Russia, Prussia, and Austria supported the invasion of Spain by a French army of 200,000 men. Ferdinand was restored once again to the throne, and once again he renounced the liberal constitution of 1812. The liberals not only lost this struggle, but they also suffered bitter reprisals from the government, which tortured and executed their leaders.

The Nationalist Revolt of 1821 in Greece

A revolt in Greece in 1821, inspired more by nationalism than liberalism, achieved greater success than did the rebellions of 1820 in Spain. It succeeded because other members of the Concert of Europe, not just Britain, lent their support to the revolt. Greece had long been a province in the sprawling Ottoman Empire, but a nationalist movement, organized by Prince Alexander Ypsilantis (1792–1828), created a distinct Greek national identity and inspired the demand for a separate Greek state. In 1821 a series of revolts against Ottoman rule took place on the mainland of Greece and on some of the surrounding islands. These rebellions received widespread support in Europe from scholars who considered Greece the cradle of Western civilization and from religiously inspired individuals who saw this as a struggle of Christianity against Islam. Hundreds of European volunteers joined the Greek rebel forces. Thus the insurrection became not only a liberal and national revolt but also a broad cultural encounter between East and West.

The Greek revolt placed the powers allied in the Concert of Europe in a quandary. On the one hand they were committed to intervene on behalf of the established order to crush any nationalist or liberal revolts, and they condemned the insurrection on those grounds when it first erupted. On the other hand they were Western rulers who identified the Ottoman Turks with everything that was alien to Christian civilization. The European powers eventually took the side of the Greek rebels, who in 1833 finally won their independence and placed a Bavarian prince, Otto I (r. 1833–1862), on the throne. Thus the Greek war of

CHRONOLOGY

1820	Liberal Revolt in Spain
1821	Beginning of Greek revolt against the Ottoman Empire
1825	Decembrist Revolt in Russia against Nicholas I
1830	Revolution in Paris, Louis-Philippe I becomes king of France; beginning of the Polish Rebellion
1848	
February	Revolution in Paris
March	Insurrection in Berlin; revolutions in Milan and Venice
May	Meeting of the Frankfurt Parliament; meeting of the Prussian Assembly
December	Election of Louis-Napoleon as president of the Second French Republic; Frederick William dissolves Prussian Assembly

■ Eugène Delacroix, *The Massacre at Chios* (1824)

In 1821 the Greeks on the Aegean Islands rebelled against their Turkish rulers, and in April 1822 Turkish reprisals reached their peak in the massacre of the inhabitants of Chios. Romantic paintings were intended to evoke feelings, in this case horror, at the genocide perpetrated by the Turks against the Greek rebels. The painting reveals the close association of romantic art with the causes of liberalism and nationalism.

independence effectively ended the Concert of Europe. Originally intended to crush nationalist and liberal revolts, the Concert had in this case helped one succeed.

The Decembrist Revolt of 1825 in Russia

The least successful of the early liberal revolts took place in Russia, where a number of army officers, influenced by liberal ideas while serving in western Europe during the Napoleonic wars, staged a rebellion against the government of Tsar Nicholas I (r. 1825–1855) on the first day of his reign. The officers, together with other members of the nobility, had been meeting for almost a decade in political clubs, such as the Society of True and Faithful Sons of the Fatherland in St. Petersburg, where they pursued their goals of establishing a constitutional monarchy and emancipating the serfs.

When Tsar Alexander I died suddenly in 1825, the rebels, who were known as Decembrists° for the month in which their rebellion took place, hoped to persuade his brother Constantine to assume the throne and establish a representative form of government. Their hopes were dashed when Constantine refused to tamper with the succession and accepted the reign of his brother Nicholas. The reactionary Nicholas had no difficulty suppressing the revolt, executing its leaders, and leaving Russian liberals to

struggle against police repression for the remainder of the nineteenth century.

LIBERAL AND NATIONALIST REVOLTS, 1830

A second cluster of liberal and national revolts in 1830 achieved a greater measure of success than the revolts of the early 1820s. These revolutions took place in France, the kingdom of the Netherlands, and the kingdom of Poland.

The French Revolution: The Success of Liberalism

The most striking triumph of liberalism in Europe during the early nineteenth century occurred in France, where a revolution took place fifteen years after the final defeat of Napoleon at Waterloo. This liberal success did not come easily. During the first few years of the restored monarchy conservatives had their way. Louis XVIII had approved a Charter of Liberties in 1814, but he was hardly receptive to any further liberal reforms.

During the reign of the conservative Charles X (r. 1824–1830) liberals gained support from merchants and manufacturers, as well as from soldiers who still kept the memory of Napoleon alive. When liberals feared that Charles would claim absolute power, and when a serious economic crisis afflicted the country in 1829, liberals at last gained a majority in the Chamber of Deputies, the French legislature.

Charles then embarked upon a perilous course. In what became known as the July Ordinances he effectively undermined the principles of the Charter of 1814. These ordinances dissolved the new Chamber of Deputies, ordered new elections under a highly restrictive franchise, and censored the press. The public reaction to this maneuver caught the king by surprise. Thousands of students and workers, liberals and republicans alike, poured onto the streets of Paris to demonstrate. Skirmishes with the king's troops only made the situation worse, and when the tricolor flag of the French Revolution appeared on top of Notre Dame Cathedral, protesters blocked the streets with barricades. Unable to restore order, the king abdicated in favor of his grandson, but the liberals offered the crown instead to the Duke of Orléans, who was crowned as Louis-Philippe I (r. 1830–1848).

Louis-Philippe accepted a revised version of the Charter of 1814 and doubled the franchise, giving the vote to middle-class merchants and industrialists. The king catered to this bourgeois constituency by encouraging economic growth and restricting noble privilege. His reign, which is often referred to as the "bourgeois monarchy," also achieved a measure of secularization when the Chamber of Deputies declared that Roman Catholicism was no longer the state religion. In keeping with mainstream liberal ideals, however, he did nothing to encourage republicanism or radical democracy, much less socialism.

The Belgian Revolution: The Success of Nationalism

The French Revolution of 1830 triggered the outbreak of a liberal and nationalist revolution in the neighboring country of Belgium. At the Congress of Vienna the Austrian Netherlands were united with the Dutch Republic in a new kingdom of the Netherlands. This union of the Low Countries did not work out, and soon after the formation of the new kingdom the Belgians began pressing for their independence as a nation. With a Dutchman, William I, as king and with the seat of government in Holland, the Dutch were the dominant partner in this union, a situation that caused considerable resentment in Belgium. Belgians spoke Flemish or French rather than Dutch, which had become the kingdom's official language. Moreover, most Belgians were Catholics, whereas the majority of Dutch people were Protestants. With their own language, religion, and culture, as well as their own history, Belgians thought of themselves as a separate nation.

When the news of the Revolution in Paris reached Brussels, fighting broke out between workers and government troops. A national congress gathered to write a new constitution, and when the Dutch tried to thwart the rebellion by bombarding the Belgian city of Antwerp, Britain assembled a conference of European powers to devise a settlement. The powers agreed to recognize Belgium's independence, and they arranged for a German prince, Leopold of Saxe-Coburg, to become king. The Dutch, however, refused to recognize the new government, and they renewed their military attacks on Belgium. Only in 1839 did all sides accept the new political arrangement.

The Polish Rebellion: The Failure of Nationalism

The French Revolution of 1830 triggered a second uprising, this one unsuccessful, in the kingdom of Poland. Poland had suffered many partitions at the hands of European powers during the eighteenth century, and in 1815 the Congress of Vienna had redefined its borders once again. After incorporating much of the eastern portion of the country into the Russian Empire, the Congress established a separate Polish kingdom, with Warsaw as its capital and the Russian Tsar, Alexander I, as its king (r. 1815–1825).

Alexander had approved a liberal Polish constitution in 1815, but he grew to regret this decision, and his rule as king of Poland gradually alienated Polish liberals within the national legislature, the *sejm*. The accession of Nicholas in 1825 only aggravated those tensions, and in 1830 a revolt that began within the school of army cadets quickly gained the support of the entire army and the urban populace. The revolt appealed to both liberals and nationalists, and it drew inspiration from a group of romantic poets who celebrated the achievements of the Polish past. When the powers of western Europe refused to intervene on behalf of this liberal cause, however, Nicholas was able to crush the rebellion, abolish the *sejm*, and deprive the kingdom of Poland of its autonomous status. His brutal repression set back the cause of liberalism and nationalism in Poland for another two generations.

LIBERAL REFORM IN BRITAIN, 1815–1848

The challenges that liberals faced in Britain were somewhat different from those they confronted in most other European countries. Having maintained the status quo during the era of the French Revolution, the forces of British conservatism remained formidable. At the same time, however, Britons already enjoyed many of the rights that liberals on the European continent demanded, such as freedom of the press and protection from arbitrary imprisonment. The power of the British monarchy was more limited than in almost any other European country. The ideology of liberalism, which had deep roots in British political and social philosophy, defined the political creed of many Whigs, who formed the main opposition to the ruling Conservative or Tory party after 1815.

In this relatively favorable political climate, British liberals pursued three major goals, which amounted to a program for reform rather than revolution. The first was parliamentary reform and the expansion of the franchise, which they achieved when a Whig prime minister, Lord

Grey, who came to power in 1830, pushed the Great Reform Bill through Parliament in 1832. The bill expanded the franchise to include most of the urban middle class, created a number of new boroughs in heavily populated areas, and established a uniform standard for the right to vote in all parliamentary boroughs. In keeping with the principles of liberalism, however, the bill restricted the vote, and hence active citizenship, to property owners. It rejected the demands of radicals for universal male suffrage and it denied women the vote.

The second liberal cause was the repeal of legislation that denied political power to Catholics and also to Protestants who did not attend the services of the Anglican Church. Liberals were opposed on principle to religious discrimination, and many of them belonged to Protestant nonconformist congregations. Conservatives opposed the repeal of this legislation, but they feared a civil war in Ireland if Catholics were not allowed to sit in the British Parliament. The Tory prime minister, the Duke of Wellington, eventually agreed to liberal demands. The Protestant nonconformists were emancipated in 1828, while the Catholics had to wait until one year later.

The third liberal cause was free trade. The target of this campaign was a series of protective tariffs on the import or export of hundreds of commodities, including raw materials used in production. The most hated protective tariff was on grain (known in Britain as corn), which kept the price of

basic food commodities high in order to protect the interests of landlords and farmers. In 1837 a group of reformers formed the Anti–Corn Law League with the purpose of bringing about the repeal of the Corn Law of 1815, which greatly restricted the importation of foreign grain into Britain. This campaign against protectionism did not succeed until 1845, when the Tory prime minister, Sir Robert Peel, brought about repeal by securing the votes of some of his own party and combining them with those of the Whigs, all of whom favored free trade.

Unlike the liberals, socialists and radical democrats achieved little success in Britain during the first half of the nineteenth century. In 1837 members of the London Workingman's Association, in collaboration with a few radical Members of Parliament, drew up a People's Charter, calling for the implementation of a program of radical democracy. Their demands included universal male suffrage, annual parliaments, voting by secret ballot, equal electoral districts, the elimination of property qualifications for Members of Parliament, and the payment of salaries to those same members. The workers who supported this cause became known as Chartists.

In 1848 the Chartists decided to draft a new charter and threatened to form a revolutionary national assembly if Parliament were to reject the new document. Within the next few years, however, the Chartist movement died. British workers revealed, as they would throughout the re-

The Last Great Chartist Rally in Britain, April 10, 1848

Government precautions, including the appointment of special constables to handle the crowd, and rain kept the number of demonstrators in London lower than anticipated. The government ordered the leader of the movement, Feargus O'Connor, to stop the planned march to Parliament.

mainder of the nineteenth century, that they had little inclination to take to the streets, especially after good economic times returned. The government's reduction of indirect taxes during the 1840s also helped prevent Britain from experiencing revolution in 1848.

THE REVOLUTIONS OF 1848

Unlike Britain, almost every country in Europe experienced revolution in 1848. A wave of revolutionary activity spread rapidly throughout the Continent. The revolutions took place during a period of widespread economic discontent. European countries had suffered bad harvests in 1845 and 1846 and an economic recession in 1847, leading to a temporary decline in the standard of living among industrial as well as agricultural workers. Discontent took the form of mass protests and demonstrations, which increased the likelihood of violent confrontation. The revolutions of 1848 were more widespread than the revolts of the 1820s and 1830, and they involved greater popular participation. These revolutions also gave greater attention to both nationalist and socialist issues.

The French Revolutions of 1848

The first of the revolutions of 1848 took place in France, where the liberal government of Louis-Philippe faced mounting criticism. A series of demonstrations in Paris in favor of the right of workers to vote and to receive state assistance for their trades was the final precipitant. When troops from the Paris National Guard fired on the demonstrators and killed forty people, the barricades once again appeared in the streets and the rebels seized government buildings. In an effort to save his regime, Louis-Philippe abdicated in favor of his grandson, but the revolutionaries abolished the monarchy and declared the Second French Republic.

A provisional republican government that included liberals, radical democrats, and two socialists offered French socialists the first opportunity to realize their goal of a democratic and socialist republic. The socialist agenda included not only universal male suffrage, which was granted immediately by the government, but also active support for the masses of unemployed workers. National workshops were set up to give the unemployed jobs on public projects, while ordinances reduced the length of the workday to ten hours in the city and twelve hours in rural areas.

These bold socialist initiatives did not last long. The elections held in April 1848 to constitute a new National Assembly and write a new constitution seated an overwhelming majority of conservative monarchists and only a small minority of republicans and socialists. Resentment of the provisional government's assistance to urban workers and anger at the levying of a surtax to pay for government programs revealed the lack of broad popular support for radical political programs. Tension between the new conservative assembly and the forces of the left mounted when

the government closed the workshops and Parisian workers were either drafted into the army or sent to the provinces.

These newly adopted policies led to further working-class violence in Paris in June 1848. When General Louis Cavaignac, known as "the butcher," was called in to suppress this insurgency with regular army troops, there was a devastating loss of life. No fewer than 1,500 insurgents were killed in the streets or in summary executions, while another 4,000 were sent into exile in French colonies. These confrontations appeared to Karl Marx to constitute class warfare, a prelude to the proletarian revolution he predicted for the future. The socialist Louis Blanc, who was implicated in these uprisings, fled to England, where Marx himself would soon arrive and spend the rest of his life.

The revolution ended with the election of Napoleon's nephew, Louis-Napoleon Bonaparte (1808–1873), as the president of the Second French Republic in December 1848. As president, Louis-Napoleon drew support from conservatives, liberals, and moderate republicans. He also benefited from the legend that his uncle had created and the nationalist sentiment it inspired. The younger Napoleon followed in his uncle's footsteps, seizing power in December 1851 and proclaiming himself emperor of the French one year later. He called himself Napoleon III, in deference to the dynastic rights of the uncrowned Napoleon II, the son of Napoleon I who had died in 1823. During the Second Empire, which lasted until 1870, Napoleon III pursued moderate liberal policies and restored a semblance of parliamentary government, but he never satisfied the demands of republicans and socialists. Having been defeated in 1848, these radicals attempted to achieve their goals once again in 1870 with the establishment of the Paris Commune, as discussed at the beginning of this chapter.

The Revolutions of 1848 in Germany, Austria, Hungary, and Bohemia

Until French revolutionaries built barricades in the streets of Paris in 1848, liberalism and nationalism had achieved little success in Germany. German university students, inspired by the slogan "Honor, Freedom, Fatherland," had staged a number of large rallies during the early years of the nineteenth century, but the forces of conservatism had kept them in check.

A major opportunity for the liberal cause in Germany came in 1848 in the immediate wake of the revolution in France. As in France, however, this opportunity was complicated by the more radical demands of democrats and socialists for universal suffrage, including equal rights for women. German radicals also demanded government assistance for artisans and workers who had suffered economic hardship as a result of industrialization. In Berlin, the capital of Prussia, these discontents led radicals to barricade the streets. The situation became more serious after troops fired into the crowd, killing some 250 people. The violence spread to the countryside, where peasants demanded that landlords renounce their privileges and grant them free use

Prostitution, Corporal Punishment, and Liberalism in Germany

In March 1822 Gesche Rudolph, a poor, uneducated 25-year-old woman from the northern German city of Bremen, was arrested by municipal authorities for engaging in prostitution without registering with the police. Ever since the days when troops from five different European nations had occupied her neighborhood, Rudolph had been selling her sexual services as her only form of livelihood. After her arrest she was not given a formal trial but was summarily expelled from the city and banned from ever returning. Unable to earn a living through prostitution in a village outside the city, where she resided with a brother who physically abused her, Rudolph returned to the city, where she was arrested once again for prostitution. This time she was sentenced to fifty strokes of the cane and six weeks in jail, after which she was once again expelled from the city. Returning again to Bremen, she was arrested in a drunken stupor in a whorehouse and subjected to a harsher sentence of three months' imprisonment and 150 strokes before another expulsion. This pattern of arrest and punishment, expulsion and return occurred repeatedly during the next two decades, with the number of strokes rising to 275 and the period of imprisonment to six years. During a portion of her prison sentence she was given only bread and water for nourishment.

Rudolph's arrest in 1845 at the end of a six-year imprisonment and her subsequent expulsion and return to Bremen led to the appointment of a liberal lawyer, Georg Wilhelm Gröning, to represent her. After reviewing her case and calculating that she had been whipped a total of 893 times and imprisoned for a cumulative period of eighteen years, Gröning appealed her sentence to the senate of Bremen on the grounds that her treatment was not only futile but immoral. His appeal addressed an issue that went far beyond this particular case or even the prosecution of the crime of prostitution. Gröning's action raised the highly controversial issue of the legitimacy and value of corporal punishment, an issue that pitted liberals and conservatives, who had different notions of justice.

Until the eighteenth century the penal systems of Europe had prescribed corporal punishments, administered publicly, for most crimes. These punishments ranged from whippings and placement in the stocks for minor offenses to mutilation, hanging, and decapitation for felonies. They were justified mainly on the grounds that they provided retribution for the crime and deterred the criminal and those who witnessed the punishment from committing further crimes. These two main functions of retribution and deterrence are the same functions that capital punishment allegedly serves today. Corporal punishments were also intended to humiliate the criminal both by violating the integrity of the body and by subjecting the prisoner to the mockery and sometimes the maltreatment of the crowd. The torture of suspects to obtain evidence also served some of these functions, although judicial torture took place during the trial, not as part of the sentence.

The entire system of corporal punishment, as well as that of torture, came under attack during the eighteenth century. In Prussia torture was abolished in 1754, and the General Law Code of 1794 eliminated many forms of corporal punishment. The General Law Code reflected the concern of Enlightenment thinkers that all such assaults on the body were inhumane and a denial of the moral dignity of the individual. Because corporal punishments in Prussia and elsewhere were administered mainly against people from the lower classes, they also were a violation of the liberal principle of equality before the law.

Despite these efforts at reform, the illegal administration of corporal punishment by public and private authorities continued in Prussia and the other German states. Conservatives, who had a different notion of justice from that of the liberals, defended these sentences on the grounds that all punishment, including imprisonment, was intended to deny the criminal freedom and hence his or her dignity. For them any reference to natural rights and human dignity were "axioms derived from abstract philanthropic speculation." The president of the Prussian police, Julius Baron von Minutoli, expressing the conservative position on the issue, claimed that corporal punishment was more effective than imprisonment in preventing crime, since it alone could instill terror in the criminal.

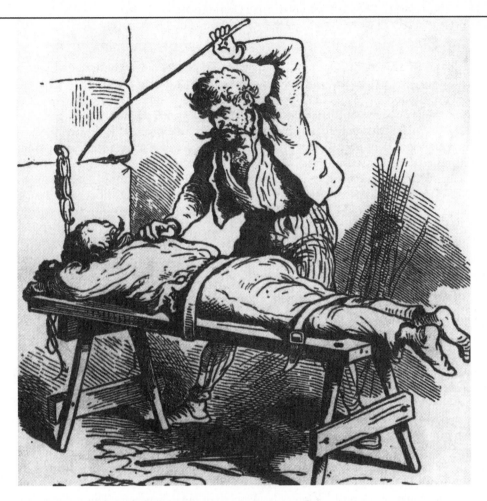

■ **Corporal Punishment in Nineteenth-Century Germany**
Whipping in prisons continued long after public corporal punishment was abolished in the middle of the nineteenth century.

It was apparent that in the case of Gesche Rudolph, 893 strokes had not instilled terror in her or brought about any transformation of her spirit. The Senate made the young woman Gröning's ward and suspended her sentence. Gröning arranged for Rudolph to live in the countryside under the strict supervision of a competent countryman. This compromise solution at least broke the cycle of expulsion, return, and punishment that had failed to reform her. We do not know whether she gave up her life of prostitution.

Soon after Gesche Rudolph became Gröning's ward, the liberal critics of corporal punishment in Germany celebrated a victory. King Frederick William IV of Prussia formally abolished the practice in his kingdom in May 1848. Shortly thereafter the Frankfurt Parliament included freedom from physical punishment by the state in its *Declaration of the Basic Rights of the German People.* Most German states and municipalities, including Bremen, wrote this right into law in 1849. The failure of the Frankfurt Parliament, however, and the more general failure of liberalism in Germany after 1849 led to a strong campaign by conservatives to reinstate corporal punishment in the 1850s. They succeeded only in maintaining corporal punishment within the family, on manorial estates, and in the prisons. Liberalism had not succeeded in completely establishing its standard of justice, but it did end exposure to public shame as a punishment for crime. ■

Questions of Justice

1. What elements of liberalism led those who adhered to this ideology in the nineteenth century to object to corporal punishment?

2. In addition to inflicting physical pain, corporal punishment produces social shame. What is the difference between social shame and legal guilt? In what ways does shame still play a role in punishments today?

Taking It Further

Evans, Richard. *Tales from the German Underworld: Crime and Punishment in the Nineteenth Century.* 1998. Provides a full account of the prosecution of Gesche Rudolph.

of their lands. In response to these pressures, King Frederick William IV summoned an assembly, elected by universal male suffrage, to write a new Prussian constitution.

As these events were unfolding, the contagion of revolution spread to Austria, the other major German kingdom, which formed the nucleus of the sprawling Habsburg Empire. News of the revolution in Paris led to demonstrations by students and workers in Vienna. An assortment of Austrian liberal aristocrats, middle-class professionals, and discontented workers demanded an end to the long rule of the conservative minister, Clemens von Metternich. In response to the demands of these groups, Emperor Ferdinand I (r. 1835–1848) summoned a constitutional assembly and installed a moderate government.

The main difference between the revolutions of 1848 in Austria and the other German lands was that events in Vienna awakened demands of Hungarians and Czechs for national autonomy within the empire. In Hungary the nationalist leader Lajos Kossuth (1802–1894) pushed for a program of liberal reform and national autonomy. This initiative created further tensions between the Magyars and the various national minorities within the kingdom of Hungary. Similar problems arose in Bohemia, where a revolution in Prague led to demands from the Czechs for autonomy within the Habsburg Empire. In June 1848 the Czech rebels hosted a Pan-Slav Congress in Prague to advance a nationalist plan for achieving unity of all Slavic people within the empire. This idealistic proposal could not be realized, for there were many distinct Slavic nationalities, each of which had a desire to preserve its autonomy. In addition, there was a large German-speaking population within Bohemia that identified with other German territories in the Confederation.

The most idealistic and ambitious undertaking of the revolutions in central Europe was the meeting of the Frankfurt Parliament in May 1848. Some 800 middle-class liberals, many of whom were lawyers, officials, and university professors, came from all the German states to draft a constitution for a united Germany. In December 1848 this parliament promulgated a *Declaration of the Basic Rights of the German People,* which recognized the equality of all German people before the law; freedom of speech, assembly, and religion; and the right to private property. Like so many liberal assemblies, however, the Frankfurt Parliament failed to address the needs of workers and peasants and therefore failed to win broad popular support.

In April 1849 the Frankfurt Parliament drafted a new constitution for a united Germany, which would have a hereditary "emperor of the Germans" and two houses of parliament, one of which would be elected by universal male suffrage. King Frederick William of Prussia, however, refused the parliament's offer of the new imperial crown, which he referred to as coming from the gutter and "reeking of the stench of revolution." At that point the Frankfurt Parliament disbanded and the efforts of German liberals to unite their country and give it a new constitution came to an inglorious end.

By the middle of 1849, conservative forces had triumphed in the various German territories and the Habsburg Empire. In Prussia the efforts of the newly elected assembly to restrict noble privilege triggered a reaction from the conservative nobles known as *Junkers.* Frederick William dismissed his liberal appointees, sent troops to Berlin, and disbanded the assembly. In Austria Prince Alfred Windischgrätz, who had crushed the Czech rebels in June, dispersed the rebels in Vienna in October. When Hungary proclaimed its independence from the empire in April 1849, Austrian and Russian forces marched on the country and crushed the movement.

The Revolutions of 1848 in Italy

The revolutions of 1848 also spread to Austrian possessions in the northern Italian territories of Lombardy and Venetia. In Milan, the main city in Lombardy, revolutionary developments followed the same pattern as those in Paris, Berlin, and Vienna. The success of the insurgents in Milan triggered rebellions in other towns in Lombardy, in Venice, and in the southern Kingdom of the Two Sicilies. The spread of these revolts inspired the hope of bringing about the unification of all Italian people in one state.

The ruler who assumed the nationalist mantle in 1848 was Charles Albert of Piedmont-Sardinia, the most economically advanced of the Italian states. This initiative began successfully, as Charles Albert's army, which included volunteers from various parts of Italy, marched into Lombardy and defeated Austrian forces. Instead of moving forward against Austria, however, Charles Albert decided to consolidate his gains, hoping to annex Lombardy to his own kingdom. This decision alienated republicans in Lombardy and in other parts of Italy as well as the rulers of the other Italian states, who feared that Charles Albert's main goal was to expand the limits of his own kingdom at their expense. By August 1848 the military tide had turned. Fresh Austrian troops defeated the Italian nationalists outside Milan. The people of that city turned against Charles Albert, forcing him to return to his own capital of Turin. The Italian revolutions of 1848 had suffered a complete defeat.

National Unification in Europe and America, 1848–1871

Prior to 1848 the forces of nationalism, especially when combined with those of liberalism, had little to show for their efforts. Besides the Greek rebellion of 1821, which succeeded largely because of international opposition to the Turks, the only successful nationalist revolution in Europe took place in Belgium. Both of these nationalist movements were secessionist in that they involved the separation of smaller states from larger empires. Efforts in 1848 to form nations by combining smaller states and territories, as in Italy and Germany, or by uniting all Slavic people, as proposed at the Pan-Slav Congress, had failed. Between 1848 and 1871, however, movements for national unification succeeded in Italy, Germany, and the United States, each in a different way. In the vast Habsburg Empire a different type of unity was achieved, but it did little to promote the cause of nationalism.

ITALIAN UNIFICATION: BUILDING A FRAGILE NATION-STATE

The great project of Italian nationalists, the unification of Italy, faced formidable obstacles. Austrian military control over the northern territories, which in the end had thwarted the nationalist movement of 1848, meant that national unification would not be achieved peacefully. The dramatic economic disparities between the prosperous north and the much poorer south posed a challenge to any plan for economic integration. A long tradition of local autonomy within the kingdoms, states, and principalities made submission to a strong central government unappealing. The unique status of the papacy, which controlled its own territory and which influenced the decisions of many other states, served as another challenge. Despite these obstacles, the dream of a resurgence of Italian power, reviving the achievements of ancient Rome, had great emotive appeal. Hatred of foreigners who controlled Italian territory, which dates back to the fifteenth century, gave further impetus to the nationalist movement.

The main question for Italian nationalism after the failure of 1848 was who could provide effective leadership of the movement. It stood to reason that Piedmont-Sardinia, the strongest and most prosperous Italian kingdom, would be central to that undertaking. Unfortunately the king, Victor Emmanuel II (r. 1849–1861), was more known for his hunting, his carousing, and his affair with a teenage mistress than his statesmanship. Victor Emmanuel did, however, appoint as his prime minister a nobleman with liberal leanings, Count Camillio di Cavour (1810–1861). Cavour was deeply committed to the unification of the Italian peninsula, but only under Piedmontese leadership, and preferably as a federation of states. In many ways he was the antithesis of the republican Giuseppe Mazzini (1805–1872), the other central figure in Italian unification. Mazzini's idealism and romanticism led him to think of national unification as a moral force that would lead to the establishment of a democratic republic, which would then undertake an extensive program of social reform.

Mazzini's strategy for national unification involved a succession of uprisings and invasions. Cavour, however,

adopted a diplomatic course of action intended to gain the military assistance of France against Austria. In 1859 French and Piedmontese forces defeated the Austrians at Magenta and Solferino and drove them out of Lombardy. One year later Napoleon III signed the Treaty of Turin with Cavour, allowing Piedmont-Sardinia to annex Tuscany, Parma, Modena, and the Romagna, while ceding to France the Italian territories of Savoy and Nice. This treaty resulted in the unification of all of northern and central Italy except Venetia in the northeast and the Papal States in the center of the peninsula (see Map 21.1).

The main focus of unification efforts now turned to the Kingdom of the Two Sicilies in the south. A rebellion against the Bourbon monarch Francis II, protesting new taxes and the high price of bread, had taken place there in 1860. At that point the militant republican adventurer Giuseppe Garibaldi (1807–1882) intervened with decisive force. Garibaldi was determined no less than Cavour and Mazzini to drive all foreigners out of Italy and achieve its unification. Originally a supporter of Mazzini's republican goals, Garibaldi gave his support in the 1860s for Italian

■ **Giuseppe Garibaldi**
The uniform he is wearing was derived from his days as a guerilla fighting in the civil war in Uruguay, 1842–1846. Garibaldi also spent two years in asylum in the United States.

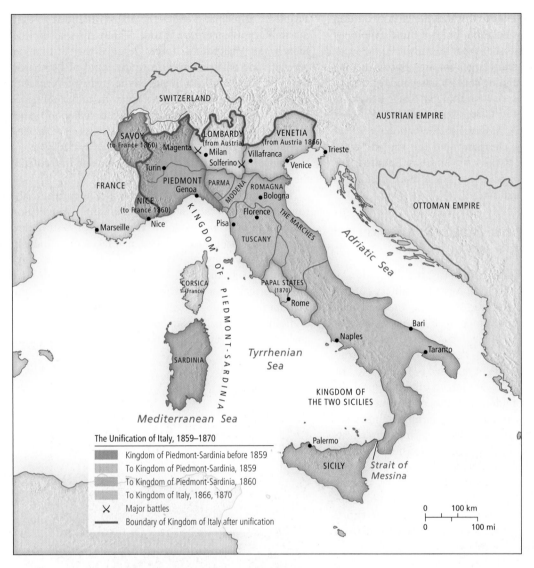

■ **Map 21.1 The Unification of Italy, 1859–1870**

The main steps to unification took place in 1860, when Piedmont-Sardinia acquired Tuscany, Parma, Modena, and the Romagna and when Garibaldi seized control of the Kingdom of the Two Sicilies in the name of King Victor Emmanuel of Piedmont-Sardinia.

unification within the framework of a monarchy. A charismatic military leader, Garibaldi put together an army of volunteers, known as the Red Shirts for their colorful makeshift uniforms. In 1860 he landed in Sicily with an army of 1,000 men, took the main Sicilian city of Palermo, and established a dictatorship on behalf of King Victor Emmanuel. He then landed on the mainland and took Naples. Shortly thereafter the people of Naples, Sicily, and most of the Papal States voted their support for union with Piedmont-Sardinia. In March 1861 the king of Sardinia assumed the title of King Victor Emmanuel of Italy (r. 1861–1878). Complete unification was achieved when Austria ceded Venetia to Italy in 1866 and when French

troops, which had been protecting a portion of the Papal States, withdrew from Rome in 1870.

GERMAN UNIFICATION: CONSERVATIVE NATION BUILDING

Like Italy, Germany experienced a successful movement for national unification after the disappointments of 1848. The German movement, like the Italian, benefited from the actions of crafty statesmen and from the decisions made by other states. Unlike Italy, however, Germany achieved unification under the direction of highly conservative rather than liberal forces.

The main dilemma regarding German unification was whether Prussia or Austria would form the nucleus of any new political structure. In the end, Prussia, with its almost entirely German-speaking population, its wealth, and its strong army, assumed leadership of the movement. The key figure in this process was Count Otto von Bismarck (1815–1898), a lawyer and bureaucrat from an old *Junker* family whom King William I of Prussia appointed as his prime minister in 1862. By birth, training, and instinct Bismarck was an inflexible conservative, but he did not hes-

itate to make alliances with any political party, including the liberals, to achieve his goals.

Bismarck pursued the goal of national unification through the exercise of raw military and political power. He did not share the romantic devotion of other German nationalists to the fatherland or their desire to have a state that embodied the spirit of the German people. His determination to achieve German national unification became synonymous with his goal of strengthening the Prussian state. This commitment to the supremacy of Prussia within a

■ **Map 21.2   The Unification of Germany, 1866–1871**

Prussia assumed leadership in uniting all German territories except Austria. Prussia was responsible for the formation of the North German Confederation in 1866 and the German Empire in 1871.

united Germany explains his steadfast exclusion of the other great German power, Austria, from his plans for national unification.

Bismarck's achievement of German unification was based mainly on Prussian success in two wars. The first, the Austro-Prussian War of 1866, resulted in the formation of a new union of twenty-two states, the North German Confederation, which had its own legislature, the *Reichstag* . The second war, which completed the unification of Germany, was the Franco-Prussian War of 1870–1871. Napoleon III was responsible for beginning this conflict, but Bismarck welcomed the opportunity to take on the French, who controlled German-speaking territories on their eastern frontier and who had cultivated alliances with the southern German states. Bismarck played his diplomatic cards brilliantly, guaranteeing that the Russians, Austrians, and British would not support France. He then used the army that he had modernized to invade France and seize the towns of Metz and Sedan. The capture of Napoleon III during this military offensive precipitated the end of France's Second Empire and the establishment of the Third French Republic in September 1870.

As a result of the war Prussia annexed the predominantly German-speaking territories of Alsace and Lorraine. Much more important, it led to the proclamation of the German Empire with William I of Prussia as emperor. Officially the structure of the new empire was that of a federation, just like that of the North German Confederation that preceded it. In fact the government of the empire, like that of Prussia, was highly centralized as well as autocratic, and the liberal middle classes did not participate in it, as they did in the governments of Britain, France, and Italy. The German imperial government won the support of the middle class by adopting policies supporting free trade, but the ideologies that underpinned the new German Empire were those of conservatism and nationalism, which encouraged devotion to "God, King, and Fatherland."

UNIFICATION IN THE UNITED STATES: CREATING A NATION OF NATIONS

At the same time that Italy and Germany were achieving national unification, the United States of America engaged in a bitter process that preserved and strengthened the federal union it had instituted in 1787.

Throughout the early years of the republic Americans thought of themselves as citizens of particular states more than as members of a single national community. Nationalist sentiment, such as had developed in European countries on the basis of a common language and culture, had difficulty materializing in the United States, especially as the young republic began to incorporate new territories into the federal union. This process of unification, which proceeded in a piecemeal fashion, took much longer than the unifications of Italy and Germany in the 1860s. Florida

was annexed in 1819, while Texas, an independent republic for nine years, was admitted in 1845 and California in 1850.

The great test of American national unity came during the 1860s, when eleven southern states, committed to the preservation of the economic system of slavery, and determined that it should be extended into new territories acquired by the federal government, seceded from the union and formed a confederation of their own. The issue of slavery had helped to polarize North and South, creating deep cultural and ideological divisions that made the goal of national unity appear even more distant. In 1861 these divisions led to the outbreak of civil war between the northern and southern states.

The constitutional issue underlying the Civil War was the preservation of the union. When the war ended in 1865, and slavery was abolished, that union was not only preserved but strengthened. Amendments to the U.S. Constitution provided for equal protection of all citizens under the law. The South, which had its own regional economy, was integrated into the increasingly commercial and industrial North. The whole process of national unification, both economic and social, was greatly facilitated by the building of railroads. Gradually the people of the United States began to think of themselves as a united people, drawn from many different nations of the world. The United States became "a nation of nations."

NATIONALISM IN EASTERN EUROPE: PRESERVING MULTINATIONAL EMPIRES

The national unifications that took place in Germany, Italy, and the United States formed part of a *western* European pattern in which the main units of political organization would be nation-states. Ethnic minorities would of course always live within the boundaries of these states, but the state itself would encourage the growth of a national identity among all its citizens.

In *eastern* Europe a very different pattern prevailed, especially in the Habsburg and Russian empires. Instead of becoming unified nation-states, these two empires remained large, multinational political formations, embracing many different nationalities. This pattern was most obvious in the large, sprawling Habsburg Empire, which encompassed no fewer than twenty different ethnic groups, each of which thought of itself as a nation. The largest of these nationalities were the Germans in Austria and Bohemia and the Magyars in Hungary, but the Czechs, Slovaks, Poles, Slovenes, Croats, Rumanians, Bulgarians, and Italians (before 1866) all formed sizable minority populations. National unification of the empire would have presented a much more formidable task than the ones that confronted Cavour and Bismarck.

During the era of national unification the ideology of nationalism threatened to tear apart this precariously unified empire. It awakened demands of Hungarians, Czechs, and

■ **Map 21.3   Nationalities Within the Habsburg Empire**
The large number of different nationalities within the Habsburg Empire made it impossible to accommodate the demands of all nationalities for their own state.

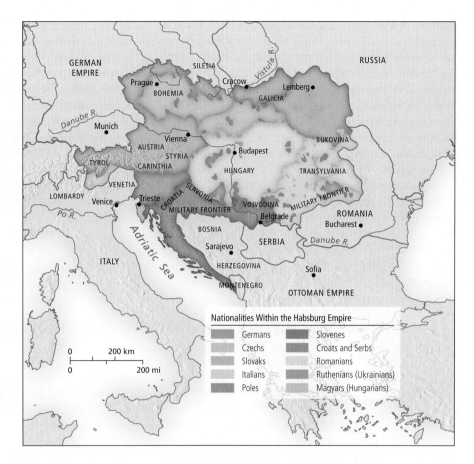

others for national autonomy and also spawned a movement for the national unity of all Slavs. The emperor, Francis Joseph, recognized the danger of nationalist ideology. He also feared that liberalism, which was often linked to nationalism, would at the same time undermine his authority, which he had reasserted with a vengeance after the failure of the revolutions of 1848. He therefore repressed these nationalist aspirations at every turn. This policy had disastrous consequences for the future history of Europe, since Slavic nationalism and separatism have remained a source of political instability of southeastern Europe until the present day.

The one concession that Francis Joseph did make during this volatile period was to establish the Dual Monarchy of Austria-Hungary in 1867. This significant increase of Hungarian power within the empire came in the wake of the disastrous defeats of Austrian forces by the French and Piedmontese in 1859 and the Prussians in 1866. Austrian liberals took this opportunity to call for the introduction of constitutional government, while the second-largest ethnic group within the empire, the Magyars, demanded more autonomy for Hungary. The *Ausgleich* (Settlement) of 1867, which was proposed by the wealthy Hungarian nobleman and lawyer Ferenc Deák (1803–1876), created a dual monarchy in which Francis Joseph would be both king of Hungary and emperor of Austria. This arrangement represented a

concession to Magyar nationalism but gave very little to all the other nationalities within both kingdoms. The *Ausgleich* officially recognized the equality of all nationalities within the empire, and allowed schooling to be conducted in the local language, but it permitted only Germans in Austria and Magyars in Hungary to acquire their own political identity. Instead of a unified nation-state the emperor now presided over two multinational monarchies.

Throughout this period Russia also remained a multinational empire, and it threatened to bring more nationalities under its control by pursuing a policy of imperial expansion. The Crimean War (1853–1856), which was the first major international conflict since the Congress of Vienna, was the direct result of this expansionary policy. The war, which claimed almost a million casualties on all sides, began when Russia occupied the principalities of Moldavia and Wallachia (present-day Romania) in the Ottoman Empire in order to gain access to the Straits of Constantinople and thus to the Aegean and Mediterranean seas. Russians justified this incursion by claiming they were protecting the Orthodox Christianity of people in the Balkans from their Turkish Muslim oppressors. They also claimed that they were promoting the national unity of all Slavic people under Russian auspices. This Russian version of Pan-Slavism differed from that developed by Czech

Slavs at the Pan-Slav Congress of 1848. In effect it was an extreme form of Russian imperialism that rivaled the nationalism of individual Slavic nationalities. It owed nothing to genuine nationalist ideology.

Britain resisted the Russian occupation of Moldavia and Wallachia, ostensibly to protect its trade with the Turks but more urgently to prevent Russia from becoming too powerful. The underlying British fear was that Russia might invade India, Britain's most important colony. When the Turks declared war on the Russians, therefore, the British followed suit and were joined by the French. The poorly trained British forces suffered staggering losses, more of them from disease than from battle. Nevertheless, the British, French, and Turks prevailed, handing Russia its most humiliating defeat of the nineteenth century. The defeat led to a curtailment of Russian expansion for the next twenty years and preserved the balance of power in Europe. Within Russia the defeat contributed to a crisis that led to a series of liberal reforms during the rule of Tsar Alexander II (1855–1881). Alexander, an indecisive man who had inherited the throne in the middle of the Crimean War, was hardly a liberal (he once referred to the French system of government as "vile"), but he did yield to mounting liberal pressure to emancipate the serfs in 1861. Even in this highly conservative regime, therefore, liberal ideology gained a small victory.

CONCLUSION

The Ideological Transformation of the West

··································· ▬ ···································

The ideological encounters that took place between 1815 and 1871 resulted in significant changes in the political culture of the West. As the early nineteenth-century ideologies of liberalism, conservatism, socialism, and nationalism played out in political movements and revolutions, the people who subscribed to these ideologies often redefined their political objectives. Many British and French socialists, for example, recognizing the necessity of assistance from liberals, abandoned their call for creating a classless society and sought instead to increase wages and improve working conditions of the lower classes. The demands of socialists for greater economic equality pressured liberals to accept the need for more state intervention in the economy. The realities of conservative politics led liberal nationalists in Germany and Italy to accept newly formed nation-states that were more authoritarian than they had originally hoped to establish. Recognizing the strength of the ideologies to which they were opposed, conservative rulers like Emperor Napoleon III and Tsar Alexander II agreed to adopt liberal reforms. Liberals, conservatives, socialists, and nationalists would continue to modify and adjust their political and ideological positions during the period of mass politics, which began in 1870 and which will be the subject of the next chapter.

The Western ideologies that underwent this process of adaptation and modification had a broad influence on world history. In the twentieth century, three of the four ideologies discussed in this chapter have inspired political change in parts of the world that lie outside the geographical and cultural boundaries of the West. Liberalism has provided the language for movements seeking to establish fundamental civil liberties in India, Japan, and several African countries. In its radical communist form, socialism inspired revolutions in Russia, a country that for many centuries had straddled the boundary between East and West, and in China. Nationalism has revealed its explosive potential in countries as diverse as Nepal, Thailand, and Zaire. Ever since the nineteenth century, Western ideologies have demonstrated a capacity both to shape and to adapt to a variety of political and social circumstances.

Suggestions for Further Reading

For a comprehensive list of suggested readings, please go to www.ablongman.com/levackconcise/chapter21

Anderson, Benedict. *Imagined Communities: Reflections on the Origin and Spread of Nationalism.* 1991. A discussion of the ways in which people conceptualize the nation.

Clark, Martin. *The Italian Risorgimento.* 1999. A comprehensive study of the social, economic, and religious context of Italian unification as well as its political and diplomatic dimensions.

Gellner, Ernest. *Nations and Nationalism.* 1983. An interpretive study that emphasizes the social roots of nationalism.

Hamerow, Theodore S. *Restoration, Revolution, Reaction: Economics and Politics in Germany, 1815–1871.* 1966. An investigation of the social basis of ideological encounters in Germany.

Honour, Hugh. *Romanticism.* 1979. A comprehensive study of romantic painting.

Hunczak, Tara, ed. *Russian Imperialism from Ivan the Great to the Revolution.* 1974. A collection of essays that illuminate Russian nationalism as well as imperialism over a long period of time.

Lichtheim, George. *A Short History of Socialism.* 1970. A good general treatment of the subject.

Nipperdey , Thomas. *Germany from Napoleon to Bismarck, 1800–1866.* 1996. An exploration of the creation of German nationalism as well as the failure of liberalism.

Onuf, Peter S. *Jefferson's Empire: The Language of American Nationhood.* 2000. A study of Jefferson's expansionary nationalism.

Pflanze, Otto. *Bismarck and the Development of Germany: The Period of Unification, 1815–1871.* 1963. The classic study of both Bismarck and the unification movement.

Pinckney, David. *The French Revolution of 1830.* 1972. The best treatment of this revolution.

Seton-Watson, Hugh. *Nations and States.* 1977. A clearly written study of the nation-state.

Sperber, Jonathan. *The European Revolutions, 1848–1851.* 1994. The best study of the revolutions of 1848.

Tombs, Robert. *The War Against Paris, 1871.* 1981. A narrative history of the Paris Commune.

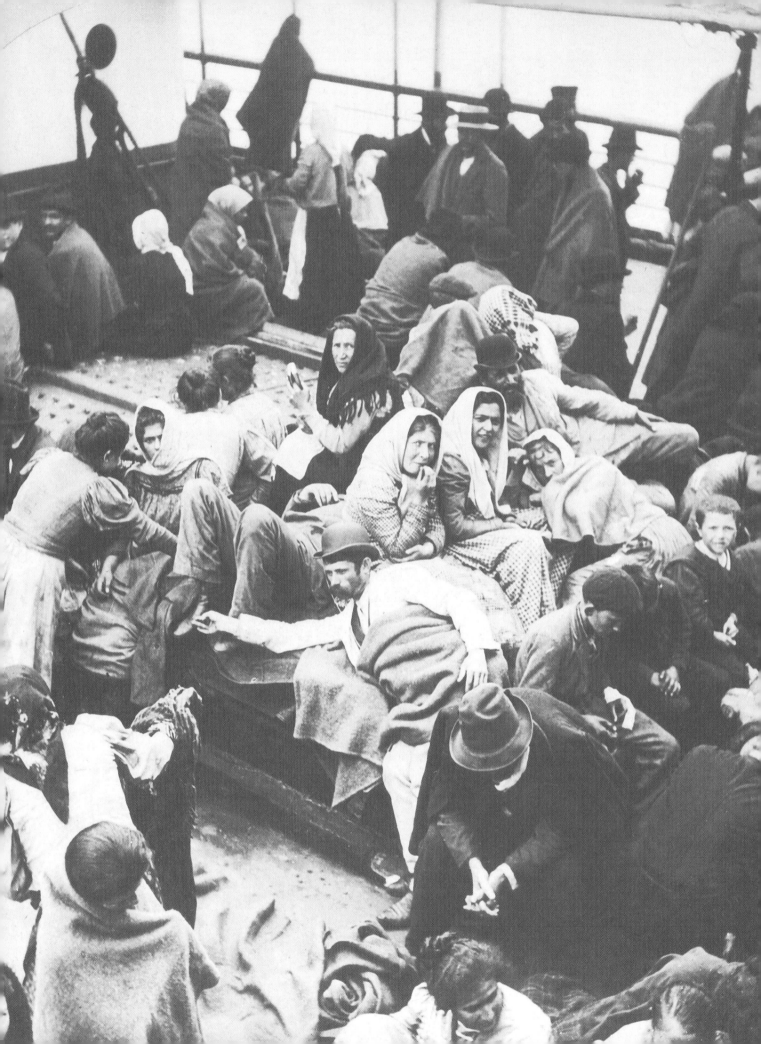

The Coming of Mass Politics: Industrialization, Enfranchisement, and Instability, 1870–1914

I N THE SPRING OF 1881, A HARROWING SCENE TOOK PLACE IN ST. PETERSBURG, capital of the vast Russian Empire. A 28-year-old woman, Sofiia Perovskaia, was scheduled to be executed for her part in the assassination of Tsar Alexander II. Born into the ranks of wealth and privilege, Perovskaia had rejected her traditional role in order to join the revolutionary socialist movement. She became a leader of the People's Will, a small revolutionary group that sought to undermine the tsarist regime through a program of sabotage and assassination. These revolutionaries dared to set their sights on assassinating the tsar himself, and on March 1, 1881, they achieved this goal. Led by Perovskaia, six People's Will members (all under age 30) stationed themselves at prearranged points along the streets of St. Petersburg. At Perovskaia's signal, they released their bombs and assassinated one of the most powerful men in Europe.

Despite the death of the tsar and the audacity of the crime, however, the tsarist regime did not crumble. The six assassins were quickly arrested and sentenced to death by hanging. (One of the six was pregnant and therefore allowed to live.) On the day of Perovskaia's execution, she mounted the scaffold calmly, but when the noose was placed around her neck, she grabbed hold of the platform below with her feet. It took the strength of two men to pry her feet loose so that she could hang.

The image of Sofiia Perovskaia clinging to the platform with her bare feet while her two executioners strained to push her to her death captures the ferocity of political struggle not only in Russia but throughout Europe at the end of the nineteenth century. As Chapter 21 explained, the ideological competition among liberalism, conservatism, socialism, and nationalism shaped the political culture of the West in the nineteenth century. Economic developments after 1870 both intensified and widened this competition. Individuals and groups that had traditionally been excluded from power demanded a voice in political affairs. Even in

Mass Society on the Move: European immigrants arriving in the United States, New York Harbor, 1906.

authoritarian Russia, the political nation could not long remain the preserve of the titled and wealthy. Neither economic modernization nor the coming of mass politics ensured the victory of democracy, however. Like Sofiia Perovskaia's executioners, the governing classes often struggled hard to pry newcomers off the platform of political power—and they often won.

Four questions will structure our exploration of this period:

- How did the economic and social transformation of Europe after 1870 help shape the encounters between established political elites and newcomers to the political process?
- How did the ruling classes of the Western powers respond to the new threats and opportunities provided by mass political participation?
- What was the relationship between modern nationalism and the emergence of mass politics?
- In what ways did the emergence of feminism in this period demonstrate the potential as well as the limits of political change?

Economic and Social Transformation

Europe's political development between 1870 and 1914 is inextricably linked to its economic and social transformation. Technological advances expanded both the speed and scale of industrialization; increasingly regional and national economies found themselves enmeshed in a global web of production, trade, and consumption. These economic changes altered Europe's demographics and exacerbated social tensions.

ECONOMIC DEVELOPMENTS AFTER 1870

Three important developments helped shape European actions and attitudes during these years: the onset of economic depression in 1873, the expansion of the Industrial Revolution into new geographic regions and economic sectors, and the emergence of new patterns in the production and consumption of industrial goods.

In 1873, Europe's economy tilted sharply downward—prices, interest rates, and profits all fell, and remained low in many regions until the mid-1890s. Contemporaries referred to this as the Great Depression in Trade and Agriculture°. In hindsight, "Great Depression" may seem an inaccurate label for a period that saw a continuing rise in world production and growing levels of foreign investment in new industrial economies, but to many Europeans living in these decades, this Great Depression seemed depressing indeed. Both agriculture and business were hit hard. By the 1890s, the price of wheat had fallen to only one-third of what it had been in the 1860s. Businessmen found that their profit margins were squeezed as the prices of finished products fell, often by as much as 50 percent, while labor and production costs tended to remain much more static.

What caused this depression? Ironically, it was rooted in the very success of the Industrial Revolution. Cheaper transportation costs opened the breadbaskets of the American Midwest and Ukraine to European consumption. With wheat and other agricultural goods now flooding the market, farmers were forced to accept increasingly lower prices for their products. More generally, as regions and nations industrialized, they of course produced more goods. Yet many industrial workers, agricultural laborers, and land-owning peasants still stood on the very edge of subsistence, with little money to spend on industrial products. Thus in many regions of Europe production exceeded consumption, and the result was a long-term agricultural and industrial depression.

The onset and impact of economic depression is closely linked to the second important economic development of this period—the continued expansion of the Industrial Revolution. Between 1870 and 1914 the world's rail network grew by 500 percent. The expanded railway system began to meld Europe's diverse regions into a single economic region. During the 1880s, even peasants still farming in traditional ways were caught up in the momentum of the industrial economy.

The expansion of the Industrial Revolution coincided with a shift in the processes of industrialization itself. The decades after 1870 witnessed a new phase in the techniques and technologies of both production and consumption: the "Second Industrial Revolution°."

The electrical, steel, and chemical industries shaped the Second Industrial Revolution. In 1866 the English scientist Michael Faraday (1791–1867) designed the first electromagnetic generator and thirteen years later the American Thomas Edison (1847–1931) invented the lightbulb. These developments sparked a huge new energy-producing industry and transformed both domestic life and industrial production. Similarly, a series of scientific and technological innovations in the 1870s ensured that for the first time steel could be produced cheaply and in huge quantities. The availability of steel, more durable and more flexible than iron, expanded production in industries such as railroads, shipbuilding, and construction. At the same time, discoveries in chemistry made possible the production of synthetic dyes, as well as advances in the production of fertilizer and petroleum refining.

In the Second Industrial Revolution, unlike the first, governments played an active role. The challenge posed by

14 Août 1888   14 Septembre 1888   26 Décembre 1888   20 Janvier 1889

■ **The Eiffel Tower Reaches to the Sky**

The inventions of the mechanical crane and stone cutter, combined with technological advances in the production of steel, iron, cement, and plate glass, allowed architects and builders to reach to the skies. Gustave Eiffel designed the Eiffel Tower for the Paris World's Fair of 1889. Ridiculed by critics as a "truly tragic street lamp," the Eiffel Tower soon came to symbolize both Paris and the new modern age.

the depression hastened this retreat from the free-trade principles of economic liberalism. As profits declined, businessmen demanded that their governments act to protect domestic industries from foreign competition. In this period, only Britain, Denmark, and the Netherlands refused to construct tariff walls designed to overprice the goods of outside competitors.

Declining profits also led business owners to develop new organizational forms. They turned to both *vertical integration*—buying up the companies that supplied their raw materials and those that bought their finished products—and *horizontal integration*—forming cartels or trusts with companies in the same industry to fix prices, control competition, and ensure a steady profit.

The marketing of goods also changed. During these decades, a revolution in retailing occurred, one that culminated in a new type of business aimed at middle-class customers—the department store. This new type of commercial establishment offered a vast array of products in large quantities at low prices. To stimulate sales, the department store provided huge, well-lighted expanses filled with appealing goods sold by courteous, well-trained clerks. Another innovation, mail-order catalogs, offered the store's delights to potential customers stranded in distant rural regions. Advertising became a crucial industry in its own

right, as business sought to persuade potential customers of new needs and desires.

ON THE MOVE: EMIGRATION, URBANIZATION, AND SOCIAL CONFLICT

These economic developments accelerated already existing patterns of urbanization and immigration. The depression hit agricultural regions particularly hard, at just the same time that continuing population growth exerted greater pressure on land and jobs. Industrial expansion also undercut rural manufacturing and handicraft production, crucial sources of income for rural populations. In response, men and women from the countryside sought new economic opportunities in the industrializing cities of Europe, or further abroad, in the United States, Canada, South America, and Australia.

As a result of this immigration, European cities grew dramatically after 1870. In 1800, only twenty-three European cities had more than 100,000 inhabitants. By 1900, 135 cities of such a size had sprung up. Most urban immigrants came to the cities from the surrounding countryside, but inhabitants of industrially underdeveloped regions crossed state borders to create an international workforce. Italians headed

A LETTER HOME

For immigrants to the United States, the "new world" offered the chance to break free from the cultural and religious restraints that had governed their lives in their villages at home. Many found the changes unsettling and distressing. Others were thrilled with their new freedom, as this letter reveals. The letter never made it to Goodstein's "auntie," but was instead confiscated by Russian tsarist authorities in an effort to discourage illegal emigration from its Polish territories.

San Bernadino [California], 28 November 1890

Dearest Auntie!

How happy I was a little while ago when finally I received a letter from You. Reading it and hearing about your good health gave me great pleasure and joy. . . .

This past 4 November, it was exactly one year since I left home. On 4 December I arrived in New York and on the 12th I reached San Bernadino. I can tell You for sure that I should have left home 15 years earlier. It would have been much better for me, a thousand times better because I am not able even to describe it to You, how I looked at first and how different I look now. I do not want to write about it because if I start I may never finish with it. I would like to ask the people at home just this one question: why is it forbidden for a young man to take a walk with a girl, to talk to her and to become acquainted with her. I do not consider it a sin. . . . Only You [the Jews in Poland]. . . are so backward. . . .

I do not mean to insult You, but it is especially true that in Your small towns within a half hour everything is known all over and becomes gossip. And so when a young man from there arrives here, what kind of an impression does he make?. . . when he gets together with people, he does not know how to behave and how to have a good time. . . . He also does not know how to hold a knife or a fork or a table napkin. And he does not know how to sing or raise a toast in company. At home we only used to say, "*Lehayim*." At home we only sang *zmires*.*

. . .

In our store, we also sell women's dresses and even underwear. And it may happen that a young man has to sell to some young girl some such things or whatever. We also sell, here, undershirts, shirts, collars, fine ties, pocket watches, top hats and overcoats. All this the young man was not acquainted with at home. . . .

Be well, Dear Auntie, and please write again to Your forever loving nephew.

Your nephew,
M. Goodstein

———
* *"Lehayim"* = "to life"; a toast. *"Zmires"* = sabbath songs.

Source: From Witold Kula et al., *Writing Home: Immigrants in Brazil and the United States 1890–1891*, edited and translated by Josephine Wtulich (New York: Columbia University Press, 1986). Reprinted by permission of East European Monographs.

to France and Switzerland, while the Irish poured across the Irish Sea into Liverpool and Glasgow.

Some immigrants headed not for the nearest city, but for an entirely different continent. Between 1860 and 1914, over 52 million Europeans crossed the ocean in quest of a better life. Seventy-two percent of these transoceanic immigrants traveled to North America, 21 percent to South America, and the rest to Australia and New Zealand.[1] Rapid economic change, combined with accelerated urbanization and immigration, heightened social tensions and destabilized political structures. The freefall in prices that characterized the depression eroded capitalist profit margins and increased middle-class resistance to workers' demands. Class hostilities rose as businessmen sought to protect their profit margins by both reducing the number of their employees and increasing labor productivity. In rural regions such as Spain and Ireland, the devastating collapse in agricultural prices fostered serious social and economic crises. Increasingly desperate, agricultural laborers and peasants turned to violence to enforce their calls for a fairer distribution of land.

The flow of immigrants into Europe's cities also sent social and ethnic tensions soaring. Cities were often unable to cope with the sudden and dramatic increases in population, despite the spread of public health provisions such as water and sewer systems. Housing shortages and poor living conditions exacerbated social tensions as newcomers battled with established residents for jobs and apartments. The mixture of different nationalities and ethnic groups often proved particularly explosive.

Defining the Political Nation

Faced with rising social tensions, political leaders sought ways to quell social discontent and to ensure the political loyalty of their populations. They faced a new world of mass politics—a new political culture characterized by the participation of men outside the upper and

■ **The Bicycle Revolution**

The bicycle revolutionized daily life for ordinary Europeans. Mass industrial production made the bicycle affordable, and for the first time, ordinary individuals, far too poor to afford a horse or motorcar, could dare to purchase their own private means of transportation, which would get them where they wanted to go in one-quarter of the time that walking required. No longer confined to their village for work opportunities or social contacts, bicycle owners discovered that their daily world had widened fourfold.

middle classes. Across Europe in the decades after 1870, those in power had to figure out how to stay there. They had to devise ways to incorporate the newly politicized masses into the nation while at the same time suppressing actual and potential unrest.

RUSSIA: REVOLUTION AND REACTION

As the example of Russia illustrates, failure to construct a common national identity threatened political rulers with revolutionary consequences. To catch up with the West, the tsarist regime adopted Western industrialization but it had no intentions of accepting Western ideas of representative government. It could not, however, completely

block the flow of these ideas into the Russian Empire. By the 1880s, many members of Russia's small but growing middle class espoused liberal political goals such as a written constitution and limited representational government. Other Russians embraced socialism. Both liberalism and socialism constituted revolutionary ideological challenges to tsarist absolutism. With the use of repressive legislation and an ever-expanding secret police force, the tsars Alexander III (r. 1881–1894) and Nicholas II (r. 1894–1917) drove political dissenters underground or into exile.

They could not, however, quell the social unrest produced by economic change. By the turn of the century, rapid, state-sponsored industrialization had built an industrial structure in Russia, but it stood on a very faulty foundation. Heavy taxation and rapid population growth increased competition for land and heightened economic anxiety among the peasant masses. Within the industrial cities, social unrest also simmered. Factory workers labored more than twelve hours a day in wretched working conditions for very little pay. Any protest against these conditions was regarded as protest against the tsar and was quickly repressed.

In 1905, popular discontent flared into revolution. Across the Russian Empire, cities came to a standstill as workers went on strike and demanded both economic and political rights. Regions on the fringes of the empire, such as the Baltic states, rose up in revolt against imperial rule, and middle-class liberals demanded representative government. In October, Tsar Nicholas II acceded to demands for the election of a legislative assembly. The Revolution of 1905 appeared to be a success.

By 1910, however, the tsar had regained much of his autocratic power. Revolutionary fervor dissipated as rival groups jostled for political influence. The tsar, with his army still loyal, refused to carry out many of the promised reforms. Tsarist autocracy remained intact, but so too did the causes of the discontent that had led to the revolution. The divided Russian Empire would not survive the pressure of World War I.

GERMANY: IDENTIFYING THE ENEMY

In contrast to Russia's tsarist government, political rulers in Germany made a concerted effort to build a national community, despite the authoritarian nature of Germany's political structure. We saw in Chapter 21 that real power lay in the hands of William I (r. 1861–1888), the first emperor (or *kaiser*) of the unified Germany, and his chancellor, the conservative aristocrat Otto von Bismarck. Appointed by the emperor, Bismarck did not answer to the legislature or the electorate. He could not entirely ignore the Reichstag, however, because it had to approve the budget and appropriate the funds necessary to run the government. Bismarck thus faced the task of ensuring a sympathetic majority in the Reichstag while at the same time maintaining the emperor's

■ **The Revolution of 1905 in the Movies**

On a day that became known as "Bloody Sunday" (January 22, 1905), a group of 100,000 Russian workers and their families attempted to present to the tsar a petition calling for higher wages, better working conditions, and the right to participate in political decision making. Government troops opened fire on the unarmed crowd; at least 70 people were killed and more than 240 were wounded. The massacre horrified and radicalized much of Russian society, and sparked the Revolution of 1905. This photograph, supposedly of the moment when the tsar's troops began to shoot the demonstrators, is one of the most familiar images of the twentieth century—yet it is *not* in fact a documentary record. Instead, it is a still taken from *The Ninth of January*, a Soviet film made in 1925.

authority, protecting the social and political privileges of the aristocracy, and pacifying the masses.

One way to unite these disparate interests was by identifying a common enemy. Arguing that loyalty to the Roman papacy compromised German Catholics' loyalty to the new state, Bismarck in the 1870s initiated the *Kulturkampf* (the "struggle of civilization"), a series of measures designed to limit the power of the Catholic Church in Germany. But Bismarck lost this battle. Catholics organized into an opposition political party and resisted Bismarck's efforts to marginalize them or to paint them as "non-German." In 1878, then, Bismarck shifted his aim to a new target: German socialists. He outlawed the German Social Democratic Party (SPD) and authorized the federal police to disband all socialist meetings and organizations.

This attack on the SPD appealed to antisocialist groups such as conservative landowners, Roman Catholics, and liberal businessmen, and thus gave Bismarck the Reichstag majority that he needed. The antisocialist strategy, however, risked alienating the growing urban working class. To attract the support of this vital social segment, Bismarck introduced some of the most thoroughgoing social welfare measures yet seen in Europe. He initiated sickness benefits in 1883, coverage for industrial accidents in 1884, and old-age pensions and disability insurance in 1889. Even so, the outlawed SPD continued to attract growing numbers of working-class supporters.

In 1890, however, the new German emperor, William II (r. 1888–1918), fired Bismarck and let the antisocialist legislation lapse. William II believed he could cement a sense of common German national identity among its various social groups—Catholics and socialists, aristocrats and workers, liberals and military officers, industrialists and landowners—through aggressive militarization and imperial expansion. These policies helped clear the way for World War I, a war that would at first unify but then destroy the German imperial state.

ITALY: THE ILLUSION OF TRANSFORMATION

The development of national unity in Italy ran up against two key obstacles: the papacy and poverty. After the Italian army marched in and claimed Rome as the capital of Italy in 1870, Pope Pius IX (r. 1846–1878) shut himself within the Vatican and refused to recognize the new state. The hostility between the papacy and the new government undermined the state's legitimacy. Severe levels of poverty and economic underdevelopment, particularly in southern Italy, also obstructed the development of an Italian national community. Dominated by huge, inefficiently run agricultural estates, the south was unable to support its expanding population. Immigration to France, Switzerland, South America, and the United States relieved only some of the pressure. Economically desperate and receptive to radical political ideas, the rural poor demanded the breakup of large landholdings.

Italian political life deepened the social crisis. No single party had a majority in the national assembly. Instead, Italian politicians developed a system of *trasformismo*, building and maintaining coalition governments by transforming opponents into allies through bribery and patronage. Because political leaders needed the votes of southern landowners to stay in power, the system stifled any chance to implement programs of economic development or land reform.

■ **Map 22.1 Europe at the End of the Nineteenth Century**

A comparison of this map with Map 19.2 ("Europe After the Congress of Vienna in 1815," p. 418) shows the impact of modern nationalism on European political geography. The most striking change is the formation of the new states of Italy and Germany (the German Empire). In addition, nationalist movements succeeded in carving away large chunks of the Ottoman Empire's European territories. By the 1880s, Bosnia and Herzegovina were under Austrian administration, and Greece, Serbia, Montenegro, Rumania, and Bulgaria had all achieved independence.

In a vain attempt to build national consensus through military glory, Prime Minister Francesco Crispi (1819–1901), one of the heroes of Italian unification and a dominant figure in post-unification politics, authorized a disastrous invasion of Ethiopia. Italy's defeat in Ethiopia led to the fall of the Crispi government in 1896 and to a period of political confusion. Anarchist bombings, socialist-led urban uprisings, violent labor strikes, and agricultural riots escalated.

In the first decade of the twentieth century, however, Italy appeared to take a new course under the premiership of Giovanni Giolitti (1842–1928). Alarmed by the growing appeal of Italy's revolutionary socialist parties, Giolitti embarked on a policy of improving workers' lives and so convincing them that real change did not require revolution. Giolitti legalized trade unions, nationalized the railroads, established public health and life insurance programs, cracked down on child labor, established a six-day workweek, and in 1911 introduced universal manhood suffrage. Like Crispi, he turned to imperial expansion to foster a sense of "Italianness" among diverse groups. Unlike Crispi's humiliating failure in Ethiopia, however, Giolitti's colonial venture succeeded. In 1912 Italy annexed Libya.

Yet Giolitti's efforts to create a more inclusive political nation in Italy faltered. During "Red Week" in June 1914, anarchist and socialist-inspired revolts spread across northern Italy. Like his predecessors, Giolitti relied on the support of southern landowners in the assembly and therefore ignored the crying need for economic development in the south. On the eve of the First World War, Italy remained seriously divided between north and south, between peasant and landowner, between industrialist and worker.

FRANCE: A CRISIS OF LEGITIMACY

Unlike Germany and Italy, France had long existed as a nation-state, but a century of almost continuous political revolution ensured that in the final decades of the nineteenth century no consensus existed on who or what France actually was. Born in the humiliation of military defeat, the French Third Republic faced a crisis of legitimacy.

This crisis of legitimacy was worsened by the failure of French politicians to generate much enthusiasm. A dozen different parties jostled for control of the legislature. Because no single party controlled a majority, the only way to form a government was through forging coalitions, and thus political wheeling and dealing, financial corruption, and constant reshuffling of officeholders became the common tools of parliamentary politics. The lackluster nature of French politics accentuated the appeal of those who wished to destroy the French Republic—monarchists who wanted a king back on the throne, Bonapartists longing for the glory days of Napoleonic empire, Roman Catholics disturbed by republican efforts to curb the political power of the Church, aristocrats opposed to democracy.

CHRONOLOGY

1867	National Society for Women's Suffrage founded in Britain
1871	Unification of Germany; formation of French Third Republic
1873	Onset of Great Depression in Trade and Agriculture
1881	Assassination of Russia's Tsar Alexander II
1890	German chancellor Bismarck dismissed by Emperor William II; SPD legalized
1894	Captain Alfred Dreyfus convicted of treason in France
1896	Italian invasion of Ethiopia defeated; publication of Herzl's *The Jewish State*, founding text of Zionism
1897	Karl Lueger elected mayor of Vienna on anti-Semitic platform
1898	Formation of Sinn Fein in Ireland
1905	Revolution in Russia
1906	Formation of British Labour Party
1914	Red Week in Italy

This fundamental lack of consensus about the nature or shape of France was strikingly revealed by the eruption of the Dreyfus Affair°. In 1894, on the basis of hearsay evidence and forged documentation, a French military court convicted Captain Alfred Dreyfus (1859–1935) of espionage. Prominent French intellectuals took up Dreyfus's case. Support for Dreyfus, who was Jewish, became linked to support for the secular and egalitarian ideals of the Republic; the anti-Dreyfusards, in contrast, saw Dreyfus's Jewishness as a threat to France's Catholic identity and argued that to question the army hierarchy was to undermine France's military might.

The Dreyfus Affair revealed the strength of anti-republicanism in France, and so drove the Republic's supporters to seize the offensive. The government placed the army under civilian control and removed the Catholic Church from its privileged position in French political life. With these measures policymakers aimed to define France in secular and republican terms.

In 1914, the success of this effort at redefinition remained unclear. National political life was dominated by the Radical Party, which represented the interests of small shopkeepers and independent artisans in rural and small-town constituencies. Radicals opposed the taxes necessary to establish social welfare programs and dragged their feet on social legislation such as the ten-hour workday (not passed until 1904) and old-age provisions (not established until 1910). As a result, workers increasingly turned to violent ideologies and actions, such as anarchism and sabotage.

BRITAIN: NATION, CLASS, AND RELIGION

Unlike Germany and Italy, Britain was not a new nation; unlike France, it did not have to reconstruct its political structures after the humiliation of military defeat. Yet in Britain, too, the upper classes faced the task of responding to working-class demands for a political voice. They also confronted the problem of a regional divide even wider than the gap between north and south in Italy—that between Ireland and the rest of the less-than-United Kingdom.

In 1867, many urban working men in Britain won the right to vote, and in 1884 this right was extended to rural male laborers. Both the Conservative and the Liberal parties sought the support of these new working-class voters with programs designed to benefit ordinary people. The most substantial foundations of Britain's welfare state were, however, constructed in the early twentieth century by a Liberal government. Between 1906 and 1912, the Liberals enacted a series of welfare measures, including pensions for the elderly and sickness and unemployment benefits for some workers. As with Bismarck's pioneering social measures in Germany and Giolitti's reforms in Italy, this legislation was intended not only to attract workers' votes, but also to ensure working-class loyalty to the nation and its political leaders. In 1906, however, the formation of the working-class Labour Party signaled that many workers wanted an independent political voice.

Suffrage reform, welfare measures, and the formation of the Labour Party all ensured that by the end of the century the British political nation had expanded to include working-class men. It proved incapable, however, of embracing the Irish Catholic peasantry. In Ireland, economic grievances fused with resentment fueled by centuries of political and religious repression, and convinced many Irish Catholics of the need for independence from Britain.

Faced with growing Irish nationalism, the British resorted to military rule, accompanied by attempts to alleviate peasant grievances through land reform. Then, in the 1880s, the British Liberal leader William Gladstone (1809–1898) embraced the cause of Irish "Home Rule"—limited political autonomy for Ireland. For a short time it appeared as if parliamentary measures would solve the Irish problem.

Home Rule, however, met fierce opposition not only from British Conservatives, but also from Irish Protestants. The descendants of English and Scottish settlers in Ireland, these Protestants constituted a minority of the Irish population as a whole, but made up the majority of the population in northern Ireland. Frightened by the idea of belonging to a Catholic state, the northern Irish Protestants made it clear that they would fight to the death to remain a part of Britain.

The defeat of Home Rule bills introduced in 1886 and 1893 persuaded many Irish Catholic nationalists of the futility of working with the British. In 1898 they organized themselves as Sinn Fein (pronounced *shin fane*—Gaelic for "Ourselves Alone"), a political movement devoted to complete independence for Ireland by any means necessary. Sinn Fein grew rapidly, and by 1914 could call to arms a paramilitary force of 180,000 fighters. As the success of Sinn Fein demonstrated, Irish Catholics were developing their own sense of nationhood, one that refused to be subordinate to any competing notion of "Britishness."

Broadening the Political Nation

A cross Europe in the last third of the nineteenth century and the opening decades of the twentieth, both aristocratic and middle-class politicians enacted measures extending the vote to lower-class men. The expanded franchise and the new technologies of mass communication created a new age of mass politics, one that saw the emergence of socialist working-class political parties on the left, and the rise of racist and radical nationalist parties on the right.

THE POLITICS OF THE WORKING CLASS

In the decades after 1870, socialism established itself as a powerful force in European parliamentary politics, the means by which workers sought to claim a place in the political nation. By 1914, socialist parties had been formed in twenty European countries.

Why socialism? As we saw in Chapter 21, by 1870 Karl Marx had published a series of books outlining his theory of revolutionary socialism. Not many workers had the time, education, or energy necessary for the study of Marx's complex ideas. But Marx's basic points, presented to workers by socialist party activists and organizers, resonated with many workers. Quite simply, most workers had already identified their boss as the enemy, and Marx assured them that they were right. His insistence that class conflict was inherent within the industrial system accorded with their own experience of social segregation and economic exploitation.

The most dramatic socialist success story was in Germany. By 1914, the German Social Democratic Party (the SPD) held 40 percent of the seats in the Reichstag, and served as the model for socialist parties founded in the Netherlands, Belgium, Austria, and Switzerland. The rapid growth of socialist parties such as the SPD persuaded many

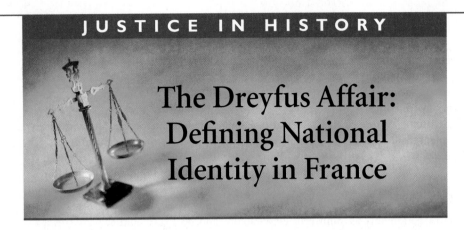

The Dreyfus Affair: Defining National Identity in France

On September 27, 1894, the five officers that made up the counterespionage section of France's War Ministry examined a disturbing document—an unsigned, undated, torn piece of paper that had clearly served as a cover letter for a packet of documents containing information on French military equipment and training. The officers found no envelope, but they concluded that the letter was intended for Lieutenant Colonel Maximilian von Schwartzkoppen, the German military attaché in Paris. Thus, this torn piece of paper constituted evidence of treason. Someone in the French officer corps was selling military secrets to the Germans.

After a brief investigation and a cursory comparison of handwriting samples, the French investigators concluded that the traitor was Captain Alfred Dreyfus, a candidate officer on the General Staff. An unlikely traitor, Dreyfus had compiled a strong record during his military career and, by all accounts, was a staunch French patriot. Moreover, because of his marriage to a wealthy woman, he had no need to sell his country for money. He was, however, an aloof and arrogant man, disliked by most of his fellow officers and without a strong backer among his superiors. He was also a Jew.

Despite the lack of solid evidence, Dreyfus was convicted of treason. After a ceremony of military degradation, he was exiled in 1895 to a specially constructed prison hut on Devil's Island, a former leper colony twelve miles off the coast of French Guyana. Many French men and women believed he had gotten off too lightly. Both public and press clamored for his execution.

With Dreyfus safely imprisoned on his island, his case seemed closed. But in July 1895, Major Marie-Georges Picquart was named chief of the Intelligence Bureau. An ambitious man determined to make a name for himself, Picquart soon discovered that the sale of military secrets to the Germans had continued even after Dreyfus's imprisonment. Ignoring his superiors' instructions to leave the Dreyfus case alone, Picquart set out to trap the man he first believed to be Dreyfus's accomplice. The evidence he uncovered, however, led him to conclude that Dreyfus was in fact innocent.

Picquart's investigations raised serious doubts about Dreyfus's conviction. These doubts were transformed into sensational charges on January 13, 1898, when one of France's most famous authors, Émile Zola, alleged in a Paris daily newspaper that the French military was engaged in a colossal cover-up. In an article headlined *"J'accuse!"* ("I accuse!"), Zola charged that the General Staff had knowingly convicted an innocent man. Zola's accusations aroused enormous public attention, and over the next six weeks, riots broke out in French cities.

Retried before a second military court in 1899, Dreyfus was again found guilty—although this time "with extenuating circumstances," a ridiculous verdict (there are no extenuating circumstances for the crime of treason) concocted to salvage the military's position despite Dreyfus's obvious innocence. In the subsequent riots that broke out in Paris, 100 people were wounded and 200 jailed. Ten days later, the French president pardoned Dreyfus in an effort to heal the divisions opened by the trial. Finally, in 1906, a French high court set aside the court-martial verdict and exonerated Dreyfus. Not until 1995, however, did the French military acknowledge the captain's innocence.

The Dreyfus Affair drew international attention, polarized French politics, and tore apart Parisian society. It sparked not only violent protests but also numerous duels and a series of related trials for assault, defamation, and libel. To uphold Dreyfus's conviction, high-ranking military officials falsified evidence, even to the point of forging entire documents. The question "Are you for or against Dreyfus?" divided families and destroyed friendships. During the height of the controversy, for example, the painter Edgar Degas spoke contemptuously of paintings by Camille Pisarro. When reminded that he had once admired these very same works, Degas said, "Yes, but that was before the Dreyfus Affair." Degas was a passionate anti-Dreyfusard; Pisarro believed Dreyfus was innocent.[2]

What about the Dreyfus Affair so aroused personal passion as to alter one painter's perception of another's work? What made this trial not simply a case, but an *affair,* a matter of public debate and personal upheaval, a cause of violent rioting and political turmoil?

To comprehend the Dreyfus Affair, we must understand that it was less about Captain Alfred Dreyfus than about the very existence of the French Third Republic. The intellectuals and politicians who rallied in support of Dreyfus were defenders of the Republic, men and women who sought to limit the army's involvement in France's political life, who linked both monarchy and empire to national disaster rather than national glory, and who believed in a secular definition of

The Dreyfus Affair
Captain Alfred Dreyfus before his judges, 1899.

the nation that would treat Roman Catholics no differently from Protestants, Jews, or atheists. Dreyfus's opponents, in contrast, regarded the establishment of the Third Republic as a betrayal of the true France—a hierarchical, Roman Catholic, imperial state, steeped in military traditions. Defending the military conviction of Dreyfus became a way to express support not only for the army, but also for the authoritarian traditions that the Republic had jettisoned. The Dreyfus Affair was thus an encounter between competing versions of French national identity.

The question "What is France?," however, could not be answered without considering a second question: "Who belongs in France?"—or more specifically, "What about Jews?" France's small Jewish community (less than 1 percent of the total population) had enjoyed the rights of full citizenship since 1791—much longer than in most of Europe. Yet the Dreyfus Affair clearly demonstrated that even in France, the position of Jews in the national community was far from

assured. Although anti-Semitism probably played little role in the initial charges against Dreyfus, it quickly became a dominating feature of the affair. More than seventy anti-Semitic riots ravaged France during this period. Anti-Semitic politicians and publications placed themselves in the vanguard of the anti-Dreyfus forces. For many anti-Dreyfusards, Dreyfus's Jewishness explained everything. The highly acclaimed novelist and political theorist Maurice Barres insisted, "I have no need to be told why Dreyfus committed treason . . . That Dreyfus is capable of treason I conclude from his race."[3]

Anti-Semites like Barres regarded Jewishness as a kind of genetic disease that made Jews unfit for French citizenship. To the anti-Semitic nationalist, the Jew was a person without a country, unconnected by racial or religious ties to the French nation—the very opposite of a patriot. As a symbol of rootlessness, "the Jew" came to represent for many anti-Dreyfusards the forces of unsettling economic and political change that appeared to be weak-

ening the French nation. Anti-Semites pointed to the successes of assimilated Jews such as Dreyfus—not only in the army but also in the universities, the professions, and business life—as evidence of what they perceived as the threat of Jewish "domination" of French culture.

Declared innocent in 1906, Dreyfus resumed his military career and served his country with distinction in the First World War. Like Dreyfus, the Third Republic survived the Dreyfus Affair. It was probably even strengthened by it. Outrage over the army's cover-up led republican politicians to limit the powers of the military and so lessened the chances of an anti-republican military coup. Anti-Semitism, however, remained a pervasive force in French politics and cultural life well into the twentieth century.

Questions of Justice

1. What does the Dreyfus Affair reveal about definitions of national identity in late-nineteenth-century Europe?
2. Once Dreyfus was convicted, many French men and women believed that for the sake of the national interest, his conviction had to be upheld. In what situations, if any, should "national interest" override an individual's right to a fair trial?

Taking It Further

Cahm, Eric. *The Dreyfus Affair in French Society and Politics.* 1994. A wide-ranging history.

Kleeblatt, Norman, ed. *The Dreyfus Affair: Art, Truth, and Justice.* 1987. This richly illustrated collection of essays explores the cultural as well as political and legal impact of the case.

Lindemann, Albert S. *The Jew Accused: Three Anti-Semitic Affairs (Dreyfus, Beilis, Frank) 1894–1915.* 1991. An illuminating comparative study.

Snyder, Louis L. *The Dreyfus Case: A Documentary History.* 1973. An accessible collection of primary documents.

socialists that working-class revolution was just around the corner. In 1891 SPD leader August Bebel (1840–1913) told SPD congress delegates, "I am convinced that the fulfillment of our aims is so close, that there are few in this hall who will not live to see the day."[4]

By the time Bebel made this promise, however, economic and political developments were creating serious problems for Marxist theory and practice. The expansion of the franchise seemed to indicate that workers could gain political power without violent revolution. Socialists faced crucial and often divisive questions: Should they work for gradual reforms that would make life better for the worker—and risk making capitalism more acceptable? Could socialists participate in coalition governments with nonsocialists—and so lend legitimacy to parliamentary systems they condemned as oppressive and unequal?

The quest for answers to these questions led some socialists to socialist revisionism°, a set of political ideas most closely associated with the German theorist Eduard Bernstein (1850–1932). Bernstein rejected Marx's faith in inevitable violent revolution and argued instead for the gradual and peaceful evolution of socialism through parliamentary politics. Bernstein called for German socialists to abandon their commitment to revolution, to form alliances with liberals, and to carry out immediate social and economic reforms.

In 1899, the SPD congress condemned Bernstein's revisionism and reaffirmed its faith in working-class revolution. Bernstein had lost the battle—but he won the war. For regardless of its socialist theory, in practice the SPD acted like any other parliamentary party. It focused on gradually improving the lot of its constituency through legislative change. Its effect, although not its aim, was to make the existing political system more responsive to the needs of working-class constituents.

Despite the almost hysterical fears of many middle- and upper-class Europeans, the successes of socialist political parties probably worked less to foment revolution than to strengthen parliamentary political systems. To many at the end of the nineteenth century, however, revolution appeared a genuine possibility. The depression led businesses to look for ways to cut costs. As management sought to reduce the number of laborers, to increase the rate of production, and to decrease wages, workers began to organize themselves in new and threatening ways.

Trade unions, for example, grew more radical. The unions of the 1850s and 1860s had tended to be small, craft-based groupings of highly skilled workers. In contrast, the new unions aimed to organize all the male workers in an entire industry—for example, all male textile workers, rather than just the skilled weavers. These new unions were also much more willing to resort to large-scale strikes and to violence.

In the first decade of the twentieth century, the European labor movement became further radicalized by

■ **The Unions' Challenge**

In 1911 the British government deployed troops in the city of Liverpool to put down working-class labor unrest. In one confrontation, two people were killed.

its encounter with the new ideology of syndicalism°. Syndicalists worked to overturn the existing social and political order by marshaling the economic might of workers. In the syndicalist vision, if every worker in a nation went on strike, the resulting disruption of the capitalist economy would lead to working-class revolution. According to the French syndicalist theorist Georges Sorel (1847–1922), workers had to embrace violence to destroy the capitalist state. Sorel did not actually believe that a general strike was possible, but he believed that the idea of the general strike was crucial. In Sorel's view, the general strike served as an essential myth, an inspirational idea that would give workers the motivation and self-confidence they needed to overthrow the state.

In their rejection of parliamentary politics and in their willingness to utilize violent means to achieve their revolutionary ends, syndicalists were heavily influenced by anarchism°. Opting for direct and violent action such as street fighting and assassination, anarchists aimed to destroy rather than control the state. The Russian anarchist Mikhail Bakunin (1814–1876) insisted that the great obstacle to achieving a just and egalitarian society was the state itself, not capitalism or the industrial middle class.

The combined impact of both syndicalism and anarchism created a climate of social unrest and political turmoil in much of Europe before 1914. In the 1890s, French anarchists terrorized Paris with a series of bombings and the fatal stabbing of President Sadi Carnot. Other prominent victims of assassination included Empress Elisabeth of Austria-Hungary in 1898, King Humbert of Italy in 1900, and U.S. president William McKinley in 1901.

NATIONALIST MASS POLITICS

Mass politics was not confined to the left. Socialism possessed little appeal in areas that industrialized late and so still contained a large peasant class profoundly threatened by the continuing Industrial Revolution. Socialism also failed to attract members of the lower middle class (or "petty bourgeoisie") who regarded the Marxist vision of working-class rule as a frightening nightmare. Instead, they turned to the new mass politics of nationalism. In the age of the masses, the right-wing ideas offered by nationalist, racist, and anti-Semitic parties also answered the demands of many ordinary people for a political voice.

Unlike socialists, who placed great faith in intellectual debate and rational persuasion, nationalist politicians did not recruit supporters with reasoned arguments. Nationalist politics relied more on visual imagery and symbolism than on the written word, and utilized emotional appeals rather than intellectual debate. By waving flags, parading in historical costumes or military uniforms, and singing folk songs, nationalists tapped into powerful personal and communal memories to persuade voters of their common identity, one based not on shared political ideas or economic interests but rather on ethnic, religious, or linguistic ties. This was as much a politics of exclusion as of inclusion—it defined the nation by identifying who was "not in" as well as who belonged.

The Appeal of Anti-Semitism in the Age of Mass Nationalism

Defining a common energy often serves as an effective tool for forging national unity. Many nationalists targeted Jews as anti-Semitism became a dominant theme in nationalist politics. In the final third of the nineteenth century, nationalists charged Jews with causing the depression, masterminding terrorist conspiracies, and fostering the rise of socialism. As anti-Semitism grew, so too did anti-Jewish violence. In Russia, this violence often took the form of pogroms, mass attacks on Jewish homes and businesses, sometimes organized by local government officials. Although pogroms did not occur in western Europe, Jews in France, Britain, and other industrialized nations also experienced increasing hostility.

Three developments explain this heightened anti-Semitism. First, the new nationalism meant new perceptions of common "racial roots." Ideas about "the English race" or of the shared racial heritage of the French had no scientific basis, but these perceptions of racial links nonetheless proved extremely powerful. Nationalists increasingly defined "Jewishness" as a racial identity as well as a religious belief. As a racial marker, Jewishness was not a matter of choice but of blood—something that could not be changed. If national identity grew from supposedly racial roots, then in the eyes of many Europeans, Jews were foreign plants, outsiders whose very presence threatened national unity.

The growth in immigrant Jewish urban populations after 1881 exacerbated this perception of Jews as outsiders and serves as the second factor that explains heightened anti-Semitism. After the assassination of his father in 1881, Tsar Alexander III blamed Russia's Jewish community for his father's death. He responded by reimposing restrictions on Jewish economic and social life with the May Laws of 1882. Fleeing this repression, Jews from the Russian Empire settled in Paris, London, Vienna, and other European cities. These new, impoverished, clearly identifiable immigrants were easily blamed for unemployment, the spread of disease, soaring crime rates, and any other difficulty for which desperate people sought easy explanations.

Many anti-Semites, however, associated Jews not with poverty but with wealth and power. One of the most striking developments of nineteenth-century history was what one historian has labeled the "rise of the Jews," the third element in explaining anti-Semitism in this era.[5] Most Jewish communities did not gain civil and political rights until the second half of the nineteenth century. As relative newcomers to the mainstream of European societies, Jewish businessmen tended to move into economic sectors associated with the emerging modern economy. In Germany, for example, almost all the large department stores were owned by Jewish businessmen, and in the cities of Frankfurt, Berlin, and Hamburg all the large daily newspapers were in the hands of Jewish proprietors. As a result, the small craftspeople and artisans with a great deal to lose from economic modernization often linked big-business capitalism—which they feared—to Jewishness. Jews became the embodiment of threatening change to many newly enfranchised European voters. Across Europe, explicitly anti-Semitic parties emerged, while established conservative parties adopted anti-Semitic rhetoric.

Austria-Hungary: The Politics of Division

Political conflict in the industrially underdeveloped Habsburg Empire demonstrates the appeal of nationalist politics. Straining under the social and economic pressures of late industrialization, Austria-Hungary contained numerous ethnic and linguistic groups competing for power and privileges. This competition intensified as the franchise was gradually widened. Language became a key battleground. In a multilingual empire, which language would be taught in the schools? Which language would guarantee career advancement? Not surprisingly, individuals tended to agitate for the primacy of their own native language. In the Austrian half of the empire, Germans protested against Czech success in gaining official support for the Czech language. By 1900 the struggle over language laws in Austria had become so intense that no party could establish a majority in the legislative assembly, and Emperor Francis Joseph (r. 1848–1916) resorted to ruling by decree.

Anti-Semitic politics proved particularly powerful in Vienna, the capital of the Austrian half of the Empire. As the city attracted both Austrian Jews from the surrounding countryside and Jewish emigrants fleeing Russian pogroms, Vienna's Jewish population climbed from 118,000 in 1890 to 147,000 in 1900. This growing Jewish presence provided the opportunity for Karl Lueger (1844–1910), a lawyer, self-made man, and ambitious politician. Lueger's Christian Social party demonstrated how hate-based politics could overcome social and economic divisions among members of a single ethnic or religious community. Lueger used both anti-Semitism and promises of social reform to unite artisans and workers with conservative aristocrats in a German nationalist party. His proposals to exclude Jews from political and economic life proved so popular that he was elected mayor of Vienna in 1897 over the opposition of Emperor Francis Joseph. Lueger was still the mayor in 1908, when 18-year-old Adolf Hitler moved to Vienna. Hitler remained in the city for several years, soaking in the anti-Semitic political culture.

Zionism: Jewish Mass Politics

The heightened anti-Semitism of the last quarter of the nineteenth century convinced some Jews that the Jewish communities of Europe would be safe only when they gained a political state of their own. The ideology of Jewish nationalism was called Zionism°, as Jewish nationalists called for a return to Zion, the biblical land of Palestine. Most Jews in western nations such as France and Britain viewed Zionism with skepticism, but it had a potent appeal in eastern Europe, home to more than 70 percent of the world's Jewish community—and to the most vicious forms of anti-Semitism.

Zionism became a mass movement under the guidance of Theodor Herzl (1860–1904). An Austrian Jew, Herzl was living in Vienna when Karl Lueger was elected mayor. Confronted with the appeal of anti-Semitism to the mass electorate, Herzl began to doubt whether Jews could ever be fully accepted as citizens. His experience as a journalist reporting on the Dreyfus Affair convinced Herzl that Jews would always be outsiders within Europe. In 1896, he published *The Jewish State*, a call for Jews to build a nation-state in Palestine. Through newspapers, popular publications, large rallies, and his own enthusiasm, Herzl made Zionism into an international mass movement. By 1914, about 90,000 Jews had settled in Palestine, where they hoped to fulfill the Zionist dream.

Outside the Political Nation? The Experience of Women

T he extension of suffrage to men outside the middle and upper classes called attention to gender differences, as middle-class women demanded that they, too, be made part of the political nation. The campaign for women's suffrage, however, was only part of an international feminist movement°. At the core of nineteenth-century feminism stood a rejection of the liberal ideology of separate spheres—the insistence that both God and biology destined middle-class men for the public sphere of paid employment and political participation, and women for the private sphere of the home. In seeking a place in the political nation, feminists sought not just to enter the public, masculine sphere, but in fact to obliterate many of the distinctions between the public and private spheres altogether and so to reconfigure political and social life.

CHANGES IN THE POSITION OF MIDDLE-CLASS WOMEN

During this period the feminist movement remained largely middle-class in its membership and its concerns. Politically active working-class women tended to agree with Karl Marx that class, not gender, constituted the real dividing line in society. For help in bettering their lives, they turned to labor unions and to working-class political parties rather than middle-class feminist organizations.

Changing economic and social conditions provide the background for the emergence of middle-class feminism. In the last third of the nineteenth century, middle-class men and women began to limit the size of their families. The depression cut into business profits and made economic ventures more precarious. At the same time, the tendency to keep both boys and girls in school longer meant added financial obligations for the middle-class family. Limiting births, through the use of already well-known methods such as abstinence, withdrawal, and abortion, enabled the middle-class family to cut expenses and yet maintain a middle-class lifestyle. In Britain in the 1890s, the average middle-class family had 2.8 children, a sharp contrast to the 1850s, when the typical middle-class family had 6 children. Middle-class married women no longer spent much of their married adult life pregnant or nursing. This change not only meant better health, it also freed women for other pursuits, including feminist activism. In contrast, working-class women continued to have large families: Their children left school and began earning an income at a young age, and so were economic assets.

The expectations of unmarried middle-class women were also transformed during this period, as the expan-

■ Women at Work

The expansion of local and central government interference in daily life created many opportunities for women's paid employment. Here government health inspectors check a schoolgirl for head lice.

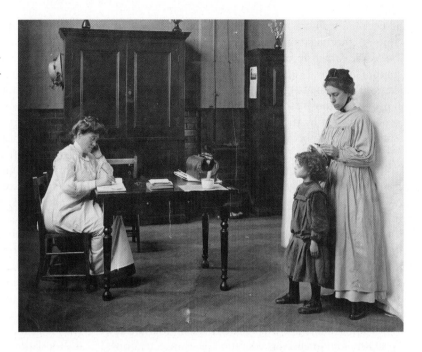

sion of the state and the Second Industrial Revolution widened their options. In the final decades of the nineteenth century, local governments took over many tasks traditionally assigned to churches and charities, such as feeding and educating the poor. Middle-class women quickly claimed positions in the new local bureaucracies, on the argument that women's expertise in managing households and raising children could be directly translated into managing poorhouses and running schools. Women served on school and welfare boards, staffed government inspectorates, voted in local elections, and were elected to local office. At the same time, the emergence of new technologies and the retail revolution created new jobs for women. Middle-class women moved into the work world as typists, telephone and telegraph operators, sales clerks, and bank tellers. During the 1860s in England, the number of women working as commercial clerks and accountants increased tenfold.

Middle-class women thus found new ways to make a living; they did not, however, find the same opportunities as their male counterparts. A woman earned an average of between one-third and two-thirds less than a man working in the same job. The entry of large numbers of women into any job was certain to result in a recasting of that position as unskilled and low-paying. Unlike men, women lost their jobs when they married and found most supervisory positions closed to them.

THE FEMINIST MOVEMENT

By the 1880s, an international feminist movement had emerged to challenge the legal, political, and economic disabilities facing European and American women. Consisting of a vast web of interconnected organizations, publications, and correspondence networks, the middle-class movement sought to challenge the ideology of separate spheres and to establish a new basis for both private and public relations. Its multifaceted campaigns focused on four fronts: the legal impediments facing married women, employment opportunities and higher education for girls and women, the double standard of sexual conduct enshrined in European laws, and national women's suffrage.

Women and the Law

European legal systems strongly reinforced the liberal ideology of separate spheres for men and women. Law codes often classified women with children, criminals, and the insane. Article 231 of the Napoleonic Code, the legal system of France and the basis of the legal codes of much of western and central Europe, declared that the wife was the dependent of the husband; hence, "the husband owes protection to his wife; the wife owes obedience to her husband." English common law, based on tradition and precedent rather than on a single, systematized code, proclaimed much the same idea. As William Blackstone explained in his famous *Commentaries on the Laws of England* (1765–1769), "the husband and wife are one person in law," and that person was the husband. A married woman simply disappeared in the eyes of the British common law. Most property brought into a marriage, or given to her or earned by her while married, became the property of her husband.

From the middle of the nineteenth century on, women's groups fought to improve the legal rights of married women. By the end of the 1880s, English married women had won rights to own property, control their income, and keep their children when divorced. In contrast, the German women's movement suffered a sharp defeat with the promulgation of the Civil Code in 1900. The Civil Code, which formulated a single uniform legal system for Germany, proclaimed that "the husband takes the decisions in all matters affecting married life." It granted all parental authority to the husband, and declared that all property owned by the wife before marriage or given to her after marriage became the husband's.

Finding a Place: Employment and Education

In addition to their legal campaigns, feminists also worked to widen women's educational and employment opportunities as part of their effort to enter the public sphere. Feminists' educational campaigns in the second half of the nineteenth century sought to improve girls' secondary education and to open universities to women. The fight to upgrade the quality of girls' secondary schooling was often difficult. Many parents opposed an academic curriculum for girls, a position reinforced by medical professionals who argued that girls' brains simply could not withstand the strain of an intellectual education. In France, feminists achieved their goal of a state-funded and state-run system of secondary schools for girls in the 1880s. They lost the battle for a university-preparatory curriculum, however, which made it difficult for girls to pass the exams necessary to enter the French university system. Not surprisingly, the number of women in French universities remained very small throughout this period. Opportunities for university education for women varied enormously. In the United States, women accounted for one-third of all students in higher education as early as 1880, while in Germany, women were not admitted to full-time university study until 1901.

Feminists also campaigned to broaden the range of jobs open to women. In 1900, French women won the right to practice law, and in 1903 a woman lawyer in Toulouse presented a case in a European court for the first time. In 1906, the physicist and Nobel Prize winner Marie Curie became the first woman to hold a university faculty position in France. By the opening decades of the twentieth century, women doctors, although still unusual, were not unheard of. In Russia, women accounted for 10 percent of all physicians by 1914.

Moral Reform

Both the campaigns for women's legal rights and the expansion of employment and educational opportunities helped women move out of the private and into the public sphere. But the third goal of feminist activity—to eradicate the double standard of sexual conduct—posed a more radical challenge to nineteenth-century middle-class culture and its ideology of separate spheres. By arguing that the same moral standards should apply to both men and women, feminists questioned whether two separate spheres should exist at all.

The ideology of separate spheres glorified women's moral purity and held that the more aggressive, animal-like natures of men naturally resulted in such male pastimes as heavy drinking and sexual adventurism. The laws as well as the wider culture reflected these assumptions. For example, in France, a woman with an illegitimate child could not institute a paternity suit against the father: Premarital sex was a crime for the woman, but not for the man.

In their effort to erase the moral distinctions between men and women, feminists fought on a variety of fronts. One key area of struggle was the regulation of prostitution. By the 1870s, many European countries, as well as the United States, had established procedures that made it safer for men to hire prostitutes, while still treating the women involved as criminals. In England, the Contagious Diseases Act, passed in 1870 to address the problem of venereal disease, declared that any woman suspected of being a prostitute could be stopped by the police and required to undergo a genital exam. For almost twenty years feminists such as Josephine Butler (1857–1942) campaigned both to repeal the legislation that regulated prostitution and to focus public attention on the lack of employment opportunities for women.

Abuse of alcohol was another key battleground for the women's movement. Feminist activists argued that the socially accepted practice of heavy male drinking had devastating consequences for women, in the form of both family poverty and domestic violence. The temperance or prohibitionist cause thus became a feminist issue. The movement triumphed in the United States in 1919 when decades of agitation from groups such as the Women's Christian Temperance Union led to the passage of the Eighteenth Amendment prohibiting the manufacture and sale of alcoholic beverages. "Prohibition," however, did little to transform gender relations; instead, it simply created new ways for organized crime syndicates to make money. The American prohibition experiment ended in 1933 with the repeal of the Eighteenth Amendment.

In general, feminist moral reform campaigns achieved only limited success. The regulation of prostitution did end in Britain in 1886 and in the United States, France, and the Scandinavian countries by 1914, but remained in effect in Germany. In all European countries and in the United States, the sexual double standard remained embedded in both middle- and working-class culture far into the twentieth century.

THE FIGHT FOR WOMEN'S SUFFRAGE

The slow pace and uneven progress on both the legal and moral fronts convinced many feminists that they would achieve their goals only if they possessed the political clout of the *national* suffrage. In 1867 the National Society for Women's Suffrage was founded in Britain; over the next three decades suffrage societies emerged on the Continent and in the United States.

These suffragists had little success. Only in Finland (1906) and Norway (1913) did women gain the national franchise in this period. The social upheaval of World War I brought women the vote in Russia (1917), Britain (1918), Germany (1919), Austria (1919), the Netherlands (1919), and the United States (1920). Women in Italy had to wait until 1945; French women did not gain the vote until 1946, Greek women not until 1949. Women in Switzerland could not vote until 1971.

Feminists faced a number of significant obstacles in their battle for the national franchise. In Catholic countries such as France and Italy, the women's suffrage movement failed to become a political force not only because the Church remained fiercely opposed to the women's vote, but also because in Catholicism—in its veneration of the Virgin Mary and other female saints, in its exaltation of family life, in the opportunity for religious vocation as a nun—women found a great many avenues for emotional expression and intellectual satisfaction. Feminism had a much harder time taking root in these countries. In central and eastern Europe the obstacles were even greater. In much of this region, economic development was far behind that of the western areas of Europe, and thus middle-class culture—the social base of feminism—was also underdeveloped.

In contrast to eastern Europe, in Britain the middle class was both large and politically powerful, and the political structure had shown itself capable of adaptation and evolution. Yet even in Britain, the site of the first and the strongest European female suffrage movement, women failed to win the vote in the nineteenth century. As a result, a small group of activists resorted to more radical tactics. Led by the imposing mother-and-daughters team of Emmeline (1858–1928), Christabel (1880–1958), and Sylvia Pankhurst (1882–1960), the suffragettes° formed a breakaway women's suffrage group in 1903. The Pankhursts were convinced that the mainstream suffragists' tactics such as signing petitions, publishing reasoned arguments, and lobbying politicians would never win the vote. "Deeds, Not Words" became the suffragette slogan. The suffragettes broke up political meetings with the cry "Votes for Women!" They chained themselves to the steps of the Houses of Parliament, shattered shop windows, burned churches, destroyed mailboxes, and even, in a direct attack on a cherished citadel of male middle-class culture, vandalized golf courses.

In opting for violence, the suffragettes staged a full frontal assault on a central fortification of middle-class culture—the ideal of the passive, homebound woman. The fortress they were attacking proved well-defended, however. Their opponents reacted with fury. Police broke up suffragette rallies with sexually focused brutality: They dragged suffragettes by their hair, stomped on their crotches, punched their breasts, and tore off their blouses. Once in jail, hunger-striking suffragettes endured the horror of forced feedings. Several jailers pinned the woman to her bed while the doctor thrust a plastic tube down her throat, often lacerating her larynx in the process, and pumped in food until she gagged.

CONCLUSION

The West in an Age of Mass Politics

The clash between the British suffragettes and their jailers was only one of a multitude of encounters, many of them violent, among those seeking access to political power and those seeking to limit that access, in the era from 1870 to the start of World War I in 1914. At the same time, changing patterns of industrialization and accelerated urbanization gave rise to other sorts of encounters—between the manager seeking to cut production costs and the employee aiming to protect his wages, for example, or among the newly arrived immigrants in the city, struggling to survive in an unfamiliar culture, and the long-established residents who spoke a different language.

Out of such encounters emerged key questions about the definition of "the West." Where, for example, did the West end? Did it include Russia? The expansion of the franchise and the processes of making nations raised even more fundamental questions. Was the West defined by democracy? Should it be? Was it synonymous with white, western European men or could people with olive-colored or black skin—or women of any color—participate fully in Western culture and politics? Was "the West" defined by its rationality? In the eighteenth century,

Enlightenment thinkers had praised the power of human rationality and looked to reason as the path to social improvement. The rise of a new style of politics, based on emotional appeal and often irrational racist hatred, challenged this faith in reason. But at the same time, developments in industrial organization and technologies, which helped expand European national incomes, seemed to point to the benefits of rational processes.

As we will see in the next chapter, the expansion of Western control over vast areas of Asia and Africa in this period led an increasing number of Europeans and Americans to highlight economic prosperity and technological superiority as the defining characteristics of the West. Confidence, however, was accompanied by anxiety as these years also witnessed a far-reaching cultural and intellectual crisis. Closely connected to the development of mass politics and changes in social and gender relations, this crisis slowly eroded many of the pillars of middle- and upper-class society and raised searching questions about Western assumptions and values.

Suggestions for Further Reading

For a comprehensive list of suggested readings, please go to www.ablongman.com/levackconcise/chapter22

Evans, Richard. *The Feminists: Women's Emancipation Movements in Europe, America, and Australasia 1840–1920.* 1977. A helpful comparative overview.

Kern, Stephen. *The Culture of Time and Space 1880–1918.* 1983. An innovative work that explores the cultural impact of technological change.

Lidtke, Vernon. *The Alternative Culture: Socialist Labor in Imperial Germany.* 1985. Looks beyond the world of parliamentary politics to assess the meaning and impact of working-class socialism.

Lindemann, Albert. *Esau's Tears: Modern Anti-Semitism and the Rise of the Jews.* 1997. A comprehensive and detailed survey that challenges many assumptions about the roots and nature of modern anti-Semitism.

Mayer, Arno. *The Persistence of the Old Regime: Europe to the Great War.* 1981. Argues that landed elites maintained a considerable amount of economic and political power throughout the nineteenth century.

Milward, A. S., and S. B. Saul. *The Development of the Economies of Continental Europe, 1850–1914.* 1977. A helpful survey.

Moch, Leslie. *Moving Europeans: Migration in Western Europe Since 1650.* 1992. Filled with maps and packed with information, Moch's work explodes many easy assumptions about the movement of Europeans in the nineteenth century.

Nord, Philip. *The Republican Moment: Struggles for Democracy in Nineteenth-Century France.* 1996. Illuminates the struggle to define and redefine France.

Pilbeam, Pamela. *The Middle Classes in Europe, 1789–1914: France, Germany, Italy, and Russia.* 1990. A comparative approach that helps clarify the patterns of social change.

Richards, Thomas. *The Commodity Culture of Victorian England: Advertising and Spectacle 1851–1914.* 1990. Fascinating study of the manufacturing of desire.

Stearns, Peter N. *Lives of Labor: Work in a Maturing Industrial Society.* 1975. Explores changing economic and social patterns.

Steenson, Gary P. *After Marx, Before Lenin: Marxism and Socialist Working-Class Parties in Europe, 1884–1914.* 1991. Examines both ideology and political practice within Europe's socialist parties.

Weber, Eugen. *Peasants into Frenchmen: The Modernization of Rural France, 1870–1914.* 1976. A very important work that helped shape the way historians think about "nation making."

Notes

1. Leslie Moch, *Moving Europeans: Migration in Western Europe Since 1650* (1992), 147.

2. Norman Kleeblatt, *The Dreyfus Affair: Art, Truth, and Justice* (1987), 96.

3. Quoted in Eric Cahm, *The Dreyfus Affair in French Society and Politics* (1994), 167.

4. Quoted in Leslie Derfler, *Socialism Since Marx: A Century of the European Left* (1973), 58.

5. Albert Lindemann, *Esau's Tears: Modern Anti-Semitism and the Rise of the Jews* (1997).

The West and the World: Cultural Crisis and the New Imperialism, 1870–1914

I N THE AUTUMN OF 1898, BRITISH TROOPS MOVED INTO THE SUDAN IN NORTHEAST Africa to claim the region for the British Empire. On September 2, the British Camel Corps faced an army of 40,000 fighters. The Sudanese soldiers, Islamic believers known as dervishes who possessed a reputation for military fierceness, were fighting on their home ground against an invading force. Nevertheless, after only five hours of fighting, 11,000 dervishes lay dead. Their opponents lost just forty men. While the dervishes, armed with swords and spears, surged forward in a full-scale frontal assault, the British troops sat safely behind fortified defenses and, using repeating rifles and Maxim guns (a type of early machine gun), simply mowed down their attackers. According to one participant on the British side, the future prime minister Winston Churchill, the biggest danger to the British soldiers during the battle of Omdurman was boredom: "the mere physical act [of loading, firing, and reloading] became tedious." The dervishes had little chance of boredom. Churchill recalled, "And all the time out on the plain on the other side bullets were shearing through flesh, smashing and splintering bone; blood spouted from terrible wounds; valiant men were struggling through a hell of whistling metal, exploding shells, and spurting dust—suffering, despairing, dying."[1]

The slaughter of 11,000 Sudanese in just over five hours formed but one episode in what many historians call the age of new imperialism, a period that witnessed both the culmination of, and a new phase in, Europe's conquest of the globe. This often-violent encounter between Europe and the regions that Europeans emphatically defined as non-Western was closely connected to the political and economic upheavals examined in Chapter 22. An understanding of

Paul Gauguin, *Matamoe* ("Peacocks in the Country"), 1892: The Fauvist painter Paul Gauguin fled Europe for Tahiti in an effort to restore to his art the strong colors and emotions that he believed characterized non-Western cultures. The sights, sensibilities, and symbolism of Tahitian society profoundly affected his painting—and helped shape modernist art.

the new imperialism, however, demands a close look not only at political rivalries and economic structures, but also at scientific, intellectual, and cultural developments in the last third of the nineteenth century. At the same time that European and American adventurers risked life and limb to chart Africa's rivers, exploit its resources, and subjugate its peoples, Western artists and scientists embarked on explorations into worlds of thought and perception far deeper than the surface reality accessible to the senses, and in so doing challenged the social order and even the meaning of reality itself.

The final decades of the nineteenth century and the opening years of the twentieth thus constituted an era of internal fragmentation and external expansion. The scientific, artistic, and physical explorations that are the subject of this chapter redefined the West and its relationship with the rest of the world. As Western dominance over Africa and Asia expanded, states such as Russia and Japan embarked on conscious efforts to westernize their societies and thereby compete successfully with the West's industrial and military might. Areas of white European settlement such as South Africa and the United States moved more firmly inside Western boundaries. The tendency to color the West white, however, marginalized nonwhite inhabitants of these regions.

This chapter addresses three questions:

- How did scientific developments during this period lead to not only greater intellectual and cultural optimism but also deepened anxiety?
- What factors led many Europeans in this period to believe they were living in a time of cultural crisis?
- What were the causes and consequences of the new imperialist ideology for both the West and non-Western societies?

Scientific Transformations

Advances in medicine, physics, and the social sciences during the last third of the nineteenth century helped improve the health and hygiene of Western societies and transformed understandings of the connections between individuals, their communities, and the physical world. Many Europeans and Americans believed that these changes confirmed the West's cultural superiority and made future progress inevitable. Others, however, found these developments profoundly unsettling.

MEDICINE AND MICROBES

Throughout the nineteenth century, expanding urban populations served as fertile seedbeds for contagious ill-nesses. In the 1860s, however the chemist Louis Pasteur (1822–1895) discovered that microscopic living organisms—bacteria—pass disease from one host to another. Following Pasteur, Robert Koch (1843–1910), professor of public health in Berlin, isolated the tuberculosis bacillus in 1882 and the bacteria that cause cholera in 1883. The work of Pasteur, Koch, and other scientists in tracing the transmission of disease transformed Western medical practice. Between 1872 and 1900, the number of European deaths from infectious diseases dropped by 60 percent. Once physicians and surgeons accepted that microscopic organisms caused disease, they began to develop techniques to control their spread. The development of antiseptic surgery in the later 1860s improved the patient's chances of surviving the operating table. The increasing use of anesthetics in the second half of the nineteenth century also improved those odds.

These medical advances gave Europeans genuine confidence that the conquest of nature through science would create a healthier environment. But the widespread awareness of germs also heightened anxiety. Isolation of the bacilli that caused an illness did not immediately translate into its cure, and viral infections remained often lethal. After the 1870s, Europeans were aware that they lived in a world populated by potentially deadly but invisible organisms, carried on the bodies of their servants, their employees, their neighbors, and their family members.

THE REVOLUTION IN PHYSICS

The decades between 1890 and 1910 also witnessed a revolution in physics. At the core of this scientific revolution lay the question, "What is matter?" For most of the nineteenth century, the answer was simple: Matter was what close observation and measurement, as well as common sense, showed it to be. A series of discoveries and experiments challenged this commonsense view of the universe and offered in its place a much more mysterious and unsettling vista. The discovery of the X ray in 1895 disrupted prevailing assumptions about the solidity and predictability of matter. They were shaken even further in 1898 when the Polish-French chemist Marie Curie (1867–1934) discovered a new element, radium, which did not possess a constant atomic weight. Two years later, the German scientist Max Planck (1858–1947) theorized that a heated body radiates energy not in a continuous, steady, predictable stream, but rather in irregular clumps, which he called *quanta*. Although at first dismissed by most scientists as contrary to common sense, Planck's quantum theory accorded with the emerging picture of a changeable universe.

These scientific discoveries provide the context for the work of Albert Einstein (1879–1955). Bored by his job as a patent clerk, Einstein passed the time speculating on the nature of the cosmos. In 1905, he published an article that introduced to the world the theory of relativity. Einstein's

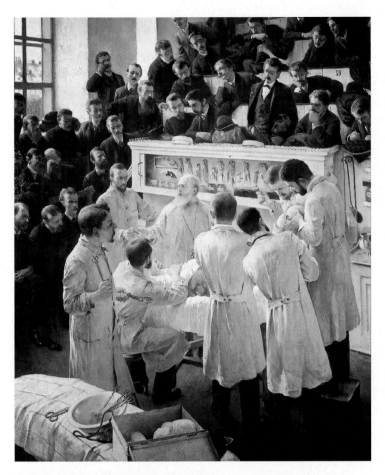

■ **Adelbert Seligmann, *German Surgeon Theodor Billroth at Work in Vienna* (1890)**
Modern surgery in the making: The patient has been anesthetized, but the modern operating room does not yet exist, nor are the doctors wearing gloves or masks. Billroth, the director of the Second Surgical Clinic in Vienna, pioneered surgical techniques for gastrointestinal illnesses and cancer.

social scientists in the last third of the nineteenth century began to formulate troubling theories about the nature of human society. As Chapter 21 explained, the mainstream of nineteenth-century thought was positivist: It placed great faith in human reason and therefore in the validity of applying methods drawn from the natural sciences to the study of human affairs. In the last decades of the century, however, social scientists began to emphasize the role of nonrational forces in determining human conduct.

For example, the French theorist Gustave LeBon (1841–1931) inaugurated the discipline of crowd or collective psychology in this era when he showed how appeals to emotion, particularly in the form of symbols and myths, can influence crowd behavior. In LeBon's view, democracy relinquished political control to the easily swayed masses and so would lead only to disaster.

The German philosopher and poet Friedrich Nietzsche (1844–1900) dared to challenge the rationality of science itself. Nietzsche was trained as a classical philologist; his study of language convinced him that everything we know must be filtered through a symbolic system—through language or some other means of artistic or mathematic representation. Because we can know only the representation and not the thing itself, scientific observation and analysis cannot uncover "reality." Even the style of Nietzsche's publications worked to expose the limits of reason. Rather than write carefully constructed essays that proceeded in a logical, linear fashion from fact to fact, Nietzsche adopted an elusive, poetic style characterized by disconnected fragments, more accessible to intuitive understanding than to rational analysis.

theory rejected the nineteenth-century assumption of the absolute nature of time and space. Instead, Einstein argued, time and space shift relative to the position of the observer. Similarly, matter itself shifts. Mass depends on motion, and thus time, space, and matter intermingle in a universe of relative flux.

With this revolution in physics, much of science became incomprehensible to ordinary men and women, even educated ones. The new science also challenged the basic assumptions that governed nineteenth-century thought by offering a vision of the universe in which what you see is *not* what you get, in which objective reality might well be the product of subjective perception.

THE REVOLT AGAINST POSITIVISM

Just as the revolution in physics presented a new and potentially more disturbing picture of the physical universe, so

The highly influential work of the Viennese scientist and physician Sigmund Freud (1856–1939) also highlighted the power of nonrational forces in shaping human conduct. Freud argued that the conscious mind plays only a very limited role in shaping the actions of each individual. His effort to treat patients suffering from nervous disorders led him to hypnosis and dream analysis, and to the conviction that behind the conscious exterior existed a deeper, far more significant reality—the unconscious. In *The Interpretation of Dreams* (1900), Freud argued that beneath the rational surface of each human being surge all kinds of hidden desires, including such irrational drives as the longing for death and destruction.

As a scientist, Freud believed that he could understand human behavior (and treat mental illness) by diving below the rational surface and exploring the submerged terrain of unconscious desire. Yet the emergence of Freudian psychology convinced many educated Western individuals not that the irrational could be uncovered and controlled, but rather that the irrational was *in* control.

THE TRIUMPH OF EVOLUTIONARY THEORY

During the same period in which social scientists were outlining new ways to understand human behavior and raising serious doubts about the essential rationality of that behavior, developments in geology and biology also led to both confidence and anxiety. Evolutionary theory provided a scientific framework in which educated Europeans could understand and justify their own superior social and economic positions. It also, however, challenged basic religious assumptions and depicted the natural world in new and unsettling ways.

Traditionally, Europeans had relied on the opening chapters of the Bible to understand the origins of both nature and humanity. By the 1830s, however, the work of geologists challenged the biblical account. Geologists such as Charles Lyell (1797–1875) argued that the Earth had formed over millions of years. Lyell refuted the orthodox Christian position that geological change and the extinction of species could be explained by supernatural intervention. Instead, he and others argued that the material world must be seen as the product of natural forces still at work, still observable today.

But how could one explain the tremendous variety of plant and animal species in the world today on the basis of natural processes? In 1859, the British scientist Charles Darwin (1809–1882) answered this question in a way that proved quite satisfying to large numbers of educated Europeans—and quite horrifying to others. Darwinian evolutionary theory° rested on two basic ideas: *variation* and *natural selection.* Variation refers to those small but crucial biological advantages that assist in the struggle for survival: A bird with a slightly longer beak, for example, might gain access to scarce food supplies. Over generations, the individuals more adapted for survival displace those without the positive variation. Variation, then, provides the means of natural selection, the process by which new species evolve.

Darwin's theories proved extraordinarily influential. Published in 1859, *The Origin of Species* aroused immediate interest and controversy. This controversy intensified when, in 1871, Darwin published *The Descent of Man,* in which he firmly placed humanity itself within the evolutionary process. Many Christians reacted with horror to a theory that they believed challenged the biblical narrative of Creation and undercut their understanding of nature as a harmonious, well-ordered system that revealed the hand of God. Many middle-class Europeans and Americans, however, welcomed Darwin's ideas as providing a coherent and appealing explanation of change. They argued that evolution did not banish divine purpose from the universe but instead showed God at work in the gradual development of more perfect species. They saw Darwin's work as a scientific confirmation of their faith in the virtues of competition and in the inevitability of progress.

The British writer Herbert Spencer (1820–1902) saw evolution as the key to social progress. A self-confident, eminently practical thinker, Spencer coined the phrase "the survival of the fittest." In Spencer's view, human societies evolve like plant and animal species, and only the fittest, those able to adapt to changing conditions, survive.

Spencer's essentially biological vision of society shaped the theories of Social Darwinism°. Arguing that racial hierarchy was the product of natural evolution, the Social Darwinists applied Spencer's ideas about the importance of individual competition and the survival of the fittest to entire races. They concluded that the nonwhite races in Africa and Asia had failed to compete successfully with white Europeans and thus displayed their biological inferiority.

In their effort to construct a scientifically based racial hierarchy, Social Darwinists used not only Darwin's and Spencer's ideas but also the theory of "recapitulation," first proposed by the German zoologist Ernst Haeckel (1834–1919). According to Haeckel, as an individual matures, he or she moves through the same stages as did the human race during the course of its evolution. The idea of recapitulation enabled scientists to fill in the gaps left by the fossil record. By observing the development of children into adults, they argued, we can witness the evolutionary maturation of the human race. Social Darwinists used the theory of recapitulation to argue that only white European males had reached the pinnacle of evolutionary development. They contended that nonwhite men, as well as all women, embodied the more primitive stages of evolution through which the white European male had already passed.

Such ideas spread beyond the ranks of the social Darwinists. Sigmund Freud, for example, argued that "the female genitalia are more primitive than those of the male," while Gustave LeBon compared the average female brain to that of a gorilla.[2] Nineteenth-century scientists and large sections of the European public welcomed evolutionary theory as scientific proof of deeply embedded cultural assumptions, such as the benefits of competition, the rightness of white rule and male dominance, and the superiority of Western civilization. Yet evolutionary science also worked to undermine European confidence because it threatened to erase the boundaries between humanity and animality, and so made civilization itself seem more vulnerable.

Cultural Crisis: The Fin-de-Siècle and the Birth of Modernism

The sense that Western civilization was endangered, that degeneration and decay characterized the contemporary experience, was summed up in a single

French phrase: *fin-de-siècle*°. Literally translated as "end of the century," *fin-de-siècle* served as a shorthand term for a mood of cultural pessimism and even despair that characterized much of European society in the final decades of the nineteenth century and the opening years of the twentieth. Yet exhilaration as well as anxiety characterized this time of cultural crisis. Fast-moving economic and social change, coupled with the new scientific ideas, convinced many Europeans that old answers were no longer sufficient. The quest for new answers fostered the birth of what would become known as modernism, a broad label for a series of revolutionary developments in thought, literature, and art.

FIN-DE-SIÈCLE ANXIETIES

As the nineteenth century drew to a close, many Europeans and Americans believed that Western civilization was seriously, perhaps even fatally ill. Popular works of fiction depicted Western culture as diseased or barbaric. In a twenty-volume work, the French novelist Émile Zola (1840–1902) traced the decline of a once-proud family to symbolize the decay of all of France. In *Nana* (1880), Zola used the title character, a prostitute, to embody his country. Watching as French soldiers march off to defeat in the Franco-Prussian War, Nana is dying of smallpox, her face "a charnel-house, a heap of pus and blood, a shovelful of putrid flesh."[3] Novels such as *Dr. Jekyll and Mr. Hyde* (1886) and *Dracula* (1897) showed that beneath the cultured exterior of a civilized man lurked a primitive, bloodthirsty beast.

The concept of the "inheritance of acquired characteristics," associated with the work of the French scientist Jean-Baptiste Lamarck (1744–1829), played a crucial role in fostering fears of cultural and physical degeneration at the fin-de-siècle. More than fifty years before Darwin published his *Origin of Species*, Lamarck theorized that acquired characteristics (traits that an individual develops in response to

■ **A page from *Criminal Man* (1876), by Cesare Lombroso**

An Italian physician, Lombroso established the new social science of criminology. In *Criminal Man,* he argued that individuals with certain physical characteristics, such as a narrow forehead or linked eyebrows, are likely to be criminals. According to Lombroso, the criminal body is the result of evolutionary regression. In the face, skull, and physique of the criminal we can see evidence of a reversion to a more primitive evolutionary state. The images shown here are grouped alphabetically as follows: A: shoplifters; B, C, D, F: swindlers; E: murderers; G: fraudulent bankrupts; H: purse-snatchers; I: burglars.

experience or the environment) could be passed on to the individual's offspring. Because the process of genetic reproduction was not understood until the twentieth century, Lamarck's theories remained very influential throughout the nineteenth century and possessed deeply disturbing implications. Middle-class Europeans began to speculate that the conditions of urban industrial life were producing undesirable characteristics among urban workers, characteristics that their children would then inherit. In the middle-class view, the transmission of physical weakness, sexual promiscuity, and violent criminality from one generation to the next threatened to reverse the evolutionary ascent of Western civilization.

The fear of degeneration evident throughout fin-de-siècle culture resulted in efforts to tighten the boundaries around accepted definitions of "maleness" and "femaleness" in order to bolster both the moral and physical strength of Western societies. Both scientists and lawmakers, for example, worked to identify homosexuals as threats to the social order. Traditionally, Europeans and Americans had viewed same-sex sexual practice as a form of immoral behavior, indulged in by morally lax—but otherwise normal—men. (Few considered the possibility of female homosexual behavior.) In the last third of the nineteenth century, however, the emphasis shifted from *actions* to *identity*, from condemning a specific type of sexual behavior to denouncing a certain group of people now considered abnormal and dangerous. Scientists argued that "the homosexual" was diseased—and that he could communicate this disease to others. This moral and medical condemnation of male homosexuality became enshrined in legislation. The penal code of the new Germany stipulated severe punishment for homosexuality, while the British government in 1885 made illegal all homosexual acts, even those between consenting adults in the privacy of their own home.

The new science of sexuality also heightened concern about sexual behaviors and gender roles. During the final decades of the nineteenth century, scientists invaded the most intimate areas of human behavior and made important breakthroughs in the understanding of human reproduction and sexual physiology. In 1875, a German physiologist discovered the basic process of fertilization—the union of male and female sex cells. Four years later, scientists for the first time witnessed, with the aid of the microscope, a sperm cell penetrating an egg. The greater understanding of sexual *physiology* went hand in hand with the effort to apply the scientific method to sexual *practice*. With data drawn from biology, anthropology, and human physiology, scientists in Europe and the United States sought to define "normal" sexual behavior. The German scientist Richard von Krafft-Ebing labeled homosexuality a pathology in 1886, while many publications condemned masturbation and frequent sexual intercourse. Other works offered support for antifeminism by arguing that female physiology incapacitated women for public life.

■ **Gustav Klimt,** *Medicine* **(1901)**
Klimt was commissioned by the University of Vienna to create a work that would celebrate medicine's great achievements. Not surprisingly, the painting he produced provoked great controversy. The woman in the forefront is Hygeia, the Greek goddess of health, but behind her swim images of female sexuality and death. Klimt's paintings often featured women as alluring but engulfing elemental forces.

Heightened concern about gender boundaries even pervaded the visual art of late-nineteenth-century Europe. Women often appeared as elemental forces, creatures of nature rather than civilization, who threatened to trap, emasculate, engulf, suffocate, or destroy the unwary man. In *Medicine,* by the Austrian painter Gustav Klimt (1862–1918), the liquid portraits of women flow between and into images of sex and death in a disturbing and powerful painting. Such images recur even more graphically in the work of Klimt's student Egon Schiele (1890–1918). In his very short life Schiele created more than 3,000 works on paper and 300 paintings, many of these depictions of the dangerous female. In works such as *Black-Haired Girl with Raised Skirt* (1911), harsh colors and brazen postures present an unsettling vision of female sexuality.

THE BIRTH OF MODERNISM

Schiele's disturbing paintings exemplify the new modernist movement. Although the term modernism° was not commonly used until the 1920s, the main developments it embraced were well underway by 1914. Modernist art and literature expressed a set of common attitudes and assumptions that centered on a rejection of established authority. In the final decades of the nineteenth century, many artists tossed aside accepted standards and rules and embarked on a series of bold experiments. At the core of modernism was a questioning of all accepted standards and truths, particularly those that shaped the middle-class liberal worldview.

In that liberal worldview, the arts served a useful purpose and were a vital part of civilized society. Modernism rejected this idea of art as an instrument of moral or emotional uplift. Modernists argued that art is autonomous—it stands alone, of value in and of itself rather than for any impact it may have on society. Modernist painters, for example, did not seek to tell a story or to preach a sermon, but rather to experiment with line, color, and composition.

Modernists also challenged middle-class liberalism by insisting that history is irrelevant. Fascinated with the process of change over time—with the evolution not only of species but also of ideas and societies—most middle-class men and women viewed history as the orderly forward march of progress. In contrast, modernists argued that fast-moving industrial and technological change had shattered the lines connecting history and modernity. Painters such as the Futurists in Italy (one of the many artistic movements that clustered under the modernist umbrella) reveled in the new machine age, a world cut off from anything that had gone before. In their paintings they depicted human beings as machines in motion, moving too fast to be tied down to history.

Modernism also rejected the dominant nineteenth-century faith in the power of human reason and observation, and instead emphasized the role of individual emotion and experience in shaping human understanding. In Paris, a group of artists centered on the Spaniard Pablo Picasso (1881–1973) dared to juxtapose different perspectives and points of view on a single canvas. They called themselves Cubists°. Just as Albert Einstein revolutionized physics by arguing that time and space shift as the position of the observer changes, so Cubism transformed Western visual culture by revealing the incompleteness and even incoherence of individual perception. Their fragmented, jagged, energetic works no longer reflected the world "out there," but instead revealed the artist's fluid and contradictory vision.

This emphasis on art as a form of personal expression is also seen in the Expressionist° movement, centered in central and eastern Europe. Expressionists such as the Russian painter Wassily Kandinsky (1866–1944) shattered artistic boundaries and splashed their emotions all over the canvas. Kandinsky sought to remove all form from his painting, to create a universe of pure color that would express a fundamental spiritual reality. In the process, he produced the first purely abstract paintings in Western art.

Because they so radically challenged middle-class and liberal standards and assumptions, modernist works were greeted with incomprehension and outrage. Most middle-class men and women remained firmly within a cultural milieu in which paintings revealed pretty scenes, novels told a moral tale, and music offered harmonious charm. These audiences condemned modernism as sick, pornographic,

■ **Wassily Kandinsky, *Composition VII* (1913)**
Kandinsky's experiments in color and form led him to pure abstraction.

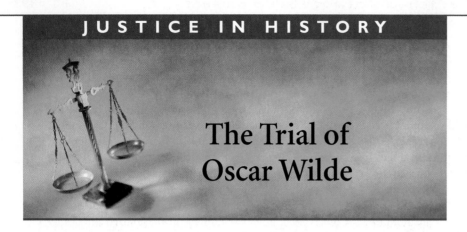

The Trial of Oscar Wilde

In March 1895 the Marquis of Queensberry left a message with the porter of a gentleman's club in London. The message, written on Queensberry's calling card, read "To Oscar Wilde, posing as a *somdomite.*" What Queensberry meant to write was *sodomite,* a common term for a man who engaged in sexual relations with other men. By handing the card to the porter, Queensberry openly accused Wilde, a celebrated novelist and playwright, of homosexual—and therefore criminal—activity. Ten years earlier the British Parliament had declared illegal all homosexual activity, even consensual relations between adults in a private home. Queensberry's accusation, then, was extremely serious. Oscar Wilde responded by suing Queensberry for libel—and set in motion a legal process that led to Wilde's imprisonment, and indirectly, to his early death.

Wilde made a reckless mistake when he chose to sue for libel, for in fact Queensberry had not libeled him. Wilde was a homosexual, and he and Queensberry's son, Lord Alfred Douglas, were lovers. Why, then, did Wilde dare to challenge Queensberry? Perhaps the fact that he was married, with two children, seemed to provide a certain shield against the charge of homosexuality. Or perhaps Wilde's successes as a novelist and playwright gave him a misguided sense of invulnerability. With two of his plays currently appearing on the London stage to favorable reviews, Wilde stood at the pinnacle of his career in the spring of 1895.

Wilde had built that career on a deliberate flouting of middle-class codes of morality. He saw himself as an artist, and insisted that art should be freed from social convention and moral restraint. His "High Society" comedies about privileged elites living scandalous lives and exchanging witty epigrams were far from the morally uplifting drama expected by middle-class audiences. He also used his public persona to attack the conventional, the respectable, and the orthodox. Widely recognized for his outrageous clothing and conversation, Wilde had consciously adopted the mannerisms of what nineteenth-century Britons called a "dandy"—a well-dressed, irreverent, artistic, leisured, and most of all, effeminate man. Before the Oscar Wilde trial, such effeminacy did not serve as a sign of, or a code for, homosexual inclinations, but it did signal to many observers a lavish—and loose—lifestyle. Oscar Wilde, then, was a man many British men and women loved to hate.

Even so, when his trial opened Wilde appeared to be in a strong position, the prosecutor rather than the defendant. Because Wilde had Queensberry's card with the "sodomite" charge written right on it, Queensberry faced certain conviction unless he could show that Wilde had engaged in homosexual activity. Wilde knew, of course, that Queensberry would not risk bringing the legal spotlight to bear on his own son's homosexuality.

At first, Queensberry's attorney, Edward Carson, focused on Wilde's published works, trying to use Wilde's own words against him. It proved an ineffective strategy. On the witness stand Wilde reveled in the attention and ran circles around Carson.

On the second day of the libel trial, however, Wilde's witticisms proved insufficient as Carson began to question him about his frequent visits to a male brothel and his associations with a number of young, working-class men who worked as male prostitutes. Suddenly the issue was no longer the literary merit or moral worth of Wilde's published writings, but rather his sexual exploitation of working-class boys. At this point, Wilde withdrew his libel charge against Queensberry, and the court declared the marquis not guilty.

If Queensberry was not guilty of libel in calling Wilde a sodomite, then by clear implication, Wilde was guilty of homosexual activity and therefore a criminal. Within days he was charged with "gross indecency" with another male. The jury in that case failed to reach a verdict, but the state was determined to obtain a conviction and brought the charges again. Wilde was refused bail, and on May 20 he was back in court.

On May 25, 1895—just three months after Queensberry had left his misspelled message with the club porter—Wilde's promising literary career ended. He was found guilty of seven counts of gross indecency with other men. The presiding judge, Sir Alfred Wills, characterized the trial as "the worst case I have ever tried," and declared, "I shall under the circumstances be expected to pass the severest sentence the law allows. In my judgment it is totally inadequate for such a case." He sentenced Wilde to two years at hard labor. The physical punishment took its toll. Wilde died in 1900 at age 46.

In sentencing Wilde, Wills described him as "the centre of a circle of extensive corruption of the most hideous kind." How do we account for the intensity of Wills's language, as well as the severity of Wilde's sentence? Homosexual activity had long been condemned on religious grounds, but this condemnation grew more fierce in the closing decades of the nineteenth century. In a time of rapid and threatening change, the marking of gender boundaries became a way to create and enforce social order. Wilde crossed those boundaries, and so had to be punished. Moreover, by the end of the nineteenth century, the state had assumed new responsibilities. Desperate to enhance national strength in a period of heightened international competition, governments intervened in areas previously considered the domain of the private citizen. By the turn of the century, western European governments were compelling working-class parents to send their children to school, regulating the hours adults could work, supervising the sale of food and drugs, providing limited forms of old-age pensions and medical insurance—and policing sexual boundaries.

The policing of sexual boundaries became easier after the Wilde trial because it provided a homosexual personality profile, a "Wanted" poster to hang on the walls of Western culture. For many observers of his very well-publicized trial, Wilde became the embodiment of "the homosexual," a particular and peculiar type of person and a menace to cultural stability. The Wilde trial linked "dandyism" to the new image of the homosexual. Outward stylistic choices such as effeminacy, artistic sensibilities, and flamboyant clothing and conversation became, for many observers, the telltale signs of substantial inner corruption. Thus the Wilde case marked an important turning point in the construction, as well as the condemnation, of a homosexual identity. ■

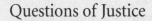

■ **Oscar Wilde and Lord Alfred Douglas**

Although the British government pursued its case against Wilde, it made no effort to put together a case against Douglas.

Questions of Justice

1. How does this trial illustrate the role of medical, legal, and cultural assumptions in shaping sexual identity?
2. Did the trial of Oscar Wilde achieve justice? If so, of what kind and for whom?

Taking It Further

An Ideal Husband. 1999. Film adaptation of Oscar Wilde's very funny play, which exemplifies his lighthearted but devastating critique of conventional manners and morals.

Ellman, Richard. *Oscar Wilde.* 1988. An important biography of Wilde.

Hyde, H. Montgomery. *The Trials of Oscar Wilde.* 1962. Includes extensive quotations from the trial transcripts as well as photographs of some of the documentary evidence.

McLaren, Angus. *The Trials of Masculinity: Policing Sexual Boundaries 1870–1930.* 1997. Places the Wilde trial within a wider cultural context.

anarchic, and often simply insane. For many, then, modernist art exemplified the degeneration of Western civilization and thus contributed to a growing sense of cultural crisis.

POPULAR RELIGION AND SECULARIZATION

The fin-de-siècle was also a period of religious transformation. Developments in geology and biology undermined the orthodox Christian view of a harmonious, divinely directed, natural world; at the same time, medical advances worked to narrow the appeal of traditional religion. Tragedies once accepted as "acts of God," such as epidemic disease, now appeared to be curable and controllable. Increasingly, scientists seemed able to answer questions once thought the province of the theologians.

The Christian response to such challenges varied. Some Christians embraced the scientific method as a gift from God and argued that the Christian faith must adapt to the ongoing expansion of human knowledge. To many theologians as well as ordinary believers, the study of the Bible as an historical and literary document promised to free Christians *from* antiquated beliefs impossible to sustain in the new scientific age, and *for* a more reform-oriented religious life.

Other Christians, however, resisted accommodations to the scientific age. Protestant fundamentalists insisted on retaining a belief in the literal, historical, and scientific accuracy of the Christian scriptures, a stance that often led them to oppose science as the enemy of religion. Similarly, the Roman Catholic papacy adopted a defiant pose. In 1864, Pope Pius IX (r. 1846–1878) issued a *Syllabus of Errors*, which condemned not only materialism but also the idea that the pope should "harmonize himself with progress, with liberalism, and with modern civilization." Five years later, a church council proclaimed the doctrine of papal infallibility: Any decrees issued by the pope with regard to faith and morals were free from error and good for all time and all places.

The most significant challenge faced by Christianity after 1870, however, emerged not from scientific laboratories but rather from the department stores and playing fields. In the growing industrial cities, both working- and middle-class individuals enjoyed new, secular sources of entertainment, inspiration, and desire. Whereas shared religious worship had once cemented community life, the increasingly elaborate rituals of spectator sports now forged new bonds of loyalty and identity. At the same time, the delectable array of colorful products displayed in shop windows promised fulfillment and satisfaction in the here and now, an earthly paradise rather than a heavenly reward.

Yet even in the face of such challenges and despite a growing sense of crisis among many clergymen, religious belief remained a powerful force in the decades after 1870.

In Britain, regular Sunday worship continued to be a central aspect of middle-class culture, and the still-strong Sunday School movement as well as religious instruction in state schools ensured that working-class children were taught the fundamentals of the Christian faith. On the Continent, many Europeans connected revolutionary anarchy with unbelief after revolutionaries executed the Archbishop of Paris in 1871 (see Chapter 21). The excesses of the Paris Commune thus contributed to a religious revival. Much of this popular Catholic religiosity focused on the cult of the Virgin Mary: By the 1870s, the shrine at Lourdes, site of Mary's miraculous appearance in 1858, was attracting hundreds of thousands of Catholic pilgrims.

Three additional factors contributed to the religiosity of late-nineteenth-century Europe. First, the high rate of immigration fostered attachments to the religious cultures of the homeland. In English cities, for example, Irish immigrants looked to the local Roman Catholic Church for spiritual solace, material support, and social contacts. Second, nationalism also shored up religious belief and practice in many regions. Hence, for Polish nationalists dreaming of independence from Russian rule, Roman Catholicism was a key part of a separate national identity. Finally, as we shall see in the next section, imperialism became interwoven with Western Christianity. Missionary publications and societies gave Western Christians a sense of both purpose and power.

The New Imperialism

For many Europeans—particularly the British, who presided over the largest empire in the world—imperialist domination served as reassuring, even incontrovertible evidence of the superiority of Western civilization. Social Darwinism supplied a supposedly scientific justification for the conquest of peoples deemed biologically inferior; swift and decisive victories over other lands and societies helped quell anxiety about European degeneration; and the onward march of Christian missionaries seemed incontrovertible proof of God's favor.

UNDERSTANDING THE NEW IMPERIALISM

Imperialism was not, of course, new to Europe. In the fifteenth century, Europeans had embarked on the first phase of imperialism, with the extension of European control across coastal ports of Africa and India, and into the Americas. In the second phase, which began in the late seventeenth century, European colonial empires in both Asia and the Western Hemisphere expanded as governments sought to augment their profits from international trade.

After 1870 and particularly after 1880, Europe's expansion into non-European territories became so much more aggressive that historians label this third phase the age of new imperialism°. In just thirty years, European control of the globe's land surface swelled from 65 to 85 percent. What factors lay behind this new imperialism?

Technology, Economics, and Politics

Part of the answer lies in the economic developments examined in Chapter 22. The new technologies characteristic of the Second Industrial Revolution meant that industrial Europe increasingly depended on raw materials available only in non-Western regions such as Asia, Africa, and South America. Rubber, for example, was essential not only for tires on the new automobiles, but also for insulating the electrical and telegraph wires now encircling the globe. Palm oil from Africa provided the lubricant needed for industrial machinery. Increasingly dependent on these primary resources, European states were quick to respond to perceived threats to their economic interests.

Competition for markets also accelerated imperial acquisition. With the onset of economic depression in 1873 (discussed in Chapter 22), industrialists were faced with declining demand for their products in Europe. Imperial expansion seemed to provide a solution, with annexed territories seen as captive markets.

A global investment boom in the 1890s accelerated imperial expansion. Western European capital spread across the globe, underwriting railway lines, digging mines, and erecting public utilities in the United States, Latin America, Russia, Asia, and Africa. With each railroad or coal mine or dam, European interests in non-European regions expanded, and so did the pressure on European governments to assume formal political control should those interests be threatened, whether by the arrival of other European competitors or by local political instability.

New imperialism intertwined with both domestic and international politics as well as economics. As suffrage expanded, political leaders needed to find issues that would appeal to new voters. Imperialism was one such issue. It assured ordinary men that they were part of a superior, conquering people. Tales of dangerous explorations and decisive military victories engaged the emotions and prodded the ordinary individual to identify more closely with the nation. In addition, newly formed nations such as Italy and Germany sought empires outside Europe as a way to gain both power and prestige within Europe. Similar concerns about international status and military and strategic advantages motivated nations such as Britain and France both to defend and expand their existing empires.

The Imperial Idea

New imperialism functioned as a belief system, as an idea that permeated middle-class and mass culture in the decades after 1870. Images of empire proliferated, appearing in boys' adventure stories, glossy ads, picture postcards, cookie tins, and cheap ceramic plates and mugs. At exhibitions and world's fairs, both goods and peoples from conquered regions were put on display to educate the crowds of viewers about the "imperial idea."

At the center of this idea stood the assumption of the *rightness* of white European dominance over the world. What led white Europeans to believe they had both the right and the responsibility to take charge of other cultures and continents?

One key factor was the perceived link between Western Christianity and "civilization." Christian missionaries served as a vanguard of Western culture throughout the nineteenth century. Missionary societies acted as powerful interest groups that often lobbied for Western territorial expansion to promote the spread of Christian missionary activity.

Europeans also pointed to their advanced technologies as evidence of their material and moral superiority, and as a justification for their imperial rule. Before the nineteenth century, the technological gap between European and non-European societies had not loomed large; in some cases, such as China, non-European societies had held the technological advantage. Industrialization, however, gave Europe the technological edge.

Finally, Social Darwinism lent a seemingly scientific authority to the imperial idea by supposedly proving the mental and moral superiority of white Europeans over all peoples of color. Thus the British Lord Milner (1854–1925) explained in a speech in South Africa in 1903: "The white man must rule, because he is elevated by many, many steps above the black man; steps which it will take the latter centuries to climb, and which it is quite possible that the vast bulk of the black population may never be able to climb at all."

Many Europeans, however, rejected the imperialist assumption of Western superiority. Some modernist artists, for example, looked to non-Western cultures for artistic inspiration and argued that these societies had much to teach the West. The Fauves ("wild beasts"), a Paris-based circle of artists that included Henri Matisse (1869–1954) and Paul Gauguin (1848–1903), condemned most Western art as overrefined and artificial, and sought in their own brilliantly colored works to rediscover the vitality that they found in non-Western cultures (see page 486).

Critics of empire often focused on its domestic political and economic implications. The British economist J. A. Hobson (1858–1940) charged that overseas empires benefited only wealthy capitalists while distracting public attention from the need for domestic political and economic reform. Hobson argued that unregulated capitalism led almost inevitably to imperialist expansion. While impoverishing the masses, the capitalist system generates huge surpluses in capital for a very small elite, who must then find

■ **Pablo Picasso, *Les Desmoiselles d'Avignon* (1907)**

Many art historians argue that Cubism was born with this painting. One of Picasso's sources of inspiration was an exhibition of African masks held in Paris. Like many modernists, Picasso saw in primitive art a passion and an elemental clarity that he sought for in his own work.

somewhere to invest these surpluses. Hobson's ideas proved very influential among European socialists, who condemned imperialism along with capitalism.

Many liberals also condemned imperialism. The British prime minister William Gladstone (1809–1898) clung fast to the liberal belief that free trade between independent nations fostered international peace. Yet between 1880 and 1885—while Gladstone headed the British government—the British Empire expanded at the rate of 87,000 square miles per year, with Gladstone himself ordering the bombardment of Alexandria and the military occupation of Egypt. When Gladstone did hold firm to his anti-imperialist ideals and ordered British troops to withdraw from the Sudan in 1885, he outraged the British public. Critics of empire were in the minority, not only in Britain but throughout Europe. The imperial idea permeated European and much of American culture in the final decades of the nineteenth century.

THE SCRAMBLE FOR AFRICA

New imperialism reached its zenith in Africa. In 1875 European powers controlled only 11 percent of the African continent. By 1905, about 90 percent of African lands and 110 million Africans were under European control. The conquest of the African continent was so rapid and dramatic that as early as 1884 mystified Europeans began to talk about the Scramble for Africa°.

Overcoming the Obstacles

When the nineteenth century began, a vast and profitable trading network between European merchants and Africa's coastal regions existed, centering on the exchange of European goods for African gold and slaves. European efforts to establish settlements in the interior, however, faced three key obstacles—the climate, disease, and African resistance.

Africa was known as "the white man's grave," deservedly so. Seventy-seven percent of the white soldiers sent to West Africa in the early nineteenth century died there. Temperatures of over 100 degrees Fahrenheit in some regions and constant rainfall in others made travel extremely difficult. The mosquito and the tsetse fly made it deadly. Mosquito bites brought malaria, while the tsetse fly carried trypanosomiasis, or sleeping sickness, an infectious illness that began with a fever and ended in a fatal paralysis. Sleeping sickness also killed off livestock such as horses and oxen and so aggravated the problem of transportation within the African interior. Despite the dangers posed by the climate and disease, Europeans endeavored to establish inland settlements but then faced the obstacle of African resistance. In the seventeenth century, for example, the Portuguese set up forts and trading centers in modern Zimbabwe but were driven out by local populations.

In the first half of the nineteenth century, however, various forces destabilized Africa's political structures and so weakened the African ability to withstand conquest in later

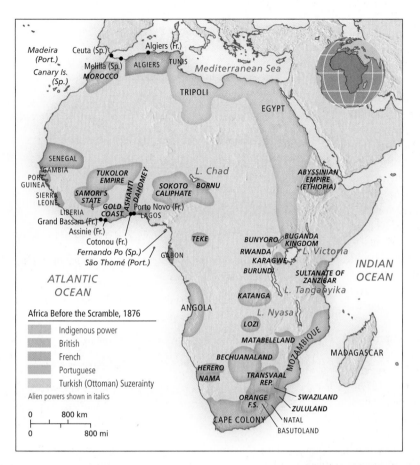

(a)

Madeira (Port.)

Canary Is. (Sp.)

Ceuta (Sp.)
Melilla (Sp.)
MOROCCO
ALGIERS
Algiers (Fr.)
TUNIS
Mediterranean Sea
TRIPOLI
EGYPT

SENEGAL
GAMBIA
PORT. GUINEA
SIERRA LEONE
LIBERIA
Grand Bassam (Fr.)
Assinie (Fr.)
TUKOLOR EMPIRE
SAMORI'S STATE
ASHANTI
DAHOMEY
GOLD COAST
Porto Novo (Fr.)
LAGOS
Cotonou (Fr.)
Fernando Po (Sp.)
São Thomé (Port.)
GABON
L. Chad
SOKOTO CALIPHATE
BORNU
TEKE
ABYSSINIAN EMPIRE (ETHIOPIA)
BUNYORO
RWANDA
KARAGWE
BURUNDI
BUGANDA KINGDOM
L. Victoria
SULTANATE OF ZANZIBAR
L. Tanganyika
INDIAN OCEAN

ATLANTIC OCEAN

ANGOLA
KATANGA
L. Nyasa
LOZI
MATABELELAND
BECHUANALAND
HERERO NAMA
TRANSVAAL REP.
ORANGE F.S.
ZULULAND
SWAZILAND
CAPE COLONY
NATAL
BASUTOLAND
MOZAMBIQUE
MADAGASCAR

Africa Before the Scramble, 1876

	Indigenous power
	British
	French
	Portuguese
	Turkish (Ottoman) Suzerainty

Alien powers shown in italics

0   800 km
0   800 mi

■ **Map 23.1a** **(a) Africa Before the Scramble, 1876, and (b) Africa After the Scramble, 1914**

A comparison of these two maps reveals the dramatic impact of the new imperialism on African societies. Indigenous empires such as the Sokoto Caliphate in West Africa came under Western rule, as did tribal societies such as the Herero. Even indigenous states ruled by whites of European descent came under European rule, as the examples of the Transvaal and the Orange Free State in South Africa illustrate. Only Ethiopia preserved its independence.

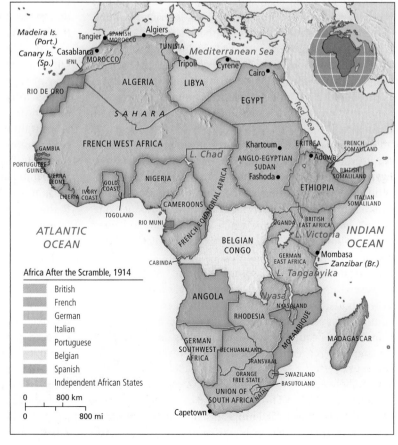

(b)

Madeira Is. (Port.)

Canary Is. (Sp.)

Tangier
SPANISH MOROCCO
Algiers
Casablanca
IFNI
MOROCCO
TUNISIA
Tripoli
Cyrene
Cairo
Mediterranean Sea

RIO DE ORO
ALGERIA
LIBYA
EGYPT
S A H A R A
Red Sea

FRENCH WEST AFRICA
GAMBIA
PORTUGUESE GUINEA
SIERRA LEONE
LIBERIA
IVORY COAST
GOLD COAST
TOGOLAND
NIGERIA
CAMEROONS
RIO MUNI
L. Chad
Khartoum
ANGLO-EGYPTIAN SUDAN
Fashoda
ERITREA
Adowa
FRENCH SOMALILAND
BRITISH SOMALILAND
ETHIOPIA
ITALIAN SOMALILAND

FRENCH EQUATORIAL AFRICA
CABINDA
BELGIAN CONGO
UGANDA
BRITISH EAST AFRICA
L. Victoria
GERMAN EAST AFRICA
Mombasa
Zanzibar (Br.)
L. Tanganyika
INDIAN OCEAN

ATLANTIC OCEAN

ANGOLA
L. Nyasa
RHODESIA
NYASALAND
MOZAMBIQUE
GERMAN SOUTHWEST AFRICA
BECHUANALAND
TRANSVAAL
ORANGE FREE STATE
NATAL
SWAZILAND
BASUTOLAND
UNION OF SOUTH AFRICA
Capetown
MADAGASCAR

Africa After the Scramble, 1914

	British
	French
	German
	Italian
	Portuguese
	Belgian
	Spanish
	Independent African States

0   800 km
0   800 mi

decades. Although the precise nature of the destabilizing forces varied by region, one common denominator prevailed—the unsettling impact of early encounters with the West. In the 1830s, for example, Britain and other European powers, pressured by humanitarian and missionary lobby groups, embarked on an effort to stamp out the West African slave trade. They succeeded, but only in West Africa. The slave trade shifted to the central and eastern regions of the continent and wreaked havoc with political arrangements there. African slaving nations relied on frequent military raids to obtain their human merchandise. These raids—carried out by Africans against Africans—disrupted agricultural production, shattered trade networks, and undermined the authority of existing political rulers. With political systems in disarray, many African regions were vulnerable to European encroachment.

At the same time, three specific developments shifted the balance of power in the West's favor—the steamship, the "quinine prophylaxis," and the repeating, breech-loading rifle. By the 1820s, steamships were widely in use on European lakes and rivers. Steam proved crucial in enabling Western imperialists to overcome the obstacles to traveling through Africa by allowing them to use the continent's extensive but shallow river system. Steam enabled Westerners to penetrate the African interior; quinine helped them survive once they got there. In the 1850s, a series of chance discoveries revealed the importance of taking quinine prophylactically—of saturating the system with quinine before any risk of infection. By the 1860s, Westerners were routinely ingesting quinine in preparation for postings in Africa—and their death rates dropped dramatically.

African death rates, however, soared because of the third crucial technology of imperialism—the repeating, breech-loading rifles carried by Europeans from the 1870s on. Before the invention of these rifles, Europeans used muskets or muzzle-loading rifles that had to be loaded one ball or cartridge at a time while standing up, and were prone to foul easily, particularly in damp weather. Such weapons did not provide Europeans with much of a military advantage, even over spears. With the repeating rifle, however, "any European infantryman could now fire lying down, undetected, in any weather, fifteen rounds of ammunition in as many seconds at targets up to half a mile away." The repeating breech-loader and its descendant the machine gun made the European conquest "more like hunting than war."[4]

Slicing the Cake: The Conquest of Africa

In the decades after 1870, European states moved quickly to beat out their rivals and grab a piece of the African conti-

CHRONOLOGY

1859	Darwin's *Origin of Species* outlines theory of evolutionary development
1868	Meiji Restoration in Japan: onset of rapid modernization
1869	Proclamation of doctrine of papal infallibility
1882	Tuberculosis bacillus isolated
1884	Berlin Conference: Scramble for Africa accelerated
1885	Russia establishes control over central Asia
1895	Trial of Oscar Wilde in England; discovery of the X ray
1898	Spanish-American War: United States expands holdings in Pacific and Caribbean
1900	Death of Nietzsche; publication of Freud's *Interpretation of Dreams*
1905	Publication of Einstein's theory of relativity
1907	First exhibition of Picasso's *Les Desmoiselles d'Avignon*
1911	Revolution in China: overthrow of Manchu Dynasty

nent. As King Leopold II of Belgium (r. 1865–1909) explained in a letter to his ambassador in London in 1876, "I do not want to miss a good chance of getting us a slice of this magnificent African cake."[5]

Leopold's slice proved to be enormous. Presenting himself as a humanitarian whose chief concern was the abolition of the slave trade, he called on the other European leaders to back his claim to the Congo, a huge region of central Africa comprising territory more than twice as large as central Europe. After a decade of controversy and quarreling, representatives of the European powers met in Berlin in 1884 and agreed to Leopold's demands. At the same time, they used the Berlin Conference to regulate the partition of Africa. According to the terms established in Berlin, any state claiming a territory in Africa had to establish "effective occupation" and to plan for the economic development of that region.

But as the history of the Congo demonstrated, colonialism in Africa was far from a humanitarian endeavor. By claiming all so-called vacant land, Leopold deprived villagers of the grazing, foraging, and hunting grounds they needed to survive. He levied impossibly high rubber quotas for each village, forcing villagers to harvest wild rubber for up to twenty-five days each month while their families starved. Brutal punishments ensured compliance: Soldiers chopped off the hands of villagers who failed to meet their rubber quota. At the same time, the Belgians forced black Africans to serve as human mules to transport rubber and other goods. This practice spread sleeping sickness from the western coast into the interior. Between 1895 and 1908, an epidemic of sleeping sickness decimated the already weakened population. An estimated three million people died from the combined effects of forced labor, brutal punishments, starvation, and disease.

King Leopold's personal brand of imperialism proved so scandalous that in 1908 the Belgian government replaced Leopold's personal rule with state control over the Congo. Yet the king's exploitation of the Congo differed only in degree, not in kind, from the nature of European conquest elsewhere in Africa. Forced labor was common throughout European-controlled areas, as were brutal punishments for any Africans who dared resist. Faced with tribal revolt in Southwest Africa, the German colonial army commander in 1904 ordered that the entire Herero tribe be exterminated. Twenty thousand Africans, including children, were forcibly driven from their villages into the desert to die of thirst.

African Resistance

As the Herero rebellion demonstrates, Africans frequently resisted the imposition of these often-brutal imperial regimes, but to no avail. The only successful episode of African resistance to European conquest occurred in northern Africa, in the kingdom of Ethiopia (also called Abyssinia). After four centuries of isolation, Ethiopia modernized in the 1850s. By the time of the European Scramble for Africa, Ethiopia had developed not only a modern standing army but also an advanced infrastructure and communications system. These factors enabled the Ethiopians to defeat the Italian army at the battle of Adowa in 1896, and so to remain independent of Italian imperial control.

Adowa, however, was the exception. Most African resistance was doomed by the technological gap that yawned between the indigenous peoples and their European conquerors. A booming arms trade developed between European rifle manufacturers and African states desperate to obtain guns. Frequently, however, the arms shipped to Africa were inferior models—muskets or single-firing muzzle-loaders rather than the up-to-date and deadly efficient repeating rifles and early machine guns possessed by the European invaders.

Even African resistance leaders who adopted modern military weapons could not stand for long against the industrial might of Western powers. The most famous African resistance leader, Samori Turé (1830–1900), built a vast West African empire of 115,000 square miles and held off the forces of French imperialism for fifteen years. But he, too, was conquered in the end. Samori Turé armed his elite cavalry troops with 6,000 repeating rifles, used with deadly effect against the French in a series of battles in the 1880s. He was one of the first military commanders to conceive of the tactics of modern guerilla warfare—hit-and-run attacks, night battles, the crucial advantage of knowing the land. Yet 6,000 repeating rifles and guerilla tactics could

not hold off the vast weight of French imperialism. Ambushed in 1898, Samori Turé died in exile two years later, with his empire in European control.

ASIAN ENCOUNTERS

Unlike most of Africa, many of the diverse states of Asia had already been woven into the web of the Western economy well before 1870. Pacific states such as Java and Malaysia formed a part of the eighteenth-century mercantilist empires established by Dutch, British, Portuguese, and French trading companies As in Africa, however, a number of factors accelerated the pace of imperialist acquisition after 1870. First, new industrial processes often heightened the economic value of many of these regions. The development of a process for producing dried coconut, for example, made Samoa so valuable that Germany, Britain, and the United States competed for control over the tiny islands. Second, imperialist gains by one power led to anxiety and a quicker pace of expansion by its rivals. Finally, the steady erosion of Chinese political stability—itself a result of encounters with the West—intensified this Asian scramble.

American and Russian Imperialism

The U.S. embrace of an Asian empire may seem surprising, given its own history of rebellion from British colonial rule. Yet much of nineteenth-century American history was the story of imperial expansion. In 1853, Commodore Matthew Perry used the potent threat of his squadron of four warships to force the opening of Japan to American commerce. During the 1860s and 1870s the United States participated with the European powers in chipping away at China's national sovereignty to ensure favorable terms of trade there. By the end of the century, the United States had annexed Hawaii and part of Samoa, and as a result of the Spanish-American War had acquired Guam, the Philippines, Cuba, and Puerto Rico.

Russia was also a key player in the game of Asian empire during this era. The tsarist regime expanded its control southward into central Asia, primarily as a preemptive response to the expansion of British power in India. Fearing that the British might push northward, the Russians pushed south. By 1885, the Black Sea region, the Caucasus, and Turkestan had all fallen to Russian imperial control. Over the next three decades the oil fields of the Caucasus would become a crucial part of the Russian industrial economy.

As the tsarist regime expanded its Asian empire, it increasingly encroached upon Chinese territory, a move that contributed to the destabilization of China and to growing hostilities between Russia and Japan. By 1860, Russia had gained from China a sizable chunk of land along the Pacific coast and began pressing into Manchuria. Manchuria, however, was a region also coveted by Japanese imperialists. The growing antagonism between Russia and Japan led to the outbreak of the Russo-Japanese War in 1904, which ended a year later in a dramatic Japanese victory. Military defeat by a people regarded as racially inferior shocked Russians and led to demands for radical political change. With Tsar Nicholas II's regime clearly weakened and his troops tied up in Manchuria, this domestic discontent exploded in the Russian Revolution of 1905. (See Chapter 22.) The return of his soldiers from the Manchurian front enabled Nicholas to withstand this challenge to his authoritarian rule. His regime, however, was fundamentally weakened: Imperialism could be a risky business.

Japanese Industrial and Imperial Expansion

Japan's victory over Russia in 1905 vividly illustrated its remarkable rise to global power and its emergence as an imperialist player. Japan had remained largely sealed off from the West until 1853, when Commodore Perry's warships forced Japan to open two of its ports to American ships. The next fifteen years were tumultuous, as Western powers pushed to expand their economic influence in Japan and as Japanese elites fought over the question of how to respond to the West. Anti-Western terrorism became endemic, civil war broke out, and a political revolution ensued.

In 1868, Japan emerged from this turbulent time with a new government. For more than 200 years effective political control had rested in the hands not of the Japanese emperor, but rather of the "Shogun," the military governor of Japan. When the Shogun adopted pro-Western policies, Japan's warrior nobility tossed him from power and restored the young Emperor Mutsuhito (1867–1912) to effective rule—the Meiji Restoration.

■ **Map 23.2   Imperialism in Asia, 1914**

The impact of the new imperialism on Asia was not as dramatic as in Africa, but the spread of Western rule is significant nonetheless. This map shows a key development: the entry of non-European powers—Japan and the United States—into the imperialist game. What it does not show is the extent of Western and Japanese influence in China. Profoundly destabilized by foreign intervention, China in 1914 was in the midst of revolution.

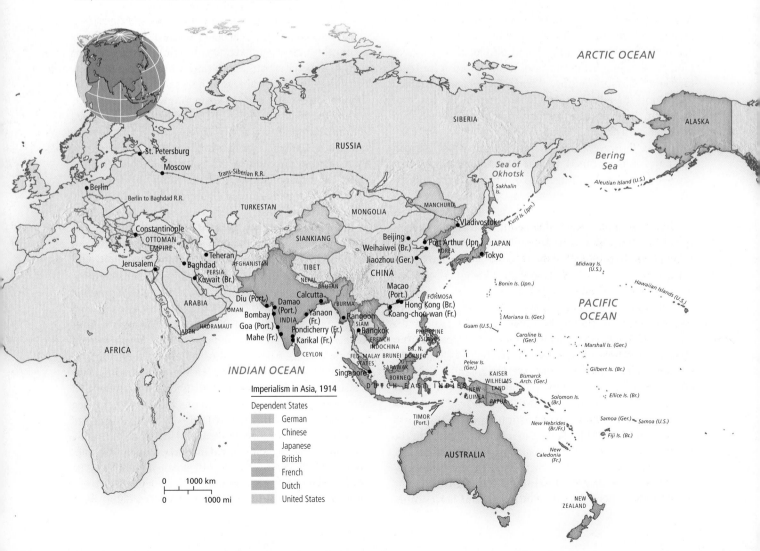

"A DREAM OF THE FUTURE"

In 1878, Tachibana Mitsuomi published his "Dream of the Future" in Hochi Shimbun, *the newspaper that he edited. Tachibana's dream is a nightmare. It reveals the anxiety prevalent in Japan during its time of rapid modernization and increasing contact with Western economies and ideas. In this excerpt, Tachibana projects the consequences of an imaginary decision to lift regulations on the importation of Western capital. In actual fact, no such decision was made. The Japanese government borrowed technology, techniques, and institutions from the West, but restrained the inflow of Western capital, thus retaining control over the Japanese economy.*

Tachibana's story opens with his bewilderment at suddenly finding himself on a busy street in Tokyo in 1967:

"The houses in the surrounding streets were splendidly built and some of them three, and others five stories high; flags from every merchant's house were waving in the air; all kinds of precious articles were displayed in the shops and carriages and horses were incessantly passing to and fro. Indeed, a most flourishing trade was actually before my eyes. Greatly puzzled at this, I went into a shop and found that the master of the shop was a White man with blue eyes and red hair, wearing handsome clean clothes and sitting in an easy position by a desk; and that those wearing scanty and torn apparel and in the employment of the master of the house, were none but the yellow-coloured and high-cheek-boned brethren of ours. . . . I was informed that . . . all the large houses in the main streets [were] occupied by the Whites. . . .

". . . I then passed into the [side] streets and on looking at the state of the houses, I saw none but immense numbers of my countrymen flocking together like sheep or pigs, in a few poorly-built houses . . . their scanty dress leaving portions of their body uncovered . . . their wives were weeping from the cold, and the children crying from hunger, the husbands being employed by the Western people, and were earning scarcely sufficient wages to fill the mouths of their families. . . .

"I, seeing this, could hardly keep from weeping and was sorely puzzled why my countrymen should have fallen to such misery . . . I saw a respectable looking gray-haired old man standing on the bridge . . . I approached him and after bowing to him, I asked, 'Is this country Japan? Is this the capital, Tokei [Tokyo]? How is it that the Western people alone are enjoying such great wealth, whilst the Japanese are in such a miserable state? . . .'"

The old man explains to Tochibana that the Japanese "were outdone by the superior strength of capital and intellect" from the West. As a result of lifting regulations on Western investment and ownership within Japan, "those who have control over the wealth of Japan . . . are none but the Western people." Tochibana concludes, "At this, I was very sad and deeply affected, and I was on the point of bursting into tears, when I suddenly awoke and found that it was all a dream."

Source: From Tachibana Mitsuomi, "A Dream of the Future," *Hochi Shimbun,* October 17, 1878. For the full version and a commentary, refer to Ian Inkster, *Japanese Industrialisation: Historical and Cultural Perspectives* (Routledge: London and New York, 2001), pp. 1–6.

Even more dramatically, these anti-Western elites determined that the only way to resist Western domination was to adopt Western industrial and military technologies and techniques. The next four decades witnessed a thoroughgoing revolution from the top as Japan's feudalist political system was dismantled, replaced by a modern centralized state modeled on France. Funds poured into building a modern navy, modeled on Britain's, and a powerful conscript-based army, modeled on Germany's. Beginning in the 1890s, Japan used its now formidable military force to push its way into the imperialist game. War with China in 1894 and Russia in 1904 led to the Japanese seizure of Taiwan and Korea, and to expanded Japanese economic influence in Manchuria.

Scrambling in China

While Japan used its encounter with the West to modernize and militarize its society, China proved far less successful in withstanding Western encroachment. Throughout the nineteenth century, Chinese national sovereignty slowly eroded, as European powers, soon joined by the United States and Japan, jostled for access to China's markets and resources. Competition for access to Chinese markets actually determined the course of Western imperialism throughout much of Asia. France's quest for a protected trade route to China, for example, led to the French empire in Indochina. By 1893, the Union of French Indochina included the formerly independent states of Laos, Cambodia, Annam, and Tonkin—the latter two better known by the contemporary name of Vietnam.

For much of the nineteenth century, China's encounter with the West worked to diminish the sovereignty and independence of its government. Low customs duties ensured that the profits flowed out from rather than into China. Even more significant, the principle of "extraterritoriality" declared foreign residents subject only to their own country's laws and so placed Westerners entirely outside the Chinese legal system, while granting Chinese residents in Western countries no such equivalent rights.

Western actions after 1895 further weakened China's central government. The Sino-Japanese War of 1894–1895 revealed China to be far weaker than the Western powers had realized. Over the next five years, these powers scrambled to create spheres of influence throughout China. The European powers and the United States agreed in 1899 to back the American "open door" policy, which opposed the formal partitioning of China (as had just occurred in Africa), but Western economic and political involvement continued to expand.

Chinese opposition to this intensified Western encroachment provoked greater outside interference—and the collapse of the Manchu dynasty that had governed China since the seventeenth century. In 1900, a secret society devoted to purging China of Western influence began attacking foreigners. This "Boxer Rebellion" received the covert support of the Chinese government. With more than 200 missionaries and several thousand Chinese Christians killed, the West responded in fury. A combined European, American, and Japanese military force crushed the rebellion and sacked Beijing. Required to pay a large indemnity to the West and to grant further trade and territorial concessions to its invaders, the Chinese central government was fatally weakened. In 1911, revolution engulfed China and propelled it into four decades of political and social tumult.

"White Australia"

The story of imperialist conquest in Asia also extends to the island continent of Australia. Discovered and claimed for Britain by Captain James Cook in 1770, Australia became a dumping ground for British convicts for several decades. But as the British textile industry expanded, the six British colonies established in Australia became vital suppliers of wool and a center of British immigration.

European settlement interrupted the nomadic way of life for the estimated 500,000 inhabitants of Australia, living in scattered tribal groupings. British policy toward the Aborigines shifted over time. Many settlers saw the Aborigines as a clear and violent threat that had to be eradicated. Massacres of Aborigines resulted. Christian and humanitarian groups, as well as the British government in London, opposed this sort of violence and insisted that the Aborigines should be westernized and Christianized. For most of the nineteenth century, British officials forcibly removed Aboriginal children from their homes and placed them in mission stations where they were educated and then farmed out as apprentices and servants. Few, however, assimilated to the Western way of life. Thus the final decades of the nineteenth century saw a shift in official policy from assimilation to "protection." Aborigines and mixed-race individuals were declared legal wards of the state and required to live on reserves. Aborigines did not receive Australian citizenship until 1967.

White Australians also perceived Asian immigrants as a threat to their Western identity. By the 1850s, tens of thousands of Chinese had migrated to Australia. Arriving as indentured servants, they worked under brutal conditions. Chinese gold miners, for example, received one-twelfth of the wages paid to a European. As the numbers of Chinese immigrants grew, so, too, did anti-Chinese sentiment. Most British immigrants and white native Australians, often fiercely divided in their vision of what sort of nation Australia should be, agreed that it should be colored white. In 1888, the Australian government turned back ships containing Chinese immigrants; restrictive immigration legislation soon followed.

In 1901, the six Australian colonies joined together in the Commonwealth of Australia, part of the British Empire but a self-governing political entity—and a self-defined "Western" nation. For many Australians, including the first prime minister, Edmund Barton, "West" meant "white." Barton, who campaigned on a platform calling for a "White Australia," regarded his country as an outpost of Western civilization in the Eastern hemisphere.

CONCLUSION

Reshaping the West: Expansion and Fragmentation

Africans and Asians who saw their political and social structures topple under the imperialist onslaught would probably have agreed with the Austrian poet Hugo von Hoffmansthal (1874–1929) when he wrote in 1905 that "what other generations believed to be firm is in fact sliding." Hoffmansthal, however, was commenting not on Africa or Asia or any other region of imperialist conquest, but rather on the Western cultural and intellectual landscape, which, like colonial political boundaries, underwent enormous and disturbing change in the period between 1870 and the outbreak of World War I in 1914. In this era, matter itself began to slide, as the Newtonian conception of the world gave way to a new, much more unsettling picture of the physical universe. At the same time, changes in medical practice, the revolt against positivism, and the triumph of Darwin's evolutionary theory helped undermine established assumptions and contributed to the sense that the foundations of Western culture were shifting. So, too, did the birth of modernism as well as broader cultural changes such as the move of middle-class women into the public sphere and the redefinition of sexual boundaries.

In the decades after 1870, then, a series of encounters reshaped the West. Its geographic boundaries expanded as non-European regions such as the United States emerged as significant economic and imperial powers. With Australians claiming Western identity, "the West" even spilled over into the Eastern Hemisphere. Yet fragmentation as well as expansion characterized the Western experience after 1870. At the same time that some social thinkers were proclaiming white cultural superiority, European artists such as Gauguin and Picasso were embracing the visual forms of Asian and African societies in an effort to push open the boundaries of Western culture. While scientific and technological achievements convinced many Europeans and Americans that the West was destined to conquer the globe, others regarded these scientific and technological changes with profound uneasiness.

The next chapter will show that the sense that old certainties were slipping led some Europeans to welcome the outbreak of war in 1914 as a way to restore heroic values and clear purpose to Western society. The trenches of World War I, however, provided little solidity. Many nineteenth-century political, economic, and cultural structures slid into ruin under the impact of total war.

Suggestions for Further Reading

For a comprehensive list of suggested readings, please go to www.ablongman.com/levackconcise/chapter23

Adas, Michael. *Machines as the Measure of Men: Science, Technology, and Ideologies of Western Dominance.* 1989. A superb study of the way in which the ideology of empire was inextricably connected with cultural and intellectual developments within the West.

Betts, Raymond F. *The False Dawn: European Imperialism in the Nineteenth Century.* 1975. A general survey that looks at the ideas that underlay imperialism as well as the events that shaped it.

Bowler, Peter. *Evolution: The History of an Idea.* 1989. Looks at the development of evolutionary theory both before and after Darwin.

Butler, Christopher. *Early Modernism: Literature, Music, and Painting in Europe, 1900–1916.* 1994. Wide-ranging and nicely illustrated.

Dijkstra, Bram. *Idols of Perversity: Fantasies of Feminine Evil in Fin-de-Siècle Culture.* 1986. This richly illustrated work shows how anxiety over the changing role of women permeated artistic production at the end of the nineteenth century.

Dodge, Ernest. *Islands and Empires: The Western Impact on the Pacific and East Asia.* 1976. A useful study of Asian imperialism.

Ellis, John. *The Social History of the Machine Gun.* 1975. Lively, nicely illustrated, and informative.

Gould, Stephen Jay. *The Mismeasure of Man.* 1996. A compelling look at the manipulation of scientific data and statistics to provide "proof" for racist and elitist assumptions.

Headrick, Daniel R. *The Tools of Empire: Technology and European Imperialism in the Nineteenth Century.* 1981. Highlights the important role played by technology in determining both the timing and success of Western imperialism.

Hochschild, Adam. *King Leopold's Ghost.* 1998. Blistering account of Leopold's imperialist rule in the Congo.

Pick, Daniel. *Faces of Degeneration: A European Disorder c. 1848–1918.* 1993. Argues that concern over degeneration formed a central theme in European culture in the second half of the nineteenth century.

Showalter, Elaine. *Sexual Anarchy: Gender and Culture at the Fin de Siècle.* 1990. An illuminating look at the turbulence that characterized gender relations in the fin-de-siècle.

Sperber, Jonathan. *Popular Catholicism in Nineteenth-Century Germany.* 1984. A look at the religious dimensions of popular culture.

Thornton, A. P. *The Imperial Idea and Its Enemies: A Study in British Power.* 1959; reprinted 1985. An older but still-important look at imperialist ideology and opposition.

Vandervort, Bruce. *Wars of Imperial Conquest in Africa, 1830–1914.* 1998. An up-to-date study by a military historian.

Wesseling, H. L. *Divide and Rule: The Partition of Africa 1880–1914.* 1996. A solid survey of complex developments.

Notes

1. Winston Churchill, *The River War: An Account of the Reconquest of the Sudan* (New York, 1933); quoted in Daniel Headrick, *The Tools of Empire: Technology and European Imperialism in the Nineteenth Century* (1981), 118.
2. Quoted in Anne McClintock, *Imperial Leather: Race, Gender, and Sexuality in the Colonial Contest* (1995), 50.
3. Quoted in Shearer West, *Fin de Siècle* (1993), 24.
4. Headrick, *The Tools of Empire,* 101. Headrick is the historian who identified the crucial role of the steamship, the quinine prophylaxis, and the repeating, breech-loading rifle in the conquest of Africa.
5. Quoted in Thomas Pakenham, *The Scramble for Africa 1876–1912* (1991), 22.

The First World War

O N THE MORNING OF JULY 1, 1916, IN THE FIELDS OF NORTHERN FRANCE near the Somme River, tens of thousands of young British soldiers crawled out of ditches and began to walk across a muddy expanse filled with shards of metal and decomposing human bodies. Encumbered with backpacks weighing more than sixty pounds, the men trudged forward. For the past week their heavy artillery had pummeled the Germans who lay on the other side of the mud. Thus they expected little opposition. In less than sixty seconds, expectations and reality horribly diverged. The German troops, who had waited out the bombardment in the safety of "dugouts"—fortified bunkers scooped from the earth beneath the trenches—raced to their gunnery positions and raked the evenly spaced lines of British soldiers with machine-gun fire. The slowly walking men made easy targets. Those who were lucky enough to make it to the enemy lines found their way blocked by barbed-wire fences—still intact, despite the bombardment. Standing in front of the wire, they were quickly mown down. Over 20,000 British soldiers died that day, thousands within the first minutes of the attack. Another 40,000 were wounded. Yet the attack went on. Between July 1 and November 18, 1916, when the Battle of the Somme finally ended, almost 420,000 British soldiers were killed or wounded. Their French allies lost 200,000 men to death or injury. German casualties are estimated at 450,000.

Such carnage became commonplace during the First World War. At the Battle of Verdun, which began before the Somme conflict and continued after, the French and Germans suffered total casualties of at least 750,000, while in the disastrous Gallipoli offensive of 1915, ANZAC (Australia and New Zealand) troops experienced a casualty rate of 65 percent. Between 1914 and 1918, European commanders sent more than eight million men to their deaths in a series of often futile attacks. The total number of casualties—killed, wounded, and missing—reached over 37 million.

Chapter Outline

- The Origins of the First World War
- The Experience of War
- The Home Front
- War and Revolution

Death on the Western Front: This movie still comes from *The Battle of the Somme,* a documentary filmed during the battle and the first "war movie" shown in Britain.

These casualty figures were in part the products of the Industrial Revolution. Between 1914 and 1918 the nations of the West used their factories to churn out ever more efficient tools of killing. The need for machine guns, artillery shells, poison gas canisters, and other implements of modern warfare meant that World War I was the first total war°, a war that demanded that combatant nations mobilize their industrial economies as well as their armies, and thus a war that erased the distinction between civilian and soldier. In total war, victory depended on the woman in the munitions factory as well as the man on the front lines.

The First World War challenged many core assumptions of Western culture and reshaped economic and political structures. By shattering the authoritarian empires of eastern and central Europe and integrating the United States more fully in European affairs, the war ensured that commitment to democratic values became central to one dominant twentieth-century definition of "the West." But the war also strengthened antidemocratic forces: It catapulted into power a communist regime in Russia, intensified eastern Europe's ethnic and nationalist conflicts, and undermined many of the economic structures on which Western stability and prosperity rested. The years after the war, then, would see an acceleration of the cultural and social fragmentation already underway in the prewar period.

Four questions inform this chapter's examination of the origins and experience of the First World War:

- What factors led Europe into war in 1914?
- What were the characteristics of the war experience on the front lines?
- What was the war's impact on the home front?
- What were the consequences of this war for the European and the global social, political, and international order?

The Origins of the First World War

On June 28, 1914, the heir to the throne of Austrian-Hungarian Empire, Archduke Franz Ferdinand (1863–1914), was assassinated by ethnic Serbian terrorists. One month after the archduke's death, Austria declared war on Serbia. One week later, Europe was at war, with the Central Powers°—Germany and Austria—squared off against the Allies° (Russia, France, and Britain). By the time the war ended in late 1918, the conflict had embraced nations from around the globe.

Why did the murder of one man on the streets of a Balkan city lead to the deaths of millions in theaters of war ranging from muddy ditches in northern France to the deserts of northern Africa and the depths of the Atlantic? To understand the war's origins, we need to examine four interlocking factors: eastern European nationalism, the creation of rival alliance systems, the requirements of an industrialized military, and a strengthening conviction among both policymakers and ordinary people that war would provide a resolution to social and cultural crisis.

NATIONALISM AND THE ALLIANCE SYSTEM

The roots of the First World War extend deep into the soil of nationalist conflict in eastern Europe. As a multiethnic, multilinguistic empire, Austria-Hungary's very survival depended on damping down the fires of nationalism wherever they flamed up. Yet much of Serbian politics centered on fanning the nationalist flame. Radical Serbian nationalists sought the unification of all Serbs in eastern Europe into a Greater Serbian state. With over seven million Serbs living in Austria-Hungary, the Austrian monarchy regarded Serbian nationalism as a serious threat.

The hostile relations between Serbia and Austria-Hungary led directly to the outbreak of World War I. Austrian officials charged that the ethnic Serbian terrorist group responsible for assassinating Archduke Franz Ferdinand had links to the Serbian government. When Serbia failed to comply with a lengthy set of demands, Austria-Hungary declared war.

But why did war between Austria-Hungary and Serbia mean war across Europe? To understand what transformed this Austro-Serbian conflict into a continental war, we need to look to the heightened international competition that divided Europe into rival alliance systems. The spread of mass nationalism and the creation of new states such as Italy and Germany destabilized international relations. To protect and expand their national security and influence, governments sought alliance partners. In 1882, Germany, Austria-Hungary and Italy formed the Triple Alliance, which stood against the Franco-Russian Alliance, formalized in 1894.

At the same time, Kaiser William II's new "world policy" for Germany pushed Britain toward closer diplomatic relationships with Russia and France. William and many prominent Germans wanted to see Germany claim its "place in the sun" as a global imperial and naval power. From the British point of view, a strong German navy challenged British national security, just as an expanding German empire was bound to come into conflict with British imperial interests. In response, Britain concluded a series of military, imperial, and economic arrangements with both Russia and France. These arrangements cleared the way for the formation of the Triple Entente° among France, Russia, and Britain. An informal association rather than a formal alliance, the Triple Entente did not require Britain to join in a war against Germany, but British officials clearly viewed Germany as the major threat to British interests.

By the first decade of the twentieth century, then, Europe had split into two opposing camps: the Triple Alliance versus the Triple Entente. To German policymakers, it appeared that Germany stood surrounded by hostile powers. With Italy regarded as unreliable, Germany's alliance with Austria-Hungary took on greater and greater importance. Strengthening this crucial ally became paramount. These considerations guided German policymaking in July 1914. When Austrian officials debated their response to the as-sassination of Franz Ferdinand, Kaiser William and his chancellor Theobold von Bethmann-Hollweg (1856–1921) urged a quick and decisive blow against Serbia. In what some historians have described as an act akin to issuing a "blank check," the kaiser assured the Austrian ambassador that Germany would stand by Austria, even at the risk of a war with Russia, which had for decades sought to expand its influence in the Balkans by claiming the position of Serbia's advocate and protector.

■ **Map 24.1   Europe, August 1914**

In August 1914 each of the Central Powers faced the challenge of war on two fronts, but the entry of the Ottoman Empire into the war on the side of the Central Powers in November 1914 blocked Allied supply lines to Russia through the Mediterranean.

Europe, August 1914

The "Central Powers"

States formerly associated with the Central Powers, but remaining neutral on the outbreak of war, and later joining the Allies

The "Entente" or "Allies", following the German attack on Belgium and the Austrian attack on Serbia

Neutral, later joining the Central Powers

Neutral, later joining Allies

THE INDUSTRIALIZED MILITARY AND THE WILL TO WAR

Alliances alone do not explain the transformation of the Austro-Serbian conflict into a European war, however. No alliance *required* either Russia or Britain to enter the fray. To understand why these powers entered the war when they did, we need to look at a third factor in the origins of World War I—the demands of an industrialized military.

In the decades before 1914 military planning was dominated by a new reality, the railroad. The speed with which nations could now throw armies into battle almost obliterated the distinction between mobilization and actual war. *Mobilization* refers to the transformation of a standing army into a fighting force—calling up reserves, requisitioning supplies, enlisting volunteers or draftees, moving troops to battle stations. Traditionally, mobilization required months and could be halted if the diplomats succeeded in avoiding war. But the railroads accelerated the mobilization process and thereby changed the very nature of military plans. Aware that the enemy could also mobilize quickly, military planners stressed the importance of striking before being struck. Once a nation mobilized, therefore, the momentum toward war became almost irresistible.

These factors help explain the origins and impact of the military blueprint that structured German actions—and Allied reactions—in the summer of 1914. This scheme was the Schlieffen Plan°. The Franco-Russian Alliance meant that beginning in 1894, German military planners had to prepare for the possibility of a two-front war. The Schlieffen Plan aimed for a quick knockout blow against France, which would then allow the German army to concentrate on defeating the much larger force of Russia. The rationale here was that Russia's territory was so vast, and its industrial infrastructure so underdeveloped, that Russian troops would not pose an immediate threat to German borders. According to the Schlieffen Plan, the smaller Austrian army would hold off the slowly mobilizing Russians while the German army moved with lightning speed against France.

The need for speed dictated the next step in the plan—an attack against France via Belgium. German planners knew that the French expected any German attack to come through France's heavily fortified northeastern provinces. The Schlieffen Plan called for the bulk of the German army to swing to the west instead. Moving rapidly in a wide arc, the German army would flood into France through Belgium, encircle Paris, and scoop up the French forces before their generals knew what had hit them.

The need for speed—the key factor in the Schlieffen Plan—placed enormous pressure on German politicians to treat a Russian declaration of mobilization as a declaration of war itself. And that is what happened. Only two days elapsed between Russia's order of mobilization and the

German declaration of war. Moreover, the plan for a speedy thrust into France meant that Germany went ahead with its invasion of Belgium—a decision that brought Britain into the war. Belgian neutrality was guaranteed by Britain under a long-standing treaty. Germany's unprovoked and brutal invasion of Belgium provided the British government with the public-pleasing moral justification it needed to enter the war with mass support. Thus, just six weeks after an Austrian archduke died in Sarajevo, British and German soldiers were killing each other in the mud of northern France.

Unable to rein in the new forces of industrial warfare, diplomats also faced new pressures from public opinion. This public pressure, or the "will to war," also helps explain the outbreak of World War I in 1914. Two developments created a new mass interest in foreign affairs. First, the rise of the popular press—cheap newspapers marketed to a semiliterate public—and new technologies such as the telegraph, telephone, and camera collapsed distances and made international news much more immediate and accessible. Second, the emergence of mass nationalism played an important role in shaping public opinion. Well-schooled in national identity, the European masses by 1914 viewed international relations as a vast nationalistic competition. They wanted evidence that "we" were ahead of "them."

Public opinion, therefore, constituted a real, although impossible-to-measure factor in the war's outbreak. In the last weeks of July, pro-war crowds gathered in large cities. Middle-class men and women, particularly students, predominated in the cheering crowds. In the countryside, farmers and villagers were more fearful, while in working-class neighborhoods anti-war demonstrations received solid support in July. But after August 1914, opposition to the war was very much a minority movement, even among working-class socialists. Socialist parties throughout Europe voted overwhelmingly to approve war appropriations as national loyalties proved far stronger than class solidarity.

What made the idea of war so appealing to many men and women in 1914? As Chapter 23 explained, the years before 1914 witnessed a widespread cultural crisis in Europe, marked by fears of racial degeneration and gender confusion. War seemed to provide an opportunity for men to reassert their virility and their superiority. It also offered them the chance to be part of something bigger than themselves—to move beyond the boundaries of their often-restricted lives and join in what was presented as a great national crusade. For political leaders, war provided the opportunity to displace domestic hostilities onto the battlefield. We saw in Chapter 22 that worsening political divisions and social conflicts characterized the decades before 1914. As the future British prime minister Winston Churchill explained, war united societies with "a higher principle of hatred."

Most anticipated a short war. The men who marched off in August 1914 expected that they would be home by Christmas. Instead, if they survived, which few of them did, they would spend not only that Christmas, but the next three, in the midst of unspeakable and unprecedented horror.

The Experience of War

·····························■·····························

This would be a war that shattered expectations, a war of revolutionary possibilities and devastating slaughter, a war that extended beyond Europe into Africa, across Asia, and out into the Atlantic Ocean. As the economic demands of total war escalated, governments assumed unprecedented powers, women stepped into new roles, and social tensions rose. Thus at the same time the war spread beyond European borders, it also transformed relations within Europe.

THE WESTERN FRONT: STALEMATE IN THE TRENCHES

Implementing a modified version of the Schlieffen Plan, the German troops swept into Belgium in August 1914. By the first week of September the German troops had swung into France and seemed poised to take Paris. The Germans had overstretched their supply lines, however. French and British forces turned back the German offensive at the Marne River and saved Paris, but they were unable to push the German army out of France. By the middle of October, the German, British, and French forces were huddling in trenches that eventually extended more than 300 miles from the Belgian coast to the borders of Switzerland. There they stayed for the next four years.

The trenches were defensive fortifications, and the long stalemate on the Western Front shows that they worked well. Despite numerous attempts between the fall of 1914 and the spring of 1918, neither side was able to break through the enemy line. Attacking infantry units faced the dreadful task of walking forward against troops armed with machine guns and sheltered behind wide barbed-wire fences and a thick wall of dirt and sandbags.

A discussion of trench strategy, however, conveys nothing of the appalling misery summed up by the term "trench warfare." Imagine standing in a ditch that is about seven or eight feet deep and about three or four feet wide. The walls of the ditches are packed mud, propped up with sandbags.

■ **French Soldiers**

These French soldiers are stationed in a listening post near the front lines. Note the typical trench features: barbed wire at the top, the sandbag walls, the omnipresent and always necessary shovel.

EXPECTATIONS VERSUS REALITY

Written by two young upper-middle class British writers, the following poems illustrate the shift from the initial enthusiasm for the war to later disillusionment and despair. In the first poem, written just as the war began, Rupert Brooke welcomes the war as an ennobling and purifying force that will bring genuine peace. In contrast, Wilfred Owen's later piece flatly describes a soldier asphyxiated by poison gas. Brooke died of blood poisoning on his way to Gallipoli in 1915; Owen was killed in battle in 1918, just days before the war ended.

1914. *PEACE* BY *RUPERT BROOKE*

Now, God be thanked Who has matched us with His hour,
And caught our youth, and wakened us from sleeping,
With hand made sure, clear eye, and sharpened power,
To turn, as swimmers into cleanness leaping,
Glad from a world grown old and cold and weary
Leave the sick hearts that honor could not move,
And half-men, and their dirty songs and dreary,
And all the little emptiness of love.

DULCE ET DECORUM EST BY *WILFRED OWEN*

Bent double, like old beggars under sacks,
Knock-kneed, coughing like hags,
We cursed through sludge,
Till on the haunting flares we turned our backs
And towards our distant rest began to trudge.
Men marched asleep. Many had lost their boots

But limped on, blood-shod. All went lame; all blind;
Drunk with fatigue; deaf even to the hoots
Of tired, outstripped Five-Nines that dropped behind.
Gas! Gas! Quick, boys!—An ecstasy of fumbling,

Fitting the clumsy helmets just in time;
But someone still was yelling out and stumbling
And flound'ring like a man in fire or lime . . .
Dim, through the misty panes and thick green light,
As under a green sea, I saw him drowning.
In all my dreams, before my helpless sight,
He plunges at me, guttering, choking, drowning.

If in some smothering dreams you too could pace
Behind the wagon that we flung him in,
And watch the white eyes writhing in his face,
His hanging face, like a devil's sick of sin;
If you could hear, at every jolt, the blood
Come gargling from the froth-corrupted lungs,
Obscene as cancer, bitter as the cud
Of vile, incurable sores on innocent tongues,—
My friend, you would not tell with such high zest
To children ardent for some desperate glory,
The old Lie: "Dulce et decorum est
Pro patria mori."*

———————
"It is good and right to die for one's country."

Sources: From "Peace" from *"1914" Five Sonnets* by Rupert Brooke. London: Sidgwick & Jackson, 1915; "Dulce et Decorum Est" from *Poems* by Wilfred Owen, with an Introduction by Siegfried Sassoon. London: Chatto and Windus, 1920.

Wooden boards cover the floor, but the mud squelches between them. The top side of the ditch facing the enemy is reinforced with piled sandbags and barbed-wire barricades, thus deepening your sense of being underground. Moreover, the trenches zigzag at sharp angles, ensuring that everywhere you look you see a wall of mud. Because you are in northern France, it is probably raining. Thus you are standing not on but *in* mud—if you are lucky. In some parts of the line, soldiers stand in muddy water up to a foot deep. On the other side of your sandbag defenses stretches no-man's-land°, the territory dividing the British and French trench systems from the German. Pocked with deep craters from heavy shelling, often a sea of mud churned up by the artillery, no-man's-land is littered with stinking corpses in various states of decomposition. Your constant companions are lice (the term *lousy* was coined on the Western Front) and rats. If you are in the trenches after 1915, you also face poison gas, with its threat of blinded eyes, blistered skin, seared lungs, and death by asphyxiation.

With the gas mask a standard part of every soldier's uniform, military companies resembled hordes of insects. And, like insects, they were easily squashed. In the summer of 1915 an average of 300 British men became casualties on the Western Front every day, picked off by snipers, felled by an exploding shell, or wasted by disease brought on by living in the mud amid putrefying corpses.[1]

The offensives, the attacks launched by both sides on the Western Front, sent the numbers of dead and wounded soaring. None of the elderly commanders—the Germans Helmut von Moltke and Erich von Falkenhayn, the French Joseph Joffre and Ferdinand Foch, and the British Douglas Haig and John French—knew what to make of trench warfare. Schooled to believe that war is about attacking, they sought vainly to move this conflict out of the ditches by throwing vast masses of both artillery and men against the enemy lines. But time and time again the machine gun foiled these mass attacks.

The Battle of the Somme, described in the opening of this chapter, provides a classic illustration of a failed offensive. The Somme, however, was just one of many fruitless attacks launched by both sides on the Western Front. By the end of 1917, the death tolls on the Western Front were astonishing, yet neither side had gained much ground. Soldiers, who enlisted not for a specific term or tour of duty but "for the duration"—until the war ended—became convinced that only the dead escaped from the trenches.

THE WAR IN EASTERN EUROPE

The Western Front was only one in a number of theaters of war. Floundering in the snows of the Italian Alps, the Italian and Austrian armies fought each other along a stationary front for two brutal years after Italy, enticed by the promise of territorial gain, joined the war on the Allies' side. Characterized by futile offensives and essential immobility, the war in Italy mirrored the conflict on the Western Front. In eastern Europe, however, a different plot unfolded. For three years, massive armies surged back and forth as the plains and mountains of eastern Europe echoed with the tumult of spectacular advances, headlong retreats, and finally political revolution.

■ **Paul Nash, *We Are Making a New World* (1918)**
During the war many modernist artists abandoned "art for art's sake," the idea that art had no moral purpose or social responsibility. Instead, they used their art to communicate their moral outrage against the war. Paul Nash (1889–1940), a British landscape painter and army volunteer, explained in 1918, "I am no longer an artist, interested and curious, I am a messenger who will bring back word from the men who are fighting to those who want the war to go on forever. . . . may it burn their lousy souls."[2] Before the war, Nash had painted pastoral scenes; his wartime experience, however, pushed him to employ modernist techniques. Nash's *We Are Making a New World* (1918)—a title dripping in irony—is one of the finest of the war's paintings. Nash transformed the landscape genre from an evocation of natural beauty into a cry of pain.

The Eastern Front: A War of Movement

When the war began in August 1914, Russia shocked its enemies by fielding a much stronger army more quickly than German and Austrian military planners had expected. Surprised by the speed of the Russian advance, German troops in East Prussia at first fell back, but brilliant maneuvering by the German commanders Paul von Hindenburg (1847–1934) and Erich von Ludendorff (1865–1937) turned the Russian tide at the Battle of Tannenberg at the end of August. Within two weeks the Germans had shoved the Russian troops back across the border. In the subsequent months, the Germans advanced steadily into Russian imperial territory. Over the next two years the pattern of Russian advances and retreats continued. Russian soldiers pushed into Austria-Hungary in June 1916, but could not sustain the attack. The summer of 1917 saw another initially successful Russian advance, but it too soon disintegrated into a retreat.

These defeats revealed that Russia's economic and political structures could not withstand the pressures of total war. Demoralized by defeat and by the daily grind of life without adequate rations, uniforms, or ammunition, Russian soldiers began to desert in ever-larger numbers. On the home front Russian workers and peasants grew ever more impatient with wartime deprivations and demands. This disaffection led to revolution. As we will explore in detail later in this chapter, the tsar was forced to abdicate in March 1917.

In November, the Bolsheviks, a small group of socialist revolutionaries, seized control and proceeded to pull Russia out of the war. Signed in March 1918, the Treaty of Brest-Litovsk° ceded to Germany all of Russia's western territories, containing a full one-third of the population of the prewar Russian Empire. Germany now controlled the imperial Russian territories in Poland, the Baltic states, and part of Byelorussia. But because it had to commit large numbers of troops to controlling this new territory, Germany reaped less advantage from this victory than might have been expected.

THE WORLD AT WAR

The imperialist expansion of the later nineteenth century ensured that as soon as the war began, it encompassed much of the globe. The British and French Empires supplied the Allies with invaluable military and manpower resources. Australia, New Zealand, Canada, India, South Africa, and Ireland supplied no less than 40 percent of Britain's military manpower during the war.

Fighting fronts multiplied as the major combatants struggled for imperial as well as European supremacy (see Map 24.2). Portugal joined the Allies in hopes of expanding its colonial possessions in Africa, while Japan seized the opportunity to snatch German colonial possessions in China. In return, Japan contributed to the Allied war effort by using its navy to protect Allied troop and supply ships in both the Pacific and the Mediterranean.

The Middle East also became a key theater after the Ottoman Empire joined the war on the side of the Central Powers in 1914. To defeat the Ottomans, the Allies joined

■ Map 24.2 The World at War

Imperialist relationships and global economics ensured that a European conflict became a world war. In Africa both Portuguese and South African troops fought a bush war against German and native soldiers. The entry of the Ottoman Empire on the side of the Central Powers in November 1914 extended the conflict into the Middle East. Japan, the first non-European power to enter the war, occupied German colonial territories in Asia and the Pacific region. When the United States joined the Allies in April 1917, a number of Latin American countries also declared war on Germany.

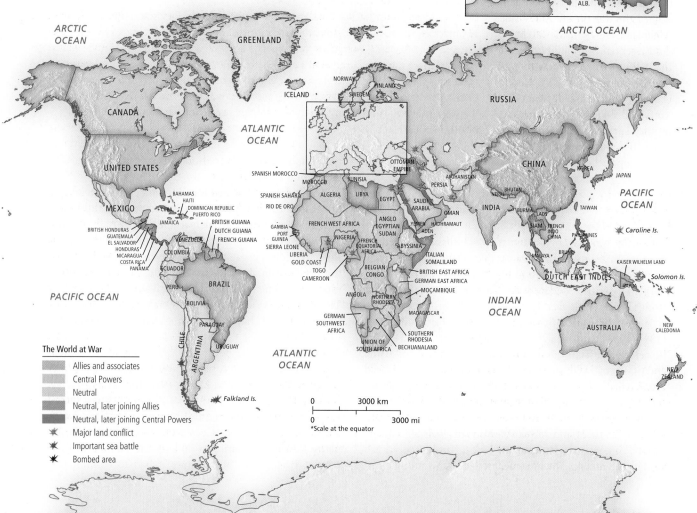

The World at War

- ▨ Allies and associates
- ▨ Central Powers
- ▨ Neutral
- ▨ Neutral, later joining Allies
- ▨ Neutral, later joining Central Powers
- ✳ Major land conflict
- ✳ Important sea battle
- ✳ Bombed area

0   3000 km
0   3000 mi
*Scale at the equator

■ **Sikh Cavalry Officers**
Sikh cavalry officers from India patrol on the Western Front. India provided 1.3 million men to assist the British war effort. Indian troops fought—and more than 49,000 Indian soldiers died—in battles in the Middle East, in East Africa, and on the Western Front.

with Arab groups seeking to free themselves from Ottoman rule. Led by a British soldier named T. E. Lawrence (1888–1935)—better known as "Lawrence of Arabia"—and inspired by British promises of support for an independent Arab state, Arab nationalists used guerilla warfare to attack the Ottoman forces on the Arabian peninsula. By 1917 British troops had pushed Ottoman forces out of Sinai, Arabian nationalists had lifted Ottoman control from almost the entire coastal region of the Arabian peninsula bordering the Red Sea, and Lawrence and his Arab allies had captured Jerusalem.

THE END OF THE WAR

Despite the losses of its ally in the Middle East, in the spring of 1918 Germany looked to be in winning position. With Russia out of the war and both Serbia and Romania occupied by their forces, the Central Powers could claim to have won the war in eastern Europe. Yet Germany was far weaker than any map of its eastern conquests in early 1918 could indicate. Germany was being strangled from the sea.

The War at Sea and the Entry of the United States

While infantrymen rotted in trenches and struggled in the sands of the Middle East, the German and British navies fought a critical war at sea. German submarines sought to cut Britain's imperial lifeline and starve out its civilian population by sinking ships before they could reach British ports. In turn, British naval vessels stretched a blockade across all ocean and sea passageways to Germany and its allies. The Allied blockade proved effective in preventing food

and other essential raw materials from reaching Germany. Food shortages sparked riots in more than thirty German cities in 1916.

Under pressure from this domestic unrest, German policymakers in 1917 took a huge gamble when they decided to up the tempo of their submarine war against Britain. Suspecting that supposedly neutral American passenger ships were delivering essential war materiel to Britain, they ordered their submarines to sink without warning any ship heading for British shores.

The German policy of unrestricted submarine warfare resulted in the entry of the United States into the war in April 1917. Three other factors, however, also played a role in the U.S. declaration of war against Germany. First, Franco-British news stories about German atrocities during the invasion of Belgium persuaded many Americans that right rested on the Allied side. Second, the American economy had become thoroughly intertwined with that of the Allies. Trade between the United States and the Allied nations had grown from $825 million in 1914 to more than $3 billion in 1916, and American bankers had loaned more than $2 billion to the Allied governments. Finally, the German government committed a serious blunder in the spring of 1917 when it offered to back Mexico in recovering New Mexico, Arizona, and Texas in exchange for Mexican support should war break out between Germany and the United States. British interception of a telegram sent by the German foreign minister Arthur Zimmermann exposed this offer and inflamed anti-German sentiment in the United States. The German resumption of unrestricted submarine warfare, then, simply put flame to kindling that was already in place.

The U.S. declaration of war provided an immediate psychological boost for the Allies, but several months passed before American troops arrived on the battlefield in significant numbers. By July 1918, however, the United States was sending 300,000 fresh soldiers to Europe each month. The Allies now had access to a seemingly unlimited supply of materiel and men. Eventually nearly two million American soldiers were sent to Europe and 112,000 American soldiers died, approximately half of these from disease, half in battle.

Back in Motion: The Western Front in 1918

Faced with the prospect of having to fight fresh American forces, the German army launched a massive ground assault against British and French lines on March 2, 1918—before the bulk of the U.S. army had been deployed. In just thirty minutes the German troops broke through the British front line; in seven days, German soldiers advanced forty miles; by April the German army stood just fifty miles from Paris.

What explains this sudden shift on the Western Front from a conflict characterized by stalemate and deadlock to a war of rapid movement? The answer is that the German High Command in 1918 finally developed strategies that matched offensive techniques with industrialized killing technology. As we have seen, in the first years of the war commanders remained committed to offensive techniques suited to an age of preindustrial warfare—the mass charge, the cavalry attack.

In 1918, however, the Germans came up with a new offensive strategy. Rather than throwing masses of men against machine guns, they mounted a series of small group attacks that aimed to cut behind British and French positions rather than charge straight on against them. In addition, they scrapped the massive preliminary artillery barrage that signaled when and where an attack was about to begin, and instead employed sudden gas and artillery bursts throughout the offensive. The rapid German advance in the spring of 1918 showed that technique had caught up with technology.

In July, however, the Allies stopped the German advance; in August they broke through the German lines and began to push the German army backward. Throughout the summer the push continued. By September the Western Front, which had stood so stationary for so long, was being rolled eastward at a rapid clip.

The final German gamble failed for three reasons: First, the German advance was so rapid that it overstrained German manpower and supply lines; second, the Allies learned from their enemies and adopted the same new offensive strategies; and third, the Allies figured out how to make effective use of a new offensive technology—the tank. Developed in Britain, the tank obliterated the defensive advantages of machine-gun-fortified trenches. A twentieth-century offense met a twentieth-century defense, and the war turned mobile. Reinforced with fresh American troops and the promise of more to come, the Allied forces surged forward against the hungry and demoralized Germans. When the Bulgarian, Ottoman, and Austrian armies collapsed in September and October, Germany stood alone. On November 11, 1918, German leaders signed an armistice and the war ended.

The Home Front

The term "home front" was coined during World War I to highlight the fact that this war was fought not only by soldiers on the front lines, but also by civilians at home. On the Eastern Front, civilian death tolls were very high. Hundreds of thousands of Serbs, Montenegrins, Romanians, and others died from starvation, disease, and brutal military occupation. In the Armenian lands in the heart of the Ottoman Empire, over one million men, women, and children died as a consequence of the Ottoman government's decision to deport the entire Armenian population as a security measure. In both western and eastern Europe, four years of warfare transformed societies. Total war recast and in some cases revolutionized the economic, political, and social relations of combatant nations.

SOCIAL TRANSFORMATION

World War I was the first industrial war. Poison gas, the machine gun, barbed wire, shovels, canned foods, uniforms, and boots all poured out of Europe's factories and helped shape this distinctive style of warfare. Even more important, industrialization made it possible for governments to deploy the vast masses of men mobilized in this conflict. Contrast the 170,000 men who fought the Battle of Waterloo in 1815 with the one million combatants in the first Battle of the Marne in September 1914. Only industrialized production could keep these huge armies supplied with weapons, ammunition, and other necessities.

At first, no government realized the crucial role that industrial labor would play in this war. Governments practiced "business as usual"—letting the free market decide wages, prices, and supply—with disastrous results. Soaring rates of inflation, the rapid expansion of the black market, growing public resentment over war profiteering (the practice of private businessmen making huge profits off the war), and, most crucially, shortages of essential military supplies, including ammunition, proved that a total war economy needed total regulation. Beginning in 1915, both the Allied and Central Powers governments gradually assumed the power to requisition supplies, dictate wages, limit profits, and forbid workers to change jobs. Such measures greatly expanded the size and power of the central governments in the combatant states.

The war's reliance on industrial production also greatly empowered industrial producers—the workers. In 1915 both France and Britain abandoned political party competition and formed coalition governments, which included socialist and working-class representatives. At the same time, political leaders welcomed labor unionists as partners in shaping the wartime economy. In return, French and British union leaders agreed to a ban on labor strikes and the "deskilling" of certain jobs—a measure that allowed unskilled laborers, particularly women, to take the place of skilled workers at much lower rates of pay.

Despite these "no strike" agreements, both Britain and France saw a sharp rise in the number of labor strikes in 1916 and in 1917. Faced with the potential of disintegration on the home front, political leaders in Britain and France reacted similarly. Both countries witnessed the emergence of war governments committed to total victory. In Britain, David Lloyd George (1863–1945) became prime minister at the end of 1916. A Welsh artisan's son who had fought hard to reach the top of Britain's class-bound, English-dominated political system, Lloyd George was not a man to settle for a compromise peace. One year later, Georges Clemenceau became prime minister of France. Nicknamed "the Tiger," Clemenceau demanded victory. When asked to detail his government's program, he replied simply, "*Je fais la guerre!*" ("I make war!").

Making war, however, was not possible without public support. The British and French governments recognized that if civilian morale were to be sustained, the basic needs of ordinary citizens had to be met. Both governments intervened regularly in the economy to ensure that workers received higher wages, better working conditions, and a fair distribution of food stocks. As a result, living standards among employed workers in France and in Britain rose during the war.

The situation in Germany differed significantly. The parliamentary political voice of the working class, the Social Democratic Party (SPD), was not invited to participate in a coalition government. Instead, the aristocratic generals Hindenburg and Ludendorff—the heroes of the Battle of Tannenberg—assumed a significant political role, and the army and big industrial firms seized control of German economic life. Industrialists' incomes soared, while ordinary workers were ground down by escalating inflation and chronic food shortages. By 1918, industrial unrest had slowed German war production, and the success of the Allied blockade meant Germans were starving. Germany stood on the brink of revolution.

GENDER UPHEAVALS

Total war also brought significant changes to women's roles in the workforce. By 1916, labor shortages in key military industries, combined with the need to free up as many men as possible for fighting, meant that governments on both sides actively recruited women for industrial and agricultural jobs. In eastern Europe, the agricultural labor force came to consist almost entirely of women. In western Europe, women joined labor unions in unprecedented numbers. They took on extremely dangerous positions in

■ **Women in the War**
Women often served at the front in extremely dangerous conditions. The two women in this photograph set up a dressing station to treat the wounded just five yards behind the trenches.

munitions factories; they worked just behind the front lines as ambulance drivers and nurses; and they often led the way in walking off the job to demand better conditions.

The impact of the war on women's roles should not be exaggerated, however. Throughout the war, more women continued to work in domestic service—as cooks, maids, and nannies—than in any other sector of the economy. Most women who did move into skilled industrial employment were not new to the world of paid employment. Before 1914 they had worked in different, lower-paying jobs. And they certainly were not treated as men's equals. In government-run factories in Britain, women were paid as little as 50 percent of men's wages for the same work.

Nevertheless, for many women, the war constituted a profoundly liberating experience. With their husbands away, many wives made decisions on their own for the first time. The average wages of female munitions workers in Britain were three times their prewar earnings. Middle-class women also testified to the freedom the war brought. Before 1914, the position of middle-class women in Europe had undergone important changes, as Chapter 22 detailed. Yet the predominant idea remained that women were biologically suited for the private confines of home and family, and men for the public arena of work and politics. The war, however, threw women into the public space. The middle-class girl who before 1914 was forbidden to travel without a chaperone might be driving an ambulance, splashing through mud and blood, or washing the bodies of naked working-class soldiers.

At the same time that the war smashed many of the boundaries to which women had been confined, it sharply narrowed the world of the middle-class male soldier. While women were on the move—driving buses, flying transport planes, ferrying the wounded—men were stuck in the mud, confined to narrow ditches, waiting for orders. Expecting to be heroes, men of action, they found themselves instead living the sort of immobile, passive lives that had characterized the prewar middle-class women's experience.

Many of these radical changes proved temporary. When the war ended, the movement of women into skilled factory jobs and public positions such as bus drivers and train conductors was rapidly reversed. Other changes appeared more permanent. In France in 1919, there were ten times as many female law students and three times as many female medical students as there had been in 1914. British women over age 30 received the vote on a limited basis while in the United States, Germany, and most of the new states in eastern Europe, the achievement of female suffrage was more complete. (Women in France, Italy, Switzerland, and Greece remained unenfranchised.) Cultural changes also seemed to signal a gender revolution. Women began to smoke in public; trousers became acceptable female attire; hemlines rose dramatically; and the corset and bustle disappeared for good.

War and Revolution

The machinery of total war tore at the social and political fabric of European societies. Many welcomed what they saw as the opportunity to tear apart the old cloth and create something entirely new. Marxists aimed to build a socialist world order, while nationalists sought to assert the rights of their ethnic or linguistic group. The peace settlement, however, fell far short of creating a new Europe. Many of the conflicts that had caused the war remained unresolved, with disastrous consequences for the next generation.

THE RUSSIAN REVOLUTIONS

The war brought political chaos to Russia. Tsar Nicholas II (r. 1894–1917), a man of limited intelligence and a remarkable capacity for self-delusion, insisted on going to the front and commanding his army, while his government disintegrated at home. Observing this political disarray, the French ambassador wrote to his government in January 1917, "I am obliged to report that, at the present moment, the Russian Empire is run by lunatics."[3] The lack of effective political leadership, combined with Russian losses on the battlefield, brought to a boil the simmering disaffection with the tsarist government. Almost two million Russian soldiers had died and many more had been wounded or taken prisoner. Economic and communications networks had broken down, and people were hungry. Even members of the tsarist government began to ask not *if* revolution would occur, but *when*.

The Popular Revolution

The answer came in March 1917. A group of women workers in Petrograd staged a demonstration to protest against inadequate food supplies. This demonstration sparked others, and governmental orders quickly lost all authority. One week later Tsar Nicholas was forced to abdicate. The Russian Revolution had begun.

Who now controlled Russia? Two competing centers of power soon emerged: the Provisional Government and the Petrograd Soviet. On March 12, the Russian parliament created a Provisional Government from among its members. Members of the gentry and middle classes dominated the new Provisional Government. These men tended to be liberals who wished to remake Russia as a parliamentary democracy. They quickly enacted important reforms such as universal suffrage, the eight-hour workday, and civic equality for all citizens.

But at the same time, across the empire industrial workers and soldiers formed soviets°, or councils, to articulate their grievances and hopes. As Russian revolutionary socialists returned from exile in the weeks after the tsar's overthrow, they joined these soviets. The Petrograd Soviet soon became a powerful political rival to the less radical Provisional Government.

The revolution, however, did not originate with nor was it controlled by either the liberals in the Provisional Government or the socialists in the Petrograd Soviet. A popular revolution overthrew Nicholas II, and at the core of this popular revolution stood a simply stated demand: "*Peace, Land, Bread.*" Soldiers—and most Russians—wanted an immediate end to a war that had long ceased to make any sense to them. Peasants, as always, wanted land, their guarantee of survival in a chaotic world. And city dwellers wanted bread—food in sufficient quantities and at affordable prices.

The Provisional Government could not satisfy these demands. It did promise the gradual redistribution of royal and monastic lands, but peasants wanted *land* immediately. *Peace* appeared impossible. Not only did Russia have commitments to its allies, but German armies stood deep within Russian territory. A separate peace with Germany would mean huge territorial losses. The war therefore continued, but the continuation of the war meant no *bread*: Russia no longer had the resources both to wage war and to reconstruct its economy. The population of the cities began to dwindle as food disappeared from the shops, factories ceased operation because of shortages of raw materials, and currency had little value.

The Provisional Government's inability to supply "peace, land, and bread" meant that the revolution continued. Peasants effected their own land reform by simply seizing the land they wanted. Soldiers declared their own peace by deserting in huge numbers. The Provisional Govern-

ment grew increasingly unpopular. Not even the appointment of the popular socialist and Petrograd Soviet member Alexander Kerensky (1881–1970) as prime minister could stabilize the government's position.

The October Revolution

This tumultuous situation created the opportunity for the Bolsheviks°, one of the socialist factions in the Petrograd Soviet, to emerge as a powerful revolutionary force. In April 1917, the Bolshevik leader, Vladimir Lenin (1870–1924), returned from almost twenty years in exile. Iron-willed and ruthlessly pragmatic, Lenin argued that a committed group of professional revolutionaries could force a working-class revolution on Russia. On November 9, Bolshevik fighters captured the Winter Palace in Petrograd, where the Provisional Government had been sitting. (By the old-style Russian calendar, the Bolshevik coup occurred in the month of October; hence the label the "October Revolution").

With the October Revolution, a *second* Russian Revolution was underway. The Bolsheviks declared a policy of land and peace—land partition with no payment of compensation to estate owners and an immediate peace with Germany, regardless of the cost. (And as we have seen, the cost was high: According to the terms of the Treaty of Brest-Litovsk, signed with Germany in 1918, Russia lost its western territories.)

Not everyone in Russia was won over by promises of peace and land, however. Confronted with a diverse array of opponents, the Bolsheviks turned to the methods of terror. Over the next two years, the Bolsheviks waged a brutal war against domestic and international opponents of their Communist Revolution. This civil war killed off more combatants than had World War I. In the resulting famine,

■ **Red Square**

Lenin inspires the crowds gathered in Moscow's Red Square on May Day 1918.

Revolutionary Justice: The Nontrial of Nicholas and Alexandra

On July 16, 1918, Bolshevik revolutionaries shot and killed Nicholas II, Tsar of Russia; his wife, the Tsarina Alexandra; his heir, 14-year-old Alexei; their four daughters—Olga (age 23), Tatiana (age 21), Maria (age 19), and Anastasia (age 17); their three servants; and their physician. When news of the deaths reached other countries, the killings were condemned as murders. The Bolsheviks, however, termed them executions, acts of revolutionary justice.

When Nicholas II abdicated on March 15, 1917, after twenty-three years on the throne, he expected to embark on a life of exile in Britain. Instead, the Provisional Government placed the tsar and his family under house arrest and appointed a Commission of Inquiry to investigate the persistent rumors that the tsar's German-born wife had conspired with Germany to destroy Russia. The commission found no evidence to convict the tsar or his wife of treason, but by the autumn of 1917, its findings were irrelevant. The war with Germany was effectively over, whereas the war against all that the tsar had stood for had just begun.

The civil war that followed the Bolshevik Revolution proved fatal for the royal family. Faced with counterrevolutionary challenges on all sides, the Bolsheviks feared that if Nicholas escaped, he would serve as a symbolic center for these antirevolutionary forces. They decided to move him to a region firmly under Bolshevik control. In April 1918, a special train transported the tsar and his family to Ekaterinburg (about 900 miles east of Moscow), where they were placed in the hands of the Bolshevik-dominated Ural Regional Soviet. Meanwhile, the revolutionary Bolshevik government prepared to try Nicholas publicly for his crimes against the Russian people. The charge was no longer secret contacts with Germany—the Bolsheviks themselves had negotiated with Germany and ended Russia's participation in the war—but rather the tsar's both real and symbolic leadership of a politically repressive regime. Leon Trotsky, the head of the Petrograd Soviet, planned to present the case against Nicholas.

But the case was never made. By July, an anti-Bolshevik army was approaching Ekaterinburg from the east. If these troops freed the imperial family, they would score a crucial victory. Told that Ekaterinburg might fall to the enemy within days, the Ural Soviet decided to execute the tsar and his family immediately. The soviet acted most likely with Lenin's approval.

Pavel Medvedev, one of the tsar's guards, later offered a detailed account of the events of the evening of July 16. His interviewer recorded what Medvedev had told him:

> [He said,] The Tsar, the Tsaritsa [Tsarina], the Tsar's four daughters, the doctor, the cook and the lackey came out of their rooms. The Tsar was carrying the heir [Alexei] in his arms. . . . In my presence there were no tears, no sobs and no questions. . . .

Medvedev then testified that he was ordered out of the room. When he returned a few minutes later:

> . . . he saw all the members of the Tsar's family lying on the floor with numerous wounds to their bodies. The blood was gushing. The heir was still alive—and moaning. [The commander] walked over to him and shot him two or three times at point blank range. The heir fell still.[4]

What Medvedev's understated account did not relate were the more gruesome details of the execution. In an effort to preserve part of the family fortune, the tsar's daughters were wearing corsets into which had been sewn diamonds. When they were shot, the bullets, in the words of one eyewitness, "ricocheted, jumping around the room like hail."[5] Even after several pistols were emptied, one of the girls remained alive. The guards resorted to bayonets.

The killing of not only the tsar but also his wife and children was a startling act, as the Bolsheviks themselves recognized. The Ural Regional Soviet announced the tsar's execution, but said nothing about his family, while the official statement from Moscow reported that "the wife and son of Nicholas Romanov were sent to a safe place."[6]

These omissions and lies reveal the Bolsheviks' own uneasiness with the killings. Why, then, was the entire family shot? The Bolsheviks' determination to win the civil war regardless of the cost provides part of the answer. According to Trotsky, Lenin "believed we shouldn't leave the Whites [the anti-Bolshevik forces] a live banner to rally around."[7] Any of the tsar's children could have served as such a banner. The rapid approach of the White army meant the royal family had to be disposed of quickly. But Trotsky also viewed the killings as an essential and absolute break with the past. In his words, "the execution of the Tsar's family was needed not only to frighten, horrify, and to dishearten the enemy, but also in order to shake up our own ranks, to show them that there was no turning back, that ahead lay either complete victory or complete ruin."[8] For the Bolsheviks, there was no middle ground.

The killing of Tsar Nicholas and his family thus forms part of the pattern of escalating violence that characterized the First World War's revolutionary aftermath. But in the blood of these killings we can also see reflected two ideas that had a powerful impact on postwar political life—first, the subordination of law to the revolutionary state; second, the concept of collective guilt.

The Bolsheviks offered a different idea of justice. As a Bolshevik publication explained in a discussion of the tsar's killing:

> Many formal aspects of bourgeois justice may have been violated. . . . However, worker-peasant power was manifested in the process, making no exception for the All-Russian murderer, shooting as if he were an ordinary brigand. . . . Nicholas the Bloody is no more.[9]

In the Bolshevik model, the law was not separate from but rather subordinate to the state. Legal rights and requirements—the "formal aspects of bourgeois justice"—could be suspended in the service of "worker peasant power," as embodied in the revolutionary state.

This concept of the law subordinate to the state helps us understand the tsar's execution without trial; the concept of collective guilt provides a context for the killing of his children. The Bolshevik model of socialism assumed that *class* constituted objective reality. Simply by belonging to a certain social class, an individual could be—and was—designated an enemy of the revolution. The Bolshevik constitution equated citizenship with social class. Workers and peasants received the vote, but seven categories of people, such as those who lived off investment interest, were disenfranchised. For the next two decades, aristocratic and middle-class origins served as an indelible ink, marking a person permanently as an enemy of the revolutionary state—regardless of that person's own actions or inclinations. Thus, from the Bolshevik perspective, the tsar's children bore the taint of their royal origins. When their continuing existence threatened the revolution, they were shot. Over the next four decades, the concept of collective guilt would result in the deaths of millions in the new Soviet Union.

When World War I ended and representatives of the Allied victors met in Paris in 1919 to build the new postwar world, they sought to establish nationalist-based democracies, in which the rule of law would guarantee the rights of individuals. These two interlinked concepts of law and human rights became for many the defining features of "the West," of democracy, and of civilization itself. The Bolsheviks challenged this definition. They offered instead a definition of democracy based on class and an understanding of the law resting on the demands of continuing revolution. ■

Questions of Justice

1. In what ways was the murder of the Russian royal family the by-product of total war rather than the result of any revolutionary ideals?

2. Were the Bolsheviks correct in arguing that "justice" is never blind, that legal systems always reflect the interests of a society's dominant groups? Is there such a thing as impartial justice?

Taking It Further

Kozlov, Vladimir, and Vladimir Khrustalëv. *The Last Diary of Tsaritsa Alexandra.* 1997. Translation of the tsarina's diary from 1918.

Rosenberg, William, ed. *Bolshevik Visions: First Phase of the Cultural Revolution in Soviet Russia.* 1990. The section on "Proletarian Legality" explores the Bolsheviks' effort to develop a legal system that embodied their revolutionary ideals.

Steinberg, Mark, and Vladimir Khrustalëv. *The Fall of the Romanovs.* 1999. Detailed account of the last two years of the tsar and his family, based on recently opened archives.

■ **Tsar Nicholas II and Family**
Tsar Nicholas II, the Tsarina Alexandra, and their family.

death tolls reached as high as five million. Yet, as the next chapter shows, the Bolsheviks emerged victorious. The Russian Empire was remade as the Soviet Union, a communist state.

Spreading the Revolution

The victory of the Bolsheviks in Russia inspired socialists across Europe and around the world. Strikes, riots, and attempts at revolution punctuated the immediate postwar era. The most important of these attempts to mimic the Russian Revolution occurred in Germany. Disillusion with the kaiser's regime had set in long before Germany had lost the war. Defeat simply accentuated the desire for radical political change.

Inspired by the success of the Bolshevik Revolution, a socialist faction called the Spartacists (after Spartacus, the gladiator who led a slave revolt against Rome in the first century B.C.E.), wanted Germany to follow Russia down the path to communist revolution. Directed by Karl Liebknecht (1871–1919) and Rosa Luxemburg (1870–1919), the Spartacists opposed the moderation and gradualism of the Social Democratic Party (SPD), which now controlled Germany's postwar government. By November 1918, thousands had rallied behind Liebknecht and Luxemburg in Berlin, German communists had declared the province of Bavaria a Soviet republic, and the Red Flag—the symbol of communism—was flying over eleven German cities. Civil war raged until the spring of 1919, when the SPD defeated the communists for control of the new Germany.

THE NATIONALIST REVOLUTIONS

In both Germany and Russia, the war created the opportunity for *social* revolution. In other areas, the war kindled the fires of *nationalist* revolution. In Europe, nationalist revolutions coalesced with military defeat to tear apart Austria-Hungary. When the war turned decisively against the Central Powers in 1918, the army erupted in mutiny, as Slovenian, Ruthenian, Serbian, and Czech troops rebelled. By the end of October, nationalist leaders had declared the formation of independent governments in the Hungarian, Czech, Polish, and Balkan regions.

The combined impact of total war and nationalist revolution also had a profound impact on the Middle East. By the late nineteenth century, Arab intellectuals had begun to dream of overthrowing Ottoman rule and establishing independent Arab states. After the Ottoman Empire joined the Central Powers in 1914, the British recruited Arab nationalists for the Allied war effort with promises of Arab political independence after the war. In 1915, Sir Henry McMahon exchanged letters with Sharif Husayn (Hussein) ibn Ali, head of the Hashemite dynasty that acted as traditional guardian of Islamic holy sites. McMahon promised Husayn control over all the Arab areas liberated from Ottoman rule. This "McMahon-Husayn Correspondence,"

however, was not legally binding, nor did it establish precisely the actual boundaries under discussion. The situation grew even more complicated when Britain also promised to support a Jewish state in the same region. Eager to win the backing of the international Jewish community, particularly Jews in the United States, the British government in 1917 issued the Balfour Declaration°, a pledge of British support for a Jewish national homeland in Palestine. These contradictory promises made to both Arabs and Jews set the stage for disaster in future decades.

The Middle East was not the only region in which the war heightened nationalist aspirations. Throughout Europe's global empires, nationalist movements grew stronger as the war changed economic relationships. Germany's submarine warfare and the Allies' blockade sharply limited both imports of colonial raw materials and foods into Europe and exports of European industrial products to the imperial territories. The war thus stimulated the development of more diversified and industrialized—and therefore more independent—economies in regions such as Australia, India, South Africa, and much of South America.

In countries such as India, which lost almost 50,000 of its soldiers in the war, more and more people began to question the right of a small group of men in a government far away to involve their people in such a disastrous conflict. As the war was drawing to a close, Mohandas Gandhi (1869–1948) introduced India and the world to a new form of revolution. He called on his followers to fight the British not with armed weapons but with moral force—with nonviolent protest and civil disobedience. Gandhi transformed Indian nationalism from the preserve of Western-educated intellectuals to a mass movement. By the end of the war, he and his followers stood ready to challenge British rule over India.

THE FAILURE OF THE PEACE SETTLEMENT

At the beginning of 1919, the representatives of the victorious Allied nations gathered in Paris to draw up the treaties that would outline the peace settlement. Yet their aims were far higher than simply ending the war; they wished to construct a new Europe and to reconfigure the conduct of international affairs.

At the center of this high endeavor was the American college-professor-turned-president Woodrow Wilson. In what he called his Fourteen Points, Wilson identified the elements needed for a new international order. In Wilson's vision, the ideal of national self-determination could transform Europe into a collection of peaceful, prosperous, independent nation-states. As Wilson explained, the multinational empires should be broken up and "every people should be left free to determine its own polity, its own way of development, unhindered, unthreatened, unafraid; the little along with the great and powerful." The cornerstone of this new world order would be a new organization, the League of Nations°, that would have the power to resolve international disputes. All states, big and small, European and non-European, would have a voice in the league and negotiations would be conducted openly and democratically.

In the Wilsonian vision, then, the peace settlement would ensure that World War I was "the war to end all wars." Instead, the settlement that ended this first total war played a central role in preparing the ground for the next.

By the terms of the Versailles Treaty°, between Germany and the Allied nations, Germany lost all of its overseas colonies, 13 percent of its European territory, 10 percent of its population, and its ability to wage war. The treaty limited the German army to a defensive force of 100,000 men, with no aircraft or tanks, and declared the Rhineland a demilitarized zone, emptied of German soldiers and fortifications. The Versailles Treaty also ceded the coalfields of the Saar region to France for fifteen years. Most significantly, the treaty declared that German aggression had caused the war, and therefore that Germany must recompense the Allies for its cost. In 1921, the Allies presented Germany with a bill for reparations° of 132 billion marks ($31.5 billion). As we will see in the next chapter, this reparations clause set up an economic cycle that was to prove devastating for both global prosperity and German democratic politics. In addition, the German people bitterly resented the entire peace settlement, which they perceived as unjustly punitive.

In eastern Europe, the peace settlement redrew the regional map but there too failed to create the foundations of stable democracies. Poland once again became an independent nation, with pieces carved out of the German, Austrian, and Russian Empires. One entirely new state was formed out of the rubble of the Austrian-Hungarian Empire—Czechoslovakia. Romania, Greece, and Italy all expanded, while Serbia became the heart of the new Yugoslavia. Hungary was reduced to one-third of its prewar size. All that remained of the Habsburg Empire was Austria; all that remained of the Ottoman Empire was Turkey.

These changes were heralded as the victory of national self-determination. But as Woodrow Wilson's own secretary of state, Robert Lansing, complained, "This phrase is simply loaded with dynamite. It will raise hopes which can never be realized." No fewer than 30 million eastern Europeans remained members of minority groups. Over nine million Germans resided in countries other than Germany; one-third of the population of Czechoslovakia was neither Czech nor Slovak; and the new state of Yugoslavia contained an uneasy mixture of several ethnic groups. Rather than satisfying nationalist ambitions, the new boundaries served to inflame them, thus creating a volatile situation for the post–World War I world.

Like the ideal of national self-determination, the League of Nations also failed to fulfill Wilson's dream of making war obsolete. Three factors help explain the league's failure. First, it did not represent every state. When the league met for the first time in 1920, three significant world powers had no representative present: Germany and the Soviet Union were excluded, and, in a stunning defeat for President Wilson, the U.S. Senate rejected membership. The failure of these three states to participate in the league at its beginning stripped the organization of much of its potential influence. Second, the league had no military power. Although it could levy economic sanctions against states that flouted its decisions, it could do nothing more. Finally, the will to make the league work was lacking. With Wilson removed from the picture, European leaders were free to pursue their own rather more traditional visions of what the league should be. French politicians, for example, believed that the league's primary reason for existence was to enforce the provisions of the Versailles Treaty—in other words, to punish Germany rather than to restructure international relations.

CONCLUSION

The War and the West

·························· ▬ ··························

Sparked by nationalist fervor, international competition, and a widespread will to believe that in war lay the solution to political divisions and cultural fears, World War I quickly slipped out of the control of both the diplomats and the generals. Industrialization changed the face of combat. Total war smashed the boundaries of the battlefield, eroded the distinction between soldier and civilian, and demanded an overhaul of each combatant nation's political, economic, and social structures.

The idea of "the West" also changed as a result of the impact of this war. The entry of American forces in the final year of the war signaled that in the twentieth century, the United States would have to be factored into any definition of "Western culture" or "Western civilization." At the same time, the spread of the war to the Middle East and Africa and the significant role played by soldiers from imperial territories such as Tunisia, India, and Australia demonstrated the global framework that complicated and constrained Western affairs. The war's revolutionary aftermath also had profound consequences for formulations of "Western identity." With the triumph of the Bolshevik Revolution, two versions of modernity now presented themselves—one associated with the United States and capitalism, and the other represented by the new Soviet Union and its communist ideology. Soviet communism's intellectual roots lay in Marxism, a quintessentially Western ideology, one shaped by Western ideals of evolutionary progress and the triumph of human reason. But after the Russian Revolution, communism was increasingly viewed by many in the West as something foreign, the Other against which the West identified itself.

The carnage of World War I also challenged the faith of many Europeans that through industrial development the West was progressing morally as well as materially. In the final decades of the nineteenth century, European and American soldiers had used repeating rifles and machine guns to conquer huge sections of the globe in the name of Western civilization. In 1914, European and American soldiers turned their machine guns on each other. The world the war had created was one of unprecedented destruction. Millions lay dead, with millions more maimed for life. Vast sections of northern France and eastern Europe had been turned into giant cemeteries filled with rotting men and rusting metal. Across central and eastern Europe, starvation continued to claim thousands of victims, while a worldwide influenza epidemic, spread in part by the marching armies, ratcheted up the death tolls even higher. In the new world shaped by relentless conflicts such as the Battle of the Somme, the pessimism and sense of despair that had already invaded much of the arts in the decade before the war became more characteristic of the wider culture. For many Europeans, the optimism and confidence of nineteenth-century liberalism died in the trenches.

Yet, paradoxically, the war also fostered high hopes. Wilson declared that this had been the war to end all wars. The fires of revolution burned high and many in the West believed that on top of the ashes of empire they would now build a better world. The task of reconstruction, however, proved immense; as we shall see in Chapter 25, in many areas, retrenchment replaced revolution. Seeking stability in an increasingly unsettled world, many Europeans and Americans did their best to return to prewar patterns. The failure of the peace settlement ensured that the "war to end all wars" set the stage for the next, far more destructive total war.

Suggestions for Further Reading

For a comprehensive list of suggested readings, please go to www.ablongman.com/levackconcise/chapter24

Cork, Richard. *A Bitter Truth: Avant-Garde Art and the Great War.* 1994. A beautifully illustrated work that looks at the cultural impact of the war.

Eksteins, Modris. *Rites of Spring: The Great War and the Birth of the Modern Age.* 1989. Explores the links among modernism, the war experience, and modernity.

Ferguson, Niall. *The Pity of War.* 1999. A bold reconsideration of many accepted interpretations of the origins and experience of the war.

Fitzpatrick, Sheila. *The Russian Revolution, 1917–1932.* 1994. As the title indicates, Fitzpatrick sees the revolutions of 1917 as the opening battle in a more than ten-year struggle to shape the new Russia.

Gilbert, Martin. *The First World War: A Complete History.* 1994. A comprehensive account, packed with illuminating detail.

Gilbert, Martin. *The Routledge Atlas of the First World War.* 1994. Much more than a set of maps, Gilbert's atlas provides a very clear and useful survey of both the causes and results of the war.

Higonnet, Margaret. *Lines of Fire: Women's Visions of World War I.* 1998. An important study of women's experiences.

Joll, James. *The Origins of the First World War.* 1984. One of the best and most carefully balanced studies of this complicated question.

Read, Christopher. *From Tsar to Soviets: The Russian People and Their Revolution, 1917–1921.* 1996. An up-to-date study of the popular revolution and its fate.

Winter, J. M. *The Experience of World War I.* 1989. Despite the title, this richly illustrated work not only covers the war itself but also explores the factors that led to its outbreak and outlines its chief consequences.

Winter, J. M., and R. M. Wall, eds. *The Upheaval of War: Family, Work and Welfare in Europe, 1914–1918.* 1988. A series of essays examining the home front experiences.

Notes

1. Figure from Tony Ashworth, *Trench Warfare 1914–1918* (1980), 15–16.
2. Quoted in Richard Cork, *A Bitter Truth* (1994), 198.
3. Quoted in W. Bruce Lincoln, *Red Victory: A History of the Russian Civil War* (1989), 32.
4. Quoted in Edvard Radzinsky, *The Last Tsar*, trans. Marian Schwartz (1993), 336.
5. From the written account of Yakov Yurovsky, quoted in Radzinsky, *The Last Tsar*, 355.
6. Quoted in William Henry Chamberlin, *The Russian Revolution, 1917–1921. Volume 2. From The Civil War to the Consolidation of Power* (1987), 91.
7. Quoted in Lincoln, *Red Victory*, 151.
8. Ibid., 155.
9. Quoted in Radzinsky, *The Last Tsar*, 326.

Diese Hand
führt das Reich

deutsche Jugend folge ihr
in den Reihen der H.J.!

Reconstruction, Reaction, and Continuing Revolution: The 1920s and 1930s

ON SEPTEMBER 14, 1927, AN OPEN CAR ACCELERATED DOWN A STREET IN Nice in southern France. In its passenger seat sat a woman, who let her long silk shawl whip in the wind. This woman in free-flowing clothing, speeding down the streets in a convertible, provides a fitting image for aspects of Western culture in the decade after World War I. Entranced by the automobile, Americans and Europeans embraced its promise of mobility and freedom. They perceived themselves as moving ahead, breaking through traditional barriers and heading off into new directions. Even more fitting was the identity of that female passenger: Isadora Duncan, by 1927 one of the most famous artists in Europe. In the years before World War I, the American-born Duncan had rejected classical ballet as an artificial form that restricted and deformed the female body. She cast aside ballet's confining toe shoes and tutus, and opted for bare feet and simple tunics. For Duncan, dance was not a force imposed on the body from outside; instead, dance flowed from the body itself. In her break with the highly regulated system of classical ballet, her quest for more natural forms, and her desire to liberate women, both physically and artistically, Duncan serves as an apt symbol for modernity. Moreover, as an American, Duncan appeared to personify the new culture that for many Europeans represented the world of the future. Even her clothing—loose tunics, free-flowing scarves, fluid shawls—symbolized a love of freedom and movement.

Yet freedom is sometimes dangerous and movement can be violent. On that autumn day in 1927 Duncan's long scarf became entangled in the wheel of her car and strangled the dancer. Gruesome as it is, the image of Duncan's sudden death serves as an appropriate introduction to the history of the West in the

"This Hand Guides the Reich: German Youth Follow It in the Ranks of the Hitler Youth": In this German propaganda poster from the 1930s, the Nazi government promises order and strong leadership, and at the same time allies itself with youth and vigor. During the 1930s, governments from across the political spectrum borrowed techniques from mass advertising to spread their ideas and win support.

1920s and 1930s, the turbulent interlude between two tragic world wars. The American president Woodrow Wilson had hailed World War I as the "final war for human liberty." Many Europeans agreed; they thought that the war would propel their society down a new road, yet in much of Europe the drive toward freedom ended quickly. The interwar period saw the strangulation of democracy in eastern and southern Europe and the rise of political and cultural ideologies that viewed human liberty as an illusion and mass murder as a tool of the state.

These developments had profound implications for the idea of the West. In the Wilsonian vision, "the West" stood as a culture that promoted individual freedom through democratic politics and capitalist economics. But the success of antidemocratic and anticapitalist ideologies in capturing the hopes and allegiances of large numbers of Europeans illustrated that Wilson's definition of the West was only one among many, and that the link between "Western" and "democratic" remained fragile.

Understanding the developments that shaped the interwar era demands close consideration of the way Europeans responded to the revolutionary aftermath of World War I. Hopes for radical social and political change often clashed with the desire to restore the prewar order.

Four questions will guide our examination of these decades:

- In what ways did reconstruction rather than revolution characterize the postwar period?
- What circumstances explain the emergence of the Radical Right?
- What factors led to the polarization of European politics in the 1930s?
- How did the interaction between Europe and the world outside the West change after the war?

Out of the Trenches: Reconstructing Culture and Politics in the 1920s

As we saw at the end of Chapter 24, in the years immediately following World War I Europe stood on the brink of revolutionary change. The war toppled empires and redrew the map of eastern and central Europe. Gender roles turned upside down, imperial patterns shattered, and social expectations were raised. Despite these expectations and fears, however, reconstruction rather than revolution characterized much of the immediate postwar period. In many areas, World War I was the turning point that failed to turn.

UTOPIA OR THE WASTE LAND?

To many Europeans, the devastation of World War I offered the promise of a clean start. The Bauhaus, established in Berlin in 1919 as a school for architects, craftsmen, and designers, epitomized the near-utopianism of much of European culture after the war. Its founder, Walter Gropius (1883–1969), hoped his students would become nothing less than "the architects of a new civilization."[1] Many interwar architects saw themselves as part of a glorious new machine age. The Swiss architect Le Corbusier (1887–1965) called a house simply "a machine for living in." Le Corbusier and his fellow modernist architects stripped a building of ornament and frequently exposed its "machinery" such as heating ducts and elevator shafts.

Closely related to the worship of the machine in the interwar period was a celebration of movement and speed. The automobile evolved from a rich man's toy to a middle-class necessity, made possible by the assembly-line techniques developed in Henry Ford's Detroit factories. The assembly line, which reduced the entire industrial workforce of a factory to a single efficient machine, crossed from the United States into Europe in the later 1920s. The airline industry also took off in this era. In 1919 the first air passenger service between London and Paris began; the next decade saw Europe's major cities linked by air networks. In 1927, when the American Charles Lindbergh (1902–1974) became the first person to fly across the Atlantic alone, he was hailed not only as an international hero, but also as an icon of human resourcefulness and technological mastery.

Many Europeans, however, rejected the optimism and utopianism of much of postwar culture. In the English-speaking world, the American expatriate poet T. S. Eliot (1888–1965) supplied the most evocative portrait of postwar disillusion. In 1922, Eliot published a lengthy poem called "The Waste Land," which became a widely used metaphor for the senselessness of the war. Like a Cubist collage painting, "The Waste Land" comprises fragments of conversation, literary allusions, disjointed quotations, and mythological references, all clashing and combining in a modernist cry of despair.

The heightened anxiety that characterized much of Western literature after the war is also clear in the realms of theology and philosophy. In his postwar writings, the Swiss theologian Karl Barth (1886–1968) emphasized human sinfulness and argued that an immense gulf separated humanity from God. Reaching God demanded a radical leap of faith. In the philosophy of existentialism taught by Martin Heidegger (1889–1976), the human condition is one of anxiety and alienation. To overcome this alienation, Heidegger argued, the individual must struggle to rise above mere existence to a consciousness of the genuine and authentic.

A sense of anxiety as well as anger dominates much of the visual art of the period. War veteran Otto Dix

■ Otto Dix, *Flanders* (1934–1935)
In this painting, the Flanders landscape is literally shaped by the bodies of soldiers. Like these soldiers—and much of postwar European culture—Dix could not escape the war. His paintings reveal a man permanently wounded.

(1891–1969) filled his canvases with crippled ex-soldiers. In *Flanders,* painted in 1934, Dix depicted a nightmare of trench soldiers, rotting like blasted trees. Many war veterans such as Dix had hoped that the war would bring radical social and political change. Instead, prewar patterns soon reasserted themselves. Stuck in the mud, the soldiers in Dix's *Flanders* provide a haunting image of European society in the interwar years.

THE RECONSTRUCTION OF GENDER

An examination of women's roles in the interwar period illustrates the way radical change dissipated and prewar patterns re-emerged. At first sight, the era seems to be one of profound change in gender relations. By 1920 women in the United States and many European countries had received the right to vote in national elections and to hold national office. Expanding health care and service sectors meant new jobs for women as nurses, social workers, secretaries, telephone exchange operators, and clerks. Women's higher-education opportunities also widened, and the practice of family limitation spread into working-class households. Thus, the "New Woman" dominated films, novels, and popular music of the 1920s. She lived, worked, and traveled on her own. Even her clothes reflected her new freedom: She wore trousers and shorter skirts, and chopped off her long hair.

■ The "New Woman"
Almost every aspect of the "New Woman" captured in this 1928 French photograph caused offense to traditionalists: short skirts and bobbed hair, smoking in public, the association with a car and therefore with mobility and illicit sex—all crossing the border into masculine terrain.

Despite these important changes, however, women's roles actually altered little in the two decades after World War I. A greater percentage of women worked, but they tended to be barred from management positions, assigned to the most repetitive tasks, and paid by piecework, with the result that the wage gap between male and female laborers remained wide.

These years also witnessed a concerted effort to reconstruct nineteenth-century masculine and feminine ideals. Both the war's lengthy casualty lists and the drop in the average family size provoked widespread fear about declining populations. Governments and religious leaders joined together to convince women that their destiny lay in motherhood. Sale and purchase of birth control devices became illegal during the 1920s in France, Belgium, Italy, and Spain. France outlawed abortions in 1920. In Britain after 1929, a woman who had an abortion could be sentenced to life imprisonment. To encourage population growth, governments also expanded welfare services such as family allowances, subsidized or state-provided housing, school lunches, health insurance, and prenatal and well-baby clinics.

THE RECONSTRUCTION OF NATIONAL POLITICS

As World War I drew to a close, U.S. President Woodrow Wilson envisioned a new international order based on democratic politics. Such hopes went unrealized. Pre-1914 economic, political, and social relationships survived the war and helped weaken the new democratic states. Even in revolutionary Russia, many aspects of the prewar tsarist regime re-emerged in the 1920s.

The Defeat of Democracy in Eastern Europe

After the peace negotiations concluded in 1922, postwar eastern Europe certainly looked markedly different from its prewar counterpart (see Map 25.1). The Russian, Austrian-

■ **Map 25.1 Europe in the 1920s and 1930s**
The map shows the consequences of not only World War I but also such successor conflicts as the Irish-English struggles, which resulted in the formation of an independent Ireland; the war between Bolshevik Russia and its enemies, which widened the western frontiers of the Soviet state; and the Turkish uprising, which kept Turkey intact and independent.

Hungarian, and Ottoman Empires had all disappeared, replaced by a jigsaw puzzle of small independent nations. But lines on the map did not change key political and economic realities.

First, nationalist-ethnic divisions continued to haunt postwar political structures. In the new Yugoslavia, for example, ethnic struggles dominated interwar politics. Croat representatives refused even to sit in the new Serb-dominated parliament. Second, much of eastern Europe remained a world of peasants and aristocratic landlords. With little industrial growth and few cities to absorb labor, unemployment rates and land hunger were both high.

Ethnic divisions and economic underdevelopment helped destabilize eastern Europe's new democratic political systems. With the exception of Czechoslovakia, every eastern European nation returned to authoritarian politics during the 1920s or early 1930s. In Yugoslavia, for example, escalating ethnic violence peaked in 1928 when a popular Croatian political leader was shot to death on the floor of the legislature. The ensuing ethnic unrest gave King Alexander (a Serb) the excuse he needed to abolish the constitution and replace parliamentary democracy with a royal dictatorship. A brutal repression of Alexander's opponents followed.

The Weakness of the Weimar Republic

In Germany, too, the appearance of radical change masked crucial continuities between the pre- and postwar eras. The kaiser's empire gave way to the Weimar Republic°, led by a democratically elected parliamentary government. This democratic political structure, however, sat uneasily atop antidemocratic social and political foundations.

The survival of authoritarian attitudes and institutions resulted in part from the civil war that raged throughout Germany in the fall of 1918 and the first months of 1919. Anxious to impose order, the moderate socialists (SPD) in the Weimar government left untouched the civil service, judiciary, and army. The bureaucrats, judges, and officers in these institutions represented the old Germany. Continuing in positions of authority and influence, they constituted a formidable antidemocratic force at the very heart of the Weimar Republic. In addition, the SPD leaders deployed the "Free Corps," volunteer paramilitary units. The 400,000 men in these units, many of them ex-soldiers, regarded democratic ideals and the new German republic with contempt—"an attempt of the slime to govern."[2] In 1920 and in 1923, Free Corpsmen participated in violent rebellions against the Weimar government. The second attempted "putsch" was led by an ex-army corporal named Adolf Hitler.

These antidemocratic forces in the Weimar Republic fed on the widespread resentment among Germans aroused by severity of the Versailles Treaty. Many Germans blamed the moderate socialist government that signed the treaty for agreeing to a humiliating settlement. They argued that

Germany's surrender had been premature: No Allied troops stood on German soil in November 1918 and so Germany had not really been defeated. Army officers encouraged the idea that Germany could have kept on fighting had it not been "stabbed in the back" by its socialist government. This "stab-in-the-back" legend helped undermine support not only for the SPD's moderate socialism but even for democracy itself.

The shaky foundations of democracy in Weimar Germany were eroded further by the dramatic events of 1923. In that year, the German mark collapsed completely and paper money ceased to have any value. This hyperinflation° was the unintended by-product of the Weimar government's effort to force the Allies to reconsider reparations. In 1922, the Weimar government halted payments and demanded a new economic settlement. The French retaliated by sending troops into Germany's Ruhr Valley to seize coal as a form of reparations payment. German laborers in the Ruhr valley resisted the invasion by going on strike. Already relying on a policy of inflationary spending to meet its budget deficit, the German government began printing money with abandon to pay the striking Ruhr workers. The inflation rate surged upward. By January 1923, the mark, which in 1914 could be traded for the American dollar at a rate of 4:1, had plummeted to an exchange rate of 22,400:1. By October, the exchange rate from mark to dollar was at 440,000,000:1. Families who had scrimped for years found they had only enough savings to buy a loaf of bread.

As a result of this disaster, the French army pulled out of the Ruhr Valley and in 1924 Allied and German representatives drew up the Dawes Plan, which renegotiated reparations. By the end of 1924, the German economy had stabilized; the later 1920s were years of relative prosperity. Yet for many Germans, the memory of hyperinflation tainted the Weimar Republic. Many Germans concluded that democracy meant disorder and degradation. They looked with longing back to the prewar period, an era of supposed social stability and national power.

The Reconstruction of Russia

Even in the newly formed Soviet Union, the nation that epitomized revolution, important aspects of prewar society re-emerged in the postwar period. By 1922, the Bolsheviks had established their authority over most of the regions of the old tsarist empire—and had re-established many features of the authoritarian tsarist regime.

The impact of civil and international war partly explains the continuity of authoritarian rule. Fearing the spread of communist revolution, fourteen countries (including the United States) sent more than 100,000 soldiers to support the anti-Bolshevik forces in the Russian civil war. The need to win this war led the Bolsheviks to adopt increasingly authoritarian measures. Like the Jacobins during the French Revolution, the Bolsheviks turned to terror to defeat their enemies, both domestic and foreign. In the first six years of

The Trial of Adolf Hitler

On February 24, 1924, Adolf Hitler appeared in court in Munich to confront a charge of high treason following his pathetic attempt three months earlier to overthrow the Weimar government by armed rebellion. The trial marked a crucial point in Hitler's career. It gave him a national platform and, even more important, convinced him of the futility of an armed offensive against the state. From 1925 on, Hitler would work through the parliamentary system in order to destroy it. But the trial of Adolf Hitler is also significant in what it reveals about the power of antidemocratic forces in the new Germany. The trial made clear that many in positions of authority and responsibility in the Weimar Republic shared Hitler's contempt for the democratic state. By treating Hitler not as a traitorous thug but rather as an honorable patriot, his prosecutors helped weaken the already fragile structures of German democracy.

Hitler's attempt to overthrow the Weimar Republic by force occurred at the height of hyperinflation and the ensuing political chaos. By November 8, 1923, when Hitler took up arms, the German mark was worth only one trillionth of its prewar value. As its currency eroded, the Weimar Republic saw its political legitimacy seeping away as well. Separatist movements in several states threatened the sovereignty of the central government in Berlin. Separatist politics attracted the

support of many men from aristocratic backgrounds, members of the traditional conservative elite who viewed Weimar democracy as a foreign and unwelcome import.

Hitler had little interest in the separatist movement, but he believed he could channel its antidemocratic sentiments into a national revolution. He attracted a number of supporters, including one of the most important men in Germany, the World War I hero General Erich von Ludendorff. Seeking to avoid the blame for Germany's defeat in 1918, Ludendorff insisted that his army could have won the war had it not been stabbed in the back by the Social Democratic politicians who now ran the government. Like many German conservatives—and like Hitler—he viewed the Weimar Republic as illegitimate.

On November 8 Hitler made his move. His men surrounded a Munich beer hall where 2,000 supporters of Bavarian separatism had gathered. Hitler declared that both the Bavarian and the national governments had been overthrown and that he was now the head of a new German state, with Ludendorff as his commander in chief. Around noon the next day, Hitler, Ludendorff, and several thousand of their followers marched toward the regional government buildings located on one of Munich's main squares. Armed police blocked their passage. In the ensuing firefight, seventeen men were killed. Despite the bullets

whizzing through the air, Ludendorff marched through the police cordon and stood in the square awaiting arrest. Hitler ran away. Police found him two days later, cowering in a supporter's country house about thirty-five miles outside Munich.

The Beer Hall Putsch had clearly, utterly, completely failed. In jail awaiting trial, Hitler contemplated suicide. Yet later he described his defeat as "perhaps the greatest stroke of luck in my life." The defeat meant a trial; the trial meant a national audience—and an opportunity for Hitler to present his case against the Weimar Republic.

In his testimony, Hitler admitted that he had conspired to overthrow the democratically elected Republican government, but he insisted he was not therefore guilty of treason. The real treason had occurred in November 1918, when the Social Democratic government had surrendered to the Allies: "I confess to the deed, but I do not confess to the crime of high treason. There can be no question of treason in an action which aims to undo the betrayal of this country in 1918. . . . I consider myself not a traitor but a German."

Hitler argued that he was not aiming for personal power: "In what small terms small minds think! . . . What I had in mind from the very first day was a thousand times more important than becoming a minister. I wanted to become the destroyer of Marxism." Thus Hitler depicted himself as a patriot, a

Hitler in Landsberg Prison, 1924
This photo of Hitler during his short imprisonment was made into a postcard, to be purchased by his supporters.

nationalist motivated by love of Germany and hatred of communists and socialists. "The eternal court of history," according to Hitler, would judge him and his fellow defendants "as Germans who wanted the best for their people and their Fatherland, who were willing to fight and to die."[3]

Despite Hitler's own admission of conspiring against the government, the presiding judge could convince the three lay judges (who took the place of a jury) to render a guilty verdict only by arguing that Hitler would most likely be pardoned soon. The reluctance of the judges to convict Hitler highlights the extraordinary sympathy shown to him and his political ideas throughout the trial and during his imprisonment. The chief prosecutor offered a rather surprising description of an accused traitor: "Hitler is a highly gifted man, who has risen from humble beginnings to achieve a respected position in public life, the result of much hard work and dedication. . . . As a soldier he did his duty to the utmost. He cannot be accused of having used the position he created for himself in any self-serving way." In delivering the verdict, the judge emphasized Hitler's "pure patriotic motives and honorable intentions." Rather than being deported as a foreign national convicted of a serious crime (Hitler was still an Austrian citizen), Hitler was given a slight sentence of five years, which made him eligible for parole in just six months.

The favorable treatment continued in prison, where Hitler received special privileges: He was exempted from work and exercise requirements, provided with prisoners to clean his rooms, even given a special table, decorated with a swastika banner, in the dining hall. When he was released in September, his parole report described him favorably as "a man of order."[4]

Hitler's gentle treatment reveals the precarious state of democratic institutions in Germany after World War I. Many high-ranking Germans in positions of power and influence (such as judges and prosecutors) viewed parliamentary democracy with loathing. The trial also reveals the willingness of conservative aristocrats to ally with Radical Right groups such as the Nazis. Still not very strong, the Nazis in 1923 were easily reined in. A decade later, however, the conservatives who thought they could ride Hitler to

power suddenly found that they were no longer in control.

Questions of Justice

1. Imagine you are a German war veteran reading about this case in the newspaper in 1924. Why might you be attracted to the party of Adolf Hitler?
2. Hitler appealed to the "eternal court of history." What do you think he meant? How would Hitler have defined "justice"?

Taking It Further

Gordon, Harold Jr. *Hitler and the Beer Hall Putsch*. 1972. This lengthy study (over 600 pages) provides a detailed account of the putsch and its aftermath.

The Hitler Trial Before the People's Court in Munich, trans. H. Francis Freniece, Lucie Karcic, and Philip Fandek (3 vols.). 1976. English translation of the court transcripts.

Bolshevik rule, the Cheka (the secret police force) executed at least 200,000 people.

Ideology is the second factor that helps explain the continuity of authoritarian rule in post-tsarist Russia. Faced with the task of building a communist state in an economically backward society, the Bolshevik leader Vladimir Lenin modified Marxist theory. In a peasant society, Lenin argued, the agent of revolutionary change could not be the industrial working class. Instead, the Bolshevik or Communist Party, an elite of highly disciplined, politically aware and committed individuals, would be the "vanguard" of revolution.

In the Bolshevik view, the masses could not be trusted to make their own decisions; instead, communist officials made these decisions for them. These officials became a privileged caste, with access to the best jobs, food, clothing, and apartments. The rule of the tsar had been replaced not with democracy but with the rule of the commissar, the Communist Party functionary.

In the economic sphere, as in the political system, important continuities shaped the Russian experience. By 1921 famine in the countryside and widespread peasant unrest forced Lenin to backpedal from communist economics and announce a New Economic Policy (NEP)°. Under NEP, peasants were allowed to sell their produce for profit. Although the state continued to control heavy industry, transport, and banking, NEP encouraged the proliferation of small private businesses and farms—just as the tsar's economic policymakers had done before the war.

The Rise of the Radical Right

A very different sort of revolution occurred in Italy, a region long on the periphery of European power., The fascist revolution introduced Europe to a new politics, the politics of the Radical Right.

THE FASCIST ALTERNATIVE

Conceived in the coupling of wartime exhilaration and postwar despair, fascism° offered an alternative to the existing political ideologies. Fascism was more than a set of political ideas, however. As presented by its creator, Benito Mussolini (1883–1945), fascism was an ongoing performance, a spectacular sound-and-lights show with a cast of millions.

Mussolini's Rise to Power
Mussolini joined the Italian army in 1915 and fought until he was wounded in 1917. When the war ended, he sought to

■ **The March on Rome, October 28, 1922**
The fascist march on Rome was not an armed rebellion but rather a carefully orchestrated show of power, a piece of street theater designed to demonstrate Mussolini's mass support. The king had already asked Mussolini to become prime minister.

THE CULT OF THE LEADER

The personality cult characterized not only the Radical Right ideologies of Italian fascism and German Nazism, but also the ideological system that stood at the opposite end of the political spectrum: Stalinist communism. Searching for a way to mobilize the masses without granting them actual political power, Mussolini, Hitler, and Stalin erected around themselves leadership cults. Their own images came to embody the nation. As the following set of excerpts shows, the cults of Mussolini, Hitler, and Stalin took on religious dimensions, with all three men adored as secular saviors.

I. Description of Mussolini's Visit to Trieste in 1938

Finally we have seen and heard Him! . . . These first reactions, expressed with indescribable joy, eyes moved to tears and an ineffable, agonizing joy . . . It is not easy to describe the expression on most faces, on those of the little people as on those of the educated, of the mass as a whole. Expressions of wonderful contentment and pride among those who saw Him pass close by—especially among the dockworkers He visited yesterday—and those whose eyes He met, those who caught His eye. "Never such eyes! The way he looks at you is irresistible! He smiled at me . . . I was close, I could almost touch him . . . When I saw him my legs trembled" . . . and a thousand other similar statements show and confirm the enormous fascination exercised by his person.

II. Description of an Early Nazi Rally by Louise Solmitz, Schoolteacher

The April sun shone hot like summer and turned everything into a picture of gay expectation. There was immaculate order and discipline . . . the hours passed. . . . Expectations rose. There stood Hitler in a simple black coat and looked over the crowd. Waiting. A forest of swastika pennants swished up, the jubilation of this moment was given vent in a roaring salute. . . . How many look up to him with a touching faith! As their helper, their savior, their deliverer from unbearable distress—to him who rescues the Prussian prince, the scholar, the clergyman, the farmer, the worker, the unemployed, who leads them from the parties back into the nation.

III. Speech by a Woman Delegate at a Workers' Conference in the Soviet Union

Thank you comrade Stalin, our leader, our father, for a happy, merry kolkhoz life!

He, our Stalin, put the steering-wheel of the tractor in our hand. . . . He, the great Stalin, carefully listens to all of us in this meeting, loves us with a great Stalinist love (*tumultuous applause*), day and night thinks of our prosperity, of our culture, of our work . . .

Long live our friend, our teacher, the beloved leader of the world proletariat, comrade Stalin! (*Tumultuous applause, rising to an ovation. Shouts of 'Hurrah!'*)

Sources: "I. Description of Mussolini's Visit to Trieste in 1938," reprinted by permission of the publisher from *The Sacralization of Politics in Fascist Italy* by Emilio Gentile, translated by Keith Botsford, p. 147, Cambridge, Mass.; Harvard University Press. Copyright © 1996 by the President and Fellows of Harvard College. "II. Description of an Early Nazi Rally by Louise Solmitz, Schoolteacher," copyright © 1988 by Claudia Koonz. From *Mothers in the Fatherland: Women, the Family, and Nazi Politics* by Claudia Koonz. Reprinted by permission of the Charlotte Sheedy Literary Agency. "III. Speech by a Woman Delegate at a Worker's Conference in the Soviet Union," from *Stalin's Peasants: Resistance and Survival in the Russian Village After Collectivization* by Sheila Fitzpatrick. Copyright © 1996 by Oxford University Press, Inc. Published by Oxford University Press, Inc.

create a new form of politics that would translate the military camaraderie and the exhilaration of violent action from the trenches to peacetime society. The result was fascism. Mussolini condemned conservatism, liberalism, and socialism as outdated. Socialism exalted the working class; liberalism viewed the individual as the core of society; conservatism clung to social hierarchy. Fascism, however, identified the *nation* as the dominant social reality.

Just three years after the first fascist meeting in Milan in 1919, Mussolini became prime minister of Italy. His rapid rise to power occurred against a backdrop of social turmoil. In 1919 and 1920, more than one million workers were on strike and a wave of land seizures spread across the countryside. During these years, fascist squads disrupted Socialist Party meetings, vandalized the offices of socialist newspapers, broke up strikes, beat up trade unionists, and protected aristocratic estates from attack. By 1922, the fascists were a formidable political force, favored by many Italians who feared the spread of communist revolution. In October 1922, King Victor Emmanuel III (r. 1900–1946) asked Mussolini to become prime minister.

The Fascist Revolution in Italy

Over the next four years Mussolini used both legal and illegal methods, including murder, to eliminate his political rivals and remake Italy as a one-party state. By 1926, he had succeeded. Party politics, an independent press, and the trade union movement ceased to exist. The restored death penalty and a strong police apparatus stood ready to enforce Mussolini's will.

At the same time, the "Cult of the Duce" fostered public adulation of the "Leader." Carefully choreographed public appearances gave ordinary Italians the chance to see, hear, and adore Mussolini and, through contact with his person, to feel a part of the new Italy. Mussolini paid careful attention to his public image. Photograph after photograph showed him as a man of action, always on the move, always pressing forward. Huge public rallies set in massive arenas, carefully staged with lighting and music, inspired his followers. A popular fascist slogan summed up the leadership cult: "Mussolini is always right."

Yet Mussolini's many promises of radical social and economic change went unrealized. In theory, fascism promised to replace capitalist competition and the profit motive with corporatism: Committees (or "corporations") made up of representatives of workers, employers, and the state were to direct the economy for the good of the nation. In actuality, workers' rights disappeared from fascist Italy while private property and industrial profits remained untouched. Early fascist promises of land redistribution were quickly forgotten, and the traditional landed aristocracy prospered.

The Great Depression and the Spread of Fascism After 1929

During the 1930s, fascist movements emerged in almost every European state. The key factor in the spread of fascism was the Great Depression°. On October 24, 1929, the American stock market collapsed. Over the next two years, the American economic crisis evolved into a global depression. Banks closed, businesses collapsed, and unemployment rates rose to devastating levels. Even by the end of the 1930s, the production rates of many nations remained low. Desperate people looked for desperate answers. Fascism provided some of these.

Why did the depression spread so quickly? The explanation lies with the changing role of the United States in Europe. During World War I, European nations sold off their domestic and foreign assets and borrowed heavily. By the end of 1918 Allied nations owed the United States more than $9 billion. American credit became the fuel that kept the European economy burning. American investors loaned money to Germany, which used the money to pay reparations to the Allies, which in turn used the money to pay back the United States. The system worked for a short time. Fueled by loans, the German economy kicked into gear. Currencies stabilized, production rose, and American money flowed not only into Germany but into all of Europe. If these loans dried up, however, Europe faced disaster.

In 1929 that disaster struck in the form of the collapse of the U.S. stock market. Scrambling to scrape up any assets, American creditors liquidated their European investments, and European economies tumbled. The political and social disarray that accompanied the Great Depression enhanced the appeal of fascist promises of stability, order, and national strength. In the 1930s, fascist movements emerged across Europe and existing authoritarian regimes adopted many fascist trappings.

THE NAZI REVOLUTION

In Germany, the Nazi Party offered a different version of Radical Right ideology. Just as the emergence of fascism was inextricably linked to Benito Mussolini, so Nazism° cannot be separated from Adolf Hitler (1889–1945). To understand the Nazi Revolution in Germany, we need first to explore Hitler's rise to power and then to examine the impact of Nazi rule on ordinary people.

Hitler's Rise to Power

Hitler, an Austrian, had spent several years before the war in Vienna, soaking up the ideas of extremist German nationalism laced with antidemocratic, antisocialist, and often anti-Semitic imagery and ideas. When World War I broke out, he grabbed at the chance to fight the war in a German rather than an Austrian uniform. Hitler regarded army life as "the greatest of all experiences" and served for almost the entire length of the war, until he was temporarily blinded by poison gas in 1918. After the war he settled in Munich, a fertile breeding ground for far right-wing political factions.

The Nazi Party began as one of these small fringe groups, with Hitler quickly emerging as its leader. *Nazi* is shorthand for *National Socialist German Workers' Party*,

CHRONOLOGY

1918	Civil war in Russia; civil war in Germany
1921	New Economic Policy (NEP) begins in Soviet Union
1922	French occupation of the Ruhr; Mussolini becomes prime minister in Italy
1923	Hyperinflation in Germany; Beer Hall Putsch
1924	Dawes Plan
1926	Military dictatorship established in Poland
1929	Royal dictatorship established in Yugoslavia; onset of the Great Depression; Stalin orders Soviet collectivization
1933	Hitler becomes chancellor in Germany
1934	The Great Purge begins in the Soviet Union
1935	Nuremberg Laws passed in Germany
1936	Popular Front government elected in France; civil war begins in Spain

but this title is misleading. Like fascism, Nazism opposed socialism, communism, trade unionism, and any political analysis that emphasized class conflict or workers' rights. Like Mussolini, Hitler exalted the nation, but Hitler's Nazism, much more so than Mussolini's fascism, focused on *race* as the key social reality. To Hitler, all history was the history of racial struggle, and in that racial struggle, the Jews were always the principal enemy. Hitler regarded Jewishness as a biological rather than a religious identity, as a sort of toxic infection that could be passed on to future generations and that posed a threat to those he called "Aryans"—white northern Europeans.

In the elections of 1928, Nazi candidates won only 2.6 percent of the vote. The Great Depression of 1929 gave the Nazis their chance at power. As unemployment rates skyrocketed, no German politician was able to put together a viable governing coalition. In this unstable climate, political polarization accelerated. By July 1932, the Nazis had become the largest party in the parliament, winning the support of 37 percent of the German voters. Support for their communist rivals also widened.

Terrified of the threat posed by communism and convinced that Hitler could be easily controlled, a small group of conservative politicians persuaded the aged President Paul von Hindenburg to offer Hitler the position of chancellor in January 1933. One member of this group, Baron Franz von Papen, reassured a friend that Hitler posed "no danger at all. We have hired him for our act. In two months' time we'll have pushed Hitler so far into the corner, he'll be squeaking."[5] But von Papen was wrong.

Within six months Hitler had destroyed what remained of democracy in Germany and established a Nazi dictatorship. After the German parliament building burned down in February, Hitler declared that the fire was part of a communist plot and demanded the power to imprison without warrant or trial. Mass arrests of more than 25,000 of his political opponents followed. In March, German politicians, cowed by Nazi threats of imprisonment, passed the Enabling Act. This key act gave Hitler the power to suspend the constitution and pass legislation without a parliamentary majority. By the summer of 1933, parliamentary political life had ceased to exist in Germany.

National Recovery

Jews, communists, socialists, and other groups defined as enemies of the state faced the constant threat of persecution and imprisonment under the Nazi regime during the 1930s. But for many Germans not in these groups, life got better. Nazi rule brought economic prosperity, restoration of national pride, and a cultural revolution that linked the power of nostalgia to the dynamism of modernity.

Economic depression gave the Nazis the chance at power; economic prosperity enabled them to hold on to this power. Because Hitler perceived himself as a revolutionary, bound by no existing rules, he was able to adopt the aggressive and ultimately successful economic policy suggested by Hjalmar Schacht (1877–1970), his finance minister. Economic orthodoxy dictated that in times of depression, a government should cut spending and maintain a balanced budget. Schacht embarked on a program of massive state expenditure instead. The result was the most impressive economic recovery in Europe. Industrial output rose by almost 30 percent while unemployment dropped from 44 percent in 1932 to 14.1 percent in 1934 to under 1 percent in 1938. Although real wages fell under Nazi rule and independent trade unions were outlawed, the fact that jobs were now available made Hitler an economic savior to many Germans.

Many also viewed him as a national savior, a leader who restored Germany's pride and power. Payment of war reparations, demanded by the humiliating Versailles Treaty, halted in 1930 because of the global economic crisis. Hitler never resumed payment. He also ignored the treaty's military restrictions and rebuilt Germany's armed forces. By 1938, parades featuring row after row of smartly uniformed troops signaled the revitalization of German military might. For many ordinary Germans, the sight of troops goose-stepping under the German flag meant a personal as well as a national renaissance. As one Nazi song proclaimed, "And now the me is part of the great We."[6]

To create the "great We," Hitler utilized modern techniques and technology. Impressed by Mussolini's use of the radio to popularize fascism, Hitler subsidized the production of radios in Germany so that by the end of the 1930s most Germans had access to a radio—and to Hitler's radio talks. He also recognized the power of the cinema, and hired the brilliant filmmaker Leni Riefenstahl (1902–2003) to film Nazi rallies. These still-astonishing films show an overwhelming mass spectacle, in which an entire nation appears to be marching in step behind Hitler.

But Hitler also recognized the power of nostalgia for many Germans. He used modern techniques and technologies to establish the Nazis as bulwarks of tradition. In speeches, posters, and films, the Nazis painted a picture of a mythic Germany, an idyllic community peopled by sturdy blonde peasants, small shopkeepers, and independent craftsmen. At the same time, the Nazis capitalized on many Germans' fear of modernization by linking key aspects of the modern economy to "Jewishness." According to Nazi propaganda, international corporations, large department stores, and supermarket chains were all part of a vast Jewish conspiracy to deprive ordinary people of their livelihoods.

Campaigns of Repression and Terror

Part of the appeal of the "great We" that Hitler created relied on the violent repression of the "not Us," those defined as outside or opposed to the nation. The Nazis first targeted political opponents. By 1934 half of the 300,000 German Communist Party members were in prison or dead; most of the rest had fled the country. The Nazis also persecuted specific religious groups on the basis of their actual or presumed opposition to the Nazi state. Roman Catholics were banned from government service and subject to constant harassment, and about half of Germany's 20,000 Jehovah's Witnesses were sent to concentration camps.

The groups that the Nazis deemed biologically inferior suffered most severely. Beginning in 1933, the Nazi regime forced the sterilization of the Roma (Gypsies), the mentally and physically handicapped, and mixed-race children. By 1939, 370,000 men and women had been sterilized.

The Jewish community—less than 1 percent of the German population—bore the brunt of Nazi racial attacks. To Nazi anti-Semites, Hitler's accession to the German chancellorship was like the opening of hunting season. They beat up Jews in the streets, vandalized Jewish shops and homes, threatened Christians who associated with Jews, and violently enforced boycotts of Jewish businesses. In 1933, "non-Aryans" (Jews) were dismissed from the civil service and the legal profession, and the number of Jewish students in high schools and universities was restricted. Every organization in Germany—youth clubs, sports teams, labor unions, charitable societies—underwent "Nazification," which meant Jewish members were dismissed and Nazis appointed to leadership roles. In 1935, the "Nuremberg Laws" labeled as Jewish anyone with three or more Jewish grandparents. Marriage or sexual relations between German Jews and non-Jews now became a serious crime.

WOMEN AND THE RADICAL RIGHT

Much of the appeal of both fascism and Nazism lay in the promise to restore order to societies on the verge of disintegration. Restoration of order included the return of women to their proper place. Mussolini proclaimed, "Woman must obey. . . . In our State, she must not count."[7] In the Nazi realm, "the soil provides the food, the woman supplies the population, and the men make the action."[8]

One of the first actions of the new Nazi government was to dismiss women from the civil service. Women physicians could work only in their husbands' practices. By 1937, both women physicians and women Ph.D.s had lost the right to be addressed as "Doctor" or "Professor." Birth control became illegal and penalties for abortion increased while prosecutions doubled. The Nazi regime also used a series of financial and cultural incentives to encourage women to stay at home and produce babies. These included marriage loans (available only if the wife quit her job), income tax deductions, and the opportunity to participate in housewives' discussion, welfare, and leisure groups.

In Italy, Mussolini's government initiated a wide-ranging social welfare program to strengthen the woman's traditional role. To encourage the birth of healthy babies, the fascists instituted family allowances, maternity leaves, birth and marriage loans, and family health clinics. They also passed a series of laws to strengthen traditional family life.

Unmarried men over age 30 had to pay double income tax (priests were exempt), homosexual relations between men were outlawed, and fatherhood became a prerequisite for men in high-ranking public office. Quotas limited the number of women employed in both the civil service and in private business, while women found themselves excluded entirely from jobs defined as "virile," a varied list that included boat captains, high school principals, and history teachers.

The Polarization of Politics in the 1930s

To Europeans and Americans disenchanted with the response of the democracies to the challenge of the Great Depression, fascist Italy and Nazi Germany offered powerful alternatives. The Soviet Union provided yet another option. While the capitalist nations struggled with high unemployment rates and falling industrial output, communist Russia appeared to be performing economic miracles. Politics in the West thus became polarized between communism on the left and fascism and Nazism on the right. In both the United States and Europe, however, politicians and policymakers sought to maintain the middle ground, to retain democratic values in a time of extremist ideologies.

THE SOVIET UNION UNDER STALIN: REVOLUTION RECONSTRUCTED, TERROR EXTENDED

Many Europeans looked with envy at the Soviet Union in the 1930s. Unemployment had disappeared; huge industrial cities transformed the landscape; the development of new industries such as chemicals and automobiles, together with a full-scale exploitation of the Soviet Union's massive natural resources, sent production indices soaring. But this economic transformation rested on dead bodies, millions of dead bodies. During the 1930s, mass murder became an integral part of the Soviet regime under Joseph Stalin (1879–1953).

Stalin's Rise to Power

By 1928, Stalin was the uncontested head of the party. At the time of Lenin's death in 1924, however, few observers would have predicted such a development. Stalin's more charismatic, intellectually able colleagues such as Leon Trotsky (1879–1940) and Nikolai Bukharin (1888–1938) overshadowed the stalwart Bolshevik.

Two factors explain Stalin's rise to power. First, as party secretary from 1922 on, Stalin both determined the success of party membership applications and decided who got promoted to what and where. Thus, throughout the 1920s he slowly built up a broad base of support within the party. Vast numbers of ordinary communists owed their party membership, and in many cases their livelihoods, to Stalin. Unlike the original Bolsheviks, most of these new members were not well educated or well versed in communist ideology. In fact, 25 percent were functionally illiterate.

Second, while Stalin expanded his support at the grassroots, a fierce ideological struggle at the highest levels of the Communist Party distracted his rivals for the party leadership. To launch the Soviet economy into industrialization, Trotsky urged the abandonment of Lenin's New Economic Policy (NEP), which had encouraged small private farms. Bukharin, however, insisted that agricultural development should precede industrialization. By skillfully playing one side against the other, Stalin was able to seize control of the party and the state by 1928.

The "Revolution from Above": Collectivization and Industrialization, 1928–1934

As party leader, Stalin placed the Soviet Union firmly back on a revolutionary course, with the aim of catapulting the Soviet Union into the ranks of the industrialized nations. The first step in what was called "the revolution from above" was collectivization°, the replacement of private and village farms with large cooperative agricultural enterprises run by communist managers according to directives received from the central government. Collectivization had both economic and political aims. Regarded as more modern and efficient, collective farms were expected to produce an agricultural surplus and thereby raise the capital needed for industrialization. But in addition, through collectivization, Stalin sought to transform peasants into employees of the communist state.

The peasants resisted this transformation, however, and forced collectivization proved devastating for rural Russia. Rather than turn their resources over to the state, peasants burned their crops and slaughtered their livestock. In the subsequent famine, up to seven million Soviet citizens died.[9] An additional ten million peasants were deported; many of these died either on the way to or in forced labor camps.

While class war raged in the countryside, city dwellers embarked on the second stage of the "revolution from above"—industrialization. In 1931 Stalin declared that

■ **"Pictures Can't Lie. . . "**

To claim and consolidate his position as sole leader of the Communist Party and of the Soviet Union, Stalin had to falsify history and present himself as Lenin's chosen heir. Murder and mass executions could remove competitors from the present, but to erase them from the past, Stalin turned to the airbrush and the scissors rather than the gun. Pictures showing other Bolsheviks standing next to Lenin were cropped, leaving him with Stalin, or if such a pairing could not be achieved, standing alone. This illustration shows the process at work. Compare the photo shown on page 521 of Chapter 24 with the photo above. In the first photo, taken just seconds before the one shown here, Lev Kamenev and Leon Trotsky—leading Bolsheviks and rivals with Stalin for the party leadership after Lenin's death—stand to Lenin's left. But in this picture, Kamenev and Trotsky have been cut out and some steps have been drawn in. Trotsky was forced into exile in 1929 and murdered in 1940; Kamenev was executed in 1936.

Soviet industry had to catch up with the West in ten years: "Either we do it or we go under."[10] "Doing it" demanded, first, fierce labor discipline. If fired, a worker was automatically evicted from his or her apartment and deprived of a ration card. "Doing it" also demanded reducing already-low levels of personal consumption. Eighty percent of all investment went into heavy industry, while domestic construction and light industry—clothing, for example, or furniture—were ignored. Scarcity became the norm, with long lines and constant shortages part of every urban resident's existence.

While millions starved in the country side, young communists acclaimed these years of hardship and horror as an era of heroism. Babies born in this decade received names like "Little Five Years" (for girls) and "Plan" (for boys), reflecting their parents' enthusiasm for the series of Five-Year

Plans issued by the Stalinist government as outlines for the new world order. Immense publicity focused on the gargantuan engineering achievements of the era—the cities built atop swampland, the hydroelectric projects with their enormous dams and power plants, the Moscow subway system. Such publicity made party members feel part of a huge and powerful endeavor. A popular song announced, "We were born to make fairy tales come true."[11]

No propaganda campaign and no amount of effort from enthusiastic young communists, however, could provide the Soviet Union with the labor it needed to catch up with the West in ten years. Forced labor was crucial. Throughout the 1930s, approximately five million men, women, and children labored in prison camps.[12] Many of the huge engineering triumphs of the decade rested on the backs of prisoners and deportees.

Stalin's Consolidation of Power: The Great Purge and Soviet Society, 1934–1939

By the mid-1930s, most villages were collectivized and the mass violence had ended. The seventeenth Party Congress in 1934 called itself the "Congress of Victors" as the party celebrated its industrial successes and the achievement of collectivization. But within five years, half of the 2,000 delegates had been arrested; of the 149 elected members of the Congress's Central Committee, 98 were shot dead. These Congress delegates, and hundreds of thousands of other Soviet citizens, were victims of the "Great Purge°."

The earliest victims tended to be top-ranking Communist Party officials, many of whom had opposed Stalin on various issues during the 1920s. By charging these powerful men with conspiring against the communist state, Stalin reduced the chances that any competitor might oust him. In a series of three spectacular show trials attended by journalists from all over the world, leading Bolsheviks pleaded guilty to charges of conspiracy and sabotage, and were immediately executed. Numerous smaller trials replicated the process throughout the Soviet Union.

The Great Purge quickly spun out of control to embrace low-level party members, managers in state agencies, factory directors, and engineers. Family members, neighbors, clients, and friends all became victims. Many were killed without trial, others executed after a legal show. Many of those purged were deported to slave labor camps to be worked to death on Stalin's vast construction projects. At least 750,000 people died, with the numbers of those arrested, imprisoned, or deported running into the millions.[13]

The Great Purge consolidated Stalin's hold on the Soviet Union. It not only eliminated all potential competitors, it also tied huge numbers of people more tightly to Stalin and his version of revolution. Individuals who moved into the positions left vacant by the purge's victims had an enormous material as well as psychological stake in viewing the purge as an act of justice.

The popularity of the purge was also closely linked with the emergence of a Stalin-centered personality cult. By the time the purge began, the cult was an omnipresent part of Soviet urban life. Huge posters and statues ensured that Stalin's figure remained constantly in front of Soviet citizens. Every scientific, technological, or economic advance in the Soviet Union was linked to the person and power of Stalin. The scores of letters personally addressed to Stalin that poured into central government offices testify that to many Soviet citizens, Stalin personified the nation.

THE RESPONSE OF THE DEMOCRACIES

The apparent economic successes of fascism and Nazism on the right, and Stalinism on the left, polarized European politics. For many Europeans in the 1930s, it seemed that democracy had failed and that they had no choice but to opt for fascism or communism. The failure of "Popular Front" governments, anti-fascist coalitions made up of communists, socialists, and centrists, accentuated this polarization.

A Third Way? The Social Democratic Alternative

The effort to meet the challenge of the depression without embracing either the Radical Right or the Stalinist Left accelerated the development of the political model that would dominate the West after World War II: social democracy°. In a social democracy, a democratically elected government accepts the role of ensuring a decent standard of living for its citizens. Although social democracy did not triumph in western Europe until after the massive bloodletting of another total war, the interwar years witnessed important steps toward this third path, an alternative to the extremes on both the Right and the Left.

One of the most striking experiments occurred in the United States. Franklin Delano Roosevelt (1882–1945) became president in 1932 at the height of the Great Depression, when unemployment stood at 24 percent. Promising a "New Deal" of "Relief, Recovery, Reform," Roosevelt tackled the depression with an activist governmental policy that included agricultural subsidies, public works programs, and the Social Security Act of 1935. Unemployment, however, remained high and the gross national product (GNP) did not recover to 1929 levels until 1941.

According to the theories of the British economist John Maynard Keynes (1883–1946), Roosevelt failed to solve the problem of unemployment because he remained committed to the ideal of a balanced budget. Keynes insisted that in times of depression, the state should adopt a program of deficit spending to stimulate economic growth. The experience of Sweden after 1932 appeared to confirm Keynes's theory. The Swedish Social Democratic government allowed its budget deficit to climb while it financed a massive public works campaign, as well as an increase in welfare benefits. By 1937 unemployment was shrinking rapidly as the manufacturing sector boomed.

"Keynesian economics" would help shape social democracies after World War II. In the 1930s, however, most Western governments remained reluctant to intervene in the economy. In the areas hard hit by depression, such as coal-mining communities and port cities, the lack of government intervention meant continuing high unemployment rates and widespread poverty throughout the 1930s.

Popular Fronts in France and Spain

The limited success of democratic governments in addressing the problems of the Great Depression meant that many experienced the 1930s as a hard, hungry decade when democracy failed to deliver a decent standard of living. The examples of France and Spain illustrate both the political polarization occurring in Europe in the 1930s and the sharp limits on governments seeking both to maintain democratic politics and to improve the living conditions of their citizens.

The Great Depression hit France later than most other European nations, but by 1931 the nation was experiencing a sharp economic downturn. As the economy plummeted, social unrest rose, and so, too, did the appeal of the fascist movement. In 1934, right-wing antigovernment riots left 17 dead and more than 2,000 injured. The increasing strength of fascism, combined with the deepening national emergency, led to the formation of the Popular Front, a coalition comprising radicals, socialists, and communists.

In 1936, the Popular Front won the national elections and the Socialist Party leader Leon Blum (1872–1950) took office as prime minister. Over the next year, Blum nationalized the key war industries and gave workers further pay increases, paid holidays, and a forty-hour work week. The global financial community responded with a massive pullout of capital from France, resulting in a major financial crisis and the devaluation of the French franc. Dependent on foreign loans, Blum's government faced sharp pressure to pull back from its program of social and economic reforms. When it tried to do so, its working-class constituency rose in revolt. The Popular Front in France quickly disintegrated.

In Spain, the Popular Front was defeated not by economic pressures but by civil war. In 1931, a democratically elected republican government replaced the Spanish monarchy and in 1936, a Popular Front government, comprising both socialists and communists, took office. Army officers, led by General Francisco Franco (1892–1975), rose in rebellion and civil war began.

The struggle between the left-wing Republican government and the right-wing rebels quickly became an international issue. Both fascist Italy and Nazi Germany supported the rebellion. The Republic appealed to the democracies for aid, but the only government that came to its assistance was that of the Soviet Union. Unnerved by Soviet involvement, the governments of France, Britain, and the United States remained neutral, although 15,000 of their citizens joined the International Brigades to fight for the cause of democracy in Spain. All total, over 59,000 volunteers from fifty-five countries fought in these brigades.

The Spanish Civil War raged until March 1939, when the last remnants of the Republican forces finally surrendered. Four hundred thousand men and women died in the war; in the following four years, another 200,000 were executed. The war resulted in the death of democracy in Spain and the establishment of an authoritarian government led by Franco.

European Empires in the Interwar Era

The polarization of European politics was one important consequence of the First World War. The war also had significant—but contradictory—consequences for the structures of European empires. The war both strengthened European imperialism and accelerated the formation of mass nationalist movements that challenged imperial control.

THE EXPANSION OF EMPIRE

During the final years of World War I, the Allies claimed to be fighting for national self-determination, but they had no intention of allowing the nations under their imperial rule to determine themselves. Belgium and Portugal retained their African colonies, and Britain and France divided up Germany's African possessions. In Asia, some of the spoils went to Japan, Australia, and New Zealand (see Map 25.2). Similarly, in the Middle East the victorious Allies carved up the Ottoman Empire. France took over Syria and Lebanon; Britain established control of Iraq, Palestine, and Jordan. The British also retained a dominant influence in both Egypt and the new state of Saudi Arabia.

During the interwar period, European imperial nations placed new emphasis on the necessity and desirability of their imperial connections. The Belgian government promoted the Congo as a "model colony," while Portugal embarked on an intensive economic development campaign in its imperial territories. Throughout the 1920s and 1930s, the French government promoted colonial investments so that by 1940, over 45 percent of French overseas investment went to its empire. In Britain, a series of colonial exhibitions impressed on the British public the importance of the

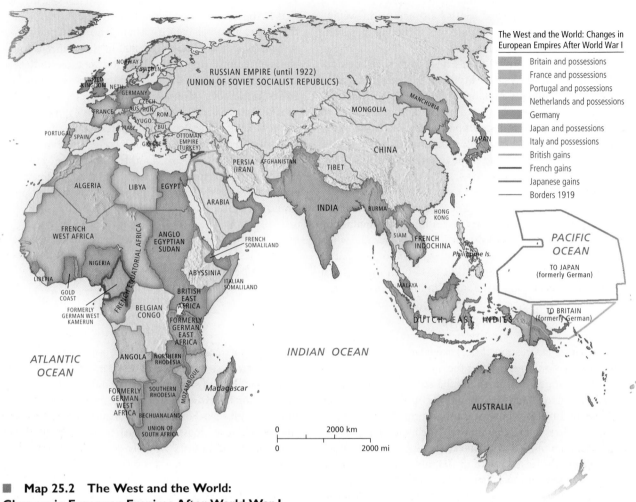

■ **Map 25.2 The West and the World: Changes in European Empires After World War I**

Britain, France, and Japan were the principal beneficiaries of Germany's loss of empire after World War I.

empire to Britain's economic prosperity, while popular British filmmakers and novelists found that imperial settings formed the perfect backdrop for tales of heroic Englishmen triumphing against all odds.

The Erosion of Empire

Yet this period also witnessed the emergence of important challenges to the imperial idea. Shifting global economic relationships and communist ideology accelerated the spread of mass nationalist movements and so eroded imperial control.

The economic demands of total war had forced Europe's imperial powers to utilize fully their colonial resources. This strategy brought with it unintended but far-reaching social changes, including the increasing migration of workers, the

expansion of cities, and the enveloping of once isolated villages in the global economic web. These unsettling changes provoked resistance, often in the form of anti-Western agitation. In African villages, anti-Western religious movements increased in number and popularity. In the growing cities, immigrants found that Islam provided an alternative cultural identity to that offered by their European rulers.

The Great Depression further accelerated the spread of mass nationalism throughout Asia and Africa. Because of the depression, the prices of primary products fell sharply. The result was disastrous for the undeveloped regions of the world that relied on income from the sales of agricultural products and raw materials. At the same time, the benefits of imperial governance diminished. Looking for ways to reduce expenditures, European governments cut funds to colonial schools, public services, and health care. Direct taxation rates rose while unemployment rates soared.

In response, nationalist movements exploded. For example, challenges to French imperial rule escalated in Tunisia, Algeria, and Indochina.

Communist ideology also played a role in the spread of nationalism in imperial territories. Lenin argued that imperialism was the logical outcome of capitalism and its quest for markets, and thus that anticapitalism and anti-imperialism went hand in hand. Under Lenin, the Soviet Union declared itself the defender of oppressed nationalities everywhere, and provided assistance to nationalist independence movements in Indonesia, Indochina, Burma, and most significantly, China, where Soviet advisers helped form the Communist Party in 1921. Led by Mao Zedong (1893–1976), the Communist Party would revolutionize Chinese society after World War II and offer a potent challenge to Western models of modernity.

THE QUESTION OF WESTERNIZATION: THE CASES OF TURKEY AND INDIA

The question of the relationship between modernity and the West was a crucial one for nationalists in non-Western regions. Nationalists sought not only political independence but also economic modernization. They wanted to establish prosperous nations on a level equal with Europe and the United States. But could modernization be achieved without westernization? Interwar developments in Turkey and India offer two different answers to this question.

To Mustafa Kemal Pasha (1881–1938), the leader of Turkey, "modernity" and "the West" seemed inseparable. A war hero, Kemal led the postwar nationalist revolt that defeated the Anglo-French plan to partition the Ottoman Empire's Turkish heartland. Kemal had no intentions of letting Western powers govern Turkey, but he was not anti-Western. To modernize Turkey, he embarked on a program of not only a state-led industrialization, but also cultural westernization. Kemal outlawed polygamy, required all Turks to take surnames (he became known as Kemal "Ataturk"—"the Turk"), and even insisted on new clothes. Western suits replaced Eastern robes, and the bowler hat replaced the fez, which Ataturk claimed was "an emblem of ignorance, negligence, fanaticism, hatred of progress and civilization."[14] This westernization did not mean democratization. Despite setting up a parliament elected by universal suffrage, Ataturk made full use of emergency executive powers to govern with an iron grip over a one-party state. He also continued the Ottoman policies of repression toward Turkey's Armenian minority.

In India, the nationalism of Mohandas Gandhi (1869–1948) offered a striking contrast to Ataturk's pro-Western approach. Gandhi transformed the Indian National Congress into a mass nationalist movement by appealing to Indian customs and religious identity. He was not opposed to modernization, but he argued that modernization did not necessarily mean westernization. Thus Gandhi (a lawyer educated in England) rejected Western dress and presented himself in the role of the religious ascetic, a familiar and deeply honored figure in Indian culture. Similarly, his insistence that the nationalist struggle be one of "moral force" rather than a physical fight drew on the Hindu tradition of nonviolence. Ordinary Indians surged into the movement, calling Gandhi "Mahatma," or "great-souled," a term of great respect. India remained the jewel in Britain's imperial crown, but the glue holding it in place was deteriorating rapidly by the end of the 1930s.

THE POWER OF THE PRIMITIVE

Just as nationalists outside the West began to challenge the idea of Western supremacy in this era, so too did westerners themselves. One of the bestsellers in Europe during the 1920s was Oswald Spengler's *The Decline of the West* (1919), which argued that western European civilization was marching along a path of inevitable decline. The poet Ezra Pound was more succinct; he described European civilization as "an old bitch, gone in the teeth."

Developments in psychology undermined the idea of Western superiority by eroding the boundaries between so-called primitive and modern cultures. In his postwar writings, Sigmund Freud (1856–1939) argued that within each individual the *id*, the unconscious force of primitive instinct, battles against the controls of the *ego*, or conscious rationality, and the *superego*, the moral values imposed by society. Although Freud taught that the continuity of civilization depended on the repression of the id, many Freudian popularizers insisted that the individual should allow his or her primitive self to run free.

The work of Freud's one-time disciple Carl Jung (1875–1961) also stressed the links between the primitive and the modern. Jung contended that careful study of an individual's dreams will show that they share common images and forms—"archetypes"—with ancient mythologies and world religions. These archetypes point to the existence of the "collective unconscious," shared by all human beings, regardless of when or where they lived. Thus, in Jung's analysis the boundary between "civilized" and "primitive," "West" and "not West," disappeared.

In the work of other thinkers and artists, that boundary remained intact, but Western notions of cultural superiority were turned upside down. The German novelist Herman Hesse (1877–1962) condemned modern industrial society as spiritually barren and celebrated Eastern mysticism as a source of power and wisdom. Similarly, the *Négritude* movement stressed the history and intrinsic value of black African culture. Founded in Paris in 1935 by French colonial students from Africa and the West Indies, Négritude condemned European culture as weak and corrupted, and called for blacks to recreate a separate cultural

■ The Power of the Primitive

When the American dancer Josephine Baker first hit the stage in Paris in 1925, her audience embraced her as the image of African savagery, even though Baker was a city kid from Philadelphia. A Parisian sensation from the moment she arrived, Baker's frenetic and passionate style of dancing, as well as her willingness to appear on stage wearing nothing but a belt of bananas, seemed to epitomize for many Europeans the essential freedom they believed their urbanized culture had lost, and that both the United States and Africa retained. As Baker's belt of bananas, designed by her white French employer, makes clear, much of this idealization of the primitive was deeply embedded in racist stereotypes. But it is also clear that both Baker's blackness and her Americanness represented a positive image of liberation to many Parisians.

and political identity. The movement stole the white racists' stereotype of the "happy dancing savage" and refigured it as positive: Black culture fostered the emotion, creativity, and human connections that white Western industrial society destroyed. More generally, a new openness to alternative intellectual and artistic traditions characterized interwar culture. This era, for example, saw a lasting transformation of popular music as the energetic rhythms of African American jazz worked their way into white musical traditions.

CONCLUSION

The Kingdom of Corpses

In 1921, the Goncourt Prize, the most prestigious award in French literature, was awarded not to a native French writer but to a colonial: René Maran, born in the French colony of Martinique. Even more striking than Maran's receiving the prize was the content of the novel for which he was honored. In *Batouala*, Maran mounted a fierce onslaught against Western culture: "Civilization, civilization, pride of the Europeans and charnel house of innocents . . . You build your kingdom on corpses."[15]

For many in the West, Maran's description of Europe as a kingdom of corpses seemed apt in the aftermath of total war. The 1920s and 1930s witnessed a dramatic re-evaluation of Western cultural and political assumptions. Both Soviet communism on the left and Nazism and fascism on the right rejected such key Western ideals as individual rights and the rule of law. Such extremist ideologies seemed persuasive in the climate of despair produced not only by the war, but by the postwar failure of democracy in eastern Europe and the collapse of the global economy after 1929. As a result, the kingdom of corpses grew: in Nazi Germany, in Spain, and most dramatically in the Soviet Union. The kingdom of corpses was, however, a particularly expansionist domain. When the 1930s ended, the West and the world stood on the brink of another total war, one in which the numbers of dead would spiral to nearly incomprehensible levels.

Suggestions for Further Reading

For a comprehensive list of suggested readings, please go to www.ablongman.com/levackconcise/chapter25

Bookbinder, Paul. *Weimar Germany: The Republic of the Reasonable.* 1996. An innovative interpretation.

Brendon, Piers. *The Dark Valley: A Panorama of the 1930s.* 2000. Fast-paced but carefully researched and comprehensive overview of the histories of the United States, Germany, Italy, France, Britain, Japan, Russia, and Spain.

Carrère D'Encausse, Hélène. *Stalin: Order Through Terror.* Vol. 2, *A History of the Soviet Union, 1917–1953.* 1981. A brief but convincing account of the way Stalin seized and held power in the Soviet Union.

Fischer, Conan. *The Rise of the Nazis.* 1995. Summarizes recent research and includes a section of primary documents.

Fitzpatrick, Sheila. *Everyday Stalinism. Ordinary Life in Extraordinary Times: Soviet Russia in the 1930s.* 1999. Explores the daily life of the ordinary urban worker in Stalinist Russia.

Fitzpatrick, Sheila. *Stalin's Peasants: Resistance and Survival in the Russian Village After Collectivization.* 1995. Superb history from the bottom up.

Getty, J. Arch, and Oleg V. Naumov. *The Road to Terror: Stalin and the Self-Destruction of the Bolsheviks, 1932–1939.* 1999. Interweaves recently discovered documents with an up-to-date interpretation of the Great Purge.

Gilbert, Bentley Brinkerhoff. *Britain 1914–1945: The Aftermath of Power.* 1996. Short, readable overview, designed for beginning students.

Jackson, Julian. *The Popular Front in France: Defending Democracy, 1934–1938.* 1988. A political and cultural history.

Kershaw, Ian. *Hitler.* 1991. A highly acclaimed biography.

Mack Smith, Denis. *Mussolini: A Biography.* 1983. An engaging read.

Pedersen, Susan. *Family, Dependence, and the Origins of the Welfare State: Britain and France, 1914–1945.* 1993. Shows how welfare policy was inextricably linked to demographic and eugenic concerns.

Rothschild, Joseph. *East Central Europe Between the Wars.* 1974. An older source, but still one of the best accounts of this tumultuous region in this tumultuous time.

Thomas, Hugh. *The Spanish Civil War.* 1977. An authoritative account.

Whittam, John. *Fascist Italy.* 1995. A short synthesis of recent research. Includes a section of primary documents and an excellent bibliographic essay.

Notes

1. Quoted in Peter Gay, *Weimar Culture* (1970), 99.
2. Quoted in Michael Burleigh, *The Third Reich: A New History* (2000), 36.
3. Quoted in Joachim Fest, *Hitler* (1973), 190–193.
4. Ibid., 192, 218.
5. Quoted in Claudia Koonz, *Mothers in the Fatherland* (1987), 130.
6. Ibid., 194.
7. Ibid., 56; Victoria DeGrazia, *How Fascism Ruled Women: Italy, 1922–1945* (1992), 234.
8. Quoted in Koonz, *Mothers in the Fatherland,* 178.
9. See J. Arch Getty and Roberta Manning, *Stalinist Terror: New Perspectives* (1993), 11, 265, 268, 280, 290.
10. Quoted in Mark Mazower, *Dark Continent: Europe's Twentieth Century* (1998), 123.
11. Quoted in Sheila Fitzpatrick, *Everyday Stalinism* (1999), 68.
12. See Stephen G. Wheatcroft, "More Light on the Scale of Repression and Excess Mortality in the Soviet Union in the 1930s," in Getty and Manning, *Stalinist Terror,* 275–290.
13. "Appendix 1: Numbers of Victims of the Terror," in J. Arch Getty and Oleg V. Naumov, *The Road to Terror: Stalin and the Self-Destruction of the Bolsheviks, 1932–1939* (1999), 587–594.
14. Quoted in Felix Gilbert, *The End of the European Era* (1991), 162.
15. Quoted in Tyler Stovall, *Paris Noir: African Americans in the City of Light* (1996), 32.

World War II

IN THE WEEKS IMMEDIATELY PRECEDING AND FOLLOWING THE END OF THE SECOND World War in Europe, many Allied soldiers faced their most difficult assignment yet. Hardened combat veterans, accustomed to scenes of slaughter and destruction, broke down and wept as they encountered a landscape of horror beyond their wildest nightmares: the world of the Nazi concentration and death camps. As one American war correspondent put it, "we had penetrated at last to the center of the black heart, to the very crawling inside of the vicious heart."[1] The American soldiers who opened the gates of the camp in Mauthausen, Austria, never forgot their first sight of the prisoners there: "By the thousands they came streaming . . . Hollow, pallid ghosts from graves and tombs, terrifying, rot-colored figures of misery marked by disease, deeply ingrained filth, inner decay. . . . squat skeletons in rags and crazy grins."[2] Similarly, the British troops who liberated Bergen-Belsen in Germany were marked indelibly by what they encountered within the camp's walls: 60,000 emaciated and diseased prisoners. Bergen-Belsen had become the dumping ground for tens of thousands of prisoners evacuated from camps in eastern Europe, as the Nazi SS desperately retreated in front of the advancing Soviet army. Already sick and starving, these prisoners were jammed, 1,200 at a time, into barracks built to accommodate a few hundred. By March 1945, both drinking water and food had disappeared, human excrement dripped from bunk beds until it coated the floors of the barracks, and dead bodies piled up everywhere. In these conditions, the only living beings to flourish were the microorganisms that cause typhus. Floundering in this sea of human want, British soldiers, doctors, and nurses did what they could; even so, 28,000 of Bergen-Belsen's inmates died in the weeks following liberation. The photographs of the mass graves taken by the Allies when they opened the camps produced an enduring image of mass killing, one that has become emblematic of what is now called the Holocaust°, the murder of approximately

Wilhelm Becker, *Bombing Raid in Berlin* (1943): The intentional and intensive bombing of civilian centers was one of the defining characteristics of the Second World War.

six million European Jews, and three to five million other victims, including Polish and Russian Christians, Jehovah's Witnesses, Roma (Gypsies), homosexuals, and political opponents of the Nazi regime.

A few months later, in August 1945, U.S. planes dropped two atomic bombs on the Japanese cities of Hiroshima and Nagasaki. Tens of thousands died within seconds. Another compelling image, the mushroom cloud, immediately seared itself on Western consciousness. As Europeans and Americans encountered the awesome destructive power of first-rate physics allied to military might, they were forced to confront the possibility of mass killing on an unprecedented, even incomprehensible, scale.

The Holocaust and the atomic bombings in Japan were not equivalent acts. Both, however, ensure the centrality of mass killing in any discussion of World War II—and in any discussion of the experience or meaning of the twentieth-century West. The assembly-line techniques of mass murder developed by the Nazis and, in very different ways, the sheer efficiency of the atom bomb in obliterating urban populations forced both individuals and their political leaders to confront the destructive potential of modern industrial technologies and techniques. In their use of Western science and technology to achieve fundamentally irrational and evil ends, the Nazi death camps upset settled assumptions about the benevolent role of intellectual and industrial endeavors in society, as well as the supposed moral superiority of Western civilization. The Bomb, too, caused widespread questioning about basic Western ideals and values. Originating in the desire to save the West from Nazi domination, its use against Japan continues to provoke heated controversy about Western motivations and to raise important questions about the implications of advanced technology for democratic decision making.

Both the Holocaust and the Bomb occurred within the context of World War II. In Hitler's quest to conquer the European continent, he joined hands with an unlikely ally: Japan. Japan's desire for a Pacific empire clashed with American and British interests in the region and transformed a European war into a global conflict. Understanding World War II, then, demands that we look not only at Germany and the results of the twisted perversions of Nazi ideology but also at global power relations, patterns of economic dependency, and the changing relationship between the West and the rest of the world.

To examine this second round of total war, this chapter focuses on five questions:

- What were the expectations concerning war in the 1920s and 1930s, and how did these hopes and fears lead to armed conflict in both Europe and Asia?
- How did Nazi Germany conquer the continent of Europe by 1941?
- Why did the Allies win in 1945?

- How and why did the war against the Jews take place, and what were its consequences?
- What did total war mean on the home fronts?

The Coming of War

The 1914–1918 war had been proclaimed the "war to end all wars." Instead, a little more than twenty years later, total war once again engulfed Europe and then the world. Adolf Hitler's ambitions for a German Empire in eastern Europe account for the immediate outbreak of war in September 1939. But other, longer-term factors also contributed, and help explain the origins of World War II. During the 1930s, a series of military conflicts underlined the fragility of the post–World War I international settlement and foreshadowed the horrors to come in World War II.

THE 1930s: PRELUDE TO WORLD WAR II

The origins of the Second World War are closely tied to the First. The treaties negotiated after 1918 created an uneasy peace, one that could not be sustained. The redrawing of eastern and central European boundaries failed to fulfill the nationalist ambitions of many groups and created new territorial resentments, while the League of Nations proved too weak to serve as the basis of a new international order.

The onset of the Great Depression in 1929 heightened this international instability. Economic nationalism intensified as nations responded to economic collapse by raising tariff walls to protect their own industries. In addition, some political leaders sought escape from economic difficulties through territorial expansion. In Japan, for example, the collapse of export markets for Japanese raw silk and cotton cloth made it difficult for the Japanese to pay for their imports of oil and other industrial resources. Japanese nationalists pushed for aggressive imperialist expansion to ensure access to vital resources. In 1931, Japanese forces seized Manchuria. Similarly, Mussolini proclaimed empire as the answer to Italy's economic woes. Seeking to expand Italy's North African holdings, Mussolini ordered his army into Ethiopia in 1935.

The Italian forces inflicted on the Ethiopian people many of the horrors soon to come to the European continent, including the saturation bombing of civilians, the use of poison gas, and the establishment of concentration camps. Yet the democracies did not act, nor did they respond the following year when Franco's military rebellion against Spain's democratically elected government sparked the Spanish Civil War. The democracies' inaction seemed to signal that aggressors could act with impunity. In 1937 the

Japanese resumed their advance in China. The Japanese conquest was brutal. In what became known as the Rape of Nanking (Nanjing), soldiers used babies for bayonet practice, gang-raped as many as 20,000 young girls and women, and left the bodies of the dead to rot in the street. The League of Nations had condemned Japan's seizure of Manchuria in 1931 but could do little else.

Against this backdrop of military aggression and the democracies' passivity, Hitler made his first moves to establish a German Empire in Europe (see Map 26.1). In 1933, he withdrew Germany from the League of Nations and two years later announced the creation of a German air force and the return of mass conscription—in deliberate violation of the terms of the Versailles Treaty. In 1936, Hitler allied with Mussolini in the Rome-Berlin Axis° and again violated his treaty obligations when he sent German troops into the Rhineland, the industrially rich region on Germany's western border. Yet France and Britain did not

respond. Two years later, in March 1938, Germany broke the Versailles Treaty once more by annexing Austria after an intense Austrian Nazi propaganda campaign punctuated by violence.

After the successful *Anschluss* ("joining") of Germany and Austria, Hitler demanded that the Sudetenland, the western portion of Czechoslovakia inhabited by a German-speaking majority, be joined to Germany as well. With France and the Soviet Union pledged to protect the territorial integrity of Czechoslovakia, Europe stood on the brink of war. The urgency of the situation impelled Britain's prime minister Neville Chamberlain (1869–1940) to fly to Munich. After intense negotiations that excluded the Czech government, Chamberlain and French prime minister Edouard Daladier agreed to the immediate German occupation of the Sudetenland. Assured by Hitler that this "Munich Agreement" satisfied all his territorial demands, Chamberlain claimed to have achieved "peace in our time."

■ **Map 26.1 The Expansion of Germany in the 1930s**

Beginning with the remilitarization of the Rhineland in 1936, Hitler embarked on a program of German territorial expansion. This map also indicates the expansion of the Soviet Union into Poland as a result of the secret terms of the German-Soviet Non-Aggression Pact.

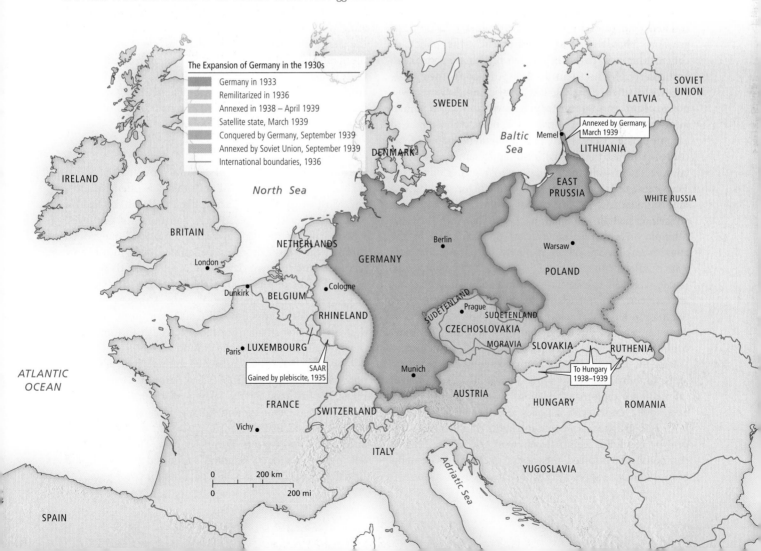

"Peace in our time" lasted for six months. In March 1939, German troops occupied the rest of Czechoslovakia. Four months later, Hitler liberated Germany from the threat of a two-front war by persuading Stalin to sign the German-Soviet Non-Aggression Pact°. The pact publicly pledged the two powers not to attack each other; it also secretly divided Poland between them and promised Stalin substantial territorial gains in the Baltic regions.

On September 1, 1939, German troops invaded Poland. The British and French declared war against Germany on September 3. Two weeks after German troops crossed Poland's borders in the west, the Soviets pushed in from the east and imposed a regime of murderous brutality. The Second World War had begun.

EVALUATING APPEASEMENT

Could Hitler have been stopped before he catapulted Europe into World War II? The debate over this question has centered on British policy during the 1930s. With the United States remaining aloof from European affairs, the communist Soviet Union regarded as a pariah state, and France weakened by economic and political crisis, Britain assumed the initiative in responding to Hitler's rise to power and his increasingly aggressive actions.

After World War II broke out, one term came to be equated with passivity and cowardice in the face of aggression. That term was appeasement°—the policy of conciliation and negotiation that British policymakers, particularly Neville Chamberlain, pursued in their dealings with Hitler in the 1930s. Chamberlain, however, was not a coward and was far from passive. Convinced he had a mission to save Europe from war, he actively sought to accommodate Hitler. For Chamberlain, and many of his contemporaries, the alternative to appeasement was a total war that would surely destroy Western civilization. They remembered the last war with horror, and agreed that the next war would be even worse. The horrendous civilian casualties inflicted by the Italian air force in Ethiopia and by the bombing of Spanish cities in the Spanish Civil War convinced many Europeans that war was completely unacceptable.

Motivated by the desire to avoid another horrible war, appeasement also rested on two additional pillars—first, the assumption that many of Germany's grievances were legitimate; second, the belief that only a strong Germany could neutralize the threat posed by Soviet communism. During the 1920s, British policymakers sought to renegotiate reparations and draw Germany back into the network of international diplomatic relations. Hitler's rise to power gave added impetus to a policy already in place. British leaders argued that they could rob Hitler of much of his appeal by rectifying legitimate German grievances. Fear of communism reinforced this desire to stabilize Germany. Many politicians applauded Hitler's moves against German

communists and welcomed the military resurgence of Germany as a strong bulwark against Soviet Russia. But in the summer of 1939, the startling announcement of the German-Soviet Non-Aggression Pact revealed the hollowness of this bulwark, just as the German invasion of Czechoslovakia in March had exposed Hitler's promises of peace as worthless.

Europe at War, 1939–1941

German soldiers crossed the Polish border on September 1, 1939; just two years later, Hitler appeared to have achieved his goal of establishing a Nazi Empire in Europe. By the autumn of 1941, almost all of continental Europe was either allied to or occupied by Nazi Germany.

A NEW KIND OF WARFARE

During these two years, the German army moved from triumph to triumph as a result of its mastery of the new technology of offensive warfare. Executing a strategy of attack that fully utilized the products of modern industry, the German military demonstrated the power of a mobile, mechanized offensive force. Germany's only defeat during these years came in the Battle of Britain, when Germany confronted a mobile, mechanized defense. Like Germany's victories, this defeat highlighted the central role of industrial production in modern warfare.

Blitzkrieg

Germany's swift conquest of Poland provided the world with a stunning demonstration of this new offensive strategy. Most of the German army, like the Polish, moved on foot or by horseback, as soldiers had done for centuries. Fast-moving motorized divisions, however, bludgeoned through the Polish defenses, penetrated deep into enemy territory, and secured key positions. While these units wreaked havoc on the ground, the Luftwaffe—the German air force—rained ruin from the air. Thirteen hundred planes shrieked across the Polish skies and in just one day destroyed the far smaller, less modern Polish air force, most of whose planes never left the ground.

Newspaper reporters christened this new style of warfare blitzkrieg°—lightning war. Western Europeans experienced blitzkrieg firsthand in the spring of 1940. The German army invaded Denmark and Norway in early April, routed the French and British troops sent to aid the Norwegians, and moved into western Europe in May. The Netherlands fell in just four days; Belgium, supported by French and British units as in World War I, held out for two weeks.

On May 27, 1940, the British army and several divisions of the French force found themselves trapped in a small pocket on the northern French coast called Dunkirk. Their destruction seemed certain. But over the next week, the only Allied success in the campaign unfolded. The British Royal Air Force (RAF) held off the Luftwaffe while the British navy and a flotilla of fishing and recreational boats helmed by British civilians evacuated the troops. By June 4, 110,000 French and almost 240,000 British soldiers had been brought safely back to Britain. But, as the newly appointed British prime minister Winston Churchill (1874–1965) reminded his cheering people, "wars are not won by evacuation."

Over the next two weeks the Germans steadily advanced through northern France, and on June 14 they marched into Paris. The French Assembly voted to disband and to hand over power to the World War I war hero Marshal Philippe Pétain (1856–1951), who established an authoritarian government. On June 22 this new Vichy regime° (named after the city Pétain chose for his capital) signed an armistice with Germany that pledged French collaboration with the Nazi government. Germany occupied France's western and northern regions, including Paris, as well as the Atlantic seaboard. One million French soldiers became prisoners of war. Germany, with its allies and satellites, held most of the continent.

■ **Victory Celebration, July 1940**

Young German girls in Berlin prepare a carpet of flowers for Hitler.

The Battle of Britain

After the fall of France, Hitler hoped that Britain would accept Germany's domination of the continent and agree to a negotiated peace. But the British government was now headed by Winston Churchill, a vocal critic of Britain's appeasement policy since 1933. In his first speech as prime minister, Churchill promised, "Victory—victory at all costs."

Faced with the British refusal to negotiate, Hitler ordered his General Staff to prepare for a land invasion of Britain. But placing German troops in the English Channel while the RAF still flew the skies would be a certain military disaster. Thus, a precondition of invasion was the destruction of the RAF. On July 10, German bomber raids on English southern coastal cities opened the Battle of Britain, a battle waged in the air—and in the factories. In the summer of 1940, British factories each month churned out twice the number of fighter aircraft produced by German plants. The British had also constructed a string of anti-aircraft gun installations and radar stations. These preparations, Britain's higher production rates of aircraft, and the fact that RAF pilots were fighting in the skies above their homes gave the British the advantage. On September 17, 1940, Hitler announced that the invasion of Britain was postponed indefinitely.

THE INVASION OF THE SOVIET UNION

War against Britain had never been one of Hitler's central goals, however. His dreams of the "Third Reich," a renewed Germanic European empire that was to last a thousand years, centered on conquest of the Soviet Union and the acquisition of its rich agricultural and industrial resources.

Hitler had planned to send his troops into the Soviet Union in April 1941, but postponed the invasion for two crucial months while German troops reinforced Italian offensives in the Balkans and North Africa. Economic considerations explain this decision. Germany received 50 percent of its cereal and livestock from the Balkan region, 45 percent of its aluminum ore from Greece, and 90 percent of its tin from Yugoslavia. Most crucially, the oil fields of Romania constituted Germany's chief source of this vital war-making resource. Without oil, there would be no *blitz* in *blitzkrieg*. By the summer of 1941, Hitler's forces succeeded in protecting German access to these important resources with dramatic victories in North Africa, Greece, and Yugoslavia. But these victories came at a high price. In the winter of 1941, the delay in beginning the Soviet invasion would imperil the German army.

On June 22, 1941, three million soldiers, the largest invading force the world had yet seen, began to cross the Soviet borders. In a matter of days, most of the Soviet air force was destroyed. In just four months, German tanks were within eighty miles of Moscow, Kiev had fallen, and Leningrad was besieged. Germany not only governed an astonishing 45 percent of the Soviet population, it also controlled access to much of the Soviet Union's natural and industrial resources, including more than 45 percent of its grain and 65 percent of its coal, iron, and steel. On October 10, Hitler's spokesman announced to the foreign press corps that the destruction of the Soviet Union was assured. German newspapers proclaimed, "CAMPAIGN IN THE EAST DECIDED!"[3]

But within just a few months, the German advance had stalled. Three obstacles halted the German invasion: stiffening Soviet resistance, the difficulty of supplying the Germans' overstretched lines, and the Russian weather. German troops rapidly squandered the huge reserves of anti-Stalinist sentiment in occupied Soviet territory by treating the local populations with fierce cruelty. German atrocities in the occupied territories strengthened the will to resist among the Soviets still in the Germans' path. Anti-German partisan units worked behind the German lines, sabotaging their transportation routes and murdering their patrols. They found the Germans especially vulnerable to this sort of attack because of their overstretched supply lines. Since June the Germans had advanced so far so fast that they overstrained their supply and communication lines. The weather worsened the logistical problems. An early October snowfall, which then melted, turned Russia's dirt roads to impassable mud. When the ground froze several weeks later, the German forces, like Napoleon's army 130 years earlier, found themselves fighting the Russian winter. By the end of the winter, the casualty list numbered more than 30 percent of the German East Army.

In the spring of 1942 the Germans would resume their advance, but the failure to deal the Soviets a quick death blow in 1941 gave Stalin and his military high command a crucial advantage—time. In zones soon to be occupied by the German army, Soviet laborers dismantled entire factories and shipped them eastward to areas out of German bombing range. Between August and October 1941, 80 percent of the Soviet war industry was in pieces, scattered among railway cars. But by 1943, these factories were rebuilt in the east and Russia was outproducing Germany: 24,000 tanks versus 17,000; 130,000 artillery pieces versus 27,000; 35,000 combat aircraft versus 25,000. In a total war, in which victory occurs on the assembly line as well as on the front line, these were ominous statistics for Hitler and his dreams of a German Empire.

The World at War, 1941–1945

The West's imperialist legacy ensured that World War II was not confined to Europe. Britain would never have been able to stand alone against the German-occupied continent without access to the resources of its colonies and Commonwealth. Britain also drew heavily on the resources of the still neutral United States. In March 1941, the U.S. Congress passed the Lend-Lease Act°, which guaranteed to supply Britain all needed military supplies, with payment postponed until after the war ended. Lend-Lease gave first Britain and then the Soviets access to the incredible might of American industry. German efforts to block British access to these resources spread the war into the Atlantic, where British merchant marines battled desperately against German submarines. At the end of 1941, however, an astonishing Japanese offensive in the Pacific fused together the previously separate Asian and European conflicts, drew in the United States, and made World War II a truly global war.

Throughout the 1930s both Britain and the United States had watched warily as Japan embarked on its expansionist moves. Then in 1941 the Japanese occupied Indochina, and the United States responded by placing an embargo on trade in oil with Japan. Japan's imperial ambitions demanded that it move decisively before its oil ran out. The South Pacific, a treasure house of mineral and other resources, beckoned. Between December 7 and 10, 1941, Japanese forces launched successful attacks against American, British, and Dutch territories in the Pacific. The U.S. Pacific fleet base of Pearl Harbor, Hawaii, was gutted; Guam, Wake Island, and Hong Kong fell quickly; by the end of February both Malaya and Singapore were defeated as well. By May, the Japanese cemented this astounding success with the conquest of Indonesia, Burma, and the Philippines. In just a few months, Japan had established itself as imperial overlord of the South Pacific, with its wealth of raw materials (see Map 26.2).

The audacity of the Japanese attack impressed Hitler, who declared war on the United States on December 11, 1941. In Europe Germany now faced the alliance of Britain, the Soviet Union, and the United States. Even against such an alliance, Germany appeared to occupy a strong position. By January 1942, German troops in North Africa stood within two hundred miles of the strategically vital Suez Canal and in the spring the German army resumed its advance in the Soviet Union. With Germany on the move in the east and Japan controlling the Pacific, the Allies looked poised to lose the war.

FROM ALLIED DEFEAT TO ALLIED VICTORY IN EUROPE

Twelve months later the situation had changed, and the Allies were on the road to eventual victory. This road, however, proved long and arduous. The period from 1942 through 1945 was marked by horrendous human suffering and cataclysmic military battles. Yet in the end American and Soviet industrial supremacy, allied with a superior military strategy, pushed the balance in the Allies' favor.

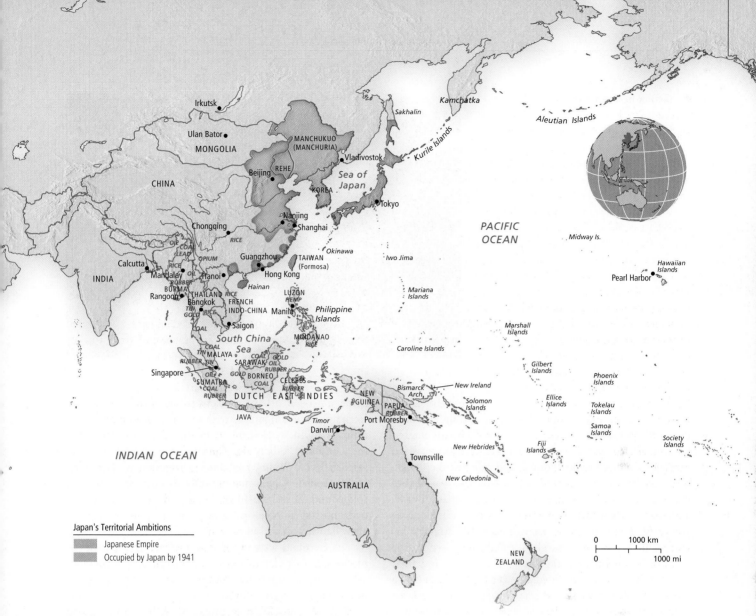

■ **Map 26.2 Japan's Territorial Ambitions**

Lacking its own supply of natural resources, Japan embarked on imperial conquest.

The Turning Point:
Midway, El Alamein, and Stalingrad

The second half of 1942 proved the turning point as three very different battles helped transform the course of the war. In the Pacific, victory at the Battle of Midway gave the U.S. forces a decisive advantage. In North Africa, British forces experienced their first battlefield victory at El Alamein, and in Europe, the Battle of Stalingrad dealt Germany a blow from which it never recovered.

The Battle of Midway was the result of the Japanese effort to ensure its air supremacy by drawing the U.S. Pacific fleet's aircraft carriers into battle. To do so, the Japanese attacked Midway Island, a U.S. outpost, on June 4, 1942. By midmorning the Japanese had shot down two-thirds of the American planes. But then an American dive-bomber group that had gotten lost suddenly found itself above the main Japanese carriers. Caught in the act of refueling and rearm-

ing the strike force, their decks cluttered with gas lines and bombs, the carriers made remarkably combustible targets. In five minutes, three of Japan's four carriers were destroyed; the fourth was sunk later in the day. Japan's First Air Fleet was decimated. The destruction of the Japanese fleet dealt Japan a blow from which it could not recover. The United States possessed the industrial resources to rebuild its lost ships and airplanes. Japan did not. In five explosive minutes at Midway the course of the Pacific war changed.

In contrast, the battle of El Alamein marked the culmination of more than two years of fighting in North Africa. In September 1940, Mussolini had ordered his troops to advance from Libya (an Italian colony) into Egypt, as part of his effort to establish an Italian empire in the Mediterranean. That winter British and Australian troops not only pushed the Italians back but drove far into Libya itself. The stakes were too high for Hitler to let his Italian ally lose:

555

■ Stuck in the Mud

Climate and geography proved unbeatable foes for the German army in the Soviet Union. The thaw following an October snowfall turned the roads to mud and greatly slowed the German advance. The onset of real winter the following month brought far worse conditions.

Whoever held North Africa would control both the strategically and economically vital Suez Canal and the southern shipping lanes of the Mediterranean. The Germans entered the conflict and by June 1941, the German Afrika Korps, led by Field Marshal Erwin Rommel, had muscled the British back into Egypt. For more than a year the two armies pushed each other back and forth across the desert. But finally British Field Marshal Bernard Montgomery, an abrasive, arrogant man whose meticulous battle strategy included the leaking of false plans, caught the Germans by surprise at El Alamein in October 1942.

One month later combined British and American forces landed in Morocco and Algeria, and over the next six months pushed Germany out of North Africa. The following year North Africa served as the Allies' jumping-off point for their invasion of southern Italy in July 1943. El Alamein thus marked a crucial turning point in the war. Churchill said of it, "It is not the beginning of the end, but it may be the end of the beginning."[4]

Churchill's apt description fits the third turning point of 1942, the Battle of Stalingrad, as well. In July the German army was sweeping southward toward the oil-rich Caucasus. Hitler ordered the southern offensive split into two, with one arm reaching up to conquer Stalingrad on the Volga River. The conquest of Stalingrad would give the Germans control over the main waterway for the transport of oil and food from the Caucasus to the rest of the Soviet Union: The Soviet lifeline would be cut. But by dividing his offensive, Hitler widened his front from 500 to 2,500 miles. By the time the German Sixth Army reached Stalingrad on August 23, German resources were fatally overstretched.

Recognizing Germany's vulnerability, Stalin's generals assured him they could attack the exposed German lines and then encircle the German Sixth Army—but only if Stalingrad's defenders could hold on for almost two months while they assembled the necessary men and ma-

chinery. An epic urban battle ensued, with the Russian and German soldiers fighting street by street, house by house, room by room. By November, the Russians had surrounded the Germans. When the German commander, General Friedrich von Paulus, requested permission to surrender, Hitler replied, "The army will hold its position to the last soldier and the last cartridge."[5] Paulus finally disobeyed orders and surrendered on January 30, 1943, but by then his army had almost ceased to exist.

The Germans were never able to make up the losses in manpower, material, or morale they suffered at Stalingrad. The colossal struggle turned the course of the European war. Beginning in the summer of 1943, the Russians steadily pushed westward. By the spring of 1944 the Red Army had reached the borders of Poland. In August Soviet troops turned south into Romania and Hungary. By February 1945 they were within 100 miles of Berlin (see Map 26.3).

The Fall of Germany

As the Red Army closed in on Germany from the east, the British and Americans pushed in from the south and the west. Responding both to Stalin's pleas for a "Second Front" in Europe to relieve the pressure on Soviet troops and to Churchill's desire to protect British economic interests in the Mediterranean, the Allies invaded Italy. On July 10, 1943, Anglo-American forces landed in Sicily, prepared to push up into what Churchill called the "soft underbelly" of German-controlled Europe. Within just fifteen days, Mussolini had been overthrown and his successor opened peace negotiations with the Allies. But then German muscle hardened that soft underbelly: The German army occupied Italy. British and American soldiers faced a long, brutal, slow-moving push up the peninsula. Ridged with mountains and laced with rivers, Italy formed a natural defensive fortress. In an eight-month period, the Allied forces advanced only seventy miles.

The real "Second Front" did not open up for another year, when the Allies carried out the largest amphibious operation the world had ever seen. On June 6, 1944, American, British, and Canadian troops crossed the English Channel and landed on beaches in northern France. The "D-Day" landings illustrated the Allied advantage in key resources. Against the Allies' eight divisions, the Germans had four; against the Allies' 5,000 fighter planes, the Germans could send up 169. The Allies, however, faced the formidable task of uprooting the Germans from territory where they had planted themselves five years earlier. For ten long months, the British, American, Canadian, and imperial troops fought a series of hard-won battles. But by mid-April the British and American armies stood within fifty miles of Berlin.

The Allies agreed to leave the conquest of Berlin to the Soviet Army. In this climactic battle of the European war, 320,000 Germans, many of them young boys, fought three million Soviet troops. Even so, it took eleven days before the city's commander surrendered on May 2. Two days earlier, Hitler had taken a cyanide capsule and then shot himself with his service pistol. On May 7, 1945, General Alfred Jodl (1890–1946) signed the unconditional surrender of German forces.

THE AIR WAR, THE ATOM BOMB, AND THE FALL OF JAPAN

When Germany surrendered, the war in the Pacific was still raging. After the Midway battle of 1942, the United States slowly pushed the Japanese back island by island. While U.S. troops moved closer to the Japanese mainland, British and Indian troops rebuffed a Japanese attempt to invade India and pushed the Japanese out of Burma. Australian forces, with American assistance, held the line at New Guinea and forestalled a Japanese invasion of Australia. By February 1945, then, when U.S. Marines landed on the small island of Iwo Jima, just 380 miles from Japan's home

■ **Map 26.3   Allied Victory in Europe, 1942–1945**
Beginning in late 1942, Allied forces moved onto the offensive.

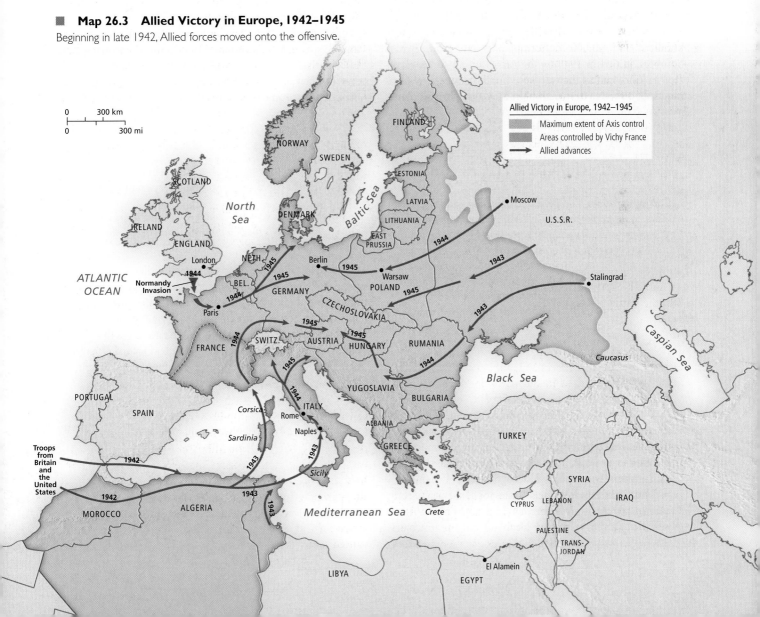

islands, the Japanese war effort was in tatters and an Allied victory was ensured. Obtaining this final victory, however, proved far from easy. In the month of fighting for the island of Iwo Jima, one-third of the American landing force died or suffered injury. The April conquest of Okinawa was even more hard-won. Outnumbered two to one, the Japanese endured unbelievable losses—110,000 of the 120,000 soldiers on the island died. Yet they still inflicted serious damage on the attacking force, killing or wounding 50,000 Americans before the fight was over.

The Air War

Despite the high price exacted to win them, the battles of Iwo Jima and Okinawa were significant victories: The United States now had the bases it needed to bomb Japanese cities. This air war utilized tactics and technologies developed over the previous five years in Europe. For many European civilians, World War II was the war of the bomber. In Britain, until late 1941, civilian deaths outnumbered military, and most civilians died in bombing raids. During autumn 1940, Londoners endured the "Blitz"—seventy-six consecutive nights of mass bombing. By May 1941, almost every main industrial city in Britain had been bombed, and 43,000 noncombatants lay dead. British bombers, joined in 1943 by the American air force, retaliated in kind, and as the war wore on, developed new techniques of airborne destruction. In May 1942, British planes

destroyed Cologne with the world's first 1,000-bomber raid, and one year later, introduced the world to the horror of the firestorm with the bombing of Hamburg. In this human-made catastrophe, fires caused by incendiary bombs combine with winds to suck the oxygen out of the air and raise temperatures to combustible levels. As one survivor recalled, "The smallest children lay like fried eels on the pavement."[6] In a single night, 45,000 of Hamburg's residents were killed. In total, more than 500,000 German civilians died in bombing attacks. Twenty percent of the dead were children.

In 1945 the conquests of Iwo Jima and Okinawa enabled the U.S. air command to adopt the tactics perfected in the skies over Germany as a key strategy to defeat Japan. On one March evening, American bombs and the ensuing firestorm killed 85,000 residents of Tokyo. Over the next five months, American bombers hit sixty-six Japanese cities, burned 180 square miles, and killed approximately 330,000 Japanese. At the same time, a U.S. naval blockade cut Japan off from its supply lines.

The Manhattan Project

While American bombers pulverized Japanese cities during the spring and summer of 1945, a multinational group of scientists fought a very different sort of battle in a secret military installation in New Mexico. The Manhattan Project°, the code name for the joint British-American-

---

LIVING UNDER THE BOMBS
·················

During the 1930s, European statesmen and politicians condemned the aerial bombing of civilian populations as an act of barbarity and criminality. Once World War II began, the targeting of civilians in order to break home-front morale and impede industrial production became commonplace. Analysts disagree about the military effectiveness of urban bombing, but no one can dispute the human horror.

In this first excerpt, an elderly air warden from Hull, one of Britain's northern port cities, is speaking. One night, when he returned from his post, he found that his street:

Was as flat as this 'ere wharfside—there was just my 'ouse like—well, part of my 'ouse. My missus were just making me a cup of tea for when I come 'ome. She were in the passage between the kitchen and the wash'ouse, where it blowed 'er. She were burnt right up to 'er waist. 'Er legs were just two cinders. And 'er face—The only thing I could recognize 'er by was one of 'er boots—I'd 'ave lost fifteen 'omes if I could 'ave kept my missus. We used to read together. I can't read mesen [myself]. She used to read to me like. We'd 'ave our armchairs

on either side o' the fire, and she read me bits out o' the paper. We 'ad a paper every evening. Every evening.

In the following excerpt, a German woman, 19 years old on July 28, 1943, recalls the bombing of Hamburg and the firestorm it induced:

We came to a door which was burning just like a ring in a circus through which a lion has to jump. . . . I struggled to run against the wind in the middle of the street but could only reach a house on the corner. . . . We got to the Loschplatz [park] all right but I couldn't go across the Eiffestrasse [street] because the asphalt had melted. There were people on the roadway, some already dead, some still lying alive but stuck in the asphalt. They must have rushed on to the roadway without thinking. Their feet had got stuck and then they put out their hands to try to get out again. They were on their hands and knees screaming.

Sources: Excerpt from a Mass-Observation typescript report, filed at Mass-Observations offices, no. 844, August 23, 1941. Copyright © by the Trustees of the Mass-Observation Archive. Reprinted by permission; and from Martin Middlebrook, *The Battle of Hamburg*, Allen Lane, 1980. Reprinted by permission of the author.

Canadian effort to construct an atom bomb, was an extraordinary endeavor, the biggest and most expensive weapons research and development project up to that point in history. Comprising thirty-seven installations in nineteen American states and in Canada, it employed 120,000 individuals. Yet this gargantuan effort was top-secret, unknown even to American vice president Harry Truman, who first learned of the project only after President Roosevelt died.

The Manhattan Project originated as part of the war against Germany, not Japan. When the European war began, a number of scientists—many of them eastern and central European émigrés who had fled the Nazis, many of them Jewish—feared that Germany, with its stellar tradition of scientific research and state-of-the-art laboratories, possessed the potential for developing an atom bomb. They pressured the British and American governments to build the Bomb before Hitler did so. Britain took the initial lead by creating a committee to oversee atomic research in the spring of 1940. By the following summer, British research had persuaded the Americans that an atom bomb could be constructed. In October 1941—two months before Japan bombed Pearl Harbor—Roosevelt and Churchill agreed to create an atomic partnership.

For three years the Manhattan Project scientists labored to unlock the atom's power. They finally succeeded on July 16, 1945, when the world's first atomic explosion—the Trinity test—detonated over the desert of New Mexico. The date of the Trinity test is crucial because by the time of the test, Nazi Germany had already fallen to the Allies, and Japan was staggering under the combined effects of the American naval blockade and nightly bombing raids. Given this situation, the decision to use atom bombs against Japan generated controversy from the very start. Many of the scientists on the Manhattan Project opposed the decision, as did important American military officials such as General Dwight Eisenhower (1890–1969), supreme commander of the Allied forces in Europe; General Douglas MacArthur (1880–1964), supreme commander of the Allied forces in the Pacific; and Admiral William Leahy (1875–1959), chairman of the U.S. Joint Chiefs of Staff.

Advocates of dropping the atom bomb on Japan argued that the fierce Japanese resistance encountered by Americans at Iwo Jima and Okinawa and by the British in Burma signaled that an invasion of Japan's home islands would result in horrifying casualties. Leahy noted to Truman that if casualty rates were as high as those on Okinawa, then the numbers of Americans killed in the first phase of the invasion could reach 50,000. An invasion of Japan was, however, not a foregone conclusion in the spring and summer of 1945. Leahy and others argued that the naval blockade would end the war *without* an invasion, and in 1946, the U.S. Strategic Bombing Survey concluded that "in all probability prior to 1 November 1945, Japan would have surrendered . . . even if no invasion had been planned or contemplated." Survey officials, of course, had the bene-

fit of hindsight, an advantage denied to Truman and his advisers in the summer of 1945. But more important, from Truman's perspective, continuing to blockade and to drop conventional bombs on Japan meant continuing to put American soldiers in harm's way, a cost he was unwilling to pay. The atom bomb's appeal was not in its potential to kill tens of thousands in a single night; conventional bombs were already doing that, and doing it rather effectively. But the idea of massive casualties, caused by a single atomic bomb, dropped by a single plane, promised to have an enormous psychological impact on the Japanese, and so to end the war more quickly and to bring American servicemen home.

A Light Brighter Than a Thousand Suns

As a result, at 8:15 A.M. on August 6, 1945, an American plane named the *Enola Gay* (after the pilot's mother) dropped an atom bomb above the city of Hiroshima. A light "brighter than a thousand suns" flashed in the sky.

■ The Mushroom Cloud

The detonation of the atomic bomb over Hiroshima on August 6, 1945, produced what would become one of the most familiar images of the post–World War II age.

Temperatures at the site of the atomic explosion reached 5,400 degrees Fahrenheit. All those exposed within two miles of the center suffered primary thermal burns—their blood literally boiled and their skin peeled off in strips. Scientists calculated that the atom bomb produced casualties 6,500 times more efficiently than an ordinary bomb. Of Hiroshima's wartime population of 400,000, 140,000 died by the end of 1945, with another 60,000 dying in the next five years.

The Japanese reacted to the atomic bombing of Hiroshima with incomprehension and confusion. They literally did not know what had hit them. Within the high levels of the Japanese government, gradual realization of the atomic bomb's power strengthened the position of those officials who recognized that Japan must now give up. A hardline faction of the military, however, wished to fight on. Then, on August 8, the Soviet Union declared war on Japan. The next day American forces dropped an atom bomb on the city of Nagasaki and killed 70,000 outright, with another 70,000 dying over the next five years. On August 10, Emperor Hirohito told his military leaders to surrender. Viewed in the West as an implacable warlord, Hirohito was actually a man with fairly limited political power who had been pressing for peace since June. Negotiations between the Allies and the Japanese continued until August 15, when hostilities ended.

In Hiroshima and Nagasaki, however, another war was raging, this time against an unseen and at first unrecognized enemy—radiation. The lingering horror of radiation sickness, accounts of which were at first dismissed by many Americans as Japanese propaganda, signaled that the atom bomb was not just a bigger weapon, not simply more bang for the buck. In the months after the war's end, Europeans and Americans came to recognize that the revolutionary new force of atomic power had introduced the world to new possibilities—and new horrors.

The War Against the Jews

In the months following the war's end, the world confronted a very different sort of horror, as people began to piece together the story of Hitler's war against the Jews. For European Jews, World War II brought unprecedented terror and, for millions, death. Chapter 25 explained that hatred of the Jewish people stood at the heart of Hitler's world view and Nazi ideology. Yet anti-Semitism alone cannot explain the mass murder that we now call the Holocaust, nor was the Holocaust the product of a detailed plan carefully plotted by Hitler long before he came to power. The decision to murder Europe's Jews evolved over time, in the context of total war.

FROM EMIGRATION TO EXTERMINATION: THE EVOLUTION OF GENOCIDE

During the 1930s, Nazi policies focused on forcing German Jews to emigrate. By 1938, these policies had driven out about 25 percent of Germany's Jewish population. At the same time, however, the unification of Germany and Austria, followed by the seizure first of the Sudetenland and then all of Czechoslovakia, meant 300,000 more Jews in the expanded Germany. These numbers skyrocketed with the outbreak of the war. The invasion of Poland brought almost two million more Jews under German control. Pushing Jews to emigrate no longer seemed a workable solution to what the Nazis defined as the "Jewish Problem." But even more important, the fact of war itself made a radicalization of policy and a turn toward murderous violence much more acceptable.

The German occupation of Poland marked the first step toward the Nazi construction of a new racial order in Europe. Hitler intended the Slavic populations, defined in his racist hierarchy as biologically inferior, to serve as a vast labor pool for their German superiors. To reduce the Polish people to slaves, the Nazis embarked on a wholesale destruction of Polish society and culture. They seized businesses and bank accounts; replaced Polish place names with German; closed universities and high schools; and murdered Polish intellectuals and professionals. By the time the war ended in 1945, more than 20 percent of Poland's population had died.

Within the context of their larger plan of racial reordering, Nazi officials talked about "eliminating" Jews from Poland. At this point, however, "elimination" did not yet mean total extermination but instead referred to vaguely articulated plans for mass deportations. Thus German policy toward the Jews in Poland initially focused on "ghettoization." The Nazis forcibly expelled Jews from their homes and confined them in ghettos sealed off from their non-Jewish neighbors. Packed into overcrowded apartments, with inadequate food rations and appalling sanitary conditions, the ghetto populations lived in a nightmare of disease, starvation, and death.

In the almost two-year period between the invasion of Poland and the invasion of the Soviet Union, an estimated 30,000 Jews died, killed outright by German soldiers or dying a more lingering death from starvation and disease as a result of deportation and ghettoization. Yet the suffering had only begun. In the summer or fall of 1941, the Nazis decided on what they termed the Final Solution° to the "Jewish Problem": genocide.

The German invasion of the Soviet Union helped shape the "Final Solution." Marching with the forces of the regular army were special mobile units of the SS called Einsatzgruppen° ("strike forces"). With the army providing logistical support, these small motorized units (about 3,000 men in all) took on the task of liquidating those designated as enemies of the Nazi Reich—which meant killing communists and Jews.

Most of these murders followed the same general pattern: SS soldiers rounded up all of the Jewish men, women, and children in a town or village and marched them in batches to a field or woods. They ordered the first batch to dig a large ditch. They then stripped their victims of their clothing, lined them up on the edge of the ditch, and shot them at point-blank range. Subsequent batches were lined up and shot as well, so that by the end of a day's worth of killing, dead and dying bodies filled the ditch. A thin layer of soil was then thrown on top, transforming the ditch into a mass grave. Estimates of the final death count of the Einsatzgruppen actions range from 1.5 to 2 million.

In their war against the Jews, the Einsatzgruppen found ready allies among large sectors of the occupied population. Recall that the earliest stages of the German invasion of the Soviet Union took place in the territories that had been seized by the Soviets in 1939 as a result of the German-Soviet Non-Aggression Pact. Hence the local populations often welcomed the German troops as liberators and aided the SS in hunting down and killing Jews. In Lvov in eastern Galicia, for example, anti-Soviet Ukrainian fighters turned on the large Jewish community and in two days of violence killed at least 7,000 Jews—*before* the Einsatzgruppen had even arrived.

THE DEATH CAMPS: MURDER BY ASSEMBLY LINE

On January 20, 1942, senior German officials met in a villa in Wannsee, outside Berlin, to finalize plan for killing every Jew in Europe. SS Lieutenant Colonel Adolf Eichmann (1906–1962) listed the number of Jews in every country; even the Jewish populations in neutral countries such as Sweden and Ireland showed up on the target list. The Wannsee Conference marked the beginning of a more systematic approach to murdering European Jews, one that built on the experience gained by the Einsatzgruppen in the Soviet war.

To accomplish mass murder, the Einsatzgruppen had become killing machines. By trial and error, they discovered the most efficient ways of identifying and rounding up Jews, shooting them quickly, and burying the bodies. But the Einsatzgruppen actions also revealed the limits of conventional methods of killing. Shooting took time, used up valuable ammunition, and required large numbers of men. Moreover, even the best-trained and carefully indoctrinated soldiers eventually cracked under the strain of shooting unarmed women and children at close range. A systematic approach was needed, one that would utilize advanced killing technology and provide a comfortable

distance between the killers and the killed. This perceived need resulted in a key Nazi innovation: the death camp.

The death camp was a specialized form of a concentration camp. From 1933 on, Hitler's government had sentenced communists, Jehovah's Witnesses, the Roma, and anyone else defined as an enemy of the regime to forced labor in concentration camps. After the war began, the concentration camp system expanded dramatically. Scattered throughout Nazi-controlled Europe, concentration camps became an essential part of the Nazi war economy. Some firms, such as the huge chemical conglomerate I. G. Farben, established factories inside or right next to camps, which provided vital supplies of forced labor. All across Europe during the war, concentration camp inmates died in huge numbers from the brutal physical labor, torture, and diseases brought on by malnutrition and inadequate housing and sanitary facilities. But it was only in Poland that the Nazis constructed *death* camps, specialized concentration camps with only one purpose—murder, primarily the murder of Jews.

The death camps marked the final stage in a vast assembly line of murder. In early 1942 the trains conveying Jewish victims to the death camps began to rumble across Europe. Jewish ghettos across Nazi-occupied Europe emptied as their inhabitants moved in batches to their deaths. Individuals selected for extermination followed orders to gather at the railway station for deportation to "work camps" farther east. They were then crammed onto cattle cars, more than 100 people per car, all standing up for the entire journey. Deprived of food and water, with hardly any air, and no sanitary facilities, often for several days, many Jews died en route. The survivors stumbled off the trains into a nightmare world. At some camps, SS guards culled stronger Jews from each transport to be worked to death as slave laborers. Most, however, walked straight from the transport trains into a reception room, where they were told to undress, and then herded into a "shower room"— actually a gas chamber. Carbon monoxide gas or a pesticide called Zyklon-B killed the victims. After the poison had done its work, Jewish slaves emptied the chamber and burned the bodies in vast crematoria, modeled after industrial bake ovens.

The Nazis thus constructed a vast machine of death. In this machine, slave laborers constituted key components, each with identification numbers tattooed onto their forearms, a type of human "bar coding." Along a murderous assembly line the human raw material moved from arrival through selection to the undressing rooms to the gas chamber to the crematoria. Approximately three million Jews died in these factories of death. The death camp victims joined the millions who starved or died of disease in the ghettoes, suffocated in the cattle cars, were shot in mass graves, or worked to death in the labor camps. Children were especially vulnerable. Of the Jewish children living in

■ **Mass Grave at Bergen-Belsen**

This concentration camp was liberated by British soldiers on April 15, 1945.

1939 in the regions already or soon to be under German control, only 11 percent survived.

In total, the Holocaust claimed the lives of approximately six million Jews. The number of Roma victims remains unclear. Somewhere between 200,000 and 600,000 died in what the Roma call the *Porajmos*—the Devouring. Jews and Gypsies were the only groups singled out for total extermination based on their supposed biological identity. But Hitler's drive to create his new Germany claimed three to five million other victims as well. Five to fifteen thousand homosexuals perished. So, too, did as many as three million Polish Christians.

THE ALLIES' RESPONSE

Allied leaders had access to surprisingly accurate information about the Holocaust from very early on. British code breakers translated German military radio transmissions throughout the summer of 1941 so that as the German army—and the Einsatzgruppen—moved into the Soviet Union, British officials confronted intercepted messages such as this one from August 27: "Regiment South shot 914 Jews; the special action staff with police battalion 320 shot 4,200 Jews." By June 1942, Allied leaders knew that death camps existed.

Such information quickly became accessible to ordinary people. British and American newspaper readers and radio listeners received numerous reports about Jewish massacres; after 1942, these reports told about the death camps.

But this information had to compete with other war news and many of these articles were written in a skeptical tone, as both reporters and editors had a difficult time believing that such atrocities could be taking place. Pressure from Jewish and non-Jewish public-interest groups did succeed in pushing the British and American governments to issue an inter-Allied declaration in December 1942 that in no uncertain terms announced and condemned Hitler's effort to exterminate European Jewry. This declaration was broadcast all over the world.

Despite this official acknowledgment of the mass murder of Jews, the Allies did not act directly to stop the killings. Should the Allies then be considered bystanders in the crime of the Holocaust? Some historians contend that anti-Semitism in both British and American society structured the Allies' military priorities and prevented leaders from exploring strategies such as sending in commando units, bombing the rail lines into the death camps, or even bombing the camps themselves. Other historians argue that these alternatives were not militarily feasible, and that the Allies did the only thing they could do on the Jews' behalf—win the war as quickly as possible.

In the months after the war ended, Allied leaders struggled to bring Nazi leaders to trial to account for their crimes. What one participant called "the greatest trial in history" opened on November 14, 1945. For eleven months, a tribunal of four judges—American, British, French, and Soviet—sat in a courtroom in the German city of Nuremberg to judge nineteen prominent German military, political, and industrial leaders. The Nuremberg trials°, broadcast by the crowds of journalists packed into the courtroom, offered the world its first encounter with the Holocaust. The trials highlighted the Nazi onslaught against European Jewry as one of the most horrendous of the Nazis' many "crimes against humanity," a category first introduced into international law at Nuremberg.

The Home Fronts: The Other Wars

As the Holocaust made vividly clear, for many Europeans during World War II the home front was not a place of safety or normalcy but a place where other wars were fought. The spreading resistance against the Nazi regime, as well as bombing raids and forced labor obligations, obliterated the distinction between combatant and noncombatant, blurred gender roles, and provoked calls for radical social change.

THE LIMITS OF RESISTANCE

Throughout the war individuals and groups in occupied Europe performed heroically, hiding Jews and others on the run, sabotaging equipment, disrupting transportation systems, and relaying secret information to the Allies. In the Soviet Union and in mountainous regions of Yugoslavia, Italy, and southern France, where the terrain offered shelter for guerillas, anti-Nazi fighters formed partisan groups that attacked German army units. In one of the best-known cases of resistance, the Jews in the Warsaw ghetto rose up in the spring of 1943. Armed with only one or two submachine guns and a scattering of pistols, rifles, hand grenades, and gasoline bombs, Jewish fighters held off the far superior German military force for more than a month. In the end, however, the ghetto was leveled and all its survivors deported to Nazi death camps.

The deaths of the Warsaw Ghetto rebels illustrates why only a minority of Europeans served in the Resistance. Concerned for their own and their families' safety, most Europeans hoped simply to keep their heads down and survive the war. The German practice of exacting collective retribution for Resistance actions particularly undercut mass support for anti-German efforts. In 1942, for example, British intelligence forces parachuted Czech agents into German-held Czechoslovakia. The agents assassinated the chief SS official in the region, Reinhard Heydrich (1904–1942), but they were immediately betrayed by one of their own. In retaliation, the Germans massacred the entire population of the village of Lidice.

CHRONOLOGY

1931	Japan invades Manchuria
1936	Spanish Civil War begins
1938	Germany annexes Austria; occupies the Sudetenland
1939	
March 15	Germany invades Czechoslovakia
August 23	German-Soviet Non-Aggression Pact
September 1	Germany invades Poland
September 3	Britain and France declare war on Germany
1940	Germany conquers western Europe
1941	
June 22	Germany invades Soviet Union; Einsatzgruppen begin mass killings of Jews
December 7	Japan bombs Pearl Harbor
1942	
January 20	Wannsee Conference: "Final Solution" agreed on
June 4	Battle of Midway
August 23	German Sixth Army reaches Stalingrad
October 23	Battle of El Alamein begins
1944	D-Day landings
1945	
May 7	Official German surrender
July 16	Trinity test
August 6	Atomic bombing of Hiroshima
August 9	Atomic bombing of Nagasaki
September 2	Official Japanese surrender

Divisions within the Resistance also limited its impact. In many regions, conservatives fighting to preserve the prewar status quo clashed with guerilla groups that espoused radical political goals. The fiercest struggle occurred in Yugoslavia, where political and ethnic divisions split both the country and the Resistance. Parts of the country such as Slovenia and Macedonia were occupied by German or German-allied armies and endured brutal repression. In Croatia, a Nazi-sponsored fascist regime embarked on a

The Trial of Adolf Eichmann

On May 23, 1960, David Ben-Gurion (1886–1973), the prime minister of Israel, made a spectacular announcement: Israeli secret service agents had kidnapped Adolf Eichmann, a wanted Nazi war criminal, and smuggled him into Israel to await trial. Eichmann, the head of the Gestapo's Jewish Affairs unit, had implemented Nazi policies on Jewish emigration and deportation. His office sorted through the complicated bureaucratic procedures to ensure that the trains laden with Jews kept to their schedules and delivered their human cargo to the gas chambers on time. It was to Eichmann that Jewish leaders came to plead for emigration visas and for work permits. It was with Eichmann that Jewish leaders negotiated about the timing, size, and composition of deportations. For many Jews, then, Eichmann represented German power and came to personify Nazi evil. He had disappeared in the chaotic final days of World War II and eventually made his way to Argentina, where, as "Ricardo Klement," he lived a quiet, respectable life with his wife and children—until 1960.

From the moment of Ben-Gurion's sensational announcement, the Eichmann case occupied the attention of the world. Six hundred foreign correspondents attended the trial, which was one of the first to be filmed by television cameras. More than 1,500 documents were submitted and 120 witnesses testified in the 114 sessions held between April 11 and August 14,

1961. Three judges, each of whom had been born in Germany and had emigrated to Palestine in 1933, heard the evidence. On December 15, they sentenced Eichmann to death. He died by hanging on May 31, 1962, the first execution in Israel, which had abolished capital punishment for all crimes except genocide.

The Eichmann trial told the story of Jewish suffering during World War II to the widest possible audience. Both Ben-Gurion and the chief prosecutor, Gideon Hausner, stated publicly that the trial aimed to construct "a living record of a gigantic human and national disaster," and so educate both young Israelis and the entire world in the causes and consequences of the Holocaust.[7] As Hausner explained in his emotional opening statement, he saw himself as the spokesman for "six million accusers . . . [whose] ashes were piled up in the hills of Auschwitz and in the fields of Treblinka, or washed away by the rivers of Poland."[8] Hausner (who, like many Israelis, had lost most of his relatives in the Nazi death camps) called more than 100 witnesses, many of them death camp survivors. Their testimony, published or broadcast throughout the world, painted an unforgettable and detailed picture of the horror of genocide.

By the time the prosecution rested its case, no one could doubt that Eichmann was a guilty man, one who had played an essential role in the murder of millions. Yet the Eichmann trial attracted an enormous amount of criti-

cism, and continues to arouse great controversy. Critics charged that to achieve moral justice for Holocaust victims and survivors, the Israeli court committed a legal injustice against Eichmann. The trial was not only made possible by a violation of international law (Eichmann's kidnapping), it also was filled with irregularities, including the introduction of testimony that did not pertain to the specific crimes charged. Critics also disputed Israel's legal right to try Eichmann: The crimes had not occurred in Israeli territory, nor were Eichmann's victims Israeli citizens. (Israel did not exist until 1948.)

In reply to these critics, Hausner and other supporters of the prosecution insisted that justice demanded that Eichmann be brought to trial, and that the Israeli government had pursued the only course of action open to it. In the Eichmann trial, then, we confront a case in which what was legal on the one hand and what was just on the other appeared very much at odds. There is no doubt that Eichmann was guilty of horrendous crimes; there is also no doubt that the Israeli government stepped beyond the boundaries of international law in kidnapping Eichmann.

The Eichmann trial also raised important questions about the nature of the Holocaust. Was it a crime perpetrated by a few very evil men, or did the evil penetrate deep into German, and European, society? The prosecution's case sought to depict Eichmann as a monster, a brilliant and demonic mas-

■ **Eichmann on Trial**
Eichmann sits on the left in a cage of bulletproof glass.

termind responsible for the deaths of millions of Jews. As Hausner contended, "it was [Eichmann's] word that put gas chambers into action; he lifted the telephone, and railway trains left for the extermination centers; his signature it was that sealed the doom of tens of thousands."[9] Such a depiction provided a comforting explanation for the Holocaust—it was perpetrated not by ordinary human beings but by monstrous devils.

Yet many trial observers and subsequent historians argued that such a depiction was simply wrong. This argument appeared in forceful terms in the most well-known critique of the prosecution—Hannah Arendt's *Eichmann in Jerusalem: A Report on the Banality of Evil,* published in 1963. Arendt (1906–1975), a Jewish philosopher who had fled Nazi Europe in 1941, argued that the evidence provided in the trial showed Eichmann to be a fairly commonplace man, motivated by ambition as much as by ideology, a rather plodding bureaucrat obsessed with trivial details—in other words, an ordinary man, capable of extraordinary evil.

Must ordinary men be held responsible for following evil orders? This is the final question raised by the Eichmann trial. Defense attorney Robert Servatius insisted that the Holocaust was an "act of state," a crime carried out by a political regime, for which no civil servant could bear the blame. Eichmann only followed orders. Servatius concluded his arguments by asking Eichmann how he viewed "this question of guilt." Eichmann replied,

> Where there is no responsibility, there can be no guilt. . . . The questions of responsibility and conscience are for the leadership of the state. . . . I condemn and regret the act of extermination of the Jews which the leadership of the German state ordered. But I myself could not jump over my own shadow. I was a tool in the hands of superior powers and authorities.[10]

Eichmann's judges disagreed. In declaring Eichmann guilty of genocide, they argued,

> We reject absolutely the accused's version that he was nothing more than a "small cog" in the extermination ma-

chine. . . . He was not a puppet in the hands of others. His place was among those who pulled the strings.[11]   ■

Questions of Justice

1. Even if Eichmann's assertion that he was simply "a tool in the hands of superior powers and authorities" could be proven correct, to what degree was he culpable for his actions?

2. In the Eichmann case, the letter of the law and justice appeared to be at odds. In what situations—if any—must the law be broken to ensure that justice prevails? Who has the authority to make such a judgment?

Taking It Further

Laqueur, Walter. "Hannah Arendt in Jerusalem: The Controversy Revisited," in Lyman H. Legters, ed., *Western Society After the Holocaust.* 1983. Examines the impact of Arendt's critique of the trial.

The Trial of Adolf Eichmann: Record of Proceedings in the District Court of Jerusalem. Vols. 1–9, 1993–1995. The basic primary source.

savage program of ethnic homogenization with a campaign of terror against Jews, Bosnian Muslims, and Serbs. Guerilla bands of Serbian soldiers called *Chetniks,* who supported the now-exiled Yugoslav monarchy, fought back. Like the Croatian fascists, however, the Chetniks also slaughtered both Muslims and Jews.

In the midst of this bloody free-for-all, a second Resistance group emerged. Led by communist Josip Broz (1892–1980), alias "Tito," these partisans saw the war as a chance for social revolution and promised equality for all in a reunited Yugoslavia. Tito's partisans focused on fighting Germans (diverting ten German divisions from the eastern front), but they also battled against the Croatian fascists and the royalist Chetniks, both of whom opposed Tito's aim of a communist state.

In Germany itself and in countries allied to rather than conquered by the Germans, potential resisters had to convince themselves that patriotism demanded working against their own government. In France until 1943, resistance meant opposing the lawfully instituted but collaborationist Vichy government of Marshal Pétain. As a World War I hero, Pétain was popular even with those who did not share his authoritarian conservatism. By 1943, however, an alternative focus of national loyalty had emerged: the Free French headed by General Charles De Gaulle (1890–1970). At the end of 1942, De Gaulle declared himself the head of a Free French provisional government. French patriots could declare themselves loyal to this alternative government and fight in the Resistance against both Nazi rule and Vichy collaboration.

UNDER OCCUPATION

In occupied Europe, Nazi racial ideology shaped the experience of both soldiers and civilians. The Nazis drew a sharp line between the peoples of western Europe—the Dutch, Norwegian, Danes, and Flemish, all considered of racially superior "Germanic stock"—and the Slavs of eastern Europe. The ferocity of Nazi brutality increased exponentially in the eastern occupied regions. In the conquered areas of the Soviet Union, for example, conditions reached barbaric levels. Almost 63,000 Soviet civilians were killed in the first five weeks after the German invasion. In planning for the invasion, German policymakers made clear that they intended to strip the conquered nation of its food, with no provision made for feeding the defeated Soviets. Although German plans for a quick conquest in the Soviet Union were soon shattered, German willingness to regard the Soviet population as expendable remained unchanged.

The German occupation of western Europe was less heavy-handed, particularly during the first half of the war. The Nazis believed that "Germanic" peoples such as the Dutch could be taught to become good Nazis and therefore spared them the extreme brutality that characterized the German occupation in the east. Moreover, in western Europe the Germans sought to work with rather than to annihilate political and economic elites. For example, in both Belgium and the Netherlands civil servants continued to do their prewar jobs.

The German occupation in the west, even in the first two years of the war, was, however, far from lenient. The Nazis forced occupied countries to pay exorbitant sums to cover the costs of their own occupation. In addition, they were required to sell both manufactured products and raw materials to Germany at artificially low prices. Anyone who spoke out against the Nazis faced imprisonment or death. The occupation grew even more harsh after 1943 as German military losses piled up, stocks of food and essential supplies dwindled, and German demands for civilian labor increased.

For millions of European men and women in German-occupied Europe, the war meant forced labor in Germany. Within days of the invasion of Poland, Polish POWs were working in German fields. By August 1944, German farmers and factory owners employed more than 5.7 million foreign civilian laborers (one-third of them women) and almost two million POWs. These foreign workers accounted for more than half the labor in German agriculture and in German munitions plants, and one-third of the labor force in key war industries such as mining, chemicals, and metals. They worked grueling hours for very little pay.

THE WOMEN'S WAR

As we have seen, women joined the ranks of the Resistance and were forced to labor in German industries. Women also tended to bear the brunt of home front deprivation, as they were the ones who had to get a meal on the table and clothe their children in the face of severe rationing. Only the Soviet Union, however, mobilized women for military combat. By 1944, 246,000 women were in front-line units. Soviet women also constituted 80 percent of the agricultural and 50 percent of the industrial labor force. All Soviet women under age 45 who were not engaged in essential war work were required to work eleven hours a day constructing defenses. For all Soviet citizens, male and female, life on the home front meant endless labor, inadequate food supplies, and constant surveillance under martial law.

Unlike the Soviets, British women were not combat soldiers, but they were drafted for service in civilian defense, war-related industry, or the armed forces. Women accounted for 25 percent of the civilians who worked in Britain's Air Raid Protection services as wardens, rescuers, and telephone operators. All citizens working less than 55 hours per week had to perform compulsory fire-watching duties from 1941 on. The numbers of British women employed in male-dominated industries such as metals and chemicals rose dramatically. Only the Soviet Union mobilized women more fully.

■ The Women's War

Russian women dig trench defenses at the outskirts of Moscow in 1941. No other state mobilized its women as fully as did the Soviet Union.

Until 1943, the German home front contrasted sharply with that of Britain and the Soviet Union. In the first years of the war, the Nazi government rationed clothing and food supplies but did not dramatically cut consumption levels. Most significantly, Hitler hesitated to conscript middle-class German women for industrial labor. He believed that the future of the "German race" depended on middle-class women being protected from the strains of paid labor so that they could bear healthy Aryan babies. Thus in Germany the use of foreign labor took the place of the full-scale mobilization of women. The number of women in the German workforce actually fell by 500,000 between 1939 and 1941.

The fall of Stalingrad marked a turning point in Nazi policy toward German women at work. With losses on the Eastern front averaging 150,000 men per month, the German army desperately needed more soldiers. At the same time, the German war economy demanded more

workers. In response, Hitler's deputy Joseph Goebbels (1897–1945) declared that Germany must fight a total war, which meant total mobilization of the home front. The final, desperate year of the war saw a concentrated use of female labor in Nazi Germany.

Of all the combatant states, the United States stands out as unique with regard to the home front. The United States never fully mobilized its economy, and more than 70 percent of its adult women remained outside the paid workforce. Rationing was comparatively minimal and consumption levels in the United States high. In fact, for many families, the war years brought prosperity after years of economic depression. But most important, American cities were never bombed, and thus the United States was able to maintain a clear distinction between soldier and civilian, man and woman—a distinction that was blurred in other combatant nations.

WHAT ARE WE FIGHTING FOR?

To mobilize their populations for total war, governments had to convince their citizens of the importance of the war effort. Maintaining morale and motivating both civilians and soldiers to endure deprivation and danger demanded that leaders supply a persuasive answer to the question: What are we fighting for?

All nations—democratic or authoritarian—rely on myths, stories of national origins and identity, to unify disparate individuals, classes, and groups. In all the combatant nations, governments enlisted artists, entertainers, and the technologies of the mass media for myth making and morale building. The British artist Henry Moore's (1898–1986) drawings of ordinary people in air raid shelters (completed under an official commission) evoke the survival of civilized values in the midst of unspeakable degradation. Perhaps the most famous musical work from the war is Dmitri Shostakovich's (1906–1975) *Seventh Symphony*—now universally known as the *Leningrad Symphony* and a symbol of human resilience. Shostakovich composed the early drafts of this work in Leningrad while German shells were falling, and it was actually performed in Leningrad in August 1942, while the city was still under siege.

During the war, film came into its own as an artistic form capable of creating important myths of national unity. Laurence Olivier's version of Shakespeare's *Henry V* (1944) comforted British moviegoers with its classic story of a stirring English military victory against huge odds. In Italy, a group of filmmakers known as the Neo-Realists created a set of films that dramatized the Resistance spirit of

■ **Henry Moore, *Tube Shelter Perspective* (1941)**
Inadequate public provision of air raid shelters forced working-class Londoners to take matters into their own hands. They began to use London subway stations for shelter during nighttime bombing raids. Impressed by the resilience and good humor of these ordinary people, Moore paid homage to their courage in a series of striking drawings.

national unity. Shot on location, with amateur actors and realistic sets, films such as Roberto Rossellini's *Open City* (1945) depicted lower-class life with honesty and respect and called for the creation of a better society from the rubble of the old.

Rossellini's call for the creation of a new society was echoed throughout Europe during the war. As early as December 1942, a government committee set out a radical plan for a new Britain. In rather unusual language for an official document, the committee's report identified "five giants on the road to reconstruction": Want, Disease, Ignorance, Squalor, and Idleness. To slay these giants, the committee recommended that the state assume responsibility for ensuring full employment and a minimum standard of living for all through the provision of family allowances, social welfare programs, and a national health service. The Beveridge Report (named after the committee's chairman) became a bestseller in Britain and the basis for a number of postwar European social welfare plans. Across Europe a consensus emerged on the need for social democracy, a society in which the state intervenes in economic life to ensure public welfare.

Four factors explain this radical reorientation of European politics. First, and most important, as the war dragged on and the death tolls mounted, European men and women demanded that their suffering be worthwhile. They wanted to know that they were fighting not to rebuild the depressed and divided societies of the 1930s, but to construct a new Europe. Second, the war (and the ongoing revelations of Nazi atrocities) discredited the politics of the far right. This sort of politics, whether fascist, Nazi, or conservative-authoritarian, disappeared from legitimate political discussion. But in Europe (although not in the United States) the liberal ideal of the free and self-interested individual competing in an unregulated economy also lay in ruins, the victim of the prewar Great Depression. The new Europe, then, had to be built along different lines. Third, Europeans observed the combatant nations' success in mobilizing their economies for total war, and began to ask themselves and their political leaders, if governments can regulate economies to fight wars, why can they not regulate economies for peacetime prosperity? Finally, the important role of socialists and communists in the Resistance enhanced the respectability of radical political ideas. Out of the Resistance came a determination to break the mold of prewar politics and build something better.

CONCLUSION
The New Europe, The New West

Adolf Hitler had promised his allies and his enemies that he would create a new Europe. And so he did. As Europeans emerged from their bomb shelters, returned home from their army units, and searched desperately for family members, they faced an uncertain future in a radically changed world. As Chapter 27 shows, World War II succeeded in creating a new European (and a new global) order, but one dramatically different from that envisioned by Hitler. The war also reshaped the dominant idea of the "West." Hitler offered a set of ideas that promised a dramatic reconfiguration of Western values along racist, authoritarian lines. In the Nazi vision, the West comprised white, northern Europeans, marching in step to the dictates of the antidemocratic state. The wartime encounter with this vision was crucial; from it emerged a sharpened commitment within the West to the processes and values of democracy.

But to present the Second World War as a conflict between democracy and Nazism is to oversimplify. To defeat Nazi Germany, the democracies of Britain and the United States allied with Stalin's Soviet Union, a dictatorial regime that matched Hitler's Germany in its contempt for democratic values and human rights and that surpassed it in state-sanctioned mass murder. The Soviet Union emerged from the war as the dominant power in eastern Europe; as we will see in the next chapter, the presence of the Red Army obliterated any chance to establish democratic governments in this region.

The tensions inherent in the Anglo-American alliance with the Soviets led directly to the Cold War, the ideological and political conflict that dominated the post–World War II world and that once again forced a redefinition of the West. From 1949 until 1989, it was easy to draw the West on any map: One simply shaded in the United States and those countries allied to it. But at the same time a new division emerged. World War II marked the beginning of the end of European imperial control over the non-European world. As a result, the postwar era would see growing tensions between "North" and "South"—between the industrially developed nations and the underdeveloped regions seeking to shrug off their colonial past.

Suggestions for Further Reading

For a comprehensive list of suggested readings, please go to www.ablongman.com/levackconcise/chapter26

Alperovitz, Gar. *Atomic Diplomacy: Hiroshima and Potsdam. The Use of the Atomic Bomb and the American Confrontation with Soviet Power.* 1994. The first edition of this book, published in 1965, sparked an ongoing scholarly debate about the role of Cold War concerns in shaping U.S. decision making at the end of World War II.

Browning, Christopher. *Ordinary Men: Reserve Police Battalion 101 and the Final Solution in Poland.* 1992. A powerful account of the participation of a group of "ordinary men" in mass murder.

Calder, Angus. *The People's War: Britain, 1939–1945.* 1969. Lengthy—but worth the effort for students wishing to explore the war's impact on British society. (Those who want a shorter account

can turn to Robert Mackay, *The Test of War: Inside Britain 1939–45* [1999].)

Frayn, Michael. *Copenhagen.* 1998. A remarkable play in which Frayn dramatizes a meeting (that actually did occur) between the German atomic physicist Werner Heisenberg and his Danish anti-Nazi colleague Niels Bohr. Contains both extremely clear explanations of the workings of atomic physics and a provocative exploration of the moral issues involved in the making of the atom bomb.

Friedlander, Saul. *Nazi Germany and the Jews, 1933–1939.* 1998. An important study of the evolution of Nazi anti-Semitic policy before the war.

Hilberg, Raul. *Perpetrators, Victims, Bystanders: The Jewish Catastrophe, 1933–1945*. 1992. As his title indicates, Hilberg looks at the three principal sets of participants in the Holocaust.

Iriye, Akira. *The Origins of the Second World War in Asia and the Pacific*. 1987. Part of Longman's "Origins of Modern Wars" series aimed at university students, this short and readable study highlights the major issues and events.

Keegan, John. *The Second World War*. 1989. Provides clear explanations of military technologies and techniques; packed with useful maps and vivid illustrations.

Kitchen, Martin. *Nazi Germany at War*. 1995. A short and nicely organized survey of the German home front.

Marrus, Michael R. *The Holocaust in History*. 1987. A clearly written, concise account of historians' efforts to understand the Holocaust. Highly recommended.

Moore, Bob, ed. *Resistance in Western Europe*. 2000. A collection of essays that explores recent research on this controversial topic.

Overy, Richard. *Russia's War: A History of the Soviet War Effort, 1941–1945*. 1997. A compelling account, written to accompany the television documentary *Russia's War*.

Paxton, Robert. *Vichy France: Old Guard and New Order, 1940–1944*. 1972. A now-classic study of the aims and evolution of France's collaborationist government.

Rhodes, Richard. *The Making of the Atomic Bomb*. 1986. A lengthy but very readable account; very good at explaining the complicated science involved.

Rhodes, Richard. *Masters of Death: The SS-Einsatzgruppen and the Invention of the Holocaust*. 2002. Compelling account of the Einsatzgruppen actions during the German invasion of the Soviet Union.

Rock, William R. *British Appeasement in the 1930s*. 1977. A balanced and concise appraisal.

Weinberg, Gerhard. *A World at Arms: A Global History of World War II*. 1994. Places the war within a global rather than simply a European context.

Notes

1. Quoted in Robert H. Abzug, *Inside the Vicious Heart: Americans and the Liberation of Nazi Concentration Camps* (1985), 19.
2. Quoted in Gordon Horwitz, *In the Shadow of Death, Living Outside the Gates of Mauthausen* (1991), 167.
3. Quoted in Richard Overy, *Russia's War* (1998), 95.
4. Quoted in Peter Clarke, *Hope and Glory: Britain, 1900–1990* (1996), 204.
5. Quoted in Joachim Fest, *Hitler* (1973), 665.
6. Quoted in Richard Rhodes, *The Making of the Atomic Bomb* (1988), 474.
7. Gideon Hausner, *Justice in Jerusalem* (1966), 291.
8. Ibid., 323–324.
9. From Hausner's opening statement; quoted in Moshe Pearlman, *The Capture and Trial of Adolf Eichmann* (1963), 149.
10. Ibid., 463–465.
11. Ibid., 603; Hausner, *Justice in Jerusalem*, 422.

INFORMATION
LIBRE

Redefining the West After World War II

ON ONE APPARENTLY ORDINARY DAY IN AUGUST 1961, WESTERN EUROPEAN television viewers witnessed a dramatic scene. While the news cameras rolled, policemen from East Berlin played tug-of-war with firemen from West Berlin—but between them was not a length of rope, but rather a middle-aged German woman. This horrifying contest had been set in motion by an important episode in the Cold War: the construction of the Berlin Wall. Appalled by the growing numbers of East German citizens who were fleeing communist rule through the gateway of West Berlin, the East German and Soviet authorities decided in 1961 to block that gate by building a wall. In the early morning hours of August 13, East German workers erected a barbed-wire fence along Berlin's east-west dividing line. In some cases, this line ran right through apartment buildings. For the next few weeks, these apartments provided literal "windows to the West." West Berlin firemen waited with blankets ready to catch anyone willing to jump out a window—and out of communist eastern Europe. These windows closed quickly. The communist authorities bricked them up; later they leveled entire apartment buildings to create a moat in front of what was now the armed fortress of East Berlin. The barbed-wire fence became a concrete wall buttressed by gun towers, lit by searchlights and patrolled by armed guards with "shoot to kill" orders.

The unidentified woman in this scene, literally caught between West and East, serves as an appropriate symbol for Europe during the 1950s and 1960s. In these decades, the Cold War between the United States and the Soviet Union influenced European politics, culture, and society. The woman's desperation to reach the West reminds us that American influence in western Europe should not be equated with Soviet control of eastern Europe: Not many Europeans tried

Chapter Outline

- A Dubious Peace, 1945–1949

- The West and the World: Decolonization and the Cold War

- The Soviet Union and Eastern Europe in the 1950s and 1960s

- The West: Consensus, Consumption, and Culture

Protest Poster, Paris (1968): Many of the protest movements of the 1960s questioned the democratic nature of Western governments. Protesters in Paris in 1968 used posters such as this one to articulate their sense that, despite constitutional guarantees and universal suffrage, Western political systems actually suppressed free speech.

■ **Tug-of-War at the Berlin Wall**
Caught by the television cameras, this woman sought to escape through her window into West Berlin. She succeeded.

to run *into* the Soviet bloc. Cultural and economic dominance are not the same as political tyranny. Nevertheless, many Europeans in the West as well as the East felt that they no longer controlled their own societies.

In the Cold War two ideologies clashed against each other; the Cold War was as much a battle of ideas and values as weapons and warriors. Both sides laid claim to universal cultures—to have achieved a way of life that would benefit *all* human societies. This ideological encounter forced a redefinition of "the West." Previous chapters have described the way in which this cultural construct shifted over time. By the late nineteenth century, Christianity, although still important, played a less central role in defining "the West" than did a mix of other factors, including the possession of industrial technology, the illusion of white superiority based on pseudoscientific racist theorizing, and faith in both capitalist economics and liberal political values. The Cold War added an anti-Soviet stance and a fear of communist ideology to the mix. These additions at times eroded the Western commitment to democracy, particularly within the developing world.

Significantly, the Cold War turned "hot" not in Europe but in places such as Korea, Cuba, and Vietnam. The postwar years witnessed the widening of the economic gap between "North" and "South"—between the industrialized nations, largely located in the Northern Hemisphere, and the economically underdeveloped regions (many but certainly not all of which were situated south of the equator), now shrugging off colonial rule and seeking both political independence and economic prosperity. Thus, as Europeans encountered each other across the Cold War divide, they also encountered non-Europeans across a huge economic gulf. Two very different contests—North versus South and West versus East—quickly became entangled with each other as the Cold War moved beyond Europe's borders to the developing regions.

These encounters created postwar Western culture. To understand their impact, this chapter addresses four questions:

■ Why and how did the world step from World War II to the Cold War?
■ What was the impact of decolonization and the Cold War on the global balance of power?
■ What patterns characterized the history of the Soviet Union and eastern Europe after the death of Stalin?
■ What patterns characterized the history of western Europe in the 1950s and 1960s?

A Dubious Peace, 1945–1949

World War II ended in the spring of 1945, but the killing did not. Postwar purges and deportations ensured that the death totals continued to mount, while in many regions world war gave way to civil war. Most significant, as the "hot" war waned, the Cold War between the Soviet Union and the United States began.

DEVASTATION, DEATH, AND CONTINUING WAR

If there was peace in Europe and Asia in 1945, it was the "peace of a graveyard," with an estimated 55 million people dead. In the immediate postwar period, the death statistics continued to rise as the victors turned with vengeful fury against the vanquished. In Czechoslovakia, purges killed 30,000 collaborators between 1945 and 1948. In Yugoslavia, Tito ordered the massacre of anticommunists. No one knows how many died; some estimates range as high as 60,000.

Those left alive faced the overwhelming task of reconstruction. Throughout Europe, the bombers had rendered most highways, rail tracks, and waterways unusable. With laborers, seed, fertilizer, and basic equipment all in short supply, agricultural production in 1945 stood below 50 percent of prewar levels. Less visible, but just as devastating, was the destruction of the financial system. Few European currencies were worth much. In occupied Germany, cigarettes replaced marks as the unit of exchange.

One of the most serious problems facing Europe was that of the refugees or displaced persons (DPs). The war and Hitler's attempt at racial reordering had uprooted millions from their homes. The DP problem grew even larger as a result of the peace settlement. The Soviet Union kept the Polish territories it had claimed in 1939 and Poland received a large chunk of what had been prewar Germany. The new Polish government then expelled the German inhabitants from this region. In Czechoslovakia, Romania, Yugoslavia, and Hungary, too, ethnic Germans were forced out. More than 11 million Germans suffered from these deportations. As many as two million died en route to Germany. Ethnic Germans were not the only ones to endure deportation. Between 1945 and 1948, eastern European governments forcibly transferred an additional seven million refugees, in a brutal solution to the ethnic divisions that had destabilized prewar political structures.

Forced deportation can be understood as a continuation of war—a war carried out by governments against groups marked as dangerous because of their ethnic makeup. Other forms of war also continued after 1945. Ukrainian nationalists kept up a guerilla war against the Soviets until the early 1950s. In Greece civil war between communist and anticommunist forces raged until 1949, while in Trieste (along the Italian-Yugoslav border) civil war continued until 1954. In the forests and marshes of Poland, anticommunist guerilla groups fought against the new communist regime until 1956.

FROM HOT TO COLD WAR

The conflict that aroused the most alarm and posed the greatest threat to the dubious peace after 1945 was the Cold War°, the struggle for global supremacy between the United States and the Soviet Union. Within just a few years of the defeat of Germany and Japan, the allies became enemies, and what Winston Churchill called an "Iron Curtain" dropped between eastern and western Europe. The divisions of the Cold War were rooted in World War II, nurtured by the fears and hopes it aroused.

Interests, Aims, and Armies, 1943–1945

Each of the Allied leaders had different aims and interests. Stalin demanded ultimate control over the eastern European political settlement: To ensure his own and his state's security, he demanded communist-controlled governments in the states bordering the Soviet Union. In contrast, U.S. president Franklin D. Roosevelt believed that global international security and economic prosperity de-

pended on the establishment of democracies, committed to capitalist economic principles and practices, throughout Europe. British prime minister Winston Churchill possessed a third set of aims. Concerned about the postwar balance of power in Europe and the maintenance of the British Empire, Churchill recognized that once Germany was defeated, a power vacuum would exist in central and eastern Europe. He feared that the Soviets might prove too eager to fill that vacuum. A permanent Soviet presence in the Balkans particularly threatened British military and economic interests throughout the Mediterranean.

These conflicts among the Big Three became apparent as early as 1942. To prevent Soviet domination of eastern Europe, Churchill pressed for an Anglo-American invasion of the Balkans. When the Allied leaders met for their first summit in Tehran in 1943, however, Stalin and Roosevelt overruled Churchill and agreed that the Anglo-American invasion would be a single, concentrated attack across the English Channel into France (the D-Day invasion of June 1944). This decision left the Balkans open to the Red Army. By the time the Big Three met in Yalta in February 1945, the communist partisans under Tito controlled Yugoslavia, and the Soviet Army had occupied Romania, Bulgaria, Hungary, and much of Czechoslovakia.

The presence of the Red Army in eastern Europe weakened the negotiating positions of Churchill and Roosevelt at Yalta. Roosevelt's desire to obtain Stalin's commitment to enter the war against Japan also reduced his bargaining power. A series of problematic compromises resulted. Stalin signed a declaration promising free elections in eastern Europe; at the same time, Roosevelt and Churchill agreed that such freely elected governments should be pro-Soviet. Germany's future remained undecided although the Big Three agreed to share the postwar occupation by dividing Germany, as well as the symbolically and strategically vital city of Berlin, into occupation zones controlled by the United States, the Soviet Union, France, and Britain.

The final Big Three summit in the German city of Potsdam in July 1945 did not bridge the gap between the Soviet Union and its partners. At this summit, Stalin faced two unfamiliar negotiating partners. The new U.S. president Harry Truman (1884–1972) replaced Roosevelt, who had died in April, and midway through the summit, the new British prime minister, Labour Party leader Clement Attlee, arrived to take Churchill's place. The change of personnel made little difference, however. Stalin was determined to maintain control over those territories occupied by his armies, while the British and Americans increasingly saw Stalin's demands as a threat to both democratic ideals and the European balance of power. Moreover, during the summit Truman received a telegraph informing him of the successful Trinity test in New Mexico. The atomic bomb meant that the war in Japan would soon be over—and that the Americans and British no longer needed or wanted Stalin to join the war in the Pacific. With western incentives for placating Stalin now removed, the tone of the negotiations became more hostile. Nevertheless, at Potsdam, Truman and Attlee agreed to Stalin's demands for German reparations to help the Soviet Union recover from the war.

The Cold War Begins, 1946–1949

Within just a few years of the war's end, clashing aims and interests had shredded the wartime alliance. Three key developments—the breakdown of cooperation over Germany, the Truman Doctrine°, and the Marshall Plan°—exposed the breach between the former allies.

Economic developments shattered allied cooperation over Germany. In 1946, British and American authorities became convinced, first, that unless radical measures were taken, Germans faced mass starvation, and second, that European economic prosperity depended on German economic prosperity. To stabilize Germany's economy, they combined their zones into a single economic unit and, much to Stalin's fury, stopped reparations deliveries to the Soviets.

The announcement of the Truman Doctrine the following year made clear the hostilities between Stalin and the West. In February 1947 Attlee's government informed Truman's administration that it could not afford to continue its fight against communist rebels in Greece. The United States immediately assumed Britain's role in Greece, but more important, Truman used this development to issue the Truman Doctrine, which committed the United States to the policy of containment°, resisting communist expansion wherever in the world it occurred.

The Marshall Plan further exposed the division of Europe into two hostile camps. In June 1947, U.S. secretary of state General George Marshall (1880–1959), alarmed that hungry Europeans might turn to communism, proposed that the United States underwrite Europe's economic recovery. British foreign secretary Ernest Bevin (1881–1951) and French foreign minister Georges Bidault (1899–1983) welcomed Marshall's proposal. With representatives from twelve other European states, Bevin and Bidault devised a four-year plan for European economic reconstruction. In 1948, the first food shipments from the United States reached European ports. Eventually $17 billion in aid poured into Europe, while a new international body, the Organization for European Economic Cooperation (OEEC), worked to coordinate aid, eliminate trade barriers, and stabilize currencies.

The Marshall Plan helped stabilize and integrate the economies of western Europe and accelerated Europe's leap into postwar prosperity. Stalin's response to the plan, however, cemented the division of East and West. The United States offered aid to any country that chose to accept it, including the Soviet Union and the states of eastern Europe, but required participating governments to join the OEEC. Stalin viewed the OEEC as an instrument of American economic domination and so refused to allow eastern European governments to accept Marshall aid. When the Czechs tried to do so, he engineered a communist coup that destroyed what remained of democracy in Czechoslovakia.

In 1949, the basic Cold War pattern that would hold for forty years took shape. The British and American zones of occupied Germany, joined with the French zone, became the western-allied state of West Germany. The Soviet zone became communist East Germany. In April 1949 nine western European nations[1] allied with the United States and Canada in NATO (North Atlantic Treaty Organization)°, a military alliance specifically aimed at repelling a Soviet invasion of western Europe. Months later, on August 29, 1949, the Soviet Union tested its own atomic bomb. Over the next few years, Stalin forced his eastern European satellites into an anti-Western military alliance (finalized as the Warsaw Pact° in 1955) and both the United States and the Soviet Union developed hydrogen bombs. Europe stood divided into two hostile military blocs, each dominated by a superpower in possession of a nuclear arsenal.

The West and the World: Decolonization and the Cold War

While the conflict between East and West dominated much of the postwar period, it soon blended with a very different struggle, that between the peoples of the developing nations and European imperialism. By the end of the 1960s, the age of the vast European overseas empires had finally ended. As decolonization became entangled with Cold War rivalries, superpower influence often replaced European imperial control. The Soviet Union and the United States used economic and military aid, as well as covert action, to cajole and coerce newly independent nations into choosing sides in the global Cold War conflict. The superpowers served as magnetic poles, drawing toward themselves competing nationalist forces and so entangling Cold War concerns with nationalist independence struggles throughout the world (see Map 27.1).

THE END OF THE AGE OF EUROPEAN EMPIRES

Faced with the reality of superpower domination in Europe, nations such as Britain and France looked to their imperial possessions to give them international power and prestige. In the economic hard times following World War II, moreover, European governments regarded their empires as more crucial than ever. The war, however, had aroused nationalist demands for independence from European rule to a fever pitch. In the Pacific region, many colonial nationalists had sided with the Japanese against the British, Dutch, and French, whom they regarded not as defenders of democracy but as imperial overlords. They pointed to the inherent contradiction between the Allies' claim to be fighting for democracy and the fact that many Allied states denied democratic rights to their imperial subjects.

When the war ended, these nationalists resisted European efforts to reimpose imperial rule, and a series of bloody colonial conflicts resulted. In Indonesia, for example, war raged from 1945 to 1949, as the Dutch fought bitterly to keep hold of a region they viewed as vital to their economic survival. In 1949, however, the nationalist Ahmed Sukarno (1949–1966) led his country into independence.

Like the Dutch, the British found their empire in revolt in the postwar period. Throughout the war Churchill had placed a high priority on preserving the British Empire, but the economic and military demands of total war significantly weakened Britain's ability to control its far-flung possessions. Clement Attlee, who succeeded Churchill as prime minister in July 1945, sought to retain Britain's hold on its essential imperial interests by jettisoning those that Britain no longer needed—or could no longer afford.

The British first jettisoned the Indian subcontinent. During World War II, the refusal of Indian nationalists to cooperate with the British war effort made clear that Britain could no longer rule India. After the war, therefore, Attlee's government opened negotiations with nationalist leaders. Muslim nationalists led by Muhammad Ali Jinnah (1876–1948) refused to accept citizenship in an independent state dominated by Hindus, and won from the British the creation of a separate Muslim state—Pakistan. India and Pakistan, as well as Burma, received independence in August 1947.

Just as the redrawing of boundary lines in eastern Europe resulted in brutal deportations and mass death, so the partition of the Indian subcontinent sparked widespread devastation. More than ten million people fled their homes and became refugees—Muslims fearing Hindu rule, Hindus fearing Muslim rule, Sikhs fearing both. Mahatma Gandhi traveled from village to village in some of the most afflicted areas and begged for an end to the killing, but the death tolls reached 250,000—and included Gandhi himself, who was shot by an assassin just six months after India achieved independence.

In Palestine, too, British retreat led to bloodshed in 1948. After the war in Europe ended, European Jewish refugees, persuaded by Hitler that a Jew could be safe only in a Jewish state, poured into British-controlled Palestine. Many soon found themselves waging guerilla warfare against the British, who sought to maintain regional political stability by limiting Jewish immigration. Faced with mounting violence as well as growing international pressure to grant

CHRONOLOGY

1947	India, Pakistan, and Burma achieve independence from British rule
1948	Formation of Israel
1950	Outbreak of the Korean War
1954	Defeat of French forces in Indochina; beginning of Franco-Algerian War
1955	Khrushchev's Secret Speech: de-Stalinization underway
1956	Hungarian uprising
1957	Formation of European Economic Community (EEC)
1958	De Gaulle era begins in France
1961	Berlin Wall built
1962	Cuban missile crisis
1964	Beginning of Brezhnev era in Soviet Union
1968	Prague Spring

Jewish demands for statehood, the British turned the problem over to the new United Nations. At the end of 1947, the UN adopted a plan calling for the partition of Palestine into Jewish and Arab sectors forming a Jewish and Arab state. The British, however, pulled out their troops in May 1948 without transferring authority to either Jews or Arabs. Jewish leaders immediately proclaimed the new state of Israel, and the region erupted into all-out war. After nine months of fighting, an uneasy peace descended, based on a partition of Palestine among Israel, Jordan, and Egypt. Approximately 750,000 Palestinian Arabs became stateless refugees.

By withdrawing from hot spots such as India and Palestine, the British hoped to preserve and stabilize what remained of the British Empire. During the 1950s, successive British governments sought to diminish the force of nationalism throughout their colonial territories by diverting it down channels of constitutional reform and systems of power sharing—and then fiercely stomping down on nationalists who broke out of these channels. Neither compromise nor coercion could stem the tide of nationalism, however, and by the end of the 1960s, the British Empire had been reduced to an assortment of island territories.

France, too, saw its empire disintegrate in the postwar decades despite fierce efforts to resist nationalist movements. In Indochina, the nationalist leader Ho Chi Minh (1890–1969) adopted the U.S. Declaration of Independence for his model when he proclaimed independence in September 1945. The stirring rhetoric, however failed to convince the French, who fought for almost a decade to

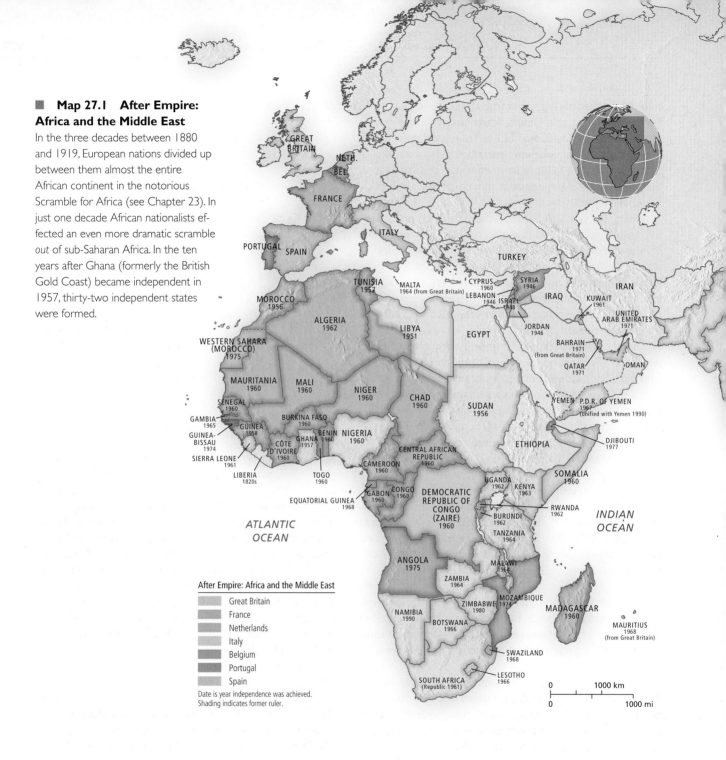

■ **Map 27.1 After Empire:
Africa and the Middle East**

In the three decades between 1880
and 1919, European nations divided up
between them almost the entire
African continent in the notorious
Scramble for Africa (see Chapter 23). In
just one decade African nationalists effected an even more dramatic scramble
out of sub-Saharan Africa. In the ten
years after Ghana (formerly the British
Gold Coast) became independent in
1957, thirty-two independent states
were formed.

After Empire: Africa and the Middle East

- Great Britain
- France
- Netherlands
- Italy
- Belgium
- Portugal
- Spain

Date is year independence was achieved.
Shading indicates former ruler.

retain their hold in Southeast Asia. But in 1954, the French
army suffered a decisive defeat at Dien Bien Phu in
Vietnam, and French rule in Indochina ended.

Humiliated by this defeat, French army officers responded ferociously to the outbreak of a nationalist revolt
in Algeria that same year. Many prominent politicians and
ordinary men and women shared the army's view that
France had been pushed too far, and must now stand fast.
The result was the Franco-Algerian War, a brutal fight that
raged from 1954 until the early 1960s. By the time Algeria
claimed independence in 1962, approximately 200,000
Algerian nationalist fighters had been killed or imprisoned.

Fifteen thousand French soldiers and auxiliary forces were
dead, as were almost 23,000 civilians in both France and
Algeria.

The Franco-Algerian War seriously divided French society, called into question the meaning of French democracy,
and resulted in profound political change. Supporters of
the French army in Algeria saw it as a force fighting on behalf of Western civilization against barbarism (both
Muslim and communist). Critics, pointing to the evidence
that the French army used torture against its enemies, argued that the war threatened to corrupt French society. In
1958, France teetered on the brink of civil war, with French

army officers preparing for an assault on Paris. The World War II hero Charles De Gaulle forced through a new constitution, which sharply tilted the balance of power in French domestic politics toward the president (conveniently De Gaulle himself).

The end of the European age of imperialism signaled an important shift in global power relations, and in the relationship between the West and the rest of the world. Declarations of political independence, however, did not always or often change the economic balance of power. European states lost their monopoly on the raw materials and markets of their one-time colonies, yet in the postcolonial era, many newly independent regions, particularly in Africa, grew more economically dependent than ever on the West. Desperate for income, governments focused not on industrial development but on production of primary products for export markets: cash crops such as coffee and sugar, and mineral resources such as uranium, copper, gold, and diamonds. These choices made the new states' economies extremely vulnerable to fluctuations in Western demand and prices while at the same time ever more dependent on Western imports of manufactured goods.

THE GLOBALIZATION OF THE COLD WAR

During the early decades of the Cold War, many Europeans feared that World War III would break out in divided Berlin. But in fact, the Cold War turned hot only in the developing nations, at the intersection of superpower rivalries and nationalist conflicts.

The Korean War, 1950–1953

The first such intersection occurred in Korea. Once part of the Japanese empire, Korea, like Germany, was divided after World War II. A Soviet-allied communist regime assumed power in North Korea, and an anticommunist state propped up by the United States controlled the south. In 1950, North Korean troops invaded South Korea in an attempt to unite the country under communist rule. This civil war, a struggle between rival groups of Korean nationalists, was quickly swallowed up by the Cold War. A UN-sponsored, largely American army fought alongside South Korean troops, while the Soviet Union supplied arms and Communist China provided soldiers to support North Korea.

The Korean War accelerated the globalization of the Cold War. As a result of the Korean conflict, the French government was able to persuade Truman's administration to support its struggle against Ho Chi Minh and the communist nationalists in Indochina, thus drawing the United States onto the path that would lead to its war in Vietnam. The conflict in Korea also welded Japan firmly into the Western alliance. As the U.S. army turned to the Japanese for vital military supplies, more than $3.5 billion poured

into and rejuvenated the Japanese economy. Transformed from an occupied enemy to a staunch ally and an economic powerhouse, Japan became the dam holding back "the red tide that threatens to engulf the world."[2] Thus, in a curious way, Japan—geographically as far "East" as one can get—became a part of the "West."

The Korean War also fostered intense political controversy within western Europe. Fearing that the war's outbreak signaled a more aggressive Soviet policy in Europe as well as Asia, western European leaders pushed for the transformation of NATO from a loose defensive alliance to a coordinated fighting force. In return, Truman's administration demanded that its European allies permit the rearmament of West Germany. With the trauma of German conquest and occupation so recently behind them, many Europeans were horrified by the prospect of a militarily rejuvenated Germany. But after four years of controversy and a failed effort to create a western European army, West Germany rearmed under the NATO umbrella.

Changing Temperatures in the Cold War, 1953–1970

In 1953, both sides in the Cold War changed leaders. Stalin died in March, just a few months after a new Republican administration headed by President Dwight Eisenhower (1890–1969) took office in the United States. This change of leadership heralded a new phase in the Cold War. When Eisenhower took office, he condemned Truman's policy of *containing* communism as defeatist, and instead committed the United States to *roll back* communism. This newly aggressive American stance was matched on the other side of the Cold War divide. Nikita Khrushchev (1894–1971), who emerged in 1955 as Stalin's successor, played a dangerous game of nuclear bluff, in which he persistently and often successfully convinced allies and foes alike that the Soviet Union possessed a far stronger nuclear force than it actually did.

Both Khrushchev and Eisenhower recognized, however, that nuclear weapons made total war unwinnable and both sought ways to break out of the positions into which they were frozen by Cold War hostilities. Thus the period from 1953 until 1964 was characterized by thawing superpower relations followed by the icy blasts of renewed hostilities. In 1955, for example, representatives of Britain, France, the United States, and the Soviet Union met in Geneva for the first summit of the Cold War, but this initial thaw ended one year later when Khrushchev sent tanks into Hungary to crush a nationalist rebellion—a clear demonstration that he would permit no challenge to Soviet authority in eastern Europe. The Soviets' successful launch of the first human-made satellite, *Sputnik,* in 1957 was even more chilling because it revealed the Soviet capability to launch intercontinental ballistic missiles (ICBMs)—not only European but also American cities now lay vulnerable to a nuclear

■ **"We Will Bury You!"**

In sharp contrast to the reserved, taciturn Stalin, Khrushchev often exploded in anger. This *Time* magazine cover from September 1961 shows Khrushchev in a familiar bombastic pose, as the Soviet Union announced that it was resuming above-ground testing of its hydrogen bombs. One of Khrushchev's most memorable lines was his warning to the West about the coming economic supremacy of the Soviet system: "We will bury you!"

strike. Yet just one year later the Soviet Union announced a voluntary suspension on nuclear testing and nuclear test ban talks began. In 1959 Khrushchev even spent twelve days touring the United States.

These warming relations, however, turned frosty in 1960 after the Soviet Union announced it had shot down an American spy plane and captured its pilot. This announcement aborted a planned second superpower summit and initiated one of the most dangerous periods in the post–World War II era, during which the construction of the Berlin Wall° provided a concrete symbol of the Cold War divide. As we saw at the beginning of this chapter, the continuing outflow of east Germans to the West through Berlin led the East German communist leader Walter Ulbricht (1893–1973) and Khrushchev to take dramatic action in 1961. Two weeks after the wall went up, the Soviet Union ended a three-year moratorium on nuclear testing. The new American president John F. Kennedy (1917–1963) increased military spending and called for an expanded

civil defense program to prepare for nuclear war. Across Europe men and women feared that their countries would become a nuclear wasteland.

Such a war was narrowly avoided in the fall of 1962 as once again the Cold War intersected with a nationalist struggle. In 1959, a nationalist revolutionary movement led by Fidel Castro (b. 1926) had toppled Cuba's pro-U.S. dictator. Castro quickly aligned Cuba with the Soviet Union. In 1962, Kennedy learned that the Soviets were building nuclear missile bases in Cuba. What Kennedy did not know was that the Soviet forces in Cuba were armed with nuclear weapons— and with the discretionary power to use these weapons if U.S. forces attacked. Some of Kennedy's advisers urged just such an attack, but instead the president used secret diplomatic channels to broker a compromise. Khrushchev removed the missiles and in exchange, Kennedy withdrew NATO's nuclear missiles from Turkey and guaranteed that the United States would not invade Cuba.

The Cuban missile crisis in some ways marked a watershed in the history of the Cold War. In its aftermath, both the United States and the Soviet Union backed off from nuclear brinkmanship. In 1963, the superpowers agreed to stop aboveground nuclear testing with the Nuclear Test Ban Treaty, and set up between them the "hotline," a direct communications link to encourage immediate personal consultation in the event of a future crisis.

Yet relations between the superpowers remained tense throughout the 1960s, as the Vietnam War made clear. After the defeat of French imperial forces at Dien Bien Phu in 1954, rival Vietnamese nationalists had fought to control the Indochinese peninsula. But just as in Korea a decade earlier, this nationalist struggle soon merged with the Cold War. Ho Chi Minh and his communist regime in North Vietnam relied on the Soviet Union and China for support, while American military and economic aid propped up an anticommunist government in South Vietnam. American assistance eventually came to look like outright intervention: By 1968, more than 500,000 American soldiers were fighting in Vietnam. Fifty-eight thousand GIs died during the war—as did well over one million Vietnamese.

The Soviet Union and Eastern Europe in the 1950s and 1960s

Divided by the Cold War, the peoples of western and eastern Europe in the 1950s and 1960s followed separate paths. For the citizens of eastern Europe and the Soviet Union, the end of World War II brought renewed terror rather than peace. Stalin's death in 1953 inaugurated a period of political reform and the seeming promise of prosperity, but by the end of the 1960s, economic stagnation and political discontent characterized life in the Soviet bloc.

STALINIST TERROR, DE-STALINIZATION, STAGNATION

As the Red Army slowly pushed the Germans out of Soviet territory and then back through eastern Europe in the final years of World War II, many of the inhabitants of these regions found that liberation from German occupation did not mean freedom, and that the end of the war did not mean peace. Within the Soviet Union Stalin accused entire ethnic groups, such as the Chechens, of collaborating with the Germans. Soviet soldiers loaded hundreds of thousands of men, women, and children onto freezing freight cars without adequate supplies of food, water, or warm clothing, and shipped them eastward. An estimated 25 percent of these people died on the journey or in the first few years of barren existence in their new homes. These deportations continued into the early 1950s.

Terror also marked the daily lives of eastern Europeans in the late 1940s and early 1950s, as a result of Stalin's response to developments in Yugoslavia. In 1948, Yugoslavia's communist leader, Tito, broke with Stalin and refused to let

■ **Map 27.2   Europe in the Cold War**
As this map shows, during the Cold War the "West" was defined culturally and politically, rather than in geographic terms. Greece and Turkey stand far to the east in Europe, yet their membership in NATO placed both within the "West."

Show Time: The Trial of Rudolf Slánský

On the night of July 31, 1951, Rudolf Slánský—general secretary of the Communist Party of Czechoslovakia (CPC) and the second most powerful man in Prague—left his 50th birthday party, and headed home, a frightened man. Outwardly, nothing was wrong. The CPC had celebrated the day in style. The communist president, Klement Gottwald, presented to Slánský the medal of the Order of Socialism, the highest honor awarded in Czechoslovakia. Telegrams of congratulations poured in from all over the country. But the huge stack of congratulatory telegrams contained no greeting from Stalin. Slánský knew he was in trouble.

At another place and in another time, Slánský's fear could be dismissed as mere paranoia. But in the upper ranks of the Communist Party in Czechoslovakia in 1951, signs of Stalin's approval or disapproval were literally a matter of life or death. The Stalinist purge of eastern Europe was well underway, with thousands arrested, tortured, imprisoned, or killed.

Slánský knew he was vulnerable on three counts. First, he held a rank high enough to ensure a spectacular show trial. As the Soviet Great Purge of the 1930s had demonstrated, trials and executions of leading communists worked both to terrorize Stalin's potential rivals and, by rousing ordinary citizens to perpetual vigilance, to cement mass loyalty to the regime. But for a trial to be a genuine show, the defendant had to be worth showing.

Slánský, as the CPC general secretary, was the perfect defendant.

Slánský was a target for Stalin's purge, second, because he was a Czech, and Stalin viewed his Czech colleagues with particular suspicion. Czechoslovakia was the only state in eastern Europe with a history of successful democracy and without Soviet troops in occupation after 1945. Moreover, the CPC had participated with noncommunists in a coalition government longer than any other eastern European communist party.

Such differences linked the CPC to the ideology of "national communism," which taught that the Soviet path to communism was not the only one, that each nation must find its own route. "National communism" became a heresy in Stalin's eyes after his break with the Yugoslav communist leader Tito in 1948. Tito had dared to lead Yugoslavia down a different path, and had dared to defy Stalin's leadership. Determined to prevent any additional defections from his eastern European empire, Stalin embarked on a quest for real or potential "titoists." To save his own skin, CPC leader Klement Gottwald needed to demonstrate his willingness to uproot titoism from his party and his government. Slánský became that demonstration.

Finally, Slánský was vulnerable because he was a Jew. When the purges in eastern Europe began in 1948, anti-Semitism played no prominent role, but by 1950 the intersection of Middle Eastern power plays, Cold War hostilities, Stalin's paranoia, and the still-

powerful tradition of Jew-hating in eastern European culture made Jewish communists particularly suspect. Aiming to establish a Soviet presence in the Middle East after the war, Stalin had tried to persuade the new state of Israel to align with the Soviet Union by offering the new Israeli government diplomatic recognition and arms deals. But Stalin's efforts failed. By 1950, Israel had become an ally of the United States. Stalin responded with fury. All Jews came under suspicion of "Zionist" (that is, pro-Israel and therefore pro-Western) tendencies.

Stalin's failure to send Slánský a birthday telegram signaled that Slánský was now on the list of suspects. Over the following months Soviet advisers and homegrown Czech torturers pressured prisoners already caught in the net of the purge to confess that they were part of a Slánský-led conspiracy to overthrow the communist government and to turn Czechoslovakia against the Soviet Union. These torture-induced confessions were then used to prepare a flimsy case against Slánský and thirteen other men (eleven of them Jews).

Shortly before midnight on November 24, 1951, security agents arrested Slánský at his home. A lifelong atheist, Slánský could say nothing except "Jesus Maria." He knew what was coming. Instrumental in initiating the Stalinist purge in Czechoslovakia, Slánský had approved the arrests and torture of many of his colleagues. Ironically, he had drafted the telegram asking Stalin to send Soviet advisers to

■ **Rudolf Slánský on Trial**
Slánský, already a broken man, bows his head as he hears his death sentence on November 27, 1952.

the party. As one experienced interrogator noted about a different defendant, "He'll confess; he's got a good attitude toward the party."[4] In addition, Slánsky may have been promised, as were other show trial defendants, that his life would be spared and his family protected if he confessed.

In his closing statement, Slánský said, "I deserve no other end to my criminal life than that proposed by the state prosecutor."[5] The prosecutor demanded the death penalty. Slánský was executed on December 3, 1952. Ten of his co-accused also hanged. Their families were stripped of their party memberships and privileges, deported with only the barest essentials to designated districts, and assigned to manual labor. ■

assist in the Czech purge—the very same advisers who decided to target Slánský.

For the next year, Slánský endured mental and physical torture, directed by these advisers. Common torture tactics included beatings and kickings; prolonged periods without sleep, food, or water; all-night interrogation sessions; and being forced to stand in one place or march in circles for days on end. One interrogator recalled, "Instead of getting evidence, we were told that they were villains and that we had to break them."[3] Breaking Slánský took six months; the remaining months were spent defining and refining the details of his imaginary crimes against the communist regime, and rehearsing for the all-important show trial.

Slánský's trial, which began on November 20, 1952, was in every sense a show. Before the trial began, party officials had already determined the verdict and the sentences. Prosecutors,

defense attorneys, judges, and the accused spoke the lines of a script written by security agents. Thus, one year after his arrest, Slánský stood up in court and pleaded guilty to the crimes of high treason, espionage, and sabotage. A founding member of the CPC, he said he had conspired to overthrow the communist government. A resistance fighter during World War II, he confessed to working with the Nazis against the communists. A zealous Stalinist, he announced that he was a titoist-Zionist who had plotted to hand Czechoslovakia to the Americans.

Why did Slánský make such a ludicrous confession? Fear of further torture is clearly one motive, but other factors also came into play. Communists such as Slánský believed that the interests of the party always came first, ahead of individual rights, ahead of abstractions such as "truth." Slánský may have believed that his confession, false though it was, served

Questions of Justice

1. In what ways did Cold War concerns shape Slánský's trial?
2. What sort of justice was served in the trial of Rudolf Slánský?

Taking It Further

Lukes, Igor. "The Rudolf Slánský Affair: New Evidence." *Slavic Review* 58, 1 (Spring 1999): 160–187. Illuminating study of the role of Cold War intrigue in determining Slánský's fate.

Kaplan, Karel. *Report on the Murder of the General Secretary.* 1990. Kaplan emigrated from Czechoslovakia to West Germany in the late 1970s, with a stack of hidden documents, and wrote this report.

the Soviets dictate Yugoslavia's foreign and domestic policies. Alarmed by his loss of control over Yugoslavia, Stalin strove frantically to consolidate his control over the rest of eastern Europe by eliminating any potential Tito imitators from these societies. As he had in the Soviet Union in the 1930s, he turned to terror—mass arrests, show trials, torture, imprisonment, and death—to achieve his aims. The Cold War provided Stalin with additional incentives to battle against any possible threat to his personal power. Stalin insisted that a Western conspiracy to divide and conquer the Soviet bloc could be defeated only by a thoroughgoing purge of communist ranks.

Labor and prison camps soon dotted eastern European maps. Between 1948 and 1953, many more communists were killed by their own party members than had died at the hands of the Nazis during World War II. Soviet-trained security forces targeted not only prominent communists but anyone remotely connected to "the West," including veterans of the Spanish Civil War and members of international organizations (such as the Boy Scouts). Jews, considered "cosmopolitan" and therefore potentially pro-Western, were particularly suspect. Only Stalin's death in 1953 caused the wave of persecution to recede.

Soviet leaders jostled for power after Stalin's death but by 1955 Nikita Khrushchev had triumphed over his rivals and claimed control. A true communist success story, Khrushchev was born to illiterate peasants, began work as a coal miner at age 14, and rose to the top of the Soviet system. Convinced by his own experience of the superiority of communism over capitalism, Khrushchev believed that the Soviet Union could win the Cold War on the economic rather than nuclear battlefield—but only if Soviet living standards substantially improved, and only if the Stalinist systems of terror and rigid centralized control were dismantled.

Khrushchev's determination to set communism on a new course became clear in February 1956 when, in a lengthy speech before the Twentieth Congress of the Communist Party, he shocked his listeners by detailing and condemning Stalin's crimes. This "Secret Speech" marked the beginning of de-Stalinization°, a time of greater openness in the Communist bloc when for the first time in years dissent and debate reappeared in public life. De-Stalinization meant the loosening of economic controls as well, as Khrushchev sought to outproduce the capitalist West.

Khrushchev's rivals, however, equated de-Stalinization with destabilization; in 1964, high-ranking communists forced him from office. After a short period of collective leadership, Leonid Brezhnev (1906–1982) emerged as the new Soviet leader, a position he held until his death in 1982. Fifty-eight years old and already physically ailing when he assumed the party leadership, the increasingly decrepit Brezhnev matched his era. During the Brezhnev years the Soviet economy stagnated, and rigid censorship and repression once again characterized Soviet society. Those who expressed dissident views soon found themselves denied employment and educational opportunities, imprisoned, or confined indefinitely in a psychiatric ward.

Yet dissent did not disappear. Soviet society may have resembled a stagnant pond by the 1970s, but beneath the surface churned dangerous currents that, in the late 1980s, would engulf the entire communist system. Nationalism among the non-Russian populations served as the source of much discontent. Non-Russians increasingly equated the centralized economic and political control emanating from Moscow with colonialist dominance rather than with communist solidarity. By the mid-1960s, clandestine nationalist political organizations operated in almost every non-Russian republic of the Soviet Union.

DIVERSITY AND DISSENT IN EASTERN EUROPE

Despite the uniformity imposed by Soviet-style communist systems during these decades, the nations of eastern Europe developed in different ways. De-Stalinization contributed to this diversification. In his "Secret Speech" of 1956, Khrushchev declared, "it is ridiculous to think that revolutions are made to order"[6] and so indicated that communist nations could follow paths diverging from the road traveled by the Soviet Union.

1956 and After

But just how far from the Soviet road could those paths go? The contrasting fates of Poland and Hungary in 1956 provide the answer. In Poland, popular protests against rigid Stalinist controls proved strong enough in 1956 to bring back into power Władysław Gomułka (1905–1982). An influential Polish communist who had been purged in the Stalinist terror of 1951, Gomułka succeeded in establishing a uniquely Polish brand of communism, one that abandoned collective farming and efforts to control Polish Catholicism and yet remained loyal to the Warsaw Pact. During these same years, Hungary also pursued a de-Stalinizing "New Course" under the leadership of a reformist communist. Unlike Gomułka, however, Imre Nagy (1896–1958) proved unable to resist demands for a break with the Soviet Union. By October 1956, hundreds of thousands of Hungarians were on the streets of Budapest, chanting, "We will never again be slaves." On October 31, Hungary withdrew from the Warsaw Pact—or tried to. Four days later, Khrushchev sent in the tanks. As many as 20,000 Hungarians may have died as the Red Army crushed all resistance.[7] Nagy was executed in 1958.

The repression of the Hungarian revolt defined the limits of de-Stalinization in eastern Europe: The Soviet Union's satellite states could not follow paths that led out of the Warsaw Pact. Within the confines of this structure and of the one-party state, however, the governments of eastern Europe continued to pursue different courses. East Germany became the most industrially advanced and urbanized country in eastern Europe, while Poland's countryside was dotted with family farms. Perhaps most surprisingly, post-1956 Hungary became the most liberal country in the Eastern bloc under Nagy's successor, János Kádár (1912–1989), a reformist communist who, like Gomułka, had survived torture and imprisonment during the Stalinist terror of the early 1950s. Kádár encouraged debate within the Communist Party, loosened censorship on film studios and publishers, and permitted private business ventures. In sharp contrast, Romanians endured the reign of the "mini-Stalins." Gheorghe Gheorghiu-Dej (1901–1965) and Nikolai Ceauşescu (1918–1989) imposed not only one-party but one-man control over the country through Stalinist methods of terror.

Within the diverse experiences of eastern Europeans, certain commonalities characterized the post-1956 era. Except in Romania and even more oppressive Albania, living standards improved. Educational opportunities expanded, the supply of consumer goods increased, and political repression became less overt. Even so, overcentralization, bureaucratic mismanagement, and political corruption ensured that living standards remained below those of the West. Moreover, the very consumer goods that were supposed to persuade eastern European citizens of the superiority of the communist system instead demonstrated its deficiencies. With a radio, a Hungarian teenager could tune into Radio Free Europe and hear of a livelier, more abundant society in the West. In East Germany, television watchers could view West German networks and catch a glimpse of Western prosperity.

The Prague Spring

Discontent and dissent simmered throughout the eastern bloc during the 1960s and then, in 1968, boiled over in Czechoslovakia. In the years leading up to 1968, a reform movement within the Czech Communist Party brought to power the communist reformer Alexander Dubček (1921–1992). Dubček sought "socialism with a human face." This more humane socialism included freedom of speech, press, assembly, and travel; the removal of Communist Party controls from social and cultural life; and decentralization of the economy. Dubček's effort to reform the system from the top quickly merged with a wider popular protest movement that had arisen among intellectuals, artists, students, and workers. The result was the Prague Spring°—the blossoming of political and social freedoms throughout Czechoslovakia, but especially in the capital city of Prague.

By the summer of 1968, many of the ideas of the Prague activists were filtering through to other eastern European countries. Frightened communist leaders throughout the eastern bloc demanded that Brezhnev act to stifle the Prague Spring. On the night of August 20–21, 80,000 troops—drawn not only from the Soviet Union but also from

■ **Crushing the Prague Spring, 1968**
Confronted with the overwhelming might of the Warsaw Pact armies, many Czechs tried to reason with the invading soldiers, who could do little but shrug and say they were only obeying orders.

Poland, Hungary, and East Germany—crossed the Czech border and reimposed repressive control.

Brezhnev acknowledged that Soviet domination in eastern Europe rested on force alone when he articulated what came to be known as the "Brezhnev Doctrine." Formally a commitment to support global socialism, the Brezhnev Doctrine was essentially a promise to use the Red Army to stomp on any eastern European effort to achieve fundamental change.

After 1968 eastern Europeans recognized the futility of attempting to reform a system that had now been revealed as beyond reform. Many, perhaps most, retreated to private worlds of friendship and family life (or to the easy escape provided by alcohol). Others refused to give up or give in to a system they now viewed as utterly corrupt. They sought, in the words of the Czech playwright, dissident, and future president Václav Havel (b. 1936), to "live in truth" in the midst of a society based on lies.

The West: Consensus, Consumption, and Culture

······················· ▬ ·······················

As in eastern Europe, in western Europe both the experience of total war and Cold War concerns helped shape postwar societies. The desire to make the suffering of the war years worthwhile, as well as fear of communism, furthered the integration of Europe's economies and helped define the political centrism characteristic of western Europe in the 1950s and 1960s. The dominant fact of the postwar years was, however, material prosperity as western European economies embarked on two decades of dramatic economic growth and consumer spending.

THE TRIUMPH OF DEMOCRACY

In sharp contrast to the interwar years, the parties in power in western Europe in the 1950s and 1960s, and the voters who put them there, agreed on the viability and virtues of parliamentary democracy. The new constitutions of France, West Germany, and Italy guaranteed the protection of individual rights, and French and Italian women achieved suffrage. The democratic ideal of the universal franchise had finally been realized in most of western Europe. Citizenship, though, meant more than the right to vote. It also meant the right to a decent standard of living—to social as well as political democracy. Through the nationalization of key industries, the establishment of public agencies to oversee and encourage investment and trade, and the manipulation of interest rates and currency supplies, governments assumed the task of ensuring full employment, as well as access to an extensive welfare system, for their citizens. The postwar years thus saw the triumph of social democratic politics in Europe.

Postwar Political Consensus

As we saw in Chapter 26, the triumph of social democracy was rooted in the suffering of World War II, as Europeans grew determined to create a better world out of the rubble of total war. This determination remained, but much of the radicalism of the wartime spirit quickly receded as the Cold War constricted the parameters of political debate. The mainstream political parties—Christian Democrats or Conservatives on the right, Social Democrats or Socialists on the left—agreed in refusing to allow Communist Party members to participate in governing coalitions. In France and Italy, communist parties consistently drew 20 to 30 percent of the vote, but their exclusion from office after 1948 effectively marginalized them.

With the communists isolated, and with the ideologies of the extremist right such as fascism and Nazism discredited by the horrors of the war, western European politics took on a new and marked stability during the 1950s and early 1960s. Christian Democratic° parties dominated the political landscape of continental Europe. For example, the Christian Democrats governed West Germany between 1949 and 1969 and provided every prime minister except two in Italy between 1945 and 1993. These parties, which drew on a Roman Catholic base for their support, combined their largely conservative social ideology with a progressive commitment to the welfare state.

Economic Integration and Affluence

These political developments unfolded against an economic backdrop of increasing prosperity. In the first half of the 1950s, Europeans moved rapidly from the austerity of the immediate postwar years to an age of unprecedented affluence.

One important factor in this new prosperity was the greater coordination of western European economies. World War II provided the impetus for this economic integration. Fighting in conditions of unprecedented horror, Europeans looked for ways to guarantee a lasting peace. In 1943, Jean Monnet (1888–1979), who would oversee French economic planning in the postwar era, declared, "there will be no peace in Europe, if the states are reconstituted on the basis of national sovereignty." In July 1944, Resistance leaders from France, Italy, the Netherlands, and a number of other countries met in Geneva to embrace Monnet's vision and declare their support for a federal, democratic Europe.

No such radical restructuring of Europe occurred, but the push toward greater European union moved forward in the years after 1945, impelled by Cold War concerns. Opposition to Stalin helped western Europeans see themselves as part of a single region with common interests. At the same time, American postwar planners—anxious to restore economic prosperity to Europe in order to lessen the appeal of communism—urged their European colleagues to dismantle trade barriers and coordinate national economic plans.

The first step toward economic unification came in 1950 when the French foreign minister Robert Schuman (1886–1963) proposed the merger of the German and French coal and steel industries. The resulting European Coal and Steel Community (ECSC), established in 1952, comprised not only Germany and France, but also Italy, Belgium, the Netherlands, and Luxembourg. It proved to be an economic success, stimulating economic growth throughout the member economies.

Heartened by the success of the ECSC, the six member nations in 1957 formed the European Economic Community° (EEC) or Common Market°. The EEC sought to establish not only an enormous free trade zone across member boundaries, but also to coordinate policies on wages, prices, immigration, and social security. Between 1958 and 1970, trade among its six member states increased fivefold.

If a European living in 1930 had been transported by a time machine to the Europe of 1965, he or she would probably have been most astonished, however, not by European economic integration but by the cornucopia of consumer goods spilling over the lives of ordinary Europeans. After years of wartime rationing, Europeans went on a spending spree and did not stop. A swift and unprecedented climb in real wages—by 80 percent in England, for example, between 1950 and 1970—helps explain why. So too does the construction of the welfare state. With full employment and comprehensive welfare services offering unprecedented financial security, Europeans shrugged off habits of thrift.

This spending spree transformed both the interiors of European homes and the exterior environment. The postwar period witnessed a boom in housing construction. The annual volume of construction rose by 80 percent between 1950 and 1957. With new houses came new household goods. Items such as refrigerators and washing machines, once unaffordable luxuries, now became increasingly common in ordinary homes. In France, the stock of home appliances rose by 400 percent between 1949 and 1957. At the same time, the automobile revolutionized much of both the rural and urban landscape. Highways, few and far between in 1950, cut across the countryside, and parking meters, unknown in Europe before 1959, dotted city streets.

WESTERN CULTURE AND THOUGHT IN THE AGE OF CONSUMPTION

Cultural developments in Western society highlight a shift from an era structured by the memories of World War II to a period shaped by prosperity. Existentialism and modernism retained their dominant cultural position in the later 1940s and 1950s. By the beginning of the 1960s, however, artists began to retreat from engagement with the horrors of World War II and the overwhelming challenges of the Cold War. Instead, they produced works that reflected, commented on, and reveled in the cascade of consumer abundance that was transforming Western culture.

Finding Meaning in the Age of Auschwitz and the Atom Bomb

Forged in the despair of the 1930s and hammered into shape by the horrors of the Second World War, existentialism remained a powerful cultural force in the early postwar era. Jean-Paul Sartre's conviction that existence has no intrinsic meaning, and yet that the individual retains the freedom to act and therefore make meaning, resounded loudly in a world that had experienced both the Holocaust and the Resistance. Hence existentialist themes echoed throughout the visual arts in the 1950s. The sculptures of the Swiss artist Alberto Giacometti (1901–1966), for example, epitomize existentialist anguish—fragile, insubstantial, they appear ready to crack under the strain of being.

In this period, the terrors of the nuclear age also helped shape cultural consciousness. Because figurative painting seemed utterly incapable of capturing the power and terror of the atomic age, the Bomb reinforced the hold of abstract art over the avant-garde. But abstract art itself changed. Formal geometric abstractions had characterized much of prewar art; after the war, a new modernist movement, Abstract Expressionism, displayed more spon-

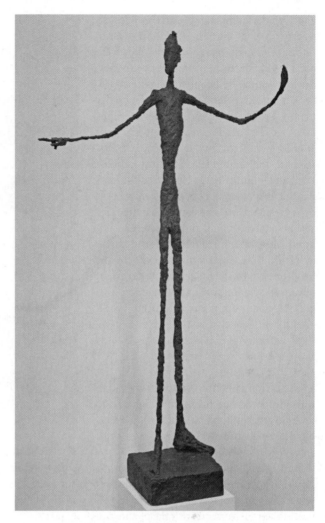

■ **Alberto Giacometti, *Man Pointing* (1947)**
Giacometti's sculptures embodied existentialist anguish. His account of this piece's creation seems to be lifted from one of Jean-Paul Sartre's novels: "Wanting to create from memory [the figures] I had seen, to my terror the sculptures became smaller and smaller, they had a likeness only when they were small, yet their dimensions revolted me, and tirelessly I began again, only to end several months later at the same point."

taneous styles. The Abstract Expressionist Jackson Pollack (1912–1956), for example, invented an entirely new way of painting. Placing the canvas on the ground, he moved around and in it, dripping or pouring paint. In Pollack's works, the canvas has no clear center, no focal point. Instead, it disintegrates, like matter itself. As Pollack explained, "New needs need new techniques . . . The modern painter cannot express his age, the airplane, the atom bomb . . . in the old forms."[8]

Most people confronted their nuclear fears not in art galleries, but rather in movie theaters and popular fiction. In the movies, various nuclear-spawned horrors, including giant spiders, ants, and turtles, wreaked weekly havoc on the Western world. Fittingly enough, many of these films were produced in Japan. Throughout the 1950s, nuclear war and the postnuclear struggle for survival also filled the pages of popular fiction. Probably the most important "nuclear" novel, however, confined mention of atomic bombs to a single sentence. In *The Lord of the Flies* (1954), British author William Golding (1911–1993) told the simple but brutal story of a group of schoolboys stranded on an island after they flee atomic attack. Their moral deterioration poses basic questions about the meaning of civilization, a question brought to the forefront of Western society by its use of advanced science and technology to obliterate civilian populations during World War II.

Culture and Ideas in the World of Plenty

By the early 1960s, however, artists began to turn away from such big questions and to focus instead on the material stuff of everyday existence. In works such as the British artist Richard Hamilton's *Just What Is It That Makes Today's Homes So Different, So Appealing?* (1956), artists satirized and yet celebrated postwar materialism, and revealed their fascination with the plethora of material objects pouring off assembly lines.

■ **Richard Hamilton,** *Just What Is It That Makes Today's Homes So Different, So Appealing?* **(1956)**

British artist Richard Hamilton was one of the leading figures in the Pop art of the 1950s.

This artistic sensibility helped shape Pop art°. Pop focused on the material rather than the spiritual, spoke in the vocabulary of mass material culture, and even relied on mass production and mass marketing. It thus challenged accepted ideas about the role of both art and the artist in Western society. When Gerhard Richter (b. 1932) placed himself in the furniture display of a West German department store and called the resulting "piece" *Living with Pop* (1963), he turned the artist, as well as art, into a commodity, something to be bought and sold just like anything else. In the age of consumption, Pop advocates declared, the individual artist's intentions were unimportant, and concepts such as artistic genius were irrelevant.

Similar themes also characterized developments in social thought. Existentialism had elevated the individual as the only source of meaning in an absurd universe. In the late 1950s, however, a new social theory, structuralism°, pushed the individual off center stage. Structuralism, which French anthropologist Claude Lévi-Strauss (b. 1908) first introduced to a wide audience, transformed a number of academic disciplines, including literary criticism, political theory, sociology, and even history. Lévi-Strauss argued that the myths told in all cultures, whether those of Brazilian Indian tribes still using Stone Age tools or medieval French peasants or contemporary Londoners, shared certain "deep structures," repeated patterns that help give order to the cultural world. In the structuralist view, all human beings exist within a ready-built structure that shapes and dictates the way they perceive the world. Thus in structuralism, as in Pop art, the individual becomes less significant.

Science and Religion in the Age of Affluence

While Lévi-Strauss sought to decipher human culture, biologists embarked on the task of decoding humanity's genetic structure. In 1953, the British biologist Francis Crick (1916–2004) and his American colleague James Watson (b. 1928) discovered the structure of DNA, the basic building block of genetic material. Crick and Watson's model of the "double helix," the intertwined spirals of chemical units that, in a sense, issue the instructions for an individual's development, caught the attention of the world. As biologists and geneticists furthered their investigations into human genetic inheritance, they raised exciting yet potentially disturbing possibilities, such as the cloning of living organisms and genetic manipulation, and added a new dimension to the perennial debate about individual freedom.

Other scientific developments assured human beings more freedom from their physical environment than ever before. Motivated by the Cold War, the space race launched humanity beyond the confines of Earth, culminating in 1969 with the American astronaut Neil Armstrong's moon walk. Medical breakthroughs in this era seemed to promise that infectious diseases could be eradicated. Large-scale production of penicillin transformed ordinary medical care, as did rapid development of vaccines against many childhood killers such as measles. In 1953, the American Jonas Salk announced the first successful clinical trial of a polio vaccine. In this era, blood transfusions become more commonplace, along with the development of organ transplants, following the first successful kidney transplant in Chicago in 1950. Like washing machines and television sets, a long and healthy life suddenly appeared accessible to many people in the West.

While scientists were claiming more control over the physical environment, the organized churches continued to offer spiritual authority and sustenance. Church attendance, which had declined in most Western countries in the interwar period, rose during the 1950s. Throughout Catholic Europe, the vibrancy of Christian Democratic politics reflected the vital position of the Catholic Church in society.

In the 1960s, however, the situation changed dramatically. Europeans abandoned the church sanctuary in favor of the department store, the sports stadium, and the sofa in front of the television set. Declining rates of church attendance, a growing number of civil rather than religious marriage ceremonies, and an increased reluctance to obey Church teaching on issues such as premarital sexual relations all pointed to the secularization of European society. By the 1970s, churchgoing rates in both Protestant and Catholic countries were in freefall. In what had once been called "Christendom," the fastest-growing religious community was Islam.

The churches did not remain stagnant during this time of change. A number of Protestant theologians argued that Christianity could maintain its relevance in this more secular society only by adapting its message to a modern context. The biggest change occurred in Roman Catholicism. In 1963 the Second Vatican Council—widely known as Vatican II°—convened in Rome, the first catholic council to meet since 1870. The Church emerged from Vatican II less hierarchical and more open, with local and regional councils sharing more power with the papacy. For ordinary Catholics, the most striking changes occurred in the worship service. The priest moved from in front of to behind the altar, so that he could face the congregation, and he spoke in the vernacular rather than in Latin.

Vatican II was less revolutionary in its approach to sexual issues and gender roles. The council said nothing about homosexuality, reaffirmed the traditional doctrine of clerical celibacy, and insisted that only men could be ordained as priests. The council left open the question of birth control but three years later, the pope declared contraceptive use to be contrary to Church teaching. The issues of clerical celibacy, women's ordination, and contraceptive use would bedevil the Church for the rest of the century.

SOCIAL ENCOUNTERS IN THE AGE OF AFFLUENCE

With the unprecedented prosperity of the postwar years came a series of encounters between different cultural and social groups. As trade and production increased, so, too, did the volume and variety of goods imported from elsewhere, particularly the United States. The demand for laborers rose as well, bringing with it a rising tide of immigration and of women's employment. Affluence also permitted more young people than ever before to attend colleges and universities. The encounters that resulted from these developments both shaped and were shaped by western Europeans' efforts to make sense of the new material world.

Americanization and Coca-Colonization

For many Europeans, this new world seemed overwhelmingly American, as U.S.-based corporations scattered branch offices throughout western Europe, and U.S.-produced goods filled the shelves of European shops. The U.S. presence in science and technology was also formidable. The United States invested more in scientific research and development, produced more graduates in the sciences and engineering than all other Western countries combined, and came out on top in terms of numbers of papers published and patents registered. American domination of popular culture was even more striking. Immediately after World War II, the U.S. government forced European states to dismantle quotas on American film imports by threatening to withhold much-needed loans. By 1951, American productions accounted for more than 60 percent of film showings in western Europe. American television, too, quickly established a central position in European mass culture. The popular *Lone Ranger* series, for example, appeared in twenty-four countries. Language itself seemed subject to American takeover. Words such as *babysitter* and *comics* entered directly into German, while French children coveted *les jeans* and *le chewing-gum*.

Europeans differed in their response to the new American presence. Many enthusiastically embraced American culture, equating it with greater openness and freedom. Others, however, feared that American products such as Coca-Cola would not only conquer European markets but degrade European tastes. Europeans spoke with alarm about the "brain drain" as scientists and academics headed across the Atlantic to the richer universities of the United States. They argued that even as Europe was losing its colonial possessions, it was itself undergoing colonization, or at least "coca-colonization."[9]

Europeans across the political spectrum feared Europe's becoming a secondhand version of the United States, yet the cultural history of this era was one of reciprocal encounters rather than one-way Americanization. Europeans consumed American products with great gusto, but in the process they adapted these products to suit their own needs. In the late 1950s, for example, four young working-class men from the northern British seaport of Liverpool latched on to the new American rock and roll, mixed in their own regional musical styles, and transformed popular music not only in Europe but also in the United States. The impact of the Beatles testified to the power of European culture to remake American cultural products. Even McDonald's, when it arrived in European cities in the 1960s, made subtle changes to the composition of its fast food to appeal to the differing tastes of the new markets.

Immigration and Ethnic Diversity

A second set of encounters that transformed European societies during this era resulted from the presence of rising numbers of immigrants, who brought with them new and in many cases non-Western cultural traditions. Immigration was the by-product of both decolonization and economic prosperity. As European imperial control collapsed, white settlers retreated back to their country of origin, and colonial "losers"—indigenous groups that had allied with the now-defeated colonial powers—fled because they feared discrimination, retribution, or perhaps simply a loss of status. At the same time, as northern and western European states experienced both soaring economic growth figures and a slowing rate of population increase, governments recruited foreign labor. By the beginning of the 1970s, the nations of northern and western Europe were home to approximately nine million immigrants, half of these from the less prosperous Mediterranean states of Portugal, Spain, Italy, and Greece. The other half came from Turkey, Yugoslavia, and countries in Asia, Africa, and the Caribbean.

These workers did the dirtiest, most dangerous, least desirable jobs. They worked the night shifts, emptied the bed-

■ **Immigrants Arriving in Britain, 1956**
Many immigrants from regions within the British Empire had been taught that Britain was the "mother country" or "home." They were shocked to discover that once in Britain, they were regarded as foreign and as inferior.

pans, dug the ditches, and cleaned the toilets. They lived in substandard housing, often confined to isolated dormitories or inner-city slums, and accepted low, often illegally low, pay rates. Yet despite discrimination and exploitation, western Europe offered greater economic opportunities than were available in the immigrants' homelands.

The majority of the early immigrants were single men. They tended to see themselves, and were seen by their host countries, as "guest workers," temporary laborers who would earn money and then return home to their native lands. By the mid-1960s, however, families were beginning to join these men, and a second generation of "immigrants" was being born. This generation changed the face of Europe. By the 1980s European societies had become multiethnic.

The emergence of urban ethnic subcultures immeasurably enlivened European cultures and economies (and diets); it also complicated domestic politics and raised challenging questions about the relationship between national and ethnic identity. Racism became more overt as the white settler groups who returned "home" in the wake of decolonization often brought with them hardened racist attitudes, and the presence of nonwhite minority groups, clustered in certain cities, sparked resentment in societies unused to cultural diversity.

The Second Sex?

In 1949, the French writer Simone de Beauvoir (1908–1986) published *The Second Sex*. In this influential critique of gender divisions in Western industrial society, de Beauvoir argued that women remained the "second sex"— that despite changes in their political and legal status, women were still defined by their relationship to men rather than by their own actions or achievements. Over the next two decades, the new prosperity pushed women into higher education and the labor force and so, in the long run, worked to undermine the traditional gender roles that de Beauvoir described. In the short run, however, affluence accentuated women's domestic identity.

A number of changes both reflected and reinforced postwar domesticity. The most important were demographic. Marriage rates rose and the marriage age dropped in the postwar years. In the United States, between 1940 and 1957, the fertility rate rose by 50 percent. Europe experienced a baby "boomlet" rather than a baby boom. European birth rates rose in the late 1940s but dropped again in the 1950s (whereas U.S. fertility rates remained high into the 1960s). Nevertheless, although family sizes were small, a higher percentage of western European women than ever before had children.

By exalting women's maternal identity, both religion and popular culture provided a potent ideology for these demographic changes. The Roman Catholic Church of the 1950s placed renewed emphasis on Mary, the paragon of motherhood. Pope Pius XII (r. 1939–1958) particularly encouraged the growth of devotion to Mary. He proclaimed in 1950 that Mary had ascended bodily into heaven (the Doctrine of the Assumption) and designated 1954 as the Year of Mary. This Marian devotion encouraged women to regard motherhood as a holy calling and the very core of female identity. Popular culture reinforced this religious message, with its glossy images of what families should look like and how they should interact. In television programs and in the articles and advertisements of women's magazines, the woman stayed at home, presiding over an expanding array of household machines that, in theory, reduced her housework burden and freed her to focus on the satisfactions of motherhood.

The domestic ideal, however, remained removed from the reality of many women's lives in the postwar era. In the poorer social classes, women by necessity continued to work outside the home, as they always had. At the same time, the new culture of consumption demanded that many women, clinging precariously to the middle rungs of the social ladder, take on paid employment to pay for the ever-expanding list of household necessities.

A new pattern of employment emerged that reconciled the new domesticity with the needs of expanding economies. Increasingly, single women, including those in the middle class, worked until they married. Many continued to do so until the first child arrived, and resumed paid employment after the last child had left home or at least started school. This work was regarded, however, as secondary to their main job—the making of a home and the rearing of children. Part-time employment, with lower wages and few or no benefits, expanded accordingly. Everywhere pay rates remained unequal.

Inequalities in legal status continued as well. Until 1964 and the passage of the Matrimonial Act, for example, a married French woman could not open her own bank account, run a shop, or apply for a passport without her husband's permission. Traditional gender roles remained firmly intact, despite the material and political changes of the postwar era.

The Protest Era

The unprecedented prosperity of the West in this era permitted a dramatic expansion of higher education systems. By the later 1960s, the expanding university campuses became the center of powerful protests as political demonstrations exploded in almost every Western country and in the developing nations well. In France, a student demonstration blossomed into a full-scale social revolt. Within a few days, eight million French men and women were on strike. "Paris '68" came to symbolize the political and social discontent of many in the West, particularly the youth, during these years.

Much of this discontent focused on the New Left° argument that ordinary people, even in democratic

ROCK AND REVOLUTION

·················

In 1967, the Beatles, already global superstars, released Sgt. Pepper's Lonely Hearts Club Band. *Called the "most influential rock album ever produced,"* Sgt. Pepper's *revolutionized rock music. The complexity of its compositions impressed serious music critics, who for the first time acknowledged that rock music was worth listening to. The album's lyrics, too, received unprecedented praise, with one reviewer comparing the last song on the album ("A Day in the Life") to T. S. Eliot's modernist masterpiece, "The Waste Land" (see Chapter 25). Although not overtly political,* Sgt. Pepper's *illustrates many of the themes of the protests that marked the era in which it was produced. Infused with a sense of playfulness and celebration, the album called its listeners to burst out of the confines of order, authority, and rationality, and embrace instead the values of human community and emotional liberation.*

SHE'S LEAVING HOME

Wednesday morning at five o'clock as the day begins
Silently closing her bedroom door
Leaving the note that she hoped would say more
She goes downstairs to the kitchen clutching her
    handkerchief
Quietly turning the backdoor key
Stepping outside she is free.
She (We gave her most of our lives)
is leaving (Sacrificed most of our lives)
home (We gave her everything money could buy)

She's leaving home after living alone
For so many years. Bye, bye
Father snores as his wife gets into her dressing gown
Picks up the letter that's lying there
Standing alone at the top of the stairs
She breaks down and cries to her husband
Daddy our baby's gone.
Why would she treat us so thoughtlessly
How could she do this to me.
She (We never thought of ourselves)
is leaving (Never a thought for ourselves)
home (We struggled hard all our lives to get by)
She's leaving home after living alone
For so many years. Bye, bye
Friday morning at nine o'clock she is far away
Waiting to keep the appointment she made
Meeting a man from the motor trade.
She (What did we do that was wrong)
is having (We didn't know it was wrong) fun
Fun is the one thing that money can't buy
Something inside that was always denied
For so many years. Bye, bye
She's leaving home bye bye

societies, possessed little power. Appalled by the excesses of Stalinism and concerned about the growth of large corporations and of the state itself in the West, New Left thinkers such as the German philosopher Herbert Marcuse (1898–1979) warned that expanding corporate and state power threatened the individuality and independence of the ordinary citizen. They argued that debate might seem open, but that experts and elites, not ordinary people, made the actual choices. Hence the protesters demanded "participatory" rather than parliamentary democracy, the revitalization of citizenship through active participation in decision making.

Discarding orthodox political solutions went hand in hand with overturning traditional social rules. In their demand for "liberation," the students focused as much on cultural as on economic and political issues. Commentators

began to talk about a sexual revolution as practices became commonplace that in the 1950s were labeled immoral or bohemian—couples living together before marriage or individuals engaging in sexual relationships with a variety of partners.

The protests of the later 1960s were also linked to the wider context of decolonization and the Cold War. Protesters identified their struggle for a more open politics with colonial independence movements. Rejecting both Soviet-style communism and free-market capitalism, they turned for inspiration to the newly emerging nations of Latin America and Asia. Seeking to break free from the confines of the Cold War, they fiercely criticized American involvement in Vietnam, in which they believed the United States served not as "the leader of the free world" but rather as an imperialist oppressor.

CONCLUSION
New Definitions, New Divisions

····························· ▬ ·····························

The Cold War was in part an ideological encounter, with both sides laying claim to the title "democratic." When Soviet tanks rolled through the streets of Budapest in 1956, they flattened not only the Hungarian Revolution but also any illusions about the democratic nature of Soviet-style communism. Yet the hope that the communist system could be reformed, that Marx's original concern for social justice and political equality could be reclaimed, remained—until twelve years later when the tanks rolled again in an eastern European city. The crushing of the Prague Spring destroyed any hope of a democratic eastern Europe within the confines of the Cold War.

In contrast, democracy took firm root in western Europe during the postwar era, even in nations with antidemocratic cultural traditions such as West Germany and Italy. Yet in 1968, protesters in Paris and in cities throughout the world challenged the easy linkage of "the West" with democracy. They pointed out that the increasing scale and complexity of industrial society deprived ordinary people of opportunities for genuine participation in political decision making. And they pointed to the way that Cold War divisions superseded democratic commitments. Despite its abandonment of democratic practices to reinforce racial apartheid, for example, South Africa considered itself, and was considered by other powers, as part of "the West." Within the Cold War context, "the West" sometimes seemed to mean simply "anti-Soviet."

By the early 1970s, the sharp bipolarities of West versus East had begun to break down. Over the next three decades, economic crisis, combined with revolutionary changes in eastern European and Soviet affairs, would reshape the contemporary world. By the early 1990s, the Cold War was over and nationalist conflicts, often fueled by vicious ethnic and religious hatreds, once again played front and center, after twenty years of being upstaged by superpower hostilities.

Suggestions for Further Reading

····························· ▬ ·····························

For a comprehensive list of suggested readings, please go to www.ablongman.com/levackconcise/chapter27

Ansprenger, Franz. *The Dissolution of Colonial Empires.* 1989. A clear and comprehensive account (that unfortunately includes no maps).

Castles, Stephen, et al. *Here for Good: Western Europe's New Ethnic Minorities.* 1984. A useful exploration of the impact of postwar immigration, despite the rather rigid Marxist analysis.

Crampton, R. J. *Eastern Europe in the Twentieth Century–and After.* 1997. Detailed chapters on the 1950s and 1960s, including a substantial discussion of the Prague Spring.

Cronin, James. *The World the Cold War Made: Order, Chaos, and the Return of History.* 1996. An intelligent and thought-provoking overview of the impact of the Cold War.

Fineberg, Jonathan. *Art Since 1940: Strategies of Being.* 1995. A big, bold, lavishly illustrated volume that makes the unfashionable argument that individuals matter.

Fink, Carole, et al. *1968: The World Transformed.* 1998. A collection of essays that explores both the international and the domestic political context for the turmoil of 1968.

Gross, Jan T., ed. *The Politics of Retribution in Europe: World War II and Its Aftermath.* 2000. This series of essays makes clear that war did not end in Europe in May 1945.

Isaacs, Jeremy, and Taylor Downing. *Cold War: An Illustrated History.* 1998. The companion book to the CNN television series. Filled with memorable photographs.

Judge, Edward, and John Langdon. *A Hard and Bitter Peace: A Global History of the Cold War.* 1999. An extremely useful survey for students. Excellent maps.

Keep, John. *Last of the Empires: A History of the Soviet Union, 1945–1991.* 1995. Looks beyond the Kremlin to explore social, cultural, and economic developments.

Mazrui, Ali, and Michael Tidy. *Nationalism and New States in Africa.* 1984. Offers a thematic rather than chronological account of African state building.

Poiger, Uta. *Jazz, Rock, and Rebels: Cold War Politics and American Culture in a Divided Germany.* 2000. Explores the interplay among youth culture, Americanization, and political protest.

de Senarclens, P. *From Yalta to the Iron Curtain: The Great Powers and the Origins of the Cold War.* 1995. A look at the diplomatic, political, and military concerns that created the Cold War.

Stromberg, Roland. *After Everything: Western Intellectual History Since 1945.* 1975. A swiftly moving tour through the major intellectual developments.

Urwin, Derek. *A Political History of Western Europe Since 1945.* 1997. Readable, reasonably up-to-date, and comprehensive.

Wyman, Mark. *DPs: Europe's Displaced Persons, 1945–1951.* 1989. An important study of an often-neglected topic.

Zubok, Vladislav, and Constantine Pleshakov. *Inside the Kremlin's Cold War: From Stalin to Khrushchev.* 1996. A close examination of the Cold War on the Soviet side.

Notes

1. The original signatories of the NATO treaty were Iceland, Norway, Great Britain, Belgium, the Netherlands, Luxembourg, France, Italy, and Portugal. Greece and Turkey joined the alliance in 1951, West Germany in 1954, Spain in 1982. Sweden, Finland, Switzerland, Austria, Yugoslavia, and Albania remained nonaligned with either the United States or the Soviet Union.
2. Quotation from *Time,* 1950; quoted in Martin Walker, *The Cold War and the Making of the Modern World* (1993), 66–67.
3. Quoted in Karel Kaplan, *Report on the Murder of the General Secretary* (1990), 159.
4. Ibid., 242.
5. Ibid., 231.
6. Ibid., 105.
7. Official Hungarian statistics reported 3,000 dead. John Lewis Gaddis places the number at 20,000 in *We Now Know: Rethinking Cold War Evidence* (1997).
8. Quoted in Jonathan Fineberg, *Art Since 1940: Strategies of Being* (1995), 89.
9. Reinhold Wagnleitner, *Coca-Colonization and the Cold War: The Cultural Mission of the United States in Austria After the Second World War* (1994).

The West in the Contemporary Era: New Encounters and Transformations

O N THE EVENING OF NOVEMBER 9, 1989, EAST GERMAN BORDER GUARDS stationed at the wall that divided East and West Berlin gazed out nervously at an unprecedented sight. Thousands of their fellow citizens had gathered in front of the gates and were demanding to be let through into the western half of the city. This demand was extraordinary; in the twenty-eight years that the Berlin Wall had stood, over 200 people had been shot trying to cross it. But the autumn of 1989 was no ordinary time. A radically reformist regime had emerged in the Soviet Union and publicly proclaimed that its eastern European allies could no longer rely on the Soviet army to assist them in putting down domestic dissent. Poland and Hungary were in the process of replacing communist governments with pluralist parliamentary systems. And in East Germany itself, 200,000 disaffected citizens had taken advantage of relaxed border controls in Hungary and Czechoslovakia to flee to the West in just a few weeks, while over one million had joined illegal protest demonstrations.

On November 9, in response to overwhelming public pressure, the East German government announced that it would drastically relax the requirements for obtaining an exit visa to visit or emigrate to the West. In a press conference to announce the upcoming changes, the East Berlin Communist Party boss Gunter Schabowski gave a carelessly worded reply to a reporter's question about the new travel policy. Schabowski indicated, incorrectly, that as of the next morning, anyone who wanted to head to the West could obtain an automatic exit visa at the border. The news spread quickly, and huge crowds gathered at the checkpoints that dotted the Berlin Wall. The nervous border guards had no idea what to do. Neither did their superiors, who refused to issue the guards any clear instructions. As the crowds pressed forward, the guards gave in and opened the gates. While television cameras broadcast the scene to an astonished world, tens of thousands of East Germans walked, ran, and danced across the border that had

Chapter Outline

- Economic Stagnation and Political Change: The 1970s and 1980s

- Revolution in the East

- In the Wake of Revolution

- Rethinking the West

And the Wall Came Tumbling Down: Berliners celebrate the fall of the Berlin Wall in November 1989.

for so long literally and symbolically divided West from East. Elated with their new freedom and energized with a sense of power and possibility, they then turned on the wall itself. Jumping on top of it, they transformed it from an instrument of coercion and division into a platform for partying. Caught, the East German government saw no way to close the gates. Within a few days, and again without any official approval, ordinary Germans, equipped with hammers and chisels, began to dismantle the wall that the politicians had erected almost three decades earlier.

As extraordinary as the fall of the wall was, the events that followed over the next two years proved even more dramatic—the collapse of communist regimes throughout eastern Europe, the end of the Cold War, the disintegration of the Soviet Union, and the onset of civil war in Yugoslavia and in many formerly Soviet regions. Over the next decade, both governments and ordinary people—not only throughout Europe but across the globe—struggled to build new structures to suit the vastly changed geopolitical landscape. With the collapse of communism and the sundering of the Iron Curtain that had once divided Europe, the meaning of "the West" itself changed, as new enemies emerged to take the place of the Soviet Union. Clearly, then, the dramatic developments of 1989–1991 deserve close study, but they must be set within a context of causes and consequences.

To explain that context, this chapter will address four questions:

- How did economic and political developments in the 1970s and 1980s interact to end the international structures of the postwar era and create a volatile situation within the Soviet bloc?
- What factors explain not only the outbreak but also the success of the revolutions of 1989–1991?
- What were the consequences of these revolutions for the societies of eastern Europe?
- What were the implications of these developments for the meaning of "the West" itself?

Economic Stagnation and Political Change: The 1970s and 1980s

A s the 1960s drew to a close, the risk of nuclear war seemed to recede with the onset of detente°, the effort to stabilize superpower relations through negotiations and arms control. But stability remained elusive. Economic crisis heightened political and social polarization, while the renewal of the Cold War at the end of

the 1970s destabilized both international and domestic relations.

THE 1970S: A MORE UNCERTAIN ERA

In the early 1970s, the United States and Europe—both East and West—entered a new era. Detente signaled a relaxing of the Cold War tensions that had structured so much of international relations since the end of World War II, while economic developments warned that the easy affluence of the postwar era had ended.

The Era of Detente

Changes in the Cold War climate were first felt in West Germany. In 1969 the West Berlin mayor and Social Democratic Party (SPD) leader Willy Brandt (1913–1992) became chancellor. This first non-Christian Democratic government in over twenty years proceeded to implement a new *Ostpolitik* or "Eastern policy"—the opening of diplomatic and economic relations between West Germany and the Soviet Union and its satellite states. In the triumphant climax of Ostpolitik, East and West Germany recognized the legitimacy of each other's existence in 1972 and in the next year, both Germanys entered the United Nations.

During this era, the leaders of the superpowers also acted to break down the bipolarities of the Cold War. By the end of the 1960s, both the Soviet Union and the United States faced stagnating economies, and both were spending $50 million per day on nuclear weapons. These economic pressures led Soviet and American leaders to embrace détente. In November 1969 Soviet and American negotiators began the Strategic Arms Limitation Talks (SALT). Signed in 1972, the agreement froze the existing weapons balance.

Important changes within the communist world also contributed to detente. Throughout the 1930s and 1940s, the Chinese Communist leader Mao Zedong was an obedient disciple of Stalin. In the 1950s, however, relations cooled when Mao challenged Khrushchev's aim of "peaceful co-existence" with the West. Khrushchev, in turn, opposed Mao's "Great Leap Forward." This effort to transform a peasant society into an industrial powerhouse in one year led to the deaths of an estimated 30 million Chinese, victims of starvation and Mao's fantasies. Horrified, Khrushchev suspended economic aid to China in 1960. By the time the first Chinese atomic bomb exploded in 1964, the split between China and the Soviet Union was open and irrevocable. U.S. president Richard Nixon (1913–1994) and his national security adviser Henry Kissinger (b. 1923) decided to take advantage of this Sino-Soviet split. In 1971, Nixon announced the lifting of travel and trade restrictions with China, and then sent shock waves through the world by visiting China himself. Nixon's reconciliation with communist China was a turning point: In the 1950s and 1960s, "East versus West" had formed a basic building block of international relations. In the 1970s, the shape of international politics looked much less clear.

Economic Crisis and Its Consequences

The economic outlook also blurred in this era as the 1970s brought an unprecedented combination of high inflation and high unemployment rates. Commentators labeled this new reality stagflation°—the escalating prices of a boom economy combined with the joblessness of an economy going bust. Between 1974 and 1976 the average annual growth rate within western European nations dropped to zero.

War and oil played important roles in creating this economic crisis. In October 1973, Egyptian and Syrian armies attacked Israel. In retaliation for American military aid to Israel, the oil-producing states, or OPEC (Organization of Petroleum Exporting Countries), imposed an embargo on sales to the United States and drove up prices from $3 to $16 per barrel of oil. In 1979 political revolution in Iran sparked an even more dramatic price rise—up to $35 per barrel by 1981. These price increases vastly accelerated the inflationary spiral.

International competition contributed to the crisis. Western societies possessed a politicized workforce that demanded relatively high wages and extensive social services. Increasingly, manufacturing concerns moved south and east, to take advantage of the lack of labor regulation and protection in the developing world.

As the economic pie grew smaller, competition for slices grew fierce. The 1970s saw a resurgence of industrial unrest in western Europe. Racial and ethnic conflict also worsened. We saw in Chapter 27 that postwar governments struggling to cope with labor shortages had encouraged immigration. With the onset of economic crisis, these immigrant communities soon found themselves under attack. By 1975 West Germany, France, the Netherlands, Britain, Belgium, Sweden, and Switzerland had all banned further immigration. Because it explicitly (although incorrectly) linked the presence of immigrants to unemployment, anti-immigration legislation helped solidify racist attitudes among many sectors of the European population. Violence against immigrants began to escalate.

Explicitly racist political parties capitalized on the new anti-immigration sentiment. In France, for example, Jean-Marie Le Pen (b. 1928), a veteran of the Algerian war, created the *Front National* in 1974 as an anti-immigration party. Appealing particularly to young, male working-class voters, Le Pen's party remained a threatening political presence for the next three decades.

THE 1980S: THE END OF CONSENSUS IN THE WEST

The economic crisis of the 1970s called into question the social democratic assumptions that had governed political life since World War II. Discontented voters looked for

■ **The New Conservatism**
Britain's first female prime minister, Margaret Thatcher, called herself a "conviction" rather than a "consensus" politician. She held office from 1979 to 1990—the longest term of any British prime minister in the twentieth century.

radically new answers. In Spain, Portugal, and Greece, they turned to socialist parties. Throughout most of western Europe and in the United States, however, New Conservatism° dominated political society.

The New Conservatives

Three leaders epitomized the New Conservatism: the Republican Ronald Reagan in the United States (1911–2004), the Christian Democrat Helmut Kohl in West Germany (b. 1930), and the Conservative Margaret Thatcher in Britain (b. 1925). New Conservatives rejected the postwar emphasis on social improvement in favor of policies intended to create less governmental control and more opportunities for individual achievement. Thus they sought to privatize state-owned industries and to dismantle the welfare state. In the New Conservative analysis, rising social expenditures, funded by rising taxes, lay at the heart of the economic crisis.

Yet New Conservative fiscal policies did not actually break sharply from their social democratic predecessors. Reagan, for example, used deficit spending to finance skyrocketing military budgets (up by 40 percent during his administration). The real break lay in the New Conservatives' willingness to tolerate high unemployment rates. By imposing high interest rates on their economies, Thatcher and Reagan brought inflation under control. High interest rates, however, overvalued the British pound and the American dollar. As a result, manufacturers found it hard to sell their products abroad and many went under. In Britain, 13 percent of the workforce was unemployed by 1984. In West Germany, too, Kohl's policies of holding down taxes and government expenditures were accompanied by unemployment rates of over 9 percent in the mid-1980s.

By the end of the 1980s, as a result of falling global oil prices and the Reagan military spending spree that primed the pump of the global economy, Western economies returned to growth. But the average late-1980s growth rates of 2 to 3 percent per year were lower than those of 5 to 6 percent that had characterized Western economies in the 1950s and 1960s. At the same time, unemployment rates tended to hover between 5 and 7 percent—levels that would have been regarded as unacceptably high in the earlier period. A new political culture, based on lowered expectations, had come into being.

Even Europe's leftist parties had to adapt to this new political culture. Socialist and social democratic governments in Sweden, Italy, Greece, and Spain during the 1980s also followed the path of reduced health and social security expenditures and wage cuts. The most dramatic example of the adaptation of the left occurred in France. In 1981, French voters elected Socialist Party leader François Mitterrand (1916–1996) to the presidency. In his first year in office, Mitterrand implemented a series of radical social democratic measures, including a rise in the minimum wage, a reduction in the workweek, expanded social welfare, and higher taxes for the wealthy. But in 1982, Mitterrand was forced by a series of economic catastrophes—falling exports, rising trade and budget deficits, soaring inflation rates—to cut social spending and to let unemployment rates rise.

New Challenges and New Identities

The triumph of New Conservatism demonstrated that economic crisis had shattered the post-World War II social democratic consensus. The protests of the 1960s also helped break apart this consensus, and in the 1970s, two offshoots of these protests—new feminism and environmentalism—offered new cultural and political alternatives.

New feminism° emerged directly out of the student protest movement of the 1960s. Female activists, eager to connect analyses of political subordination to their own experiences of sexual repression, grew frustrated at being denied a voice in the protests. Their efforts to liberate women from political and cultural limits and expectations gave birth to what was, by the 1980s, an international feminist movement.

Economic and demographic changes buttressed the new feminism. The numbers of women working outside the home rose in these decades—up by 50 percent in Italy between 1970 and 1985, for example. By the late 1970s, women in France accounted for over 34 percent of the labor force; in Britain, 31 percent; in West Germany, 37 percent. During the same decade, the age at which men and women first married began to climb and birth rates continued to fall.

Western politics gradually responded to the changes in women's roles. In the British general elections of 1992, twice as many women stood as parliamentary candidates compared to 1979. By the mid-1980s, women averaged about one-third of the members of parliament in Sweden, and women members accounted for approximately half of Norway's cabinets. Feminists sponsored legislation that outlawed spousal rape and legalized abortion. They also achieved greater access to educational and professional opportunities for women, as well as more generous parental leave policies, family allowances, and child care provisions.

Environmentalists added their voice to the political cacophony of the 1970s and 1980s. They challenged the fundamental structures of industrial economies (whether capitalist or communist), particularly their inherent emphasis on "more, bigger, faster, now." The movement embraced the ideas of unorthodox economists such as Britain's E. F. Schumacher (1911–1977), who insisted that quantitative measures of economic growth (such as the GNP) failed to factor in environmental destruction and social dislocation, and that in many contexts, "small is beautiful." Drawing on the protests of the 1960s, they demanded a new politics, one that would draw ordinary citizens more directly into the political process.

Green politics° drew its ideas not only from environmentalism but also from feminism. The Greens contended that the degradation of the natural environment stemmed from the same root as discrimination against women—an obsession with physical power and an unwillingness to tear down hierarchical structures. By the late 1980s Green Parties had sprouted in fifteen western European countries. The Greens were the most successful in West Germany, where they sat in the legislature from 1983 and formed an important voting bloc.

From Detente to Renewed Cold War

At the same time that economic crisis, feminist protest, and the new environmental awareness undermined political consensus, rising superpower tensions put an end to the era of detente and caused greater rifts within western European societies. In the first half of the 1970s, detente had appeared to be flourishing. In 1975 representatives of 32 European states, Canada, the United States, and the Soviet Union signed the Helsinki Accords. They declared their acceptance of all existing European borders, agreed to a policy of joint notification of all major military exercises (thus reducing the chances of accidental nuclear war), and promised to safeguard the human rights of their citizens.

Yet the Helsinki Accords marked not only the culmination but also the beginning of the end of the detente era. First, eastern European and Soviet dissidents used the Helsinki human rights clauses to publicize the human rights abuses committed by their governments and to demand fundamental reforms. Second, U.S. president Jimmy Carter, who took office in 1976, chose to place human rights at the center of his foreign policy. Carter's approach infuriated Soviet leaders, who resented what they regarded as his meddling in their internal affairs. As detente crumbled, the arms race accelerated, with both the Warsaw Pact and NATO increasing their defense budgets and deploying intermediate-range nuclear missiles.

Detente finally died in December 1979, when Soviet troops invaded Afghanistan. Calling the invasion "the most serious threat to peace since the Second World War," Carter warned that if the Soviets moved toward the Middle East, he would not hesitate to use nuclear weapons.

With the election of New Conservatives such as Thatcher in 1979 and Reagan in 1980, the renewal of the Cold War took on a greater intensity. Reagan labeled the Soviet Union the "Evil Empire"—a reference to the popular *Star Wars* film series that was first released in the 1970s—and revived the anticommunist attitudes and rhetoric of the 1950s. Thatcher strongly supported Reagan's decision to accelerate the arms buildup begun by Carter. Her hard-line anticommunism won her the nickname "The Iron Lady" from Soviet policymakers.

The renewal of the Cold War, like the end of economic prosperity, opened up large rifts within western European societies. NATO's decision to deploy its new generation of nuclear missiles drew hundreds of thousands of protesters into the streets of London, Bonn, Amsterdam, and other cities. Many of these protesters demanded not only the cancellation of the cruise missiles but also a withdrawal from NATO's nuclear umbrella.

Revolution in the East

Between 1989 and 1991, revolution engulfed eastern Europe and the Soviet Union. The appointment of Mikhail Gorbachev (b. 1931) as Soviet Communist Party Secretary in 1985 proved pivotal. Gorbachev's efforts to reform the Soviet system led to a series of breathtaking changes: Soviet control over eastern Europe ended, the Cold War came to an abrupt halt, the Soviet Union itself ceased to exist. Ironically, Gorbachev set in motion the first two of these developments precisely to avoid the third.

THE CRISIS OF LEGITIMACY IN THE EAST

While Western countries in the 1970s struggled with stagflation and disappearing economic growth rates, the Soviet Union posted record-breaking production figures. By 1984, for example, the Soviet Union was producing 80 percent more steel and six times as much iron ore compared to the United States. But Soviet prosperity was an illusion. Published growth and productivity statistics had little to do with actual economic performance. The Soviet economy continued to be hampered by overcentralization. "Success" in Soviet industry meant fulfilling arbitrary quotas, regardless of the quality of goods produced, the actual demand for the product, or the cost of producing it. By the 1980s, the only growth sectors in the Soviet economy were oil and vodka—and then the bottom dropped out of the oil market. After 1981, oil prices began a steady fall. For the Soviet economy, the results were catastrophic.

The Soviet leadership was incapable of responding to the economic crisis. Throughout the 1970s, Soviet leader Leonid Brezhnev's increasing physical frailty mirrored that of the country at large. Like many of his colleagues, Brezhnev had been a child at the time of the Russian Revolution; he knew only Soviet rule and had risen into major office very young because of the employment opportunities created by Stalin's Great Purge. In 1982, the average age of members of the Politburo was 68. These men had a vested interest in maintaining the status quo, not in carrying out fundamental reform.

The Soviet Union's satellite states in eastern Europe also lurched from apparent prosperity into economic crisis during this period. During the 1970s, the Soviets provided oil to their eastern European satellites at prices far below the market value and so shielded these economies from some of the tensions afflicting their western European rivals. At the same time, eastern European governments borrowed heavily from Western banks. Western loans did not, however, solve fundamental problems such as overcentralization and the divorce of prices from production costs.

In the 1980s, the debt-laden economic structures of eastern Europe began to collapse. Two factors were crucial. First, governments found they had to borrow simply to service their existing debt. Second, as oil prices fell, the Soviet Union responded by charging market value for its oil sales to its satellites, thus depriving these economies of a crucial support. Ordinary people soon felt the impact of this economic crisis as governments restricted the flow of consumer goods and imposed higher prices.

Events in Poland at the end of the decade illustrated how economic discontent and political dissent could create a revolutionary situation. Faced with negative economic growth rates, the Polish government announced price increases for meat and other essentials in July 1980. Poles hit the streets in angry protest. This protest gave birth to Solidarity.° Led by a charismatic and politically savvy electrician named Lech Wałęsa (b. 1943), Solidarity was both a trade union and a political movement. It demanded not only the right to unionize and strike, but also the liberation of political prisoners, an end to censorship, and a rollback of the state's power. Within just a few months, ten million Poles had joined Solidarity's ranks.

Fearing Soviet military intervention, the Polish communist government cracked down. In December 1981 Prime Minister Wojciech Jaruzelski declared martial law and arrested more than 10,000 Solidarity members (including Wałęsa). Like the Hungarian Revolution in 1956 and the Prague Spring of 1968, Solidarity seemed to be one more futile and defeated protest in eastern Europe. The Solidarity story, however, ended very differently. As Poland's economic crisis deepened, its debt to the West climbed inexorably, food shortages became endemic, unemployment rates rose, and real wages fell.

But Solidarity refused to be defeated. Both in prison and out, its members resolved to act as if they were free. They met in small groups, published newspapers and ran a radio station, and organized election boycotts. Solidarity remained a political presence and a moral force in Polish society throughout the 1980s, and in 1989 it emerged to lead Poland into democracy.

GORBACHEV'S RADICAL REFORMS AND THE REVOLUTION IN EASTERN EUROPE

In 1982, the decrepit Leonid Brezhnev died—and so, very quickly, did his two successors, Yuri Andropov (1982–1984) and Konstantin Chernenko (1984–1985). The time had come for a generational change. When Mikhail Gorbachev succeeded Chernenko, he was 54 years old. Compared to his elderly colleagues on the Politburo, he looked like a teenager.

Gorbachev came to power in 1985, convinced that the Soviet system was ailing, and that the only way to restore it to health was through radical surgery. What he did not anticipate was that such surgery would in fact kill the patient. His surgical tools were glasnost and perestroika, two Russian terms without direct English equivalents.

Glasnost°, roughly translated as "openness," "publicity," or "transparency," meant abandoning the deception and censorship that had always characterized the Soviet system, for a policy based on open admission of failures and problems. Through glasnost Gorbachev aimed to overcome the alienation and apathy that he perceived as endemic in Soviet culture, to convince citizens of the importance of participating in the structures of political and economic life.

At the same time, he sought to change those structures through perestroika°, often translated as "restructuring" or "reconstruction." Gorbachev believed he could reverse his nation's economic decline only through a series of reforms focusing on modernization, decentralization, and the introduction of a limited market. He knew, however, that even limited reforms threatened the vested interests of communist bureaucrats. Thus the success of economic perestroika depended on political perestroika. The culmination of political restructuring came in May 1989, when Soviet voters entered the voting booths to elect the Congress of People's Deputies, and for the first time in Soviet history they had a choice of candidates. True, all of these candidates were Communists, but just one year later, Gorbachev ended the Communist Party's monopoly on parliamentary power, and the Soviet Union entered the brave new world of multiparty politics.

■ **Glasnost**
Mikhail Gorbachev meets with workers in Moscow in 1985.

Restructuring Soviet economics and politics also demanded restructuring international relations. By the 1980s, at least 18 percent of the Soviet GNP was absorbed by the arms race; Gorbachev concluded that the Soviet Union simply could not afford the Cold War. As soon as Gorbachev took office, then, he signaled to the West his desire to resume arms control negotiations. In December 1987, Gorbachev and U.S. president Ronald Reagan signed the INF (Intermediate Nuclear Forces) Treaty, agreeing to the total elimination of land-based intermediate-range nuclear missiles. In 1991, the superpowers agreed to reduce their stockpiles of intercontinental ballistic missiles (ICBMs).

The need to reduce military spending also led to the Soviet retreat from eastern Europe. In his first informal meetings with eastern European leaders in 1985, Gorbachev told them they should no longer expect Soviet tanks to enforce their will on rebellious populations. By the time Gorbachev addressed the UN General Assembly at the end of 1988 and declared that the nations of eastern Europe were free to choose their own paths, dramatic changes were already underway.

Hungary and Poland moved first toward jettisoning communist rule. Even before Gorbachev took power, economic crisis had driven both governments to experiment with limited market economies and political liberalization. With Gorbachev in power, the pace of reform in Poland and Hungary accelerated rapidly. In January 1989, Hungary took the leap into political pluralism by legalizing noncommunist political parties and trade unions. In February, Solidarity and Polish communist officials began "roundtable talks" aimed at restructuring Poland's political system. In June, Poland held the first free elections in the Soviet bloc. Solidarity swept the contest and formed the first noncommunist government in eastern Europe since 1948.

When Gorbachev refused to send in the tanks to stop the Polish revolution, communist governments in the rest of eastern Europe were doomed. In November 1989, the Berlin Wall fell. In December, after a year of ever-widening protest demonstrations, the communist government in Czechoslovakia resigned. Alexander Dubček, the hero of the Prague Spring of 1968, returned in triumph to assume the leadership of parliament, and the playwright and leading dissident Václav Havel became the Czech president. In March 1990, the Christian Democrats took over the government from the communists in East Germany; seven months later the states of East and West Germany ceased to exist, and a single Germany was reborn. At the end of the year, reform-minded Communist Party members in Bulgaria overthrew the government of Todor Zhivkov, who had been in power for thirty-five years.

All of these revolutions occurred with very little bloodshed. The pace of change in Czechoslovakia was so smooth, in fact, that the events earned the nickname "the Velvet

CHRONOLOGY

1967	Six-Day War in the Middle East
1973	Yom Kippur War in the Middle East; era of stagflation begins
1979	Soviet invasion of Afghanistan; revolution in Iran; first meeting of European Parliament
1980	Solidarity forms in Poland
1985	Gorbachev takes power in Soviet Union
1989	Revolution in Eastern Europe: communist governments collapse
1990	Reunification of Germany
1991	Gulf War; civil wars in former Yugoslavia begin; Soviet Union dissolved
1998	Russian economy bankrupted
2001	Terrorist bombings in New York City and Washington, D.C.
2003	American-British forces invade Iraq; eastern European countries join EU

Revolution." But in Romania, the revolutionary cloth came soaked in blood. In December 1989, Romania's dictator Nikolai Ceauşescu ordered the army to fire on a peaceful protest; hundreds died. In a matter of days, however, the soldiers turned against Ceauşescu. On December 25 televised pictures of the execution of Ceauşescu and his wife were broadcast around the world. The reformist communist Ion Iliescu (b. 1930) formed a new government.

FROM SUCCESS TO FAILURE: THE DISINTEGRATION OF THE SOVIET UNION

By 1990, Gorbachev was one of the best-known leaders in the Western world. His leadership was seen as pivotal in accomplishing radical change in eastern Europe with a minimum of bloodshed and in ending the Cold War. For Gorbachev, these changes in the international structure were means to an end—freeing the Soviet economy for prosperity and thereby saving Soviet communism. But prosperity eluded his grasp, and the system he sought to save disintegrated. Between 1985 and 1991, Gorbachev's administration started and stopped twelve different national economic plans. Yet these reforms seemed only to worsen the economic crisis. By 1990, food and other essential goods were scarce, prices had risen by 20 percent since the year before, and productivity was falling. Dramatic increases in the numbers of prostitutes, abandoned babies, and the homeless signaled a society in the midst of breakdown.

This economic crisis ensured that Gorbachev faced fierce opposition not only from hard-line communists who opposed his reforms, but also from more liberal reformers who wanted to accelerate the shift to a capitalist economy. These men and women found a spokesman in Boris Yeltsin (b. 1931), a charismatic, hard-drinking, boisterous politician who became the president of Russia (as distinct from the Soviet Union) in 1991. When communist hard-liners attempted to overthrow Gorbachev in August 1991, Yeltsin led the popular resistance movement that defeated the coup attempt.

Gorbachev was finally beaten not by a political coup but by the power of nationalism. Glasnost had allowed separatist nationalist movements within the Soviet Union to surface from the underground. Gorbachev tried to halt the breakup of the Soviet Union by deploying troops to quell nationalist uprisings in Azerbaijan, Georgia, and the Baltic states, but he was unwilling to wage all-out war, and the Soviet Union broke apart. On December 25, Gorbachev resigned his office as president of a state that no longer existed.

For many ordinary Russians, the ending of the Soviet regime meant freedom of the worst kind—freedom to be hungry, freedom to be homeless, freedom to be afraid. In January 1992, Yeltsin applied "shock therapy" to the ailing Russian economy. He lifted price controls, abolished subsidies, and privatized state industries. By mid-1994, the state sector of the Russian economy had shrunk to under 40 percent. But the economy did not prosper. Prices climbed dramatically and unemployment rates soared upward, while cuts in government spending severed welfare lifelines. By 1995, 80 percent of Russians were no longer earning a living wage. The economic situation worsened in 1998, when Russia effectively went bankrupt. The value of the ruble collapsed and the state defaulted on its loans. Even Russians with jobs found it difficult to make ends meet. Workers in state jobs simply were not paid at all. In contrast, managers of state industries were often able to manipulate privatization for their own private enrichment, so they grew fabulously wealthy.

The economic and social collapse that followed the end of the Soviet Union fostered a climate of desperation in which extremist nationalism flourished. Georgia, Armenia, and Azerbaijan experienced civil war in the 1990s. In Russia itself, Yeltsin faced strong opposition from nationalist groups who viewed the breakup of the Soviet Union as a humiliation for Mother Russia.

The sharpest nationalist challenge to Yeltsin came from Chechnya, one of twenty-one autonomous republics within Russia. Chechen nationalists declared Chechnya independent in 1991. The Chechen-Russian dispute simmered until 1994 when Yeltsin committed 30,000 troops to forcing Chechnya back within Russia's embrace. In the ensuing twenty-month conflict, 80,000 died and 240,000 were wounded—80 percent of these Chechen civilians. Yeltsin negotiated a truce in the summer of 1996, but four years later his successor, Vladimir Putin (b. 1952), renewed the war and Chechen nationalists returned to terrorism.

In the Wake of Revolution

Like the former Soviet Union, the countries of eastern Europe found the path from communist rule to democracy far from easy. All the former Soviet satellite states in eastern Europe experienced high inflation rates, high unemployment, and economic instability in the wake of the revolution. Many faced nationalist hostilities from minority groups; some confronted the ultimate challenge of civil war.

EASTERN EUROPE: STUMBLING TOWARD DEMOCRACY

The dissolution of the Soviet bloc meant that economic networks established over the last four decades suddenly disintegrated. In addition, Western advisers and the International Monetary Fund, which controlled access to much-needed loans, insisted that the new governments follow programs of "austerity" aimed at cutting government spending and curbing inflation. The result was economic hardship far beyond what any Western electorate would have endured. In Poland, for example, the new Solidarity-led government instituted the "Big Bang" on New Year's Day 1990. Controls disappeared and overnight prices jumped between 30 and 600 percent. The inflation rate for 1990 in Poland was a remarkable 550 percent. Even in 1995, when the economy had stabilized, inflation remained at 20 percent, while joblessness stood at 15 percent.

But by the second half of the 1990s, it was clear that Poland was succeeding in moving from communism to capitalism. With some measures of market reform already in place before 1988, both Poland and Hungary were the best prepared for the transition from a command to a capitalist economy. The Czech Republic and the Baltic nations also moved fairly rapidly through the most difficult stages of this transition. In countries such as Romania, Bulgaria, and Albania, economic instability continued, with the majority of their populations experiencing hardship.

Political stability was also hard-won during this decade. The revolutionary coalitions that had led the charge against communist rule in 1989–1990 quickly fragmented as their members moved from the heady idealism of challenging authoritarianism to the nitty-gritty of parliamentary politics. In addition, voters who were fed up with economic hardship turned to the people who represented a more stable past. Between 1993 and 1995, ex-communists returned to power in Lithuania, Hungary, Bulgaria, and Poland. In Romania, they had never left. Yet the revolutions of 1989 were not reversed. Ex-communists continued with the economic liberalization programs of their opponents, although in many cases opting for a more gradual transition. No former communist regime returned to authoritarian rule or a centralized state-run economy.

A far greater threat to eastern European democracy was posed by the revival of pre–World War II political ideas and styles. Much of eastern Europe witnessed a resurgence of ethnic hostilities in the 1990s. In Czechoslovakia, Havel's government could not bridge the regional-ethnic divide that opened up between the Czech half of the country and Slovakia. In 1993, Czechoslovakia ceased to exist, replaced by the separate nations of the Czech Republic and Slovakia. The breakup of Czechoslovakia occurred peacefully, but ethnic divisions turned violent in much of eastern Europe. Anti-Semitic rhetoric returned to political discourse and discrimination against the Roma minority populations grew sharp.

The problems that engulfed Germany after its eastern and western halves reunited in October 1990 illustrated the difficulties faced by eastern Europeans as they struggled to adjust to a post–Cold War world. When the two Germanys united, Chancellor Helmut Kohl trusted that West Germany's economy was strong enough to pull its bankrupt new partner into prosperity, but he proved overly optimistic. By 1997, unemployment in Germany stood at 12.8 percent—the highest since World War II. In the eastern regions, over 20 percent of the population was out of work. Economic despair fueled racial violence. Attacks against foreign workers escalated, as did support for neo-Nazi organizations.

In 1998, these economic and social problems led German voters to reject Kohl and the Christian Democrats. The Social Democrats, out of office since 1982, took charge under the leadership of Gerhard Schroeder (b. 1944). Schroeder, however, was unable to reverse the economic slide. By 2001, the German economy was standing still, with a GDP growth rate of little over zero. The gap between the former West and East Germanys remained wide, with easterners enduring the worst of the German economic crisis.

THE BREAKUP OF YUGOSLAVIA

The postrevolutionary decade proved most difficult in Yugoslavia. There the revival of nationalist hostilities led to civil war and state-sanctioned mass murder, to scenes of carnage and mass atrocities not seen in Europe since the 1940s.

When the communist guerilla leader Tito seized control of the Yugoslav state after World War II, he sought to construct a united nation with two tools—federalism and communism. A federal political structure consisting of six equal republics prevented Serbia, or any other of the republics, from dominating Yugoslavia. Communism served as a unifying ideology, a cluster of ideas that transcended the divisions of race, religion, and language. Ethnic identities and rivalries were part of the bourgeois past that had supposedly been left behind.

Yugoslavs often said, however, that their nation consisted of "six nationalities, five languages, four religions, . . . and one Tito." According to this folk wisdom, Tito—not communism, not federalism—was the glue that held together this diverse state. In 1980, Tito died. Ominously, the year after his death saw the outbreak of riots between ethnic Albanians and Serbs in the province of Kosovo. Even more ominously, Tito's death coincided with the onset of serious economic crisis. By 1987, inflation was raging at 200 percent per year and two years later it had burst through into hyperinflation—200 percent *per month*.

In 1989, the revolutions that swept through the Soviet satellite states shattered the hold of communism on Yugoslavia as well. Ethnic nationalism, long simmering under the surface of Yugoslavian political life, poured into the resulting ideological void. Croats, Muslims, and other groups that had long resented ethnic Serbian domination in Yugoslavia called for the breakup of the Yugoslav federation. Nationalist Serbs, however, recognized that relatively poor Serbia could remain powerful only in the context of a larger Yugoslavia and so opposed any talk of destroying the Yugoslav federation. They found a popular spokesman in Slobodan Milosevic (b. 1941), a former communist functionary who transformed himself into an aggressive Serbian nationalist. Milosevic possessed a powerful weapon—the Serb-dominated Yugoslav army, the fourth-largest fighting force in Europe.

Thus, when the Croatian republic declared independence from Yugoslavia in June 1991, the result was civil war as Milosevic mobilized the army to defeat the separatists. In 1992 the war spread to Bosnia-Herzegovina after its government, too, declared independence.

The Croatian and Bosnian wars introduced the world to the horrors of ethnic cleansing° and rape camps. To create all-Serb zones within Croatia and Bosnia, Serb paramilitary units embarked on a campaign of terror designed to force Muslims and Croats to abandon their homes and villages. They burned mosques, closed schools, and vandalized houses. Most villagers fled; the paramilitaries tortured and often killed those who stayed. An estimated 20,000 women, most of them Muslim, were placed in special camps where they were subjected to regular, systematic rape. By 1994, all sides within the Bosnian war were practicing ethnic cleansing, although it is clear that Serbs initiated the practice and used it most extensively.

With Serbia assisting the Bosnian Serbs and Croatia assisting the Bosnian Croats, the Muslim community within Bosnia suffered the most intensely and begged Western governments to abandon their positions of neutrality and

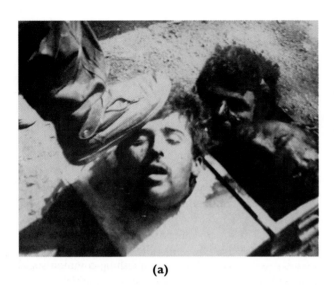

(a)

(b)

■ **Bosnian War Atrocities**

(a) Serbian heads, found after Serb fighters raided a Muslim base in northern Bosnia in 1993. (b) The mass grave of Muslim civilians, Pilica, northwest of Srebrenica, in the spring of 1996. Twelve thousand of the men and boys of Srebrenica tried to flee to safety—about half made it; many of those that did not were forced by Serb fighters to dig their own graves and then shot in front of them. The citizens of Srebenica who did not flee were told by Bosnian Serbian general Ratko Mladic, "No one will harm you." Mladic then ordered his soldiers to shoot all Muslim men age 17 to 60. Reviewing the evidence against Mladic, the UN tribunal noted, "These are truly scenes from hell, written on the darkest pages of human history."

A GLOBAL YOUTH CULTURE?

The following excerpt, from an interview with rock singer and Serbian nationalist Sonja Karadzic, first appeared in a Serbian magazine in September 1992, at the height of the war in Bosnia. Daughter of Radovan Karadzic, the political leader of the Bosnian Serbs, Sonja Karadzic condemned her fellow Serbs who had fled the war in Bosnia for the safety of Serbia. Her use of the term chetnik *demonstrates the power of historical memory: The chetniks were World War II guerillas who fought against the Nazi-backed Croatian regime. In this piece, Karadzic offers a disturbing definition of Western civilization: one characterized not by democratic freedom and the protection of human rights, but rather by a culture of violence fostered by American television and films.*

If the Americans come to Bosnia, they'll see that our soldiers look at the world like theirs do. We aren't Vietnamese or Iraqis, we are fighters who think in terms of the same images and music as their soldiers do. The Serbian chetnik fighters have grown up with a Coke in their hand and watching the same TV spots as someone their own age in Alabama, and we're into the latest styles just the way guys or girls from Florida are. Together we got our battle ethics from the movies about Mad Max and Terminator, Rambo and Young Guns. And what happened when the war began—we started identifying with the media images and heroes. Our fighters got into battle dress, short Rambo boots and modern weapons of destruction. They call themselves chetniks—but Mad Max Chetniks, Serbian Terminators. And most important, it doesn't matter what sex you are. Nobody is dirty or sloppy or smelly or unshaven—we're still into good cigarettes and Coca-Cola, nice perfume and makeup, and we're up on the latest movies and music. And we still like a good laugh—not the Moslem nonsense down in town. We're building a new lifestyle in a new country.

Fortunately for us only the best fighters, the real ones have stayed. The others have helped us perform a natural selection by running away from the homeland they weren't prepared to defend and build up . . .

For us the Serbian chetniks . . . will always be our heroes, our Serbian Terminators. With fighters like them we are already the victors in this war and leaders in the creation of a new civilization.

Source: From an interview with Sonja Karadzic, by Nenad Stefanovic, *Duga* (Belgrade), September 12–26, 1992. Excerpted and translated by Ann Clymer Bigelow. Reprinted by permission.

to stop the atrocities. Finally, in 1994, NATO planes began bombing Serb positions, the first time in its history that NATO had gone into combat. One year later, the Dayton Accords, signed in Dayton, Ohio, brought an uneasy peace to Bosnia.

Peace eluded Serbia during this period, however. In 1998, large-scale fighting between Serbs and Albanians erupted in the province of Kosovo. Ethnic cleansing, mass rape, and a huge exodus of refugees began once again. After a second NATO bombing campaign, NATO and Russian troops moved into Kosovo, and in 2001, a police helicopter transported Milosevic to the Netherlands to be tried for genocide before the International War Crimes Tribunal.

Rethinking the West

At the start of the 1990s, a sense of triumphalism characterized much of Western culture—at its simplest, expressed as "we won the Cold War." But who was "we"? For forty years, the Cold War had provided a clear enemy and thus a clear identity: The West was anticommunist, anti-Soviet, anti–Warsaw Pact. Communism's loss of credibility, the disintegration of the Soviet Union, and the dismantling of the Warsaw Pact all demanded that the West revise itself. But so, too, did other important social, political, and cultural changes that occurred in the wake of the tumultuous events of the later 1960s and the economic downturn of the 1970s.

THE EUROPEAN UNION

With the ending of the Cold War, the nations of western Europe, united under the umbrella of the European Union° (EU), moved to take on a much more important role in global affairs. We saw in Chapter 27 that the EU began in the 1950s as the Common Market or EEC (European Economic Community), an economic free-trade organization of six western European nations. By the end of the millennium, this organization had become a powerful entity possessing not only economic but also political clout, a potential counterweight to the United States.

During the 1970s and 1980s, the EEC widened both its membership and its areas of cooperation. Britain, Denmark, and Ireland joined in 1973, Greece in 1981, Spain and Portugal in 1986. (Austria, Finland, and Sweden joined in the 1990s.) In 1979, a European Parliament chosen directly by European voters met for the first time. Throughout these decades, the European Court of Justice gradually began to assert the primacy of the European Community over national law, thus pushing western Europe down the road toward political integration. The EEC—the European Economic Community—became the

EC—the European Community (EC), a political and cultural as well as economic organization.

The pace of change accelerated in the 1980s and 1990s as the Single European Act of 1985 and the Maastricht Agreements of 1991 replaced the European *Community* (EC) with the European *Union* (EU), defined by France's President Mitterrand as "one currency, one culture, one social area, one environment." The establishment of the EU meant visible changes for ordinary Europeans. They saw their national passports replaced by a common EU document, and border controls eliminated. The creation of a single EU currency—the euro, which replaced national currencies in 2002—tore down one of the most significant economic barriers between European countries. At the same time, the powers of the European Parliament expanded. Member states moved toward establishing common social policies (such as labor rights) and a common defense system, with an EU rapid-reaction force of 60,000 men created in 2003.

This process of European unification was controversial, however. Small traders and independent producers opposed the seemingly endless stream of orders and regulations issued by EU bureaucrats and the way in which economic integration privileged large, international firms over small, local shops. "Euro-skeptics" questioned the economic value of unification. They pointed out that throughout the 1990s, the U.S. economy continued to outperform that of the EU, and European unemployment rates were often high. Britain, Denmark, and Sweden refused to join the conversion to the euro, fearing a loss of national sovereignty and economic independence.

The end of the Cold War posed an even sharper challenge to the EU. Should the European Union (often called simply "Europe") include East as well as West? To be recognized as belonging to "Europe," nations applying for EU membership had to meet a set of complex financial requirements that demonstrated both the essential stability of their economies and their commitment to market capitalism. Thus "Europe" was defined, first of all, as capitalist. But a set of political requirements made clear that "Europe" also meant a commitment to democratic politics. Applicants' voting processes, treatment of minority groups, policing methods, and judicial systems were all scrutinized as the EU used its considerable economic clout to nurture fledgling democratic structures in eastern Europe. In 2003, the EU parliament voted overwhelmingly in favor of expanding the union to include Estonia, Latvia, Lithuania, Poland, the Czech Republic, Slovakia, Slovenia, and Hungary, as well as Cyprus and Malta (see Map 28.1).

ISLAM AND EUROPEAN IDENTITY

Significantly, the expansion of the EU in 2004 did not include Turkey, although talks on its membership application began in 1995. Turkey had sought membership in the EU for over forty years, but a number of obstacles stood in the way, including its support of Turkish Cypriots' claim to independence, the clash between Turkey's repressive penal system and EU human rights legislation, and its poverty. If Turkey joined the EU, it would immediately become the most populous and the poorest state in the Union. Opponents to Turkey's bid for membership feared that the European economy could not absorb the expected massive influx of impoverished Turkish migrant workers. They also, however, opposed full membership in "Europe" for Turkey because most Turks are Muslim, and for many Europeans, "European" and "Islamic" described clashing cultures.

The struggle over Turkish membership in the EU was just one of many controversies in contemporary Europe resulting from an ongoing battle to reconcile European identity with a growing Islamic cultural and political presence. By 2004, the number of European Muslims stood at 20 million—5 percent of the EU's population. Because the European Muslim birth rate is three times higher than that of non-Muslims, the percentage of Muslims within Europe is likely to continue to expand.

Muslim Communities in Europe

There is, of course, no single "Muslim Europe." In eastern European countries such as Bulgaria, Albania, and Bosnia, Muslims were part of the indigenous nation, the descendants of those who converted to Islam centuries earlier during the era of Ottoman rule. In western Europe, by contrast, most Muslims were immigrants or the children or grandchildren of immigrants, drawn to the West by greater economic and educational opportunities.

Even in western Europe, the Muslim experience varied. The majority of Britain's two million Muslims had roots in India or Pakistan, and thus received citizenship because of their Commonwealth inheritance; in contrast, until the

■ **Map 28.1 Contemporary Europe**

The revolutions of 1989 and their aftermath mark a clear turning point in European history, as a comparison of this map and that of "Europe in the Cold War" (p. 581) will show. Significant changes include the breakup of the Soviet Union and Yugoslavia, the replacement of Czechoslovakia by the Czech Republic and Slovakia, the unification of Germany, and the expansion of the EU.

passage of new citizenship laws in 2004, few of the three million Muslims living in Germany—most of them Turks or of Turkish descent—could claim the rights of citizenship. Many Muslims were highly educated and prosperous, but overall, the Muslim standard of living throughout Europe lagged behind that of non-Muslims: Muslims were far more likely to be unemployed; to work in low-paying, dead-end jobs; to live in substandard housing; and to possess fewer educational qualifications than their non-Muslim neighbors.

As minarets began to poke through the skylines of European cities, some non-Muslim Europeans argued that their own cultures were under threat. The decision of Iran's Ayatollah Khomeini to issue a death sentence against the Anglo-Indian writer Salman Rushdie in 1989 forced many of these tensions and hostilities into the open but provided no easy answers.

Terrorism and Islamism

This textbook has traced the way in which "the West" changed meaning, often in response to places and peoples defined as "not West." With the ending of the Cold War, the West lost its main enemy, but a replacement stood readily at hand. Terrorism in many ways replaced communism as the new foe against which the West defined itself. Because terrorists seek to achieve political ends through violence and intimidation, terrorism short-circuits the democratic process: Decision-making power shifts from the ballot box to the bomb. Thus terrorism directly opposed what many regarded as the bedrock of Western culture—a commitment to democracy and the rule of law.

Yet the equation of the West with law and democracy conveniently ignored other, less palatable, products of Western political culture such as fascism, Nazism, and terrorism itself. Terrorism grew out of late nineteenth-century anarchism, which advocated violence as a means of political change (see Chapter 22). Like the assassins who killed Tsar Alexander II in 1881, contemporary terrorists belonged to groups lacking access to political power. Unable to achieve their goals through political persuasion (lobbying, campaigning, winning votes), they endeavored to destabilize the governments they opposed through acts of terror. Thwarted nationalism provided especially fertile soil for the growth of terrorism. In Spain, the Basque separatist group Eta engaged in three-decades of terror to achieve its aim of an independent Basque state. In Northern Ireland, assassinations and bombings became commonplace after the Irish Republican Army (IRA) turned to terror to pressure the British government to relinquish its control over the province.

Terrorism is thus one of the negative aspects of "Western civilization." But by the 1980s, terrorism was often perceived as the antithesis of the West, an outside threat, usually bearing an Arabic face. Popular perceptions linked "terrorism" and "Islam," with Islam defined as emphatically "not West"—fanatical, violent, and antidemocratic.

Terrorist activity sparked by the Palestinian-Israeli conflict helped forge this link. Frustrated by the failure of the United Nations to implement its 1947 resolution promising a Palestinian state, Palestinian nationalists in 1964 formed the Palestine Liberation Organization (PLO). Like the IRA in Northern Ireland or Eta in Spain, the PLO saw violence as the only means to its nationalist ends. The PLO's commitment to terrorism deepened after the Six-Day War of 1967, which led to Israel's occupying East Jerusalem, all land west of the Jordan River (the West Bank), and the Golan Heights (see Map 28.2). During the subsequent decades the PLO took its campaign of terror around the world and Israel continued to receive more aid from the United States than did any other country. As Israel went on the offensive against not only Palestinian terrorism but also popular Palestinian uprisings in the 1980s and 1990s (the first and second "intifadas"), many Muslims came to the conclusion that the United States was bankrolling a repressive regime.

The Israeli-Palestinian conflict strengthened Western perceptions of a link between Islam and terrorism because it not only engendered the PLO but also fostered the development of Islamism°. Also called Islamic fundamentalism or *jihadism* (after the Islamic idea of *jihad,* or holy war), Islamism is explicitly anti-Western—and is rejected by many Muslims as a corruption or negation of Islamic values. Islamism views Western culture as a threat to Islamic identity, regards the United States as the standard-bearer of the West and thus as the particular enemy of Muslim interests, and accepts violence, including the murder of civilians, as an acceptable means to its ends.

A confluence of developments, in addition to the Israeli-Palestinian conflict, helped form the Islamist tide. First, modernity itself created in its wake a fundamentalist surge, not only within Islam but within other religious traditions as well. In times of often confusing change and growing secularization, men and women sought clear answers and the guarantee of order through rigid religious systems. The dislocation, discrimination, and disempowerment that characterized the Muslim immigrant experience for many young men in particular transformed European cities into breeding grounds for Islamism.

The West's willingness during the Cold War to prop up unpopular and corrupt governments also helped foster anti-Western forms of Islam. In Iran, for example, the popular revolution of 1979 that overthrew the autocratic, U.S.-backed Shah and vaulted the Ayatollah Khomeini (1901–1989) into power was explicitly anti-Western and anti-American. Khomeini rapidly reversed the westernizing and modernizing policies of the Shah and decried the United States as the "Great Satan."

A third development that helped swell the surge of Islamism occurred over a decade later, in the aftermath of the Gulf War of 1991, in which a twenty-eight-country coalition defeated an Iraqi invasion of Kuwait. After the war ended, U.S. forces remained in Saudi Arabia. In the Islamist

The Sentencing of Salman Rushdie

In February 1989, the Ayatollah Khomeini, political leader of Iran and spiritual head of the Shi'a Muslim community, issued a death sentence against the novelist Salman Rushdie and offered an award of $2.5 million to any faithful Muslim who succeeded in killing him. Rushdie, a British citizen who had never been tried in any Iranian or Islamic court, immediately went into hiding, where he remained for several years. His death sentence ignited the "*Satanic Verses* Affair," a tumultuous international crisis caused by a resounding clash of cultural assumptions and expectations.

The crisis centered on a book. In the early autumn of 1988 Viking Penguin published Rushdie's *The Satanic Verses*, a difficult novel about the complexities and contradictions of the modern immigrant experience. Born in India and raised in an Islamic home, Rushdie wrote *The Satanic Verses* to describe "migration, metamorphosis, divided selves, love, death, London, and Bombay."[1] The novel received immediate critical acclaim, with reviewers praising it as an astonishing work of postmodernist fiction.

Other readers judged it differently. Many Muslims around the world regarded the book as a direct attack on the foundations of their religious faith. One scene in the novel particularly horrified devout Muslims. In this episode, the central character has a psychotic breakdown and falls into a dream: Muhammad appears as a corrupt businessman and prostitutes in a brothel take on the names of the Prophet's wives.

The novel aroused intense controversy from the moment of its publication. The government of India banned it almost immediately; within a matter of weeks, several other states followed suit. Anti-Rushdie demonstrations in both India and Pakistan turned violent, resulting in fifteen deaths. Bookstores selling the novel received bombing and death threats. In western Europe, hostilities between Muslims and non-Muslims intensified. Then, on February 14, 1989, an announcer on Radio Tehran read aloud the text of a *fatwa*, or decree, issued by the Ayatollah Khomeini:

> I would like to inform all the intrepid Muslims of the world that the author of the book entitled The Satanic Verses, *which has been compiled, printed and published in opposition to Islam, the Prophet and the Koran, as well as those publishers who were aware of its contents, have been sentenced to death. I call on all zealous Muslims to execute them quickly, wherever they find them . . . Whoever is killed on this path will be regarded as a martyr, God willing.*

Western governments reacted quickly against Khomeini's call for Rushdie's death. The twelve nations of the European Community, the United States, Sweden, Norway, Canada, Australia, and Brazil all condemned Khomeini's judgment, recalled their ambassadors from Tehran, and cancelled high-level diplomatic contacts with Iran. British prime minister Margaret Thatcher provided police protection for Rushdie and dismissed British Muslim demands to ban the book: "It is an essential part of our democratic system that people who act within the law should be able to express their opinions freely."[2]

Large numbers of Muslims, including many who spoke out against Rushdie's book, also condemned Khomeini's fatwa. Some Muslim scholars contended that the Ayatollah's fatwa was a scholarly opinion, not a legally binding judgment; others argued that Rushdie could not be condemned without a trial, or that because Rushdie lived in a society without an Islamic government, he was not bound by Islamic law.

But many ordinary Muslims ignored these high-level theological and legal disputes and greeted the Ayatollah's fatwa with delight. The news of the Ayatollah's fatwa brought crowds of cheering Muslims into the city streets. In Manchester and Bradford, young British Muslim men insisted they would kill Rushdie if given the chance. In Paris, demonstrators marched to cries of "we are all Khomeinists!"

Why did Khomeini's fatwa arouse such popular enthusiasm within Western Muslim communities? A partial answer is that many Muslims were frustrated with what they regarded as the unequal application of the laws of censorship. Faced with what they saw as a hate-filled, pornographic caricature of Islam, they demanded that Western governments use

the laws censoring pornography and banning hate crimes to block the publication of Rushdie's book. In Britain, Muslims were particularly outraged that the existing law against blasphemy protected only Christianity, the official state religion.

But the controversy was not simply a dispute about censorship. For some Muslims, Rushdie's *Satanic Verses* epitomized Western secular society, with its scant regard for tradition or religious values. As Dr. Kalim Siddiqui of the pro-Iranian Muslim Institute in Britain proclaimed, "western civilization is fundamentally an immoral civilization. Its 'values' are free of moral constraints."[3] From this perspective, Khomeini's fatwa condemned not just one book or one author, but an entire culture that seemed inherently opposed to Islam. Khomeini had already proven himself a forceful leader in the Iranian hostage crisis of 1979–1980, when he successfully thumbed his nose at American power. Now once again he seemed willing to take on the West to defend Islam.

The anti-Western stance of some radical Muslims was mirrored by the anti-Islam position soon occupied by some Rushdie supporters. In one of the most ironic twists in the entire *Satanic Verses* Affair, Rushdie's books, which condemned the endemic racism in British society and exposed the falsehood of Western claims to cultural superiority, were championed by individuals who articulated precisely the sort of Western cultural chauvinism against which Rushdie had written so passionately. For example, Robert Maxwell, a multimillionaire communications tycoon, offered $10 million to any individual "who will, not kill, but civilise the barbarian Ayatollah" by forcing him to recite publicly the Ten Commandments.[4] Many western Europeans agreed with the conclusion drawn in this letter to a British daily newspaper: "The lesson of the Rushdie affair is that it was unwise to let Muslim communities establish themselves in our midst."[5] The lines were drawn, with Islam standing for irrationalism, barbarity, intolerance, and ignorance, while the "West" was linked to democracy, reason, freedom, and civilization. At precisely the moment when the crumbling of communism and the ending of the Cold War deprived the West of one of its defining attributes, the *Satanic Verses* Affair offered up a new Other against which the West could define itself. ■

Questions of Justice

1. On what grounds are publications censored in secular Western societies? Given the existence of this censorship, should Rushdie's book have been banned?

2. In what ways does the *Satanic Verses* Affair illuminate the tensions within many European societies since the 1970s, as communities struggled to adapt to the challenges of ethnic and religious diversity?

Taking It Further

Bowen, David G., ed. *The Satanic Verses: Bradford Responds*. 1996. This collection of essays and documents helps explains why many British Muslims viewed the British government's failure to censor Rushdie's book as an act of injustice.

view, the proximity of American-controlled bases to some of the most holy sites in Islam both sullied Islamic purity and insulted Arabic political independence.

In 1995, a series of terrorist attacks in the form of bombs planted on the subway trains and hidden in the wastebaskets of Paris revealed the danger of Islamist terrorism. Significantly, some of the men involved in these attacks came out of European Muslim communities. An even more dramatic demonstration of Islamist rage occurred on September 11, 2001. Three jets hijacked by Islamist terrorists smashed into the World Trade Center in New York City and the Pentagon (the U.S. military headquarters in Washington, D.C.), while a fourth crashed in Pennsylvania. Almost 3,000 people died. In response to the horrifying attack, U.S. president George W. Bush (b. 1946) declared a "war on terrorism." This war led to air attacks against Afghanistan in October 2001, and then, in March 2003, to an Anglo-American invasion of Iraq.

In the years after 9/11, the question of Western identity was more troublesome than ever. European and American Muslims found their loyalties questioned, their religious beliefs regarded as grounds for suspicion. The long, complex history of Islam in the West was often ignored, replaced by a simplistic "Them" versus "Us" mentality.

■ **Map 28.2   The Middle East in the Contemporary Era**

Although placed under Palestinian self-rule in 1994, the West Bank and Gaza Strip remain contested areas, sites of frequent confrontations between Palestinians and Israelis.

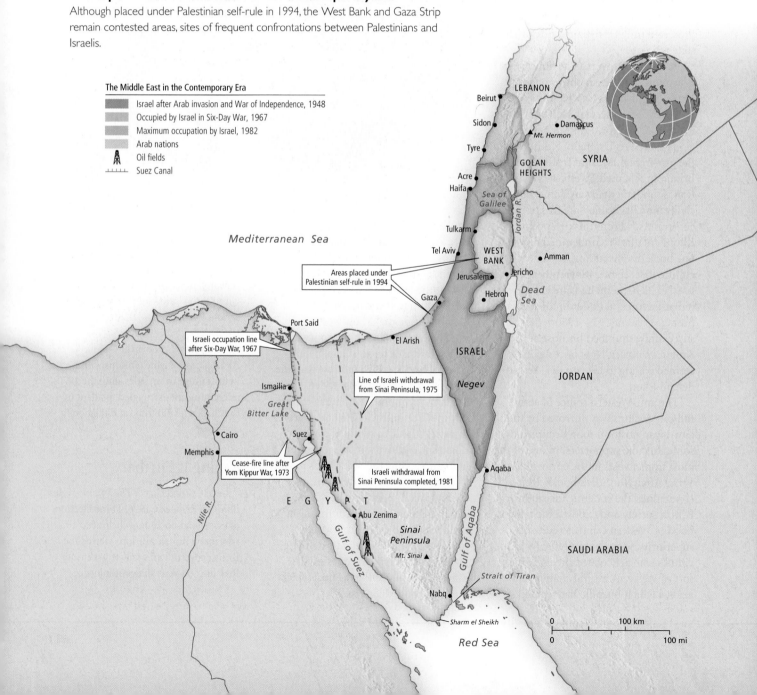

Euro-Islam

Yet the encounter between Islam and Europe was far from wholly negative. The majority of European Muslims rejected Islamism. Many, particularly those of the second and third generations of immigrant families, saw themselves as creators of a new culture: Euro-Islam°. Regarding themselves as fully Muslim and fully European, these individuals insisted that no contradiction existed between Islam and what many westerners view as the core values of the West—democratic politics, respect for individual differences, and civil liberties guaranteed by law to all, regardless of race and gender.

Euro-Islam has produced significant theological innovations. Traditional Islamic theology cuts the world in two: *dar al-Islam,* or "house of Islam," and *dar al-harb,* or "house of war." In *dar al-Islam,* Islamic law prevails. In *dar al-harb* (most of the contemporary world), Muslims cannot properly practice Islam and so live in a state of constant spiritual war. But Euro-Islamic proponents such as the Swiss scholar Tariq Ramadan argue that there is a third "house": *dar ash-shahada,* or "house of testimony," those regions—such as western Europe or the United States—where Muslims can profess and live their faith in community with non-Muslims.

European Muslim women have also played an important role in shaping Euro-Islam. Muslim women such as the members of the French group *Ni Putes Ni Soumises* ("neither whores nor submissives") have been at the forefront of campaigns to eradicate such traditional practices as female circumcision and the forced marriage of young girls to men from their parents' or grandparents' homelands.

INTO THE POSTMODERN ERA

The end of the Cold War, the formation of the European Union, and the growth of significant Muslim communities within western Europe all demanded a re-evaluation and redefinition of West. So, too, did a number of intellectual, artistic, and technological developments that together helped create the postmodern era. A grab-bag term covering a huge array of styles and stances, postmodernism° at its core constitutes the rejection of Western cultural supremacy, and more particularly, a challenge to the idea that Western science and rationality

had constructed a single, universally applicable form of "modernity."

The Making of the Postmodern

Postmodernism in this general sense resulted from the joining of postmodernist art and the literary theories of post-structuralism. By the early 1970s, a significant number of artists who worked in a wide variety of media had moved out from under the modernist umbrella. These postmodernists attacked the modernist idea of the "avant-garde," an elite of artistic geniuses fighting on the frontiers of aesthetic excellence. Feminists, especially, questioned the way modernism dismissed traditionally female art forms—weaving, for example—as mere "crafts" rather than "real art." Postmodernists also rejected the modernist ideal of "art for art's sake," and instead insisted that art had to say something to the world around it. To communicate with a wider public, they plundered both the past and popular culture for familiar forms and material.

These postmodernist practices in art paralleled a growing body of literary and cultural theory often called

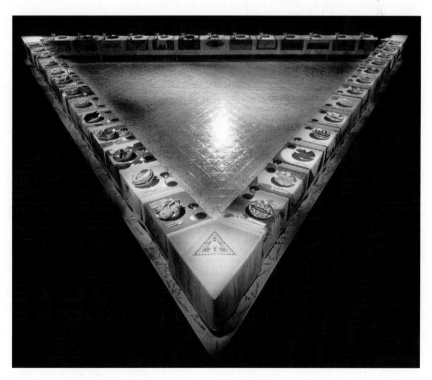

■ Judy Chicago, *The Dinner Party* (1973–1979)

This installation sits on 2,300 white porcelain tiles, across which run the names of 999 women from Western history. Each of the thirty-nine place settings includes a ceramic or painted china plate and a needlework runner that use symbols to portray historical or mythological female figures. Like Chicago's work, much of the feminist art of the 1970s focused on celebrating femaleness, the ways in which women's bodies and experiences set them apart from men. Later in the era, many younger feminists criticized this work for reducing women to some sort of mythic female essence, and instead focused their art on exposing the dynamics of power and oppression in modern societies.

poststructuralism. In very different ways, poststructuralists argued that because the world we see and experience is structured by language, and because all communication produces a variety of meanings and interpretations, we must abandon the idea of universal truth. The literary theorist Roland Barthes (1915–1980), for example, denied the existence of fixed truth when he declared the "Death of the Author," by which he meant that the purpose of literary study is not to ask "What does the author mean?" but instead to explore the way in which the reader creates his or her own meanings.

The postmodernist view of cultural values as always in flux disturbed many more traditional critics, who continued to insist that criteria of aesthetic excellence ("Beauty") and objective standards of knowledge ("Truth") did exist. Yet postmodernist concerns with communication, interpretation, and authority certainly seemed appropriate for an era that many called "the Information Age" and others called the postindustrial society°. The industrial phase of economic development was characterized by an emphasis on production. But in the postindustrial phase, the *making* of things becomes less important than the *marketing* of them. A postindustrial society, in fact, is characterized less by *things* in general than by *images, ideas, and information.* If the factory symbolized industrial society, then the epitome of the postindustrial era is the personal computer, with its capacity to disperse information, market products, and endlessly duplicate yet constantly alter visual and verbal images. Governments scrambled to impose control on the proliferating technologies of the postindustrial age, but in true postmodern fashion the centers of authority broke down. Existing laws that regulated pornography, for example, proved difficult to apply to the Internet, the vast global communications web.

Similarly, developments in medical technologies raised important questions about authority and ownership. In 1978, Louise Brown was born in Britain, the world's first "test-tube baby." Over the next twenty years, assisted fertility treatment resulted in the births of more than a million babies. As the technology grew more sophisticated, so too did the ethical and political questions. Societies struggled to determine the legality of practices such as commercial surrogate motherhood, in which a woman rents her womb to a couple. Genetic research provoked even more debate about which authorities or what principles should guide scientific research. The announcement in February 2001 that the human genome had been decoded—that scientists had mapped the sequencing of the human genome, or set of instructions in every cell in the human body—immediately raised such questions as, Who owns this information? Who has the authority to decide how it is to be used?

Religion in the Postmodern Era

Postmodern patterns—the fragmentation of cultures, the collapse of centers of authority, the supremacy of image—

also characterized Western religious faith and practice after the 1970s. Christianity no longer served as a common cultural bond. In a time of increasing immigration and cultural diversity, Islam was the fastest-growing religious community in western Europe. By the end of the twentieth century, established Protestant churches in western Europe faced a serious crisis, with regular churchgoers now a small minority of the population—less than 5 percent in most countries. Religious faith became a private matter, the mark of subcultures (often defined by an "Us versus Them" mentality), rather than a bond tying together individuals and groups into a cohesive national culture.

At the same time, however, the long-reigning Pope John Paul II (r. 1978–2005) experienced unprecedented popularity. The most well-traveled and populist-oriented of twentieth-century popes, John Paul II became a media star. Much of his popularity rested on his intimate connection with Poland's Solidarity, and therefore with an image of liberation. Born Karol Wojtyla, John Paul was the first non-Italian pope since 1523 and the first-ever Polish pope. Twelve million people—one-third of the Polish population—greeted the pope in Warsaw in 1979 when he made the first visit by any pope to a communist country. Many Solidarity members testified to the importance of this visit in empowering them to challenge the political order fourteen months later. But the pope's support for Solidarity did not mean he supported other forms of rebellion against authority. He adopted a firmly authoritarian approach to church government and took an uncompromising stand against birth control, married clergy, and the ordination of women. Yet the pope was unable to bring into line an increasingly rebellious flock throughout Europe and the United States. By the 1980s, Catholic Italy boasted the second-lowest birth rate in the world (after China): Clearly Italian Catholics were using birth control no matter what the pope dictated. It was hard to avoid the conclusion that in western Roman Catholicism, as in much of postmodern society, image ruled while authority dissipated.

The Global Economy and Environment

Authority also seemed to dissipate from elected governments as non-elected individuals and institutions increasingly determined the course of national economies. In the 1990s, currency speculators moved their money in and out of currency markets with astonishing rapidity and often-devastating consequences for the countries involved. In 1997, for example, Thailand was forced to devalue its currency; the economic catastrophe of collapsing currencies and stock markets quickly spread to Indonesia, Malaysia, the Philippines, and South Korea.

Similarly, the World Bank and the International Monetary Fund (IMF) possessed far more power than did many elected officials. Created to stabilize the global economy in the aftermath of World War II by representatives of

Western governments, these institutions embodied the confidence characteristic of the postwar West. Outside economists and agronomists, who tended to ignore local traditions and expertise, believed that an infusion of Western economic and technological expertise would set the rest of the world on the path to economic growth. By the 1990s, the widening gap between "North" and "South," the rich and poor nations of the world, called into question these easy assumptions.

The urgency of the environmental crisis also revealed the limitations of Western expertise. By 1985, some 257 multilateral treaties mandated various forms of environmental protection—restrictions on trade in endangered species, wetlands preservation, forest conservation, regulation of industrial emissions. Almost half of these had been signed since 1970. Yet the degradation of the planet proceeded apace. The environmental crisis in eastern Europe was particularly urgent. For decades, the conquest of nature had been a key part of communist ideology. The most basic environmental precautions were ignored within Soviet and eastern European cities; untreated sewage and radioactive material were often dumped directly into lakes and rivers.

The danger of environmental breakdown extended beyond eastern Europe. Many scientists regarded global warming (climate change as the result of industrial activity) as a threat to not only European or Western but also

■ **North versus South**
An Ethiopian farmer wages a losing war against drought and famine.

worldwide economic stability. If they are correct, then the citizens of the West in the new millennium face the necessity of moving beyond the boundaries of "American" or "European" or "Western" to a far more global sense of identity.

CONCLUSION

Where Is the West Now?

In England, the most popular fast food is not fish and chips, long the quintessential English national supper, nor is it the Big Mac, as opponents of economic globalization might predict. Instead it is curry, the gift of the minority South Asian immigrant community. In the new millennium, "the West" may no longer serve as an important conceptual border marker. By many of the criteria explored in this textbook—economic, technological, political, and cultural—Tokyo would be defined as a Western city. So, too, would Melbourne—or Budapest or Warsaw. Nevertheless, the economic and social trauma that afflicted Russia and the poorer nations of the former Soviet bloc such as Romania and Bulgaria in the 1990s and after demonstrates that the "West" retains its distinct identity, for clearly the gap between it and the "East" remains wide. The admittedly hesitant, still incomplete spread of the Western ideal of democracy has thrown a fragile bridge across that gap. But perhaps the real divide for the twenty-first century stretches between "North" and "South"—the huge and growing difference between the global Haves and the Have-Nots. Whether any bridge can stretch across that span remains to be seen.

Suggestions for Further Reading

For a comprehensive list of suggested readings, please go to www.ablongman.com/levackconcise/chapter28

Ardagh, John. *Germany and the Germans: The United Germany in the Mid-1990s.* 1996. A snapshot of a society in the midst of social and economic change.

Hughes, H. Stuart. *Sophisticated Rebels: The Political Culture of European Dissent 1968–1987.* 1988. A perceptive and imaginative exploration of "dissenters," ranging from Solidarity and Soviet dissidents to German Greens, Welsh nationalists, and an assortment of novelists and philosophers.

Kavanagh, Dennis. *Thatcherism and British Politics: The End of Consensus?* 1987. Kavanagh answers the question posed in his title with a convincing "yes."

Kotkin, Stephen. *Armageddon Averted: The Soviet Collapse, 1970–2000.* 2001. Vivid account of this crucial story.

Lewis, Jane, ed. *Women and Social Policies in Europe: Work, Family and the State.* 1993. A series of essays exploring the position of women in western Europe. Packed with statistics and useful tables.

McNeill, John. *Something New Under the Sun: An Environmental History of the Twentieth Century.* 2000. Argues that twentieth-century human economic activity has transformed the ecology of the globe—an ongoing experiment with a potentially devastating outcome.

Ost, David. *Solidarity and the Politics of Anti-Politics: Opposition and Reform in Poland Since 1968.* 1990. Although the bulk of this account was written before the revolution of 1989, it provides a compelling study of Solidarity's emergence, impact, and ideology.

Rogel, Carole. *The Breakup of Yugoslavia and the War in Bosnia.* 1998. Designed for undergraduates, this work includes a short but detailed historical narrative, biographies of the main personalities, and a set of primary documents.

Rosenberg, Tina. *The Haunted Land: Facing Europe's Ghosts After Communism.* 1995. Winner of the Pulitzer Prize, this disturbing account focuses on the fundamental moral issues facing postcommunist political cultures.

Sandler, Irving. *Art of the Postmodern Era: From the Late 1960s to the Early 1980s.* 1996. Much more broad-ranging than the title suggests, this well-written, blessedly jargon-free work sets both contemporary art and the theories of the postmodern within the wider historical context.

Stokes, Gale. *The Walls Came Tumbling Down: The Collapse of Communism in Eastern Europe.* 1993. A superb account, firmly embedded in history.

Young, John W. *Cold War Europe 1945–1991: A Political History.* 1996. A solid survey.

Notes

1. Salman Rushdie, "Please, Read *Satanic Verses* Before Condemning It," *Illustrated Weekly of India,* October 1988. Reprinted in M. M. Ahsan and A. R. Kidwai, *Sacrilege versus Civility: Muslim Perspectives on The Satanic Verses Affair* (1991), 63.

2. Quoted in Malise Ruthven, *A Satanic Affair: Salman Rushdie and the Wrath of Islam* (1991), 562.

3. Quoted in Ruthven, 100.

4. *Bookseller,* London, February 24, 1989. Quoted in Lisa Appignanesi and Sara Maitland, *The Rushdie File* (1990), 103–104.

5. *The Sunday Telegraph,* June 24, 1990. Quoted in Ahsan and Kidwai, 80.

Glossary

absolutism (p. 314) A form of government in the seventeenth and eighteenth centuries in which the ruler possessed complete and unrivalled power.

acropolis (p. 60) The defensible hilltop around which a polis grew. In classical Athens, the Acropolis was the site of the Parthenon (Temple of Athena).

Aeneid (p. 109) Written by Virgil (70–19 B.C.E.), this magnificent epic poem celebrates the emperor Augustus by linking him to his mythical ancestor, Aeneas, the Trojan refugee who founded the Roman people. Considered by many to be the greatest work of Latin literature, the poem has had enormous influence in the West.

agrarian capitalism (p. 265) A form of economic organization characteristic of European colonialism in which Europeans organized the production of certain kinds of commercial crops (such as sugar, tobacco, and indigo) on land expropriated from native peoples and with slave labor.

agricultural revolution (p. 167) Refers to technological innovations that began to appear during the eleventh century, making possible a dramatic growth in population. The agricultural revolution came about through harnessing new sources of power with water and wind mills, improving the pulling power of animals with better collars, using heavy plows to better exploit the soils of northern Europe, and employing a three-field crop rotation system that increased the amount and quality of food available.

alchemy (p. 339) A form of learned magic that was intended to turn base metals into precious ones.

aldeias (p. 260) Settlements for natives who had converted to Christianity in Brazil. In these settlements the Jesuit fathers protected the natives from enslavement.

Allies (p. 510) During World War I, the states allied against the Central Powers of Germany and Austria-Hungary. During World War II, the states allied against the regimes of Nazi Germany, fascist Italy and imperial Japan.

Anabaptism (p. 280) Meaning "to rebaptize"; refers to those Protestant radicals of the sixteenth century who rejected infant baptism and adopted adult baptism. Anabaptists treated the Bible as a blueprint for reforming not just the church but all of society, a tendency that led them to reject the authority of the state, to live in self-governing "holy communities," and in some cases to practice a primitive form of communism.

anarchism (p. 478) Ideology that views the state as unnecessary and repressive, and rejects participation in parliamentary politics in favor of direct, usually violent, action.

Antonine Decree (p. 105) In 212 C.E. the emperor Aurelius Antoninus, called Caracalla, issued a decree that granted citizenship to all the free inhabitants of the Roman Empire. The decree enabled Roman law to embrace the entire population of the empire.

Apologists (p. 114) Christian writers in the second and third centuries C.E. who explained their religion to learned non-Christians. In the process they helped Christianity absorb much of Hellenistic culture.

appeasement (p. 552) British diplomatic and financial efforts to stabilize Germany in the 1920s and 1930s and so avoid a second world war.

Arians (p. 125) Christians who believe that God the Father is superior to Jesus Christ his Son. Most of the Germanic settlers in western Europe in the fifth century were Arians.

aristocracy (p. 382) A term that originally applied to those who were considered the most fit to rule and later identified the wealthiest members of society, especially those who owned land.

Asceticism (p. 126) The Christian practice of severely suppressing physical needs and daily desires in an effort to achieve a spiritual union with God. Asceticism is the practice that underlies the monastic movement.

Babylonian Captivity of the Church (p. 211) Between 1305 and 1378 seven consecutive popes voluntarily chose to reside in Avignon, France, in order to escape anarchy in the streets of Rome. During this period the popes became subservient to the kings of France.

Babylonian Exile (p. 56) The period of Jewish history between the destruction of Solomon's temple in Jerusalem by Babylonian armies in 587 B.C.E., and 538 B.C.E., when Cyrus of Persia permitted Jews to return to Palestine and rebuild the temple.

balance of power (p. 319) An arrangement in which various countries form alliances to prevent any one state from dominating the others.

Balfour Declaration (p. 524) Declaration of 1917 that affirmed British support of a Jewish state in Palestine.

baroque (p. 317) A dynamic style in art, architecture, and music intended to elicit an emotional response. It was closely associated with royal absolutism in the seventeenth century.

Battle of Kadesh (p. 39) The battle between Egyptian and Hittite armies in Syria in 1274 B.C.E. that set the territorial limits of both empires in Canaan and the Middle East for a century during the International Bronze Age.

Berlin Wall (p. 580) Constructed by the East German government, the wall physically cut the city of Berlin in two and prevented East German citizens from access to West Germany; stood from 1961 to 1989.

blitzkrieg (p. 552) "Lightning war;" offensive military tactic making use of airplanes, tanks, and motorized infantry to punch through enemy defenses and secure key territory. First demonstrated by the German army in World War II.

boers (p. 360) Dutch farmers in the colony established by the Dutch Republic in South Africa.

Bolsheviks (p. 521) Minority group of Russian socialists, headed by Lenin, who espoused an immediate transition to a socialist state. It became the Communist Party in the Soviet Union.

bourgeoisie (p. 387) A social group, technically consisting of those who were burghers in the towns, that included prosperous merchants and financiers, members of the professions, and some skilled craftsmen known as "petty bourgeoisie."

bronze (p. 41) An alloy of tin and copper that produces a hard metal suitable for weapons, tools, ornaments, and household objects. Bronze production began about 3200 B.C.E.

bubonic plague (p. 206) An epidemic disease spread from rats to humans via flea bites. The infection enters the bloodstream, causing inflamed swellings called buboes (hence, "bubonic" plague) in the glands of the groin or armpit, internal bleeding, and discoloration. Although disputed by some, most experts consider bubonic plague the cause of the Black Death, which killed at least one-third of the population of Europe between 1348 and the early 1350s. Bubonic plague reappeared recurrently in the West between 1348 and 1721.

caliph (p. 175) After Muhammad's death in 632, the ruler of the Islamic state was called the caliph. The sectarian division within Islam between the Shi'ites and Sunni derived from a disagreement over how to determine the hereditary succession from Muhammad to the caliphate, which combined governmental and some religious responsibilities.

caliphate (p. 147) The Islamic imperial government that evolved under the leadership of Abu Bakr (r. 632–634), the successor of the prophet Muhammad.

calling (p. 276) The Calvinist doctrine that God calls the Elect to perform his will on earth. God's calling gave Calvinists a powerful sense of personal direction.

canon law (p. 187) The collected laws of the Roman Catholic Church. Canon law applied to cases involving the clergy, disputes about church property, and donations to the Church. It also applied to the laity for annulling marriages, legitimating bastards, prosecuting bigamy, protecting widows and orphans, and resolving inheritance disputes.

capital (p. 428) All the physical assets used in production, including fixed capital, such as machinery, and circulating capital, such as raw materials; more generally the cost of these physical assets.

caravels (p. 249) Hybrid three-masted ships developed about 1450 in the Iberian peninsula by combining the rigging of square with triangular lateen sails. These ships could be sailed in a variety of winds, carry large cargoes, be managed by a small crew, and be defended by guns mounted in the castle superstructure.

Carnival (p. 297) The most popular annual festival in much of Europe before modern times. Also known as Mardi Gras, the festival took place for several days or even weeks before the beginning of Lent and included all kinds of fun and games.

Carolingian Renaissance (p. 164) The "rebirth" of interest in ancient Greek and Latin literature and language during the reign of the Frankish emperor Charlemagne (r. 768–814). Charlemagne promoted the intensive study of Latin to promote governmental efficiency and to propagate the Christian faith.

Catholic Reformation (p. 282) A series of efforts during the sixteenth century to purify the Church that evolved out of late medieval spirituality and that included the creation of new religious orders, especially the Society of Jesus.

Central Powers (p. 510) Germany and Austria-Hungary in World War I.

Chalcedonians (p. 125) Christians who follow the doctrinal decisions and definitions of the Council of Chalcedon in 451 C.E. stating that Christ's human and divine natures were equal, but entirely distinct and united in one person "without confusion, division, separation, or change." Chalcedonian Christianity came to be associated with the Byzantine Empire and is called Greek Orthodoxy. In western Europe it is known as Roman Catholicism.

chinoiserie (p. 374) A French word for an eighteenth-century decorative art that combined Chinese and European motifs.

Christendom (p. 199) Collectively refers to the many Christian kingdoms of western Europe that used Latin as the language of worship, diplomacy, and law during the Middle Ages.

Christian Democratic (p. 586) Conservative and confessionally based (Roman Catholic) political parties that dominated much of western European politics after World War II.

Christian humanists (p. 270) During the fifteenth and sixteenth centuries these experts in Greek, Latin, and Hebrew subjected the Bible to philological study in an attempt to understand the precise meaning of the founding text of Christianity.

circuit court (p. 193) Established by King Henry II (r. 1154–1189) to make royal justice available to virtually anyone in England. Circuit court judges visited every shire in England four times a year.

civic humanism (p. 234) A branch of humanism introduced by the Florentine chancellor Leonardo Bruni who defended the republican institutions and values of the city. Civic humanism promoted the ethic of responsible citizenship.

civilization (p. 12) The term used by archaeologists to describe a society differentiated by levels of wealth and power, and in which religious, economic, and political control are based in cities.

civitas (p. 103) The Roman term for a city. A city included the town itself, all the surrounding territory that it controlled, and all the people who lived in the town and the countryside.

clans or kin groups (p. 154) The basic social and political unit of Germanic society consisting of blood relatives obliged to defend one another and take vengeance for crimes against the group and its members.

class (p. 383) A large and often cohesive social group that was conscious of its shared economic and political interests.

classicism (p. 385) A style in art, architecture, music, and literature that emphasizes proportion, adherence to traditional forms, and a rejection of emotion and enthusiasm.

Cluny (p. 172) A monastery founded in Burgundy in 910 that became the center of a far-reaching movement to reform the Church that was sustained in more than 1,500 Cluniac monasteries, modeled after the original in Cluny.

Cold War (p. 575) Struggle for global supremacy between the United States and the Soviet Union, waged from the end of World War II until 1990.

collectivization (p. 541) The replacement of private and village farms with large cooperative agricultural enterprises run by state-employed managers.

colons (p. 375) White planters in the French Caribbean colony of Saint Do mingue (Haiti).

Columbian exchange (p. 262) The trade of peoples, plants, animals, microbes, and ideas between the Old and New Worlds that began with Columbus.

Common Market (p. 586) Originally comprising West Germany, France, Italy, Belgium, Luxembourg, and the Netherlands, the Common Market was formed in 1957 to integrate its members' economic structures and so foster both economic prosperity and international peace. Also called the European Economic Community (EEC).

communes (p. 171) Sworn defensive associations of merchants and workers that appeared in north-central Italy after 1070 and that became the effective government of more than a hundred cities. The communes evolved into city-states by seizing control of the surrounding countryside.

communism (p. 447) The revolutionary form of socialism developed by Karl Marx and Friedrich Engels that promoted the overthrow of bourgeois or capitalist institutions and the establishment of a dictatorship of the proletariat.

Concert of Europe (p. 447) The joint efforts made by Austria, Prussia, Russia, Britain, and France during the years following the Congress of Vienna to suppress liberal and nationalist movements throughout Europe.

Conciliar Movement (p. 211) A fifteenth-century movement that advocated ending the Great Schism and reforming church government by calling a general meeting or council of the bishops, who would exercise authority over the rival popes.

Confessions (p. 295) The formal sixteenth-century statements of religious doctrine: the Confession of Augsburg for Lutherans, the Helvetic Confessions for Calvinists, the Thirty-Nine Articles for Anglicans, and the decrees of the Council of Trent for Catholics.

Congress of Vienna (p. 418) A conference of the major powers of Europe in 1814–1815 to establish a new balance of power at the end of the Napoleonic Wars.

conquistadores (p. 254) Spanish adventurers in the Americas who explored and conquered the lands of indigenous peoples, sometimes without legal authority but usually with a legal privilege granted by the king of Spain who required that one-fifth of all things of value be turned over to the crown. The conquistadores extended Spanish sovereignty over new lands.

conservatism (p. 446) A nineteenth-century ideology intended to prevent a recurrence of the revolutionary changes of the 1790s and the implementation of liberal policies.

containment (p. 576) Cold War policy of blocking communist expansion; inaugurated by the Truman Doctrine in 1947.

Corpus of Civil Law (p. 132) The body of Roman law compiled by the emperor Justinian in Constantinople in 534. The Corpus became a pillar of Latin-speaking European civilization.

cosmology (p. 336) A theory concerning the structure and nature of the universe such as those proposed by Aristotle in the fourth century B.C.E. and Copernicus in the sixteenth century.

counties (p. 164) Territorial units devised by the Carolingian dynasty during the eighth and ninth centuries for the administration of the empire. Each county was administered by a count who was rewarded with lands and sent to areas where he had no family ties to serve as a combined provincial governor, judge, military commander, and representative of the king.

courtly love (p. 200) An ethic first found in the poems of the late twelfth- and thirteenth-century troubadours that portrayed the ennobling possibilities of the love between a man and a woman. Courtly love formed the basis for the modern idea of romantic love.

creoles (p. 361) People of Spanish descent who had been born in Spanish America.

crusades (p. 184) Between 1095 and 1291, Latin Christians heeding the call of the pope launched eight major expeditions and many smaller ones against Muslim armies in an attempt to gain control of and hold Jerusalem.

Cubism (p. 493) Modernist artistic movement of the twentieth century that emphasized the fragmentation of human perception through visual experiments with geometric forms.

cultural relativism (p. 265) A mode of thought first explored during the sixteenth century to explain why the peoples of the New World did not appear in the Bible. Cultural relativism recognized that many (but not necessarily all) standards of judgment are specific to particular cultures rather than the fixed truths established by natural or divine law.

culture (p. 12) The knowledge and adaptive behavior created by communities that helps them to mediate between themselves and the natural world through time.

cuneiform (p. 17) A kind of writing in which wedge-shaped symbols are pressed into clay tablets to indicate words and ideas. Cuneiform writing originated in ancient Sumer.

Curia (p. 187) The administrative bureaucracy of the Roman Catholic Church.

Cynic (p. 82) Cynics followed the teachings of Antisthenes (ca. 445–360 B.C.E.) by rejecting pleasures, possessions, and social conventions in order to find peace of mind.

Darwinian theory of evolution (p. 490) Scientific theory associated with nineteenth-century scientist Charles Darwin that highlights the role of variation and natural selection in the evolution of species.

Decembrists (p. 452) Russian liberals who staged a revolt against Tsar Nicholas I on the first day of his reign in December 1825.

de-Christianization (p. 412) A program inaugurated in France in 1793 by the radical Jacobin and former priest Joseph Fouché that closed churches, eliminated religious symbols, and attempted to establish a purely civic religion.

deduction (p. 340) The logical process by which ideas and laws are derived from basic truths or principles.

deists (p. 346) Seventeenth- and eighteenth-century thinkers who believed that God created the universe and established immutable laws of nature but did not subsequently intervene in the operation of nature or in human affairs.

Delian League (p. 64) The alliance among many Greek cities organized by Athens in 478 B.C.E. in order to fight Persian forces in the eastern Aegean Sea. The Athenians gradually turned the Delian League into the Athenian Empire.

demand (p. 429) The desire of consumers to acquire goods and the need of producers to acquire raw materials and machinery.

democracy (p. 54) A form of government in which citizens devise their own governing institutions and choose their leaders; began in Athens, Greece, in the fifth century B.C.E.

demonic magic (p. 347) The invocation of evil spirits with the goal of utilizing their supernatural powers to change the course of nature or to alter human behavior.

de-Stalinization (p. 584) Khrushchev's effort to decentralize political and economic control in the Soviet Union after 1956.

detente (p. 598) During the 1970s, a period of lessened Cold War hostilities and greater reliance on negotiation and compromise.

dialectic (p. 447) The theory that history advanced in stages as the result of the conflict between different ideas or social groups.

dialectical materialism (p. 447) The socialist philosophy of Karl Marx according to which history advanced as the result of material or economic forces and would lead to the creation of a classless society.

Diaspora (p. 110) The dispersion from its homeland of a population who nevertheless retains a sense of ethnic identity, most notably the Jewish dispersion after the Roman sack of Judaea.

division of labor (p. 426) The assignment of one stage of production to a single worker or group of workers to increase efficiency and productive output.

domestication (p. 13) Manipulating the breeding of animals over many generations in order to make them more useful to humans as sources of food, wool, and other byproducts. Domestication of animals began about 10,000 years ago.

Dreyfus Affair (p. 474) The trials of Captain Alfred Dreyfus on treason charges dominated French political life in the decade after 1894 and revealed fundamental divisions in French society.

dualistic (p. 341) A term used to describe a philosophy, such as that of René Descartes, in which a rigid distinction is made between body and mind or between the material and the immaterial world.

Dutch Revolt (p. 305) The rebellion against Spanish rule of the seven northern provinces of the Netherlands between 1579 and 1648, which resulted in the independence of the Republic of the United Provinces.

Edict of Nantes (p. 304) Promulgated by King Henry IV in 1598, the edict allowed the Huguenots to build a quasi-independent state within the kingdom of France, giving them the right to have their own troops, church organization, and political autonomy within their walled towns, but banning them from the royal court and the city of Paris. King Louis XIV revoked the edict in 1685.

Einsatzgruppen (p. 560) Loosely translated as strike force or task force; SS units given the task of murdering Jews and Communist Party members in the areas of the Soviet Union occupied by Germany during World War II.

empire (pp. 18, 358, 622) Large political formations consisting of different kingdoms or territories outside the boundaries of the states that control them.

enclosure (p. 428) The consolidation of scattered agricultural holdings into large, compact fields which were then closed off by hedges, bushes, or walls, giving farmers complete control over the uses of their land.

encomienda (p. 256) The basic form of economic and social organization in early Spanish America, based on a royal grant awarded to a Spaniard for military or other services that gave the grantee and his successors the right to gather tribute from the Indians in a defined area.

enlightened despots (p. 396) The term assigned to absolute monarchs who initiated a series of legal and political reforms in an effort to realize the goals of the Enlightenment.

Enlightenment (p. 387) An international intellectual movement of the eighteenth century that emphasized the use of reason and the application of the laws of nature to human society.

Epicureans (p. 81) Followers of the teachings of the philosopher Epicurus (341–271 B.C.E.). Epicureans tried to gain peace of mind by choosing pleasures-rationally.

ethnic cleansing (p. 605) A term introduced during the wars in Yugoslavia in the 1990s; the systematic use of murder, rape, and violence by one ethnic group against members of other ethnic groups in order to establish control over a territory.

Etruscans (p. 85) A people native to Italy, the Etruscans established a league of militaristic cities in central Italy that grew rich from war and trade. Etruscans had a great influence on the formation of the Roman state.

Eucharist (p. 189) Also known as Holy Communion or the Lord's Supper, the Eucharistic rite of the Mass celebrates Jesus' last meal with his apostles when the priest-celebrant consecrates wafers of bread and a chalice of wine as the body and blood of Christ. In the Middle Ages the wafers of bread were distributed for the congregation to eat, but drinking from the chalice was a special privilege of the priesthood. Protestants in the sixteenth century and Catholics in the late twentieth century began to allow the laity to drink from the chalice.

Euro-Islam (p. 613) A European-Muslim culture that believes that no contradiction exists between Islam and the core values of the West.

European Economic Community (EEC) (p. 586) Originally comprising West Germany, France, Italy, Belgium, Luxembourg, and the Netherlands, the EEC was formed in 1957 to integrate its members' economic structures and so foster both economic prosperity and international peace. Also called the Common Market.

European Union (EU) (p. 607) A successor organization to the EEC; the effort to integrate European political, economic, cultural, and military structures and policies.

excommunication (p. 187) A decree by the pope or a bishop prohibiting a sinner from participating in the sacraments of the Church and forbidding any social contact whatsoever with the surrounding community.

Expressionism (p. 493) Modernist artistic movement of the early twentieth century that used bold colors and experimental forms to express emotional realities.

factories (p. 359) Trading posts established by European powers in foreign lands.

fascism (p. 536) Twentieth-century political ideology that rejected the existing alternatives of conservatism, communism, socialism, and liberalism. Fascists stressed the authoritarian power of the state, the efficacy of violent action, the need to build a national community, and the use of new technologies of influence and control.

federalists (p. 407) The name assigned by radical Jacobins to provincial rebels who opposed the centralization of the state during the French Revolution.

feminism, feminist movement (p. 480) International movement that emerged in the second half of the nineteenth century and demanded broader political, legal, and economic rights for women.

Fertile Crescent (p. 14) Also known as the Levantine Corridor, this twenty-five mile wide arc of land stretching from the Jordan River to the Euphrates River was the place where food production and settled communities first appeared in Southwest Asia (the Middle East).

feudalism (p. 166) A term historians use to describe a social system common during the Middle Ages in which lords granted fiefs (tracts of land or some other form of income) to dependents, known as vassals, who owed their lords personal services in exchange. Feudalism refers to a society governed through personal ties of dependency rather than public political institutions.

fief (p. 166) During the Middle Ages a fief was a grant of land or some other form of income that a lord gave to a vassal in exchange for loyalty and certain services (usually military assistance).

Final Solution (p. 560) Nazi term for the effort to murder every Jew in Europe during World War II.

fin-de-siecle (p. 491) French term for the "turn of the century"; used to refer to the cultural crisis of the late nineteenth century.

First Triumvirate (p. 91) The informal political alliance made by Julius Caesar, Pompey, and Crassus in 60 B.C.E. to share power in the Roman Republic. It led directly to the collapse of the Republic.

Forms (p. 69) In the philosophical teachings of Plato, these are eternal, unchanging absolutes such as Truth, Justice, and Beauty that represent true reality, as opposed to the approximations of reality that humans encounter in everyday life.

Forum (p. 86) The political and religious center of the city of Rome throughout antiquity. All cities in the empire had a forum in imitation of the capital city.

freemasons (p. 395) Members of secret societies of men and women that flourished during the Enlightenment, dedicated to the creation of a society based on reason and virtue and committed to the principles of liberty and equality.

French Wars of Religion (p. 302) A series of political assassinations, massacres, and military engagements between French Catholics and Calvinists from 1560 to 1598.

German-Soviet Non-Aggression Pact (p. 552) Signed by Stalin and Hitler in 1939, the agreement publicly pledged Germany and the Soviet Union not to attack each other, and secretly divided up Poland and the Baltic states between the two powers.

Girondins (p. 407) The more conservative members of the Jacobin party who favored greater economic freedom and opposed further centralization of state power during the French Revolution.

glasnost (p. 602) Loosely translated as openness or honesty; Gorbachev's effort after 1985 to break with the secrecy that had characterized Soviet political life.

Gothic (p. 201) A style in architecture in western Europe from the late twelfth and thirteenth centuries, characterized by ribbed vaults and pointed arches, which drew the eyes of worshipers upward toward God. Flying buttresses, which redistributed the weight of the roof, made possible thin walls pierced by large expanses of stained glass.

grand jury (p. 193) In medieval England after the judicial reforms of King Henry II (r. 1154–1189), grand juries were called when the circuit court judge arrived in a shire. The sheriff assembled a group of men familiar with local affairs who constituted the grand jury and who reported to the judge the major crimes that had been committed since the judge's last visit.

Great Depression in Trade and Agriculture (p. 468) Downturn in prices and profits, particularly in the agricultural sector, in Europe from 1873 through the 1880s.

Great Depression (p. 538) Calamitous drop in prices, reduction in trade, and rise in unemployment that devastated the global economy in 1929.

Great Persecution (p. 121) An attack on Christians in the Roman empire begun by the emperor Galerius in 303 C.E. on the grounds that their worship was endangering the empire. Several thousand Christians were executed.

Great Purge (p. 542) Period of mass arrests and executions particularly aimed at Communist Party members. Lasting from 1934 to 1939, the Great Purge enabled Stalin to consolidate his one-man rule over the Soviet Union.

Great Schism (p. 211) The division of the Catholic Church (1378–1417) between rival Italian and French claimants to the papal throne.

Green politics (p. 600) A new style of politics and set of political ideas resulting from the confluence of environmentalism, feminism, and anti-nuclear protests of the 1970s.

guilds (p. 210) Professional associations devoted to protecting the special interests of a particular trade or craft and to monopolizing production and trade in the goods the guild produced.

haciendas (p. 256) Large landed estates that began to be established in the seventeenth century replaced encomiendas throughout much of Spanish America.

Hallstatt (p. 84) The first Celtic civilization in central Europe is called Halstatt. From about 750 to about 450 B.C.E., Hallstatt Celts spread throughout Europe.

helots (p. 62) The brutally oppressed subject peoples of the Spartans. Tied to the land they farmed for Spartan masters, they were treated little better than beasts of burden.

heresies (p. 125) Forms of Christian belief that are not considered Orthodox.

hetairai (p. 66) Elite courtesans in ancient Greece who provided intellectual as well as sexual companionship.

Holocaust (p. 549) Adolf Hitler's effort to murder all the Jews in Europe during World War II.

Homo sapiens sapiens (p. 13) Scientific term meaning "most intelligent people" applied to physically and intellectually modern human beings that first appeared between 200,000 and 100,000 years ago in Africa.

hoplites (p. 62) Greek soldiers in the Archaic Age who could afford their own weapons. Hoplite tactics made soldiers fighting as a group dependent on one another. This contributed to the internal cohesion of the polis and eventually to the rise of democracy.

Huguenots (p. 301) The term for French Calvinists, who constituted some 10 percent of the population by 1560.

humanists (p. 231) During the Renaissance humanists were writers and orators who studied Latin and sometimes Greek texts on grammar, rhetoric, poetry, history, and ethics.

Hundred Years' War (p. 213) Refers to a series of engagements (1337–1453) between England and France over England's attempts to assert its claims to territories in France.

hyperinflation (p. 533) Catastrophic price increases and currency devaluation, such as that which occurred in Germany in 1923.

Iconoclasm (p. 144) The destruction of religious images in the Byzantine empire in the eighth century.

icons (p. 144) The Christian images of God and saints found in Byzantine art.

ideologies (p. 446) Theories of society and government that form the basis of political programs.

Ideologues (p. 608) A group of liberal writers and philosophers in France who objected to Napoleon's religious policy on the grounds that it would inaugurate a return of religious superstition.

induction (p. 340) The mental process by which theories are established only after the systematic accumulation of large amounts of data.

indulgences (p. 211) Certificates that allowed penitents to atone for their sins and reduce their time in purgatory. Usually these were issued for going on a pilgrimage or performing a pious act, but during the Babylonian Captivity of the Church (1305–1378) popes began to sell them, a practice Martin Luther protested in 1517 in an act that brought on the Protestant Reformation.

industrial capitalism (p. 435) A form of capitalism characterized by the ownership of factories by private individuals and the employment of wage labor.

intendants (p. 316) French royal officials who became the main agents of French provincial administration in the seventeenth century.

Investiture Controversy (p. 187) A dispute that began in 1076 between the popes and the German emperors over the right to invest bishops with their offices. The most famous episode was the conflict between Pope Gregory VII and Emperor Henry IV. The controversy was resolved by the Concordat of Worms in 1122.

Jacobins (p. 405) A French political party supporting a democratic republic that found support in political clubs throughout the country and dominated the National Convention from 1792 until 1794.

Junkers (p. 322) The traditional nobility of Prussia.

justification by faith alone (p. 272) Refers to Martin Luther's insight that humanity is incapable of performing enough religious good works to earn eternal salvation. Salvation is an unmerited gift from God called grace. Those who receive grace are called the Elect.

knight (p. 166) During the Middle Ages a knight was a soldier who fought on horseback. A knight was a vassal or dependent of a lord, who usually financed the knight's expenses of armor and weapons and of raising and feeding horses with a grant of land known as a fief.

Koine (p. 80) The standard version of the Greek language spoken throughout the Hellenistic world.

La Tène (p. 84) A phase of Celtic civilization that lasted from about 450 to 200 B.C.E. La Tène culture became strong especially in the regions of the Rhine and Danube Rivers.

laissez-faire (p. 446) The principle that governments should not regulate or otherwise intervene in the economy unless it is necessary to protect property rights and public order.

lapis lazuli (p. 41) A precious, deep-blue gemstone found in the Middle East that was traded widely for jewelry during the International Bronze Age.

latifundia (p. 108) These huge agricultural estates owned by wealthy Romans, including the emperor, often used large slavegangs as labor.

lay investiture (p. 172) The practice of nobles, kings, or emperors installing churchmen and giving them the symbols of office.

League of Nations (p. 525) Association of states set up after World War I to resolve international conflicts through open and peaceful negotiation.

Lend-Lease Act (p. 554) Passed in March 1941, the act gave Britain access to American industrial products during World War II, with payment postponed for the duration of the war.

Levantine Corridor (p. 14) Also known as the Fertile Crescent, this twenty-five mile wide are of land stretching from the Jordan River to the Euphrates River was the place where food production and settled communities first appeared in Southwest Asia (the Middle East).

liberalism (p. 446) An ideology based on the conviction that individual freedom is of supreme importance and the main responsibility of government is to protect that freedom.

linear perspective (p. 237) In the arts the use of geometrical principles to depict a three-dimensional space on a flat, two-dimensional surface.

lord (p. 166) During the Middle Ages a lord was someone who offered protection to dependents, known as vassals, who took an oath of loyalty to him. Most lords demanded military services from their vassals and sometimes granted them tracts of land known as fiefs.

Macedonian Renaissance (p. 173) During the Macedonian dynasty's rule of Byzantium (867–1056), aristocratic families, the Church, and monasteries devoted their immense riches to embellishing Constantinople with new buildings, mosaics, and icons. The emperors sponsored historical, philosophical, and religious writing.

Magisterial Reformation (p. 274) Refers to Protestant churches that received official government sanction.

Magna Carta (p. 193) In 1215 some English barons forced King John to sign the "great charter," in which the king pledged to respect the traditional feudal privileges of the nobility, towns, and clergy. Subsequent kings swore to uphold it, thereby accepting the fundamental principle that even the king was obliged to respect the law.

Manhattan Project (p. 558) Code name given to the secret Anglo-American project that resulted in the construction of the atom bomb during World War II.

marches (p. 263) Territorial units of the Carolingian empire for the administration of frontier regions. Each march was ruled by a margrave who had special powers necessary to defend vulnerable borders.

Marshall Plan (p. 576) The use of U.S. economic aid to restore stability to Europe after World War II and so undercut the appeal of communist ideology.

mechanical philosophy (p. 341) The seventeenth-century philosophy of nature, championed by René Descartes, holding that nature operated in a mechanical way, just like a machine made by a human being.

mendicant friars (p. 188) Members of a religious order, such as the Dominicans or Franciscans, who wandered from city to city and throughout the countryside begging for alms rather than residing in a monastery. Mendicant friars tended to help ordinary laypeople by preaching and administering to the sick and poor.

mercantilism (p. 318) The theory that the wealth of a state depended on its ability to import fewer commodities than it exported and thus acquire the largest possible share of the world's monetary supply. The theory encouraged state intervention in the economy and the regulation of trade.

metropolis (p. 358) The parent country of a colony or imperial possession.

Mishnah (p. 127) The final organization and transcription of Jewish oral law, completed by the end of the third century C.E.

Modern Devotion (p. 212) A fifteenth-century religious movement that stressed individual piety, ethical behavior, and intense religious education. The Modern Devotion was promoted by the Brothers of the Common Life, a religious order whose influence was broadly felt through its extensive network of schools.

modernism (p. 493) Term applied to artistic and literary movements from the late nineteenth century through the 1950s. Modernists sought to create new aesthetic forms and values.

monastic movement (p. 126) In Late Antiquity, Christian ascetics organized communities where men and women could pursue a life of spirituality through work, prayer, and asceticism. Called the monastic movement, this spiritual quest spread quickly throughout Christian lands.

monotheism (p. 38) The belief in only one god, first attributed to the ancient Hebrews. Monotheism is the foundation of Judaism, Christianity, Islam, and Zoroastrianism.

Montagnards (p. 407) Members of the radical faction within the Jacobin party who advocated the centralization of state power during the French Revolution and instituted the Reign of Terror.

mosque (p. 146) A place of Muslim worship.

Napoleonic Code (p. 414) The name given to the Civil Code of 1804, promulgated by Napoleon, which gave France a uniform and authoritative code of law.

nation (p. 448) A large community of people who possess a sense of unity based on a belief that they have a common homeland and share a similar culture.

nationalism (p. 448) The belief that the people who form a nation should have their own political institutions and that the interests of the nation should be defended and promoted at all costs.

national self-determination (p. 689) The doctrine advanced by nationalists that any group that considers itself a nation has the right to be ruled only by the members of their own nation and to have all members of the nation included in that state.

nation-state (p. 448) A political structure sought by nationalists in which the boundaries of the state and the nation are identical, so that all the members of a nation are governed by the same political authorities.

NATO (North Atlantic Treaty Organization) (p. 576) Defensive anti-Soviet alliance of the United States, Canada, and the nations of western Europe established in 1949.

natural magic (p. 343) The use of magical words and drawings to manipulate the occult forces that exist in nature without calling on supernatural beings for assistance.

nawabs (p. 372) Native provincial governors in eighteenth-century India.

Nazism (p. 538) Twentieth-century political ideology associated with Adolf Hitler that adopted many fascist ideas but with a central focus on racism and particularly anti-Semitism.

neoclassicism (p. 385) The revival of the classical art and architecture of ancient Greece and Rome in the eighteenth century.

Neoplatonism (p. 341) A philosophy based on the teachings of Plato and his successors that flourished in Late Antiquity, especially those of Plotinus. Neoplatonism influenced Christianity in Late Antiquity. During the Renaissance Neoplatonism was linked to the belief that the natural world was charged with occult forces that could be used in the practice of magic.

NEP (New Economic Plan) (p. 536) Lenin's economic turnaround in 1921 that allowed and even encouraged small private businesses and farms in the Soviet Union.

New Conservatism (p. 599) Political ideology that emerged at the end of the 1970s combining the free market approach of nineteenth-century liberalism with social conservatism.

new feminism (p. 600) Re-emergence of the feminist movement in the 1970s.

new imperialism (p. 497) The third phase of modern European imperialism, that occurred in the late nineteenth and early twentieth centuries and extended Western control over almost all of Africa and much of Asia.

New Left (p. 591) Leftwing political and cultural movement that emerged in the late 1950s and early 1960s; sought to develop a form of socialism that rejected the over-centralization, authoritarianism, and inhumanity of Stalinism.

nobility (p. 382) Members of the aristocracy who received official recognition of their hereditary status, including their titles of honor and legal privileges.

no-man's-land (p. 514) The area between the combatants trenches on the Western Front during World War I.

Nuremberg trials (p. 563) Post-World War II trials of members of the Nazi Party and German military; conducted by an international tribunal.

Old Regime (p. 402) The political order of eighteenth-century France, dominated by an absolute monarch and a privileged nobility and clergy.

oligarchy (p. 66) A government consisting of only a few people rather than the entire community.

orthodox (p. 125) In Christianity, the term indicates doctrinally correct belief. Definitions of Orthodoxy changed numerous times.

paganism (p. 124) The Christian term for polytheist worship (worshiping more than one god). In the course of Late Antiquity, the Christian church suppressed paganism, the traditional religions of the Roman empire.

panhellenic (p. 61) This word means open to all Greek communities. It applies to the athletic games, such as the Olympic Games, in which competitors came from all over the Greek world.

papacy (p. 123) The bishop of the city of Rome is called the Pope, or Father. The papacy refers to the administrative and political institutions controlled by the Pope. The papacy began to gain strength in the sixth century in the absence of Roman imperial government in Italy.

paradigm (p. 343) A conceptual model or intellectual framework within which scientists conduct their research and experimentation.

parlements (p. 316) The highest provincial courts in France, the most important of which was the Parlement of Paris.

patricians (p. 86) In ancient Rome, patricians were aristocratic clans with the highest status and the most political influence.

patrons and clients (p. 89) In ancient Roman society, a powerful man (the patron) would exercise influence on behalf of a social subordinate (the client) in anticipation of future support or assistance.

Pax Romana (p. 98) Latin for "Roman Peace", this term refers to the Roman Empire established by Augustus that lasted until the early third century C.E.

perestroika (p. 602) Loosely translated as "restructuring;" Gorbachev's effort to decentralize, reform, and thereby strengthen Soviet economic and political structures.

personal rule (p. 326) The period from 1629 to 1640 in England when King Charles I ruled without Parliament.

phalanx (p. 62) The military formation favored by hoplite soldiers. Standing shoulder to shoulder in ranks often eight men deep, hoplites moved in unison and depended on one another for protection.

philology (p. 231) A method reintroduced by the humanists during the Italian Renaissance devoted to the comparative study of language, especially to understanding the meaning of a word in a particular historical context.

philosophes (p. 386) The writers and thinkers of the Enlightenment, especially in France.

pilgrimage (p. 127) Religious journeys made to holy sites in order to encounter relics.

Pillars of Islam (p. 146) The five basic principles of Islam as taught by Muhammad.

plantation colony (p. 250) First appearing in the Cape Verde Islands and later in the tropical parts of the Americas, these colonies were established by Europeans who used African slave labor to cultivate cash crops such as sugar, indigo, cotton, coffee, and tobacco.

plebeians (p. 86) The poorest Roman citizens.

polis (p. 60) Or city-state, developed by Greeks in the Archaic Age. A polis was a self-governing community consisting of a defensible hilltop, the town itself, and all the surrounding fields farmed by the citizens of the polis. Poleis (plural) shared similar institutions: an assembly place for men to gather and discuss community affairs, a council of elders, and an open agora, which served as a market and a place for informal discussions.

polytheistic (p. 23) Refers to polytheism, the belief in many gods.

pop art (p. 588) Effort by artists in the 1950s and 1960s both to utilize and to critique the material plenty of post-World War II popular culture.

popular sovereignty (p. 602) The claim that political power came from the people and that the people constituted the highest political power in the state.

portolanos (p. 249) Books of sailing directions that included charts and descriptions of ports. Portolanos appeared in the Mediterranean in the Late Middle Ages.

positivism (p. 449) The philosophy developed by August Comte in the nineteenth century according to which human society passed through a series of stages, leading to the final positive stage in which the accumulation of scientific data would enable thinkers to discover the laws of human behavior and bring about the improvement of society.

postindustrial society (p. 614) A service rather than manufacturing-based economy characterized by an emphasis on marketing and information and by a proliferation of communications technologies.

postmodernism (p. 613) Umbrella term covering a variety of artistic styles and intellectual theories and practices; in general, a rejection of a single, universal, Western style of modernity.

Pragmatic Sanction of Bourges (p. 240) An agreement between the pope and king of France made in 1438 that guaranteed the virtual autonomy of the French Church from papal control.

Prague Spring (p. 585) Short-lived popular effort in 1968 to reform Czechoslovakia's political structures; associated with the phrase "socialism with a human face."

predestination (p. 276) The doctrine promoted by John Calvin that since God, the all-knowing and all-powerful being, knew everything in advance and caused everything to happen, then the salvation of any individual was predetermined.

prerogative (p. 326) The set of powers exercised by the English monarch alone, rather than in conjunction with Parliament.

Price Revolution (p. 294) After a long period of falling or stable prices that stretched back to the fourteenth century, Europe experienced sustained price increases between about 1540 and 1640, causing widespread social and economic turmoil.

priesthood of all believers (p. 273) Martin Luther's doctrine that all those of pure faith were themselves priests, a doctrine that undermined the authority of the Catholic clergy over the laity.

proletariat (p. 447) The word used by Karl Marx and Friedrich Engels to identify the class of workers who received their income from wages.

protectionism (p. 365) The policy of shielding domestic industries from foreign competition through a policy of levying tariffs on imported goods.

Radical Reformation (p. 275) Refers to Protestant movements that failed to gain official government recognition and were at best tolerated, at worst persecuted, during the sixteenth century.

Raiders of the Land and Sea (p. 45) The name given by Egyptians to the diverse groups of peoples whose combined naval and land forces destroyed many cities and kingdoms in the eastern Mediterranean and Anatolia, thereby bringing the International Bronze Age to an end.

Reign of Terror (p. 407) A purging of alleged enemies of the French state between 1793 and 1794, superintended by the Committee of Public Safety, that resulted in the execution of 17,000 people.

relics (pp. 127, 277) In Christian belief, relics are sacred objects that have miraculous powers. They are associated with saints, biblical figures, or some object associated with them. They served as contacts between Earth and Heaven and were verified by miracles.

Religious Peace of Augsburg (p. 274) In 1555 this peace between Lutherans and Catholics within the Holy Roman Empire established the principle of *cuius regio, eius religio,* which means "he who rules determines the religion of the land." Protestant princes in the Empire were permitted to retain all church lands seized before 1552 and to enforce Protestant worship, but Catholic princes were also allowed to enforce Catholic worship in their territories.

Renaissance (p. 226) A term meaning "rebirth" used by historians to describe a movement that sought to imitate and understand the culture of antiquity. The Renaissance generally refers to a movement that began in Italy and then spread throughout Europe from about 1350 to 1550.

reparations (p. 525) Payments imposed upon Germany after World War I by the Versailles Treaty to cover the costs of the war.

republicanism (p. 226) A political theory first developed by the ancient Greeks, especially the philosopher Plato, but elaborated by the ancient Romans and rediscovered during the Italian Renaissance. The fundamental principle of republicanism as developed during the Italian Renaissance was that government officials should be elected by the people or a portion of the people.

requeriemiento (p. 254) A document read by conquistadores to the natives of the Americas before making war on them. The document briefly explained the principles of Christianity and commanded the natives to accept them immediately along with the authority of the pope and the sovereignty of the king of Spain. If the natives refused, they were warned they would be forced to accept Christian conversion and subjected to Spain anyway.

revisionism, socialist revisionism (p. 478) The belief that an equal society can be built through participation in parliamentary politics rather than through violent revolution.

rhetoric (p. 231) The art of persuasive or emotive speaking and writing, which was especially valued by the Renaissance humanists.

Roman Republic (p. 85) The name given to the Roman state from about 500 B.C.E., when the last king of Rome was expelled, to 31 B.C.E., when Augustus established the Roman Empire. The Roman Republic was a militaristic oligarchy.

Romanesque (p. 200) A style in architecture that spread throughout western Europe during the eleventh and the first half of the twelfth centuries and characterized by arched stone roofs supported by rounded arches, massive stone pillars, and thick walls.

romanization (p. 104) The process by which conquered peoples absorbed aspects of Roman culture, especially the Latin language, city-life, and religion.

romanticism (p. 449) An artistic and literary movement of the late eighteenth and nineteenth centuries that involved a protest against classicism, appealed to the passions rather than the intellect, and emphasized the beauty and power of nature.

Rome-Berlin Axis (p. 551) Alliance between Mussolini's Italy and Hitler's Germany formed in 1936.

Schlieffen Plan (p. 512) German military plan devised in 1905 that called for a sweeping attack on France through Belgium and the Netherlands.

scholasticism (p. 198) A term referring to a broad philosophical and theological movement that dominated medieval thought and university training. Scholasticism used logic learned from Aristotle to interpret the meaning of the Bible and the writings of the Church Fathers, who created Christian theology in its first centuries.

Scramble for Africa (p. 498) The frenzied imposition of European control over most of Africa that occurred between 1870 and 1914.

scriptorium (p. 156) The room in a monastery where monks copied books and manuscripts.

Second Industrial Revolution (p. 468) A new phase in the industrialization of the processes of production and consumption, underway in Europe in the 1870s.

Second Triumvirate (p. 94) In 43 B.C.E. Octavian (later called Augustus), Mark Antony, and Lepidus made an informal alliance to share power in Rome while they jockeyed for control. Octavian emerged as the sole ruler of Rome in 31 B.C.E.

seigneur (p. 386) The lord of a French estate who received payments from the peasants who lived on his land.

separate spheres (p. 393) The theory that men and women should conduct their lives in different social and political environments, confining women to the domestic sphere and excluding them from the public sphere of political involvement.

sepoys (p. 372) Indian troops serving in the armed forces of the British East India Company.

Septuagint (p. 81) The Greek translation of the Hebrew Bible (Old Testament).

serfs (p. 170) During the Middle Ages serfs were agricultural laborers who worked and lived on a plot of land granted them by a lord to whom they owed a certain portion of their crops. They could not leave the land, but they had certain legal rights that were denied to slaves.

settler colony (p. 250) A colony authorized when a private person obtained a license from a king to seize an island or parcel of land and occupied it with settlers from Europe who exported their own culture to the new lands. Settler colonies first appeared among the islands of the eastern Atlantic and portions of the Americas.

simony (p. 172) The practice of buying and selling church offices.

Social Darwinism (p. 490) The later-nineteenth-century application of the theory of evolution to entire human societies.

social democracy (p. 542) Political system in which a democratically elected parliamentary government endeavors to ensure a decent standard of living for its citizens through both economic regulation and the maintenance of a welfare state.

Solidarity (p. 601) Trade union and political party in Poland that led an unsuccessful effort to reform the Polish communist state in 1981; survived to lead Poland's first non-communist government since World War II in 1989.

Sophists (p. 69) Professional educators who traveled throughout the ancient Greek world, teaching many subjects. Their goal was to teach people the best ways to lead better lives.

soviets (p. 520) Workers' and soldiers' councils formed in Russia during the Revolution of 1917.

Spanish Armada (p. 304) A fleet of 132 ships, which sailed from Portugal to rendezvous with the Spanish army stationed in the Netherlands and launch an invasion of England in 1588. The English defeated the Armada as it passed through the English Channel.

spiritualists (p. 281) A tendency within Protestantism, especially Lutheranism, to emphasize the power of personal spiritual illumination, called the "inner Word," a living form of the Scriptures written directly on the believer's soul by the hand of God.

stagflation (p. 599) Term coined in the 1970s to describe an economy troubled by both high inflation and high unemployment rates.

states (p. 358) Consolidated territorial areas that have their own political institutions and recognize no higher political authority.

Stoicism (p. 82) The philosophy developed by Zeno of Citium (ca. 335–ca. 263 B.C.E.) that urged acceptance of fate while participating fully in everday life.

structuralism (p. 588) Influential post-World War II social theory that explored the common structures of language and thought.

Struggle of the Orders (p. 86) The political strife between patrician and plebeian Romans beginning in the fifth century B.C.E. The plebeians gradually won political rights and influence as a result of the struggle.

suffragettes (p. 483) Feminist movement that emerged in Britain in the early twentieth century. Unlike the suffragists, who sought to achieve the vote for women through rational persuasion, the suffragettes adopted the tactics of violent protest.

supply (p. 429) The amounts of capital, labor, and food that are needed to produce goods for the market as well as the quantities of those goods themselves.

Syncretism (p. 109) The practice of equating two gods and fusing their cults was common throughout the Roman Empire and helped to unify the diverse peoples and religions under Roman rule.

syndicalism (p. 478) Ideology of the late nineteenth and early twentieth century that sought to achieve a working-class revolution through economic action, particularly through mass labor strikes.

Talmuds (p. 127) Commentaries on Jewish law. Rabbis completed the Babylonian Talmud and the Jerusalem Talmud by the end of the fifth century C.E.

Tetrarchy (p. 119) The government by four rulers established by the Roman emperor Diocletian in 293 C.E. that lasted until 312. During the Tetrarchy many administrative and military reforms altered the fabric of Roman society.

thomism (p. 199) A branch of medieval philosophy associated with the work of the Dominican thinker, Thomas Aquinas (1225–1274), who wrote encyclopedic summaries of human knowledge that confirmed Christian faith.

Time of Troubles (p. 309) The period from 1604 to 1613 when Russia fell into chaos, which ended when the national assembly elected Tsar Michael Romanov, whose descendants ruled Russia until they were deposed in 1917.

total war (p. 510) A war that demands extensive state regulation of economic production, distribution, and consumption.

trading posts (p. 254) Built by European traders along the coasts of Africa and Asia as a base for trade with the interior. Trading posts or factories were islands of European law and sovereignty, but European authority seldom extended very far beyond the fortified post.

transubstantiation (p. 189) A doctrine promulgated at the Fourth Lateran Council in 1215 that explained by distinguishing between the outward appearances and the inner substance how the Eucharistic bread and wine changed into the body and blood of Christ.

Treaty of Brest-Litovsk (p. 515) Treaty between Germany and Bolshevik-controlled Russia, signed in March, 1918, that ceded to Germany all of Russia's western territories.

trial by jury (p. 193) When disputes about the possession of land arose after the late twelfth century in England, sheriffs assembled a group of twelve local men who testified under oath about the claims of the plaintiffs, and the circuit court judge made his decision on the basis of their testimony. The system was later extended to criminal cases.

Triple Entente (p. 510) Informal defensive agreement linking France, Great Britain, and Russia before World War I.

triremes (p. 63) Greek warships with three banks of oars. Triremes manned by the poorest people of Athenian society became the backbone of the Athenian empire.

troubadours (p. 199) Poets from the late twelfth and thirteenth centuries who wrote love poems, meant to be sung to music, which reflected a new sensibility, called courtly love, about the ennobling possibilities of the love between a man and a woman.

Truman Doctrine (p. 576) Named after U.S. president Harry Truman, the doctrine that in 1947 inaugurated the Cold War policy of resisting the expansion of communist control.

Twelfth-Century Renaissance (p. 198) An intellectual revival of interest in ancient Greek philosophy and science and in Roman law in western Europe during the twelfth and early thirteenth

centuries. The term also refers to a flowering of vernacular literature and the Romanesque and Gothic styles in architecture.

tyrants (p. 62) Political leaders from the upper classes who championed the cause of hoplites in Greek city-states during the Archaic Age. The word "tyrant" gained its negative connotation when democracies developed in Greece that gave more political voice to male citizens than permitted by tyrants.

Unitarians (p. 281) A religious reform movement that began in the sixteenth century and rejected the Christian doctrine of the Trinity. Unitarians (also called Arians, Socinians, and Anti-Trinitarians) taught a rationalist interpretation of the Scriptures and argued that Jesus was a divinely inspired man, not God-become-man as did other Christians.

universal law of gravitation (p. 339) A law of nature established by Isaac Newton in 1687 holding that any two bodies attract each other with a force that is directly proportional to the product of their masses and indirectly proportional to the square of the distance between them. The law was presented in mathematical terms.

universal male suffrage (p. 406) The granting of the right to vote to all adult males.

vassals (p. 166) During the Middle Ages men voluntarily submitted themselves to a lord by taking an oath of loyalty. Vassals owed the lord certain services—usually military assistance—and sometimes received in exchange a grant of land known as a fief.

Vatican II (p. 589) Popular term for the Second Vatican Council that convened in 1963 and introduced a series of changes within the Roman Catholic Church.

Versailles Treaty (p. 525) Treaty between Germany and the victorious Allies after World War I.

Vichy, Vichy regime, Vichy government (p. 553) Authoritarian state established in France after defeat by the German army in 1940.

Warsaw Pact (p. 576) Military alliance of the Soviet Union and its eastern European satellite states in the Cold War era.

Weimar Republic (p. 533) The democratic German state constructed after defeat in World War I and destroyed by the Nazis in 1933.

wergild (p. 155) In Germanic societies the term referred to what an individual was worth in case he or she suffered an injury. It was the amount of compensation in gold that the wrongdoer's family had to pay to the victim's family.

witch-hunt (p. 300) Refers to the dramatic increase in the judicial prosecution of alleged witches in either church or secular courts from the middle of the sixteenth to the middle of the seventeenth centuries.

Zionism (p. 480) Nationalist movement that emerged in the late nineteenth century and sought to establish a Jewish political state in Palestine (the Biblical Zion).

Zoroastrianism (p. 58) The monotheistic religion of Persia founded by Zoroaster that became the official religion of the Persian Empire.

Credits

Unless otherwise acknowledged, all photographs are the property of Pearson Education, Inc. Page abbreviations are as follows: (T) Top, (B) Bottom, (L) Left, (R) Right, (C) Center.

What Is the West?
2 Canali Photobank; 4 European Space Agency/Photo Researchers, Inc.; 5 Courtesy of Adler Planetarium & Astronomy Museum, Chicago, Illinois (W-264); 8 American Museum of Natural History Library (AMNH#314372)

Chapter 1
10 Victor R. Boswell, Jr./National Geographic Image Collection; 12 Augustin Ochsenreiter/South Tyrol Museum of Archaeology; 17 (L) Courtesy of the Trustees of the British Museum, London (BM116730); 17 (R) Courtesy of the Trustees of the British Museum, London (WA15285); 19 Robert Harding Picture Library; 21 Erich Lessing/Art Resource, NY; 23 Scala/Art Resource, NY; 27 Roger Ressmeyer/Corbis

Chapter 2
30 National Archaeological Museum, Athens/Dagli Orti/The Art Archive; 35 British Museum, London/Bridgeman Art Library; 36 Egyptian Museum Cairo/Dagli Orti/The Art Archive; 38 Osiride Head of Hatshepsut, originally from a statue. Provenance: Thebes, Deir el Bahri. Limestone, painted. H. 64 cm. H. with crown 124.5 cm. The Metropolitan Museum of Art, Rogers Fund, 1931, (31.3.157) Photograph © 1983 The Metropolitan Museum of Art. All rights reserved, The Metropolitan Museum of Art; 41 Nimatallah/Art Resource, NY; 44 Hirmer Verlag; 48 (T) Erich Lessing/Art Resource, NY; 48 (B) Oriental Institute, University of Chicago

Chapter 3
52 Erich Lessing/Art Resource, NY; 56 Collection, Israel Museum, Jerusalem. Photo © Israel Museum/David Harris; 59 State Hermitage Museum, Moscow, Russia; 61 (All) American Numismatic Society; 66 Staatliche Äntikensammlungen und Glyphtothek, Munich; 67 Robert Harding Picture Library; 71 Scala/Art Resource, NY

Chapter 4
74 Scala/Art Resource, NY; 80 Réunion des Musées Nationaux/Art Resource, NY; 82 Erich Lessing/Art Resource, NY; 84 (T) Erich Lessing/Art Resource, NY; 84 (B) Staatliche Museen, Berlin/BPK, Berlin; 85 Robert Harding Picture Library; 88 Statue of Cybele, Roman, II Century A.D., Bronze, Length 139.1 cm. The Metropolitan Museum of Art, Gift of Henry G. Marquand, 1897. (97.22.24) Photograph by Schecter Lee, Photograph © 1985 The Metropolitan Museum of Art. All rights reserved, The Metropolitan Museum of Art; 93 Alinari/Art Resource, NY

Chapter 5
96 Erich Lessing/Art Resource, NY; 100 SEF/Art Resource, NY; 101 Erich Lessing/Art Resource, NY; 102 Vasari/Index s.a.s.; 106 akg-images; 110 Scala/Art Resource, NY; 112 Courtesy of the Trustees of the British Museum, London (BMC Vespasian 16)

Chapter 6
116 Österreichische Nationalbibliotek, Vienna; 119 SEF/Art Resource, NY; 120 Erich Lessing/Art Resource, NY; 124 Victoria & Albert Museum, London/Art Resource, NY; 133 (T) Erich Lessing/Art Resource, NY; 133 (BL) Courtesy of the Trustees of the British Museum, London (1918-5-1-62/K93196); 133 (BR) Courtesy of the Trustees of the British Museum, London (1918-5-1-62/K93195); 135 Réunion des Musées Nationaux/Art Resource, NY

Chapter 7
138 Art Resource, NY; 142 David and Goliath, Byzantine, Made in Constantinople, 629–630; Early Byzantine, Silver, D. 1 ½ in. (3.8 cm); Diam. 19 ½ in (49.4 cm); The Metropolitan Museum of Art, Gift of J. Pierpont Morgan, 1917 (17.190.396) Photograph © 2000 The Metropolitan Museum of Art. All rights reserved, The Metropolitan Museum of Art; 144 Courtesy of His Eminence Archbishop Damianos and the Holy Council of the Fathers, Saint Catherine's Monastery. Photograph © Idryma Orous Sina, Mt. Sinai Foundation; 147 AP/Wide World Photos; 149 Freer Gallery of Art, Smithsonian Institution, Washington, D.C.: Purchase, F1930.60a; 153 British Museum/Eileen Tweedy/The Art Archive; 156 By permission of the British Library (Cotton.Nerod.iv. fol. 211)

Chapter 8
160 Art Resource, NY; 165 Erich Lessing/Art Resource, NY; 167 Bodleian Library, Oxford University (Ms Bodl. 624 fol. 81r); 169 akg-images; 170 Réunion des Musées Nationaux/Art Resource, NY; 171 Chitter Åhlin/The Museum of National Antiquities, Sweden; 177 Scala/Art Resource, NY

Chapter 9
182 Giraudon/Art Resource, NY; 186 Dagli Orti/The Art Archive; 191 Bibliothèque Nationale, Paris, France/Bridgeman Art Library; 195 Bibliothèque Nationale de France, Paris; 200 Courtesy Achim Bednorz; 201 (L) Marc Garanger/Corbis; 201 (R) Courtesy Achim Bednorz

Chapter 10
204 Snark/Art Resource, NY; 213 Honourable Society of Inner Temple London/Eileen Tweedy/The Art Archive; 214 Bibliothèque Nationale de France, Paris (MS. Fr. 2644 fol. 135); 217 Bibliothèque Nationale de Rouen (MS U 49 fol. 1); 218 Tomb Effigy of Jean d'Alluy, mid-13th century, Limestone, 83 ½ × 34 ¼ in. (212.1 × 87 cm) The Metropolitan Museum of Art, The Cloisters Collection, 1925. (25.120.201) Photography © 1979 The Metropolitan Museum of Art. All rights reserved, The Metropolitan Museum of Art; 219 Réunion des Musées Nationaux/Art Resource, NY; 220 Réunion des Musées Nationaux/Art Resource, NY

Chapter 11
224 Scala/Art Resource, NY; 229 Ravenna/Index s.a.s.; 233 Kunsthistorisches Museum, Vienna/Art Resource, NY; 236 (Both) Orsi Battaglini/Index s.a.s.; 237 Art Resource, NY; 238 Alinari/Art Resource, NY; 239 Brancacci Chapel, Santa Maria del Carmine, Florence, Italy/Bridgeman Art Library

NY/© 2005 Artists Rights Society (ARS), New York/ADAGP, Paris; **588** Kunsthalle, Tubingen/Bridgeman Art Library/© 2005 Artists Rights Society (ARS), New York/DACS, London; **590** Hulton Archive/Getty Images

Chapter 28
596 AP/Wide World Photos; **599** Reuters/CORBIS; **606 (L)** Gyori Antoine/Corbis Sygma; **606 (R)** Scott Peterson/ Getty Images; **611** Hulton Archive/Getty Images; **613** Through the Flower/© 2005 Judy Chicago/Artists Rights Society (ARS), New York; **615** Neil Cooper/Panos Pictures

Index

Contemporary Political Map of the World

CANADA

ALASKA (U.S.)

UNITED STATES

MEXICO

GREENLAND (KALAALLIT NUNAAT) (Den.)

Arctic Ci

ICELAND

UN KINGI

IRELAND

FRA

PORTUGA

AZORES (Port.)

ATLANTIC OCEAN

CANARY IS. (Sp.)

WESTERN SAHARA (Mor.)

MOROC

MAURITANI

CAPE VERDE

SENEGAL

MA

THE GAMBIA

GUINEA-BISSAU

GUINEA

SIERRA LEONE

LIBERIA

CÔTE D'IVOIR

BURKINA FAS

GHA

BAHAMAS

CUBA

HAITI

DOMINICAN REPUBLIC

PUERTO RICO (U.S.)

ST. KITTS AND NEVIS

ANTIGUA AND BARBUDA

DOMINICA

ST. VINCENT AND THE GRENADINES

BARBADOS

GRENADA

TRINIDAD AND TOBAGO

GUYANA

SURINAME

FRENCH GUIANA (Fr.)

JAMAICA

BELIZE

GUATEMALA

HONDURAS

EL SALVADOR

NICARAGUA

GUADELOUPE (Fr.)

MARTINIQUE (Fr.)

ST. LUCIA

COSTA RICA

PANAMA

VENEZUELA

COLOMBIA

ECUADOR

GALÁPAGOS IS. (Ec.)

PERU

BRAZIL

BOLIVIA

PARAGUAY

CHILE

URUGUAY

ARGENTINA

HAWAII (U.S.)

PACIFIC OCEAN

WESTERN SAMOA

AMERICAN SAMOA (U.S.)

TONGA

FRENCH POLYNESIA (Fr.)

ATLANTIC OCEAN

FALKLAND IS. (U.K.)

Antarctic Circle

Tropic of Cancer

0° Equator

Tropic of Capricorn

80°N

60°N

40°N

20°N

20°S

40°S

60°S

80°S

160°W 140°W 120°W 100°W 80°W 60°W 40°W 20°W

0   1,500   3,000 Miles

0   1,500   3,000 Kilometers